$57.95

12-2-98

EARTH SCIENCES
REFERENCE

EARTH SCIENCES
REFERENCE

MARY McNEIL

FLAMINGO PRESS

Lake San Marcos, California

Publisher's Cataloging in Publication
(Prepared by Quality Books Inc.)
McNeil, Mary.
The earth sciences reference/Mary McNeil.
p. cm.
Includes bibliographical references, cross references, and indexes.
ISBN 0-938905-01-5
1. Earth sciences — Dictionaries — English. 2. Physical sciences — Diction-
aries — English. 3. Ecology — Dictionaries — English. I. Title.
QE5   550'.3   QB190-89
                                                              MARC

PUBLISHED BY FLAMINGO PRESS
             2958 State Street
             Carlsbad, CA 92008

Cover Photographs:

Left: Coral Reef — Sipadan Island, Borneo
           Courtesy of V. Nicholas Galluzzi, MD
Center: Apollo 17 View of Earth —
           Courtesy of NASA
Right: Kilauea — in eruption
           Courtesy of US Geological Survey

Cover Design & Production:
Moog & Associates, Inc.

ACKNOWLEDGEMENTS

This is a thank you to all those friends and colleagues who helped in the shaping of this volume. Though too numerous to mention individually, each is special.

A particular thank you to those numerous librarians who worked so hard to obtain those many books and articles necessary to such a reference..

Thank you, Mary Beth Arkell, for going that extra mile to get the manuscript to the printer.

FOREWORD

Planet Earth appears smaller than at any other time in human history. As populations and tensions grow the finiteness of the Earth and its resources must be considered. The interdependence of all life is becoming more evident. Small insects affect the gases of the atmosphere and contribute to 'Global Warming' and climate change. How much greater is the human contribution.

The information explosion has made us all aware that problems, formerly considered local, have often far wider effect, sometimes global. The air we breathe, the water we drink, the food we eat, our shelters, and way of life all relate to the distribution and quality of the elementary components of the planet. These include the great oceans, the fabulous drifting continents with forests, grasslands, wetlands, and deserts all dependent upon a lithosphere of rocks and minerals.

We need the ability to view the planet as a whole, to see its uniquness, its seemingly endless variety, and the fragility of its ecosystem. We must, perforce, become more caring stewards.

Mary McNeil
San Marcos, California

USER'S GUIDE

The Earth Sciences Reference is an introductory research tool to answer questions and stimulate interest for further investigation. In an age of information overload and specialization, many scientists may find it useful to explore another branch.

The complex interactions of physical, chemical, and biological forces on Planet Earth are introduced in an expanded glossary form for ready reference. The generous bibliography opens further avenues of research. Many individual entries are supplemented by one or more others.

A main entry may have the notation (q.v.) Latin for 'see', or the word 'see' may follow a paragraph. The indices, general and geographical, may also note additional references.

The metric system is used throughout but the English equivalent is given in parenthesis. Weights, measures, and other dimensional information are only meant to be approximate and are primarily for perspective. Also, Appendix III notes the equivalents.

Some parts of the world have been selected for more detailed description based upon the need for an over-view or because the area is especially important in some way. Some special emphasis has been given to the Southern Hemisphere since it has often been under-represented.

Minerals in major world markets and of importance to life and present technology are included. In many cases the reserves are given in the order of the major holders. The U.S. Bureau of Mines has recently changed its system of reporting and the reserves given are those which can be economically extracted and processed as of the date of the report.

For those information buffs, it is hoped the Reference will provide a pleasurable and useful paperchase.

CONTENTS

	Page
ACKNOWLEDGEMENT	iii
FORWARD	v
USER'S GUIDE	vii
AA - AZURITE	1
BABA GURGER - BY-PRODUCT	47
c - CYPRESS SWAMPS	85
DACITE -DZUNGARIAN PLAIN	147
E LAYER - LAKE EYRE	173
F LAYER - MOUNT FUJIYAMA	195
g - GYROSCOPE	217
HABITAT -HYPSOMETRIC CURVE	257
IAPETUS - ITURI FOREST	275
JACUPIRANGITE - JUVENILE WATER	293
K:AR - KYANITE	299
L WAVE - LYSOCLINE	311
MAAR - MYLONITE	331
LAKE NAIVASHA - NYIRAGONGO CALDERA	373
OASIS - OZONE LAYER	397
P WAVE - PYROXENES	417
QATTARA - QUINTA	461
RAD - RWANDA	465
S WAVE - SYZYGY	491
TAAL VOLCANO - TYPHOON	553
U-SHAPED VALLEY - UYUNI SALAR	585
VADOSE WATER - VULTURE MINE	593
WAD - WULFENITE	605
XENO- - X-RAY	621
YAKUTIA DIAMOND FIELDS -YUNNAN PLATEAU	624
ZAIRE BASIN - ZUIDER ZEE	629

CONTENTS (Continued)

	Page
GEOLOGICAL TABLE - APPENDIX I	635
CHEMICAL TABLE - APPENDIX II	636
WEIGHTS AND MEASURES - APPENDIX III	637
BIBLIOGRAPHY	639
GEOGRAPHICAL INDEX	657
GENERAL INDEX	677

ILLUSTRATIONS

Page

Ellsworth Mountains and Icecap - Antarctica .... Frontispiece

Borborema Pegmatite Dike - Northeast Brazil 84

Dunes - Namib Desert, Southwest Africa 146

Loma Prieta Earthquake Damage - San Francisco/Oakland 172

Central Cascade Glacier - Washington 216

The Himalayan Mountains - Pakistan 256

Itatiaia Massif - Rio De Janeiro (State), Brazil 292

Kilauea - Mountain of Fire 330

Aluminum Waste Lagoon, East St. Louis 396

San Andreas Fault 490

Uranium Mine - Date Creek, Arizona 552

Mount St. Helens - Washington - Before and After Eruption ... 604

Waterfall - Poças De Caldas, Brazil 628

Ellsworth Mountains and Icecap — Antarctica
Courtesy of Dr. Richard Ojakangas, Dept. of Geology, University of Michigan, Duluth

A

AA 'Aa' is Hawaiian for dark, viscous, clinkery, basaltic lava common in the Islands. It cools rapidly on the surface while remaining hot and fluid within for long periods of time. This difference in cooling rate causes jagged blocks with a thin and friable crust. The lava, when it finally escapes, leaves tubes and tunnels. Tubes and tunnels of this origin are found in many places around the world.

AARDVARK The aardvark with its burrowing nose is an insect-eating mammal. It developed in isolation after the breakup of Pangaea (q.v.). Its range today is from Ethiopia to South Africa. The aardvark is about 1.8 meters (6 feet) long. Locally known as 'earth pig', it is a natural control over termites and ants in areas plagued by these insects.

ABDUCTION The Earth's Crust is segmented into plates. An oceanic plate can be thrust beneath a continental one by forces operating within the Mantle (q.v.). This is 'abduction' in plate tectonics (q.v.).

ABERS 'Abers' are estuaries in Brittany, northwest France. They occur where streams cut across the sea cliffs. Abers were strategic locations during World War II.

ABIOTIC An abiotic environment is a sterile one. Abiotic means without life.

ABLATION Ablation is the wasting away of the surfaces of glaciers by direct vaporization caused by sun, wind, and rain. Glaciers thin and waste in the lower part of the ice mass. In Spain, ablation erosional forms are 'neve penitente' or remorseful snows. Different rates of ablation create these cone structures.

ABORIGINE Native inhabitants of an area are aborigines. They are tribes or natives that have inhabited an area for long periods of time and are different from later groups. The American Indian is aboriginal to North and South America.

ABRASION Abrasion is wearing away of rock surfaces by friction, milling, rock grinding, or other mechanical action. Ice, pebbles, and sand can abrade a stream channel. Roundness reflects the violence through which the material has traveled. In streams and in the sea, rocks are transported at varying velocities. This results in collisions and opportunities for abrasion.

ABRASIVES Industrial minerals used to abrade, sharpen, hone, grind, and smooth are abrasives. Corundum, emery, and sand are the most used.

ABSOLUTE DESERT Outside the Arctic and Antarctic, there are 2 absolute deserts: Atacama of Chile and Namib of South Africa. These are regions of no rainfall for years on end. In one area of Atacama 2.5 centimeters (1 inch) was reported in a 29-year period.

ABSOLUTE HUMIDITY The amount of water vapor (in grams per cubic meter) found in a volume of air is its absolute humidity.

ABSOLUTE TIME Age is calculated in years of any organism, object, or event. Rock ages are usually calculated from ratios of radio active elements. The most commonly used method is the ratio of potassium-40 to argon-40. These are relative calculations. There is no absolute time known for rock ages. See **AGE DATING**.

ABSOLUTE ZERO Absolute zero temperature is set at -278.18° Celsius (-459.69° Fahrenheit). Lord Kelvin set absolute zero at the point where all temperature-induced motion of atoms or molecules ceased.

ABSORBER An absorber takes up ionizing radiation. A sheet of paper absorbs alpha rays (q.v.) and most beta rays (q.v.). Steel and concrete absorb gamma rays (q.v.) and neutrons. Hafnium and cadmium are used as rods in nuclear reactors because they are effective absorbers.

In the Atmosphere, an absorber takes up the Sun's heat and energy. Absorbers may be of carbon dioxide or particulate matter such as dust, water droplets, or volcanic ash. Some absorbers take up radiation from the Earth. Others absorb sound waves.

ABSORPTION A sponge taking up a solution demonstrates the process of absorption. Fluid molecules enter into a solid sorbent (q.v.). This process is important in mineralization, especially of clays.

ABYSSAL The very deepest parts of the ocean are 'abyssal', Greek for bottomless. Abyssal depths are greater than 5,000 meters (16,500 feet). These regions account for 3% of the World Ocean.

ABYSSAL PLAINS Abyssal (q.v.) plains are the flattest parts of the sea floor as well as the deepest. All features on the abyssal plains are abrupt, whether seamounts or canyons. In the North Atlantic some abyssal plains are:

• Sohm Plain - South of Newfoundland. 3 seamounts rise from ocean floor. Milne Seamount is 4,545 meters (15,000 feet).

• Hatteras Plain - Off eastern United States.

• Blake-Bermuda Plains - Western Atlantic off the Carolinas. Blake and Bermuda plateaus rise from the plains.

ACACIA Acacia trees, common in semi-arid African savannas, have a double-root system enhancing survivability in climates of extremes of wet and dry. Their tap roots may be several meters. Their near-surface root system captures run-off. Acacia leaves roll back on themselves creating a thorn-shape with a reduced area for evapo-transpiration (q.v.). Acacia are 'Leguminaceae' and nitrogen-fixing.

'Acacia tortilis' (umbrella acacia) provides food and its flat-topped, leafy canopy shelter to the East African elephant. It blossoms with a white flower that appears just before the rains. Dry, yellow seed pods are disseminated by elephant and antelope spoor. The animal's digestive tract may be critical to germination or may only provide seed transport out of the parental shade.

ACCELERATION Acceleration is an increase in velocity rates. In biology, an assumption is made that evolutionary changes occur earlier and earlier in successive generations. This is the acceleration of evolution.

Acceleration of gravity relates to the speed of falling objects at 980.665 centimeters (32.174 feet) per second per second. Gravity aceleration varies with altitude, latitude, and density.

The acceleration of erosion can be caused by earthquakes or conditions in the regolith (q.v.).

ACCELERATOR The accelerator is an electrical or magnetic instrument used to increase the velocity of elementary particles such as electrons and protons. Some particle velocities approach the speed of light. In an accelerator, atomic nuclei are bombarded by atomic particles, usually protons.

ACCESSORY MINERALS Important minerals contained in a rock, but used to define it, are accessory. These may be classed as minor or occasional (the French say 'accidental'). Common minor accessories are apatite, hematite, or zircon. Some occasional minerals are titanium, topaz, and tourmaline.

Accessory minerals form less than 2% of sedimentary rocks. They are more evident in igneous rocks, where they may be 'primary' or 'secondary'. If primary, they crystallized from the lava or magma. If secondary, they were probably introduced in solutions.

ACCIDENTED LANDSCAPE Repeated abrupt changes in elevation create a regionally accidented landscape. Any form of relief contrasting in elevation with its immediate area is accidented.

ACCLIMATION Acclimation is adaptation of individual organisms to climatic or environmental changes. It may be a physiological adjustment or simply acquiring greater tolerance. Natives of the high Andes have enlarged breathing capacity to survive the oxygen deficiency.

ACCORDANT LEVEL When relief of an area has the same maximum elevation level, the landscape is accordant. Mountain-tops are of the same height. Plateaus have been leveled off at the same elevation. Tributaries find the mainstream at an accordant level for the valleys.

Parts of the Appalachians (the Poconos) are accordant as are the lateritic plateaus of the Guiana Highlands. Accordant landscapes appear to represent terrains that were peneplaned and subsequently uplifted.

ACCRETION Aggregation of rock particles into a mass to enlarge it is accretion. The particles may be of any size. Cements vary coming from the original adjacent material or from a foreign source.

It was long considered that accretion built up continents by adding to cratons or continental shield areas. Mountains were welded on to ancient cratons. Accretion also describes continental growth by joining up areas that drifted separately. Land formed by this accretion is called 'suspect terrain'. Parts of Alaska are considered suspect terrain. See **CONTINENTAL DRIFT**.

In milling ores, the process of accretion controls many sludges and slags. Cementing materials may be introduced or natural.

ACCRETION BAR A low level deposit of sand and/or gravel forms a bar on a stream bed. Bars form on the inside of curves. Accretion bars are important in placer mining as collectors of heavy minerals.

ACCUMULATION Glaciers increase in size by 'accumulation'. Snows are incorporated into ice fields. The accumulation zone is the upper portion where annual increments of snow and ice are greater than wastage or ablation (q.v.).

ACCUMULATOR PLANT Plants often acquire abnormal metal content from metals in the soils, some deleterious. Some selectively absorb certain metals. These are accumulator plants, excellent geobotanical indicators. Locoweed, toxic to cattle, accumulates selenium.

ACICULAR Very fine acicular or needle-like crystals can be found as inclusions in rocks and minerals. Rutile needles are often found in quartz crystals, which are said to be rutilated.

ACID The number of hydrogen-plus ions in a solution is a direct measure of its acidity. All acids contain hydrogen, but many compounds with hydrogen are not acids (water is an example). On the pH scale (q.v.) an acid will be less than 7 and anions will predominate.

ACID LAVAS Acid igneous rocks contain more than 10% visible quartz and are rich in alkali feldspars. Acid lavas are molten equivalents of the magmas that gave rise to acid igneous rocks.

Acidic lavas rarely travel far as they are relatively more viscous than basaltic lavas (q.v.). They tend to form plugs in craters causing gases to be pressurized and explosive. Gases are steam, carbon dioxide, nitrogen, and sulfur.

The product of an acidic flow may be rhyolite, a rock similar to granite in composition. If very gaseous, pumice results. If the lava cools rapidly, noncrystalline, glass or obsidian forms.

ACID RAIN A weak acidity (pH 5-6) is natural to rainfall. It is caused by carbonic acid from small amounts of carbon dioxide and water in the Atmosphere. Sulfur and nitrogen can increase acidity. Natural acid rain is reinforced by additional carbon dioxide and sulfur from auto emissions and industrial output. Acid rain has become a severe political problem between the United States and Canada.

Toxic acid rain is becoming a major health hazard. In the Baltimore area, the pH of acid rain can reach as low as 2.9. Spawning of some fish has been affected. Bass will reproduce best in waters with a pH of 8. Below pH 7, their survival is impaired.

Acid rain is an erosional factor in dissolving limestone and releasing calcium and carbonate ions. Intense damage may result to buildings from acid rain. In Athens, Greece, acid rain is contributing to the destruction of famous marbles, including the Parthenon and Erechtheum. In Agra, India, the Taj Mahal is being severely damaged by acid rain. Complete destruction is forecast within 50 years.

Forests have been adversely affected by acid rain. In Europe, the acidity is 30 times that of natural rain or snow. Much of Germany's many forests have been affected. Trees in New England are showing the stress caused by acid rain.

ACID ROCKS Leucocratic (light-colored) igneous rocks containing more than 65% silica are acidic. Granite and rhyolite (q.v.) are acidic. Some other well-known acidic rocks are leucite, muscovite, nepheline, and sodalite.

ACID SOILS Soils deficient in exchangeable bases, particularly calcium, are considered acidic. These soils require additions of lime to be suitable for agriculture. The pH (q.v.) is below 6.

Humid tropical soils are usually acidic, as are the red and yellow forest soils of tropical and semi-tropical climates. Because they are subject to excessive leaching, these soils require special management.

ACIDIFICATION Europe's major environmental problem is the acidification of its land and waters. Between the 1940's and 1980's over half the fish have disappeared from Norwegian lakes. See **ACID RAIN**.

ACONCAGUA Aconcagua Volcano, a landmark on the Chilean-Argentinian border, has an elevation of 7,223 meters (23,835 feet). It is the highest peak in the western hemisphere. An extinct volcano, Aconcagua's crest has been flattened by erosion. On its south slope is Uspallata Pass, one of the few across the Andes.

ACOUSTIC WAVES Acoustic waves contain and transmit sound energy. They travel through air, water, rock, and sediment. Acoustic waves are important in geophysics for sonar, seismic, and other applications.

ACOUSTIC WELL LOGGING Acoustic well-logging is used in the petroleum industry to determine well levels and other conditions. Sound is transmitted down the well and an echo returns to activate a recorder.

ACRE An acre is a surface measure equivalent to 43,560 square feet. It is in common use in Britain, Canada, and the United States. The acre is 10 square chains (q.v.) or 660 x 660 feet, a common measure for surveyors. In the U.S. there are 640 acres to a section, or 1 square mile and there are 36 sections in a Township. The acre equals 0.405 hectares in the metric system.

ACREFOOT Water over an area of an acre to a depth of 1 foot is an acrefoot. This is an irrigation measure equal to 1,235 million liters (325,850 gallons).

ACTINIDE SERIES The Actinide Series on the Periodic Table of Elements begins with actinium and ends with lawrencium (Nos.89-103). The series includes uranium and the transuranium elements. Beyond uranium, the elements do not occur naturally. All are metals and all have radioactive isotopes (q.v.).

ACTIVATOR An activator is a substance causing a mineral to fluoresce (q.v.). The activator may be an accessory or an inclusion.

ADAPTATION Long-term evolutionary changes of plant and animal populations may be adaptations to environment. The environmental changes probably occurred over sufficient time to allow for adaptation.

ADIABATIC CHANGE Air rises and expands because the weight exerted upon it is lessened with elevation. At 5,500 meters (18,000 feet) pressure is only half that at sea level. Compression of descending airmasses accounts for some famous warm winds. (Chinook of the Rockies and the Foehn of Europe).

The cooling rate of rising dry air is the adiabatic dry rate, 5.5° Fahrenheit/1,000 feet (10° Celsius/kilometer). Normal air temperature cools with elevation at the adiabatic lapse rate, an average of 3.6° F/300 meters (1,000 feet) of elevation. Pilots use this unit to estimate temperature effects on their instruments.

ADIT An adit is a mine entrance that is almost horizontal. The tunnel beyond the opening is a drift.

ADOBE Natural adobe is the clayey-silty material found in desert basins. Bricks are made by adding water and extraneous organic material, often manure. Once mixed, adobe is baked in the Sun.

ADRIATIC SEA A long arm of the Mediterranean Sea cutting into Europe is the Adriatic Sea. It is joined to the Ionian Sea through the Strait of Otranto. Venice on the Adriatic was a launching point of many explorations to the Orient in the 14th and 15th Centuries.

The Adriatic separates Italy from Yugoslavia and is relatively uniform in width. It subdivides into 2 distinct basins. The northern one is 240 meters (790 feet) deep and the southern, 1,240 meters (4,100 feet). The sea is 820 kilometers (493 miles) long and 164 kilometers (98 miles) wide.

ADSORPTION Substances sometimes adhere to surfaces with which they have no chemical combination. This is adsorption. Charcoal will remove dye from solutions by adsorption. Adsorption is also a characteristic of many molecular sieves (q.v.).

ADVECTION Weather changes result from heat transfer, or advection from airmass to airmass. Advection is a lateral transfer of energy and moisture. It is the 'great weather maker' of the Mid-Latitudes. It operates in coastal areas between onshore and offshore winds.

ADVECTION FOG Mild humid air moving over a colder surface creates an advection fog. The airmass is cooled by radiation and conduction. Fog is common along coasts in summer and over a snowy surface in winter.

AEGEAN SEA The Aegean Sea flanks the west coast of Turkey and the east coast of Greece. It has many fabled islands, high points of a landmass that sank beneath the sea at the end of the Tertiary (q.v.).

About 10 million years ago the land connection between Europe and Asia was broken and seas invaded as the land sank. Today the sea has a depth of 2,000 meters (6,500 feet) at the southern end of what was formerly the landmass.

AEGEAN VOLCANIC LINE The Aegean Vocanic Line forms a belt across the Aegean Sea (q.v.). It begins with the volcanic islands of Susaki Aegina and Mathana, passes through Milos, Santorini (q.v.), Nisyros, Hyali, and Kos. The active volcanoes are Santorini and Nisyros.

AEOLIAN DEPOSITS The most famous of all aeolian deposits are the loess deposits (q.v.) of China. These deposits of dust-size materials were blown into China from deserts to the north and west.

Sand dunes are the commonest form of aeolian deposits. They are moved and shaped by the winds. See **DUNES**.

Few wind-derived or aeolian placers exist. Light material is winnowed and heavier detritus remains. Gold has been found in aeolian placers in California, Mexico, and Australia.

AERATION ZONE The aeration zone in a soil is the unsaturated area above the water table. Water in this zone is held in the pores of the soil by capillary tension. See **CAPILLARITY**.

AERIE An aerie is a nest perched on a cliff or mountain top. Usually, it is the nest of an eagle, condor, or other bird of prey.

AEROBIC Living organisms are classed as aerobic or anaerobic. If they live in air and intake oxygen they are aerobic. Atmospheric weathering of the terrain is aerobic.

AEROSOL An aerosol is a suspension of fine solid or liquid particles in a gas. Some natural aerosols are fog, mist, and smoke. They are concentrated in the lower 3,000 meters (10,000 feet) and washed out of the Atmosphere by rains.

Volcanic and nuclear particulates which reach high into the Stratosphere are not affected by rains and will stay in suspension for years. They return to the Troposphere on the jet streams.

The presence of warming aerosols, primarily hydrocarbons, is considered to be greater than that of cooling particulate matter such as dust. If aerosols continue to build up in the Atmosphere, a major global warming may occur by the end of the century (Schneider, American Climatological Society).

Aerosols have been banned in the United States as the gases used contribute to the Greenhouse Effect (q.v.). See **CFC's**.

AESTIVATION Animals sometimes go into a dormant state in hot dry seasons. This is aestivation and is not unlike hibernation in cold winters. It is a protective measure against the adverse effects of climate.

AFAR TRIANGLE Afar Triangle is the desert area where East Africa and the southwestern tip of the Arabian Peninsula almost touch. The triangle is between 2 branches of the East African Rift. It is also the lowest and most geologically active area on the African continent. See **DANAKIL DEPRESSION**.

AFFLUENT If a tributary greatly increases the volume of discharge of the river system it joins, it is affluent. The Missouri River is an affluent to the Mississippi.

AFFORESTATION Allowing or encouraging tree growth is afforestation. The United Nations has many on-going programs, primarily in North Africa and on the west coast of South America in the 'fog desert'.

AFGHAN DESERT The Afghan Desert of Asia is really composed of 3 deserts. These are wide deserts flanking the Hindu Kush Mountains.

AFGHANISTAN Afghanistan is bounded by China, Iran, Pakistan, and the USSR. It is divided by high mountains that trend east-west. The major range is Hindu Kush with elevations up to 7,273 meters (24,000 feet).

Geologically, Afghanistan is mainly in a mobile mountain belt comprised principally of geosynclinal marine sediments intruded by basic igneous rocks and granites. Major events have occurred in every age since the Archaen and the axis of the belt has progressed to the south with each.

The North Afghan Platform is east of the Hindu Kush and Bandakshan ranges and north of the Safed Koh which is cut by the Khyber Pass (q.v.). Lapis lazuli (q.v.) is found in the Bandakshan. Not far from the Sar-e-Sang mine, uraninite was identified.

AFRICA Africa is the 2nd largest continent encompassing 20% of the Earth's landmass. It is 11,500 kilometers (6,900 miles) long by 7,833 kilometers (4,700 miles) wide at the bulge. Supported by the African Plate, it is almost completely surrounded by oceanic ridges.

The African Shield or craton, making up the African basement, is a platform of ancient rocks. Radioactive dating (q.v.) puts these shield rocks in the Proterozoic.

South of Europe and connected to southwest Asia, Africa is made up of deserts, savannas, and forested tropical lowlands. It also contains one of the few tropical rainforests and the world's largest swamp area, the Sudd (q.v.). The continent is a tableland with few mountain ranges. Kilmanjaro, East Africa, is the highest peak at 5,861 meters (19,342 feet). Generally, the surface is lower than that of the Western Hemisphere or Eurasia.

The Holocene (Recent) has been marked by erosion and Africa is eroding at an accelerated rate. It loses a minimum of 715 tons per year from its surface as a result wind and water activity.

There are 2 carbonatite (q.v.) belts related to the East African Rift. The eastern in Kenya can be traced south to the Transvaal via Malawi. The western in Uganda extends to Tanzania, Zambia, and South Africa. A 3rd carbonatite belt in Angola is related to the rift zone of the continental margin (q.v.).

AFRO-BRAZILIAN LANDMASS In the Mesozoic Era, part of Gondwana (q.v.) was fragmented off from the main continental landmass. Theory contends that Afro-Brazilia was the portion cut off by rifting.

LAKE AGASSIZ Lake Agassiz arose when the Continental Ice Sheet dammed north flowing drainage. An enormous glacier resulted. At the end of the Ice Age, Agassiz Lake covered northwest Minnesota, eastern Dakotas, and most of southern Manitoba, Canada. The lake covered 250,000 square kilometers (100,000 square miles).

Agassiz was shaped by glacial moraines (q.v.) which also cut flow to Hudson Bay. Rich farmlands, created from fine silts formed at the bottom of Lake Agassiz, mark the area today. The area is a flat plain cut by the Red River. Remnants of Agassiz are: Lake Manitoba, Winnipeg, Winnipegosis, and Lake of the Woods.

AGATE Agate is a variety of fine-grained and clouded quartz called chalcedony. Often there are spectacular zones of color due to mineral impurities. The colors may be white-gray, green, orange, red, or brown.

Agate deposits, widely distributed around the world, are most famous in southern Brazil. There agate is found over an area of a million square kilometers (600,000 square miles). This agate is famed for its quality, nodule size, and quantity of material. It is reputed to have spurred much of the German immigration to the region. Many migrants were lapidary artists.

AGE Geological time is subdivided into eons, eras, periods, and epochs. Age is an alternate name for era.

AGE OF THE EARTH The latest estimate of the Earth's age is 4.6 to 5.0 billion years. It is based upon radioactive dating (q.v.) and the uranium to uranium ratio found in rocks. Measurements were made on the African Shield, Greenland, and Australian rocks.

Sediment ages in lower Archaen rocks of Barberton Plateau, South Africa are 3.5 billion years old. These sediments eroded from even more ancient crustal rocks.

AGGLOMERATE Agglomerate is a mixed collection of compacted and cemented volcanic rocks. It is composed of ash, bombs, lapilli, and other debris. Another name for this cemented sediment is volcanic breccia.

Agglomerate is often found in the neck of a volcanic vent or crater having formed from the ejecta of a previous eruption.

AGGRADATION Aggradation is the process of sediment accumulation. Dunes are aggradation deposits. Material eroded from one area may be found in an aggrading deposit to which it was transported. Deltas and marine sediments are aggradation deposits.

AGGREGATE Inert materials such as sand, gravel, rock, and shell used in paving are aggregate.

AGONIC LINE The line of zero magnetic declination traced on a map is the Agonic Line. It is a great circle (q.v.) passing through both True and Magnetic poles. The North Magnetic Pole and the rotational pole, or tip of the Earth's Axis, are not the same.

Anywhere along the Agonic Line the magnetic compass points to True North. The line wanders with polar shifts and maps giving its location must be periodically updated. Variation east and west of the line is shown in degrees. Today, the line is roughly Lake Superior to South Carolina but 200 years ago it was in the Atlantic.

AGULHAS Needle-like peaks in Latin America are 'agulhas', Spanish for needle. They are common in the Chilean Alps where glacial plucking is active.

In Brazil, acicular rutile fragments found in diamond-bearing sediments are 'agulhas'. They are indicator minerals to diamond-bearing sediments.

AGULHAS CURRENT The coastal Agulhas Current is an offshoot of the South Equatorial Current which touches Africa north of Malagasy (Madagascar). The current is very well defined below 30° South Latitude. It is reputed to be one of the swiftest of oceanic currents.

MOUNT AGUNG Indonesian Agung Volcano is on Bali and is a neighbor of Krakatoa. Agung erupted in 1963 sending volcanic ash into the Stratosphere.

The greenhouse effect (q.v.) from the dust and ash clouds caused a 2-3° Celsius (5° Fahrenheit) temperatures increase between 40° South and 20° North Latitude. It was 8 years before conditions returned to those prevailing before the eruption.

AIR The Earth's atmospheric envelope is made up of constantly moving molecules. They move faster when heated and bounce farther apart. Warm air has fewer molecules and weighs less per unit of volume than cold.

The Earth is a great radiator having been heated by the Sun. It also has its own internal heat source though it is minor in comparison. Heated surface air rises and circulation begins. Dry air at sea level is composed of:

Nitrogen	78.08%
Oxygen	20.94%
Argon	0.93%
Carbon Dioxide	0.03%
Other	0.02%

AIR POLLUTION Until very recently, air pollution was considered a local problem. Global wind systems, however, are capable of wafting pollution hundreds, even thousands of miles from their source. The annual firing of grasslands in Argentina and southern Brazil bring a SMOG (q.v.) and haze to Rio de Janeiro.

Pollution may be natural or produced by people. Chemicals released into the Atmosphere can combine with others already there and create dangerous conditions. Other chemicals can destroy the protective quality of the Atmosphere by disturbing the radiation shield. Air pollution needs more study, and great effort should be made to eliminate harmful combinations.

AIR PRESSURE A column of air will exert a pressure of 14.7 pounds per square inch (psi) on the Earth's surface at sea level. The unit of measure for air pressure is the atmosphere.

AIRMASS An airmass is a large, homogeneous atmospheric body that is moved by surface winds. The airmass has a relatively uniform temperature and moisture content at a given elevation. It may be warm or cold, wet or dry. Airmasses bring changes in temperature and humidity that affect weather. They also adapt to and are affected by conditions and topography on the Earth's surface.

Airmasses affecting the United States emanate from Canada and are cold and dry. Those from the Gulf of Mexico are warm and wet, from the Gulf of Alaska cold and moist.

Airmasses are named for their sources areas: Polar Pacific, Polar Atlantic, Tropical Atlantic, Tropical Gulf, Tropical Pacific. They may be propelled by jet streams (q.v.) allowing them to cross a local area rapidly.

Airmasses often collide and heavier colder air pushes up warmer, lighter air. Airmasses may be extremely large, measuring hundreds of kilometers across and thousands of meters thick. This means that even with strong winds propelling it, an airmass may remain long enough to cause a deep cold or heat wave.

AKOSOMBO DAM Akosombo Dam on the Volta River in Ghana created a lake that is more than 250 miles long, one of the largest of artificial lakes.

ALABASTER Alabaster is a variety of gypsum and limestone compressed hard. It is a smooth rock suitable for sculpture. Alabaster is clear to white with yellow and grey banding. It is softer than marble, so less difficult to carve.

ALASKA Alaska is a peninsula of the North American Continent. It is separated from the USSR by the narrow Bering Strait. The Arctic Ocean is its northern boundary.

Brooks Range and the North Slope are part of the North American Craton but the rest of Alaska appears to be made up of a collection of micro-continents and oceanic crustal material. Between 135 and 110 million years ago, part of the North America Continent made a 90° swing about a hinge point at the Mackenzie Delta in Canada. Barrow Arch beneath Prudhoe Bay was a response to continental shift. Today the steeply dipping sediments of the arch hold fantastic petroleum reserves, presently being exploited.

Alaska has the largest number of glaciers in North America, mostly in the Wrangell-St. Elias mountains. The state is rich in mineral resources and scenic wonders.

ALASKAN EARTHQUAKE On Good Friday, 1964, an earthquake shook Anchorage with the force of 200,000 megatons for 4 to 7 minutes. 130 acres of land slid into the sea and the town of Valdez was destroyed. The quake was felt 1,330 kilometers (800 miles) away. The reading was 8.5 on the Richter Scale. It has since been revised to 8.7.

ALASKAN PIPELINE A pipeline carries petroleum from Prudhoe Bay in the Arctic to the port of Valdez in Southern Alaska. The distance is 1,280 kilometers (768 miles) across Alaska. Half the line is above ground and half buried. The line makes 800 stream crossings. It can carry 1.5 million barrels of crude per day. During the winter, the line is heated to keep the oil flowing.

Controversy surrounded its construction because of fears for its environmental impact. Long-term effects on ecology are still unknown.

ALBATROSS PLATEAU Albatross Plateau is a remnant of a mountain range. In the Pacific off Mexico, it is part of the East Pacific Rise. There are 2 subsidiary ranges off South America: Chile Rise and Nazca Ridge.

Soundings show a valley in the plateau similar to the valley in the Carlsberg Ridge in the Indian Ocean. The rift responsible for the valley also created the Gulf of California. Spreading has been occurring in the Gulf for over 4 million years. The Salton Sea Basin and Death Valley were created by the rift. On land, the rift becomes San Andreas Fault (q.v.).

ALBEDO Solar radiation reflected back into the Atmosphere is the albedo. Snows and glaciers have the greatest amount but tropical forests, desert sands, and vegetation also have albedo. The ice sheets (q.v.) exert the greatest albedo from their 13 million cubic kilometers (8 million cubic miles) of ice. This is predominantly in the Southern Hemisphere.

If global warming occurs melting will be more rapid as the radiation reflector becomes smaller. See **ICE SHEETS**.

ALBITE Albite is plagioclase feldspar. It is often found in volcanic rocks. Usually, it is found as white triclinic crystals. They are of sodium aluminum silicate. See **FELDSPAR**.

ALBITIZATION When molecules of potassium feldspar are substituted 1 by 1 with sodium, the process is albitization. It is often an indication of wide-spread rock alteration and mineralization. The Russians have studied their Precambrian rocks and claim albitization is a guide to their gold and uranium deposits.

ALCAN HIGHWAY The 2,530 kilometer (1,520 mile) highway from Dawson Creek, British Columbia to Fairbanks, Alaska was built in 1942. The Canadian Government gave the United States Army Corp of

Engineers permission to create the land route to Alaska. It was built as insurance for the security of the territory during World War II.

ALCHEMY The art of alchemy, forerunner of modern chemistry, began with attempts to convert base metals into gold. Alchemy is derived from Arabic 'Al Kimia', from Kimia the ancient name of Alexandria, Egypt. Alchemy flourished there from the time of the Ptolomies to the 18th Century. Many alchemists worked with plants and herbs to achieve remarkably useful medicines and materials.

ALEUTIAN TRENCH The Aleutian Trench associated with the island arc southwest of Alaska is 3,700 kilometers (2,220 miles) long, 50 kilometers (30 miles) wide and 7.7 kilometers (4.6 miles) deep. Islands form a single chain and the trench is on the outer or seaward side. The Aleutian Basin is landward.

ALGAE 'Algae', simplest of all plants, are common seaweeds though they may be found in freshwater. They have no true leaves, stems, or roots. Color is useful for geologists and oceanographers. Algae are red, blue-green, green, or brown. Algae range from micro to macro and are colonizers. Blue-green Algae are the oldest and most widespread living organisms and the most primitive. After the Krakatoa eruption, blue-green Algae were the first lifeforms. They were rapidly succeeded by more complex forms.

Algae produce chlorophyll (q.v.) and are great oxygen producers. There are conjectures of blue-green Algae's role in the Precambrian (q.v.) and the change to an environment of increased oxygen. Fossil Algae have been found in 3.6 billion year old rocks (Schopf, UCLA).

In many parts of the world, Algae are food. East Indian rice farmers introduced blue-green Algae into their paddies for their nitrogen-fixing character. Agar is used in laboratories to nurture Bacteria and Fungi. Iodine, potassium chloride, organic acid, and algin (a plastic) are produced from Algae.

ALGAL BLOOM Sudden and abundant growth of Algae as in a Red Tide (q.v.) is an algal bloom. It may be sufficient to destroy marine life. The rapid life cycle of the Algae tends to build up hydrogen sulfide as organisms decompose. The sulfide, in turn, kills off other organisms.

ALGAL REEFS Many reefs are algal rather than coral as 'Algae' make up a much larger portion of the organic residue than do corals. See **REEFS**.

ALGERIA The North African nation of Algeria is physiographically divided into the Saharan Shield, a peneplaned (q.v.) surface covered with Cretaceous limestones, and marine sediments.

The Atlas Mountains are composed of geosynclinal marine sediments which were uplifted, folded, and faulted in continental collision between the Shield and ancient Tyrrhenia. The mountains are in 2 ranges, the Maritime and the Saharan. The latter has long valleys between high plateaus.

The Maritime Atlas are a segment of the mountains that extend from Morocco to Tunisia. The Saharan Atlas extend from the High Atlas of Morocco to the Aures Massif and the Tunisian frontier. The range effectively cuts off the northern part of the country from the south.

The Sahara Desert in Algeria is a plateauland culminating in the Ahoggar Mountains. Limestone sinks provide water for the occasional oasis (q.v.).

ALICE SPRINGS BASIN   In mid-Australia, Alice Springs Basin is drained by the ephemeral Todd River. The interior basin, south of the MacDonnell Range has a mean elevation of 1,200 meters (3,960 feet). It is one of the few areas in the Outback (q.v.) where limited settlement occurs.

ALKALI   Soil salts formed in arid to semi-arid areas are alkali or alkaline. Alkali salts are water soluble compounds of the alkali metals.

Solubility is the reason the alkali salts are not found in humid soils. Alkali soils are basic with a pH greater than 8.5. Their high sodium content is sufficient to interfere with plant growth.

ALKALI FLATS   Alkali salts derived from plant ash contain potassium and sodium carbonates. A buildup of these salts is detrimental to soils. When the salt content is extreme, alkali flats develop. Rapid evaporation of alkaline waters on basin floors causes precipitation of sodium carbonate, sodium chloride, and other salts.

ALKALI LAKES   Alkali lakes result when potassium and sodium carbonate content are in excess of normal. Mono Lake, California (q.v.) is an alkali lake. Many smaller alkali lakes are found in Nevada and elsewhere in the southwest desert. Alkali Lakes are important in the United States, Canada, and Egypt as sources of useful minerals.

ALKALINE   A substance is alkaline when its pH (q.v.) is greater than 7 and there is a concentration of sodium and potassium base cations.

ALKALINE ROCKS   Igneous rocks (q.v.) with a high percent of alkalis in relation to silica and aluminum are alkaline. The rocks are free of calc-alkalic feldspars (q.v.). Alkaline rocks include syenite, nepheline, leucite, and sodalite. Syenites have little or no quartz.

ALLOCHTHONOUS   Deposits transported into a region are allochthonous. Glaciers and thrust sheets have transported great quantities of material from their point of origin. Allochthonous deposits are recognizable when they differ in kind and age from the country rock.

In plate tectonics theory, rafted micro-continents that have been welded together are allochthonous. Portions of Alaska are considered as 'suspect terrain' because they appear to fit the model.

ALLOWED ORBITS Electrons orbit the nucleus of an atom at well-defined distances. The electron in hydrogen can be at R-1 or R-2, where R stands for radius. The electron may not be in-between.

ALLOY Metals can be combined to form a new metal or alloy. Some ores naturally contain 2 or more metals but most alloys are artificial.

Copper mixed with tin results in bronze. The Bronze Age was probably introduced by an accidental discovery of this combination. Brass, a common alloy, results from mixing copper with zinc.

ALLUVIAL Alluvial or stream-borne sediments form major part of the Pleistocene and Recent geological columns (q.v.). Great floodplains of mature and old age streams were built by alluvium deposited by streams. Lacustrine or lake sediments are also classed as alluvial.

ALLUVIAL CONE Rock detritus is washed from steep slopes to form a conical heap or alluvial cone at the base. The cone is not unlike an alluvial fan but the gradient is steeper and deposits tend to be thicker. Alluvial cones are common in mountainous deserts. The cones at Banff, Canada, are considered classic.

ALLUVIAL FAN Streams flowing from mountains form delta-shaped or fan-shaped deposits at the base. Gradient changes, from steep to relatively gentle, slow a stream's velocity and cause it to lose its sediment load. Larger rocks are dropped first. The waters tend to spread or fan out as the deposit advances toward the valley. Intermittent streams in arid to semi-arid climates build thick fans because sediments are not carried far. These thick fans coalesce to form aprons.

ALLUVIAL GOLD Placers of gold and other heavy minerals are alluvial (q.v.). They are distinct from vein or lode deposits. Most placers are Tertiary or Recent in age, but some of the richest are Precambrian (q.v.). Among these are Witwatersrand, South Africa and Jacobina, Brazil.

ALLUVIUM Alluvium is a general term for all stream-borne sediments. These include gravel, sand, silt, clay, and mud. Lake deposits of similar composition are lacustrine as well as alluvial. Alluvium is designated as Ancient or Recent. Older sediments are often found on terraces along a stream or strand.

ALMAGEST Ptolomy, a savant of ancient Alexandria, wrote the 'Almagest'. It contained the concept that the Earth was located at the center of the Universe. This idea held until the Middle Ages.

ALPHA PARTICLE An alpha particle is positively charged and identical to the helium atom, with 2 protons and 2 neutrons. The alpha particle is emitted by some radioactive elements.

ALPHA RAYS Streams of alpha particles with 2 protons and 2 neutrons bound together form alpha rays. Due to the protons, these particles have a double charge. Alpha rays, the least penetrating of common radiation (alpha, beta, gamma), are stopped by a sheet of paper. Bombardment at close range can be hazardous to human tissue.

ALPINE TUNDRA Mountains with high elevations and low latitudes have zoned vegetation according to prevailing temperatures. A community of plants and animals develops to withstand conditions above the timberline. These conditions are Tundra and the plants are all low to the ground to avoid the worst winds. Included in the community are grasses, lichen, moss, and wildflowers. Within this Alpine Tundra Ecosystem rocks tend to be sorted downslope ranging from sand to boulders in accordance with gravity. Each sediment type has its own community of plants and animals.

ALPS Alpine mountain-building was initiated by the collision between the European and African Plates. The pressure gave rise to a vice-like effect when Africa subducted below the European Plate. The suture is marked by volcanoes along the Mediterranean Rim.

Intense folding caused shortening of sedimentary layers by 1/4 to 1/8 of their original length. The Alps arch northeast extending from France through Austria for 1,000 kilometers (600 miles).

The Carpathian Alps are a 1,000 kilometers (600 miles) extension which stretches from Czechoslovakia and Rumania to the Black Sea. The Apennines in Italy and the Dolomites in Yugoslavia developed at right angles to the main cordillera (q.v.).

Although most of the high Alps are in Switzerland, Mont Blanc, in France is the highest peak at 4,807 meters (15,863 feet). Other famous high Alps are the Matterhorn and Jungfrau.

ALTERATION Alteration is a chemical or weathering process that transforms rocks. Deeply buried rocks undergo alteration from both heat and pressure. This subaerial process results in metamorphosis and the class of rocks called metamorphic (q.v.). Weathering (q.v.) is alteration which occurs under atmospheric conditions.

ALTIPLANOS Between the ranges of the Andes are high valley floors or plains. In Chile and Bolivia these plains, over 3,000 meters (10,000 feet), are 'altiplanos' or high plains.

ALTITUDE Vertical distance from sea level upward is altitude. Any land is measured from the sea level datum (q.v.). Alexander Von Humboldt (1842) was the first to estimate average elevation or altitude for high mountains. Depressions on the Earth's surface are measured from sea level downward.

ALTOCUMULOUS Altocumulous clouds are high, very puffy, and gray with water vapor. They often bring thunder and hailstorms.

ALTOSTRATUS Altostratus clouds are blankets of gray or blue masses of water vapor at relatively high altitudes. They may bring rain or snow.

ALUMINA Aluminum oxide, alumina, can occur naturally as corundum. Alumina is a constituent of bauxite (q.v.), the major ore of aluminum.

ALUMINUM Aluminum is a silvery, metallic element that is never found alone. The metal is chemically active and has many uses, especially because of its light weight accompanied by strength. Its chief ore is bauxite (q.v.).

Aluminum in rocks resists corrosion because a transparent film of aluminum oxide forms on the surface. Aluminum is common in soils and in the regolith (q.v.).

ALUNITE Alunite is a hydrated sulfate of aluminum and potassium. It occurs in veins, in sedimentary rocks, and is disseminated in igneous rocks.

Vein and bedded deposits rarely contain great tonnages. In these deposits alunite results from feldspar alteration by volcanic sulfur emanations.

Exceptional alunite deposits in Utah contain 100 million tons of 20-30% alumina. Potash is produced from them. In Toffa, Italy, alunite has been a source of potash since the 15th Century.

ALVIN Alvin is a research submarine used in deep ocean exploration. One of the early modules succeeded in recovering an H-bomb lost in Spanish waters. Alvin's hull is of titanium.

AMARANTH Amaranth was a staple in Pre-Columbian America. It is a tall, leafy, grain with a red flower and black seeds. The plant ranged from Arizona to Argentina. Popped amaranth seeds, 'alegria', are still a favored sweet in Mexico. A coffee-like beverage is also brewed from the plant. 'Huatli', the Aztecs' amaranth grain, was used as tribute. The tumbleweed is of the Amaranth Family.

AMAZON BASIN The Amazon Basin lies between the Guiana and Brazilian Highlands in South America. The drainage area covers 5,712,000 square kilometers (2,284,000 square miles). The basin has been sinking since the Paleozoic (300 m y) and now slopes gently to the east. The Upper Basin flanks the Andes and has many lacustrine sediments.

Seasonally, the basin is 95% inundated. There is much lateral erosion from streams and tides. Undercut banks and extensive rockfalls erode 'Terra Firma' or firm ground.

Tributaries draining the basin include some of the world's largest rivers and most have great rapids. A huge fall-line encircles the basin. Flood areas, several times as wide as the Amazon River (q.v.) support a special forest, the 'Igapo'. Slopes and terraces support grasslands and gallery forest (q.v.). Plant speciation is enormous. In the northwest basin, Indians have discovered medicinal value in more than 1,300 plants.

Temperature in the basin does not vary greatly either seasonally or diurnally, ranging from 92 to 98° Fahrenheit.

AMAZON BORE The tidal bore entering the Amazon Estuary can reach a height of 7.6 meters (25 feet). It has been described as 'a waterfall' several kilometers across and 1.5 kilometers (1 mile) long moving upstream. It has been clocked at 21.5 kilometers (12 miles) an hour over a 500 kilometer (300 mile) distance. The roar of this wall of water can be heard for 25 kilometers (15 miles). The Brazilians call the bore 'pororoca'.

AMAZON DELTA The Amazon Delta is 270 kilometers (160 miles) across and still forming. A large part is beneath the sea. The force and impact of the silts are great. They color the sea for a great distance offshore. Mixing of seawater with fresh is slow. Freshwater is found on the sea surface very far from shore.

Delta coastal swamps are virtually impenetrable. Dense mangrove, palm thicket, and grasses all intertwine. This is the habitat of the American crocodile or 'cayman'.

AMAZON HYDROLOGIC CYCLE The Amazon is the wettest area on Earth. It holds 75% of the world's freshwater supply. The river discharges 20% of all river runoff.

Climate is tropical humid or wet. Iquitos, on the Upper Amazon receives an average 250 centimeters (103 inches) of rain a year. Nowhere on the Amazon are rainfall averages as high as in West Africa and Southeast Asia.

Some Amazon water is from atmospheric circulation but 88% is recycled moisture. Moisture returns to the Atmosphere through evapotranspiration almost as fast as it falls.

The climatic importance of this recycled moisture is great. When the vegetation is cut, local climate becomes drier as it has in Belem and Manaus. Deforestation can also jeopardize the Brazilian Cerrados (q.v.) to the south and contribute to further drying out of the Northeast.

AMAZON RAINFOREST The Amazon Rainforest covers 5% of the Earth's surface but has 75% of the world's timber resources. The tree canopy begins in the Andean foothills and stretches east thousands of kilometers. The forest extends from the Guiana Highlands in the north to the slopes of the Central Plateau of Brazil in the south. Mid-river, the forest narrows. It broadens again at the Delta.

Evapotranspiration (q.v.) from this vast forest profoundly affects world climate patterns. This is primarily because of its enormous moisture contribution. An immense quantity of oxygen is also produced by the forest and this is important to atmospheric balance of gases.

AMAZON RIVER The Amazon is both the longest and widest of the world's rivers. These statistics have only been recently confirmed. Its length depends upon which Andean source is considered principal. A major source of the Amazon is a glacier at 4,758 meters (15,700 feet) in the Andes. Its melt flows into Lake Ninococha, Peru. The drainage to the Pacific is blocked by very high mountains.

The Amazon is navigable for ocean-going vessels for 3,600 kilometers (2,000 miles). At Iquitos, 1,600 kilometers (1,000 miles upstream, the river is nearly 3.3 kilometers (2 miles) wide. The fall from Iquitos to the Atlantic is only 91 meters (300 feet).

Fluctuations in the main river due to floods and tides are often extreme. At Manaus, where special floating docks handle shipping, the range is from 7-13 meters (23-43 feet). See **AMAZON BORE**.

The annual discharge is 1,594 cubic kilometers (770 cubic miles) of water into the Atlantic. This is 20% of the world's freshwater budget. The Amazon drains 7 countries in addition to Brazil. They are Bolivia, Colombia, 3 Guianas, Peru, and Venezuela.

AMAZON TRIBUTARIES Amazon tributaries from the west, north, and south draining the entire basin. Of these, 21 are longer than 1,160 kilometers (700 miles) and some are up to 5,000 kilometers (3,000 miles). The greatest of all is the Madeira (q.v.).

The great Tocantins, Xingu, Tapajos, and Madeira rivers flow north to the Amazon from the Central Brazilian Plateau. The Jari, Trombetas, and Negro flow south from the Guiana Highlands.

The Urubamba-Ucayali System rises in the Andes southeast of Cuzco and flows by Macchu Picchu, the Inca archaeological site. It then flows through a 1,200 meter (4,000 foot) gorge to join the Maranon, the upper part of the main Amazon. The confluence of the Ucayali and Maranon is west of Iquitos, Peru.

Hundreds of rivers, many of them very large and important, feed the tributary system from the Andes. The Beni in Bolivia rises north of La Paz and feeds the Marmore which in turn is part of the Madeira System. The whole is a great water network.

The middle Amazon, known as the Solimoes, is joined below Manaus by Rio Negro. The Solimoes and the Negro merge very slowly. The different colored waters are visible for a great distance. With their merger, the river becomes the Lower Amazon to the sea. See **MADEIRA RIVER and RIO NEGRO**.

AMAZON WATERS The Amazon-Solimoes complex is referred to as 'whitewater'. It is really a clay-yellow color due to the sediment load from the Andes. Rio Negro, like all 'blackwater' rivers, carries a load of organic material from forest soils. The mixing of black and white waters occurs below Manaus. It is a prolonged mixing process which is readily discernible for kilometers.

The only truly clear waters flow over older eroded areas. The Tapajos and Xingu rivers from the Brazilian Highlands have a greenish cast to their transparent waters and they are the purest.

AMAZONITE Amazonite is a green variety of feldspar suitable for jewelry. Its use goes back many centuries. Brazilian Indians made earplugs, 'tembetas', from amazonite.

AMBER Amber is the fossilized resin or sticky sap from trees, particularly the conifer. Conifers were exceptionally abundant 30-40 million years ago.

The fossil resin material may contain the preserved organic remains of insects and plants. These have helped to date the amber.

New Jersey amber, found in clays, dates from 100 million years. It contains some perfectly preserved ants.

The Greek name for amber is 'elektron' because it has a charge when rubbed. The fossil has a range of colors but yellow and brown are the most common. Quality material is found in the Baltic Sea, near Kallingrad, USSR.

AMBIANCE The French word 'ambiance' refers to the environment around a body or organism. The term encompasses all physical and chemical effects.

AMERICAN CORDILLERA The mountain chains from Alaska to Tierra del Fuego form the American Cordillera. In North America, these are the Rockies, in Mexico and Central America the Sierras, and in South America the Andes.

The cordillera is the true 'El Dorado' of the New World. It contains 50% of the world's copper as well as a wealth of other minerals.

The Andes are mainly of andesitic rocks (q.v.). In the Northern Hemisphere the rocks are more varied. The mountains are intruded by many great batholiths (q.v.). Transverse volcanoes in Central America are also part of this cordillera system, which has been called the 'Spine of the Americas'.

AMETHYST Amethyst is a purple variety of quartz (q.v.). The color comes from inclusions of manganese oxide. The Greeks believed amethyst gave an immunity to drunkeness so wine was served in amethyst goblets.

The Germans considered amethyst a symbol of sovereignty and the most valued material was and is royal purple. In the Roman Catholic Church, amethyst is the symbol of peace and power. It is used in the Bishop's ring.

AMINO ACIDS Amino acids are chemical compounds containing the amine radical, NH-2. At least 8 amino acids are essential to nutrition. The alpha-amino acids are important constituents of protein.

AMMONIFICATION In the process of ammonification, nitrogen-bearing compounds are broken down, releasing ammonia.

AMMONIUM NITRATE When gaseous ammonia is introduced into a nitric acid solution, ammonium nitrate is formed. The generated heat evaporates any water that may have been present. The compound is used as fertilizer.

AMMONITE The ammonite is a fossil mollusk. There are about 7,500 species. The ammonite was abundant in Jurassic-Cretaceous seas. Nautilus found in Pacific waters today is a close relative.

In Saudi Arabia, there is an 'Ammonite Wall' forming a valley rim that has an extraordinary number of the fossils. Huge ammonite fossils have been found atop the Himalayas.

AMOEBA Unicellular amoeba is a Protozoan, the smallest of all known animals. It lives in water and ingests food and oxygen from it. The amoeba cell wall is so thin, water easily passes through it. Reproduction is by simple cell division.

Intestinal parasitic amoebas are endemic in many tropical and subtropical areas. Amoebic dysentery caused more deaths than enemy action in some South Pacific areas during World War II.

AMORPHOUS Minerals with randomly arranged atoms and molecules are amorphous. Usually they are formed by hardening of colloidal gels or lavas. Some examples are agate, obsidian, and opal.

AMPHIBOLE Amphibole is an anhydrous silicate of iron oxide, calcium, and magnesium. The Amphibole Group is close to the Pyroxene (q.v.). White to dark-green in color, the crystals may be acicular or blunt. Amphiboles are glassy or satiny and have a hardness of 5-6 on Moh's Scale (q.v.). They are common in igneous and metamorphic rocks.

AMPLITUDE Amplitude is the maximum value or strength of a wave. It also is the height of an ocean wave. In a sound wave, loudness reflects amplitude and brightness reflects amplitude in a light wave.

AMUR RIVER For much of its course, the Amur River forms the boundary between the USSR and China. Its course is southeast from the junction of the Shilka and Argun rivers for 2,960 kilometers (1,780 miles) to empty into Tatar Strait. In China, the river is known as Heilung-Kiang. In China, much of its passage is across a marshy plain.

At Khabarovsk, Siberia, 830 kilometers (500 miles) from the sea, the Amur turns north. The river mouth is ice-bound 5 months of the year. An effort is underway to rechannel the river to create a more southerly outlet.

AMYGDALE A vesicle or small, thin-walled cavity usually lined with crystalline material is an amygdale. Amygdales are formed by gas bubbles in lava. The name is from the Greek 'amygdala' or almond.

The crystal filling of an amygdale is usually of calcium, quartz, or zeolite. These minerals are sometimes stratified and indicate the original lava flow.

ANADROMOUS Some fish, such as the salmon, leave the sea to spawn in freshwater. Such fish are anadromous.

ANAEROBIC Environments in which organisms may live without atmosphere or oxygen are anaerobic. Some bacteria flourish in such an environment.

ANAK KRAKATOA 'Anak Krakatoa' is Indonesian for child of Krakatoa. A volcano broke the sea surface January 25, 1925 on the site of the Krakatoa's collapsed crater. The new volcano grew steadily and by 1970 it had reached 100 meters (330 feet).

ANASTOMOSING A braided river, one forming an intertwined network, is anastomosing. Delta areas and lower reaches of most great rivers are classic examples.

ANATEXIS Magma can form from pre-existing rocks engulfed in a magma chamber. Subjected to heat and pressure, rock is reworked or recombined. The 'new' rock is anatectic or resmelted.

Anatectic rocks are also termed 'palingenetic'. If the rock is only partly reworked it is a 'migmatite'. Migmatites are hybrids and often found in pegmatites (q.v.). Some granites are considered entirely anatectic.

Anatexis can also occur within the bottom sediments of a geosyncline when temperatures and pressures reach sufficient magnitude.

ANATOLIA In the ancient world, much of Turkey was in Anatolia, a region that once covered the Asia Minor Peninsula. It was known as the 'Ante-Chamber of Asia'.

ANAVILHANAS STATION The ecological station of Anavilhanas is on the Rio Negro in Brazil. It is in a stretch of the Amazon tributary where trees and shrubs are adapted to living in water for up to 10 months a year.

Black and clearwater rivers tend to lack nutrients so fish depend upon plants for food. This is the situation on this part of the Negro. The Indians have named the fish for the plants they eat.

Goulding stated that 75% of the 150 fish species sold in the Manaus markets depend on the 'Igapo' forest (q.v.) for survival. He estimates there are 700 fish species in Rio Negro.

ANCHOVY Anchovy, a small herring-like fish, made up to 15% of the world's catch until 1972. For years between 7 and 8 million ton of anchovies were fished off the Peruvian Coast. In these waters, a natural upwelling of water from the deeps allowed phyto- and zooplankton to flourish, providing food for large fish populations.

Upwellings (q.v.) depend upon a specific wind pattern. The winds in Peru were interrupted by El Nino (q.v.) events which became more frequent. Fish populations fell off tremendously. They were also greatly over-fished. The fisheries have not yet recovered.

ANCIENT BEACH PLACERS Valuable minerals are found in ancient beach placers. Deposits often are on elevated terraces which are remnants of ancient shores. Florida's Trail Ridge titanium deposits are a good example.

Deeply buried gold in South Africa and Brazil are ancient beach placers of Precambrian Age.

ANDEAN SALARS Salars, salt-encrusted playas containing brines, are numerous in the high Andes. The largest are in a million square kilometer (400,000 square mile) area extending from northern Chile and northwest Argentina to Bolivia. Freshwater Lake Titicaca bounds the northern end of the salar area.

The salar area is one of interior drainage with over 100 basins and 75 large salars. The largest is Salar Uyuni, Bolivia (q.v.).

ANDES MOUNTAINS The Andes are part of the American Cordillera (q.v.). This chain, 2nd highest in the world, is located on the western side of South America. Many peaks exceed 6,000 meters (20,000 feet). The Andean Divide exceeds 3,000 meters (10,000 feet) for 3,300 kilometers (2,000 miles).

The Andes flank the west coast with only a small coastal strip between the mountains and sea. From Ecuador to Tierra del Fuego, the mountains extend 6,400 kilometers (4,000 miles). The width ranges from 32-800 kilometers (20-500 miles). In the north the Andes split into 3 main arms between which are high valleys or 'altiplanos'.

The mountains are mainly of andesite (q.v.), a light-colored igneous rock. In the north a granitic batholith is exposed by erosion. The high mountains, even at the Equator, are glacier-capped.

The Andes are a storehouse of mineral wealth, of copper, tin, gold, and silver.

ANDESITE Andesite is a light-colored igneous rock that is fine-grained and crystalline. It ranges in color from gray-pink to red-brown, even purple. Andesite is intermediate between acidic and basic rocks, having a 60% silica content. Extruded from the volcanics of the Pacific Belt, it is considered a volcanic counterpart of diorite.

Andesite is composed of plagioclase, augite, hornblende, and biotite with a texture similar to that of rhyolite. The texture also may be porphyritic (q.v.) as it is in some Paleozoic examples. Most andesites, however, are Tertiary extrusives.

Dacite is a variety of andesite with small crystals of feldspar and quartz. The color may range from pale pink through gray to almost black. Felsite is of andesite, dacite, and rhyolite.

ANDESITE LINE The Andesite Line traces the line between the oceanic basalts of the Pacific Rim and the andesite-rhyolite rocks of the adjacent continent. It also marks a suture line between crustal plates.

ANDROMEDA Andromeda, a constellation in the Milky Way Galaxy (q.v.), is in the northern sky just south of Cassiopeia. Looking at this star through a telescope reveals the Andromeda Galaxy (q.v.).

ANDROMEDA GALAXY The Andromeda Galaxy is similar to the Milky Way Galaxy (q.v.). Andromeda is 2 million light-years from Earth and is spiral-shaped. It is the closest galaxy to the Milky Way and is made up of 150 billion stars.

ANEMOMETER An anemometer is an instrument used to measure wind speeds. It is equipped with cups on a rod. These fill with wind causing the rod to turn. The velocity of the turns is recorded on the dial.

ANEMONE Anemones are organisms that are known as 'flowers of the sea'. They belong to the Polyp Group. Anemones are anchored in place. They trap and sting their prey as it floats by. They are provided with tentacles for this purpose.

ANGARALAND According to Suess, a great continent existed north of the Tethys Sea (q.v.). The landmass is the nucleus of the Siberian Shield. Suess named it for a river in Siberia, the Angara.

According to theory, Asia was formed by the disappearance of Tethys and the linking of Angaraland with Gondwanaland (q.v.). Tethys (q.v.) once extended from Central America to Asia.

ANGEL FALLS The highest waterfall in the world is Angel Falls in southeastern Venezuela. It was discovered by the pilot and soldier of fortune, Jimmy Angel, in 1935. He was prospecting this part of the Guiana Highlands for gold.

The falls emerge from Anyatepui Massif which rises 2,500 meters (8,250 feet) above sea level. The total drop of the falls is 973 meters (3,212 feet). One drop alone is 802 meters (2,648 feet).

The base of the falls is 150 meters (495 feet) in elevation.

ANGIOSPERMS Angiosperms are the highest order of plants. Some 125,000 species have been identified. Angiosperms differ from earlier seed-bearing plants in that their seeds are protected by pods or ova.

Angiosperms were discovered in the Jurassic of Scotland but really show up in abundance in the Lower Cretaceous (125 m.y.). All true flowering plants and deciduous trees are angiosperms.

ANGLE OF REPOSE The limiting angle of any slope is the angle of repose. It is the angle at which unconsolidated material can maintain equilibrium. The angle of repose for dry sand is approximately 33°.

ANGSTROM Angstrom (Å) is a unit of measure for wavelengths of light. It is equal to 0.01 millionth of a centimeter (10^{-8} centimeters).

ANGULAR MOMENTUM Angular momentum is a vector perpendicular to the plane of rotation. Conservation of angular momentum causes the Earth to rotate and is responsible for generation of the jet streams.

ANHYDRITE The hydrous form of calcium sulfate is anhydrite. It is often found in evaporite deposits (q.v.) in bands, alternating with gypsum.

ANIMAL PHYLA The main divisions of the Animal Kingdom are Phyla. These are:

Protozoa	Single-celled animals (Amoeba, Flagellates)
Porifera	The sponges
Coelenterata	Coral, jelly-fish
Platyhelminthes	Flatworms
Nematoda	Round worms
Annelida	Segmented worms
Bryozoa	Moss animals
Arthropoda	Insects, spiders, trilobites
Mollusca	Snails, clams
Echinodermata	Crinoids, starfish
Chordata	Vertebrates, graptolites

ANION An anion is a negatively charged ion (q.v.). An atom or a compound will be the sum of its electrical charge. In an electrolytic solution, an anion will migrate to the positive pole or the anode.

ANKERITE When considerable iron replaces magnesium in dolomite, the mineral becomes ankerite. Ankerite is a constituent of some carbonatites (q.v.) and has helped to identify highly weathered examples.

ANNIHILATION Annihilation occurs in particle physics when a particle (electron) and an anti-particle (positron) meet. The total is converted to photons and the original particle disappears.

ANNUAL FLOOD Annual flood is the average of the highest flow over the years for a given river system. This is not necessarily flood-level since the highest flow may not over-top the banks. The number of years included in the statistic is between 30 and 50.

ANNUAL PLANT A plant reaching full reproduction in a year is an annual. The vegetative part of the plant dies in winter at the cold-limiting temperature of the individual plant. Regeneration is from a cold-resisting seed.

ANOMALY Any deviation from normal is an anomaly. Some anomalies have become very useful in exploration to define structures and ore bodies. Anomalies of gravity, magnetics, and seismicity are important.

ANORTHOSITE Anorthosite is a variety of gabbro (q.v.) primarily composed of coarse crystals of calcium plagioclase feldspar. It is high in aluminum content (25-30%). Magnetite and pyroxene are accessory minerals.

Anorthosite is a white to dull-gray igneous intrusive rock which resembles marble. There are major masses in the Adirondack Mountains that exceed 1,600 square kilometers (1,000 square miles). The aluminum reserves are estimated in billions of tons. Anorthosite has been worked for aluminum in Norway and Canada.

Some moon rocks, brought back by astronauts, are anorthosite.

ANTARCTIC CIRCLE The Antarctic Circle is a line parallel to the Equator at 66°30' South Latitude. It divides the South Temperate Climate Zone from the South Polar Zone. At the Circle, the Sun is above the horizon 24 hours a day in mid-summer, below 24 hours in mid-winter.

ANTARCTIC GLACIATION On the Antarctic Continent, glaciation began in the Paleocene (65-53 m.y.), well before its onset in Europe. In Antarctica there were no interglacial epochs during which the cover melted. Glaciation has continued with different levels of intensity throughout this time.

The Ice Sheet is up to 5 kilometers (3 miles) thick. Only the very highest peaks break through. These are called 'nunataks'. A number of glaciers of great magnitude emanate from the mountains. The Antarctic Coast is marked by a number of great ice shelves. See **ROSS ICE SHELF**.

ANTARCTICA Antarctica is the least known of the great continents. It is larger than Europe. Like Africa, it rides on a plate surrounded by active oceanic ridges. The continent is on a 4,000 meter (13,000 foot) platform. The tectonics are only partially understood.

The only active subduction zone is between Antarctica and South America. The Peninsula Mountains are an extension of the Andes. There is a subsurface island arc making the connection.

The South Pole is in the center of 13 million square kilometers (5.5 million square miles) of snow and ice. Temperatures on this ice pack can go to 100° below zero Fahrenheit.

One of the world's largest coal fields is found in Antarctica. This indicates that a warm climate prevailed over a long enough period in the past to produce the abundant organic material. See **OZONE HOLE**.

ANTECEDENT STREAM An antecedent stream is older than the current landscape, or relief. If a fault cuts across a stream without diverting it, the stream is considered antecedent to the fault.

The Columbia River is antecendent through Columbia Gorge. The Danube, cutting its way through the Transylvanian Alps, is antecedent. The Arun and Brahmaputra are antecedent through the Himalayas where the land has been uplifted. The streams kept pace in cutting their channels.

The Colorado is a good example of a river that is antecedent for only part of its long course. The river cut Grand Canyon while the Colorado Plateau was being uplifted.

ANTHRACITE Coal that is hard and dense is anthracite. Its carbon content may reach 90%. It burns slowly without giving off a great deal of ash and smoke.

Anthracite is found only in highly folded rocks where compression contributed to its formation. It is found along the eastern margin of the Appalachians where folding was extreme.

ANTI-MATTER Atomic particles that differ from ordinary ones by having an opposite charge are referred to as 'anti-matter'. Protons have positive charges, anti-protons have negative charges.

ANTICLINE The upward folding of the Earth's Crust results in an anticline. Beds are folded as a unit and the bedding planes diverge from the axis of the fold. An upthrusted group of beds will create a fold that is open at the bottom. The most recent sediments are on the outer flanks, older rocks are at the center. Anticlines often alternate with downfolds or synclines (q.v.).

Natural gas and petroleum in marine sediments migrated to the highest part of anticlinal folds. Hydrocarbons are less dense than seawater. If conditions are favorable for deposition, anticlines are excellent petroleum exploration targets. In fact, for many years the industry only concentrated on these targets.

An anticlinorum is an anticline of immense proportions. It is composed of many minor folds with independent axes. These axes are convexly curved about the major axis. The anticlinorum is a regional feature while the anticline (q.v.) is a local one.

ANTICYCLONE When an airmass has its zone of highest pressure at the center, it is an anticyclone. Airflow is away from the High, and is divergent. Wind blows clockwise away from the center in the Northern Hemisphere. High pressure airmasses move more slowly than low pressure ones or cyclones (q.v.). Highs bring clear skies and extremes of temperature.

Anticyclones have less subsidence on the east side of the oceans (west side of continents) between 25-30° of Latitude. This airmass configuration causes west coast dry climates.

ANTIMONY Antimony is one of the semi-metals, intermediate between true metals and nonmetals. The chief ore of antimony is stibnite, a sulfide. Silver-white antimony is hard and brittle. It is a strategic mineral (q.v.) used in bullets and batteries. It has some use as a fire retardant. Antimony can be alloyed and used in ceramics.

Antimony is often found in veins with gold. There are large deposits in China and Bolivia and important ones in Mexico.

China produces 80% of the world's supply of antimony. The United States consumes about 30% but only produces 10%. Total world reserves are estimated at 5.1 million metric tons (1989).

ANTIPODES 'Antipodes' is a British expression meaning the opposite ends of the Earth. Sometimes, it is applied to Australia. The poles are truly antipodal.

ANTS Ants are social insects and have a highly structured life cycle. They are especially abundant in tropical and subtropical zones. Brazil has been referred to as 'one great ant's nest' and it has been suggested that the ants are the real conquerors of the country.

Ants present problems in many areas. In South America, the Parasol, or leaf-cutter, excavates huge chambers in the soil. The colony will have hundreds of thousands of members. In the ant hill, workers will set out leaf cuttings on which they place fungal spores, to create fungus gardens to feed their larvae.

Where the ants are, crops are constantly being destroyed. A field can be completely consumed overnight. At the same time, ants aerate the soils.

Ants are also miners. One of the most productive diamond deposits (Soldier Hill Mine) was discovered when ants turned over the earth in search of nutrients.

APACHE TEARS Apache Tears are small obsidian pyroclasts (q.v.) with a tear-drop shape. They were first noted in Apache Territory in southwestern United States.

APATITE Apatite is the commonest phosphate mineral. White, green, or brown it has a hardness of 5 on Moh's scale (q.v.). It is a common constituent in all rock types (igneous, metamorphic, and sedimentary). Primary apatite as large beautiful crystals is sometimes found in pegmatites and in association with veins of wolframite (tungsten) and tin.

Bedded calcium fluorapatite is found in many evaporite deposits. For years the United States supplied 50% of the world's phosphate from sedimentary deposits in Florida. Today phosphates are being produced in many countries and from apatite sources in igneous and metamorphic rocks. The development of carbonatite (q.v.) sources has grown greatly in the last decade.

APHANITIC Aphanitic is a textural term for a dark, fine-grained rock. Constituents are microscopic and the rock tends to be dense.

APHELION The aphelion is that point in the orbit of a planet or comet when it is farthest from the Sun.

APHOTIC ZONE The oceanic zone where photosynthesis (q.v.) no longer can function due to the lack of light is the aphotic zone. Its depth is variable and can depend on such factors as water clarity, season, and time of day.

APLITE Aplite is a light-colored granitic rock with a fine-grained, sugary texture. It is composed almost entirely of quartz and feldspar. Aplite in small dikes is often associated with pegmatites. The mineral is resistant to weathering due to its grain size.

APOGEE The apogee is that point in the orbit of a satellite when it is farthest from the center of the Earth.

APOPHYSIS Apophysis is the penetration by an intrusive mass into an enclosing body. Many apophyses are mineral lenses.

APPALACHIAN MOUNTAINS The Appalachian System has many ranges and extends 6,600 kilometers (4,000 miles) north to south in eastern North America. They are very old mountains with origins in a Precambrian volcanic chain that developed in the ocean, west of the present east coast. Today's mountains are the result of uplift and erosion. They divide into belts: Piedmont, Precambrian Highlands, Appalachian Valley, Folded Mountains, and Allegheny Plateau.

In the west, drainage is dendritic (q.v.) creating a complex of hills and low mountains. In the east, structures were more complex although the pattern is still dendritic. Bedded sediments eroded to create the Ridge and Valley Province. Glaciation played a major role in the north.

APPALACHIAN OROGENY A Precambrian volcanic chain in the sea west of the present east coast formed the nucleus of the Appalachians. Remnants of the ancient range stretch from New England to Georgia. When the range emerged from the sea, erosion accelerated. Detritus was deposited around and between volcanoes and in the geosyncline (q.v.) to the west.

By the beginning of the Paleozoic Age (600 m.y.) the ancient range had been folded, faulted, and uplifted, and was again eroding. Volcanoes on the eastern fringe persisted. By the end of the Paleozoic Era (200 m.y.), the mountains were again subjected to major folding. Since that time, they have been eroding with only intermittent uplift.

The oldest part of the Appalachian System is now under the coastal plain and foothills. Radioactive dating shows it to be a billion years old, with younger intrusions.

APPALACHIAN PLATEAU The Appalachian Plateau is on the western side of the mountains. The Plateau extends from Maryland south and is very dissected. Its eastern fringe is the Cumberland Escarpment and the Allegheny Front. The northern scarp was dissected to create the Poconos and the Catskill Mountains.

APPALACHIAN VALLEY The Appalachian Valley extends with few breaks from Newfoundland, Canada to Alabama. Champlain, Shenandoah, and Tennessee are among its many valleys. Its sediments are mainly carbonates.

APRON An apron is created at the base of a desert mountain slope by coalescing alluvial fans (q.v.). Streams emerging from mountains drop their sediment loads due to an abrupt change in slope. Fans extend and merge to form the apron.

GULF OF AQABA The Gulf of Aqaba is an arm of the Red Sea providing an ocean port for Jordan. The Gulf, at the northern end of the Sea, forms a 'V' with the Gulf of Suez to enclose the Sinai Peninsula.

The trench filled by the Gulf of Aqaba, is an extension of the Great Rift System of East Africa.

AQUA REGIA Alchemists combined nitric acid and hydrochloric acid to form a 'Aqua Regia', royal water. It was used in the attempt to create gold and platinum from other minerals. See **ALCHEMY**.

AQUACULTURE Aquaculture is the cultivation of plants and animals in water. Many efforts to raise food in this manner are being conducted, some very ancient. Oysters grown for pearls are an example of aquaculture. See **HYDROPONICS**

For 2,000 years, South East Asians have been raising fish, mostly carp, in rice paddies. It makes up about 25% of all fish consumed in the region. Fish larvae must be collected and the paddies stocked. Because of pollution and overfishing, larvae are increasingly hard to find and the culture is threatened.

AQUAMARINE Aquamarine is a blue gem variety of beryl. It is found as an accessory mineral in pegmatites (q.v.). Only the most perfect crystals are gem quality. Color is imparted by iron inclusions.

AQUATIC Plants and animals that spend all or part of their life-cycles in water are aquatic.

AQUEDUCT An aqueduct is a channel for transporting water. It may be a canal or an enclosed pipeline. The Romans built some famous aqueducts to bring water over great distances. The arched structures built to support the channels are found throughout Europe. Some are still functioning.

In western Asia, water is transported in aqueducts which are true tunnels. These are constructed so that excessive evaporation is prevented.

AQUEOUS SOLUTION Any mixture with water whether in a gas, liquid, or solid state is an aqueous solution. The classic is champagne with all 3 states of matter: Alcohol, carbon dioxide, and sugar.

AQUIFER An aquifer is a source of water. In geology, the term is usually reserved for rock formations or unconsolidated sediments with sufficient storage capacity to allow them to be tapped for groundwater.

The water-bearing layer or stratum is of permeable rock, sand, or gravel underlain by a more impermeable material. The aquifer is also capped by an impermeable layer. Less permeable layers are of clay or shale. Within the aquifer water moves easily.

The source is where aquifer sediments outcrop and receive runoff water or come in contact with a spring line. The source is always higher and the aquifer dips, usually fairly gently, to a lower level where it may again crop out. Water is obtained at the outlet from a well which may have artesian (q.v.) flow.

AQUITARD An aquitard is an impervious rock formation retarding water flow. Usually the sediments are shales and clays.

ARABIAN DESERT The subtropical desert of the Arabian Peninsula is subject to the dry airmasses prevailing over western Asia. The Arabian is really 3 deserts: Naferd or Nefud in the north, Dahoma in mid-peninsula, and Rub' al Khali or 'Empty Quarter' in the south.

Of all the world's deserts, the Arabian has the most sand. In the interior, seif (q.v.) dunes have developed parallel to prevailing winds. These dunes have a 6:1 ratio of width to height. In Rub' al Khali, seifs have developed ranging up to 167 kilometers (100 miles) long. This 'Empty Quarter' is a 65,000 square kilometer (25,000 square mile) sand sea. It is the largest continuous sand mass in the world.

ARABIAN PENINSULA The Arabian Peninsula of western Asia is a mountainous desert from the Red Sea to the Persian Gulf, and from the Gulf of Aqaba to the Indian Ocean. Mountains rim the desert on 3 sides. The largest alluvial fans in the world are at the base of these mountains.

ARABIAN SHIELD The Arabian or the Arabian-Nubian Shield is an old stable platform split by the Great Rift of East Africa (q.v.). About 30% of the Arabian portion of the Shield is composed of granites. There have been many younger granitic intrusions with accompanying mineralization. The Saudi Arabians and the U.S. Geological Survey have been conducting many fruitful mineral explorations in the area.

ARABLE Land suitable for agriculture is arable. Only 7% of the Earth's surface is arable. Of this, about 26% is farmed. The elements making land suitable for agriculture are: Topography, soil texture, nutrient availability, seasonal temperatures, and precipitation.

Some factors may be altered increasing the arable land. Usually modifications are in the nature of energy subsidies and contour farming. These could increase arable lands by 30%.

ARAGONITE Aragonite, a calcium carbonate, is similar to calcite but has a different structure. Mother-of-Pearl in mollusk shells is aragonite. The name comes from Aragon, Spain.

Aragonite may form attractive twinned orthorhombic crystals. The needle-like crystals often are of a fibrous metamorphic calcium formed under high pressure.

ARAGUAIA RIVER The Araguaia-Tocantins is the 3rd largest tributary of the Amazon. Upper reaches of the Araguaia are in the boundary zone between rainforest and Sertão (q.v.) or semi-arid backland of Brazil.

The river rises in the Central Plateau. It flows north on a parallel course with Tocantins separated by the São Francisco Mountains until the confluence. The confluence is at Maraba in Para State at 7° South Latitude. Araguaia is even less muddy than Tocantins (q.v.), considered the purest of Amazon streams.

MOUNT ARARAT Mount Ararat figures in the biblical story of Noah. It is in Turkey, 75 kilometers (45 miles) from Ervan, capital of Soviet Armenia. The mountain is in the Caucasus Range. Ararat rises to 5,135 meters (16,946 feet). Its glacial conditions have hampered expeditions seeking the Ark of Noah.

ARAUCARIA The conifer genus, 'Araucaria', is one of the oldest and most primitive of living trees. It is related to trees that flourished 2 million years ago. The Monkey Puzzle Tree is of this genus.

The modern range of the Araucaria Pine is southern South America and Australia. In the Chilean Alps at about 30° South Latitude, it is dominant on western slopes between 910 and 1,364 meters (3,000 and 4,500 feet).

ARBAIN 'Arbain' is Arabic for 40, a symbolical number in the Middle East. It has mystical meanings to both Christians and Mohammedans.

The ancient caravan track from El Fasher, Sudan to Assuit, Egypt is the 'Arbain'. It takes approximately 40 days by camel.

ARBOREAL Animals that are tree dwellers or live in treetops are arboreal. The treetop is a popular habitat in the rainforest as the canopy is relatively closed and travel from treetop to treetop is easy.

American rainforests, particularly the Amazon, have the most arboreal species. Madagascar (Malagasy) has exceptional speciation. It also has some exotic specimens in its remnant forest.

ARCH Arching of sediments gave rise to positive areas when surrounding sediments subsided. Some developed in the Paleozoic (570-225 m y) and persist as areas of relatively old rocks encircled by younger ones. These areas were never highlands.

The Cincinnati Arch is a broad structure paralleling the Appalachian Geosyncline on the west. Arches have been described from other areas. One of the largest is the Ponta Grossa Arch in the Parana Basin of Brazil.

Arches are also landforms of semi-arid to arid regions. A stream cutting a canyon wall creates an alcove. Where the high area between streams is narrow, an arch is carved when eroded material falls out. Beautiful natural arches are found in Canyonlands of Utah, especially in Arches National Park.

Sea caves, collapsing from wave action, can result in some beautiful arches and columns.

ARCHAEN ERA The Archaen, also known as the Archaeozoic Era, is the oldest geological time division. With the Proterozoic, it makes up the Precambrian.

The Archaen began 4.6-5 billion years ago or even earlier. The Era is characterized by 2 major environments, the Greenstone Belts (q.v.) and vast granite-gneiss regions. In Australia zircon crystals have been dated 4.2 billion years and were older than the rocks that contained them.

The Archaen Era gave way to the Proterozoic (2.5 b.y.). See **PROTEROZOIC**.

ARCHIPELAGO Groups of related islands form a chain known as an archipelago. The islands are surface expressions of related volcanoes. Some important archipelagos are Indo-Malaysia, Antilles, and Fuego.

ARCTIC The region around the North Pole above 66°30' North Latitude is the Arctic. Most of the region is uninhabited cold desert.

Temperatures are extremely cold. In the Alaskan Arctic in winter, temperatures can hover at -20° Fahrenheit. Temperatures of -60° have been recorded at Verkhoyansk in Siberia. Arctic has become an adjective for extreme cold. Arctic climate is found above the timberline on high mountains, even at the Equator.

ARCTIC CIRCLE The Arctic Circle is a line drawn parallel to the Equator through 66°30' North Latitude. This line divides the North Polar Climate Zone from the Temperate Zone.

In the Polar Zone the Sun is above the horizon for 24 hours a day in mid-summer and below the horizon for 24 hours a day in mid-winter.

ARCTIC OCEAN The Arctic is part of the World Ocean. It lies between northern North America and northern Eurasia. In winter the ocean is covered in pack ice (q.v.) over most of its extent.

A sill separates the Arctic Ocean waters from the North Atlantic and bottom waters do not mix. The Bering Sea, which also has a sill, connects the Arctic Ocean with the Pacific Ocean.

ARCTIC SILL The Arctic Sill separates the Arctic Ocean from the Atlantic. It was discovered by Nansen on the voyage of the Research Vessel Fram'. The sill is a sediment build-up on the ocean floor. It is sufficiently high to prevent mixing of bottom ocean waters.

ARDEB The 'ardeb' is a Middle East capacity measure especially used for grains. Weights differ by grain, an ardeb of dura is 336 rotls, of simsim (sesame) 264 rotls. The 'rotl' also varies from 0.5-3.0 kilos (1 to 6 pounds). In Egypt, the ardeb is 5.619 United States bushels, equivalent to 198 liters.

ARENACEOUS Arenaceous rocks are composed of sandy particles. Sandstone, gritstone, and siltstone are examples.

ARETE The 'arete', French for fishbone, is an extremely rugged and narrow rock ridge formed by glacial plucking (q.v.). The ridge separates glaciated valleys.

ARGENTITE Argentite is a relatively rare but very valuable ore of silver. Its metal content may be as high as 87%. Usually encountered in veins with other silver ores, this sulfide has a hardness of 2 on Moh's Scale (q.v.) and a specific gravity of 7.3. Argentite has been mined at Potosi, Bolivia; Comstock Lode, Nevada; and in Mexico.

ARGILLACEOUS Rocks containing a high percentage of clay are called argillaceous. In this category are mudstones, argillites, shales, and flagstones. Flagstones are shales with a high sand content.

ARGILLITE Argillite is a hard shale, high in silica. It has been metamorphosed from clay. The cementing agency may be colloidal silica.

ARGON Argon is one of the noble (q.v.) or inert gases. These gases were considered rare but argon makes up 1% of the Atmosphere, a far greater abundance than carbon dioxide. Argon-40 captured in ancient rocks has allowed scientists to date these rocks using a potassium:argon ratio of the isotope (q.v.).

Argon is now used to fill some light bulbs. Argon crystals are being grown in laboratories to create crystal transistor shields.

ARID CLIMATE 'Arid' is limited to climates where rainfall is below what vegetation requires. Atmospheric precipitation is low and evaporation is greater. Endogenous streams are intermittent and lakes are confined to interior basins. Winds are highly erosive.

ARKOSE If particles in a conglomerate exceed 2 millimeters, the conglomerate (q.v.) is arkosic. Arkose is the weathered product of decomposing granite or gneiss in dry climates. It has not been transported far from its source rocks.

Arkosic sandstone has more feldspar particles than sandstone, more than 35%. The feldspar is mostly orthoclase and microcline. The texture is also different since it is made up of poorly sorted angular grains ranging from 0.02-2.0 millimeters.

ARRANGEMENTS Landforms are often arranged in patterns that are peculiar to their areas. The streams, valleys, and mountains of the Ridge and Valley Province of the Appalachians is an example.

Patterns give a region character and are clues to its geological history. They are important in forming soil types and vegetation.

ARRESTING FACTOR The 'arresting factor' in an ecosystem may be anything causing the vegetation to be stunted and maintained in a subclimax stage.

ARROYO The channelway of an intermittent stream in semi-arid Southwest United States is given the Spanish name 'arroyo'. Channels are characteristically steep-sided with flat floors.

ARSENIC Arsenic is a semi-metal and rarely found alone. Tin-white, arsenic tarnishes on the surface when exposed to air. Its luster is metallic and hardness is about 3.5. Rare crystals are rhombohedral with perfect basal cleavage.

Arsenic anomalies have led to the discovery of gold in what are known as arsenical gold belts. See **CARLIN GOLD BELT**.

Arsenic is produced as a smelting by-product. One of its major uses is the hardening of lead.

Gallium arsenide, with crystals in a 1:1 ratio, is used in micro-wave communications. Gallium arsenide is also used in lasers and for optical display systems.

ARTESIAN BASIN An artesian basin contains a large aquifer (q.v.) in its sediments. The aquifer is subject to compaction but is protected by an aquitard (q.v.), normally a clay or shale. Confined waters when released will rise higher than the local water table. Often, they flow to the surface.

The Great Artesian Basin in Australia contains huge quantities of water under artesian conditions. The famous oases of the northern Sahara are nourished from water tapped in artesian basins.

ARTESIAN WATER Underground water trapped under pressure in a permeable layer of sediments between 2 impermeable layers, is in an aquifer. If the water is tapped and flows freely without being pumped, it is artesian water. A fault intersecting such a layer will produce a spring. Artesian water is named for the Artois Region of France, where such flowing wells were common. See **PERMEABILITY**.

Artesian water is held in some sandstones in western United States. The water is taken up by the sandstone in the northern Great Plains. The formations dip to the east. They are tapped by many wells to serve farms. Few today are still free-flowing.

ARTHROPODA The phylum Arthropoda includes the joint-legged invertebrates with external skeletons. These fall into 3 classes:

- Trilobites (q.v.) - 3-lobed marine organisms. Abundant in the Paleozoic (570-225 m.y.). 60% of Cambrian (570-500 m.y.) marine fauna.
- Crustacea - Crabs, lobsters (marine and freshwater).
- Insecta - The first insects are detected from the Paleozoic.

ARTIKA In 1977, Artika, a Soviet atomic icebreaker, broke through to the North Pole. It took 13 days to make the voyage from Murmansk and back, 3,852 nautical miles (4,436 statute miles and 7,393 kilometers). Of this distance, 1,200 nautical miles were of solid ice.

The Soviets have a fleet of icebreakers. In 1988, when whales were entrapped in ice off northern Alaska, a Soviet icebreaker took part in the rescue operations

ASBESTOS A fibrous amphibole (q.v.), asbestos or chrysotile is a satiny mineral. When drawn into fibers, asbestos bends easily. It has been used for fireproofing.

Dust from asbestos is toxic to humans. Recently its use has been restricted in buildings in the United States. Asbestos from processing plants has caused pollution in the Great Lakes. Clean-up efforts are costly.

ASCENSION ISLAND   Ascension Island near the Equator is volcanic and related to the Mid-Atlantic Ridge (q.v.). The island served as a refueling point between Natal, Brazil and Dakar, Senegal during World War II. Today it is a satellite tracking station.

Ascension Island is special to the large green, sea turtles. The turtles, when grown, attain 90 kilograms (200 lbs) in size. They swim from South America annually to nest. It is a journey of 3,300 kilometers (2,000 miles). It takes the turtles 2 months at sea. The young turtles swim back to South America.

One zoologist relates the migration to continental shifts that allowed the jaguar and other animals of the Americas to prey on the turtles. The turtles turned to the sea for safety and happened on Ascension, which at that time was closer to the American continent. Over time the turtles built up the stamina to cross the widening sea.

ASEISMIC RIDGE   The Earth's spreading crust at a hot spot (q.v.) creates an aseismic ridge. At present such a ridge is forming at Tristan Volcano.

ASHFLOW TUFFS   When an explosive volcano ejects a gas cloud of up to 1,000° it will carry aloft ash particles. The base of the cloud will be dense with pyroclastic fragments. It will hug the ground and deposit its cargo in a flow. When cooled this ashflow forms a white or gray-green tuff due to their chlorite content.

The tuffs are rich in silica, a glass, that is so jagged it creates a difficult landscape to transit. When the tuffs are fused or welded they become ignimbrites (q.v.). Large deposits are found in Nevada and New Mexico.

Ashflow tuffs can be in great sheets. Such tuffs are common in Scotland, New South Wales, and in the Cascades of the Pacific Northwest.

ASIAN CORDILLERA   The Asian Cordillera includes the Caucasus Mountains between Europe and Asia, the Kara Kum, the Himalayas, and the Tien Shan. There are also many less well-known ranges. The Cordillera forms a continuous belt across Asia. It formed as the continents collided.

The highest continental mountain on Earth is Everest in the Himalayas (q.v.). It rises to 8,796 meters (29,028 feet).

ASPEN   The aspen tree is a poplar with flat leaves that are ruffled by the slightest wind. This deciduous tree is found in the Rockies between 2,400 and 2,800 meters (7,900 and 9,250 feet) of elevation.

In the Mackenzie Delta (q.v.) at the edge of the Beaufort Sea, above the Arctic Circle, the aspen grows at sea level.

ASPHALT The heaviest petroleum product, asphalt, hardens as it cools. Asphalt may be found as a hard black mineral. It is mined in blocks or in a more fluid form. Its principal use is as a paving additive.

Asphalt was used by the Babylonians as a cement. Nebuchadnezzar's workmen used it on the great wall around Babylon. The wall supported the famous Hanging Gardens, 1 of the 7 'Wonders of the Ancient World'.

ASSAY An assay is a chemical and physical test to determine the amount of metal in an ore, For gold, a fire assay is used. This is virtually a small smelter operation.

ASSIMILATION Foreign material may be incorporated into a magma (q.v.). It is blended and assimilated to become an integral part of the magma.

ASSOCIATION Association is the characteristic assemblage of plants found in a particular uniform environment. The association, an ecological unit, is dominated by one or more species.

ASTEROID Between the orbits of Mars and Jupiter there are millions of chunks of orbiting rock material smaller in size than planets. These masses are asteroids. They are thought to have developed from the same gaseous clouds from which planets formed.

Asteroids are of varying sizes and orbits and they may collide creating smaller bodies. These have a different orbit. When asteroids cross planetary orbits, they are considered meteorites (q.v.).

Free-swimming, star-shaped echinoderms (q.v.) are asteroids.

ASTHENOSPHERE The plastic layer below the Earth's Crust is the Asthenosphere. It is the Upper Mantle and extends to a depth of 250 kilometers (150 miles). It is a region of inferred convective activity and such mass flows relate to isostatic adjustments. See **ISOSTASY**.

ASTROLABE The astrolabe is an instrument used to measure the altitude of stars and other heavenly bodies.

ASTRONOMY Astronomy is devoted to the study of the Cosmos, its energy, objects, and events. Mapping and identifying stars in our own and neighboring galaxies takes a great deal of dedication on the part of astronomers.

ASWAN DAM A dam to control the Nile's flow is located in the Aswan area of Egypt. A new High Dam, replacing an earlier one, holds back Nile water in a 270 kilometer (162 mile) long reservoir, Lake Nasser. The dam is 245 meters (810 feet) high and the wall is 3.2 kilometers wide (2 miles) wide. With the dam an additional 7,500 square kilometers (3,000 square miles) of desert was brought under cultivation.

Changes in agricultural practices have created problems. Nile silts are deposited behind the dams and weirs rather than in the floodplain and delta, a process begun with the first dams on the Nile and made more evident with Aswan.

Since the advent of the Nile dams, fertilizers have had to be used increasingly and crop prices rose forcing out marginal producers. Many new hectares have been added to the farmland but it is costly to maintain high production.

Irrigation canals have furthered disease, especially malaria and bilharzia. Canals have increased with the new dam and the problem has been compounded. Water losses from evaporation in irrigation ditches and canals increase salinity of the remaining water with deleterious effect on the soils.

Evaporation from Lake Nasser is a major problem. Losses were anticipated from the high temperatures prevailing in the area but the dessicating effect of high-velocity winds over the lake was not taken into consideration. 15 billion cubic meters of water are lost each year. Water is also lost to the porous Nubian Sandstone along the lake's western shore.

The Nile Delta has been altered in its growth. On its seaward side, the balance of nutrients reaching the sea has been altered and adversely affects fisheries in the Eastern Mediterranean.

The Toshka Canal project upstream from Aswan is an attempt to link Lake Nasser to the Toshka Depression. The waters could sink through the floor of the 40 kilometer (24 mile) wide valley, where it can leach the evaporites of salts and contaminate the underlying Nubian Aquifer which serves New Valley.

Aswan, in the construction phase caused considerable disruption to the Nubian populations of both Egypt and Sudan. Relocation of the entire population was necessary. It split the Nubian Nation.

Part of the population moved to the Blue Nile area in Sudan, the rest were scattered in Egypt. The Pharaohs through centuries tried to dismember Nubia. Ironically, modern technology succeeded where the Pharaohs had failed.

ATACAMA DESERT Atacama Desert along the west coast of South America for 3,200 kilometers (2,000 miles) straddles the border between Peru and Chile. Atacama, one of the dryest deserts on Earth, is long and narrow. At its widest, it is 320 kilometers (200 miles).

Annual precipitation is less than 1.25 centimeters (0.5 inches). Much of the desert only gets 2.54 centimeters (1 inch) over 7 years, and some parts receive none. One station reported no rain in more than 100 years. This is 'absolute desert'.

The Humboldt Current (q.v.) offshore creates an inversion (q.v.) layer for 6 months with cloudy, gray skies, and fog. The fog is the only moisture the area receives with the exception of a few streams from the Andes which cross the desert.

The United Nations is attempting to reforest a portion of Atacama with 'fog forest' trees. Once the forest takes hold it can become somewhat self-sustaining through evapotranspiration (q.v.).

ATLANTIC/GULF COAST PLAIN The plain fringing the eastern and southern United States emerged only a few million years ago. The sediments are from the Appalachians (q.v.). These mountains were eroding for over 100 million years and the sediments deposited overlie a sunken piedmont (q.v.). In Georgia, sediments are up to 4,500 meters (15,000 feet) thick.

The Gulf of Mexico has been the dumping ground for the Mississippi, Rio Grande, Chatahoochee, Appalachicola, and other rivers. Louisiana is totally formed from accumulated sediments from the Mississippi System.

ATLANTIC HOT SPOTS Hot spots (q.v.) in the World Ocean have been increasingly studied. In 1985, Atlantic hot spots were discovered with thick deposits of sulfides of copper, iron, and zinc. These were found to support a biota with bacteria at the base of the food chain. The deposits are described as being as large as the Houston Astrodome.

The sulfide mounds are located 3,000 kilometers (1800 miles east of Miami. The Alvin (q.v.) crew described 'smoking geysers' of different temperatures which related to different minerals and which were different colors. Blue (400° Fahrenheit) geysers were of calcium sulfate and black (600°) with iron pyrite. Boiling was suppressed by the great depth. The deposits are of copper, zinc, silver, and gold.

ATLANTIC OCEAN The Atlantic, a part of the World Ocean, separates the Eastern and Western Hemispheres. It extends into the Arctic and reaches the Antarctic. The average depth is 3,940 meters (13,000 feet). It is this shallow due to the extent of the continental shelves.

Relatively young, Ewing estimated its age as no older than 100 million years. No older fossils have been discovered.

There are 3 major seas in the Atlantic. These are the Caribbean, the Mediterranean, and the Baltic. The main contributors of freshwater are the Amazon and Zaire (Congo) rivers. Together, these account for 25% of all the freshwater runoff in the world.

ATLANTIC TRENCHES In the Atlantic, there are 2 marginal trenches. One is north of Puerto Rico in the volcanic belt of the Caribbean. The other is the Romanche Trench off West Africa. The average depth of these trenches is 8,000 meters (27,000 feet).

ATLANTIS The mythical lost continent, Atlantis, has been related to the Island of Crete in the Mediterranean Sea. Another Minoan Island was destroyed by Santorini Volcano and it appears to fit the legend as well. See **SANTORINI**.

ATLANTIS I 'Atlantis I', a Woods Hole Oceanographic Institute research vessel, made a number of discovery voyages, especially in the Atlantic. In 1949, the Lamont crew discovered the Mid-Atlantic Rift (q.v.).

During I.G.Y. (International Geophysical Year) the crew determined that the floor of the Atlantic was of igneous rock.

ATLANTIS II Research Vessel 'Atlantis II' investigated the 'funny water' of the Red Sea in 1963. At 1,800 meters (6,000 feet) of depth, the crew encountered 135° Celsius water with a salinity 10 times that of normal. The water was also extremely high in metal ions.

The crew determined that there are 3 distinct pools and that overlying water did not mix with pool waters. The largest pool is 11 x 5 kilometers (7 x 3 miles) across. It is called Atlantis II Deep. These pools may be in calderas (q.v.).

ATLAS MOUNTAINS The Atlas Mountains in northwest Africa reach 4,240 meters (14,000 feet) and are snow-capped on the north slopes. The Sahara Desert begins on the southern flank. The Atlas ranges form a wall between the desert and the Mediterranean Sea.

ATMOSPHERE A gaseous envelope surrounds Planet Earth creating our Atmosphere. It is composed of 78% nitrogen, 21% oxygen, and small amounts of other elements. The Atmosphere provides a shield for the Earth from electromagnetic and particle radiation. There are windows in it but most ultra-violet photons (q.v.) are absorbed.

The density of the Atmosphere 100 kilometers (60 miles) from the Earth's surface is only l/millionth that at sea level. 90% of the air is in the Troposphere, a 16.5 kilometer (10 mile) thick layer above the Equator and 8.3 kilometers (5 miles) thick over the Poles. The Stratosphere, the layer above the Troposphere, is dry and the density is weak.

A warmer layer with the Stratosphere is the Ozone Layer (q.v.). Above the Stratosphere, is a Thermosphere in which is contained the Ionosphere (q.v.). The Thermosphere is capped by the Exosphere.

In the Troposphere, temperatures drop with altitude. They rise again beginning at an altitude of 48 kilometers (30 miles) at the Mesopause in the Mesosphere. Mesopause temperature is -93° Celcius (-135° Fahrenheit). Orbiting masses do not warm up, however, as the air is too thin.

ATMOSPHERIC PRESSURE Standard atmospheric pressure is 760 millimeters (29.921 inches) of mercury at sea level. This is a pressure of 1.0133×10^6 dynes per square centimeter or 1,013.3 millibars.

There are 14.7 pounds per square inch (psi) or 1 atmosphere of pressure at sea level and only 5.5 pounds atop Mount Everest.

ATOLL An atoll is a circular coral reef enclosing a lagoon. The lagoon maintains a connection with the sea by means of a channel. Many reefs enclose volcanic islands that have undergone subsidence or are subsiding.

The reef is made up of skeletons of marine organisms. Coral grows on the rim and builds upward as organisms die and decompose. The reef grows as it subsides. See **REEF**.

ATOM The fundamental particle of matter that cannot be subdivided by chemical means is the atom. About 1 billionth of it is solid mass and most of this is nucleus. A single drop of water contains billions of atoms of hydrogen and oxygen.

The atom has a nucleus with electrons in motion around it. The nucleus has positively charged protons and particles with no charge. These are neutrons. Protons and neutrons have about the same mass.

The number of protons impart special characteristics to the atom. Each element has a definite number affecting among other things its mass. The number of protons of an atom gives it its atomic number. For hydrogen, the number is 1; for helium, 2.

The positive charge of the nucleus must be balanced by an equal negative charge from electrons. An electron's mass is 1/2,000th that of a proton. Every atom has an average weight. This weight is given a number equal to the total of protons and neutrons. The scale has been set around the carbon atom. The commonest isotope (q.v.) of carbon has been given an atomic weight of 12. The unit on the scale is 1/12th the weight of carbon-12, or the mass of 1 proton or 1 neutron. This is a relative weight.

ATTRITION Attrition is wearing-away in size and the smoothing of angularity by abrasion (q.v.). It is a slow process which removes particles bit by bit.

AUGEN Local stresses from faulting and shearing can result in cataclastic rocks (q.v.). Since all rocks do not resist stress in the same way, lenses of more resistant ones are found in banded or layered material. Some rocks are so lenticular the German word 'Augen' for eye is used. Banded gneisses (q.v.) often contain such resistant lenses and are 'augen-gneiss'.

AUGITE One of the most abundant minerals in basaltic lavas is augite. It is a ferromagnesium mineral of the Pyroxene Group (q.v.). It is also common in other igneous rocks and can be found in marbles.

Augite is very dark and greenish-black. It has short crystal prisms and imperfectly developed pyramids. It differs from other silicates in its aluminum content.

AULACOGEN An aulacogen is the remnant arm of a 3-armed rift system or a triple-junction fault. Trenches related to fold mountains on the Russian and Siberian Platforms are such remnants. They were inland rifts of a new coast that was later blocked by mountain chains.

The Soviet mountains were recognized by Shatsky as having accompanied continental collisions. These aulocogens date from the Paleozoic (225-500 m.y.). A similar structure dating 2 billion years is found in Canada east of Great Slave Lake (Athapuscow Aulacogen). South of the Oachitas is another such remnant of major continental shifting.

AURIFEROUS A placer or lode rock that is gold-bearing is auriferous.

AURORAE Aurorae are streams of charged particles that enter the Earth's Magnetic Field through windows (q.v.) between 65-70° of latitude. In the Northern Hemisphere, their reflection is seen as the Northern Lights. These lights appear on 2 out of 3 nights. On rare occasions, they may be seen at lower latitudes.

The light waves are particle streams which are emitted from the Sun and related to solar flare (q.v.) activity. The rays react with the Earth's Magnetic Field 75-1,000 kilometers (50-600 miles) up in the Atmosphere.

AUSTRALIA The island continent of Australia encompasses 7,419,353 square kilometers (2,967,741 square miles) of territory. It is a 'shadeless land' with relatively few forests.

Australia contains the 2nd largest desert in the world. It covers 1/3 of the continent, blanketing the interior plains. The desert conditions are due to rain shadow effects, latitude, and distance from the sea. The region is extremely dry and windy. In one drought, a billion tons of soil was eroded and transported widely by the winds.

In gross terms Australia is relatively flat-lying and generally smooth-surfaced, the result of peneplanation (q.v.). The major Australian landforms:

- Interior or Central Basin - Desert of low relief.
- West Plateau- Series of tablelands on the Australian Shield.
- Eastern Highlands - A mini-cordillera of moderate elevation.
- Coastal Plain - A thin strip flanking the Eastern Highland and tropical vegetation on the Timor Sea Coast.
- Great Barrier Reef (q.v.) - Off northeast Queensland.

Australian pastures are largely served by deep bores (q.v.). There are few permanent streams.

Great mineral reserves have been discovered on the continent. Among them gold, iron ore, nickel, and uranium.

AUSTRALOPITHECUS   Australopithecus is a species of Hominid which has become extinct. Fossils were unearthed in South Africa in 1925. The indications are of teeth similar to humans but with a smaller brain. The advanced Hominid lived about 1 million years ago.

AVALANCHE   An avalanche is a landslide moving great masses of snow or ice downslope. It may also contain earth and rock from the slopes or precipices. Snow melting and refreezing increases the pack.

When the snowmass becomes heavy enough, it begins to move, slowly at first, then accelerating. Rock and mud will also be moved by avalanches. Snow and sediment has been sufficient to engulf villages in the Alps and elsewhere.

Different kinds of avalanches have been classified in Alpine studies. They fall into 3 general classes: Rolling and sliding; pure or completely airborne; and common, which is intermediate.

The greatest recorded avalanche occurred in Peru in 1962 from ice-capped Huascaran, South America's 2nd highest mountain. The avalanche began at 6,300 meters (21,000 feet) and ended in the valley at 2,400 meters (8,000 feet) covering a distance of 16 kilometers (10 miles). It was clocked at 15 minutes.

The icemass contained 2.5-3 million cubic meters (3.27-3.9 million cubic yards) of material. It pushed a wall 55 meters (180 feet) high.

Deforestation (q.v.) of mountain slopes has increased avalanche danger in many parts of the world. Slopes around Urserental Valley in the Alps were once covered by dense forest. By 1870, the forest was gone and the valley became famous for its avalanches.

AVICENNA   Persian writings on mountain building, erosion, and deposition are dated from 1021-1023 A.D. They have been attributed to Avicenna (Ibn Sina), an Arab physician, who lived from 980-1037 A.D.

AVROGADRO'S LAW   Count Amadeo Avrogadro determined that equal volumes of different gases contain the same number of molecules when held at the same temperature and pressure.

AYERS ROCK   The Australian symbol, Ayers Rock, is a monadnock (q.v.). It is in the Central Australian Desert 402 kilometers (250 miles) south of Alice Springs. Dome-shaped it stands 250 meters (1,143 feet) high and is 7 kilometers (4 miles) long.

Ayers Rock is considered the largest monolith in the world, although not monolithic. It is composed of bedded sediments that are primarily arkosic (q.v.) sandstones. The monument was transferred back to the Aborigines, who regard it as a holy place. They have leased it back to the Government for tourism.

AZIMUTH   The angle between a meridian and a great circle is the azimuth. It is expressed in degrees on the horizon, clockwise from north. To establish the meridian for an azimuth reading, it is necessary to make an astronomical observation. Mariners express bearings in degrees of azimuth.

AZONAL SOIL   There are 3 great orders of soils:

- Zonal - well developed and mature.
- Intra-zonal - well developed, local conditioned. Immature.
- Azonal - No development of soil profile. Recent alluvium.

THE AZORES   The Azores are 9 small volcanic islands in the North Atlantic Ocean belonging to Portugal. They served as a refueling station during World War II. Subsequently trans-Atlantic flights to Europe used the base until longer range aircraft came into use. Today the islands are a favorite vacation spot for Europeans.

The Azores are habitable to some extent because a water supply is provided by streams and valley hot springs. Like other islands in the Atlantic, the Azores are exposed summits of volcanoes. They are over a hot spot (q.v.) and not a spreading zone.

In the Atlantic offshore of the islands, Cape St. Vincent Ridge and the Gloria Fault were discovered in 1971. The fault is 330 kilometers (200 miles) long and 300 meters (1,000 feet) deep in the ocean floor.

SEA OF AZOV   The Sea of Azov is really a bay in the Black Sea. This sea goes inland between the Caucasus and Crimean Mountains. It is shallow but the Russians keep it navigable to Rostov and the coal port of Mariupol by dredging channels in the sea floor.

AZURITE   The copper mineral azurite is associated with malachite (q.v.). Azurite is a copper carbonate with a hardness of 3.5-4 and a specific gravity of 3.77. Its luster is vitreous. Long blue crystals in prisms are responsible for its name.

Azurite often occurs in a more granular or earthy form and is light blue in color. Azurite is 55% copper but since it is not common, it is not considered a major ore.

B

BABA GURGER The site of the first major oil strike in Iraq. was at Baba Gurger. The flow was so copious, it took 9 days to set the Christmas Tree (well-head valve). Reservoirs had to be built to protect the Tigris River from the flowing oil. The strike was only 5 miles from the 'Eternal Fires of Babylon', mentioned in the Bible.

BACKDEEP The deep on the concave side of an island arc (q.v.) is the backdeep.

BACKGROUND RADIATION Low-level background radiation is always present. Its source is the Cosmos and the Earth itself. Gamma or X-Rays result from radioactive decay of unstable elements like potassium, thorium, and uranium. These are found in rocks and minerals nearly everywhere.

Background radiation differs in various parts of the world depending upon latitude, elevation, and rock assemblages. Polar regions receive more cosmic radiation than lower latitudes. Radiation is greater at higher elevations than at sea level. Older exposed formations and igneous rocks are more likely to emit radiation than are more recent sediments.

There are locations with levels currently considered unsafe. Nearness to the surface of radioactive minerals affects greatly the amount of detectable background. Levels 10 times greater than 'safe' are found in Brazil, Canada, Congo, India, West Africa, South Africa, and the USSR. All are shield (q.v.) areas.

People living in these areas do not appear to have special health problems associated with radioactivity, nor do they manifest obvious genetic ill-effects. Radioactivity is accepted as a cause of sterility but some of these locations have very high population growth rates. See **RADON**.

BACKSHORE The portion of the beach above the high tide line is the backshore. Often the backshore forms a berm (q.v.).

BACKSLOPE The backslope is the gently-sloping side of a ridge. On a dune it is the leeward side.

BACKWASTING The weathering process of backwasting is one of valley slope recession. Streams extend erosion headward by plucking off the slopes.

BACKWATER A backwater is made up of interconnecting streams or lagoons. The lagoons are separated from the sea by narrow land barriers. There are occasional openings to the sea through which tides may run.

BACTERIA   Bacteria are microscopic plant-life. They may be free-living or parasitic (q.v.). Some are pathogenic (disease producing). Bacteria have a single-celled or non-cellular structure. Their life-form is often colonial. As a rule, they do not possess a nucleus.

Bacteria are important decomposition agents. They contribute to both the life- and chemical cycles. See **NITROGEN CYCLE**.

BADDELEYITE   A major oxide ore of zirconium is baddeleyite. The Pocos de Caldas Plateau in Minas Gerais, Brazil, has been an important source. The deposits are illuvial (q.v.) placers, or accumulated elluvial (q.v.) sediments.

BADLANDS   Semi-arid terrain with deep gully development are called badlands. Most interfluves have collapsed making the land difficult to cross.

Badlands have a stark beauty which makes them a tourist attraction in the Dakotas and in the Colorado Desert of California.

BAGAGEIRA   Bean-like pebbles of titanium, or 'bagageira', are common indicator minerals in Brazilian diamond fields. The blue-gray stones are found in streams draining the Diamond District of Minas Gerais, and especially in the vicinity of the Bagagem River.

BAHIA   The Spanish name for a large bay is 'bahia'. It is used a great deal in Florida and California.

Carbonados or industrial diamonds have been given the trade name 'Bahia' since many come from that Brazilian state.

BAHRAIN   Oil-rich Bahrein is an archipelago (q.v.) in the Persian Gulf. Surface sediments are of limestones and sand dunes.

LAKE BAIKAL   Lake Baikal, Siberia, is the deepest lake in the world reaching 800 meters (2,640 feet) below sea level. It is 700 kilometers (420 miles) long and 75 kilometers (45 miles) wide. The lake is in a huge graben (q.v.) produced by a Jurassic or Early Tertiary (150-50 m.y.) rift. The portion of the lake above sea level has an outlet through the Angara River to the Yenesei Drainage System. Inflow is from the Upper Angara, Selenga, and Barguzin Rivers. Baikal is ice-bound from January to May.

BAIKAL DEPRESSION   The Siberian Baikal Depression is located at the junction of the Sayan and Yablonovy Mountains. The graben is a great rift valley, a continuation of the Himalayan Suture. Lake Baikal (q.v.) is on the floor of the rift.

BAJA CALIFORNIA   Lower or Baja California, Mexico, is the peninsula portion of California. It is surrounded by waters of the Pacific and Gulf of California, or Sea of Cortez. The peninsula was part of mainland Mexico about 25 million years ago, before it rifted away. The Cape Mountains are part of the Rockies. They form a spine for the peninsula.

Climate is semi-arid to arid with Vizcaino Desert in the south. This desert was almost impassable until recently. There is now a modern highway from Tijuana to La Paz at the southern tip.

BAJADA A series of coalescing alluvial fans deposited by intermittent streams forms a 'bajada' in basins of interior drainage. The name comes from the Spanish for a dip-slope. Sediments dropped at the break-in-slope have combined to form an aggradational plain.

Alluvial fans merge at their lower ends into gently sloping deposits of sandy gravels. These gravels may attain great thickness, (hundreds of feet) and form an apron along the mountain front.

The confluence of alluvial fans may contain a bajada placer of heavy minerals. These are mainly detrital deposits that fill gulches and low places on the slopes. The bajada placer has natural riffles catching minerals when sheet-flooding occurs. Many desert gold placers are of this type.

BAKU Baku, on the shores of the Caspian Sea, was the first Soviet oil field. In the 19th century, it was 'awash with oil' and caviar-producing sturgeon were threatened. Other Apsheron Peninsula fields soon joined Baku. The fields are still producing gas and oil.

BALL CLAY Granite can decompose to form ball clay. It is similar to kaolin (q.v.) in chemical composition. Ball clay is workable, but is excessively sticky and has many impurities. It is used in bonding china. Another name for ball clay is pipe clay.

BALL LIGHTNING Balls of bright flame skipping over the Earth's surface and associated with electrical storms are energized plasma (q.v.). Ball lightning is relatively common where iron is present in large amounts in surface rocks. The phenomenon is common over banded iron formations in Brazil. It is much reported from the Canadian Shield.

BALTIC SEA The Baltic is almost an inland sea. In northern Europe, it washes the shores of the USSR, Poland, and Finland. Its coastline is rising 1 meter (3 feet) per year, presumably from glacial rebound.

BALTIC SHIELD The stable land surface of the Baltic Shield is a remnant of ancient Fennoscandia (q.v.). The Scandinavian Peninsula, Finland, and the Kola Peninsula (q.v.) in the USSR are on this shield.

BAMBOO Bamboo, the largest of the grasses, is of great economic importance in the Orient. It grows in clumps and some reach 60 meters (200 feet) tall. In tropical Asia and America there are about 200 different species.

Small, young shoots of some bamboo varieties are edible. The pulp is used for paper and the wood for furniture.

Since grasses were widespread in the Miocene (20 m.y.) it is assumed bamboo developed earlier in the Tertiary. Higher Mid-Holocene (q.v.) temperatures allowed bamboo groves in Northern China to flourish. The shoots are a favorite food of the Giant Panda.

BANANAL ISLAND The largest river island in the world is Bananal. It is located in the Araguaia River (q.v.) in Central Brazil. Bananal is homeland to the Chavante Indians, who became noted for shooting down aircraft with spears (1940's). The Araguaia River joins the Tocantins to form a great tributary emptying into the Amazon.

BAND THEORY Band Theory in quantum physics explains to some extent the nature of conductors, insulators, and semiconductors.

It is theorized that electrons are in different orbital shells with different energy levels. There are insufficient electrons to fill the available energy levels and the number of energy levels multiplies when atoms join to become molecules. The number of energy levels is the sum of those in all the atoms. Semiconductors are defined as 2-banded with 1 full energy level and 1 empty. See **SEMICONDUCTORS**.

BANK High ground flanking a stream or river is a bank. Right and left banks are defined by the flow from source to sea. A bank is usually above the high water line. Floods over-reach the banks.

A submerged elevation on the sea floor is a bank. Grand Banks off Newfoundland, Canada are famous as fishing grounds.

BANYAN The Banyan (Ficus bengalensis) is one of the greatest shade trees in the world. Shrines are often set up under them in India. Legend has it that one tree sheltered an army of 10,000. The Emperor Asoka had hundreds planted in the Ganges Delta 2,000 years ago.

The banyon seed germinates in a palm or other tree. Rope-like shoots reach the ground and take root. Each tendril thickens to become a buttress up to 6 meters (20 feet) in diameter. An individual tree resembles a miniature forest. Its canopy is formed of branches with heart-shaped leaves. The banyan canopy (q.v.) is extraordinarily compact.

BAOBAB Remarkably well-buttressed by its multiple root-trunks, water-loving baobab (Adansonia digitata) is found in the African Savanna. It has very small leaves for its size. The tree has a large trunk giving it a 'pot-bellied look'. Some are 3 meters (10 feet) in girth. These trees can live a 1,000 years.

Baobab has extraordinary importance for savanna dwellers for its water storage. In recent times, desperate searches for fuelwood have resulted in destruction of baobabs with the resultant loss of a water source.

The baobab is said to have been the tree that so angered God, He planted it upside-down. Its soft trunk provides a home for many birds and for the Bush Baby. Bats are the pollinizing agents.

BAR A levee is created by longshore currents transporting sediments. They become a bar when high enough to break the water's surface. Off-shore bars are well-developed along the Atlantic and Gulf coasts of the United States.

A bar is joined to the mainland when the intervening water is filled with sediment.

Bars develop in stream channels wherever sediment is dropped.

In meteorology, a bar is a unit of pressure. It equals 1 million dynes per centimeter^2. On the mercury barometer, zero is set at 750.076 millimeters (29.5306 inches) of mercury at 0° Celsius (32° Fahrenheit).

BARCHAN Traveling, crescent-shaped dunes are barchans. On the Great Erg of the Sahara, barchans reach 150 meters (500 feet) due to winds and available sand. Dunes form where sand is limited but the wind direction must be constant. Horns or points are always away from the wind. Dunes near Moses Lake, Washington, are barchans.

BARITE Barite is an ore of barium that occurs primarily as veinlets in sedimentary rocks. Petrified barite roses or rosettes are found in desert areas. In carbonatites like Araxa in Brazil (q.v.), barite is in small veinlets spread throughout the matrix.

The ore is used as drilling mud in petroleum operations.

BARK Bark is the outer covering or cortex of land plants. Bark covering the cambium is especially well-developed in trees.

BAROMETER The barometer used to measure air pressure was invented by Torricelli in 1643. It is a glass tube filled with mercury. Mercury is 13 times heavier than water and a useful indicator. At sea level mercury indicates 750 millimeters (29-30 inches) at 0° Celsius. The measure is of air pressure on water vapor.

BAROMETRIC EFFECT The Barometric Effect occurs when cosmic radiation increases as atmospheric pressure decreases. There is a greater influence of ultra-violet and other cosmic radiation at high altitude.

BAROMETRIC PRESSURE Barometric pressure is the pressure exerted by the Atmosphere upon the Earth. This amounts to 14.7 pounds per square inch (psi) at sea level or 29.92 inches of mercury. Pressure varies with both altitude and airmass. In general, pressure decreases with altitude. See **BAROMETER**.

In a storm there may be so much velocity at the vortex that barometric pressure drops considerably. In the 'eye of a storm', pressure at sea level can drop as low as 26.35 inches of mercury. These storm centers are low pressure areas (q.v.).

BARREIRAS   Cliffs along the Brazilian Coast from north of the Amazon to Rio de Janeiro are 'barreiras'. On average, they are 50-60 meters (155-200 feet) and composed of a friable sandstone intercalated with decayed or decomposing shales. In some places they come to the shore, in others there are recent beaches between the cliffs and the sea.

The cliff-forming Barreiras Formation has been dated from the end of the Mesozoic (225-65 m.y.) to the Quaternary (q.v.). Sands are buff to red, while the shales are of varying hues. Barreiras is non-fossiliferous and eroded from rocks of the ancient Brazilian Shield. Detrital minerals from a Precambrian source found on Brazilian beaches were held for a time by Barreiras.

BARREL   The barrel is the most quoted unit in the international crude oil trade. King Edward IV set the standard of the 'barrel' for herring. The standard then, and now, is 42 gallons or 159 liters. In recent years, shipments have been made in 55 gallon oil drums but quotations are still made in 'barrels of crude'.

The barrel is also used for measuring cement. In this case, the barrel is equivalent to 372 pounds or 181 kilos.

BARRENS   Barrens is a British term describing stretches of thinly vegetated areas. The Pine Barrens of New Jersey are widely spaced pines.

BARRIER REEF   Reefs separated from the mainland by deep water form a barrier reef. Intervening waters do not have the conditions for reef development, especially of coral. The reefs may be continuous or a string of small ones. Some barrier reefs break the surface forming islands, others are partially or totally submerged.

The most famous is Great Barrier Reef in Australia. It only has an occasional gap allowing inland waters to mix with the ocean.

BARYON   The baryon is a class of subatomic particle characterized by its mass and radioactivity. A baryon is the decay product of a proton and requires great energy to form. It is relatively short-lived and contains 3 quarks (q.v.).

BASAL CONGLOMERATE   Basal conglomerate is an accumulation of rock, pebble, gravel, and sand, silica-cemented above an unconformity (q.v.). It is coarse-grained and well-sorted. The conglomerates display a fining upward of grain size.

A basal conglomerate results from a slowly advancing shore where wave action has stripped the soil and loose particulates from the sediment, leaving the pebbles and coarser material. See **CONGLOMERATE**.

BASALT A dark, heavy, fine-grained rock of volcanic origin, basalt is wide-spread. It has almost equal amounts of feldspar and ferromagnesium minerals with up to 52% silicon dioxide. The composition is of plagioclase feldspar (labradorite, bytownite, and anorthosite), with pyroxene. The dominant pyroxene is augite. Iron and olivine are present in the groundmass and as phenocrysts (q.v.). Augite may also appear in phenocrysts. The color is from green to black.

Basalt is found primarily on ocean floors, but there are extensive flows on continents. It emerges from the Earth about 2,000° Fahrenheit. The magma slows quickly in the sea where pillow lava can form. Vescicles in pillow lava may show concentric banding. Some pillow lavas are dated 3 billion years.

On land, basalt cools more slowly and can travel very far. When it does cool, it shrinks and forms hexagonal or pentagonal patterns. These mark joints or zones of weakness that progress from the surface downward and erosional columns result.

Some of the prismatic columns are huge and form interesting landscape features. Ireland and Scotland have coasts littered with basaltic columns. Giant's Causeway, Northern Ireland is made up of broken columns. In Senegal, West Africa. basaltic columns form cliffs several tens of meters high.

BASALT WEATHERING Basalt flows in the sea alter to spilites in which labradorite is replaced by albite. Pyroxene and olivine will be replaced by chlorite. Basaltic glass in deep sea sediment is hyaloclastite or palagonite. Hyaloclastite is stable in seawater but palagonite alters to a zeolite (phillipsite) or to montmorillonite clay. Phillipsite can make up to 50% of some deep sea sediments.

Subaerially olivine weathers easily to serpentine and other minerals while the pyroxenes go to chlorite. The weathering is onion-skinned. That is, the surface takes on a reddish tone and breaks off in layers.

BASALTIC LAVAS Some great lava flows issued from rifts in the Earth as well as from volcanoes. The flows have been continental or sub-continental in magnitude. Some lava plateau remnants are Deccan, India; Columbia Plateau, United States; and Parana, Brazil. See **BASIC LAVAS**.

BASE A chemical that reacts with an acid to form a salt is a base. It has positively charged ions (cations) and contains the hydroxide (OH) radical. The compound gives off hydroxide ions in solution.

BASE EXCHANGE CAPACITY Many clays possess a capacity for base exchange. This is a process whereby cations and anions may be exchanged. This is an important chemical phenomenon in mineral alteration.

BASE LEVEL In any given area, base level is the lowest point to which a stream can erode its valley. Sea level is used for base level in general but many streams in basins of interior drainage have a base level higher than sea level. These streams may flow into lakes or drain away into the basin floor to become part of the groundwater.

BASELINE In land surveys, baselines are set. A grid or network is drawn with meridians east and west and parallels north and south of a base-line that is the Prime Meridian or Prime Parallel. The system gives rise to blocks. These are coded in western United States as Townships and Ranges and are numbered from the baseline.

A precise baseline is the first step to accurate surveying. The starting and ending points are fixed astronomically. The advantage of government surveys is that the astronomical points are already located and marked. These are noted on base maps and topographical sheets. Physical markers are in place on location.

BASELINE PROFILE In ecology (q.v.), a survey of environmental conditions is made prior to disruption of natural conditions. This survey is the Baseline Profile included in every Environmental Impact Statement (EIS). Statements are now required for all development.

BASE MAP A base map is a working map. It is developed from whatever information is available. Upon the base map, the scientist will overlay or add data. The most useful base maps are topographical such as supplied by the U.S. Geological Survey. Other countries have similar agencies. Aerial photography is available for much of the Earth from NASA and other governmental agencies.

BASE METALS Base metals are chemically active metals. Excluded from this group are gold, silver, and platinum.

BASIC LAVAS Basic lavas originate in magmas rich in iron, magnesium, and calcium. They emerge at high temperature (2,000° Fahrenheit) and can travel up to 67 kilometers (40 miles) before cooling.

Basic lavas are less gaseous than acidic lavas (q.v.). They tend to be more liquid and flow more easily. This ease of flow gives rise to a ropy lava the Hawaiians call 'pahoehoe' (q.v.).

When lava cools in seawater, it forms pillow lava. On the continent, when the surface of the flow cools more quickly than the interior, a jagged surface results. If the lava is gassy, scoria forms. See **BASALT** and **BASALTIC LAVAS**.

BASIC ROCKS Rocks with a silica content from 45-52% are considered basic.

BASIN A basin is a depression of great areal extent. Depression size and complexity vary depending upon the degree of erosion. Sometimes there are basins within basins. In the Great Basin of the United

States in addition to basins within basins there are ranges of mountains with even smaller hills and basins.

The floor of a depression is flat or gently sloping. The basin may be occupied by a stream or a lake. The lake may be of fresh or saline water, or even have been replaced by an evaporite pan.

In more humid areas, land drained by a river and its tributaries is a river basin. The basin encompasses all of the watershed and the basin may be ringed by a fall-line (q.v.).

BASIN AND RANGE PROVINCE   The Basin and Range in Western North America is a physiographic province with distinctive characteristics. The province extends from Oregon to Mexico City. It is sheltered from the Pacific by the Cascade Range in the north; Sierra Nevada, in the middle; and Sierra Occidental in the south.

The region is one of intermontane plateaus and basins, parallel fault-block north-south ranges, scattered volcanic centers, and dry lakes. It is about equally divided between mountain and plain. There are very few flowing rivers.

BATEA   The 'batea' is a prospector's shallow pan fashioned from wood. It is used for hand-washing gold and heavy minerals. Introduced in Brazil in the 1700's, it is still in use there by itinerant prospectors ('garimpeiros').

The pan was imported to California in 1849 and has since been replaced by metal or plastic. The essential design has not changed.

BATHOLITH   The batholith is a structure resulting from a great injection of magma into pre-existing rocks. A batholith may cover a great area. Some are enormous as is the California Batholith. Many batholiths form the core of folded mountains. Surrounding rocks frequently show signs of metamorphism.

BATHYAL   Very deep waters in lakes or in the ocean are bathyal. The zone begins around 300 meters (1,000 feet) for lakes. The submarine region extending from the continental platform and slope to 1,000 meters (3,300 feet) is the Bathyal Zone. Bathyal deposits are finer in grain size than neritic deposits (q.v.), but are coarser than abyssal (q.v.) ones.

BATHYMETRY   Bathymetry is measuring and outlining the contours of the depths of oceans and lakes.

BATHYSCAPH   The bathyscaph is a vessel used for deep sea exploration. The first piloted descent was June 6, 1930. Below 450 meters (1500 feet) fish with their own headlights or other mechanisms for illumination were encountered. 30 years later, Trieste explored the Marianas Trench (q.v.).

BAUXITE　Bauxite is the major ore of aluminum. It is an earthy material, yellow to red in color, the red depending upon iron content. Bauxite is residual and forms in place. Typically, economic bauxite ores will contain 55-65% aluminum oxide. Ores are all impure and require up-grading at the source.

Major suppliers are Australia, Guinea, Jamaica, and Surinam. Brazil joined these ranks in 1986-7. The United States imports 94% of its bauxite. The government stockpile goal of 7 million tons is rarely met.

There are 4 main classes of bauxite deposits. They appear to be related and many show a transition. The deposits are:

Bedded　-　With a definite structure.

Blanket　-　At or near surface. Nearer regolith (q.v.) than bedded.

Pocket　-　In limestones and clays.

Detrital　-　Transported and redeposited.

Bauxite conversion to alumina is energy-expensive making bauxite deposits in the United States anti-economic. Alternative sources such as alunite are also energy-expensive.

Bauxite is the major source of gallium. It is recovered from Indian bauxites that have approximately 60 parts per million (ppm). Czechoslovakia also recovers gallium from processing bauxite. Many other minerals are present in bauxites but are too costly to recover. Process tailings or red muds (q.v.) are reserves.

BAUXITIZATION　Bauxitization, a weathering process converts country rock to bauxite by leaching and capillarity under tropical to subtropical climatic conditions. Residues are rich in aluminum, iron, and silica. The process is a form of laterization (q.v.).

BAY　Indentations along coastlines where the sea flows between the landforms are bays. A bay is similar to but smaller than a gulf.

In the Carolinas, United States, there are bays whose origin has not been satisfactorily explained. Some geologists think they may be the result of meteoritic impact.

BAYOU　A bayou is a channel of slow-moving water. There are many such channels in the Mississippi Delta.

BEACH　A shoreline deposit around a lake or along the coast bordering the ocean is a beach. Beaches may be sandy or detrital deposits and may have sediments of any size from cobble to mud. Willard Bascom defines a beach 'as an accumulation of rock fragments subject to movement by ordinary wave action'.

In some parts of the world there are long continuous sandy stretches of beach. Where the Sahara meets the sea in Mauritania and along the south coast of Brazil such expanses can be found.

BEACH PLACERS There are 2 types of beach placers. These are stream placers where the river meets the sea and wave-built placers.

Additional concentration by waves reworking stream placers gives rise to richer deposits. Some are important sources of diamonds (South Africa, Sierra Leone) and heavy minerals (Australia and Sierra Leone).

BEACH SANDS Beach sands are the weathering product of coastal rock. The type of sand depends upon the source rocks. Color is often a clue. In most of the United States beach sands are gray due to their high quartz content. In Florida, sands are white due to the high lime and coral origin.

There are black sand beaches. These have different origins. In Hawaii, black sands are decomposed basic lavas. In Australia, Brazil, India, and Sierra Leone they are of heavy mineral concentrations, principally of rutile and ilmenite.

BEAM A stream of atomic particles flowing in the same direction forms a beam. Beams may be of light or electromagnetic radiation.

BEARDSLEY METEORITE There is evidence that the Beardsley, Nebraska, meteorite impacted solid rock. This is important since its age is estimated at 4.8 billion years. The accepted age of the Earth is 4.5-4.6 billion years. This is the oldest known meteorite.

BEARING A compass bearing or direction is taken from a fixed point. The initial point is fixed astronomically even for dead-reckoning.

BEAUFORT SCALE The scale developed by Beaufort is used to describe wind velocity. It is used in Britain and the United States. The scale indicates the level of intensity from calm to hurricane in 12 stages, each with a specific velocity range. Hurricane, 12 on the scale, is any velocity over 65 knots (125 kilometers or 75 miles) per hour.

BEAUFORT SEA The Beaufort Sea is an arm of the Arctic Ocean, north of Alaska and Canada. The sites of North Shore oil explorations are the inlets in the sea of Prudhoe Bay (q.v.), Mackenzie Bay, and Mackenzie Delta (q.v.). Off Tuktoyaktut Peninsula, artificial islands were constructed among the ice floes at a cost of billions of dollars.

BED A bed is the smallest unit in the stratigraphic column (q.v.). It is a discreet layer of sediment.

To the miner, bed is an ore or coal seam. These normally contain many beds.

BED LOAD Detrital material carried along the bottom by the current is bed load, a portion of the total sediment. The rest is in suspension.

BEDROCK Solid fresh or bedrock underlies the weathered surface. Depths to bedrock vary from a veneered surface to many meters, depending on weathering.

Rock beneath gold placer gravels is bedrock to miners though there are other layers between it and true bedrock.

BENCH Any terraced level in an open-pit mine or quarry is a bench. A wave-cut platform at the foot of a cliff is a bench. Its upper portion is out of water at low tide.

BENCH MARK Official government survey parties leave markers or monuments. These are clearly marked as BM (Bench Mark), PBM (Permanent Bench Mark), or TBM (Temporary Bench Mark). Local altitude above sea level may also be shown. Markers serve as survey initiation points.

BENCH PLACERS Bench placers are terrace deposits along stream channels. They represent the location of earlier stream beds before the river cut further into the valley floor. Many bench placers have ancient gravels in place and these are sometimes worked for gold.

BAY OF BENGAL Bengal Bay is an arm of the Indian Ocean between Burma and India. It is fed by the Ganges, Brahmaputra, and Irrawaddy rivers (q.v.).

About twice a century, mud deposits suddenly shift from the shelf to the deep sea floor creating huge submarine canyons. The triggering device for these turbidity currents (q.v.) is not well defined. The river deltas spread well to the middle of the bay and the force and weight of the sediments are important factors.

BENGUE TROUGH In Nigeria, the Bengue Trough is a 600 kilometer (360 mile) northeast-southwest trending mineral belt. It is a graben, 80-90 kilometers (48-54 miles) wide filled with 5,000 meters (16,500 feet) of Cretaceous sediments. The trough cuts a plateau 50 meters (165 feet) above sea level. The major mineralization is lead-zinc.

Plate tectonic specialists think the rift is a 'failed arm' of a triple junction. 2 arms opened to form oceanic basins while the 3rd is left as a fissure on the continent.

BENGUELA CURRENT The Benguela Current in the South Atlantic Ocean flows in a northerly direction along the west coast of Africa. Like its counterpart off western South America, it is a cold current. Benguela brings fog, the only moisture source for some South African deserts.

Off the Angolan Coast, the current is farther offshore. It flows north until the shape of the continent influences it, then it curves west to merge with the South Equatorial Current (q.v.).

BENIOFF ZONES Earthquake foci in the Pacific define the Benioff Zones. The name is given to subduction zones (q.v.). One dips to the north beneath the Alaskan Peninsula.

The Alaskan zone is an area where the oceanic plate is shoved against the relatively rigid North American continental margin. The zone disappears beneath the Bering Sea at a depth of 150-200 kilometers (90-120 miles). The western limit of the zone is the Aleutians. Denali Fault in Alaska may be a suture line.

The Lithosphere in a Benioff Zone moves downward at about 45°. This is demonstrated in the Tonga Region where the zone slopes away from the Trench on a northwest strike. The earthquake epicenters are progressively deeper.

BENTHIC Sea floor environment from inshore to the deeps is benthic. Lake bottoms have also been called benthic.

Marine life is either pelagic or benthic. Plants and animals, attached, free-swimming, or crawling are benthic when they depend upon the bottom for sustenance. Shallows and intertidal areas have the greatest number of smaller organisms. Reef builders are benthic.

BENTONITE Bentonite is a member of the Montmorillonite Group of clays. It is produced by the devitrification (q.v.) of volcanic ash. Bentonite may be a swelling or a non-swelling clay. Swelling bentonite is sodium-rich. Wyoming clay is of the swelling type.

The Wyoming deposits are widespread and shallow. When fresh, they are bright yellow-green grading to blue with depth. At Colony, Wyoming, the deposits are 2.1 meters (7 feet) thick. Wyoming clay is used as drilling mud (q.v.) in petroleum production. It is also used in pelletizing taconite iron ore.

Mississippi or non-swelling bentonite is used for bleaching coloring matter from oil.

BERGSCHRUND A Bergschrund is a very large crevasse (q.v.) at the head of an alpine glacier. The crevasse separates moving snow and ice from relatively fixed snow and ice clinging to the valley headwall.

BERING LAND BRIDGE A land bridge connected Alaska to Siberia in the Pleistocene. The land, Beringia, was exposed by a lowering of sea level by about 85 meters (280 feet). It created a land bridge that provided a migration route for animals and humans.

Migration was mostly from Siberia to Alaska into North and ultimately South America. It occurred over a 5 million year period:

4.7-2.5 m.y. -	Temperate climate and steppe animals (deer, bear lemmings, moles).
1.8 m.y. -	Mammoths.
Most recent -	Bison, caribou, musk ox, sheep, and humans.

Beringia was subcontinental in extent and in its last 150,000 years was 1,200 kilometers (720 miles) north-south and 2,200 kilometers (1,320 miles) east-west. Fossil indications are that it was covered in vegetation that was transitional between Tundra and Steppe.

BERING SEA   The Bering Sea is a part of the Pacific Ocean and separates Asia from North America. The sea is 1,600 kilometers (1,000 miles) north-south and 2,166 kilometers (1,300 miles) east-west. It is connected to the Arctic Ocean by Bering Strait and Chukchi Sea. Both separate Alaska from the Soviet Union.

The Bering is a very cold sea with an average temperature most of the year of only -3° Celsius (27° Fahrenheit). The Bering Sill impedes bottom water interchange between the Sea and the Pacific.

BERM   A small horizontal, almost level platform on a slope is a berm. It creates greater slope stability and provides drainage control. The berm can result from terrace formation by an eroding stream or by stream rejuvenation. A berm can also be formed by wave action. Because of their stabilizing effect and erosion control, berms are often artificially produced.

BERMUDA HIGH   In summer, in the Northern Hemisphere, a semi-permanent high pressure develops over the Atlantic from the Azores to Bermuda. The Bermuda High forces weather to follow the Northeast Trades around its southern edge.

BERMUDA RISE   There are 3 rises in the North Atlantic Ocean isolated from the Mid-Atlantic Ridge (q.v.). They are the Bermuda, the Muir, and the Kevin.

The Bermuda Rise is 1,000 kilometers (600 miles) north-south and 500 kilometers (300 miles) east-west. The central Bermuda Islands are on a pedestal rising 4,000 meters (13,000 feet) from its base on the floor of the Atlantic.

BERMUDA TRIANGLE   The Bermuda Triangle is a portion of the Atlantic Ocean which has as points to the triangle, Miami, Bermuda, and Puerto Rico. It is in the western part of the Sargasso Sea (q.v.), an area of sudden storms, violent air currents, and waterspouts. Not all of the phenomena have been satisfactorily explained. Ships and aircraft have been lost in the area.

The nature of the Sargasso Sea and its complex of deep water currents probably have much to do with the mystery surrounding the Bermuda Triangle. MODE, Mid-Ocean Dynamic Experiment was set up to study these currents.

BERYL   Beryl is a metal of unusual stability and elasticity along with hardness (8 on Moh's Scale). It has many commercial and Space Age uses. The metal is 'strategic' due to its use in the atomic piles of some nuclear reactors and other high technology applications.

Beryl or beryllium ore is found in veins and pegmatites (q.v.). Commercial grade beryllium oxide is 12%. Rarely can deposits be found that are rich enough to be worked exclusively for beryl.

India has the largest proven pegmatite reserves. Brazil's proven reserves are small (15,000 tons) but the vast unexplored pegmatite provinces make it likely these will be augmented. In 1987, Brazil produced an estimated 850 tons of 10% ore.

Until the 1970's, the United States was dependent upon imports from Brazil and elsewhere. The discovery of bertrandite in a topaz rhyolite extrusive at Spor Mountain, Utah, made the country largely self-sufficient in beryllium.

Emerald, aquamarine, morganite, and golden beryl are gemstones of beryl. They are imported from Brazil, Colombia, India,and USSR.

BETA RADIATION Beta radiation is a stream of Beta particles (q.v.) or rays. A Beta particle has a single electrical charge emitted from the atomic nucleus during decay. If the charge is negative, it is an electron; if positive, a positron. Decay occurs within the nucleus and neutrons yield a proton, an electron, and a neutrino.

Beta radiation is dangerous but a thin metal shield offers protection. Beta emissions can be deflected by inducing a magnetic field normal or perpendicular to them. See **COSMIC RADIATION**.

BEZYMIANY VOLCANO In Kamchatka, USSR, Bezymiany Volcano violently exploded in 1956. It was monitored by Kliutchi Station (Soviet Geophysical Center). The energy output was 40,000 billion kilowatts. A cubic kilometer of rock weighing 2.4 billion metric tons was ejected at a speed of 2,000 kilometers (1,250 miles) per hour. Initial pressure was 3,000 atmospheres.

Bezymiany ash (500 million cubic meters) was 'vacuumed up' by the jet stream and deposited in England 4 days after the eruption. Ash fell for 7 months as far away as 250 kilometers (150 miles).

A volcanic cloud 8,000 meters (26,000 feet) thick reached an altitude of 36 kilometers (22 miles). It sent gas to 45,000 meters (147,000 feet) in a matter of minutes. Bezymiany affected world climate for over a year.

The volcano collapsed and was transformed into a caldera (q.v.) within which a dome rapidly built. This dome grew 58 meters (190 feet in a single month.

BIFURCATION Bifurcation is the merging of 2 or more major river systems. It occurs where slopes are gentle and the country relatively flat. One of the best examples is the linking of the Orinoco to the Amazon via the Casiquiare River in south Venezuela. The Casiquiare feeds into the Upper Rio Negro in Brazil in high-water seasons.

BIG BANG THEORY The Big Bang Theory relates to the origin of Planet Earth. Fragments of a previously existent Universe coalesced into a mass and subsequently exploded. This explosion is dated between 13 and 20 billion years ago. It was created by a thermonuclear fusion. The mass was composed primarily of hydrogen and helium. All matter and space then expanded and is continuing to do so.

Remnants of the exploded mass formed galaxies. The Sun, a star in the Milky Way Galaxy, formed 10 billion years ago and is estimated to last another 10 billion.

The dust cloud that began rotating about the Sun coalesced to give rise to the planets. Earth evolved at least 4.5 to 5 billion years ago.

For practical purposes, the age of the Universe begins with the Big Bang. The Big Bang Theory does not contradict an infinite existence of the Universe. It refers only to its form.

BIGHT   A bight is a small crescent-shaped bay following a coastline curve. A deep, narrow bight is a cove. Both are inlets connected with the sea by narrow channels. The California Bight provides a natural lee to the prevailing winds where the coast below Point Conception is more east-west.

BIKINI ATOLL   Bikini is a coral atoll in the Pacific built up on a volcanic basement. Seimic surveys confirm coral limestone at 4,500 meters (15,000 feet), establishing the correctness of Charles Darwin's assumption that the Pacific floor sank while the atolls grew.

Bikini was the site of an atomic test blast, which forced the indigenous population to move. Attempts to sanitize Bikini environment are underway to allow the people to return.

BILLION   Billion, for Americans is equal to 10 to the 9th power. For the British, billion is 10 to the 12th power (the American trillion). Ancient rocks dated 2 billion years in the United States would be written as 2 b.y. while in England it would be 2,000 m.y. (million years).

BILMA ERG   The Erg of Bilma, an enormous sand sea, extends from Tibesti Massif to the Air Mountains in southwest Sahara. The erg is of dunes blown from Tibesti, Libya by the Harmattan (q.v.), the prevailing wind in the region. The central part has high dunes flanked on the east by barchans (q.v.). In the southern part of the sand sea, the dunes are seifs with long ridges up to 180 kilometers (110 miles) with an average of 1,000 meters (3,300 feet).

Yardangs (q.v.) are a special feature. They permit passes through the Erg which caravans use to cross the wasteland.

BILMA MARSHES   For centuries, the Bilma Marshes in West Africa have been a traditional source of salt. A famous caravan route passes them.

A mineral salt crust develops on the marshes under the high evaporation of the area. It is broken up, raked, and packed onto camels. A camel can carry up to 110 kilograms (250 pounds).

BINARY ALLOY A binary alloy is composed of 2 metallic elements. Bronze, an alloy of copper and tin is an example.

BINGHAM COPPER MINE Bingham, Utah, was the largest copper mine in the world, an open-pit operation in a granite pluton. The granite stocks are several hundred kilometers in diameter. The pit covers 636 hectares (1,400 acres) from which 3,355 million metric tons were removed.

Secondary chalcocite replaced other sulfides resulting in a workable porphyry (q.v.) copper ore of 2-3%. By 1977, 11 million tons had been produced. The mine accounted for most U.S. production during the years of its operation. Production from the mine has been halted.

Microbial mining has been used recently to extract low-grade ore from the dumps. Acidic waters are poured over the dumps to encourage bacterial growth to accelerate leaching. This is a form of 'heap leaching'.

BINOMIAL SYSTEM A binomial system was developed for naming organisms. The names are in Latin, the scholars' language at the time the system began.

In the classification, the generic name is given first, then the species, e.g.: Ricinus communis L. This is the scientific name for the castor bean. The initial is for an honoree, in this case the famous biologist, Linnaeus.

BIOCHEMICAL CYCLE In the biochemical cycle elements essential to life are traced from the inorganic phase to the organic and back again.

BIOCHEMICAL OXYGEN DEMAND The amount of oxygen required to remove organic matter from industrial wastewater is the biochemical oxygen demand or BOD.

BIOCLASTIC Fragments of organic remains are bioclastics. The prefix is from 'bios' meaning life. A coral reef is composed of bioclastics.

BIOCOENSIS The biological community found within a given habitat is a biocoensis, a group of organims living together.

BIODEGRADABLE In pollution control, materials are biodegradable if they can be broken down into simple inorganic substances through bacterial or fungal activity.

Many manufactured chemicals are not biodegradable in the short term and thus present serious ecological problems. This is particularly true of a number of plastics.

BIOFACIES The biological aspect of a sediment is its biofacies. The facies may be restricted to a horizon or stratum or encompass the entire strata. With lateral and vertical variations, organisms may share time horizons but have different ecologies.

BIOGENOUS SEDIMENT   A sediment composed of 30% organic material is biogenous. Most biogenous sediments are of organic material composed of calcium carbonate, silicate, or phosphatic minerals.

BIOGEOCHEMICAL CYCLE The biogeochemical cycle is made up of the movement of minerals and other elements, particularly gases, through organic and inorganic realms. These cycles are critical to a geochemical balance on the planet. The most important ones are of carbon, nitrogen, phosphorus, oxygen, and the hydrologic or water cycle.

BIOHERM A bioherm is an organic reef formed by an aggregation of organic debris (Algae, Coral). Bioherms develop in rough water and materials are poorly sorted.

BIOLOGICAL DIVERSITY In ecology, biological diversity is an important variable of organisms found within a unit area. The great number of species found in the tropics is an example of biological diversity.

BIOLUMINESCENCE Bioluminescence is a chemical reaction of organisms causing them to emit light without measurable heat. A beautiful expression of the phenomenon is the phosphorescent light in the sea seen at dusk or at night.

BIOMASS The total of organic matter, alive or dead, is the biomass. It is expressed in grams per square meter. Biomass often refers to agricultural products or by-products. The biomass can be an important energy resource. Experimentation into its use is on-going.

BIOME Earth is divided into ecosystems or biomes governed by climate. They grade into each other but are distinct habitats with special flora and fauna. Tropical rainforests, deserts, and wetlands are examples of biomes.

Between biomes there are transitional zones in which may be found specialized lifeforms or merely representatives from adjoining zones.

BIOSPHERE The biosphere is that part of the Earth's surface sustaining life. It is a very thin layer and includes the land surface and subsurface, the World Ocean and a thin part of the Troposphere (q.v.).

BIOTA All living matter or 'Biota' are subdivided into 2 major kingdoms: Animal (Fauna) and Plant (Flora).

BIOTITE Biotite is a variety of mica, a hydrated silicate of aluminum, potassium, magnesium, and iron. It is an important constituent of igneous rocks. It is found in some metamorphic and sedimentary rocks as well.

Biotite is dark-brown to black and often referred to as 'black mica'. It weathers to chlorite and phlogopite.

BIRCH DISCONTINUITY The Birch seismic discontinuity is found at a depth of about 900 kilometers (540 miles) into the Earth's Mantle. It is assumed to indicate a marked change in physical or chemical composition.

BIRD The bird is a member of the Aves Class of Vertebrates. Most are feathered and all are winged, but not all are capable of flight. There are about 28 orders, 150 families, and 9,000 species.

Birds are a natural control of insect populations. They also contribute to the distribution of pollen and seeds.

BIRD MIGRATION Semi-annually there is a passage or bird migration. In the Northern Hemisphere birds fly south to avoid winter. Migrations may even be from hemisphere to hemisphere for the reversal of seasons or from the polar regions to the tropics.

The Golden Plover is an example of sophisticated migration. It has 2 major routes. In the fall, it flies east from Labrador into the Atlantic, then south. It flies 4,000 kilometers (2,400 miles) over water to South America. In the spring, it takes the direct route over land to Labrador.

Sophisticated migrations are not exclusive to the Western Hemisphere. The seabird, the tern, flies from offshore Angola to the Minch in Scotland to nest and produce its young on the rocky isles.

BIRD-FOOT DELTA A river system may develop a delta in the form of a bird's foot. Natural levees grow into this form beginning from 2 original ones. The pattern is digitate or inter-fingering.

BIREFRINGENCE Minerals crystallizing in a non-Cubic System may have light passing through which vibrates in 2 planes at right angles to each other.

The velocity of one light ray relative to the other is less, and 2 indices of refraction (q.v.) result.

BISCUIT BOARD TOPOGRAPHY The graphic British term 'biscuit board topography' describes cirques (q.v.) that look as if carved by a biscuit or cookie cutter. The topography is of rolling uplands in early stages of glaciation.

BISMUTH Bismuth is the heaviest of the naturally occurring elements. It has 83 protons and 126 neutrons. Bismuth-214 is radioactive. All elements heavier than bismuth are subject to radioactive decay.

BIT A bit is a boring device attached to a pipe (stem) and used to drill wells or bore holes in hard rock. Bits are often made from tungsten carbide and have jagged teeth. Even though bit materials are quite hard, replacement has to be frequent and is costly.

BITTER LAKE   A saline lake with a high sodium sulfate content is a bitter or bittern lake. Many are found in southwestern United States.

The Red Sea crossing point for Moses and the Israelites was Egypt's Bitter Lakes. These are rich in sulfates and carbonates.

BITTERN   Residues from evaporation (q.v.) leave crystalline salt in a magnesium-rich liquor, or bittern. Evaporation and precititation is in a more advanced phase than in the bitter lake (q.v.). The soluble minerals are late phase evaporites derived from saline waters.

BITUMEN   Naturally occurring tars and resins with a high hydrocarbon content are bitumens. They may be liquid (petroleum) or tar (asphalt). Oil shale and bituminous coal are also bitumens.

BITUMINOUS COAL   A rock is considered bituminous if its bitumens (q.v.) can be recovered by heating. Coal from which 40% of high volatile bitumens can be recovered is bituminous.

Bituminous coal is soft and is transitional between lignite and anthracite (q.v.). These soft coals are the most used for industrial and home heating.

BITUMINOUS SANDS   Bituminous sands are an alternative energy source by reason of their bitumen (q.v.) content. The Murray Formation, Alberta, Canada is a major source of these sands. See **TAR SANDS**.

BIVALVE   The pelecypods, or clams, are bivalved mollusks. The typical mollusk's shell has 3 layers, one of which is an organic film protecting the others. The outer inorganic shell is calcite lined with aragonite or mother-of-pearl.

Primitive pelecypods first appeared in the Ordovician Period (500-430 m.y.). See **MOLLUSKS**.

BLACK BODY   A black body is an absorber of radiation. There is no reflection from it. On Earth, soot (q.v.) is nearest to a true black body.

BLACK GOLD   Gold ore may be coated with a thin veneer of black manganese oxide. Miners call it 'black gold'.

Petroleum is 'black gold' because of the wealth associated with it.

BLACK HILLS   The Black Hills of South Dakota and Wyoming are brown sandstone ridges with shale overlying a gray granite batholith. The batholith was intruded 1.46 billion years ago. The evidence seems to be that millions of years later the batholith was again pushed up into the sediments. See **BATHOLITH**.

Intrusive activity also left a series of laccoliths (q.v.). Black Hills granite pegmatites have produced some extraordinarily large crystals of feldspar and spodumene. See **PEGMATITES**.

Structurally, the Black Hills are the result of arching which occurred in other parts of the Rockies during the same period. The structure is easy to see where the domes have been breached. Sheer cliffs always face the center of the Hills.

BLACK HOLE The location in the Universe of a collapsed giant star is a 'black hole'. There are an estimated billion black holes in our galaxy making up about 90% of our Universe. They are thought to be sources of cosmic energy.

BLACK LIGHT A black light is an ultra-violet ray gun used to illuminate minerals in a dark area. Some minerals take on quite different colors under this light and many are very beautiful. Minerals that change color are 'fluorescent'.

BLACK MUD Fine-grained, deep black or dark brown muds containing organic residues are often found in marshes and lagoons. Organic material may be decaying enough to give off hydrogen sulfide which kills other organisms, adding to the organic accumulation.

BLACK RAPIDS GLACIER During a particularly heavy snowfall in Alaska in 1936-37 Black Rapids Glacier advanced 35 meters (115 feet) per day. See **GLACIERS**.

BLACK SANDS Black sands containing heavy minerals such as ilmenite, rutile, and magnetite are found in stream placers and on beaches. Sometimes the deposits are economic. On a beach the placer is the result of mineral concentration by wave action.

Black sand deposits have been found on Recent and Ancient beaches in workable placers. Some of the best are in Australia, Brazil, Ceylon, Florida, India, and Sierra Leone. See **PLACERS**

Hawaiian black sands are made up of tiny grains of black lava. Beaches of this black sand are an important tourist attraction.

Some black sands contain monazite with a small amount of thorium and are radioactive. Guarapari in Espirito Santo, Brazil, is such a black sand beach. It is considered a health resort based on the therapeutic effect of the sands.

BLACK SEA The Black Sea is (2,000 meters) deep, very saline, and hydrogen sulfide builds up in its depths. The sea connects with the Mediterranean via the Bosporus, Sea of Marmora, and Dardanelles. Current flow is 2-way. Surface waters flow from the Black Sea while bottom current is from the Mediterranean.

BLAKE PLATEAU Blake Plateau rises from the floor of the Atlantic Ocean and is not a part of the Continental Shelf. Blake is 250 kilometers (150 miles) wide and extends from off South Carolina to the Bahamas. The top of the plateau is between 400 and 600 fathoms. (There are 6 feet or 1.8 meters to a fathom).

The eastern edge of the plateau has a 45° slope away from the continent to the sea floor at 1800 fathoms. On the west it merges into the Continental Slope. The surface is covered with mud, ooze, and organic debris. An unexpected artesian freshwater source was encountered in drilling. Phosphates and manganese nodules of mineable grades were also discovered.

BLIZZARD Blizzards are windstorms of great intensity accompanied by snow, sleet, low temperatures, and very low visibility. On the Great Plains, the force results from a collision of cold Arctic air out of Canada and warm air from the Gulf of Mexico. The storms are propelled from southwest to northeast by the jet streams (q.v.).

BLOCK CAVING Block caving is under-cutting ore in a mine section and allowing it to collapse. Overburden, or cover rock, can come with the ore and cleaning is necessary. Underground block caving is sometimes used to mine support pillars after the rest of the ore has been mined.

BLOCK LAVA Block lava is partially crystallized material from which gases have exploded in small bursts. Its surface is scoriated, or pockmarked. Surface lava cools more rapidly than the fluid mass within. The lava breaks off in sharp-cut chunks due to the differential cooling. A 'malpais' (q.v.) landscape is created.

BLOCK MOUNTAINS Mountains bounded by faults that have moved vertically relative to each other are block mountains. If land is raised in relation to the terrain on both sides, it is a horst. If the block drops relative to both sides, it is a graben. Block mountains with these structures are common in the Basin and Range Province.

BLOOM To bloom is to flower and minerals flower with efflorescenses on the surface of rocks. Cobalt bloom is one of the more common types. Surface evaporites may bloom after the rains.

BLOW HOLE Sea caves along a shore often have collapsed roof structures. Waves breaking within caves send high sprays up through the openings or blow holes.

BLOWOUTS Broad, shallow, enclosed depressions created by the wind are blowouts. They are relatively common in arid and semi-arid areas. Sometimes the blowout stabilizes and plants are sheltered there.

BLUE CLAY Blue or greenish clay is a semi-pelagic sediment limited to ocean depths of at least 250 meters (825 feet). The clay is rich in detrital minerals and always has a percentage of calcium carbonate. It also is high in organic material and iron sulfate. Blue clay covers about 37 million square kilometers (22 million square miles) of ocean floor. See **PELAGIC.**

BLUE-GREEN ALGAE Blue-green Algae are considered one of the oldest forms of life on the planet. It is a single-celled plant with a colonial habit. These are true plants, capable of photosynthesis (q.v.).

Algal traces are found in Precambrian rocks to such an extent, their abundance in Precambrian seas is undisputed. Algae (q.v.) may have greatly contributed to the increase in oxygen in the Atmosphere so oxygen-breathing lifeforms became viable.

BLUE GRAVEL Some deep, water-saturated Tertiary (65-2 m.y.) gravels in California gold country have a blue-gray cast. They are the unoxidized portions of gold-bearing gravels. Near surface gravels take on red from iron oxide.

BLUE GROUND The common name for weathered kimberlite is 'blue ground'. It is slate-blue to slate-green micaceous pyroxene and it often hosts diamonds. Blue ground is primarily found in volcanic necks or plugs. Kimberlite weathers to yellow ground at the surface.

Recently, kimberlite has been found in some United States locations, but none with significant diamonds.

BLUE JOHN A form of fluorspar found in Derbyshire, England, is known locally as 'Blue John' and internationally as Derbyshire Spar. It is massive with blue bands on a relatively colorless background. See **FLUORSPAR.**

BLUE NILE RIVER The Nile River has 2 main sources. One is in the headlands of Abay Creek which feeds into Lake Tana in the Ethiopian Highlands. This part of the Nile is called Blue Nile for its especially clear water. The other major source is in East African lakes and is the White Nile (q.v.). At Khartoum, Sudan, the rivers merge to form the Nile which flows through northern Sudan and Egypt.

The Blue Nile has cut a gorge about a 1.5 kilometers (1 mile) deep through the Ethiopian Highlands. It was a spectacular barrier to explorations seeking the source of the Nile.

The Blue Nile Dam has been built in Sudan to generate power and create new agricultural land in that part of the Sahara. See **WHITE NILE RIVER.**

BLUE WHALE The blue whale ('Sibbaldus musculus') is the largest mammal. It measures 30 meters (100 feet) and weighs up to 90 metric tons. Its newborn are 7 meters (23 feet) long.

The enormous blue whale feeds on plankton (q.v.) and krill, a tiny shrimp. They consume a ton or 2 at a time. The whale is toothless and filter feeds. Blue whales live in polar waters. See **KRILL**.

BLUESCHISTS Blueschists are composed of a blue amphibole, glaucophane. It is a fine-grained metamorphic rock derived from basic igneous rock. It contains as accessories actinolite, clino-pyroxenes, garnet and rutile.

BLUFF The relatively steep, stable slope at the outer edge of a floodplain is a bluff. Bluffs can also form along coasts above marine terraces.

BOD BOD, an acronym for Biochemical Oxygen Demand, is the aquatic micro-organisms' requirement for oxygen. Eutrophication (q.v.) is correlated with a high BOD.

BODY BURDEN The amount of radioactive material present in humans and animals is the body burden. Its biological half-life differs and is less than the natural radioactive half-life (q.v.).

BOG A bog is similar to a swamp but is incapable of supporting trees. There is a great deal of vegetation, primarily of mosses and low-growing plants and shrubs. Because the terrain is water-logged, decayed vegetation can accumulate to form peat.

Bogs are found in glacier scoured areas and in the vicinity of aging lakes. A number of them can be found in the high Rockies and Sierra Nevada.

Scotland and Ireland's peat bogs are famous and have been extensively mined for fuel for centuries. About 1/7th of Ireland is made up of bog. The most famous is Bog of Allen.

BOG IRON Bog iron, hydrated iron oxide (limonite), formed in lakes and bogs is a spongy mass with clay. Iron was precipitated by bacterial activity in the anaerobic environment.

Sweden and Finland have large reserves of bog iron ore. The only known bog iron being deposited today is in the eastern Baltic area.

BOG SOILS Bog soils are intrazonal and result from poor drainage. They are rich in organic material of bog or marsh origin. Because of the high organic content, they are black or dark-brown in color.

LAKE BOGORIA Lake Bogoria, former Lake Hannington, is in the Great Rift Valley of East Africa. It is an alkaline-saline lake just north of the Equator and was formed 10,000 years ago. Bogoria is shallow, 17 kilometers (10 miles) by 500 meters (1,650 feet). Spring and stream fed, its north end is in Loboi Swamp. In the 1920's it was still a habitat for crocodiles but today it only supports Algae.

BOILING POINT When the gaseous and liquid phases of matter are in equilibrium, they have attained the boiling point. The temperature of this occurrence differs with the materials.

BOLIVIA Land-locked Bolivia has long been a major supplier of tin. The tin was first discovered below silver in Bolivia's famous Potosi MInes (q.v.).

Bolivia divides naturally into 4 physiographic provinces:

- Andes - 3 great chains across Bolivia for 500 miles trending NW-SE. Average, elevation 6,600 meters (20,000 feet). Among them are 4 of the world's highest mountains.

- Altiplanos - High mountain plateaus above 3,600 meters (12,000).

- Rainforest - Beni River Basin was notorious for slavery and death during the rubber boom of the early 1900's. The Beni is a major tributary of the Amazon System.

- Llanos (savannas) - Lowlands in southeast slope to Paraguay Basin.

The Santa Cruz area of Bolivia is an oil producer. Other parts of the country are also rich in natural resources. High altitude, geographical isolation, and political problems have contributed to the poverty of the country.

BOLAS DE PLATA 'Bolas de plata', Spanish for silver balls, was the name given nuggets totaling 1,633 kilograms (4,000 pounds), some were more than 200 kilograms (500 pounds). It was a spectacular bonanza (q.v.).

BOMBS Large rock fragments ejected from a volcano are bombs. They are primarily liquid when ejected. During their trajectory they cool and take shape due to atmospheric contact.

BONANZA An exceptionally rich strike of gold or silver ore is a 'bonanza'. a word from the Spanish meaning prosperity.

BONDING Bonding is atomic attraction. Atoms of the same or different elements bond ionically by a transfer of electrons. Bonding is covalent, meaning electrons are shared as with hydrogen and oxygen in water.

LAKE BONNEVILLE Bonneville was the largest of the Great Basin's Pleistocene lakes. It covered 140,000 square kilometers (54,000 square miles). Sevier, Provo, and Great Salt Lake are remnants of Bonneville. Great Salt Lake today is a brine.

Many mountains composed of Paleozoic marine limestones were islands. Ancient shorelines are easily discernible. When the area became more arid, Sevier Playa and Great Salt Lake Desert formed.

BOOKCLIFFS The Bookcliffs, sediments up to 300 meters (1,000 feet) high form the boundary between Cretaceous and Cenozoic horizons (65 m.y.) in Utah and Colorado. They form a broad arc of 330 kilometers (200 miles) long and are composed of eroded sandstone and shales.

Light-colored sandstone overlies 910 meters (3,000 feet) of Mancos Shale. The sandstone thins to the east. The Bookcliffs contain 12-17 billion tons of mineable bituminous coal. It is one of the world's major coal reserves.

BORA The Bora is an adiabatically warmed wind. It warms moving down Alpine slopes at the head of the Adriatic Sea. The wind is generated in the Danube Basin and is originally cold. Its warmth is relative. It brings chill weather to a normally subtropical area. The Bora can attain up to 160 kilometers (100 miles) per hour.

BORAH PEAK EARTHQUAKE A quake felt in Thousand Springs Valley, Idaho in 1983 was traced to the Borah Peak gravel fan. The quake registered 7 on the Richter Scale. The epicenter was on the Lost River Fault which had shown no movement for 10,000 years.

The reaction on the fault was along 40 kilometers (25 miles) and the epicenter was at a depth of 16 kilometers (10 miles). The quake was felt 2 minutes later in Salt Lake City and 4 minutes later in Seattle.

The energy force is estimated at 30 times that of Mt. Saint Helens. In 1 second, a hillside rose while another dropped a meter (3 feet). Geysers spouted to (6 meters) 20 feet. The earthquake also released 400 billion gallons of water.

Borah Peak rose a 0.3 meter (1 foot) and the valley dropped 1.2 meters (4 feet).

BORBOREMA BELT The Borborema Belt of pegmatites in Northeast Brazil follows structural lines created in the early Precambrian. The pegmatites were intruded 800-900 million years ago and were recrystallized 550-450 million years ago. Many interesting and economic minerals are present. See **PEGMATITES**.

BORE A tidal bore is created by the sea pushing into a narrow channel or up an estuary. Large bores are known from the Adriatic Sea, the Amazon, the Gulf of California, and the Bay of Fundy, between Nova Scotia and New Brunswick, Canada. See **AMAZON BORE**.

The Bay of Fundy (q.v.) has tides that differ by 12 meters (40 feet). Attempts are being made to channel this energy into a source of power.

BOREAL FOREST The boreal forest is a sub-polar biome (q.v.). It is located south of the Tundra and north of the mixed deciduous forests and grasslands. It is a fragile ecosystem.

Parts of the Siberian boreal forest are threatened by pollution from the industrialization of the region. See **TAIGA**.

BORNITE Bornite is a copper mineral that is rarely an ore. When weathered, it takes on a purplish irridescence, 'peacock ore' to miners. When Bisbee Copper mine first opened, bornite was common. A much prized specimen mineral, modern copper mining methods do not allow its easy collection.

BORON Boron is mined in Death Valley, California. The ore is volcanic and associated with thermal springs. Sodium borates are found in Miocene (26-12 m.y.) marls while calcium borates are in Pliocene (12-2 m.y.) muds.

The lenticular deposits found in a continental basin are related to Late Tertiary (q.v.) tectonics. The main minerals are colemanite, tincal, and ulexite. Quaternary or Recent brines hold redeposited mineral.

Turkey has 60% of the world's boron reserves which are set at 600 million metric tons. Turkey and the United States are the prime producers.

Marco Polo brought boron from Tibet and with it techniques for glass-making. This is still a major use of the mineral. Boron combines with carbon, nitrogen, and silica to form borides. These have melting points up to 3,000° Celsius, are extremely hard, and have high conductivity.

Boron-10, the isotope, has special uses in atomic physics. It can capture neutrons from a nuclear reactor and convert them to the stable isotope, Boron-11. See **ISOTOPE**.

BORT Bort is an industrial diamond formed from a ball of carbon. It may also be a black diamond or an inferior stone. The Bahian Diamond Fields, Brazil, produce many borts or 'carbonados'. The hardest ones, however, are from New South Wales, Australia.

BOSS A stock, or boss, is a an igneous Intrusive that is rounded or elliptical in shape. Overlying or surrounding rocks have eroded away.

Many stocks and bosses have been found to be mineralized. Some are porphyrys with economic sulfide ores.

BOTRYOIDAL 'Botryoidal' from the Greek for a bunch of grapes is used to describe the shape or form of some minerals.

BOTTOM QUARK The discovery of the Upsilon Particle in atomic physics indicated the existence of a bottom quark, another subatomic particle. The role of these particles is still under study. See **QUARKS**.

BOUDINAGE The 'boudinage' weathering pattern resembles the French sausage links that gave it its name. Tectonic activity broke up the rock and shaped it into elongated forms. Smoothed fractures often have a pillow-like structure.

BOUGUER ANOMALY In gravity surveys, corrections to a predetermined datum have to be made. The resultant value is the Bouguer Anomaly. The correction considers altitude and lithology at the point of observation.

BOULDER A boulder is any block of rock with a diameter greater than 25 centimeters (10 inches). Usually boulders are rounded by abrading and rolling and have been moved a distance from the parent rock. Many have been transported and deposited by glaciers.

BOULDER CLAY Glacial produced clay contains some rocks and boulders. Usually blue-gray or brown, boulder clay is found in morainal (q.v.) material. In Scotland, deposits are up to 60 meters (200 feet) thick.

BOULDER TRAIN A boulder train is debris left by glaciers in transit. It may be fan-shaped. Often more than one path is recorded in the train.

Boulder float in a boulder train may indicate mineral deposits that are not too far away. A major copper deposit was discovered in Finland by mapping boulder float. Uranium float in a boulder train led to rich Canadian deposits. See **FLOAT**.

BOUNDARY CURRENTS Surface north-south parallel oceanic currents flow close to the continental margins. These are boundary currents. Continental masses deflect east-west prevailing current flow. The boundary currents are strongest on the western sides of the oceans.

BOWEN'S REACTION SERIES Bowen determined the order and form of mineral reactions in a magma or melt. He established a continuous and a discontinuous series. He showed that crystallization relates to the cooling sequences of different igneous rocks.

In igneous rocks, the earliest minerals precipitate are under very high temperature and pressure and are the most easily weathered out of the rocks. Labradorite and pyroxene are in this class and will weather more easily than mica and orthoclase feldspar. Quartz, a later phase, is most resistant to weathering.

BOX CANYON A steep-sided valley, so narrow it appears enclosed, is a box canyon. Numerous in southwestern United States, the canyons are divided by very narrow ridges. Travel is difficult and dangerous as canyons can fill quickly during flash floods.

BRACHIOPODS Brachiopods are small crustaceans with thick shells and leaf-like appendages for swimming and feeding. Shells are of chitin and calcium phosphate.

Brachiopods are present in all seas. They first appeared in the Cambrian (570-500 m.y.) with a well-developed structure indicating a long evolution prior to that time. They were diminished during the Permian (280-225) Extinction but were not eliminated.

BRACHIOSAURUS The vegetarian dinosaur, Brachiosaurus, one of the largest of land animals, averaged 100 tons. One author noted that this was equivalent to the weight of 16 large elephants.

BRACKISH WATER When salinity of water is between fresh and salt, it is brackish. Water becomes saline when it has access to the sea or is subject to evaporation. Seawater averages 35 parts per thousand (ppt) of dissolved salts. Brackish has 0.05 to 17 parts per thousand.

BRAHMAPUTRA RIVER The Brahmaputra River originates in the Tibetan Himalayas. It flows through the Indian State of Manipur to Bangladesh where it joins the Ganges. Through the Ganges-Brahmaputra Delta (q.v.) it empties into the Bay of Bengal, an arm of the Indian Ocean.

The annual discharge is 382 cubic kilometers (185 cubic miles) of water. The sediment load contributes to the great delta at the annual rate of 550 million metric tons.

BRAIDED STREAM Several different channels in the lower course of a mature river appear braided. The waters come together and separate. Sedimentary bars separating channels are deposited as the river slows. Unlike meandering streams, braided streams extend over the floodplain.

In arid areas, streams lose carrying capacity as the inflow decreases and a braided pattern can develop upstream. Glacial streams develop the pattern when flow is halted by freezing. A stream subject to great velocity differences due to periodic flooding or estuarine effects may develop the braided pattern. Below Manaus, the Amazon is a braided stream.

RIO BRANCO The Rio Branco, tributary of the Rio Negro, is an important part of the Amazon System. It originates in the Guiana Highlands on the triple border of Brazil, Guyana, and Venezuela.

Rio Branco drains Roraima Territory in Brazil. It flows through a large graben (q.v.) for most of its 563 kilometer (350 mile) course to the confluence with Rio Negro. The Negro joins the Solimoes or Upper Amazon.

BRASILIA-BELEM HIGHWAY   The highway linking the capital of Brazil to Belem at the mouth of the Amazon crosses the southern watershed of that great river. The road is a 2,500 kilometer (1,500 mile) artery cut through savanna and forest. Hopes for agricultural colonies along the strip were abandoned primarily because the rainforest and 'cerrado' soils are not productive.

The Central Brazilian Highlands have been opened up and an outlet to the sea has been established. The highway was asphalted and in constant use by 1975. Communities along the route are almost all dedicated to serving the transport net.

BRASS   Brass is an alloy composed of 70% copper and 30% zinc. It has been a prized metal alloy for centuries. The major use is in plumbing fixtures, ship fittings, and cartridge shells.

BRAZIL   Brazil, the 5th largest country in the world occupies the central and northeast of South America. The country extends over 8.5 million square kilometers (3.3 million square miles) or almost half the continent.

Most of the Amazon Basin is within Brazil where it makes up the northern 1/3 of the nation. The Amazon Valley is densely forested covering thousands of kilometers from the Guiana Highlands to the Central Plateau. The forest stretches from the Andean foothills to the Atlantic Ocean. The Basin produces 20% of the world's freshwater and a 3rd of the world's oxygen. It is literally a lung for the planet.

In sharp contrast to the Amazon Valley is the Northeast drought triangle which forms the Brazilian Bulge. From the babacu palm forests of Maranhão south, the land ranges from semi-arid to arid. It is plagued by extended droughts and torrential rains. See **SERTÃO**.

The eastern Brazilian littoral is fringed with mountains from the Rio Doce to Uruguay. Behind the coastal range in the south is the Parana Plateau, which drains to the La Plata System of Argentina. This Plateau descends in steps to the coastal range.

The Central Plateau of Brazil is the continental divide between the Amazon and the Parana-La Plata systems. The plateau covers 3,087,500 square kilometers (1,187,500 square miles) in Minas Gerais, Goias, and Mato Grosso. It is dissected by great rivers.

In the southwest, the plateau gives way to the 'pantanal'. That lowland covers a part of Mato Grosso which is in the Paraguay Basin. Mountains rise from this lowland on its western edge. Among them are famous mountains of manganese and iron ore, Urucum (q.v.) and Rabicho.

BRAZIL CURRENT   The South Equatorial Current splits off the Brazilian Bulge. One arm flows into the North Atlantic, the other south along Brazil's coast as the Brazil Current.

The Brazil Current turns east at about Latitude 30° South where it and the Falklands Current join to merge into the West Wind Drift (q.v.) of the South Atlantic.

BRAZIL NUT The fruit of the Brazil nut tree (Bertholetia excelsa Lecythidaceae) is edible. Unlike most Amazonian species, the tree grows in clusters in the wild. It attains a height of up to 50 meters (150 feet) and has a triangular shape. It is widespread in and almost exclusive to the Amazon Basin.

The trees produce 15-30 hard nuts in a pod weighing about 2.5 kilograms (5 pounds). These nuts develop on the crown of the tree and are usually over 30 meters (100 feet) up in the tree. When they fall they can be lethal missiles.

Production of nuts has been down over the past 5 years due to the influx of refugees from the northeast harvesting the nuts and felling the trees.

The Brazil nut is unique in having the highest known natural radiation of any food. Radiation is 14,000 times that of common fruits. Radiation levels differ with tree locations. Up to 5.10 ppm (parts per million) of radioactive mineral are recorded.

BRAZILIA The continental shield or ancient cratonic area upon which much of modern Brazil rests is known as 'Brazilia'.

BRAZILIAN COMPLEX Brazilian rocks of Archaen Age were called 'Brazilian Complex' by Branner (1917). The name is still in general use. The rocks make up the crystalline basement found at the core of the eastern mountains, Serra do Espinhaco (Backbone Mountains) and the Serra do Mar. The Serra do Mar forms an almost solid barrier along the Atlantic Coast.

BRAZILIAN HIGHLANDS Part of the southern perimeter of the Amazon Basin is formed by the Brazilian Highlands. South of the Amazon Plains these highlands rise gradually from the lowlands.

In the south, the highlands drop by a series of abrupt steps into the South Atlantic. The Highlands are separated from the Andes by the uplands or 'chapadas' (q.v.) of the Central Plateau.

BRAZILIAN MATA The Brazilian Mata is separate from the Amazon Forest although it was once a part. It is a small tropical rainforest stretching along the Brazilian coast of Bahia. It is its most dense near Ilheus. There are outliers in Espirito Santo, São Paulo, along the Rio de Janeiro coast and into Minas Gerais. These forests are rapidly disappearing.

The forest was and is cut primarily to create farmland and for fuel. The advent of railways burning fuelwood hastened its destruction.

Brazil is reforesting a large portion of this area, but the trees being planted are rarely tropical hardwoods.

BRAZILIAN OIL SHALE Brazil has vast areas of oil shale reserves, second only to the United States. The Irati Shale which forms an enormous S-shaped formation in the Parana Basin extends from São Paulo to Uruguay. It appears to be the richest in retortable oil.

In the sub-Amazon Basin in Maranhão, Piaui, and Goias, an area of 385,000 square kilometers (230,000 square miles is underlain by Paleozoic shales. Also in Maranhão, the Codo Formation contains kerogen (q.v.). The Longo Shales appear to be the most widespread.

For years, Brazil has been operating a pilot plant operation for the extraction of oil from shale. Based upon the success of the process, a plant is proposed closer to the Irati source area.

BRAZILWOOD Brazilwood, 'pau Brasil' is a variety of 'Caesalpina' from which a reddish-purple dye, brazilin, is produced. Trade in this wood caused the first interest in this part of the New World and gave Brazil its name.

BREACHED ANTICLINE An anticline (q.v.) eroded along its axis is breached. Erosional scarps face the central gap and each other.

BREADFRUIT The breadfruit tree ('Artocarpus altilis') is seedless and reproduces from the root. Originally from Malaysia, it was introduced into Polynesia where its fruit has become a staple.

BREAKER A wave approaching the shore will break and dissolve. The break is usually at the crest. There are 4 types of discernible breakers:

Spilling   - A wind wave that takes a great distance to dissolve.

Plunging - Swell produces combers or plungers that curl and dissolve with a crash. A hollow forms in front of the wave.

Surging   - The wave peaks before spilling or plunging.

Collapsing- The wave breaks in the middle or at bottom.

BREAK-IN-SLOPE A break-in-slope is an abrupt gradient change on an arid mountain-side. The mountain rises from the pedimented (q.v.) lower slope. The abrupt break-in-slope is also called the knickpoint.

BREAKS 'The breaks' is a term used to describe terrain bordering uplands that are deeply eroded and ravined.

BRECCIA Angular fragments of rock cemented by similar material of finer grain are 'breccia', Italian for broken material. Breccia retain their angularity. The fragments have not traveled far.

Breccia can result from mechanical friction on faults and joints, or be of volcanic origin. Often breccia plug the throat of a volcano. Then, it is termed a breccia pipe.

Mechanical weathering products contributing to talus are often called breccia.

BREEDER REACTOR A breeder reactor produces fissionable material in excess of immediate needs. The excess may be used as a future fuel.

BRICK Brick is the result of the heating and compression of muds or clay. It may be natural or manufactured, as is adobe (q.v.).

When a brick is baked, the magnetic particles within it align themselves with the Earth's Magnetic Field.

BRIDALVEIL FALLS Bridalveil falls are cataracts of water which almost dissipate before reaching the valley floor. The spray is reminiscent of a bride's veil.

Bridalveil falls are found in glacially scoured areas where a tributary stream was cut off when a glacier carved the deep U-shaped valley. The tributary mouth was left high above the mainstream and water now cascades over the edge. Bridalveil Falls in Yosemite, California, had this origin.

BRILLIANT CUT The brilliant cut diamond has 58 facets, 33 above and 25 below the girdle of the gem. The pyramid was the basis for the brilliant cut.

BRIMSTONE Brimstone is another name for sulfur (q.v.). Usually, brimstone is associated with volcanoes, with invisible flames, and choking fumes. Ejected sulfur has all these characteristics.

BRINE A brine is saline water, less salty than seawater. It is impregnated with soluble salts. Lagoonal waters are often brines, since seawater is diluted by freshwater.

Evaporation increases the salt content of lakes in arid and semi- arid regions and brines develop. Great Salt Lake became a brine in this way. Brines often contain valuable minerals. The brines may be worked for these. Many are simply worked for salt (q.v.).

BRIQUET (BRIQUETTE) A briquet is a compact mass of coal or metal. It is composed of dust-size particles in an aggregate. Briquettes form under heat but may naturally cement without being heated.

BRISTLECONE PINE The Bristlecone Pine growing in the White Mountains of California, is the oldest known living tree. According to tree ring counts, it is 5,000 years old. This age agrees with the carbon-14 dating. Comparatively, redwoods at 2,000 years are young. Bristlecone pines grow in Precambrian soils derived from limestone or dolomite.

There are Bristlecones in Colorado and New Mexico that are not so old. They generally grow sheltered by Aspen. These Bristlecones appear to be a different species.

BROKEN HILL   Broken Hill Mine, New South Wales, Australia, produces lead and zinc. The ore is in relatively unaltered sediments that are not associated with volcanics. Discovery was made during a major gold rush.

BROMELIADS   Bromeliads ('Bromeliaceae') are widespread tropical plants. It was the largest plant family found only in America until 'Pitcairnia' was discovered in South Africa. A third of all bromeliad species are found in Brazil. The family includes epiphytes and some herbs.

Pineapples are bromeliads. Along coastal Brazil, pineapples were almost completely uprooted because they were providing a breeding ground for malaria- and yellow fever-carrying mosquitoes. Pineapples were introduced into Hawaii where they flourished.

BROMINE   The non-metallic halogen element, bromine, a reddish liquid, is noted for its bad but distinctive odor. Bromine is used in photography and in the production of gasoline.

Bromine is one of the chemicals implicated in the depletion of the Ozone Layer (q.v.) although it is not nearly so important as chlorine (q.v.).

BRONTOSAURUS   One of the largest animals that ever lived, Brontosaurus, the Thunder Lizard, was a vegetarian. The reptile averaged 85' long.

BRONZE   Bronze, one of the oldest alloys of human creation, is 90% copper and 10% tin. It is stronger and more durable than copper alone. In order to give church-bells better tone, copper is 70% and tin 30%.

The Romans used bronze extensively as did other cultures during the Bronze Age. Fine bronze sculptures have been unearthed in Benin, Africa.

BROOKITE   Brookite, a brownish-black mineral, is a titanium oxide ore. It is found in commercial deposits at Magnet Cove, Arkansas. Brookite is a constituent of many carbonatites (q.v.).

BROWN AIR   Brown air is the photochemical SMOG (q.v.) found in some cities (Los Angeles, Mexico City, Tokyo). Dry climate coupled with nitrogen dioxide emitted by industry and automobile exhaust are the cause of the yellow-brown color in the air.

BROWN ALGAE   Brown Algae ('Phaeophyceae') is also yellowish to blue-green in color. It contains a pigment which disguises its chlorophyll. It is usually found in cool, deep water. Sargassum weed is an exception, being found in the warm Sargasso Sea (q.v.).

On more northerly coasts, brown rockweed and intertidal kelp are common. The range is from low-tide to 12-15 meters (40-50 feet) of depth. Many are sources of iodine. See **ALGAE**.

BROWN FOREST SOILS Brown forest soils form a great intrazonal soils group. They are calcium-rich and found beneath deciduous forests. There is no real development of an illuvial (q.v.) horizon.

BROWN SOILS Brown soils are lighter in color than brown forest soils. They support grasses and shrubs and are found in temperate to cool, semi-arid climates. The color grades to lighter with depth. Often brown soils grade into carbonates. See **BRUNIZEMS**.

BROWNIAN MOTION Brownian motion is the ceaseless, random movement of particles in a gas or liquid. The particles held in suspension are surrounded by molecules of the liquid or gaseous medium.

BROWNSTONE Brownstone is a dark-brown Triassic (225-190 m.y.) sandstone from the Connecticut River Valley. The sandstone grains are coated with iron oxide which is responsible for the brown color.

Once a prized building stone, many famous old houses in New York City were constructed of brownstone.

BROWSE Plants eaten by cattle and herbivorous animals are browse. Browse includes leaves, buds, and shoots of low trees and shrubs.

BRUNIZEM SOILS Brunizems are zonal soils with a distinctive A-horizon of brown soil grading into a lighter color. Calcium carbonate may be present. These soils are found in semi-arid grasslands.

BRUNSWICK MAGNETIC ANOMALY A magnetic anomaly along a 78 kilometer (40.8 miles) suture (q.v.) was detected off the northeast coast of North America. It yielded 2 traces indicating that the suture zone ended at the Mohorovicic Discontinuity at a depth of 35 kilometers (21 miles).

BRUNTON COMPASS The Brunton Pocket Transit combines 3 survey instruments: Compass, clinometer, and level. It can be hand-held and is used to measure strike and dip on layered sediments, veins, and faults.

BRYOPHYTES Bryophytes are tiny plants with a 2-stage life-cycle, one of which is parasitic. They include liverworts and mosses, plants lacking in xylem and phloem.

Bryophytes first appeared in the Devonian Period (395-345 m.y.) and are presently found in the Tundra and at high elevations on mountain slopes.

BRYOZOA Bryozoa are aquatic organisms which formed colonies on seamount lavas. They include moss animals and sea laces, and some resemble seaweeds. Bryozoa have a complete digestive system, a body cavity, and a very simple nervous system. Bryozoa date from the Cambrian Period (570-500 m.y.).

'Archimedes', a species of Bryozoa shaped like a screw, is an indicator fossil for the Pennsylvanian (300-280 m.y.). There are about 3,000 marine species and some 35 freshwater.

BUBBLE MEMORY The tiny area of magnetic bubbles on silicon chips form the memory bank used for computers.

BUFFALO GRASS When the pioneers crossed the Great Plains, they encountered a pasture grass so high it almost hid the wagons. This was buffalo grass.

As the climate became warmer and rainfall in the area decreased, the grass ceased to flourish. It is likely that the near extinction of the buffalo was due as much to diminishing grass as over-hunting. Hunting accelerated a process already underway.

BUFFALO WALLOW 'Buffalo Wallow' graphically describes the shallow depressions found on uplands. They are solution-weathered areas that fill with rainwater. The size increases with each successive storm. Often, they are intermediate in gully development.

BULK SAMPLE To determine the value of metallurgical ores, bulk samples from tons to hundreds of tons are necessary. They are put through a pilot plant and are analyzed and evaluated at each stage.

BULLION Bullion is unrefined gold, melted and molded into bars. Gold sponge from placer operations is often formed into bullion bars. To make the gold more pourable, a flux of boron (q.v.) is added.

BURGESS SHALE Middle Cambrian (535 m.y.) Burgess Shale on Mount Wapta, British Columbia, has a remarkable fossil assemblage, particularly of soft-bodied organisms.

The formation is a calcareous shale lens in a basin limestone. There are many faunal genera, some related to modern ones. A pelagic (q.v.) and a benthic (q.v.) community are present.

BURIED PLACERS Ancient placers may be covered by younger sediments or volcanic material. Some have become very deep mines as in South Africa. Similar deposits have been found in Brazil.

BUSH Bush is widely used in Africa for areas of secondary growth in rainforests. The growth is usually not as dense as jungle (q.v.). It consists of shrubs, bushes, low-creeping vines, and small trees, all matted together. A similar area can be found on the South American coast from the Orinoco Delta to the Amazon, just inland from the mangrove swamps.

In Australia, bush is used interchangeably with outback (q.v.). In Alaska, inaccessible and mountainous areas are called bush. In the contiguous United States, bush implies a wilderness area.

BUTTE 'Butte', French for tableland, is the counterpart of mesa (q.v.). American geologists consider the butte smaller than the mesa.

Buttes are common in northwestern United States, while mesas abound in the southwest. Both are isolated, steep-sided, and flat-topped. They are usually capped by erosion-resistant materials, commonly lava.

BUTTE COPPER The copper mines at Butte, Montana, were consistently worked up until the 1980's. Butte began in 1875 as a silver mine. It was known as the 'Richest Hill on Earth'. Before becoming a copper mine, 4,000 tons of silver and 20 tons of gold were produced.

BY-PRODUCT Mineral produced other than of primary output is by-product. Many mines produce by-product base metals (q.v.) that would not be economic if produced alone. This is especially true of gold.

By-product is the term used for the fissionable product of nuclear fission.

Borborema Pegmatite Dike — Northeast Brazil

C

c The symbol 'c' is a mathematical constant for the speed of light, which is expressed as c = 310,000 kilometers (186,000 miles) per second.

CAATINGA The sparse thorn forest of the Sertão (q.v.), Northeast Brazil, is called 'caatinga'. Caatinga is a Brazilian word for the bad odor exuded by some of the vegetation. Caatinga composed of stunted trees and thorny shrubs is a xerophytic vegetation adapted to this semi-arid land.

CABOCHON The cabochon is a very popular gemstone cut. It has an oval-shaped dome, is polished but not faceted. The cut is used for soft, semi-precious stones.

CADASTRAL MAP Cadastral maps give the boundaries of areas, subdivisions, and individual tracts. They are used primarily for tax purposes. Ownership of dwellings and appurtenances (outbuildings) are shown. Cadastral is from the French 'cadastre', to register.

CADMIUM The bluish-white metallic element, cadmium is becoming more important in modern industry. The ductile and malleable metal is found associated with zinc. The zinc ore sphalerite, especially black sphalerite, contains minor amounts of cadmium and manganese in addition to up to 18% iron.

Cadmium is used in electro-plating. Of late it has found increased use in nickel-cadmium batteries. When material containing the metal is scrapped and burned cadmium is released as an oxide.

Cadmium is toxic and has a usage twice that of mercury to which it is related. Cadmium also has a tendency to accumulate. It could become a serious environmental hazard.

CAIRNGORM In Scotland the Cairngorm Mountains were host to the smoky quartz crystals used in traditional Scottish jewelry. The deposits are mostly worked out. Today, citrine crystals are imported from Brazil to replace the cairngorms.

CALC- The prefix calc- denotes lime. It is used to describe rocks and minerals containing calcium carbonate.

CALC-ALKALINE Magmatic rocks with an alkaline to lime content of 55-61% are considered calc-alkaline.

CALCAREOUS A substance that contains more than 50% calcium carbonate is calcareous. Marine fossils in coral limestones are calcareous.

CALCAREOUS OOZE Calcareous ooze formed since the Jurassic (135 m.y.) covers up to 50% of the ocean floor. It is made up of deep sea sediments made up of Algae ('Coccolithophores') and Foraminifera. The organisms lived near the surface as plankton and their remains rained to the seafloor after death. Long burial transforms ooze into limestone (q.v.).

Ooze does not form on shelf areas because there are terrestrial erosional products making up the bulk of the shelf sediments.

CALCIC SERIES Igneous rocks with an alkaline to lime index greater than 61% are members of the Calcic Series.

CALCITE The principal mineral in limestone or dolomite is calcite, a crystallized calcium carbonate.

Calcite appears in many forms and is a very common mineral. It is colorless and transparent with a hardness of 3 on Moh's Scale (q.v.). Crystalline calcite has perfect rhombohedral cleavage. If broken, fragments will be rhombohedrons with smooth shiny sides.

Icelandic Spar, a rare and transparent form of calcite, is economically important. Travertine and marble are massive calcite.

CALCIUM Calcium, a silvery-white metal, is an alkaline earth element. It occurs naturally only in combination with other elements.

CALCRETE Cemented calcareous soil horizons are calcrete. In Southwestern United States indurated calcareous horizons or caliche may be developing into calcrete. They are unlike calcrete horizons found in Australia or South Africa. See **CALICHE**.

Massive Kalahari limestone, a calcium carbonate formed in an ephemeral (q.v.) lake in South Africa, is calcrete. Calcium carbonates mixed with tuffs at Olduvai Gorge, East Africa, are also calcretes. Calcretes are found in valleys and along stream channels in Australia and South Africa.

The link among these different deposits is climate, which in all cases is, and was when the calcrete developed, arid to semi-arid. Differences may be attributed to age, local conditions, and phase of development.

Some valley-type calcretes are uraniferous. The most important so far discovered are at Yeeleerie, Australia and Langer Heinrich, Southwest Africa.

CALDERA A large crater formed by the explosion and collapse of a volcano is a 'caldera', Spanish for kettle or cauldron. The great cavity of Las Canadas, Canary Islands, is a caldera. At Asosan, Japan, the caldera is 23 x 16 kilometers (14.3 x 10 miles).

Collapse and subsidence of the volcano followed when material from former eruptions plugging the volcanic neck was explosively ejected and pulverized. Repeated eruptions can destroy newly developed crater walls. Further collapse enlarges a caldera.

Most calderas are lake filled. The pressure that brought about the collapse of huge mountains, caused the development of domes, new cones, smaller craters, and vents. These structures rise from the floor of the huge, newly created depressions.

The caldera is a landform that is becoming increasingly well-known. Calderas are found in the Rockies and in the Great Basin. Yellowstone is the largest in the United States. It is 67 kilometers (40 miles) in diameter. Krakatoa, Ngorongora, and Santorini are a few of the famous calderas.

Mount Mazama, in southern Oregon exploded and collapsed 6,500 years ago. The mountain was 3,600 meters (12,000 feet) high. The new crater formed by the collapsed volcano filled with rainwater to form Crater Lake. Wizard Island is the erosional result of a small dome.

CALEDONIAN MOUNTAINS The Caledonian Orogeny culminating in the Caledonian Mountains began over 600 million years ago at the end of the Proterozoic. The mountains have been eroding since.

Remnants like the Scottish Highlands are found in Europe, North America, and West Africa. These Caledonian remnants extend from Scotland to Scandinavia and North Ireland. The mountains appear in Greenland but the connection through Iceland is missing. In Newfoundland, Caledonian System mountains form the Older Appalachians.

Once the Caledonians were as high as the Himalayas. They are composed of very hard, metamorphic rocks. Its southwest-northeast orientation is evident in the Great Glen of Scotland. The Caledonian System was built on the great continental landmass of Laurasia (q.v.). This continent subsequently broke apart, recollided, and separated again.

CALICHE Gravel and detritus cemented with calcium carbonate form hardpans in desert and semi-desert soils. These caliches are widespread and represent fossil soil horizons.

On the High Plains of Kansas, Oklahoma, and Texas, caliches are prevalent. The Mescalero Caliche of New Mexico forms ledges and caps.

Impure nitrates from Chile and Peru are called 'caliche'.

CALIFORNIA CURRENT South of Vancouver, Canada, the Japanese or Kuro Shio Current becomes the California Current. It is a cold boundary current paralleling the continent. It accounts for the famous San Francisco fogs.

The main current leaves the California Coast at Monterey and heads southwest towards the Equator. Its circuit is completed when the California Current merges into the North Pacific Equatorial Current.

A minor limb of the current bathes the Southern California Coast and accounts for the famous Southern California marine layer.

CALIFORNIA DESERT From Lake Tahoe on the north into Baja California, Mexico, California is desert. It extends from Antelope Valley to Death Valley and it represents about 25-30% of the state.

Within this region, there are 5 distinct physiographic provinces:
- Basin and Range
- The Mojave Desert
- The Salton Trough
- The Peninsula Ranges

Elevations range from 85 meters (280 feet) below sea level in Death Valley to 4,333 meters (14,200 feet) in the White Mountains. Rock types range from Precambrian (2.3 b.y.) to Recent.

CALORIE The calorie is a measure of heat. A gram of water raised 1° Celsius under 1 atmosphere of pressure requires 1 calorie of heat.

CALVING Calving is a glacial weathering process. Great chunks of ice break off glaciers at zones of weakness. Icebergs originate this way. Up to 15,000 icebergs are estimated to calve off the Greenland Ice Cap each year.

CAMBIUM Soft tissue found between the wood and bark of a tree is the cambium. From it secondary growth is produced. Tree rings mark annual growth in the cambium of temperate climate trees.

CAMBRIAN The earliest period of the Paleozoic Era (570-225 m.y.) is the Cambrian (570-500 m.y.). It was named for Wales in Great Britain.

In the Cambrian slow transgressions invaded the continent. These are estimated at 16 kilometers (10 miles) per million years. Warm, shallow, epicontinental seas resulted in which life flourished.

The first shelled invertebrates arose in the Cambrian. Trilobites (q.v.) abounded and late in Cambrian, Nautiloids were present. Shelled brachiopods, whose early skeletons were of phosphate, preceded the trilobites. Graptolites appeared in Mid-Cambrian. Wide, shallow continental shelves of limestone, sandstone, and shale built up. Continental areas are presumed to have been desert. The Taconian Orogeny ended the period.

CAMEL A great caravan animal, the camel, has endurance and is adapted to harsh steppe and desert climates. It is related to the llama, alpaca, and vicuña, all found in the Andes. The Arabo-African camel has 1 hump,the Bactrian of Central Asia 2.

Camels were imported into the United States early in the century for service in the southwest desert. The experiment was not successful.

Camels were also introduced into Australia during the gold rush and were successful. Afghan drovers were brought in with the camels and they may have made the difference. Some trains still are in existence. The camels today contribute to tourism.

CAMEROON Cameroon in west-central Africa is geographically transitional between Savanna and Rainforest. Its southern boundary is within 2° of the Equator.

Southern Cameroon reaches to the Congo Basin in the east and is host to part of the Ituri Rainforest (q.v.). The Adamaoua Plateau is in central Cameroon with elevations between 700-1,000 meters (2,300-3,300 feet) covered by savanna and gallery forest. Its core is the Adamaoua Batholith. See **BATHOLITH**.

Benoue River Basin is in the north as is part of the Chad Basin (q.v.). Savanna gives way to desert as Lake Chad is approached. Along the west coast a volcanic range traces an old rift system. Its major activity was in the Cretaceous (130-65 m.y.) and Tertiary (65-2 m.y.) when its effusions covered the plateaus of Adamaoua and western Cameroon. See **CAMEROON VOLCANO**.

The Precambrian (q.v.) metamorphics of the area were intruded by granite, diorite, and gneiss. The major outcrops are Precambrian since the sedimentary cover laid down in later series have all but eroded away. They are most evident today in the Benoue Basin.

CAMEROON VOLCANO Cameroon is an active volcano on the West African Coast. Separated from the rest of the range. Cameroon has 2 peaks and no craters. Eruptions are from fissures. Great Cameroon is 4,000 meters (13,350 feet) high and Little Cameroon, 1,760 meters (5,820 feet). The latter is smothered in tropical forest and its southwest flank extends to the Atlantic.

CAMPOS 'Campos', Latin for fields, cover a large part of Latin America. They are broad grasslands, usually on upland terrain. In Brazil, campos are found along the coast and on the Central Plateau.

CANADA Canada extends over almost 10 million square kilometers (4 million square miles). Its boundary with Alaska is the 141st Meridian. With the contiguous United States, the 54°40' parallel of North Latitude is the line. The Arctic Ocean separates it from the USSR.

Canada is the world's 2nd largest country and covers 6 times zones. It is endowed with the largest supply of freshwater in the world.

There are 3 major physiographic subdivisions:

- Canadian Shield (q.v.) - From Labrador to Lake Winnipeg. Precambrian (q.v.) rocks.
- Downfolds - West Central Canada. Young folded mountains.
- Cordillera - West. The Canadian Rockies.

Canada leads the world in the production of asbestos, nickel, silver, and zinc. It is 2nd in gypsum, potash, sulfur, and uranium. It is also a leading producer of aluminum from nepheline.

There is major production of copper, iron, gold, platinum, and titanium. Canada is well endowed with coal on both coasts and petroleum in mid-continent and in the Mackenzie Delta on the Beaufort Sea. Major production of oil from tar sands (q.v.) began in Athabasca in 1986.

CANADIAN SHIELD The Canadian or Laurentian Shield extends from Eastern and Central Canada into Minnesota, Wisconsin, Michigan, and New York. It is the largest exposed Precambrian surface in the world.

The shield is 80% composed of granite-gneiss. The Archean Greenstone Belt was surrounded by various Proterozoic (q.v.) mountain ranges which have since eroded away. The almost sea level or peneplained relief shows the roots of these ancient ranges. See **GREENSTONE BELTS** and **PRECAMBRIAN**.

CANANEA COPPER DISTRICT Cananea Copper District produced 1.5 billion pounds of copper and 25 million ounces of silver in its first 100 years of operation. The deposits are in porphyry (q.v.), in breccia pipes, in limestone replacements, and in contact metamorphic rocks. The main copper minerals are bornite and chalcopyrite. The district is between Nogales and Naco in Mexico in the Cavanca Range.

CANARY CURRENT The Gulf Stream branches so one arm curves about the Subtropical Convergence Zone and is influenced by the Northeast Trades. This branch becomes the North Atlantic Current, which again branches off Iberia to form the cold Canary Current that flows along the African Coast.

The Canary Current also branches so one arm joins the Guinea Current flowing south at the African Bulge and the other joins the North Equatorial Current flowing west.

CANARY ISLANDS The Canaries are off Northwest Africa, 50 seamiles from Morocco. These are the 'Fortunate Isles' discovered in the 15th century some 1,160 kilometers (700 miles) south of Spain.

There are 7 islands of volcanic origin. Las Canadas on Tenerife is a caldera, 12.5 kilometers (7.5 miles) across. The lava of Lanzarote is likened to that of the Moon. Among its sparse vegetation, there is the so-called Dragon Tree which is 3,000 years old.

CANGA 'Canga', Brazilian for aggregates of iron fragments, hematite and itabirite. These are cemented iron oxides and hydroxides together with other minerals. Many plateaus and stream valleys in Brazil are literally paved with canga. Sir Richard Burton (1868) described canga as 'the ground rang as if iron-plated'.

Canga has other names in different parts of the tropics and semitropics. It maybe laterite cap in the making or eroding.

CANOPY The uppermost, leafy crown in the multi-tiered forest is the canopy. It is so interlaced that sunlight is restricted to vegetion below. The canopy contributes to the closed life-cycle of the rainforest as the chief source of evapotranspiration. Taller trees above the canopy are emergents. In the Amazon, these are mostly palms.

The canopy is especially important in a tropical rainforest where it supports an abundant arboreal population.

CANYON A canyon is a narrow valley with exceptionally steep, high side walls. Canyons are common in youthful (q.v.) terrain. They result from block faulting or other tectonic activity as well as from stream erosion. The steep sides are enhanced by stream cutting through sediments. The Grand Canyon (q.v.) is a good example.

CAPACITY Capacity is the ability of a stream to transport detritus. It is a measure of the velocity at which material moves (about 20% of stream velocity).

Capacity should not be confused with load, which is the material actually being transported.

A soil's capability to retain moisture is its capacity. It is expressed as the ratio of water-bearing soil weight to that of dry soil.

CAPE A cape is a bulging coast. It is larger than a point but smaller than a peninsula. Its elevation is the same as the surrounding terrain.

Most capes form bluffs. These may be of any rock type. Cape Manuel near Dakar on the African Coast is of basalt while Cabo Branco, Northeast Brazil, is of Barreirras Sandstone.

CAPILLARITY Capillarity is a physical phenomenon of molecular attraction. Water is raised or lowered in a volume by surface contact with a solid. This attractive force between a solid and a liquid is important in clay mineralogy.

Important in rock weathering, capillary water can be raised above the water table and in some cases the height can be relatively great. It varies according to sediment type:

Sand	-	Up to 0.5 meters (1.65 feet)
Silt	-	Up to 5.0 meters (16.5 feet)
Clay	-	Up to 50 meters (165 feet)

The intermittent wetting of sediments accelerates weathering.

Plants obtain nutrition from soils through their roots by means of capillarity. The nutrient-bearing solution is moved upward through the plant, molecule by molecule.

CAPILLARY FRINGE The transitional area between the zone of saturation and zone of aeration in groundwater is the capillary fringe.

Water is held in sediment interstices by surface tension. Pore spaces are too small for water to pour out but it can seep upward.

CAPILLARY MIGRATION Solutions may rise to the soil surface by capillarity (q.v.). The process is capillary migration. It is important in the formation of saline crusts, laterites, and bauxites (q.v.). Capillarity functions in seasons when leaching rainfall is at a minimum.

CAPILLARY WAVES Small ripples on the sea surface are caused by a gentle breeze of less than 2 knots (3.8 kilometers or 2.3 miles) per hour. These are capillary waves. The wind must increase above this level to induce gravity waves.

EL CAPITAN The great cliff of El Capitan in Yosemite National Park is on the western slope of the Sierra Nevada. It exposes the oldest and strongest of the 7 different granite types making up the California Batholith. The cliff is thought to be the tallest unbroken cliff on Earth. It rises to 1,000 meters (3,000 feet). See **BATHOLITH**.

CAPROCK Resistant rock directly overlying a less resistant material is a caprock when exposed at the surface. Caprocks may be of congealed lava, quartzite, or any other relatively hard rock.

Laterites (q.v.) frequently form caprocks on ancient peneplaned surfaces in tropical and subtropical areas. Congealed basalt flows form common caprocks. These preserve the structure of mesas and buttes in many of the western United States.

CAPTURE A stream naturally detoured to another drainage channel is said to be captured. Capture can result from headward erosion that destroys a divide area. Tectonics can change stream flow and shift it to another system. Volcanic eruptions and flows have altered many channels. In glaciated terrain, moraines block and alter flow. Even the beaver can change the drainage with their dams.

CARAT Carat is the unit of weight for precious stones and gold. The carat or carot bean from the lotus pod tree ('Ceratonia') was used as the standard unit for centuries. 142 carats = 1 ounce.

The metric carat is 200 milligrams (0.2 grams). 1 gram = 5 carats. The metric carat is now internationally accepted as standard. It was adopted because each center had a different unit. The London carat was 205.3, the Amsterdam 205.7, and the Florentine 197.2 milligrams.

CARBIDE A compound of carbon with another element is carbide. It has a hardening effect on metals. Often the combining element is tungsten. Tools used for cutting and drilling are usually of carbide.

CARBOHYDRATE The product of photosynthesis (q.v.) is carbohydrate. It contains the basic sugars, starches, and cellulose essential to animal life.

CARBON The carbon atom has 6 protons, 6 neutrons, and 6 electrons, 4 in the outer shell, This outer shell is only 1/2 full. To be complete, the outer shell needs 8 electrons. To complete the shell, carbon forms a compound by bonding with a metal or non-metal.

Carbon is found in all living organisms. The mineral makes up 0.1% of all rocks and exists in them in 3 forms. These are:

- The pure crystal - Diamonds
- Crystalline of amorphous - Graphite
- Massive - Coal.

CARBON CYCLE Most carbon is tied up in the Atmosphere or Ocean as carbon dioxide. Carbon dioxide is taken up by vegetation during photosynthesis (q.v.). It returns to the Atmosphere through transpiration and in decay to the Earth and Atmosphere. Vegetation gives off oxygen and animals respire it, giving off carbon dioxide. Bacteria play an important role in the decomposition phase. See **CARBON DIOXIDE**.

Some carbon combines with calcium to form limestone. In the seas life-forms selectively take calcium carbonate from the ocean to form shells and hard parts. After death these become incorporated into rocks such as limestone and dolomite. From these the calcium carbonate is released through solution and erosion to recombine or return to the Atmosphere. The carbon cycle can take millions of years.

CARBON DIOXIDE Carbon dioxide or the compound of carbon and oxygen makes up only 0.03% of the Atmosphere. It is, however, critical to the biosphere. The colorless, odorless gas is 1.5 times heavier than air. Carbon dioxide accumulates in caves and mines, or other confined areas. Since it displaces air, asphixiation can result.

Carbon dioxide is the main contributor to the Greenhouse Effect (q.v.). Transparent carbon dioxide is an effective screen against ultra-violet light rays. It also traps infra-red radiation from the Earth. An excess can trap heat in the Earth's atmospheric envelope and cause global warming.

Mauna Loa Observatory monitors carbon dioxide in the Atmosphere. In 1958, the level was 315 ppm (parts per million). By 1984, the level had increased to 340 ppm. Pre-industrialization levels have been estimated at 265 ppm.

Deforestation (q.v.) rivals fossil-fuel burning as a source of atmospheric carbon dioxide. Raging forest fires, almost continental in scope, occur in dry seasons. Most are left to burn out. Fires of great magnitude have occurred in recent years in Africa, Brazil, and Australia accounting for 1/2 the added carbon dioxide from this source since 1950. In the past 50 years, atmospheric carbon dioxide has increased 15%.

If atmospheric carbon dioxide were to double from 0.03% to 0.06%, a tropical climate would prevail all over the globe. Icecaps would melt and oceans rise an estimated 200 feet, increasing moisture over the Earth. In turn, this would reduce the carbon dioxide.   The cycle is however exceedingly long.

CARBON MONOXIDE When insufficient oxygen is available to form carbon dioxide, carbon monoxide is formed. It is a product of poor combustion. From 200 to 300 million tons a year are released into the Atmosphere, 1/3 in the United States.

In some congested city streets, 50 ppm (parts per million) is not an uncommon amount. It is much higher in tunnels and underground garages. In the Troposphere (q.v.), carbon monoxide is 0.1-0.2 ppm (parts per million).

Carbon monoxide is a colorless, odorless gas that is lethal. It combines with hemoglobin in the red cells of humans and animals displacing oxygen. An impairment of mental faculties occurs after 15 minutes at 200 ppm.

CARBON RATIO The percentage of fixed carbon in coal is the carbon ratio. The higher the percentage of fixed carbon, the greater the degree of metamorphism. The greater the carbon ratio, the harder the coal.

CARBON-14 Carbon-14 is a radioactive isotope of elemental carbon. Carbon-14 is forming all the time from atmospheric nitrogen as a nuclear reaction caused by cosmic rays. All organisms absorb carbon-14 while alive and cease to do so at death. This fact is useful to archaeologists dating carbonaceous materials younger than 30,000 years.

Carbon-14 unites with oxygen to form radioactive carbon dioxide which mixes with ordinary carbon dioxide. Carbon from carbon dioxide becomes living plant tissue and is, together with carbon-14, passed on to animals via the food chain.

The ratio of ordinary carbon, or carbon-12, to carbon-14 is important for dating. Half the carbon-14 decays to carbon-12 in 5,570 years.

CARBONADO A 'carbonado' is a black diamond of inferior quality unsuitable for a gem. It is very useful industrially. Carbonados were first produced from Jacobina Range, Bahia, Brazil. Most are aggregated black carbon and average 2 ounces. Australia is now a major producer.

CARBONATE MINERALS Carbonate is a salt or ester of carbonic acid, a compound of the metal with carbon and oxygen. Calcium carbonate is found in calcite and aragonite. Calcium carbonate, or carbonate of lime, is the major constituent of chalk, limestone, and dolomite and is a cementing agent in many other rocks.

Dolomite is calcium carbonate with magnesium. Magnesite is magnesium carbonate and siderite is iron carbonate. The chalk cliffs of Dover are calcium carbonate from phytoplankton remains.

Corals and mollusks form hard parts from secreted aragonite. Aragonite is not as durable as calcite. Some mollusks have shells of low magnesium calcite. Echinoderms and Foraminifera are formed of high magnesium calcite in shallow seas.

CARBONATE PIPES Carbonate pipes or vents have been described from many locations in eastern and southern Africa. They are often associated with ring-dikes and carbonatites (q.v.). The Chilwa Series of Malawi has diameters between 1 and 5 kilometers across.

CARBONATITES Carbonatites are associated with alkaline igneous rocks (q.v.). They were considered metamorphic until carbonate flows were observed at Oldoinyo Lingai in the Great Rift Valley, East Africa. Carbonatites contain phosphates, Rare Earths, titanium, thorium, and vermiculite.

Carbonate material solidifies as a kind of limestone or dolomite. Ankerite, a carbonate of iron is often present. Carbonatites occur as lava flows, tuffs, breccia pipes, plugs, ring dikes, or cone sheets. The carbonate material is very eroded in most of the known carbonatites. Ankerite is sometimes the only clue.

Phalaborwa, South Africa, is an unusual carbonatite with a major copper and phosphate mineralization. In addition there are Rare Earths and other mineral suites.

Carbonatites around the world are now major sources of apatite, a raw material of phosphate fertilizers. The most important producers from carbonatites are Brazil, Finland, South Africa, and the USSR. Production from Kola Peninsula, USSR, has been increasing steadily.

Carbonatite at Araxa, Brazil, is the world's major source of niobium. It supports a phosphate operation as well. There are niobium deposits in Canadian carbonatites also. The most well-known carbonatites in the United States are at Magnet Cove, Arkansas and Mt. Pass, California. Brookite, a titanium oxide mineral, is produced at Magnet Cove and bastnaesite, an ore containing Rare Earths, is produced at Mt. Pass.

CARBONIFEROUS The Carboniferous Period (345-280 m.y.) in the Paleozoic Age (570-225 m.y.) was preceded by the Devonian and followed by the Permian. In the United States, the Carboniferous is divided into Mississippian and Pennsylvanian; in Europe Westphalian and Stefanian.

The Carboniferous is economically important. Forests began in the Devonian, but became luxuriant and widespread in the Carboniferous. Toward the end of the period, the forests began to diminish. Fossilization of vast amounts of vegetation began and gave rise to great coal seams. These have been especially important in North America and Europe.

CARBONIZATION Plants can be transformed into rocks by carbonization. It is a process in which plants composed primarily of carbon, hydrogen, oxygen, and nitrogen are subjected to heat and pressure. The hydrogen, oxygen, and nitrogen are driven off leaving the carbon. Many organic structures were preserved in this process.

CARBORUNDUM Carborundum is a compound composed of carbon and sand. It is particularly noted for toughness as well as for its abrasive nature. Carborundum is widely used as an abrasive (q.v.) in industry.

CARIBBEAN SEA The Caribbean Sea, part of the Atlantic Ocean occupies 2,800 x 1,000 kilometers (1,700 x 600 miles). The sea is separated from the Gulf of Mexico by Yucatan Peninsula. Cuba, the Lesser Antilles, and Puerto Rico are on the east. Venezuela is to the south.

The Caribbean Basin floor is a complex of ridges and trenches. The Cayman Trench between Cuba and Jamaica has a depth of 3,800 meters (23,000 feet). Smaller basins are separated by ridges. The ridges host oil, gas, and a variety of fish fauna.

CARLIN GOLD BELT Disseminated fine gold characterizes the Carlin Gold Belt of Nevada. ASTM-80 fractions (American Society for Testing Materials) revealed anomalously high gold values when examined by atomic absorption. Tests also revealed high anomalies in arsenic, stibnite, mercury, and tellurium. The analyses led to the discovery of the rich gold belt. Fine gold is completely missed in ordinary placer and lode operations.

Carlin may be in an even larger belt of arsenical gold ores that extends, according to Joralemon, from the mercury rich region of the McDermitt Caldera in Nevada to Ballarat in California. Mercury, then silver, diminish to the south.

CARLSBERG RIDGE The Carlsberg Ridge extends from the Indian Ocean into the Gulf of Aden. Profiles taken of the ridge by Heezen show it to be identical to the Mid-Atlantic. This means that there is also a central rift. The earthquake activity is the same.

An extension of the ridge creates both the Gulf of Aqaba and the Jordan Valley. Another extends into Africa and the Rift Valley.

CARNOTITE The uranium-vanadium ore mineral, carnotite, is canary yellow and fine-grained. Found in economic amounts on the Colorado Plateau, it is especially abundant in the Ura-Van Belt. The Morrison Formation (q.v.) is the major host. These sandstone uranium deposits are rare elsewhere in the world.

CARPATHIAN ALPS The mountain system called the Carpathians is an extention of the Alps. It forms the boundary between Czechoslovakia and Poland and is in north and central Rumania. The Bucegi Range in Transylvania is of limestone, sandstone, shale, and conglomerate.

The range was folded when the crustal plate collision resulted in uplifting of the 100 million-year old sediments. Plate convergence is still progressing as the great earthquakes in the area testify. The Carpathians were glaciated in the Pleistocene.

CARRARA MARBLE Marble from Carrara, Italy, is blue-white and of very fine grade. It is especially suited for sculpture.

The marble has been quarried from the Apuan Alps along the Serchio River for 2,000 years.

CARRYING CAPACITY Carrying capacity is the maximum population a given area can support. The entire ecological system is involved. Carrying capacity may only affect a particular population, a species with particular requirements, or it may affect the whole community.

The Taylor Grazing Act in the United States was based on the estimated carrying capacity of the southwestern range. In sub-Saharan Africa, the carrying capacity of the land has been exceeded in many ways. The result, sometimes not reversible, has been desertification (q.v.), chronic drought, and famine.

CARSWELL LAKE A Precambrian crater in Canada has become Carswell Lake. The crater is thought to have been created by meteoritic impact. Crater diameter is 30,000 meters (100,000 feet). Valuable uranium deposits have been found in the area.

CARTOGRAPHY Claudius Ptolomy, the first geographer, is credited with inventing cartography or map-making. He represented the Earth at a precise scale to its size. Since his time hundreds of different types of map presentations have come into use. Special conventions, or symbols, have become universally used. See **PTOLOMY**.

CASCALHO 'Cascalho' is conglomerate and alluvial material in which diamonds are found in Brazil. It is also called 'sopa' or soup, which it resembles, when mixed with water.

Cascalho are also mill tailings, or residues from hand-cobbing operations much used in Brazilian pegmatite mining.

CASCADE RANGE The Cascades form a coastal range of 15 volcanoes in Northwest United States and into British Columbia. The range, was created by subduction (q.v.) of the Juan de Fuca Plate beneath the North American Plate.

The range includes Mount St. Helens (q.v.) which erupted in 1984 and Lassen which erupted in 1914. Mounts Hood and Baker are being monitored. These are the only presently active volcanoes in the United States outside of Alaska or Hawaii.

The Cascades are crossed by 3 major rivers, the Frazer in Canada and the Columbia and Klamath in the United States. The mountains were named for the rapids on the Columbia River.

CASING Pipe inserted into drilled wells to keep the walls from collapsing is casing. Cement slurry is pumped into the well and forced between the pipe and well-wall. When set, a casing is in place.

CASIQUIARE RIVER The Casiquiare River rises in flood stage from a gap in the south bank of the Orinoco River, 20 kilometers (12 miles) west of Esmeralda, Venezuela. The Casiquiare picks up 100 or so tributaries on its 400 kilometer (250 mile) course to join the Rio Negro of the Amazon System. It is a classic example of bifurcation (q.v.).

CASPIAN SEA The Caspian Sea is the world's largest lake. It is 1,250 kilometers (760 miles) long covering 438,697 square kilometers (169,381 square miles). In size it is comparable to the Mediteranean Sea.

The Caspian is bounded on the south by Iran. The Soviet Union borders the rest of the sea. Europe's longest river system, the Volga, feeds into the Caspian.

The inflow is not sufficient to prevent the sea from growing smaller and saltier each year. Water from rivers that empty into the sea is being used for irrigation and is contributing to the shrinkage.

The famous oil deposits of Baku, USSR (q.v.), are onshore of the sill between the north and south basins. A major portion of the world's caviar comes from the north basin. Sturgeon find the cold waters a good habitat. There are ice floes in winter.

The Caspian is a remnant of the ancient Tethys Sea (q.v.). The central trench closed by continental movement left smaller seas and inland lakes. The 20 kilometer (12 mile) pile of sediments that floor the Caspian testify to its former position along a continental margin (q.v.).

CASSITERITE Cassiterite is tin ore or tinstone. About 79% of the world's tin production is from cassiterite. It crystallizes into tetragonal columns with a hardness between 6 and 7 (Moh's Scale). It may be massive and granular, fibrous, or disseminated (greisen). It is associated with molybdenite and wolframite.

About 33% of cassiterite production is from placers on the Malay Peninsula. There are large primary deposits of cassiterite in Bolivia, China, and the USSR. Tin placers are being worked in the Brazilian Amazon, in Rondonia.

CAT CAT (Clear Air Turbulence) occurs most frequently in the vicinity of jet streams. A layer of air extends below the jet core and contains a great deal of turbulence. Warm air overlying cold, with wind shear between causes the turbulence.

Vertical shears set off long waves of turbulence. Turbulent waves are set in motion when an airmass encounters high mountains. These are lee waves and jet streams favor their formation. Cold and warm layers provide for the wind shear. The lee wave of the Colorado Front Range is noted for its clear air turbulence.

CATACLASTICS Cataclastics are rocks subjected to pressures of crustal upheaval. They are greatly shattered or fragmented. 'Cata' implies deep zones in the Crust with high temperatures and pressures.

CATACLASTITES Metamorphic rocks with evidence of crushing and fragmenting induced by great crustal disturbance are cataclastites. Serpentinite and soapstone, both derived from olivine-rich igneous rocks, are cataclastites. So, too, is mariposite, California's state rock.

CATENA The sequence found in the soil profile from top to bottom is related to topography and climate. Soils in the same area developing under different conditions form a catena. The parent rock is the same but conditions of drainage and relief are different.

The catena concept is akin to the geological one of facies (q.v.). Rock type, microclimate, angle of slope may vary, or drainage alter. Subtle differences are high-lighted by treating the soils as a unit, or catena. The concept has contributed to soils mapping, especially in East Africa.

CATHODE RAYS The negative terminal or electrode of a battery is a cathode. It emits a ray composed of negatively charged particles or electrons. The television tube is a cathode ray emitter. Geophysical instrumentation uses cathode ray emissions for a variety of displays.

CATION A cation is a positively charged ion (q.v.). Its opposite is the negatively charged anion.

CAUCASUS MOUNTAINS The Caucusus have long been considered part of the boundary between Europe and Asia. The high, narrow range is without low passes, although the USSR has managed to create the Georgian Military Highway through these mountains. The Caucusus are linked to the Crimean range and are part of the great Alpine Chain.

On the western flanks, in the Black Sea area, the mountains receive much more rainfall than the eastern side facing the Caspian. South facing slopes are also more exposed to precipitation.

The Caucusus have 2,000 or so glaciers, less than 10% in the eastern part. The highest peak is Elbrus at 5,633 meters (18,480 feet).

CAVERNS Caverns are large caves, usually found in limestone terrain. These result from dissolution of country rock by water and mineral-bearing solutions. Solution phenomena work quickly in karst (q.v.) regions. Many huge caverns in the United States have been created in this way. Among them are Mammoth Cave, the Kentucky Caverns, and Carlsbad Caverns of New Mexico.

Although caverns in limestones are the most well-known, there are some famous gypsum and marble caverns as well. Gypsum caverns in Turkey are sometimes used as dwellings. See **CAVES**.

Some extraordinary volcanics have produced caverns. Perhaps the most well known are on the Canary Islands (q.v.).

CAVES There are different types of caves of which the solution cave giving rise to caverns (q.v.) is one. Caves have been created by water, wind action, wave action, volcanism, and ice. New caves can be created by wave action at the base of a cliff in a matter of days and they can change rapidly also. Sea caves result when fractured coastal rocks produce large cracks into which waves swirl and eddy. The crack enlarges to become a cave. Rocks are gouged out by wave abrasion with erosional fragments as milling agents. The largest sea cave in the United States is in Oregon.

Glacial action gouged out many areas that later became large caves (Athabasca, Canada). Freezing and thawing allowed enlargement and glacial movement created a further milling action. Swift streams in melt phase contributed to enlargement.

Underground rivers carve caves along the course by water reacting with surrounding rocks as in Lebanon's Jeita Cave.

Caves can be created by rain action on cliff walls. Rain sweeps into porous rock and creates a cave in a relatively short time. Natural rainfall is slightly acidic and so carbonate rocks are particularly vulnerable to this type of erosion.

In canyonlands, in western United States, there are examples of wind-derived caves but the major portion of these have been amplified by flash-flooding from canyon streams.

Volcanic caves are found in lava tubes where the surface lavas cooled faster than the interior. When the magma flowed out a cavity was left behind. There are many beautiful lava caves in Hawaii like that near Kilauea Iki. The cave is 100 meters (300 feet) long. The largest volcanic cave is on the Canary Islands (q.v.).

CAVITATION Cavitation is an erosional process. When a vacuum is created in a closed channel, water will rush to fill the vacuum. The erosive force from the created energy is great. Air and water bubbles collapse from decreased pressure accompanying increased velocity. Prolonged cavitation can cause corrosion and metal fatigue. It is a special problem with aircraft and ships.

CAY 'Cay' is another word for key. Both refer to a small island, usually of coral. The island is the exposed portion of a barrier reef.

CEMENT Material binding rocks or grains in a conglomerate is a cement. There are a variety of natural cements. Calcium carbonate or silica are the most usual. High temperature lavas also act as cement.

Industrial cement is made by mixing powdered limestone, silica, aluminum, and clay. The mix is then calcined. Gypsum is added to aid the setting process.

CENOTE 'Cenote' is Mexican Spanish for a sink-hole. Cenotes are the only source of water in Northern Yucatan. This karstic (q.v.) region has a slightly dipping limestone plain, pock-marked with sink-holes. Underground caves abound due to solution weathering.

In a cenote the collapsed surface opens up the water to the surface. The Maya Sacred Well at Chichen Itza is such a cenote. The treasure found there had been sacrificed to the gods.

CENOZOIC ERA The Cenozoic or era of recent life began about 60 million years ago. It includes the Tertiary and Quaternary Periods.

CENTESIMAL SYSTEM The circumference of a circle is divided into 400 points, or grads. Each grad has 100 centesimal minutes and each minute has 100 centesimal seconds. The superscript 'c' or 'cc' denotes the minutes and seconds.

CENTI The 'centi' is 1/100th the distance on a graduated scale from freezing to boiling water. It is equal to a degree Celsius.

CENTRAL AMERICA Central America is the southernmost part of the North American Continent. The Panama Isthmus provided a natural land bridge between the American continents at various geological times. The bridge allowed fauna to be exchanged. The major traffic headed south. The latest land bridge was disrupted by the Panama Canal.

The West Indies are a line of submerged volcanoes of which Pico Duarte is the highest. A chain of volcanic islands extends from Florida to Venezuela. Other Central American volcanoes form a great chain paralleling the Pacific Ocean from Mexico to Costa Rica, where Irazu periodically raises havoc. In Guatemala, Fuego is most active.

Volcanoes dominate the Central American landscape. Within the relatively small continental area, there are 42, only 18 of which are considered dormant. The volcanoes are on the suture or rift line between crustal plates.

Central America was once covered by lush rainforest. Population pressures have virtually destroyed it. The forest is best preserved in Costa Rica on the Osa Peninsula around Golfo Dulce.

CEPHALOPODS In the Cephalopod Phylum are included gastropods and cephalopods. Gastropods (q.v.) are represented by the snail and slug; cephalopods by nautilus, octopus, and squid.

Most cephalopods are benthic (q.v.) and most have a planktonic stage. The giant squid is the largest invertebrate. It can be 1.7 meters (5.5 feet), including the arms. Cephalopods first appeared in Late Cambrian (37 m.y.) and fossils are rare. In the Devonian (395-345 m.y.) primitive ammonites (q.v.) appeared. They were almost extinct at the end of the

Permian (225 m.y.) but rose to a dominant position in the Mesozoic (225-65 m.y.). Only 2 species survived to Cretaceous (135 m.y.).

CERAMIC CLAY Special clays used in the fabrication of china and pottery are the ceramic clays. Kaolin (q.v.) is the most important.

CEREAL GRASSES Cereal grasses include barley, corn, millet, oats, rice, rye, and wheat, All are major staples in some part of the world. Cereals together with bamboo, pasture grass, and sweet grass make up the 4 major grasses.

CERIUM Cerium, a Rare Earth element is produced primarily from bastnaesite. Formerly, the major source of cerium metal was monazite, mined from beach sands in India and Brazil.

Cerium was strategic during the Korean War. The metal is especially resistant to high heat so it was used in jet engine cowlings. Later, it was replaced by zirconium and titanium. See **RARE EARTHS**.

CERRADO The vegetation of the Central Brazilian Plateau, or 20% of the country, is 'cerrado'. It is richer in species than comparable African transitional flora.

Although xeromorphic (q.v.) or drought resistant, cerrado vegetation is found in forests with both closed and open canopies, in woodlands of trees and scrub, and on grasslands with scrub and shrubs. It is not confined to the classical savanna.

In 1972, in Central Brazil, cerrado vegetation was so dense it was difficult to transit even in a jeep or other off-road vehicle. Settlements and clearing have somewhat changed that landscape.

Continuous cerrado covers almost all of Goias, western Bahia, eastern Minas Gerais, and Mato Grosso. There are patches in Northeast Brazil, Sao Paulo, and Parana. Within the Cerrado Province are a great number of gallery forests.

Cerrado vegetation is almost always distinguished by thick bark, twisted trunks and limbs, and thick twigs. Leaves are usually large. Many plants are legumes. Broadleaf shrubs are common and palms are in ubiquitous stands. Most of the grasses, sedges, and herbs have siliceous leaves. There is complete intergradation.

Cerrado soils are poor in minerals, acidic, and contain only small amounts of humus. A great deal of research has been carried out to develop viable farms in this province. There have been many improvements in productivity.

CERRO AZUL When Cerro Azul #4 oil well in the Tampico Field came in, it was considered the world's greatest well. It produced 60 million tons of oil before reaching salt water.

CERRO DE PASCO Cerro de Pasco Mine is 5 kilometers (3 miles) above sea level in the Peruvian Andes. Originally it was worked by the Incas for silver.

Copper was discovered about 30 meters (100 feet) below the silver. The huge deposit has a similar association between the metals as that found at Butte (q.v.), Montana.

Cerro de Pasco was particularly productive with an output of hundreds of millions of pounds of copper annually. Political and economic conditions have eroded its market position.

CERRO MATOSO Cerro Matoso, a Colombian mountain with nickel laterite, is 415 kilometers (250 miles) northwest of Bogota. Reserves are estimated at 70 million metric tons of 2.7% nickel. The laterite is the residual product of the weathering of ultrabasic harzburgite.

CESIUM Cesium is an element that loses an electron from its outer shell very easily when exposed to light. One of the Alkali Metal Group (q.v.), it melts at 83° Fahrenheit and so is liquid on hot days.

The principal cesium ore is pollucite, which contains about 20%. Canada has 80,000 short tons, Zimbabwe 25,000 and Namibia 20,000 of reserves.

Cesium is found almost exclusively in pegmatites (q.v.). The United States has no reserves and only 1 processor. There is no stockpile provision.

Cesium is used in photoelectric cells to convert light to electricity. Cesium compounds are used in the research and development of magnetohydrodynamic (MHD) generators. They are also used in other energy converters. The compounds are used to produce the different colors in television. They are important in biological research.

Cesium-137 was discovered during a nuclear explosion. It is especially dangerous as it emits gamma radiation. The half-life of cesium-137 is 30 years. The biological half-life is 70 days.

Human and animal organisms will accept radioactive cesium in lieu of calcium. The isotope can cause bone damage and lead to leukemia. Cesium-137 can be transmitted by milk to humans. The dairy herds feeding on irradiated ranges transmit the radioactivity. The damage to pasturage from the Chernobyl cesium leakage is of grave concern. Radiation affected areas as far away as Scandinavia.

The Tundra area of Norway and Sweden may be protected to some extent by lichen (q.v.) which acts a radiation sponge. Lichen has no underground root system so it gets all its nutrients from the Atmosphere. However, it provides the only forage for reindeer.

Radioactive Cesium is measured in bequerels per kilo of body weight. Norway has set 6,000 bequerels as the maximum safe level. After

Chernobyl the dosage reached 137,000 bequerels per kilo in Central Norway. A bequerel = 1 nuclear disintegration per second.

CHABAZITE   Chabazite is a natural zeolite and acts as a molecular seive when it is chemically activated. Chabazite rapidly absorbs water, methyl, or ethyl vapors.

An economic deposit of chabazite is located near Bowie, Arizona. See **ZEOLITE**.

LAKE CHAD   Lake Chad (Tchad) is the remnant of what was once a series of lakes. About 240 meters (800 feet) above sea level, it is at the south edge of the Bodele-Djourab Depression in the Sahara, where the savanna begins.

Lake Chad is fed by the Shari River from highlands to the southeast. The lake's average size is 16,000 square kilometers (6,200 square miles). There is no outlet from the present lake. The valleys have been filled with sand dunes. The landscape shows a series of transgressions by Chad alternating with dune build-up. Silts from the former lake fill the yardangs (q.v.).

The Paleochadean Sea covered 544,000 square kilometers (210,000 square miles) of Central Africa and old shorelines are evident. The Chad Basin is about a billion square kilometers (390,000 square miles) between the desert and the huge savanna belt, the Sahel (q.v.). The Bhar el Ghazal River, once a major artery flowing to Chad, is now dry.

Fish indicate that there was a connection between the Nile and Chad Basins in the Late Pleistocene. Also, Greater Lake Chad, at 320 meters (1,056 feet) elevation spilled water to the Benoue River System that joins the Congo (Zaire) on its way to the Atlantic.

CHAGOS FRACTURE   55 million years ago the Chagos Fracture, a transform fault, split the Indian Ocean floor into 2 segments. The fracture extends from the Carlsberg Ridge (q.v.) to the South East Indian Ridge. The plate, carrying the Indian subcontinent, moved away at about 16 centimeters (6.4 inches) per year.

CHAIN   A chain is a series of mountain ranges that form a system. A group of chains is a cordillera (q.v.).

The chain is a measuring device with 100 links each 7.92 inches long for a total of 66 feet. An acre (q.v.) is equal to 10 square chains (660 x 660 feet). Surveyors once used the chain to verify baseline (q.v.) measurements.

CHAIN REACTION   In a given period, self-sustaining fission chains emit neutrons. Radioactive elements give rise to a series of 'daughter' elements, each with a specific natural half-life before decaying to another daughter or radiogenic end product. See **RADIOACTIVE DECAY**.

Non-explosive reactions have occurred spontaneously. The most well-known is at Oklo, Gabon. It was initiated 1.8 billion years ago, when the U-235:U-238 ratio was high enough to react. See **OKLO**.

CHALCEDONY Chalcedony is a variety of quartz with many different forms. It may be tiny needle-like crystals, as micro-crystalline quartz or amorphous as in opal. Agate and carnelian are common forms. Chalcedony is also found in a variety of colors and is much prized for specimens and ornaments.

CHALCOPYRITE Copper-iron sulfide, chalcopyrite, is a common copper ore. It crystallizes in the cubic system. It is wedge-shaped, brassy-yellow, and contains 35% copper.

CHALK Chalk is a white, friable, calcareous rock composed of a great number of small marine fossils, often Radiolaria. Outcrops are fractured and permeable leaving them open to solution erosion. The White Cliffs of Dover are primarily of fossil Foraminifera (q.v.).

During the Cretaceous Period (136-65 m.y.) chalk, or limestone, was deposited in great epicontinental seas. These seas are estimated not to have exceeded 300 meters (1,000 feet) in depth. Cretaceous limestone deposits around the world indicate these seas must have persisted for a very long time.

H.M.S. CHALLENGER In the 1870's, the H.M.S. Challenger carried out a 4-year scientific voyage around the world. The ambitious purpose was to discover 'everything about the sea'. It took many volumes to report all the findings.

Among other wonders, a range of mountains was located in the middle of the Atlantic Ocean. The crew had discovered the first indications of the Mid-Atlantic Ridge (q.v.). Many of the deep sea sediments they obtained indicated great climate changes through time.

CHAPADA A Brazilian tableland is known as 'chapada'. It is a horizontal surface over 600 meters (2,000 feet) high. A succession of them is a 'chapadão'. Sakamoto noted that the steep-walled canyons of these chapadãs create a polygon pattern when viewed from the air.

Important chapadas are found in the Sertão (q.v.) of Northeast Brazil and in Minas Gerais. In the northeast they are especially important sources of water. In Minas Gerais and Bahia, some are hosts for gold- and diamond-bearing conglomerates (e.g. Chapada de Diamantina).

The Central Brazilian Divide is an extensive area of these plateaus which are capped by Cretaceous red sandstone. Chapadas are watershed areas for major drainage. They are the source areas for many major north-flowing rivers. They form the Continental Divide between the Amazon and Parana-La Plata rivers. In the southeastern part of the basin, they create a divide between the Amazon and the São Francisco (q.v.).

CHAPARRAL Chapparal is a climax vegetation in the semi-arid, subtropical Mediterranean climate of Southern California. It is composed of scrub oak, small trees, and brush. It is the result of little rainfall, dry summers, and hot days and cool nights.

In the European Mediterranean, chaparral vegetation is called 'maqui'. The name was taken by the members of the French Resistance in World War II. The maqui is dominated by cork oaks. It is also the producing area for olives, almonds, and figs.

The Arizona Chapparal differs from California's in species composition and climate. It is found in the Bradshaw Mountains between 3,000 and 5,800 feet. The Arizona species are made up of scrub live oak, manzanita, ceanothus and sumac. The Chapparal gives way to Ponderosa Pine at 6,000 feet.

CHARCOAL Charcoal is a black, porous carbon of vegetable origin. It is produced by heating wood to high temperatures in an oxyen-free atmosphere. Charcoal has long been used for fuel and for firing clay.

CHARGED PARTICLES An ion is an elementary particle with a positive or negative charge. Cosmic radiation, penetrating the Earth's Atmosphere, contains charged particles or ions. These may be of high or low energy.

Low energy particles are scattered by collisions with atmospheric molecules. High energy particles are absorbed or their energy is dispersed but the mass remains.

Lost kinetic energy is reflected as light and seen in aurorae and afterglows. High energy particles can smash nitrogen and oxygen nuclei into subatomic particles that smash other nuclei.

CHATOYANCY Chatoyancy, or cat's eye is a property of translucent minerals with a fibrous structure. This structure disperses and scatters light.

CHELATION Chelation is the process of bonding metal ions and compounds into a ring structure. The metal remains in the center. The structure is formed by more than one bond between the metal and the compound. Chelation is important in soil formation where biological processes play an important role.

Chelated compounds excreted by lichen and moss on Tundra rock are important in rock weathering.

CHEMICAL POLLUTION There are about 60,000 different chemical products now on the market in the United States. Of this number, the government has found 35,000 of them hazardous to human health.

In 1986, new chemicals were being produced at the rate of 1,000 a year. 70% of the existing ones have not been tested for toxicity or environmental damage, so control is limited. The caution required with hazardous chemicals is a major problem.

Society has to contend with chemical wastes. These have been released into rivers and lakes increasingly since the 1940's. Toxic waste dumps threaten groundwater supplies.

Lagoons have been created to solve some of the problem but these are not entirely satisfactory since chemicals may seep into the groundwater. In dry periods these sites can evaporate or concentrate minerals. Moving groundwater is filtered by soil, but not all groundwater moves.

Dioxin and other toxins can bond with clay and aluminum in the soils. There are chemical means to create the necessary controls but the cost is great. No real determination of who should bear this cost has been made.

Chemical waste in the form of gases are also at apparently critical levels. The release of Chlorofluorocarbons (CFC's) has been banned in the form of aerosols. The CFC's are used as coolants and discarded refrigeration equipment still presents a problem.

CFC's are known to have a destructive effect on atmospheric ozone. The Ozone Layer (q.v.) has undergone a 6% reduction since 1979. This depletion is probably not all related to CFC's. They are, however, implicated in the enlargement of the Ozone Hole over Antarctica. The chemicals release chlorine into the Stratosphere and it is the chlorine which is responsible for the increase in ozone destruction.

CFC's are not the only gases affecting the Atmosphere. NASA has been conducting a study of atmospheric chemistry for 20 years. This research should be continued and results made more available to scientists seeking remedies to pollution.

The complex of atmospheric gases creates a special environment for life on Earth and long-term alteration could be dangerous.

CHEMICAL PRECIPITATION Metals can be recovered by chemical precipitation. It is the usual method of dissolving metals from water. Lime and caustic soda are used to raise pH (q.v.). With pH at 8 or 9, a foam precipitate results. Sludge is disposed of or reclaimed.

CHEMICAL REACTIONS Interactions and combinations of elements and compounds result from chemical reactions. These reactions are of many different kinds, but all can be described by chemical equations or diagrams. Some are reversible and others are not.

CHERNOBYL NUCLEAR DISASTER The Chernobyl Nuclear Plant at Kiev in the USSR is composed of 4 RBMK 1,000 megawatt nuclear reactors. The upper portion of a reactor building was destroyed in a nuclear explosion in May, 1986. Superheated steam reacted with the graphite core releasing carbon monoxide, hydrogen, and other gases.

The accident caused radioactive leakage. Radiation levels in Belgrade, Yugoslavia, rose to 10 times normal. Higher than normal radiation levels were detected as far away as Sweden. No plutonium was detected so a complete meltdown did not occur but radioactive iodine and cesium escaped. Kiev is located in an important agricultural area. Grain and cattle in the vicinity were affected. Actual numbers of persons killed or injured were not released and long term radiation effects will take years to assess. See **CESIUM-137**.

CHERNOZEMS 'Chernozems', Russian for black earths, are a great soils group. The soils are found on the Russian Steppes and on prairies (q.v.) of subhumid areas. They support grasses, which contribute to their color. Chernozems have a high organic content down to a meter or more (3-4 feet) of depth.

CHERT Chert is a fine-grained, light-colored chalcedony or form of quartz (q.v.). Fracture is conchoidal and luster is greasy. Chert is usually white but may contain impurities lending it a gray cast.

Silica is precipitated in the sea, especially in the vicinity of volcanoes. It occurs as a replacement mineral in silicious limestones and may be nodular or massive.

The silica or chert replacing cells in petrified wood is precipitated from groundwater.

EL CHICHON El Chichon (Chiapas, Mexico) erupted March 28 and April 3rd, 1982. It ejected 16 million tons of material. The explosive blast killed 2,000 people. A high sulfurous ash cloud rose 16 miles in the air. This was the most powerful eruption of El Chichon's 20-year history following a 1,000-year dormancy.

A 60-mile an hour avalanche of hot ash and pumice mixed with atmospheric and volcanic gases flowed from the mountain. Sulfur (10 million tons) mixed with atmospheric moisture and created a sulfuric acid rain. There were hot surge clouds up to 800° Fahrenheit. The sulfur content was 200 times that of Mount St. Helens.

Mauna Loa Observatory reported a sunlight decrease of 25-33%, but the cooling effect was not as great as expected. Upwelling in the oceans was affected by an El Nino (q.v.) so seas stayed warm. Other El Nino global effects were present which are thought to have offset the effect of El Chichon on global climate.

CHILE Chile has 6,435 kilometers (3,860 miles) of coast bordering the Pacific, but is only 400 kilometers (240 miles) wide.

The Andes Mountains (q.v.) rise abruptly from the narrow coastal plain. The Southern Alps are glaciated and create a beautiful scenery. Many of its peaks are needle-sharp from glacial plucking (q.v.).

Many of Chile's volcanoes are active. The country has had an average of 100 major earthquakes a year since 1575 and not infrequent volcanic eruptions. Where Chile borders the Pacific Plate is a major subduction zone (q.v.).

Chile holds about 18% of the Free World copper reserves and has 2 of the world's largest copper mines: Chuquicamata (q.v.), an open pit, and El Teniente, an underground mine. Copper reserves are estimated at 120 million metric tons. Production in 1986 was 1.42 million tons.

CHIMBORAZO Chimborazo in the Ecuadorian Andes is 6,267 meters (20,561 feet). If it were measured from the center of the Earth, it would be the highest of all mountains. The Equatorial Bulge causes the mountain to reach higher than Everest.

CHIMNEY A pipe-like replacement orebody is a chimney. It is roughly circular in cross-section. Mineralized volcanic plugs, such as some kimberlites are often referred to as chimneys. Carbonatite mineralizations in pipe-like deposits are also chimneys.

CHINA The world's 3rd largest country is made up of high mountains and high, dry plateaus in the western 2/3rds of the nation. It is isolated from the eastern 1/3 by a north-south mountain range. There are 5 distinct climate zones from Tundra to Tropical Rainforest.

The most fertile part of China is Manchuria, which is made up of gently rolling plains. Manchurian coal and iron are produced in its Changpai Range. Manchuria contributes about a 3rd of China's coal and steel. Dams on the Yalu River provide electric power for North Korea and China.

Oil has been produced in China for many years and today is being produced from the rich Taching Fields. Tin, tungsten, and phosphates are worked in southern Yunnan Province.

Economically important brine deposits have been put into production. A railway to the high Tibetan Plateau to access these deposits has been completed. Reserves are said to be capable of yielding 1-2 million tons per year. In addition to the usual brines, the Chinese deposits are said to have viable uranium.

CHINOOK 'Chinook', American Indian for snow-eater, is a warm wind blowing down the east slope of the Rockies. It is warm enough to melt snow and create access to grazing feed for animals. It causes avalanches.

The velocity of the downslope wind can be up to 160 kilometers (100 miles) per hour. It is developed by the compression of subsiding air. Chinooks can cause temperatures to rise greatly in a few minutes as it did in 1943 in Spearfish Canyon, South Dakota. Temperature went from -4 to +45° Fahrenheit in 2 minutes.

CHLORINE Chlorine, the most abundant of the Halogen Group (q.v.) of elements, is a greenish-yellow gas. Highly toxic, it was the gas used in chemical warfare during World War I. It was banned by the Geneva Convention.

Chlorine has many industrial uses. It is used in water purification, bleaching newsprint, and as a solvent. As a compound, it is relatively common. Combined with sodium, it is table salt.

Chlorine is a component of chlorofluorocarbon, the CFC's which have been outlawed as threat to the global environment. The role of chlorine in the depletion of the Ozone Layer (q.v.) is just beginning to be understood. The Stratosphere is normally so dry no clouds form. Ice clouds do form, however, in the Antarctic. It has been discovered that chlorine in the presence of ice clouds destroys ozone. As a result, chlorine monoxide is 100 times greater than in the rest of the world.

CHLOROBIUM   Chlorobium is a from of bacteria used to assist some chemical reactions. In an anaerobic environment with a lack of oxygen, Chlorobium absorbs carbon dioxide and hydrogen sulfide releasing carbonates and free sulfur.

CHLOROPHYLL   Chlorophyll, the leaf-green color of plants, results from photosynthesis (q.v.). Inorganic matter is converted to organic blue-black and dark green esters in the presence of sunlight.

CHONDRITE   A chondrite is a carbonaceous or stony meteorite. One of the first discovered was found on the Nullabar Plain, Australia. It contained traces of diamond. It was dated at 4.6 billion years, which is the accepted age of the Earth. It is presumed it impacted a solid surface already in place.

CHORDATA   Chordata are vertebrates. The earliest were graptolites which lived from the Cambrian to the Ordovician Period (570-430 m.y.). They had a nervous system which warranted inclusion in the Chordata Phylum. They were not, apparently, precursors of vertebrates.

CHOTTS   Large shallow basins created by wind deflation in the southern Sahara Desert are 'chotts'. Temporary salt lakes or marshes may fill these depressions. There are many in North Africa and particularly in Tunisia.

CHROMITE   Chromite, iron-chromium oxide, is the chief ore of chromium, an important alloying metal. Chromium ore classes are:

Chemical	- High iron content
Metallurgical	- High chromium andlow iron content
Refractory	- High aluminum content.

South Africa produces chrome from large basic intrusives of the Bushveld Complex. The chrome is in pods and related to slow crystallization which segregated it out in the Great Dyke (q.v.).

Metallurgical grade chrome ore is a hard and lumpy. It contains 46% chromium. The chromium:iron ratio is 2.8:1 or better. This quality ore is becoming scarce. Charge chrome is an alloying metal produced from low-grade chrome ore.

The main producers of chromium are the Soviet Union, South Africa, Turkey, and Zimbabwe. Chromite is found in the United States in Oregon placers and the Montana Stillwater Complex. Neither is presently economic.

The United States is still the world's largest consumer. 12% is used in refractories and 76% for stainless and heat-resistant steels. Of the total world reserves (33 billion metric tons), 99% are in southern Africa. The USSR has 202 million tons and Turkey 74 million.

CHROMOSPHERE The Chromosphere is the glowing gas halo at the surface of the Sun.

CHRONOLOGY Geological time is divided into Eras, Periods, and Epochs. This is a relative chronology based on stratigraphic relationships, section comparisons in all parts of the world, and the presence or absence of fossils. Radioactive dating has become important in establishing dates, especially of Precambrian rocks.

CHRYSOBERYL Chrysoberyl is a relatively hard gemstone. Composed of beryl aluminum oxide, the color depends on available light. The most famous variety is alexandrite owing its distinction to the rare presence of chrome. Brazil is the major source of chrysoberyl.

CHUQUICAMATA MINE Chuquicamata was already in production in preconquest Chile. In the high Andes 150 kilometers (90 miles) from the coast, the Indians used llama trains to transport ore from their surface mine.

The present open pit copper mine is more than 2 by 0.8 kilometers (1.5 by 0.5 miles) by 73.6 meters (243 feet) deep. Values run 0.4 kilogram to 0.9 metric tons (1 pound/short ton).

CHZ In 1978, Hart defined a 'Continuously Habitable Zone (CHZ)' within the Solar System. Its radius is 1% larger to 5% smaller than that of the Earth's orbit. He noted that only 'G' stars like the Sun have a CHZ.

If the Earth were less massive, there would be no Ozone Layer (q.v.). If it were closer to the Sun, it would be too hot and if farther away, too cold for surface water to exist. To remain a continuously habitable planet, these conditions must persist.

CINDER A cinder is a solid particle ejected from a volcano. The projectile is 0.4-3.75 centimeters (0.16-0.6 inches). These are pea-sized bits of spongy, porous lava.

CINDER CONE Ash and pyroclastics create a cone around a bowl-shaped, steep-sided crater. The cinder cone is common and often appears on the flanks of a shield or composite volcano.

The difference between a cinder and a composite cone results from alternation of eruption types in the latter. Lava flows alternate with cinder and ash flows.

Paricutin (q.v.), a Mexican volcano, is a cinder cone which grew very quickly. In western United States, there are many examples of cinder cones, among them Sunset Crater, Arizona. Rubble covered slopes at Amboy, California, are remnants of a cinder cone.

CINNABAR Natural vermillion or cinnabar is a compound of mercury and sulfur. Cinnabar is the major mercury ore with about 86% metal. It is found in veins or gossans (q.v.) overlying other ore bodies. The largest mercury deposits in the United States are in Nevada. See **MERCURY**.

CIRCADIAN RHYTHMS Organisms have internal clocks synchronized with daylight and related to their location on Earth. The natural responses to these clocks are called the circadian rhythms.

Circadian Rhythms approximate the average solar day. They are disrupted by violent changes in time such as occur with jet travel and they account for 'jet-lag'.

CIRCLE A circle is an enclosed curve with all points on that curve equidistant from the center. The connected curved line is the circumference. A straight line bisecting the circle is the diameter, and a line from the center to the circumference is the radius.

CIRCUM-PACIFIC OROGENY The Circum-Pacific Orogeny or epic of mountain-building began in North America in the Cretaceous. Activity continued in North America and throughout the Pacific Rim through the Tertiary to the Present.

The Circum-Pacific Orogeny gave rise to the Andes, Rockies, Cascades, and the mountains of Kamchatka among others. It was and is related to the relative motion of oceanic and continental plates.

The activity circles the Pacific from Chile to New Zealand in the so-called 'Ring of Fire'. Benioff Zones (q.v.) are known off Alaska and-Chile.

CIRCUM-POLAR VORTEX Around the North Pole, there is a huge mass of cold air blocking any warm winds from moving north. Jet streams hem the southern edge of this cold airmass in a Circum-Polar Vortex.

When the jet streams dip into lower latitudes they carry cold airmasses with them. They establish patterns which they can follow for years. Such a dip in the jet stream pattern brought about the 'Little Ice Age' in Europe and North America from 1400-1850 A.D. See **LITTLE ICE AGE**.

CIRQUE The circular amphitheater at the head of a valley is a cirque. To create a cirque, a glacier, as it begins its descent, plucks at the mountainside. The cirque or bowl-shaped basin has very steep-sided walls. Glacial plucking on all sides can create a needle-like peak.

CIRROCUMULOUS CLOUDS High, wispy cirrus and puffy cumulous together form cirrocumulous clouds. The combination gives rise to the 'Mackerel Sky'.

CIRROSTRATUS CLOUDS Cirrostratus are high clouds in thin layers. They create a halo effect around the Sun or Moon. Cirrostratus are usually thin enough for the Sun to shine through. Some weather watchers feel the halos portend a spell of bad weather.

CIRRUS CLOUDS Very high cirrus clouds have been called 'mares tails' because they look that way to farmers. Formed from ice crystals, cirrus clouds are usually 6,000-12,000 meters (20,000-40,000 feet) up in the Atmosphere.

CITRINE Yellow-brown, smoky quartz, or citrine, is prized as a semi-precious stone. The most valued is golden-yellow. The yellow color is imparted to the quartz by its iron content. The principal source of citrine is Brazil. See **CAIRNGORM**.

CLARKE Each element has a calculated abundance in the Earth's Crust. This is its Clarke number.

CLASTICS Clastics are disaggregated fragments of rocks. They result from erosion or structural upheaval such as folding and faulting. The name is from the Greek 'klastos' for broken.

Accepted fragment diameter limits are in the table below:

AGGREGATE	LIMITS (mm)	EQUIVALENTS (in.)
Boulder Gravel	>256	>10
Pebble Gravel	4-256	0.3-10
Sand	1/16-4	0.002-0.3
Silt	1/256-1/16	0.00015-0.002
Clay and mud	<256	<0.00015

(Adapted from Compton, 1962)

CLAY Clay is very fine-grained material composed of hydrous aluminum silicate. Derived by weathering and chemical alteration, clay is finer than silt. See **CLASTICS**.

Primary clay forms in place from rock alteration. Primary clay tends to be chemically pure, though particle size may vary. The origin may be in the alteration of volcanic ash. Kaolinite, derived from igneous and metamorphic rocks, is purest.

Secondary, or transported, clays tend to be more uniform in size though smaller than primary. These clays may be composites from different source rocks. Impurities are added in transport.

Many clays are used as filters. Kaolin is used in ceramics. Bentonite (q.v.), of volcanic origin, is used as a drilling mud. High alumina clays are found in many parts of the United States and they are nearly all in very large deposits. Those of Utah are being carefully studied as an alternative source of aluminum.

CLEAVAGE　Cleavage is a characteristic of crystals to divide into parallel planes. It creates a relatively clean break imparted by structural regularity and molecular arrangement. Cleavage occurs where the bonding is weak.

Cleavage is classed according to perfection. Perfection is defined by the amount of light reflected per unit of area. Sheetlike breaks of uni-directional cleavage are found in micas; 2-directional cleavage in feldspars.

Many other minerals have an identifying cleavage. Cleavage is important in cutting gemstones. The diamond has 4-directional cleavage giving 8 smooth sides (octahedral). This same cleavage is found in fluorite crystals. 6-directional cleavage gives rise to a dodecahedron (sphalerite).

CLIFF　The cliff, a steep-sided slope, may develop in many ways. Some cliff types are:

Coastal	-	Undercut by waves
Escarpment	-	Derived from erosion or faulting
Valley wall	-	Deeply cut valleys in arid areas
Glaciated mountain sides		
Glaciated channels.		

Cliffs have grades of 40° or more. They face into valleys and out to sea. Weathering products drop directly to the base.

The same forces that create a cliff contribute to the cliff's retreat. Erosion is progressing at different rates in different environments. In California coastal cliff retreat is an environmental problem. The soft sediments are undercut severely at times of storms and abnormally high tides.

CLIMATE　Climate is the average prevailing weather over a given region for a considerable period of time. Earth's temperature range is only about 100° Celsius.

Climate is latitude dependant, but altitude affects it. A temperate or cold climate will prevail at high elevations even near the Equator. An area may be sheltered, interfering with normal airmass movement, or climate may be modified by nearness to the sea. Global climates have been broadly classified. See **KÖPPEN CLASSIFICATION**.

To establish a definite climate pattern, time must be sufficiently long so that weather swings will average out. Winds and airmass circulations determine the weather.

Climate changes alter vegetation patterns. Forests and grasslands shift. As climates become more arid, forests retreat and give way to grasslands. With even greater aridity, the grasslands yield to the desert. This pattern also operates in reverse with increased humidity and precipitation. This shift takes longer because soils need time to recoup nutrients. This shifting back and forth occurs most frequently in the tropical and subtropical latitudes.

When global climates are modified, the most probable cause is activity on the Sun. The relationship of continents with regard to the Sun is one that has changed through geological time. Climates of the past are not those prevailing today. Ultimately, it is the relationship of locations on the Earth to the Sun which determines the underlying climate. One scientist points out that 'the future of the Earth (as a viable planet for life) is at the mercy of tiny loops and flares on the Sun'. See **SOLAR FLARES**.

Climate between 1931 and 1960 in relation to the past 1,000 years has been abnormally warm. Global variation in surface temperatures in the last 100 years has been 5° Celsius. From 1890 to the mid 1940's temperature increased 0.5°. Since then it has dropped 0.3° Celsius per year. In the late 1980's slight warming has been noted and it has been related to a possible Greenhouse (q.v.) buildup.

CLIMAP studying long-range climate found sea surface temperature between a glacial and interglacial is 1.7° Celsius in summer and 1.4° in winter (3.1° and 2.5° Fahrenheit).

CLIMAX Climax refers to the state of the final stable community of individuals in a given ecospace. Individuals will be capable of reproduction and continuity as long as the same conditions prevail.

Great vegetation groups correspond to major climates. They are at climax. Tropical rainforests have a humid, low-latitude climate, while conifers are climax vegetation in the sub-Arctic. Climax communities are in dynamic equilibrium with climate and soils.

CLINE A cline is a regular change in gradient over a considerable distance. At the Equator the cline is:

CLIMATE	ALTITUDE	TEMPERATURE (° Celsius)
Tropical	Sea level	24-30
Subtropical	Foothill	18-24
Temperate	Mountain	6-18
Boreal (Taiga)	Sub-Alpine	3-6
Sub-Polar (Tundra)	Alpine	1.5-3
Polar	Snow Level	0-1.5

CLIPPERTON FRACTURE The Clipperton Fracture in the Pacific Ocean begins 830 kilometers (500 miles) off Central America on the crest of the East Pacific Rise. The fault strikes southwest in an almost straight line for 10,000 kilometers (6,000 miles). Soundings in the rift show depths up to 7,575 meters (25,000 feet). South of Clipperton is a ridge face measuring 5,450 meters (18,000 feet). No continental cliff is this high.

CLOSED SYSTEM A system that requires no input to maintain itself and has no output is closed. In nature, there are no true closed systems but there are approximations.

The Amazon Rainforest is virtually a closed system. Trees are sustained by recycled nutrients. Dropped foliage provides the humus, the root system forms a mat to store the humus and minerals. Even the rainfall is largely produced by the forest itself through evapotranspiration. A disruption of any part of the system risks endangering the whole.

CLOUD A cloud is formed when trillions of tiny water droplets are nucleated around minute ice crystals floating in the Atmosphere. Particulate aggregations are buoyed by winds.

There are 3 major cloud types: Cumulus, cirrus, and stratus. These combine to form varieties. Clouds disappear when broken up by wind and airmass circulation and by precipitation when moisture droplets have sufficient weight.

CLOUD CHAMBER A cloud chamber is an enclosed volume where cosmic ray ionization may be measured. The chamber led to advances in particle physics and revealed the bending of the Earth's Magnetic Field.

COAL Mineral coal results when buried plant-life is carbonized. Many coal deposits began when masses of vegetation were buried in swamp muds. With time, the organic material became deeply buried and the heat and pressure drove off oxygen and hydrogen leaving behind dense carbon material, or coal.

Great coal basins are found in some complex structural areas. They date from the Paleozoic (Permo-Carboniferous), 300 million years ago, when conditions were ideal for abundant plant life. Coal environments prevailed in Europe, the United States, South America, and South Africa.

Metamorphism varied the coals resulting in different hardnesses. The hardest coal, anthracite, is found in the highly folded Appalachian basins. Cyclothems or rhythmic sequences of bedding are prominent in some Appalachian basins (Black Warrior, Alabama). They relate to the differences in the depositional environment.

Some of the largest coal fields are of softer bituminous coals. Beds of these coals and lignites (q.v.) are found covering great expanses in the American west. Mining these presents some environmental problems which are being carefully studied.

Most brown coals developed during the Tertiary (65-2 m.y.)later than other coals. There are peats of Recent or Pleistocene origin. Some very few are forming today in Finland and in high mountainous regions.

COAL GASIFICATION Underground gasification of coal is successfully carried out in France and in the Soviet Union. Wells tap the coal seams which are ignited. The combustion gas is piped to the surface. The method produces a high yield of gas without mining or transporting the coal.

A coal gasification plant is operating at Daggett, California and producing 100 megawatts of electricity. The gas and steam is produced by heating coal. Once fired, the unit is self-firing.

COAL TAR Coal tar, a coal derivative is produced in making coke. It has many varied uses (dye production, pharmaceuticals, and explosives).

COALIFICATION Coalification is the natural process of transforming vegetable matter into mineral carbon. Diagenesis (q.v.) begins with the break-down of cellulose and lignum (peat). Coal, or graphite results at different stages. See **CARBON**.

COAST AND GEODETIC SURVEY This bureau, formed in 1807, has had its scope broadened. It is devoted to cartography, geodesy, geomagnetism, gravimetry, photogrammetry, and seismology.

To date, the Survey has produced more than 30 million aeronautical and nautical charts. The Survey operates the worldwide Earthquake Net with 125 stations in 63 countries and participates in the Pacific Sea Wave Warning System with 60 tidal stations around the Pacific Basin.

COASTAL EROSION Coastal cliffs are undercut by wave action and break off in slumps or slabs depending upon their composition. The dip of a sea cliff is important. Layered sediments with well-defined bedding planes tilting only slightly seaward can cause a landslide by being undercut. The bedding plane can become a glide plane. If an absorbent clay is involved water enchances the process. The sea cliffs of Palos Verdes and Pacific Palisades, California demonstrate this type of erosion. Expanding clays contribute to the process.

Seas erode soft clay up to 2 meters (6.5 feet) a year. Waves cut notches and the material above falls leaving a bench to become a depositional site. Waves tend to sort sediments by weight and grain size. With current and wind shifts, a new bench may be created higher up on the cliff. This terraced effect is observed on the Norwegian Coast.

COASTAL PLAIN Lowlands from the sea's edge to the first major relief form the coastal plain. It is relatively level and undissected. It may be a recently emergent portion of the Continental Shelf.

A coastal plain may develop as a result of uplift or a decrease in sea level. The sediments are marine or continental. The plain is smooth due to stream erosion and wave activity.

COASTAL SWAMPS Wetlands along coasts are mainly on lagoonal fringes. They are flooded periodically by rains or tides. In drought, they become very dry.

Many coastal swamps support mangrove (q.v.) forests. These skirt many tropical and subtropical areas. The swamps are breeding areas for many sea creatures. See **WETLANDS**.

COASTAL ZONE The zone between emergent terrain and submerged land along continental edges is coast. It is beach and shore above the high-tide line, and zone of rapid change.

Emerging coastlines such as Norway and Maine are due to glacial rebound. As the ice melted, the land rose in relation to the sea. The process is continuing and can be seen in the Gulf of Bothnia between Sweden and Finland. The area has been rising for the past 10,000 years and there are now 6,500 islands which are rooted in billion year old granite.

Volcanic activity has been responsible for great coastline change especially in Hawaii, the Aleutians, Indonesia, and Iceland. In Siberia, coastal erosion of Tundra cliffs is estimated at 100 meters a year. The cliffs are weakened by permafrost which compounds the effects of erosional activity.

Despite the emerging areas, there has been a net retreat of the world's coastlines over the last century.

COBALT Cobalt is a silvery-white metallic element. The name is from 'Kobald', German for gnome. Cobaltite the chief ore is associated with the nickel arsenide, niccolite, and sulfides in basic igneous rocks such as found at Cobalt, Ontario. It is also found in veins. Zaire produces about 50% of the world's cobalt.

The world's reserves of cobalt are 75% contained in garnierite, a nickel laterite (q.v.). Garnierite reserves are greatest in New Caledonia and Brazil. The United States has intermittently operated the Idaho cobalt deposits.

As an alloy, cobalt is used in steels. A radioactive isotope of cobalt is used for cancer treatment. About 80 kilograms (200 pounds) of cobalt are used in the production of a jet aircraft.

COBBLE Cobble is rounded rock ranging between 64 and 256 millimeters (2.5-10 inches) in diameter. It is larger than a pebble but smaller than a boulder.

Cobbles once were used to pave streets. They now frequently form the roadbed. Nantucket Island's famous streets are built of the cobbles brought to the island as ballast in the days of sailing vessels.

COCCOLITHS Coccoliths are minute marine organisms, platelets of single-celled algal plants. Magnification several thousand times is needed to see them. They are among the nannoplankton of today's seas.

Coccoliths are primarily in tropical waters where their calcium carbonate readily precipitates. In these waters coccoliths replace silica-secreting diatoms (q.v.).

Coccoliths are abundant in deep sea oozes and are found as fossils in many chalks and marls of Mesozoic to Cenozoic (q.v.) Age. Several million fossils per cubic centimeter are in these rocks. The earliest fossil coccoliths are Lower Jurassic (175 m.y.).

COCKROACH The cockroach first appeared 300 million years ago in the Carboniferous Period and has not altered much. It was the first creature to fly.

There are billions of cockroaches, primarily in tropical forests. They can eat almost anything, run fast, as well as fly. The cockroach has 440 sensing hairs on its tail and can sense the wind. It can be activated in 10 milliseconds.

COCOS PLATE The Cocos crustal plate off Central America, moving easterly into the Caribbean Plate, has broken into 7 parts. Managua, Nicaragua, is on a major one. The latest earthquake activity was in 1972.

COELACANTH Marine Coelacanth ('Latimer chalumnae') was considered extinct. It developed in the Cambrian (570-500 m.y.) and flouished 50 million years ago. A specimen was netted in the Indian Ocean in 1938. The living fossil had fins, was 1.5 meters (5 feet) long and weighed 68 kilograms (150 pounds). Other specimens have since been fished from the deeps.

COELENTERATES Coral and jellyfish belong to the Coelenterate Phylum of radial and symmetrical marine invertebrates. Coelenterates are not very different from sponges in having a body wall and no internal organs.

Coral and sea anemone belong to the Anthozoa. Coral excretes an external skeleton of calcium carbonate. The living animal is a polyp and its skeleton is the coral.

The phylum includes Hydrozoa which are more evolved than sponges. They have a muscular tissue, stinging cells, and are mobile.

COESITE Natural coesite, an ultra-high temperature quartz, is of meteoritic origin. It was first found at Meteor Crater, Arizona. Coesite has been identified from among the rocks brought to the Earth from the Moon.

COKE Coke is produced in air-tight ovens from bituminous coal (q.v.). Tars are removed as by-products. Coke is used in smelting metals.

COL A col is a pass or saddle resulting from glacial plucking. The glacier carves a cirque (q.v.) from the mountain slope. The glacier also removes material from both sides of a mountain and an arete (q.v.) may form. If the arete is scoured through, a col results.

COLD FRONT The leading edge of a cold airmass is a cold front. Cold air pushes under warmer air, which it is replacing. Usually rapid changes of weather occur with snow or rain together with high winds. In the summer, thunderstorms mark the advance of a cold front. Cool, clear air follows the cold front.

COLLAPSED STAR At the end of a star's lifetime, it becomes smaller and collapses in upon itself by the force of gravity.

COLLIMATION Collimation is the alignment of lenses as in a telescope or microscope. To achieve a correct 'line of sight', a transit or theodolyte is collimated.

COLLOID A colloid is a particle, usually larger than a small molecule. It will not pass through a semi-permeable membrane and will not precipitate from its medium, except under unusual conditions.

Clay particles in colloidal form are carried in solution and precipitated as gels. These are important in soil formation. Opals are thought to be hardened colloidal silica which was precipitated as a gel.

COLOMBIAN ANDES The Andes Mountains in western Colombia split into 3 ranges. These are oriented north-south and fan out to the northeast. Between the ranges are very high plateaus or 'paramos'. These are flat, high mountain valleys.

COLOMBIAN ECOSYSTEMS Colombia has great ecological variety. There are more bats in Colombia than anywhere else in the world. There are over 3,000 species of birds. The major ecosystems are:

- Andean - Western 1/3 of country
- Amazon Basin - Eastern Colombia is in the Amazon watershed
- Llanos - Savannas of the East Andean slopes
- Paramos - High mountain meadows.

Each ecosystem has its own complex of flora and fauna.

COLONY A colony is an aggregate of organisms. Reef coral are good examples of colonialism. Inhabitants of the colony are of the same species or are in symbiosis (q.v.) with each other.

COLOR Visible light of different wavelengths and frequencies yields different colors. Each color has a specific wavelength and frequency. Red has the longest wavelength and lowest frequency while violet has the shortest wavelength and highest frequency.

Color is an identifying characteristic of rocks and minerals. Some have only one, being monochromatic, others have more and are bi- or polychromatic.

Minerals with a metallic luster do not vary greatly in their color. Usually any change is related to its weathering pattern. Many minerals with non-metallic luster do vary greatly. Slight variations in chemistry sometimes cause radical differences in color.

COLORADO DELTA The Colorado Delta extends from the mouth of the Gila River in Arizona to the Peninsula Mountains in California. Not too long ago, Yuma, Arizona was a port.

The Delta is between 32-33° North Latitude and 114.3-115° West Longitude. A large portion of the Delta extends into the Gulf.

COLORADO DESERT The Colorado Desert of Southern California extends from the Peninsula Mountains to the Arizona border. It continues into Baja California, Mexico.

The Salton Basin area includes the Salton Trough (q.v.) or southern portion of the San Andreas Fault. Through the area, the fault is marked by a line of 'Washingtonia filifera' palms served by the extensive spring-line. The area is especially noted for its earthquake swarms.

The largest lake in California, Salton Sea, is located in the basin where many Pleistocene lakes once existed. These ancient lakes are collectively known as Lake Cahuila.

The arid Colorado Desert is a low-lying area. It is covered by sand dunes and stony flats. From the south end of the Salton Sea to the edge of the Colorado River are the spectacular Algodones Dunes or Yuma Sand Hills. The dunes are continuous over 65 kilometers (39 miles) with a width of from 5-10 kilometers (3-6 miles). In addition to the seif-like (q.v.) dunes, there are Salton barchans (q.v.). They form a group of 47 moving dunes of varying sizes.

COLORADO LINEAMENT The Colorado Lineament is a northeast-southwest series of Precambrian faults crossing the Rockies. The Colorado River traces part of the lineament. It has been charted onto the Colorado Plateau in Utah.

The affected area is about 1,100 x 160 kilometers (660 x 90 miles). Mullen Creek-Nash Fork Shear Zone is on the northern edge in Wyoming. The lineament appears to define a huge wrench fault (q.v.). See **COOK'S FAULT**.

The Colorado Mineral Belt is on the northeast end of the Colorado Lineament in north-central Colorado.

COLORADO RIVER The Colorado System drains 8% of the United States. It extends into 5 physiographic provinces:

- Middle Rocky Mountains
- Southern Rocky Mountains
- Colorado Plateau
- Wyoming Basin
- Basin and Range.

The river rises in the Phantam Valley area of Rocky Mountain National Park on the Continental Divide. It forks quickly. North Fork flows through a series of dams, tunnels, and lakes to supply water to the eastern slope and 99% of Colorado's population. South Fork flows 1,500 kilometers (900 miles) southwest to join the Green River from Wyoming and Utah. San Juan River from New Mexico meets the Colorado at Four Corners. In the lower basin, the river flows through Marble Canyon to Grand Canyon on its way to the Gulf of Mexico.

John Wesley Powell explored and mapped the drainage area. He found 3 types of streams:

   Synclinal - Flowing over bedrock

   Anticlinal - Flowing off the divide

   Radial   - Flowing from the volcanoes.

The 647,000 square kilometer (250,000 square mile) area has 14 dams with water for 3 years. The river is 2,300 kilometers (1,400 miles) long and discharges 31 cubic kilometers (15 cubic miles) of water annually.

The Colorado serves the water needs of communities along its course. In addition water is transported into Arizona, California, and Mexico.

COLUMBIA GLACIER Columbia is a spectacular blue-white, almost irridescent glacier. It is located where the Chugach Mountains meet the sea at Prince William Sound, not far from the terminus of the Alaskan Pipeline.

Columbia is the last Alaskan tidewater glacier. Recently, it has been calving (q.v.) and melting. Columbia has been retreating at about 500 meters (1,650 feet) per year. It is still about 65 kilometers (39 miles) long.

COLUMBIA ICEFIELD High in the Canadian Rockies above 3,500 meters (11,500 feet) is a massive icefield. It straddles the Continental Divide between Banff and Jasper national parks. Ice up to 1,000 meters thick (3,300 feet) covers 310 square kilometers (120 square miles).

The icefield spawns some huge alpine glaciers (q.v.) among them Athabasca and Saskatchewan. The latter is the source of the Saskatchewan River which feeds into Hudson Bay. Athabasca gives rise to the Athabascan River, a feeder stream for the Mackenzie (q.v.). Other glaciers contribute to streams emptying into the Pacific.

COLUMBIA PLATEAU Columbia Plateau is a great lava-capped landform extending over 5 northwestern states, or 375,000 square kilometers (225,000 square miles). Successive layers of basalt erupted from volcanoes and thousands of fissures.

Between flows, there were long periods of relative quiet. Forests grew and erosion created mountains to be later buried by lava. Windows (q.v.) reveal the granite Steptoes of Oregon.

Gorges cut by the Snake and Columbia Rivers reveal 1,210 meters (4,000 feet) of 10 meter (30 foot) lava flows with intermittent sediments. Most sediments are Miocene (26-12 m.y.) but in the Cenozoic (q.v.), 100,000 cubic kilometers (60,000 cubic miles) were laid down. The flows are similar to the Deccan trap of India and the Parana flows of southern Brazil.

COLUMBIUM Columbium, or niobium, often occurs in combination with tantalum. Columbium has a lower atomic weight than tantalum and is more reactive chemically. Columbium melts at 2,415° Celsius.

Columbite, an important mineral of columbium also contains tantalite and cassiterite. It is found in pegmatites (q.v.) and in placers. Pyrochlore, found principally in carbonatites (q.v.), is now the most important source of the metal. Columbium is an important alloy. Ferrocolumbium is 50-60% columbium, 5% or less manganese, 8% silica, minor carbon, and the rest iron. See **NIOBIUM**.

COLUMNAR BASALT Basaltic lava cools into hexagonal or pentagonal blocks that split apart. When eroded, the blocks form spectacular columns and pillars. They may have up to 10 sides but most are hexagonal.

Columnar jointing and columns are found covering parts of North Ireland. Wave-eroded columns form the Giant's Causeway, a tourist attraction. This feature has 40,000 columns. Most have been leveled to the ground but still others tower to 6 meters (20 feet). The basalts are 50 million years old.

COMBER A comber is a deep-water wave with the crest pushed forward by strong winds. Larger than a whitecap, it is a 'spilling breaker'.

COMET Comets have been labeled the 'dirty snowballs of Space'. They measure up to 83 kilometers (50 miles) across and are masses of rock, dust particles, and ice orbiting the Sun. There are an estimated billion comets in Space beyond Pluto.

Occasionally one is forced nearer the Sun by the energy of a passing star. As the comet approaches the Sun, the ice becomes gas and swells. This ball forms 'a coma' made up of gases ionized by ultra-violet radiation. Ionization gives rise to 2 particle streams away from the coma, and to the curved tail, which is thousands of miles long.

The rock particles glow yellow and the gas is blue from carbon monoxide. Solar wind (q.v.) exerts such pressure on a comet, the tail is always facing away from the Sun.

A comet's orbit is stretched and parabolic as it nears the Sun. Planetary orbits affect it and the course becomes elliptical. After many passes near the Sun, the gases dissipate. Rock and dust remain to become meteorites and meteor showers occur. See **HALLEY'S COMET**.

COMMENSALISM In a community, unlike organisms may live in a symbiotic relationship. This relationhip may be commensalism, where one organism is benefited and the other appears unaffected. In the sea, sponges and discarded shells provide shelter for other creatures in a different form of commensalism. See **SYMBIOSIS**.

COMMUNISM PEAK Communism Peak is the highest in the USSR. The mountain is in the Pamir Range of Tadzhik Province in Soviet Central Asia. Communism Mountain has an elevation of 7,495 meters (24,590 feet).

COMMUNITY A biological community is composed of interrelated plants and animals inhabiting a given area. It is usually a complex association of all members sharing the same ecospace (q.v.).

COMPACTION Compaction, or reduction of volume, is accompanied by an increase in density and a reduction of porosity (q.v.). It occurs where the load is greatly increased as in a geosyncline (q.v.).

COMPASS The Chinese were the first to utilize the north-seeking property of the lodestone (q.v.). The discovery was made sometime in the 11th Century. The Chinese used the lodestone to represent the Great Bear Constellation on the chess board. The purpose was to tell fortunes. The chess-piece was cut so the tail pointed to the North Star. How the pieces fell was interpreted by a seer.

At a later date this north-seeking phenomenon was used in the wind-roses of navigators. The horizon was represented by a circle of 360° and the instrument was known as the 'sailor's compass'.

COMPOSITE CONE The composite cone is a combination of cinder cone and shield volcano. Most large and famous volcanoes are composite cones. Fujiyama in Japan and Vesuvius in Italy are examples. Some composite cones are also strato-volcanoes (q.v.) because of alternations of lava and cinders

COMPOUND A compound is a chemical blend of 2 or more kinds of atoms to form a molecule. Some common compounds are water (hydrogen and oxygen), carbon dioxide (carbon and oxygen), and salt (sodium and chloride).

COMSTOCK LODE Comstock Lode in Virginia City, Nevada, was one of the deepest silver mines in the world and one of the richest. It produced about 10 million tons of silver a year. It was abandoned not because the ore ran out but because production became too costly. Recently, there have been efforts to reopen the mine.

CONCENTRATION Heavy minerals may be concentrated by streams into placers or by wave action into beach placers. Sorting is carried out by gravity.

Precipitated minerals are also concentration products. Deposition has sequence and order. The precipitates are deposited in veins, fractures, cavities, or as impregnations in rocks.

Concentration is also used as a processing technique to enrich the mineral content or an ore. The process may only consist of washing away impurities, or it may include flotation or leaching.

CONCRETIONS Cemented masses of mud, soil, and or mineral are concretions. Concretions are often concentric with onion-skin layering.

Deep sea nodules of manganese and other minerals are examples of concretions. Others are the limonite concretions common in many lateritic soils and mineral deposits.

Concretions can form around a nucleus in a loosely cemented sandstone. The nucleus can be a mineral or a shell which will contribute to the cementation process. The concretion takes on the form of a ball. When of mud and clay, a concretion can be intercalated within strata and along contact zones. Concretions are often a stage in lithification (q.v.).

CONDENSATION The change of water vapor to liquid is condensation. Dew is a natural condensate of water vapor.

CONDUCTOR A material providing a channel or path for electrons and electrical current is a conductor. Copper is an excellent natural conductor since it has an unattached electron. Most minerals with 'loose' electrons are good conductors.

CONFLUENCE Where 2 major rivers meet is a confluence. Perhaps the most famous confluence is that of the Blue and White Nile at Khartoum, Sudan. The relatively clear Blue Nile waters merge slowly into the more muddy waters of the White Nile.

Another famous confluence is that of Solimoes and Rio Negro, near Manaus, Brazil. The merging of these rivers to create the Amazon is not rapid. Each river maintains its integrity for many kilometers and each is readily discerned by color. The Solimoes or Upper Amazon is mocha-colored while the Negro is black with organic material.

CONGLOMERATE Conglomerate results when pebbles or fragments of rock are cemented. The clastics (q.v.) are larger than sand (2 millimeters). Carboniferous, ferriferous, siliceous, or other mineral solutions may be cementing agents.

Stream-rounded pebbles are found in 'puddingstone conglomerate' along present or ancient stream channels. If the fragments are large, rounded stones, the formation is a cobble conglomerate. Breccia conglomerate is made up of cemented, angular fragments that have not traveled far from their source. See **BRECCIA and COBBLE**.

On Mount Olga, a monadnock (q.v.) in Australia, cobble conglomerates abound.

CONGO BASIN The Congo (Zaire) Basin straddles the Equator between 4° North and 4° South Latitude, covering 10% of Africa. It is a saucer-like depression with the Cameroon Highlands on the north rim. The Crystal Mountains, a series of limestone hills, are on the west. Lake Tanganyika and the snow-capped Ruwenzoris (q.v.) are on the east. The African Copper Belt occupies the south rim.

The basin is known to the French as a 'cuvette' (q.v.). The Congo Basin floor is a great plain containing lacustrine sediments deposited in Tertiary (q.v.) and Recent times.

CONGO RAINFOREST The equatorial rainforest in the Congo (Zaire) Basin (q.v.) is one of 3 major rainforests in the world. In the Congo Rainforest, canopies reach 60 meters (200 feet). Among the varied tree species are ebony, mahogany, red cedar, rubber, and walnut.

Temperatures hover around 30° Celsius (90° Fahrenheit) all year and rainfall exceeds 400 centimeters (100 inches) a year. See **ITURI RAINFOREST**.

CONGO RIVER Congo (Zaire) River is the 6th longest and one of the great rivers of the world. It originates in Zambia south of Lake Tanganyika, 1,600 kilometers (1,000 miles) south of the Equator. The river system drains 3.4 million square kilometers (1.5 million square miles) or 13% of Africa.

Feeders come out of the Ruwenzori Mountains in the northeast and the Mitumbas in the southeast. Beginning at 1,500 meters (5,000 feet) elevation at a distance of 1,600 kilometers (1,000 miles) from the coast, the river's course is 5,000 kilometers (3,000 miles) long.

Born as the Chambezi River, the Congo flows southwest to disappear temporarily in Lake Bangweolo. It emerges at the south end of the lake and forms the border between Zaire and Zambia. Then it runs northwest 330 kilometers (200 miles) to join the Lualaba River and become the Upper Congo.

The Middle Congo is blocked by the Cameroon Highlands and turns west in a wide arc. Here, the river is fed by many tributaries, among them, the Ubangi. The Congo loops and recrosses the Equator on its southwest course. This stretch of river has a network of navigable waterways and 4,000 islands due to the many stream braids.

Congo Republic is on the right bank and Zaire on the left. The Lower and Middle Congo are separated by Livingston Falls. From the falls, the river flows 160 kilometers (100 miles) over coastal plain to the Atlantic.

The Congo's flow is 2nd only to the Amazon's. It discharges 2.5 million cubic kilometers (1.5 million cubic miles) of freshwater annually. This is 1/4 the annual discharge of the Amazon. The silt discharged is 560 cubic kilometers (340 cubic miles) per year.

CONGO SUBMARINE CANYON In the Atlantic, the Congo Canyon is offshore the mouth of the Congo (Zaire) River. The canyon, 1,200 meters (4,000 feet) deep, appears to be a continuation of the river.

Turbidity currents (q.v.) are active in the canyon and these contribute to the sculpture of the canyon.

CONIFER The conifer is the evergreen plant group which includes the cedar, fir, hemlock, pine, and spruce. Conifers are among the last surviving gymnosperms (q.v.). According to fossil evidence, conifers first appeared at the end of the Carboniferous Period (250 m.y.).

The conifer is the dominant vegetation in Taiga (q.v.) forests. In the North American Taiga, the dominant conifer is the spruce. In non-Taiga regions, the timberpine in southeastern United States is the loblolly and in the west it is the lodgepole pine.

CONNATE WATER Water retained in pore spaces and interstices of rocks since the rock formed is connate. It is inactive fossil water and may be interstitial or interstratal.

Connate water holds a potential for use on Space missions. Moon or planetary rocks would be the source.

CONODONT Conodonts are marine microorganisms useful as fossil indicators of petroleum and minerals. Conodonts left their hard parts in limestones and dolomites.

The conodont was world-wide at the beginning of the Paleozoic and vanished by its end (570-225 m.y.). Anita Harris' work established the usefulness of the conodont in exploration, and emphasized the importance of color in the interpretation of the fossils. She found color in conodonts to be thermally controlled.

The 'geological windows' for petroleum are the brown and yellow conodonts. If it is white, that can lead to some metals since white indicates the highest temperatures.

CONRAD DISCONTINUITY The upper and lower crusts of the Earth are separated by a marked discontinuity called the Conrad. Its depth varies between 10 and 30 kilometers (6 and 18 miles). The Upper Crust beneath continents is made up of a mix of sedimentary, igneous, and metamorphic rocks of lesser density than rocks of the Lower Crust.

Geologists are agreed that the rocks at depth are probably gabbro (q.v.). Oceanic crust differs from continental in that the Upper Crust has a thin sedimentary layer overlying basalt. Below the basalt is the denser gabbro.

CONSEQUENT STREAM A consequent stream follows topographic contours over a newly created landscape. They cut soft sediments more rapidly than hard ones. The stream carves a new topography that it then follows. Consequent streams may have subsequent (q.v.) tributaries forming at right angles.

On coastal plains where slopes are gentle, parallel drainage patterns develop.

CONSERVATION OF ENERGY A law established in physics states that energy can neither be created nor destroyed. Energy may change form, and often does, but the total ration of energy in the Universe remains the same.

This law is a workable hypothesis with reference to the Earth. It does not necessarily describe a true condition of our Universe's or Cosmic energy.

CONSTELLATION A cluster of stars with a definite pattern is a constellation. By international agreement there are 88 acknowledged constellations. Individual stars vary in distance from the Earth and each other. They also vary in brightness.

CONTACT Rock types and strata are separated from each other by boundaries or contacts. These are marked by changes in rock type, changes in grain sizes in similar rock types, changes in color or mineralogy. Rocks may differ in type but have a similar origin as in the case of volcanic flows. Flows of different periods are separated by a contact sometimes evident by color alone.

Sediments or flows separated by erosional contacts indicate a lapse of time, sometimes a long time. Smooth transitional contacts are conformities. Those following a period of erosion are usually very irregular. These are unconformities (q.v.).

CONTACT METAMORPHISM The contact between an intrusion and country rock may be metamorphosed and the mineralogy changed. An intrusion is often surrounded by an aureole (q..v.) of metamorphic rock. Massive igneous intrusives such as the batholith (q.v.) generate an encasing layer of metamorphic rock because of the enormous heat and pressure involved in the formation phase. The accompanying mineralization may be rich and large enough to be mined as ore.

Metamorphic changes result from the confining pressure and heat. They also occur because gases and solutions can emanate from intrusions still in a magmatic state. At the contact zone the alteration halo is very evident.

CONTINENT Continents are great landmasses bounded by oceans and seas. They are cratonic areas with aggregated margins that have sometimes been transformed into mountain ranges. The continent includes the shelf area below the high-tide line. Landmasses cover 36% of the globe and 7% are underwater.

Some continental rocks are as old as 4.0 million years. This is in sharp contrast to oceanic crustal rocks which are all less than 200 million years old.

Continents are made up of 3 major parts. These are the continental shield, the stable platforms, and the mountainous belts. Plain and steppe overlie shields and platforms. The greatest exposed shield area is in Canada.

The following landmasses are continents: Africa, Antarctica, Australia, Eurasia, North America, and South America. Australia is the smallest of the continents, or the world's largest island.

CONTINENTAL DESERTS Continental deserts are also mid-latitude deserts. They cover great expanses and in Central Asia and Australia. In Australia, the desert makes up a great portion of the continent.

North America has mid-latitude rain shadow deserts where the Coast Ranges and Rockies act as barriers.

Patagonia in Argentina is a mid-latitude desert in the Southern Hemisphere. It is also a rain-shadow desert flanked by the Andes. See **DESERT**.

CONTINENTAL DIVIDE The highest point on a continent from which water can flow in opposite directions is a divide. The long, high ridge of the Rockies divides waters between the Pacific and the Atlantic.

In South America, the divide between Atlantic and Pacific is the crest of the Andes. The most spectacular dividing range is the Cordillera Blanca in Peru.

Of lesser elevation is the continental divide between waters flowing to the Amazon and those flowing south to Rio de la Plata. This divide is the Central Plateau of Brazil.

In Europe, the Alps divide north and south flowing rivers. In Asia, the most important divide is provided by the Himalayas.

CONTINENTAL DRIFT Continental Drift theory contends that continents have moved relative to each other through geological time. Wegener, the author of the theory, supposed the continents were once a single landmass, Pangaea (q.v.).

Pangaea remained intact to the Middle Paleozoic (400 m.y.) when it became 2 continents. These were separated by the Tethys Sea. The continents were Laurasia in the north and Gondwana in the south. These were later rifted apart to form other landmasses.

Through time, Gondwana (q.v.), became Africa, Antarctica, Australia, India, and South America. In the Northern Hemisphere, North America separated from Eurasia and the Atlantic Ocean came into being.

Dislocations and continental collisions caused great mountains to be thrust up. Among these were the Alps, Andes and Himalayas. The mountains continue to rise as the crustal plates crush into each other.

Validation of the continental drift concept has come from a great body of data, most of it from deep sea sediments. It is a concept now widely accepted by geologists.

Continental drift continues and Greenland only recently separated from the mainland. It is still drifting at 20-30 meters (65-100 feet) per year. North America is drifting west away from Eurasia.

Australia moves away from Antarctica at 5 centimeters (2 inches) a year covering 5,660 kilometers (3,400 miles) in 100 million years. Movements are not always steady, but are in spasms.

The molten core of Earth may have expanded about 200 million years ago causing convective cells or eddies that moved continents. This could have also occurred at other times in the past. There is evidence of Precambrian rifting between North America and Eurasia that subsequently closed to be reopened again in Mid-Paleozoic.

CONTINENTAL GLACIER A glacial mass covering a large portion of a continent in the form of an icecap is a continental glacier. There are at present only 2, the Antarctic and Greenland icecaps. See **ANTARCTICA**.

Continental glaciers cover 9.5 million square kilometers (5.7 million square miles) of the Earth's surface. If they were to melt, the seas would rise about 60 meters (200 feet).

Greenland's icecap is 2,400 meters (8,000 feet) thick and Antarctica's 4,200 meters (14,000 feet). Only a few of the highest mountains show through the ice. The barren peaks are 'nunataks'.

CONTINENTAL ISLANDS Continental islands rise from the continental shelf and are a part of the continental landmass. Tasmania, Great Britain, and New Zealand are in this class. They have been separated from the mainland long enough to develop distinctive plant and animal life.

CONTINENTAL MARGINS Ocean basins are bounded by continental margins. These may or may not coincide with the edges of crustal plates. There are 3 different types of continental margins:

Divergent	- (49%) In interior of crustal plates. Formed by rifting. Oceanic rock is at spreading edges
Translational	- (33%) At crustal plate edges. Axes of new coordinates are parallel to the former ones.
Convergent	- (18%) At plate edges, continents are underthrust by oceanic material.

Most divergent margins have thick prisms of sediments which develop into continental rises. Convergent margins border deep trenches. Translational margins are between the divergent and convergent margins and have smaller continental rises.

CONTINENTAL SHELF Continents extend offshore from the low-tide line. They often slope gently to 182 meters (600 feet or 100 fathoms). This undersea area is variable in width, ranging from 17 to 500 kilometers (10-300 miles).

Along the Atlantic Coast of the United States the continental shelf averages 64 kilometers (40 miles) in width. The lower 48 states have 500,000 square kilometers (300,000 square miles) of shelf while Alaska has 916,000 (550,000).

Continental shelves may be dissected by submarine canyons (q.v.). The most prominent off the Atlantic Coast is Hudson Canyon.

CONTINENTAL SLOPE The Continental Slope extends from the edge of the shelf at 180 meters (600 feet) to depths of 900 to 3,000 meters (3,000 to 10,000 feet). The width averages 25 kilometers (15 miles).

CONTOUR Lines drawn through points of equal value are contours. On a topographic map, they are lines of equal elevation. Contours on weather maps are drawn through points of equal pressure. These outline the airmasses. See **ISOBARS**.

CONVECTION Convection is vertical transfer of heat. Air rises when warm and expands, losing density in relation to the surrounding air. Cool air descends and contracts.

A warm airmass will continue to rise, although cooling, until it reaches another airmass with compatible temperatures, moisture content, and atmospheric pressure.

Convection forms currents or thermals of air turbulence and is important to the development of thunderclouds. Clear air turbulence, CAT (q.v.), is convective air of thermals with insufficient moisture or nucleation particles to create clouds and rain.

Temperature can result in density changes and contrasting densities can, in turn, cause convection (q.v.). Convection results when warm air rises at the Equator and descends near the Tropics of Cancer and Capricorn. These convection cells are known as Hadley cells. They maintain the Trade Winds and moderate climate.

Similar exchanges between the Polar Regions and Mid-Latitudes are less effective modifiers. Overturn of seawater creates convection cells when cold polar air mixes with warmer water at lower latitudes.

Scientist theorize that the core of the Earth is very hot. Some of the heat is from radioactive sources. The rest is the result of chemical heating and pressure. Energy created by these different sources generates convection, or rising and descending currents, of heated magma (q.v.) within the Mantle. The geothermal gradient is 1° per 30 meters. At the Core, it is 4,000° Celcius (7,200° Fahrenheit).

CONVERTER REACTOR Any nuclear reactor producing fissionable material different from the original fuel is a converter reactor. The amount of fissionable material produced is less than the amount consumed to generate energy and the reactor must be refueled.

MOUNT COOK The highest peak in New Zealand, Mount Cook is in the Southern Alps. Cook is 3,742 meters (16,349 feet) in elevation and is glaciated.

The most important of Cook's glaciers is Tasman, which is up to 600 meters (2,000 feet) thick. Tasman mantles the eastern slope for 27 kilometers (17 miles). It is moving at the rate of 50 centimeters (20 inches) per day. Attrition from melting and evaporation at the snout is great.

COOK'S RIFT In addition to the San Andreas System, there may be another great rift system in western United States. Dr. Cook (University of Utah) speculates that this rift also enters the continent from the Gulf of California. It includes some major faults in Arizona, Utah, Idaho, Wyoming, and Montana. This system supposedly joins the Rocky Mountain Trench in British Columbia.

COPPER Copper was one of the metals known to ancient craftsmen. To the Romans, copper was 'aes Cyprium' or metal from Cyprus. The island still continues to produce.

The Egyptians thought so highly of copper, they gave it the symbol of Eternal Life, the 'Ankh' which is a circle above a cross.

Copper is the only pure metal commonly found. It is reddish-brown and does not easily rust or corrode. The metal is relatively reactive, is malleable, and is an excellent conductor. Its hardness is 2-3 on Moh's scale (q.v.). In electronics, pure copper is important. Nothing but silver exceeds it in conductivity. More than 50% of all copper production is used in electronics.

Copper is found in veins and in sedimentary beds or lenticular pods. Some leading copper minerals are bornite, chalcopyrite, pyrite, arsenopyrite, and copper carbonates (malachite, azurite).

Low grade sulfide deposits in the United States, Chile, and Peru are some of the main producers. Zaire and Zambia both produce substantial copper carbonates. Many countries produce copper but only 8 figure in world trade.

COPPER BELT The 167 x 33 kilometer (100 x 20 mile) African Copper Belt is on the south rim of the Congo (Zaire) Basin (q.v.). Organic matter in the sea helped precipitate copper from eroded Precambrian rocks. Glaciation and further erosion led to additional deposition. A 3,200 meter (10,560 foot) pile of sediments resulted. The area contains 25% of world's known reserves (880 million metric tons). The deposits were discovered about 5,000 years ago.

COPPER CANYON The Uruque River in Sonora, Mexico, has cut a deep canyon through the Sierra Madre Occidental. The steep wall of Mount Mohinara flanks the canyon. Little explored, it appears that there is a complex of 3 canyons deeper than Grand Canyon or Hells Canyon (q.v.). Like the Grand Canyon, the area continued to rise while the river continued to cut into the sediments.

COPPER PROCESSING Paul Revere is credited with establishing the first rolling and sheet copper mill in the United States. He fabricated the cannons for the USS Constitution, 'Old Ironsides'.

Today, milling begins with screening to less than 15 centimeters (6 inches), followed by crushing. Ore is then put into a rod or ball mill (depending upon the required output). Final milling results in a powder that is smelted and poured into ingots.

COQUINA Coquina is a form of limestone. It is generally of relatively recent geological origin and composed of a shelly aggregate. Coquina is used as a roadbed material along the Texas south coast.

CORAL The living coral organism is in the Anthozoa Class of Coelenterate Phylum. It is cup-shaped and has tentacles to trap food. It requires shallow, warm, clear seas with a temperature above 20° Celsius (69° Fahrenheit). Salinity must be low, not above 35%. Coral does not thrive below a depth of 15 meters (50 feet).

Oxygen and plankton are required for coral and often they are in symbiosis with Algae. Coral provide carbon dioxide for the Algae and the reef provides the anchor. Algae, in turn, provide the coral with oxygen through photosynthesis (q.v.).

Limestone reefs are formed from the remains of coral and other animals and plants. Reefs appear in the inter-tropical zones where the environmental conditions needed for coral and associated biota are found. Reefs can grow 5-7.5 centimeters (2-3 inches) per year.

Atlantic reefs are found in the Antilles and around Florida. The most northern reefs are off Bermuda where the Gulf Stream warms the waters.

Reefs are more widespread in the Southwest Pacific, where there are about 300 large coral atolls. In the Indian and Western Pacific there are 330,000 square kilometers (220,000 square miles) of reefs supporting 200,000 species of coral. Coral are endanged by shipping and other human endeavors such as dredging. See **REEFS**.

CORAL SEA The Coral Sea in the western Pacific off Northeast Australia lies between the Great Barrier Reef and New Hebrides. The sea is bounded on the north by New Guinea and the Solomon Sea with its islands.

The warm waters of the Coral Sea have much reef development. The sea was the scene of strategic naval engagements in World War II.

CORDILLERA The mountain chains of western North and South America form a 'cordillera', Spanish for mountain chain. The American Cordillera is continuous from Alaska to Tierra del Fuego.

In the United States, it includes the Rockies, Sierras, and Cascades and in Canada, the Canadian Rockies. The South American Andes are split into parallel north-south ranges with altiplanos (q.v.) between. In Mexico, there are 2 main branches, Oriental (east) and Occidental (west). Between is a high central plateau. The mountains are built on continental margins (q.v.). They are surface expressions of crustal plate movement at the Pacific Rim.

CORDILLERAN ICE SHEET During the last Ice Age a glacial ice sheet was centered in British Columbia. The ice spread northwest into the Aleutians, bypassing the Yukon Valley. It also spread into northwest United States.

CORE The Core of the Earth is its dense interior. It is estimated to begin at a depth of 5,154 kilometers (3,075 miles) and continue to the center of the Earth at 6,371 kilometers (3,822 miles). The Outer Core is the lower boundary of the Mantle (q.v.).

Core density ranges from 9.71 to 16 grams/cubic centimeter at its maximum. The Earth as a whole is 5.519 gm/cm^3, while the average for surface rocks is 2.7. Temperature is estimated at 4,000° Celcius (7,200° Fahrenheit. The Core is roughly 1/3 the Earth's mass. By its density, it is assumed to be of iron and nickel with the greatest concentration in the Inner Core. Iron alone makes up 38% of the Earth's mass.

Core is material brought up from a borehole. The structure and the strata of subsurface beds is maintained intact. The data obtained is used to construct a stratigraphic column, sometimes from surface to basement rocks.

CORIOLIS EFFECT As the Earth turns on its axis, there is a deflection of matter to the right in the Northern Hemisphere. This is the Coriolis Effect. It operates in reverse in the Southern Hemisphere.

Coriolis affects airmass movement and is reflected in climate and weather. The effect is more intense near the Equator, bending winds so the Trades are from the northeast and southeast.

Long distance trajectories are also affected. To reach a distant target, the Coriolis Effect must be considered.

CORNICHE A prominent bluff capped by a resistant layer of rock is a 'corniche'. It is named for bluffs along the Mediterranean Coast.

Ferruginous, laterized, and peneplained plateau caps of canga (iron ore) are also called 'corniches'.

CORONA The gaseous halo around the Sun is the Corona. In this layer, temperatures are estimated at a millions degrees (Kelvin). The halo is very broad, extending several radii beyond the Sun.

The Corona is especially visible when the Moon covers most of the Sun. These eclipses give us an exceptional view of the Corona and they occur every year or so. The Corona emits cosmic rays, including X-rays, some of which reach the Earth.

CORRASION Mechanical erosion, or corrasion, is primarily caused by winds. The most obvious examples are the wind-blown relief structures in deserts. Other elements than wind play a role in corrasion. Boulders smash into each other, glaciers scour, and rivers abrade channels by dragging bed loads.

CORRELATION Unless there is evidence of overturn, the oldest sedimentary horizons are at the bottom of a geological section being studied. Flat-lying sediments are often broken by valleys and irregular topography. Tracing sediments across topographic gaps, regions, and even continents is done only after detailed study of the individual horizons being correlated.

Correlation of stratigraphic horizons from one location to another is based on inference. This depends upon the relative ages of the rocks, their mineral content, and on plant and animal fossils found in the particular strata (q.v.).

Correlation of igneous rocks is more difficult. Correlations are made based upon mineral content, relative age, and degree of metamorphism. Although igneous rock correlations are more illusive, some have been made from continent to continent. The Nigerian and and South American tin granites are an example. Igneous rock correlations also rely heavily on radioactive dating (q.v.).

CORROSION Corrosion is chemical breakdown, usually from waters containing carbonic acid. Limestone reacts and is dissolved by waters containing acidic chemicals. Other rocks react but not so readily.

CORUNDUM An aluminum silicate, corundum, is second only to diamond in hardness. This characteristic makes it a valuable industrial abrasive.

Emery, a fine-grained mix of corundum and magnetite, is widely used in abrading and polishing. Manufactured industrial corundum is a combination of sand and carbon.

Gem corundum is highly prized. Ruby and sapphire are among the most valuable stones. High quality gems come from Burma, Sri Lanka (Ceylon), and Thailand.

COSMIC RADIATION Cosmic radiation penetrates Earth's Atmosphere through the gap in the magnetic shield at the poles. Aurora Borealis and Aurora Australis (q.v.) of the northern and southern hemispheres are reflections of the energy given off by cosmic rays.

Cosmic rays are streams of elementary particles emanating from the Sun and other stars.They are caused by the bombardmentof subatomic particles that also come from the Sun and stars. The primary particles produce secondary particles when they pass through the Atmosphere and are deflected by the Earth's Magnetic Field (Latitude Effect).

Effective radiation is about 0.03 Rems (q.v.) per year at sea level. For every 1,500 meters (5,000 feet) of elevation, the value doubles. The dose at sea level is increased by a factor of 50 with solar flare activity.

High energy particles are mostly protons and alpha rays (q.v.) although they contain heavier particles, electrons, and gamma rays. Particles travel at or near the speed of light and reach the Earth mainly as protons (q.v.). Skylab identified some uranium nuclei. Cosmic ray bombardment has been related to explosions of supernovae (q.v.).

COSMIC ABUNDANCE Recent studies put elemental abundance in the Cosmos and in cosmic rays as follows:

ELEMENT	COSMOS	COSMIC RAYS
Oxygen	24.0%	5.0%
Carbon	13.0	7.0
Nitrogen	2.4	2.0
Neon	2.4	1.0
Magnesium	1.0	1.2
Silicon	1.0	1.0
Iron	0.9	0.9
Argon	0.2	0.4
Aluminum	0.1	0.2
Chromium	0.01	0.6
Manganese	0.01	0.6
Beryllium	0.00007	0.8
Lithium	0.000045	1.2

Evidence for cosmic abundance is based on meteoritic data. The extraordinary amounts of lithium and beryllium in cosmic rays as compared with the Cosmos is noteworthy.

COSMIC RAY AVALANCHE High energy cosmic rays penetrate the Earth's Atmosphere. It is estimated that a particle travels at 0.8 kilometers (0.5 miles) before colliding with another nucleus. Collision results in stored or kinetic energy being converted to mass and a shower of particles results.

A photon (q.v.) striking a nucleus results in an electron, a positron, and debris. If the positron and electron collide, they disappear (annihilation) and high energy photons are created. If the energy is high enough, another shower or cascading 'avalanche' occurs.

COTOPAXI VOLCANO The equatorial volcano of Cotopaxi, Equador, is snow-capped all year. Its height is 5,850 meters (19,300 feet). It is the world's highest active volcano. The present peak grew up in the caldera of the ancient volcano, Picacho, which blew up 70,000 years ago and then collapsed in upon itself. See **CALDERA**.

Cotopaxi has erupted explosively many times. The worst was in 1877 when ash and pumice were expelled and the eruption triggered disastrous mudflows in which thousands died. The event was similar to that which destroyed the early capital of Guatemala.

COULEE Coulee is a local name for a canyon cut into the Columbia Plateau. It is a steep-sided gash in thick lavas of glassy rhyolite or obsidian. Grand Coulee is a large one carved by the Columbia River. Most coulees are dried river channels.

COUNTRY ROCK Country rock is a generic term for rock surrounding a mineralized zone. It is also the host rock for a vein, dike or sill from which it is profoundly different.

The term in mining signifies all rock but that containing ore or economic mineral.

COVALENT BONDING Atoms lacking any of the 8 electrons in the outer shell may share electrons in covalent bonding. Water with 6 oxygen electrons is sharing 2 hydrogen electrons in a covalent bond.

CRAB NEBULA A supernova explosion observed in China in the 16th Century resulted in the formation of electrons and electromagnetic fields that were 10's of kilometers across. The generated energy measured 10 to the 31 watts. The event was located in Crab Nebula.

Supernovae are sources of all types of radiomagnetic energy. They demonstrate how neutron stars can be converted to particle energy. See **SUPERNOVA**.

CRATER A crater forms from ejected debris around the neck of a volcano. The crater is a circular depression the outer walls of which are covered with ash and other pyroclastics. The inner crater bowl may be very large. In a live volcano, as in Hawaii, the crater may be filled with molten lava.

Subsidiary cones or craters form on the flanks of the central crater. Vesuvius has about 30 such craters, Etna close to 700.

Where the cone and volcano have collapsed inward a gigantic crater or caldera (q.v.) can develop. When the volcano becomes dormant, the crater may fill with water. This is the origin of Crater Lake (q.v.) in Oregon.

CRATER LAKE About 6,500 years ago the volcano, Mount Mazama, erupted and collapsed. It was 3,600 meters (12,000 feet) in elevation before the explosive eruption.

Mazama, in Oregon, ejected pumice over a 58 kilometer (35 mile) radius. In some areas, there were 16 cubic kilometers (10 cubic miles) of debris.

When the volcano collapsed a caldera 10 kilometers (6 miles) across with a depth of 670 meters (2,200 feet) formed. Present walls are between 150 and 600 meters (500 and 2,000 feet). The caldera filled with rainwater to form Crater Lake.

Wizard Island appeared 1,000 years ago. It is now 231 meters (763 feet) above water level. Maximum lake depth is 585 meters (1,932 feet).

Lake level is well above the local water table. Crater Lake is the deepest lake in the United States.

CRATERS OF THE MOON Lunar craters were long a subject of controversy. Since the successful Moon missions, scientists agree that many are volcanic and others are impact craters resulting from meteoritic impact.

In Idaho, stiff lava cones stand on pahoehoe (q.v.) flows. These cones have craters up to 20 meters (60 feet) deep. The area is known as 'Craters of the Moon'.

CRATON A craton is the old Precambrian shield or stable area of a continental landmass. Cratons are portions of the Earth's Crust that have achieved stability and have not altered much since the Precambrian. Mountain masses on cratons are not of recent origin. Cratonic margins are normally ringed by mobile belts (q.v.).

CREEP Creep, or solifluction, is slow mass movement downslope of soil or decomposed rock. It occurs on the surface and in the Upper Mantle. It may result from alternation of freezing and thawing. When topsoil freezes, it expands pushing surface boulders upward. When thaw occurs, the boulders slip downhill.

Creep results from gravity but may be initiated by water. Movement is not violent as in a landslide and is often discontinuous. It can be insidious as it is not always readily observable.

Creep can adversely affect structures, especially dams and bridges. The movement may be revealed by stress signs such as arching, fissuring, and vegetation growing at an unusual angle.

CREST The crest is the maximum height of a river in flood. Usually after cresting, there is a rapid decrease in flow.

The high point of a wave is its crest. This point is used to measure wavelength, the distance from crest to crest. Wave height is measured from trough to crest.

CRETACEOUS The Cretaceous Period (125-65 m.y.) is the latest in the Mesozoic Age. It was succeeded by the Paleocene Period of Tertiary Age and underlain by the Jurassic Period. 'Creta' is Latin for chalk.

The Cretaceous was a period of great plant development. Monocotyledons and dicotyledons, as well as angiosperms, came into being. Cicads were abundant. Marine life flourished and Foraminifera were widespread.

Cretaceous transgressions by the seas exceeded those of the Ordovician (500-430 m.y.). In the Cretaceous great chalk or limestone deposits were laid down in the worldwide, episodic seas. During the transgressions, continents were flooded for periods up to 2 million years.

Marine transgressions occurred during the relatively long breakup of Pangaea (q.v.). Seas linked the Arctic to the Gulf of Mexico and the Utah to the Great Lakes area.

The buildup of the seas and fluctuations of sealevels were related to the changing topography of ocean basins and the material from spreading ridges. Enormous basalt flows built up on ocean floors. Volcanic activity probably increased global temperatures causing proliferation of life and some species extinction.

In the Northern Hemisphere, there were 2 great continental landmasses and in the Southern, there was one. Great mountain building occurred. The Rockies were thrust up and the Andes rose.

At the end of the Cretaceous Period (65 m.y.), there was a great species extinction of both plants and animals. It was of great biological importance to the evolution of lifeforms. The extinction is a great geological mystery. Dr. Alvarez (Chicago) believed anomalous iridium found at Cretaceous-Tertiary boundary clays is the result of asteroid impact with a force 1,000 times Krakatoa. Other evidence of cosmic events is being collected.

Dr. Zollar found Kilauea ejecta enriched in iridium up to 20,000 times normal levels. However, this evidence does not completely explain the widespread nature of the iridium-bearing clays, found as far apart as Italy and Australia.

CRETACEOUS CONTINENTS From the end of the Precambrian to the Cretaceous (500-65 m.y.) there were 2 great continental landmasses. Angara which included Scandinavia; the Algonquin Region of North America, and Sino-Siberia was in the Northern Hemisphere. A continent that broke up into Afro-Brazilia and Madagascar was in the Southern Hemisphere.

CREVASSE Great glacial fissures develop as a result of differential movement and tension in the ice. These crevasses are deep cracks. They can be 45 meters (150 feet) or more deep and will occur if the valley widens spreading the ice. They can occur if ice moves over ledges or knobs and is stretched and broken.

A break in a natural levee system is a crevasse. Sediments will break a levee (q.v.) in floodtime. Coarse deposits are found at the exit end of deltas, where crevasses build in weak levees.

CRINOIDS Crinoids are a class of Phylum Echinodermata (sea lilies). Members of this class have central cups with an attachment for holding them in place and food gathering arms. Individual species are important indicator fossils.

CRIPPLE CREEK The rich mines of Cripple Creek, Colorado, are on the site of an ancient caldera (q.v.). These deposits yielded as much bullion gold as all the other mines in the Colorado Mineral Belt put together. In recent years some of the mines have been reopened.

CRITICAL MASS A critical mass is defined as the smallest amount of fissionable material that will undergo and sustain radioactive decay (q.v.) under special conditions.

CRITICAL MINERALS Metals and minerals considered important for defense are critical if the nation can only meet part of the demand. This may be the result of a lack of reserves or of market conditions.

Minerals remain in this category if they can be supplied from a friendly and available foreign source. Copper, nickel, and vanadium are so considered.

CROCIDOLITE Crocidolite, an asbestos mineral is marketed as 'mineral wool'. South Africa is the major producer from the Asbestos Mountains near the Orange River.

Under certain conditions, crocidolite alters to a hard, solid material. Its blue color changes to a golden yellow and silica or quartz replaces the fibers. The result is the famous 'tiger eye' or yellow 'cat's eye' semi-precious stone.

CROSS-BEDDING Sediments, particularly sandstones, reflect the currents that deposited them. Cross-bedding will be produced when currents scour out the stream bed and grains move up shallow slopes to drop into the trough. The steep side is in the direction of the flow. Sediments dip in the direction of flow where they form at an angle.

Wind blown sands will form cross-bedding in dunes reflecting the wind direction at the time of deposition. Some spectacular cross-bedding can be found in the Jurassic (195-136 m.y.) sandstone of the Entrada Formation in Colorado and New Mexico.

CROSSCUT A crosscut is an offshoot from the main shaft of a mine. Tunnels are cut from it to reach the ore body or veins.

CRUDE OIL Petroleum pumped from the Earth is referred to as 'crude oil'. It is black or greenish black, rarely amber. Crude is divided into 3 classes:

- Asphalt - A tarry substance
- Paraffin Base - With high paraffin, almost no asphalt
- Mixed - Both paraffin and asphalt. A wide range of viscosities from liquid thin to thick and ropy.

Crude oil, in addition to oil, can contain water, salt and gas. If the sulfur content is high (over 1%), it is 'sour crude'. The constituents affect refining. A barrel (42 gallons, 159 liters) of crude can yield:

PRODUCT	PERCENT
Gasoline	46.2%
Gas, oil, distillates	22.0
Jet fuel	7.4
Fuel oil	6.6
Kerosene	2.1
Residues and losses	15.3

CRUST The outer layer of the Earth's Mantle is the Crust, or Lithosphere. It is measured from the surface to the Mohorovicic Discontinuity (q.v.). The discontinuity is an abrupt break where seismic waves indicate a change in density.

Continental crust is thicker than oceanic. It is thicker beneath mountains and thinner beneath continental shelves.

Oceanic crust forms at rises or mid-oceanic ridges from seafloor spreading. Basalt erupts filling fissures and new crust spreads over the ocean floor.

CRUSTACEANS Crustaceans are in the Arthropod Phylum. The class is usually aquatic, both marine and freshwater, but is not restricted from the land. Crabs, lobsters, and shrimp are crustaceans.

CRUSTAL PLATES The Earth's surface is segmented into great rigid masses, or plates. These are supplied with crustal material of Mantle origin. Additions are usually along great oceanic rifts (Mid-Atlantic Ridge and East Pacific Rise). The plates move, and as some support continental areas, continents move. Movement is very slow, only a few centimeters a year but it may be spasmodic and over a great distance in a single event.

There are 7 major plates separated by oceanic trenches and rift valleys. Plate boundaries are marked by rifts and plates may move in opposing directions. When plate collisions occur, one is forced down and the other over-rides.

Some crustal material is resorbed into the Mantle. It may rise to the surface again as a mountain chain or volcanic islands. Occasionally, a 'welded zone' such as the Himalayas occurs. Almost all major earthquakes relate to plate boundaries. See **PLATE TECTONICS**.

CRYPTOVOLCANIC Some volcanic structures are cryptovolcanic because surface evidence is missing. 'Crypto-' is from the Greek for hidden. Many basins are thought to be cryptovolcanic.

CRYPTOZOIC The Cryptozoic is one of the major Eons of geological time. It encompasses all of the Precambrian (q.v.). The Cryptozoic is much longer than the Phanerozoic (q.v.), its counterpart.

CRYSTAL The word crystal comes from the Greek 'krystallos' which means cold as ice. The rock structure called crystal is a solid with a definite geometry. This geometry is a reflection of the ordered internal arrangement called the crystal lattice. The repeating patterns of atomic structure within a mineral create 7 different forms 1 of which is amorphous. Once the pattern develops, it replicates itself and the crystal grows.

An imaginary line may be drawn from the center of a crystal face to the center of the opposite crystal face. This line is the crystal axis. Axes define crystal structure, or habit. The 7 major crystal classes are based upon axes, See **CRYSTAL SYMMETRY** and **CRYSTAL SYSTEMS**

CRYSTAL SYMMETRY Crystal symmetry refers to the arrangement of crystal faces. They are defined as a:

Plane	- A crystal divides into symmetrical halves
Symmetry axis	- Imaginary line about which a 360° turn returns crystal to original position
Center of symmetry	- Imaginary line from any point to one on an opposite face.

The symmetry axis is named for the number of faces encountered in rotation: Diad, triad, tetrad, and hexad. There are 32 classes, when crystals are arranged by number and kind.

CRYSTAL SYSTEMS The 6 major crystal systems and a 7th amorphous one are:

Isometric	- 3 equal axes at right angles (diamond, fluorite)
Tetragonal	- 3 unequal axes, 1 at right angles (zircon)
Hexagonal	- 3 horizontal axes at 60° plus a vertical axis at right angles to others (beryl, quartz)
Orthorhombic	- 3 unequal axes at right angles to each other (barite, topaz)
Monoclinic	- 2 unequal axes at right angles (orthoclase, spodumene)
Triclinic	- Unequal axes, none at right angles (feldspar)
Non-symmetric	- Amorphous (gels, opal).

CRYSTALLINE STATE The crystalline state is that of solid material with an internal structure of molecules and ions. A crystal is physically and chemically identical with others of the same combination. Often growth is established in a particular direction.

Water is an integral part of the chemical composition of some crystals. The water is in an hydroxide compound.

CUESTA The cuesta is the predominant relief in sedimentary basins and on old platforms. It is similar to the hogback (q.v.) with a steeply-scarped slope and an opposite gentle one (30° maximum) but the hogback dip is greater. The steep cuesta scarp faces into the valley.

For a cuesta to form there must be gently dipping beds, an alternation of resistant and non-resistant sediments, and a resistant capping material. Caps are usually lava or sandstone.

CUMMULOUS CLOUDS Cumulous clouds are thunder clouds. They are puffy, gray, and may be anvil-shaped. Thunderheads have flattened bottoms but under convectional heating grow to great heights. The base remains low in the Atmosphere. The clouds bring showers and lightning that can flash from cloud to cloud as well as to the ground. See **LIGHTNING**.

CUIRASS The indurated horizon or hardpan is a 'cuirasse' in West Africa. It is a rock-hard horizon of iron or aluminum hydroxides. The texture may be rough and sharp. The laterite (q.v.) cuirass may degrade to gravel.

Indurated horizons are found near plateau edges and slope breaks. They may also be recemented alluvials. In Africa and South America, the indurated cap is most often iron ore.

CULLINAN DIAMOND The Cullinan diamond found in South Africa in 1905 weighed 3,106 carats (over 500 grams or 1.25 pounds). It yielded 1,063 carats in gems including the Star of Africa now in the British Sceptor. The Star weighs 530 carats.

CURIE The curie is a radioactivity measure equal to 3.7 billion disintegrations or particle emissions per second from nuclides. A curie will be produced by a gram of radium. It was named for Marie Curie, the discoverer of radium.

CURIE POINT Substances lose permanent magnetism under different sets of conditions for each material. The 'loss' temperature is the Curie Point, named for its discoverer, Pierre Curie. Igneous rocks when cooled below this point assume a permanent orientation related to the time of cooling. This characteristic is useful for studies of paleomagnetism (q.v.).

CURRENTS Current is from the Latin verb 'to run'. Air, rivers, seas, and the Earth's Atmosphere and Mantle all have currents or flows.

Ocean currents are caused by a number of factors. Some of these also affect air, Mantle currents, and rivers. The factors are:

- Coriolis Effect (q.v.) and Earth's rotation
- Temperature/salinity differences - From local climate or inflows of freshwater
- Surface wind energy - Transmitted to depths by friction
- Solar heat - Water rises inches at Equator, sinks at Poles.

Currents travel at different speeds than the surrounding ocean and have broad generally circular patterns. These are affected by continents. They are influenced by and have an influence on climate. Currents aerate the seas and act to exchange heat and cold.

Atmospheric currents are responsible for the redistribution of 80% of the Earth's energy, the ocean 20%. Atmospheric currents are warmed and rise at the Equator, cool and sink toward Poles.

Mantle currents are only slightly affected by solar heating. Chemical and physical forces that cause temperature and pressure variations and internal radioactivity are more important sources of convective energy.

CUVETTE 'Cuvette' is widely used in Africa to describe large sedimentary basins. Characteristically, they contain many smaller basins. Congo (Zaire) Basin is a cuvette. The Anglo-Parisian Basin in Europe is also a cuvette.

CYANIDE TREATMENT Low-grade gold ore is crushed, aerated, and immersed in potassium cyanide and lime to extract the element. Gold combines with the cyanide and is later released by zinc. Up to 90% recovery is possible using this process.

CYANOPHYCEAE These blue-green Algae appeared 2.6 billion years ago and are among the most ancient forms of life. They are widely distributed and occur in hot springs. Their gelatinous coating makes them temperature resistant. They proliferate with sunlight and seawater.

In Cyanophyceae, every time the cell splits a molecule of hydrogen dioxide results and oxygen is released. These Algae undoubtedly contributed to the oxygenization of the Atmosphere in the Precambrian (q.v.).

CYBERNETICS Cybernetics is concerned with the importance and design of feedback mechanisms in living organisms and machines. Comparisons have been made between reactions of the automatic nervous system in humans and animals and electronically designed systems.

'Cybernetics' is from the Greek, to govern. The science is relevant to all human-machine interfaces.

CYCADOPHYTES Cycadophytes evolved in the Permian (280-225) but reached maximum in the Mesozoic (225-65 m.y.). Cycadophyta make up 40% of Jurassic (q.v.) plant fossils. Cycadeoids differed from cycads in that they grew large flowers. From Greenland to Antarctica they flourished and were the oldest of flower-bearing plants.

Triassic (q.v.) forests were dominated by conifers, cycads, and cycadeoids. These last are now extinct. Cycads grew in upland areas and in slope forests. Their characteristic pinnate leaves are found in dark shales, such as the Newark.

Cycadophytes, to which the sago palm belongs, were probably a link between seed ferns and angiosperms.

CYCLONE Cyclones form in low pressure areas where winds move counter-clockwise in the Northern Hemisphere; clockwise in the Southern. The birth and development of these storms is cyclogenesis. A low pressure area alone is insufficient to create a cyclone.

Low pressure areas may be huge, hundreds of miles across. They bring much rain and snow. Temperate climate inclement weather is a succession of low pressure systems moving from west to east in the belt of the

Westerlies. The systems are a few days apart and move rapidly due to high winds.

Cyclonic development occurs in airmass convergence. It begins along a front and east of it (Northern Hemisphere). Cold air over-takes it and an eddy develops. Cyclones appear to strengthen under jet streams (q.v.) and are propelled by them. Cyclones, hurricanes, and typhoons arise from these convergences.

Cyclogenesis occurs along the east slope of the Rockies, in the Gulf Coast area, and in waters off the Carolina Outer Banks.

CYCLOTRON The cyclotron has allowed a greater investigation of the atom. It is an accelerator (q.v.) within a chamber where particles are excited to high energies.

CYPRESS Swamps, where cypress trees flourish, are found along the Atlantic Coast of the United States. Cypress trees can attain great heights, some 45 meters (150 feet). Their root systems form a buttress. This buttress supports their great height against currents, tides, and winds.

Cypress roots and cypress swamps are important breeding grounds for many organisms. See **WETLANDS.**

Dunes — Namib Desert, Southwest Africa
Courtesy of Dr. Donald Carlisle, Earth & Planetary Sciences, UCLA

D

DACITE Dacite, a volcanic rock composed of plagioclase feldspar, biotite, and hornblende, is associated with andesite (q.v.). The rocks are similar but dacite is more siliceous and lighter in color. It is derived from a more viscous magma than andesite. The texture is aphanitic (q.v.).

DAKOTA BADLANDS Dakota badlands are incredibly rugged. They are made up of closely spaced jagged ridges, ravines, and gullies. The badlands were created from easily eroded, silty sands in a semi-arid environment. No vegetation was present to protect the terrain. The area continues to erode.

DALLES In northwest United States, canyons or gorges with vertical sides are 'dalles' French for dells. They are youthful landforms with canyons cut by boulder-strewn streams with strong rapids.

DAMS Natural dams may form by volcanic flows blocking a stream, by landslides, by fallen trees or debris, or the tireless beaver's construction. Excess sediment dropped by tributaries form inland deltas that may ultimately dam the stream.

There are many artificial dams constructed across major rivers around the world. In Siberia, Nurek (q.v.) and Rogun serve new industrial-metallurgical complexes. Tarbela, in Pakistan, is now completed. It is designed to hold back 121,720 million cubic meters of water. Both Itaipu and Tucurui have been completed in Brazil. These are all mammoth constructions. See **HYDROPOWER**.

DANAKIL DEPRESSION The hottest and lowest part of the Great Rift Valley (q.v.) is the Danakil Depression. The depression is in the Afar Triangle of the Ethiopian Desert. The Triangle forms a wedge into the Ethiopian Highlands where the Awash Gorge widens. Afar is separated from the Red Sea by low hills.

In the deepest part of the depression, 155 meters (510 feet) below sea level, surface rock temperatures are the highest on Earth.

The Awash River rises in the Ethiopian Highlands and spreads out onto the depression floor. The main river system flows into swampy Lake Adabada, 133 kilometers (80 miles) from the Red Sea. Other stream channels disappear in the desert.

To the south of Danakil is a northeast-trending group of 5 volcanoes with hot springs, the 'Erta-ale' or Flaming Mountains. The volcanoes rise abruptly from salt flats. Lake Assal is in these flats. It has the saltiest of all the world's brines.

The salt flats are worked by Afar Tribesmen who have traded the salt for necessities for centuries. Salt is taken by caravan to the highlands where it is sold for many times its original price.

DANUBE RIVER The Danube, Europe's 2nd longest river, rises from springs in the Black Forest of Germany, about 850 meters (2,800 feet) above sea level. Fed from the Alps, it flows southeast into Austria, Hungary, Czechoslovakia, Yugoslavia, Rumania, and Bulgaria, then turns north into Rumania again before reaching the Black Sea.

The Danube Delta has 4 major distributaries. The delta area is a broad swampy fan. Discharge is about 66 cubic meters (218 cubic feet) per second.

DARCY The Darcy is a unit of permeability. Rocks have permeabilities measured in fractions of darcys. Brazil's Botucatu Sandstone, an average sandstone, has a permeability of 200 millidarcys.

DARWIN Charles Darwin produced the controversial book, 'Origin of the Species' from natural history data he collected while on a 5-year voyage of HMS Beagle. He developed theories of natural selection and survival.

Darwin's work gave impetus to the Theory of Evolution (q.v.). He was the first to detail adaptation of plants and animals to their environ-ments.

DATUM A datum is an item of information, and the singular of data.

A datum is also a reference point, or base for mapping and surveying. Sea level is the datum for calculations of elevation and depth.

DATE PALM The date palm 'Phoenix dacatylifera' has according to one author 'its head in the sun and its feet in water'. The palm grows to great heights and may be hundreds of years old.

Date palms have 2 sexes and must be pollinated. Natural pollination is by wind but cultivated trees are hand pollinated. There is a delicate balance in the weather required for fruit to develop. A little moisture in the air at the wrong time may kill a crop.

The date palm has been the survival base for many tribes in the deserts of Africa and Arabia. The famous oasis of Siwa in Egypt's Western Desert has over 200,000 palms.

DAUGHTER ELEMENT In radioactive decay, a nuclide or element emits other nuclides or elements. In a radioactive chain reaction, the next produced element is a daughter. See **DECAY CHAIN**

DAVIS TANK A mile underground in Homestake Mine at Lead, South Dakota, the Davis Tank measures neutrinos created by nuclear reac-tions. In the tank radioactive material is passed through a chemically clean fluid to create new isotopes. Argon-37 is one.

DAWSONITE Dawsonite makes up 10% of the shale found in Piceance Creek Basin, Colorado. The basin hosts valuable oil shales (q.v.) as well.

Dawsonite contains up to 3% aluminum. Before this resource can be developed, a number of problems must be resolved. These relate to capital investment, energy, water, and environmental concerns over waste disposal.

The shales are considered an alternative source of aluminum. From just the Green River Formation (q.v.), there is a potential for 5.9 billion tons of aluminum oxide.

DDT Dichloro-diphenyl-tri-chloro-ethane (DDT) is a chlorinated hydrocarbon that is used as a pesticide. It is a crystalline compound which is not soluble.

DDT was used extensively during World War II as a mosquito repellant. Most tropical and subtropical countries have used it as a control on yellow fever and malaria. Although the pesticide is effective in controlling and in some cases eradicating the diseases, it has deleterious side effects which have became known after these efforts were initiated. It is toxic to some vertebrates. Its use has been greatly curtailed but not stopped.

DEAD SEA Dead Sea or 'Bhar Lut' is not a sea but a salt lake. This lake between Israel and Jordan has no natural outlet. It is fed by the Jordan River.

The Dead Sea occupies the Syrian-African Graben at the north end of the Great Rift Valley (q.v.). The water surface is 395 mters (1,300 feet) below sea level at its deep northern end, It is the lowest recorded surface on Earth.

Water levels in the sea remained about the same for centuries. Lately, both Jordan and Israel have taken so much water from the Jordan River the inflow to the Dead Sea is greatly reduced and the level in the Sea is dropping.

In the southern Dead Sea where depths are about 2.5 meters (8 feet), the sea has been converted into ponds from which Jordan and Israel are producing potash, magnesium, bromine, and salt. Solar evaporation is an important part of this process.

DEBRIS 'Debris' is French for ruins. It graphically describes rock waste composed of larger boulders and rocks. It differs from detritus (q.v.) only in fragment size.

Large debris flows occur on desert mountain slopes. They do a great deal of damage as components are large and move rapidly.

Along beaches, storm activity often leaves a line of debris on the strand. The debris line contains shells, organic remains, usually kelp and other seaweeds, driftwood, and many bits of human refuse which had been dumped at sea.

Debris lines also define the maximum high-tide lines.

DECAY CHAIN A radioactive decay series results from atom splitting or particle collision. Emitted isotopes belong to the radioactive decay chain. The series from radioactive uranium to radiogenic lead is such a decay chain. There are others not so well-known. See **URANIUM.**

DECCAN PLATEAU The lava-topped Deccan Plateau of southeast India is all below 600 meters (2,000 feet) in elevation. The flat- topped hills rise in steps. They are in the path of the monsoon (q.v.) winds that dry the surface from November to April. With the shift in wind to the southeast, from the Arabian Sea and Indian Ocean, the rains come, making the plateau productive.

Basalt flows cover about 334,000 square kilometers (200,000) square miles). Deccan flows together with those of the Columbia Plateau (northwestern United States) and Parana Plateau (Brazil) are among the greatest known out-pourings of lava. Near Bombay, the flows are 3,000 meters (10,000 feet) thick, thinning to the interior. Lava soils are good, deep, and relatively fertile.

Deccan flows have congealed to a traprock, a dark, fine-grained basalt that fractures into blocks resembling stairs. The flows are Cretaceous to Eocene (136-40 m.y.) in age.

DECIDUOUS Trees and bushes that shed leaves at a definite season are deciduous. In the autumn, many shed foliage, usually with dramatic color changes. New foliage only appears the following spring. The temperate forests of Europe and North America are deciduous.

DECOLLEMENT 'Decollement' is French for a fold and thrust movement from lateral stress. Sediments move laterally while the basement rocks remain in place.

DECOMPOSITION Decomposition is a chemical and/or biological weathering process. All organisms die and decompose. The process is assisted by bacteria. Decomposition is part of the life-cycle of plants and animals.

DECREPITATION When minerals are broken down by heat application, the process is accompanied by an explosive crackling noise called decrepitation.

DEEP SEA SEDIMENTS Only 10% of the sediment carried by rivers ends in the deep sea. Other sediments are produced on the deep seafloor. Deep sea or abyssal sediments are classed as:

    Biogenic   - Of biological or organic origin.

    Nonbiogenic - Sediments mechanically settling.

In biogenic sediments, marine organisms are deposited as hard or soft parts. Organic material forms oozes with calcium, silica, and phosphate. Nonbiogenic deposits are transported by turbidity currents. The nonbiogenic sediments may be marine volcanics.

DEEP STAR The submersible Deep Star was developed to study ocean depths. By 1971, it had already completed over 200 dives in the Pacific and Caribbean. Among its studies was that of the deep scattering layer (q.v.). This is a zone of great plankton (q.v.) density.

DEFLOCCULATION The separation of compounds by physical or chemical means is deflocculation. In the process particles disperse. Colloids (q.v.) in the dispersed phase are suspended in the fluid.

DEFLATION Deflation is wind action on the surface of rocks and sediments. Wind carries off loose particles resulting from mechanical erosion caused by freezing, thawing, or other types of friction.

Deflation removes all loose material and has a winnowing affect, especially in desert areas. Winnowing (q.v.) contributes to aeolian or wind erosion from alluvial deposits. See **CORRASION**.

DEFORESTATION Global forests are decreasing at an alarming rate, 11 million hectares (25 million acres) per year at last count by the United Nations. Forest still covers about 20% of the globe, 10% is open woodland. Deforestation is most rampant in subtropical and tropical areas. It is considered the most serious of the world's present environmental problems. About 1/2 of all the original forests have disappeared since 1950.

There are 5 major modern causes of deforestation:
- Agricultural expansion
- Timbering without controls and reforestation
- Fire
- Fuelwood collection
- Industrial pollution, particularly acid rain.

Forested areas of Central America have been reduced by about 40% since 1960. The forests have been converted to pasture for cattle raised for export beef. In Costa Rica, a hurricane and other natural disasters have destroyed additional forest.

In Ghana cocoa and other forests are being cut to clear for farm plots because the cocoa market has been depressed. It takes 20 years for a cocoa tree to become productive. Shade canopy is a requirement for young cocoa trees and this shade takes a comparable period to mature. Soils being exposed to the sun are lateritic (q.v.) and not particularly suitable for farming. Ghana has virtually no rainforest left where once it was 30% covered.

In West Africa, 25% of a family's income is spent on fuelwood and there is a desperate gathering of this valuable commodity.

In the Philippines, deforestation has been declared a national disaster and emergency. It has been the cause of major destructive flooding and water supplies are threatened.

The slopes of the Himalayas are being deforested to a critical point in Nepal, espcially in the Arun Valley area. On the Ganges Plain deforestation has increased the vulnerability of 500 million people to flooding. The floods of 1988 were particularly disastrous to Bangladesh.

Deforestation leads to erosion, flooding, siltification, and species extinction. In transitional areas, it leads to desertification (q.v.).

Long-term effects on global climate are unknown. Convection patterns are changing and deforestation has caused an increase in albedo (q.v.). Local effects on climate have been disastrous. Rains in Panama have decreased 42.5 centimeters (17 inches) in the past 50-year period. See **FOREST FIRES.**

DEGASSING The process of degassing or the release of volatiles allows some common oceanic gases to escape into the Atmosphere. Among these are carbon dioxide and chlorine.

Degassing may have been the process by which sufficient gas escaped from the Earth's Mantle to form the atmospheric envelope about the planet. Degassing occurred when temperatures fell below the boiling point. It is a continuing process.

DEGRADATION The erosional process of degradation wears down rocks and sediments by the forces of air, ice, water, and wind. It is controlled only by rock resistance. It is the opposite of aggregation (q.v.).

Degradation of a stream channel occurs when the carrying capacity of the stream exceeds the load being carried. This allows water to flow more rapidly and cut channels more deeply.

DEGREE DAY Fuel requirements are assessed in a given area in terms of heating degree days. Mean temperature for a day is subtracted from 65° Fahrenheit. If the average January day is 35°, the degree day is 30.

The cooling degree day is calculated based upon the degrees above 65 for the average summer day. Forecasting temperature ranges allows for energy planning. This is especially important if raw material supplies are scarce or high priced.

DELTA A delta is an alluvial deposit at the mouth of a river. A main river may divide into smaller streams and there may be several mouths. Some rivers debouch directly into the sea, others form huge alluvial fans. These fans progressively advance to the sea. The delta shape is usually arcuate or bird-foot.

For a delta to form, certain conditions are required. Among them is a smooth basement, abundant detritus, and an absence of offshore currents. By the weight of its accumulating sediments a delta may be lowered as much as 0.5 millimeters per year.

Many rivers empty into lakes and larger streams forming inland deltas. Some of these have become important agricultural areas, such as the Gash Delta in arid Sudan.

Growing deltas cause a rapid build-up of sediments. On the southwest limb of the Mississippi, accretion is as much as 80 meters (250 feet) per year. This is also true of the new Brazos Delta in Texas. The addition of coastal land is even greater in some of the deltas of Southeast Asia where they are growing as fast as 180 meters (600 feet) a year.

Other delta coasts are suffering attrition. The Nile is the most obvious. Since the construction of dams and redistribution of the river's flow, especially since 1964, erosion has been reducing the delta.

Since most of the major rivers of the world now have large dams, there will be a diminution of the buildup of delta coasts.

DELTA FLANK DEPRESSION Many deltas have bordering bays in flank depressions. Lake Pontchartrain, Louisiana, fills one on the Mississippi Delta. Abu Qir Bay, where Nelson defeated Napoleon, is in a flank depression of the Nile Delta. Zuider Zee (q.v.) fills one on the Rhine.

DELTAIC STRATIGRAPHY The simplest delta has 3 beds: Topset, foreset, and bottomset. Topset beds are composed of coarse material, sand, and pebbles. Generally they are subhorizontal. Foreset beds are of coarse materials also but are inclined. The dip on foreset or frontal beds may be 20-35°. Bottomset beds are composed of silt and clay and are horizontal.

Compound delta stratigraphy, produced under unstable conditions may truncate foreset beds in the upper layers. A series of new beds may cover the original deposits. The new ones may be oriented in the same or a different direction.

DENDRITIC DRAINAGE The dendritic drainage pattern reminded earth scientists of tree branching. The pattern is common on crystalline rocks. It is also found on some sediments, particularly heavy clays.

DENDROCHRONOLOGY Tree rings and other annual growth phenomena make up the study of dendrochronology. Age-dating of flora (plants) has been greatly enhanced by this science and art.

DENITRIFICATION The biochemical process of denitrification transforms nitrogen to a form available to plants. The conversion process is usually performed by bacteria, and some plants play host to nitrogen-fixing bacteria, among these plants are legumes.

DENSITY Density, the concentration of matter, is a physical attribute of the Earth. It is expressed as mass per unit volume (grams per cubic centimeter). The average density of the Earth is 5,520 kilograms per cubic meter. Water is 1 gram per cubic centimeter.

Seawater is more dense than fresh, cold water more dense than hot. This is important as density differences cause convection (q.v.). It is also important to coastal dwellers where freshwater wells may be encroached by seawater.

Freshwater tends to overlie saltwater. Where streams are involved, a heavily sedimented river will have greater density than seawater.

DENSITY CURRENTS Density currents result from contrasts in fluid density. They may arise from differences in temperature or different quantities of material in suspension. Density currents in the ocean containing great sediment loads are turbidity currents (q.v.).

DENUDATION Wearing away, or erosion, of rocks toward base level (q.v.) is denudation. An erosional cycle is a single denudation period. All human life has been confined to the last and present denudation.

There have been many geological periods of denudation, or great levelings, as many peneplaned (q.v.) surfaces testify. Denudation is surface erosion on a grand scale.

DEPLETION ALLOWANCE The depletion allowance, a tax benefit in the United States, favors mining and petroleum industries. Income free from taxation is based upon production and is for depletion of reserves. Originally it was designed to stimulate exploration and investment.

DEPOSIT The complex of material accumulated through erosion and deposition is a deposit. Deposits are alluvial (water-borne), glacial, marine, or wind blown. They may be described by location as 'deltaic'.

In economic geology, a deposit contains sufficient ore to be a potential mine as opposed to a prospect (q.v.).

DEPOSITIONAL BASINS Depositional basins are lake or river basins, basins of interior drainage, or structural basins. They can be classified as:

Alluvial	- Alluvium fills low places and lakes.
Dune	- Wind created dunes dam streams creating lakes
Lava	- Flows congeal to form barriers across streams
Structural	- A down-dropped block creates a basin (Baikal in Siberia).

Alluvium, wind created dunes, and lava flows dam streams. They can create lakes. Lake Moses in Washington is a the result of damming by dunes. Flows have created many of the lakes in the Rift Valley of East Africa. The block faulting originally created the basin. Often the weight of sediments and flows can result in compaction which lowers a basin floor.

DEPRESSION A depression is a surface area below the level of surrounding relief or below sea level. Those below sea level are absolute depressions. Examples are: Dead Sea, Baikal, and Death Valley.

Some major depression types are the:

- Glacial Depression - Many are large and water-filled (Finland, the Great Lakes).
- Volcano-tectonic Depression - Caldera (q.v.) or graben (q.v.). Some water-filled (Crater Lake).
- Deflation Depression - Large wind scoured basins. An enormous one in the Sahara holds Lake Chad (q.v.).
- Structural Depression - Synclines (q.v.) from regional warping. In arid areas subject to deflation (Southern Sahara).
- Delta Flank Depression - Bordering major deltas. They fill with water (Lake Pontchartrain).

DESALINIZATION Removal of salts from saline waters especially seawater is desalinization. Evaporation is a process that has been used for centuries. There are many desalinization processes, but the most popular is distillation or the trapping of steam.

So much energy is required to heat seawater to obtain domestic water suppies, it is uneconomic for any but an oil-rich area. Kuwait and Qatar produce drinking water from the sea. In the process, at Qatar, salt is put back into the sea, endangering marine life in the triangle between Bahrein, Qatar, and Saudi Arabia.

DESERT Arid regions, or deserts are in special geographic areas related to latitude and airmass movement. Deserts are found in a belt stretching along the west coasts of continents between 10 and 30° North and South Latitude, influenced by tropical anticyclones.

In central parts of continents in Mid-Latitudes, climate is dominated by cold polar-born anticyclones. Wide swings of diurnal temperature are the rule and relative humidity is low. Mid-Latitude deserts are caused by continentality or remoteness from oceans or the blocking of airmasses by high mountains.

Eurasia has some of the world's greatest deserts caused by continentality. The Sahara in Africa is affected by its position on the west coast and by its continentality.

Other than in the Polar Regions, there are 3 big cold deserts. These are Gobi in Asia; Patagonian in South America; and Nevada in North America.

Insufficient rainfall to sustain any but specialized plant and animal life is the rule over 25% of the globe. These areas are desert or semi-desert. Rainfall is less than 12.5 centimeters (5 inches) per year. Many deserts receive well under this. Where evaporation from vegetation and soils exceeds precipitation per year over a period of time, a desert develops.

Permanent streams rarely originate in deserts. The Nile, the most famous desert stream, is exogenous with origins in Equatorial Africa and Ethiopia.

DESERT LANDFORMS There are 5 main desert landforms (adapted from Small, 1970):

- Mountain-ringed basins
- Plateaus or mesas
- Pediplains
- Sand accumulations
- Stony deserts

In mountain-ringed basins there is centripetal drainage. They are surrounded by steep-sided, boulder-strewn, deeply dissected plateaus. The floor is often a dry lake. (Basin and Range Province).

Plateaus and mesas rise from the desert floor. Slopes are nearly vertical and canyons have flat floors. In Libya and Egypt, plateaus are cut by branching wadis (q.v.). Grand Mesa, Colorado, is the largest mesa in United States.

Pediplain surfaces of coalescing pediments. Inselbergs (q.v.).appear to be prominent features of the deserts of the Southern Hemisphere. In South Africa these surfaces have their relief broken by inselbergs. Structures of this type are found in Australia and South America.

The great accumulations of sand are found on ergs (q.v.) and dunes. The Great Erg of the Sahara is a group of ergs from the Ahoggar Mountains to Tibesti, Libya.

In addition to the ergs, the Sahara is famous for its stony desert areas. These deserts are made up of stone pavements winnowed of fines by the wind. These are the hammadas and regs of the Sahara.

DESERT SURFACES In desert areas on igneous and volcanic rocks a pavement develops from pebbles and small stones that are tightly compacted by wind and rain. The stones settle on alluvium with the longest axis parallel to the surface. They take on desert varnish (q.v.) and resemble a mosaic. Mosaics often appear where the bedrock is limestone.

A cobblestone pavement can result as wind and water erosion remove light or fine material leaving lag gravels (q.v.). A great source of these gravels can lead to a stony desert.

Desert rocks sometimes acquire a patina or glaze. The veneer of iron and manganese oxides was once thought to be solely from mineral solutions. The evidence shows an interaction with micro-organisms. These include Algae, lichen, and pollen. Rocks are solution pitted and the agency carries the varnishing material. Lichen is known to have a high iron and manganese content and is erosive in solution.

A desert patina in Egypt took 2,000-3,000 years to acquire a light-brown layer. Black layers took 20,000-50,000 years. The carbon base of these varnishes made it possible to take radiocarbon readings and age date them.

DESERTIFICATION An estimated 6.36 million hectares (14 million acres) per year become desert or semi-arid. If the process continues at this rate, 33% of the Earth's potentially arable lands will be lost by the turn of the century. In the Sahel, a 6,670 kilometer (4,000 mile) wide strip across Africa, the land has become virtually sterile.

In Sudan, the desert grew to the south 100 kilometers (60 miles) in a 17-year period (1958-1975). The trend is continuing. Climate studies indicate the rate is faster than any lowering of precipitation would cause. The natural situation is aggravated by over-population and over-grazing of the lands.

The Sahara is spreading at the rate of 1.5 million hectares (3.3 million acres) a year.

DETRITUS Sediments or fragments of loose disaggragated rock are detritus. These fragments are angular and of varying sizes, and are easily transported. They accumulate at the base of slopes.

DEUTERIC A late phase alteration of igneous rocks as a magma consolidates is described as a deuteric alteration.

DEUTERIUM Deuterium is a naturally occurring hydrogen isotope. It has a neutron as well as a proton. With a mass twice ordinary hydrogen, there is 1 atom of deuterium for every 6,500 atoms of hydrogen.

Deuterium occurs in seawater and is non-radioactive. The combination gets the name 'heavy water' from its mass. Deuterium is the raw material of fusion nuclear reactors. See **ISOTOPE**.

DEVITRIFICATION Natural volcanic glass is not stable over time (several million years). Microlites, small, thin, fibrous crystals, replace the glass growing outward from the center of the glass shard. The crystals radiate outward in a process called devitrification.

DEVONIAN The Devonian Period in the Paleozoic Age (395-345 m.y.) overlies the Silurian and precedes the Carboniferous or Mississippian.

The Acadian Orogeny of great volcanic activity occurred in Mid-Devonian (370 m.y.) in what is now New England. In this period of great activity the Appalachians were raised in the Taconian Orogeny. In Europe, the Caledonides resulted from the Caledonian Orogeny. These events were accompanied by intense metamorphism and great granitic intrusions. See **OROGENY**.

Great erosion accompanied and followed the mountain-building. It created thick sequences of sediments, particularly of redbeds. One important section of red, continental sands is in New York. The Old Red Sandstone in Britain is a massive sequence of redbeds.

Amphibians first appear in the Devonian as did the first seed plants. Fish were abundant in Devonian seas. The graptolites (q.v.) became extinct.

DEW   Dew is natural condensation of warm moisture in the air encountering a cooler mass. Vegetation cools at night, but the air holds the warmth radiated by the Earth.

When water vapor in an airmass equals the capacity of the airmass to hold moisture, that airmass is saturated. The colder the airmass, the less moisture it can hold.

Temperature, when vapor begins to precipitate, is at dewpoint. Dewpoint varies depending upon relative humidity (q.v.). When local relative humidity reaches saturation, or 100%, condensation occurs on vegetation and on surface objects. Because dew is pure water, it has a flushing effect on soils and helps to retard salt build-up.

Dew is particularly common in the United States in late summer and early autumn when the Atmosphere contains a great deal of moisture. Longer nights allow increased radiation cooling and temperatures fall below the dewpoint.

In Peru and Chile, 40 centimeters (16 inches) of dew precipitation is added to the low rainfall. Experiments are underway to plant a 'fog forest'. Eucalyptus and Aleppo Pines do well.

In Israel's Negev Desert (q.v.) where rainfall is 2.5-20 centimeters (1-8 inches), dew is carefully collected. Dew precipitates 250 nights a year and heavily in 140. Up to 0.96 gallons of water can be collected on a small plastic sheet angled to a plant's roots.

DIABASE   Diabase is a dark green, eruptive, basic rock composed of feldspar (labradorite) and pyroxene (augite). It is a common igneous rock found in veins, dikes, and stocks. Its chemical composition is similar to gabbro's (q.v.), but its texture is ophitic (q.v.) due to late-phase augite enclosing plagioclase feldspar laths.

Diabase weathers readily at its surface due to a lowering of pH and Eh (q.v.) and an increase in oxygen. River water, which is more neutral than air, is less destructive. This is the reason given for the fact that diabase in the Amazon Basin is only found forming falls on some tributary streams.

Diabase sills of great magnitude are associated with some basalt flows. See **SILL**.

DIAGENESIS   The complex process of diagenesis begins transforming sediments as soon as they are deposited. Sands are ultimately converted to sandstone from the periphery to the center. Cementing and compaction are important agencies. Diagenesis may be both chemical and mechanical. Heat and pressure due to compaction play a big role.

DIAMOND Diamond, the hardest mineral, is composed entirely of carbon. The diamond is hard but can be extremely brittle. It is usually octaoctahedral in crystal form but some Brazilian diamonds are dodecahedron.

The most common diamonds are white, blue-white, and yellow. Apple green is only known from India and is rare. The most famous blue diamond is the Blue Tavernier.

Diamonds were first discovered in bank gravels of the Kristna River, India. India has produced some famous stones. Among them are the 'Great Mogul' (793 carats) and the 'Kohinoor' (800 carats). All Indian diamonds are alluvial and their source is unknown.

South Africa's first diamonds were alluvial. Beneath gravels, diamonds were found in yellowish earth. About 15 meters (50 feet) below was 'blue ground' which contained a greater number. Host yellow and blue grounds were kimberlite (q.v.). The discovered structure was a diamond pipe. Some pipes are more than 300 meters (1,000 feet) in diameter.

Special thermodynamic conditions and a narrow range of pressures create diamonds. Pipes are volcanic chimneys that were connected to deep-seated magma chambers. Magma rose to the surface at Mach 2 speed and pressure rose to 100,000 psi (q.v.). Some gems disintegrated to graphite others disappeared into the air as carbon dioxide.

Brazilian diamonds are found in Precambrian alluvial sediments and gravels. Some kimberlites have been discovered but none containing diamonds. Brazil has produced very high grade stones, and some very large diamonds such as Getulio Vargas (726 carats), Darci Vargas (460 carats) and Coromandel (400 carats).

Industrial or black diamonds are widely used. Also bort, an amorphous or semi-crystalline carbon, is used in industry. Industrial use consumes 80% of all diamond production. Major diamond production is from the Orange River Estuary and Kimberley, South Africa, Sierra Leone, Brazil, and Australia. Diamond discoveries have been reported from the USSR. In the United States, no economic deposits have been found.

By simulating the conditions under which diamonds are formed naturally, synthetic diamonds have been produced.

DIAMOND CUT The diamond, or brilliant, cut is the most chosen for precious gems, especially the diamond, ruby, and sapphire. The cut has 58 facets around its girdle, 33 above and 25 below. Inspiration for the cut was the Great Pyramid.

By 1978, Israel was cutting and finishing half the gem diamonds being produced in the world.

DIAMOND SATELLITES Indicator minerals associated with diamonds are 'satellites'. Some 56 different accessory minerals have been identified in secondary diamond deposits. Most common are rutile and anatase needles and pebbles. Gold and rubies are often present. Diamond prospectors have local names for the minerals and use them as exploration guides.

DIAMOND WEIGHTS Diamonds are measured in carats (q.v.) and points. 100 points is 1 carat and 1 carat = 0.2 grams or 20 milligrams. 142 carats = 1 English ounce. Standards were set by international agreement.

The original carat weight was arbitrary and based on the weight and size of a locust tree seed. See **CARAT**.

DIAPHANEITY The optical characteristic, diaphaneity, relates to the transparency of gemstones. Most precious gems are transparent. Diaphaneity measures the degree of that transparency.

DIAPIR A diapir is a structure resulting from the rupture of rocks overlying a dome, or anticlinal fold. Plastic core material is squeezed upward under great pressure. Diapiric activity is thought to bring Mantle material to the surface at spreading ridges. The forces of convective heating provide the energy for diapiric activity.

Sedimentary rock diapirs often have a core of salt or shale. Off the Gulf Coast of the United States, a number of giant salt domes of diapiric origin have collapsed to form submarine basins. These are being filled with sediment. The structures, both on and offshore, are important as petroleum reservoirs and are worked for chemical salts and sulfur.

DIASPORE Diaspore is a rare mineral sometimes cut for collectors. It is transparent to semi-translucent, gray to yellow or violet, and is composed of aluminum hydroxide. Diaspore results from the decomposition of corundum (q.v.) and is found in bauxite, an ore of aluminum.

DIASTEM A diastem is a depositional break in the stratigraphy (q.v.) of a sedimentary formation. Less pronounced than a disconformity (q.v.), a diastem is usually intraformational.

DIASTROPHISM Diastrophism includes all the processes of crustal deformation. The Crust may be uplifted, lowered, warped, folded, or rifted.

Diastrophism involves major movement. The processes alter rocks chemically and physically. Crustal disturbances, including mountain-building, are found in zones of crustal weakness, particularly around major rifts and in volcanic belts. The processes may act abruptly as in earthquakes and eruptions or more slowly as in glacial rebound (q.v.).

DIATOMACEOUS EARTHS Vast accumulations of fossil diatoms and Algae gave rise to deposits of diatomaceous earth. The organisms lived in both freshwater and seawater. The earthy material is composed of siliceous skeletons of small aquatic plants. A single cubic inch of diatomite contains as many as 40 million tiny plant skeletons. See **DIATOMS**.

Deposits of diatomite are found in California and Oregon. In Northeast Brazil, there are large deposits along the coast. The major use is in filtering. See **DIATOMS**

DIATOMACEOUS OOZE Marine sediments composed almost entirely of diatom remains in muds are diatomaceous oozes. These cover 38 million square kilometers (22 million square miles) of the Antarctic Ocean floor. Diatomaceous ooze is also abundant on the Pacific floor. See **DIATOMS**.

DIATOMIC MOLECULES Some atoms pair up to form elemental compounds or diatomic molecules. The compounds most involved are hydrogen, nitrogen, and oxygen.

DIATOMS Diatoms are tiny, aquatic, yellow-green algal plants with siliceous cell walls. Individuals live near the water surface as plankton. When the organism dies the siliceous skeletons sink and accumulate on the seafloor. Skeletons in great quantity become deposits of diatomaceous earth (q.v.).

Diatoms first appeared in the Cretaceous (136-65 m.y.). They have been abundant in fresh and seawater ever since. These phytoplankton are a nutrient and are of major importance in the food chain.

DIFFERENTIAL WEATHERING Different rock and mineral compositions weather at different rates. Ridges, columnar structures, and erosional monuments are the result of this differential weathering (q.v.).

DIFFRACTION The optical phenomenon of diffraction occurs when white light is passed through the opaque edges of a mineral or through narrow slits. The light is broken into the color spectrum.

Diffraction is useful in the identification of some gemstones.

DIKE When an intrusive igneous rock fills fractures and seams, it is called a dike. A dike that is concordant with bedding is a sill (q.v.). Dikes frequently are narrow wedges cutting across igneous or sedimentary rocks. Some dikes form pegmatites (q.v.) which cut across igneous rocks and can extend for kilometers.

On Spanish Peak, Colorado, lava cooled in cracks of earlier rocks creating a dike. In Northeast Brazil, a great series of pegmatites cut across the Borborema Chapada (q.v.).

Some dike swarms radiate from a central source to form ring dikes. Many are related to acidic igneous rock and carbonatites (q.v.). Precambrian ring dikes like Vredefort (q.v.) are continuously under study in an attempt to understand their nature.

During the Proterozoic (q.v.) there were dike swarms in the great shield (q.v.) areas. An important one, the Great Dyke of South Africa, is dated 2.55 billion years. It extends across the Archaen (q.v.) of Zimbabwe.

Eras of dike intrusion may be related to continental breakup. The Jurassic Karroo Dike (dolerite swarms) appears related to the break-up of Gondwana (q.v.). In the Cenozoic (65 m.y. - Present), dike swarms are associated with the spreading of the North Atlantic Ocean.

DINOFLAGELLATES Microscopic dinoflagellates have characteristics of both plants and animals. Flagella or thread-like appendages propel the organisms in their planktonic existence. These organisms create food by photosythesis (q.v.).

Dinoflagellates are an important nutrient source in the marine and freshwater food chains. They can redden seawater with their cell pigmentation and contribute to Red Tide (q.v.). The species, 'Noctiluca', can cause large phosphorescent displays.

DINOSAURS During the first 100 million years the climate of Panagea (q.v.) was favorable to vegetative growth and the rise of great reptiles. The reptiles were cold-blooded and therefore more efficient the larger they grew.

Dinosaurs appeared in the Jurassic (193-136 m.y.) and were widespread. Not all were large. They had mammal-like bones and some authorities say some may have had the beginnings of warm-bloodedness. They were largely vegetarians and browsers. They laid eggs in nests. Their peak was reached during the first 70 million years after Panagea (q.v.) broke up. When the climate cooled, the dinosaurs could no longer survive. As a comparison: It takes a modern alligator many hours to raise its temperature even 1° Celsius.

Although the passing of the dinosaur from the geological scene appears sudden, many paleontologists do not believe in wholesale extinction. Others find evidence of a great mass extinction of lifeforms at the end of the Cretaceous when the majority of the reptiles appear to have disappeared. See **EXTINCTIONS**.

The Morrison Formation on the Colorado Plateau has a wealth of dinosaur remains. The last giant dinosaur, Triceratops, a 3-horned reptile, left fossils on the flanks of Green Mountain in Utah. These were discovered in 1887. The United States has set aside Dinosaur National Park on the Colorado Plateau. It includes Green Mountain.

DIORITE Diorite is a dark, gray-green crystalline rock made up of plagioclase feldspar and hornblende, ferromagnesium silicate, and other minerals in minor amounts.

Diorite is similar to diabase, but differs in texture. It is medium to course-grained and darker than acidic igneous rocks and syenites (q.v.). Quartz diorite (2-3% quartz) tends to be lighter in color. Diorite may be porphyritic with phenocrysts (q.v.) of plagioclase, hornblende, or biotite. It is a transitional rock, often grading to granite.

Diorites are usually small intrusives or plugs as in the Choisica Pluton, Peru. Occasionally dikes or sills are diorites. Granodiorites are found in Norway and in southeast Alaska.

On the island of Corsica, diorite has unusual concentric bedding which is called 'orbicular diorite'.

DIOXIN Only a few molecules of dioxin, an herbicide, is considered a health hazard. It has been linked to both nervous disorders and cancer.

Such high levels were found in the soil of Times Beach, Missouri, the Environmental Protection Agency monitored the removal of the entire town. See **CHEMICAL WASTE**.

DIP A dip is a rock surface that slopes from the horizontal. It is the angle the slope-line makes with the horizontal. This angle may be up to 90°. The dip angle is formed by a bedding plane, dike, or fracture. Dip is measured perpendicular to the line of strike, or orientation.

A dip slip is the dislocation of a fault parallel to its dip.

DIRECTIONAL DRILLING Some sites cannot be reached by straight drilling. Sometimes, it is possible to angle drill to intercept the desired location. Another term for directional drilling is slant drilling.

Petroleum exploration economics are such that a slant drilling capability is valuable. A platform is set up from which several sites can be reached. This technique is especially useful in offshore operations.

DIRTY SNOW Snow with a large quantity of waste rock is 'dirty snow'. An avalanche can acquire great quantities of waste in transit and the snows are called 'dirty'. They move rapidly causing more destruction than usual because of their abrasiveness.

DISCHARGE Water passing a particular point in a definite period of time, whether surface or subsurface, is discharge. Discharge is also the term used for the volume of water emptying from a stream into a lake or ocean.

In the United States, it is expressed in feet per second.

DISCOASTERS Discoasters are star-shaped marine nannofossils (q.v.). They flourished from Late Paleocene to Late Pliocene (55-3 m.y.) and became extinct during the Pleistocene, about a million years ago. Many geologists think their extinction was due to a cosmic event.

The fossils are useful in transoceanic correlations.

DISCONFORMITY A disconformity is an unconformity between parallel layers in a stratigraphic section (q.v.). It is characterized by erosional relief in the underlying bed. A disconformity is usually noted toward the close of a geological period.

DISCONTINUITY A number of discontinuities, abrupt material changes, have been described in the Earth's Mantle. These are detected changes in density. Among these is the Mohorovicic Discontinuity (q.v.) defining the lower limit of the Earth's Crust.

DISPERSION The optical phenomenon, dispersion, occurs when white light is separated into colored rays. Transparent gemstones show dispersion.

DISPLACEMENT Displacement in chemistry occurs when a more active element in a reaction pushes out a less active one from the molecule. In the creation of sulfates, hydrogen is the element displaced.

DIVERGENCE In the ocean, especially near continents, horizontal water flow may originate from a central point and move outward. This is divergence. Displaced waters are replaced by upwelling (q.v.) which brings cold waters sometimes from great depths.

DIVERGENT MARGIN Continental Margins surrounding ocean basins are divergent, convergent, or translational.

Divergent margins are the most common. They occur in the interior of crustal plates. These margins are formed by spreading belts of rifting landmasses. They continue to spread apart and new mantle rock is deposited at the spreading edge.

Because a long time is involved in development and low continental areas have been overrun by seas, continental shelves will be wide, as in the Atlantic. Most divergent margins have great accumulations of sediments that form into rises (q.v.). See **CONTINENTAL MARGINS**.

DIVINING ROD A forked stick grasped while witching for water is a divining rod. The water-witch grasps the tines and holds it straight out. When the rod bends towards the ground, supposedly of its own energy, it is said to have sought and found water. See **DOWSING**.

DODECAHEDRON The dodecahedron crystal form has 12 faces. It is a member of the Isometric System. Diamonds sometimes form as dodecahedrons. If the crystal faces have 4 edges of equal length they are rhombic dodecahedrons as in sphalerite. See **CRYSTAL SYSTEMS**.

DOLDRUMS Areas of calm or light breezes on both sides of the Equator are 'Doldrums'. These are low pressure areas of great thunderstorm activity. The doldrums presented a great challenge to sailing vessels as they could be becalmed there for months.

DOLERITE Dolerite is a dark-colored basic igneous rock composed of medium-grained, ferromagnesium minerals. It is similar to gabbro (q.v.), but has a finer grain. Dolerite is coarser than basalt.

Dolerite is composed of feldspar, pyroxene, and olivine with very little if any quartz. It is often found at the edge of gabbroic massifs and forms in dikes and sills. Some famous dolerite complexes are the Great Whin Sill in Great Britain, the Karroo dolerites of South Africa, the Palisades Sill of New York, and Mt. Wellington Sill, Tasmania.

DOLINE Dolines are karstic landforms. They may be short closed valleys, or depressions ranging from a few meters to hundreds in diameter. In general, they have a saucer-like shape.

Many caves in karst (q.v.) country have an entrance in a doline. Roswell, New Mexico's bottomless lake is a water-filled doline among 20 steep-sided ones of which 12 hold water.

DOLOMITE Calcium magnesium carbonate, dolomite, is similar to limestone, except some calcium has been replaced by magnesium. Usually the number of calcium and magnesium atoms is equal.

Dolomite is darker than limestone, harder, and denser. It may form as an evaporite as have some recent dolomites in Solar Lake, Israel where dolomite results as a reaction of brine with aragonite (q.v.).

The Dolomites are a range of mountains in the Italian Alps. They are composed mainly of dolomitic limestone which was uplifted from a shallow sea 200 million years ago. The dolomite was sufficiently resistant to form great saw-toothed masses with sheer cliffs. They are usually not much over 3,300 meters (10,000 feet).

DOMING Doming occurs when an igneous body pushes the overlying mass upward. Domes may be single peaks or ranges. Doming also occurs as a result of squeezing, as in a diapir (q.v.). When pressure is removed the crust may rebound as after glacial retreat. See **IGNEOUS ROCKS**.

DOPPLER SHIFT Wavelengths of light or sound shift as they move. When the source moves away from the observer in a visible wavelength, there is a shift to the red or long end of the spectrum. If the source approaches the observer, the shift is to the blue end. This phenomenon is Doppler Shift, or Doppler Effect.

New equipment for aircraft instrument approaches to landing will use the characteristics of Doppler to assist pilots.

DOUBLE DISPLACEMENT When 2 chemical compounds combine to form another by exchanging some molecules, it is a double displacement. Usually, there is a preferred replacement as in silver nitrate plus sodium chloride yielding silver chloride and sodium nitrate.

DOVER STRAITS Northern France and Southern England are on the Dome of the Weald. The Straits of Dover are in the central part of the dome providing a narrow passage between the countries. The North Downs come to the coast and form the White Cliffs of Dover.

DOWNS In England, rolling hills are downs. They are usually meadow-covered. The downs were formed from dunes deposited by the wind. In Middle-English, they were called 'douns'.

DOWSE To dowse is to seek water below the Earth's surface using a 'divining rod'. The rod is of beech or birch and the dowser is a 'water-witch'. The rod will, apparently of its own accord, bend toward the Earth when above water. Drilling is then recommended.

The success of dowsing has never been really explained. A dowser is undoubtedly a natural prospector with subconscious knowledge of the terrain.

DRAG FOLDS Strata bend to form drag folds as a fault or dike is approached. These features may reveal the direction of movement along a fault. A later disturbance can, however, render them unreliable.

DRAINAGE BASIN A stream with all its tributaries, drains a wide area referred to as a basin because of its usual bowl shape. The drainage basin includes all of the watershed as well as the lower reaches of the river system. The 2 classical drainage basins ringed by high ground are the Amazon and the Congo (Zaire).

DRAINAGE PATTERNS River courses are described as dendritic (resembling a trellis), parallel, rectangular, or radial. Factors affecting the forms are:

- Topography over which the stream flows
- Rock types and their relative resistance
- Relationship of tributaries to each other
- The climatic regime of the area.

DRAKENSBERG RANGE The highest and most spectacular part of the Great Escarpment of South Africa (q.v.) is a range of rugged, sheer volcanic cliffs. These fringe the interior plateau from the Transvaal to the Cape Province. Known as the Drakensberg Range, its highest part is in land-locked Lesotho.

Drakensberg, or 'Dragon Mountain', has earned its name. Its peaks suggest a dragon's outline and in the past it spurted fire. The NE-SW trending range has many peaks over 3,300 meters (10,000).

Drakensberg's foundation is of thick sandstone beds ranging in age from Upper-Paleozoic to Triassic (150-200 m.y.). Great lava flows began emerging from fissures in these rocks. Individual lavas are up to 50 meters (165 feet) thick and the whole sequence above the sandstone is 1,350 meters (4,500 feet). On the eastern slopes, basalt cliffs drop directly and steeply to the coastal plain fringing the Indian Ocean.

DREDGE A dredge is an important piece of placer mining equipment. It is a mechanical shovel-arm fixed on board a vessel or floating platform and used to scoop earth from a stream bed or the seafloor.

One of the most spectacular dredging operations was for diamonds off South Africa. The seas proved too rough for the operation to continue.

DREIKANTER 'Dreikanter' is German for 3-sided. It aptly describes rock fragments resulting from glacial erosion.

DRIFT Drift denotes sorted and unsorted detrital material of glacial origin. Unsorted drift is also known as till (q.v.).

Drift has a variety of other meanings. In a mine, a drift is a small tunnel branching from a main channel. It is used to block out ore or facilitate operations. A drift usually follows a vein or an orebody.

Winds cause snow or sand to pile up into drifts. Snow and sand in motion are said to be drifting.

In the sea, major currents are due to wind and other forces such as internal waves. These great systems are referred to as drifts.

In navigation, drift is instrument variation due to changes in wind direction and velocity. This drift must be corrected to stay on-course.

Deviation in a drill hole is drift.

DRILL STRING On an oil rig, the pipe or 'drill-string' is passed through the floor of a rotary turntable or platform. The pipes are joined together in sections to attain lengths up to thousands of feet. Handling these great pipe lengths requires much skill.

DRILLING MUD Drilling mud is a necessity for oil well operations. A mixture of mud, clay, and chemicals is pumped into a drill hole through the drill string (q.v.). The bit is cooled and cleaned by the mud and the cuttings are flushed out. Mud also serves as a lubricant.

Drilling muds contain special clays. Bentonite (q.v.) is the most important.

DRIPSTONE The stalagmites and stalactites found in caves are dripstones. The are formed from calcium carbonate solutions precipitated from the cavern walls, ceiling, and floor. They appear as great icicles hanging from the cave ceiling or they tower up from the cavern floor.

DROUGHT Drought is a prolonged period of dryness in non-arid or semi-arid areas. It occurs when there is a shift in airmass movement in the Upper Atmosphere causing disruptions in rainfall. These in turn affect plant and animal life.

Droughts of great magnitude occur in mid-continent areas when 'normal' jetstream patterns change. Some droughts are cyclical and appear related to the 22-year solar flare cycle. Others are not wholly explicable. See **SOLAR FLARES**.

A shift in the Intertropical Convergence (ITC) upsets normal monsoonal patterns in West Africa and India with sometimes disastrous results. A continuous drought tends to set up its own cycle, since water-retaining vegetation gets destroyed. In 1970, Africa was almost self-sufficient in food. The drought ended that enviable position. In a 15-year period there were 2 great droughts. By 1984, 1/4 of the continent had to be fed from imported grain.

Other factors serve to compound the drought problem and cause them to be increasingly more severe. Among them are:

- Large population increases
- Political unrest
- Neglect of good agricultural practices
- Over-grazing
- Soil erosion.

When 'normal weather' is again in place, it tends to amplify the potential for disaster. Populations of people and domestic animals increase rapidly when a drought passes. This pattern prevails in the Sahel and other semi-arid areas. Since the carrying capacity (q.v.) of the land is exceeded, vegetation is destroyed, sometimes permanently. The next drought event is more disastrous than the last. This cycle leads to desertification (q.v.).

The drought of 1983 was the most disastrous in Australian history and it persisted many months. Its origin was in the pattern of atmospheric circulation which affected not only Australia but the whole Southern Hemisphere. There is a probable relationship to El Nino (q.v.) events. High pressure over eastern Australia and New Zealand persisted and successfully blocked the rain-bringing airmasses from Antarctica.

Droughts of great magnitude have occurred in the United States. That of the 1930's led to the Dust Bowl (q.v.). The drought of 1988 covered an even wider area and substantially affected the crop yield and water supplies.

DROWNED VALLEY The lower end of a valley can become sediment-laden. The sediment is dropped farther and farther upstream. The increased weight of this sediment lowers the valley floor, allowing the sea to invade. The process is gradual.

The Hudson River below Albany is a drowned valley. It extends offshore to become a submarine canyon. Chesapeake Bay is the drowned valley of the Susquehanna River.

DRUMLIN A drumlin is an elongated hill of glacial drift (q.v.). The shape results from ice pressure exerted on the sides and from above after a glacier has dropped its load.

Ice riding over a moraine (q.v.) picks up debris and molds it around obstacles. Hills created in this manner are oval. Some are quite large. Drumlins can be up to 160 meters (500 feet) high and several kilometers long. They tend to be in groups with their axes in the direction of glacial flow.

Near Boston, Bunker Hill, a battle site of the Revolutionary War, is a drumlin. It is one of a drumlin field in eastern New England. The largest drumlin field in the United States is in up-state New York. Syracuse is on and among these drumlins. The largest of all known drumlin fields is in northwestern Canada.

DRUSE A druse is a crystal cluster growing from a common base in an oval rock cavity. The cavity can be any size and is lined by crystals of quartz. Infrequently, the crystals grow to large size. Amethyst druses from southern Brazil have exceptionally large crystals.

DRY ADIABATIC RATE The dry adiabatic is the rate at which air cools or warms due to expansion and compression. It is about 1° Celsius per 100 meters of of altitude (5.5° Fahrenheit per 1,000 feet).

DRY FARMING Farming under conditions of little rainfall and no irrigation is dry farming. The crops sown are usually barley, sorghum, and wheat. The selected crops must be drought resistant and attain most of their growth in the short wet season.

Techniques for successful dry farming include contour plowing to prevent erosion and protect the tilth (q.v.); carrying out mulching to enrich the soils; and assiduous weeding. Weeds transpire water needed for the crops. It is important to have periods of fallow (or land rest) to allow nutrients and soil water to accumulate.

DRY PLACERS Dry placers, also known as dry diggings, are located in ravines where water is unavailable. Some placers are worked by using air blowers to winnow out the ore. Others use wool fleece (Golden Fleeces) to capture gold. The wool captures the gold blown up with the sands. This is a use of electrostatic principles. Other materials than wool are now used.

DTA Differential Thermal Analysis (DTA) is used to determine the energy associated with chemical reactions, with physical changes in crystals, and with alteration phenomena under uniform heat conditions. DTA is especially useful in the study of clays and other earths.

DUCKBILL PLATYPUS The Duckbill Platypus is considered by many evolutionists as a possible link between reptiles and mammals. Its present habitat is southern Tasmania. Indications are that the animal dates from 2 million years.

Platypus is an egg layer and supplies its young with milk, although not from mammary glands. Its bill is soft and used in working streambeds for food and to make burrows. The duckbill is fur-bearing and up to 0.6 meter (2 feet) long. It can eject poison from its back legs for defense.

DUMP The tailings storage area of an ore processing mill is a 'dump'. It is a specially prepared area. Material is reworked or it may remain a reserve if grades are not high enough for recovery under existing market conditions.

DUNE A dune is a wind-derived erosional landform. It develops where there is no vegetation to interfere with saltation (q.v.). The most likely locations for development are on beaches and in deserts. Dunes are moving mounds of sand and the individual grains are in motion. Beach dunes are sometimes sculpted by wave action.

There are 2 important desert dunes related to wind and terrain. They are the 'barchan', a crescent-shaped dune on a flat surface, and a longitudinal dune, the 'seif', an Arabic word for sword.

Barchans curve into the wind and the horns point away. They are found where the wind is unidirectional. The La Joya dunes on a high plateau in Peru are 'walking half moons'. They move north 16-20 meters (50-60 feet) a year.

Seifs form long, high ridges parallel to the prevailing winds. They are common where crosswinds are frequent. The seif dune type is characteristic of the Arabian Desert.

Coastal dunes are common. Those on the North Sea Coast of West Germany were once invading the country at a very rapid rate. Today, they are fixed by marram, a grass that manages to grow faster than the dunes. This grass is being tried on Oregon beaches.

DUNG Dung, cattle excrement, is used extensively for fuel in Third World countries. In Asia and Africa the amount burned annually is about 400 million tons. If this same amount were used as fertilizer it would increase yield by about 20 million tons of grain.

The major problem with dung as fuel is the smoke it creates. This smoke is responsible for much eye infection, which is especially prevalent in desert areas. It is a major cause of blindness second only to that caused by sand insects.

DUNITE Dunite is a realtively rare ultra-basic igneous rock. 90% of the rock is made of olivine and other mafic minerals. The type locality is Mt. Dun, New Zealand.

DURICRUST Duricrusts are hard rock cappings on ancient peneplaned (q.v.) surfaces. These are surfaces which have been uplifted. They are a common landform in Australia where they extend over thousands of square kilometers in Queensland and elsewhere.

Duricrusts are of 3 types and are not restricted to Australia although most common there. These types are aluminous or ferruginous, siliceous, and calcareous or magnesian. They can overlie leached bedrock, but do not appear to be due to the same climate variations as laterites (q.v.).

DUST The Atmosphere holds huge amounts of dust particles. They serve to reduce solar radiation. They also provide a nucleation source necessary to precipitation. Dust sources are many, they include:

- Volcanic eruptions

- Deflation by winds
- Meteoroid collisions with the Earth.

There are explosive volcanoes which impel dust and ash into the Atmosphere. Sometimes the force is so great the particulates are in the path of high altitude jets and can even circumnavigate the globe. Huge eruptions have caused a version of 'nuclear winter' (q.v.).

In desert areas sands are winnowed out by strong winds which can become eddying bores. These winds can scour a desert of its sands and expose the bedrock below. The famous sandstorms of the Sahara and Arabian deserts are agencies in deflation.

The impact or explosion of an astral body gouges out a crater in the surface of the Earth and forcing showers of dust and sand particles into the Atmosphere.

DUST BOWL Large portions of the Mid-United States suffered enormous wind deflation (q.v.). Topsoil was blown many hundreds of miles away and much of it ended in the sea.

Deflation is initiated by prolonged drought (q.v.). Soil erosion, disruption of grasslands, and deep plowing all contribute. The deflation period was from 1931-1940.

DUST VEIL INDEX A climatic effect of volcanic eruptions is enormous dust clouds circling the globe. The clouds are found at 2 levels, one of low elevation, 20-27 kilometers (12-16 miles), and the other above 50 kilometers (30 miles).

Dust clouds can be dense, high in sulfuric acid, and prevail for a long period. Their effect is measured by the Dust Veil Index. This Index set Krakatoa at 1,000.

In 1783, there were 2 major eruptions where the temperature dropped over the Northern Hemisphere by 5° Celsius. Relative warming during the early and and mid-20th Century is thought to have been the result of atmospheric clearing of volcanic dust. With events like El Chichon (q.v.) which occurred in 1982, this could change.

DYNE A dyne is a unit in the cgs (centimeter-gram-second) system. It is the force needed to accelerate 1 unit of mass 1 centimeter per second per second.

DWYKA TILLITE In South Africa during the Permian or Pennsylvanian (300-225 m.y.) or both, great deposits of glacial till were laid down in the Southern Hemisphere. Some of the Dwyka sediments are 600 meters (2,000 feet) thick. Beneath the tillite of primarily large faceted boulders, the basement rock shows the passage of glaciers.

Ice covered almost all of southern Africa and southern Madagascar, which was then part of the African continent. Similar tillite thicknesses are found correspondingly in Australia and in South America.

Loma Prieta Earthquake — San Francisco/Oakland, 1990
Courtesy of US Geological Survey

E

E LAYER The E Layer is an irregular zone in the Ionosphere (q.v.). It is about 150 kilometers (190 miles) thick and is intensely ionized (q.v.).

EARTH Earth, a planet in the Solar System, is an oblate spheroid, flattened at the poles and bulging at the Equator. The equatorial diameter is 12,756 kilometers (7,926 miles). The total area is 517 million square kilometers (190 million square miles). From Pole to Pole, the distance is 12,714 kilometers (7,900 miles). Earth is the 5th largest planet in the Solar System.

Earth orbits the Sun in the plane of the ecliptic (q.v.) at the rate of 105,000 kilometers (65,000 miles) per hour. Measurements from satellites indicate the North Pole is 24.4 meters (80 feet) more off center than the South. The Northern Hemisphere is longer and more lopsided than the Southern.

The position of the Earth in the Solar System is especially important for life on the planet. It is just the right distance from the Sun for the water to exist on its surface. Water makes up 72% of that surface. If the Earth were closer to the Sun, water would vaporize. If it were more distant, water would all be ice. The heat energy of the Earth is only 1/2,000th that of the Sun.

The planet is made up of an outer Crust, an inner Mantle, and a Core. The Crust (q.v.) is 10-50 kilometers (6-30 miles) thick. It is thicker beneath the continents than beneath the ocean. The Mantle (q.v.) is 3,000 kilometers (1800 miles) thick and is of molten rock or magma (q.v.). Within the Earth, temperatures and pressures increase with depth. The Earth's Core is of nickel-iron.

Scientists believe the Earth originated from a cosmic dust cloud. They estimate the cloud to be 8 trillion kilometers (5 trillion miles) across. The Sun acted as a thermonuclear reactor and produced a fusion reaction to create the cloud. The cloud later coalesced to produce the planets. See **BIG BANG**.

EARTH AXIS The Earth's axis extends from Pole to Pole and the globe revolves around it once every 24 hours or so. The direction of spin is to the east. The axis is tilted 23.5°, an angle that varies between 22-25°.

Earth's tilt gives rise to seasons. These relate to the angle at which the Sun's rays hit the Earth. Areas receiving the most direct rays are warmest. Earth is closer to the Sun in January than in July. Southern Hemisphere summers are about 7% weaker.

Over a 22,000 year period the orbit around the Sun has an axial precession, 'the Wobble Cycle'. A complete cycle takes about 41,000 years. In the extreme position, the Earth leans farther from the Sun than if no precession took place. This means the colder seasons become deeper. Milankovitch and others believe this wobble leads to colder winters and provides a clue to the onset of Ice Ages (q.v.).

The Earth's axis now points to the North Star. 4,000 years ago navigators steered by a point between the Big and Little Dippers (Ursa Major and Ursa Minor). In another 16,000 years the position will have reversed.

EARTH CRUST The Crust or outer layer of Earth is an estimated 33 to 66 kilometers (20-40 miles) thick. On the continents, it is veneered by rocks, soil, sand, and clay. The Crust is thinner beneath the oceans (5-33 kilometers (3-20 miles). The Mohorovicic Discontinuity (q.v.) marks the lower boundary of the crustal layer.

Crustal relief is uneven. The highest mountains reach 8 kilometers (5 miles) and the deepest trench in the ocean is about 9.5 kilometers (6 miles).

Magnesium silicate, perovskite, is the most abundant of crustal building blocks. Many Upper Mantle minerals are converted to perovskite under high pressure (240,000-1.3 million atmospheres).

EARTH CURRENTS Electrical currents in the Earth's Crust are related to cosmic currents of the Electromagnetic Field, of auroras, and solar flares. These internal Earth currents are called telluric.

EARTH MAGNETISM The Earth's Magnetic Field functions as though it were a great bar magnet with horizontal and vertical components. Field intensity decreases proportional to the distance from the magnetized sphere.

A few Earth radii from the center of the planet, Magnetic Field intensity is small. Around the Earth there are magnetic fields called the Van Allen Belts (q.v.).

Secondary magnetic fields may be set up in certain rocks, depending upon the rock's susceptibility. Great masses of magnetite have strong magnetic fields.

EARTH ORBIT Earth's orbit of the Sun is almost elliptical due to the pull of other planets. Every 100,000 years there is a complete cycle from circular to elliptical. This phenomenon is 'orbital eccentricity' and accounts for long periods of polar climate in Mid-Latitudes. The change alters the position of the Earth in relation to the Sun by about 4-5 million miles, thus affecting solar radiation. See **PERIODICITY**.

EARTHENWARE The majority of potteries are of earthenware, a common clay fired at less than 1,200° Celsius. Iron is an important flux.

EARTHQUAKE Rupture of the Earth's Crust and the movements accompanying it make up an earthquake. Rupture may occur along an already deeply faulted and fractured zone. Results can be relatively minor adjustments among rock blocks, or major dislocations.

Epicenters or quake foci are located at the intersection of 3 distance curves, recorded by different seismic stations. Distance is calculated using the lag time between 'p' and 's' waves (q.v.). The epicenter is above the hypocenter, or quake center, within the Earth's Crust.

Earthquake intensity is measured on various scales relating magnitude to potential damage. These measure the physical shaking of the Earth at a given point. In the United States, the Richter Scale (q.v.) is used. Intensities greater than 5 or 6 are life-threatening. Only wars and plagues have taken toll of more lives than devastating earthquakes and accompanying tsunamis (q.v.).

In 1962 long or L wave (q.v.) vibrations from the Chilean Earthquake were 6,660 kilometers (4,000 miles) in length. The Earth vibrated for 24 hours. The Chile Quake was 8.9 on the Richter, the greatest magnitude recorded.

Prior to major earthquakes, lights have been reported. It may be that strain sets up an electrical charge not unlike the piezo-electric effect (q.v.) on a crystal. Changes in ground electrical conditions allowed prediction of a Kamchatka earthquake.

During an earthquake, radon (q.v.) in deep water wells is known to increase and water levels drop. Using this information, the Russians predicted by 6 hours the Altai Quake in Central Asia, November, 1978.

EAST AFRICAN LAKES A number of lakes are associated with the Great Rift Valley (q.v.) of East Africa. The lakes are sources of some important rivers, among them the White Nile, the Congo (Zaire), and the Zambezi.

The major lakes are Albert, Edward, George, Kivu, Naivasha, Nyassa or Malawi, Rudolph, Ruwenzori, Tanganyika, and Victoria. All the lakes are in Rift Valley trenches except Victoria which is in a collapsed basin between the East and West Rifts.

EAST AFRICAN RIFT Great trench-like valleys formed along parallel faults in East Africa. The Rift Valley System extends from the Red Sea and the Dead Sea (both in rifts) to Malawi in the south and beyond to meet the Global Rift System (q.v.). The East African is the greatest continental rift yet defined.

EAST PACIFIC HIGH A semi-permanent high pressure area is located over the east-central Pacific Ocean. Known as the East Pacific High, it is comparable to the Bermuda High (q.v.) in the Atlantic.

EAST PACIFIC RISE The 'Downwind Expedition' of the IGY (q.v.) (International Geophysical Year) measured heatflow from the Pacific Ocean floor on a ridge near Easter Island. The heatflow was 5 times normal. Sound patterns were similar to those of the Mid-Atlantic Ridge (q.v.) implying a similar topography. Additional evidence has been collected.

A mountain range rises 4,545 meters (15,000 feet) from the ocean floor, with peaks within 212 meters (700 feet) of the surface. The Rise or range is 1,600 kilometers (1000 miles) long and up to 320 kilometers (200 miles) wide.

Seafloor spreading in the area is 4.5 centimeters (1.8 inches) per year. A series of eruptions in the central rift pushes older rocks away and a definite pattern, discernible by magnetic stripes with reversing polarities, is imprinted on the seafloor.

EASTERLY WAVE When the Bermuda High airmass is weak and located in a position more south than usual, a trough pushes toward the Tropics. This is a Polar Trough, a low pressure area, in the Mid-Latitude Westerlies. The trough is pushed by a Polar Front and is trapped by the Trades. As a result, shearing occurs.

This shearing is basic to hurricane development. If a hurricane does not develop, an Easterly Wave does.

The Easterly Wave is an elongated low pressure area with deep vertical development. Moving off the North African Coast, it may form a vortex with clouds up to 9,000 meters (30,000 feet). As the wind convection increases the airmass picks up more moisture, fueling more clouds.

What the exact trigger is that converts an Easterly Wave into a hurricane is not known but a great drop in atmospheric pressure occurs.

EASTERN BOUNDARY REGIONS The world's fisheries are greatest in the upwelling (q.v.) areas of oceanic eastern boundaries. Upwelling off California, the Canary Islands, and Chile are examples. Since the species are similar, there is probably a relationship between species and the food chains in these currents.

These favorable areas represent only a fraction of the World Ocean yet they supply 1/3 of the world's commercial fish.

EASTERN RIFT BELT A portion of the Great Rift System of East Africa is the Eastern Rift Belt. It is in western Kenya and northeastern Tanzania. Lavas of this belt show great carbonatite (q.v.) activity.

EBB-TIDE Tides turning and waters receding from the shore are ebb-tide. See **TIDES**.

ECHINODERMATA In the Echinodermata Phylum the main classes are Pelmatazoa and Eleutherozoa. Crinoids, or Pelmatazoa, were abundant in the Paleozoic (570-225 m.y.). The only presently living members are the sea lilies (800 species) attached to the ocean floor by long stems. Most of these are found in the East Indian Ocean, with a few in the West Indies and off Cape Hatteras.

There are about 5,000 species of marine invertebrates belonging to Eleutherozoa, or mobile Echinoids. The group have been around since the Cambrian (570-500 m.y.). One species, the sand dollar, is useful to Cenozoic (Tertiary and Recent) interpretation.

Echinodermata have only rudimentary arms, are globular or flat with 5-fold symmetry, as in the starfish. Their skin is spiny with ossicles of calcium carbonate. Almost every ossicle consists of a single crystal of magnesium calcite.

ECHO-SOUNDING Depth measurements in the sea are made with an echo sounder. The time interval between sending a signal and receiving an echo from the bottom is calculated. A signal may be sonic or ultrasonic.

The Scattering Layer (q.v.) affects soundings. The velocity of sound is affected by temperature, pressure, and salinity of the sea. All records must be interpreted using these factors.

ECLIPTIC The planets of the Solar System all move about the Sun in a single plane. The line they trace is the ecliptic. This imaginary surface through the Sun and Earth remains constant all throughout the Earth orbit. The Earth's axis inclines 23.5° from the ecliptic. This inclination combined with rotation and revolution (q.v.) governs the amount of solar energy received at any location on Earth.

ECLIPSE An eclipse is the total or partial obscuring of light. The Moon receives its light from the Sun as does the Earth. As the Moon turns we see more or less sunlit area, giving us phases.

As the Earth turns a shadow is cast into Space. When the Earth is between the Sun and the Moon, the shadow falls on the Moon eclipsing it. A partial eclipse occurs 2 to 5 times a year. Every 5 years, a total eclipse is observed from some location on Earth. See **SOLAR ECLIPSE.**

ECLOGITE Eclogites are dark, dense, basic rocks composed primarily of garnet and pyroxene. Eclogites are not widely distributed but they are known from South Africa and California. South African eclogites occasionally have included diamonds.

Kimberlite pipes have eclogite xenoliths, an indication the pipes originated at great depth. Eclogite results from regional metamorphism under conditions of high temperatures and pressures.

Hot liquid basalt erupts to form ridges. Upon cooling eclogite forms from a portion of the magma. Complete transformation of basalt to eclogite occurs between 70-100 kilometers (42-60 miles) into the Mantle. This is the origin of the Eclogite Layer. The Layer may be important in identifying the energy source for continental drift (q.v.).

ECOLOGY Ecology, the study of the inter-relations of lifeforms and their environment, emphasizes the interdependence of all organisms and their niches (q.v.).

The environment is now understood to be inclusive of the continent, seas, and the Atmosphere. Ecological problems are now understood to be global problems. See **ECOSYSTEM**.

ECOSPACE   The dynamic environment in which a community of populations lives, evolves, and interacts is an ecospace. All are members of the same ecosystem. Planet Earth is an ecospace.

ECOSYSTEM   The ecosystem is the fundamental unit in ecology (q.v.). Size is irrelevant. A single drop of water is a complete ecosystem for some single-celled plants and animals. The ecosystem is a collection of communities (q.v.) within an ecospace. There is a living and a non-living component to every ecosystem. The non-living includes, among other things, the energy source directly or indirectly from the Earth and Sun.

There are important variables. Temperature may be restricted to a special range, as with corals. Pressure is usually from gravity. Gases (oxygen, carbon dioxide, and nitrogen) play a vital role. Water, if only as vapor, is important. Rocks, soils and physiographic features define the geography. Every ecosystem has producers, consumers, and decomposers.

ECOTONE   An ecotone is the zone between ecosystems or biomes (q.v.). A great variety of organisms can be found in the ecotone drawing sustanence from each ecosystem. Lagoonal environments are ecotones.

In an ecotone, climates may be borderline and subject to change. In this case the ecotone may be a less favorable area for members of an adjacent ecosystem. The Sahel of Africa is such an ecotone. 'Sahel' is Arabic for edge.

ECUADOR   Named for the Equator, Ecuador is 75% within the Andean Cordillera (q.v.). The balance is of small coastal plains and islands. The most important islands form the Galapagos Archipelago (q.v.). The Cordillera is separated into 2 ranges and the intermontane valley between is separated by lava flows into 11 different basins.

Ecuador's boundary with Peru is still in dispute

EDDY   An eddy is a current of water, air, wind, or any fluid that moves in a circular manner. An eddy will be off to the side from the main flow. If the eddy is closed and rapid, it is a whirl (whirlpool or whirlwind).

EDENTATA   The Great Anteater or Hairy Tamandua is of the Order Edentata, a group of mammals without teeth but with great claws. It feeds on termites and ants and is a natural control. The Tamandua can clean out an ant colony using its claws and long sticky tongue.

The Great Anteater is found in South America where it plays an important role in the savanna and rainforest in keeping down the ant and termite populations. Its sole enemy is the jaguar.

EDIACARA ASSEMBLAGE There is a complex of fossils found in the Ediacara Hills, Australia, that is a testament to the great proliferation of lifeforms in the Precambrian (700+ m.y.). The fauna include, among other forms, Algae, jellyfish, and worms. Similar complexes have been located in the British Isles, South Africa, and USSR.

LAKE EDWARD Located in the West Rift, Edward is one of the major lakes in the Great Rift System. It is connected to Lake George via a 40 kilometer (24 mile) channel. The western shore is in Zaire, the eastern in Uganda. The lake is 65 x 38 kilometers (39 x 22 miles) and at its deepest is 112 meters (369 feet).

Edward is fed by Nyamgasani River draining the Ruwenzoris (q.v.). Streams from the Rwanda and Kigezi Highlands and Virunga Volcanoes also enter the lake. The outlet is the Semliki River which flows northeast 250 kilometers (150 miles) to Lake Albert and the Albert Nile. See **NILE RIVER.**

EFFLUENT Effluent, meaning 'to flow from',is used to describe the discharge from sewage systems. Hydrologists refer to streams flowing out of and draining an area as effluent. An effluent stream remains above the water table, but may be seasonal.

EGYPT Egypt occupies the northeast corner of Africa. The physiography naturally divides into 4 main regions:

- Nile Valley and Delta
- Eastern Desert - From the Nile to the Red Sea.
- Western Desert - From the Nile to Libyan border.
- Sinai Peninsula - Separated by Gulf of Suez and Suez Canal.

Sinai and the Eastern Desert are a part of the Arabo-Nubian Massif. The Precambrian Basement crops out in Sinai and along the mountains of the Eastern Desert. West of them, Tertiary sediments (65-12 m.y.) make up the desert floor. In the south, these give way to Cretaceous sediments (135-65 m.y.) and Nubian sandstone (q.v.).

The Western Desert is the site of the Great Erg (Sand Sea). Very recently water has been discovered at depth and it is being tapped for agricultural development. The area will also receive water from Lake Nasser (q.v.).

Eh The standard symbol 'eh' for the potential for the reduction-oxidation 'redox' process. It is especially important in soil analysis and mineral exploration. It is a climate and favorability key and is considered with pH (q.v.).

EJECTA Ejecta are pyroclastic materials erupted from a volcano. They may be of molten lava, ash, gas, cinders, and rock in any combination.

EKMAN SPIRAL The Ekman Layer exists where frictional forces are strong enough to create the Ekman Spiral. The Spiral is the effect of the force of a layer of the sea upon the subjacent level to it.

Wind blown seas turn to the right in the Northern Hemisphere due to the Coriolis Effect (q.v.). This affects surface layers and the friction is communicated to the next layer below causing water to be pushed further to the right, initiating a spiral.

ELASTICITY An elastic body will strain in response to stress. All the strain is recoverable if the stress is removed. It is unlike plastic or viscous material that does not recover when freed from stress. Thin sheets of mica demonstrate elasticity, after bending they spring back to their original shape.

ELECTRICITY Negatively charged particles or electrons, are attached to atoms in the static state. If the outer shell is negative, the atom may lose an electron to become positive. This movement, or current, of electrons is electricity.

ELECTROLYTES Electrolytes are readily ionized substances. They are conductors of electricity, or electrical energy.

ELECTROMAGNETIC FORCE The force emitted from an electromagnetic field will react with any charged particle or object. It will not react with a neutral object such as light. See **MAGNETIC FIELD**.

ELECTROMAGNETIC RADIATION Oscillating electric and magnetic fields produce electromagnetic radiation in Space. The radiation is generated when energy moves away from a charged particle.

ELECTROMAGNETIC SPECTRUM The electromagnetic spectrum is the entire known range of electrical energy. At one end are extremely long radio waves. At the other, extremely short X-rays. The spectrum includes visible light.

ELECTROMAGNETIC WAVES There are many types of electromagnetic waves, each defined by wavelength and frequency or oscillations per second. Length is in centimeters.

ELECTROMAGNETISM The Danish physicist, Oersted, discovered that electrical current has a magnetic field. The current is responsible for magnetism but magnetism can also set up an electrical current.

The direction of the force exerted by an electromagnetic field is perpendicular to current direction. Planetary motion is fundamental to the creation of electrical current. See **MAGNETISM**.

ELECTRON An electron is an elementary particle with a negative electrical charge. Normally, it orbits the nucleus of the atom. Its mass is equivalent to 0.522 MeV (million electron volts). It has axial spin as well as current.

All elements or atoms have specific electrons restricted to particular orbits. The orbital plane is called a shell. The distance between shells is increased with increased atomic weight (q.v.).

The relationship between chemical properties and atomic structure is determined by electron arrangement in the shells. Behavior is governed by the outer shell.

The shells have order and arrangement. There are a maximum of 2 electrons in the 1st shell, 8 in the 2nd, 18 in the 3rd, 18 in the 4th, 18 in any additional excepting the outer. The outer does not contain more than 8. See **ELECTRON CLOUD**.

Hydrogen has 1 shell and 1 electron. Lithium has 2 shells and 2 electrons, 1 in the inner and 1 in the outer shell. The electron shell (q.v.) has a zero magnetic moment with a half spin upward and a half spin downward, or in opposing directions.

ELECTRON CLOUD Electron orbitals composed of millions of electron passes around the nuclei are electron clouds.

The innermost shell has only 's' orbitals. They are spherical and the simplest. The 'p' orbital is a rough, single figure 8, 'd' a double 8. 'f' orbitals are found in rare earths and are more complex. Electrons in the cloud govern interactions and bonding (q.v.). Every orbital can hold a maximum of 2 's', 6 'p', and 10 'd' electrons.

ELECTRON VOLT The electron volt is the amount of energy gained by an electron from a potential difference of 1 volt. This is minute, equal to 1.6×10^{-12} ergs.

An electron passing through 1 volt difference in potential transmits this energy to the particle. A single electron moving from one battery pole to the other needs 12 electron volts of energy in a 12-volt battery.

ELEMENT An element is matter composed of similar atoms. Substances which cannot be broken down to simpler forms by chemical means are considered elementary, thus the name.

There are 92 naturally occurring elements on Earth. Of these 65 are metals (q.v.). There are additional elements, which are unstable bringing the total to 103.

All atoms of a particular element have been given the same atomic number. Elements have been given symbols and arranged on a table so that those most similar are grouped together. See **PERIODIC TABLE**.

Every mineral is either an element or a compound of chemical elements. The rocks that compose the Earth's crust are made up of these elementary substances.

ELEVATION Elevation is the measure of relief above sea level. Maximum elevations of continental landmasses are:

CONTINENT	MAXIMUM ELEVATION		MOUNTAIN
	Meters	Feet	
Asia	8,840	29,172	Everest
South America	7,040	23,232	Aconcagua
North America	6,040	19,932	McKinley
Africa	6,010	19,833	Kilmanjaro

CONTINENT	MAXIMUM ELEVATION		MOUNTAIN
	Meters	Feet	
Europe	4,807	15,863	Mont Blanc
Antarctica	4,603	15,189	Markham
Australia	2,211	7,296	Townsend

ELFIN FOREST A forest of miniature gnarled trees and shrubs is an elfin forest. The Chaparral of Southern California has low scrub elfin forest representatives. These are usually found at slightly higher elevations than the semi-desert scrub. See **CHAPARRAL**.

MOUNT ELGON One of the world's highest volcanoes, Mount Elgon is on the border between Kenya and Uganda. The volcano, which last erupted 3 million years ago, has a base that is 80 kilometers (50 miles) in diameter. Its caldera is 8 kilometers (5 miles) across and 600 meters (2,000 feet) deep. The floor of the caldera is marshy. Elgon's rim reaches 4,320 meters (14,175 feet).

The slopes of Mt Elgon are of weathered volcanic material which produced some of the richest soils of the region. The Giant Lobelia found on Kilmanjaro also is found on Elgon. Rivers drain from the crater and the area has many productive coffee and tea plantations.

ELUVIAL PLACER An eluvial placer develops where a slope is eroded and gravity has moved debris downhill. Many economic mineral deposits are formed in this way. They include some Malayan tin placers and the zirconium (baddeleyite) deposits of Pocos de Caldas, Brazil.

ELUVIATION Material transported in solution or suspension through soil is eluviated. Elluviation occurs when precipitation exceeds evaporation.

In equatorial parts of the globe, where rainfall is very heavy as in the Amazon, eluviation plays an important role. Clay and colloidal material are carried in descending waters and deposited lower in the profile. Humid tropical soils are eluviated as well as leached.

Detrital material or detrital capping resulting from rock break-up in place is eluvium. It contrasts with alluvium (q.v.)

EMBAYMENT An embayment is a coastal feature. Submergence from rising seas or sinking land can result in an embayment or drowned valley. It can also occur when a depression is invaded by the sea. San Francisco Bay is such an embayment.

The Mississippi Embayment was once a coastal feature. It is now located far upstream. Sediments fill it to a great depth.

EMENDATION Emendation allows the free flow of waters from one basin to another. It occurs when watersheds are not definite. The classic example is the link between the Orinoco and Casiquiare Rivers that allows water in Rio Branco, a sub-basin of the Amazon, to also flow into the Orinoco Basin of Venezuela.

Emendation also occurs with the Upper Paraguay River and the tributaries of the Amazon in Mato Grosso and Rondonia. The meeting of these waters effectively turns Brazil south of the Amazon into an island during heavy rainy seasons.

EMERALD Emerald is a silicate of aluminum and beryl. It ranges in color from intense green to yellow green. The color is imparted by chromium oxide.

A fine emerald is a precious gem. The finest come from Colombia, Brazil, and India. The Soviet Union also produces the gemstones.

In ancient Peru, emeralds were the symbol of royalty among the Incas. The high priests wore emeralds as symbols of the Sun.

EMERALD CUT Emerald cut is a step-cut chosen to enhance color over brilliance. It has elongated, rectangular facets on the crown and pavillion. The girdle is similar. Corners are often faceted. Tiny stones are not cut in this fashion since the tables would be too small.

EMERGENCE Emergence is the elevation of a continent, coastal zone, or island in relation to sea level. The shift in elevation can be due to tectonic disturbance, subsidence of bordering oceanic area, or glacial rebound (q.v.).

Uplift of an emergent coast is slow and a gentle shelving can result. The Southern California Coast at Palos Verdes has as many as 13 terraces. In Scandinavia glacial rebound is continuing with terracing and raised beaches. Longshore bars are developing off Finland and Sweden. Islands are appearing in Baltic bays.

EMERY Abrasive emery is a dark, granular aggregate of corundum, magnetite, and one or more other minerals. Most emery deposits are of magnetite, corundum, and spinel. Peekskill, New York, deposits contain magnetite, sillimanite, and alumino-silicates of magnesium and iron (cordierite or sapphirine).

EMF SERIES The order in which metals replace each other in salt solutions is the Electromotive Force Series (EMF). The order is of decreasing potential (voltage difference). It is potassium, sodium, calcium, magnesium, bivalent iron, zinc, trivalent iron, and copper.

ENDOMORPH An included mineral contained in a crystal of a different mineralogy is an endomorph. Rutile contained within quartz is common.

EMI KOUSSI CALDERA The highest point in the Sahara is the ancient volcano of Emi Koussi on the southern edge of the Tibesti Massif (q.v.). It is 3,415 meters (11,204 feet) above the desert floor.

The volcano erupted and collapsed 5 million years ago. The cones within the caldera testify to activity after the collapse. The caldera is 20 kilometers (12 miles) in diameter and 900 meters (3,000 feet) deep.

ENERGY Physicists define energy as the ability to do work. Work is defined as the force acting upon a body multiplied by the distance over which the body moves. Motion is an integral part of work.

All forms of energy are interchangeable. Some forms are: Chemical, electromagnetic, heat (solar), mechanical, and nuclear. Energy in motion is kinetic. Stored or at rest energy is potential.

Present energy sources powering industry are primarily the hydrocarbons including coal. Nuclear energy has been slow to develop for a variety of social and economic reasons. For broad industrial use, solar energy has not yet been proven economic. See **SOLAR ENERGY**.

A doubling of energy demand occurs about every 10 years. Known petroleum resources are sufficient to meet demand for up to 50 years at present rates of population and industrial growth. Not all these resources are readily available.

ENERGY BUDGET The Sun's energy strikes the Earth through direct rays. The Earth receives this energy as light and expels it as heat. On the average about half is absorbed by the oceans and land, the rest is reflected back into Space. Energy absorbed by the Earth is returned to the Atmosphere and about 25% of this is held in the Atmosphere as latent heat.

ENERGY SOURCES The world's present energy needs are met in the following ways:

- Petroleum Based - Oil, natural gas, oil shale, tar sands
- Coal - largely bituminous, also brown coal and lignite
- Nuclear - Uranium, thorium, hydrogen
- Solar
- Sea - Waves and tides
- Weather - Temperature inversions, winds
- Geothermal - Hotsprings and volcanoes
- Hydroelectric - Waterfalls, dams
- Organic - Peat, wood, animal and vegetable matter.

The hydrocarbons (q.v.) are the major sources. 10% of natural gas supplies in oilfields is still being 'flared off'. Using flared off gas and opening new natural gas fields could increase the supply. The only country self-sufficient in natural gas at the present time is the USSR. See **NATURAL GAS**.

Less than 10% of all energy is produced by nuclear reaction. The use of hydropower (q.v.) has increased in recent years, particularly in the USSR and South America.

ENGLISH CHANNEL The narrow strip of sea between the Atlantic Ocean and the North Sea is the English Channel. It was once a river valley that became, an embayment, then a strait.

ENIWETOK ATOLL Elugelab Island in Eniwetok Atoll, South Pacific Ocean, was the site of a fusion bomb test, the H-Bomb in 1952. The blast created a crater 3.2 kilometers (2 miles) deep with a diameter of 1.6 kilometers (1 mile), equivalent to a small caldera (q.v.).

ENNEDI PLATEAU The Greater Lake Chad Basin is rimmed to the northeast by sandstone cliffs of the Ennedi Plateau. The plateau is perched above the granite basement rocks. The cliffs rise to 1,450 meters (4,756 feet).

Ennedi resulted from surface doming which occurred 100 million years ago. It is highly dissected by stream erosion. The area still receives 200 millimeters (8 inches) of precipitation a year. Ennedi Plateau with the Ahoggar Range (q.v.) are among the few positive structures in the vast Sahara.

ENTRENCHED STREAM Large desert rivers, including those flowing through a landscape rejuvenated by uplift, deeply incise their canyons. They are limited in periods of flow, but the volume of sediments is high, so abrasion is rapid.

The well-defined trench that is cut into the flat bottom of the stream bed results from a sustained increase of velocity and bed-load. Downcutting is violent but not necessarily long-lived.

ENTROPY Entropy is energy within a thermodynamic system that is unavailable for conversion to any other form of energy. Entropy is said to describe the 'degree of disorder of any physical system'.

ENVIRONMENT The Earth's environment has changed in a number of major ways over the 4.6 billion years of its lifetime. Perhaps the most important changes have to do with the Sun's activity.

Sun luminosity is estimated to have increased by 25%. How that has affected the Earth depended upon a number of interrelated factors affected by Earth physics.

The major change in the Earth's Atmosphere made possible the present lifeforms. Oxygenation was brought about presumably by photosynthesis (q.v.) of Algae. The released oxygen destroyed several gases inimical to aerobic life. See **CHZ**.

The sum of physical, chemical, and biological conditions create the 'environment of deposition' of a sedimentary rock. Principal depositional environments are:

- Continental - Terrestrial, desert, glacial, aquatic, alluvial, fluvial, lacustrine, and paludal
- Marine - Neritic, bathyal, and abyssal
- Intermediate - Deltaic, lagoonal, and littoral.

Environments also have been classed structurally:

- Basins - Geosynclinal, epeirogenetic, and fault induced
- Oceanic basins - Bathyal and abyssal
- Montane areas
- Volcanic areas
- Non-tectonic areas - Gradational.

In the biological world environments are described in terms of ecosystems and biomes (q.v.).

EOCENE The Eocene Epoch is a part of the Tertiary Period (65-2 m.y.). The Eocene (54-37 m.y.) followed the Paleocene and was overlain by the Miocene. North American Eocene fossils indicate a link with Europe that subsequently disappeared. There was also a temporary link between North and South America, providing a land bridge for the transfer of animals between hemispheres.

Eocene was an epoch of great tree development, oak, banyan, and fig among others. Magnolias flourished in Alaska and cypress forests in Greenland. Both are subtropical trees.

Toward the end of the Eocene (27 m.y.) mountain building began in the Tethys Sea (q.v.). The Pyrenees and Alps originated and continued to grow well into the Miocene.

EOLIAN (AEOLIAN) Eolian is derived from 'Eolus', Roman god of winds. It describes wind transported and deposited sediments.

Stratigraphy resulting from eolian cross-bedding demonstrates the great variability in wind directions and velocities. Remarkable crossbedding is evident in such famous formations as the Navajo Sandstone.

EON (AEON) Eon is the major division of geological time. There are 2 eons, the Cryptozoic and the Phanerozoic. The Cryptozoic coincides with the Precambrian and the Phanerozoic encompasses the Paleozoic to Recent (570 m.y. - Present).

EPEIRIC SEA Epeiric or epicontinental seas are large and shallow. They covered continental areas in great transgressions throughout geological time. Hudson Bay and the Baltic Sea are present epeiric seas.

At the beginning of the Paleozoic (570 m.y.), a broad epeiric sea covered the São Francisco and Paranaiba River basins in Brazil.

EPEIROGENESIS Uplift or subsidence on a continental scale is epeirogenic. In the process the landmass is not folded, though it may be tilted.

Epeirogenesis is a diastrophic process on a great scale, dominated by slow vertical movements giving rise to continents. The process is characterized by isostatic (q.v.) adjustments.

Epeirogenesis differs from orogeny or mountain-building. The latter is the result of tangential movement and proceeds relatively quickly. See **DIASTROPHISM**.

EPHEMERAL Ephemeral streams are intermittent in their flow. In arid areas these streams flow only in response to precipitation within the area. Usually, they are triggered by thunderstorms in the headwaters which can result in flash flooding.

EPICENTER The focal point of seismic activity during an earthquake is its epicenter. Seismologists determine it from 3 reporting stations which plot wave transits. Where seismic waves intersect is the epicenter.

Most epicenters are located in narrow belts along crustal plate boundaries. Relatively few are within a plate. The intensity may, however, be as great. The New Madrid Quake (q.v.) is an example.

EPIDOTE Epidote is a silicate of calcium, aluminum, and iron found in igneous and metamorphic rocks. It appears generally as small, thin, yellow-green crystals. Relatively hard, it is 6-7 on Moh's Scale (q.v.). Epidote is characteristic of the greenschist facies (q.v.) such as found in Otago, New Zealand.

EPIGENETIC DEPOSIT An epigenetic mineral deposit is formed later than the rock enclosing it. The deposits may be formed from invading mineralized solutions. Some pegmatites, the late phase of magmatic crystallization, are epigenetic in relation to the enclosing granites. Usually, these deposits occur at or near the surface.

EPILIMNION The layer of lake water between the surface and the thermocline (q.v.) is the epilimnion. The lower level of the epilimnion changes markedly with the seasons. This can be an area of pronounced cooling.

EPIPHYTES Epiphytes are aeroid plants growing attached to trees and shrubs but not connected with the ground. Roots dangle in mid-air and collect moisture.

Trees and epiphytes have a commensal (q.v.) relationship. Some orchids, bromeliads, cacti, and ferns are epiphytes.

EPOCH An Epoch is a subdivision of a Period on the geological time column. Rocks formed during an Epoch are often a unified Series.

EQUATOR The Equator is an imaginary line forming a Great Circle girdling the globe midway between the poles. This line is perpendicular to the Earth's rotational axis. It is the geographical line between the Northern and Southern hemispheres. The Tropics (q.v.) straddle this line from 30° N to 30° S Latitude.

In the Pennsylvanian Period (300 m.y.) the Equator bisected the Earth between the poles. It traced a line from Newfoundland to the Gulf of

California. During this period, coral formed on the edge of the Arctic Ocean.

EQUATORIAL COUNTER CURRENT In the Southern Hemisphere, the Doldrums Current is counter to the Equatorial. It is near Surinam and French Guiana in winter. In summer it flows to meet the Guinea Current off Africa.

EQUATORIAL CURRENT Equatorial Latitudes are dominated by a westerly flow of water generated by the Trades. These currents are separated by a narrow easterly current.

The North Equatorial in the Atlantic curves to join the Florida Current or Gulf Stream. In the Pacific it curves to the right blending into the Kuro Shio Current. The current splits again and one arm swings into the Indian Ocean, the other curves north.

The South Equatorial Current flowing from African waters hits the Brazilian Bulge. Then, as the Brazil Current it flows south hugging the coast to Cabo Frio. It then gently curves east to join the West Wind Drift off Argentina.

The current flowing south from the Equator off northern South America is the southern arm of the North Equatorial Current. It brings warm air with rain to the cooler land.

EQUATORIAL TROUGH A low pressure area of tropical convergence, the Equatorial Trough brings with it numerous weather disturbances. It is particularly noted for violent thunderstorms.

EQUILIBRIUM PROFILE The hyperbolic curve described by a stream in equilibrium denotes hydrostatic stability. The equilibrium profile shows a river no longer cutting into its bed, and no longer depositing alluvium.

EQUINOX Twice a year, any given point on the Earth will have 12 hours of daylight and 12 hours of darkness. This phenomenon is 'Equinox' from the Latin for equal night. It occurs on March 21st and September 23rd when the Sun is overhead at noon along the Equator.

ERA The Era is a division of geological time. There are 5 great Eras, divided into Periods and Epochs beginning 4.6 billion years ago:

> Archaeozoic - 4.6 b.y. to 1.6 b.y.
>
> Proterozoic - 1.6 b.y. to 570 m.y.
>
> Paleozoic   - 570 m.y. to 225 m.y.
>
> Mesozoic   - 225 m.y. to 75 m.y.
>
> Cenozoic   - 75 m.y. to the Present.

The first 2 Ages are linked in the Precambrian, which coincides with the Cryptozoic Eon and represents 83% of all Earth history. The Proterozoic ended in the Caledonian Orogeny (q.v.).

There is no evidence of terrestrial life during the Precambrian. The Paleozoic was a time when the first land plants and animals appeared. This Period closed with the Appalachian Orogeny. See **APPALACHIANS**.

The Mesozoic is known as the 'Age of Reptiles'. This was the era in which the dinosaurs and other giant reptiles flourished. The era concluded with the Laramide Orogeny (q.v.).

The Cenozoic Era on-going in the Present includes the Tertiary with its volcanism and the Pleistocene with the most modern of the Ice Ages (q.v.).

MOUNT EREBUS The only active volcano on the continent of Antarctica is Mount Erebus. It rises to 4,024 meters (13,202 feet) and has a crater that is 800 meters in diameter (2,600 feet). The crater contains a lake of lava.

LAKE ERIE Lake Erie is one of the Great Lakes derived from glaciation. It is the only one of them still freezing completely in winter. This is due to its shallowness and its location in relation to storms.

Lake Erie is greatly polluted as a result of population density and massive industrial activity on its shores. Efforts are underway to clean up the lake, but it will be a very long and expensive process.

ERG Great sand sheets in desert areas are ergs. 1/5 of the Sahara is made up of them or 9 million square kilometers (3.5 million square miles). One of the greatest ergs is in the Sahara, Great Sand Sea. The Libyan Erg alone covers an area the size of France. Sand sheets making up these ergs are enormous and have great depths. The largest continuous sand surface is in Saudi Arabia.

The erg surface is virtually lifeless and distinguished by dunes. 'Erg' is Berber for a not entirely flat sandy desert and one that is greatly wind-blown.

'Erg', a Greek word for work, is used as a unit of measure. It is equivalent to the work done by 1 dyne (q.v.) of energy over 1 centimeter of distance or length.

EROSION Erosion is a weathering process at work to degrade the Earth's surface by physical, chemical, and mechanical forces. Billions of tons of rock waste are removed annually by the erosional agencies of water, waves, wind, gravity, and glaciation. These agencies remove and transport surface material to new locations.

The Earth is undergoing a great denudation in the geological period of the Present. There is an average global lowering of the continental areas of 30.5 centimeters (1 foot) every 30,000 years. The Colorado and Mississippi Rivers together remove a cubic mile of sediment to the sea every year. In the case of the Colorado it is depositing enormous amounts behind its dams.

The global rainfall average is 30 inches which means the present landscape could be reduced to sea level in 25 million years.

EROSIONAL BASINS   There are a variety of erosional basins and many of them are basins of interior drainage. The major types are: Aeolian, fluvial and solution.

The aeolian basin is a wind-derived basin. Perhaps its greatest expression is the Qattara Depression of Egypt and Libya. This basin makes up the eastern 1/3 of the northern Sahara.

The fluvial basin is usually a small scour basin caused by flash flooding and eddying. These are 'tinajas' in southwestern United States.

The solution basin is created by water over soluble rock. Lakes constantly eat away at rock bottoms, deepening them.

ERRATIC BLOCK   An erratic block is a glacially transported boulder. It is often found on rock of a very different type.   These boulders may weigh tons. One in the Rockies is thought to have originated in the Hudson Bay area. These erratics are very obvious in glaciated terrain. It was boulders such as these that helped Agassiz to describe the process of glacial erosion.

ERTS   The Earth Resources Tracking Satellite (ERTS) is a major source of new data on mineral resources, vegetation distribution, flood and drought data, and crop and soil conditions.

The series of ERTS satellites has produced imagery of many otherwise inaccessible areas. They have also given us a global view of some of the planet's resources.

ERUPTION   An eruption is a violent volcanic emission of lava, pyroclastics, and gas from a crater or fissure. Magmatic material is channeled to the surface. Often ejecta build up around the crater.

Ejecta may be propelled explosively, usually by steam, or more quietly in flows. Widespread ashfalls may be erupted. In 1888, Bandai-san, Japan, erupted so violently it blew off the side of the mountain.   The ejected material was already rock.

EURASIAN TAIGA   The Eurasian Taiga is the largest single forested area on Earth. It stretches from Scandinavia to Siberia in the Sub-Polar Region. The forest has both evergreen and broadleaf trees but is dominated by conifers, especially fir and spruce. The vast area is noted for its permafrosted (q.v.) soils.

EUROPEAN EELS   The European eel has a remarkable life cycle. Leaf-like larvae are produced from pea-size eggs. From the spawning area in Sargasso Sea, the larvae drift on the Gulf Stream toward Europe. The 5,000 kilometer (3,000 mile) journey takes up to 3 years during which time larvae develop into elvers. When adult they will make the return journey to spawn and die.

EUSTATIC MOVEMENT Worldwide, there are changes in sea level due to many causes. Glacial advance or retreat is prominent among these. Many changes are almost imperceptible, others drastic.

Off some shores, such as the Pacific Rim, tectonic activity plays a great role in land and sea relationships. All global sea level changes are eustatic.

EUTROPHICATION The normal aging of a lake results in eutrophication. This is a process by which the body of water becomes enriched in minerals, nutrients, and organic detritus. The source of these may be natural or from treated and untreated effluents. As the materials build up, dissolved oxygen is depleted and more organisms die. This process progresses more rapidly In shallow waters. Pollution has caused the process to be accelerated in many important lakes.

In lakes where there is seasonal overturn these materials are brought to the surface waters. Decomposition of organic material leads to the formation of hydrogen sulfide which causes more death and decay.

When excess nutrients result in algal proliferation, a scum or mat forms. The oxygen level of the water drops as the algal mat shuts off air causing more organisms to die. The oxygen produced by the Algae (q.v.) is insufficient to compensate.

EVAPORATION Evaporation is the change in phase from liquid to vapor. Heat absorption can trigger the change. Warm moist air rises from the sea or land and warm, moist airmasses form. These are moved by global winds.

Evaporation from the ocean surface is the major source of rainfall. Evaporation is proportional to wind velocity and heat radiation over a damp soil.

In desert areas, evaporation is a special problem for water storage in open reservoirs. Annual losses from evaporation are great. The evaporation rate at Tucson, Arizona, is about 360 centimeters (90 inches) per year, greatly in excess of precipitation.

EVAPORITES Evaporites are created when evaporation causes salts to precipitate and concentrate. The principal sedimentary deposits created by this process are anhydrite, gypsum, potassium, salt, and at times calcium and magnesium (limestone and dolomite).

Evaporites are formed in sequence with the least soluble precipitating first. From seawater, calcium carbonate and iron oxide are first. These are usually found lowest in an evaporite sequence. They are followed by gypsum, a sulfate of calcium, then by salt or halite. Sulfates of magnesium and sodium are more soluble, so precipitate last.

Evaporites appear in the fossil record in the Precambrian (2 b.y.). Evaporites are forming today along the Arabian Coast, the Texas Coast, and in Australia. The most common evaporites are anhydrite, dolomite, gypsum, and halite. See **SABKHAS**.

EVAPOTRANSPIRATION   The temperature dependent process of evapotranspiration is an important part of the hydrologic cycle (q.v.). It is the evaporation that occurs from the surfaces of plants and animals. These transpire moisture into the Atmosphere.

MOUNT EVEREST   Everest, a peak in the Himalayas on the Nepal-Tibet border, is 8,830 meters (29,140 feet) high. It is the highest continental peak on Earth. Mauna Loa, Hawaii (q.v.) has a greater total elevation.

The slopes of Everest are covered by some of the largest alpine glaciers (q.v.) in the world. One of the largest is Khumba on the northwest flank.

EVERGLADES   The Everglades, the largest subtropical wilderness in the United States, is also one of the largest freshwater marshes in the world. It covers 8,330 square kilometers (5,000 square miles) in Southern Florida.

The main freshwater source is Lake Okeechobee. The drainage net is a complex system of rivers to which many canals have been linked.

Within the region there are higher locations which support pine and other tree growth. Sawgrass, a serrated sedge, is however, the dominant vegetation of the Everglades. It grows to 1.8 meters (6 feet) and is in a 108 kilometer (65 mile) wide band. Within the marsh area, there are low islands of palmettos and shallow ponds where the bald cypress is found. Along the coast is a dense mangrove growth in brackish waters.

The region is a habitat for 300 species of birds and many animals including the American alligator and otter.

That the Everglades Region is an emerging coastal plain is the consensus among geologists. However, Professor Petuch, Florida International University, believes the Everglades is a 2,830 square kilometer (1,700 square mile) impact crater.

The asteroid supposedly impacted the area 38 million years ago excavating the limestone. There are fractures in the limestone and intimations of a metallic core in the impact area 58 kilometers (35 miles) southwest of Miami, from which high magnetic readings are received through the mud. In this area, the Ocala Formation has been blasted away. The rim of the crater shows vestiges of coral.

EVOLUTION   Evolution is a concept of how lifeforms changed and developed through geological time. It is based on fossil evidence and upon knowledge of species' changes through breeding of animals and plants.

The changes are gradual and orderly and organisms grow from simple to complex to specialized. Often this last quality has resulted in an inability to survive through further environmental change.

Evolution presupposes that all life is related. It does not negate creation, as so often implied, rather it expands the form that creation takes and sees it as an continuum rather than a single event.

EXCLUSIVE ECONOMIC ZONE The Exclusive Economic Zone (EEZ) is a belt in which a nation has the right to the fruits of the ocean for 300 kilometers (200 miles) offshore. Many nations have stipulated that their frontiers are at this limit.

Agreements have been made to respect these limits for fisheries, but disputes still abound.

EXFOLIATION Exfoliation is gradual unloading of pressures stored in granite or gneiss. These pressures built up in the rock formations when the batholiths (q.v.) were intruded. Rocks spall off due to expansion as the overlying weight is removed.

Although exfoliation is a characteristic means of decomposition in granite and gneiss, it can also occur with sandstones and other resistant, homogeneous, or very fine-grained rocks.

Variations in temperature are responsible for changes in the rock permeability allowing moisture to collect and ferrosilicic solutions come to the surface by capillary action (q.v.). The solutions produce a veneer on the underside of the separating section and a build-up of clay occurs which furthers the detachment process. The onion-like peeling off of these rocks still has not been completely explained.

Exfoliation was formerly attributed only to temperature extremes. Experiments show these, by themselves, would result in grain-by-grain disintegration rather than the scaling off of concentric layers.

Exfoliation is obvious in the granitic terrains of the world where the resulting rounded forms are prominent. Some spectacular examples of exfoliated landforms are Half Dome in Yosemite, California, and Sugarloaf in Rio de Janeiro Harbor.

EXPLORER MISSIONS In 1986, the spacecraft Explorer flew by the planet Uranus obtaining photographs and data. Preliminary examination of the information has led scientists to speculate that planetary theory must be reevaluated. See **URANUS**.

The Explorer II Mission completed its fly-by of Neptune in 1989 and the data received will take years to assimilate. See **NEPTUNE**.

EXPLOSIVES The use of compact, instant sources of energy is often required in the extraction of petroleum and minerals. Explosives, like TNT (tri-nitrotoluene), require delicate handling, especially underground. Mineral extraction would be impossible without the explosives.

Explosions from both natural and induced sources create seismic waves. These waves are omnidirectional and are mostly 'p' waves (q.v.). Induced waves are the basis for seismic surveys.

EXTINCTIONS Species extinctions have occurred throughout geological history from varying causes. Statistics compiled in 1983 indicate that mass extinctions occur every 26 million years.

It is estimated that in the next 50 years, we will witness the destruction of 25% of all plant species and many animal ones. This is being caused largely by the impact of human activity on the global environment.

Evidence shows that 440 million years ago much marine life disappeared, while 250 million years ago 96% of all life disappeared including the last trilobites. The extinction of 65 million years ago, in which the dinosaurs disappeared, is called the 'Great Extinction' (q.v.).

LAKE EYRE Typical of many desert lakes, Eyre in Central Australia, is ephemeral. It is Australia's largest dry lake. The salt flat covers an area 150 x 83 kilometers (150 x 50 miles). The lowest part of the lake is 12 meters (40 feet) below sea level. The lake is a remnant of the inland sea that existed in wetter Tertiary times.

In size, Lake Eyre is one of the largest in the world. The present dry surface is covered with a film of salt. The lake only rarely fills. This event has been documented only twice since 1840. The drainage basin is 1,300,000 square kilometers (500,000 square miles).

The basin is a downwarp in the Earth's Crust which has been deepened by deflation (q.v.). The major rivers, the Diamantina and Coopers, normally die out in the desert before reaching the lake.

F

F LAYER The F Layer in the Atmosphere reflects high frequency (100 meter band) radio waves back to the Earth. It is the highest layer in the Ionosphere. The lower part of the Layer, the Appleton Layer, varies in thickness from 155 kilometers (93 miles) over Australia to 415 kilometers (250 miles) over England.

FACE In an open pit mine, surface wall rock with ore is called the face. The face is drilled in a grid pattern for the emplacement of explosive charges needed to break up the ore. A similar pattern is used underground on the ore-bearing wall, which also is referred to as the face.

FACIES Facies is the special composite of rock and fossils (when present) that makes up a particular sedimentary formation. Within a formation, the facies may change horizontally or vertically to reflect changes in the depositional environment or metamorphism. These changes may be transitional or abrupt.

Igneous rock facies refer to variations in texture or mineral composition. The facies reflects conditions in the magma (q.v.) at the time of cooling, later intrusions, or the presence of metamorphism.

FAIRWEATHER FAULT The Fairweather Fault may be traced from Lituya Bay in Alaska southeast across the Pacific Ocean to a spreading ridge (q.v.) off Vancouver Island. The fault continues to a junction off Point Arena on Cape Mendocino, California. The total distance is about 2,000 kilometers (1,200 miles).

Fairweather joins Mendocino Fault (q.v.) at a 'triple junction' with the San Andreas (q.v.). Both San Andreas and Fairweather trace a seam between the Pacific and North American plates. West of the faults, movement is northwesterly. The eastern plate is relatively stationary.

FALKLAND CURRENT In the South Atlantic, the Falkland Current breaks off from the West Wind Drift between Tierra del Fuego (q.v.) and Antarctica. It has been likened to the Labrador Current in the North Atlantic.

The current forms an eddy into the curve of the South American continent. It then flows north to merge with the Brazil Current which in turns returns the waters to the the West Wind Drift.

FALKLAND ISLANDS The Malvinas Isles are better-known as the Falkland Islands. They are in the South Atlantic Ocean east of the Argentinian tip. The islands, together with Sandwich, Shetlands, and South Orkney, are British.

Tundra climate prevails over the Falklands Islands. There are 59 species of birds that nest there and 5 types of penguins including the

King and Magellanic. A pastoral world, the islands are given over to sheep-herding.

There have been rumors of possible petroleum reserves offshore the Falklands. This may have been the real reason for the War between Argentina and Britain that broke out in the 1980's. Argentinian claims go back to colonial times.

FALL-LINE An escarpment or plateau edge is often marked by streams cascading to the plain in a series of waterfalls. The falls originate at roughly the same elevation.

A fall-line around a basin can be horseshoe-shape, or simply rectilinear. There is a striking, relatively straight fall-line along the Appalachians between the mountains and the coastal plain. A classical horseshoe fall-line rings the Amazon Basin.

FALLOUT Airborne particles settling out of the Atmosphere are 'fallout'. They may be radioactive material from a nuclear blast, volcanic ash, wind-blown sand, or other particulates.

FALLOW Good agricultural practice involves leaving ground uncultivated to recuperate minerals and nutrients. Often, the ground is seeded to hold and enrich the soils during this rest period. A favored rest crop in the American southwest is alfalfa.

The idle period, or fallow, varies geographically but is rarely under 3 years. Because of heavy leaching with rainfall, tropical and subtropical soils need much more than 3 years to be effective.

FALSE BEDROCK In many placers, a hard or tight formation is encountered well above bedrock. This horizon is usually a gravel cement. Gold may be found in the interstices and pockets of this false bedrock.

In some placers more than one cemented horizon is encountered depending upon the weathering and depositional history of the area. True bedrock may or may not be gold-bearing.

FAMILY Closely related plants and animals form a Family in the Taxonomic or Binomial Classification. Family subdivides into Genera and Species.

FANGLOMERATE Fanglomerate is a consolidated deposit found in the piedmont area of mountain ranges. Material varies from clay and silt to large blocks. Fanglomerate fragments are angular and sub-rounded indicating they have not traveled far. Fanglomerate is sometimes mistaken for glacial till (q.v.).

FAMOUS FAMOUS is the acronym for French-American Mid-Ocean Undersea Study (1974). 3 submersibles were used: Alvin (q.v.), Archimedes, and Cyana. Exploration between 2,180 and 2,900 meters (7,200 and 9,600 feet) of depth yielded evidence of new crustal material.

Studies concentrated on the inner floor of a 3.3 kilometer (2 mile) wide rift on the Mid-Atlantic Ridge. It was the area first noted as significant by the Glomar Challenger crew and Dr. Maurice Ewing. The small submarines made 44 dives photographing and continuously recording.

The rift's inner floor had parallel fractures varying from 15-90 meters (50-300 feet) wide and up to 0.8 kilometer (0.5 mile) long. From the fractures, the crew concluded the seafloor was being pulled rather than pushed apart. All material was basaltic.

FATA MORGANA Fata Morgana is a mirage or optical illusion. The original Fata Morgana was the image of spectacular city high over the Straits of Messina, Italy. It was named for Morgan La Fey, King Arthur's sister. She was the enchantress, who lured sailors to death.

FAULT A fault is a fracture in the Earth's surface along which there can be movement of one block in relation to another. They may occur anywhere. There are many types, such as normal or block, lateral, thrust, and transform.

A faultline is an intersection of a fault plane with the Earth's surface. Faultlines and attendant earthquakes, are often near continental margins (California and Chile).

The fault plane is the surface where movement occurs. A scarp (q.v.) can result. Usually, fault scarps are steep but later erosion can alter them. Most scarps result from normal faulting or blocks moving vertically in relation to each other.

FELDSPAR Feldspars are a group of alumino-silicate rocks made up of lime, potash, and soda. Feldspar is found in almost all igneous and metamorphic rocks. It is the most abundant mineral after quartz. The feldspar crystals have been called 'oblong packages', which they resemble. They are colorless to pink, yellow, or green. The difference between the 2 major groups is the predominance of either potash or soda-lime.

The Groups are the Potash and the Plagioclase. Orthoclase and microcline make up the potash feldspars. Their crystal structures are different. Orthoclase is monoclinic while microcline is triclinic. The Plagioclase Group is an isomorphous series from albite to anorthite. The end member, albite, is a sodium mineral. Anorthite, the other end member, is a calcium mineral. The group is also called the Soda-Lime Feldspars.

Feldspars weather to clay. Aluminum goes into solution and stays there if the pH (q.v.) is less than 4 or greater than 9. (Aluminum hydroxide will precipitate only from a neutral and saturated solution). Silica from feldspar remains in solution reacting with aluminum to form the clay.

Industrial feldspar is commonly mined from pegmatites (q.v.). Crystals can be large. Some from the Black Hills and Carolinas have been spectacular.

Moonstone, a popular gemstone, is orthoclase and albite. It is sometimes in the gangue of ruby mines. Amazonite is mostly microcline. It is a blue-green stone found in India and not in the Amazon.

FELDSPATHOIDS Feldspathoids are similar to feldspars but are alkaline aluminum silicates. They are found in igneous rocks with leucite, a potassium aluminum silicate, and nepheline, a sodium aluminum silicate. Sodalite and lazurite are feldspathoids.

FELLFIELDS Alpine Tundra 'fellfields', or stony fields on high mountain slopes, are also sometimes classed as Felsenmeer (q.v.). Fellfield rocks are medium-sized and are accompanied by sand and gravel. They host mountain wildflowers.

FELSENMEER Great aggregates of large broken rocks created by glacial plucking are 'Felsenmeer', German for rock sea. Felsenmeer are found on high mountain slopes above the timberline. They differ from Fellfields (q.v.) in rock size.

Boulder fields can be found on the White Mountain summits of New Hampshire. Fellfields are common in Scandinavia and in the Alps.

FELSITE Felsite is a very fine-grained igneous rock of alkali feldspar and quartz. It is a compact, relatively dense rock which has resulted from devitrification (q.v.). The color range is from pale pink to gray.

FEN 'Fen' is British for a saltmarsh or wetland. Most English fens have been drained to make way for farms and pastures. Originally they were salty peat bogs.

FENCE DIAGRAM Geologists use the fence diagram to illustrate the subsurface. Connecting lines are drawn between similar horizons found in wells, bore-holes, and outcrops. These reveal a 3-dimensional picture.

FENNOSCANDIA SHIELD The Fennoscandia Shield is the Precambrian (q.v.) continental platform extending from Norway and Sweden into Finland, and the Kola Peninsula and Karelia in the USSR. It is also called the Baltic Shield.

This shield area is comparable to the Canadian Shield, but is smaller. See **SHIELD**.

FENNOSCANDIA UPLIFT The tremendous load of glacial ice during the Pleistocene caused the Lithosphere to be depressed beneath Fennoscandia. About 10,000 years ago, the ice began melting and the Crust unloading. The area rose and is still rising. Numerous shorelines and islands attest to this uplift.

Western Sweden, where the icecap was assumed thickest, has risen 2 centimeters a year for at least 5,000 years. The uplift has been 60 meters (200 feet). The greatest rebound occurred in the Gulf of Bothnia. It amounted to a meter a century.

The region was ground down by glacial activity and the landscape is of hilly plains and low mountains alternating with lake basins. The predominant vegetation is northern Taiga Forest with the pine in the more rocky terrain; the spruce and birch on the less rocky. On the Kola Peninsula the vegetation is Tundra (q.v.) with only scattered birch.

FENSTER An erosional gap in an overthrust sheet or recumbent anticlinal fold is a 'Fenster', German for window. The gap exposes the underlying rock or sediments.

FERMI The 'fermi' is a unit equal to 10^{-13} centimeters. This is the approximate diameter of a proton (q.v.).

FERN A fern reproduces by spores rather than seeds. A single fern can have a billion spores. The plants have delicately traced fronds rather than leaves, They are found in sheltered areas of humid forests. In the Carboniferous (q.v.) some were seed-bearing.

FERRALITIC SOILS Ferralitic soils are humid tropical soils with aluminum or iron in the near-surface profile. They are very old, deeply weathered, and have developed under abundant rainfall and good drainage.

FERROCHROME Ferrochrome is a metallurgical product of chrome ore. Practically every chrome producer is converting to ferrochrome.

South Africa leads with an installed capacity of 800,000 metric tons per year. Transvaal chrome ore is low grade, made economic to convert to ferrochrome by low-priced electricity. Enormous coal reserves in the region make this possible.

Soviet production of ferrochrome is high, based on relatively high-grade but declining chrome deposits in the Urals.

The non-communist world had capacity to produce 2.27 million tons of high carbon ferrochrome by 1982. Actual production reached 1.7 million metric tons in that year.

In the United States, the General Services Administration converted 142,000 tons of stockpile chromite to high-carbon ferrochrome in 1982 and 92,000 in 1986. Congress has mandated the continuation of conversion of not less than 53,000 tons per year through 1993.

FERROMAGNESIUM Iron and magnesium minerals are generally dark and dense. In this group are rock-formers like augite, biotite, hornblende, and peridotite.

FERROMAGNETIC ELEMENTS The ferromagnetic elements include iron, nickel, cobalt, gadolinium, and dysprosium. They differ from other elements in that their atoms have incomplete inner shells (electrons in orbital planes). Iron, for example, begins to fill its outer shell with electrons before the inner one is complete.

In these elements the net electron spin is affected and 5 of the 6 outer electrons spin in one direction. This is the 'Ferromagnetic Effect'. It causes iron atoms to line up to form a permanent magnet in the presence of a magnetic field.

FERTILE CRESCENT The Fertile Crescent, a great arc stretching from Egypt through Jordan to Mesopotamia and the Persian Gulf, was the center of an ancient culture. The society was based on agriculture and was supported by great river systems. These were the Nile and its Delta and the Tigris-Euphrates System with its broad and muddy plains.

FERTILIZERS Fertilizers are important to increase crop yields and reliability. The major fertilizers are nitrogen, phosphate, and potassium.

Natural fertilizers are not sufficient for the high volume production needed for growing populations. So fertilizers are manufactured in large quantities. This production is larger than the production of common minerals like aluminum and copper.

Misused fertilizers can become pollutants. If nitrogenous fertilizers are excessive they can dissolve in wet weather and enter the rivers and lakes where they fertilize the Algae and upset the ecological balance. Excessive phosphates can also disturb this balance.

FETCH Fetch is the maximum distance over which wind blowing in a constant direction can generate ocean waves. From wind speed, direction, and fetch, wave heights are predicted.

FIELD CAPACITY The percentage of water retained in soil, despite gravity, is its field capacity. Water is held on soil particles by surface tension and is available to vegetation by capillary action (q.v.).

FIFTH FORCE A 'fifth force' is hypothesized to explain some of the effects of gravity on the Electromagnetic Field.

FILTER A filter separates materials from air, light, or liquid. Many minerals are used as filters, especially clays and zeolites.

FINENESS Fineness is the amount of pure gold contained in bullion (q.v.) or in a natural alloy. California placer gold averages 885 fine. Pure gold is 1,000 fine. Gold coins are usually 900 fine. English coins, however, are 917 fine.

Fine gold also describes gold that will pass through a 20-mesh screen, but will be contained by a 40-mesh. Screens are standard units of the American Society for Testing Materials (ASTM).

FINGAL'S CAVE Great basaltic flows once covered Scotland and Ireland. On Staffa Island, off Western Scotland, weathering has carved into the flows and created caves. The caves have pillars of basalt for walls.

The most well-known is Fingal's Cave, named for the legendary giant, protector of the islands. The cave is 18 meters (60 feet) above the sea and is cut 60 meters (200 feet) into the cliff. The walls give off a blue-grey sheen.

FIRE ASSAY A small scale smelting process for analysis is a fire assay. It is primarily used for gold and silver. The assay gives the metal content but not the purity. The use of the fire assay is very ancient. They were performed by the early Egyptians.

The assays are only guides. All reported gold may not be recoverable as it may be locked up with other minerals.

FIRE CLAY High temperature clays are used to line crucibles and furnaces. They are referred to as fire or refractory clays.

FIRE FOUNTAIN Rhythmic gas eruptions, common on Hawaii, come from rifts and fissures. This is especially true of Mauna Loa (q.v.). The gas eruptions create fountains of fire.

FIREDAMP Mine gases are called firedamp because they extinguish or damp the flames of miners' lamps. These lamps with open flames were used as mine sensors as well as for light. The lamps have saved many lives by indicating the presence of dangerous gases. The lamps begin to fade thus alerting the miner. Another system was to carry canaries into the mines. It was time to get out when the canary died. The lamps were more humane.

Modern mines have sophisticated sensors for mine gases but lamps are still in use in more primitive situations. Methane (q.v.) is the most common mine gas.

FIRN A firn is made up of unconsolidated glacial snows not yet ice. As the snow becomes more dense, crystals become more granular. Firn forms from snow that has survived one or more ablation (q.v.) periods.

In a firn basin, development of melt-freeze cycles occur with temperature changes, diurnally and seasonally. As firn freezes, ice crystals tend to be large and connect to form a crustal ice layer known to the Russians as 'nast'.

FIRTH 'Firth' is the Scottish equivalent of a fjord, or glacial valley that has been invaded by the sea. Firths are long sea arms resembling estuaries, but are narrower and deeper. Firth of Forth is Scotland's most famous inundated valley. See **FJORD**.

FISH Fish are cold-blooded vertebrates that first appeared in the Devonian Period (395-345 m.y.) which is known as the 'Age of Fishes'.

True fish are aquatic and cylindrical in shape. They are gilled for oxygenation, have a tail fin, and are often scaled. There are about 450 orders, 4,000 genera, and 20,000 fish species with a wide variety of habitats from small ponds to ocean depths. About 1/3 live in fresh-water. The temperatures that fish can tolerate range from -0° Celsius in Antarctica to 40° Celsius in hot springs. Deep sea fish are usually small and must rely upon falling plankton (q.v.) for food. Small species are prey for larger fish.

Prior to true fish development, the species coelacanth (q.v.) appeared with lungs and gills. Coelacanth is a creature between the fish and amphibian. It was considered extinct until a specimen was netted in the Indian Ocean in 1938.

FISHERIES Many societies depend upon fishing to subsist but the largest fleets belong to the more affluent nations. The annual catch is about 75 million tons. The 4 largest fleets and the percentage of each are:

> Japan 14%
> USSR 13
> China 6
> United States 5

Fisheries are confined to a narrow belt around continents. This belt is characterized by depths which are not too great for light penetration. This is important for photosynthesis (q.v.) to occur. Also, in this confined belt the species are more abundant because the food-chain is longer than in the open ocean.

The catch itself is from relatively few over-fished species. The types sought depend upon tradition and market conditions. Modern fisheries are not only over-fishing favorable areas but are extreme wasteful of the unpreferred species. In recent years, there has been a growing tendency to use drift-nets. These huge net scoop up everything and when fish and sea mammals become entrapped they are often slaughtered. There are no size restrictions. The latest depradations of these fisheries has been in the Mediterranean Sea.

Reduction of a particular population can profoundly affect others. Over-fishing anchovies off Peru caused the demise of the industry. The anchovy virtually disappeared due to over-fishing and the adverse effects of El Nino (q.v.). The rhythmic exchange between anchovy and sardine was not taken into account.

Not only were species numbers diminished, but birds and other fish populations dependent upon them were also reduced.

Rivalry among fishing fleets has led to political confrontation. The institution of the Fish Conservancy Zone in 1977 created a 300 kilometer (200 mile) national preserve has reduced the pressures but violations are constantly reported.

FISHING A driller's term, 'fishing' is the attempt to retrieve drill-pipe and bits lost in a well. This is an extremely critical operation, especially if the loss could cause expensive well-abandonment.

FISSILE Extremely thin beds in sedimentary or metamorphic rocks are fissile. The bed thickness is under 2.0 millimeters. Fissile rocks are prone to flaking, as the micas; or to collapse, as with shales.

FISSION Fission is splitting the nucleus of an atom heavy enough to yield 2 lighter elements. A vast amount of energy is released together with neutrons.

Fission can occur spontaneously but it is usually triggered by nuclear absorption of gamma rays, neutrons, or particles. The most notable natural fission was at Oklo, Gabon and it began billions of years ago in the Precambrian. See **OKLO**.

FISSURE A natural rift in the Earth's Crust longer than wide is a fissure. Rifts in cooled lavas are fissures; in other rocks faults. Giant cracks in the Earth's Crust have released floods of lava. Flow remnants form plateaus covering hundreds of square kilometers. See **DECCAN PLATEAU**.

The most voluminuous basalt flows in the Recent were in Iceland and in Kamchatka, USSR. See **FLOOD BASALTS**.

FITZ ROY MASSIF The Fitz Roy Massif in the southern Andes is a batholith (q.v.). It has exposed spires, needles, and pinnacles above the snow-fields. These features resulted from vertical fracturing of the exposed granite and exfoliation (q.v.).

FJELD Barren, upland or plateau country, in Scandinavia is called 'Fjeld'. It is a Tundra landscape on the Fennoscandia Shield (q.v.) with outcrops of Precambrian (q.v.) rocks.

FJORD The fjord is a narrow arm of the sea extending inland an average of 40 kilometers (24 miles) with depths up to 600 meters (2,000 feet). The longest is Nordvest Fjord in Eastern Greenland which extends inland for 313 kilometers (194 miles).

The fjord is the seaward end of a glacial valley and is narrower than an estuary. Glaciers cut into elevated shorelines and submerged the land. Depression of the land level under the weight of the ice allowed marine transgression. Fjords are U-shaped, as are all glacial valleys.

FLAGSTONE Flagstone, often used for decorative pavement, is a thin-bedded sandstone, split into slabs. Flagstones are often selected for their natural colors.

FLASK The unit of measure for mercury is the flask. The standard iron flask contains 76 pounds (34 kilos) of mercury, or quicksilver.

FLINDERS RANGE In South Australia Flinders Range is composed of folded sandstones and siltstones that reflect abrupt shifts of climate. Today, the area is dry and hot in summer.

The 700 million year old sediments show annual depositions for about 900 years. These sediments were deposited by glacial meltwaters.

There is regular banding with dark clays, 1.3 centimeters (0.5 inches) apart with sandier material between. These are thought to reflect cycles of the Precambrian Sun.

Flinders Range has a saw-toothed ridge of resistant quartzite on the once-domed mountains. The mountains first appeared with thrusting 500 million years ago and were again thrust upward about 60 million years ago. They created the oval bowl, Wilpena Pound, when the dome broke. In all, the peaks rise 1000 meters (3,000 feet) above the arid plain.

FLINT Compact nodules of silica or chalcedony are flint. They are fossils of sponges and other marine organisms. Flints are dull in color, sharp-edged, and have angular cleavage. They are found in chalk beds where they are black to dark gray. The chalks of England are rich in flint.

Flints were mined by American Indians, particularly the Iroquois, who used them for tools. Rubbing 2 pieces of flint together produces a spark. This provided early man with a ready fire source.

FLOAT Float are erratic pieces of ore or rock from a known or unknown source. Some have been transported over a great distance. Float can be vein rock or mineral found far down-stream of its source.

Float specimens give indications of a past or present source of minerals. Glaciers transported material over great distances so the mapping of 'float trains' has been useful. In Finland this technique has been especially so.

Seeking the source of float, especially material rich in economic ores, is the task of prospectors, geologists, and geophysicists.

It is usually done without the aid of geochemistry although it is greatly enhanced by geochemical mapping.

FLOES Blocks of ice or 'floes' break off from the pack ice or ice sheets. These blocks range from very small to kilometers cubed. Floes are in continuous movement. When they collide they form ridges.

Floes move in tune with the pack ice (q.v.). Within the Arctic Ocean, they move clockwise. Floes can escape into the North Atlantic.

FLOOD BASALTS Highly fluid basaltic lavas erupted from large fissures in the Earth's surface. These flows were widespread, especially during the Mesozoic Age and Tertiary Period. Flood basalts are correlated with major rifting. Great basaltic plateaus were built by repeated lava flows covering up to 300,000 square kilometers (200,000 square miles). They averaged 500 meters (2,500 feet) thick. Flow remnants form great plateaus in Africa, Brazil, India, Siberia, and the United States.

FLOODPLAIN A periodically flooded level valley floor is a floodplain. Streams drop sediments as they spread out and lose velocity. As the area close to the main channel becomes smoothed, floodwaters tend to spread farther out, enlarging the plain.

FLOODS Floods result from torrential rains which cannot be absorbed by the soils so runoff swells rivers over their banks. Seasonal snow-melts also cause flooding, especially if a great warming follows particularly heavy winter snows.

In the United States there have been some spectacular floods in the Mississippi-Ohio drainage area. Many precautions and flood control projects have been instituted.

In California in 1861 a great deluge turned the San Joaquin and Sacramento Valleys into a 500 kilometer (300 mile) long lake, the width varying between 35-100 kilometers (20-60 miles). Sacramento was so flooded, the capital moved to San Francisco.

Not only the Sacramento Valley was affected but Santa Barbara's lowland as well. The city of Ventura had to be abandoned. The event was so devastating, California went bankrupt.

The following year the Los Angeles, San Gabriel, and Santa Ana rivers merged and the area between Signal Hill, near Long Beach, and Huntington Beach was inundated. This was caused by a storm that formed at sea and arrived without warning.

Similar events are recorded in 1884-1891 and attributed to weather changes caused by the Krakatoa eruption. It was a time of torrential rains and violent cyclonic storms at sea. In 1891, the Colorado River at Yuma, Arizona was 33 kilometers (20 miles) wide.

FLORIDA PENINSULA The Florida Peninsula is a limestone shelf composed of marine organisms. It grew in warm subtropical waters where the environment met the needs of coral (q.v.) and other marine life. The shelf is partly emerged and is a wedge dipping south. See **EVERGLADES**.

FLOTATION The process of floating objects or ore in water and other fluid media is flotation. Archimedes discovered that if an object weighs less than an equal volume of water, it will float in it; if more it will sink.

Flotation is the favored chemical process of ore separation. Agitated ore is floated in an acid or caustic soda solution until it can be taken off as a froth or precipitated.

Mineral separation was only by gravity until 1911 when flotation was introduced. With copper concentration, 67% is recovered by gravity; 90% can be recovered by flotation.

FLOW BANDING Silicious lavas often show layering or flow banding. The flows may be alternations of different mineralogical layers. Each represents a different time frame.

FLUORINE Fluorine is a pale yellow, gaseous element, never found free in nature. It reacts with nearly all elements. It forms fluorides with metals. Excessive fluorides in natural waters can be toxic.

FLUORITE Fluorite is an isometric mineral crystallizing in cubic form. Fluorite has perfect octahedral cleavage. It can be of different colors, among them purple, yellow, and red. The mineral fluoresces under ultra-violet light.

Flourite is widespread and often associated with metal deposits as part of the gangue (q.v.). The major ore is fluorspar, a massive, crystallized fluorite. It is often found in limestones.

The world's fluorspar resources are 362 million metric tons. Of these the USSR holds 30%. The breakdown of proven and indicated reserves for 1987 are compared with the proven economic reserves of 1989* (in millions of metric tons) is:

	1987	1989
USSR	104.0	61.68
Mongolia	65.0	49.89
South Africa	40.0	29.02
China	25.0	17.23
Mexico	24.0	18.14
United States	11.0	NA
France	10.0	6.35
Spain	9.0	6.35
Brazil	8.0	NA
Italy	8.0	6.35
Kenya	3.0	1.81
United Kingdom	3.0	1.81
Thailand	2.0	.91

DNPM, Brazil (1988)

U.S. Bureau of Mines 1990

* The discrepancies relate to Bureau's new approach to reserves.

Production in the United States is largely from the Fluorspar District of Illinois and Kentucky, once the world's largest producer. Production is from fissure veins, sedimentary replacement deposits and residual gravels.

Today the world's major production is from Mexico and Mongolia. Both produce 15%. Much of Mexico's production comes from the deposits in the Sierra de Encantada, Coahuila, where the fluorspar is in 'manto' or blanket deposits.

Fluorspar is used as a flux in metallurgy. When especially pure, above 90%, it is used in acid production. With the increasing concern for the Ozone Layer's (q.v.) deterioration, production of chlorofluorocarbons, CFC's (q.v.), has been reduced in the United States.

FLUORESCENCE Fluorescence is the quality of minerals to absorb ultra-violet rays and alter them to slower rays. The effect is a color change. White calcite will turn rose red. Ultra-violet lamps used in darkened areas pick up this phenomenon. Fluorescence can be used to identify some minerals. The color displays can be beautiful.

FLUVIATILE PLACERS Stream or fluviatile placers are commonly found on the convex side of meanders. Placers develop where stream flow is diminished.

FLUX 'Flux' is from the Latin for flow. Flux or energy flow across a unit area at right angles to the lines of force of the Electromagnetic Field (q.v.) is flux density, or magnetic induction. It is measured in webers (q.v.) per meter squared.

In metallurgy, a flux is an additive used to increase the fluidity of a melt and reduce the melting point.

FLY ASH Fly ash is soot and ash in flues or in the air above coal-burning plants. Fly ash particulates are often radioactive. The Environmental Protection Agency (EPA) released new emission standards in 1985 to reduce fly ash emissions into the Atmosphere.

FLYSCH Marls, clays, shales and sandstones bordering the Alps on the north and south flanks are 'flysch'. The deposits, derived from the uplifting and eroding mountains, are sandy and calcareous. Flysch is made up of thin, regular, and cyclical bedding.

Flysch sediments were laid down in intermontane basins created during the folding episodes. Interbedded marine shale and greywacke (q.v.) were probably deposited by turbidity currents (q.v.) from the rapidly uplifting mountains.

FLYWAYS Migrating birds have distinctive flyways. There are 4 major flyways in the United States:

Atlantic	-	Follows the Appalachians from Maine to Georgia
Mississippi	-	Follows river system to the Gulf
Central	-	Follows the Front Range from Montana to New Mexico
Pacific	-	Broad belt from the Pacific to eastern Idaho, Utah, and Arizona.

Along these various flyways, the government has set up many preserves and the waterfowl use them extensively.

FOCUS The origin area of an earthquake is its focus; a region never a point. Earthquakes are classified with reference to focal depth:

Shallow	- Up to 60 kilometers (37 miles) are Crustal
Intermediate	- 60-310 kilometers (37-86 miles) are Mantle
Deep	- Greater than 310 kilometers (86 miles).

The deepest earthquakes recorded at 745 kilometers (447 miles) were below Flores Sea in Indonesia between Flores Island and Celebes.

FOEHN Cyclonic systems cross mountainous terrain, cooling and warming airmasses. Warm, dry wind blowing down the lee slope is a 'Foehn' in Europe. In the United States, it is a 'Chinook'(q.v.).

The Foehn on the north slopes of the Alps originated as a moist wind blowing over southern slopes. As the airmass rose it cooled and the clouds became moisture-laden. As it flowed down the north slope it heated under compression.

With a Foehn, snows melt and avalanches ensue.

FOG Any cloud of water vapor at ground level is a fog. Commonly, it is the result of cool air passing over the warm Earth during the nighttime hours.

In Central California, this results in 'Tule Fog', found found in low places. It rarely exceeds the height of the vegetation. It is hazardous for road travel.

Offshore cold currents along the South African, Californian, and Chilean coasts are responsible for virtually all moisture in the Atmosphere over these arid and semi-arid lands. Moisture is transported inland as a fog or marine layer.

FOLD Rock strata compress and fold from internal forces and pressures. Folding is part of the mountain-building process accompanying the collision of continental plates, possible diapiric (q.v.) activity, or sedimentary compaction.

Folds range from infinitesimally small to gigantic. They may be downfolds, or synclines, where central rocks are pushed down in relation to the limbs. Up-folds, or anticlines, are opposite. A reclining fold with one limb above the surface, is a monocline. The folds themselves may be referred to as symmetric, assymetric, and overthrust.

FOLD BELTS Throughout geological time great regional folding has occurred resulting in some huge mountain ranges. These events were episodic and date from the Early Proterozoic.

Fold belts are often mineralized. Some have been traced from continent to continent. See **APPALACHIANS**.

FOOD CHAIN The food chain highlights the biological interdependence among plants and animals. In the ecosystem, one organism supports another. Humans obtain food from both animals and plants. Animals feed on other animals or plants. In general, less complex animals are food for the more. Ultimately all depend upon plants.

The food chain transfers solar energy in the Biosphere. There are 3 chains of energy transfer:

      Predator Chain -   From plant to plant-eater to carnivore

      Parasite Chain -   An animal or plant is attached to a host and draws nourishment from it

Saprolite Chain - From decomposing plants and animals to micro-organisms.

A delicate balance is maintained in all these systems. A parasite can kill the host. In general, the shorter the food chain, the more population an area or region can support.

In Southeast Asia rice is used and, instead of meat, small fish are preferred to large. Less energy is required for the shorter food chain.

FOOTWALL In a mine or quarry, the footwall is the sediment or rock just below the ore-bearing layer, or vein.

The down-dropped fault block surface is a footwall in relation to the parent rock.

FORAMINIFERA Foraminifera are plankton, marine organisms of the Phylum Protozoa (q.v.). They have calcium carbonate skeletons. 'Forams' are small enough to escape being ground by drilling equipment. Some are so minute, a gram of sand can contain 50,000 shells. Fossil forams have been very useful markers in petroleum exploration.

Skeletons make up a considerable part of the calcareous ooze covering the floor of the western Indian Ocean, the South Pacific, and 2/3 of the Atlantic. In the Atlantic, Foraminifera ooze is up to 3,600 meters (12,000 feet) thick.

Most chalk deposits are of Foraminifera. There was a great development of forams in the Paleozoic (570-225 m.y.) and another in the Cretaceous (136-65 m.y.). Globergerina species (q.v.) is predominant in the Cenozoic (65 m.y. - Present).

Foraminifera, coral, and Algae are significant calcium carbonate reef builders. These organisms make up most of the 1.5 billion tons of calcium carbonate deposited each year. The Rubrum species is responsible for the sands of some pink tropical beaches.

Studies show Foraminifera are useful for determining relative water temperatures of the past. If they have a left coil, the waters were cold; if right, the waters were warm. See **FOSSILS**.

FOREDUNES Foredunes are coastal features with mounds averaging 3 meters (10 feet). Dunes are immediately behind the high-tide line. U-shaped ridges are common in Britain and along the east coast of the United States. These ridges are created from blowouts in the foredunes.

FORESTS Forests, great aggregations of tree growth, began 335 million years ago. Some 20% of the Earth's present forested areas are in the Amazon Basin. Most of the rest is in the Taiga Region (q.v.) which extends across Canada, Scandinavia, and the Soviet Union. The USSR holds 20% of the world's timber trees, 80% in Siberia. Timbering is not feasible in the tropical rainforests as the preferred species are normally dispersed and not in stands.

Once Europe was densely forested but the trees were felled for farms and fuel. In the United States, most forest is secondary growth and covers only a fraction of its original extent.

During the Ice Age, most of Africa was forested. Since, then climate especially of North and West Africa has become drier. The desert began encroaching on the savanna and continues to advance. Cutting fuel-wood (q.v.) and felling trees for agriculture have accelerated this desert advance in modern times. Remnants of subtropical and tropical forest are now threatened by over-population by humans and animals. See **DEFORESTATION**.

Forests are water reservoirs and a major part of the hydrological cycle (q.v.). They conserve water in the vegetation and in the soils. Continued deforestation threatens the world's water balance.

FOREST FIRES Forest fires destroy millions of hectares annually, causing massive disruption of watershed areas. Timber is destroyed which requires decades for regrowth. With forest fires gene pools are lost, sometimes forever. The terrain is opened to erosion and dessication.

Many fires are the result of violent thunderstorms, but more recently they are often caused by human action, accidental or deliberate.

Natural fire, if early enough, clears undergrowth and helps maintain greater safety for full-grown trees by removing the 'fuel ladder' created by the understories. Ash and mineral residue enrich soils for a short period and do help new growth. Letting a forest burn under adverse wind conditions, however, can create a disastrous situation such as occurred in Yellowstone in 1988.

In California, the Chaparral becomes tinder-dry and is subject to frequent burnings. Unusually heavy rainfall leads to a lush growth of brush and increases fire danger. After a fire, if the land is reseeded early, even with temporary grasses, erosion from the next rains may be curtailed.

FORMATION A formation is a complex of rocks and minerals with distinctive characteristics. It may be of sedimentary sequences or of regionally metamorphosed sediments.

Formations may be combined into Groups and Series and subdivided into Members. They are often set apart by unconformities (q.v.).

Formation members have a similar origin, age, and composition. Facies (q.v.) changes reflect the depositional environment or origin. There may be structural differences. A formation extends over a wide area and represents a definite time period.

It is the custom in North America and Australia to name formations for the locality where they were first or best described. This is the 'type locality'.

FOSSILS Fossils are preserved vestiges of organisms that are found in geological time horizons. They are useful for correlation, age dating, and some are distinctive to a single horizon.

Fossils are composed of the durable parts of organisms. These include shells, stems, tree trunks, and skeletons of animals. A fossil may also be an impression, or cast of an organism's soft parts made in damp sediments that later hardened. A fossil impression may be of a leaf or small organism with excellent or partial detail. Most casts are found in fine-grained consolidated silts and clays.

Petrified forests are excellent examples of fossils. Silica has replaced and altered wood and transformed it to stone, but cell structure and banding remain. The largest petrified forest in the United States is in Arizona.

Many exciting and interesting fossils of land animals have been discovered. These include the dinosaurs and the mammoth. In most instances the replacement material of the cells has been silica and the detail is excellent. Ice crystals preserved the mammoth in a virtually intact condition.

Marine fossil organisms have contributed much to our understanding of life in the seas both past and present. The numbers of marine fossils are staggering. Today they can be found atop the Alps and Himalayas as well as in basin sediments.

The oldest fossil of complex plants are possibly from the Siberian Cambrian (570-500 m.y.) rocks. The next oldest are found in the Australian Silurian (435-395 m.y.).

The oldest identifiable fossils are bacteria and blue-green Algae, both in the Prokaryota Super-Kingdom of one-celled organisms with no single nucleus. Fossils of this nature have been found in the Precambrian of Australia, North America, and South Africa in rocks over a billion years old.

FOSSIL FUELS Coal, oil, natural gas, and peat are fossil fuels. They developed from organic material deposited in the geological past. In the decaying process, hydrogen and carbon were released. These have resulted in huge hydrocarbon (q.v.) reserves.

Great forests covered large portions of the globe during the Pennsylvanian Period (300-280 m.y.). These forests decayed to become coal seams. Plant imprints are found in many of these seams. See **COAL**.

FOSSIL GROUNDWATER Water retained in the ground from an earlier geological time is fossil water. It is water trapped by rock arrangement and structure.

In areas of little rainfall, fossil groundwater is sometimes tapped for agricultural or industrial use. In many desert areas water supplies are from these fossil water sources. This is 'mined water' and the source can be depleted. Replenishment from rainfall or snow does not reach this supply. See **GROUNDWATER**.

FOUTA DJALLON Fouta Djallon, a west African massif, abuts the Guinea coastal plain. It is a sandstone plateau covering 78,000 square kilometers (30,000 square miles). It overlies the basement granite of the African Shield (q.v.). The plateau is cut by valleys and deep canyons.

Fouta Djallon is the source area of the Senegal and Gambia Rivers which flow to the north. It also supplies tributary streams to the Niger en route to the Gulf of Guinea. See **NIGER RIVER**.

FRACTURE A fracture is a structural break or a small fault. Fractures usually accompany faulting and jointing and reflect the shears involved. They may be almost microscopic as well as quite large.

A fracture zone is a great linear belt on the ocean floor with all the characteristics of faulted areas. It includes troughs, steep ridges, and subsidiary fractures. There are great fracture zones in the eastern South Pacific and Mid-Atlantic.

Fracture is also the way in which a mineral breaks. It is referred to as earthy, even, or uneven and is related to cleavage (q.v.). The most distinctive fracture is conchoidal. It can be seen in quartz and flint.

FRACTIONATION Fractionation separates crude oil into components by distillation. Each fraction has its own boiling point allowing separation. Heated crude is pumped into towers. Lighter components vaporize readily and seek the tower top where they cool and condense at different levels. These lighter components include gasoline, kerosene, and light fuel oils which are drawn off.

FRAM STRAIT The strait between the Greenland Sea and the Arctic Ocean is the Fram. It is the main outlet for ice from the Arctic. It is also the northern extreme of one Gulf Stream branch.

Fram Strait is where cold Arctic waters meet the relatively warm Atlantic waters. SAR (Synthetic Aperture Radar) is being used to study the area to determine whether sea ice is an indicator of climate change.

FRANCIUM A radioactive alkali metal, francium is obtained through the bombardment of thorium. It is a daughter (q.v.) element of actinium and not found in nature.

FRANZ JOSEF GLACIER The Southern Alps of New Zealand form a high mountain wall on the west coast of South Island. They receive sufficient precipitation and are high enough to be glacier capped.

One of the glaciers is Franz Josef, named for the Austrian Emperor. It originates in a cirque at 2,700 meters (8,850 feet). The ice stream is 500 meters (1,600 feet) wide and it extends to 300 meters (1,000 feet) above the sea. Its movement is marked by advances and retreats. The overall velocity of movement is 1.5 meters (5 feet) per day. The glacier feeds into Waiho River and a subtropical valley with luxuriant rain-forest growth.

FRASCH PROCESS The Frasch Process is a system for extracting sulfur from deep reservoirs. Concentric pipes are driven into a deposit and superheated water (180° Celsius) is poured into an outer ring. Compressed air is forced down the center and molten sulfur is forced up a middle ring. The dried product is pure sulfur.

FRASER RIVER From its source in the Canadian Rockies the Fraser River crosses the British Columbia Plateau. Its headwaters are near the United States border.

The north flowing Fraser has cut a spectacular 160 kilometer (100 mile) canyon through the Coast Mountains along an ancient fault line. Vegetation and climate change dramatically from one end of the canyon to the other. The transformation is from a semi-arid sagebrush region to a dense rainforest.

After emerging from the canyon, the Fraser River flows west and south to Vancouver and the Pacific Ocean.

FREAK WAVE When ocean waves collide at an angle, they break and reform into a particularly forceful or 'freak wave'. Many freak waves are found off Cape Mendocino, California, an area of upwelling (q.v.).

FREE FALL We have 'free fall' when acceleration goes to zero and a constant velocity is reached. The actual point of free fall depends upon air density and the shape and density of the falling body. It varies with temperature and altitude. Objects in free fall move in a straight line.

FREE-MILLING Gold and silver readily released by crushing and mixing are 'free-milling'. They do not require roasting or chemical treatment.

FREQUENCY Frequency is the number of complete waves passing a given point per second. The oscillations may be of water, sound, or electricity. Frequency is a measure of vibration or revolutions per second.

FRESHWATER The most essential resource for most non-marine life is freshwater. To be designated as 'fresh', it must have less than 1,000 milligrams per liter of dissolved solids. Freshwater has a density of 1 gram per cubic centimeter.

Only 1/3 of 1% of all freshwater is available and much of this is lost since precipitation is unevenly distributed. Water is impure in the Polar areas so at McMurdo Sound, Antarctica, water is distilled using nuclear power. See **RAINWATER**.

FRIABLE Rocks that readily fractionate are friable. This property is used to identify rocks and minerals. If friable, the simplest pressure will cause them to break apart.

FRONT The boundary zone between airmasses is a front. It is named for the displacing airmass, whether warm or cold. If neither airmass displaces the other, a 'stationary front' occurs and the weather remains unchanged.

FRONT RANGE A range of mountains in a chain rising directly from a plain is called a 'front range'. In the United States, the most well-known is the Colorado Front Range.

FROST Crystalline ice coating objects or bodies when temperatures go below freezing is frost. Moisture coating on leaves will turn to frost at freezing. Sometimes, this outer coating protects plants. Frosts are described as light, heavy, or killing.

Rock weathering can be caused by repeated freezing and thawing, or frost action. Ice crystals form in tiny fissures causing pressures that are released abruptly when thaw occurs. The fissures grow and the rock surface is fractured. This process is assisted by the roots of small plants creating wider cracks in the rocks.

Frost lifts the ground surface and the humps that result are 'frost heaves'. These usually occur at thawing. Soils saturated with water again freeze and expand. In cold climates and mountain areas frost heaving is responsible for the many breaks in roads. Annual repair costs are enormous in the United States.

'Frost hollows' are small valleys or basins where cold air settles. Near-surface air, cooling at night, becomes dense and tends to flow downhill as gravity wind, causing frost to develop in low areas.

FUEL CELLS Fuel cells operate very like batteries but they do not have to be recharged. The most common fuel cells are operated with hydrogen and oxygen. These form water and the transformation releases energy.

Fuel cells as a source of power are still under study. A fuel cell built by United Technology had 400-500 stacked cells giving off 11 megawatts of power. This was sufficient for half a million homes.

FUELWOOD In Third World countries 2 billion people suffer from a fuelwood shortages. In 65 countries, supplies do not meet demands. In some countries fuelwood cost reaches $200 a year or about 40% of total income. 50% of the fuel is used for cooking, which is essential to health. A kilo of rice requires a kilo of fuelwood.

In some countries, gathering of a day's needs requires a minimum of a day's work. This collection usually falls to women and children.

Fuelwood is being harvested faster than the regrowth rate. In many subtropical woodlands or savannnas, the ecosystem is under great pressure. Savannalands are not the only areas in peril. Tropical rain-forests are also being cut for fuel.

The fuelwood deficit by the year 2,000 is estimated at 860 million cubic meters or 50% of the demand (United Nations). Its cost is estimated at $2.6 billion a year. See **DEFORESTATION**.

MOUNT FUJIYAMA Japan's highest mountain is Fujiyama volcano. It is 3,776 meters (12,388 feet). Fuji is on the south coast of Honshu Island 100 kilometers (60 miles) from Tokyo. The beautiful cinder cone (q.v.), which is considered classic, forms the crater wall.

Fujiyama is a stratovolcano (q.v.) composed of alternations of lava extrusions and the residue of more violent eruptions. The present volcano is built on material from 2 known prior ones. It last erupted in 1707.

FULGURITE Glassy, slender, tubular, fused quartz grains are fulgurite. They have a branched shape and are sometimes a meter long.

It is conjectured that fulgurites were fused by lightning. They are usually found on mountain tops and atop crags. The greatest number of fulgurites have been found in Libya and Tunisia. It appears that fulgurites fused long before the Present.

FULLER'S EARTH Fuller's Earth is attapulgite or montmorillonite clay with accessories (q.v.) of kaolin, illite, and halloysite. The primary minerals make up 90% or more of the clay. These clays have low plasticity, high water content, and most have a high silica to aluminum ratio. They are good decoloring agents. Their most important characteristic is their adsorptive (q.v.) power.

FUMAROLE A vent in the Earth's Crust from which gas and steam can escape is a fumarole. The gases and vapors may come from great depths. Some bring minerals to the surface. Examples are found in Yellowstone National Park in Wyoming and in the Valley of Ten Thousand Smokes in Alaska.

BAY OF FUNDY The world's highest recorded tides are in the Bay of Fundy, between New Bruswick and Nova Scotia in Canada. Tides are high twice a day. They pile water up to 12-15 meters (40-50 feet). An attempt is being made to harness the tides as an energy source.

Fishermen string their nets across the mouth of the bay to catch the fish the tidal force brings in.

FUSION Fusion, the opposite of fission, occurs when 2 small atoms are joined to form a larger atom. In the process some matter is lost as energy. Greater energy is released by fusion than by fission (q.v.).

South Cascade Glacier — at foot of Sentinel Peak, Washington
Courtesy of US Geological Survey

G

'g' The universal gravity constant, 'g', represents the gravitational force of a mass, or body, at rest. The attractive force is reflected as weight. The accepted 'g' value for the Earth is 5,519 grams per cubic centimeter.

When a spaceship reenters the Atmosphere, a braking force is exerted. In the case of Apollo, the force on the astronauts was 7 g's, or 7 times their own weight. See **GRAVITY**.

GABBRO Gabbro is a basic igneous rock composed of plagioclase feldspar, clinopyroxene (labradorite and augite), with some olivine or hornblende. The dark minerals give it a dark gray-green color. It is coarsely grained and of granitic texture. Gabbro contains no quartz. Common accessories are apatite, iron, and magnesium.

Consolidated at depth, gabbro can be found in such structures as lopoliths, dikes, and dike complexes.

GABON Located in equatorial West Africa, Gabon is underlain by Precambrian shield rocks upon which sedimentary basins have developed. The Ogooue River Basin covers the eastern 2/3 of the country. The river rises in the lakes south of Lambarene. The Chaillu Massif separates the basin from the south coastal plain. The massif forms a series of plateaus which merge into the Crystal Mountains.

Gabon was once 2/3 covered by rainforest. Where the forest is accessible to the coast and the Trans-Gabon Railway, it is being rapidly logged off, especially of its hardwoods. The coastal forests are almost gone.

The mineral reserves of Gabon include the world's 4th largest reserves of manganese, 200 million metric tons of economic grade. In addition, there are 500 million metric tons of high grade (65%) iron ore. Other important minerals are uranium, gold, and diamonds. See **OKLO**.

Petroleum is responsible for 2/3 of Gabon's exports and 60% of its GNP (Gross National Product). The petroleum reserves are estimated at 480 billion barrels (66 million metric tons) and the natural gas at 14 billion cubic meters (490 billion cubic feet).

GABON ESTUARY The Gabon Estuary is formed by the Como and Mbei rivers which rise in the Crystal Mountains. They form the drowned valley which is an arm of the Gulf of Guinea. The estuary once was noted as the best harbor on the West African Coast. See **ESTUARY**.

GADOLINIUM The Rare Earth (q.v.), gadolinium has the characteristic of ferromagnetism when below 16° Celsius. This low Curie point (q.v.)

above which ferromagnetism cannot survive, makes the metal important for heat sensitive magnetic components.

GALAPAGOS HOT SPOT In the Galapagos Rift at a depth of 2,500 meters (7,500 feet) the Alvin (q.v.) crew found '5 oases in a wasteland of basalt pillows'. Each has a vent exuding hot mineralized waters rich in hydrogen sulfide, a food for bacteria which in turn produce carbohydrates (q.v.). They are the beginning of a food chain (q.v.).

Associated with the hot spots or vents is a spreading zone in the geologically young ocean floor. Continental crust near the zone is thin, and is being added to by basalt ejections from the rift.

GALAPAGOS ISLANDS The Galapagos Islands, south of the Equator are part of Ecuador. Land area is 5,000 square kilometers (3,000 square miles) in 38,300 square kilometers (23,000 square miles) of sea.

The Islands are a refuge for giant sea turtles and many birds. The oldest islands have fossils dating from 2-3 million years.

GALAXY An enormous collection of stars, planets, gas, and dust moving through Space is a galaxy. The whole is held together by gravity (q.v.). The galaxy is the largest known grouping of matter in the Universe. Galaxies form groups or clusters. Giant elliptical galaxies, contain trillions of stars. Some emit radio waves.

Milky Way (q.v.), home galaxy for the Earth, has 100 billion stars. The Milky Way and Andromeda are spiral galaxies. They are hundreds of thousands of light years (q.v.) across. Astronomers think there are a greater number of planets than stars in these galaxies.

In 1987, 2 brilliant galactic arcs of blue light were discovered. It was conjectured that it would take 100 million supernova exploding simultaneously to create that arc effect over hundreds of trillions of miles.

GALE Wind is at gale force on the Beaufort Scale (q.v.) when its velocity exceeds 50 kilometers (30 miles) per hour.

GALENA The richest lead ore, galena, is a compound of lead and sulfur. The dense, gray mineral crystallizes in the cubic habit. Galena is found in calcareous rocks and veins. It is often in association with silver.

Lead production in the United States is mostly from the southeast Missouri lead-zinc deposits. Other important producers are Poland's Silesia and Australia's Broken Hill (q.v.).

Lead has many uses. It is particularly important because accumulated sheets of lead provide protection against radiation, particularly from X-rays and gamma-rays.

GALILEO Galileo (1564-1638) performed experiments to test the force of gravity. He dropped cannonballs from the top of the Tower of Pisa (Italy) to check velocity. A heavy ball and a lighter one were dropped. Both took the same time to hit the ground.

Galileo's astronomical observations proved Copernicus correct in his deduction that Earth revolves around the Sun and is not the center of the Universe.

GALLERY FOREST The forest fringe along a stream channel in tropical grasslands is a 'gallery forest'. Cottonwoods and willows grow where flooding is frequent. Acacia and other savanna trees are on higher banks.

GALLERIES Galleries (kanats, ganats, qanats) are underground tunnels for transporting water in the arid Middle East. Many of them are very ancient.

Iran has 30,000 such tunnels. From North Africa to Central Asia there are about 500,000 kilometers (300,000 miles) of galleries. Some are still in use.

These remarkable works of engineering not only transported water but also protected it from evaporation by solar radiation.

GALLIUM The 'dispersed element', gallium, is widespread in occurrence, but no ore exists. Gallium metal is recovered as a by-product from some bauxite aluminum production.

In 1986, consumption in the United States was 15,000 kilos (33,500 pounds) and 17,000 kilos were imported primarily from France. Previously, Switzerland had been the major supplier. Japan's production was expected to reach 10,000 kilos by the end of 1986. Elkem, the Norwegian firm, will produce at the Bremanger Smelte-verk 5,000 kilos a year of 99.95% gallium from aluminum waste. The output will be 10% of world production (1987).

The United States has begun gallium production from Utah copper tailings. It expects to produce 10,000 kilos of gallium, which will about meet U.S. demand in 1990. This facility will also recover germanium (q.v.).

The major gallium use is in electronics for light-producing diodes and visual display panels. It is a valued semiconductor (q.v.). Gallium is non-toxic but can be toxic when alloyed with arsenic in gallium-arsenide.

GALVANOMETER A galvanometer is a charge measuring device. The instrument uses electromagnetism to detect currents. Seismologists set off a dynamite charge and measure the generated waves as they pass through the Earth. Wave velocities indicate rock densities.

GAMMA RAYS High energy protons associated with atomic break-up are gamma rays. They have the shortest and highest wavelengths of the known Electromagnetic Spectrum. The particle stream is considered a cosmic ray (q.v.).

Gamma rays are released as atoms disintegrate. They travel at the speed of light and have no mass or charge. Gamma rays are penetrating and protection, or shielding, is needed against the radiation. Lead is the most common form of protective shielding.

GANGES RIVER Originating in the Gangotri Glacier (Cow's Mouth Cave) at 3,927 meters (12,960 feet) in the Himalayas, the Ganges River drops about 3,300 meters (11,000 feet) to the plain. The river slopes another 300 meters (1,000 feet) to the Bay of Bengal. In the last few hundred kilometers the gradient is negligible.

The Ganges is one of the world's big rivers. It is 2,500 kilometers (1,500 miles) long. Its valley is between the Himalayas and the hills of central India. The Kosi River, a tributary, rises near Everest.

The Hooghly contributes to the Delta of the Ganges-Brahmaputra Rivers. The Hooghly and the West Delta are in India, the East Delta is in Bangladesh. See **BRAHMAPUTRA RIVER**

The Ganges-Brahmaputra Delta is the world's largest (75,000 square kilometers (30,000 square miles). Delta alluvium is 900 meters (2,970 feet) thick. The sediments are built up well into the middle of the Bay of Bengal. The delta area has been depressed over time. Land animal fossils have been found in cores retrieved from 100 meters (300 feet beneath sea level.

In the 1988 flooding of the delta, 1/3 of Bangladesh was underwater. Since the area is the world's most populous in terms of density per square kilometer the affect of the enormous flood was devastating.

GANGUE The uneconomic part of a vein is gangue. Much gangue is devoid of even potential value, so ore-to-gangue ratios are critical in any economic analysis of a mine.

GARNET Garnet is a group of aluminum silicate minerals with 6 related subspecies with a similar isometric crystal habit. They are found dispersed in igneous rocks and are common erosional products in stream and beach placers.

Garnet is a natural abrasive and has many industrial uses. The most valued abrasive is almandite, an iron-aluminum silicate, found in contact metamorphic zones in limestones, schists, and serpentine. The major economic source in the United States is from Gore Mountain, New York.

Some garnets are prized as gemstones. During the 18th and 19th centurys pyrope garnets from Czechoslovakia were fashionable. The pyrope garnets are red and of magnesium-aluminum silicate. Demantoid garnets from the Urals are green and have more fire than diamonds. A green garnet found in South Africa is 'Transvaal Jade', and a red one, 'Cape Ruby'. Accessory minerals determine the color and type of garnet.

GARNIERITE Garnierite, an important nickel ore, is a secondary product from nickel-bearing olivine rocks, the result of lateritic weathering.

The major producer of garnierite has been New Caledonia. There are large deposits in Brazil, Colombia, Cuba, and Central America. See **LATERITE**.

GAS The vapor phase of matter is gas. Of the many gases in the Atmosphere the most important are oxygen, carbon dioxide, and nitrogen.

In gaseous diffusion, a gas can be separated by passing it through a membrane. The separation can be atomic or molecular. See **NATURAL GAS**.

GASAHOL Gasahol is a gasoline substitute of largely organic origin. Brazil was one of the leaders in converting automobiles to use gasahol with successful results. By 1986, 1 in 10 cars was burning gasahol, a saving of $2 billions in annual petroleum cost. This really means a savings in foreign exchange since the gasahol was produced from the natural biomass of the country.

Conversions in the United states have been relatively few although we have a large biomass waste and gasahol has been proven to be an effective fuel.

GASOLINE The petroleum distillation product, gasoline, requires 20 times as much water as petroleum to produce. A barrel (q.v.) of crude oil will yield 17.8 gallons of gasoline.

Gasoline is the fuel of choice for cars in the United States. It has been shown that 15% ethanol mixed with gasoline makes an excellent fuel and may be more used in the future. See **PETROLEUM**.

GASTROLITH Gastroliths are well-rounded, highly polished stones. They are believed to have been ingested by dinosaurs as a digestive aid. They are also called 'gizzard stones'.

GASTROPODS Members of the Mollusk Phylum, gastropods include snails and slugs. Gastropods are found in seas, in brackish water, in freshwater, and on land. Marine gastropods are benthic (q.v.). Some gastropods secrete from the mantle a shell-forming material.

Gastropods first appeared in the Cambrian (570-500 m.y.) and were particularly abundant in the Carboniferous (345-280 m.y.). Some are useful indicator fossils.

GeV The notation for the giga-volt is GeV. It is equal to a billion electron volts. It is the energy required to move 1 electron through 1 volt. This is a unit used in atomic energy.

GEANTICLINE Great arching of the Earth's Crust results in a geanticline. A geanticline contains both anticlines and synclines superimposed on the main fold. The counterpart of geanticline is geosyncline (q.v.).

GEIGER COUNTER The battery operated Geiger-Muller Counter measures radioactivity. Positive ions are attracted to a long metal tube wall and are ionized by helium contained in the tube. The positive charge of new electrons causes the characteristic click. The charge is about 1,000 volts.

Alpha particles are stopped by the metal of the counter. Some beta particles penetrate the tube but it is mostly penetrated by the gamma particles. See **GAMMA RAYS**.

The Geiger Counter was a potent and inexpensive tool used in uranium exploration. It still finds favor for its use in the detection of radioactivity. Scintillometers are more precise.

GELIFLUCTION Gelifluction is downslope flow of material in areas where permanent ground ice persists. See **PERMAFROST**.

GENE The gene is the unit of germ plasm that controls heredity and by which characteristics are passed from the parent organism to its offspring. Chromosomes in genes determine the kind and quantity of inherited traits.

Genes are all-important in the species evolution. Genetic engineering by altering gene structure and the sequence of DNA (deoxyribonucleic acids) has altered some traits. The opportunity to correct many inherited disorders is promised in this work. Ethical problems associated with human genetic engineering are just being considered and are awesome.

Plants developed for agriculture depend upon wild gene pools for occasional crossing in order to keep the plants healthy and disease proof. Wild forms of staples may only make up a small percent of the gene structure but it can be critical to survival of a hybrid. Biological banks are being set up in some national parks and preserves.

It is well-known that healers in some forested areas use up to 10% of the known flowering plants as medicine. Only a minor number have been scientifically examined. Meanwhile, the plants are disappearing rapidly. The Central American gene pool is such an area and it is disappearing. See **GERM PLASMA**.

GEOBOTANICAL EXPLORATION It is widely known that some plants are indicators of specific minerals. They thrive in soils rich in these minerals. The profusion of a particular plant may indicate the presence of an ore body.

Geobotanical exploration in the United States has been limited to an accessory role. Its potential has not been developed.

Dunn, of the Canadian Geological Survey, has determined that the black spruce concentrates gold and platinum in the outer bark and in the twigs. The twigs also collect uranium. Arsenic, which is a pathfinder for gold, collects in the bark of the alder. Gold and platinum also concentrate in the pollen of fireweed.

Arctic carnations indicate copper. Yellow violets are good lead and zinc indicators. Locoweed in the American Southwest selectively accumulates selenium, a toxin that can kill cattle.

Root systems accumulate nutrients and minerals from the soils. The different root systems are adapted to their biomes (q.v.) and make of the plants visual indicators to soil horizons. Traditionally, soils have been analyzed but these only reveal the insoluble metals. It is very cost effective to analyze the vegetation.

GEOCHEMISTRY In recent oceanographic work, geochemistry has proven a valuable geological discipline. Ore-forming processes observable in many deep sea locations require geochemical interpretation. Geochemists have long contributed to the understanding of origin and development of rocks and minerals. The composition of planetary materials is their province.

Recent eruptions and earthquakes have presented some challenges. Some have been preceded by relatively large emissions of hydrogen gas, as much as 10 times normal. There are radon (q.v.) releases, particularly in wells, and an increase in chlorine in some mineral springs along faults. The environmental importance of all these dynamics require geochemical interpretation.

GEOCHRONOLOGY The geological time scale and its subdivisions are involved in the study of geochronology. In addition to correlation and paleontology this study is assisted by radioactive age dating (q.v.).

GEODE Geodes are hollow, sub-spherical rocks usually ranging in size from 2.5 to 30.5 centimeters (1 inch to a foot). The hollow is filled with druzy crystals of quartz or calcite. See **AMETHYST**.

GEODETIC SURVEY When continental surveys are made, the Earth's curvature is taken into account. Surveys of this type are 'geodetic'. The United States carries out coastal and geodetic surveys (q.v.) which support the mapping of the nation.

GEOGRAPHY Geographical studies include study of the physical planet as it relates to human activity. Biogeography, climate, the environment, and urban planning are given special attention.

A knowledge of the world and the forces operating in the natural, economic, and political arenas is becoming more important as global interaction becomes more and more a fact of life. It is the role of geography to address these issues as well as provide the information base for many of the decisions to be made by individuals, businesses, and nations.

Cartography or map making, one of the earliest activities of geographers, is an integral part of geography and is a fundamental tool in all geoscience. Today, the capability of computer enhancement of photographs from Space has added a new dimension to an ancient art.

GEOLOGICAL COLUMN The geological column is a graphic presentation, in gross terms, of the Earth's formations. They are presented with their relative ages as understood to date. The column graphically represents the relationship of rock units to each other through time. The column begins at the bottom in the Precambrian (4.6-5.0 b.y.) and progresses upward to the Recent and Present.

A particular portion of the column, given in more detail is a Geological Section. It identifies the ages and types of rock in a given area. It becomes more specific as it relates to smaller and smaller areas. Sections also present the oldest formation on the bottom unless the strata have been overturned by structural upheaval. The information reflected in a geological section is the result of the following:

- Review of all earlier work available on an area
- Data gathered in the field and direct work on the formations
- Interpretation of aerial photographs and other remote sensing
- Many laboratory studies of rock samples and cores if available.

GEOLOGICAL MAP The geological details of an area are presented in the form of a geological map. It ignores soils and the weathering mantle. Map information is from field work, aerial photography, and other studies.

Data are super-imposed on a base map. The base map may be topographic. The United States Geological Survey provides updated topographical sheets for most areas. If such a base map is not available, data may be plotted directly on aerial photographs and then converted to maps. All important geological phenomena are recorded to scale.

GEOLOGY The basic Earth Science from the physical point of view is geology. The word itself means 'study of the Earth'. Geology requires a unified approach to this planetary study. The mission is to look at the Earth as a whole, as part of the Solar System, and to become intimately aquainted with its smallest particles. The knowledge of many other disciplines is necessary. Particular emphasis is placed on physics and chemistry.

Geology is not only the study of the physical planet as it presently exists but it asks what it was like throughout its 4.6-5.0 billion years of history.

Geology includes the study of rocks and minerals both continental and oceanic, past and present. Biology throughout time is important. The past Biosphere and its ecosystems are recorded in the rocks. Paleontology, a branch of geology, studies and interprets these records.

GEOMAGNETIC FIELD The Geomagnetic Field surrounding the Earth extends into Space for many Earth radii. The Field is confined to the Magnetosphere. The Magnetopause, the upper surface of the Geomagnetic Field is very irregular as it is affected by solar wind (q.v.).

The present location of the North Geomagnetic Pole is 70° North, 101° West. The South Geomagnetic Pole is 67° South, 143° West. During the last 150 years the geomagnetic poles have stayed at the same latitude but have shifted longitude at the rate of 0.04° per year.

Earth has had a Geomagnetic Field for at least 2.6 billion years according to paleomagnetic studies. In the last 2,000 years dipole intensity has decreased 50%. The record shows that in the past the field has reversed in polarity. Reversals were rapid, in less than 10,000 years.

The dipole has decreased 7% in strength over 130 years which suggests it may disappear by A.D. 4,000. It may, however, increase again.

The Geomagnetic Field is thought to originate in the fluid of the Outer Core of the Earth which results from convective currents in the iron Inner Core. See **CONVECTIVE CURRENTS**.

GEOMETRY The mathematical field of geometry is the study of lines, points, and planes. Rules set forth by the Greek, Euclid, have been its foundation. Einstein's 1916 theory of gravity as a curvature in space-time, gave geometry new meaning.

A knowledge of geometry is necessary to the geoscientist, who must be capable of viewing a 3-dimensional Earth and a multi-dimensional Universe.

GEOMORPHOLOGY Relief forms on the Earth's surface and investigation of their origins and evolution are geomorphic studies. Modern computer technology has made it possible to model many processes working together to create results similar to those seen on the landscape.

GEOPHYSICS Geophysics is the study of physical phenomena directly affecting the planet (gravity, seismicity, electromagnetics, etc.). Planetary studies include not only the surface with its continents and seas but the Inner Earth, the Atmosphere, and Outer Space.

The portability of instruments to measure Earth phenomena made them popular. Airborne equipment allowed studies of the Earth from a platform bettered by satellites. Scientists can study cosmic rays, storms, clear air turbulence, and other phenomena.

Oceanography progressed enormously with the development of geophysical equipment and with remote sensing. Geophysics contributed to the fundamental knowledge of the deep ocean floor and the dynamics of the Earth. Much of the corroboration of Continental Drift and Plate Tectonics was contributed by geophysics.

Using satellite and astronomical information geophysicists are able to study the other planets and contribute to our knowledge of the Universe.

GEOSTILL Metal is precipitated from seawater and the processes are considered a geostill. The discovery of 'hot spots' on the ocean floor with extrusions of metalliferous solutions shows the geostill to have been an important agency of metal deposition.

GEOSYNCLINE A downfold in the Earth's Crust of regional proportions is a geosyncline. It may be a great compression-caused trough that infilled with huge masses of marine and shore sediments.

Geosynclines tend to form along continental margins (q.v.). Long periods of erosion with sediments filling marine embayments and troughs are followed by metamorphism related to general downwarp and mountain building.

Thick sediments sink in the trough and are compressed by weight. Temperatures rise with pressure and sediments are altered. Continuous accumulation and sagging result in compressive folds.

Folded and distorted sediments emerge from the sea to become mountain ranges. Sediments related to these orogenies (q.v.) are molasse, flysch, and greywacke. Silicious deposits, salt, gypsum, and thick coal-bearing formations also result.

Emergence may be caused from crustal plate collision or rebound. In the Gulf of Mexico, the Earth's Crust will support 12,000 meters (40,000 feet) of sediments before it regurgitates them.

In North America the major geosynclines are Appalachia, Oachita, and Cordillera. Sediments are quartzose feldspathic sandstones and mudstones. On the oceanic side of geosynclines there are geanticlines composed mainly of Precambrian crystalline rocks.

Plate tectonics (q.v.) has altered some geosynclinal theory. The relationship of geosynclinal sediments to plate sutures is being studied.

GEOTHERMAL BRINES Brines (q.v.) with salinities 10 times seawater have been found in great rifts. Water leached from sediments penetrates a geothermal source area. Mineralized waters are propelled by the geothermal source to a zone of accumulation.

A geothermal brine was discovered in the Salton Trough (q.v.) at 1,400 meters (4,620 feet). Temperatures at the bottom of the well were about 340° Celsius. The brine contained more heavy metals than found in pools on the Red Sea floor, where temperatures are between 44 and 56° Celsius. Usual bottomwater is 22°. See **RED SEA HOT SPOTS**.

GEOTHERMAL ENERGY The surface of the Earth's Crust and the first 15 meters (50 feet) within are roughly at atmospheric temperature. Mantle rocks have greater temperatures as a result of pressure and radioactivity.

Heat within the Earth is geothermal and appears in 3 ways:
- As water trapped within rocks
- Hot springs and hot waters that can be tapped by wells
- Steam.

The chief disadvantage to the use of these energy sources is that the water and vapor contain some undesirable minerals, many of them corrosive.

In both Iceland and New Zealand, geothermal energy is an important energy source. Some work is being done in Hawaii to utilize similar resources. In California, geysers are being tapped for their energy. The brines of the Salton Trough are too corrosive to be fully utilized. See **GEOTHERMAL BRINES**.

GEOTHERMAL GRADIENT There is a gradual increase in temperature from the Earth's surface to its center. The gradient varies in different parts of the Earth. The average is 1° Celsius per 30 meters (100 feet). Recent measurements of heat flow support this value for the Crust and Upper Mantle.

The actual temperature at a given location depends on the:

- Thermal conductivity of the rock
- Proximity to active volcanos
- Structure - Gradients increase more rapidly in dipping than in horizontal strata
  - Morphology - Gradients increase in mountains, decrease in valleys.

In Morro Velho, a deep gold mine in Brazil, the gradient is 1° Celsius per 55 meters (180 feet).

GERMANIUM Germanium, a metalloid (q.v.), is akin to silicon. and is an important semiconductor. Its crustal abundance is small, only 0.001%.

Although, germanium is not a conductor, small impurities introduced into the metal (doping) allows it to become charged. The most used doping products are aluminum, arsenic, and boron. Controlling the amounts gives direction to the current flow.

Germanium is recovered from coal ash and flue dust. In 1986, an operation began in Utah to recover gallium and germanium from the Bingham copper tailings. United States germanium production in 1989 was 22,000 kilograms (49,280 pounds). This germanium production was used 65% in infra-red optics and sensing devices, 15% in fiber optics, and only 5% in semiconductors and 5% went to catalytics, chemotherapy, and metallurgy.

Recent growth in fiber optics and other uses for germanium have increased the importance of the element. Silica can be substituted for some uses but for elevated power and high frequency needs, germanium is more reliable.

GERM PLASM Modern crops are products of selective breeding. To maintain production at a high rate, expand it, improve quality, or raise resistance to disease, new genetic material must be introduced and new hybrids developed. Wild germ plasm is needed for these purposes.

Without cross-breeding with wild teosinte from time to time, the United States corn crop would fall off.

A few years ago the United States sugar crop was blighted by a mosaic caused by aphids. A tolerant sugar strain from Java was crossed and the production was saved. In 1970, Brazilian coffee was affected by rust that threatened production as far north as Central America. A rust-resistant plant from the Ethiopian Highlands was the source of germ plasm.

Germ plasm acquisition from wild sources is becoming increasingly difficult as source areas like the Central American Rainforest diminish in size and productivity. Many crops have their origins in tropical and subtropical areas which are threatened with population pressures and deforestation.

Germ banks are being set up today to preserve germ plasm. In many cases it may be too late. Economic, social, and political considerations make it imperative that major producers of individual crops have their own specialized germ banks. See **GENE**.

GEYSER 'Geyser' in Icelandic means roarer. It describes the continuous or intermittent jets of hot water erupting from vents in the Earth's Crust. The force behind the geyser is steam. Rain and snowmelt provide the water which infiltrates into the hot volcanic rocks beneath the Earth's surface. There, it is converted to the steam which energizes the geysers and creates the fountains.

Geyser eruptions may have periodicity like Old Faithful in Yellowstone National Park. In the Valley of Geysers, Kamchatka, USSR, there are 20 active geysers erupting more or less regularly at intervals ranging from 10 minutes to 5 hours. First Born erupts hourly with an ejection of waters to 12 meters (40 feet) with a steam cloud to 150 meters (500 feet).

GEZHOUBA DAM China's largest dam is Gezhouba. It was designed to produce 14 gigawatt (q.v.) hours of electricity per year. The dam is sited in a gorge of the Yellow River (q.v.).

GEZIRA Gezira, Sudan, is the world's largest farm under a single management system. There are 892,000 hectares (2 million acres) under cultivation. Cotton is the major crop.

The Gezira is the world's longest-running ecological experiment. In 1911, the British started the scheme (q.v.) to raise irrigated cotton in 1911 in the triangle between the Blue and White Nile. In 1975, there was some crop diversification. The Gezira today is beset by economic and management problems.

GHANA In West Africa, Ghana was once known as 'The Gold Coast'. It is on the shores of the Gulf of Guinea into which Ghana's major river, the Volta, empties. Ghana is primarily made up of a low plain which gives way to the Ashanti Plateau in the central part of the country and the Atakora Range in the south. Once Ghana was covered by tropical rainforest but this has been almost completely felled.

Ghana is underlain by the West African Craton which is composed of Precambrian rocks of the Archaen-Proterozoic boundary (2.2-1.9 b.y.). These are altered sediments of phyllites and slates. The phyllites contain up to 6% carbon, an unusually high amount. Late-Proterozoic horizons overly the altered phyllites.

The craton is crossed by a NE-SW Greenstone Belt and intruded by Eburian granites. Eastern Ghana borders on the Katangan-Damaran (Pan-African) Mobile Belt. See **GREENSTONE**.

Ghana produces diamonds and was for a while 2nd in world caratage. The nation also produces manganese and bauxite (q.v.). Gold-bearing Precambrian conglomerates occur in Late-Proterozoic sediments. These are considered to have been favorable also for the deposition of uranium. Quartz pebble conglomerates elsewhere are producers. (Brazil, Canada, South Africa).

GHAR PARAU The deepest cave in Asia is Ghar Parau in the Zagros Mountains of western Iran. The cave was only discovered by speliologists in 1971. They reached a depth of 742 meters (2,434 feet) in the huge limestone solution cavity and only did not go deeper because of flooding.

GIANT SQUID The giant squid is a Cephalopod (q.v.) measuring up to 15 meters (50 feet). Found in the deep sea, the squid sometimes surfaces at night in search of food. Squid are food for the sperm whale.

GIANT'S CAUSEWAY A huge natural pavement of basaltic lava blocks forms the Giant's Causeway which legend says extended from Antrim, Ireland to the Scottish Island of Staffa. The original flows (50 m.y.) were widespread in Great Britain. The blocks resulted from the columnar (vertical) jointing common to basalt (q.v.).

Lava cools from the surface inward causing shrinkage into polygonal patterns. This gives rise to vertical jointing and columns. Most columns are hexagonal, but some are up to 10-sided. Sea erosion gave the Causeway the step-like structure and the process is continuing.

GIBRALTAR SILL A rocky sill across the entrance to the Strait of Gibraltar at a depth of 300 meters (1000 feet) restricts bottom flow between the Mediterranean Sea and Atlantic Ocean.

GIBRALTAR STRAIT The Strait of Gibraltar is 15 kilometers (9 miles) wide. It separates the Iberian Peninsula of Europe from North Africa and connects the Mediterranean Sea to the Atlantic Ocean.

GILGAI RELIEF Gilgai relief is hummocky with elevations between 5 and 15 centimeters (2 to 6 inches). It is caused by expanding clays that push soils upward. Dried polygon cracks become depressions. Gilgai is a micro-relief typical of predominantly clay soils.

GINKGO The oldest living tree type is the 'Ginkgo bilboa' a gymnosperm (q.v.). It is a maidenhair tree fern with fan fronds and it bears a yellow fruit. The ginkgo can attain a height of 30 meters (100 feet). It is cultivated in eastern China today.

The Ginkgo is the only survivor of the Ginkgoales that appeared in the Triassic (225-190 m.y.) and were abundant in the Jurassic (190-136 m.y.). Every reconstruction of 'dinosaur environment' includes these tree ferns.

GLACIAL DRIFT Glacial drift applies to all detrital deposits of glacial origin. Large parts of North America and Europe are covered by erratic materials or glacial clays. The blocks vary in size.

GLACIAL MILL A glacial mill is a hole carved in glacial ice by cascading water flowing over a precipice or edge of a crevasse. Milling action enlarges the crevasse.

GLACIAL MOVEMENT Glacial flow is plastic and discontinuous. There have been repeated advances and withdrawals, some greater than the present.

Glacial movement, especially of alpine glaciers. is stream-like. The center moves fastest. Surface ice, however, is faster than bottom ice. Glaciers move at different rates, a few centimeters to hundreds of meters in a day. Black Rapids Glacier, moved 60 meters (200 feet) in a single day, while Rhone Glacier moved 10 meters (30 feet). In Greenland, glaciers have moved 30 meters (100 feet) or more per day.

GLACIATION Advance and retreat of glaciers (q.v.) enormously affects the Earth's water budget. The ratio of sea to land is affected as well as sea level. Glacial weight affects the amount of land in relation to the sea as land tends to rise as glaciers unload. Glaciers are among the Earth's most powerful erosional forces.

There were 3 major Ice Ages, the Precambrian, Carboniferous (Paleozoic), and Pleistocene. Evidence for the Precambrian Ice Age has been found in rocks of the Fennoscandia Shield (q.v.), and other shield areas around the globe. Evidence in Australia indicates at least 2 Ice Ages in the Precambrian.

The Carboniferous Ice Age (2 m.y.) occurred on all continents except Antarctica. Most of the evidence however for a Carboniferous glaciation is from South America.

In the Pleistocene, 29% of the continental area of the globe was glaciated. The Age was marked by epochs of advance and retreat. During the last glacial advance, the World Ocean was lowered 60 meters (200 feet). In prior Pleistocene advances, they were lower. In Interglacials, sea level was 15-30 meters (50-100 feet) higher than at present. In both hemispheres, the last glacial maximum was 18,000-20,000 years ago.

GLACIER A glacier is a massive buildup of ice that occurs when snowfall exceeds melt and runoff. Snow turns to ice and the ice spreads. The ice-mass will begin to move when impelled by pressure from its own weight.

A glacier is a great erosive agent. Hudson Bay and the Great Lakes are in depressions caused by ice scour.

In present glaciers and ice floes there are 6.7 cubic kilometers (4 cubic miles) of water. These amount to 6 billion metric tons per square kilometer (9 billion per square mile). When the last great melting occurred, seas rose 120 meters (400 feet).

There are 2 main types of glaciers, continental ice sheets and valley or alpine glaciers. Continental ice is confined to Antarctica and Greenland today. In Greenland, the ice sheet is 3,000 meters (10,000 feet) thick at its center. Marie Byrd Land Glacier in Antarctica is 4,250 meters (14,000 feet) thick.

Valley glaciers do not attain great thicknesses. Formed on mountain tops and ridges they have flow generated by gravity and they scour U-shaped valleys. Glacial deposits of loose rock and sand at the melting front are moraines (q.v.). Cape Cod and Long Island in the United States are moraines of glacial outwash.

In Alaska, glacial ice is distributed over 48,070 square kilometers (28,842 square miles). The greatest glacier concentration is in the Alaska Range which extends from the Alaskan Peninsula to the Yukon. There are many in the Wrangell, Brooks, and coast ranges of Chugach, Coast, Elias, and Kenai.

The weight of glacial ice affects the Earth's wobble as it spins. This may have a long term climate affect if the Earth's position in relation to the Sun is changed. See **EARTH'S AXIS**.

GLADE A glade is a natural open space in a woodland or forest. It is an indication of plant succession between savanna and woodland or woodland and forest. They are large 'windows' allowing sunlight to penetrate to the forest floors.

GLASS Glass, contrary to what is usually thought, is not a solid. It is a fluid with sufficient viscosity (q.v.) to behave as a solid. It may take centuries, but even leaded cathedral windows show flow. Glass occurs when energy is abruptly reduced and there is insufficient time for crystals to form and grow. This abrupt drop occurs in volcanic flows when they encounter the Atmosphere.

Natural glass is formed from volcanic silica. Obsidian, Iceland agate, pitchstone, and pumice, all types of volcanic glass, are associated with rhyolitic flows.

The most well-known volcanic glass is obsidian. It is found abundantly on Lipari Islands, Italy, in the Siskiyous of California, in Yellowstone

National Park, and on Mount Hecla in Iceland. There is a large obsidian flow in the Newberry Caldera in Oregon.

Glass-making was an art learned early in human history. About 1,000 BC, the Phoenicians had a thriving glass trade. They used heated sand, sodium oxide, and lime to produce it.

Glass has many uses. The ability to weave filaments of glass has expanded this use. Modern manufactured glass contains 16% soda ash (q.v.). See **OBSIDIAN**.

GLAUCONITE   Glauconite, or greensand, is mica-like. It is an iron-potassium silicate mineral formed on the seafloor. Due to its potassium content, glauconite can be used for radiactive dating (q.v.).

GLEN   In Scotland, 'glens' are long valleys that may or may not be secluded. Many glens are fault troughs. The most famous of these is the Great Glen Moor. Glen Moor is in the graben (q.v.) of Glen Moor Fault.

Glen Moor Fault is a shear zone from the Firth of Lorn to Moray Firth. It separates the Northern Highlands by a deep northeast-southwest trench. Loch Ness and Loch Locky are in the valley. The Caledonian Canal connects the lochs and the sea.

GLEY   'Gley' is Russian for sticky clay a name for soils that are often water-logged. Gleys are fine-grained, of blue-gray sometimes mottled color from the lack of oxygen. The process of gleization produces gley soils.

GLOBAL RIFT SYSTEM   In the Mid-Atlantic the Global Rift has been fairly well explored. Other portions have not been as extensively studied but sufficiently so that its continuity is known.

The Global Rift is 65-75,000 kilometers (40-45,000 miles) long and extends through the Mid-Atlantic, East Pacific, Pacific-Antarctic, and Indian oceans. Enormous faults make up the Rift in the Earth's Crust creating boundaries for major crustal plates.

The rifts may be over 1,800 meters (6,000 feet) deep and several times as wide. Rift valleys accompany underwater mountain ranges which extend more than twice around the world. The Global Rift is found on portions of continents. They are represented by huge fault systems such as the San Andreas, East African, and Syrian Rifts.

GLOBAL TEMPERATURE   In the past 150,000 years temperatures have fluctuated greatly. From an average of 55° (Fahrenheit), there was a drop to 52° and an Ice Age developed. Temperatures rose again 125,000 years ago to an average of 60°, dropping to the high 50's in the next 50,000 years. They dropped still further 75,000 years ago to 50° and another Ice Age ensued. This sequence recurred again about 25,000 years ago.

These temperature changes are relatively small, a few degrees, 2-3° Celsius (4-5° Fahrenheit). Graphs of these changes point out how fragile is the line between an Ice Age and the Present.

Fluctuations are apparently related to the axial tilt and wobble of the Earth. Warming of the Atmosphere by carbon dioxide may tend to slow cooling. See **GREENHOUSE EFFECT**.

GLOBERGERINA OOZE   Pelagic (q.v.) Globergerina ooze is white to gray in color. It is 30% composed of Foraminifera shells, predominantly 'Globergerina bulloides'. The skeletons were deposited in relatively deep seas, not over 3,600 meters (12,000 feet).

Sediments contain up to 6,000 specimens per gram and cover 128 million kilometers (77 million square miles) of seafloor. About 2/3 of the Atlantic floor is covered by the calcareous ooze.

Globergerina has been a useful fossil indicator in petroleum research. See **FORAMINIFERA**.

GLOMAR CHALLENGER   The research vessel, Glomar Challenger, was designed as a floating drilling platform. Its voyages have provided sediment cores and geophysical evidence of seafloor spreading.

The data show that North America separated from Europe no more than 200 million years ago. Africa and South America were later (150 m.y.). Separation between the continents is widening at the rate of 5 centimeters (2 inches) a year.

Glomar Challenger detected an east-west spreading ridge in the eastern Mediterranean Sea with Cyprus on one end. The crew found the muds from the Nile dated less than 2 million years.

GLORIA   The British developed side scanner, GLORIA (Geological Long Range Inclined ASDIC) can cover 27 square kilometers (10,000 square miles) in a day. It emits sound which fans out 30 kilometers (20 miles) on either side of the vessel. It has revealed 200 formerly unknown undersea volcanoes, vents, faults, and canyons.

GLORY HOLE   A glory hole is the opening up to the surface of an underground mine. Dimensions of the pit are much smaller than those of a true open pit mine. Glory holes are usually made in pegmatites.

GLOSSOPTERIS   Glossopteris flora have been preserved in the Angolan part of Congo (Zaire) Basin and in Zambezi Basin, Mozambique. Glossopteris was a giant tongue fern, characteristic of the Permian (250 m.y.). Rocks containing fern fossils have been placed in the Upper Carboniferous to Permian (Lower Gondwana) Period.

GNEISS   Undulating, foliated, coarse-grained, banded, metamorphic rocks are gneiss. They are composed of quartz, orthoclase, and microcline or hornblende. Gneiss is crystalline with much the same composition as granite

Gneisses have orientation, or schistocity (q.v.). They range in color from gray to pink and have a streaky appearance. The rock type forms from altered shale or igneous rock. It is widespread, especially in Precambrian rocks. Archaen gneiss from Greenland is dated 2.8 billion years.

GOBI DESERT The Gobi is one of the world's most legendary deserts. It is a part of the Central Asian Desert and merges with the Takla Makan Desert of Western China.

Gobi is, in general, a stony desert, barren, and high. A railway crosses part of it from China to Ulan Bator, Mongolia. The route is through salt basins and scrub desert and a slightly less arid region.

The Dzungarian Basin of Mongolia is the famous 'Gate to Gobi'. It opens into a wide, flat valley that gives way to the desert.

GOBLET VALLEYS A goblet valley is a drainage feature in arid terrain. Major uplift carried valleys aloft but streams continued to cut into the slopes. Valley debris on the Panamint Escarpment in Death Valley looks as though it were poured from wine goblets. At least this was what the eminent geomorphologist, William Morris Davis imagined.

GOETHITE Goethite is hydrated iron-oxide not unlike limonite, with which it is often associated. The minerals differ in that goethite is crystallized and limonite is not.

Goethite is about 63% iron and is an important ore in Alsace-Lorraine, France. It has been mined also in Cuba. Much of what was once considered limonite has proven to be microcrystalline goethite.

GOLCONDA Golconda, near Hyderbad, India is the site of famed diamond fields. All deposits are placers derived from Precambrian conglomerates. These have yielded some of the world's most famous diamonds. Among these are Star of India and Kohinoor.

GOLD The precious metal element, gold, is unreactive, durable, and not subject to rust. It is almost always in a free elemental state. It has a specific gravity of 19, or some 8 times that of sand. This is why it can so readily be separated from the tons of sand associated with it in stream placers.

Gold has been mined for thousands of years. In Solomon's time, it was the wealth of Ophir, now in Saudi Arabia. Egyptians used gold for ornamentation. Later gold became the major coinage of the world.

Gold has a cubic crystalline habit, yellow color, and metallic brilliance. Because it is soft (2.5-3 on Moh's Scale), gold is often alloyed to be workable.

18-carat gold is an alloy containing 750 thousandths of a gram (18/24ths) of fine gold and 250 thousandths of a gram (6/24ths) of copper. Gold is calculated in 'fineness'. This signifies how many parts per thousand are gold. If the gold were 75% pure, it would mean it has a fineness of 750 as in 18 carat gold. United States gold coins are 90% gold and 10% copper. They are 900 fine.

Gold leaf is created when the soft gold is pounded to a thin sheet. Smithsonian's Desautel tells us 1/3 million such sheets would only measure an inch if they were stacked. An ounce of gold this thin could cover 13 square feet. Gold is found in alluvium (placers), in igneous rocks, and veins like the Motherlode of California. Rich placers are located down-stream of some major gold deposits. In plate tectonic theory, some gold deposits are associated with convergent plate boundaries. Many famous deposits are associated with Precambrian reefs.

GOLD PRODUCTION AND RESERVES (millions of Troy ounces)

Note: 1,000 kilograms = 32150.7 Troy ounces.

Production	1984	1985	1986	1987	1988	1989*
SouthAfrica	681.17	670.9	653.17	NA	618.3	610.0
USSR	269.05	270.6	273.71	NA	279.9	280.0
United States	64.07	74.65	111.97	NA	200.9	240.0
Australia	52.88	56.92	74.65	NA	152.0	200.0
Canada	81.18	85.53	99.53	NA	127.8	150.0
Brazil	55.99	40.43	34.21	34.0	100.1	100.0
China	NA	NA	NA	NA	77.8	80.0

* Estimated
Source: US Bureau of Mines and DNPM of Brazil.

The major holders of Gold Reserves are: (in metric tons)

South Africa	20,000
USSR	6,220
United States	4,840
Australia	1,800
Brazil	930
Canada	1,700
China	NA

Source: US Bureau of Mines, 1990

Reserves are estimated by Companhia Vale do Rio Doce (CVRD) at 3.2 billion ounces or as much as all gold produced up to 1982. This amount is greater then total world reserves set at 2.4 billion ounces (149.2 metric tons).

In 1982 Pelado production was 6,192 kilograms (192.6 thousand Troy ounces or 5.99 metric tons). In the same region CVRD has put Volta Grande into operation geared for 30 kilograms per year from reserves of 30 metric tons of gold. At Serra Pelada, as the deposit becomes deeper and mining more difficult, more 'garimpos' (prospects) are deserted. When a sufficient number have reverted to the Government, the deposits will be rationalized into a mine and worked by more modern methods.

20% of all present world gold production is from by-product sources. Relatively few nations possess appreciable amounts of gold ore, with South Africa leading with about 50%. If Brazil's estimates of Pelada and the rest of the Amazon Basin are correct, the position of Brazil may improve enormously.

In Alaska, stream pollution problems resulting from many small gold mining operations are creating a major problem. Elsewhere in the United States, gold production is concentrated at the Homestake mine and in the arsenical gold belt of Nevada. Here the gold is extremely fine-grained and ordinary mining methods would be uneconomic.

To 1986 3 billion Troy ounces of gold had been produced, 50% mined in the last 30 years. Of today's production, 1/3 is held in central banks, 1/3 is used for jewelry and industry, and the final 1/3 is in personal reserves.

GOLDEN FLEECE Jason's search for a golden fleece is a legend based on fact. Fleeces were used to collect gold from streams. The custom has continued along the Ingur River in Georgia, USSR. Ingur gold is in tiny particles and this gold adheres to wool, the oilier the better. Fleeces sunk in the river trap the gold.

In Brazil, cowhide was substituted for the fleece when so many took to streams to try their luck during the Great Depression.

GONDWANA Gondwana, an ancient landmass composed of Antarctica, Australia, India, South Africa, and South America, was bordered on the north by the Poseidon Sea. Godwana was fragmented in the Mesozoic Age.

Seuss named Gondwana for an Indian province that had unusually ancient geology. It was apparently the heartland of an old continent. Fossils are similar to those of South Africa. The only coal in India is in this area, as are most of the iron and manganese deposits.

GORGE A fast flowing stream will rapidly cut a steep-sided valley in resistant rock. A tributary of the Rhine has cut a gorge 600 meters (2,000 feet) deep and so narrow in places, it can be jumped.

The soft rocks of the Grand Canyon have been sculpted by wind, rain, and blowing sand. The canyon is now 1,7 kilometers (1 mile) deep and 13 kilometers (8 miles wide). The river fills the bottom of the gorge. Many gorge areas have been uplifted during cutting, contributing to some extraordinary depths. The 3 deepest gorges in North America are Hells Canyon on the Snake River, Copper Canyon in Sonora, Mexico, and Grand Canyon. In Central China, on the Yangtze Kjang River are 3 gorges. The longest, 75 kilometers (45 miles), cuts through 12 mountains. One of the biggest dams in the world, Gezhouba (q.v.), has been sited in this area.

GOSSAN A gossan is a zone of secondary enrichment of iron oxide (limonite or hematite) and other oxides. These are often found above an ore body. Gossans result from weathering, capillarity (q.v.) and selective deposition. The gossans are important mineral indicators.

Iron oxide caps form from iron-rich veins and sulfide deposits. Many iron-rich gossans are found in Wadi Wassat volcanics in Saudi Arabia.

A crustal nickel gossan led to a significant mineralization in the same region.

Australia has concentrated on duricrust and gossan exploration for nickel.

GOUGE Brecciated, fractured, or softened rock in fault zones is gouge. It results from pressures and frictions exerted by mass movement.

GOWGANDA TILLITE Huronian (q.v.) Gowganda Tillite is composed of coarse sediments of unsorted glacial debris. Named for a coarse conglomerate in India, the tillite is thought to represent the oldest known Ice Age.

In the Upper Peninsula, the tillite is overlying an older soil horizon on the north shore of Lake Huron. A similar conglomerate, the Coleman, is located near Cobalt, Ontario.

GRABEN 'Graben' is German for trough or ditch. A down-dropped fault block is a graben. The graben is between 2 blocks that are thrust upward. The overall topographic effect is of an elongated depression or valley. Many are corridors for major streams.

The Rhine Valley is a graben 300 kilometers (180 miles) long and 33-42 kilometers (20-25 miles) wide. It is between the upthrust blocks, or 'Horsts' of the Black Forest in Germany, and the Vosges Mountains of France. Death Valley in California is a graben.

The Global Rift System has many grabens, among them Jordan Valley, Dead Sea, and the East African lakes, The widest graben is the Danakil Depression (q.v.) which is below sea level.

GRADIENT A gradient is the profile of the rate of change over a distance in a definite direction.

In surveying, the gradient is the incline of a bedding plane, river bed, or slope. It is expressed as a percent, in degrees, or in fractions. The gradient describes the slope over which a river flows from its source to the sea.

Horizontal pressure gradients in the Atmosphere are 90° to the isobars (q.v.) and toward lower pressure.

GRADIENT WIND A gradient wind blows parallel to curved isobars (q.v.) in a steady field of air pressure. Gradient wind speed is attained when centrifugal force or Coriolis Force (q.v.), and the pressure gradient are balanced. Gradient wind occurs at about 455 meters (1500 feet) in altitude since wind is retarded by friction close to the Earth's surface.

GRAIN An individual particle or crystal making up sand, sediment, or rock is a grain. It may be coarse, medium, or fine in size.

A grain is a seed of a cereal grass. Present usage includes soybeans and other commodities in the grains. Grain has come to signify the entire plant in some usage. Grains are the dietary mainstay of humans and many land animals.

A grain is also a unit of weight equal to 0.648 parts of a gram (q.v.). It is 0.04167 parts of a pennyweight (q.v.).

GRAM The basic unit of the metric system is the gram. It is the mass or weight of 1 cubic centimeter of water. A liter is 1,000 cubic centimeters of 1,000 grams (1 kilogram).

GRAN CHACO Gran Chaco is a great marshy lowland west of the Paraguay River in South America. It is between the Paraguay River and the Bolivian Andes. The name is derived from 'Chacu' of the Guarani Indians. It means an abundance of wildlife.

The Chaco plain is composed of alluvium with gravel, silt, and clay. There is a mirror image in the Pantanal (q.v.) of Brazil. It also is similar to the Chaco of Argentina.

Gran Chaco is a virtually treeless plain subject to flooding in the rainy season. The Quebracho tree used for tanning leathers and the Carnauba palm, which produces a latex tapped for wax, are among the few trees. Carnauba flourishes in the marshes near the Paraguay River.

The Verde and Montelindo Rivers flow from Gran Chaco to the Paraguay which in turn empties into the Alto Parana. The Parana flows to the La Plata which empties into the Atlantic. The waters of the rivers and ponds contain the rare lungfish and the voracious piranha. The South American crocodile (cayman) has been greatly hunted for skins in recent years.

There are reptiles in the area ranging from the coral snake to the anaconda. The latter can attain 10 meters (30 feet) in length and is amphibious. The boa constrictor is ubiquitous.

The tapir, South America's largest land animal, is a hoofed creature related to the horse and rhino. It is nocturnal and uses its snout to forage. The foraging tends to create paved paths to favorite watering points as the tapir turns over stones and tamps them with its feet. The tapir's only enemy is the jaguar. The jaguar ('onca' in Brazil) and ocelot are the most important cats of the area. There are also anteaters ('tamandua'), deer and the very vicious wild boar.

The world's largest rodent, the partially web-footed 'capyvara', is also found in this area. It can be up to 1.2 meters (4 feet) and weigh up to a 45 kilos (100 pounds).

The Gran Chaco is an area of enormous insect activity. The most injurious to humans are the anopheles mosquitoes and the gnats. The termite constructs mounds some of which are 1.5 meters (5 feet) or more. They seem invariably to pick the center of the only track around.

GRAN SABANA Gran Sabana is the plains area or savannaland of Venezuela between the Andes and the Orinoco Delta. A small extension of the savanna is found in Brazil.

GRAND BANKS The Grand Banks are a rise on the continental slope in the North Atlantic Ocean off Newfoundland, Canada. The seas above the Banks are relatively shallow and famous for fisheries.

The waters are warmed to a considerable extent by the Gulf Stream. This became apparent in 1882 when gales pushed the Gulf Stream further offshore and an enormous fish-kill resulted from the too cold waters.

GRAND CANYON The deepest and most spectacular of the many canyons along the Colorado River (q.v.) is Grand Canyon. It is 1.7 kilometers (1 mile) deep and from 11.7 to 25 kilometers (7-15 miles) from the North to South Rim. The canyon cuts across 462 kilometers (277 miles) of northwestern Arizona through sediments that range from the Permian (Kaibab Limestone) down the stratigraphic column to Precambrian (Brahmin and Vishnu) schists and granitic intrusions. A billion years of geological history is revealed.

The Colorado River probably took less than 10 million years to carve the canyon revealing the great age sequences. It is probable that uplift accompanied the down-cutting, hastening the process. Most of the sediments are marine and were deposited when the region was beneath the sea.

GRAND CAUSSES Plateaus in the central-south of the French Massif Central are known as the Grand Causses. They are of limestone that accumulated in a geosynclinal (q.v.) gulf during the Jurassic (199-136 m.y.). The limestones are up to 1,500 meters (5,000 feet thick.

Causses sediments were uplifted and dissected in the Cretaceous and Tertiary. Erosion resulted in a series of high plateaus 900-1,200 meters (3,000-4,000 feet). The plateaus are separated by gorges and the area has some notable rivers, among them the Tarn, Jonte, Dourbie, and Vis. Rock pinnacles abound. See **PINNACLES**.

GRANITE Granite is an igneous, intrusive rock composed of quartz, alkaline feldspar, and mica. Its texture is granular, or coarse to medium-grained but even. Granite may be light gray or pink to reddish.

There is at least 10% of visible quartz but it may range as high as 30%. However, feldspar is the predominant mineral. There is a variable amount of biotite mica with some muscovite. Rarely, there is some hornblende as in New Hampshire's Conway Granite.

Microcline (q.v.) is most common in granite pegmatites, which are dikes of coarser granitic material. Quartz is an essential mineral (q.v.) of granite, but usually only makes up 10% of the rock. Often the quartz is in veins or cavities.

Granites are grouped based on feldspar content and type:

        Alkali granites - 66% or more of alkali feldspars
        Adamellites   - Almost equal alkali and plagioclase feldspars
        Granodiorites - 66% or more of plagioclase.

Granite is the commonest of igneous rocks. High in silica, it was formed at depth from Mantle material. Final cooling and solidification released gases such as boron and fluorine. Some gases were trapped in joints and cracks and altered the granite. Some alteration processes are greisenization, kaolinization, and tourmalinization.

Granites are mountain formers. Granite batholiths (q.v.) make up the core of many great ranges, including the Sierra Nevada. Granite uplands have rounded summits and steep-sides. These are the result of the weathering process of exfoliation (q.v.).

There are great granitic outcrops in Western Australia, West Africa, Arabia, Brazil, Europe, and North America, all shield areas (q.v.). The largest known single granitic mass is in Finland where it covers 23,000 square kilometers (13,800 square miles).

GRANITIC GRUS Granite may be shattered to great depths by weathering and fracturing which caused alteration of many minerals. Disaggregation of the granite by weathering yields a granitic grus.

Biotite mica and plagioclase feldspar may alter to clay resulting in a volume increase, This creates pressure on other minerals and causes further alteration. Biotite altering to vermiculite results in a 40% volume increase.

GRANITIZATION The process which transforms pre-existing rocks to rocks of a granitic character without an intermediate magmatic stage is granitization. It was the subject of debate for a long time, especially in Europe. It is now accepted that many Proterozoic sedimentary rocks have been altered to granite. Some of the best examples have been found in the ancient Caledonian Mountains of Scotland.

GRANULAR The textural term, granular, describes the aggregation of grains of approximately equal size. These are not large, but macroscopic.

GRAPHIC GRANITE Quartz fills the spaces of some smooth-sided feldspar blocks in granite. When the quartz forms a zig-zag pattern resembling ancient Cuneiform writing, the rock is 'graphic granite'. It is a pale gray, buff, or pink in color.

GRAPHITE Graphite is a soft, greasy, pure carbon mineral. Its atomic structure is unlike that of the diamond, which also is of pure carbon. In graphite, carbon atoms are held loosely and lie in planes so each is at the corner of a hexagon. The layers can easily slip by each other accounting for graphite's softness. Graphite is usually soot-colored.

The primary use of graphite is as pencil 'lead'. For this purpose it is combined with a clay. The mineral is also an important industrial lubricant.

Graphite blocks were used as modulators in a now obsolete type of nuclear reactor. These blocks were used at Hanford which has been redesigned. This type of reactor is still in use in the USSR in the RBMK units of the water-cooled types.

At Chernobyl, Kiev, there are 4 of these 1,000 megawatt reactors. One was involved in a major accident in May, 1986. Radiation levels of 10 times normal, were reported as far away as Belgrade, Yugoslavia. Radioactivity was from cesium, not plutonium. A complete meltdown was averted. See **CHERNOBYL**.

GRAPTOLITES In Devonian and Silurian sandstones and limestones, there are fossil colonies of tiny graptolites. Graptolites were abundant and distributed worldwide. They were non-sessile though they may have been attached with thick stems in the Paleozoic. Fossil graptolites were preserved by carbonization (q.v.).

GRASSES Thousands of varieties of wild and cultivated grasses exist and in almost every climate zone. Grasses are the largest of all present plant families. They tend to enrich the soils and prevent erosion.

Humans and animals use cereal, pasture, and sweet grass and even some special shoots of bamboo for food. Grasses first appeared 70 million years ago.

GRASSLANDS Grasslands are an ecosystem extending over much of the tropics and temperate zones. They cover 25% of the world land area. In the Tropics, they are found where there is a definite rainy season. The grasses can then tolerate the dry periods. They are coarser and thicker in the Tropics and they also grow grow faster.

Grasslands are found on every continent except Antarctica. On most continents, great areas once grasslands have been turned into farms and pastures. There are still great grassland areas and areas once farmed returning to grassland.

Grasslands can continue to exist if the upper soil layer is moist a good part of the year and the root systems are not over-grazed. If the area becomes too wet, forest begins to take over, if too dry, a semi-desert develops.

Perennial grasses are dominated by great groups of bunchgrass and sodgrass. Grazing animals and grasslands were balanced in the Grassland Ecosystem for long periods of time. Animals first were browsers, then transformed into grazers about 12 million years ago.

In the United States, for 2 generations, grasslands were over-grazed. This caused soil erosion and subsequent deflation (q.v.). The Dust Bowl (q.v.) of the 1930's was brought on by drought in an already damaged ecosystem. Tractor farming, and the changes in plowing methods as well as over-grazing all contributed.

In the Middle East, grasslands were destroyed in the 7th Century, when the Arabs moved in with their sheep and goats and over-grazed the area. Range mismanagement together with climatic shifts caused desertification. A similar situation occurred in much of the Mediterranean Rim.

The remnant of grassland in the African Sahel (q.v.) is being subjected to the same pressures and the area is undergoing much desertification (q.v.).

GRAVEL Rock fragments between 2 and 256 mm (0.125 and 6 inches) are gravel. The gravel is a weathering product and stream deposited. It is sized as granule, pebble, cobble, or boulder. Roughly 54 kilos (120 pounds) = 1 cubic yard, the standard American measure.

Gravel is made mechanically by crushing stone or rock. Such manufactured gravel is widely used in construction, especially where stream gravels are not readily available.

Gravel fans abound at the foot of the Panamint Range in California's Death Valley testifying to torrential stream activity.

GRAVIMETER A gravimeter measures variation in the Gravitational Field at the Earth's surface. Large masses of dense rock increase the pull of gravity at particular locations. Sensitive gravimeters can detect differences in gravitational acceleration between very separate locations.

To use the gravimeter effectively, corrections have to be made for the distance to the Earth's center from the particular location and altitude. See **GRAVITY**.

GRAVITY All things are pulled toward the Earth's center by gravity. All freely moving objects fall to Earth. The force of the Earth's Gravitational Field extends some distance into Space.

Gravity depends upon mass, the greater the mass the greater the force exerted as weight. The force differs with distance between the masses.

Sir George Everest, in a survey of the Himalayas, found that his results differed from astronomical observations by 150 meters in 600 kilometers. The plumbline was deflected toward the Himalayas instead of toward the Earth's center. When mass was calculated, the deflection was 300 meters less than for gravity alone.

It was found that Mount Everest was not denser, but rather had deeper roots than suspected. Bouger found the same situation in the Andes.

On average, gravity measurements of highlands are less than those of lowlands. After correcting for altitude, the measurements are subtracted from a theoretically estabished value for the Earth and a Bouger anomaly is obtained. It is usually negative. The higher the station, the higher the negative value. Anomalies at sea are slightly positive due undoubtedly to the denser material below. See **ISOSTASY**.

An object falling toward the center of the Earth increases speed as the field force increases. This gravity acceleration is greater at the poles because the distance to the Earth's center is less due to the Earth's shape. Centrifugal Force is also less.

The force of gravity remains almost constant through the Earth's Mantle and only drops off at the Core where 33% of the mass is located. The Core represents only 16% of the volume.

GRAY AIR 'Gray Air' is a type of SMOG (q.v.) that results from a mixture of sulfur, oxides, and particulates in the Atmosphere. It occurs frequently from the excessive burning of coal and oil.

Pilots flying the Arctic Region as long ago as the 1950's reported gray haze. Arctic Haze has been building up since that time. Pollution was and still is emanating from coal-based heavy industry in Europe and the USSR.

GREAT ALPINE FAULT New Zealand's major rift zone is the Great Alpine Fault. It is in a ridge on the Global Rift System (q.v.). The rift turns south and east in the Indian Ocean and passes between Australia and Antarctica. A branch appears in the mountains of New Zealand.

GREAT BASIN The Great Basin in Nevada and western Utah is a large area of lake sediments in intermontane basins and valleys. The Wasatch Front Range shows ancient shorelines of Pleistocene Lake Bonneville (q.v.). Today the shorelines are 300 meters (990 feet) above Great Salt Lake. See **BASIN AND RANGE PROVINCE**.

GREAT CIRCLE Geometrically any intersection of a plane and a sphere results in a circle of 360°. If the intersecting plane includes the center of the sphere, it is a great circle. The Equator is a great circle as are the meridians of Longitude.

A great circle bisects the Earth into hemispheres. There are any number of great circles and they can bisect one another. A circle that does not pass through the center of the sphere is a small circle. Parallels of latitude other than the Equator are small circles.

Great circles are the shortest distance between 2 points on the globe and are used extensively in navigation.

GREAT ESCARPMENT The eastern edge of the South African Plateau extending from Zimbabwe to Cape Province is known as the Great Escarpment. It is a great wall paralleling the Indian Ocean for 1,125 kilometers (700 miles). Its highest portion is in the Drakensberg Range (q.v.) in Lesotho.

GREAT LAKES In North America between Canada and the United States, there are 5 ancient river valleys that are millions of years old. The Great Lakes (Superior, Ontario, Huron, Michigan, and Erie) that fill the valleys are much younger, only 8,000-10,000 years old.

Ice sheets deeply gouged the valleys, then left behind their meltwater. The lake floors are below sea level and are partly dammed by moraines. More than 25% of the freshwater in all the lakes and rivers of the world is held in the Great Lakes.

Lake levels have risen and fallen over time. There has been record high water for the last few years. For the first time in 100 years the lakes have all been receiving high precipitation at the same time. The record low occurred about 23 years ago. In the 1960's eutrophication (q.v.) was so great in Lake Erie the lake was green and opaque, and its aquatic life was endangered. Today, a number of polluted rivers are emptying into Erie and the other lakes, some of which are worse off than Erie. A harbor near Chicago is said to have a an extremely high PCB content. The asbestos pollution of Lake Superior is well-documented. A great effort is underway to reverse the damage.

A water quality agreement between the United States and Canada was signed in 1972 for the prevention of pollution. A former pact joined the lakes and the St. Lawrence River into a Seaway.

GREAT PLAINS The Great Plains make up 20% of the United States. They follow along the foothills of the Rockies for 2,600 kilometers (1,600 miles) and extend east about 1,250 kilometers (750 miles).

The average elevation of the Great Plains is 450 meters (1,500 feet). It increases as the Rockies are approached. Close to the mountains, the Great Plains are known as the 'High Plains'.

The Great Plains have a grasslands (q.v.) ecosystem and are in a delicate balance between forest and semi-arid scrublands. With good land management and sufficient water the soils of the Great Plains are productive. The region, however, receives only about 50 centimeters (20 inches) of rainfall per year and suffers from periodic drought. Presently, these plains produce much of the wheat harvested in the United States.

There are indications that there was an especially severe drought lasting from 1200-1400 A.D. Indians farming the area were forced to abandon it. Severe drought again occurred in the 1930's. The latest severe drought was the summer of 1988. Whether this is the beginning of a serious drought cycle is not yet known.

GREAT RIFT SYSTEM The Great Rift extends from Southwest Asia to Mozambique in Southeast Africa. Secondary faults and volcanoes are on either side of the main rift with branching valleys.

The Great Rift is a continental portion of the Global Rift (q.v.). The Red Sea fills a part of this 10,000 kilometer (6,000 mile) segment.

Rift profiles are identical to those made by Heezen of the Mid-Atlantic Rift. It has been concluded that the rifts formed in the same way. Rifting is small in comparison to the Global Rift System but some geologists feel the region is an ocean in the making.

In East Africa, the Rift Valley is bordered by highlands like the Ruwenzoris (Mountains of the Moon), the Marimbas, and some of Africa's highest peaks (Kenya and Kilmanjaro). Lakes dot the rift north to south.

From the Red Sea to Lake Manyara in Tanzania, there has been deep subsidence and rifting. In Danakil Depression (q.v.) the rift is 500 kilometers (300 miles) across.

The Rift is active with volcanoes and hot springs. In Kenya, there is a colossal trench with walls 600 meters (2,000 feet) high. The floor has subsided over the last 20 million years. Plateaus on both sides of the rift are composed of highly eroded ancient shield rocks. All the younger rocks are in the rift.

The Asian extension of the Great Rift from the Gulf of Aqaba to southwest Turkey is the Great Syrian Rift. From Baalbek at 1,150 meters (3,800 feet) the rift slopes to the Dead Sea and 392 meters (1,294 feet) below sea level.

The Rift is extraordinarily visible on Apollo 17 photos taken from 140,000 kilometers (90,000 miles) in Space.

GREAT SALT LAKE In Utah, in the eastern part of the Great Basin is Great Salt Lake. It is a remnant of Pleistocene (Glacial) Lake Bonneville (q.v.). The present lake is 1/6 the size of the ancient one.

Water in Great Salt Lake is saline with 14-27% dissolved salts. From 1959 to 1963, the lake became nearly saturated with dissolved solids at 24-28%.

GREAT WHIN SILL In Northumberland, England, is a black intrusive sill that forms a 160 kilometer (100 mile) escarpment in a crescent from the Pennines to the sea. The steep side faces north. The sill is 30 meters (100 feet) thick and in some places twice that.

Unlike Karroo Sill of South Africa, the Great Whin does not have many other sills associated with it.

GREEN MUD Green mud is oceanic ooze composed mainly of glauconite (q.v.). The ooze is found near the edge of the continental shelf at depths between 90 and 2,275 meters (300 and 7,500 feet). See **GREEN-SANDS**.

GREEN RIVER FORMATION The Eocene Green River Formation of Utah, Colorado, and Wyoming is a lacustrine and evaporite sequence. The sediments were laid down in ancient Lake Gosiute, a vast shallow Middle Eocene lake. Lake beds on the basin rim grade to fluvial sediment of the Bridger and Wasatch Formations.

Laminated Green River oil shales have an average thickness of 600 meters (2,000 feet). Their deposition took 6.5 million years. An estimated 7 trillion barrels of hydrocarbon reserves are locked in these oil shales. The Green River is considered the largest single concentration in the world. It is rivaled only by the Brazilian Longo and Irati shales. See **IRATI**.

GREENHOUSE EFFECT The Earth, when there is no snow cover, readily absorbs short-wave solar radiation and gives off long-wave radiation. The Atmosphere is capable of absorbing 90% of the long-wave radiation but only 14% of the short-wave energy.

There are about 30 trace gases in the atmospheric envelope. These gases allow ultraviolet and visible light to pass through. Radiated infra-red from the Earth is absorbed by the gases causing a thermal blanket or 'Greenhouse Effect'. The effect is to warm the lower, but cool the upper Atmosphere. The present temperature of the Troposphere (q.v.) is 288° Kelvin (15° Celsius). This is 35° warmer than prior to the Industrial Revolution.

Carbon dioxide in the Atmosphere measured about 270-290 parts per million in 1860. In 1987, it was 339 ppm. This resulted from the burning of an estimated 5 billion tons of fossil fuel. These figures are only estimates as careful carbon dioxide measurements have only been available since 1958 when awareness of the Greenhouse Effect on the planet became widespread in the scientific community.

Of the greenhouse gases, carbon dioxide is major. Some others are methane, nitrous oxide, chlorofluorocarbons, and water vapor. It is known that a methane molecule traps heat 20 times better than carbon dioxide, but all the included gases have a warming effect.

Tropical forests contain 340 billion tons of carbon, equal to 50% of the carbon in the Atmosphere. Deforestation releases carbon to the Atmosphere and contributes to the build-up. Increased carbon dioxide would increase photosynthesis and decrease moisture through evaporation. The balance is delicate and a warming of a few degrees could destabilize glaciers. Deforestation has been referred to as a 'time bomb' particularly with the phenomenal increase in 'slash and burn' cultures.

Due to the Greenhouse Effect, Earth surface temperatures are higher than normal. A warming of 5° Celsius is estimated by 2100 A.D. The increase could trigger climatic changes, cause a rise in sea level, and generally alter the environment and agriculture.

If compensating glacial oscillations are real and a new cycle is impending, some of these Greenhouse Effects may be blurred. See **GLACIATION**.

GREENLAND Greenland is the largest island in the world. It is mostly covered by the remnant of a continental ice sheet. There are only 2 ice sheets left on the globe, The other is in Antarctica. Together they cover 10% of the globe with continental ice.

As in Antarctica, the base of Greenland's ice is below sea level. The highest elevation is 3,000 meters (10,000 feet) but the ice has a thickness of 3,300 meters (10,890 feet).

In Greenland it snows all year, more in the south than in the north. The largest of Greenland's glaciers is at Jacobshaven on the west coast. It is advancing at the rate of 30 meters (100 feet) a day. When it reaches the sea, it calves into huge icebergs. Up to 15,000 icebergs are calved off every year.

Greenland was the site of some of the very first studies of alkaline igneous rocks. Illimaussaq was one of the important uranium discovery locations. The carbonatites of Greenland are rich in tantalum and niobium and they are being worked for phosphates.

An eastern extension of the Canadian Shield (q.v.), Greenland has some of the world's oldest rocks. 3.8 billion year old gneiss (q.v.) is found on Greenland.

GREENSANDS   Greensands, or greensand marls, are micaceous minerals of iron potassium silicate known as glauconite. Dark green glauconite grains form on the deep sea floor as a weathering product of biotite. Glauconite is abundant in Cretaceous rocks.

Cretaceous greensands of New Jersey were once quarried for potassium. Production only ceased with the discovery of the rich German potash deposits.

Glauconite is useful for potassium-argon dating as its crystal structure permits a ready diffusion of argon.

GREENSCHIST   Greenschist is basic igneous rock that has been metamorphosed at low temperatures. Abundant chlorite is responsible for the color and schistosity.

Seawater alters basaltic lavas to greenschist. Metalliferous hot water in a rift in an oceanic spreading zone, such as in Red Sea deep pools, suggests a source for the metals contained in the greenschist. Greenschist often has veins of iron, nickel, and copper. Metal-rich muds from weathered greenschist are often found atop sulfide orebodies.

GREENSTONE The metamorphic rock known as greenstone contains hornblende, epidote, and serpentinite, all alteration products of pyroxene. In Canada and elsewhere, greenstone is the metamorphic product of andesite, rhyolite, or basalt. Much of the material flowed into the sea and formed pillow lavas (q.v.). These lavas as well as sediments were altered. Many of the original minerals were converted to green-colored secondaries. Greenstone Belts are found in Precambrian shield areas. Long narrow belts of greenschists are found in the central parts of large continental masses. Although widely distributed, greenstone belts are found most extensively in gneissic terrain.

Commonly, the greenstone belts are basin-shaped, elongated, and generally parallel to linear belts of altered volcanic rock. The older they are, the less linear they are. The volcanics are bounded by gneiss and granite domes.

The gneiss is typically banded by severe metamorphism. In addition to gneiss and the highly metamorphosed sediments, there is often anorthosite (q.v.). Anorthosites are not very common and are limited to the Precambrian. Interestingly enough, they form a great deal of the lunar crust.

Cycles of greenstone formation have been identified between 3.9 and 2.7 billion years ago. Some identified in South Africa are:

Group	Unit	Age
Shamvaian		2.7 b.y.
Bulawayan	Upper Greenstones	2.8 b.y.
Bulawayan	Lower Greenstones	3.0 b.y.
Sebakwian		3.5 b.y.

Barberton Belt, South Africa, has been dated at 3.4 billion years while the Ivory Coast greenstones are 2.2. A similar belt in Chile (Rocas Verdes) is thought to be Cretaceous.

Some geologists think greenstones are remnants of an Archaen oceanic crust. These rocks differ from modern oceanic basalts. They formed from volcanics in down-warping ocean basins when the heatflow was 3-4 times greater than at present due to the level of radioactivity. A softer Archaen Crust allowed diapiric activity which resulted in gneissic domes.

The Precambrian Albiti Greenstone Belt in Canada is gold-bearing. The komotitic (q.v.) pile of South Africa is nickel-bearing and the Great Dyke in Zimbabwe has platinum, nickel, and copper.

GREISEN   Metasomatized granite impregnated with minerals is greisen. It contains quartz, tourmaline, topaz, cassiterite, wolframite, and fluorite.

Granites which have undergone greisenization are composed principally of quartz and muscovite, and a metamorphosed feldspar. Occasionally the mica will be lithium- or fluorine-bearing. Sometimes topaz greisen can be up to 90% of the rock. Greisens are present in many tin-tungsten deposits and are found with other mineral suites such as in molybdenum deposits. See **METASOMATISM**.

GRENVILLE FRONT   The Grenville Front, a high shear zone, is an ancient fault system (1-1.2 b.y.). It is traced by the St. Lawrence Valley. The zone passes through the Labrador Trough.

There are indications of an extension of the Grenville in northwest Ireland, the Scottish Highlands, and Scandinavia. Grenville projects west into the United States. Some scientists believe it may connect to the ancient New Madrid System (q.v.).

GREYWACKE   Poorly decomposed detrital material from basic rocks is greywacke. It is of quartz (less than 75%), feldspar, and other minerals. The fragments are dark gray-green to brown, poorly sorted, angular and of clay and sand size. Greywackes resemble sandstones that were rapidly unloaded in their original environment.

The depositional environment of greywacke is inshore with turbidity currents. Greywackes often host marine fossils. The greywacke beds are not very thick.

GRIT Sandstone with small, angular grains is grit. Its angularity is an indication that the sand grains do not travel far from their source before being consolidated. Grit is a natural abrasive (q.v.).

GROOVES Glacial ice moves slowly, centimeters per day. It takes a long time to cut long deep grooves such as found on many glacially scoured rocks. Extraordinary ones, like those on Australian Precambrian rocks and on granite overlooking the Alaskan Inland Passage are very deep and very smooth.

GROUND ICE Large masses of permafrost (q.v.) ice develop in Tundra soils. The ice melts and thaws superficially, refreezing with accompanying expansion and contraction. Permafrost soils form tundra polygons and pingos due to the presence of ground ice.

GROUNDNUT SCHEME Many attempts have been made to develop Tropical Africa. At the end of World War II, the British mounted a scheme (q.v.) to grow groundnuts, or peanuts, in East Africa on an industrial scale. Its purposes were to develop agricultural technology, help the African economies, and alleviate shortages of margarine and cooking oil in Britain.

High enthusiasm led to a large scale operation in which 3.2 million acres were put into production. This was in Tanganyika (Tanzania), Kenya, and Northern Rhodesia (Zambia). It was divided into 30,000 acre blocks from which it was expected there would be an annual yield of 600,000 tons of peanuts.

Economically and socially the natural balance in the area was upset, The machinery, much of which was second hand, failed to cope with the long root systems found in bush scrub. The machinery also tended to pack the sandy soils and rendered them unfit for peanut cultivation. First yields did not replace the seed.

It has been conjectured that had the scheme initiated by pilot projects, it might have met with some success. It was instead a major fiasco and costly to the British. Later work showed that a 50% greater peanut yield resulted from the ancient African system of fallowing after 'slash and burn' cultivation.

GROUNDWATER Water infiltrates soil and sediment to the hydrostatic level of the locale. This level is the water table, or top of the phreatic lense. The surface conforms to topography. Groundwater is often tapped for domestic use.

Underground water is 30 times more plentiful than surface water in rivers and lakes. In the United States, 20% of all domestic water is groundwater, in Israel 54%, and in Germany 70%. Groundwater may be near surface and readily tapped or, it may be at great depth as in parts of Arizona. To reach this deep water is very expensive. Deep wells are needed and a constant energy source to lift the water.

In some areas groundwater is being used faster than the replenishment rate. This is groundwater mining. It results in a general lowering of the water table. Such sources are eventually abandoned because it becomes too expensive to obtain the water.

One of the major groundwater sources in the United States is the Ogallala Formation. It supplies irrigation water to major agricultural areas. The Ogallala is being mined out. The aquifer was considered full 40 years ago. One authority said its water supply was equal to that of Lake Huron.

There is another type of groundwater not so readily reached. It is water bound up within soils, sediments, and rocks. The rocks may be at great depths. It is estimated that between 2 and 3 million cubic kilometers of water are tied up in this manner.

GROWING SEASON The growing season in temperate climates is measured from the last killing frost of spring to the first of autumn. The number of days varies widely in the United States.

On the Florida Keys, the growing season is 100% of the year. In California's productive area, it is 260 days, while elsewhere it may be 100 days or less. The kinds of crops planted depend upon the length of the growing season in a particular area.

GUANO 'Guano' is Quechua Indian for bird excrement. It is a rich source of nitrogen, phosphorus, and potash. Guano is a natural fertilizer found on islands along the Chilean and Peruvian coasts.

The high nitrogen content is probably due to the following:

- The bird types producing the guano
- Prevailing atmospheric conditions
- Age of the guano
- The oceanic contribution.
- Dry desert air which protects nitrogen.

On some of the California coastal areas and islands, guano is accumulating. These areas were set aside as sea bird sanctuaries.

Bat guano is found in many caves and caverns. The guano they produce has been critical to the United States throughout its history. During the War of 1812, when the British blockaded the country, bat guano or 'earth niter' for gunpowder was mined from caves. The bat guano was important to the Confederate Army also and they found it in Texas caves.

GUAYULE The guayule shrub ('Parthenium argentatum') is native to the Sonoran Desert of Mexico and Big Bend country of Texas. It is a gray-green shrub that reaches 60-90 centimeters (2-3 feet).

Guayule produces a latex suitable for making synthetic rubber. The latex is used as a subsitute for Hevea latex. Guayule has a high resin content, but there is now a process to deresinate it.

Quayule latex plants can be mowed rather than harvested, thus increasing the potential. Guayule rubber adheres extremely well to fabric and so is suitable for many types of hoses and belts.

An experimental acre of 5-year old guayule plants produced about 725 kilos (1,600 pounds) of latex. During World War II, the United States used 1.3 million kilos (3 million pounds) principally as a sealant for tanks.

GUIANA HIGHLANDS The Guiana Highlands bound the Amazon Basin on the north. They are ranges of low mountains and plateaus. The Guianas have a long history of erosion, uplift, peneplanation, uplift again, followed by the present erosion cycle.

The Highlands are generally flat-topped as a consequence of peneplanation (q.v.). They range in elevation from 900-2,700 meters (3,000-9,000 feet) and have steep sides. Roraima, on the Brazil, Venezuela, and Guyana boundary is the highest plateau.

The basement complex of the Guiana Highlands is of Precambrian crystalline rocks. Gold and diamonds are in alluvial deposits eroded from the basement. Gold lodes have been found but to date no kimberlite pipes as sources of the diamonds.

Uplifted sediments are plateaus, often with preserving laterite caps. The plateaus tend to be on the north or Guiana side of the divide and are rich in economic minerals, particularly bauxite.

Together with the Brazilian Highlands on the south flank of the Amazon Basin, the Guianas are the oldest mountains in South America (600 m.y.).

GUIANAS There are 5 Guianas between the Orinoco River and the Amazon. Besides the 3 nations, there are the Venezuelan and Brazilian Guianas. Most of the region is tropical rainforest, but there is a broad savannaland, part of the Venezuelan Gran Sabana. It extends some 250 kilometers (150 miles) into Brazil.

The Sabana supports one of the largest cattle ranches in the world, Dadonaw, a half million hectares. The ranch is watered by the Rupununi River. The region has a very low carrying capacity (q.v.), however, because the grass is nutritionally poor, reflecting the poor soils.

'Guiana', Indian for land of waters, has 600 navigable rivers flowing to the Atlantic. Several rivers connect the Amazon and Orinoco Systems. The Essequibo River and its tributaries drain a very large area. Much of the Guiana shoreline on the Caribbean is of wetlands and swamps which are dominated by mangrove. See **EMENDATION**.

GUINEA The West African nation of Guinea has 4 major physiographic provinces:

- The Coastal Plain, islands and lagoons.

- Fouta Djallon Massif (q.v.).
- Upper Niger Plain.
- Southwestern Highlands.

The important rivers of West Africa, the Niger, Senegal, and Gambia all rise in the Fouta Djallon.

Guinea is 45% rainforested and some of the major trees are teak and mahogany. This rainforest, like other African rainforests, is being heavily timbered to earn foreign exchange and is endangered.

Guinea is famous for its lateritic soils. Only about 6% of its land is arable. The buildup of laterites (q.v.) has led to mineral reserves of iron ore and bauxite. It is estimated that bauxite reserves amount to 7.45 billion metric tons from which 240 million metric tons of alumina can be produced. Iron ore and diamonds accounts for 1/5 of the GNP (Gross National Product).

GULF OF GUINEA The Gulf of Guinea, an arm of the Atlantic, includes the bights (q.v.) of Benin and Biafra. The Gulf receives the outflow from the Niger and Volta rivers. It abuts the African Coast at the edge of the African Plate. An island arc (q.v.) is aligned with Mount Cameroon (q.v.). The geology of this part of the African Coast corresponds to that of the stretch from Brazil to the Guianas in South America.

GULF A gulf is a portion of the sea extending into the land such that the land appears to envelope the sea. This definition fits the Gulf of California, but not so aptly the Gulf of Mexico. A gulf is much larger than a bay, but is smaller than a sea.

GULF STREAM The Gulf of Mexico may be the true source of the Gulf Stream but the Stream gains integrity as the Florida Current. As such, it flows between the West Indian Platform and the continental coast.

The path traced by the Stream is a variable one. It has been known to vary in a single month as much as 160 kilometers (100 miles). There are indications that the Gulf Stream changed course in the early 1600's. It shifted from northeast to a more easterly direction.

By 1780 it was flowing slightly to the southeast. The Sargasso Sea (q.v.) was pushed south and Arctic waters came in from the north. The great shift coincided with the Little Ice Age (q.v.) and certainly Britain felt the lack of the warmer water. Only in the 1900's did the Stream resume the course it held almost 400 years earlier.

This course is north along the United States coast to Cape Hatteras, then northeasterly. In this segment, it is 60 kilometers (40 miles) wide and 600 meters (2,000 feet) deep. Surface temperature are as high as 80° Fahrenheit. The Stream in this segment moves 6 kilometers (4 miles) an hour and carries 100 billion tons of water.

After the current moves away from Hatteras, it loses speed and is called the Eastern Drift or Atlantic Current. The Stream meets the cold Labrador Current off the Grand Banks.

Midway across the Atlantic, the current splits and the Canaries Current, powered by the Northeast Trades is born. The other arm impelled by southwest winds becomes the North Atlantic Drift.

The Drift passes between the British Isles and Iceland warming western Europe to Norway, where surface water temperatures are 45° Fahrenheit. At this point the Gulf Stream has traveled 8,330 kilometers (5,000 miles). The temperature effect is such that in some areas on the western coast of Scotland and Ireland there are pockets of subtropical vegetation.

Stream velocity varies. Overall it is the fastest current in the open ocean, up to 18 kilometers (11 miles) per hour, averaging 8 kilometers (5 miles). Over Blake Plateau, flow is 1-2 kilometers (4-5 knots) per hour and it has scrubbed the Plateau clear. Maximum current depth is 788 meters (2,600 feet).

A slow-moving cold counter-current has been charted moving beneath the Gulf Stream on the western edge of the Sargasso Sea.

Gulf Stream waters are indigo colored. In the open ocean, they are slightly darker than those of the Atlantic. This is due to its density. Glowing streaks of 'white water' appear on the Stream from time to time. These were mentioned by Columbus and have been an enigma since.

Ponce de Leon, Spanish discoverer of Florida, was first to note the Gulf Stream. His ships in full sail cruising off Canaveral were propelled backwards. The Stream was first charted by Benjamin Franklin in 1770.

GUMBO Gumbo is an especially sticky soil when wet. In Missouri, the putty-like clays are associated with the lead-zinc deposits.

GUYANA The largest of the Guianas (q.v.), Guyana is typical of the 3 nations with its narrow coastal plain fringing a tropical rainforest. In the southern part of the country are some of the world's most beautiful waterfalls, among them Kaieteur with its 224.5 meter (741 foot) drop followed by another of 30 meters (100 feet). The falls are 36 meters wide (120 feet).

Guyana produces bauxite from weathered Precambrian terrain and has been the world's major source of metallurgical bauxite. In the highlands bordering Brazil, there have been some major diamond discoveries which led to border disputes. See **GUIANAS**.

GUYOTS Guyots are flat-topped seamounts. They probably once had peaks that were eroded off by wave action. A volcano rising from the seafloor, breaking the surface would be flattened.

Volcanoes arose in the Cretaceous (136-65 m.y.) and then sank beneath the sea. There is a great chain of these undersea, flat-topped mountains in the Pacific.

It is difficult to explain the almost 1,000 meters (3,000 feet) of sea overlying these mountains, some of which rise nearly 4,000 meters (13,000 feet) from the ocean floor. The average height is 1,200 meters (3,600 feet). Plate tectonics may hold the solution to what appears to be a great subsidence of the ocean's floor.

GYMNOSPERM The ancestors of modern land plants probably emerged from the ocean between 400 and 500 million years ago. They are assumed to have been simple marine organisms not unlike modern Algae. All plants are thought to have been descended from these primitive forms of Algae, Fungi, and Bacteria. These forms are grouped in the Thallophyta Phylum.

The descendents of the Thallophytes were more complex but still relatively simple plants. They were spore-bearing and have been grouped in the Pteridophyta Phylum. The group became the dominant vegetation in the Paleozoic. The enormous coal seams found in the Carboniferous horizons testify to this dominance. The period closed with great forests of ferns, giant horsetails and club mosses.

From the same Thallophytes that produced the Pteridophytes or from the Pteridophytes seed-producing plants appeared. Later these seed-producers out-distanced the Pteridophytes.

Seed producing plants are divided into the unprotected seed of the gymnosperms and the protected angiosperms, or flowering plants. Conifers are the most widespread of the gymnosperms. Conifers appeared before the end of the Carboniferous. By the Eocene, however, the dominant vegetation was of the angiosperms.

GYPSUM White to yellowish gypsum is a hydrated calcium sulfate found in many parts of the world interstratified with limestones and anhydrite. Gypsum originally weathered out of igneous rocks as iron pyrite and calcite. These went into solution in epicontinental seas. Later in the cycle of transgression and regression, they were precipitated in evaporative basins as calcium sulfate. In the United States, impressive gypsum deposits are associated with evaporites left upon the regression of the Sundance Sea.

Clear transparent calcium sulfate crystals are selenite. These crystals can be found in many areas of the southwestern desert of the United States.

Gypsum is often encountered in caves and caverns. Sometimes the crystals are bent. As they grow out from the base they can take on flower-like shapes. The famous Snowball Dining Room in Mammoth Cave has masses of gypsum on its walls. Gypsum is precipitated as a by-product of the phosphate fertilizer production. The gypsum waste generated presents a problem because the calcium sulfate may leach into the groundwater.

Gypsum is used as wallboard or as an additive for cement. Some is used in plaster of Paris. Fine-grained translucent calcium sulfate is alabaster. It is a popular carving medium.

GYRE In the Atmosphere a gyre is an eddy born of a cyclonic storm. Gyre centers are coincident with subtropical high pressure zones.

Main oceanic currents form enormous elliptical loops that are gyres. Motion in the Northern Hemisphere is clockwise, in the Southern, counter-clockwise as a result of the Coriolis Force (q.v.).

It is thought the shape of the continents also play a role in the generation of gyres. The Falklands Eddy in the curve of the Argentinian coastal area shows this phenomenon. Gyre energy probably helps maintain the integrity of the Sargasso Sea (q.v.). It is suggested that eddies preserve its oval shape and prevent the waters from mixing with the rest of the Atlantic.

GYROSCOPE A gyroscope is an instrument based on the Earth's rotation. The Gyroscope can resist induced torque that would alter spin. Gyroscopes are subject to precession or drift. The Earth itself is a great gyro and is subject, as are all gyros, to precession (q.v.).

The gyroscope principle is used in the gyrocompass which has a spinning axis parallel to the horizon. It is more stable than a magnetic compass. It must be reset at frequent intervals, however, because of the precession.

Himalayan Mountains — Pakistan
Courtesy of Dr. Carlisle, Earth & Planetary Sciences, UCLA

H

HABITAT The living space or immediate environment of a particular group of organisms is the habitat. It is an ecospace within the ecosystem (q.v.) and includes all facets of the local environment.

HABOOB Whirlwind in Arabic is 'haboob'. It is a violent and destructive sandstorm. Periodically, it affects Egypt, Sudan, Arabia, and the Indian Plains. The coalescing and eddying clouds of dust and sand are propelled by strong winds.

The haboob airmass can reach 1,500 meters (5,000 feet) into the Atmosphere. Visibility is reduced to zero or almost.

The storms do not last long but a settlement can be buried in sand very quickly. In some areas the haboob is followed by heavy rain. In northern Sudan, it almost invariably rains mud.

HACHURES Topographic map symbols indicating depressions are hachures. These are short marks made from a closed contour line. They point to the center of the depression.

HADLEY CELL There is an exchange of airmasses in the tropics. This exchange occurs in a semi-enclosed area, or Hadley Cell, that is located between Latitude 30° and the Equator.

Warm moist air rises in the tropics and moves to the Mid-Latitudes where it sinks. The airmass is transported back toward the Equator by the Trade Winds.

HADRON The hadron is a strongly interactive subatomic particle that decays to stable particles (protons, electrons, photons, and neutrinos). The end product of cascading emission energy is a proton of the baryon type, or a heavy proton. Other particles may be produced such as leptons and photons.

HAIL Hail is a form of solid precipitation. Its occurrence is occasional and restricted in distribution. Hail is composed of ice pellets (hailstones) that are larger than sleet (q.v.).

Hailstones develop during intense thunderstorms from ice-layering on frozen water droplets. Droplets are carried upward by convective currents. When they reach below freezing temperatures, the ice coating forms.

If the updraft is overcome by gravity, the pellet sinks. It may then be coated with additional water and carried aloft again in another updraft. It mixes with snow, refreezes, and the pellet grows. Precipitation occurs when updraft forces no longer can overcome pellet weight.

Hail, although associated with thunderstorms, is practically unknown in the tropics where thunderstorms abound. It is also rare in warm subtropics where thunderstorms are at a maximum, as in Florida and along the Gulf Coast.

Hail and hail damage are local occurrences on the Great Plains and in the Rocky Mountains. It is the most destructive type of precipitation. In the United States, hail costs at least $200 million per year in crop and property damage.

HALF-GRABEN When there is assymetrical movement of a fault block a half-graben forms. The half-graben is characteristic of intracontinental rifts, such as the Mid-Continent in the Lake Superior area.

Copper and nickel mineralization in layered mafic intrusions of the Duluth Complex are found in the Lake Superior half-graben.

HALF-LIFE The time it takes for half the atoms of a parent radioactive element to disintegrate through 'daughter elements' (q.v.) to their end product is its 'half-life'. Each stage has its individual half-life and the half-life differs for each decaying element. The process may take from a millionth of a second to billions of years. The half-life of uranium is 4.5 billion years. It takes that long for half its atoms to be converted to radiogenic lead. See **RADIOACTIVITY**.

HALITE Halite, composed of sodium chloride, is rock salt. Its crystal habit is cubic and it has 3 directions of cleavage. Halite is usually translucent and has a distinctive taste. It can occur in massive formations and is widespread.

Massive halite deposits are found in New York State. Halite deposits in Poland have enormous underground workings. Salt today is, however, more commonly recovered from brines and seawater. See **SALT**.

HALLEY'S COMET Halley's Comet is visible from the Earth every 76 years. It was seen passing the Earth in 1910 and again in 1986. In March, 1986, it was especially observable in the Southern Hemisphere.

The Comet's tail measured 10° of arc, or 20 times the width of the Moon. In 1910, the tail was reported as 90°. Its center is a tiny mass of ice.

The Comet was photographed by Explorer and some satellites. These photographs are being carefully studied. The comet will orbit the Earth again in 2061. See **COMET**.

HALMROLYSIS The process of weathering submarine sediments by the removal of certain ions and through chemical exchange is halmrolysis.

HALO Ice-bearing cirrus clouds very high in the sky have a halo effect observed as a ring around the moon. The effect is an optical illusion.

A rainbow effect can be noted as the Sun's rays pass through the ice crystals in the clouds. A much less observed effect is 'the ring around the Sun'.

HALOCLINE The halocline is a segment of the oceanic water column which reflects a great change in salinity. The halocline moves up and down as salinity increases or decreases.

The halocline is more observable in higher latitudes due to a reduction in surface heating and increased precipitation.

HALOGEN Chemically, halogens are producers of salts. They make up a group on the Periodical Table (q.v.). Halogens have 7 electrons in the outer atomic shell and are capable of accepting 1 more.

Metals readily lose electrons so they easily form salts with the halogens. The best known example is table salt formed from sodium and the halogen chlorine.

HALOMORPHIC Intrazonal, alkaline and saline soils are halomorphic. They are usually found in semi-arid areas where drainage is confined to interior basins. These soils include Solonchaks, or saline soils, that are common in Central Asia.

HALOPHYTE Salt-loving or salt-tolerant vegetation is halophytic. It resembles desert vegetation in having thorns or fleshy leaves, as well as other adaptive characteristics. The Australian saltbush is a halophyte.

HAMMADA The 'Hammada', Berber for rocky desert, is a landform of low relief. All fine material has been removed by wind deflation leaving bare rocks. These rocks are broken into boulders and stones of varying sizes creating a chaotic landscape.

HANGCHOW BAY Hangchow Bay is an arm of the East China Sea. It has a famous tidal bore. The bay is funnel-shaped and wave heights can rapidly build. The bore affects shipping from Shanghai.

HANGING VALLEY The valley of a tributary stream is not cut as deeply by glacial scour as the main stream. Differential cutting sometimes leaves the mouth of the tributary far above the valley. Height differences can be so great, the tributary must join the main stream by a cascading waterfall.

There are 2 beautiful cascades over 300 meters (1,000 feet) in Yosemite, California. Hanging valleys with such cascades are also found in Colorado and Chile, among other glaciated areas.

HANGING WALL The exposed face of a block-faulted rock is the hanging wall. It is above the separated portion.

HARD ROCK MINING Mining of ores in igneous or metamorphic rocks is referred to by miners and geologists as 'hard rock' mining. These rocks are hard because they have been welded by heat and pressure. They solidified from a hot melt or magma. Sedimentary rocks are considered 'soft rocks'.

HARD WATER   Water with a high mineral content is known as 'hard water'. Water with calcium and magnesium as carbonates is common where calcareous rocks abound. These carbonates may be removed and the water 'softened'. When the included minerals are sulfates, chlorides, and nitrates, the water is permanently hard.

HARDNESS   One of the identifying characteristics of minerals is hardness. This hardness depends upon the strength of atomic bonding within the crystal structure. Harder minerals are more tightly bonded.

To test hardness, the Moh's Scale (q.v.) is in common use. In the field, a geologist or miner may use a fingernail, a piece of steel or glass to determine relative hardness. See **BONDING**.

HARDPAN   Hardpan is the name given to crusts appearing in the Lower A or B Horizons of a soil profile. It is formed of cemented soil particles. The cementing agent may be of silica, sesquioxides (q.v.), or calcium carbonate.

Iron hardpan forms from sesquioxides and is cemented by them. Silcrete (q.v.) forms when silica cements silicate detritus. Calcrete and calcareous hardpans are cemented by calcium carbonate. In this case, the matrix may or may not be calcareous.

In the desert southwest of the United States, hardpan is almost universally a calcareous crust at or near the surface. In Australia hardpan or 'duricrust' (q.v.) may refer to any near surface indurated horizon.

HARLECH DOME   The Harlech Dome is an ancient structure which split when the continent of Pangaea (q.v.) broke up (60 m.y.). Part of the dome is found in the mountains of northwest Wales. A complement of the Welsh Dome is found on Avalon Peninsula in southeast Newfoundland, 2,200 kilometers (1,320 miles) away.

The areas are equidistant from the Mid-Atlantic Ridge. Sediments are similar and date from 570-500 million years. They contain similar trilobites.

HARMATTAN   A seasonal wind blowing from the Saharan High to West Africa as far south as Liberia is called the 'Harmattan'. It has strong, constant, dust-laden winds which blow for 8 months of the year. These winds carry sands from as far east as Tibesti (q.v.), in Libya. The dry wind reaches into the Atlantic as far as the Madeira Islands.

HARZ MASSIF   The Harz Mountains rise from the north German Plain to a height of 700 meters (3,000 feet). They trend NW-SE across West and East Germany for 100 kilometers (60 miles) in a 32 kilometer (20 mile) swath.

The landscape is deeply ravined. Granites have intruded the sediments which are metamorphosed. The mountains have quartzite ridges. The cycles of uplift and erosion took 250 million years.

In the west, the Harz are steplike and lower slopes are covered by spruce and fir. Above them are the mountain meadows. Valleys host peat bogs noted for their marsh gas (q.v.) buildup. In the eastern or Lower Harz, the landscape is gentler and the lower slopes support deciduous trees like oak and beech.

HAWAII In Mid-Pacific, the 8 Hawaiian Islands are part of a great volcanic chain. This chain extends from the coral island of Kure, northwest of Midway, through 30° of Longitude. It traces an arc to the southeast covering 2600 kilometers (1600 miles) of the Pacific Ocean. See **ISLAND ARCS**.

Hawaii was formed of basalt flows from volcanoes and vents. These volcanoes are not related to the Pacific Rim of Fire. They are in the center of the Pacific Plate, over a series of hot spots or plumes (q.v.).

There are presently 2 active volcanoes on the islands, Mauna Loa and Mauna Kea. Others are active beneath the sea. Maui is the world's largest dormant volcano.

Climate on the islands is dependent on location, whether in a rain shadow or not. There are water shortages on some islands. Leeward on Mauna Kea is an arid area which receives only 10 centimeters (4 inches) of rain a year. There is a trough between Mauna Loa and Mauna Kea that is one of the world's driest areas. Other island locations receive abundant rainfall. Kauai averages 195 centimeters (475 inches) per year.

There are varied vegetation patterns resulting from the great climate variability. Windward slopes of the main islands support rainforests. Outlying atolls support grass, palms, shrubs, and thistle.

Because of its uneven distribution, the water budget of Hawaii presents problems with a growing population and increased agriculture. The destruction of rainforest to create pasturage will only increase the problems. See **HAWAIIAN RAINFOREST**.

HAWAIIAN ARCH The Hawaiian Chain developed as a part of the Hawaiian Arch. This geological structure is built about a central moat with flanking arches. The arches have a maximum height of 1.5 kilometers (1 mile) and a wavelength of 500-600 kilometers (300-360 miles). The Hawaiian Arch is similar to the Cretaceous Ponta Grossa Arch of South America, with its great axial dike swarms.

HAWAIIAN RAINFOREST The Hawaiian Rainforest has an ecosystem that supports many flowering plants. About 300 of these are trees. There are 140 different species of ferns, some towering enough to be trees. The forest is laced with vines and orchids are common.

Of the 125 bird species indigenous to the Islands, the majority live in the rainforest. This rainforest, like all tropical rainforests, is being destroyed. At present a 3,300 acre tract of myrtle wood reaching 30 meters (100 feet) in height is being cut to make wood chips. Then the area will be converted to pasture.

Since the rainforest plays an important role in moderating climate and stabilizing water supplies on the Islands, its destruction means environmental changes and some species extinctions. See **HAWAII**.

HAWAIIAN RIDGE The Hawaiian Ridge in the Pacific Ocean extends from the Kure Islands to the Hawaii volcanoes, a distance of 2,600 kilometers (1,600 miles) with its high point at Mauna Kea. Maximum present activity is concentrated at Mauna Loa and Kilauea Crater on its flank at the southeast end of the Hawaiian Ridge.

Volcanism progressed from northwest to southeast. The Molokai Fracture in the Pacific Plate extends 5,000 kilometers (3,000 miles) from the East Pacific Rise to the Hawaiian Ridge.

HAZE The atmospheric condition known as haze is the optical effect of light on aerosol particulates. These particulates are typically 1-10 micrometers in radius (1 micrometer = 0.00004 inches). Winds are capable of carrying small particulates hundreds of thousands of kilometers, sometimes keeping them aloft for months.

Haze from an airmass replete with particulates is different from local haze which is often the result of fuel-burning. Haze on the East Coast of the United States has in addition to wafted particulates a component of residual heavy oil rich in nickel and vanadium. In other areas, coals rich in arsenic, selenium, and other elements release particulates of these elements into the Atmosphere.

Throughout the country, lead is being added to atmospheric haze from auto exhaust fumes, although less so with unleaded gasoline. Zinc and antimony have been detected from burning refuse. Dark brown or orange color in much western haze is due mostly to these elements. See **SMOG**.

HEADWARD EROSION Stream erosion eats into a headwaters area, tending to enlarge it and cut it down. Headward erosion may result in the disappearance of the divide and the capture and alteration of stream flow.

HEADWATERS Collection areas where streams and water courses form are headwaters. It is an ill-defined area, but is the source of the feeder rivers of a drainage system. Usually it is the highest part of a basin.

HEATFLOW Heat is a form of energy which when added to matter results in evaporation, expansion, fusion, and a rise in temperature producing other physical changes. The 3rd Law of Thermodynamics states that heat moves but not cold since cold is only the absence of heat. Heat flows only from hot to cold.

The major source of heat within the Earth is radioactive decay. Some of this radioactive heat is residual from planetary formation. The internal heat is estimated at 10^{21} joules per year. (Average is 0.06 joules/square meter/second or 60 milliwatts per square meter).

Within the Earth's crust hot material rises to form new oceanic crust. This is a known phenomenon at oceanic ridges and rifts such as the East Pacific Rise. The seafloor is rapidly spreading and the heat is removed by the circulation of seawater within the crustal material. This creates chemically rich 'smokers', or hot spots. See **HOT SPOTS**.

HEAVY METALS All heavy metals have high specific gravities. This leads to their ready separation by gravity. The heavy metals include cobalt, iron, lead, mercury, nickel, titanium, and uranium.

HEAVY MINERALS Relatively rare and heavy minerals found in placer concentrations are indicator minerals of continental sediments. Magnetite and rutile are most common.

HEAVY WATER Water contains an isotope of hydrogen called deuterium (q.v.). The fraction containing deuterium is called 'heavy water'. Heavy water has higher boiling and freezing points than ordinary water. It is more viscous also. Seawater is a source of deuterium.

Deuterium is used as a raw material for fusion nuclear reactors. It acts as a moderator, slowing down neutron activity.

HECTORITE Hectorite is a clay composed of a sodium magnesium silicate and lithium. Its primary importance has been in filtering beer. The type locality is Hector, California.

HELIUM Helium is the second most abundant element in the Universe. The universal mass is 75% hydrogen and 23% helium. The Sun produces helium from hydrogen by nuclear reaction.

Helium escapes from the Earth because it is so lightweight. The amount being released from the Crust and the amount escaping into the Atmosphere are in a steady-state since helium is constantly being produced from radioactive decay.

Helium atoms are stable and don't combine even with other helium atoms. Helium gas, is composed of atoms, not molecules. It has the lowest of all boiling points, only a few degrees above Absolute Zero (q.v.). It liquifies at $4°$ Kelvin at which point it becomes a superconductor (q.v.).

All radioactivity releasing Alpha Rays produce helium. Helium nuclei, which are positively charged alpha particles, are released in great amounts by radioactive decay of uranium or thorium. A single helium atom has 28 MeV (million electron volts). As much as 2% helium is recorded from natural gas wells.

As a lighter than air gas, helium is used to propel balloons. It is non-inflammable. Helium is now used by divers since it causes less difficulty with 'the bends' than nitrogen. Industrially helium is used in laser technology.

HELLS CANYON Hells Canyon is one of the deepest gorges in North America. It is 2,394 meters (7,900 feet) deep. The Snake River cuts through 200 kilometers (125 miles) of volcanics to create the steep-sided canyon on the Oregon-Idaho border. Hells Canyon and Copper Canyon in Sonora, Mexico, are deeper than the Grand Canyon. Hells Canyon is also called the Grand Canyon of the Snake River.

HEMATITE Hematite is a dark-colored iron oxide mineral that gives a blood-red streak. It is a common mineral and gives a red tone to many soils and rocks. Laminated hematite is known as itabirite (q.v.),

Hematite is found as an earthy ochre (q.v.), as a compact or massive ore, and as oolitic or fossil iron ore. As oolite, it has an affinity for manganese and is found in deep sea nodules.

HEMISPHERE When a great circle bisects the Earth, the created halves are hemispheres. The Equator separates the Northern Hemisphere from the Southern. Custom has decreed that Europe, Asia, Africa and Australia are in the Eastern Hemisphere while North and South America are in the Western.

HERCYNIAN OROGENY The Hercynian Orogeny was the folding of the Earth's crust during the Carboniferous Period (345-280 m.y.). Mountain-building was accompanied by granitic intrusions which are still evident in Europe. The Hercynian Woods of the Black Forest, Germany, gave the orogeny its name.

HERODOTUS The Greek historian, Herodotus, 480-420 B.C., speculated that the Nile Delta was built in a former Mediterranean gulf. Sediments had been deposited by the Nile (q.v.) for over 20,000 years. Herodotus named the distribution plain a 'delta', for the triangular-shaped letter of the Greek alphabet.

HIATUS Any gap in a sedimentary sequence is considered an hiatus. It represents a time of no deposition. The hiatus is distinct from an unconformity (q.v.) and usually represents a narrower span of time.

HIGH PRESSURE SYSTEM A high pressure system is a very large airmass with high internal barometric pressure (q.v.). The airmass may be up to a 1,600 kilometers (1,000 miles) in diameter. Air subsides within the mass due to density.

Winds diverge from the center of the High. The resulting airmasses are responsible for a variety of weather including the extremely cold air in mid-continental United States that originates in the Arctic.

The high pressure system airmass can also act as a heat pump, as does the Bermuda High. High pressure areas can block storms, even hurricanes. They can also prolong a storm's intensity by preventing its movement.

It was such a 'stalled' high pressure zone which caused and prolonged the drought on the plains of the United States in 1988. This drought ruined the year's corn crop.

HILL A hill is a landscape prominence of lower elevation than a mountain. It is less than 300 meters (1,000 feet) above the terrain. Hills are often formed by dissection of uplands, plateaus, or volcanoes. They do not result directly from uplift.

HIMALAYAS The Himalayas form a vast wall in Afghanistan, Kashmir, India, Nepal, Pakistan, and Tibet. They are the highest continental mountains on Earth. At the western end are the Hindu Kush and Karakorum ranges. The Hindu Kush Range alone is 1,000 kilometers long (600 miles) and has 20 peaks over 7,000 meters (23,000 feet) high.

There are few passes over the Himalayas. The most famous is Khyber Pass, a 53-kilometer (33 mile) gap in the Safed Koh Range. It links Pakistan and Afghanistan.

Himalayan foothills are jungle-covered to 900 meters (1,000 feet) and forested to 2,575 meters (8,500 feet). The subsequent scrub forest gives way to Alpine Tundra. Most of the mountains are snow-capped. Everest, the highest, is 8,796 meters (29,028 feet). Several others reach 7,880 meters (26,000 feet). The mountains are composed of fossiliferous marine sediments including limestones, some dating from the Cambrian (570-500 m.y.).

3 great rivers rise in the Himalayas. These are the Indus to the Arabian Sea, the Ganges, and the Brahmaputra. These last 2 deposit their loads onto the same delta in the Bay of Bengal.

HISTORICAL GEOLOGY Historical geology is devoted to landscape evolution and the history of lifeforms on Earth. The development of geological chronology is due in part to this study.

The historical geologist synthesizes and interprets data in terms of time and interrelationships. Paleontology, the study of past lifeforms, is very important to this interpretation.

HOAR Sublimation (q.v.) occurs when the surface crust of snow is colder than the air. Minute hoar frost crystals form which are more fragile than snow. Hoar forms as a result of the temperature difference between the snow and the air. This difference may be considerable. In Switzerland, 15° Fahrenheit has been recorded.

Since hoar crystals are weaker than snow crystals, they can break when overloaded by new snowfall. Since they present a weak base, they can trigger an avalanche (q.v.).

HOBA WEST METEORITE Hoba West, at 60-80 tons in weight, is the largest known meteorite. This extraterrestrial rock is embedded in sandstone in Botswana, southwest Africa. See **METEORITES**.

HOGBACK Steep, narrow, elongated hills of resistant rock are hogbacks. Tilted sediments of different resistances have built a set of ridges and valleys. In western United States, these landforms reminded the early settlers of razor-backed hogs.

Hogback sediments generally dip more than 30°. The hogback is similar to the cuesta (q.v.) but the angle of dip is greater.

HOLOCENE Holocene is the name given to recent geological time. including the Present. It corresponds to the Neolithic Age for its onset and encompasses the last 10,000-12,000 years. Recent alluvial deposits, beach and dune sands, and volcanic sediments make up the Holocene deposits.

HOMEOSTASIS Inherent stability, or the capacity of a system to self-regulate, is homeostasis. It is the ability of a system to resist external change. Homeostasis does allow a system to maintain itself and also to subtly change. It is extremely important to biological systems.

In homeostasis, there is at all times a controlled feedback which allows for new conditions. It is this mechanism that allows the system to interact with the environment.

HOMESTAKE MINE Homestake, one of the deepest gold mines in the Western Hemisphere, began with surface operations. The vein was part of a mile-wide gold belt. Gold content dropped off with depth.

About a ton of earth must be moved to obtain 0.3 Troy ounces. By 1963, a billion dollars worth of gold had been produced. The mine at Lead, South Dakota, opened in 1878.

HOMESTEAD ACT In 1862, Congress enacted the Homestead Act to assist settlement of Western United States. Originally, settlers were awarded 160 acres. This was found inadequate because of the semi-arid nature of the climate and was amended to 640 acres.

HOMOCLINE A group of sedimentary beds dipping in the same direction at about the same angle creates a homocline.

HOMOPOLAR BONDING Homopolar bonding is covalent bonding or sharing of electrons with adjacent atoms of the same element. Fluorine has 7 electrons in the outer shell. 6 of these are paired. The 7th pairs with a 7th electron from an adjacent fluorine atom to form a molecule. This is an example of homopolar bonding.

Carbon has 4 electrons in the outer shell and can form 4 homopolar bonds. Diamonds show this homopolar bonding. See **BONDING**.

MOUNT HOOD Mount Hood, a volcano in the Cascade Range in northwestern United States, is the highest point in Oregon. It is 60 miles from Mount St. Helens (q.v.). Hood has been dormant since 1865. There were 160 earthquakes registered at Hood in 1980. The volcano is being monitored by the U.S. Geological Survey.

HOOGHLY RIVER The Hooghly River, a distributary of the Ganges System, flows from the Himalayas to the Bay of Bengal. Calcutta, a port on the Hooghly, experiences a tidal bore that tends to keep the channel open to the sea. At times water moving upstream is destructive.

HORIZON 'Horizon' is Greek for boundary. The line, in the distance, where Earth and sky appear to meet is the horizon.

A stratigraphic level in sedimentary rocks is called an horizon.

Layers in a soil profile are also horizons.

HORN When a headland is shaped by erosion to form a pyramid, it is called a horn. The landform is found in glaciated areas where the erosion has been in the form of glacial plucking (q.v.).

CAPE HORN A glacially eroded headland on Isla Hornos is known as Cape Horn. The island is 110 kilometers (70 miles) south of Tierra del Fuego. It is the tip of South America and where that continent is closest to Antarctica.

Cape Horn became famous in the days of sailing vessels. 'Round the Horn' was a hazardous journey from the Atlantic to the Pacific. The great Westerlies (q.v.) had to be faced.

Today, supertankers, too large for the Panama Canal are making the long voyage 'round the Horn'.

HORNBLENDE The ferromagnesium mineral, hornblende is dark green or black and is the most common of the Amphibole Group (q.v.). It is found in igneous, metamorphic, and sedimentary rocks. Hornblende crystals have a satiny luster and long, narrow prisms. The mineral is sometimes mistaken for pyroxene (q.v.).

HORNFELS Hornfels forms from shale baked under great heat and pressure. A metamorphic rock, it is fine-grained and forms into a 'mosaic' of interlocking minerals.

HORSE LATITUDES The belts of high pressure known as the Horse Latitudes receive warm air brought by the Trade Winds. The air cools and sinks in these belts which hover about 30° North and South Latitude. The Horse Latitudes are characterized by calm, light, and variable winds. Precipitation in these latitudes is less than on either side of the belts.

The origin of the name is disputed. Some think that sailors considered the Horse Latitudes as unpredictable as an old mare. The Spaniards are reputed to have thrown many horses overboard in these latitudes. When they were becalmed, it is assumed their horses died from a lack of freshwater.

HORSESHOE CRAB The horseshoe crab ('Limulus polymus') is not a crab. It is, instead, the evolutionary predecessor of the spider and scorpion. It is a 'living fossil' that first appeared about 250 million years ago. It is related to the trilobite (q.v.) that became extinct about 300 million years ago.

Larvae of the horseshoe crab look like trilobites. The adult organism has 2 pairs of eyes, one of which can see polarized light.

In Delaware Bay, the crab was so common there were over a million crabs on a mile of beach at mating time. The crab was over-harvested for feed and fertilizer. It is now an endangered species.

HORSETAIL VEIN A reasonably thick vein of ore may spread out into thin veinlets running every which way. Miners were reminded of a horse's tail when it fanned, so they gave the vein its name.

HORST 'Horst' is German for an elongated uplifted block bounded by steep linear scarps. The upthrust block between down-dropped blocks is the horst. It is opposite to the graben (q.v.). Block faulting will give rise to 'horst and graben' terrain such as found in the Basin and Range Province in the United States.

HOSS HOSS is an acronym for High Volume Open Sea Skimmer. It is a special vessel designed to skim oil spills from the sea surface. It has an intake capacity of 2,000 gallons per minute.

HOT SPOTS Hot Spots are volcanic centers located mid-plate or near the junction of crustal plates. They result from convective activity in the Mantle. Hot spots are over relatively stationary plumes (q.v.).

The Iceland Plume is believed to have been in existence when Pangaea (q.v.) rifting began. Under Iceland, it is estimated that there are 25 or more magma chambers in a line with the Reykjanes Ridge. Reykjanes is a surface expression of the Mid-Atlantic Ridge (q.v.).

In the hot spots, rifting does not appear to be continuous but is by eruption from individual magma chambers. Seafloor spreading creates a volcanic ridge bounded by faults in the hot spot areas.

The Juan de Fuca Hot Spot off Oregon is above metalliferous hot plumes. The hot spots in the Red Sea and beneath the East Pacific Rise also are highly mineralized and related to seafloor spreading. The average spreading rate is centimeters per year.

Alvin (q.v.) investigations show that seafloor organisms deplete sulfur and oxygen around the vents over the hot spots. These elements provide the energy source for these lifeforms.

The number of known hot spots has grown since the 1976 count of 122. NASA recently discovered an anomalously high temperature over what is probably a hot spot in the Atlantic, 3,000 kilometers (1,800 miles) east of Miami.

HOT SPRINGS When springs are above the ambient water temperature of an area, they are 'hot springs'. Geysers are intermittent hot springs with temperatures well above that of local water.

Yellowstone Park has about 3,000 hot springs. Spring waters are heated by pressure and molten rock beneath the surface. Many hot springs around the world have temperatures about 37° Celsius and have been heated by radioactivity. Many of them are famous health spas.

Hot springs are a source of geothermal energy. In New Zealand and Iceland, hot springs are economically useful. In Iceland the hot waters are pumped into greenhouses to grow fruits, vegetables, and flowers. They are also used to heat homes.

HOWLING 50's There is a belt of westerly winds between 50 and 60° South Latitude. The winds are so strong, the belt is referred to as the 'Howling 50's'. In the days of sailing vessels, the wind in the rigging was said to howl.

HUAYCO AVALANCHE The collapse of natural dams high in the Andes released glacial meltwater and an aqueous mudslide occurred. The collapse at Huayco was triggered by an earthquake. The avalanche of mud was so great it buried a number of Andean villages with an enormous amount of rock and earth.

HUBBARD GLACIER Hubbard Glacier in southern Alaska on Yakutat Bay is a surge glacier given to sudden movements of great velocity. The speed can reach 250-660 kilometers (150-400 miles) per hour. Movement is lubricated by water beneath the glacier.

Hubbard Glacier, named for the Jesuit glaciologist, Father Hubbard, began surging about 90 years ago and has been on the move since. The average distance covered in a year has been 25 meters (80 feet) but in 1986 the giant glacier, moved much faster. By late August it had moved 12.5 meters (40 feet) a day. It then slowed to almost half that velocity.

Hubbard is the 3rd largest glacier in North America and it is in the St. Elias Range. It is 150 kilometers (90 miles) long by 10 kilometers (6 miles) wide and 90 meters (300 feet) thick. The west branch is 125 kilometers (75 miles) long. Hubbard is the longest valley glacier so far measured.

The glacier is calving off up to 60 meter (200 foot) blocks of ice into Yakutat Bay. Its lateral morainal ice has converted Russell Fjord into Russell Lake, making it one of the largest of glacier-dammed lakes.

The effect Hubbard Glacier is having on the Lake, Situk River, wildlife, and forest as it moves is as yet unknown. Yakutat town is threatened by the massive glacier.

HUDSON BAY Hudson Bay is the largest bay in the world and is bounded by Quebec, Ontario, Manitoba provinces, and the Northwest Territories of Canada. It was named for Henry Hudson, whose Hudson Bay Company opened up the area.

Hudson Bay is connected to the Atlantic by Hudson Strait between Baffin Island and the Ungava Peninsula of Quebec. Cutting into Ontario and Quebec in the south is James Bay. Hudson Bay is ice-bound a good part of the year.

The shores of the Bay are a favored polar bear habitat. They find it a prime area for fishing in summer.

HUDSON CANYON The submarine canyon off the Hudson River is a drowned portion of the river valley. The canyon is 15-30 meters (50-100 feet) deep and 1.6 kilometers (1 mile) wide at Sandy Hook. From the edge of the Continental Shelf southeast, it is 180 meters (600 feet) wide.

The Canyon extends 240 kilometers (150 miles) into the Atlantic from the mouth of the river. The canyon's end is marked by a nearly perfect volcanic cone, Caryn Seamount.

HUDSON RIVER Henry Hudson, when he sailed up the Hudson River thought he had discovered the legendary 'Northwest Passage'. The river has such a low gradient from Albany, New York, to the sea that Atlantic tides are present with a range of 1.5 meters (5 feet).

The Hudson rises in glacial Lake Tear of the Clouds on Mount Marcy, which is New York's highest. The river separates Taconic Range on the east from the Catskills. In the lower reaches, the river is flanked by the Palisades Sill (q.v.) on the west and Manhattan Island on the east.

HUMBOLDT CURRENT The Humboldt Current is cold, swift, and wide. It originates off Antarctica at the tip of South America. Humboldt flows north to become the Peru Current. Off Ecuador it turns west. It is so cold, penguins are found in its waters near the Equator.

The Humboldt Current is the weather-maker of western South America. Its winds bring 508 centimeters (200 inches) of rain to Chile's south coast annually. Farther north, where the land is warmer, clouds absorb the available moisture and the deserts of Chile and Peru receive no rain but do have fog.

Offshore winds sweep surface waters out to sea and subsurface cold waters rise to replace it. This upwelling (q.v.) brings nutrients to the surface waters and marine life abounds.

Once every 12 years or so, although presently more often, the winds shift and storms hit the coast. Such a storm is El Niño (q.v.). Its warm current forces the cold Humboldt-Peru away from the coast. The effects on fish are tremendous and populations are depleted. See **EL NINO**.

HUMIDITY The amount of water vapor or humidity retained by an air-mass depends upon temperature. Warm air retains much more than cold. Humidity is greatest at the Earth's surface and in low latitudes.

Humidity at a specific temperature and pressure is referred to as:

Absolute - When a direct measure

Specific - Water vapor weight in air

Relative - Percent of total humidity that could be held.

HUMUS Humus is decayed plant and animal matter in soils. Humus adds to the mineral and nutrient content of the soil. It also assists soils to retain moisture. The presence of humus causes the pore space in soil to increase, which allows for greater aeration.

HURONIAN OROGENY The Huronian Orogeny was a time of uplift and mountain building in the Precambrian (q.v.). It marked the change from the Archean to the Proterozoic.

HURRICANE The hurricane is a violent, cyclonic, tropical windstorm. The storm path can be 330 to 660 kilometers (200 to 400 miles) wide. The minimum speed is about 123 kilometers (74 miles) per hour (Beaufort Scale). Near the eye or center of the storm, speeds can reach over 250 kilometers (150 miles) per hour. The eye may be as much as 40 kilometers (25 miles) across.

These storms are accompanied by heavy rains and high seas. For a hurricane to be born, sea temperatures must be at least 78° Fahrenheit.

The source of Gulf Coast and Atlantic hurricanes is off the North African Coast. The Harmattan's (q.v.), hot desert winds provide the nucleation dust. The resulting airmass picks up moisture over the Atlantic and can be identified by a line of thunderstorms in the Northeast Trades. Most storms will remain as Easterly Waves (q.v.). A few become tropical storms and the rare one becomes a hurricane.

'Hurakan' is Nahuatl Indian and describes storms in the Gulf of Mexico, Caribbean, and southeastern Atlantic. Hurricanes also are spawned off the West Indies or Cape Verde Islands. Similar storms generated in the Pacific are typhoons, unless off the Mexican Coast.

The Caribbean, Florida, and the Gulf Coast from Yucatan to Florida are periodically hit by hurricanes. The majority diminish to tropical storms when they approach land. The few that retain intensity are extremely destructive.

'Hugo', in the fall of 1989, created havoc along the Carolina Coast of the United states. The preliminary estimate of the damage is 10 billion dollars.

The hurricane with the lowest recorded pressure was 'Gilbert'. It occurred in September, 1988 and devastated the Island of Jamaica. It also created enormous damage on Yucatan and great flooding around Monterey in Mexico after it was down-graded to a storm.

HWANG HO RIVER One of the world's great rivers, the Yellow, or Hwang Ho, has a long history of disasters. It rises in the Nan Shan Mountains and crosses Central China on its passage to the sea at Shanghai. It discharges 1.6 billion tons of sediments per year into the sea. See **YELLOW RIVER**.

HYDRAULIC MINER The hydraulic miner is a double-bottomed box built to rock like a cradle. It sloshes water over the minerals to be separated from the sands. Called a 'rocker' it has been much used in the gold fields.

HYDROCARBONS Compounds of hydrogen and carbon, or hydrocarbons, have a special chemical linkage. They are described by their structural arrangements instead of the usual chemical formulas. Different compounds have the same numbers of atoms but these are arranged differently. These compounds are 'isomers'.

Petroleum is a major hydrocarbon. The development of hydrocarbon chemistry led directly to the enormous petrochemical industry so important to modern life.

In addition to petroleum, other important hydrocarbons are natural gas, oil, tar sands, and oil shales.

HYDROGEN Hydrogen is the simplest element. It exists as a gas, is odorless and tasteless. It is rarely encountered in the free state, but it abounds in combination. The hydrogen atom has 1 proton and 1 electron. Hydrogen combined with oxygen yields water.

Hydrogen is the most abundant gas in the Sun and through nuclear reaction gives off helium (q.v.).

Hydrogen is a nuclear fuel. It is used in fusion nuclear reactors. The atomic fusion creates energy. The reaction reaches a heat of over 100 million degrees Celsius. To contain such a reaction, a magnetic field is necessary.

HYDROGEN SULFIDE Hydrogen sulfide is a colorless, poisonous gas with an odor of rotten eggs. Formed on lake bottoms from organic debris, the gas rises during seasonal lake overturn. It can kill large numbers of fish and other organisms, thereby adding to the decomposing debris producing the hydrogen sulfide.

In August of 1986, a cloud of gas believed to be hydrogen sulfide and carbon dioxide rose from the crater lake of Nios in Northwest Cameroon, Africa. Gases normally trapped in the bottom waters bubbled to the surface and escaped. It is likely that carbon dioxide was the major cause of the more than 1,200 deaths. Hydrogen sulfide was an important contributing factor.

A similar event, but less disastrous, occurred in 1984 from nearby Lake Monoun. It had been assumed that a landslide had caused a sudden overturn of that lake.

HYDROGRAPHIC BASIN An area drained by a principal river and its tributaries is a hydrographic basin. It may be large, as the Amazon Basin, or fairly small and local. The basin is fed from the watershed that is usually high and rims the area.

Basins may be asymmetrical. In the Amazon, drainage from the left bank tributaries is appreciably shorter than from the right bank.

HYDROLOGIC CYCLE Water circulation between the sea, land, air, and back to the sea is the Hydrologic Cycle. Some 580 trillion tons of water are exchanged each year between the Ocean and Atmosphere. The water turn-over is 150,000 cubic kilometers (90,000 cubic miles) every 12 days. This is generated by evaporation and condensation.

Most water is directly from the seas. Direct evaporation from the land is minimal. It is significant though in terms of desert and forest climates.

HYDROLYSIS When water interacts with compounds and new substances are formed, the process is termed hydrolysis.

HYDROPONICS The process of growing plants in nutrient-rich solutions is hydroponics. Plants are grown without soil. They are planted in a base of sand or gravel to lend mechanical support. The water to which nutrients have been added is combined with inert material. See **AQUACULTURE**.

HYDROPOWER Hydropower is not evenly distributed around the world but as follows:

	Percent	Megawatts
Africa and Australia	29	N/A
Asia	28	618,000
South America	20	431,900
North and Central America	16	323,924
Europe	7	154,500

Most Asian hydropower is in the Soviet Union. In South America, the lion's share is in Brazil.

Europe has developed only 59% of its potential, South America only 8% before Itaipu and Tapajos dams. South America, however, supplies 73% of its electricity from hydropower.

Total megawatts from Africa and Australia are not available but include the production from Aswan, Blue Nile, Kariba, and others.

HYDROSPHERE All water on the planet is part of the Hydrosphere.

This is true whether locked in glacial ice and snow or in rocks and groundwater though these are not as obvious as the flowing rivers and streams, the lakes and the seas. That portion of the Earth's surface made up of the World Ocean is continous around the world and covers 72% of the globe. The average depth of the the Ocean is 3 kilometers (1.5 miles).

HYPABYSSAL ROCKS Rocks formed at medium depth in the Mantle between the plutonic and abyssal (q.v.) are hypabyssal. Volcanic rocks, laccoliths, and some veins are hypabyssal. Rocks formed under hypabyssal conditions tend to be microgranular or porphyritic (q.v.) in texture.

HYPOGENE The hypogene is the zone or mineral just below a deposit that has been enriched by surface oxidation. The superficial or supergene portion of the deposit has been altered. The primary mineralization or hypogene deposit is unaltered.

HYPOLIMNION The hypolimnion is the cold, dense, lower layer of a lake. It is separated from the epilimnion by the thermocline (q.v.) where temperatures rapidly change.

HYPOTHERMAL DEPOSIT Minerals deposited at great depth, under extremes of temperature and pressure are hypothermal and many are economic. These deposits include veins and are linked to a magma source. The mineral deposits may show an alteration halo.

HYPOTHESIS The hypothesis is a scientifically developed and possible explanation for something not understood. The hypothesis, or theory, is subjected to test before acceptance by the scientific community. It does not necessarily mean that it is 'the answer'.

Frequently, an hypothesis will lead to better understanding and finally to an explanation compatible with all known facts. The hypothesis may still be subject to change when a new set of facts are discovered.

HYPSOMETRIC CURVE A graph displaying the frequency of land heights versus oceanic depths can be plotted as an hypsometric curve. It can give a generalized picture of the Earth's surface but, it is not a profile.

I

IAPETUS The ancestral or proto-Atlantic Ocean is known as Iapetus. It lasted millions of years; from the Precambrian (q.v.) to the Devonian (395-345 m.y.). Rifting that began in the Precambrian had separated North America from Europe and Africa.

Subduction (q.v.) zones formed. One off eastern New York in Mid- to Late-Devonian spawned the Taconic Range of the Appalachians.

260 million years ago, a continental collision between North America and Africa raised the younger Appalachian Mountains and the ocean was replaced by the landmass of Pangaea (q.v.). This remained intact until 200 million years ago when rifting between Africa and Antartica occurred. See **MID-ATLANTIC RIFT**.

IBERIA The Iberian Peninsula containing Spain and Portugal was rifted from its Bay of Biscay location and rotated to face Africa. Sardinia and Corsica are pieces of French Coast. The Pyrenees are the rotation hinge. The European Plate moved west, the African east.

ICE Ice, the solid phase of water, is formed by freezing the liquid or recrystallizing snow. Ice holds 75% of all the freshwater in the world. As glaciers (q.v.), it reshapes the landscape. Ice expands 10% in volume and exerts enormous pressure in all directions. A cubic foot (0.028 cubic meters) weighs 57 pounds (25 kilograms).

ICE AGE An Ice Age exists when glaciers and ice sheets cover great areas of the globe. It consists of many freezing and thawing episodes. In the the past few million years, there were 4 major advances each 10's of thousands of years in duration.

The Ice Ages were separated by Interglacials of the same length. Mini Ice Ages occurred during Interglacials whenever the average global temperature dropped a few degrees. It can be assumed that there were also times of limited warming during the Glacials.

Glaciation occurred in the Pleistocene, Carboniferous (mostly alpine) and Precambrian times. The Present may be an Interglacial Epoch in the Pleistocene to Recent Ice Age.

Mechanisms triggering glaciation may be astronomical, solar, or terrestrial, or a combination. Events which may be related are:

- Earth's orbital eccentricity (100,000-year cycle)
- Earth's axial precession (22,000-year cycle)
- Earth's change in obliquity (41,000-year cycle)
- Solar flare activity
- Volcanic activity.

Glaciation was preceded by major diastrophism (q.v.). Cycle calculations of glaciation were made by Milankovitch and others. Radioactivity data has refined them. Thousands of cores stored at Lamont Laboratory suggest the validity of a 100,000-year cycle for a Glacial Epoch.

We are approaching the end of a 100,000-year Interglacial. Snows come earlier and pile up and there is added snow cover at the Poles. The snowline is advancing 80 or more kilometers (50 miles) per year and many present glaciers have reached a preservation point. Others, as in Alaska, continue to retreat.

Lower local temperatures in periglacial areas affect a much larger area. In a recent 30-year period, the Northern Hemisphere cooled less than 1° Fahrenheit but Iceland was down 2°. Snows increased in Baffin Bay and north of Hudson Bay. New glaciers were forming, others like Norway's growing. In 1978, Boston had the heaviest snow in 100 years, 0.53 meters (21 inches).

What effect global atmospheric conditions, among them the carbon dioxide buildup and Greenhouse Effect (q.v), have on the Glacial Cycle is not known. It is known that during the Ice Age carbon dioxide in the Pacific rose and fell with oceanic circulation.

In the Pleistocene, water was locked up in ice and sea level was reduced 100 meters (300 feet). The Bering Sea was land. It is believed that humans and animals used the land bridge from Asia to North America.

ICE CAP An ice cap is a small ice sheet (q.v.). The ice cap on Vatner Glacier, Iceland, is an example. It covers 115 x 167 kilometers (75 x 100 miles) and is 227 meters (750 feet) thick.

Ice forms first in highlands where precipitation is great and temperatures low. It becomes a large mass often covering a peak. By the weight of its mass, an ice cap may begin to move. Then, it becomes a glacier (q.v.).

ICE SHEET A continental ice sheet is a thick, extensive mass of ice. Great ice sheets up to 3 kilometers (2 miles) thick dominated North America in the Pleistocene. The major one was the Laurentide which covered Eastern Canada, New England, and New York. A Cordilleran Ice Sheet covered the western high mountains. Eurasia had ice sheets, and both Poles were covered.

Only 2 ice sheets remain. They cover 14.8 million square kilometers (5.7 million square miles). The Greenland sheet is 2,500 meters (8,000 feet) thick. The Antarctic is 4,300 meters (14,000 feet). A few mountain peaks rise above the ice sheets.

If the present ice sheets melted the sea would rise an estimated 60 meters (200 feet). As if to compensate for rising sea levels, formerly glaciated areas rise in rebound when relieved of the weight of the ice. Scandinavia has been rising for several thousand years.

ICE SHELF Thick slabs of ice extend into the sea. Some are up to 600 meters (2,000 feet) thick and 600 kilometers (400 miles) wide. Such shelves are common in Antarctica.

Shelves may be attached to glaciers or to the landmass. Ice streams flow in fissures in the Antarctic Ice Shelf. Explorers have described 5 ice shelves from West Antarctica. A particularly unstable one is Ross (q.v.).

Some scientists fear that there is a possibility of sufficient warming to cause parts of the shelves to break off. This would affect the seas and cause global flooding. This breaking off of ice shelves is not to be confused with calving (q.v.).

ICE STORMS Sleet is formed from freezing rain in ice storms. The storms occur when rain from a relatively warm, moist airmass aloft passes through a colder (below freezing) airmass before precipitating. The super-cooled rain freezes on vegetation or cold surfaces and builds up ice to 2.5 centimeters (1 inch) thick in the form of a glaze.

ICE WEDGE Ice wedges form and are common in permafrosted (q.v.) soils at temperatures of -6 to -8° Celsius. They can persist at temperatures of -1 to -2°. The ice wedge freezes and expands in place causing a variety of effects and creating a micro-relief. Wedges rupture rocks. Melting wedges can create lubrication for solifluction (q.v.).

Casts are fossil indications of the former existence of an ice wedge. They show the wedges to be widest at the top, tapering down in the matrix. They can form interconnecting patterns such as found near Barrow, Alaska.

ICEBERG An iceberg is a mass of floating glacial ice found near coastal areas in high latitudes. The ice mass breaks (calves) off the terminal end of a glacier and is carried away by the ocean currents.

A relatively smooth iceberg becomes irregular from age and climate. It may calve further, or its parts may reweld. Icebergs transport large amounts of detritus and deposit erratic boulders.

Icebergs are a great threat to navigation. The emergent part is only about 10% of the total mass. Icebergs with as much as 100 meters (300 feet) above the sea are common. Each year under the present climatic regime, 1,792 cubic kilometers (430 cubic miles) of ice are calved off.

Some icebergs travel extraordinary distances. From the Arctic, they have been recorded as far south as Bermuda. One spectacular one made its way from Antarctica 5,500 kilometes (3,420 miles) almost to the harbor of Rio de Janeiro.

Only a small percentage of the total mass of icebergs reach the shipping lanes of the North Atlantic. The number fell considerably during the recent warm interlude. They are again being reported in the shipping lanes. Since the sinking of the Titanic, the United States has maintained an Ice Patrol.

ICEFALL   Chunks of ice moving downslope, or over a cliff form an icefall. Icefalls are often found in crevassed areas. See **CREVASSE**.

ICEFLOE   An icefloe differs from an iceberg (q.v.) in its origin. While the iceberg was part of the continental ice sheet, the icefloe forms of freezing oceanic waters. Such freezing begins close to coastal areas. Icefloes tend to be smaller than icebergs.

ICELAND   Iceland is a topographic expression of the Mid-Atlantic Ridge and Rift System (q.v.). It is midway between the Faroe Islands and eastern Greenland just below the Arctic Circle.

In the last 1,000 years there have been 150 volcanic eruptions. In 1783 a huge eruption resulted in 220 square miles of lava that covered much of the arable land and led to famine. Surtsey erupted in 1957, Eldfell in 1976, and Hecla is still active.

Present activity began about 13 million years ago. Since 1,500 A.D. 30% of the world's known lava flows poured out over Iceland. Earthquakes are numerous and heatflow from geysers is sufficient to be an energy source for the country.

The Mid-Atlantic Rift in Iceland is a discernible graben (q.v.) many kilometers long and 12 meters (40 feet) deep and growing wider. The graben is especially visible at Almannagja in Southwest Iceland. The oldest rocks are on its extreme east and west flanks.

ICELANDIC LOW   A semi-permanent low pressure area exists over the North Atlantic in the vicinity of Iceland. The Icelandic Low has a marked effect on the climate of Europe. See **LOW PRESSURE SYSTEM**.

ICHTHYOSAURUS   Ichthyosaurs, dolphin-like reptiles, first appeared in Triassic (225-190 m.y.) seas. Mary Ann Anning, a 10-year old shell collector found the first fossil ichthyosaur in cliff sediments near her home in Lyme Regis, England. In 1821, 10 years later, she found the first fossil 'Plesiosaurus' also a marine reptile.

The finds were so spectacular, they captured the imagination of the British people and a folk song was created, 'She sells seashells down by the seashore, Mary Ann'.

ICICLE   A conical shaped ice pendant or icicle, is formed from dripping supercooled and freezing water. The pendants form on eaves when roof snow begins to melt under a warm Sun and runoff begins. As the day's warmth is short, the icicle refreezes before thaw is completed.

IGNEOUS ROCKS Rocks formed by consolidation of molten Mantle material, or magma are igneous. The magma may consolidate below the Earth's surface or be ejected from fissures and volcanoes.

Igneous rocks are classified according to their silica content. There are 4 main groups. In order of increasing density, these are acidic, intermediate, basic, and ultra basic.

In acidic igneous rocks. silica is greater than 66%, or quartz is more than 12%. Granite is an intrusive acidic rock and rhyolite is its extrusive counterpart. Granite batholiths (q.v.) often form the core of mountains.

Basic and ultra-basic igneous rocks have a silica content below 52%. The important minerals are iron, magnesium, and calcium. Continental rocks tend to be acidic while basic and ultra-basic rocks are found on the ocean floor, and on many islands. Some enormous basaltic flows are found on continental plateaus in the United States, India, and Brazil.

IGNIMBRITE An ignimbrite is an acidic igneous rock formed by the suspension of very fluid, fine fragments of magma in ultra-hot gases. The high temperatures exceed the melting point of glass.

The ignimbrite is a pyroclast from an explosive volcano. It looks like lava. There are thousands of square miles of ignimbrite in Nevada.

IGUAÇU The Iguaçu River rises in the Serra do Mar coastal range of Brazil and flows west 1,320 kilometers (820 miles) to join the Parana. 'Iguaçu' is Guarani Indian for great waters.

Just before the confluence with the Parana River (q.v.), on the boundary of Brazil and Argentina where the river falls off the Parana Plateau, 300 individual falls cascade over the crescent-shaped cliff into a 5 kilometer (3 mile) wide gorge. Along its course the Iguaçu collects uncounted streams. It has over 70 forming the Falls.

The cascades are separated by lush forest. Some fall directly, a drop of 82 meters (270 feet). Others bounce off ledges. Sun shining through the mists gives off a beautiful rainbow effect.

Iguaçu Falls are in a miniature tropical Eden. The forest, mainly of bamboo, palm, and tree ferns, is host to many kinds of orchids and bromeliads (q.v.). Parrots and bright-colored macaws are ubiquitous.

Iguaçu Falls are most spectacular at high water (rainy season). They shrink greatly in the dry season. In 1934 and again in 1978 the Falls dried up.

IGY The International Geophysical Year, (IGY), was established to unite the world's geophysicists in combined activities. 1957-1958 was chosen as especially interesting because of sunspot (q.v.) activity. It was the mid-point of the 14-year cycle.

Efforts were made to study Inner and Outer Space. The oceans were subjected to extensive study and deep oceanic trenches were explored. The United States had 8 vessels on long voyages and a number of others making shorter cruises. The USSR had 9 research vessels, mainly in the Pacific.

IKURSK GOLD   The Ikursk Goldfields in the USSR are reputed to be extremely rich. They are located at Bodaibo on the Vitim River, a tributary of the Lena in Siberia. Lena Goldfields Company had concessions on the deposits before the Russian Revolution.

ILLAMPU & ILLIMANI   The 2 highest mountains of Bolivia's Cordillera Oriental rise above the 3,650 meter (12,000 foot) high Altiplano (q.v.). Illampu with its twin peaks overlooks Lake Titicaca, while tri-peaked Illimani forms a backdrop for La Paz.

Both mountains were intruded by a batholith (q.v.) 20 million years ago and the sediments uplifted and eroded. The area was again uplifted 2 million years ago.

These mountains are only 320 kilometers from the Pacific but the meltwaters from their glaciers are part of the Amazon watershed.

ILLITE   The clay, illite, is derived from potassium feldspar. Illite makes up an intermediate hydrous mica in a weathering process that leads to kaolin (q.v.) or china clay.

In the North Pacific, large deposits of illite and quartz have been discovered. These sediments originated in the steppe and desert areas of Europe and Asia and were held as loess (q.v.) for a time before being transported to the sea.

ILLUVIATION   Illuviation is the proceess whereby clays, sesquioxides (q.v.), and carbonates are leached from the soil's A-Horizon and concentrated in the B-Horizon. The material is transported by gravity and is in solution. It is precipitated in the lower horizon together with other fine-grained materials.

IMBRICATION   Shingling of flat pebbles on a stream bed is imbrication. The pebbles overlap so the upper edge is oriented in the direction of current flow. This over-lapping of rock edges occurs on some beaches, or 'shingles', of the British Isles.

IMMATURE SOIL   Where erosion exceeds the rate a soil builds downward, the result is an immature soil. The profile will be poorly defined and no distinct horizons will appear. It is an azonal soil.

IMMISCIBLE   When 2 or more phases of matter at mutual equilibrium cannot dissolve completely in one another, they are immiscible. The most well-known example is of oil and water.

THE EARTH SCIENCES REFERENCE

IMPACT CRATER A crater resulting from a meteorite hitting the Earth, Moon, or other planet is an impact crater. Lake Acraman, South Australia, is an example. A meteorite struck the area 600 million years ago. Its velocity is estimated at 1,000 kilometers (600 miles) a second. There are shatter cones resulting from the high velocity shock. The crater has a diameter of 160 kilometers (96 miles).

Lake Acraman was the first meteoritic impact crater. It is recognized as older than the Cenozoic (70 million years).

There are many impact craters around the globe. Among those of relatively recent origin is Meteor Crater in Arizona (q.v.).

IMPERMEABLE Impermeable rocks and terrain only allow water to flow through them with great difficulty. There are degrees of impermeability. Clay materials tend to be more impermeable than sands.

IMPLOSION An implosion is the opposite of explosion and is an inward blast. The principle is used in atomic bombs. Plutonium driven inward forms a ball, creating a chain reaction.

IMPREGNATION The introduction of a mineral into a rock after its formation is impregnation. The process occurs when mineral solutions are introduced into an area and absorbed by the rock.

INCLUSION Any strange body, gas, liquid, or solid, that is included within the mass, rock, or mineral is termed an inclusion. A particularly obvious and beautiful example is the presence of rutile needles in some quartz crystals. Water is a common inclusion in quartz. Mineral inclusions often lend color as chrome does to emerald.

INDEX FOSSIL A fossil that is exclusive to a definite geological horizon may be an index fossil. The ideal index fossil is widely distributed, abundantly present, but restricted to a relatively short period of geological time.

A fossil which fulfills all the requirements is 'Mesosaurus'. a great reptile, found in the Irati Shales of the Brazilian Permian. The trilobite (q.v.) is an index fossil that had worldwide distribution in the Paleozoic and then became extinct.

INDIAN DIAMOND FIELDS The first diamond mining occurred in India at Golconda. The richest fields were near the Kistna River in southern India. Some of the biggest and most beautiful diamonds have been found in these ancient placers. The source of the diamonds is still unknown.

INDIAN OCEAN The World Ocean is divided into 3 major parts, the Pacific, Atlantic, and Indian oceans. The Indian Ocean is bounded by Africa on the west. To the north are the Arabian Peninsula and India, and on the east are Indonesia and Australia.

The Indian Ocean contains the Arabian Sea, Red Sea, Persian Gulf, and Bengal Bay. In the ocean, there are deep basins, 3 ridges, 1 rise, and abyssal plains. There are also small pieces of the continental landmass left behind when Gondwana broke up. These form plateaus, mostly below sea level. The highest point on one of the continental remnants forms the Seychelles.

The only deep trench is Java, bordered to the north by a line of large volcanoes, among them Krakatoa (q.v.).

The Ganges and Indus rivers carry great sediment loads into the Indian Ocean as did the Zambezi before Kariba Dam. Thousands of feet of sediments have built up. The Ganges Delta reaches to the middle of Bengal Bay.

INDIAN OCEAN CURRENT Current in the Indian Ocean is anti-clockwise all year, forming a great eddy which is the Indian Ocean Current. The Agulhas Current, an arm of the Indian Ocean Current, flows between Malagasy and Southeast Africa. Another branch converges with the West Wind Drift at about 35° South Latitude.

From November to March, the North Equatorial Current flows west just north of the Equator. It disappears when the Southwest Monsoon blows. There is then a general easterly flow across the Mid-Indian Ocean.

INDIAN PLATE The Indian Plate moved across a part of the Tethys Sea (q.v.) and obliterated it. As this occurred, the Indian Ocean was opened up behind the Indian Plate.

The Indian Plate collided with Asia about 50 million years ago and the Himalayas have risen along the suture line. In the past 50 million years marine sediments have been uplifted 8.3 kilometers (5 miles) above the sea. The northern Himalayan High Range is rich in ammonite (q.v.) shells. No fossils are found to the south.

INDIAN SUMMER Indian summer is a sudden warming after the first cold spell of autumn. It may last for a few days or weeks, or may not occur.

INDIGENOUS PLANTS A plant is indigenous if native to an area. Some indigenous New World plants are corn, cassava, potatoes, rubber, and tobacco.

INDONESIA Indonesia encompasses 13,000 islands between the Indian Ocean and the Pacific. Some islands have tropical rainforest plants and animals not found elsewhere. The islands also have some of the most explosive volcanoes on earth, 77 are presently active.

INDRICOTHERIUM Fossils of a huge hornless rhinoscerus were found in Khazakhstan, in Central Asia. They proved to be of the largest of land mammals. The estimated weight of 'Indricotherium' was 16 tons. It measured 5.5 meters (18 feet) to the shoulders. The mammal was at home in both dry and damp forests and in Pleistocene (q.v.) bogs.

INDUS RIVER The Indus, a major stream, rises in the Himalayas in Tibet and flows over a 3,000 kilometer (1800 mile) course through West Pakistan into the Sea of Oman.

Before the river changed its course, it left a delta in what is now Punjab, This ancient delta has 5 million acres of alluvium.

The evidence in the Indus River Gorge is that the river is older than the mountains. It cut quickly enough to keep pace with the uplift caused by the collision of the Indian and Asian Plates.

Along the Indus are vestiges of ancient agrarian societies, among them Mohenjo-Daro (q.v.).

INDUSTRIAL WASTE WATER Industrial waste water presents a great problem in environmental management. Problems have become more and more acute as quantities and varieties of waste have increased. Cleaning up pollution caused by industrial waste waters expelled into rivers and the ocean requires billions of dollars and inventiveness.

For the treatment of industrial waste water some tests have been developed to measure the biochemical oxygen demand (BOD). This is necessary as a forerunner to removing organic matter. Testing for trace and minor elements, overlooked in the past, is now being implemented. Time is running out for some streams and bays and the waste waters must be treated before release.

INERT GASES Inert gases, sometimes called noble or rare, are relatively unreactive elements. They include helium, neon, krypton, xenon, and radon.

These gases do not form diatomic (q.v.) molecules. They will react only under very special conditions.

INERTIA For a body or mass to move, sufficient force must be exerted upon it to overcome its natural tendency to stay put. This same mass once moved has a tendency to stay in motion. Sir Isaac Newton was the first to state this physical law.

INFILTRATION Infiltration is the penetration of rainwater into the soil. Water soaks into soil and rock to become part of the groundwater. Infiltration capacity and its effectiveness depend upon the porosity and permeability of the soil and rock. See **POROSITY** and **PERMEABILITY**.

INFLUENT STREAM Any stream feeding into the groundwater table is influent. The water table is below the stream bed, and may be far below in semi-arid areas where streams are seasonal.

INFRA-RED RAYS Infra-red rays are invisible radiation from waves longer than visible light. They are a part of the Electromagnetic Spectrum (q.v.).

INFRA-RED SENSING Infra-red sensing is a useful geophysical exploration tool. Photographs are made on special sensitive film capable of capturing infra-red waves. Differences in temperature can be detected indicating many types of phenomena.

Infra-red sensing has led to the discovery of ideal fishing grounds in the sea and minerals on land. Vegetation differences are picked up by satellite imagery making global maps possible.

INGOT An ingot is a molded form of metal. The form is set for a particular metal allowing for easy recognition.

INGRESSION A slow advance of the sea onto the continent is an ingression. Sediments deposited during an ingression are characterized by local and shallow gradations from fluvial to marine environments.

Ingression sediments differ from transgression (q.v.) suites in that they lack the typical transgression conglomerates.

INJECTION WELL An injection well to pump water or gas into an oilfield is drilled to promote secondary recovery. Sometimes it is also used to establish a pressure balance in a field.

INLIER An inlier is an elliptical area of older rocks surrounded by younger ones. Older sediments are revealed by the erosion of an anticline.

INNER CORE The Earth's Inner Core, because of its density, has long been thought to be composed of nickel and iron. Evidence for this assumption has been mathematical. It is confirmed by the nature of many meteorites. Today there is a growing assumption that the Earth's Inner Core is in a plasma (q.v.) state. See **CORE**.

INSELBERG An isolated, massive, hill or mountain on an eroded pediplain (q.v.) is an 'Inselberg', Dutch for isolated mountain. Inselbergs are common in arid South Africa, Arabia, and southwestern United States.

Most inselbergs are shaped by exfoliation (q.v.). The onion-skin weathering is believed caused by chemical activity and a daily heating and cooling. These lead to a splitting off of outer layers and a rounded outcrop.

INSOLATION Insolation is the solar radiation reaching the Earth's surface. The quantity varies with latitude and with the presence or absence of protective layers in the Atmosphere.

Some mechanical destruction of rocks is due to daily fluctuations in insolation and the heating and cooling that results. It is not now considered as great a weathering agency as previously.

INTERGLACIAL The period of glacial retreat between great advances is the Interglacial. Lakes in the United States indicate 3 or 4 interglacials during the last glaciation. The basins of the Great Basin were as dry as at present. Some stages were warmer than the present. It appears we may be in the 5th Interglacial.

If this Interglacial is coming to a close, the effects will be global. Crop failures could cause great disruptions in human society. A cooling trend has been responsible for crop failures already. Both the Glacial and Interglacial epochs have been subject to great swings of climate. It is the global effect over a long period that defines the epoch.

Should a buildup in glaciation continue over a prolonged period, major shifts in global winds could increase energy needs. Global wind shifts also cause precipitation patterns to change and many wet areas become drier and subject to drought and some formerly dry areas receive increased precipitation.

The transition to an Ice Age is not linear. There are climatic swings with fluctuating temperatures but the overall trend is down. Ice advance is triggered by a drop in temperature of a few degrees. Past interglacials have been warmer than the present. From 1940-1960 there was a drop of 5° Fahrenheit. The trend was about 0.3° per year.

How much a cooling trend would be offset by increased Greenhouse Effect (q.v.) and depletion of the Ozone Layer (q.v.) is as yet unknown. It is the present subject of computer modeling. Both conditions are thought to be creating a global warming. See **ICE AGES**.

INTERMITTENT STREAM Streams originating in arid environments are ephemeral or intermittent. These streams only come to life with a sudden storm accompanied by flash flooding. These streams disappear into the ground or evaporate almost as rapidly as they appear.

INTERNAL WAVE Any wave motion within a fluid mass is an internal wave. Internal waves result from density changes within fluids. Internal waves in the sea are encountered at the thermocline (q.v.) or in turbidity currents. Sharp discontinuities, or density changes, at current boundaries can cause internal waves.

Internal waves may be enormous and dangerous. An internal wave 75 meters (260 feet) from crest to trough has been recorded. USN Thresher, a submarine, was a possible victim of a disasterous internal wave triggered by a storm in the Gulf of Maine.

INTERNATIONAL DATELINE There are 24 time belts around the world. It is therefore possible to lose or gain a day circumnavigating the globe.

By international agreement, the 180th Meridian of Longitude was chosen as the official Dateline. The line does not faithfully follow the Meridian, but is drawn to avoid any land area.

INTERTIDAL Intertidal areas between high- and low-tide lines vary greatly. They are affected by daily, neap, spring tides, and storms.

INTERTROPICAL CONVERGENCE The Intertropical Convergence (ITC) occurs where the Trade Winds converge from northeast and southwest. The ITC shifts north of the Equator during the northern summer and south during the winter. The ITC marks the boundary between humid and dry airmasses.

Southeast monsoonal winds bring rains to Sub-Saharan West Africa. These winds are sometimes blocked from the continent by the dry desert winds of the Harmattan (q.v.). The ITC can be stalled offshore, allowing the dry airmass to dominate the regional climate. Thus, the location of the ITC is of major climatic importance since humid airmasses can not pass it.

A similar situation affects the Indian subcontinent where monsoonal rains depend upon the location of the ITC. Strong loops to lower latitudes made by the Westerlies can change ITC patterns and disrupt the regional climate.

The drought of the Sahel in the early 1970's was caused by the stalling of the ITC some 2° of Latitude farther south than usual. The southern movement of jet streams limits the ITC in some summers. This is now referred to as the 'Sahelian Effect'.

In the Western Pacific, the Thermal Equator is well north of the geographic as a result of warm oceanic currents flowing north. Southeast Trades are carried across the Equator, where they change direction to southwest due to the Coriolis Force. The accompanying weather is one of violent thunderstorms and squalls.

INTRAZONAL SOILS Soils are classified as azonal, intrazonal, and zonal based on the developmental stage of the soil profile. An intrazonal soil has a minimal profile development yet reflects the influences of local relief, parent rock or material, age, vegetation, and climate.

INTRUSIVE Intrusive igneous rocks penetrate other formations while still in a molten or magmatic stage. They do not reach the surface. Their forms vary from enormous to pencil thin. Intrusive rocks form various structures, among them batholiths, laccoliths, dikes, sills, and veins.

INVERSE RELIEF Sediments in positions opposite to their usual formational structure exhibit inverse relief. Anticlinal sediments found in a valley and synclinal sediments on a ridge are examples.

INVERSION Any reversal in the normal decrease of temperature with elevation is an inversion. In many areas a blanket of warm stable air aloft acts as a trap, keeping relatively cool air at the surface. Freezing rain can result from the cold surface airmass.

In a basin, like Los Angeles or Mexico City, an inversion interferes with the dispersal of air pollutants allowing SMOG (q.v.) to build up.

INVERTEBRATE Any animal lacking a spine or backbone is an invertebrate. The Animal Kingdom is divided into Vertebrates and Invertebrates.

IODINE Normally the halogen, iodine, skips the liquid phase at atmospheric temperature. It occurs as a violet-hued vapor. As a solid, it has gray-black crystals.

The greatest source of iodine crystals is brown seaweed which concentrates iodine and bromine from seawater. Iodine in seawater is variable, from 100 to 1,299 tons per cubic mile.

Iodine is also produced as a by-product from brine and nitrate operations. Present world production is 3 million tons per year and Japan is the major producer.

Iodine is a necessary nutrient in human diet, although the amount is only 0.0001 grams per day. Its lack can lead to metabolic disorders.

Iodine-13, a radioactive isotope, is present and hazardous immediately following a nuclear blast. Its half-life is 14 days. Tiny amounts of radioactive iodine are sometimes used as a tracer to diagnose medical problems.

ION An ion is an atom with excess positive or negative electrical charges. An atom becomes an ion when it loses or gains 1 or more electrons in electron transfer.

IONIC BONDING Oppositely charged ions attract each other by electrostatic force. They join in an ionic bond.

An example of ionic bonding is found in the way sodium and chlorine atoms each search for stable outer shells with 8 electrons. Sodium will give up an electron and chlorine will accept it making both charged atoms or ions. Bonded, they form salt.

IONIZATION An atom or a molecule that has gained or lost electrons is an ion. The process is ionization. It can be triggered by chemistry, lightning, or radioactivity.

IONOSPHERE A layer in the Earth's atmospheric envelope, the Ionosphere, is a zone where oxygen and nitrogen are ionized. This zone is between 58 and 330 kilometers (35 and 200 miles) above the Earth's surface.

The Ionosphere has layers of free electrons. These ionized layers stop short-wave radiation from penetrating the Atmosphere and act as a protective shield. They also are reflectors of low-frequency radio signals.

IRAN Iran, formerly Persia, has for centuries been the crossroads of routes to Asia. The Old Silk Road was a major one.

Iran has 390,000 square kilometers (150,000 square miles) of desert, parts of which are noted for especially high sand dunes. The area between Iraq and Iran called Shatt al Arab (q.v.) was the scene of recent hostilities.

Iran's northern border is with the Soviet Union. Part of that border lies along the Caspian Sea. Oil was discovered in this region and Iran has been and is a significant producer of oil and natural gas. Iran has the 4th largest reserves in the world or 92 billion barrels of crude. See **PETROLEUM** and **NATURAL GAS**.

IRAQ Iraq was the site of great ancient agricultural societies. For more than 4,000 years there was intermittent cultivation on the Upper Tigris Plain and in Mesopotamia (between the Tigris and Euphrates Rivers). It is the location of ancient Babylon. See **FERTILE CRESCENT**.

Today most irrigated acreage is in trouble from alkalinity, salinity, and waterlogging. These problems have recurred throughout the area's history. With increased population Iraq has been an importer of grain.

Like its Middle East neighbors, Iraq is an important petroleum producer. Next to Saudi Arabia, Iraq has the world's greatest reserves or 100 billion barrels of crude oil. See **BABA GURGER** and **PETROLEUM**.

IRAZU Irazu Volcano in Costa Rica was in constant eruption from 1963 to 1965. It spewed sulfurous fumes and ash and triggered many huge mudslides.

Irazu is located 32 kilometers (20 miles) from San Jose. It is a major mountain in the Cordillera Central. Its slopes are forested up to the crater rim.

From Irazu's crater rim, at 3,432 meters (11,260 feet) in elevation, it is possible to see both the Atlantic and the Pacific Oceans.

IRIDESCENCE Iridescence is a play of colors on some minerals. It results from the interference of light by a thin film of gas or liquid. This causes a rainbow effect as the spectrum becomes visible.

IRIDIUM The platinum isotope, iridium, has been found in a worldwide clay layer at the Cretaceous-Tertiary boundary. The blue clay was first discovered in Italy. Iridium is normally only a trace mineral on Earth. It is, however, found in several thousand times the Earth's abundance in asteroids and meteors.

This phenomenon of a relatively high concentration of iridium in a single clay layer just at the time of the Great Extinction (q.v.) lead the physicist Alvarez and his geologist son to conclude that the Earth was impacted by an asteroid at that time. The impact caused massive particulate concentration in the Upper Atmosphere which engendered the enormous climate change which killed off the dinosaurs and other life forms. See **NUCLEAR WINTER**.

IRON Iron, a chemically active element, nearly always occurs as a compound. It combines with oxygen, silica, other elements, and molecules and has been one of the world's most used and useful metals.

After aluminum, iron is the most abundant of the elements. It is usually encountered as an oxide. Iron minerals include hematite, limonite, magnetite, and goethite. As a sulfate, it is most common as iron pyrite.

The world's largest reserves of iron ore are in Brazil. Before evaluations of Carajas, Brazil's reserves were billions of tons. Venezuela has large reserves at Cerro Bolivar and Bolivia at Mutum. Australia has large reserves in the Hammersleys. The USSR is a major producer.

The Mesabi Range in the United States has already produced 3 billion tons of ore and the area is still producing 90% of United States production, but grades have been falling off.

IRON FORMATIONS Assemblages of rocks rich in iron and containing layered minerals are called banded-iron formations. They contain sequences of hematite, manganese, and jasper or they are of quartz, sandstone, clay, and shale, with iron contained in the sediments.

The origin of these formations has been much debated. Both assemblages indicate formation in warm climates. They are major sources of iron and manganese ores. The iron-manganese-jasper formations appear to be limited to the Precambrian. The clay-shale-iron formations are dated Silurian. The major iron ores of South America are Precambrian.

IRON OXIDE Iron and oxygen form rust. The color, orange-brown or red is that of many tropical and subtropical soils. Terra rossa of the Mediterranean area has inclusions of iron oxide. Iron oxide in some soils occurs in mineable quantities as ocher (q.v.). Hematite (q.v.) is a common iron oxide.

IRON SANDS Iron sands are limonite or magnetite rich. They are concentrations of iron minerals due to natural washing and concentration as in a stream. These concentrates form black sands (q.v.).

IRRAWADDY RIVER The Irrawaddy River, Burma, flows through foldbelts with a parallel drainage pattern. The river has developed several mouths into the Bay of Bengal.

The Irrawaddy rises from a Himalayan glacier inside Burma on the Chinese border. The river is 90 meters (300 feet) wide as it crosses the Irrawaddy Plain on its 2,160 kilometer (1,300 mile) course.

ISLAND An island is a relatively small landmass surrounded by water. Australia may be considered the largest island or a continent. If the latter, Greenland is the largest island.

Islands may be continental fragments or volcanic. Some major islands are Borneo, Britain, Honshu, Iceland, Malagasy, and New Zealand.

ISLAND ARCS Island arcs form narrow, segmented, volcanic archipelagos (q.v.). These are great belts of andesitic or basaltic origin. They are located along continental margins. There is usually a deep-sea trench. The trenches are secondary features and earthquakes in them are common.

The average island arc is 10 kilometers (6 miles) wide and 100-150 kilometers (60-90 miles long). Many are much longer, as are the Kurile Islands.

Island arc and trench systems result when oceanic plates collide. Submerged parts rise through the overlying plate as in the case of Japan. Islands may also arise from a hot spot or plume reaching the ocean floor through a rift. The plume mechanism sets off volcanic activity that results in the growth of the islands. The plume moves slowly along the rift zone. The Hawaiian Islands (q.v.) are part of such a progressive system.

ISOBAR Plotted lines of equal pressure are isobars. Atmospheric pressure is measured in millibars on barometers. Isobars are displayed graphically on charts to show winds and airmasses. Where contour lines merge, the winds are strong.

ISOGRAD A contour on a map which indicates the first appearance of a specific mineral in a metamorphic sequence is an isograd.

ISOMER Chemical compounds with the same atomic composition but with different atomic arrangement are isomers. Many are of carbon (q.v.).

ISOMORPHOUS SUBSTITUTION In isomorphous substitution, one atom replaces another of similar size in a particular crystal lattice. Substitution does not change the crystal structure, only its chemistry.

ISOPACH Rock units on a map are contoured by lines of equal thickness. The lines are isopachs. They are especially useful in outlining the thickness of ore of mineable grade.

ISOSTASY Isostasy Theory holds that there is compensation among crustal weights to maintain the gravitational balance. The crustal blocks are unequal in depth into the Earth's Mantle. Mountains have deeper roots than basins. Smith referred to it as 'the geological version of Archimedes buoyancy principle'.

The analogy is made with an iceberg floating in a denser medium, the sea. Only a portion of the iceberg (10%) shows above the sea surface. The roots of the Sierra Nevada, California, extend 60 kilometers, (37 miles) into dense crustal material.

The Earth's Crust is constantly adjusting to isostatic balance. Fennoscandia is the region most out-of-balance at present.

ISOTHERM An isotherm is a line drawn between points of equal temperature. Atmospheric isotherms trend west to east but are deflected by cool oceanic currents towards the Equator. Warm currents deflect the isotherms to higher latitudes.

ISOTOPE An atom of a given element may have a different atomic weight or nuclear mass but the same atomic number. Such an atom is an 'isotope' of the element. The number of protons is the same but the number of neutrons is different. The chemical properties are the same but one isotope of an element may be radioactively unstable, while another is not. Atomic weight is determined by the number of neutrons.

ITABIRITE Itabirite is an ore of iron with a very high iron content, over 60%. It is a quartzitic hematite of metamorphic origin and is schistose.

The type locality is in the Itabira Formation, which is part of the Precambrian Minas Series of Brazil. Less quartzose members of the formation are iron ore, with an average grade over 60%. Companhia Vale de Rio Doce (CVRD) which produces itabirite is the world's largest iron mining company.

In the Brazilian 'Iron Quadrilateral' near Belo Horizonte, Minas Gerais, there are entire mountains of metamorphic rock with up to 70% hematite. Sawtooth crested Itabirito Mountain is characteristic of this region. The region's ore reserves are in the billions of metric tons.

ITACOLUMITE Itacolumite is a flexible sandstone that can be bent due to looseness of its sand grains. The grains rotate around each other and there is sufficient mica to serve as a glide plane.

Itacolumite sandstones have been found not only in the type locality of Minas Gerais, Brazil, but in India and the Appalachian Mountains.

In Brazil, itacolumite is associated with diamond-bearing conglomerate.

ITAIPU DAM Itaipu hydroelectrical system is located between Sete Quedas (7 cataracts) and Foz de Iguaçu (Iguaçu River mouth) on the Parana River. It is the largest such installation in the West. Itaipu went operational in 1983 and is expected to produce 70 billion kilowatt-hours annually by 1989. Paraguay presently sells back power from its share to Brazil.

Itaipu is some 1,000 kilometers (600 miles) from Brazil's major industrial centers so power will be sent over high-voltage alternating current lines. To other South American power users, transmission will be over high voltage direct current (HVDC) lines.

ITURI RAINFOREST The Ituri Rainforest in the Congo (Zaire) Basin extends from eastern Cameroon to Zaire. It is noted for its dense stands of trees.

Ituri is the home of the Pygmy tribes. It is also the habitat of the largest known beetle, Goliath. Goliath grubs sometimes provide food for the Pygmies.

Itatiaia Massif — Rio de Janeiro (state), Brazil

J

JACUPIRANGITE Jacupirangite is an alkaline igneous rock in the Soda Pyroxene Group. It is 80% titano-augite, 19% titano-magnetite, with minor amounts of nepheline and apatite. The type locality is Jacupiranga, São Paulo, Brazil. Jacupirangite is known from East Africa, Kovdozero, USSR, and Iron Hill, Colorado. See **IGNEOUS ROCKS**.

Apatite, though a relatively small percent of the rock, is sufficient to be mined for phosphate at Jacupiranga. The Brazilian deposit was one of the first apatite-bearing carbonatites (q.v.) to be economically viable.

The Brazilian intrusive was first mined for magnetite (iron ore) and was the site of the first South American iron foundry. The carbonate was used as a flux in smelting. Today, the intrusive is mined for apatite and the carbonate supplies a cement plant.

JADE Jade may be of nephrite or jadeite. Nephrite is a variety of amphibole, while jadeite is a pyroxene. The color ranges from white to deep green. The Chinese say jade was forged from a rainbow to make thunderbolts for the god of storms.

In Neolithic times, men worked nephrite from the Green Jade River (Kask Kash) and White Jade River (Yurung Kash) in eastern Turkestan, USSR. Huge jade boulders have been found in these areas. Some were over 200 kilos (500 pounds).

Nephrite is more suitable for stone carving while jadeite is used for jewelry. The Aztecs of Mexico used nephrite for ornaments and in religious ceremonies. The Maoris of New Zealand worked nephrite from South Island. They called it 'axestone' and to them it was important for ceremonial tools and jewelry.

Jade is found in Wyoming and Alaska where it is worked mainly by gem collectors and rockhounds.

JAPAN The islands of Japan are on the boundary between the Pacific and Asiatic Plates. There are 30 active volcanoes, including the famous Fujiyama, which last erupted in 1707. The islands have been subjected to many devastating earthquakes throughout their history.

The black, acidic volcanic soils are not as fertile as the volcanic soils of Southeast Asia. Rice culture has dominated the country for centuries. Recently, it has been mechanized to achieve greater yields for a growing population. Its cost has risen with the use of machinery and fertilizers.

The islands are under a humid subtropical climate regime in the south and humid continental in the north. See **ISLAND ARCS**.

JAPANESE CURRENT The Japanese, or Kuro Shio, Current flows north along the Japanese Coast and curves east to the Gulf of Alaska. Then it flows south along the North American West Coast bringing cold Arctic waters.

Along the coast it is the California Current which moderates the climate. Its associated airmasses bring little rainfall to Southern California but do bring fog and a cooling marine layer.

JARILANDIA Jarilandia is a tree farming experiment in the Amazon Basin along the Jari and Trombetas rivers. Tropical rainforests have great speciation but rarely are there stands of a particular species. Jarilandia trees were planted to supply a floating pulp mill. 60% of the area was to be maintained as natural rainforest.

The Nigerian tree, 'gmelina', was selected but after trials proved not to do well in the sandy soils. The Amazon floods did not bring in the expected nutrients. After tests, the Caribbean Pine was selected as the most suitable.

Jarilandia also has one of the largest rice growing plantations in the world. There are 2 harvests a year and the yield is 3.6 metric tons per acre. In addition, there is a kaolin operation.

The Jarilandia project was initiated by shipping magnate, D. K. Ludwig, who purchased the original tract for $3 million dollars and spent a billion in its development.

The effects of creating the pulp-wood forest and mills on the Amazon were unknowns. Soil deterioration and water pollution problems arose. Jarilandia's technicians were working on these problems when the project was taken over by the Brazilian Government.

Other Amazon tree farming projects are Fordlandia, a rubber plantation, and the pepper trees set out by Japanese colonists. These projects are now showing reasonable success, especially the pepper plantations which are designed to allow the production of crops under the shade of the pepper trees.

Both plantation operations were long and costly in their start-up phases. By comparison the 20-year gestation period at Jarilandia is short.

JASPER Jasper is an impure chalcedony with iron oxide which gives it its red color. The color may vary to brown and sometimes green. Jasper, a cryptocrystalline quartz is abundant enough to be considered a rock. This is especially so in Precambrian iron formations where jasper makes up thick horizons. A striking example is the Banda Alta Formation of Mato Grosso, Brazil.

JET Deep black, dense lignite or jet is often suitable for jewelry. It is fine-grained and easily polished.

JET DRILL The jet drill is a churn type using a string of hollow rods or pipes. Water is pumped to the bit as it chops at material. Water washes the material up between the rod and casing. It is a useful sampling device for placers.

JET FUEL A highly refined kerosene-based fuel is used in jet aviation. Only 7% of every barrel of petroleum is suitable for this purpose.

JET STREAM Jet streams are strong, relatively narrow currents of air concentrated along an almost horizonal axis in the Upper Atmosphere. Convergence and divergence of jet streams gives rise to cyclones (q.v.). These produce further jet streams.

Jet streams are characterized by strong vertical and lateral wind shears. Winds can reach 415 kilometers (250 miles) per hour. From between 10 and 50 kilometers (6 and 30 miles) into the Atmosphere there are jet streams at varying levels.

In North American summers, the jet stream usually flows north of the Canadian border. In winter, it may loop south to the Gulf of Mexico. These jets are found between 6,000 and 9,000 meters (20,000 and 30,000 feet) altitude. They blow from west to east and are dipped to a northwest-southeast trajectory by the Coriolis Effect (q.v.). The actual path changes from day to day, and season to season. A pilot riding a jet east can sometimes save fuel and gain time.

A low level jet stream at 2 kilometers (1.2 miles) altitude flows north from the Gulf of Mexico. It is a warm, moist tongue of air. It contributes to the climate of the Gulf Coast and beyond.

JOIDES The Joint Oceanographic Institutions for Deep Earth Drilling (JOIDES) was formed when Congress turned down the Mohole Project (q.v.). Lamont, Scripps, University of Miami, and Woods Hole joined to drill 6 deep holes with financial help from the National Science Foundation. JOIDES contributed greatly to the knowledge of the seafloor and plate tectonics (q.v.).

Off Blake Plateau in the Atlantic, they took cores from the mid-ocean ridge and rift. For comparison, cores were taken in the Gulf of Mexico, the Caribbean, and North Pacific away from East Pacific Rise.

In 1986, the crew of Research Vessel Resolution cored the south flank of the Costa Rican Ridge. Shallow water fossils were found at 4,000 meters (13,200 feet) below sea surface. These provided evidence of subsidence. The water contained in the marine sediments had a salinity twice that of seawater.

JOINTS Fractures or joints, micro- or macroscopic, appear in rocks as a result of tectonic activity. There is no relative displacement as in faults. Jointing may result from rock contraction during cooling. The blocky structure of basalt columnar jointing results from this contraction. Shearing and tension also produce joints.

Joints are found along bedding planes, in the direction of dip, or across the bed. The amount and type of jointing depends upon individual rock rigidity. When overburden is removed, joints parallel to the surface develop from rebound.

Jointing aids weathering as it increases the surface available for chemical activity. Vertical jointing can lead to erosional towers, horizontal jointing to a flat-topped relief.

JOJOBA The jojoba plant is a self-fertilizing desert shrub. Its seeds contain a liquid wax with physical and chemical properties very like those of sperm whale oil. It grows in saline and alkaline soils and is native to the Sonoran Desert. Because of its special properties, jojoba is considered a candidate for gasahol (q.v.).

JONGLEI CANAL The Jonglei Canal is a 362 kilometer (217 mile) bypass for the Nile River in Southern Sudan. The bypass would shorten the distance through the Sudd (q.v.) and increase the total flow of the river.

The Sudd, the world's largest swamp, takes an enormous amount of Nile water. The swamp's great expanse adds evaporative surface, so water loss is huge.

The elimination of the great bend in the Nile is expected to save 4.7 billion cubic meters of water a year. Construction began in 1976, financed by the Arab oil nations. The sponsors hope the arable land reclaimed will become a breadbasket for the Arab World. The project will increase flow to Lake Nasser and this additional flow will require the Toshka Canal (q.v.) to Western Egypt to control erosion. See **JONGLEI INVESTIGATION**.

JONGLEI INVESTIGATION The Jonglei Investigation Team was established by the British to determine the feasibility of building a canal on the Equatorial Nile to increase river flow through the Sudd (q.v.) of southern Sudan.

The projected canal would extend from Jonglei, north of Juba, to a point on the White Nile between its confluences with the Jeraf and Sobat Rivers. This would shorten the distance and ease navigating the Bahr el Jebel River as well as reduce evaporation losses in the Sudd (q.v.).

The report, 'Equatorial Nile Project, and its effect on the Anglo-Egyptian Sudan' was published in Khartoum in 1954. The Jonglei Investigation was part of a much greater study of the entire Nile System, especially the Equatorial Nile.

Possible ecological costs of the canal were discussed as well as the direct effects on Dinka, Nuer, and Shilluk tribes. The tribes use the floodplains in drier periods to pasture cattle. Diversion is expected to affect these pastures. It is also expected to affect the fish, alter soils, introduce new pests, and generally transform the environment. See **JONGLEI CANAL**.

JONKERS DIAMOND   Uncut, the Jonkers diamond found in South Africa weighed 726 carats. Egypt's last Pharaoh, Farouk, owned one of the gemstones the diamond yielded. It weighed 125 carats.

JUNGLE   A jungle is a dense, nearly impenetrable growth of vines, shrubs, small trees, and bushes. It is found along river systems in the subtropics and tropics. It is also found where tropical rainforests have been cut and burned. Jungle is a secondary growth and quite different from true rainforest (q.v.). In contrast, the rainforest is relatively clear below the canopy.

The word jungle is derived from the Sanskrit 'jangala' which means desert. In some areas, jungle is transitional to semi-arid scrublands.

JUNIPER   The conifer genus, 'Juniperus', is very widespread in the semi-arid uplands of western United States. A piñon-jupiter woodland is found scattered throughout the Great Basin.

JUPITER   The planets Saturn, Uranus, Neptune, and Jupiter are known as the Jovian planets. They are considered to have characteristics in common with Jupiter. The Jovian planets are very different from Earth. The Jupiter Atmosphere is thick with hydrogen, helium, methane, and ammonia.

Jupiter has been photographed and monitored by spacecraft and found to be the most massive of the Jovians. It has 70% of the Solar System's planetary material. The planet was also found to emit twice the energy it receives from the Sun. The excess is thought by astronomers to be from formational radioactivity.

The Voyager Mission obtained some interesting photographs of Io, the innermost of the 4 moons of Jupiter. It appears to have more eruptive activity than does the Earth. During the flyby, 7 active volcanoes were recorded.

In October, 1989, the Space Shuttle, Atlantis, launched the Galileo Probe on its mission to Jupiter. The voyage will take 6 years. It should add considerably to the knowledge of Jupiter and its satellites.

JURASSIC PERIOD   The Jurassic Period (195-136 m.y.), a part of the Mesozoic Age, followed the Triassic and preceded the Cretaceous. Great outcrops of Jurassic sediments are found in the Jura Massif of France. Britain also has thick sections.

The Jurassic is rich in fossils, primarily marine organisms. The most important of these were the ammonites which lived in deep water. In-shore fossils are Foraminifera and ostracods. The Jurassic is also the period of maximum reptile development, both in size and kind. Bird fossils appear for the first time in Upper Jurassic.

Great development also occurred in the Plant Kingdom during the Jurassic when angiosperms (q.v.) first appeared. They became abundant in the Lower Cretaceous.

During the Jurassic, Pangaea (q.v.) continued to break up and shallow seas invaded much of the land. These covered 1/4 of Europe. In North America, a seaway grew parallel to the Cordilleran Geanticline in Early Jurassic (200 m.y.). Utah and Wyoming were covered by wind-blown sand (Navaho Sandstone).

By Mid-Jurassic the Sundance Sea had extended into Idaho and Wyoming building up thick limestones. The evaporite sequences are extensive (Gypsum Spring and Carmel formations of the San Rafael Group). These extended onto the Colorado Plateau. A rising geanticline later drained to the east. See **MORRISON FORMATION**.

The Nevadian Orogeny of folded mountains and volcanoes occurred in western North America. The disturbance caused great alteration of older rocks. Strongly deformed Mariposa Formation developed in California and metamorphosed limestones in Idaho and Nevada.

JUTE Jute, a plant of the linden family is used for sacking and cloth. It is grown in the Ganges Delta where it has flourished for hundreds of years. Jute is a main cash crop of India and Bangladesh.

JUVENILE WATER Water of magmatic origin is juvenile. It usually reaches the surface through hot springs and is not normally part of the hydrological cycle (q.v.). Juvenile water is chemically derived within the Earth's Crust. It can be brought to the surface zone by igneous activity. Juvenile waters relate to the degassing (q.v.) of the Earth's Mantle.

K

K:AR The ratio, K-40:Ar-40 (potassium-40 to argon-40) is used to age-date rocks. Only a very small amount of potassium is made up of the potassium-40 isotope and 7% of that decays to argon-40. The rest decays to calcium-40. The combined decay chains have a half-life of 1.31 billion years. See **ISOTOPE**.

Using argon-40, dating accuracy is within 1-2%. This has been checked against other dating techniques. By careful analysis it was found that some of the oldest terrestrial rocks date from 4.58 billion years. These rocks are from Greenland and the Siberian Shield.

KAIETEUR FALLS Kaieteur Falls on the Potaro River in the Guiana Highlands is one of the world's most beautiful. The falls are 100 kilometers (60 miles) upstream of the confluence of the Potaro and Essequibo (q.v.) rivers in Guyana.

The Potaro drops off a 225 meter (740 foot) sandstone plateau into a heavily forested gorge. The waters are 90 meters (300 feet across) at the top of the plateau.

The setting is dense tropical rainforest mingled with savanna. It has an interesting and varied fauna. Behind the falls is a cave housing hundreds of swallows.

KALAHARI DESERT In Botswana, Southwest Africa, between the Orange River and Lake Ngami, a marshy depression, is the Kalahari Desert. It is separated by mountains from the Namib Desert (q.v.). Kalahari is plateauland covering an area 700,000 square kilometers (420,000 square miles). This 'Great Thirstland' has almost no rain and has extremely hot summers.

Kalahari sands are red with iron oxide. Among the sparse vegetation is the specially adapted 'Welwitschia mirabilis' (q.v.). The Bushmen, aborigines living in the desert, are miracles of adaptation to the rigorous environment.

KAME A kame is a small, conical hill of stratified glacial drift (q.v.) composed of ill-sorted sand and gravel. The sediments were deposited by meltwaters in a hole gouged by a stalled glacier. Kames also formed as fans at the glacier's edge.

KAO NASA's Kuiper Airborne Laboratory (KAO), a specially fitted C-141, can cruise at 12,425 meters (41,000 feet) above most water vapor in the Atmosphere. Water vapor blocks infra-red radiation.

In March,1977, over Southwest Australia while viewing the first occultation of Uranus, the crew observed a 'belt of satellites' in a 10 kilometer wide ring. It was the first planetary ring discovery in 350 years. Since then,Voyager I noted a Jupiter ring and Voyager II in the 1989 flyby discovered 8 rings encircling Neptune (q.v.).

KAOLIN Pure white clay, kaolin, is an alumino-silicate derived from the decomposition of feldspar. It is a true clay with particles less than 2 microns (0.002 mm) in size.

Economic kaolin is an aggregate of book-shaped sheets of kaolinite, an hydroxide of aluminum silicate.

High alumina (over 30%) kaolinitic clay is found in the Marysville, Utah area. There is a kaolin belt in the Eastern United States stretching from Alabama to South Carolina. Important deposits of kaolin have been found in Europe and Brazil.

Kaolin, or china clay, was first used in China where it was quarried at Kao-Lin. China clay is highly refractory, with a melting point of 1,800° Celsius. When fired, kaolin is white or nearly so.

KARA KUM Between the Caspian Sea and the Amu Darya River in the USSR is Kara Kum, a black sand desert with barchans (q.v.) up to 75 meters (250 feet) high. Kara Kum covers 300,000 kilometers (115,000 square miles). It is limited in the north by the Urt-Urt Plateau and in the south by the Kopet-Dagh and other ranges.

Kara Kum Canal transports Amu Darya water to support cotton grown on the surrounding steppe. The canal was finished in 1958. There are plans to continue it to the Caspian Sea.

KARABURAN The 'Karaburan' or black storm of Central Asia is propelled by east-northeast gale force winds. These winds pick up desert dust and transport it in great clouds. The clouds darken the skies from spring to the end of summer. See **BEAUFORT SCALE**.

KARAKORAM The 2nd highest mountain range in the world is the Karakoram north and west of the Himalayas. The range in northern Pakistan and northern India extends into Afghanistan, China, and the USSR.

The Karakoram Range merges with the Hindu Kush and Pamirs near the Afghan border. It is separated from the Himalayas by the Indus River Valley. 18 of its peaks are over 7,600 meters (25,000 feet).

KARIBA DAM The Zambezi River is dammed at Kariba, where the gorge is 1,000 meters (3,600 feet) across. Kariba Lake, 280 kilometers (168 miles) long forms part of the border between Zimbabwe and Zambia. The lake is silting rapidly and surface plant life has already appeared.

The dam was built primarily to produce hydropower. Its output is 750,000 kilowatts of electricity per year.

Ecological changes to the Mozambique Plains caused by the dam have not been evaluated. In the dam area, traditional migratory patterns of many animals were interrupted. During construction in 1955, Operation Noah's Ark rescued 6,000 animals.

THE KARROO The Karroo is a vast, arid to semi-arid, elongated structural basin. It contains steep-sided mesas of Permo-Triassic Beaufort Sediment (280-190 m.y.) capped by dolerite (q.v.). The basin is on a plateau bounded by mountains just below the main scarp of the Central African Plateau. Karroo Sediments are considered important evidence of continental drift. Similar beds are found in Brazil, India, and Western Australia, all once part of the single landmass, Gondwana (q.v.).

Sediments contain Permo-Carboniferous (300 m.y.) coal seams with plants different from those of the plants in the coal seams of Europe or North America. In Gondwana, 'Glossopteris' (q.v.) flourished and the environment of deposition must have been sub-tropical to support that fragile plant.

Today, annual precipitation in the Karroo is below 38 centimeters (15 inches), less in the west. The area supports Karroo Bush which is intermediate between tropical and subtropical vegetation and similar to maquis or chapparal (q.v.).

KARROO SILL The Karroo Sill is extrusive dolerite. It is really hundreds of dolerite sills that cap the Karroo Sediments in South Africa. The sills are Mesozoic (225-65 m.y.).

The Karroo is the largest collection of sill structures in the world. They range from a few to 300 meters (900 feet) thick. Total thickness of sill layers is thousands of meters.

In terms of volume the sill emplacement is likened to the basaltic lavas that built the great plateaus of India and Brazil, and the Columbia Plateau in Northwestern United States. See **SILL**.

KARST The landscape resulting from the dissolution of carbonate rocks by circulating groundwaters is karst. Drainage is virtually all underground as runoff disappears into porous rock and sinkholes. There are great numbers of solution caverns. Along the Dalmatian Coast of Yugoslavia, the type locality for karstic terrain, there is rainfall, but the surface is almost barren. Runoff does not remain on the surface long enough for vegetation to take hold.

In Yucatan, Mexico, the sole source of freshwater is from sinkholes or 'cenotes' in the limestone. Cenotes (q.v.) are steep-sided wells that often have appreciable depths to water.

The world's greatest area of karstic terrain is in South China. Surface rocks have eroded away leaving a special landscape. In Kwangsi Province, limestone sentinels surround basins that were once caverns. In Yunnan, there is a plain with a 'stone forest' of tall, narrow limestone towers.

Karst may host economic minerals including bauxite, clay, phosphates, iron, and sulfides. The minerals have been solution deposited. Some caverns are lined with stalagmites and stalactites (q.v.) crystallized from mineralized solutions.

KARUM SALT LAKE In the northwest of the Danakil Depression of Ethiopia, a salt lake developed on the Karum Plain. It is 75 kilometers (45 miles) wide and once was part of the Red Sea. The salt beds are 1,121 meters (3,700 feet) thick. Karum Lake is dry except for its center. Brine pools are near a crater.

Volcanic buckling has created salt hills up to 38 meters (125 feet) high. Yellow solution pinnacles are 2 meters (6 feet) high. See **DANAKIL**.

KASHMIR VALLEY A great downfold in the Earth's Crust created a trough in the sub-Himalayan range of Pir Panjal in India. The trough was filled by erosional sediments, mostly mud and clay, to a depth of 700 meters (2,300 feet). Today, the 135 x 32 kilometer (85 x 20 mile) Kashmir Valley is irrigated by the Jhelum River bringing meltwaters to the area.

This 'Vale of Kashmir' was the site of the famous Moghul gardens of Shalimar, Shahi, and Nishat. During the 'Raj', the area was used by the British as a 'hill station'. It was a @ace to recuperate from the heat of the Indian Plains.

KATMAI ERUPTION Katmai Volcano, Alaska, erupted in 1912 and covered 142 square kilometers (55 square miles) with 30 million tons of burning 'sand'. Katmai then collapsed and became a caldera. A new volcano emerged a few miles away.

Katmai type volcanoes were more common in the Tertiary and Pleistocene than in the Re Recent. They are noted for sand flows and glowing clouds. There have been 'Rains of Fire' in recent time in New Zealand, Italy, Libya, and Sumatra. Molten silica by the millions of tons has been ejected. The silica solidified to form ignimbrites (q.v.). Katmai erupted in June and was preceded by record cold weather. After the eruption, haze and fog reached Wisconsin in a very few days. There was an immediate global warming upon eruption followed by unseasonably cold weather which lead to crop failures. See **NUCLEAR WINTER**.

KATWE CRATERS East of the Ruwenzoris (q.v.) in Uganda is a graben in the west branch of the Great Rift Valley (q.v.). The graben floor is pock-marked with more than 50 rounded craters, some of which are superimposed on others. There is no evidence of lava so these must have been gaseous blowouts.

Many of the craters are now water-filled and the grassland is an attraction for the regional fauna.

KEEWEENAW PENINSULA Keeweenaw Peninsula extends into Lake Superior from Michigan. The peninsula is the south limb of a synclinal trough which contains the lake. It was the site of the greatest copper production in the United States. The copper is native copper, a metal first worked by the Indians.

Keeweenaw Peninsula hosts a 167 kilometer (100 mile) long by 5 kilometer (3 mile) wide belt of native copper in basaltic flows. The copper is concentrated on the top of the lava flows of which there are some 400. The total thickness is 6,000 meters (20,000 feet). The sequence is dated at 2 billion years. The sequence is much older than the flows of the Michigan Basin (q.v.).

The copper was brought to the surface by hydrothermal solutions in the form of copper sulfide. The sulfide came into contact with the iron oxides in the basalt. The oxygen combined with the sulfur and the copper was reduced to a metal. Keeweenaw is the largest known deposit of 'native' copper.

KELP Kelp is seaweed, an Algae (q.v.). It is a giant plant, sometimes 60 meters (200 feet) long with no roots. It is anchored by hold-fasts or tendrils up to 10 meters (30 feet) long that cling to rocks. Gas-filled bubbles on fronds act as floats keeping the kelp just below the surface.

Kelp forms mats over very large areas. These can shut off oxygen and light to the sea below. Red-brown kelp carries out photosynthesis (q.v.) and oxygenates the sea around it. But, the rate ofut, the rate of the photosynthesis is too slow to provide an off-setting supply of oxygen.

There is a kelp farming pilot project in California processing kelp for methane (q.v.).

KELVIN SCALE The velocity of atomic activity is temperature dependent. Lord Kelvin developed a scale, or thermometer, based on the point where atoms slow down to virtually no motion. This point is 0° Kelvin. Water also freezes at this temperature set at -273° Celsius, or Absolute Zero (q.v.). Room temperature on the Kelvin Scale is about 293°. The Kelvin is the astronomer's preferred scale.

At the present time, some laboratories are able to create superconductivity (q.v.) at temperatures of 230° Kelvin.

MOUNT KENYA Kenya is one of the famous peaks in East Africa. It is an extinct volcano in the Great Rift System (q.v.). Its peak rises to 5,163 meters (17,040 feet) in height, is snow-capped, and classical in form. The mountain sides are forested with Lobelia, which grows to 8 meters (26 feet), and 6 meter (20 feet) Groundsel.

The volcanic slopes of Mount Kenya are productive and tea plantations produce an important cash crop and source of foreign exchange for Kenya.

KEROGEN Kerogen is a waxy, solid organic compound. It is a 3-dimensional polymer (q.v.) of carbon, hydrogen, sulfur, and oxygen in a macromolecular form. Kerogen is embedded in fine-grained material (marlstone). It is the most important oil shale hydrocarbon and the most abundant.

In a froth flotation process, at 650° Celsius, the complex breaks down into oil, gas, carbon, and shale. Some kerogen remains in the rock and resembles coke.

KEROSENE Kerosene, a liquid, is derived from petroleum. Its major use is as jet fuel. Only 7% of a barrel of crude oil is kerosene.

KETTLE HOLE A periglacial feature, the kettle hole is a small depression. It is a relatively shallow structure of 6-15 meters (20-50 feet), a few hundred feet across. A detached block of buried glacier melted to leave the depression.

KHAMSIN 'Khamsin', Arabic for 50, is the name given to a hot, dry, southern wind blowing across the Sahara of Egypt and Sudan. It is common in the spring and causes the air to be thick with drifting dust and sand.

In Algeria, this wind is the 'Sirocco'. It is 'Shahali' in Central Sahara and 'Harmattan' (q.v.) in West Africa.

KHAZAKHSTAN The USSR Republic of Khazakhstan has enormous natural resources. The Republic contains the 3rd largest coal basin in the USSR, the Karaganda, with 46.6 billion tons in beds ranging from 1.5-15 meters (5-50 feet) of predominantly low-sulfur coal. To complement this wealth of coal, Khazakhstan has iron ore reserves of 7 billion tons. In 1970 this was 15.5% of the total of the USSR reserves.

In addition to coal, the area has petroleum reserves. These are in the Emba Basin of the Ural River in western Khazakhstan.

One of the major suppliers of chromite, USSR reserves are concentrated in the Kempyrsai Deposit of western Khazakhstan in the Atyubinsk Region. See **CHROME**.

The main copper production of the USSR is from pyrites, but there are significant porphyry (q.v.) deposits in Khazakhstan. The Republic also has non-ferrous metals. It has become an important metallurgical center.

KHUMEI DUNES In Kordofan Province, Sudan, 108 kilometers (65 miles) from El Obeid, there was once a green belt with baobab trees (q.v.). Destruction of the belt caused sand dunes near Khumei to increase in size and number.

A 6-year drought, with no rain in 1985-1986, caused almost all the vegetation to disappear. During this time, the baobab trees were sacrificed for fuel. Locusts (q.v.) invaded in 1986 completing the destruction.

KHYBER PASS The famed Khyber Pass in the Safed Koh Range of the Himalayas links Afghanistan and Pakistan. The pass is one of the few through these high mountains, the pass is 55 kilometers (33 miles) long.

KILAUEA At 1,212 meters (4,000 feet) of elevation on the flank of Mauna Loa Volcano (q.v.) is Kilauea Crater. Hawaiians call Kilauea the 'house of everlasting fire'.

There were 48 major events in 1986 and the volcano has been active in 1988-89. Kilauea can exude millions of tons of lava in a day and it has been adding to the size of the island. Many eruptions imperil villages. See **MAUNA LOA**.

KILLARNEY OROGENY The Killarney Orogeny occurred at the close of the Proterozoic Age (550 m.y.). It was the last of the great mountain-building events (Laurentian, Algonquian, Killarney) that produced the Proterozoic mountains of North America and Europe.

MOUNT KILIMANJARO Kilimanjaro, a volcano in Tanzania, rises from the Amboselli Plain. It is an expression of the Great Rift System of East Africa. The volcano is about 400 kilometers (240 miles) southeast of Mount Kenya.

Kilimanjaro is 5,929 meters (19,565 feet) high and is snow-capped all year. Its crater is ash 'rimmed by blue-white ice'. Short glaciers produced the Hemingway 'snows'.

Like Mount Kenya, Kilimanjaro is forested at its base and for a considerable way upslope. Tall Lobelia are found on these slopes. The timberline is abrupt.

KILOGRAM The kilogram is a unit in the Cgs (centimeter-gram-second) System. It equals 1 liter of water at 4° Celsius when water is at its heaviest. A kilogram, 1,000 grams = 2.245 pounds.

KIMBERLITE Kimberlite is a peridotite breccia. The type locality is at Kimberley, South Africa. Weathered, it is the famous 'blue ground' that often contains diamonds. It is found in pipe-like intrusives.

Kimberlite contains a large percent of iron and magnesium altered to serpentine. The weathered upper part of the pipe is blue ground, below it is 'yellow ground'. Yellow ground also contains diamonds but is much more difficult to work. South African kimberlites may be of Mesozoic Age (225-65 m.y.).

Recently kimberlite has been found on the Colorado-Wyoming line. No economic diamond deposit, pipe or placer, has been uncovered.

KIMBERLEY RANGE Along the west coast of Australia, the Kimberleys never exceed 700 meters (2,300 feet). Where they abut the coast small inlets have developed which are famous for their dangerous tides. The range extends over 1,000 kilometers (600 miles).

The major river system of the region is the Ord which has become harnessed for irrigation.

The gorges and canyons of the range are subject to flash flooding in the monsoon season from December to March.

In recent years the Kimberleys have been the target of some major exploration, particularly for nickel.

KINETIC ENERGY Energy related to a body in motion is kinetic. It is calculated as 1/2 the mass of the body times the velocity squared.

KING SOLOMON'S MINES The Bible reports that King Solomon and King Hiram brought a total of 1,086 talents (about 28.5 kilograms or 917 troy ounces) of gold from Ophir. That is 31 metric tons or half the known gold supply of the ancient world.

Ophir is believed to be Mahd adh Dhahab (Cradle of Gold) Mine between Medina and Mecca in Saudi Arabia. The location of King Solomon's Mines has been speculated upon for centuries. There have been many fabulous 'Ophirs'.

The Saudi deposits fulfill the legends in many ways. The deposit has been reworked many times. Radiocarbon dating shows workings from 600-900 A.D.

Between 1939-1954, Saudi Mining Syndicate produced 55 metric tons or 1.77 million Troy ounces. Production was from 9 dumps that ran 0.6 ounces/ton. Deep workings were opened up and some new, rich zones were found.

KINGDOM The Taxonomic Classification System divides all living things into 4 Kingdoms (Fungi, Protist, Plant, and Animal). The Kingdoms are divided into Phyla. In the Animal Kingdom there are 19 phyla only 1 of which is vertebrate (Chordata).

The Phyla are divided into Classes, Orders, Families, Genera, and Species. Humans (Homo sapiens) is in the class Mammalia (mammals), the order of Primate, and the family of Hominidae. There are 3 genera.

KINTA RIVER VALLEY The world's largest alluvial tin fields are in the Kinta River Valley, Malaysia, near Kuala Lumpur. They have been worked for centuries, primarily by Chinese. Indications are that the deposits may soon be exhausted.

KIRUNA Sweden produces iron ore for itself and Europe from the Kiruna Mines in Lappland. Production is 25 million metric tons annually of magnetite.

Proven Kiruna reserves are 3 billion tons of high grade ore, up to 70% iron. The ore is mined from a steeply-dipping mass of magnetite in Precambrian rocks.

KIVU LAKE Kivu, one of the lakes of the Great Rift (q.v.) East Africa, came into existence in the Tertiary. Volcanic activity in the Virunga Range dammed the Upper Nile Valley. The new outlet is via the Ruzizi (Rusisi) River to Lake Tanganyika, 110 kilometers (70 miles) downstream. This damming event changed Kivu drainage to the Congo (Zaire) and the Atlantic Ocean.

KLIPPE A klippe is part of an overthrust block cut off its main thrust sheet. 'Klippe' is German for cliff and the structure is an isolated rock assembly separated from its formation by a fault. The fault is low angle and the rocks above are older.

KNOLL On land, a knoll is a low hill. In the sea, a knoll is any elevation less than 1,000 meters (3,300 feet) rising from the ocean floor.

A knoll has a limited summit area whether on land or in the sea.

KNOT The knot is a maritime unit of length. It comes from the days of sailing vessels when speed was calculated by knots on a rope, or logline. A knot is 1 nautical mile (6,080 feet).

KÖPPEN CLASSIFICATION A broad system of macro-climate classification was developed by the geographer, Köppen. He defined 5 main groups and relatively few subdivisions. The basis of the system is the heat of summer, cold of winter, and rainfall amounts throughout the year.

KOHINOOR DIAMOND The Kohinoor Diamond, was found at Godavari, India, in 1,300 A.D. It weighed 187 carats and later became part of Queen Victoria's crown jewels. Badly cut, it had none of its reputed brilliance. Now it is in Queen Mary's crown. Recutting did not enhance it.

KOHL Kohl is a dark cosmetic used since Egyptian times. It is made from stibnite, a sulfide of antimony. Kohl was used by both Cleopatra and Jezebel as an eye cosmetic.

KOLA PENINSULA Kola Peninsula, USSR on the Finnish border, is within the Arctic Circle between the Arctic Ocean and the White Sea. The landscape is Tundra (q.v.), the Khibina Tundra.

Peninsula geology has been studied since 1920. There are 3 major intrusions of alkaline rocks (q.v.), the last 300-500 million years ago. The main belt is Mid-Peninsula and associated with large massifs (q.v.).

Because Kola is a geologically stable shield area and seismically quiet it was chosen as the site of a deep drill-hole, the deepest in the world. It is 12.066 kilometers (7.24 miles). The results of the drilling upset some long-held theories.

It had long been held that the Conrad Discontinuity (q.v.) marked a change to basalt in crustal composition. This would be encountered at a depth of 7.5 kilometers. Basalt was not present for the entire depth of the hole.

Kola has some of the richest deposits of copper and nickel in the USSR. It was a surprise to encounter these minerals at 1.6 kilometers (1 mile). They are even considered mineable. The biggest surprise was the finding of copper, nickel and lead at 2 horizons, at 6 and 11 kilometers. Fluid was encountered in fractures down to 9 kilometers and the rock was porous. This was a total surprise as the overburden was supposed to have compacted rock so such conditions would not occur.

In the Kovdozero District, carbonatite lavas and pyroclastics are widespread. Outcrops are limited to a 60 square kilometer (24 square mile) area with a subsided caldera, 8 kilometers (4.8 miles) across. It is in the northeast end of the Khibina-Kovdozero (Kontozero) Graben. Rocks are similar to those of the Uganda carbonatites (q.v.).

Labuntson, who discovered the Kola apatites, was laughed at for describing 'fictitious phenomena'. Today, the apatites are a major fertilizer raw material for the USSR. The apatite is in a 4 kilometer (2.4 mile) belt up to 200 meters (60 feet) thick. Ore reserves are in the billions of tons. See **APATITE**.

KOMODO ISLAND Komodo is one of the Indonesian Islands. It is famous as the habitat of the world's largest living lizard, up to 3 meters (10 feet).

KOPJE In south Africa, small hills, 'kopjes' are common. They are isolated stone knolls of the same origin as inselbergs (q.v.) but smaller. They are found on the plateau in South Africa and Zimbabwe.

KORDOFAN DUNES In Kordofan and Darfur Provinces, Sudan, 2 belts of fixed dunes dominate the landscape. They are the High Qoz and Low Qoz. North of El Obeid, the dune pattern is transverse to that to the south. In general, the dunes have 'snake-like ridges' up to 12 meters (40 feet). The strike is northwest-southeast and is not related to the present wind flow. See **DUNES**.

KRAKATOA In 1883, Krakatoa Volcano in the Sunda Strait, Indonesia, erupted with a force equal to 400 hydrogen bombs. The explosion was so loud it was heard in Central Australia.

The eruption was from 3 craters simultaneously, after a dormancy of 200 years. The volcano subsequently collapsed forming a great submarine caldera with 3 peaks above water.

Krakatoa ejected 21 cubic kilometers (5 cubic miles) of pyroclastics. So much pumice was floating in Sunda Strait, shipping was blocked.

The Sun was still dark in Japan 4 days after the eruption. Europe had spectacular sunsets for 3 years caused by atmospheric particulates. Dust circled the globe 3 times causing a 2-year drop in temperature equivalent to a 'nuclear winter' (q.v.).

KREEP KREEP is an acronym for lunar rocks with potassium, Rare Earths, and phosphorus. They are closest to terrestrial kimberlite (q.v.) which had erupted from depths in the Mantle greater than 200 kilometers (120 miles). Kimberlite differs from KREEP in that it has been in contact with eclogite (q.v.).

KRILL Tiny shrimp-like plankton are food for the baleen type of filter-feeding whales. The krill are rich in protein and other nutrients. They make up part of the diet of penguins, seals, and sea birds. As other plankton (q.v.), they are the initiation of a food chain and thus critical to life in the sea.

Super-swarms of krill have been found off Elephant Island in the Antarctic. The schools are hundreds of feet across. These have been fished for the past decade by the Soviets for fishmeal. The annual haul is 125,000 tons per year. Japanese and Soviet fishermen are using nets that can haul in 60 tons a day. Environmentalists and others are concerned that they are over-fishing the area.

KRUMMHOLZ Krummholz is a cluster of dwarfed and twisted trees found on high mountain slopes above or at the timberline. Trees were deformed by wind and crushed by ice. Many resemble flags as the branches grow away from the prevailing wind.

The growing season is short so krummholz or elfinwood trees have an adapted system of regeneration. They put out roots where the trees touch the ground and they reproduce by layering.

The Krummholz Zone, transitional between Taiga and Tundra (q.v.), is favored by birds and elk in the warmer seasons. Krummholz is the name given to both the ecotone and the vegetation.

KRYPTON Krypton, a gaseous element, was considered unreactive until an experiment with an electrical charge caused it to emit a blue glow. This quality has made it useful for fog-lamps. Krypton is emitted by some nuclear reactions.

Radioactive krypton is used as a medical tracer. Both krypton and argon are used in lasers employed in eye surgery.

KUPUKUPU FERN Kupukupu fern is one of the first plants to be established in the lavas of Hawaii. Its roots break apart the lava chunks, providing the plant with a base and nutrients. The fern is rapidly succeeded by typical Hawaiian vegetation.

KURO SHIO CURRENT The Japanese Current (q.v.) is Kuro Shio Current while in Japanese waters. It is warm until it transits the Gulf of Alaska and turns cold. The current curves to follow the coast of North America and finally becomes the California Current (q.v.).

KURSK MAGNETIC ANOMALY The Kursk Magnetic Anomaly is one of the largest anomalies of its kind in the world. It is given off by a huge iron and quartzite massif near Kursk, USSR. The anomaly is 600 kilometers (360 miles) long and 2-40 kilometers (1.2-24 miles) wide. The ore deposits the anomaly defines range from 40 meters (132 feet) in the north to 350 meters (1,155 feet) thick in the south. The richest ores are up to 62% but the average is 32%. The reserves are 40 billion tons of which 13 billion are half high and half medium grade.

The anomaly was first discovered because of erratic compass readings. The orebody together with nearby coals are the basis of a steel industry in the area.

KUZNETSK BASIN Kuznetsk Basin, south of Novosibirsk, is at the foot of the Altai Range in Siberia. The Kuzbas Region is rich in coal and iron ore. It is an important defence metallurgical region second only to the Don-Leningrad (Donbas) area.

In the Kuznetz Complex, there are huge basic steel mills relying on the high grade coal produced in the Basin. There are machinery and munitions plants as well. Novokuznetsk is the main center.

KWAJALEIN Kwajalein, the world's largest atoll (q.v.) is in the Marshall Islands. A reef encloses 2,850 square kilometers (1,100 square miles) of lagoon. The island is 130 kilometers (78 miles) long.

KYANITE The alumino-silicate, kyanite, is mainly a refractory mineral. With its polymorphs (q.v.) andalusite and sillimanite, kyanite belongs to the Sillimanite Group. Though chemically the same, these minerals have different crystal structures due to differences in formational temperature and pressure.

Kyanite shows differences in hardness related to its crystal axis. Parallel to the axis, the hardness is 5, while across the crystal it is 7 on the Moh's Scale (q.v.).

Long-bladed crystalline kyanite is often an accessory mineral in gneisses and schists. Occasionally, it is massive and makes up the bulk of the rock. In the United States, it is mined in North Carolina and in Georgia.

Very fine translucent blue and pink crystals are gemstones.

L

L WAVE An 'L' wave is a long, surface wave generated by a combination of 'p' and 's' waves at the epicenter of a seism or earthquake. L waves travel around the world through the outer layer of the Crust. They are the most destructive of seismic waves.

The L wave travels either in a uniform solid or as a Raleigh Wave in a non-uniform solid. Its velocity is 3.67 kilometers (2.2 miles) per second.

LABOR The old Spanish-Mexican measure, 'labor', is used in surveying. It is a land tract of 1,000 'varas' (177.14 acres or 71.74 hectares). The labor was once used extensively in southwestern United States. It appears on titles going back to the land-grant days.

LABRADOR CURRENT The Labrador or Arctic Current is developed in Davis Strait between Greenland and Baffin Island. It is an off-shoot of the East Greenland Current which skirts Greenland to Cape Farewell. A branch flows up Greenland's west coast, another south along Labrador, Newfoundland, and New England to Cape Cod. In this reach, it is the Labrador Current. Off Cape Cod, the current turns east and merges with the Gulf Stream.

The Labrador Current is responsible for some of the heaviest fog banks on Earth. This is due to cool air being further cooled by a cold sea.

LABRADOR RANGE The Precambrian Labrador Range is a large upthrust block between Labrador and Quebec. The mountains trend north-west. Only low hills remain on the east. The Labradors host iron ore and other economic minerals. The range gives off a magnetic high on the Canadian Shield.

LABRADORITE Labradorite belongs to the Plagioclase, or Soda-lime Group of feldspars. This group grades from albite to anorthite or from sodium-aluminum silicate to calcium-aluminum silicate.

Labradorite is an intermediate member composed of anorthite with 30-50% albite. It is dull, black, or dark gray and was named for the basic igneous rocks of Labrador. Wet labradorite has an iridescence (q.v.).

LACCOLITH Magma cooled below the surface to form a circular or semi-circular lense-like mass is a laccolith. It has a mushroom shape. The intrusive conforms to sediments that have arched to provide space.

The La Sal Mountains of Utah are laccoliths exposed by erosion. The Henry Mountains, also in Utah, have many laccoliths and are the type locality. In these structures there are no single conduits. They were fed laterally from large magma chambers.

Laccoliths are found also found in the Black Hills of South Dakota. Devil's Tower, Wyoming, may be a stem from an ancient laccolith rather than a volcanic neck as previously thought.

LACUSTRINE Deposits accumulated in lakes or of lake origin are lacustrine. They may be detrital or organic material as well as clays and silts. These sediments abound in formerly glaciated areas. The lakes drained leaving bottom sediments to form plains. The distinctive deposits grade to fine at the center of a basin.

Lacustrine deposits are often found in plateau or mountain basins. Great Salt Lake Basin and others which were once filled by large glacial lakes have enormous deposits. Many large lacustrine deposits are found on the eastern flanks of the Andes.

LAG DEPOSITS Wind and water erosion can winnow and wash out fine material leaving the coarser. Remaining materials or lag deposits, are usually of gravel and pebble. Some lag deposits contain heavy minerals, other have trapped gold.

LAGEOS LAGEOS (Laser Geodynamic Satellite) is NASA's vehicle to study Earth rotation and crustal movements. It is equipped with 426 reflector plates to provide it with solar energy.

The satellite is capable of measuring the relative position of Earth stations within 3 centimeters, thus crustal movements are clearly discernible.

LAGOON A lagoon is a body of relatively quiet, shallow water separated from the ocean by a barrier. The barrier may be an island, shoal, or reef. Lagoons receive freshwater and sediments from shore streams and tidal seawater. They are less saline than the sea and serve as spawning grounds for many marine animals.

Laguna Madre between the Gulf Coast of Texas and Padre Island is the largest hypersaline lagoon in the United States. As a result of semi-isolation, it is more saline than usual. It is shallow, and the evaporation rate is high. Laguna Madre is made up of a series of long, narrow, lagoons with separate basins. Hurricanes can close the narrow outlets at each end.

LAHAR 'Lahar' is the Indonesian name for a volcanic mudflow. Great columns of ash from huge volcanic explosions result in torrential rains that trigger mudflows. Lahar refers to both the flow and the deposits at the base of the volcano.

Lahar flows are of huge volume and great velocity. Destruction of crater walls leads to slides. Crater waters have also been displaced by muds causing great flooding. An event of this type occurred on Java in 1919. It resulted in an enormous loss of life.

LAHONTAN Pleistocene (q.v.) Lake Lahontan occupied a series of depressions in western Nevada. Run-off from the Sierra Nevadas fed the lake. At least 3 lake stages have been identified by ancient shorelines. During Interglacials the basins were dry, as today.

LAKE A lake is a more transient landscape feature than most. It will eventually fill with sediment or vegetation, or will drain. A lake has a lifespan of a few hundred to a few thousand years.

Most of the world's major lakes were produced by glaciation. Ice scouring the land created depressions, filled them with meltwater and dammed them with glacial moraines (q.v.).

Other lakes were created when volcanic craters were filled with meltwater or by rainfall. Volcanic flows have created lakes by damming the flow of streams. Lakes can also be formed by faulting or structural activity.

Lakes are often fed by springs and more than one stream. A river can flow from a high lake level outlet if the water is deep enough. The outlet lip will be cut down by the river and ultimately the lake will be drained.

Many processes tend toward the natural destruction of lakes:

- Climate is important - Many lakes are lost to evaporation
- Wind- and stream-borne sediments infill lakes
- Vegetation shrinks lakes with organic material
- Lava flow destroy lakes or build them
- Structural activity (faulting, folding) can destroy lakes. Stream piracy causes a lake to disappear if major inflow is lost.

There are millions of lakes in the world. They are on every continent but Antarctica. They moderate local climate and control flooding. Even Australia has a few large lakes that help modify the local climate.

Lakes are clustered in districts that were formerly glaciated or areas of major rifting. There are several major lakes along the Great Rift of East Africa. The world's largest lakes are:

LAKE	COUNTRY	SIZE (Km^2)
Caspian Sea	USSR/Iran	440,000
Superior	U.S./Canada	82,500
Victoria	Tanzania, Uganda	67,000
Aral Sea	USSR	66,000
Huron	U.S./Canada	59,525
Michigan	U.S.	58,000
Baikal	USSR	33,000

The Caspian and Aral seas are really lakes. Baikal, in a Siberian rift is the deepest (over a kilometer) in the world. The Dead Sea is the lowest at 394 meters (1,300 feet) below sea level. Lake Titicaca is the highest at 3,788 meters (12,500 feet).

Some large lakes are artificial as Bratsk Dam Lake in Siberia; Lake Nasser between Egypt and Sudan; Kariba between Zambia and Zimbabwe; and Lake Mead in the United States. They age naturally.

LAKE BIOTA Lake environment in and around the water is a habitat of abundant life. Most lakes are surrounded by water-loving vegetation, especially grasses, reeds, ferns, and moss. There are many floating plants, some prolific enough to choke the lake (water hyacinth).

Plants produce chlorophyll and oxygen that animals consume and the animals produce carbon dioxide which the plants use. The lake environment is a tight, almost closed ecological system or biome. It can be disrupted easily.

LAMBDA PARTICLE The first discovered 'strange particle' was Lambda. It is subatomic and has contributed to opening the subatomic energy field to detailed study. See **SUBATOMIC PARTICLES**.

LAMELLAR FLOW Lamellar, or layered flow is smooth with successive layers of fluid passing over each other. Non-turbulent stream flow is lamellar.

LAMINATION A sedimentary layer of less than a centimeter is a lamina. It is a distinct stratum from that above or below. Lamination is alternation of layers of different thicknesses and grain sizes. It is a type of bedding commonly found in lacustrine (q.v.) clay deposits. When the layers are not parallel to the bedding plane, they are cross-laminated.

LAMPREY The lamprey is a marine fish that spawns in freshwater. It is eel-like in structure.

The lamprey has in some instances become landlocked. It is said to have destroyed the trout and whitefish in the Great Lakes.

LAND BREEZE At night, the land surface loses heat rapidly in relation to adjacent water. Air pressure builds up and sets up a flow or breeze toward the water.

LAND BRIDGE Many continents were linked in the past by land which is now beneath the sea. Some of this land is still tracable by island remnants. Malta was formerly part of the land bridge linking Europe to North Africa.

The land between North America and Eurasia across what is now Bering Strait served as a land bridge for the migration of humans and animals.

The Isthmus of Panama constitutes a land bridge between North and South America. Cutting the Canal disrupted faunal migration between the continents.

LAND SUBSIDENCE Land movement, up or down, is only in relation to the sea or other land. Subsidence can occur for many reasons. Organic material in surface layers may decompose or dry out or water tables drop. Underground circulating waters erode sediments in place and contribute to collapse. This is especially true in karst (q.v.) regions. The effect may only be evident in local sinkholes.

Petroleum production and deep mining operations have produced land subsidence, sometimes only after a great number of years have passed. This is because the surrounding sediments had sufficient integrity to allow them to erode slowly.

Subsidence also occurs from sediment compaction and the increased weight on the Earth's Crust in a geosyncline (q.v.). Crustal disturbance can lead to the downdrop of fault blocks or grabens.

LANDFORM Any large-scale, distinctive landscape feature and some very special relief are landforms. The most important landforms are mountains, plains, and plateaus. Smaller scale features like pinnacles, pipes, and knolls are special erosional forms. Major landforms distributed on unglaciated continental surfaces (After Butzer) are:

CLASS	EARTH (%)
Depositional Plains	25
Ancient Crystalline Shields	23
Erosional Plains/Plateaus	21
Old Mountain Chains	15
Young Mountain Chains	14
Volcanic Plains/Plateaus	2

LANDSAT LANDSAT is a NASA program of computerized imagery designed to cover most of the Earth from satellites. LANDSAT enhanced photos have been successfully used to study landuse patterns, explore for new minerals, evaluate world agriculture, and study world climates.

LANDSLIDE A landslide is a mass of earth moving downslope. The energy may be purely gravitational but often the mass is lubricated by mud and water. Dipping shales and other smooth sediments are the most likely to slip.

A landslide is a powerful force as exhibited in 1971 in Quebec, Canada, A mass of earth 11 meters high (35 feet) moved at the rate of 26 kilometers (16 miles) per hour. The slide ended in the river. It moved 9 million cubic yards of earth.

LANGMUIR CIRCULATION Cellular circulation in the ocean with alternating left and right helical vortices is Langmuir Circulation. The axes are in the direction of the wind.

Langmuir circulation results when vortices are set in motion by winds blowing over the sea surface at greater than 7 knots (13 kilometers or 7.8 miles) per hour.

LANZAROTE ISLAND Lanzarote, the most easterly of the Canary Islands is famous for its 'lunar' landscape. It is devoid of freshwater and there is a desalination plant at Arrecife. The island is 300 square kilometers (120 square miles) and has 300 volcanic craters.

Lanzarote rose above sea level between 1730 and 1736. Later volcanism gave rise to badlands (q.v.) or 'malpais' topography. Ejecta from Montaña del Fuego alone covers 199 square kilometers (77 square miles).

The major rift line is northeast to southwest. In addition to craters there are caverns created from lava tubes (q.v.). One particularly large one is a tourist attraction.

LA PAZ BASIN The La Paz Basin in the Cordillera Oriental of the Andes east of Lake Titicaca is drained by 2 glacier-fed streams that join to form the La Paz River. The world's highest major city is located in the valley at 3,650 meters (12,000 feet).

The relatively short La Paz River passes the city on its 160 kilometer (100 mile) course. It, however, traverses different landscapes among them the 'quebradas' or Andean gorges, and an arid badlands called Vale de la Luna (Valley of the Moon). The river has gallery forests (q.v.) of eucalyptus.

LAPILLI Some French massifs are composed of 'lapilli', Italian for little stones. Lapilli are between 5.0 millimeters and 5.0 centimeters (0.002 and 2.0 inches). They are volcanic ejecta.

LAPIS LAZULI Since ancient Egyptian times, lapis lazuli has been a treasured gemstone. A silicate of aluminum, calcium, and sodium, lapis is often sprinkled with tiny pyrite crystals.

Deep blue lapis has been mined in Afghanistan for 4,000 years. There are deposits in the United States and the USSR.

Because of lapis scarcity, sodalite (q.v.) is used as a substitute. Non-gem quality lapis is pulverized to produce ultra-marine powders.

LAPTEV SEA Laptev Sea in the Arctic between Talmyr Peninsula and New Siberia Island is north of Yakutsk. Lena Delta is built into the Laptev Sea. See **LENA RIVER**.

LARAMIDE REVOLUTION Mountain-building occurring 80 to 40 million years ago was the Laramide Revolution. The episode helped isolate the Colorado Plateau and build the Rockies. 100 million years earlier, the ancient range at its core had been peneplaned by erosion. See **PENEPLAIN**.

During the Laramide, the Rockies were folded and arched to form a geanticline. The Precambrian basement of granites and metasediments was faulted. Mineral solutions were injected into the fractures to form the Mineral Belt that stretches from Colorado to New Mexico. At this time Pangaea (q.v.) was breaking up.

LASER Light Amplification by Stimulated Emission of Radiation (LASER) is an energy source. The light is extraordinarily bright and created by the emission of high energy super-charged atoms. The light beam is very narrow, and all the light waves have a single color.

The LASER can focus great energy onto a single spot, raising the temperature up to 6,000° Celsius instantly. LASER light emits channeled photons exciting billions of atoms. Light is directed into a single path so it is coherent. (Ordinary light emits photons in any direction).

LASER rods are made of crystals or glass. The first rods were 4 centimeter ruby crystals. The crystals are filled with liquid or gas. The rod is encased in a reflector box to channel light by mirrors. These instruments with crystal rods are pulsed with rapid on/off mechanisms so the crystals will not burn up.

With the power cut down, the LASER is now used as a surgical instrument. It is also used for industrial drilling and cutting; as a rangefinder; and in space communications.

LASSEN PEAK Lassen was the only active volcano in the lower 48 United States in historical time. It is now joined by Mount Saint Helens (q.v.) and possibly Hood. All peaks are in the Cascade Mountains of the Pacific Northwest.

Lassen was last active in 1921 when it concluded a 7-year period of eruptions. Lassen's dome formed in the Pleistocene (q.v.) on the flank of old Mount Tehama, a large stratovolcano (q.v.).

LATENT HEAT Latent heat results when matter makes a reversible change of state at a constant temperature and pressure. The water-steam system is a good example. Energy from each transition is stored to allow for reversion.

LATERAL PLANATION In lateral planation, interfluves are reduced by lateral swings of a stream. Banks are undercut and the floodplain is increased.

LATERITE Laterite is a ferruginous rock resulting from soil induration. It is the end product of tropical or subtropical weathering. Fluctuations of the water table related to seasonal rainfall play a major role in the leaching process. Seasonality is a component of humid tropical and subtropical climates as even the humid climate is subject to periods of lighter rainfall.

Residual soils develop when silica and organic materials are leached from the surface horizon. Aluminum, iron, and other minerals are deposited above the water table. A crust of indurated material may develop close to the surface. The soils above are relatively infertile.

Mineral deposits result from prolonged laterization. In a Guinea profile studied by the French Overseas Geological Team, the process from soil to indurated iron ore took less than 60 years. The process is irreversible.

At Conakry. Guinea, unusually pure laterite, equal to iron ore, is 60-90 meters (200-300 feet) thick and is developed on igneous rock, mainly olivine. In Indochina, up to 50% of the land surface is underlain by laterite developed on volcanic sediments.

Huge deposits of iron ore and bauxite have formed especially in West Africa and Tropical America. There are large deposits of lateritic nickel in Brazil, Central America, Colombia, and New Caledonia. A small remnant of lateritic nickel is found in Oregon and California testifying to a major climatic change.

Laterite in Saudi Arabia's As Sarat Mountains also testifies to a climate very different from that prevailing today. Red, yellow, and white laterite underlies a thick section of Mio-Pliocene basalt. Eocene laterite covers 1,000 square kilometers (386 square miles). See **BAUXITE**.

LATITUDE   Latitude is distance in degrees north and south of the Equator. From the Pole to Equator is 90°, 10,358 kilometers (6,215 miles). A degree of latitude is 115 kilometers (69 miles).

LATITUDE EFFECT   Measurements of cosmic radiation show how intensity decreases as the Equator is approached. This is the Latitude Effect.

LATOSOL   Latosol is a soil high in aluminum and iron oxides and low in silica. It is developed by laterization and is the red, earthy soil of the tropics and subtropics. Many 'terra rossa' soils are latosols. See **LATERITE**.

LAURASIA   Laurasia, the supercontinent, began breaking up at the end of the Carboniferous Period. North America drifted west leaving in Scotland rocks matching those found in Newfoundland, Canada.

In the Permian Period, the Himalayas rose as a result of crumpling of the Earth's Crust when India drifted north from Gondwana into the Laurasia landmass. 'Laurasia' is derived from Laurentia in North America plus Asia. The name is suggestive of its size.

LAURENTIDE ICE SHEET   The Laurentide Ice Sheet began in the snowbelt of northeast Canada and spread from Ellesmere Island into Quebec and Newfoundland. Alpine glaciers grew toward the Atlantic and the west. Ice masses converged and the sheet extended to the Great Plains. The ice sheet at maximum was up to 3.3 kilometers (2 miles) thick.

LAVA Lava is molten rock flowing from a volcanic crater, vent, or fissure. It is fluid or viscous and most of its gases have dissipated before they reach the surface. Solidified lava may be porous, vitreous, or porphyritic (q.v.) in texture. It may be acidic or basic in chemical composition.

Acidic lavas (q.v.) may be explosive and have a great effect on the local area and the Atmosphere. Basaltic lavas (q.v.) having great areal extent often built great thicknesses by many layers. Some lavas were ejected from fissures and rifts and not from central volcanoes.

Great basaltic flows formed the Columbia Plateau in the United States, Deccan Plateau in India, and Parana Plateau in Brazil. From field evidence, the greatest of these flows occurred in Brazil in Mesozoic times. The numbers of lava-capped plateaus around the world indicate that great flows are not uncommon.

A lava field recently located on the floor of the Pacific on the East Pacific Rise (q.v.) is said to be enormously thick and have a diameter of 40 kilometers (24 miles). The discovery of the field is further evidence of seafloor spreading and crustal formation.

LAVA TUBE Lava flows cool on the surface while still hot and flowing within. This results in a cavity or tube being formed. Some lava tubes are very large.

The longest in Africa is in Kenya between Nairobi and Mombasa. Originally it was 8 kilometers (5 miles) long. Subsequent rifting caused the tube to be broken into segments and the longest now is 2 kilometers (1.5 miles). The tube is called Leviathan Cave and is squat rather than round.

LEACHING Leaching is the removal of soluble material by percolating waters. In humid climates inter-tropical soils can become sterile due to leaching by heavy rains.

Liquid leached from a mass is a leachate. Solutions from solid waste dumps are leachates that may be toxic.

Leaching is used to extract minerals, especially metals, from ore or from tailings (q.v.). Special solutions are used to extract copper, uranium, and other valuable materials. Solution mining usually involves pumping solutions into the Earth under heat and pressure to extract minerals and force them to the surface.

LEMMING The lemming is a rodent that inhabits the North Polar Region. It is adapted to life in the Tundra. The lemming, a small, short-tailed animal with furred feet. It lives in a network of tunnels under the snows. It survives on roots and plant stems during the winter. When the thaw occurs it lives on the edge of bogs.

The European lemming makes remarkable recurrent migration to the sea where huge numbers drown. It is as if the animal pushes a 'self-destruct button'. It may be a genetic population control mechanism.

LEMUR Lemurs are members of the Primate Family. They are quadrupeds, with wooly fur and long, bushy tails. Lemurs abounded in the Early Tertiary (q.v.) but became almost extinct in the Oligocene (38-26 m.y.). Bush Baby in Zimbabwe and the lemur population on Malagasy (Madagascar) are the survivors.

LEMURIA Lemuria was the continental landmass between India and Malagasy (Madagascar) Island. Malagasy is the habitat of the lemur (q.v.).

LENA RIVER The Lena River crosses almost all of Siberia on its north-northeast course. 'Lena' is Yakut for big river, which the Lena is. The river rises just west of Baikal Range and travels 4,500 kilometers (2,700 miles) to empty into Laptev Sea (q.v.). A bird-foot delta forms one arm of Olenek Bay.

Along its course, there are areas where the Lena is as wide as a lake, up to 16 kilometers (9.6 miles), and others so narrow, the river flows through high gorges. Rocky cliffs and narrows occur between Ust-Kat and Yakutsk. The divide between the Lena and Yenesei (q.v.) basins is very narrow.

During the 8 winter months the Lena freezes solidly through the almost 650 kilometers (400 miles) of Tundra it traverses to the sea. This region is deeply permafrosted (q.v.).

LEPIDOLITE Lepidolite is a variety of white mica with a tinge of violet. It is a silicate of aluminum, potassium, and lithium, containing fluorite. Lepidolite is exploited primarily for its lithium content. See **LITHIUM**.

LEPTON The lepton is a subatomic particle that does not participate in strong reactions. There are 6 electrons, a muon, and a neutrino associated with each lepton. See **SUBATOMIC PARTICLES**.

LEUCOCRATIC ROCKS Igneous rocks that are high in silica and light in color are leucocratic. The rocks contain more than 65% silica. In this category are granites (plutonic rocks) and rhyolites (volcanic rocks).

LIANAS Lianas are tropical vines depending upon other plants for support. They are rooted in soil but are seeking the Sun so entwine themselves around trees. They form an important part of the canopy of some tropical forests. They put out runners and thicken that canopy.

Lianas which can be up to 60 centimeters (2 feet) thick and 150 meters (500 feet) long are called 'bush ropes'. They allow animals to swing from tree to tree without leaving the canopy.

LIAS CLAY Lias is a soft, bluish clay. Cliffs of this Jurassic clay are found along the Dorset Coast of England. They contain fossil ammonites, belemnites, and icthyosaurs.

The Lower Jurassic Period is called Liassic (225-215 m.y.) in Europe. 'Lias' means layers.

LICHEN Lichen are a community of Algae and Fungi living together in mutualism. They form veneers on rocks and live in cracks and crevices. Lichen are 'pioneer plants' found in the Tundra (q.v.) and on high mountain rocks.

Lichen color ranges from black through gray-green, some are orange, purple, or red. They obtain moisture from snow or mist and can take water from the air.

In the lichen community, Algae provide photosynthesis to produce food and Fungi produce the threads that absorb and retain the water supply for the community.

Recent work shows that lichen play a great role in weathering.

Lichen secrete solutions that contribute to chemical weathering. This chemical weathering is now thought to be of greater importance than mechanical weathering by freezing and thawing.

LIGHT Light is the infra-red, ultra-violet, visible, and X-ray portions of the electromagnetic spectrum of radiation. It is an energy transmitted to Earth from the Sun. Light makes this journey at the rate of 310,000 kilometers (186,282 miles) per second. Light is converted to heat when the Earth radiates the energy back into Space.

There are 3 levels of light penetration in minerals. These are opaque (no light), translucent (some light), and transparent (almost all light can pass through).

LIGHT YEAR Astronomical distances are so vast they are calculated in light-years. A single light-year equals 10 trillion kilometers (6 trillion miles). This is the distance light travels in a vacuum during a year at the rate of 310,000 kilometers (186,282 miles) a second. The light year is a distance not a time measure.

LIGHTNING The discharge of electricity, or lightning, from a cloud to the ground or to another cloud is accompanied by light. A bolt may be several kilometers long and have an energy of tens of thousands of amperes. Temperatures are up to 50,000° Fahrenheit causing the surrounding air to expand. The expansion is heard as thunder.

About 150 lives are lost each year from lightning and thousands injured. In dry periods, lightning causes 75% of forest fires in the western United States. Lightning storms produce 1-4 pounds of nitrogen per acre of soil per year. See **NITROGEN**.

LIGNITE Lignite is natural brown coal. It is composed of woody material and other organic debris. Lignite may fracture or disintegrate upon exposure to the Atmosphere. Intermediate between peat and coal, lignite produces low calorie heat when burned.

There are massive deposits of lignite around the world. In the United States, deposits are in the High Plains. A single Wyoming Red Desert deposit is 76 meters (250 feet) thick. Huge deposits not far from Moscow, Russia, provide energy for that city. There are massive deposits in the Upper Amazon Basin.

LIME Calcined limestone is lime, a calcium oxide, widely used in glass-making and cement. Calcination is the heating of a rock to just short of melting and fusion. Limestone is calcined to drive off carbon dioxide.

Lime is a valuable conditioner for acid soils found in humid climates, such as in Eastern United States.

LIMESTONE Limestone is a sedimentary rock of aggregated clastics or of chemical precipitation. It is primarily calcium carbonate of organic origin. In many limestones, the fossils are visible.

Limestone is usually stratified and may be crystalline or massive. It is the main constituent of many of the world's mountain ranges and makes up great portions of the Alps, Dolomites, and Himalayas.

Limestones also host economic phosphates. In the United States, these are bone phosphate deposits in Florida. In Morocco, there are vast phosphate reserves in limestones and marl (q.v.).

Limestone is soluble in pure water under certain conditions. Ordinary rain is slightly acidic and so weathers limestone relatively rapidly. As the acidity of rain increases, it erodes limestone even more rapidly. Under ordinary conditions 3 meters (10 feet of limestone will yield 1/3 of a meter (1 foot) of soil.

Sinkholes can develop in surface and near surface limestone rock. When the region is pockmarked with sinkholes, caves, and underground streams, the landscape is karstic. See **KARST**.

Limestone may contain minute or larger shells. One with the latter is 'calcaire grossier'. It was used in the construction of the cathedral at Chartres, France. In contrast, the limestone used for Notre Dame Cathedral was a compact rock with micro-fossils.

LIMESTONE REEF Reefs are built up of the calcium carbonate which is of organic origin. The hard parts of these organisms remain after their demise.

Many of these reefs are coral, others are algal. The living coral colonies require shallow and clear waters. As the reef builds upward, it subsides under its own weight or in rare cases from tectonic disturbance. Growth occurs on the top within the restricted zone of coral habitat. Coral reefs grow an estimated 4 inches per 1,000 years.

Many algal reefs date from the Precambrian. Some of these ancient limestones contain phosphates in the form of phosphorite.

Buried limestone reefs are often reservoirs for petroleum and natural gas. The Permian Basin of West Texas is such a reservoir.

LIMITING FACTOR A limiting factor may be any unfavorable element in the environment of a particular plant or animal community that endangers it. Climate is the most common limiting factor on communities.

LIMNOLOGY Limnology is the study of the physical features of lakes. It includes seasonality, depth effects, biology, and physical chemistry. Oxygen supply is one of the major factors in lake biology and is given special attention by limnologists.

LIMONITE Limonite, a hydrous brown oxide of iron ore, is an alteration product of hematite, pyrite, siderite, or other iron mineral. Limonite contains about 14% water and is poor in silica. It may be in crustal form or concretionary. Limonite can form caps, gossans, and ironstones. Sometimes goethite (q.v.) is taken for limonite.

LINEAMENT Landforms and structures reflecting an underlying linear pattern of the basement are lineaments. Topography often displays linearity of faults, lakes, and other landforms. These are enhanced in aerial and satellite photogrammetry.

Care in interpreting satellite photos is needed as some photos show apparent linearity unrelated to the features of the Earth.

LINES OF FORCE Electromagnetic Field force or flux is represented by assumed 'lines of force'. Where these lines of force are closest is the strongest field. Iron filings on a paper over a magnet will take up positions equivalent to the lines of force.

LIPARI Glass ejected by Mount Vulcano when it erupted in 1888 was named 'lipari' for the islands. A thick, silica-rich, tarry lava explosively erupted and solidified upon contact with the Atmosphere.

The last Lipari eruption continued for 2 years and covered an extensive area of the Italian Archipelago with its lava.

LISBON EARTHQUAKE The earthquake of November 1, 1755 destroyed most of Lisbon, Portugal. It was so strong it was felt in Finland and caused a seiche (q.v.) in Loch Lomond, Scotland. It cost 60,000 lives in Lisbon.

LIT-PAR-LIT 'Lit-par-lit', French for layering, is used to describe zoning in some pegmatites and schistose rocks.

LITHIUM Lithium is the lightest metal. It concentrates in some late-phase ferromagnesium minerals. As a salt, it concentrates in brines. The major economic ores are lepidolite, spodumene, and ambligonite. Spodumene in pegmatites (q.v.) is often in large crystals.

Lithium-rich brines are found in salars (q.v.) on the Andean Altiplano. Salar de Uyuni, Bolivia, is the richest. Salars in Chile and Argentina will be brought into production soon. Values in these salars range between 80 and 1,500 ppm lithium. The lithium source is volcanic and the hot springs are high in lithium.

World lithium reserves are 8.34 million metric tons, 2/3 of which are in Bolivia. Chile has a subsurface deposit with 1.36 million metric tons. This property is being worked for Lithium Carbonate. The United States has 0.36 million metric tons. Some brines in the southwest are workable. New spodumene discoveries have been made in Austria and Mali. (USBM, 1990)

Lithium is a possible fusion nuclear reactor fuel. A limiting factor may be that lithium-6, the required isotope, is only 7.42 atom percent. The world reserves of the isotope are only about 0.61 million metric tons.

If lithium reserves prove sufficient, lithium-sulfur storage batteries might become a viable alternative to combustion engines. The batteries have a high energy storage capacity and could store off-peak power.

Lithium is used in the ceramics and glass industry. Lithium also has important medical uses. It has proven valuable in the treatment of some mental disorders.

LITHOMARGE In a soil profile, the boundary between saprolite and unweathered bedrock is the lithomarge, or rock margin. The lithomarge is very evident and important in laterized soils. In many environments, including the lateritic, minerals, among them uranium, are concentrated in the lithomarge.

LITHOSOLS Lithosols are azonal soils with no clearly defined profiles. They are composed of freshly weathered materials and imperfectly weathered rock particles. Lithosols are often found in slope areas.

LITHOSPHERE The Lithosphere is the solid Crust and Upper Mantle of the Earth. Its estimated thickness is between 60 and 120 kilometers (36 and 72 miles). The Lithosphere 'drifts' over the Asthenosphere (q.v.).

The principal constituents of the Lithosphere are silica and aluminum, referred to as 'sial'. Sial floats above Mantle material or 'sima' composed of silica and magnesium. Sial is beneath the continents, sima beneath the oceans.

The elemental composition of the Lithosphere is:

ELEMENT	PERCENT
Oxygen	46.71%
Silica	27.69
Aluminum	8.07
Iron	5.05
Calcium	3.65
Sodium	2.75
Potassium	2.58
Magnesium	2.08
Other	1.42
	100.00%

LITMUS Litmus is a dye made from lichens. It turns pink in acid and blue in an alkaline solutions. Litmus paper is used for some preliminary chemical tests in geology and biology.

LITTLE ICE AGE The period from 1100-1850 is known as the Little Ice Age. Earlier cold phases are documented in the fossil evidence but historical evidence is slim. The Little Ice Age is well-documented historically.

During this period, there were intermittent warm spells. Huge reversals of weather adversely affected crops. In 1540, Rhone Glacier was 12-15 meters (40-50 feet) high with a 182 meter (600 foot) width. The present glacier is very thin and withdrawn. In 1600, alpine glaciers extended low into valleys and engulfed towns. One advanced 'a musket shot per day'.

There is evidence that the Westerlies looped far south during the 16th Century bringing with them colder climates. It is important to note that the overall drop in temperature was only about 1.5° Celsius.

Grain grew in Iceland around 870 A.D. but by the 14th and 15th centuries only barley could survive. In France, cold was so intense that many people and livestock died. The famine in 1789 was a major factor in the French Revolution.

In Belgium, a 20% decrease in the growing season was recorded, enough to destroy most crops. Conditions in Europe were so severe, Eskimos fled the Arctic following the edge of the ice pack to Scotland. In Scotland, the 1690's were so severely cold, famine lasted 8 years.

American difficulties at Valley Forge are history. Despite the hardships, extreme weather favored the colonists over the British. In 1780, every harbor on the North Atlantic froze.

LITTORAL CURRENTS Currents along coastlines are littoral currents. There are 3 types:

- Rip and density - Removes material from near-shore
- Longshore - Transports and deposits material parallel to coast
- Mass transport - Brings sediments to shore.

LITTORAL ZONE The littoral zone is a biogeographical area encompassing the shore and including the tidal and benthic zones. The benthic (q.v.) extends from the inter-tidal to a depth of 200 meters (600 feet). The littoral environment is special with distinct biomes.

LIVING FOSSIL Any plant or animal that looks and behaves as its fossil ancestors that existed millions of years ago is 'a living fossil'. Among living fossils are many plants. The California grey whale, the cockroach, and the coelcanth (q.v.) are some animal 'living fossils'.

LLANO A wide plain lacking relief features, even low ones was called a 'llano' by Spanish Americans. Their name is used in the southwestern United States where the most prominent llano is the Llano Estacado (q.v.).

In South America the llanos are the savannas found on the eastern slopes of the Andes, in the Orinoco Basin, and Guiana Highlands.

These llanos are treeless plains with gallery forests strung along streams. They are intermediate between upland savannas and lowland rainforests.

LLANO ESTACADO The Llano Estacado in western Texas and eastern New Mexico was formed by erosion and deposition of Tertiary gravels and sands. A vast alluvial apron formed at the base of the southern Rockies.

Sand and gravel of the Llano Estacado overlie Cretaceous shale. The shale acts as an aquitard (q.v.) and water in the gravels is perched (q.v.). The water containing alluvial apron is 120-180 meters (400 to 600 feet) thick.

The Llano was favorable for cotton and other crops and became a farming region using groundwater. Water levels have been dropping 1.3 meters (4.3 feet) a year. Since the development of Canadian River Canyon, the apron has been separated from its water source.

Rainfall is 50 centimeters (127 inches) annually, but rarely reaches the water table due to high evaporation. Recharge is negligible. If pumping ceased, it would take 4,000 years to restore the region to prefarming levels. It is only a matter of time before the use of this water source will have to be abandoned.

LOAD The quantity of sediment carried by a stream or current is its load. Load is composed of suspended and bottom or bed load sediments. The latter detritus is material that streams or currents drag along. The Amazon has a sediment load of 133 grams per cubic meter of water. Load is not capacity.

Load used as a unit of measure is equal to 16 cubic meters (29.6 cubic yards).

LOAM Loam is soil composed primarily of wet clay mixed with silt and sand. Usually, humus or organic content is high. Loam soils contain 7-27% clay, 28-50% silt, and less than 52% sand. Organic debris provides nutrients needed by plants. It gives loam its texture.

LOBELIA In East Africa on the slopes of Mt. Kilmanjaro and the Ruwenzoris, lobelia flourish. Under temperate climate conditions the plant is relatively small. On the lower slopes of these tropical mountains, it is 20 times taller than the temperate cousin.

Lobelia has a furry look resulting from its feathery leaves. In the Kenyan 'cloud forest' at an elevation of 3000 meters (9,840 feet) it grows up to 8 meters (26 feet) tall thriving on the fog and mist.

LOCUST The locust is a type of grasshopper that moves periodically in swarms. A swarm can be made up of 10 billion insects. Locusts are capable of traveling 3,000 kilometers (2,000 miles) in a season. They devastate all the vegetation in their path.

Africa and Asia have had many locust invasions throughout history. The Bible describes the infestation. Locust swarms appear to be worst when drought conditions are most severe.

LODE A lode is a thick ore vein, or a complex of such veins spaced closely enough to be mined as a unit. A region with lodes or vein complexes of gold ore is a 'Mother Lode'. Perhaps the most famous Mother Lode is in California.

Vein development in lodes is in stages and many show re-cementing after the mineralizing solutions cooled. Renewed faulting led to fracturing of the veins and the introduction of further mineralization.

LODESTONE Lodestone, a variety of magnetite, is capable of attracting iron. It acts as a magnet and exhibits polarity (q.v.). Magnetite is a compound of ferrous and ferric oxides.

Lodestone, if floating freely, will line up with the Earth's Magnetic Field. This north-seeking characteristic made it valuable as a compass.

LOESS Silt or loess is the product of aeolian deposition. It is homogeneous, unconsolidated, unstratified, and derived from dust. It is extremely fine-grained. yellowish, and has been moved great distances in sandstorms.

Loess particles are so small they have not mutually abraded, thus are not rounded. Loess is very quartzitic silt, although it may be rich in calcium. It is permeable with a porosity of 60% and it forms fertile soils. It is a very coherent material which can be a cliff-former. Sentinel-like relief develops with erosion.

Loess covers parts of Europe, Africa, and Asia. In China, there are steep cliffs several hundred feet high of material said to have originated in the Asian deserts. Nigeria has loess from the dust of the Sahara, although much of the Sahara's wind blown-silt ends in the ocean. Measurements of the oceanic sediments show a build-up of wind-blown material.

In the United States, loess is found in the Missippi Valley where there are cliffs 9-12 meters (30-40 feet) high. There are also loess deposits on the Columbia Plateau.

LOIRE RIVER The Loire River of France is one of Europe's longest at 1,045 kilometers (627 miles). Its origin is on the 1,425 meter (4,700 foot) basaltic Cevannes Uplift above Le Puy. Loire Valley is fabled wine country and is dotted with castles.

LONG TOM The sluice box used in California's goldfields was 'Long Tom'. It was actually relatively short and could be moved easily. Long Toms had 2 sections, one for sieving and one with riffles to allow more careful concentration. A similar box is used in dredging.

LONGITUDE Longitude is the angular distance east or west of an imaginary north-south line. The Prime Meridian is drawn through Greenwich, England. Parallel lines or meridians are drawn to 180° east and west. The distance between meridians at the Equator is 115 kilometers (69 miles). The distance narrows towards the Poles.

LONGSHORE CURRENT A longshore current or longshore drift is generated by waves reaching the coast at an oblique angle. It is strongest between the surf zone and the sea. Longshore current plays a dynamic role in the development and destruction of beaches.

LONG WAVE RADIATION Any wave exceding 4 microns in length is a long wave. Sunlight is shortwave radiation. Radiation reflected back into Space by the Earth is long wave.

LOP NOR The playa or dry lake in the southern part of China's Turfan Depression (q.v.) has altered its location by over a hundred kilometers since the 13th Century due to the instability of the desert streams that supply it. The stream loads are dropped in different locations depending upon the individual stream dynamics.

LOPOLITH When an intruding magma cools in the shape of a bowl, it is a lopolith. Lopoliths are lenticular and concordant with the bedding. They tend to bulge midway across the lens. Some famous lopoliths are the Duluth and the Bushveld.

Bushveld is 250 kilometers meters (150 miles) long and 15 kilometers (9 miles thick). The Sudbury Nickel Deposit in Canada may be a lopolith, if it is not the result of meteoritic impact.

LORAN LORAN is an acronym for Long Range Navigation system. Within transmitting distance of land, LORAN allows electrical triangulation with an accuracy of up to 1.6 kilometers (1.0 miles). It is an excellent system of coastal navigation.

LOST RIVER A river, interrupted in its course by disappearing into the groundwater is 'lost'. Such a river may flow underground and re-emerge further downstream. Rivers frequently disappear in karst (q.v.) terrain. Even where rainfall is abundant, rivers go underground in the porous limestones and become lost.

Desert rivers often are lost in the sands. Humboldt River, Nevada, is a desert lost river. So is Todd River in Australia near Alice Springs.

Rainfall in these areas is slight and the surface part of a stream dries out while underground flow continues.

LOW PRESSURE SYSTEM Cyclones, counterclockwise wind systems in the Northern Hemisphere, produce storms. Since the winds are converging, the 'Low' is smaller and more distinct than the 'High'. The maximum diameter of a low pressure area is about 830 kilometers (500 miles). Forward movement is slow but it may contain very high winds. See **CYCLONE** and **HIGH PRESSURE AREA.**

LOWLANDS Any area relatively lower than the surrounding terrain is a lowland. The term usually refers to coastal plains and floodplains. Lowlands are frequently wetlands (q.v.).

LUSTER Minerals are identified by luster or sheen. Luster depends upon the reflection and refraction of light. Minerals may be brilliant, dull, pearly, resinous, silky, or vitreous. Because of their usual shiny surfaces, metals have a typically metallic luster.

LUZON ISLAND Luzon is the largest and most important of the 7,000 islands that make up the Philippines. Its center is Taal Volcano (q.v.).

LYCOPSIDS The Lycosids are scale trees that were dominant in Paleozoic (q.v.) swamps. These swamps were the origin of the great coal seams. The trees attained heights of 30 meters (100 feet) and branched only at the top. The scales are scars where leaves dropped off. They had spreading root systems. Lycopsids had a very large number of species.

LYME REGIS Lyme Regis is the type locality of many marine fossils. It is located at the mouth of the Lym River on the south coast of England. In the early 1800's, when she was 10 years old, Mary Ann Anning discovered Ichthyosaurus in the cliffs near the town. She spent her life collecting and selling fossils to museums, naturalists, and tourists.

LYSOCLINE The Lysocline or 'snow line' in the ocean is the gradient traced by dissolved calcium carbonate. The lysocline is determined by pressure. Calcium has a 1-million year residence time in seawater.

Shell and other calcium carbonate detritus form sediments on the ocean floor. If the floor depresses to a depth greater than 4,200 meters (14,000 feet), they redissolve, thus oceanic mountains can be white-capped with calcium carbonate.

Kilauea — Fountain of Fire
Courtesy of US Geological Survey

M

MAAR The crater resulting from an explosive and violet eruption of great magnitude is a maar. The eruption is of the phreatic type, set off by steam. The crater produced is a flat-bottomed excavation. Some maars contain lakes.

MACH NUMBER Mach Number is a measure of velocity in the Atmosphere. It is the ratio of the speed of a mass to the speed of sound. When aircraft fly at the speed of sound, they are at Mach 1. Mach 2 is twice the speed of sound.

MACKENZIE DELTA Mackenzie Delta on the Beaufort Sea (q.v.) has a classical triangular shape with an 80 kilometer (48 mile) base. It is hundreds of kilometers to the apex at Separation Point. The delta is laced with channels and swamps over well-developed permafrost (q.v.). Pingos (q.v.) abound.

Sediments 15,000 meters (50,000 feet) thick have built up in the delta. These sediments consolidated and their weight depressed the basin and Beaufort Sea floor. The sediments are now a huge reservoir for oil and gas.

The Delta with its Tundra environment blooms in spring with wildflowers, particularly fireweed. The Delta is the summer home for an enormous number of waterfowl.

MACKENZIE RIVER The Mackenzie River System is second to the Mississippi-Missouri in North America. The Mackenzie begins as the Finlay River high in the Rockies of British Columbia. The Finlay flows 4,241 kilometers (4,240 miles) to empty into Great Slave Lake.

The Mackenzie flows 1,700 kilometers (1,030 miles) from Slave Lake to the Beaufort Sea, north of the Arctic Circle. Great Bear Lake and thousands of smaller lakes provide drainage from a 3.3 million square kilometer (2 million square mile) area.

In its long erosional history the Mackenzie has worn down mountains as high as the Himalayas. Ancestral sediments formed a platform on the Precambrian Basement. This platform now supports the Canadian Prairie.

MADAGASCAR Madagascar (Malagasy), 417 kilometers (250 miles) off Southeast Africa in the Indian Ocean is the 4th largest island in the world. It is 1,658 kilometers (995 miles) long with a maximum width of 600 kilometers (360 miles).

Separated from mainland Africa by rifting comparable to that of the Rift Valley, Madagascar is presently moving away from the continent at the rate of 2.5 centimeters (1 inch) per year.

The tropical island is divided into a narrow coastal plain in the east, a central plateau on ancient rocks, and low sedimentary plateaus and wide plains in the west. Western sediments are related to the Karroo (q.v.) of South Africa confirming that the island once was joined to the mainland. Both Africa and the island were part of Gondwana (q.v.).

Madagascar has 21 centimeters (54 inches) of monsoon rains a year from Southeast Trades off the Indian Ocean. Parts of the island have had periods, up to 9 years, with no rain.

Some 90% of the island's forest plant species are unique to the area. This is also true of half of its birds and bats and all of its land animals. There are 40 species of lemurs (q.v.). It is a very special ecological habitat which is endangered as the forest is being cut down.

The island is rich in beryl, chromite, Rare Earths, and uranium, all of which have been found in its granitic central range.

MADEIRA RIVER The largest Amazon tributary is the Madeira. It rises in the Bolivian Andes and flows north 3,300 kilometers (2,000 miles) to the confluence with the Amazon.

The Madeira System includes the Beni, Madre de Dios, and Marmore rivers. The headwaters are at the north-south Continental Divide. Another tributary, the Guapore flows south to join the Paraguay during the high-water season. The merging waters of the Paraguay-Parana and the Amazon systems turn Brazil into a virtual island.

Near the Brazil-Bolivia border there are about 30 waterfalls of up to 145 meters (478 feet) high between the Madeira and Marmore Rivers. The famous rapids are between Porto Velho and Guajara Mirim on the Bolivian Border. The Madeira-Marmore Railway (q.v.) was built as a bypass.

The Madeira at Porto Velho in Brazil just below the falls is 1,500 meters (4,950 feet) wide. At this point it is only 90 meters (297 feet) above sea level.

MADEIRA-MARMORE RAILWAY In the Upper Amazon Basin, a railway extending over 380 kilometers (228 miles) was begun in 1889 as part of a boundary settlement in which Bolivia ceded Acre Territory to Brazil.

The railroad by-passed rapids on the Madeira River (q.v.) between Guajara-Mirim and Porto Velho. It was to provide an outlet to the Atlantic for Bolivian rubber from the Beni Basin. The railway was never completed, but it does bypass the major falls.

Construction of the line was extraordinarily costly both in human and financial terms. A legend about it claimed it cost a 'life a tie' from malaria and other tropical diseases. The line is kept open by the Brazilian Government and makes a weekly run.

MAFIC Basic igneous rocks composed of ferromagnesium minerals are 'mafic' a word derived from magnesium and iron. They are dark and include amphibole, mica, and pyroxene.

STRAIT OF MAGELLAN The Strait of Magellan separates Tierra del Fuego from mainland South America. It is 557 kilometers (334 miles) long and ranges in width from 3.33 to 25 kilometers (2-15 miles). Inclement weather prevails and makes it a difficult passage.

Before the Panama Canal, it was the only connection from the Atlantic to the Pacific Ocean. The alternative was the voyage 'round the Horn'. See **CAPE HORN**.

MAGELLANIC CLOUDS Magellanic Clouds are collections of stars in the nearest galaxies to the Milky Way (q.v.). They were noted by Magellan's crew sailing the southern seas in 1516. The crew considered them high clouds.

The 'clouds' are in 2 irregular galaxies that are visible from the Southern Hemisphere. The larger is viewed in Constellation Dorado 21° from the South Celestial Pole. It is estimated to be 75,000 light years away and to contain 500,000 giant stars. Separated from it by 30,000 light years is a smaller cloud. See **LIGHT YEAR**.

MAGMA Magma is fused, molten matter, that consolidates to igneous rock upon cooling. The major portion of magma is non-volatile. Similar igneous rocks within an area constitute a Magmatic Province.

Lavas are magma expelled from volcanoes, fissures, and vents. They are forced to the surface largely by superheated steam, sometimes by other gases.

About 60 kilometers (40 miles) into the Mantle, the temperature is 2,200° Celsius. Rock expands during melting and volume adjustment causes movements in the overlying material.

As molten magma reaches upper crustal levels, temperatures drop and minerals are precipitated. Lighter minerals remain in the upper part of the magma chamber, while heavier ones sink. Mineral type depends upon the composition of the melt or magma.

Magma separates in a sequence determined by the chemical reaction of minerals to heat and pressure. Iron, chrome, platinum, and titanium are some of the first minerals to crystallize out. See **BOWEN'S REACTION SERIES**.

MAGNESITE Magnesite, a magnesium carbonate ore, may occur as earthy material, fine-grained and compact, or as coarse, cleavable mineral. Compact magnesite is mined from irregular veins in serpentine rocks found in California, Euboea, Greece and elsewhere. Chinese magnesite often appears on world markets in dumping operations.

MAGNESIUM Silver-white magnesium is a lighter and more reactive metal than aluminum. It is very malleable and ductile. It will tarnish when damp and will ignite easily. It is usually mined from brines and the sea.

Magnesium oxide can remove heavy metals from mine and mill solutions. When added to a solutiion of heavy mineral ions, metal hydroxides form. Magnesium in 5-15 minutes raises the pH to 10.5 (saturated). This creates large crystals and sludge. The positive charge of magnesium oxide and negative charge of most heavy metals are attracted to each other and water is expelled.

Magnesium also has many refractory uses.

MAGNET A magnet is a mass that creates a magnetic field outside itself. It has the property of attracting iron. Earth is a magnet.

MAGNET COVE Magnet Cove, a carbonatite (q.v.) near Hot Springs, Arkansas, forms a shallow, topographic basin, 5 kilometers (3 miles) in diameter. Alkaline igneous rocks (q.v.) intrude Paleozoic sediments that are overlain by Late Cretaceous and Tertiary deposits.

Magnet Cove is composed of varieties of nepheline syenite, jacupirangite (q.v.), carbonatite, and ijolite. It is enriched in titanium minerals, niobium, Rare Earths, uranium, and thorium.

MAGNETIC DECLINATION The horizontal angle formed between where a compass needle points (Magnetic North) and True North is referred to as the magnetic declination. It is also known as magnetic variation. The declination is the angle clockwise from True North.

The declination angle changes from place to place. In navigation, the error must be corrected. Charted variation must be revised periodically. See **AGONIC LINE**.

MAGNETIC DIP Magnetic dip is the angle a magnetic needle makes with the horizontal. A needle, suspended on a wire and dipping toward the attraction, is the principle of the magnetometer.

MAGNETIC DISK A ferric oxide platter is used for storing computer information in a readily accessible manner for processing.

MAGNETIC FIELD An invisible force field described by lines of force (q.v.) surrounds and permeates the Earth. It was discovered in the 18th Century that electricity and magnetism are this same field force. The Earth's Magnetic Field extends into Space for hundreds of thousands of kilometers.

Most of the Earth's Magnetic Field is produced by a simple dipole at its center. Magnetic lines of force emanate from the poles. The generating source is probably the latent heat (q.v.) of crystallization and radioactivity.

At the present time, the Magnetic Pole is 11° from the Geographic Pole about which it varies over a 22-year cycle. The Earth's dipole is 11° off center. Superimposed on the dipole field is a smaller non-dipole field. Compasses indicate the angular discrepancies.

The Magnetic Field has both magnitude and direction. It acts as a shield against incoming radiation. Charged particles heading for the

Equator are deflected by the Field but not if they are on a parallel path with the magnetic axes. This means the shield is open at the poles.

MAGNETIC LINES OF FORCE A magnetic needle points in the direction of the lines of force, perpendicular to the current of the Electromagnetic Field. Electrons move around their nuclei and produce the current. This and electron spin (q.v.) set up a magnetic field. The force individually is tiny, the aggregate is tremendous. See **MAGNETIC FIELD**.

MAGNETIC REVERSALS Igneous rocks are magnetically oriented as they cool. Reversals of magnetic polarity (N-S to S-N) have been detected from seafloor rocks associated with spreading ridges.

Mirror-image reversals occur on both sides of the ridges. Glomar Challenger collected cores that recorded 171 reversals over a period of 76 million years.

The present Magnetic Epoch began 690,000 years ago. Prior to that time, the Matuyama Reversal set off the earlier Magnetic Epoch 2.4 million years ago. There were at least 9 reversals in the past 4 million years.

Scientists believe another reversal is due. As a forerunner of the reversal, Bannerjee (Univ. of New Mexico) found the field lost up to half its intensity over the past 4,000 years. It is estimated that a 'flip' could take 2,000 years. The effect on world climate is open to conjecture.

MAGNETIC SEPARATOR Magnetic minerals separate from non-magnetic minerals when subjected to a large induced Magnetic Field, or magnetic separator. Different field strengths separate the different minerals.

Magnetic separation is used to separate heavy mineral concentrates containing such valuable ores as monazite and titanium.

MAGNETISM Magnetism has 3 types or conditions governing atomic response or behavior. All magnetic behavior relates to electrical current and is caused by electricity or energy moving in orbits around atomic nuclei. The types of magnetism are:

- Negative magnetism - Matter in Magnetic Field
- Paramagnetism - Atomic shells 'unclosed' or incomplete. Atom becomes a bar magnet aligning with the field
- Ferromagnetism - Inner shells of iron atoms are incomplete.

Paramagnetism is temperature related. When heated, atoms speed up and are less affected by the field (Curie's Law). With ferromagnetism there is a large electron spin in a single direction which builds a magnetic effect between atoms.

Earth itself is a magnet. Its Magnetic Field changes through time and reversing polarity every 700,000 years. The last reversal was 690,000 years ago.

Igneous rocks retain the record of magnetism and the direction of the Magnetic Field at the time of their origin. The original latitude location of the rocks can be calculated from magnetic dip (q.v.). Polar wandering (q.v.) can be calculated from these rocks.

MAGNETITE Magnetic iron ore, magnetite, is a ferrous oxide. It is black and often occurs in skarns in both igneous and metamorphic rocks. It has 72% iron and is a hard mineral that crystallizes in the cubic system.

Many magnetite deposits have been located because of the strong magnetic fields surrounding them. Often in recent decades, they have been found because aircraft compasses were affected. This is the history of the Russian massive magnetite discoveries.

The most notable magnetite deposits of all are in Kiruna, Sweden. These produce high grade (70%) iron ore for European consumption. Massive magnetite has been worked in New Jersey.

MAGNETOMETER The magnetometer is an instrument measuring differences in magnetic attraction at the Earth's surface. The differences are indicative of the magnetic properties of the subsurface.

In 1906, Edison used a magnetometer to confirm the presence of copper-nickel-pyrrhotite in Sudbury, Northern Ontario, Canada. He acquired the property to supply material for his storage batteries.

Magnetometers, trailed from aircraft, are useful in plotting anomalies. These define favorable rock types for future consideration.

The airborne magnetometer is an important geophysical tool.

MAGNETOPAUSE The Magnetopause is a barrier envelope around the Earth. It has the shape of a teardrop. True Space is beyond this boundary which defines the limits of the Earth's Magnetic Field.

The Magnetic Field has its origins in the Earth's Mantle. It is generated by atomic electrical currents. The Magnetopause is hundreds of thousands of kilometers above the Earth. See **MANTLE**.

MAGNOLIA TREE The magnolia ('Magnoliaceae') is a living fossil (q.v.). It flourished in the Mesozoic (225-65 m.y.). It was probably part of the dinosaur's ecosystem. Its natural habitat is humid subtropical.

MAKTESH RAMON A depression in Saudi Arabia, Maktesh Ramon is a breached anticline. The depression was warped upward or folded, then eroded along the anticlinal axis. This resulted in an east-west topographic basin 40 kilometers (25 miles) by 6.5 kilometers (3.9 miles) wide.

The basin rim is of Cretaceous limestone and the middle basin is Jurassic. The Cretaceous limestone contains ammonites up to 60 centimeters (2 feet) in diameter. The rim is known as the 'Ammonite Wall'.

Jurassic sediments yield to Triassic in the south where the basin is faulted. These sediments contain nautilus-type cephalopods.

MALACHITE The copper carbonate ore, malachite, contains up to 57% copper. It is of different shades of green. It often has a concentric pattern and it usually forms thick reniform encrustations in the copper ores.

Malachite is mined in Zaire and Zambia from the Congo (Zaire) Basin. It is also known from South Africa, Australia, and the USSR. Some malachite is of gem quality and some is used in carving.

MALASPINA GLACIER Malaspina is a piedmont glacier of Wisconsin Age. It stretches 80 kilometers (48 miles) along the Gulf of Alaska. It is in St. Elias Range. Malaspina's ice field reaches 50 kilometers (30 miles) inland. The Malaspina Complex is the largest in Alaska.

As a piedmont glacier, Malaspina is the result of the convergence of a number of glaciers at the foothills. Seward Glacier is the the most important.

MALPAIS 'Malpais', is Spanish for badlands. In southwestern United States they were formed by viscous and blocky lavas that cooled on the surface while still fluid within. They form jagged masses which are difficult to traverse.

MALAWI Land-locked Malawi (Nyassaland) is in the Great Rift Valley of East Africa. 2/3 of the country is on the west flank of the Great Rift and Lake Malawi (q.v.) is a rift lake. In the lowlands of the Rift Valley, the country has tropical forest while savanna is found on the uplands.

Precambrian rocks from Archean to Late-Proterozoic are found on the platform west of the Rift Valley. The Precambrian rocks are primarily metasediments intruded by granites and syenites. Unconformably on the metasediments is the Karroo Formation (q.v.) in basins and grabens and beneath lake sediments.

The lake basins have thick Mesozoic-Recent deposits. In the valley there are Recent sediments and volcanics.

Along the flanks of the Rift are syenite intrusives and carbonatites (q.v.). Pegmatites and fissure veins intrude the metamorphic rocks.

Chilwa Island in Chilwa Lake, bordering Mozambique has a complex of carbonatites, primarily of sövite. These have been divided petrologically depending upon the mineral suites. The minerals include uranium-bearing aegirine, apatite, and pyrochlore.

Chilwa is only one in a series that includes Tundulu, Songwe, Nkalonge Hill, and Mlanje Mountains (q.v.).

LAKE MALAWI Malawi is Africa's 3rd largest lake after Victoria and Tanganyika. It is also a Rift Valley lake. Dr. David Livingston called it the 'lake of the storms'. In Colonial times Malawi was Lake Nyassa.

Malawa Lake is more than 600 Kilometers (360 miles) long covering 30,000 square kilometers (11,776 square miles). At its deepest, it is 706 meters (2,330 feet). Malawi formed 65 million years ago, later than Lake Tanganyika. Earlier lakes in the same graben date from 120 million years.

The lake borders on Malawi, Mozambique, and Zambia. Its intermittent outlet is the Shire River to the Zambezi which empties into the Indian Ocean. Lake Malawi has 240 species of fish, more than found in any other African lake. (Tanganyika has 214). There are only 7 families, half the number found in other lakes. Salinity of Malawi is only 1/3 that of Tanganyika.

MALAYSIA Most of Malaysia occupies the south part of the Southeast Asian Peninsula. The Cameron Highlands form a spine down the central peninsula. From them come the tin-bearing streams building the placers which have been the world's most productive tin workings.

MALI Mali, West Africa, is dominated by 2 massifs (q.v.) and the Sahara Desert. A large, extremely dessicated Saharan basin is Tanez-rouft. It encroaches on almost 1/3 of the country.

The western part of Mali is dominated by the Precambrian in which is found the Birrimian Greenstone Belt. In the northwest metasediments dominate. Dolerite intrusives are assumed to be Post-Carboniferous (280 m.y.). Elsewhere there are Paleozoic and Tertiary sediments with Quaternary dominating the Niger Valley.

The climate has become increasingly more arid since the Middle Ages. Then, Mali and its civilization and culture were legendary in Europe. To support such a kingdom, a stable water supply for agriculture was an essential element.

One of the massifs forms an almost circular plateau completely isolated by the Niger River (q.v.). The Niger has formed a large inland delta where it once emptied into a lake. This is now an important agricultural area.

The only major river in addition to the Niger is the Senegal which rises in the southwest in Fouta Djallon or Mali Hills.

A few miles in from a bend in the Niger River is Timbuktu Oasis. For centuries it was a caravan halt on the great east-west trade route of gold, salt, and slaves. Gold is still important to Mali. Production is about 12,960 Troy ounces (400 kilograms) a year. Kimberlite pipes (q.v.) have been found near the Faleme River but so far no diamonds.

MALLEABLE To be malleable is a characteristic of some metals. If malleable, it can be hammered into thin sheets and easily worked.

MALTHUSIAN HYPOTHESIS Malthus theorized that populations tend to out-distance food supplies. He pointed out that populations increase geometrically while food only increases arithmetically. This means widespread famine is an ever-present human condition. He contended that unless population is checked, poverty, vice, and war are inevitable.

MAMMOTH The Pleistocene Epoch (q.v.) was dominated by huge 'game' animals, the Mastodon and the Mammoth. Both exceeded the modern elephant in size. Complete fossils of the wooly mammoth were discovered in the permafrosted soils of Siberia. The animal had lived on the Tundra (q.v.) and in the Taiga (q.v.). Its dense brown wool and black hair were perfectly preserved by the ice.

The range of the mammoth in the Pleistocene was across Eurasia into Alaska and North America as far south as Arizona.

The wooly mammoth, a relative of the elephant, stood 3.5 meters (12 feet tall and had ivory tusks 4.0-4.3 meters (13-14 feet) long. Fossil ivory from the Siberian Tundra is still finding its way into the modern ivory market.

The Imperial Mammoth was taller than the Wooly Mammoth but less bulky. Fossils of it and other species have been found in the glacial lake sediments of Pleistocene Lake Bonneville (q.v.). Ancient bogs of New York have yielded more than 200 specimens.

MAMMOTH CAVE Mammoth Cave in Kentucky is believed to be the largest single cavity in the world. So far, 320 kilometers (200 miles) of cave passages have been explored. One can travel the cave passages for 250 kilometers (150 miles).

The cave system is the result of the dissolution of limestone by slightly acidic rainwater and even more acidic snowmelt. The drainage carved chambers in the limestone. Mammoth is only part of a honeycomb of caves and caverns in the karstic (q.v.) area. Echo River flowing underground finally joins the Kentucky's Green River.

It has been estimated that stalactites and stalagmites form at different rates and at different periods depending upon the precipitation. In general, Mammoth's growth rate of these features is about 2.5 centimeters (1 inch) in 100 years in one area and 25 years in another.

MANGANESE Manganese is the 2nd most abundant heavy metal in the Earth's Crust after iron. The grey-white metal is an alloy of iron in ferromanganese. Some manganese minerals are pyrolusite, psilomelane, and manganite.

The United States has only low-grade manganese deposits. The world's largest producer has been the Soviet Union with 48% manganese from the Republic of Georgia. A new mine in the Oblast Region was geared to produced 6 million tons by 1985. The largest proven reserves of manganese (80% of the 10.9 billion metric tons) are in the USSR and South Africa.

Brazilian reserves are still being evaluated. The indicated reserves (1987) were 104 million tons and the inferred were set at 137 million. Its principal production is still from Amapa in the Amazon Basin where 1987 output was 1.2 million tons. The new operations at Carajas produced 450,000 tons.

High grade ore (60%) is produced at Morro da Mina in Minas Gerais. Reserves of this quality are only a few million tons. South Africa has about 300 million tons of high grade manganese.

Reserves of the relatively recently discovered manganese deposits in Brazil have attracted the Soviet Union. The USSR has indicated an interest in investing in these deposits for the rights to 50% of the production for a 10-year period after start-up.

The Urucum (q.v.), Mato Grosso, deposits, also in Brazil, were not considered viable until recently. The big hydroelectric complex of Itaipu (q.v.) makes the area a potentially important metallurgical center. Reserves are 138 million proven tons. The region has enormous iron ore reserves as well.

In the oceans, 'potato-sized' lumps of manganese (nodules) have been discovered. In addition to the manganese, the nodules contain cobalt, copper, and nickel. The mining potential is under study by many nations. An international commission is concerned with the legal ramifications.

On some seamounts there are manganese crusts. There is evidence that manganese has replaced phosphate on Blake Plateau in the Atlantic.

MANGROVE SWAMP Mangrove swamps along tropical and subtropical coasts are periodically flooded by the sea. The flora are especially adapted to the paludal environment.

Mangrove (Rhizophora) is the dominant tree in the swamp and a complete ecosystem has developed around it. The mangrove is adapted to saline waters. It excretes salt through its leaves and has well-developed aerial roots sticking up like spears out of the mud and water. The roots branch from the lower trunk to create a buttress. Many fauna find shelter in these root systems.

Mangrove swamps are widespread around the world. This is not surprising as seeds in 15-30 centimeter (6-12 inch) pods float a long way.

Australia is known to have at least 50 mangrove species. In Thailand, mangrove is logged for fuelwood. In the United States, mangrove swamps are found along the Florida Coast.

MANIOC 'Manioc', is a Tupi Indian word for cassava. Manioc is an edible tuber which is well-adapted to slash and burn (q.v.) cultivation. It is a staple in South America particularly in the Amazon and in West Africa. The tuber was brought there from Brazil about 1600 and became widespread in the 1700's.

In its natural state, manioc root is poisonous, containing prussic acid. It must be scraped, grated, washed 10 times, dried, then cooked. The wide usage is surprising given the complexity of preparation and the primitive conditions of the societies using the tuber.

MANTLE The Yugoslav seismologist, Mohorovicic, interpreted different seismic waves as different layers in the Earth's Mantle. He determined a boundary at about 33 kilometers into the Earth as that between Crust and Mantle. It is now known as the Mohorovicic Discontinuity.

The Mantle extends into the Earth to about 2,900 kilometers (1,740 miles), The Mohorovicic Discontinuity, or surface of the Upper Mantle is not uniform around the globe. The thickness of 33 kilometers is only an average. Upper Mantle rock materials are in a molten or semi-plastic state and have the seismic characteristics of basic igneous rocks.

The Lower Mantle between 400 and 650 kilometers appears to be material in a more plastic state and the region is marked by large increases in velocity. Discontinuities at these boundaries are not as strong as at the Mohorovicic.

Volumetrically, the Mantle makes up 80.5% of the Earth, compared to 1% only by the Crust. The rest is made up of the Outer and Inner Core.

MANTO DEPOSITS 'Manto', Spanish for blanket, describes some fluorspar deposits of northern Coahuila, Mexico. These deposits are estimated as sufficient to produce 165,000 tons of acid spar per year. Millions of tons of metallurgical spar have been produced.

Manto fluorspar is at the contact between the cliff-forming Cretaceous Georgetown Limestone and Del Rio Shale or Buda Limestone. The deposits cover 5,000 square kilometers (3,000 square miles).

Structurally, the area is dominated by the Sierranias del Burro Anticline. It is a highly faulted area and the ore is related to joints developed in the limestones. The fluorite source may be the adjacent intrusion.

MANURE Manure is excrement from grazing animals. It is a natural fertilizer since it contains many nutrients required by plants, It also contains a high organic component. The natural relationship of grasslands and grazing herds has been disrupted by humans. How essential the animals are to the grassland biome has never been assessed. See **GRASSLANDS**.

LAKE MANYARA Lake Manyara is south of the first lake cluster in the northernmost lake-filled rift of the Great Rift System of East Africa.

Along Manyara's west shore is a parkland reaching to the escarpment 5-6.5 kilometers (3-4 miles) away from the lake. The scarp is fissured by gorges with streams flowing to the lake in the rainy season. There are 5 distinct vegetative zones ranging from groundwater forest to the scrubland of the escarpment. The ecosystem distribution is characteristic of the rift lakes.

Manyara, 50 kilometers (30 miles) long has thousands of coral flamingos. Water buffalo graze in surrounding wetlands; elephants feed on acacia flanking the basin walls. The savanna produces the elephant's favored Acacia tortilis (q.v.), fig, and mahogany.

At Manyara only 20 years ago there was one of the largest known herds of elephants. The mass slaughter of elephants for ivory in the past decade has decimated not only the herds around Manyara but in all of East Africa.

MAQUIS 'Maquis', Mediterranean scrub, is similar to southern California Chaparral (q.v.). The maquis has wild oak and cork oak trees.

LAKE MARACAIBO Lake Maracaibo is an extention of the Gulf of Venezuela, an arm of the Caribbean. Maracaibo covers 16,317 square kilometers (6,300 square miles) over one of the world's great petroleum reservoirs.

MARANON RIVER The Maranon River, a major contributor to the Amazon System, rises in an Andean glacial lake in Peru and is fed by meltwater. The source is less than 160 kilometers (100 miles) from the Pacific.

The river flows northwest to join the Ucayali River (q.v.) before turning east to join the Upper Amazon System.

MARBLE Calcium carbonate in crystalline limestone can be metamorphosed and recrystallized to form marble. The Carrara Mountains, Italy, are famous for the marble which makes up the mass.

Marble has diverse colors and veins due to its mineral content. Pure marble is white. Different areas produce different colors. Connemara, Ireland, produces a light green. Bahia, Brazil, mines a deeper green. Portugal and Italy are major producers of the white marble.

MARE Lunar craters are 'mares', Latin for seas, because of their great size. The mares are of black volcanic rock and cover 50% of the Moon's surface. Volcanic activity appears to have occurred early in the life of the Moon.

Mare Imbrium, 1,000 kilometers (600 miles) in diameter, is thought to be the largest impact crater on the Moon. Mare Tranquilitatis, from Apollo II data, appears to have been bombarded by meteorites 4.8-5 billion years ago, before Earth's geological record begins.

MARGINAL OCEAN BASINS Large oceanic depressions enclosed by or adjacent to continents are marginal ocean basins. They are separated from the main ocean basin by ridges, or sills. Marginal basins are deep and bottom water is isolated. All are in regions of recent or active diastrophism (q.v.) and are:

- Adjacent to island arcs and submarine volcanoes - Pacific Ocean
- Between continental blocks - Arctic Ocean, Black, Mediterranean Seas
- Long narrow rift trenches - Gulf of California and Red Sea.

MARGINAL SEA A marginal sea is a semi-enclosed part of the ocean. It is separated from the main ocean by sills or submarine ridges.

The Arctic Ocean is a marginal sea. Communication with the Atlantic is cut off by the Arctic Sill. The Bering Sill functions the same way between the Arctic Ocean and the Pacific. A similar sill reduces communication between the Mediterranean Sea and the Atlantic.

The term marginal sea also applies to the shallower portions of the ocean over the continental shelves.

MARIANAS TRENCH The Vitiaz Deep in the Marianas trench, South Pacific Ocean, was measured by the Russians during IGY (q.v.). Vitiaz is 11.7 kilometers (7 miles) deep and 1.6 kilometers (1 mile) wide.

Picard, working for the United States Navy explored the trench in the French bathyscape, Trieste. He hit bottom at 10,848 meters (35,800 feet). At that depth, Piccard found fish and shrimp.

MARINE PLACERS Mineral deposits, found on the ocean floor well below the low-tide line are marine placers. Some are former beach placers that have been flooded due to eustatic (q.v.) changes of sea level. Others may be drowned alluvial placers.

Off Malaysia, marine tin placers are related to onshore stream placers. There are heavy mineral delta placers off the United States at Appalachicola and off Travancore, India. These were sorted by deltaic and marine activity.

MARINE PROTECTION The United States Congress enacted the Marine Protection, Research, and Sanctuaries Act in 1972. The law empowers the Secretary of Commerce to designate ocean areas of special value as sanctuaries for marine life. Channel Islands, California, are within this protection.

MARINE REGRESSION Receding seas are termed marine regression. The regression results in marine terraces along shorelines. Regression may stem from increasing glacial expansion, as in the Pleistocene, or from regional uplift.

MARINE SEDIMENTS Sediments deposited in seas are marine. They can often be distinguished from continental sediments by their marine fossils.

Cycles of transgression and regression repeated throughout geological history. The highest level of the seas appears to have been at the Cambrian-Ordovician boundary (500 m.y.) in the Paleozoic and in the Cretaceous Period (136-65). These time horizons gave rise to vast amounts of marine sediments.

MARISMAS The wetlands at the mouth or delta of the Guadalquivir River in Spain are seasonally flooded. 'Las Marismas', Spanish for swamps, are cut off from the coast by a 70 kilometer (45 mile) barrier of dunes.

The sands are known as 'Arenas Gordas' or fat sands. The Las Marisma swamps are an ecological wonderland of vegetation, waterfowl and other fauna.

MARKER BED Any horizon may be a marker bed if it is distinctive because of lithology or fossil content. The bed must be traceable over considerable extent. Marker beds are useful for stratigraphic correlation.

MARL In the United States, marl refers to unconsolidated, soft calcium carbonate clay and sand. In France, marl is compact impure limestones. Marl, in this sense, appears often in stratigraphic sections of North African phosphate deposits.

MARS The planet Mars is 1/10th the size of the Earth and has a gravity only 1/3 that of Earth. Martian atmospheric pressure is less than 1% that of the Earth. Mariner 9 photos highlighted 4 huge volcanoes.

Mars does have a similar rotation and axial position to that of the Earth and so has seasonal changes in solar radiation. The Viking Mission determined that the polar caps on Mars are of solid carbon dioxide. It is below freezing everywhere so soils would be permafrosted. Winds are extremely high so loose material must have been deflated out of basins.

Mariner 4 recorded mega-craters on Mars that show an unusual polygonal pattern. Brent Crater contains alnoite that on Earth is associated with explosive carbonatites (q.v.).

From recent data, it appears Mars is heating up from internal radioactivity. Its small mass and great distance from the Sun caused it to degas long ago and give up water.

MARSH A marsh is a wetland with bogs and scattered ponds of usually stagnant water. Marsh vegetation is almost all grasses, reeds, and sedges. Water level is usually seasonal, so there are dry surfaces part of each year.

Marshes are transitional between bogs and swamps. Many serve as wildlife refuges, especially for waterfowl.

The most extensive marshlands are in the Tundra (q.v.). Soils above the permafrost (q.v.) thaw and become marshes during the summer. In the Upper Peninsula of the Great Lakes, marshes underlain by permafrost are 'muskeg'.

A coastal marsh with daily tidal flow is an environment in which the sea deposits minerals and the marsh sends organic debris to the sea. An acre of unpolluted saltwater marsh is estimated to produce 4 times as much food, as an acre of farmland.

MARSUPIAL The marsupial is a sub-class of mammals noted for the external pouch. The young are carried in the mother's pouch until able to survive on their own. The most well-known marsupials are the kangaroo, wombat, arboreal koala, and opossum. Marsupials are almost unique to Australia. The opossum is found in the New World.

MASS Gravity exerts a force upon a body causing it to remain as an entity. The bulk of a mass includes its atomic structure and interatomic spaces. A mass is defined by its weight.

MASS SPECTROMETER A mass spectrometer is a device for detecting and analyzing isotopes or elements. Nuclei are separated by their charge-to-mass ratios.

MASS WASTING The downslope gravity movement of soil and rock is mass wasting. See **CREEP**.

MASSIF 'Massif' is French for an upthrust block bounded by faults or fractures. The word is also used to describe partially eroded mountainous regions. The Armoricain Massif, Brittany; the Guiana Massif; and Brazilian Massif are examples of such mountains. Most are of Precambrian Basement rocks.

Some American geologists to refer to granitic rock masses as massifs, without regard to whether or not they have been block faulted.

MASSIVE Unbroken, uniform rocks are referred to as massive. Minerals, as potential ores, are massive if they have microcrystalline or cryptocrystalline (q.v.) structure and the aspect of a rock or formation. Hematite (iron ore) is a good example of a massive mineral.

MATO GROSSO A great and distinctive tropical forest is found in Mato Grosso, Brazil. It is in a part of the Amazon Basin where the watershed merges with that of the Paraguay River.

'Mato Grosso' means immense forest. This forest was the inspiration for Hudson's novel, 'Green Hell'. It is a forest that Hudson never saw.

MATTER Matter describes a physical entity. Its composition has been debated since Democrites first envisioned the atom about 500 B.C. Quantum physics suggests a new space-time reality for the atom.

Atomic Theory held the atom is the smallest unit which can be separated out by chemical means. Subatomic particles require radioactive bombardment to be divisible.

MATTERHORN The Matterhorn, an Alpine peak on the Italian-Swiss Border is 4,479 meters (14,780 feet). It was formed by glacial plucking, which created cirques (q.v.). The peak has 4 smooth triangular faces and a sharp pinnacle. It has appealed to generations of mountain climbers.

MATURE LANDSCAPE Erosional forces act slowly in a mature landscape. Streams cut back into highlands and produce gentle, rolling hills. The slopes are suave. The Cumberland and Allegheny plateaus are examples of mature landscapes.

Mature streams create broad floodplains. They meander (q.v.) and create oxbow lakes (q.v.). The Mississippi Valley is mature and the river is mature in its lower reaches and delta.

MAUNA KEA Mauna Kea in Hawaii, not Everest, is the highest mountain on Earth. Mauna Kea rises from the ocean floor to a summit of 10,023 meters (33,476 feet) while Everest is 8,796 meters (29,028 feet). Mauna Kea is taller than Mauna Loa (q.v.), but Mauna Loa is a much more massive volcano. Both are active.

MAUNA LOA Like Mauna Kea (q.v.), Mauna Loa has grown from fractures in the ocean floor and has formed a shield volcano. It is estimated that Mauna Loa took about a million years to grow to its present height or from the ocean floor to 9,604 meters (31,694 feet).

Mauna Loa makes up 50% of the island of Hawaii. It is 116.7 meters (70 miles) long at sea level. Loa had its origin from vents in the ocean floor where 2 major rifts meet. About 1,212 meters (4,000 feet) above ground surface on Mauna Loa is Kilauea Crater.

The volcano has been erupting for the past 3 years and has been steadily adding to the acreage of the island. Some villages and homes in the path of the lava have had to be abandoned.

MAURITANIA Mauritania, on the West African Coast, has its desert terrain modified by cool ocean waters. Like much of West Africa it has a basement of Precambrian crystalline rocks. These are partly over-lain by Saharan dune sands. Some of these dunes are still traveling as a result of the Trade Winds, but many are stable, especially in the south. Approaching Spanish Sahara and the southeast, the basement is overlain by sandstones which form plateaus.

Away from the coastal humidity, the interior of the country suffers greatly from the Harmattan (q.v.) winds. The greatest rainfall is in the southeast or coastal province. The average is on the order of 65 centimeters (26 inches).

The major economic minerals of the country are iron ore at Fort Gouraud and Gleitat el Kadar. Copper is found at Akjoujit. The iron reserves are 100 million metric tons of high grade ore.

MOUNT MAZAMA Subsidence created the caldera of Mount Mazama 6,500 years ago. The caldera, in southern Oregon, holds Crater Lake. The lake is 10 kilometers (6 miles) across and is 667 meters (2,200 feet) at maximum depth. The caldera walls rise between 150 and 600 meters (500-2,000 feet) above the water. A cinder cone in the lake is Wizard Island. It rises 231 meters (763 feet) above water level.

LAKE MEAD Mead is one of the large artificial lakes of the world. It is part of the Colorado River System. Between Nevada and Arizona, the 192 meter (115 mile) long lake is contained by Hoover (Boulder Dam). The complex supplies water and power to states adjacent to the Colorado River and to Mexico.

MEAN FREE PATH   The average distance traveled by an atom, molecule, or particle between collisions or interruptions is the 'mean free path'.

MEANDER   A meander is a winding section of a mature or old-age stream. When a stream loses the capacity to cut through resistant rock, it must move laterally.

Erosion on the outside of the bend begins the creation of a meander because river current is less on the inside of the curve allowing a bank to build. Deposition is always on the inside of the curve. In an old-age stream, cutting is greater laterally than vertically. The process widens the valley floor.

The gradient in a meander is low and the river moves slowly. A bend or loop can be cut off to form an oxbow lake when the stream finds a new course or the loops are so tight they link and the loop is cut off.

'Meander' is from the Meander River in Turkey. The river and region became famous as a site in the Trojan Wars.

MEDICINE LAKE VOLCANO   The Pleistocene-Recent shield volcano of Medicine Lake is northeast of Shasta. It is the largest of the Cascade stratovolcanoes. A lake infills the 7 x 12 kilometer (4.2 x 7.2 mile) diameter caldera. The volcano is behind the main Cascade Volcanic Arc.

MEDITERRANEAN CLIMATE   The Mediterranean Climate, one of the most pleasant, is characterized by summer drought and winter rain. It is typical of a large portion of the Mediterranean Rim. Southern California has a Mediterranean climate with even milder temperatures than Europe.

MEDITERRANEAN-DEAD SEA CANAL   The proposed canal connecting the Mediterranean Sea and the Dead Sea is the subject of controversy between Israel and Jordan. Water would be lifted 100 meters (330 feet) and piped beneath the Gaza Strip into a 21.7 kilometer (13 mile) long canal, then tunneled under the Judea Mountains into the Dead Sea.

The objective of the canal is to bring water to the Dead Sea (q.v.) since levels there are dropping rapidly. An alternative Israeli route would miss the Gaza Strip. Jordan is considering bringing water from the Red Sea. See **JORDAN RIVER**.

MEDITERRANEAN SEA   The Mediterranean Sea is in a marginal oceanic basin (q.v.) between Europe and Africa. Its name means 'sea in the middle of the world'.

The Mediterrean is saltier than the Atlantic. Its mid-latitude location adjacent to the great African desert affects surface salinity because salinity is determined by local balances between evaporation and precipitation.

The Mediterranean Sea receives 2 million tons of water per second from the Atlantic. Full interchange is blocked by the Gibraltar Sill (q.v.). The sea is a sink. Annual loss to evaporation is greater than inflow. The deficit is made up by Atlantic and Black Sea waters.

15 million years ago the Mediterranean seafloor sediments were affected by the Atlantic and Indian Ocean currents. The sea was cut off from both oceans 10 million years ago and evaporites were built up in the basin.

MEDITERRANEAN THRUST BELTS Mediterranean thrust belts are reflected in the Alps and Appenines. The belts formed on the European crustal plate when Africa moved east and Europe west. Collision thrust up the Alps, Atlas, and Appenines. Africa is still moving against southern Europe and the Mediterranean will eventually be replaced by mountains.

MEDUSA Medusa is a free-swimming coelenterate or jellyfish. It is bell-shaped or disk-like. Medusa may be colorless, pink, or red. Some species are poisonous. Tentacles with stinging cells are used to capture prey.

MEKONG RIVER The Mekong River is the 10th largest in the world, It drains the eastern Tibetan Plateau. The river descends through a series of gorges in northwest China. It then flows through Burma, Laos, northeast Thailand, and Kampuchea (Cambodia). The southern lowland has long been an important rice producer. The delta sediments build into the South China Sea.

The river has run half its course by the Burma-Laos border. It drains a total area of 795,000 square kilometers (306,950 square miles).

The Mekong flow is affected by the monsoon regime and is uneven. The Tonle Sap, a lakelike area at Phnom Penh. acts a regulator for the river. At low-water, the flow reverses. In the monsoon season, flow to the sea recurs.

MELANGE The intermixture of continental and marine sediments is called a 'melange'. Melange is found in the continental margin areas of the globe.

MELANOCRATIC Igneous rocks with between 60 and 90% dark minerals are melanocratic.

MEMBER The member is a stratigraphic unit within a geological formation (q.v.). It consists of more than one bed or stratum. Its distinctive characteristics are readily observed. Among them are particle size, color, dip, and mineral content.

MENDELIAN THEORY The monk, Mendel, spent years working with peas, studying their genetic characteristics. He experimented with more than 10,000 plants and developed a series of laws relating to inherited traits. He related traits to genes according to mathematical ratios.

MENDENHALL GLACIER Ice-blue Mendenhall Glacier in Alaska had been retreating at the rate of 12 meters (40 feet) per year in the first half of the 1900's. Overall it has been retreating since but at a much slower rate.

MENDOCINO FAULT San Andreas Fault enters the sea above San Francisco, California. The Mendocino Fault intersects San Andreas at right angles in the Pacific about 25 kilometers (15 miles) off Cape Mendocino. Mendocino Fault extends west for thousands of kilometers. Some believe it has a land extension covered by the Sierras and Rockies.

The Fairweather Fault (q.v.) joins Mendocino at the intersection with the San Andreas. This is the 'triple junction' or boundary between the North American and Pacific Plates.

In 1956 it was discovered that the magnetic lines of force on one side of the Mendocino fracture do not match those on the other. Magnetic evidence shows the fault is displaced 1,170 kilometers (700 miles) from its position when the Magnetic Field developed.

MERAPI VOLCANO There are 128 active volcanoes in Indonesia. Mount Merapi is the most active presently. It is in central Java and rises to 2,911 meters (9,550 feet). In 1006 A.D. it blew off its entire summit and destroyed the Mataram Kingdom. Since 1820, there have been 23 recorded eruptions, that of 1930 was the most disastrous.

MERCURY Mercury is chemically inactive. It is a good thermal and electrical conductor. It is insoluble. It can dissolve metal, except iron and platinum, to form alloys or amalgams. Mercury is 13.5 times as heavy as water.

Mercury was much used in the past to separate gold from impurities. When passed over gold it forms an amalgam. The mercury is later removed by boiling. Mercury is still used in this way in some remote areas such as the Upper Amazon.

Cinnabar (q.v.), an ore of mercury, occurs with quartz, carbonates, pyrites, and marcasite. Cinnabar at Almaden, Spain has been worked for centuries. A red pigment is obtained by roasting the cinnabar to drive off the sulfur.

At Idria, California, mercury ore runs 0.5 gram/ton. Mercury is widespread in southwestern United States. It tends to accumulate near volcanoes. The most notable location is McDermott Caldera in Nevada.

Mercury can form toxic compounds and has a limited ability to penetrate living cells. Some streams have been polluted with mercury, adversely affecting fish and other freshwater fauna. Phytoplankton help return mercury to the Atmosphere.

MERIDIAN   An imaginary line projected between the eastern and western hemispheres passes through Greenwich, England. This is the Prime Meridian or 0° Longitude. East and west from it, parallel lines or meridians have been drawn to 180°.

The 180° line is the International Date Line. This line is in the Pacific Ocean. It is slightly altered to avoid any land area.

MESA   'Mesa', Spanish for table, is an isolated, steep-sided plateau or tableland in southwestern United States. Mesas are composed of stratified sediments protected from erosion by a resistant cap. Often the cap is of congealed lava flows.

MESH   In a sorting screen, the number of pore spaces per inch is the mesh. This grain-size measure was established by the ASTM (American Society for Testing Materials).

MESOCRATIC   Mesocratic rocks are intermediate between leucocratic (light) and melanocratic (dark) rocks. Mesocratic rocks contain 30-60% of either light or dark minerals.

MESON   Mesons, subatomic particles, decay to form other particles after a life-span of 10^{-6} seconds. The product is 2 neutrinos with no charge. Mesons were first discovered in the Wilson Cloud Chamber experiments.

Various names have been given to the decay particles. The Pi- Meson is only found at high elevations.

MESOPOTAMIA   Mesopotamia, or 'land between the rivers' refers to the region of southwest Asia between the Tigris and Euphrates rivers. It encompasses the entire Tigris Valley.

Once the region was a powerful part of the Fertile Crescent (q.v.). It was the location of the Sumerian civilization.

MESOZOIC ERA   The Mesozoic Era between the Paleozoic and Cenozoic began 225 million years ago and lasted 160 million years. It had 3 Periods:

- Triassic - Discovered in Germany (225-190 m.y.) Ammonites and the first mammals
- Jurassic - 'Age of Reptiles' (190-136 m.y.) The Jura Alps rose
- Cretaceous - (136-65 m.y.) Period closed with widespread species extinction, especially in the Northern Hemisphere.

Paleoclimatologists believe Mesozoic climate was 8-10° Celsius near the Poles and 25-30° in the Tropics. See **GREAT EXTINCTION**.

MESQUITE   The thorny mesquite shrub is found in southwestern United States and in the Mexican desert.

The mesquite is leguminous and especially adapted to arid conditions. Each plant has a proscribed territory for the shallow part of its root structure. No seedling may flourish in the shade of its parent. Mesquite produces a nutritious sugar.

METABOLITE Metabolites are essential to life. The metabolite requirement may be extremely small but it is, nonetheless, vital.

Vitamins, minerals, and enzymes are human and animal metabolites.

METALS Metals have special properties separating them from non-metals. All have metallic luster, are good conductors, and are fusable. If a metal, it will have a positive charge and seek a negative pole.

There are about 80 metals or about 75% of all elements. The majority crystallize in the cubic system. Most have a silvery color and a high specific gravity. Many are malleable and can be drawn into fine wires.

Potassium, lithium, and sodium are not heavier than water and are known as the 'light metals'. Calcium is not malleable, nor ductile. All metals are solids except mercury (q.v.).

The price of finished metals reflects the cost of exploration, development, mining, processing, smelting, casting, and transportation. Some metals like aluminum have very high energy costs to convert them to marketable products.

Many methods are used to recover metals from mineral process waters. Some are chemical precipitation (q.v.), reverse osmosis, ion exchange, activated carbon adsorption, and cementation. These techniques are important in purifying waste waters and recycling.

METALLIC BONDING Metallic bonding reveals closely packed, positively charged ions enclosed in a cloud of negatively charged 'free' electrons. Metal cohesion comes from electrical attraction, and electrons in the cloud can be easily agitated, accounting for conductivity.

The electron cloud of each atom has to react to 12 neighbors. Extra electrons drift about playing 'musical chairs'. This is so prevalent, it is called 'time-shared covalent bonding'.

METALLOGENIC PROVINCE A metallogenic province is a region of related mineral composition. Tin-tungsten provinces, copper belts, iron formations all make up metallogenic provinces which are often continental in scale. The Tin-Tungsten Metallogenic Province is even extra-continental. Nigerian tin is related to South American.

METALLOIDS Elements near the dividing line between metals and non-metals are 'metalloids'. They are related to metals, having the power to attract electrons and conduct electricity, although they are not good conductors. Any semiconductor will become a conductor if temperatures are high enough; if low enough, it is an insulator.

Carbon is sometimes a metalloid. Graphite is a conductor while diamond is an insulator.

Some important metalloids are arsenic, boron, germanium, selenium, silica, and tellurium. These elements have become important to the semiconductor industry, vital to computer technology.

METALLURGY The engineering art of separating metals from their ores and preparing them for use is metallurgy. The field is divided into:

- Extractive - Mineral dressing, flotation, agitation, roasting, sintering, leaching, electrolysis, or amalgamation.
- Physical or Alloy - Preparing metals for market, ingot making. Processing includes alloying of all types.

The price of finished metals reflects the cost of exploration, development, mining, processing, smelting, casting, and transportation. Some metals like aluminum have very high energy costs to convert them to marketable products.

METAMORPHIC ROCKS Rocks are divided into 3 principal groups: Igneous, metamorphic, and sedimentary. Metamorphic rocks have been transformed from their original character as igneous, sedimentary or other metamorphic rocks. The transformation to metamorphic rocks from sedimentary or igneous is induced by heat, pressure, chemical reaction, or radioactivity. Rocks range from slate through schist to eclogite as depth and accompanying pressure increases.

There are 3 grades of thermal alteration: High, medium, and low. The degree is related to temperature, depth of burial, pressure and proximity to the heat source. Shale under heat and pressure will become slate. Slate undergoing increased heat and pressure is converted to schist. Sandy shales and granites convert to coarsely foliated or layered gneisses. Crystals, grains, and even fossils take on linearity through foliation.

If the heat and pressure are released, the rock may return to its original unaltered form or be remelted into the magma. A metamorphic rock can also undergo further alteration. Temperature, pressure, and chemical reaction alter solutions as well as rocks.

Metamorphic rocks are either banded, foliated, or non-banded. Rocks converted to gneiss show strong banding. If banding is thin (6mm or less), the rock will split into thin sheets as do micas. Splitting of greater intensity results in sub-parallel sheets as in slates.

Non-banded metamorphic rocks often show a mosaic of interlocking mineral grains such as in marbles and quartzites. These rocks can also show indications of flowage.

METASEQUOIA The metasequoia of China, once considered related to the sequoia of North America, is a member of the cypress family. The tree reaches 30 meters (98 feet), is deciduous (q.v.) shedding its needles.

Metasequoia first appeared 20 million years ago. It is now found in Wanshien near the Yangtze Gorge. To the Chinese, it is 'shui- sa', the sacred waterpine.

Metasequoia seeds have been given to the Intro Garden of Glenn Dale, Maryland and seedlings have been sent to Kew Gardens in England, and to Alaska.

METASOMATISM Metasomatism is atom by atom substitution. The alteration may result from dissolution of a rock or mineral in place and deposition of another brought in by solution or magmatic gases. Metasomatism is most frequent in carbonate-rich rocks. Lead (galena) for example substitutes for calcite. Important mineral deposits originated in this way.

One of the most striking examples of metasomatism is petrified wood. Cell structure is retained but is chemically altered. Silica, in the form of opal, replaces organic material. Some granites have been formed by metasomatism. See **GRANITIZATION**.

METEOR A meteor is a celestial mass occurring as a flash, or shooting star. A very bright meteor, capable of lighting up the sky, is a 'fire ball'. A fire ball can leave a residual light or 'meteor train' lasting up to 30 minutes. A meteor should not be confused with a meteorite (q.v.).

METEOR CRATER The impact of a meteorite (q.v.) causes a crater, a circular depression. The meteorite (q.v.) is usually burned up upon impact but parts of it may remain to identify the cause of cratering. There are many known meteor craters.

The largest meteor crater in the United States is in Diablo Canyon, Arizona. The impact occurred about 50,000 years ago and resulted in a crater 1,257.5 meters (4,150 feet) across and 173 meters (570 feet) deep. The crater was caused by a huge meteorite that weighed at least 8,500 tons.

The outer walls of Meteor Crater slope gently, while the inner ones are steep. The crater which once held a lake is covered with nickel-iron meteorite fragments.

METEORIC WATER Meteoric water is derived from rain or snow and is stored as groundwater.

METEORITE Meteorites are extra-terrestrial rocks or minerals found on the Earth's surface. They are irregularly distributed.

There are 3 kinds of meteorites, pure nickel-iron, iron and stone mixed, and pure stone. Stony meteorites are chondrites and those that are a combination of nickel-iron and stone are pallasites.

A large meteorite was found in Williamette, Oregon in 1902. It weighed 14 metric tons. In Australia, 127 major meteorites have been found.

METEOROID   The meteoroid is a transitional astral body. It enters Earth's Atmosphere at a speed of 16-75 kilometers (10-45 miles) per second. Meteoroids appear as flares, or 'shooting stars'. Most meteoroids burn up completely, some only partially.

When it reaches the Earth's surface, the meteoroid becomes a meteorite. It is estimated that 400 tons of micro-meteorites appear on the ground every day.

METHANE   Methane is a gaseous hydrocarbon with 70% natural gas. It is the 5th most abundant gas in the Atmosphere, having doubled in the past 150 years. According to Zimmerman it is increasing at the rate of 2% per year. After carbon dioxide, methane is the most important gas in the Greenhouse Effect (q.v.).

Methane can form from anaerobic fermentation in organic muds and is abundant in swamps where it is known as 'marsh gas'. Rice paddies are also producers.

Methane collects in enclosed areas, particularly pockets in coal mines.

There are an estimated 200 quadrillion termites for every human. Slash and burn agriculture encourages their growth. Termites are estimated to produce 100 million tons of methane a year.

Methane is the principal activator in sewage plant digesters. Many sewage plants are using this methane and are energy self-sufficient.

METRIC TON   The measurement of mineral reserves is made using the metric ton. Some researchers in the United States still use short or long tons (2,000 or 2,200 pounds). Official figures are, however, increasingly metric.

A metric ton contains 1 thousand kilograms. The short ton equals 0.907 metric tons, the long ton 1.016 metric tons. In some reports, 'tonnes' denote the metric units.

MEXICAN VOLCANIC AXIS   The Mexican Volcanic Axis is a lateral system to the San Andreas Fault. The famous volcanoes of Iztaccihuatl and Popocatepetl are along this rift axis.

MEXICO   With the United States and Canada, Mexico is part of North America. It has 16 physiographic zones but just 3 basic landscape types:

- Narrow coastal zones - On both coasts
- Mountains - Sierra Madre Occidental, Sierra Madre del Sur, volcanoes in the central-south
- High central plateau

The plateau is covered with Cretaceous sediments and the coastal zones host Recent ones.

In western Mexico a granitic system extends from the Rio Grande to the Isthmus of Tehuantepec. The California Batholith extends into

Baja California and is the sub-base of the San Pedro Martyr Range. Cretaceous to Recent volcanism extends from Cabo Corrientes on the Pacific to Vera Cruz on the Gulf. The mountains are part of the American Cordillera that extends from Alaska to Tierra del Fuego.

Mexico City is in the heart of the Mexican Volcanic Axis (q.v.) at an elevation of 2,227 meters (7,349 feet) with mountains on both sides to 5,152 meters (17,000 feet). The city is in a lake basin. Because the basin is underlain by quick clay, it responds to Earth tremors in the Pacific as well as those centered in and around the city. Such a Pacific event triggered the disasterous quake of 1985 which measured 7.8 on the Richter Scale (q.v.) and cost 10,000 lives.

Because of its enclosed position Mexico City suffers from some of the worst SMOG (q.v.) in the world, made worse by the photochemical effect of high altitudes.

GULF OF MEXICO The Gulf of Mexico, an arm of the Caribbean, was once an inland sea. A marginal sea, it is locked between North and Central America. The Gulf is fed by major streams like the Mississippi, Appalachicola, and Rio Grande as well as many minor ones.

Spawning and development of some fish and shellfish are dependent upon the existence of barrier islands, lagoons, and estuaries. The famous Gulf shrimp are in this class. Estuarine circulation assists the shrimp from spat to adult. It permits them to swim into more favorable areas relating to salinity and their stage of development. See **LAGUNA MADRE**.

The floor of the Gulf has sunk repeatedly from the weight of deposited sediments. These are now up to 10 kilometers (6 miles) thick.

The sediments have metamorphosed into sandstones, shales, limestones, and dolomites. Gulf sediments, including salt domes (q.v.) are productive petroleum reservoirs. There are a series of basin reservoirs in the Gulf.

MICA Mica is a family of hydrated silicates of aluminum, potassium, sodium, iron, and magnesium. Mica is formed of rings of silica tetrahedra joined at the oxygen corners and linked by metal ions. The metal ions can contain lithium, titanium, chromium, or fluorine.

Mica has nearly perfect parallel cleavage (q.v.).

There are 2 mica groups:

- Potassic - Muscovite micas
- Ferromagnesium - Biotite micas.

Biotite micas are variable. Iron and magnesium sustitute for aluminum and silica. In phlogopite, magnesium substitutes for aluminum.

Mica is used in the electronics industry and for electrical insulation. Some is used in paint.

The United States imports 100% of its sheet mica needs, mostly from India. Sheet mica is more valuable that flake.

MICA SCHIST Mica schist is a metamorphic rock of mica, quartz, and some feldspar. It also contains various secondary minerals. Mica schists were mostly derived from shales and tuffs. The schists are of varying thicknesses, but always laminated. They weather to oily clays that are not good for agriculture.

MICHIGAN BASIN The Michigan Basin in the Great Lakes Region of North America is about 100 kilometers (300 miles) across and filled with 395 meters (1,300 feet) of Paleozoic sediments. The circular pattern is related to structure.

The basin sediments have been described as being in a plate-like structure with layers stacked from large to small. Green Bay, Georgian Bay, Michigan and Saugeen lakes are on the edges of the plates as is Lake Huron. The top of the sedimentary pile is the floor of the Michigan Basin.

Concentrated brines rich in iodine, bromine, chlorine, magnesium, and calcium ions are found in Michigan Basin. These brines are between 300 and 2,400 meters (1,000 and 8,000 feet) deep in remnants of ancient seas that periodically covered the area. Recovery is made by pumping the brine to the surface.

MICRO- The prefix for small, usually for anything below normal vision is 'micro-'. It is also a mathematical prefix. Any basic unit is divided by 1 million if preceded by micro-.

MICROBURST During spring and summer in subtropical United States there are intense, short-lived winds or microbursts that descend from rain clouds and fan out.

Microbursts create a very strong divergence and a dangerous wind shear can result. This occurs as a result of a quick change of direction and velocity. The shear produced can be very destructive.

The microburst phenomenon is so short-lived it is difficult to pick up on radar. New dopplar (q.v.) systems may make them more easily avoided by aircraft. Recently, they were responsible for 3 air disasters.

MICROCLIMATE A microclimate is a variation from the prevailing climate of a given area. Within a climatic region, there are different microclimates varying with elevation, orientation in relation to the Sun, sea breezes, and local topography. Variations may be small or very sharp. Each microclimate has its own ecological community of plants and animals.

Shoreline areas of the world are noted for microclimatic differences. Southern California coastal communities demonstrate these differences. Another good example is found on the Scottish Atlantic Coast where an occasional subtropical garden can be found.

MICROCLINE Microcline is a potassium feldspar and a major rock-forming mineral. The green variety, amazonite (q.v.) is used for jewelry and ornaments.

MICROCONTINENTS Continental crust is found in deep seas beyond the continental shelf. These continental fragments became separated from the main landmass early during continental rifting. Some examples are Blake-Bahama Platform, Iceland-Faroe Ridge, Galicia Bank, Sao Paulo Plateau, and Madagascar Plateau.

There are faulted continental fragments of once larger microcontinents such as the Cayman and Curaçao ridges, and the Nicaragua Rise. In the Pacific there are masses of continental crust such as New Zealand, Japan, and other islands. Their origins are related to convergence and granitization (q.v.). The granitization is believed due to the pressures in subduction (q.v.) focal points.

Microcontinents are essentially the same as continents. However, new epigenetic deposits of minerals were laid down along the margins as a result of 2-stage rifting. The rifting brought the intrusion of oceanic crustal magma through the sides and bottom of the small pieces of granitic crust.

MICROSEISM The microseism is a movement in the Earth of such low intensity only an instrument can sense it. A microseism can be caused by a passing truck on a highway. Natural microseisms result frequently from the weather.

Microseisms are felt with any volcanic activity. These are carefully monitored as it may be a precursor of more pronounced activity. Seismic activity often precedes major eruptions.

MICROTEKTITES Congealed droplets of molten rock are microtektites. These are the result of the 'splash effect' from the impact on the Earth's surface of a large meteorite.

Microtektites have been recovered from Eocene (54-38 m.y.) sediment cores taken from the ocean floor. The sediments date from the time of the Radiolaria Extinction.

MICROWAVE The microwave is a very short electromagnetic wave. Its wavelength is between 1 millimeter and a meter. See **ELECTROMAGNETIC SPECTRUM**.

The use of microwaves to cook food has become popular in the United States. The energy requirement is very much less than for the conventional electrical oven.

MID-ATLANTIC RIDGE The Mid-Atlantic Ridge bisects the Ocean between Newfoundland and France. It passes between Norway and Greenland and surfaces in Iceland and the Azores. It is part of a Global Rift System.

The Ridge is the largest topographic feature on Earth occupying a 3rd of the Atlantic seafloor. It has great width for more than a 1,000 kilometers (600 miles). It is much wider than most continental mountains. Its elevation above the ocean floor is between 2,000-3,000 meters (6,600-10,000 feet). There are 2 distinct provinces: The Crest and the Highly Fractured.

The Crest Province is split by a deep rift, the Mid-Atlantic Rift (q.v.). The Fractured Province manifested on both sides of the Crest is marked by parallel faults. These have created stepped terraces to the Abyssal Plains (q.v.).

MID-ATLANTIC RIFT The Mid-Atlantic Rift is part of the Global Rift System (q.v.) with its accompanying mountains. The Mid-Atlantic Rift in the center of the Mid-Atlantic Ridge (q.v.) is the largest single feature of the global system.

The Rift follows the Crest Province and extends from Jan Mayen Island above the Arctic Circle to Bouvet Island in the South Atlantic. The rift valley reaches 4,000 meters (13,000 feet) in depth and is up to 8.3 kilometers (5 miles) wide. Valley walls are compared with the Grand Canyon.

Iceland, along the rift has its largest surface expression. The island has 20 active volcanoes and the major rift appears in that country as a huge graben.

The Mid-Atlantic Rift is spreading at an average rate of 2.5 centimeters (1 inch) per year. Transverse to the Mid-Atlantic Rift are a number of major fractures. The largest number of these is between Africa and South America. See **GLOBAL RIFT**.

MID-INDIAN OCEAN RIDGE The Indian Ocean Ridge extends from south of the Arabian Peninsula to south of Australia half way to Antarctica. A west branch of the Mid-Indian Ocean Ridge creates an arc south of Africa. The average height of the ridge is 2,000 meters (6,600 feet) above the ocean floor.

Volcanoes are strung all along the ridge. The rift accompanying the ridge is spreading at a rate of 1.5-3 centimeters (0.5-1 inch per year). Africa and Arabia are separating at the rate of 1.5 centimeters (0.5 inch) a year. The system is a segment of the Global Rift (q.v.).

MID-OCEANIC RIDGE It is estimated that 67-75,000 kilometers (40-45,000 miles) of mountain ranges encircle continents in mid-ocean.

The Mid-Atlantic Ridge (q.v.) extends from north of Iceland to the Antarctic. At about the Equator the ridge is bent towards Africa, then orientation is south again to Antarctica.

The mountains continue through the Antarctic seas and are traced to a junction with the East Pacific Rise (q.v.). See **GLOBAL RIFT**.

MID-PACIFIC RIFT A tremendous rift has been located at Latitude 30° North in the mid-Pacific. It is 4,550 meters (15,000 feet) deep, cutting into the abyssal plains. The rift strikes northwest-southeast extending for 2,700 kilometers (1,600 miles).

Eruptions began in the northwest along this rift zone more than a million years ago. Lava built up on the ocean floor until islands formed. Activity progressed and is still progressing to the southeast. 122 volcanic islands were formed. The only volcanoes active today are Mauna Loa and Mauna Kea forming Hawaii at the southeast end of the rift. See **HAWAII**.

MIGMATITE Injection gneiss, or migmatite, is formed by deep-seated igneous intrusives. Migma is partially fluid rock penetrating a host rock. These penetrations are usually on a large scale. Migmatites are often associated with granites.

MILFORD SOUND Milford Sound, a deep fjord (q.v.) in the coast of South Island, New Zealand. The Sound is narrow and like all fjords, it is deepest at the head of the U-shaped, drowned valley. Milford Sound is 290 meters (950 feet) at its deepest.

The fjord is a very beautiful and scenic feature. Triangular-shaped Mitre Peak overlooks the usually indigo waters.

MILKY WAY GALAXY The Milky Way Galaxy is a cloud-like belt containing some 3 trillion stars moving through Space. It takes about 200 million years for a single galactic revolution.

Some stars in the galaxy are packed together forming nebulae (q.v.). There are more stars near the center of the galaxy than away from it. As a result, the galaxy is wheel-shaped with curved spokes. From edge to edge, it is 100,000 light years (q.v.) at its thickest. Milky Way Galaxy is considered medium-sized by astronomers.

The Solar System is on the outer edge of one of the galaxy spokes of the Milky Way about 30,000 light years (q.v.) from the center. Earth is within the Solar System. The Solar System's orbit within Milky Way takes 220 million years.

A billion galaxies like Milky Way are conjectured. Clusters of stars move in orbits about the Milky Way and these clusters belong to other galaxies. 20 have been identified with some new discoveries which were made in the late 1980's.

MILLET Millet, a grass with small red seeds, is important in Europe, North Africa, and the Middle East as a source of grain.

MILLSTONE A millstone is a hard rock used for grinding and milling grains and soft rocks.

The millstone was an important adjunct to milling prior to metals manufacture. Modern machinery has replaced it for the most part but the millstone is still much in use, especially in under-developed areas.

MINDANAO TRENCH The Mindanao Trench off the Philippines is 10.8 kilometers (6.5 miles) deep and was long considered the deepest oceanic trench. Marianas Trench (q.v.), measured by the Soviets during the International Geophysical Year, IGY (q.v.) proved to be deeper.

MINE A mine is an exploitation of ores in an open pit, placer, or underground operation. Even abandoned operations are still referred to as mines.

Specialized excavations and open pits can lead to underground operations. These are accessed by a main shaft and crosscuts to ore veins.

Open pits for sand, gravel, and stone are quarries rather than mines.

MINERAL A mineral is an inorganic chemical compound with a particular crystal form or habit. It can be amorphous or non-crystalline. The mineral is naturally occurring. Laboratory-made substitutes are not referred to as minerals. A few minerals are elemental (gold, copper).

All minerals have identifying characteristics. The most frequently used are color, cleavage, electromagnetics, hardness, optics, and specific gravity.

There are more than 2,000 minerals, some of them rock-forming. Of these 25 are considered crucial to modern technology. This is not surprising since only a few of the contained elements are abundant enough in the Earth's Crust to reach 1%.

Minerals are classified using physical-chemical properties. They are divided into various classes (elemental, sulfides, phosphates, and others). They are found in different phases depending upon the conditions of temperature and pressure under which they were formed.

MINERAL DEPOSIT A mineral deposit is a local concentration of one or more economic substances. The deposit may be of any mineral from asbestos to zinc. Mineral deposits are classified by mode of origin (igneous, metamormorphic or sedimentary).

Economic geologists study known mineral deposits to gain information leading to a better understanding of the origins and development, associations, structural relationships, or any other special information. The effort assists in evaluating deposits. It is also useful for the development of exploration guides for the particular mineral or association.

A mineral deposit becomes a prospect when its evaluation raises possibilities for exploitation. Only 1 prospect in 1,000 becomes a mine.

MINERAL ASSOCIATIONS Mineral combinations are explained by natural laws. Those minerals in sedimentary rocks are governed by gravity deposition, solubility sequences, water, wind, and wave concentration, or other pertinent phenomena.

Mineral associations in metamorphic rocks relate to the original rock assemblage and to the metamorphic phase or degree of heat and pressure the rocks have sustained.

Mineral associations of igneous rocks are the most complex. Combinations follow laws of crystallization affecting magmas.

These were spelled out by Bowen (q.v.). Some generalizations are:

- Quartz will not be found in rocks that contain leucite, olivine, or nepheline
- If the rock is olivine or contains more than 40% dark minerals, feldspar will be a calcic plagioclase (labradorite)
- Only 1 plagioclase (soda lime) feldspar may be present with potassium feldspar
- If the feldspars are of about equal, the plagioclase will be albite or oligoclase
- If muscovite mica is present, the plagioclase will be sodic (albite or oligoclase).

MINERAL IDENTIFICATION Minerals are recognized by their identifying properties. These properties depend upon:

- Atomic Bonding - Crystal habit, chemistry, hardness, fracture and cleavage
- Atomic Weight and Packing - Specific gravity
- Light - Transparency, color, streak, luster
- Sense - Taste, smell, and touch.

MINERAL RICH MUDS Exploration in the Pacific Ocean off northwestern United States revealed metal-rich muds and lava associated with submarine hot springs. The muds, 400 kilometers (240 miles) west of Oregon, are associated with volcanic activity. Rich in zinc sulfide, the muds also contain silver, copper, and lead.

The muds are an important discovery not only because of their economic potential but because of their similarity to the muds found in the Red Sea over the Red Sea Hot Spot (q.v.).

MINERAL WATER Water emanating from springs and carrying many minerals in solution is mineral water. Around the world, health spas have sprung up to treat all types of physical ills with these waters. Not all the minerals are beneficial.

Almost all are radioactive to some degree and all have temperatures above the usual groundwater. Some types are:

- Acidic - carbonates
- Alkaline - bicarbonates
- Magnesians - elevated magnesia salts
- Sulferous - alkaline sulfates in small amounts
- Ferruginous - iron bicarbonate

MIRAGE A mirage or floating image results from the bending of light rays. In desert terrain, air above a heated surface will cause evaporation and bending of light rays. The image may be an inverted reflection. The most common mirage is of water.

MISCIBILITY Miscibility is the property of liquids that allows 2 or more to mix forming a single homogeneous fluid.

MISSISSIPPI DELTA The Mississippi River over a period of 5,000 years has had 7 different deltas. Today the delta, because of its distributaries is of the birdfoot type.

The sediments build into the Gulf of Mexico. Every 100 years the Delta increases its length by 10 kilometers (6 miles). Long ago the Delta was at Cairo, Illinois.

The weight of delta sediments is such the outer edge is sinking 2.5 meters (8.25 feet) a century. In the sedimentary pile there are 6,660 meters (22,000 feet) of Eocene (54-38 m.y.) sediments alone.

The many channels create a labyrinth of islands and lagoons. Channels with slow moving waters are 'bayous'. There are many marshes and cypress swamps as well as some hardwood forests.

The delta continues to grow at the rate of 500 meters (300 feet) a year. Delta sediments both on and off-shore are reservoirs for oil, natural gas, and sulfur.

MISSISSIPPI EMBAYMENT In the Upper Mississippi Valley there is an ancient embayment now filled with Cretaceous (136-65 m.y.) sediments. These are to some extent phosphatic. The embayment was in an intra-cratonic basin. See **CRATON**.

MISSISSIPPI RIVER The Mississippi River begins in small Lake Itasca, in Minnesota. With its tributaries, it drains 31 states and 2 Canadian Provinces. The river has probably been in existence from 40-50 million years. Over this time, it has built the great Mississippi Valley from the Rockies to the Appalachians.

The river is on average 1.6 kilometers (1 mile) wide and up to 15 meters (50 feet) deep. It is considered navigable from the Twin Cities to the delta. Great streams feed into the Mississippi. These include the Missouri, the Red, and the Ohio. The Ohio is the greatest affluent, doubling the total flow.

The Mississippi is a mature stream and traverses a meandering path from the confluence of the Ohio at Cairo, Illinois to the delta. Its velocity is not great throughout the stretch and much silting occurs. This is one reason the reduction of flow occurred on the Ohio and other tributaries during the 1988 drought. It caused barges to become stuck at especially silted points.

Winding across the plains, the river has built up to 6 meters (20 feet) of topsoil in some places. Sediments the river has deposited in Louisiana alone are 9,000 meters (30,000 feet) thick.

The valley as it nears the delta (q.v.) is up to 100 kilometers (60 miles) across. The volume of sediment carried to the Gulf yearly is about 500 million tons. The basin is being lowered at the rate of 0.3 meters (1 foot) per 1,000 years.

MISSISSIPPIAN PERIOD The Mississippian or Lower Carboniferous Period (345-280 m.y.) of Paleozoic Age overlies the Devonian and precedes the coal-bearing Pennsylvanian.

The Mississippi Valley was submerged during this time and great limestone sequences were built up. A period of orogeny and general uplifting of the landmass occurred towards the end of the period.

MISTRAL The mistral is a cold, dry wind, originating in the central mountains of France (Massif Central) and blowing to the Mediterranean. It is a strong wind from the north that blows over the Riviera a few days at a time.

The mistral can be damaging and most farmers have cypress wind breaks planted on the north side of their plots. Some homes are built with no windows or doors on the north or west.

MIXTURE Molecules of different chemicals combine to form a mixture. The molecules are not chemically compounded as no chemical change or reaction takes place in a mixture.

MOBILE BELT A part of the Earth's Crust may be relatively mobile. A mobile belt is characterized by a greater number of faults, folds, and geosynclines (q.v.) than continental Crust in general. They are often reflected in fold belts on the edge of ancient shields.

Mobile belts are usually extremely long, sometimes continental in extent and many miles wide. Since the Precambrian, 8 major mobile belts have been recognized. In each, there was widespread tectonic activity with great mineralization.

LAKE MOBUTO-SESE SEKO Lake Albert (now Lake Mobuto-Sese Seko) on the western side of the Great Rift Valley is between Uganda and Zaire. It is a large tropical lake, 5,000 square kilometers (200 square miles) at the northern end of the West Rift. It has a depth of 55 meters (180 feet) between parallel escarpments and is at an elevation of 615 meters (2,030 feet). This rift lake is the source of the Albert Nile, which plunges over Murchison Falls (now Kabalega) and flows over 67 kilometers (40 miles) of rapids.

Albert Lake is fed by the Semliki River from Lake Edward through the western edge of the Ituri Rainforest in Zaire. Flow is increased by runoff from the northern slopes of the Ruwenzoris. Most lateral flow is seasonal.

MOGOK REGION In Burma, the Mogok Region is highly mineralized. It is rich in thorium and other minerals. It has been famous for centuries as the site of the Burma ruby fields.

MOGOLLON RIM The southern flank of the Colorado Plateau is the Mogollon Rim. The rim extends over northern Arizona and New Mexico. Besides being the limit of the Plateau, the escarpment marks the northern edge of the Arizona-New Mexico desert.

MOH SCALE OF HARDNESS The relative scale of hardness developed by Moh is accepted as a field test of minerals. Based on 10 minerals, each has the ability to scratch or flake the prior less hard mineral. Diamond, the hardest natural mineral, is 10. Down-scale are corundum, topaz, quartz, orthoclase, apatite, fluorite, calcite, gypsum and talc.

MOHAVE The Mohave or High Desert is adjacent to the Colorado Desert in Southern California. The Mohave is 1,000 to 1,410 meters (3,500-4,650 feet) in elevation. Vegetation is desert scrub but there are Joshua trees. Some parts of Mohave have been simulated lunar landscape sites.

Ancient Lake Mohave once occupied about 260 square kilometers (100 square miles) and covered the areas of Soda and Silver Lakes, now dry. The Mohave River once emptied into Mohave Lake. Ancient lake levels are evident in wave cut cliffs, terraces, beach ridges, and lacustrine sediments.

The Mohave River today flows on the surface for part of its course, then sinks underground, still following its ancient channel. For much of its course, before it is completely lost in the desert, the river can be traced by gallery vegetation.

Lake Mohave in Arizona is an artificial lake on the Colorado River and unrelated to ancient Lake Mohave.

MOHENJO-DARO The archaeological site of Mohenjo-Daro in the valley of the Indus River (q.v.) is especially interesting for its well-designed water system. The Pakistan site was the center of an advanced agricultural society. The evidence indicates that it became extinct due to major climatic changes.

MOHOLE Project Mohole was organized to drill into the Earth's Crust to the Mohorovicic Discontinuity (q.v.). Congressional funding was denied but the project was not abandoned. Universities and the National Science Foundation supported exploration. Valuable data was retrieved from deep drilling. The project had to be abandoned primarily because coring tools were too readily destroyed and project costs became too high.

MOHOROVICIC DISCONTINUITY The 'Moho' or Mohorovicic Discontinuity marks the boundary between the Earth's Crust and Mantle. The boundary is characterized by an abrupt change in density reflected in an abrupt change in seismic wave velocity.

On the average, beneath continents the discontinuity is at 40 kilometers (24 miles). Below oceans, the discontinuity is 10 kilometers (6 miles).

Below the discontinuity, the seismic waves have characteristics similar to those found in basic igneous rocks.

MOLASSE Coarse clastic sediments found in mountain depressions are 'molasse'.

The clastics result from rapid uplift and down-drop of mountain ranges. Sediments are deposited at mountain fronts on sub-montane platforms, or at the bottom of a marginal sea (q.v.). Sands and clays are coarse, as are the conglomerates. Molasse can reach 6 to 8 kilometers (10 to 13 miles) in thickness. It was first identified in the Alps.

MOLASSES REEF Molasses Reef off the Florida Coast is the only living coral reef off the United States. The reef is still building. See **CORAL**.

MOLECULAR SIEVES Some clays and zeolites (q.v.) act as molecular sieves. They selectively fill their pore spaces and channels with filtered material after activation. Activation is achieved by driving off water with heat. The molecular size of the sediment is critical.

MOLECULE The molecule is the smallest unit of a chemical compound that can exist alone. Molecules are held together by chemical bonding. They may be composed of different atoms, or a single element as hydrogen or sulfur. The usual compound is composed of 2 or more atoms of different elements.

In a 2-atom molecule there are twice as many electron orbitals. With this increase, energy gaps decrease. In solids, these energy levels form bands. Electrons, in a conductor, jump gaps to reach higher energy levels. In an insulator, the gaps are wider.

MOLLUSKS Mollusks (Phylum Mollusca) include shellfish and related animals. They are land, freshwater, or sea creatures.

Mollusks secrete shells which provide protection. Most secrete aragonite, a calcium carbonate that dissolves and is replaced by calcite.

MONADNOCK Remnants of resistant upland rocks on peneplained (q.v.) surfaces are monadnocks. They are similar to inselbergs (q.v.) on pediplaned terrain in arid areas. Mount Monadnock, New Hampshire, and Stone Mountain, Georgia are examples of such erosional remnants.

MONAZITE Monazite is a phosphate of cerium, lanthanum, and didymium with traces of thorium and uranium. It is a major Rare Earths (q.v.) ore. Monazite is an orange-yellow or reddish mineral mined primarily from placers.

Massive monazite is extremely rare. It has been found at Sao Joao del Rey, Minas Gerais, Brazil, and on the Island of Madagascar. Monazite is a constituent of Precambrian igneous rocks.

World production of Rare Earths until the advent of bastnaesite (q.v.) was mainly from wave-concentrated detrital sands along the shores of India and Brazil and as a by-product from South African gold production. The Brazilian deposits today are worked by NUCLEBRAS, the Brazilian Nuclear Energy Company.

In the Appalachians of southeastern United States, 2 major belts of monazite parallel each other. In these belts, virtually all streams contain monazite and gold placers.

MONO LAKE Mono lake is a crater lake in one of the many volcanoes in a 16 kilometer (10-mile) belt in California. The belt stretches along the eastern flank of the Sierra Nevada. Mono is becoming increasingly saline due to lack of inflow and sufficient precipitation. Environmentalists are attempting to halt the aging of the lake. They may succeed in so far as man has been contributing to the natural sequence. See **LAKE**.

MONSOON In India and Southeast Asia a seasonal weather pattern prevails called the 'Monsoon', Arabic for season. Vast areas of the semi-tropical and tropical world are affected. In these regions the winds blow 6 months from the land to the sea and 6 months from the sea to the land. Winds blowing toward the warm land under low pressure bring rain. The reverse condition creates a dry season, often a drought.

Monsoonal patterns affect West Africa and, in turn, are affected by the location of the Intertropical Convergence (ITC). Since the rain-bearing winds cannot cross the ITC, its location can prevent an area from receiving seasonal rainfall and drought will result. This is the Sahelian Effect. This situation has been one of the causes of desertification of the Sub-Saharan area. See **INTERTROPICAL CONVERGENCE**.

The monsoons are also linked to the Westerlies. When these winds dip far toward the Monsoonal Belt, the belt is pushed out of its usual pattern. This can create many diverse climatic affects by dislocating the wet and dry winds. See **WESTERLIES**.

MONTANE FOREST Mountains rising up out of tropical rainforests to great heights have a wide variety of tree growth depending upon elevation. The montane forests of East Africa are the habitat of the giant lobelia, a grass, 10 to 12 meters (30-40 feet) high. It is a type of mountain bamboo and a favorite browsing food for elephants. It is a transitional growth from rainforest. See **GRASS**.

Montane forests tend to have a broad range of species with climate ranges from the Tropics to the Tundra (q.v.). The flora reflect the various climatic zones encountered at different elevations.

MONTMORILLONITE Clays are divided into 4 major groups:
- Chlorite
- Illite
- Kaolinite
- Montmorillonite.

The clays are divided on the basis of composition and structure. Montmorillonite is second to kaolinite (q.v.) in economic importance. It is an alumino-silicate with an expanding crystal lattice of lathlike particles in 3 layers, with gibbsite (q.v.) encased between layers of silica tetrahedra.

In the gibbsite layer, aluminum may replace magnesium. Water is the binding agent for the 3 layers on a single (c) axis. The bond is precarious since the amount of water varies. Clay shrinks when dry and expands when wet. When dry, montmorillonite cracks into characteristic polygonal patterns. A polygon can be from 1-4 meters (3-12 feet) across.

In addition to water there may be calcium, sodium, or potassium ions between the clay layers. Their presence gives rise to a capacity for ion exchange (q.v.).

There are enormous quantities of highly crystalline montmorillonite on the Pacific seafloor. It is assumed to have been diagenetically derived from volcanic ejecta.

MONZONITE Monzonite is an igneous rock midway between syenite and diorite. It is gray and composed of feldspar, mica, augite, and a little quartz. When the quartz content is somewhat elevated the rock is called a quartz-monzonite.

MOON Planet Earth has 1 moon or satellite (q.v.) in orbit around it. The Moon is 384,000 kilometers (239,000 miles) away and has a diameter of 3,476 kilometers (2,160 miles). It takes roughly 29 days for it to complete 1 revolution of the Earth. At the same time the moon completes 1 rotation on its axis so the same side always faces the Earth.

The moon appears to rise 50 minutes later each evening because of the relative relation between the Earth's rotation and the orbit of the Moon.

Gravity on the Moon is 1/6 that of the Earth. The pull of lunar gravity affects Earth's oceanic tides. High tide occurs at a particular location on Earth when that location faces the Moon.

Some lunar craters have walls 6.6 kilometers (4 miles) high and great diameters. Copernicus is 92 kilometers (55 miles) across. Lunar craters often contain central peaks. Many of the largest craters resulted from meteoritic impact.

Lunar composition is much the same as the Earth's. It has no Atmosphere and is subject to full solar radiation so any water must be tied up in its rocks. Its age is considered the same as the Earth's (4.6 billion years).

Astronaut-geologist Scott reported large quantities of anorthosite in the highlands of the Moon. 'Genesis Rock' has an age date of 4.15 billion years. Volcanic activity appears to have ceased 3.6-3 billion years ago.

MORAINE Glacial debris forms lobe-shaped deposits and irregular hills or moraines, some very large. These lobe-shaped moraines are associated with alpine glaciers or glaciers of local origin.

Continental glaciers left great moraines marking their limits. Moraines changed stream patterns. Lakes and swamps formed when scours were filled with meltwater.

In North America the retreat of the glaciers left huge moraines. In New Jersey the glacier left a great rock ridge up to 15 meters (50 feet) high and 5 kilometers (3 miles wide). Long Island, New York, is built on a series of terminal moraines.

Morainal mounds or hills are composed of unsorted till (q.v.) of mud, sand, and gravel. The terminal moraines formed into ridges to create these hills. Lateral moraines line valley walls.

MOROCCO The West African country of Morocco has 1,500 kilometers (900 miles) of coastline on the Atlantic Ocean and Mediterranean Sea. From the Mediterranean coastal plain the Er Rif Mountains rise to 2,450 meters (8,000 feet). They form the headland at Tangier which is across the strait from Gibraltar. Er Rif is a continuation of European mountain ranges.

The High Atlas form 3 parallel ranges extending from the Atlantic to Algeria. They average 3,300 meters (11,000 feet). Toubkal is the highest peak at 4,140 meters (13,665 feet). The mountains form the divide between the Sahara and the sea.

The High Atlas are intensely folded, metamorphosed, and intruded locally by gabbros, diorites, and alkaline igneous rocks (q.v.). Major tectonic events from the Caledonian to the Alpine are recorded in Moroccan rocks. The Anti-Atlas, a southwestern range, is part of the African Shield and hosts Precambrian rocks covered in places by Paleozoic sediments.

Phosphate mining is the major contributor to foreign exchange. The phosphate deposits are on the Ganntour and Abdoun plateaus and in the Meshala Region. The grade is high, up to 75%. Proven and indicated reserves in 1986 were 22 billion metric tons. These were the world's largest reserves. The additional reserves of Spanish Sahara augmented them further.

Lead and cobalt are also important in Moroccan economy. Morocco is the world's 5th leading producer of cobalt. Coal is important and reserves in 1986 were 150 million metric tons. Morocco produces oil and natural gas but the production does not rival that of neighboring Algeria.

MORTAR Mortar is a mix of sand, water, and lime, or cement. It is used to cement bricks or building blocks to each other.

MOTHER LODE A complex of lodes which are inter-related constitute a 'Mother Lode'. The most famous was the site of the great California

Gold Rush of 1849. This Mother Lode is located in the western Sierra Nevada Range where the inclined ledges of the foothills dip toward the batholith (q.v.).

The treasure trove of gold was in hydrothermal veins that trended north-south for 330 kilometers (200 miles). The veins themselves are of a milky quartz. Some were up to a meter (3 feet) wide and contained the gold and pyrite (q.v.).

For the average prospector, these veins were much too difficult to work so they turned to the erosional product in the placers.

MOUNTAIN The largest landscape feature in terms of elevation is the mountain. To be classed as a mountain, the minimum elevation is 300 meters (1,000 feet) above sea level. Mountain relief is usually rugged.

A range is a long line or cluster of mountains. Several lines or ridges, in the same orientation, make up a range. Within it may be several high peaks. A series of ranges with the same orientation is a chain.

In a chain, the mountains are related to each other in composition, structure, and geological history. They have a definite alignment and extend over a great area. The Rockies are a chain.

A collection of chains is a cordillera (q.v.). All along the west coast of the Americas from the Aleutians to Chile, the mountains form a cordillera. These mountains are part of the 'Pacific Rim of Fire'. In Asia and Europe related chains of mountains stretch from the Himalayas to the Pyrenees with a loop into North Africa.

Mountains form in many ways:

- Crumpling of the Earth's Crust - Folded mountains
- Mountains uplifted as a unit - Block faulted mountains
- Erosion - Plateaulands into mountains
- Winds - Pinnacles and peaks
- Glaciers - Needle peaks
- Eruption - Volcanoes

Each force is the result of an even greater one. An example is that of the Earth's crumpling. This occurs when continents collide. Glaciers through plucking and scouring contribute to the formation of mountains.

Mountains are nature's way of balancing pressure exerted on the Earth's Crust. When crustal pressure is great, fissuring results and from many rifts and vents, volcanoes rise.

MOUNTAIN PASS Mountain Pass, a peak near the Nevada border in California, hosts the Sulphide Queen Mine. The mine is producing from the greatest known concentration of the Cerium Subgroup of Rare Earths (q.v.). The major mineral is bastnaesite.

Mountain Pass is considered a unique carbonatite (q.v.). Its lack of niobium is notable. It appears related to potassic rather than sodic igneous rocks. The area is highly faulted with volcanic dikes intruding the mass. See **CARBONATITES**.

MOUTH   Where a river empties into the sea, lake, or another stream is the mouth. A delta at the mouth results from a combination of physical forces of sedimentation at the mouth and the lack of forceful currents to remove the sediments. See **DELTA**.

Some rivers have great areas of debouchment. Among these are the Ganges-Brahmaputra (q.v.), the Mississippi, and the Amazon. The mouth of the Amazon is 300 kilometers (186 miles) across.

MOZAMBIQUE   Mozambique, the former Portuguese Colony, has two major sections wrapped about Malawi (q.v.). It is has 2,575 kilometers (1,545 miles) of Indian Ocean coastline. From the Zambezi Delta south to Lourenço Marques the northeast-southwest coastal plain is dominated by sandy beaches and swamps.

North of the delta there are coral reefs along the coast to its most easterly point. North of this, the coast is dominated by rocky cliffs. Highlands and low mountains are in the interior.

Mining is important to the economy. Coal is produced in the Upper Zambezi near Tete. Reserves are 400 million metric tons in Karroo Sediments (q.v.). Bauxite grading to 62% aluminum oxide is being mined in the Manica area. This region also has gold.

Pegmatites (q.v.) with beryl, columbite, and tantalite are found in the Tete and Zambesia. Some of the carbonatites (q.v.) have characteristic ring structures. There are three major ones in the Tete District which appear to be related to the Chilwa Series and the Mlanje Mountains (q.v.) of Malawi. They are mineralized with pyrochlore (q.v.), apatite, and iron ore.

In addition to the Zambezi and Limpopo, a number of rivers drain the interior to the Indian Ocean. The Zambezi virtually divides the country. To the south are the Mozambique Plains. The Kariba Dam (q.v.) on the Zambezi affects deposition on the plain and in the delta.

MUD   A mixture of clay, silt, and water yields mud. The particle size of the material is less than 0.6 millimeters. Deep sea muds are both silicious and non-silicious (calcareous, phosphatic). See **DIATOMS**.

Calcareous muds cover nearly half the deep sea floor to a depth of 4,500 meters (14,700 feet). They accumulate at the rate of 1-4 centimeters (0.4-1.6 inches) per 1,000 years.

Phosphatic muds are rare in the deep sea, but are found on some submarine ridges and banks (e.g. Deposits on Blake Plateau).

MUD CRACKS   Subaerial evaporation, especially in playas (q.v.) can result in a shrinkage and cracking of muds into polygonal patterns. When the floods retreat the muds dry and the cracks appear.

Cracking is characteristic of clays that are alternately wet and dry. Where they occur on floodplains, these cracks can be very deep. Some along the Nile in Sudan are up to 3 meters (10 feet) deep. Cracks are not so pronounced on tidal flats because the drying interval is so short.

MUD VOLCANO A mud volcano will create a cone by the force of escaping gases. Some gases become solids almost immediately and add to the debris forming the cone. Steam and natural gas are the main agents.

In Baku, USSR, there are many mud volcanoes, some up to 75 meters (250 feet) high. Northern California has mud volcanoes in its geyser (q.v.) area.

MUDFLATS Mudflats are the exposed floor of a bay or inlet at low-tide. The clay and silt sediments are beyond the sand line. Usually the flats are only partly exposed. Mudflats are the habitat of many small crustaceans (q.v.).

MUDFLOWS Landslides and large debris flows can be lubricated by rain and flood waters. Mudflows occur on desert mountain slopes with flash-flooding, or unusually heavy rains. Some flows can be dangerously large. The distance over which material flows can be very great. At Wrightwood, California, mud flowed on a 10-15% gradient over 5 kilometers (3 miles) doing considerable damage.

Eruptions covered Vesuvius with layers of ash, lava, and pumice. These were transformed into mudflows by rains. Mudflows buried Herculaneum in 79 A.D.

MUIR SEAMOUNT The Muir Seamount is 230 kilometers (140 miles) north of Bermuda. It is perched atop the Bermuda Rise. The seamount summit is 1,500 meters (5,000 feet) below the sea surface. It rises 3,000 meters (10,000 feet) from the ocean floor. Soundings indicate that it is 100 by 58 kilometers (60 x 35 miles).

MURRAY RIVER Australia's only big river is the Murray. It flows from the Australian Alps and traces an arc to reach the sea near Adelaide in the southeast. Its course is 2,700 kilometers (1,600 miles) long.

Murray tributaries also rise in the Alps. A large, shallow lake, Alexandrina, is at the mouth of the Murray. The river is controlled and is primarily used for irrigation.

MUSCOVITE Muscovite is a potash mica. It is also known as white mica. Muscovite is an hydrated silicate of potassium found in many Precambrian pegmatites. Muscovite weathers to sericite. See **MICA**.

The main producers of muscovite are India, Brazil, and Malagasy. The United States imports its sheet mica needs.

Economic deposits of muscovite are the source of sheet mica. Sheet mica is the isinglass that was used for windows in early motor vehicles. Most mica is now used in electronics.

MUSKEG A muskeg is a poorly drained bog, marsh, or swamp due to permafrost (q.v.) in the subsoil. 'Muskeg' is Cree Indian for swamp. The term is commonly used where such wetlands are found in north central United States, Canada, and Alaska.

The Muskeg has a distinct ecosystem in Taiga or Tundra belts. Rare trees are fir or tamarack. The permafrost prevents snowmelt drainage and water builds up in the surface layers. Moss accumulates so the soil becomes a spongy black. In some areas, this layer is so thick it will support vehicular transport. Frost heaves cause a hummocky terrain.

MUSSEL WATCH The mussel, a bivalve mollusk, is a filter-feeder, taking in and giving off great quantities of water in the process of aquiring food.

Due to pollution in coastal waters, it has been necessary to create a 'Mussel Watch'. Mussels are collected and tested. Pollutant may be hydrocarbons, including DDT, metals, or radioactive matter but are not limited to these. When toxic levels are found in the mussel population, harvesting is banned. Mussel Watch is now a worldwide program.

MUTATION Permanent genetic change from the parent is mutation. It is a change that can be transmitted by genes to future generations. Mutation is an important process in the evolution of organisms.

MUTUALISM Mutualism is a symbiotic (q.v.) relationship between 2 unlike organisms in which both benefit.

A striking case of mutualism is that of the ant and the aphid. Ants care for aphid larvae in the ant nests and transfer the young to plants. Aphids in turn supply a liquid for the ant.

Lichen (q.v.) are involved in an extreme case of mutualism. Algae and Fungi complement each other to the extent of creating a virtually new biological system called Lichen.

MYLODON LISTAI Fossils of the giant sloth (Mylodon listai) were found in an ice cave on the coast of Hope Sound, Chile. It was encased in Early Cretaceous (138-135 m.y.) sediments. The claws, bones, and even sinew were intact. Mylodon belongs to Edentata, a toothless mammal.

The sloth habitat today is tropical and subtropical.

MYLONITE 'Mylonite' is from the Greek for milling or grinding. It is a name given a metamorphic rock (q.v.) that has literally been milled by tectonic activity and then reconsolidated. Mylonite fragments are microscopic and angular. The mineral has a glassy texture and resembles obsidian.

N

LAKE NAIVASHA Lake Naivasha, Kenya, occupies a basin in the Eastern Rift Valley. At an elevation of 1,820 meters (6,100 feet), the lake perches on a flank of Longonot Volcano. The Mau Escarpment, one of the major walls of the Great Rift, is on the west. Kinanpop Plateau is to the east.

Lake Naivasha was created by lava which dammed a stream. The lake was once much larger and had an outlet at Hell's Gate. This has since been blocked by volcanic debris.

NAMIB DESERT What is believed to be the oldest of the world's deserts is the Namib of South Africa. It extends inland from for a maximum of 160 kilometers (100 miles). It is 2,080 kilometers (1,300 miles) along the Atlantic Coast from Angola to the Orange River, which is the only through-flowing river in this part of Africa. The desert is divided by the Kuiseb River which intermittently flows into Walvis Bay.

Namib is a west coast desert affected by an oceanic Eastern Boundary Region (q.v.). It is a more extreme desert than Kalahari to the east. It is one of the driest places in the world.

South of the Kuiseb River, there is a sand sea of parallel dunes with alleys or troughs between. The dunes extend well inland from the sea. They are the world's highest dunes up to 300 meters (1,000 feet).

North of the Kuiseb River are the barren rock plains of the Namib. This is the habitat of the very rare 'Welwitchia mirabilis'. It survives in this hostile environment because of its root system which is up to 3 meters (6.5 feet) and the moisture produced by the fog. It can live 1,000 years on fog moisture taken in through broad absorbent leaves.

The fog is produced when an airmass cooled by the Benguela Current encounters warm air over the land. Fog effects are felt inland for 30 kilometers (20 miles). See **NAMIBIA**

NAMIBIA Namibia on the west coast of South Africa is where 2 great Precambrian shields (q.v.) collided to form Gondwana (q.v.). The rift belt or suture line crosses central Namibia. The cratons drifted apart and were rewelded 700 million years ago.

The higher Congo Shield over-rode the southern shield and the Khomas Hochland Overlap formed. Collision upthrust the mountains. The highest peak, Naukluft, has been eroding for millions of years. In southern Namibia, spectacular gorges cut the range.

The southern and eastern part of the country are in the Kalahari Basin. Karroo Sediments (q.v.) cover this area and virtually all of the rest of southern Africa.

Strong winds blowing from the land create the upwelling (q.v.) in the offshore ocean waters. This is one of the world's great fishing grounds.

The area is famous for hosting the world's greatest placer deposit of gem diamonds. These are found in ancient gravels. The diamonds were travelers from Kimberley via the Orange River. The longshore currents deposited them near Walvis Bay. They were later covered by the sands. This is the same source for the diamonds sought by the famous deep-sea dredging operations in Walvis Bay. Gold and diamonds have been worked in the Orange River Basin.

The other major mineral is uranium. It is associated with alaskites (coarse-grained granitic rocks). These intrude the Damara and Nosib Supergroups. Uranium production began in 1977 at Rossing. In addition to this uraninite, uranium is produced from the Langer-Heinrich deposit of calcretes. See **CALCRETES**.

NANNOPLANKTON Nannoplankton are phyto- or zooplankton that are less than 50 microns in diameter. The organisms are confined mostly to oceanic depths where light can penetrate. Nannoplankton account for a great deal of the carbon fixation in the oceans.

Nannoplankton are found in the open ocean where other nutrients are scarce and they are food for filter-feeding whales. More inshore, the organisms are an important food source for small protozoans, larvae of shellfish, and for small fish.

Since nannoplankton have a large surface-to-mass ratio, they need only dilute concentrations of food. See **PLANKTON**.

NANSEN BOTTLE The Nansen bottle is a sampler specially constructed to collect seawater at a particular level. This is achieved by special valves. It is also equipped with temperature gauges.

NAPPE A nappe is a large tongue of rock with only a slight angular displacement which has been transported over a great distance. Many mountain ranges have numerous nappes. The Andes exhibit many.

NARROWS When a river channel is constricted by rock formations and stream width is greatly reduced a narrows results. There are many narrows on the world's great rivers.

On the Amazon there is a narrows at Obidos where the mighty river is only 2 kilometers (1.5 miles) wide. At Kazun, the Danube is only 148 meters (488 feet) wide. On the Rhine, a narrows is so small, one may leap across. As the river flows through the narrows, there may or may not be rapids.

LAKE NASSER Lake Nasser, the reservoir behind Aswan Dam, is in Nubia, on the border between Egypt and Sudan. The 500 kilometer (310 mile) lake is 105 meters (347 feet) deep, 500 kilometers (310 miles) long, and covers 6,000 square kilometers (2,200 square miles).

With the advent of the Jonglei Canal (q.v.) in Southern Sudan, Lake Nasser is expected to have an overflow which will be taken off to Western Egypt by the Toskha Canal. This presupposes that lake inflow will be sufficient to offset the enormous present evaporation. The present lake level is well below that projected.

With water from Lake Nasser, 6.5 million feddans (2.73 million hectares) of farmland have been added to Egypt, mostly in New Valley, west of the Nile. See **ASWAN DAM**.

NATROLITE Natrolite is a hydrous sodium aluminum silicate of the Zeolite Group (q.v.). It is a fibrous, acicular (q.v.) mineral formed by a framework of linked silica tetrahedra.

LAKE NATRON Lake Natron, Tanzania, in the East African Rift Valley is replenished by hot springs containing sodium salts. The sodium carbonate is in balance. Like the brines of Lake Magadi, Kenya, it is a source of soda ash.

Natron is located in the Eastern Rift. It is in the Carbonatite Belt containing Oldoinyo Lengai (q.v.). See **CARBONATITE**.

NATURAL GAS Natural gas is the name for a group of gaseous hydrocarbons. Methane, one of these, can be produced from a biomass (q.v.) as well as from sediments and coal seams.

Natural gas, until very recently, was flared off from most oilfields. Today, it is a prized energy resource and is transported by pipeline. Of the world's reserves of 3,200 trillion cubic feet, the major holders (in trillions of cubic feet) are:

USSR	1,400.0
Iran	480.0
United States	198.0
Saudi Arabia	125.0
Algeria	110.0
Canada	91.0
Mexico	75.0
Qatar	62.0
Norway	59.0
Venezuela	55.0
Netherlands	50.0
Malaysia	48.0
Kuwait	35.0
Nigeria	35.0
Arab Emirates	31.0
China	30.0
Indonesia	30.0
Iraq	29.0
United Kingdom	25.0
Argentina	24.0
Libya	21.0
Australia	18.0
Eastern Europe	17.0

U.S. Bureau of Mines, 1984; Cuff & Young, 1986

The geopolitical distribution of natural gas (in trillions of cubic feet) is:

East Europe & Siberia	1,417.0
Middle East	774.0
North America	364.0
Africa	190.0
Asia	163.0
Western Europe	158.0
Central & So. America	110.0
Australia & New Zealand	24.0

Butane and propane are liquified petroleum gas (LPG), and are produced from wet gas or gas not obtained under its own pressure. Ethane is a by-product. With LPG, the use of natural gas in transportation could increase from the present 3%.

In addition to the natural gas in petroleum fields, the United States has natural gas reserves locked up in shales and sandstones. These represent almost a 200-year supply.

To produce the same heat, more volume of gas is required than oil but where available, natural gas is cheaper. 80% of the production is used for heating and industry. Electricity is more costly from natural gas as the energy must be transformed. Today, electricity use is only 13% of production. In millions of tons of oil equivalent, the production and consumption in 1982 was:

	Production	Consumption
United States	478	498
Siberia	348	308
Western Europe	169	185
Canada	62	49
Indonesia	47	14
Eastern Europe	45	61
South America	29	44
China	12	66

NATURAL RADIATION   Earth has a natural background radiation from its own internal supply of radioactive materials. Surface rocks and therefore radiation vary from place to place. An average dosage at sea level is .03 Rems (q.v.) per day.

NATURAL SELECTION   Natural Selection is a law of evolution. It states that only the more favorably endowed lifeforms survive. These are the most suited to their ecological niche. Over time, whole populations may disappear because of an inability to adapt as conditions change.

If natural selection is valid, species breed for the most adaptable traits for their particular environments.

NAUTICAL MILE   The knot, or nautical mile, is approximately 6,076 feet. It is also 1 minute of arc of a great circle, or 1/60th of a degree on the globe. It is a minute of latitude at the Equator. The official nautical or seamile was set in 1954 at 1,852 meters (6,076.10333 feet). The Admiralty Mile of the British is 6,080 feet.

NEAP TIDE Neap tide occurs near the time of the quarter-moon. The pull of gravity is less when the Moon is at right angles to the Earth or in quarter-moon position. Neap tides are 10-30% less than normal.

NEBULA Named for mist in Latin, 'nebula' is a dust or gas cloud in Space. It forms from the dust and gases of dying stars. It begins as an ionized ring of gases around the star. In the Milky Way (q.v.), there are 700 identified nebulae.

Nebulae can be seen by telescope. Some mirror light from stars, others are bright from light emissions caused by high-speed particle collisions. Some are bright from absorbing ultra-violet light. Their emitted energy is visible in different colors resulting in the ring nebulae. Many, however, are dark. Some are clusters of stars, others are just gaseous clouds.

Crab Nebula, resulted from a supernova explosion in 1054. Chinese astronomers noted that event. Another supernova occurred in 1572. The event was so bright it was observable in daylight. Andromeda Nebula was described in the 10th Century by Al Sufi, the Persian astrologer.

NECK A volcanic neck is a conduit for lava. In some volcanoes lava solidifies in the chimney and is surrounded by a volcanic cone. Cone material is softer than cooled lava and may be eroded away revealing the 'plumbing'. Volcanic necks are found throughout southwestern United States. Ship Rock, New Mexico is an example.

NEEDLELEAF FOREST Needleleaf forests are made up of evergreen conifers. Their needles are leaves adapted to dry and cold conditions. Needleleaf forests are found in the Sub-Arctic. They form a wide Taiga Belt that abuts the Tundra (q.v.).

Needleleaf forests are also found on mountains at elevations with Sub-Arctic climate. In the Pacific Coast Range of the United States are the most extensive large conifers of good quality timber. These include the redwoods.

NEEDLE ICE Needle ice, or 'pipkrake', is composed of clear, thin ice crystals. It grows in bare soil. The needle-like crystals result from overnight frost where soil moisture is sufficient and the soil has a fine-grained texture.

NEFTA OASIS In western Tunisia, 400 kilometers (250 miles) from Tunis is a spring-fed artesian (q.v.) basin. It supports the productive oasis of Nefta. This was the oasis that Noah's grandson, Kostel, is supposed to have discovered. The Oasis is north and west of Djerid Chott (q.v.) and reputedly has 150 springs. The area has 350,000 date palms and other fruit trees.

NEFUD DESERT The northern Arabian Nefud Desert is 670 by 330 kilometers (400 by 200 miles) in area. It is considered one of the most beautiful deserts due to spectacular displays of reds at dawn and dusk.

NEGEV DESERT The Negev Desert of Israel stretches from the Dead Sea almost to the Mediterranean. It is bounded on the east by Wadi Araba which like the Dead Sea is an extension of the Great Rift System of East Africa. Negev is bounded by Sinai (q.v.) on the west. Like Sinai, Negev comes almost to a point in the south.

The Negev is a region greatly dissected by wadis that trend northeast-southwest. It is also marked by parallel folds and in the north by rolling hills.

In Negev, agriculture as practiced by the Israelis has been likened to that of Arizona. Like Arizona the major problems of irrigated agriculture are present. These include tenuous water supply, soil salinity, and silting channels. Annual precipitation is 305 millimeters (12 inches) slightly more than in Arizona. The Israelis have also been capturing the dew (q.v.), a labor intensive practice.

RIO NEGRO The Brazilian Rio Negro is a major Amazon tributary with headwaters in Venezuela and Colombia. Rio Branco draining the Guiana Highlands joins Rio Negro at Cavoeira. Rio del Diablo, another tributary, drains black orchid country. The river is called 'black' because of its high organic content.

Rio Negro is linked via the Casiquiari River to the Orinoco System. This connection, found by Von Humboldt in 1804, may have been used earlier by Orellano.

The volume of Rio Negro is greater than any other river except the Amazon. At high-water its volume exceeds that of the Amazon. The Negro attains 16 kilometers (10 miles) wide in some reaches. It can be up to 100 meters (330 feet) deep. It drowns the forest in many places. Stagnant lakes and 'igarapes' (q.v.) form.

Rio Negro flows into the Solimoes (Upper Amazon) just below Manaus. The waters do not readily mix and the streams can be distinguished by color for some distance from the confluence.

The Rio Negro Basin in Roraima is opening up to exploration and development. This is creating many ecological problems in addition to the over-harvesting of orchids which has been going on for decades.

NEKTON Nekton are marine organisms distinguishable from plankton because they have a locomotion capability. They are near-surface, free-swimming, diminutive lifeforms. Nekton are found in lacustrine as well as marine environments. See **PLANKTON**.

NEOGENE Miocene and Pliocene, 2 Tertiary Epochs, make up the Neogene. It is a time horizon more used in Europe than in Canada and the United States.

NEOLITHIC Neolithic is a subdivision of the Quaternary Period. It corresponds in prehistory to the Polished Stone Age of human culture.

NEON Neon has been called an inert or noble gas. When an electrical current is passed through a neon chamber, it glows orange-red. The gas is not really inert and is capable of reaction. Its chief use is in lighting.

NEOPILINA GALATHEA The oldest living fossil, 'Neopilina galathea', is a small mollusk with origins in the Cambrian (550 million years ago). It has an almost transparent, conically-shaped shell of nacre or mother-of-pearl.

'Neopilina' was dredged by a Danish research vessel off the Pacific Coast of Central America from 3,570 meters (11,778 feet). Other specimens have since been found, all from very deep waters.

NEPA The National Environmental Policy Act (NEPA) of 1970 makes an Environmental Impact Statement (EIS) mandatory. One is required for every project that might affect the environment in any way.

The responsible agency is the one most closely involved. For forestry and mining, it is the Bureau of Land Management. The statement format is set and public hearings are mandatory.

NEPHELINE Colorless nepheline, a silicate of aluminum and sodium, is related to the feldspathoids and similar to albite and potash feldspar. It contains less silica.

NEPHELINE SYENITE Nepheline syenite, an igneous rock, is similar to coarse granite. It contains nepheline, a sodium aluminum silicate, usually in small crystals. Albite and potash feldspar are present instead of the quartz and orthoclase of granite. It is darkened by augite and other ferromagnesium minerals.

Nepheline syenite usually occurs as small masses. These contain elements sometimes concentrated to 5-10 times their usual crustal abundance. Phonolite (q.v.) is the extrusive equivalent of nepheline syenite. Both rocks are associated with carbonatites (q.v.).

There are well-known deposits of nepheline syenite in Ontario, Canada. The largest single mass is at Blue Mountain. It is presently being mined for use in glass and ceramics. See **SYENITE**.

NEPHRITE Nephrite, a member of the Amphibole Group is an important variety of jade. It is often confused with jadeite, a pyroxene. Among the Aztecs of Mexico both nephrite and jadeite were highly valued.

Chinese jade is also of both nephrite and jadeite. The nephrite is usually used for carvings.

NEPTUNE The 8th of the 9 planets orbiting the Sun in the plane of the ecliptic is Neptune. It is considered a Jovian Planet with 57 times the volume of the Earth. A day on Neptune is 18 hours long and its orbit about the Sun takes 165 years.

The Voyager II flew by the planet in 1989 and sent back enormous amounts of data that will take some time to be evaluated. One of the predictions had been that there would be rings about the planet. There proved to be 8 and appear to be 6 moonlets. The methane ice clouds noted by Voyager I were confirmed. The data also showed the planet to be subject to enormous storms.

NERITIC Relatively coarse continental sediments accumulate in the seas near shore. These are neritic or shallow sea sediments. The Neritic Zone extends from the intertidal area to 200 meters (600 feet) of depth or 100 fathoms.

NEUTRINO A neutrino is an elementary or subatomic particle. The major emission energy of supernovas is in the form of neutrinos. Supernova 1987A gave off 10^{58} neutrinos in a matter of seconds. (Burrows, University of Arizona).

Cosmic ray neutrinos penetrate to the Earth. Moving at the speed of light, billions of neutrinos per second pass through anything in their path.

NEUTRON A neutron is an uncharged elemental particle slightly larger than a proton. They are in all elements except hydrogen. Free neutrons, those outside the atom, are unstable and decay in 13 minutes to an electron, a proton, and a neutrino.

Neutrons sustain fission in nuclear reactors. The energy of a neutron is 939.6 MeV (million electron volts). It has no charge.

NEUTRON STAR A neutron star is a collapsed star packed with neutrons. It may be as much as 32 kilometers across (20 miles). It will have, because of its density, a weight 2.5 times greater than the Sun

NEVADA DEL RUIZ Columbia's most dangerous volcano, Nevada del Ruiz, has destroyed many Andean villages in its history. In the 1985 eruption, the ice cap melted to create a 40 meter (130 foot) long wall of water, ash, mud, and rock. The waves that struck Armero were 3 meters (10 feet) high. That disaster took 26,000 lives and left 60,000 homeless. Nevada del Ruiz erupted again 1989.

NEVE Transitional material between snow and ice in the development of a glacier is neve. It is characterized by compaction due to the recrystallization of snow to icicles. It takes 8 meters of snow to form 1 meter of neve.

NEW GUINEA New Guinea and Irian Java, Indonesia, share an island separated from Australia by Torres Strait. The island was divided among the British, Dutch, and Germans until the end of World War I when New Guinea became an Australian protectorate.

Parts of New Guinea are inhabited by Stone Age and cannibalistic tribes. The main attraction to outsiders is gold.

New Guinea is famous for the tree kangaroo who spends most of its life in the rainforest canopy. The kangaroo can jump to the forest floor from a height as great as 18 meters (60 feet).

NEW MADRID EARTHQUAKE The largest recorded earthquake in the continental United States, occurred in Missouri in 1811-12. It began December 16th with a series of quakes felt in Boston, Detroit, and New Orleans. The severest was February 17, 1812.

The quake affected millions of square miles. There was areal subsidence, the bottomland sank 3-4.5 meters (10-15 feet). New lakes like 34 kilometer (20-mile) Reelfoot in Tennessee were formed. There were a total of 2,000 shocks recorded by a scientist in Louisville. The quake itself was so severe, folklore says the Mississippi flowed backward for 24 hours.

The river's east bank was lowered while the west rose. River banks caved in and if both caved simultaneously, it caused the river to back up.

The earthquake was caused by movement on the New Madrid Fault. The fault extends from Vincennes, Indiana through and beyond New Madrid, Missouri. It terminates in the east in west-trending faults along the south boundary of the Kentucky Coal Basin.

New Madrid Fault may be part of a greater structural break in the craton that extends northeast to the St. Lawrence River Valley. The epicenter (q.v.) of New Madrid, was above a wide, ancient graben (q.v.), which may have been a Precambrian spreading zone. Rifting occurred there between 700 and 500 million years ago. This Precambrian rift appears similar to the East African Rift. The rift is now covered by 5 kilometers (15,840 feet) of sediments.

The latest recorded activity on New Madrid was in 1968 when a quake of 5.5 was registered.

NEW ZEALAND New Zealand formed along part of the Global Rift System (q.v.). The Great Alpine Fault, an active transform fault, is a surface expression of the Global Rift. The earthquakes are infrequent but they are usually severe. The Fault extends from Marlborough through Wellington to the Bay of Plenty. The 1931 Hawkes Bay Earthquake was 7.8 on the Richter and resulted in the creation of 4,000 hectares (8,800 acres) of new land.

Rotorua District, an area of active volcanism, has many geysers and hot springs. Geothermal energy from subterranean steam is tapped by wells just as it is in Iceland (q.v.).

South Island like Chile, Norway, and Alaska is fjorded. These fjords indicate a past climate with ice at sea level. Milford Sound with its U-shaped valley is such a fjord (q.v.).

Almost 1/3 of New Zealand has been deforested to make way for pasture with the introduction of sheep. The soils have evolved from the weathering of sandstone, greywacke (q.v.), volcanic ash, and wind-blown sands. They are leached and acidic and deficient in cobalt.

LAKE NGAMI Lake Ngami in northwest Botswana, Africa, has shrunk from an inland sea to a marsh during the past 10,000 years. Dr. Livingston crossed the Kalahari Desert (q.v.) to reach this lake.

NGORONGORO CRATER The largest caldera (q.v.) in Africa, Ngorongora, Tanzania, is in the Rift Valley southwest of Kilimanjaro. It is almost round with a diameter of 20 kilometers (12 miles). The caldera is 600 meters (2,200 feet) from ridge to floor.

There is a game preserve on the crater floor called 'Africa's Garden of Eden'. It is a grassy plain with small lakes and marshes. Thousands of animals including eland, elephant, lion, rhino, water buffalo, and zebra occupy the area.

NIAGARA FALLS Niagara Falls between New York and Canada divides into American and Horseshoe Falls. On the Niagara River, the falls are about 50 meters (160 feet) high. The slightly higher Horseshoe Falls is separated from American Falls by Goat Island.

Niagara Gorge where the falls empty is not stream-cut, but cut by headward erosion of the Niagara River. The escarpment has moved upstream 10 kilometers at about a meter (3.5 feet) per year.

LAKE NICARAGUA Lake Nicaragua, or 'Mar Dulce' as the Spanish named it, is the largest lake in Central America. It is dotted with islands, the most important of which is dominated by twin volcanic peaks, Ometepe and Concepcion.

Lake Nicaragua probably was once a bay in the Pacific Ocean. The bay was dammed by lava flows and the lake was created.

A proposed alternative to the Panama Canal traces a route across Central America through Lake Nicaragua. See **PANAMA CANAL**.

NICHE A plant or animal community (q.v.) within an ecosystem has a special place, or niche. The same niche may be occupied by more than one community, but only symbiotically (q.v.), for any period of time.

If more species try to occupy a niche, they compete, causing one or more to die out. Humanity through technology has greatly broadened its niche. This has often been at the expense of other species.

On a plain like Serengeti in East Africa, each herd has its special niche. Giraffes feed on tree foliage, rhinos on brush, and wildebeest on special grasses. When red oats grass is short and fresh, wildebeest graze. When the grass is older but still moist, the zebra graze, and, finally, when it is dry, the topis eat it.

NICKEL Silver-gray nickel metal is used in various alloys and for plating. A main ore is pyrrhotite, a magnetic pyrite and sulfide of iron and nickel. Pentlandite, an economic iron-nickel sulfide, is rare. It is found associated with chalcopyrite in igneous rocks. Nickel is associated with manganese nodules (q.v.) on the seafloor. These nodules are particularly abundant in the Pacific.

Pentlandite with pyrrhotite make the Sudbury, Ontario, deposits economically viable. Sudbury's intrusion is probably a lopolith (q.v.), if it is not a meteoritic impact structure.

Nickel is also mined from the lateritic ore, garnierite. It is an earthy hydrous mineral that runs between 15-33% nickel. Cobalt is often associated as in Tocantins, Goias, Brazil. Garnierite is a weathering product of olivine-rich igneous rocks (peridotites). It is estimated that 80% of the world's nickel reserves are in laterites.

Many deposits are under development but delayed due to high costs and market conditions. Capital cost to produce a pound of lateritic nickel was about $17 per pound (1981) based on 100 million pounds of nickel matte.

The world's major nickel producers are Canada and the USSR, then Australia and New Caledonia. The United States produced 14,540 short tons in 1984 but by 1986 production was only 1,000 short tons. This production was from the laterite deposit in Oregon.

The major portion of the estimated 130 million metric tons of nickel reserves in the world are held (in thousands of metric tons) by:

Cuba	18,140
Canada	8,130
USSR	6,600
Brazil*	6,000
New Caledonia	4,540
Indonesia	3,200
South Africa	2,540
China**	730
Greece	450

U.S. Bureau of Mines, 1990
* Brazil's reserves (DNPM, 1988)
** China's reserves put at 22,000 by some authorities

Reserves are that portion of the Reserve base that can be economically produced under present conditions.

NIGER Niger is a land-locked country in West Africa in the transition zone between the Sahara and the savanna. The Niger River (q.v.) crosses its southwest corner. The land is increasingly arid north and east of the river. The Ahoggar Range of Algeria extends into Niger, where it becomes the Air Massif.

Once part of Gondwana (q.v.), the crystalline basement in the south-west disappears east of the Niger River beneath younger sandstones that form a plateau dipping toward Lake Chad (q.v.).

Uranium was discovered in 1966 in the Arlit Region and has been in production since. A number of other deposits have since been found. Reserves in 1975 were 40,000 metric tons of $15.00 ore.

NIGER RIVER   The Niger River rises in the Gambia mountains of Fouta Djallon near the Sierra Leone border and only 240 kilometers (150 miles) from the Atlantic Ocean. The Niger flows east then south near Timbuktu and southwest at Gao.

In Mali the Niger skirts the Sahara and on a southeast course crosses Niger and Nigeria to the confluence of the Benue 400 kilometers (250 miles) upstream of the Atlantic. The river then runs south to its delta on the Gulf of Guinea.

The Niger is Africa's 3rd longest river. Its course is 4,330 kilometers (2,600 miles) and the river drains relatively flat country except for the Air Mountains Uranium District. Drainage from the Ahoggar Mountains is almost extinct. The Niger flows 2,000 kilometers (1,200 miles) through desert before being joined by the Sokoto from the Nigerian Highlands.

One of the most important features of the Niger is its inland delta south of Timbuktu. The river flows very slowly through the ancient delta which covers 77,700 square kilometers (30,000 square miles) and provides Mali with a much needed oasis.

The Niger empties into the Gulf of Guinea via many distributaries within its wide delta, larger than that of the Nile. The Delta is enclosed by a great semi-circle of mangrove swamps.

The river discharges 5,420 cubic meters per second into the ocean and its sediment load is 2.62 million cubic meters of sand and silt.

NIGERIA   The Lower Niger Basin is occupied by Nigeria. It is divided into 2 provinces, one above the confluence of the Niger and Benue and the other south to the Atlantic.

The country is divided north and south by cultural differences of religion and tradition. Population has a greater concentration in the more humid south. As a result, pressure on the land there is great and serious soil erosion exists due to the shortening of fallow time and overgrazing by livestock.

The coastal plain is dominated by the swamps of the Niger Delta. Inland is a region of high plains culminating in the Udi Plateau. The crystalline basement rocks are covered by Cretaceous (q.v.) to Tertiary sediments in the Niger-Benue Basin.

To the north of the Basin is the crystalline Jos Plateau. Jos rises to 1,200 meters (4,000 feet). It is most noted for its tin granites but it also hosts gold deposits. This Plateau descends in steps to the Chad Basin.

Volcanics are found in the southeast corner where the country reaches to Mount Cameroon (q.v.).

In addition to its tin production, Nigeria is producing oil and gas. The petroleum has accelerated the industrial growth of the country. The Imo River gas field supplies energy via a pipeline to the industrial city of Aba.

NILE DELTA The Nile is the most legendary of all the world's deltas. From satellite imagery, the Nile Delta shows its remarkable shape noted by Herdotus in the 5th Century B.C.

The Nile River has created a long, narrow oasis in the Sahara. In northern Sudan and Upper Egypt it is rarely more than 25 kilometers (15 miles) wide. The strip extends to the delta at Alexandria. There, the Nile branches into many distributaries. Delta flank depressions (q.v.) set off the Delta with bays.

For centuries Egyptians have farmed rich delta soils. Silts were almost all from the Blue Nile and organic material from the Sudd (q.v.) was brought in by the White Nile. Delta sediment build-up was an annual 3.5 meters (12 feet) before the dams were created.

Skylab photographs show the drying up of some 3,800 square kilometers (1,500 square miles) of Delta. Mediterranean marine life also has deserted the area due to the loss of nutrients.

NILE RIVER The Blue Nile rises in the Ethiopian Highlands in the headwaters of the Abay Creek to Lake Tana. The Blue Nile flows through Ethiopia and Sudan to its confluence with the White Nile at Khartoum. Together the rivers form the great Nile. The Nile is one of the world's longest at 6,908 kilometers (4,145 miles).

The White, or Albert Nile River, rises in the Great Rift Valley lakes. Leaving Lake Victoria (q.v.), the Upper Nile flows north through Uganda, Sudan, and Egypt. In Sudan, it flows through the greatest wetland in the world, the Sudd (q.v.). The Sobat, Bahr el Ghazal, Bahr el Jebel, and Jeraf rivers join the Nile in the Sudd. After Malakal, Sudan, no further tributaries feed the White Nile.

North of the confluence at Khartoum, the Atbara is the only tributary to join the Nile. It rises in the Ethiopian Highlands.

After the confluence with the Atbara, the Nile crosses 2,700 kilometers (1,200 miles) of Sahara. The river is totally exotic to Egypt and only waters 4% of that country.

Between Khartoum and Aswan, there are 6 rapids, the famous Nile Cataracts. At these rapids, the river cuts through the Nubian Sandstone to the crystalline basement rock.

The water contributed from the rift lakes is only 20% of the flow in the lower Nile. Opening of the Jonglei Canal (q.v.) is expected to augment it considerably. At present, the Atbara and Blue Nile provide 80% to the Lower Nile.

The Nile System began in the Early-Tertiary (54-37 m.y.) and has undergone many changes and captures due to climate and tectonics. In Late-Pleistocene (q.v.) the river was dammed in a lake but later broke open to the north through Sabaloka Gorge to the 6th Cataract. Sediment and elevations show there were 2 Pleistocene lakes of similar size 500-600 kilometers (300-360 miles) long by 30-40 kilometers (18-24 miles) wide between Malakal and Khartoum. See **JONGLEI CANAL** and **JONGLEI INVESTIGATIONS**.

NIMBOSTRATUS Heavy, gray nimbostratus clouds hang low in the sky. These clouds bring steady rains or snows.

NINETY-EAST RIDGE An extraordinarily linear mountain range has been discovered in the Indian Ocean. It rises from the basin floor to 3,600 meters (12,000 feet) and extends for 4,300 kilometers (2,600 miles). This range is still not completely surveyed but its linearity poses questions.

EL NIÑO A warm, south-flowing current in the Pacific off Peru merges with the Humboldt or Peru Current just below the Equator. Every 10-12 years (and more frequently in recent times) the warmer current comes inshore displacing colder water and pushing it out to sea.

The current shift occurs around Christmas, thus the name, 'El Niño' for the winds accompanying the shift. These winds bring Peru and Ecuador torrential rains during an El Niño event causing landslides and mudflows which cost a high toll in lives. The deserts have received up to 3½ meters (12 feet) of rain.

The sudden rise in seawater temperature results in enormous fish-kills. Hydrogen sulfide from decomposing fish stains ships. This phenomenon is called 'The Painter' in Ecuador.

In 1982 there were abnormally high temperatures in the waters from Chile to the Gulf of Alaska. The high temperatures extended west as far as the International Dateline. (q.v.). The dramatic shifts caused by El Niño were responsible for 1,000 lives and $8 billion dollars in damage in 1982-83. The phenomenon appears to be occurring more frequently than prior to 1945. There have been 8 significant El Niños since then. Most have been milder than the 1982-83 event. The worst for California before 1982 was 1976-77 when the drought was severe and the winter bitterly cold.

The El Niño is considered by meteorologists and oceanographers as the greatest weather phenomenon on Earth. Its periodicity is not wholly predictable and the worldwide havoc it creates is extraordinary. Ecological disruption is massive with these events. Changes occur within the California Current as they do in the Peru. Sudden temperature changes bring about red tide (q.v.) and fish kill. In 1982-83 waves were 12 meters (40 feet) high and did a great deal of damage along the coast. The presence of warm waters as far north as Washington during the period created great weather shifts that were continent-wide.

El Niño's story begins far from the American coasts and is related to wind shifts. Winds blow toward the semi-permanent Low that extends from Indonesia to Darwin, Australia. The shift may be hundreds or thousands of kilometers. Normally, the tropical Trade Winds create a semi-permanent High Pressure in the Southeast Pacific. Barometric pressures rise in the Southeast Asia Low Pressure Area and many changes occur, including drought in Northern Australia.

An unusual wind from the Equator to the Tasman Sea is warmed by the South Pacific Ocean. It is a southerly jet stream known as the Southern Oscillation (ENSO). This jet stream appeared before the 1957, 1965, and 1972 El Niño events. It is conjectured that it triggers El Niño conditions.

Changes in the sea are slower than those in the Atmosphere. Seawater becomes warmer by as much as 14° Farenheit and the effect is global. In the ocean El Niño conditions are accompanied by internal waves (q.v.). These move across the Pacific at several meters per second to affect the American coasts 2 months later.

The El Niño of 1982 has been called the El Niño of the Century, so widespread were its effects. Scientists believe the El Niño warming offset to a great degree the effects of the eruption of El Chichon (q.v.), which might have been followed by a 'nuclear winter' as with other major eruptions. Volcanic dust that settled on the Pacific made it difficult to read temperature data and monitor El Niño.

El Niño's usual pattern appeared to have been broken in 1982. The Trade Winds did not intensify, therefore the waters did not pile up, yet it was the strongest El Niño recorded. See **TAHITI-DARWIN LOW**.

NIOBIUM Niobium (Columbium) is a ductile, platinum-gray metallic element, associated with tantalum in pegmatites. The major ore is pyrochlore, abundant in some carbonatites (q.v.). The principal use of niobium is in ferro-niobium, a high-temperature alloy used in air- and spacecraft and in nuclear power plants.

The major portion of world production (85%) comes from Araxa, Brazil, another 7% from Catalao in Goias, Brazil. Except for minor pegmatite production, the rest is produced in Canada.

NITRATE Natural nitrate minerals are found in commercial deposits only in the Chilean desert. They are compounds of soda, oxygen, and nitrogen.

Deposits are in a 750 kilometer (450 mile) long strip in the Atacama Desert, of northern Chile, 66 kilometers (40 miles) inland.

Lack of rain has preserved surface deposits from erosion. They are found only in depressions adjacent to the coastal mountains, on pedestals, and on isolated islands.

The nitrates are in crustal layers up to 3 meters (10 feet) thick. The ore called 'caliche' is crushed and boiled in tanks, drained, and dried. Nitrates vary greatly in composition but average 17% sodium nitrate or 'Chile Saltpeter'. Iodine, which runs 1.2-1.5% is a by-product.

NITROGEN Nitrogen, a major atmospheric gas, is generated by lightning. 40 million tons a year of nitrous oxide are produced.

Certain plant bacteria pull nitrogen from the Atmosphere and deposit it in soils thus making it avaliable to the food chain. The bacteria transform the nitrogen into salts which plants can absorb. Bacteria (q.v.) are also important in decomposition of organic matter. In the decomposition process, nitrogen is given off and returned to the Atmosphere.

Nitrogen and hydrogen at high temperatures and pressures combine to form ammonia. Ammonia gas is used as a fertilizer.

There was an increase of 6 parts per billion of nitrogen in the Atmosphere between 1970 and 1980 raising it to 301 ppb (parts per billion). Increases in the nitrous oxide content of the Atmosphere could lead to warming and contribute to the Greenhouse Effect (q.v.). It could also cause a buildup of the Ozone Layer (q.v.).

50 million tons per year of nitrous oxide are being contributed to the Atmosphere, 20 million from the United States. Half this contribution is from automobile exhaust, diesel fuel, and jet aircraft.

Nitric Acid is used in fertilizers and explosives. Metals except gold and silver dissolve in nitric acid. If hydrochloric acid is also present even these will dissolve.

NITROGEN DIOXIDE Nitrogen Dioxide is a brown poisonous gas, a constituent of photochemical SMOG (q.v.). Temperature inversions (q.v.) limit its dilution in the Atmosphere. Nitrogen dioxide does not readily combine with water. When it does, toxic nitric acid, a compound of nitrogen and hydrogen, results. This is the cause of eye irritation from SMOG (q.v.). It is also damaging to the lungs.

NITROGEN FERTILIZER Nitrogen fixation to ammonia is 2nd only to the manufacture of sulfuric acid, which is the world's most important chemical industry. The ammonium ion is converted by bacteria to nitrate which can be absorbed by plants.

The most common plant additive is Urea which is 46% nitrogen. The next most important is ammonium nitrate which is 35% nitrogen.

Increasing use of nitrogen fertilizers has created a more nitrogen-rich sewage which may have long-term environmental consequences.

NIVATION Weathering and erosional processes caused by snow either directly or indirectly are nivation. Nivation acts in the glacial melt-phase.

NOBLE GASES The Noble Gases are helium, neon, argon, krypton, xenon, and radon. Once considered chemically unreactive, radon, krypton, and xenon do combine. The not so rare gases are now known as the Helium Group.

NOCTILUCENT CLOUDS Between latitudes 45-80° North and South special clouds glow with a silvery-blue light just after sunset. These clouds hover 10-20° above the horizon.

In the Northern Hemisphere, they are normally only visible in the western sky from May to mid-August. They have been observed from Portland, Oregon, to the tip of Greenland.

These clouds are unlike weather clouds, which are usually found between 300 to 3,000 meters (1,000 to 10,000 feet) of elevation. The noctilucent clouds are 80 kilometers (250,000 feet or 50 miles) into the Atmosphere. They are composed of ice coated dust particles from meteors and comets. The particles reflect sunlight and create the cloud effect.

After the meteor event in Siberia in 1908, noctilucent clouds appeared as waves. See **TUNGUSKA**.

NODE The node is the point of least vertical and greatest horizontal motion in a standing wave (q.v.). Standing waves are found in the ocean, in lakes, and bays.

NODULE A nodule is a concretion formed in a sedimentary deposit as a result of mineral precipitation. Mineral solutions precipitate around a nucleous, about an axis, or fill a cavity. Concretions form in soils in the same way. The usual cements are calcium and silica. Manganese and iron nodules have been found in deep sea locations.

Nodules are aggregations and many are combinations of basic minerals and are cemented by similar minerals in solution. The discovery of the deep sea nodules has led to efforts to mine them.

NON-CONSUMPTIVE Non-consumptive is an ecological term for resources that allow repeated use. The resource may be recycled or transformed.

NON-METALS The group of elements classed as non-metals appear on the right hand side of the Periodic Table of Elements (q.v.). There is a step-like line from boron to astartine roughly separating metals from non-metals. Borderline elements are metalloids (q.v.).

If electron attraction is the guide, elements that are good conductors are metals. Those that are good insulators are non-metals, those between are metalloids.

NORMAL FAULT In a normal fault, displacement is vertical. The high block appears topographically thrust upward. The lower block appears dropped downward. One or both sides have moved relative to each other.

NORMAL LAPSE RATE The normal lapse rate is the average change in temperature with elevation. This rate is 6° Celsius per 100 meters (3.6° Fahrenheit per 1,000 feet) of elevation.

NORTH AMERICA The North American Continent encompasses Canada, the United States, Mexico, and Central America. It includes about 40 different physiographic provinces and sub-provinces.

The North American Cordillera is an aggregate of mountain chains stretching from Alaska to Panama. It includes the Rockies, Coast Ranges, Sierra Nevadas, Mexican, and Central American ranges.

The great Canadian shield underlies the northeastern part of the continent. It forms the basement of eastern Canada and the northern tier of states to the Great Lakes. Superposed on part of the shield are ancient and more recent mountains which extend the length of the eastern United States. These are the Appalachians (q.v.).

2 great river systems have built great sediment-filled valleys and deltas. These are the Mississippi in the United States and the Mackenzie in Canada.

The North American Desert includes the Great Basin (q.v.) and the region between it and the California Coast. To the south it extends into Sonora and Baja California in Mexico. To the north it merges into the Colorado Plateau and the Rockies. To the east of the Rockies is the area known as the High Plains.

A narrow Sub-Arctic forest stretches across the continent. The belt is between 50-60° North Latitude in Canada and comes within a short distance of the Alaskan West Coast. This is the North American Taiga which is dominated by spruce. It is comparable to the Eurasian Taiga Forest. Many mountain slopes at high elevation in lower latitudes have similar Taiga (q.v.) vegetation. One of the largest and most important of these is the Redwood Forest (q.v.).

NORTH AMERICAN PLATE The crustal plate upon which most of the North American Continent rests has been moving slowly southwest for the last 18 million years at 4.5 centimeters (1.8 inches) per year.

The North American Plate is riding over the Pacific Plate (q.v.). The rate is deceptive since movement is often spasmodic. There are a series of scars suggestive of past movement. Yellowstone (q.v.) area may be one.

NORTH AMERICAN ALLIANCE A North American Water & Power Alliance was proposed in 1964 and is still under consideration. Arctic flowing rivers would be diverted and an 800 kilometer (500 mile) long reservoir built in the Rocky Mountain Trench. The reservoir would serve the High Plains agricultural areas.

The project would take 25 years to construct. It is not unlike the USSR project to divert the Ob, Irtysh, and Yenesei rivers. The Russian project would affect Arctic Ocean salinity and have an unknown affect on climate and currents. What the effects of the diversion of Canadian waters would be is unknown.

NORTH ATLANTIC CURRENT The North Atlantic Current is an extension of the Gulf Stream. It splits into great eddies or gyres up to 310 kilometers (250 miles). It joins the North Equatorial Current to form the subtropical gyre which siphons millions of tons of water into the Sargasso Sea (q.v.). See **GYRE**.

NORTH EQUATORIAL CURRENT A portion of the North Equatorial Current is forced into the Northern Hemisphere by the bulge of South America. These waters feed into the Gulf Stream. The North Equatorial Current is separated from its southern counterpart by a slender east flowing current.

The North Equatorial Current shifts with the seasons and is especially important to the monsoons (q.v.).

NORTH PACIFIC CURRENT The North Pacific Equatorial Current begins off the Mexican Island of Revilla Gigedo and flows to the Philippines. It is the longest easterly current in the world, (12,500 kilometers or 7,500 miles) long. The current travels 20 to 30 kilometers (12 to 18 miles) a day. After leaving the Marianas, a portion flows north toward Taiwan and Southwest Japan to merge into the Kuro Shio Current (q.v.).

NORTH SEA The North Sea is a shallow extension of the North Atlantic Ocean. It is a basin receiving 90% of its inflow from the English Channel. The main outflow is along the Norwegian Coast. The sea is the habitat of over 100 different fish species. The North Sea Basin is a proven reservoir for oil and is currently producing.

NORTHER Strong, cold, north winds in winter are 'northers'. They are the southward movement of polar anticyclones in the wake of intense cold fronts. These cold winds are not infrequent in the southern United States along the Gulf of Mexico and in the Western Caribbean. A similar condition sometimes affects California.

NORTHERN HEMISPHERE The globe is divided into 2 hemispheres at the Equator (q.v.). As the Earth rotates, all flow of air and water is deflected to the right in the Northern Hemisphere and to the left in the Southern Hemisphere. This phenomenon is known as the Coriolis Effect (q.v.).

On the average the Arctic is 10° warmer than the Antarctic. In 1975 this pattern was disrupted and it was almost as cold in the Northern Hemisphere as the Southern. The largest annual range of temperatures are found on the continents of the Northern Hemisphere.

NOSE An incomplete anticline (q.v.), or dome, is a nose.

NOVA A nova is an extremely bright flash of light in the sky attributed to the break-up of a star or the birth of a new one.

NOVA is the name of a powerful laser capable of igniting a pellet of fuel and creating a miniature star from fusion reaction.

NOVA is also the name of the world's largest optical instrument.

NUBIAN SANDSTONE The widespread Nubian Sandstone covers parts of Chad, Egypt, Libya, and Sudan. Similar sands have been found on the Arabian Peninsula. The sandstone is of cross-bedded, continental sediments. Its origin and climate of deposition have not been determined. There are both evaporite (q.v.) and laterite (q.v.) sequences in the Formation. In Central Sudan, large evaporite facies are present. Depositional climates appear to have been widely varying.

It can only be concluded that 'Nubian Sandstone' is a generalized name given to sandstones of uncertain age from Paleozoic to Mesozoic. Cretaceous Nubian Sandstone is well-defined from the Aswan area of Egypt.

NUCLEAR ENERGY Atomic fission or fusion releases nuclear energy from radioactive decay (q.v.). Nuclear reaction is independent of chemical reaction but radioactivity can occur during a chemical reaction. Fission occurs when atomic nuclei are split; fusion when nuclei combine.

NUCLEAR TRACERS Radioactive minerals have become extremely important as tracers in a variety of fields. The most well-known are the medical tracers used for such things as brain scanning. For this purpose, radioactive hydrogen (tritium) is used.

Tritium has been used to detect recharge or lack of it in deep wells. If tritium is present, atmospheric water is reaching the well. If it is absent, there has been no recharge since the era of atomic explosions began. Tritium is present in fallout (q.v.).

Radioactive tracers serve many useful industrial purposes. One of the most important is the grade separation of oil in pipelines.

NUCLEAR WINTER 'Nuclear winter' describes the atmospheric conditions when there is persistant cloud cover of smoke and particulate matter interfering with solar radiation. The cloud cover is similar to one expected to occur from nuclear events. Nuclear winters have occurred in the past from huge volcanic explosions. The radioactive elements are not necessarily present in the volcanic induced cover.

The strongest winds carrying clouds around the world are the Westerlies. So, in the higher latitudes temperature below the clouds caused by eruptions can be 10-20° Celsius for many months. Some years there have been no summers. Coastal areas tend to be warmer due to the maritime effect, but the clash between cold and warm air results in violent storms.

Studies reveal that volcanic eruptions in the Northern Hemisphere result in an immediate decrease in surface temperature in the continental interiors. This reduction is up to 1.4° Celsius in winter and 0.9° in summer. The lowest temperature occurs in the 2nd month after the eruption.

In the Southern Hemisphere the temperatures have not been as carefully monitored. It is known that when Tambora (q.v.) blew up in 1815, it was then the largest eruption ever recorded. Its contribution to atmospheric particulates was enormous. When Krakatoa erupted in 1883 the contribution amounted to 50 million metric tons. According to the French officials in Martinique it caused a 20% reduction in solar radiation for a 3-year period. Its effect was global. It took months before Krakatoa's dust cloud reached Europe and North America. Recovery can require up to 2 years after a major eruption.

The effect of a nuclear winter, whether caused by a natural event or a nuclear disaster, is widespread destruction of crops and damage from storms. The psychological effect of a summer without sunshine is also great. See **KRAKATOA**.

NUCLEATION Particulates in the Atmosphere may cluster or nucleate providing surfaces for the adherence of water vapor. Raindrops form where the water vapor collects. Clouds with sufficient particulates become rain clouds. Ionization (q.v.) plays an important role.

Without nucleation, precipitation can not result. Bacteria ('Pseudomonas syringae') can also play a role. Water and ice only accumulate only on 'clean dust'. Since this is so, the problem of clean air becomes especially critical over areas which already tend to be dry.

NUCLEUS The central core of any entity is its nucleus. It is surrounded in the atom by 1 or more orbiting electrons, protons, and neutrons.

The nucleus is held together by strong interaction among the subatomic particles, whose relationship to each other is an ordered one. (The plural of nucleus is nuclei).

NUCLIDE An atom characterized by its nucleus is a nuclide. The composition is described by the number of electrons, protons, neutrons, and their energy content.

NUÉE ARDENTE A 'nuée ardente' is a charged volcanic cloud from an explosive eruption. This type of cloud with destructive gases was an important part of the eruption of Mont Pelée, Martinique (q.v.).

NUGGET Nugget usually means an aggregate of gold particles. However, it may refer to an aggregate of any mineral. Gold nuggets are normally water-worn pieces of native gold and so are very pure.

The largest gold nugget came from Welcome Stranger Mine in Ballarat, Australia. It weighed in at 2,280 ounces (Troy).

NULLABAR PLAIN   The Nullabar Plain is halfway between Sydney and Perth in Australia. It is a plain of low relief in barren karstic (q.v.) limestone terrain. The elevation is below 150 meters (500 feet).

There are many collapsed sink holes and cave passages. Mullamullang Cave is 10 kilometers (6 miles) long and 36 meters (120 feet) across with halls the same height. It slopes to a depth of 120 meters (400 feet).

Where collapsed structures intercept the water table there are lakes. In the rainy season, Nullabar is an almost impassable 'sea of mud'.

NUMMULITIC   The Lower Tertiary Period is the Nummulitic. It was a time of great development of Nummulite Foraminifera. Nummulitic limestone contains an abundance of these organisms.

The Nummulitic Foramifera have tiny chambered shells which are coin-shaped. The major species are bottom-dwellers. There are about 20 species which float in the open ocean. These organisms contribute to the great oozes. Globergina ooze covers some 130 million square kilometers (50 million square miles) of seafloor.

In 450 B.C. Herodotus, the Greek Philosopher of Alexandria, Egypt, called attention to the nummalitic limestone which was used to construct the Great Pyramid.

NUNATAK   The 'nunatak' is a relief feature formed by glacial erosion and plucking. Nunataks are barren peaks protruding through an ice cap. They are prominent in Greenland and Antarctica.

NUREK DAM   The second highest earth dam in the world is the Nurek in Tajikstan in USSR. Nurek is 317 meters (1,046 feet). Rogun in the same region overtops Nurek. Aswan (q.v.) in Egypt is 111 meters (367 feet).

Nurek is a triangular prism dam, 1.5 kilometers (0.9 miles) thick with 52 million cubic meters (68 million cubic yards) of earth. The core contains clay without gravel and is smooth, polished, and ceramic-like so outside rocks slide and bounce off.

Nurek can supply 11 billion kilowatts per year to Regar Industrial Complex which has aluminum and electrochemical plants. The energy was insufficient to meet all the Regar demand so the bigger dam upstream at Rogun was put in place.

Tajikstan has the greatest hydroelectric potential in the USSR. It could produce 300 billion kilowatts, 30% of all Soviet needs.

NUTRIENT   Any food or nourishment contributing to growth and development of an organism, plant, or animal, is a nutrient. In the developed soil profile, there is a pronounced layer of humus (q.v.) which contains most of the plants' nutrients.

NYIRAGONGO VOLCANO Nyiragongo caldera is 3,448 meters (11,380 feet) atop a shield volcano in the Western Rift Valley of East Africa. It is the youngest volcano in the very seismically active area of the Virunga Mountains of Zaire. In 1948, the volcano erupted and spewed lava as far as Lake Kivu (q.v.) 16 kilometers (10 miles) away.

The crater contained a lava lake within the 197 meter (650 foot) high wall which dated from 1928. The 1976-77 eruption caused a breach in the crater wall which allowed the lava to drain away.

The caldera is 1,250 meters (4,125 feet) in diameter and 1,100 meters (3,630 feet) deep. The inner wall has 3 terraces to the former molten lake level. In 1 year, lava levels lowered 3 meters (12 feet) as the lava solidified. The lava lake level fluctuated greatly throughout its duration.

Aluminum Waste Lagoon with desiccating Red Muds — East St. Louis
Courtesy of Zellars-Williams, Division Jacobs Engineering

O

OASIS The word 'oasis' is derived from ancient Coptic (Egyptian) meaning to dwell and to drink. In an oasis groundwater is at or near the surface allowing vegetation to flourish. The groundwater persists over a long period of time.

An oasis may be watered by streams, springs, or wells. Many are found at mountain fronts along a springline. Vegetation varies from desert to desert. In North Africa, the important oases are marked by tree growth, usually of the date palm. The date is often cultivated at the expense of other local vegetation such as the acacia. See **NEFTA**.

There are artificial oases created by importing water, sometimes over great distances. Small oases areas have been enlarged to cities using imported water. Most Southern California cities are such enlarged oases. Reliance on imported water or on desert groundwater may be precarious for large populations.

OASIS DEPRESSION Some of the largest wind-scoured depressions are low oases sites. Deflation has eroded them deeply enough to allow underground water to be tapped by vegetation. In the Sahara, the average depth of the oases depressions is 250 meters (825 feet).

Good examples are found in the Libyan Desert of Egypt where depression oases cover 27,000 square kilometers (10,000 square miles). The depressions are structurally controlled. See **QATTARA**.

OB/IRTYSH SYSTEM The Ob and its tributary the Irtysh make up the longest river system in the USSR. It flows 5,568 kilometers (3,460 miles) through Western Siberia to the Arctic Ocean. It is the main north-south artery in Siberia.

The Ob and Irtysh rivers actually come from opposite sides of the Altai Glaciers which give rise to 3 great rivers. Besides Ob-Irtysh, the Yenesei originates there.

The Ob rises in the Tien Shan Mountains on the Chinese side of the Altais. The Irtysh originates in Siberia and flows 3,541 kilometers (2,040 miles) before joining the Ob. The system empties into Ob Estuary, or the Gulf of Ob, which extends 885 kilometers (550 miles) inland from the Kara Sea.

The Ob River Dam will create a 330,000 square kilometer (200,000 square mile) lake. It will be part of the network to divert waters from the Arctic to the Aral Sea. The USSR hopes to create and irrigate an additional 50 million arable acres.

The Aral Sea has been drying out and has enormously shrunk millions of hectares as a major Soviet cotton industry used the inflow waters for irrigation. The cotton project has been on-going for 30 years. The result has been an environmental problem affecting 35 million people in Uzbekistan and Khazakhstan.

One of the most important cities in Siberia, Novasibirsk, is on the Ob. Omsk is on the Irtysh. The Upper Ob/Irtysh provide an outlet for the grains of Altai and Khazakhstan. Also Kuznetz coal, oil, and salt use the artery.

OBSEQUENT STREAM An obsequent stream flows at right angles to the sedimentary dip and consequent rivers. Obsequent streams are usually short, with high gradients. They form on cuestas (q.v.) and descend the scarp.

OBSIDIAN Volcanic lava, usually from rhyolitic flows, congealing too fast to crystallize, forms obsidian or volcanic glass. One very large flow of this type occurred from the Newberry Volcano in Oregon. In Yellowstone there is a formation called Obsidian Cliff.

Obsidian is dark green to black, sometimes transparent. It is smooth, has a vitreous luster, and conchoidal fracture. Fragments are common in southwestern United States where they were used by Indians for arrowheads, spears, and tools. The Aztecs of Mexico used obsidian as ceremonial knives in religious sacrifices.

Obsidian as it congeals takes on a tear-drop shape. Then fragments are called 'Apache Tears'.

OCCLUDED FRONT A cold airmass traveling at a rate twice that of a retreating warm airmass will overtake the warm. When the airmasses merge, they are occluded. The occluded front is accompanied by damp, dreary weather, often the forerunner of a cyclonic storm. See **CYCLONE**.

OCEAN Earth is unique in the Solar System in having a water covering. It may be unique to the galaxy. The Earth's Ocean is a single continuous watermass with large and small islands. The waters cover 72% of the surface. The composition of the large landmasses or continents (q.v.) is different from most smaller islands.

The oceanic topography is made up of (in % of the Earth):

Location	Continental Shelf/Slope	Ridge/Rise	Volcanoes	Trench
Pacific	13.1	37.6	2.5	2.9
Atlantic	19.4	39.7	2.1	0.7
Indian	9.1	35.9	5.1	0.3
World Ocean	10.8	26.8	2.2	1.2

Oceanic basins are major provinces. Making up almost a 1/3 of the ocean floor, they are 4 to 6 kilometers (2.5 to 4 miles) below sea level and usually lined with basalt. The basins are generally bounded by continental shelves (q.v.), and interrupted by ridges, rises, trenches, and volcanoes. The Atlantic, Pacific, and Indian Oceans fill the largest basins. The Pacific has the largest basin equal to 1/3 of Earth. Major ridges and rises create sub-basins.

There is constant interaction between the Ocean and the Atmosphere. The boundary layer between them is a region of great physical activity. Airflow over the water together with warmer temperatures causes evaporation. There is a continuous transfer of gases. The sea surface reflects these conditions.

Water volume is the same as it was for the early Earth. When hydrogen is released it is replaced by juvenile water (q.v.) upwelling from the seafloor.

OCEAN COMPOSITION Oceanic or seawater is salty, having on the average 35 ppm (parts per million) of dissolved salts. In the Red Sea, salinity reaches 40 ppm, while in the Arctic it is 30 ppm.

Water evaporated off the surface is fresh. The vapor circulates in the Atmosphere until precipitated as rain or snow, sometimes over land. From the land it circulates back to the sea via runoff. With runoff, the weathering product of the land is transported to the sea. Large amounts of dissolved materials are included (Calcium, magnesium, potassium, silica, and sodium). These contribute to the ocean's salinity.

The 8 elements which make up 92% of the Earth's crustal abundance in parts per million (ppm) of seawater volume are:

Oxygen	857,000.0
Silicon	3.0
Aluminum	0.01
Iron	0.01
Calcium	400.0
Sodium	105.0
Potassium	380.0
Magnesium	1,350.0

Trace elements important constituents of seawater are:

Hydrogen	108,000.0
Chlorine	19,000.0
Sodium	105.0
Carbon	28.0

Of these only sodium is found on both lists. Although the amount of carbon appears small, the sea is a carbon reservoir.

OCEAN CURRENTS Within the sea there are masses of water with definite circulation patterns. These are the currents in surface or deep waters. Currents are not similar to rivers, they are more complex. A surface current usually has a counter-current at depth.

Currents are set in motion by a variety of forces. Among these are surface winds, temperature variations, influence of the Coriolis Effect, tides, earthquakes, and turbidity flows.

Major currents move in a clockwise direction in the Northern Hemisphere and counter-clockwise in the Southern. Currents are strongest on the west side of oceans in the Northern Hemisphere and on the east side in the Southern.

OCEANIC CRUST The Earth's Crust beneath the Ocean is thinner than beneath the continents. It is on the average 10.3 kilometers (6.2 miles) thick. The material is richer in Sima (q.v.), made up of silica, magnesium, aluminum, and calcium.

The crustal material is multi-layered with mud, silt, and sand found on continental shelves together with other continental detritus. This material can be up to 0.8 kilometers (0.5 miles) thick. The deep sea plains are covered by oozes (q.v.).

At the spreading ridges the seafloor is covered by basalt emanating from the rifts. The flows can be up to 1.5-2 kilometers (0.9-1.2 miles) in thickness. See **SEAFLOOR SPREADING**.

Below the different seafloor deposits is a thick layer, mainly of gabbro (q.v.). It can be up to 5 kilometers (3 miles). The rigid Upper Mantle is below. It is composed primarily of peridotite with a predominance of olivine.

OCEANIC DENSITY The density of the ocean is determined mostly by temperature and salinity. Pure water is most dense at 4° Celsius. The density of pure water is 1.0 gram per cubic centimeter. Salt increases that density and the average sea surface density is 1.0257 grams.

Seawater is vertically stable. Unless there is some contrary force, dense water at depth will not mix with the less dense above. Vertical mixing is due to forces of friction, longshore currents, waves, and wind. Upwelling (q.v.) is induced by these.

Deep water has a high density due to low temperatures and the weight of the water column. Surface waters sink under cold airmasses and rise under warm ones, partly as the Latitude Effect (q.v.).

OCEANIC HABITAT Most of the Earth's Ocean is barren of life since most life requires light, nitrates, and phosphates. Light normally does not penetrate below 18 meters (60 feet) of water. In deep oceans, nutrients on the ocean floor are inaccessible to most organisms. Fisheries are more successful over shoals and shallow shelves.

Phytoplankton are primary oceanic producers, converting solar energy to carbohydrates by photosynthesis (q.v.). Phytoplankton exist at depths with only 1% sunlight. Attached seaweed also can subsist down to extremely low levels of light. In the Caribbean the limit is 110 meters (350 feet). Phytoplankton are the first link in the food chain (q.v.).

Deep oceanic trenches had been considered devoid of lifeforms. Picard, in the Trieste (q.v.), brought up a record of fish and shrimp from 10.8 kilometers (6.5 miles) in the Marianas Trench. These lifeforms are assumed to begin their food chain with bacteria found in the 'hot spots' (q.v.).

OCEANIC MINERAL DEPOSITS Many minerals form at continental margins, among them copper, lead, and zinc. In early stages of plate divergence or rifting, heat from eruptions supplies the energy for chemical reactions between crustal minerals and bottom water.

Metals, like copper, are leached from basalt by seawater. The sequence of events occurring in a subduction zone (q.v.) can lead to ores like those of Kuroko, Japan.

Nodules on the ocean floor contain manganese, copper, nickel, and cobalt. Distributed near fracture zones, the greatest concentration is between 2 Pacific fracture zones and above a deposit of Radiolarian ooze (q.v.). Nodules are also encountered on continental shelves and on plateaus. The Blake Plateau nodules result from replacement of phosphate by manganese.

OCEANIC RIDGES AND RISES Oceanic ridges and rises are topographic highs rising from the seafloor. They cover about 25% of the Earth's surface and form a continuous system connected from ocean basin to ocean basin. The main oceanic ridge is 79,166 kilometers (47,500 miles) long as it winds its way around the globe. It bears different names such as Mid-Atlantic Ridge, East Pacific Rise, and others.

Ridges are of high relief (Mid-Atlantic); rises are of low relief (East Pacific). In the South Atlantic, the Mid-Atlantic Ridge is flanked by deep basins. Platforms rise from the basin floors. West of the Mid-Atlantic is the Rio Grande Rise and to the east is Walvis Ridge.

The ridges and rises are accompanied by a rift system. The rifts are spreading the seafloor apart and Mantle material is accreting in them.

OCEANIC SEDIMENTS 3 billion tons of continental sediments are washed into the oceans each year. Coarser sediments of gravel, sand, shell, and clay are dropped on the continental shelves inshore. Farther out are organic debris, volcanic dust, and material dropped by turbidity currents. Multicolored muds and oozes (q.v.) are found on abyssal plains. They are underlain by basalts (q.v.).

OCEANIC TECTONICS Ocean floors are in constant movement as oceanic crust is being subducted beneath continents and new continental material is being created in oceanic rifts. This is in concert with the movement of the crustal plates carrying the oceans.

Fissures away from the Global Rift System (q.v.) eject lava onto the ocean floor and volcanoes emerge. Many of these build high enough to break the sea surface as islands. Some are semi-permanent, others disappear rapidly.

OCEANIC TRENCHES Deep canyons or oceanic trenches are usually deeper than 5,000 meters (20,000 feet) and are complementary features of island arcs (Hawaii, Marianas). Trenches are also located at the boundaries between continental blocks and ocean basins.

The greatest number and deepest trenches are in the Pacific. Trenches are foci of most submarine earthquakes. Major trenches (in kilometers) are:

Trench	Depth	Length	Width
Marianas, Pacific	11.7	2,550	70
Tonga, Pacific	10.8	1,400	55
Kurile, Pacific	10.5	2,200	120
Philippine, Pacific	10.5	1,400	60
Kermadec, Pacific	10.0	1,500	40
Bonin, Pacific	9.8	800	90
Puerto Rico, Atlantic	8.4	1,550	120
South Sandwich, Atlantic	8.4	1,450	90
Peru/Chile, Pacific	8.1	5,900	100
Romanche, Atlantic	7.9	300	60
Aleutian, Pacific	7.7	3,700	50
Java, Pacific	7.5	4,500	80
Mid-America, Atlantic	6.7	2,800	40

OCCURRENCE The presence of mineral in a rock mass or an outcrop is an occurrence. If sufficiently large, it may become a prospect (q.v.) and of potential economic importance.

OCHER Clays impregnated with iron oxides are ochers (ochres). Color is variable and may be red, brown, yellow, gray, green, or black. The color depends upon the predominant iron oxide and the presence of other metallic oxides.

Many ochers are rich enough in oxides to be mineable. Their major use is in pigment manufacture. Ocher production in the United States is largely from Georgia and Alabama. At one time ochers were mined to produce pig iron, but the economics of iron mining and production changed.

OCOTILLO ('Fouquieria splendens'), the ocotillo species found in the desert southwest of the United States, is considered one of the oldest of all living plant species. It has a series of feathery arms coming from a base at the surface of the soil. The tips may flower with red, white, or yellow blossoms.

Ocotillo is restricted to the low desert areas in the United States and northern Mexico.

Near San Felipe, in Baja California, Mexico, there is an ocotillo forest preserve. The species is 'Fouquieria peninsularis' and differs from its northern relative. The delicate arms are replaced by rugged, crooked, bushlike branches.

OFFSHORE DRILLING Offshore drilling is a highly technical type of exploration and development of oil deposits beneath coastal seas. Specialized structures, or platforms, are placed above the oil prospect and drilling is done from them. They may drill at diverse angles as well as vertically. First attempts were off Louisiana in the rich oil fields of the Gulf of Mexico.

Offshore drilling has come under criticism from environmental groups as accidents have caused major oil spills. Rigs are safer today but are not fail-safe. They have also been opposed by residents of coastal cities as a scenic blight.

OGIVES Frost heaving creates raised ridges of sediments very like pointed arches. These features are 'ogives' named for the Gothic arch.

OIL Chemically, an oil is insoluble in water but soluble in ether. It is greasy to the touch. The most important economic oil is the hydrocarbon petroleum (q.v.).

OIL RECOVERY About 30% of all oil produced is recovered from normal drilling operations. Various techniques are used to recover the rest. These include special pumping, service wells, steam injection, fracturing, and acidizing.

OIL REFINING Fractional distillation or thermal cracking of crude oil is the chief refining method used. See **PETROLEUM**.

OIL SEEPS Oil seeps are natural oozing of oil, usually from asphalt pools or tar sands. These natural seeps have been known and used for thousands of years. Oil was recovered and used for lighting and for medicine.

Seeps are common in many oil producing areas. In some, they were the first indication of the reserve below. The most famous seeps, even mentioned in the Bible, are in Iraq. They are associated with the gaseous emanations of Baba Gurgur (q.v.).

In the Amazon, seeps led to exploratory wells that became producers. In the foothills of the Andes there are many seeps, some responsible for Bolivian oil discoveries. Other foothill seeps have not been explored due to development hardships and cost.

There are many oceanic seeps along the edge of producing zones. These are often responsible for slicks on the sea surface. There have been many between the California Coast and the Channel Islands, especially in the San Miguel area. Oil seeps are slow to reach the surface and the slicks they produce spread thinly over a wide area, differing from slicks from oil spills.

OIL SHALE Oil shales are fine-grained, thinly layered, and contain the hydrocarbon kerogen. High grade reserves are found in the Green River Formation of Colorado, Utah, and Wyoming. The reserves are equivalent to 2 trillion barrels of oil.

Major problems must be resolved before oil shale mining is viable. These include the:
- Capital cost and high energy cost
- Long leadtime
- Retort water disposal and water managment
- Spent shale disposal

The investment must be made in advance of declining supplies of petroleum, a fact that becomes obscured due to short-term market economics. Diminishing supplies of world oil and its cost could change the picture. Solutions to the problems of waste disposal, toxic elements and radioactivity require an expensive investment in research and development. The problem elements are uranium, arsenic, tin, fluorine, iron and boron.

There have been oil shale projects in various countries. Most were abandoned in favor of cheaper petroleum production or import cost. Brazil has had a plant in operation for some years in the Paraiba Valley between Rio de Janeiro and Sao Paulo. The best oil shales in Brazil, however, are in the south, the Irati Shales (q.v.). Development of Irati Shales was to have begun in 1986.

OIL SPILLS Shipping accidents and weather damage to offshore rigs can cause major oil spills. These are especially threatening to birds and marine-life.

Dedicated people have devoted many hours to washing oil off seabirds after a threatening spill. The U.S. Coast Guard has a task-force for clean-up. Crews on oil rigs are now being specially trained to prevent and contain spills. The HOSS, a vessel to skim thousands of gallons of oil off the sea surface, is in use but the number of these vessels is limited.

In a major spill, these efforts are only minimally effective. The Valdez oilspill (q.v.) points up the inadequacies. 3 months after this major spill there were 3 oil spills in a 24-hour period along the East Coast of the United States. A fragile coastal ecology both off and onshore appears to be in jeopardy.

OIL WELLS There are 3 types of oil wells, the exploratory, the developmental, and the service well. Exploratory wells may be drilled in areas of known reserves or in untried areas (wildcat wells). Development wells tap producing sediments. Service wells are used to test sediments and inject them with steam to force production.

OKAPI The okapi is a living fossil. A relative of the giraffe, it lacks the elongated neck. Its present range, like that of the giraffe, is the East African plains. Okapi fossils are preserved in Greek Pliocene sediments (12 million years).

LAKE OKEECHOBEE Lake Okeechobee is one of the largest freshwater lakes in continental United States. In the Everglades, the lake has been made the recipient of much diverted water.

The surrounding land has subsided from drying out and there is an increased fire danger in the area. The farms in southern Florida have a back-drainage into the lake. These waters carry a volume of nitrogen and phosphate from fertilizers, which has lead to an increasing eutrophication (q.v.) of the lake.

OKEFENOKEE SWAMP One of the oldest swamps in the United States is on the southern border of Georgia. The Cherokee called it 'Okefenokee' for trembling earth. Vegetation is not firmly anchored, and floating islands form.

The Suwanee River to the Gulf and St. Mary's River to the Atlantic rise in this wetland. See **SWAMPS**.

OLD AGE LANDSCAPE When erosion has converted mountains to rounded hummocks and rivers are full of meanders (q.v.), the landscape is in old age. The floodplains are great and the valleys broad. The Lower Mississippi Valley and Plain are good examples of old-age terrain.

OLD FAITHFUL Old Faithful in Yellowstone National Park, Wyoming, is a geyser (q.v.) which erupts steam to a height of 45 meters (150 feet).

Rainwater and snowmelt are superheated by pressure below the surface to just short of a boil and the hot waters are pushed up through a vent. Once the pressure is released, the water converts to steam and virtually explodes.

Old Faithful erupts with seeming regularity. The explosion interval has become more irregular during the last few years. Recent earthquake activity may have interfered with the vents.

OLD RED SANDSTONE The Old Red Sandstone is characteristic of Upper Devonian (300 m.y.) sediments in Britain. The sandstone is in structural basins between ancient Caledonian ridges. Old Red is said to 'still glow with remembered warmth of the Devonian Desert'. It contains continental fossils.

OLDHAM-GUTENBERG The Oldham-Gutenberg Discontinuity is the lower boundary of Earth's Mantle with the Outer Core. The discontinuity is placed at 2,898 kilometers (1,740 miles) into the Earth. It is the assumed boundary between the Peridotite Zone and the Core.

OLDOINYO LENGAI Oldoinyo Lengai Volcano is at the south end of the Rift Valley and east of Olduvai Gorge (Tanzania). 'Oldoinyo Lengai' is Masai for 'Mountain of God'. The 2,840 meter (9,370 foot) volcano is at the south end of Lake Natron, a famed dry soda lake.

Oldoinyo Lengai is distinctive for its gaseous eruptions. It erupted in 1945 and again in 1966. The 1966 eruption was of sodium carbonate (washing soda) that turns soapy when it rains. The effusion poisoned water holes.

The 1966 eruption was a special geological event because it was the first carbonatite (q.v.) extrusion observed by scientists. White lava simmered in the crater before it blew a cloud to an elevation of 7,500 meters (25,000 feet). It rained white ash. Sodium carbonate collected and recrystallized in Lake Natron and Lake Magadi. In them, bright red Algae flourished and still does.

OLDUVAI GORGE Olduvai Gorge is a fracture in the Serengeti Plain of Tanzania. In this gorge, Dr. Leakey and his colleagues found very well preserved humanoid fossils. Interpretations of magnetic reversals put the dates of these fossils between 1.71 and 1.86 million years.

The gorge is cut into Pleistocene lake beds found on the western edge of Serengeti Plain. There is some indication that the region once may have been forested.

MOUNT OLGA In Australia's Central Desert there is a group of 30 massive domes. These isolated domes don't exceed 460 meters (1,500 feet). They are rounded and smooth and on a vast plain 32 kilometers west of Ayres Rock (q.v.). The largest dome is Mount Olga.

No satisfactory explanation of these erosional features has yet been developed.

OLIGOCENE The Oligocene (38-26 m.y.) is an Epoch in the Tertiary Period between the Eocene and Miocene.

The 12-million year Oligocene produced its best sediments in Germany. In Mongolia, there is a rich Fauna preserved in Lower-Oligocene sediments. The Fauna are related to the Oligocene of North America.

OLIGOTROPHIC Oligotrophic conditions in a lake exist when biological productivity is impaired by a nutrient deficiency. Oligotrophy also can result from the presence of noxious elements, a lack of light, or from adverse temperatures.

OLIVINE Olivine, a magnesium-iron silicate, belongs to the Peridotite Group. It contains less molecular silica than other silicates. Olivine tends to form in silica-depleted igneous and metamorphic rocks and is common to some basalts. It weathers to serpentine, smectite, or goethite.

Olivine is a source of refractory magnesium used as a blast furnace slag conditioner for pig iron. It is produced in Washington State and North Carolina. Production is 100,000 tons per year.

OLYMPIC DAM A remarkable orebody was discovered in the Olympic Dam area, Roxby Downs Station, South Australia. The deposit is a complex of copper, gold, and uranium.

Preliminary drilling estimates (1982) were 32 million metric tons of copper, 1.2 million of uranium, and 1,200 of gold ore. The overburden (q.v.) is up to 350 meters (1,150 feet) thick. The known extent of the orebody is 7 x 4 kilometers (4 x 2 miles). The gold probably originated in the nearby Greenstone Belt (q.v.).

OMO RIVER Rising in the Ethiopian Highlands, the Omo River flows to Lake Rudolf (now Lake Turkana) in the Rift Valley on the Kenya border. The Upper Omo flows over rapids and through narrow gorges. The Lower Omo cuts through rolling hills.

In the hills drained by the Lower Omo, 'Australopithecus' fossils 2.5 million years old were recovered. Quartz tools of 'Homo sapiens' dating from 100,000 years were also found.

ONYX Onyx differs from agate in that it is layered in different colors of translucent chalcedony (q.v.) and the banding is parallel. Onyx is prized for carvings and ornaments.

Cave onyx, a calcite of cryptocrystalline limestone, is found in many caves and caverns. It is precipitated by groundwaters which drain karst (q.v.) terrain.

OOLITES Small rounded concretions, mainly of carbonates, are oolites. They are found in sedimentary rocks. The cementing agent can be ferruginous as well as calcareous.

Oolites in Jura, France, are marker bed guides for the Jurassic Period (195-136 m.y.). Larger concretions of the same general nature, resembling peas, are pisolites.

Tiny oolites found in caves are referred to as 'cave pearls'. A large number have been found in Carlsbad Cavern, New Mexico. The pearls have been found in other caves as well. The largest known is 0.07 centimeters (3/16 of an inch). A cross-section of a pearl under magnification showed 54 layers of calcite. The nucleus was a grain of sand.

Limestone embedded with oolites are found in northern France. The limestone has been quarried for use in building abbeys and cathedrals. Saint Paul's Cathedral in London and Canterbury Cathedral were both built of the oolitic limestone from Caen.

OORT CLOUD A cloud of ice and dust particles envelopes the Solar System beyond the outer planets. This envelope is the Oort Cloud and believed to contain billions of comets. The existence of the Oort Cloud has not been proven. See **COMET**.

OOZE Skeletons of tiny marine organisms embedded in clay create sedimentary oozes. These are found on the deep seafloor. An ooze is any fine sediment containing 30% or more of organic material. Its type is determined by the dominant organism ('Globergerina', 'Radiolaria'). The diatom, 'Radiolaria', flourishes in phosphate-rich upwellings.

Oozes may be calcareous or siliceous. Most of the western Indian Ocean Basin is covered with calcareous ooze. The Mid-Atlantic and South Pacific floors also are covered with it. Silicious ooze has a more restricted distribution and is found in narrow strips in the Mid- and North Pacific and in a broader belt in more southern oceans.

OPAL   Opal, an amorphous variety of silica, is hydrous, vitreous, and resinous. Opal always contains some water, usually 10%. Common opal is uniform in color but some rarer types are irridescent. Opals probably originate from hot acid waters precipitating silica gel.

The best quality of gem opal is found in Australia. Australian opals have closely packed particles in a regular pattern. It is this pattern that Australians think gives color to the opal.

Most opals are a soapy white to blue-green. The Andamooka opal given to Queen Elizabeth in 1954 is blue-green. Black opals from Lightning Ridge, Australia, are really dark red, blue, and green.

The opal of Virgin Valley, Nevada, occurs as seams and irregular masses in volcanic rocks. It is especially present in opalized woods where silica replaced the cell structure. Fire opals which are prized are found in Mexican porphyrys.

OPERATION NOAH'S ARK   With the building of Kariba Dam on the Zambezi River many migration paths were cut. For many animals the dam meant extinction.

A full scale effort to remove as much of the wildlife as possible was made. In all, 6,000 animals were moved in Operation Noah's Ark. They included types as diverse as elephants and snakes.

OPHIOLITE   Fragments of oceanic crust created in conditions of subduction (q.v.) are sometimes thrust above the surface of the ocean. The fragments are made up of cherty sediments, peridotite, serpentine, and basaltic material. They may be in the form of tholeolitic pillow lavas. Such an assemblage is known as ophiolite. Some ophiolites contain blue schist, known to form only at great depth.

The ophiolitic pillow lavas of Cyprus contain pyrite and chalcopyrite. Capping them are cherty iron ores and ochers.

OPHIR   Ophir is the biblical gold mine where Solomon sent his emissaries. The mine is believed to be the one worked by the Saudi Arabians between Medina and Mecca. Ophir is a name given to many ancient lost gold deposits.

OPHITIC   A rock with an ophitic texture or fabric is one in which plagioclase feldspar laths are encased in augite (q.v.).

OPOSSUM   A pouch-bearing marsupial, the opossum first appeared in North America in the Upper Cretaceous (80-65 m.y.). Fossils are found in the Laramie Group (Wyoming).

The present population moved into North America from South America. It is a 'living fossil'.

ORANGE RIVER   The Orange and its tributaries, including the Vaal River, drain 1/2 of South Africa. The Orange does not always reach the sea. Its course, 2,250 kilometers (1,350 miles) long, begins on the African Plateau. The Orange like many great African rivers carved huge valleys in troughs lined by Karroo Sediments (q.v.).

The Orange Basin includes the southern Kalahari and Namib Deserts, among the driest in the world. Orange River country is famous for its gold and diamond placers.

ORBIT The path in Space traced by a body about another is an orbit. All bodies in the Solar System have a particular path about the Sun. Space vehicles assume orbits about the Earth. If propelled into Outer Space, they trace preset trajectories.

Many manufactured satellites, especially for communications, are now orbiting the Earth.

ORBITAL The orbital is a wave function which mathematically describes electron motion about a nucleous within an atom. The electron does not emit energy continuously but only as it moves from orbit (q.v.) to orbit (Bohr's model). The range or volume over which the electron moves is its orbital

ORCHIDS The majority of orchids ('Orchidaceae') are ephiphytes (q.v.), growing on tree branches. There were 30,000 orchid species native to tropical rainforests of America and Indo-Malaysia. By 1945, 300 of them had already become extinct as a result of forest destruction and greedy collectors. What the attrition is for the past 35 years of wholesale forest devastation is unknown.

ORDOVICIAN (500-430 m.y.) In the Paleozoic Age the Ordovician Period followed the Cambrian and preceded the Silurian. It lasted 70 million years. Epicontinental, or shallow, seas covered much of the land in the Cambrian and persisted into the Ordovician.

Marine organisms dominated the Period. Fossils were not well-preserved since the calcareous rocks were diagenetically changed to dolomites in Early Ordovician. Ornamental marble quarried in the United States comes principally from these dolostones.

There were definite Ordovician provinces and source areas of faunal development. These are found in Atlantic, Arctic, and Pacific embayments among other areas. Distinctions were blurred when interior seas became more widespread.

The Canadian Lower Ordovician has 2 distinct facies, the dark, Deep-kill Shales with graptolites and limy dolostone. The shales are found from Gaspe into New Jersey.

Black shales of muddy, bottom sediments of stagnant water environments are on the east side of the Appalachian Geosyncline. The Ordovician was a period of widespread reef construction. The fossil reefs contain graptolites and brachiopods. They are east of 'Logan's Line', a thrust fault.

True corals appear at the base of the Mid-Ordovician. Their fossils are found in the Lake Champlain, New York, area. Widely distributed limestones from the Upper Ordovician contain coral reefs. These are found from Arctic Canada to Greenland and from Alaska to New Mexico.

The temperatures of the Ordovician are recorded in its rocks. It is interesting that an Ice Age held sway 450 million years ago and North Africa was the focus.

The Late Ordovician was dominated by uplift. The Appalachians continued to rise. An enormous coastal plain, The Queenston Delta, was built in Ontario and Ohio. In the west, seas still covered the land. There were 4 major stable areas or 'domes': The Adirondack Highlands, the Cincinnati Arch, the Ozark Dome, and the Wisconsin Highlands. The Taconian Orogeny closed the period.

ORE A mineral or rock prospect (q.v.) becomes an ore when it becomes possible to mine the deposit at a profit. Economic viability of a prospect depends on a number of factors. The most important are:

- Good geology - Overburden depth, reserves, continuity
- Open pit or underground - Reflected in capital cost
- Location - Relationship to local and international markets
- Market conditions - These differ at different periods
- Technology - Ore handling techniques and state of the art.

Great mineral reserves exist that cannot be marketed economically under present conditions. These are only potential ore. Many minerals produced today were known long before they became ores.

ORE DRESSING Ore dressing is the concentration of useful minerals, the removal of undesirable ones, and the separation of by-product from waste.

The important ore dressing processes are gravity, magnetics, flotation, and chemical precipitation. The efficiency of ore dressing can determine mine economics.

ORE SHOOT Rich veins often have smaller off-shoots that can be directly or indirectly related to the main vein. The form and size of such an ore shoot can vary. Extremely rich portions of an ore shoot are 'bonanzas', because of their unexpected wealth.

ORGANIC REEF The organic reef is built of tiny, limy skeletons of marine life. Reef organisms reflect geological age. The first reef builders were Algae followed by sponges and bryozoans. The Precambrian algal reef with 'Collenia' is the 660 meter (2,000 foot) Siyeh Formation of the Beltian System of Montana. This is some of the best evidence of early life.

From the Cretaceous to the Recent (136-Present), Coral has been the major reef builder. Many types of organisms are present in a reef but the reef is named for the dominant one.

Coral grows best in shallow seas, no deeper than 45 meters (150 feet), and in clear and warm water. In today's seas, these conditions exist only in the Caribbean Sea, the Red Sea, and in the South Seas. Coral reefs grow upward 30 meters (100 feet) per thousand years. Their porosity allows for infilling with Algae, Foraminera, and chemical precipitates. Growth is below sea level but reefs may be eroded by currents. When thrust above sea level, islands form.

Some major formations among organic reefs are Capitan Reef and the Guadeloupe Mountains in New Mexico and Texas, the Great Barrier Reef, Australia, and numerous atolls in the South Pacific.

ORGANISMS Living plants and animals are biological organisms. The earliest signs of life are found in 3 billion year old rocks. Organisms with hard parts capable of becoming true fossils only appeared in the Paleozoic Age (570-600 million years). Rocks formed from organic material are limestones and shales, and hydrocarbons (oil shale and coal).

ORINOCO RIVER Venzuela's Orinoco River rises in the Guiana Highlands near the Brazilian border. It flows north along the Colombian border where it acquires tributaries from the Andes.

From the mountains to the Caribbean Sea, the Orinoco has built a broad plain ending in its delta. The total course is 2,575 kilometers (1600 miles). The delta has about 50 different distributaries into the sea.

In the high-water season, the Orinoco is linked by the Casiquiare River to the Amazon System. See **EMENDATION**.

OROGENESIS Orogenesis is mountain-building. It results from diastrophism (q.v.) and is accompanied by folding, faulting, volcanism, and crumpling from continental collision, or from erosion. Mountains are a surface expression of plate tectonics, continental drift, and other dynamics of the Earth such as convection, contraction, gravity, and electromagnetism.

ORTHOCLASE Orthoclase is a potassium aluminum silicate with a little sodium. It is the only potassium feldspar in the monoclinic crystal system, the rest are triclinic. Orthoclase is common in igneous rocks and weathers to illite, a clay.

Adularia is a glassy variety of orthoclase. Moonstones are gem quality adularia with bluish opalescence. While adularia is found in igneous rocks, another glassy orthoclase, sanidine, is found in volcanic rocks.

ORTHOGENESIS The concept that evolution has been continuing in a single direction for a considerable period of time, without dependence upon natural selection, is orthogenesis.

OSMOSIS   Osmosis is the abilty of a fluid, usually water, to pass through a porous membrane and equalize pressure on both sides. It is important in biological systems and in mineralization.

OSTRICH   The world's largest bird, the ostrich, has wings too small for flight. However, it can run. Normal speed is 50-58 kilometers (30-35 miles) per hour. Its powerful legs are used for defense.

Ostrich eggs can be up to 60 centimeters (24 inches). The shells are prized by desert dwellers, who use them for water storage. This is the custom among the Bushmen of South Africa.

OUTBACK   The Australian Outback is the inhospitable Central Australian Desert. This was its most precise meaning. It now has a more popular connotation of 'anywhere in the interior'.

OUTCROP   An outcrop is a portion of any rock in place and visible on the surface. It is an indication of the rock type below the surface.

In humid terrain, erosion is relatively rapid and usually chemical so outcrops are rare. Where they are not generally found, artificial outcrops are sought (road cuts, excavations, wells). In arid areas, complete formations are often exposed. Aerial and satellite photography have enhanced the mapping of outcrops.

OUTWASH DEPOSITS   Outwash deposits are the product of glacial dumping at the edge of an icemass as the glacier retreats and melts. The deposits are large and composed principally of gravel and pebbles. They have literally been washed out of the glacier by melt-water. The depositing stream is short-lived, of high velocity, and associated with flash-flooding. The outwash fan differs from the alluvial fan in the size, sorting, and kind of the deposited material.

Beyond the edge of the terminal moraine (q.v.) of a continental glacier is the outwash plain. As the ice retreats more and more streams deposit materials on the outwash plain. See **MORAINE**.

OVERBURDEN   Uneconomic material often overlies an orebody. It must be removed before mining can begin. This material is overburden or spoil.

Overburden is especially critical in the economics of open-pit mining. It requires an 'upfront', often huge, investment before a ton of ore can be mined. This cost includes not only actual earth removal but also the cost of roads, machinery and equipment, and overhead. Continual earth removal is necessary as new locations are opened up.

OVERDRAFT   Overdraft is the extraction of groundwater at a greater rate than that of replenishment from runoff or precipitation. Overdraft is tantamount to the mining of water.

With water mining the water table drops, sometimes alarmingly. If mining continues too long and replenishment is slow a source can become unusable. Wells have to be abandoned because they:

- Are mined out
- Have excessive energy costs for pumping
- Become too saline.

OVERFISHING With technology, the total fish catch has increased. The use of sonar, nets, and factory ships, has led to overfishing and some areas have been decimated. Overfishing in itself is counter-productive, and present practices are extraordinarily wasteful.

A stable population of fish cannot be maintained at normal reproductive rates with the present practices. Human population increase is creating even more pressure on the small number of marketable fish.

Tradition and marketing are such that only a relatively few fish are greatly sought. Many less desirable fish, from a marketing point of view, are taken in the hauls and wasted. The problem is one which can only grow if international controls are not agreed upon and enforced.

OVERGRAZING Overgrazing is the excessive use of grasslands. In many cases the type of animal allowed to graze is important as some destroy root structure more than others.

Misuse of grasslands or savannas has led to widespread desertification (q.v.). This condition is usually not reversible, and contributes to greater and longer droughts. These droughts add more destroyed grasslands as pressures from people and animals increase.

The Sahel (q.v,) of Africa is in just such a self-perpetuating cycle and is adding desert to areas already increasing naturally due to climatic shifts. See **DESERTIFICATION**.

OVERTHRUST Nearly horizontal displacement of terrain along a reverse fault is an overthrust. Some are of tremendous extent. They over-ride great sequences of rock.

In the Swiss Alps dark-colored, 250 million year old rock is overlying light-colored, 50 million year old material. Recent evidence shows that many 'basement' rocks in the Appalachians are really thrusts and not basement at all.

Some thrusts are zones of mineralization. Oil reserves are found in the Wyoming Overthrust Belt.

OXBOW An abandoned meander left when a stream changed its course becomes an oxbow. Rejuvenated mature streams have sufficient energy to carve more direct routes and thus leave behind great bends, or oxbows.

In some areas, higher velocity streams only exist in the rainy seasons, so the situation may be ephemeral. Water may be dammed within an oxbow after a stream has cut between meanders. The dammed meander may be flushed out in the next season or become a lake, even a dry one.

OXIDATION Chemically, oxidation occurs when an element loses 1 or more electrons from a component atom or ion in a compound. Normally, oxidation involves the addition of atmospheric oxygen or water.

Oxidation, as a weathering phenomenon, is limited to the zone of aeration, which moves seasonally up and down in the soil profile or regolith (q.v.). Oxidation is accelerated by bacteria.

OXIDE An oxide is a compound of oxygen and a radical or group of atoms that bond as a unit. Radicals combine with oxygen to yield oxides of important ores such as aluminum, chromium, iron, and titanium.

OXYGEN Oxygen, the most abundant element, exists primarily in the combined form. As a gas, it is odorless, colorless, and tasteless. In liquid phase, it has a bluish tinge.

In the Precambrian there was a time when free oxygen was absent. This is confirmed in the South African Witwatersrand Formation of rounded or weathered pyrite and uraninite pebbles. Both these minerals are exceedingly unstable when oxygen is present.

It is estimated that oxygen became an important atmospheric constituent about 2.0-1.8 billion years ago.

The isotope (q.v.), oxygen-16, is available in the Atmosphere and in glacial ice. Oxygen-18 is primarily found in seawater.

In ecology, oxygen demand is the amount of oxygen needed to oxidize or decompose a given amount of organic compounds. See **BOD**.

OYA SHIO CURRENT Oya Shio, a current off Japan. merges with the Kuro Shio (q.v.) in the Sea of Japan. Temperatures vary widely and cause great fogs when the currents merge. These are similar to fogs found where the Labrador Current meets the Gulf Stream.

OYSTERS Oysters are bivalves which first appeared in the Triassic (225-190 m.y.). They were abundant in the Jurassic and Cretaceous Periods. They are still found abundantly in tidal areas.

Oyster beds are made up of great numbers heaped on one another. The shells are cemented to rocks and the larvae or spat live among the shells. A female can produce millions of eggs a year but only a few grow to adulthood.

Commercial oyster fishing in Delaware and Chesapeake bays have long been important. In 1900 production began falling off considerably. At present, oyster fishing in these bays is virtually non-existent due to disease and water pollution.

Many attempts are being made to farm oysters. See **PEARLS**.

OZONE Ozone, a triatomic molecule of oxygen, is more reactive than diatomic oxygen. Ozone forms under special conditions of electrical discharge as from lightning, ultraviolet light, and some pollution.

Ozone is a toxic, irritating gas with the odor of garlic. It can be fatal in doses as low as 0.0006%. Ozone is found in some SMOG (q.v.), especially at high altitude (Denver, Mexico City).

The pines of the Blue Ridge Mountains and Great Smoky Mountains produce ozone and free radicals. They release hydrocarbons into the Atmosphere that react with lightning and ultra-violet light.

OZONE HOLE In the Stratosphere over Antarctica, there is seasonal depletion of ozone. It first appeared, or was detected, in 1975 and it returns every spring. This 'hole' in the Ozone Layer (q.v.) has 35% less ozone than the layer in general. Slabs of ozone depleted air are sandwiched between layers with less depletion. The depletion is rapid, half being gone in less than a month.

Sunspot (q.v.) activity is a factor in the depletion of the Ozone, but the presence of chlorofluorocarbons (q.v.) in the Atmosphere is considered the major cause. This depletion is of concern since it went from zero to 50% in a decade. Chlorine appears to be the major culprit.

Ice crystals contain nitrogen and normally these react with chlorine rendering it harmless to the Atmosphere. The supply of chlorine now appears to exceed the necessary nitrogen.

The 'hole' is being monitored carefully with flights from Punta Arenas in Chile and from McMurdo Sound Station in the Antarctic. The hole appears to shift over latitudes south of 45°. 1988 reports imply that ozone depletion over Antarctica is becoming even greater. If so, the implications are for increased ultra-violet radiation levels globally.

Temperature in the Antarctic Ozone Hole decreased since 1960 by 15°. The climatic effects of the cooling are not known. Nor are the global effects of increased solar radiation.

Another Ozone Hole has been reported 700 miles from the North Pole. It extends from Spitzbergen, a Norwegian Island in the Atlantic, to Leningrad in the USSR. This Arctic phenomenon is considered not to be as great as that of the Antarctic.

U-2 flights over the region have been monitoring the depletion. The fact that there are inhabited areas in this region makes the presence of this ozone hole seem more menancing for the immediate term than that of the Antarctic. However, the affect on solar insolation and on climate is serious wherever on the planet such signs of a break-down of the Earth's 'sun screen' occurs.

The latest discoveries appear to show there is depletion over the Alps as well. Swiss scientists have measured a loss of 3% over the past 10 years.

Whether ozone depletion is a transient phenomenon or a trend cannot as yet be determined. The effect on global climate is, however immediate. Increased solar radiation will not only create greater warming, it will also disturb the wind patterns and rainfall. Certainly, any contributions to ozone depletion by chlorofluorocarbons needs to be immediately halted. Other measures to decrease chlorine in the Atmosphere should also be a global effort. The use of chlorofluorocarbons has increased 7% per year world-wide since its banning in the United States.

OZONE LAYER The Ozone Layer in the Upper Atmosphere acts as a partial shield against excess cosmic radiation. It successfully blocks up to 99% of ultra-violet radiation. This protective layer is found at 15-50 kilometers (9-30 miles) into the Atmosphere. In the layer there is about 200 times the ozone at sea level.

To some extent the Ozone Layer is being destroyed by jet contrails and the discharge of aerosols, especially chlorofluorocarbons into the Atmosphere. See **OZONE HOLE.**

OZONE POLLUTION The Ozone Layer in the Stratosphere acts as a shield for the Earth. Without it, the planet would be unliveable. In the Troposphere, especially at ground level, ozone at more than minor levels is a hazard. The Air Quality Standard has been 0.12 ppm for many years.

The automobile, which makes living and working in the Los Angeles Basin possible, is the primary source of the type of air pollution called 'oxidizing'. Emissions of sulfur and lead were coming under some control when it was discovered that these emissions were the source of 'Photochemical SMOG' and that ozone is the prime component.

Fishman and Kalish describe a 'river of ozone' which in 1978 extended from Texas to the Mid-Atlantic coast for a week. It was followed by a heat wave with high ozone levels in Texas, Oklahoma and Arkansas. This event was followed by airmass movement which brought high levels of ozone to the country's north and finally to the East Coast.

Controlling ozone pollution is a problem of great magnitude. Methane (q.v.) oxidation causes ozone to form in the Troposphere and this may be a major cause.

Massive burning in the Southern Hemisphere and Asia contribute enormous amounts of Carbon Monoxide. Carbon Monoxide plus the OH (Hydrogen) radical yields Carbon Dioxide and Hydrogen with ozone as a by-product. The HO_2 (Hydrogen) radical reacts with Nitrogen and ozone is a by-product. See **SMOG.**

In Los Angeles the situation is somewhat mitigated by the onshore flow of marine air. The ozone is the product of the California sunshine and periods of temperature inversion plus the emission of millions of cars belonging to residents and visitors. The primary component of this Photochemical SMOG is ozone. The problem is not a Los Angeles problem alone. It is now a national problem.

P

P-WAVE The primary seismic wave, 'p', travels through the Earth longitudinally at 7.5 to 13 kilometers (3.9-7.0 miles) per second. The 'p' wave is compressional. It encounters resistance so its velocity depends on the type and density of the material through which it travels.

PACIFIC PLATE The Earth's Crust is broken into segments or plates, one of which is the Pacific. It occupies a major part of the Pacific Ocean and is rimmed by volcanoes that mark the plate's boundary sutures or seams.

Material from the Crust sinks into deep trenches at the Asian and American margins. The Pacific Plate is being subducted (q.v.) beneath Japan at the rate of 10 centimeters (4 inches) per year.

As the Pacific Plate slowly turns, the Hawaiian Chain drifts northwest at the rate of 5.3 centimeters (2.2 inches) annually. Hawaii is over a hot spot (q.v.) and the volcanic islands formed as the plate moved. One scientist likened the Pacific Plate to a 'conveyor belt'.

A complete revolution of the Pacific Plate would take a billion years.

PACIFIC OCEAN The Pacific Ocean is bounded by North America, South America, Asia, and Australia. It occupies 1/3 of the Earth's surface and extends 17,000 kilometers (10,000 miles) from Ecuador to Indonesia. The ocean has an average depth of 3,940 meters (13,000 feet).

Drainage into the Pacific is from 19 million square kilometers (7.6 million square miles) of continent. By contrast, the Atlantic receives drainage from 69 million (27.6 million square miles). Due to the lesser amount of sediment and its greater volume of water, the Pacific has a lower salinity than the Atlantic.

Most of the world's islands are in the Pacific. It has the greatest relief of all oceans with its mountains, rises, trenches, and volcanoes. See **OCEANIC TRENCHES**.

PACIFIC-ANTARCTIC RIDGE The Pacific-Antarctic Ridge extends from the tip of South America to New Zealand. Magnetic profiles show it to be 500 kilometers (300 miles) from the spreading axis with an age of 10 million years.

PACIFIC HOT SPOTS Seafloor geysers were discovered just south of the Gulf of California in the vicinity of the East Pacific Rise (q.v.). Some of the chimney structures are up to 23 meters (75 feet) high. They have been rusted by iron and other mineral encrustations.

Since this discovery, other Pacific 'hot spots' (q.v.) have been found.

PACK ICE Frozen seawater forms pack ice by breaking into blocks, or floes (q.v.). The Arctic Ocean becomes virtually impassable much of the year due to pack ice. Below the surface ice up to 3-4 meters (9.5-13.0 feet) thick makes up the mass.

PADDY In the Far East rice is commonly cultivated in small, flooded fields or 'paddies'. These are walled with mud to hold water and control flow among the fields. Paddies are plowed while the water is up to 30 centimeters (1 foot) deep.

In these paddies 2 crops a year of rice and carp are raised. In the Ganges Delta, less than a square kilometer (1/3 square mile) will support a 1,000 people.

PAHOEHOE 'Pahoehoe' is Hawaiian for a ropy lava. It is very liquid and can flow great distances. The downhill speed of pahoehoe is 3-30 kilometers (6-18 miles) per hour.

Pahoehoe lava coils upon itself, twisting to form shapes preserved in hardened form. Cooled lava is black and may have a shiny, bright surface. The lava is non-gaseous. When cooled in the sea, it becomes pillow lava (q.v.).

PALAEARCTIC Europe and Asia north of the Himalayas, northern Arabia, and North Africa together form the Palaearctic. It contains the Earth's largest desert area. This arid belt extends from the Atlantic Coast of Africa to Arabia and Iran, and on into Asia to encompass the Gobi in Mongolia. Some other local names are Sahara, Arabian, Iranian, Turkan, and Takla Makan.

PALEOBOTANY Paleobotany is the study of fossil plantlife, its physiology, ecology, and chemistry. Great hydrocarbon reserves which are remains of organic material converted to coal, gas, kerogen, or petroleum are studied by paleobotanists. See **PALYNOLOGY**.

PALEOCENE The Paleocene Epoch (64-53 m.y.) began the Tertiary Period. Paleocene sediments overlie the Cretaceous and are followed by Eocene. North America had more or less assumed its present size and shape by the beginning of the Paleocene. The Atlantic Coastal Plain was submerged, and an inland sea covered the northern Great Plains. Paleocene clays and sands were deposited on the Gulf Coast.

The most important Paleocene formation is the Fort Union. It is found from Utah to Alberta and as far east as Nebraska. It is composed of yellow sands, gray shales, and huge coal deposits. Fossils of small, primitive mammals have been found in the western portion of the Fort Union.

The basal Fort Union member is the Cannonball Formation. It has sediments laid down in shallow marine and lagoonal environments.

During the Paleocene, sequoias appeared in North America. Rare palms also marked the Epoch.

PALEOCLIMATOLOGY Paleoclimate reconstructions can be made from rocks, fossils, and soils. Evaporite sequences, lacustrine sediments, and laterite rocks give clues to past climates.

A knowledge of paleoclimatology reveals evidence of the Earth's past relationship to the Sun. The study has helped to unearth and explain such anomalies as fossils of tropical vegetation in what today is an Arctic environment.

PALEOMAGNETISM Magnetism is introduced in minerals during crystal formation. It gives an indication of magnetic field orientation at the time of formation. Magnetism in a body or mass does not change with cessation or a subsequent change in the magnetic field.

Detailed paleomagnetic studies show the position of the poles at various geological times. Periodicity and possible changes in Earth orbits have been suggested to explain remnant magnetism. Paleomagnetic data show all continents except Antarctica have a north component of drift.

Data also show that the Arctic Ocean is becoming smaller. In the Pacific the continents are converging yet spreading data confirms the opposite. It appears that the ocean is decreasing in overall area while increasing in circumference. It is a problem which has not been satisfactorily explained.

Magnetic anomalies on the ocean floor corroborate the Continental Drift Theory. They indicate that separation of the South Atlantic continents was more rapid than those of the North Atlantic.

Paleomagnetic data also confirm that the Pacific is spreading along its rifts much faster than the Atlantic. See **MAGNETISM**.

PALEONTOLOGY The study of fossils and the rocks containing them is paleontology. It is a link between biology and geology. Paleoclimatology, paleobotany, and paleozoology are included.

PALEOZOIC ERA The Paleozoic Era or Age overlies the Precambrian. For years it was thought to be the time of the first lifeforms. Fossils have pushed that date into the Precambrian.

The first period of the Paleozoic, the Cambrian (570-500 m.y.), lasted 70 million years. The Caledonian Orogeny at the end of the period continued into the Silurian.

Lifeforms continued to be largely marine. The Ordovician and Silurian together lasted about 100 million years. These were followed by the Devonian, the 'Age of Fishes' which endured 50 million years.

In the United States, the periods following the Devonian are the Mississippian and Pennsylvanian (Lower and Upper Carboniferous elsewhere). The Mississippian and Pennsylvanian account for 65 million years. They are notable for the great coal seams developed from the luxuriant vegetation of their wetlands.

The last Paleozoic period, the Permian, existed 55 million years. The Permian is especially important because of its petroleum producing sediments. The Permian Basin of West Texas has been one the best petroleum areas in the United States. Glaciation in the Southern Hemisphere occurred during the Permian. A great swing in climate is evident in the sediments.

PALINGENESIS Palingenesis is an ultra-metamorphic process of reworking and regenerating magma (q.v.) at great depth. It is a complete mixing and reworking of molten rock. Ultra-high temperature and pressure are necessary to palingenesis.

PALMS Palms are found in all the warmest places in the world. There are about 2,100 species belonging to several hundred genera. There were palms in the Cretaceous Period (136-64 m.y.) so they are some of our oldest trees.

The ancient palm environment was of dense, low forest along rivers. The palm can be found in such environments today. A palm gallery forest can be found in the Amazon from the Xingu Basin to Peru.

The palm is really not well-adapted to arid conditions. Where they are found in desert areas, they are tapping an underground water source. Another instance of deep tapping is found in Central Australia's Palm Valley where the 'Livingstona mariae' is found. It is related to the cabbage tree palm.

The palm, which was mentioned in Exodus, has been and is extraordinarily important to humans. The Indians of the Upper Amazon bred palms, choosing those with a high carbohydrate level and about 15% protein. Over the centuries, they bred 200 types.

Palm trees have provided shelter as well as food in tropical and subtropical environments. Desert palms that grow in oases slow the moving sands, create a healthful microclimate, provide food, and enrich the soils.

Brazil, whose national anthem extols the palm, has solid stands of fanleaf over hundreds of square kilometers. The largest has 500 million Babassus capable of supporting millions of people. Indiscriminant cutting for farm plots is widespread and threatens these palm areas.

PALSAS 'Palsas', Lapplander for ridges, are periglacial landforms. They are abundant in Sweden and Finland. Palsas are peat and ice mounds on sub-Arctic bogs. They average 7 meters (23 feet) high and 10 meters (30 feet) wide. They may join and reach 100 meters (300 feet) long. Their core is a permafrost of peat. Surfaces are dry and usually barren or with low shrubs and lichen (q.v.).

PALYNOLOGY Land-based plants have existed 150 million years. Palynology is the study of fossil plant pollen and seeds. Fossil pollen and seeds are especially important for petroleum and other research.

Palynology yields clues to past climates. Pollen and seeds are geother-mometers. Lake sediments can contain pollen laid down a few thousand years ago. This pollen reveals the plant types that were present in the assemblage and provide important paleoclimate data.

PAMIR PLATEAU One of the world's highest inhabited plateaus is Pamir, mentioned by Marco Polo. In Afghanistan, the USSR, and China, the Pamir rises 4,300 meters (14,000 feet) above sea level. Peaks of the Kunlun, Karakorum, Hindu Kush, and Tien Shan ranges over-shadow the plateau. Some 100 peaks are over 6,000 meters (20,000 feet). The inhabitants of Pamir are largely nomads with herds engaged in transhumance (q.v.).

The Pamir is on a suture line between crustal plates. Earthquakes along this line have been studied for 20 years. The surface rises and subsides. Seismic waves slow down before a quake, but immediately prior to the event, resume normalcy. There is a rise in radon gas in water wells and electrical resistance increases in deep rocks.

PAMPAS Argentinan grasslands are 'pampas', an Indian word for flat-land. The pampas stretch from La Plata River south to the Patagonian Desert and from the Atlantic to the Andean foothills. Argentinean wheat is grown on the pampas and huge cattle herds are pastured.

PAN The standard miner's pan has a diameter of 40 centimeters (16 in-ches) from rim to rim and a 15 centimeter (6 inch) bottom diameter. The depth is 6.25 centimeters (2.5 inches). Originally of wood, iron and copper were used later. Today, many are plastic. Riffles have been in-corporated to make them more efficient.

To 'pan' is to wash concentrates of gold and heavy minerals allowing the minerals to settle by gravity. A special tilt angle and technique are needed for efficient panning.

To calculate production potential of a mineral deposit a 'pan factor' is used. It is the number of standard pans required to obtain a cubic yard (0.765 cubic meters) of gravel. For the 16-inch (40-centimeter) pan, the number varies between 150 and 200. The widely used factor is 180.

ISTHMUS OF PANAMA The slender land connection between Central and South America is the Isthmus of Panama. It formed about 3-5 mil-lion years ago.

On the Atlantic shore there are mangrove swamps, sandy beaches with moderate tides, and offshore coral reefs. The Pacific Shore is rocky and built by lava flows. Waters offshore are the habitat for many species of marinelife. About 10% are in both oceans.

The Panama Canal has freshwater locks that act as an effective barrier between the oceans. The proposed new canal would allow free com-munication. Inevitably, ecological change would result.

PANGAEA The Pangaea Continent was a single landmass until the Cretaceous (136-65 m.y.). It is the supercontinent of Wegener's Continental Drift Theory (q.v.). The landmass aggregated about 240 million years ago and remained intact for 100 million years. It was surrounded by the Panthalassa Ocean which covered the rest of the Earth.

When Pangaea broke up, volcanoes arose in the rifts which widened a few centimeters a year. The landmass was split by the Tethys Sea (q.v.) into Laurasia and Gondwana. These great continents later split into 6 blocks, the present continents (q.v.).

PANTANAL The lowland plain, or 'Pantanal', of Mato Grosso, Brazil, extends into Argentina, Bolivia, and Paraguay. It is on a down-dropped block of the Andean east flank and is covered by Recent sediments. Within the plain there are upthrust blocks like Urucum and Serra do Rabicho in Mato Grosso, and Mutum in Bolivia. Urucum is a 'mountain of manganese' and Mutum a 'mountain of iron ore'.

The pantanal is subject to seasonal flooding. The Paraguay River System drains the depression. In the wet season, from June until October, its floods can extend 20 to 40 kilometers (12 to 24 miles) from the banks of the Paraguay. When the waters recede there are remnant small lakes or 'lagoas', a favorite haunt of the 'jacare', or Brazilian cayman (crocodile).

PANTHALASSA The supercontinent Pangaea (q.v.) was surrounded by the Panthalassa Ocean which covered the rest of the globe. The great ocean floor was of sediment overlying basalt. There were micro-continents or rifted fragments in the ocean.

Some scientists believe Panthalassa never existed, that the Earth was covered by continental crust in the Precambrian. They subscribe to the 'Expanding Earth Theory'.

PAPYRUS Egyptians made parchment paper from papyrus reed ('Cyperus papyrus') that grows profusely in the Upper White Nile Basin. In the vast Central and East African swamps, papyrus is the dominant plant. There have been discussions of a modern paper industry based upon papyrus but no progress has been made.

Papyrus has been made into briquettes using techniques developed to create fuel from sedge. It is thought that papyrus could become an important fuel. The United Nations has been conducting experiments in Rwanda. The role of papyrus in these wetlands needs to be understood before idustrialization is undertaken. Otherwise the ecological balance may be completely disturbed. Harvesting may be appropriate, while clearing would upset the balance. See **FUELWOOD**.

PARA RIVER The southeastern distributary of the Amazon Delta is the Para River. It is 330 kilometers (200 miles) long and Marajo Island is on its left bank.

The great Tocantins (q.v.) tributary to the Amazon empties into the Para distributary upstream from Belem at Santarem.

PARACHUTE A parachute is a safety device that opens in the Atmosphere and creates drag, slowing natural descent. Parachutes are important accessories of meteorological research. When instruments are carried aloft by aircraft or rockets and jettisoned they are equipped with parachutes. Descent is broken and the instruments have time to collect and transmit data. Some can make soft landings.

PARAGUAY RIVER The Paraguay flows more than 2,500 kilometers (1,500 miles) before joining the Parana System. Its sources are on Brazil's Central Plateau and the eastern front of the Andes. The river forms a major border between Bolivia and Brazil. The Paraguay System also drains a substantial part of the Alto Parana and Pilcomayo river basins.

In flood, June to October, the Paraguay is linked by the Beni-Guapore System to the Amazon. At this season, Brazil is actually an island subcontinent.

PARALIC DEPOSIT Nearshore deposits of sediment are paralic, meaning there are frequent intercalations of marine sediments among continental ones. Their composition reveals the transgressions and regressions of the sea.

PARALLEL The Earth's sphere is bisected by a great circle called the Equator, which is also the zero° parallel line. The hemispheres from the Equator to the poles are divided into 90° of arc, each degree having its own small circle or parallel of Latitude.

Parallels and meridians form a coordinate system which makes it possible to locate positions on a map or chart of the sphere.

PARALLEL STREAM The majority of drainage patterns are dendritic (q.v.). Some major tributaries flow parallel to the main stream for great distances before joining it (Mississippi, Yellow River Systems).

PARAMOS 'Paramos' are high mountain meadows in the Andes between 1,800 and 2,400 meters (6,000-8,000 feet) at the edge of snowfields. The land is fertile and terraced steep slopes are excellent agricultural sites when the right temperature and rainfall exist. Erosion is the major concern.

PARANA PLATEAU The Parana Plateau covers a region in South America that extends from the coastal ranges of Brazil to the eastern 1/3 of Paraguay. The Parana River system cuts deep trenches across the plateau.

Parana basalt flows are the largest plateau lavas yet identified. Similar to the Columbia Plateau flows. Parana lavas cover more than 770,000 square kilometers (300,000 square miles) and are up to 600 meters (2,000 feet) thick.

Eruptions leading to the great flows took place in Late Triassic to Middle Jurassic (220-133 m.y., Amaral). Most of the flows were from fissures or vents. See **PARANA RIVER** and **IGUASSU FALLS**.

PARANA RIVER The Parana River and its tributaries all rise in the Brazilian Highlands of Minas Gerais and Goias. This 2nd longest river in South America flows south to join the Paraguay.

The Parana flows through the northern provinces of Argentina to debouch into the Rio de la Plata which is a great estuary on the Atlantic Coast. From the confluence with the Paraguay, the Parana flows 1,300 kilometers (800 miles) to the La Plata. The Uruguay River also empties into the La Plata Estuary.

In its descent from the Brazilian Plateau, the Parana and its tributaries plunge over a spectacular fall-line. Iguassu Falls (q.v.) is a series among many plunges. See **FALL-LINE**.

PARICUTIN VOLCANO Paracutin Volcano, Michoacan, Mexico. It is in the Sierra Occidental on the western boundary of the Central Plateau. The volcano appeared with a series of earthquakes in 1943. The region had become active after a 200-year period of dormancy.

Paricutin rose to 450 meters (1,500 feet) in 8 months. Now, the cone-shaped volcano is apparently quiet.

PARIS BASIN The Paris Basin, referred to by the French as a 'cuvette' (q.v.), is a counterpart of the London Basin. The 2 basins are separated by the English Channel. The Massif Central (q.v.) separates the Paris Basin from the Aquitaine Basin. Both Paris and Aquitaine are Triassic (225-190 m.y.) in age and 200 million years ago they were invaded by the sea. They were only emergent at the end of the Tertiary (2 m.y.).

During this long period of marine existence tremendous limestones and chalks built up in the region. These chalks crop out on both sides of the Channel to form the famous Dover cliffs and those of Etretat (q.v.) in France.

PARTICLE A particle is a subatomic entity with a mass measured in electron volts. All particles are affected by the Electromagnetic Field. Strong interactions cause them to decay or become unstable.

Particles tend to form octets. This phenomenon has led to the development of the Quark Model (q.v.).

The discovery of subatomic particles is not unlike the discovery of the atom in that whole new physical worlds have opened up. A new physical chemistry was necessary to deal with the subatomic. Various particle classifications have developed.

PARTICLE ACCELERATOR Research into nuclear reactions under controlled conditions has been made possible by the particle accelerator. A particle is shot at a target within a closed cell and the emissions are photographed (millions of times a day). The photos are carefully compared, and interpreted.

PASTURE GRASSES There are 4 types of grasses: Bamboo, cereal, pasture, and sweet. There are 3 main pasture grasses in the United States. These are Bermuda, Buffalo, and Blue Grass. See **GRASSLANDS**.

PATAGONIAN DESERT The Argentinian or Patagonian desert is continental and in the shadow of the Andes. It begins south of Bahia Blanca with the Rio Negro for a northern boundary and stretches to the Antarctic.

Patagonia has a high-Temporate to sub-Antarctic climate. Its flora are mainly low shrubs with a predominant grey, thorny thicket. This thicket has leaves that emit a pungent, bitter aroma.

PATINA Color coating, or patina, produced on rock surfaces is the result of weathering. It develops under subaerial conditions and transforms the surface through oxidation. The color is from the minerals contained within the rocks.

PEACOCK THRONE The Peacock Throne of Iran (Persia) contains 26,733 gems. It is part of the crown jewels and is said to back the currency of Iran.

PEARLS Pearls are obtained from the pearl oyster, a small mollusk. Only 1 in a 1,000 produces a pearl. A pearl develops with the deposition of nacre or mother-of-pearl around a minute foreign substance. The nacre is deposited in layers, growing a pearl.

Temperature, water conditions, and food all affect the pearl's color. They may be rose, creamy white, or black. The finest rose and cream pearls come from the Persian Gulf. A good quality pearl may be worth hundreds of thousands of dollars.

Pearls have been cultured for more than 70 years. A foreign object is introduced into a young oyster to induce pearl growth. Spat or larvae were obtained for many years from the Red Sea, near Dunganab Bay, Sudan, or from the Persian Gulf. Now spat are produced in Japan and elsewhere.

PEAT BOGS Peat is partially decomposed organic material found in swampy areas. It can build to such an extent, the swamp is converted to a peat bog and is covered with a mat of decaying material.

Peat is cut and used as fuel. An estimated 2,000 gigatons of methane hydrates are now frozen in peat bogs. If the bogs thawed this methane (q.v.) would be released into the Atmosphere. Since methane is a greenhouse gas which can contribute to global warming, a thaw would deepen the Greenhouse Effect (q.v.).

There are active peat bogs in the northern British Isles and in Scandinavia. Isolated peat bogs form at high elevations on mountain slopes as in the Rockies and Sierras.

PEDIMENT The pediment is a landform found in arid and semi-arid mountainous terrain. The mountain slopes have been eroded by sheet-flooding and covered with a thin veneer of sub-angular gravel.

The pediment and the mountain meet with a sharp break-in-slope. The overall slope is gentle, terminating in a bajada (q.v.). The landform reminded geologists of the facade or 'pediment' of some famous Greek monuments.

PEDIPLAIN Pediplains, coalescing pediments (q.v.) at the base of mountains, are common in arid areas. They should not be confused with peneplains (q.v.).

PEGMATITE A pegmatite is an aggregate of crystalline material. It forms a large dike (q.v.) or veins in pre-existing plutons (q.v.). It is of granitic composition and commonly intrudes granite and syenite. It is as if the granitic material for some reason became enlarged in grain-size. Pegmatites are predominantly of feldspar and white mica. Pegmatitic quartz forms in large masses or crystals. Some important minerals, in addition to quartz, are beryl, mica, tin, tourmaline, and tungsten.

Pegmatites form in the late stage of cooling magmas. Often, a pegmatite will contain acidic and sometimes rare minerals. The large crystal size is due to a longer development period and slower cooling.

Pegmatites tend to be zoned or unzoned. They are most common in belts in Precambrian rocks. Perhaps the greatest belt of zoned pegmatites is Borborema in Northeast Brazil on the border of the states of Rio Grande do Norte and Paraiba.

In the United States the major pegmatites are in Arizona, Maine, North Carolina, South Dakota, and Southern California. Economically important pegmatites are found in Brazil, West Africa, Malagasy, and the USSR.

PELAGIC The pelagic environment is in deep ocean waters far offshore. Pelagic sediments are fine clays and oozes. The oozes are composed of the remains of tiny organisms mixed with fine clay or mud.

PELE 'Pele' is the goddess of Hawaiian volcanoes. Volcanic glass is spun into threads by the wind to create 'Pele's Hair'. Tear-shaped obsidian creates 'Pele's Tears'. See **APACHE TEARS**.

PELECYPODS Pelecypods are a class of Mollusk that includes the bivalved clam. The Pelycepod first appeared in the Devonian (395-345 m.y.). By the Cretaceous (136-65 m.y.), clams were abundant. Although most clams were able to move, the 'Chamid' was a sessile reef-building species. The clam persists to the Present.

MONT PELÉE Mont Pelée on Martinique erupted in 1902. The ejecta was a rare, complex viscous lava with a molten magma that thrust through a thick dome or plug. This plug was ruptured. Glowing gas clouds and lava spurt from the vent. The clouds moved at 500 kilometers (300 miles) per hour outward from the mountain.

The eruption was accompanied by earthquakes and a tsunami (q.v.) which drowned St. Pierre. Pelee exploded 5 days after the initial eruption. Thousands were killed by the gas clouds. The volcano continued active until 1932.

PELLICULAR WATER Water is pellicular if held in suspension by molecular attraction. It forms a film adhering to solid particle surfaces. Water in the soil's aeration zone may be taken up by roots or evaporate. Pellicular water is not affected by gravity.

PENEPLAIN Erosion that has advanced to almost base level creates a gently sloping plain or peneplain (pene- means almost).

Base level is the culmination of an erosion cycle. New cycles begin with uplift and rejuvenation of landscapes. Ridges and mountains can be carved from an uplifted peneplain.

Some of today's high surfaces are uplifted peneplains. Among them are the Katanga Highlands in Africa; the Guiana Highlands, South America; the Ardennes, Belgium; the Poconos and other parts of the Appalachians in the United States. Their ridges tend to have remarkably uniform heights.

A region may go through cycles of peneplanation and uplift. With uplift there can be an arching or doming of the Earth's Crust. The Appalachians show an arching of this type. Ahoggar in the Sahara, an uplifted peneplain, is deeply dissected by wadis (q.v.).

Most of Canada east of the Rocky Mountains is peneplaned. It is underlain by the stable Canadian Shield.

PENINSULA A peninsula is an elongated projection of land into the sea. Examples are Scandinavia, Italy, Iberia, Florida, and Baja California.

PENINSULA RANGE The Peninsula Range of Southern California is formed of many small faulted blocks. They are separated from the Transverse Range by the northwest part of the Imperial-Coachella Graben. The mountains extend into Baja California, Mexico.

The granite core of the Peninsula Range is overlain by marine sediment. The granites are intruded by a number of pegmatites (q.v.), many highly mineralized and some with high quality gemstones. The range creates a rain shadow, cutting off moisture from the coast to the hinterland.

PENNSYLVANIAN The Pennsylvanian Period or System (300-280 m.y.) in the Paleozoic Era overlies the Mississipian and underlies the Permian. Pennsylvanian is almost exclusively North American usage. Elsewhere the period is considered part of the Carboniferous (q.v.). During the Pennsylvanian much of the Southern Hemisphere was glaciated.

PENNYWEIGHT The pennyweight is a unit used in California gold-fields. It equals 24 grains or 0.05 Troy (q.v.) ounces. When gold was at $35.00 an ounce, the pennyweight was worth $1.75.

PEPITA A very small nugget of gold is given the Spanish name of 'pepita'.

PERCHED WATER Water may be retained or 'perched' above an impermeable layer of sediment. The reservoir requires replenishment by precipitation. The water also may be held in the pore spaces of the rocks.

PERIDOT The pistachio-green peridot mineral is a valued gemstone. Less valuable is the oily bottle green. Peridot is an olivine-magnesium-iron silicate and color is mainly due to its iron content.

For centuries the main source of peridot was Zeberget Island (Topazios) in the Red Sea. The island was once called St. John's Island. Peridot was originally thought to be topaz, which accounts for the island's name. Other sources are Burma and the low Arizona desert.

PERIDOTITE Peridotites are silicate rocks rich in iron and magnesium. The rock is medium-coarse grained and of olivine or pyroxene origin. Peridotite is ultra-basic and weathers to serpentine. It is associated with chrome, diamonds, nickel, and platinum.

Olivine-forsterite is a peridotite suite mineral. Forsterite is associated with phosphates. At Phalaborwa Carbonatite (q.v.) in South Africa the forsterite is being mined for its phosphate content.

PERIGEE The perigee is that point in the Moon's orbit when it is closest to the Earth.

PERIGLACIAL The region bordering the continental ice sheet in the Arctic and sub-Arctic is periglacial. It is an environment of permafrost (q.v.) and freezing temperatures most of the year.

Many high mountain areas are mini-periglacial zones due to altitude and the ebb and flow of alpine glaciers.

Periglacial weathering is mainly mechanical. Thawing can result in mass movement. There are 4 different periglacial mounds that result from freezing and thawing (hummocks, peak hummocks, pingos, and palsas).

Glaciers redistribute enormous amounts of material. Deposits of loess and glacial outwash are prominent in the Periglacial Belt. Evidence abounds of past periglacial environments at lower latitudes in both North America and Europe.

PERIHELION When the Earth's orbit is closest to the Sun, it is at perihelion.

PERIOD The Period is a fundamental unit of geological chronology. It is a division of the Era, or Age. Rocks formed during a particular Period are of a System or Series.

PERIODIC TABLE The chemical chart of the elements, or Periodic Table, is arranged horizontally by atomic number and vertically by chemical group. The chart was first developed by Dmitri Mendeleev in the 1860's when he discovered order in the elements. On the basis of his findings he predicted new elements which were subsequently found.

The chart has been modified since Mendeleev's time but it was remarkably accurate. Elements are arranged by atomic weight. The groups are of those of similar chemistry and valence (q.v.).

PERIODICITY There are many geological periodicities. Among them are geomagnetic reversals, intrusions of various igneous rock types, mass extinctions of lifeforms, and Ice Ages.

There is a theory that there is a periodicity or rhythm to comet impact upon the Earth. This periodicity is thought to result from interaction of the Solar System with interstellar clouds as the Solar System moves through the Galaxy (q.v.). Geological and biological upheavals agree with cycles of impact cratering that occurred 33 and 260 million years ago.

PERLITE Hydrated volcanic glass with 2-5% water is perlite, a very light-weight material. Upon heating, perlite expands 20 times in volume. It has a low density with low conductivity and high sound absorption. It is used as acoustical tile and for filtering.

PERMAFROST Permafrost is permanently frozen ground. It is found in all periglacial (q.v.) zones. It may be a thin band or very thick. Above the permafrost there is often an active layer of soil, up to 5 meters (16.5 feet) thick.

There are extensive marshes in permafrosted areas since the surface may thaw but the meltwaters cannot drain. Some permafrosts are thousands of years old. Many other soil profiles have ice wedges from past periods of permafrost.

Arctic ground is frozen to a depth of 15 meters (50 feet). In the Lake Baikal, USSR, area permafrost is 400 meters (1,320 feet) thick. In Alaska, permafrost begins at a depth of 3-4 meters (10-13 feet) allowing Taiga (q.v.) forest to develop.

Canada has a discontinuous permafrost zone from Labrador to British Columbia and the Yukon. The south line is at 1° Celcius (30° Fahrenheit). Around Beaufort Sea, 400-600 meters (1,300-1980 feet) of permafrost has built up. At Prudhoe Bay the permafrost is 710 meters (2,340 feet) thick.

Areas remote from the Arctic support permafrost because of elevation or other microclimatic conditions. This is true of the 'Snow Belt' in the Lake Superior Region.

PERMEABILITY The capacity to allow subsurface waters to transit via pore spaces and interstices of a rock or formation is permeability. The amount of water per unit of time is the measure of permeability.

Each soil type has a constant permeability. Of the sedimentary rocks, sandstone is most permeable and porous, clay the least.

PERMIAN The Permian Period (280-225 m.y.) is the latest in the Paleozoic Era. It overlies the Carboniferous and is followed by the Triassic. The Permian is said to be between the Age of Coal and the Age of Reptiles.

The Permian climate in western and central United States and Europe was arid. Great deposits of sand, gypsum, and salt were emplaced. In the Ural Geosyncline of the USSR, there was a dead sea in the desert basin in which the Kungurian Series formed. Near Solikamsk, these sediments mainly of salt and anhydrite are 1,360 meters (4,000 feet) thick. They contain one of the world's largest reserves of potash. Germany's famous salt deposits of Stassfurt were deposited during this Permian arid regime.

Although the Permian was among the driest of periods, rainfall was sufficient at times for large forests to accumulate in some parts of the globe. There are Permian coals in areas that also suffered glaciation, notably Brazil, Argentina, and South Africa. Notable Permian coal is also found in China and Australia.

The Permian Ice Age was a Southern Hemisphere event. The Dwyka Tillite of South Africa found at the base of the Permian includes faceted boulders and striated basement rocks. The tillite (q.v.) is 600 meters (2,000 feet) thick in southern Karroo. Elsewhere in Gondwana, Australia and South America, there is evidence of this glaciation. The Talchir tillites are found on the south flank of the Himalayas below Permian marine deposits.

The Permian was a time of marked changes in flora. These included the development of the true conifer in the Northern Hemisphere. In the Southern Hemisphere the great tongue-leaved 'glossopteris' fern flourished. This was a fragile plant of probable subtropical environment.

The Permian Basin of west Texas and New Mexico is tripartite, separated by 2 platforms. The sub-basins of Midland and Delaware, are separated by a platform with a Precambrian core. In the Late-Permian, Carlsbad Basin and Midland Basin were evaporating pans. El Capitan Reef separated Delaware Basin from the sea.

Some Permian structures have served as great oil reservoirs. The Permian Basin, with its complex structure and stratigraphy, is rich in petroleum, natural gas, and potash. Reef limestones are reservoirs.

The Permian Period was one of mass species extinctions. About 1/3 of the species present at its beginning were gone by the end. The species most affected were the plankton (q.v.) feeders. Many plants and reptiles also disappeared.

Pangaea continent (q.v.) was almost completely formed by the end of the Permian. Asia had already collided with Europe to form the Ural Mountains. As land rose, the great epicontinental seas of the earlier Paleozoic (q.v.) disappeared. This, too, resulted in extinctions.

PERPETUAL SNOWS   Snows accumulating on soils above the snowline are perpetual. These snows accumulate even in summer. The snow build-up, precursor to glaciation, is greater than the amount lost through ablation (q.v.) or to peripheral melt.

PERSIAN GULF   The Persian Gulf, an arm of the Indian Ocean, is also known as the Arabian Gulf. It is sandwiched between Saudi Arabia and Iran and separated from the Indian Ocean by the Strait of Hormuz. Tidal period through the Strait is 25 hours.

The Gulf has some of the world's warmest and saltiest waters. It is shallower than the Red Sea on the opposite side of the Arabian Peninsula. The Gulf never exceeds 100 meters (300 feet) of depth.

The seafloor is made up of a thick pile of continental sediments containing oil and gasfields which produced about 1/3 of the world's petroleum.

The Gulf resulted from the collision between Asia and the Arabian Peninsula. The collision caused the mountains of Iran and Afghanistan to be pushed up. Part of Arabia was shoved below sea level in the massive crumpling.

The long term damage resulting from major oil spills in the Gulf which have resulted from the hostilities between Iran and Iraq have not yet been assessed. It is known that the water quality and ecology have been adversely affected.

PERU   There are 3 major provinces in Peru:

- The Andes
- The coastal plain and desert
- The rainforest on the north and east flanks of the Andes.

The Andes strike northwest-southeast for 200 kilometers (125 miles) across the country. At the most, the range is only 100 kilometers (60 miles) from the Pacific, but it creates the Continental Divide (q.v.).

Many peaks are 6,600 meters (20,000 feet) or more. 52 rivers cross the narrow coastal desert to the Pacific. The major one is the Santa Clara flowing north and then west to the sea. From the eastern flank of the Andes, the Maranon and its tributaries feed into the Amazon System.

The principal Andean range in Peru is the Cordillera Blanca. It has a granite batholith (q.v.) as a core. This is estimated to be 30 kilometers (18 miles) deep.

Along the coast, the Peruvian Desert receives less than 5 centimeters (2 inches) of rain a year. From May to October, fog from the Peru Current brings a little moisture. See **EL NINO**.

The northern Sechura Desert has economic phosphate deposits. The central and southern desert plains are rich in nitrates. The Andes are the world's richest source of copper and there are many significant mines. Other important minerals are gold, silver, tin, and tungsten. Petroleum is produced in the Peruvian Amazon and is shipped via Iquitos, Peru's port on the river.

In an effort to create farms in the Peruvian Amazon, 150,000 people were relocated. The project threatens the 6,000 already precariously living in the region. Soils are poor quality and the slopes are steep and not suitable for subsistence farming.

An earlier experiment on the Upper Huallega 25 years ago was a failure. Some of the lessons learned there were taken into account, but the outlook is still not good. Ecological damage is great and probably irreversible.

PETRIFICATION Petrification occurs when organic matter is replaced by solution deposited minerals. The most important replacement mineral is silica. Organic material is converted to stone by replacement.

PETRIFIED FOREST Forests buried by volcanic flows or other mantles were protected from subaerial decay. Organic material was replaced by minerals, principally silica, and the forest was turned to stone.

In North America there are a number of petrified forests. The largest is in Arizona and has trees that date from 100 million years. The predominant tree was the ancestor of the redwoods. The only conifer of this type now extant is the monkey puzzle. The trees were floated into their present positions and are encased in Chinle shales of Triassic age.

A petrified forest in Wyoming, densely populated by evergreens and hardwoods, was buried by ash from a volcano east of Yellowstone. Ashfall was so gentle it left the trees upright. Ashfalls were repeated 27 times and the record is in the rocks.

The island of Lesbos in Greece has a petrified forest. A volcano in the Island's northwest part had pine-covered slopes during a dormant period. When the mountain exploded ash and lava covered the slopes with a 100 meter (325 foot) blanket. With erosion, the solutions within this blanket replaced tree cells with silica.

PETROCHEMICALS Petrochemicals are produced from petroleum and natural gas. Hundreds of hydrocarbons are derived from these sources.

To produce petrochemicals, an additional 3% of petroleum production is required for energy. In the United States only 5% of petroleum products are presently converted to petrochemicals. Petrochemicals have achieved broad usage in modern life although they are of relatively recent origin.

PETROLEUM Petroleum is an inflamable mixture of oily hydrocarbons (q.v.). It develops from the decomposition of organic material under great heat and pressure. These conditions are found under deep burial by overlying sediments and by pressures exerted by structural deformation.

The major source of world energy today is petroleum which is classed as a fossil fuel. See **PETROLEUM RESERVES**.

PETROLEUM REFINING Processing converts crude oil to a multiplicity of products. The process essentially has 3 steps:

- Distillation - Crude is heated to 600-700° Fahrenheit. Gas is pumped to fractionation towers to condense.

- Cracking/polymerization - Molecular breakdown with heat, pressure, and catalysts.

- Treatment to remove impurities and create purer products.

PETROLEUM RESERVES Petroleum will collect where structures are favorable. 58% of oil and gas is in sandstones because they are the most porous and permeable of rock hosts. Another 40% is in limestone and dolomite and the rest, not readily accessible, are reserves in shales and tar sands.

The United States uses 1/3 the world's annual petroleum production. In 1978 there were only 43 billion barrels of proven reserves enough for 3-5 years. Unproven reserves were 385 billion barrels. If all became proven the reserves would last 20 years.

By 1983, proven and inferred world reserves were (in billions of barrels) according to the United States Bureau of Mines:

Middle East	357.5
USSR	88.0
Africa	64.0
Mexico	48.0
Far East	36.4
South America	32.0
United States	29.7
Western Europe	16.6
Canada	6.4

Exploitation of North Sea, Prudhoe Bay, and Mackenzie Delta all contributed to increasing the proven reserves. Total reserves for 1983 are 685.5 billion barrels of crude oil and 3,322.5 trillion cubic feet of natural gas (q.v.). Soviet reserves had quadrupled due to expanded exploration.

Estimates of undiscovered oil in the United States were at 68.6 billion barrels, 56.4 onshore, in locations like the Overthrust Belt of Wyoming.

Estimated reserves were scaled down after 4 years of dry holes (100). The estimate for natural gas is at 90 trillion cubic feet.

At the height of the Persian Gulf Crisis in 1990 the Saudi government reported exploration success in the Central Provinces, south of Riyadh. Indications are that the oil is high quality super-light. The Saudis claim enough oil to supply the U.S. with 1/4 of its imports for the next 50 years. Present imports are about 36 million barrels per day or 12.96 billion a year. (The Saudi estimate must be close to 150 billion barrels of additional crude.)

Present world reserves now equal 50-75 years' supply if market and political pressures do not alter them.

PETROLOGY The branch of geology devoted to the study of rocks, their compositition, texture, physical makeup, classification, optical characteristics, and transformations is petrology.

pH A scale was devised by Sorensen, to measure acidity or alkalinity of a soil. It was derived from the concentration of the hydrogen ion, and gives the negative logarithm of the hydrogen plus (H^+) ion, corresponding to 10^{-7}. All values below 7 are acidic. Neutral soil has water measuring pH 7.

The pH scale ranges from 1-14. Soils with a pH below 4 are very acidic and those above 10 are very alkaline. Both extremes are bad for agriculture. Acidic soils require calcium, alkaline soils need sulfur.

PHALABORWA In Transvaal, South Africa, the remarkable carbonatite (q.v.) of Phalaborwa has an igneous stock centrally located in a ring structure. Phalaborwa is a unique carbonatite in having an economic copper deposit. In addition, there is a producing phosphate deposit, a variety of Rare Earths (q.v.), and other minerals.

PHANERITIC Rocks with constituents visible to the naked eye are phaneritic. The grain or crystal size is usually greater than 0.2 millimeters.

PHANEROZOIC Geological time is divided into 2 Eons (Aeons). These are Proterozoic (q.v.) and Phanerozoic. The latter is the most recent and has lasted about 600 million years. 'Phanerozoic' is from the Greek for time of visible life.

The Phanerozic has 3 Eras. They are the Paleozoic, or time of ancient life; Mesozoic, middle life; and Cenozoic, recent life.

PHASE Chemically, 'Phase' reflects a difference in atomic energy and how far apart the atoms are spaced. In a gas, the atoms are widely spaced, while in a solid the atoms are so close together they have a definite organization. In liquids, the atoms are more closely spaced than in the gaseous phase but they so active that they keep slipping by one another.

Geologically, Phase is a division or stage of an Epoch. Phase, in this sense, is only rarely used.

PHENOCRYST An igneous rock may be comprised of both small and large granules. The fine material is background, or matrix. Larger crystals contained in the groundmass are phenocrysts. Phenocrysts are characteristic of porphyries (q.v.).

PHILLIPSITE The hydrous aluminum silicate, phillipsite, is a major member of the Zeolite Group (q.v.). It is the result of a reaction between rhyolitic glass and alkaline water. Ash beds alter to phillipsite when highly saline alkaline waters are present.

Phillipsite forms in deep sea deposits. It is more common in Pacific and Indian Ocean sediments than clinotilolite (q.v.) another important zeolite. Phillipsite will react with sodic brines to produce analcime, a zeolitic alteration.

Phillipsite has proven to be an exceptionally good ion exchanger in hemodialysis systems for the removal of nitrogen. It has many uses in waste disposal systems.

PHILOSOPHER'S STONE In the Middle Ages, alchemists believed there was a philosopher's stone capable of converting rock, metal, and flint to diamond or gold. It was greatly sought but never found. Experiments made in its search were the foundation of modern chemistry.

PHLOEM Phloem is an inner tissue of land plants. It is part of the sap circulation system. Sap moves upward in the xylem and downward in the phloem.

PHLOGOPITE Phlogopite is a silicate of magnesium with iron, a variety of muscovite mica. It is transitional between potassic and ferromagnesium micas and may contain lithium or fluorine. Biotite can alter to phlogopite through metasomatism (q.v.).

PHOSPHATES Phosphates are important to fertilizer production. The Phosphate Group includes apatite, collophane, dahlite, and other less common minerals. Fluorapatite and collophane are the minerals of major economic importance.

Until recently, 95% of the phosphate reserves were in sedimentary deposits. Now at least 15% of world production is from carbonatites (q.v.). Major production from these intrusives is from Brazil, Finland, South Africa and the USSR.

Morocco has the largest sedimentary reserves and challenges the United States as a supplier. The United States production has been principally from its Florida deposits of tri-calcium phosphate derived from organic residues. They are referred to as 'bone phosphate of lime' (BPL).

Phosphorite (q.v.) deposits around the world may become viable sources as more technology is applied to processing. The United States produces from its western deposits. The world's largest phosphorite deposits are probably those of China.

World phosphate reserves in 1989 were in excess of 36 billion metric tons of evaluated ore. The major holders of phosphate measured reserves are (in millions of metric tons):

Morocco/Western Sahara	7,000
South Africa	2,500
United States	1,300
USSR	1,300
Jordan	600
Brazil*	300
China	210
Senegal	160
Togo	40
Tunisia	20

U.S. Bureau of Mines, 1990
* DNPM Brazil, 1990

World production for 1989 was estimated at 174 million metric tons.

PHOSPHOR A phosphor is an entity that emits light when stimulated by radiation. Its mass is luminous or phosphorescent.

PHOSPHORITE Phosphorite is a rock containing calcium phosphate in cryptocrystalline (q.v.) form. Rock phosphate has been produced from the Phosphoria Formation in southeastern Idaho. See **PHOSPHATES**.

PHOSPHORUS Phosphorus is a non-metallic, multi-valent element of the Nitrogen Group. It is precipitated chemically and is relatively insoluble.

Great amounts are in rocks and sediments and some is returned to the Atmosphere by erosion. If the pH (q.v). is about 6-6.5, calcium and magnesium phosphate will precipitate. If it is 5.9-6.1, the precipitate produces iron and aluminum phosphate.

Plants absorb phosphorus as a salt. They release it upon decomposition. Lichens (q.v.) are capable of releasing phosphorus directly into the Atmosphere.

As a nutrient, phosphates are brought to surface waters by upwelling (q.v.). Phytoplankton absorb phosphorus, so it enters the food chain.

PHOTON The photon is a quantum (a little package) of electromagnetic energy. It has no mass and no electrical charge. These minute particles are from the Sun and Cosmos. A photon can behave as a wave or as a particle. Most solar photons reach the Earth as sunlight. X-rays and gamma rays are high energy, short wavelength electromagnetic radiation, or photons.

PHOTOSYNTHESIS Water plus carbon dioxide, in the presence of light, yields sugar and oxygen in plants. The process is photosynthesis. The sugar produced is glucose. Photosynthesis allows the plant to produce chlorophyll which provides carbohydrate.

Oxygen produced is given off by plants and returns to the Atmosphere. Respiring animal-life inhales oxygen and gives off carbon dioxide, thus providing a symbiotic relationship between plants and animals. See **SYMBIOSIS**.

PHREATIC Phreatic is a word derived from the Greek for water that can be reached by a well. It is used to signify deep groundwater. Most underground caverns have been formed by phreatic waters.

PHREATIC ERUPTION Steam explosions containing mud and other non-incandescent material are phreatic. The eruption results from heating and expansion of groundwater by internal heat sources. Phreatic eruptions can follow main outpourings of lava where water invades areas depressed by the weight of the lava. Phreatic events occur frequently in Hawaii and New Zealand.

PHREATIC LENSE In soils, the saturation zone is the phreatic lense. The upper surface is the water table, below which all pore spaces and interstices are water-logged.

PHREATOPHYTE A water-loving plant is a phreatophyte. It has adapted to seeking the water table and has developed a long tap root. Phreatophytes are found along watercourses in deserts and semi-arid areas.

PHYLLITE Transitional rocks between slate and schist are phyllites. They are more brittle than slate and range in color from dull red through yellow to greenish-gray. Some phyllites began as shales, others as volcanic tuffs.

Phyllites are fine-grained and micaceous, often with microcrystalline pyrite or garnet. Phyllites are foliated, causing them to form thin sheets. Foliation is controlled by chlorite or other micas.

PHYSICAL WEATHERING Physical weathering is the breakdown of rocks by purely mechanical forces. They include abrasion, alternation of wet to dry or hot to cold, cavitation, crystal growth, frost, root growth, and unloading.

PHYSIOGRAPHIC PROVINCES The United States is divided into natural physiographic provinces.

Eastern United States:
- New England and Adirondacks - Glaciated metamorphic rocks and granites
- Appalachian Mountains and Plateau - Sandstones and shales with a Precambrian core.

- Atlantic/Gulf Coastal Plain - Horizontal sediments covered by un-consolidated alluvium.

Central United States:

- Mississippi Valley - Alluvium.
- Ozark/Oachita Interior Lowlands - Sandstones, shales, and lime-stone.
- Superior Uplands - Glaciated sediments and metamorphic rocks.

Western United States:

- Rockies - Folded sediments, metamorphic, and igneous rocks
- Columbia Plateau - Trap rocks (lavas), loess in valleys
- Basin and Range - Gravels, sands, playa deposits, volcanics and and igneous rocks
- Sierras/Cascades - Granites and volcanic rocks
- Pacific Coastal Ranges - Sedimentary rocks
- California Valley - Unconsolidated alluvium.

PHYTOPLANKTON   Tiny, floating plants in fresh- or seawater are phytoplankton. They are a major food source, the initiation of most food chains. Phytoplankton are more important than larger fixed plants as they directly nourish a large portion of aquatic life.

Phytoplankton are important as a source of oxygen produced through photosynthesis (q.v.). Some bodies of water are colored by phyto-plankton. These events are called 'blooms'. See **PLANKTON**.

PICO-   The prefix pico- before any unit indicates that the unit is divisible by a trillion (10^9). It is the same as micromicro-.   The pico-curie, a radiation measure, is an example.

PICRITE   Picrite is a very dark ultra-basic rock. It contains augite (35%), olivine (30%), and hornblende and biotite (25%). Apatite ores can be up to 10%.

PIEDMONT   The foothill area of a mountain range is the piedmont. It may be a gentle transitional slope or more abrupt. The Appalachian Piedmont extends along the range behind the Atlantic Coastal Plain.

PIEDMONT GLACIER   At the base of many ranges, alpine glaciers tend to merge to form a larger piedmont glacier. Alpine glaciers flow out of their valleys spreading sideways and so tend to join up. Malaspina Glacier in Alaska is a piedmont glacier along the St. Elias Range.

PIEZOELECTRICITY   The property of piezoelectricity or pressure electricity, causes a charge to develop on crystal edges. It is a small charge that dissipates when the pressure is removed.

Crystals, essential to radio broadcasting, maintain frequency control through piezoelectricity. Rock crystals are prized for this characteristic. Today the majority of crystals used are synthetic and are grown from crushed quartz.

PIEZOMETRIC SURFACE The piezometric surface is the level to which water rises under its own pressure. It is also the level to which water rises in a well.

PILE Nuclear reactors were originally constructed by piling up blocks of graphite and uranium. A number of Soviet reactors, including Chernobyl, are of this type. The reactor cores are referred to as 'the pile'. The design is now considered obsolete. See **CHERNOBYL**.

PILLOW LAVA Ropy basaltic lava cooling in seawater consolidates into a 'pillow lava'. The lavas result from rapid surface cooling preventing them from spreading. The interior may remain molten after the surface has cooled. Lavas can be from vents in the seafloor or flows.

Pillow lavas at Yellowknife, Canada, were formed 2 billion years ago. Similar Cambrian pillow lavas are found in Wales and Newfoundland. Modern pillow lavas are forming off Iceland and the Hawaiian Islands.

On Cyprus, pillow lavas form part of the ophiolite (q.v.) sequence.

PINE CREEK GEOSYNCLINE Pine Creek Geosyncline, Northern Australia, is an inlier of Lower Proterozoic (q.v.) metasediments. It is surrounded by younger sediments to the north, east, and south.

In the western part of the Geosyncline are Archaen granites and metasediments. The region is famous for economic deposits of copper, gold, tin, tungsten, and uranium. The famous uranium deposits of Rum Jungle and Alligator River are in the Geosyncline.

PINGOS Pingos are permafrost relief forms resulting from water injection. Water is forced up by hydrostatic or cryostatic pressure through unfrozen gaps in permafrost (q.v.). A cone-shaped ice mound forms. The ice is covered by a thin veneer of soil. Maximum mound height is about 100 meters (300 feet). When the ice melts, the soil forms a rimmed depression which filled with meltwater.

Pingos are widespread in the sub-Arctic forests of Alaska. Some are now growing in Central Alaska. The pingo relief form was first identified in Fennoscandia.

Collapsed pingos have been identified in Ordovician rocks (500-430 million years ago) in what is now the Sahara. Their presence indicates that the area was permafrosted during that period.

PINNACLE Needle-shaped peaks are pinnacles. They often form clusters. Pinnacles form when erosion waters percolate through vertical joints (q.v.) causing blocks of rock to spall. In Bryce Canyon, Utah, there are some excellent examples of pinnacles.

In Western Australia there are isolated pinnacles up to 1.8 meters (6 feet), which are remnants of a karst (q.v.) landscape. The pinnacles are composed of yellow limestone columns wind-streaked with pink and brown sediments.

The Pinnacles Desert was eroded from high dunes of lime-rich sands. The lime was leached from the upper parts and the lower became cemented limestone and a calcrete formed. This calcrete caps the remnant pinnacles.

PIPE The cylindrical conduit or chimney providing a volcanic outlet is a pipe. Pipes are often filled with volcanic breccia. Some South African pipes contain blue or weathered yellow kimberlite (q.v.).

PIPELINES Pipelines are the most economical of transport media for petroleum and natural gas. The major expense after laying a pipeline is the building and maintenance of pumping stations (3 miles apart).

In the United States, 50% of petroleum production is shipped by pipeline, or 10 million barrels of oil and 55 million cubic feet of natural gas in 1982. A pipeline net from Soviet Siberia is sending natural gas to Europe, including to Austria and West Germany. Iraqi oil is transported by pipeline to the ancient port of Sidon in southwest Lebanon. Bolivian oil is transported across the Andes to Chile.

Minerals are slurried and shipped via pipelines. These range from coal to phosphates. The phosphate pipeline has been a major guerilla target in Spanish Sahara.

PISOLITE A concretion, similar to but larger than an oolite (q.v.), is a pisolite. They are frequent constituents of lateritic terrain. Many bauxites and some limestones are pisolitic.

PITCH Pitch, a natural asphalt, is 'heavy petroleum' found around oil seeps. This was the 'pitch' Noah used to caulk the Ark. North American Indians used it when constructing canoes.

PLACER A secondary deposit of minerals derived from erosion is a placer. The eroded product is transported, washed, segregated, and concentrated. The agencies of deposition are the wind, streams, and the sea. Placers may be buried, eluvial, or illuvial and found on beaches, terraces, and slopes, and in stream channels both modern and ancient.

The deposits are aeolian, alluvial, or beach. Gravity separation concentrates heavy minerals. Marine placers are concentrated by it and waves that wash minerals along the coast and accumulate them.

Economic placers of diamonds, gold, ilmenite, magnetite, rutile, tin, and zirconium are worked from beach, and offshore deposits. Some gold placers are found in ancient buried sediments in both South Africa and Brazil.

PLAGIOCLASE Plagioclase is an isomorphous feldspar (q.v.) series of a solid-solution group of sodium, calcium, and aluminum. The rocks are white to gray, have a vitreous luster, and 2 cleavages at right angles to each other.

A light-colored granite containing 45% plagioclase feldspar (alaskite) is mined at Spruce Pine, North Carolina. It is used in the glass industry.

PLAIN A large area of low relief is a plain. Over half of all plains are gently sloped and all have a local relief that is below 90 meters (300 feet). Rimming continents are fringes of coastal plains. The Atlantic and Gulf Coast Plains are important examples. The great rivers of the world have built huge floodplains and deltas.

The Great Plains, Pampas, and Steppes are vast continental areas of low relief. They are almost treeless and because they are all in the lee of mountains, have semi-arid climates. They support 'seas of grass' and have become grain-growing and pastoral areas.

Pleistocene to Recent alluvium cover 1/4 of all continental plains. Plains with earlier sediments are primarily volcanic.

The deep sea or abyssal plains (q.v.) are the flattest of all plains.

PLANCK The physicist, Max Planck, held that energy is released in little bundles or 'quanta' (q.v.) and that the energy was discontinuous. He introduced Quantum Theory and changed the scientific view of the physics of matter.

PLANE TABLE The plane table is a portable survey tool. A tripod with an alidade (q.v.) is mounted on a drawing board with a ruler. It is used for short distances where the Earth's curvature is not significant. The error is minimal, amounting to 15 centimeters (6 inches) in 19.2 kilometers (11.5 miles) of arc.

PLANET A large, cooled mass or body in orbit about a central star is a planet. Earth is a planet orbiting the Sun. The Sun is a star in the Milky Way Galaxy (q.v.).

Earth has a single satellite, the Moon. With 8 other planets it is part of the Solar System. The planets orbit in the equatorial plane of the Sun. The inner ones have metal-rich cores, Earth's is nickel-iron. The outer planets are helium-rich.

Planets spin slowly. A little over a day is required for each Earth rotation.

PLANKTON Plankton are free-floating organisms borne about by currents in the sea or freshwater. Plankton are the most numerous of lifeforms and may be plant or animal.

Plankton grow in seas to a depth of 120 meters (400 feet) if light can penetrate. If murky, they will be restricted to the upper 50 meters (165 feet).

Plankton are a vital part of the food chain for more complex animals. Some whales subsist on plankton. Planktonic plants or phytoplankton (q.v.), contribute extensively to water aeration since they are capable of photosynthesis (q.v.).

Diatoms (q.v.) which are phytoplankton, can 'bloom' in the spring. Millions will cover a square centimeter of water. When they die, their silica skeletons drop to the ocean floor. See **OOZE**.

PLANTS Most life is divided into 2 major Kingdoms, Flora and Fauna (plant and animal). There are 350,000 known species of living plants (1961). 80% of these are found in Brazil. The species range from 90 meter (300 foot) rainforest trees to tiny microscopic Algae (q.v.).

Plants have existed on Earth from 3.5 to 4 billion years. The largest of the younger angiosperms or flowering plants is the Chinese Wisteria with branches up to 150 meters (500 feet).

Without the plants and the photosynthesis (q.v.) which they perform, animal life could not exist. The transformation of carbon dioxide into oxygen produced by plants makes the planet habitable by oxygen-breathing lifeforms.

There is a form of chemical warfare called allelopathy carried out by some plants. They produce chemicals which inhibit the germination of seeds, their own if too early, and of other plants that might intrude on their space. The plants can also produce chemicals which further germination.

Some plants produce chemicals which are natural insecticides that enhance their growth but may inhibit growth in other species. The salicylic acid some willows and poplars produce is an example.

PLASMA Plasma, an electrically neutral gaseous mass with positive and negative ions, has been referred to as the 4th state of matter.

Plasmas differ from solids, liquids, and gases, in that they do not occur at a definite temperature. Some are produced at a few thousand degrees.

It is estimated that the Universe is composed 95-99% of plasma. As the Earth cooled, subatomic particles in plasma were converted to atoms or elements.

PLASTIC Plastic is the physical property of being moldable. Rocks in a semi-molten phase are plastic.

Any polymer (q.v.) that can be molded under heat and pressure is a plastic. Manufactured plastics began with the search for resin substitutes. Most plastics are petroleum based.

RIO DE LA PLATA Rio de la Plata is the estuary of the combined Paraguay, Parana, and Uruguay Rivers. These rivers drain the Parana Plateau and the Paraguay Basin. The Atlantic estuary forms the Argentine-Uruguay border.

More than 5.7 million cubic meters (2 billion cubic feet) of silt a year are discharged. The Parana Delta is growing into the La Plata at the rate of 70 meters (230 feet) per year. See **PARANA RIVER**.

PLATE BOUNDARIES Seismic evidence shows that earthquake patterns outline plate boundaries. There are 3 types of plate boundaries:

- Accreting boundaries
- Consuming boundaries
- Transform boundaries.

At the accretion boundary new material comes to the surface at spreading ridges in diapiric action. Most accreting boundaries are in deep seas. One passes through Iceland. 2 centimeters (1/2 inch) a year are added to each plate. It is a divergent boundary.

In a consuming boundary, material is shoved into the Mantle by an overriding plate. Continental material, too light weight to be entirely consumed floats and collides with other continental material and a buckling occurs at the suture or seam. This is a convergent boundary.

At the transform boundary, plates grind past each other edge-to-edge as in the San Andreas Fault. This is a parallel boundary.

PLATE TECTONICS Plate tectonics, a branch of structural geology, has grown based on evidence collected since the 1960's. The Earth's Crust is broken into great segments or plates which float above the Asthenosphere (q.v.). There are 16 major plates.

Movement may be generated by isostatic (q.v.) adjustment with heat and pressure from the Mantle, or from convective currents (q.v.) within the Mantle. Combinations of a variety of physical forces are likely.

Crustal plates are relatively rigid and in constant relative motion. The motion may be extraordinarily slow or rapid with major rifting. When plates collide, a portion is consumed. If a crustal plate dives into a trench next to a continental margin, upthrusting may occur on land. Uplift can be accompanied by volcanic activity in the rift zone.

Most plate boundaries are covered by seas and marked by rifts. There are 75,000 kilometers (45,000 miles) of Global Rift as a single connected system. From it, there are innumerable smaller rifts, all accompanied by a system of ridges and trenches.

The boundary of the African and European plates is along the Mediterranean. The North and South American plates are riding over the Pacific Plate. The Pacific Ocean appears to be shrinking while the Atlantic is still spreading.

PLATEAU A plateau is an elevated flat-lying terrain. Relief on a plateau is greater than on a plain. Valleys are more deeply incised and the plateau boundaries are sharp escarpments although the plateau may abut a mountain on one side. Sometimes, plateaus are 'en echelon' like stairs (southeastern Brazil and southern India).

The central portions of continental landmasses often have large plateaus. The Central African Plateau makes up a great portion of that continent. The Brazilian Plateau is the largest physical province in that country after the Amazon Basin.

PLATEAU BASALT Basalt exuded from great cracks in the Earth's surface instead of from central craters have built up huge plateaus. These flood basalts up to 2,100 meters (7,000 feet) thick have covered vast areas in Brazil, India, and the United States.

Flood basalts are not confined to the great areas mentioned. They cover lesser areas in Northern Ireland, North Africa, and elsewhere.

PLATINUM Platinum is a dull, grey blue-black and chemically unreactive metal. An excellent catalyst (q.v.), platinum is used in catalytic converters installed in automobiles to control harmful emissions. It is also used as a catalyst in oil refining. Conversions can be up to a million times faster with the platinum catalyst than without. Platinum is also used in the conversion of ozone taken in by jet aircraft.

Since platinum is chemically inactive it is used in the electrodes of heart pacemakers. Platinum has other major medical uses and is vital to the production of high grade optical glass. It is used to create the ruby rods for lasers.

Platinum is recovered from the Merensky Reef of the Bushveld Complex of South Africa. Some of the tunnel drifts are at a depth of 600 meters (2,000 feet). Platinum is associated with ultra-basic rocks and is a by-product of Sudbury, Canada, nickel production.

The Stillwater Complex, Montana, is expected to meet 10% of the United States consumption by the 1990's. At Goodnews Bay, Alaska, platinum production began in 1981. At present the United States is purchasing 1/2 the world's supply.

Platinum is now our most precious metal. It is fortunate that only small amounts are needed for most uses. Its price has been as high as $1,000 per Troy ounce. Production of refined metal in 1986 was 3.8 million Troy ounces.

PLATINUM GROUP METALS The Platinum Group Metals (PGM) are made up of platinum, iridium, osmium, palladium, rhodium, and ruthenium. They occur together and have in common their rarity, high melting points, and the ability to resist acids. When iridium is added to platinum, an alloy is created with an even higher melting point and an increased resistance to electricity and corrosion.

The major producer of Platinum metals in 1989 was South Africa with 133,000 kilograms. The USSR produced 121,000 kilograms from the almost exhausted Ural placers.

In 1989 the world resources were estimated at 100 million kilograms. Resources in the United States were estimated at 9 million kilograms. World reserves of these rare and strategic metals are in the main located in the following countries.

The measured and indicated reserves (in thousands of kilograms) are:

South Africa	50,000
USSR	5,900
Canada	250
United States	250

U.S. Bureau of Mines, 1990

PLATYPUS The duck-billed platypus is a small mammal found only in south Australia and Tasmania. It is egg-laying, has thick fur, webbed-feet, and a duck-shaped bill.

Platypus belongs to the monotremes, a group of primitive, egg-laying mammals. They are found east of the Wallace Line (q.v.).

PLAYA Playas are dry lakes, or mudflats. They are an arid to semi-arid feature which varies in size and occupies basins of interior drainage. Many have veneers of salt, others are alkali flats. Some are mud-charged with debris from near-by mountains. When the muds dry, they crack in a characteristic polygonal pattern.

Playas are subject to wind erosion or deflation. The winds can carry fine playa sediments great distances.

PLEISTOCENE The earliest part of the Cenozoic or Quaternary Era is the Pleistocene Period, which began 2 million years ago. The Period has been punctuated by glacial and interglacial epochs. The Post-Glacial Epoch merged into the Recent only 11,000 years ago. Even the Recent has seen mini-ice ages and may truly be an interglacial.

During the Pleistocene 4 major continental ice sheets covered North America. From the most recent to oldest they are Wisconsin, Illinoian, Kansan, and Nebraskan. Glacial and interglacial epochs appear to have been varied in duration. A rough periodicity of 100,000 years is indicated by deep sea sediment cores.

PLEOCHROISM Pleochroism is the capacity of a mineral to change color. These changes occur in response to changes in light intensity; alternation from wet to dry; and other responses to environment. The most well-known changes occur with alexandrite, a valued gemstone.

PLINIAN ERUPTION Mont Pelée (q.v.) was a Plinian eruption with a large ejection of gases. The most recent plinian eruption was from Colombia'a Nevada del Ruiz (q.v.). The gas column rose 27 kilometers (16 miles) and 35 million tons of andesite and dacite were ejected. Fumaroles built up sulfur and chlorine.

The Nevada del Ruiz eruption caused rapid melting of glacial ice and mudflows which devastated the countryside. An estimated 25,000 people lost their lives.

PLINTHITE The mottled, weathered mixture of iron and aluminum oxide with quartz found in some soil profiles is plinthite. The name

derives from the Greek 'plinthus' for block or brick and refers to the irreversible transition to hardpan. A plinthite develops when the soil is
subject to alternating wet and dry seasons accompanied by the rise and
fall of the water table.

PLIOCENE (12-2 m.y.) The Pliocene Period is the latest period of the
Tertiary Era. It succeeds the Miocene and underlies the Pleistocene. In
Europe it is called Neogene.

The type locality for Neogene sediments is Po Valley, Italy. In the
United States, Pliocene sections are well-known in Los Angeles Basin
and San Joaquin Valley. Foraminifera facies are evident in both
Europe and America.

PLUCKING Plucking is an erosional process of ice weathering associated with glaciers. Ice is molded around a block of bedrock and the
moving glacier plucks the encased mass from place. The process is assisted by jointing (q.v.).

PLUGGED DOME When masses of lava cool and fill a crater they block
or plug the conduit channel, thus forming a mound or plugged dome of
magmatic material. This material may be exploded away in a subsequent eruption. Or, material around the plug may erode away leaving the hardened plug in place.

PLUMES Volcanic islands rising from the seafloor at the divergent
edges of crustal plates are above volcanic plumes. As the plume moves,
new islands appear. The oldest islands are most distant from the plume
zone. The path traced by the plume is marked by islands. Tuzo Wilson
advanced this theory for the development of Hawaii.

Basalts in plume areas are of deeper origin than those from spreading
ridges. Plumes, according to Morgan, are generated at the boundary
between the Mantle and Core and rise to the Lithosphere at a rate of 2
meters (6.5 feet) a year.

Only 1% reach the surface where the material forms aseismic ridges.
Morgan believes there is a total overturn of Mantle material every 2
billion years. The plumes or hot spots (q.v.) are thought to reach 150
kilometers (90 miles) in diameter. More than 20 plumes had been identified by 1985.

PLUNGE POOLS Large potholes developed at the base of a waterfall
are plunge pools. The impact of eddying water creates and enlarges
them. Their size is related to the energy the waterfalls generate. This,
in turn, is governed by height, volume, and rock type.

PLUTON A pluton is an igneous rock consolidated at depth. These rocks
intrude others as they are thrust upward, probably in an expanded
gaseous state. Many intrusives are huge structures such as batholiths
(q.v.). Some others are laccoliths, sills or dikes. Chemical crystallization
sequence is evident in the mineral suites and crystal sizes.

Plutonic rocks are formed deep within the Earth and are only exposed after long periods of erosion. See **IGNEOUS ROCKS**.

PLUTONIUM   Plutonium, element number 94, was created in the Laboratory. The plutonium isotope, 239, is fissionable and with uranium-233 and uranium-235 is a reactor fuel. The element presents problems in the disposal of spent reacter fuels since no feasible technology has yet been developed.

At present 6 nations are involved in the recycling of plutonium. It is estimated that there will be a surplus of 100 metric tons by 1995. Only a few kilograms provide temendous energy so keeping track of the element is essential.

PLUVIAL   Periods of extraordinarily heavy precipitation of both rain and snow are pluvial. There were long pluvial periods in the Pleistocene.

Some authorities believe pluvial periods are transitional from interglacial to glacial epochs. The additional moisture augments glaciers.

PODZOL   Podzol is a large soil group of poor and acidic soils. These soils form in moist climates under conifer forests. Clay and humus have been leached down in the soil profile (q.v.). Many lowland tropical soils of South America and Southeast Asia are podzols. They support forest and scrub vegetation on what are white, sandy, and bleached soils.

In South America these soils can be found in the Rio Negro Basin and in the Guianas (q.v.). They support the Guiana Wallaba (Eperua) Forest and a form of savanna vegetation near Manaus, Brazil. This vegetation is known as a pseudo-caatinga. See **CAATINGA**.

POINT   The point is a unit for measuring the diamond. There are 100 points in a carat (q.v.).

POLAR EASTERLIES   Cold and stormy winds from polar regions are Polar Easterlies. They affect the shipping lanes in the Northern Hemisphere in winter as they cause very rough seas.

POLAR FRONT   Cold, dry, Arctic air encountering warm, moist, tropical air gives rise to a boundary zone or Polar Front. Along this front, cloud banks are up to 200 miles wide. Within the front, winds shift from being Polar Easterlies to become the Westerlies.

POLAR FRONT JET STREAM   The jet streams flow over well developed polar fronts and transport weather-making airmasses to the central Great Plains of North America. High altitude jet streams dip south at times bringing freezing temperatures even to Florida. From the 1940's to the 1970's there was an overall decrease in temperature of 4-5%. Deep dips in the jet stream patterns have been related to great changes in climate. These appear to have occurred over Europe in the Mini Ice Age (q.v.) when Greece experienced periods of prolonged cold weather.

POLAR WANDERING The Earth's axis had a greater tilt 9,000 years ago than today. It has since been seeking a more upright position. There is a cycle of roughly 40,000 years during which the axis slowly moves to a maximum tilt and than returns to the upright.

Poles, as tips of the axis, have a wandering orbit. Polar wandering has great climatic implications. It can account for fossils of subtropical vegetation in areas now sub-Arctic.

Remnant magnetism corroborates polar shifts. Evidence shows that 400 million years ago the North Pole was mid-Pacific. Its orbit took it to Guam and Japan, and across Siberia to its present location.

POLARIS The North Star, or Polaris, has been the star closest to the North Pole zenith since about the 16th Century. This means the Earth's northern axis points most directly to Polaris. The easily identified star in the Little Dipper (Ursa Minor) Constellation is a guide to navigation.

The Earth's axis has been aligning closer to the Celestial Pole about which daily stellar movement appears to occur. It will be 1/2° of arc off in the year 2,100. See **URSA MINOR**.

POLDER The Dutch reclaim land from the sea by the construction of levees and dikes. The area is drained and used for agriculture. The Dutch introduced the polder to Surinam where coastal wetlands have been reclaimed with some success.

The 'polder' or reclaimed area is usually below sea level. In times of extreme high water, polders are threatened.

Present polder development in the Netherlands is related to the Zuider Zee Project. There is a proposal to construct polders in the Waddenzee between the Frisian Islands and the mainland. There is opposition as the 'lagoon-sea' is a major refuge for European waterfowl. See **ZUIDER ZEE**.

POLES There are 3 different north and south poles. They are the:

- Geographic Poles
- Magnetic Poles
- Geomagnetic Poles

The Geographic Pole is where the Earth's Axis meets the surface.

The Magnetic Pole is at an angle of declination (q.v.) from the Geographic Pole and attracts compass needles. As the Earth is an imperfect dipole the Magnetic and Geomagnetic poles differ. Satellite measurements show the North Pole to be 24.4 meters (80 feet) farther from the Earth's center than the South Pole, This tends to slightly elongate the Northern Hemisphere.

POLISHING POWDERS Many mineral powders have become important polishing agents for industry. Some of the most valuable are oxides of aluminum, iron (jeweler's rouge), tin, manganese, Rare Earths, and silica. Of the Rare Earths, cerium is widely used for glass and optics.

POLLINATION   Pollen transfer between plants aids germination. Many plants are self-pollinating. A number need the assistance of winds, insects, birds, and humans.

Deforestation, especially for fuelwood, has had a disastrous effect on regrowth where male and female trees are needed. The collectors of fuelwood do not take tree proximity into account.

POLLUTION   Pollution, the accumulation of unwanted industrial, domestic, or thermal waste, causes the ecological balance to be disturbed. If the pollution is beyond that system's capacity to cope, it becomes an ecological problem.

All human endeavor creates pollution of some sort. With the great increases in world population, many pollution problems have become national and even global problems. With a population of 6 billions, which is projected for the next decade, pollution will be of staggering proportions if management systems are not introduced.

By the 1980's, 27 million tons of sulfur dioxide and 21 million tons of nitrous oxides were emitted into the Atmosphere in the United States alone. 65% of this was in the eastern states. The build-up of acid rain (q.v.) is serious and damage to forests is almost irreversible.

Sulfur dioxide, nitrous oxide, and hydrocarbons are transformed in the Atmosphere into secondary pollutants like ozone and airborne fine particulates of sulfate and nitrate. A major contribution to atmospheric dust is soil and rock debris lofted by winds from arid areas. Most of this dust is in the middle latitudes. Pollution from volcanic sources is major and can affect global climate, sometimes for years after an eruption.

In the United States, stream pollution has received a great deal of attention. However, not nearly enough resources have been allocated to obviate the problem. Without vigilance water supplies can become threatened.

Of recent years oceanic pollution has become a major problem. The practice of dumping wastes into the sea, especially chemical wastes, has caused local disasters. Currents transfer pollution problems to other locations such as the problem of Mexican sewage reaching San Diego Bay.

POLYGONAL PATTERNS   As water in small pools evaporates on mud flats, small depressions are created. In the aftermath of the next wet season larger pools and larger depressions are formed. Pools and depressions link up in polygonal shapes. As drying out occurs the polygonal pattern remains. At the edges cracks appear. Sometimes these are very large as in drying mud flats along the Nile River.

Ice above permafrost melts to form pools that are enlarged with each melt season. When they freeze, they retain their polygonal shape.

When they melt again, they may merge to form shallow lakes over the permafrost.

Underground or glacial ice has a polygonal vein pattern forming a lattice-work of frost-cracked surfaces. The ice veins widen and the ground forms ogives (q.v.) around the polygons. Ice can fill the cracks and deformation occurs with thawing. Such veined ice occurs on flood-plains in sub-arctic to arctic conditions and can be found in Alaska, Canada, and the Soviet Union.

POLYMERIZATION   Polymerization is the joining of organic compounds to form complex giant molecules. The molecules have a polarity being positive on one end and negative on the other allowing them to make long chains. Rubber and cellulose are natural polymers.

The chemical phenomenon of polymerization has given rise to a multiplicity of chemical combinations, especially of carbon compounds. Hundreds of hydrocarbons, fluorocarbons, and silicones have been produced by the chemical industry. Some have become important to modern life but can be environmental hazards.

POLYMORPHISM   Some elements can take different forms. Carbon is a good example. It can be present naturally as diamond, graphite, or soot.

These forms are polymorphs and result from different temperatures, pressures, and other conditions that prevailed when they were formed. Marcasite, a polymorph of pyrite, may only form from acid solutions below 450° Celsius. The limitations for pyrite, are different.

POLYPS   Polyps are tiny invertebrate animals that group together to form a coral (q.v.). Each polyp resembles a tiny worm with tentacles to grasp food as it floats by. These tentacles are equipped with a poison which attacks certain plankton (q.v.).

The polyp secretes a calcium carbonate outer shell that hardens into a lime cup. Different species have cups of different shapes. The shapes determine the configuration of the coral.

POND   A small body of water is a pond. It may form in a variety of ways. Any obstruction of a stream may cause it to pond. Beavers can dam small streams and create ponds.

There are many ponds in low places, which were formerly glaciated. Ponds formed in kettle holes, or in depressions resulting from glacial plucking (q.v.).

POPULATION   In ecology, a population is a group of individuals sharing an environment or habitat. More than one population may inhabit the ecospace.

Human population growth is putting stress upon many parts of the globe. Present global increase is on the order of 65 million a year. It is estimated that there will by 8-10 billion people on the planet by the year 2020, half in presently underdeveloped areas. In many of these areas water, food, and fuelwood for cooking are already critical, It is calculated that fuelwood alone will be 10 times less available in 2020.

The best lands are already under cultivation and there are limited stockpiles of grain. A growing part of the world's population is dependent upon North American production. The drought of 1988 is a reminder that surpluses from that production are climate dependent.

PORCELAIN Fine kaolin is baked at 1,300° Celsius to yield porcelain, an extremely fine china. Porcelain is hard, white, and transluscent. It was introduced to Europe from China by Meissen in 1710.

PORCUPINE RIVER Porcupine River, Yukon Territory, Canada, is famous for its gold deposits. It is also a favorite haunt for paleontologists and archeologists.

The Old Crow River, tributary to the Porcupine, flows over permafrosted ground that encloses many Ice Age mammals. The area had been dated at 100,000 years, but later evidence (1982) seems to establish Old Crow at 20-30,000 years.

Some authorities consider this Porcupine River area the oldest North American human habitat. The site is a collapsed pingo (q.v.).

PORIFERA The phylum Porifera is made up of sponges, a group of multicellular animals with simple specialized cells. Sponges are living cell walls in hollowed-out sacs. The walls are 3-layered, consisting of an outer or ectoderm for protection, a middle of a gelatinous substance, and an inner or endoderm of feeding cells. The structure is supported by mineral spicules, fibers of spongin, secreted by the organisms.

POROROCA The local name for the Amazon tidal bore is 'pororoca', Tupi Indian for thundering water. At Belem on the Para, a distributary of the Amazon, the river may rise 4-5 meters (13-16 feet) in minutes. The onrushing wall of water creates a great roar. See **TIDAL BORE**.

POROSITY Rocks and soils have a percentage of open space in relation to their volume. This ratio is porosity. Porosity is affected among other factors by the:

- Form or shape of the rock grains
- Sphericity
- Packing and sorting of the grains
- Presence of colloidal material.

Some rocks are dense as are shales, others porous as are sands and gravels. Water is commonly held in the pore spaces.

PORPHYRITIC TEXTURE Magmatic rocks often have large crystals embedded in a groundmass of smaller crystals or volcanic glass. Large included crystals are phenocrysts and the texture is called porphyritic.

The rock is named for the matrix material (porphyritic rhyolite). If composition, by volume, is more than 25% phenocrysts, the rock is a porphyry. Porphyries are common in volcanics.

PORPHYRY COPPER Many copper ores are disseminated in porphyry plutons. The copper and iron sulfides are of low grade, on the order of 0.4-3% copper. Country rock may be weathered to clay and contain fine mica, some chlorite, and epidote. It has been assumed that copper mineralization occurred when the pluton was shattered by unknown forces allowing its impregnation by hydrothermal solutions.

Copper is one of the minerals found associated in hot spots (q.v.) on the ocean floor.

Some of the world's great copper deposits are porphoritic such as Bingham, Utah, Morenci, Arizona, and Chuquicamata, Chile. See **PORPHYRITIC TEXTURE**.

PORTLAND CEMENT A compound of lime, silica, and aluminum, fused and clinkered, is a cement. The cement formula is generally mixed with 25% clay. Different materials added after sintering yield different types. Gypsum mixed with water and sand speeds the setting process.

POSEIDON SEA The Proto-Atlantic. or ocean that preceded the present Atlantic, was named for Poseidon, Greek god of the sea.

POSITRON The positron is an elementary particle with the mass of an electron. It is positively charged. The positron is also called an 'anti-electron'.

POTASH Potassium carbonate, or potash, was precipitated in restricted areas of large evaporative basins. For potash to develop conditions of evaporation to almost complete dryness must prevail.

For years the world potash market was dominated by Europe. Restrictions on exports from these sources spurred the development of alternative supplies. Major North American potash deposits are found in the Devonian of Saskatchewan, Canada and the Permian of New Mexico. Brine production also began and is now important.

For centuries potash was produced by evaporating solutions from leached wood ash. Processing ash in a pot accounts for the common name. The major use is as a fertilizer. Potash is also used in soap, dye, and other household items.

POTASSIUM The silver-white metallic element, potassium, is a member of the Alkali Metal Group. It occurs commonly as a compound, and is called 'kalium' in Europe. Its chemical symbol is K. When used as a fertilizer, potassium assists photosynthesis.

Potassium salts are often called Prussian Blue Salts due to an addition of coloring to aid separation. Potassium salt is still produced from the deposits at Stassfurt, Germany.

In the Western Hemisphere the deposits of the Williston Basin of Saskatchewan, Canada are the most important. These deposits are deeply buried between 1,820 and 3,030 meters (6,000 and 10,000 feet). The deposits extend into the United States into Montana and North Dakota.

In the Paradox Basin of Utah, potash reserves are below 1,200 meters (4,000 feet) and are estimated at 2 billion tons. The Michigan Basin deposits have not been completely evaluated. They are located below 2,020 meters (7,000 feet). In all, the United States reserves are estimated to be 6 billion metric tons.

African Congo deposits and those of Brazil's Northeast are mirror images. Brazil's major deposit went into production in 1985. Reserves of 13.8 billion tons of sylvinite and carnallite are indicated.

Measured reserves of the Sergipe Basin of Northeast Brazil are 525 million tons of sylvinite with 20.14-25.47% potassium oxide and 12.9 billion tons of carnallite at 7-9% potassium oxide. These are problem ores in terms of underground mining. In 1989, the world's estimated reserves of potassium were 250 billion metric tons.

The countries with the largest potassium reserves are as follows (in millions of metric tons):

USSR	13,400
Canada	1,500
East Germany	560
West Germany	500
Israel	300
Jordan	300
United States	90
Brazil	50
Spain	40
Chile	30
Italy	30
United Kingdom	25
France	20

U.S. Bureau of Mines, 1990

POTASSIUM-ARGON DATING The ratio of Potassium-40 to Argon-40 has been useful in age-dating rocks. The dating puts limits around the probable time of deposition and serves to confirm geological chronology.

POTHOLE A stream can drill holes in bedrock by the abrasive action of its sand and gravel. The holes are roughly circular due to swirling of debris-laden water. They are usually deeper than wide. Some are natural depositories of gold and diamonds.

In Death Valley, the Pothole is a brine pool measuring a meter (3 feet) in diameter.

Shallow and sometimes not so shallow potholes are features of urban streets and highways. They result from heavy vehicles plucking up pieces of the road, or the breaking up of a frost heave. Potholes are a major cost item of highway maintenance.

POTOSI The world's most famous silver deposit, Cerro Rico de Potosi, is south of La Paz, Bolivia. It is also the richest of all silver mines yet discovered. The mine is a porphyry (q.v.) stock in rhyodacite.

Since colonial times, 30,000 metric tons of 30-40% have been recovered. It is estimated that there is now as much silver in the mine as was taken out. Rich tin deposits have been discovered below the silver. Reserves of silver are estimated at 828 million tons of ore with 150-250 grams/metric ton and 0.3-0.4% tin. The tin reserves have not been completely evaluated.

The Potosi area is so honey-combed with tunnels the hill-top has caved in. Plans are being made to rework the area using modern mining methods.

ppm The symbol for parts per million is ppm, where one million parts are equal to 100%. It is commonly used to define the mineral content of a volume. The constituents minerals of water samples are reported in ppm.

PRAIRIE The Prairie or grassland of mid-western United States once covered 30% of the nation. Since the extraordinary drought of the 1930's much of the land has been allowed to recuperate and produce native grass. This grass can be sustained under relatively dry conditions. The Prairie is the world's major grain supplier. See **GRASSES, GRASSLANDS**.

PRAIRIE SOIL Prairie soil is a sub-group of the Chernozems (q.v.). It is zonal and on the humid side of the Chernozems. It is slightly acidic with a pH of 6.

Prairie soil forms in temperate, sub-humid climates with a winter dry period. The A-Horizon may have a meter (3 feet) of thick, black humus. Prairie soils are found in the USSR, North, and South America.

PRECAMBRIAN The Precambrian Era (4.5-5 b.y. to 570 m.y.) represents a period greater than all subsequent geological time. Precambrian rocks cover 75% of the globe. They are the core of many mountains and are exposed in deep canyons (Vishnu rocks, Grand Canyon).

Shield areas of the world, stable continental cratons of Precambrian rocks, have the greatest exposure. 75% of the Canadian Shield is Precambrian granite and banded gneiss. It is found over 5 million square kilometers (2 million square miles).

The Precambrian craton of South Africa, Barberton Plateau, has 4 billion year-old rocks exposed on the surface. They were thought to be the oldest rocks until those of Greenland and Australia were dated.

The earliest record of life appears in 3.4 billion year-old rocks. The fossils of blue-green Algae and Bacteria have been identified. Precambrian fossils tend to be microscopic and unicellular. Tiny, or nannofossils, not considered Algae have also been found.

Rocks made up of clusters of algal cells and also containing Metazoa, Coelenterata, Arthropoda, and worms have formed into reefs. These are the stromatolite reefs found in Canada and in the Belt Series of Montana.

PRECAMBRIAN GLACIATION   Striations (long grooves) left by Precambrian glaciers are still visible. The best examples are in Australia. Tillites (q.v.) are also found in 3 Late-Precambrian Australian strata. Some beds are up to 180 meters (600 feet) thick.

In North America many Precambrian tillites have been identified. In South Africa, there are 3 sequences. Chinese Precambrian tillites run east to west for 1,300 kilometers.

PRECAMBRIAN ORES   Many rich mineral deposits are in Precambrian rocks. They include copper, gold, iron, mananese, nickel, and silver. A large number are in sediments such as the banded iron formations, ancient placers, and reefs. South Africa's famed Witwatersrand gold is from reefs and ancient placers.

Other deposits are in igneous and metamorphic rocks. The Canadian Shield contains large amounts of copper, gold, iron, nickel, and uranium. 70% of the world's nickel is from Sudbury, Ontario. Native copper from the Upper Peninsula of the Great Lakes Region is found in Keeweenaw volcanics.

The Precambrian minerals mentioned are the most well-known, but the list is not limited to them. In Kiruna, Sweden, there are significant iron magnetite deposits. Potentially valuable Precambrian phosphorite is found in North America and China. Rare platinum deposits are Precambrian. Many nonmetallics are also found in the Precambrian, among them graphite, mica, and talc.

PRECESSION   The tilt of the Earth's axis shifts slightly due to the gravitational pull of the Sun and the Moon. This 'Precession of the Equinoxes' has a total orbit of 26,000 years. The axis is gradually shifting toward the star Vega for half the period and toward Polaris for the other half. It is in the latter period now.

PRECIPITATION   Precipitation is a condensation of vapor from the Atmosphere. It may be fog, hail, rain, sleet, or snow. When water vapor in a cloud cools, it condenses forming droplets. Rain is made up of droplets that reach the Earth's surface.

PRESSURE   Pressure is a force exerted by gravity. Absolute pressure is the force of 1 atmosphere. This is equivalent to a weight of 1.0332 kilograms per square centimeter (14.7 pounds per square inch).

Pressure exerted on the Earth affects its solid and semi-solid structure. With other forces, pressure acts in the development of rocks and minerals. It is related to heat within the Mantle and pressure increases steadily toward the center of the Earth.

Pressure exerted on a fluid is affected by the nature and depth of the fluid. Pressure on shallow water lakes is not the same as on a shallow sea, as the sea is denser due to its salinity.

PRETORIA SALT PAN The Pretoria Salt Pan is a great South African caldera filled with brine (q.v.). The caldera has a diameter of 1,000 meters (3,300 feet) with a 30 meter (100 foot) wall. Many think the caldera was the result of meteoritic impact. See **CALDERA**.

PREVAILING WESTERLIES The prevailing westerly winds are governed by the rotation of the Earth. In the Northern Hemisphere, flow generally is toward the poles. Although the winds blow primarily from the west, they can come from any direction in a storm.

Unlike the Trades, the Westerlies are not constant. Their velocities can reach gale force (q.v.). It is such storm winds that cause the 'Roaring Forties' (q.v.).

Climate is greatly affected in the mid-latitudes by the erratic nature of the Westerlies. Winters in the United States are severe or mild depending upon the intensity of the storms the Westerlies bring. The storms themselves are born in the Siberian and Canadian low pressure areas. Westerlies carry storms to Europe from the Icelandic Low Pressure Area.

The Westerlies can affect the lower latitudes when the jet streams (q.v.) form great loops toward the Equator. This occurs when low pressure areas greatly expand.

PRIME MERIDIAN The Prime Meridian is 0° Longitude. The line passes through Greenwich, England. All longitudes are measured from it, east or west, to 180°. The Prime Meridian is recognized internationally and is used to set Greenwich Mean Time (q.v.).

PRIPET MARSHES The Pripet Marshes are famous as a battleground. These marshes are in the USSR near the Polish border. They form a huge wetland covered with reeds and coarse grass. The Pripet River flows through the Pripet or Pinsk marshes on its course to join the Dnieper, which drains to the Black Sea. See **WETLANDS**.

PRISM A prism is a wedge-shaped crystal with 3 or more similar faces parallel to a single axis. The sides form parallelograms.

Light waves will bend when they pass through a glass or crystal prism and the light will split into the spectrum of colors.

An elongated wedge of sedimentary rock is a prism. It is normally very thick and often is found in geosynclines (q.v.).

PROBABLE ORE When there are reasonable expectations of economic ore reserves they are further evaluated using geophysical and geochemical methods. If the results warrant it, the reserves are classed as probable, not yet proven reserves.

PROCESS Process in Earth Science is any mechanism which results in change. Weathering, hydrothermal alteration, rock metasomatism are all processes or agencies for change in soils, rocks, and minerals.

PROFILE A profile is a graphic presentation of a function or condition related to the Earth. The gradient of a slope or stream may be described by a curve.

Cross-sections are scaled graphic displays of the subsurface. Stratigraphic columns (q.v.) are also profiles. They are of the layered sequences encountered in a particular area.

Soil profiles (q.v.) carefully describe the soil column in a particular place. The horizons and subdivisions are detailed.

PROKARYOTIC A single-celled organism is prokaryotic. Such organisms have been detected in Precambrian rocks. Some authorities have described the group as a separate kingdom, distinct from Plant or Animal.

PROPRIA GEOSYNCLINE The Propria Geosyncline is a Precambrian structure in Northeast Brazil which has a complement in Gabon, West Africa. Propia is parallel to the coast. The sedimentary prism (q.v.) is intruded by the Gloria Batholith. On both continents, the sediments are very contorted. The evidence confirms the Continental Drift Theory. See **BATHOLITH, CONTINENTAL DRIFT**.

PROSPECT An unevaluated mineralized body is a prospect as is any new potential mining property undergoing detailed analysis. Areas are selected for study based upon a geological, geochemical, or geophysical anomaly (q.v.). When a prospect shows sizeable reserves, it becomes a deposit.

PROSPECTING Prospecting is both the art and the science of searching for minerals that may be economic. The establishment of economic worth is part of the prospecting phase. It usually comes rapidly after determination of the presence of useful minerals.

PROTEIN Proteins are varying forms of amino acids. These animo acids are the building-blocks of living cells. They are long-chained carbon molecules. 'Protein' is from the Greek meaning to come first.

PROTEROZOIC ERA The Precambrian is subdivided into the Archaeozoic and Proterozoic. Some consider this usage obsolete and reserve Proterozoic for all of the Precambrian. In which sense, it complements Phanerozoic. The Phanerozoic encompasses geological time from the Precambrian to the Present.

There is merit, however, in separating the Proterozoic from the Archaeozoic. The latter was a time of high relief and erosion which became more accelerated in the Proterozoic. The Proterozoic was the time of deposition of the great banded iron formations. See **ARCHAEOZOIC, PRECAMBRIAN**.

PROTON The proton is a sub-atomic particle with a single positive charge. Its mass is 1.8 thousand times that of an electron.

The atomic number (Z) of an element denotes the number of protons in the nucleus. This is the number of positive charges. In ordinary hydrogen, a single proton is the nucleus and hydrogen has the Z number of 1.

PROTORE A low grade metallic mineral may be of no economic value in itself. It may become an ore through superficial enrichment. This is a 'protore' which may be spacially related to an economic deposit.

Protores not only supply enriched material, they also lead to the discovery of ore deposits. The Amapa manganese deposits in the Brazilian Amazon are the result of the discovery of a protore. See **AMAPA**.

PROTOZOA The Protozoa Phylum includes many single-celled animals. They include the Amoeba, Foraminifera, and Radiolaria. Some form deep sea oozes.

PSAMMITE Clastics below pebble size are psammites. Sandstone has a psammitic texture when fine-grained, fissile, and clayey. Psammitic texture implies a degree of metamorphism (q.v.).

PSEUDO- The Greek word for false is 'pseudo'. As a prefix it may indicate something similar in form but not in substance.

PSEUDO-ANTICLINE A rock formation resembling the arch of an anticline is a pseudo-anticline if it is composed of sediments overlying a buried hill.

PSEUDO-LEUCITE A pseudo-leucite results when nepheline replaces leucite in an igneous rock. Pseudo-leucites have been detected at a number of carbonatite locations (Magnet Cove, Arkansas, Iron Hill, Colorado).

PSEUDOMORPH If the original crystal structure is retained after replacement has taken place, the crystal is a pseudomorph. Limonitized pyrites are good examples of pseudomorphs.

PTAMIGAN The ptamigan, a form of grouse, is the only bird adapted to life in the Alpine Tundra of the United States. The bird lives the entire year on the Tundra. It has feathered feet and toes to help ward off the cold of winter.

PTERIDOPHYTA The Phylum Pteridophyta is made up of spore-bearing plants. This group, which includes the ferns, is well developed and differentiated.

Most ferns are small, but some tropical ones grow to 15 meters (50 feet). They are an important part of the understory of the tropical rainforest (q.v.).

Ferns first appeared in the Early-Devonian (390 m.y.) and are among the oldest of all land plants.

PTERODACTYL Pterodactyl is a member of the Pterosauria Order of winged reptiles. It appeared in Lower-Jurassic (180 m.y.) and was present in Late-Mesozoic (q.v.). It had a long wing membrane but no feathers. Pterodactyl may have been an evolutionary link between the birds and reptiles.

PTOLOMY Ptolomy of Alexandria, a Greek philosopher, considered the Earth the center of the Universe. His view held until the Middle ages. Galileo and Copernicus changed this traditional view.

In 150 B.C., Ptolomy predicted the existence of a landmass, which appears on old maps as 'Terra Australis Incognita'. This was a great deduction on Ptolomy's part. He was vindicated by the discovery of the continent of Antarctica (q.v.).

PUDDINGSTONE Puddingstone is an aggregate of cemented sand, clay or limestone. Some puddingstones developed from glacial outwash (q.v.). Puddingstone at Roxbury, Massachusetts is of this origin.

PULSAR A star emitting pulsating radio waves, beeping regularly, is a pulsar. The beeps are short bursts. From 1967 to 1977, 150 pulsars were identified. These are rapidly rotating neutron stars made up of particles with no charge.

A pulsar was noted in Crab Nebula by Chinese astrologers in 1054. They called it the 'guest star'. The Crab Nebula Pulsar emits 2 beeps per period. The period is 32 millionths of a second. The second burst is half as bright as the first.

PUMICE Pumice is a frothy, porous volcanic glass. It forms from melted obsidian (q.v.). Gas bubbling through the rock while still molten created the many pores or holes.

Pumice is similar in composition to rhyolite (q.v.). It is very lightweight. So much so, it was floating in Sunda Strait 18 months after Krakatoa (q.v.) erupted.

After the Mount St Helens eruption in 1980, the pumice retained its high temperature of 780° Fahrenheit for 2 weeks. When flowing, the pumice was at 1,000° and its velocity was 166 kilometers (100 miles) per hour. See **SANTORINI**.

PUNA The Andean Plateau, 3,000-4,000 meters (10,000-13,000 feet) is called the 'Puna' locally. It is a broad, bleak plain below towering peaks.

PUYS The French name for the cinder cones of the Auvergne Region is 'puys'. Formed by Stromboli-type eruptions. The cones are composed of scoria (q.v.). One crater edge is lower than any other and forms a lip from which lava once poured.

The Puys are a chain of 60 eroded cones. The region is noted for its hot springs.

PYCNOCLINE   The pycnocline is the vertical density layer in a water mass. The density curve is positive with depth. In the deep sea, it forms a layer between the surface and deep water. The layer is defined by a rapid change in the density gradient.

PYRITE   Pyrite is a mineral compound of copper and sulfur. It is commonly found as iron-pyrite, an ore of sulfur.

Pyrite crystallizes in the cubic habit and is brassy yellow. It has been mistaken for gold by neophyte prospectors. Its distinquishing features are:

- A greenish-black streak
- A metallic luster
- A hardness of 5 on the Moh's Scale
- A conchoidal fracture.

Spain is a major producer of pyrites for sulfur. In Bolivia, marcasite, white iron-pyrite, is of ore quality. See **PSEUDOMORPH**.

PYROCLASTICS   Pyroclastics are fragments ejected from a volcano or have their origin in fire.

PYROPHYLLITE   Pyrophyllite is a soft hydrous aluminum silicate with a potential for greater industrial use. Combined with andalusite, pyrophyllite can sustain thermal shocks. It is the product of metamorphosed acid volcanics.

Pyrophyllite has a variety of properties which are important in the refractory and ceramic industries. It does not require calcination. It is also used in insecticides.

Production in the United States is from California and North Carolina. The North Carolina deposits have a natural high purity.

PYROXENES   The pyroxenes are a large family of calcium-magnesium-iron silicates. They are a solid-solution series and some are soda-rich. They have a higher ratio of silica to metallic oxides than olivines (q.v.). Pyroxenes are distinguished from amphiboles (q.v.) by cleavage. Amphiboles cleave at $124°$ and $56°$, pyroxenes at $93°$ and $87°$.

Augite, the most common pyroxene, is a complex compound. It is a constituent of basaltic lavas and gabbros. Augite with diopside-aegirine are the most important pyroxenes in carbonatites (q.v.).

In a few carbonatites, a high titanium pyroxene is present as at Tapira, Brazil and Kola, USSR. Carbonatite pyroxenes have a distinct zonation in the ring complexes.

Q

QATTARA In northwest Egypt extending into Libya, the Qattara Depression is separated from the Mediterranean Sea, by a narrow strip of hard Miocene (q.v.) limestone. The depression is only 66 kilometers (40 miles) from the sea. The Qattara is a huge saline trough 300 x 250 kilometers (186 x 150 miles). Its lowest part is 134 meters (436 feet) below sea level.

The main basin contains many smaller basins, some occupied by oases. The Quattara surface is a giant erg (q.v.) of unconsolidated sand and marl or it is encrusted with salt .

Subsurface water in the Depression is from the border area between Sudan and Chad. It flows underground, paralleling the Nile for 1,660 kilometers (1,000 miles). Al Kufrah Oasis, Libya, survives due to this underground water source.

The southern part of the Qattara Depression is older and was created when winds deflated the weathered hammada (q.v.). Where wind deflation eroded the Qattara floor below the water table, brine pools resulted. The evaporation created the saline crusts.

The greatest resource of the Qattara is its water but some valuable minerals have also been discovered. Phosphates have developed in some basins. Egypt is planning to channel water from the Mediterranean via El Alamein into the depression. This is to create an energy source.

In World War II, the Qattara Depression proved a barrier for Rommel's Afrika Korps. He had to attack heavily fortified El Alamein on the narrow limestone neck between the Qattara and the Sea.

QOZ A widespread Quaternary sand called Qoz is found west of the Nile in Sudan. Sands in Darfur, Kordofan, and Northern Province cover a broad belt with dunes and sheets. Sand grains are well-rounded and appear to have eroded from Nubian Sandstone (q.v.).

Qoz sands indicate a major climatic shift to aridity. Whiteman noted that the climate shift was greater than would occur through 6° of latitude.

QUANTUM The quantum is an energy unit equal to 6.625×10^{-27} ergs per second. A photon (q.v.) has a quantum of electromagnetic energy.

Quantum physics is based upon the premise that in the Electromagnetic Field there are clouds of orbiting electrons, not discreet electrons or particles.

QUANTUM LEAP When an electron moves from one allowed orbit to another, it makes a 'quantum leap'. Energy released by the leap is dissipated in photons and light.

Making a quantum leap has come to mean making an extraordinary effort, or a great shift as from one environment to another.

QUANTUM THEORY Max Planck (q.v.) theorized that energy is not emitted or absorbed continuously but in small units. Energy emission or absorption is directly proportional to frequency and is concentrated in units or 'bundles', called quanta. The electron can be viewed as a particle and as a wave. See **QUANTUM**.

QUARKS Quarks are basic units of elementary particles (q.v.). The name was taken from James Joyce's 'Finnegan's Wake'. It is pronounced as 'corks'.

Quarks may or may not be the smallest form of matter. They are referred to by particle location and by position, whether 'up', 'down', or 'strange'. All have a fractional electrical charge. A proton has 2 'ups' each with a 2/3 positive charge and 1 'down' with 1/3 negative charge. The proton charge = 1. See **PROTON**.

The quark family has 18 members. In addition to 'up', 'down' and 'strange' there are 'charm', 'truth', and 'beauty'. These 6 each have their own mass and charge and are called 'flavors'. Each combines differently and yields a 'color'.

There are 3 colors, red, blue, and green giving 18 variations. For every quark there is an 'anti-quark'. Quarks can be joined by another particle, a 'gluon' without mass or charge.

QUARRY A quarry is an open pit mine for the extraction of sand, gravel, and stone. The stone ranges from shale to granite.

QUARTZ Silicon dioxide or quartz makes up 12% of the exposed land surface and 20% of the Earth's Crust. Quartz is intruded in igneous and metamorphic rocks. It is also found in sediments.

Quartz is one of the last minerals to crystallize from a magma. Its crystal size is related to time allowed for growth. In North Carolina a crystal weighing 130 kilos (290 pounds) was found. One from the Alps weighed in at 636 kilos (1,425 pounds).

Quartz crystallizes in a hexagonal pattern and tapers to a point at one or both ends. It is subject to twinning, has a hardness of 7, a vitreous luster, and a conchoidal fracture. Quartz type depends on formation temperature. Low temperature, or ordinary quartz, forms below 573° Celsius, high temperature between 573° and 1,775° at which point silica glass forms.

Sand is made up of quartz grains. A series of sand layers can be compressed and hardened to sandstone. Further alteration yields quartzite, a resistant, ridge-forming rock.

Rock crystal or quartz is used in instruments and telecommunications systems. These uses have grown from the first 'crystal' radio sets. Today, crystals are laboratory grown from particles.

Quartz is a favored gem mineral. It comes in a variety of colors depending upon the mineral inclusions. Among quartz gems are amethyst, rose quartz, citrine, and adventurine. Cryptocrystalline varieties like agate and chalcedony are used for decoration.

Quartz watches are based on the piezoelectric quality of the mineral. It allows the quartz to vibrate regularly when activated by an electrical charge.

QUARTZ MONZONITE Quartz monzonite is an intrusive rock composed of plagioclase feldspar, orthoclase feldspar, and quartz with minor amounts of hornblende and biotite. An increase in plagioclase results in granodiorite, an increase in orthoclase yields granite.

QUARTZITE Quartzite is metamorphosed sandstone and is composed primarily of bedded sands. It is unusual in that it breaks across sand grains rather than around them.

Quartzite is composed of quartz, orthoclase and microcline feldspar, and kaolin.

QUASARS Quasi-Stellar Radio Sources (QUASARS) are star-like bodies on the edge of the Universe. They are bright and fast-moving. Quasars are beyond the known galaxies, some 12 billion light-years away.

Quasars are a powerful energy source. They are the greatest light source so far identified in the Universe. Scientists believe they are the cores of galaxies. More powerful than the radio galaxies, the energy is radiated from a source about the size of the Solar System.

A quasar, observed through Lizard Constellation, had a 300% red shift. This showed it to be moving very fast to the outer edge of the Universe. See **DOPPLER EFFECT**.

QUATERNARY PERIOD The Quaternary is the latest Period of geological history. It includes the Pleistocene and Recent, or Holocene, Epochs. In all, the Period represents only 2 to 3 million years of Earth history.

Most of the Pleistocene and Recent have been periods of degradation of the Earth's surface. A massive amount of sand and gravel has been deposited from this wholesale erosion.

Deposition of alluvium and gravels began in the Tertiary Period and has continued to date. Many gravel deposits have proven to be gold-bearing.

Humankind only appeared in Earth History in the Late-Pleistocene. Age-dating of many archaeological sites indicates the earliest humans developed in Africa.

QUICK CLAY Certain clay deposits liquify easily when jarred. These are called 'quick clays'. Jarring occurs most frequently from earthquakes. This type of jarring recently created the enormous damage to Mexico City in the recent earthquake. The city is built on lake sediment.

The effects of seismic waves great distances from their source was made very apparent in the Mexico City event. The epicenter was distant, in the Pacific Ocean off Mexico's west coast. The seismic waves created were intense enough to jar the lake clays.

QUICKSAND When water is forced upward through fine grains of sand, it fills the interstices and the surface swells. The result is quicksand.

Sand grains in quicksands are finer than normal. When the surface is dry, it will be powdery. Quicksands are often found along coasts where underground water is plentiful.

The weight of an object or a person may cause sinking. The more weight the more displacement, so sinking becomes more rapid. It is rare for these sands to have depths great enough to trap an adult.

QUICKSILVER Mercury (q.v.) in liquid form is called quicksilver. A blob of mercury will roll over a surface very quickly and will not make the surface wet. It looks silvery in color. These characteristics account for the name. See **MERCURY**.

QUINTA In colonial South America, miners were required to give 1/5th of the gold and silver production to the Crown. The tax became known as the 'quinta'.

QUMRAM A famous series of caves is located at Qumran, also known as Khirbat Qumran, in the Palestinian area of northwest Jordan. In the cave of Ain Fashkha the parchments were found that are now known as the 'Dead Sea Scrolls'. The Scrolls, wrapped in linen, were in clay casks. They were biblical in nature and more than 2,000 years old. Scholars are still working on them.

R

RAD The measure of absorbed radiation is the rad. It is equal to 100 ergs of energy per gram of absorbing matter. A rad = 1/60 of a rem, an acronym for roentgen equivalent man. A roentgen (q.v.) of radiation will deposit 1 rad in human or animal tissue. See **ERG**.

Pilots absorb 1 mr (millirad) per hour from their instruments. A dental X-ray delivers 0.5 rads per film, a diagnostic X-ray will deliver 1 rad. Natural radiation (q.v.) at sea level is equal to about 50 mr annually. At 20,000 feet elevation the dose from cosmic radiation increases to 1500 mr or 1.5 rads per year.

In some parts of the world where radioactive minerals are close to or on the surface, radiation is much higher. Morro do Ferro, in Minas Gerais, Brazil gives off 3 mr per hour.

RADAM RADAM is an acronym for the radar (q.v.) survey of the Amazon Basin. This airborne survey took 10 years to complete and the results are presented in 22 volumes. The survey was as complete a study of the natural resources of the Amazon as was possible with the state of the art. SLAR, which is side-looking radar was used to penetrate dense vegetation.

RADAR RADAR is an acronym for Radio Direction and Ranging. The device emits a signal which hits an object and is reflected back to its source. The object is projected on a screen. Its distance is measured by the time the signal takes to return. Signals are ultra-high frequency radio waves. Bat studies are reputed to have inspired the invention of radar.

RADIAL DRAINAGE Rivers adopt radial drainage when the source area is a single peak. Glaciers also show radial drainage as in the French Garonne and Adour valleys. There, a semi-circle of drainage has formed that is 160 kilometers (100 miles) across the Pleistocene fans. Streams are now cutting sharp valleys.

Volcanic cones show the radial drainage patterns. Where the volcano has collapsed into a caldera (q.v.) the drainage is radial and flows to the center of the basin usually to form a lake.

RADIATION There are 3 major kinds of radiation: Heat, light, and nuclear. The Sun radiates them all. There is a component of radiation energy from the Cosmos. Earth and Atmosphere radiate heat and a tiny component of nuclear energy into Space.

Radiation travels at the speed of light (q.v). Some wavelengths are of visible light. Others are cosmic, gamma, ultra-violet, infra-red, radio, and X-ray.

Radiation energy is measured in millirems (mrems). The average annual dose for humans is 180 mrems. Often an individual's dosage in a given year is much higher. 5,000 mrems are considered safe. See **REM**.

RADIATION FOG Ground surfaces cool due to heat loss. Water vapor in contact with cooled surfaces condenses to create fog if the dewpoint (q.v.) is reached. The cool ground causes water condensation upon contact.

RADIO ASTRONOMY Radio astronomy, a relatively new field, is the analysis of radio signals from Outer Space. Astronomers have huge radio telescopes to pick up these signals. Some of the signals, traveling at the speed of light (q.v.) took 2 billion years to reach the Earth.

The radio signals are emitted by huge star-like entities called pulsars (q.v.). Crab Nebula is a distinctive emitter. Quasars (q.v.) are also radio emitters. Radio astronomy has been able to detect noise storms accompanying solar flares.

RADIO CARBON DATING The isotope, Carbon-14, is used to age date relatively recent objects. Archaeologists use the technique. Carbon-14 decays to Nitrogen-14 in a half-life (q.v.) of 5,570 years. Sites up to 50,000 years may be dated with reasonable accuracy using the C-14:N-14 ratio. The method is accurate within 200 years.

Radio carbon dating confirmed that the linen enveloping the Dead Sea Scrolls, found in Palestine, is 1,983 years old. Thus the scrolls were dated from the 1st or 2nd Century B.C. See **QUMRAM**.

RADIO GALAXIES Disturbed galaxies were discovered in the 1940's and 50's. They formed 2 huge clouds on either side of Cygnus A (500 million light years from Earth). Some of the disturbed galaxies have the energy of a billion stars and emit radio signals.

RADIO WAVES Radio waves are of medium-length, between 200 and 1,000 meters long. They are part of the Electromagnetic Spectrum (q.v.) and tend to travel in a straight line. In the Mesosphere (q.v.) and Thermosphere, radio waves bounce off airmasses which are electrically charged.

RADIOACTIVE ARGON Argon-40 is the decay product of Potassium-40. When Potassium-40 gives up an electron, it decays to Argon-40 and Calcium-40. About 11% of the Potassium-40 becomes Argon-40 over a half-life (q.v.) of 11,850 million years. See **RADIOACTIVE DATING**.

RADIOACTIVE BERYLLIUM Produced by cosmic rays, radioactive Beryllium-10 has a half-life of 2.7 million years.

RADIOACTIVE DATING Most rocks have minute amounts of radioactivity contained in elements such as uranium, potassium, and rubidium. These elements decay to produce daughter elements at known rates.

Ratios are developed between the secondary or daughter elements and the parent. Decay rates are in half-lives so remnants allow rough estimates of the time the contained radioactive isotopes originated. The ratio of the primary isotope to the daughter yields the age with an accuracy of + or -1%.

When considering rocks of Precambrian Age, 2-3 billion year old rocks, the error can be very large and still not be significant. A premise is made that the radioactive matter was present at the time of the rock's formation and that radioactive decay began immediately.

RADIOACTIVE DECAY Spontaneous change from one nuclide (q.v.) to another of a different energy state is radioactive decay. It involves the emission of alpha, beta, and gamma rays with the capture or expulsion of electrons.

Radioactive decay occurs within the atomic nucleus and occurs only in certain unstable isotopes. Decay occurs at different rates for differnt isotopes.

During a given period, half the isotope will decay to a daughter element. In an additional equal period half the remaining parent will decay to its half-life. The process proceeds and the duration is theoretically infinite.

RADIOACTIVE ELEMENTS The most well-known of the radioactive isotopes (q.v.) are Potassium-40, Thorium-232, Uranium-234, Uranium-235, and Uranium-238. Uranium isotopes give rise to 3 different decay series that end in the lead isotopes of Pb-206, Pb-207 and Pb-208.

RADIOACTIVE POTASSIUM In a newly-formed rock, radioactive Potassium-40 amounts to 1/100th of the potassium content. Potassium-40 (K-40) will break down to form calcium and argon. The calcium is similar to ordinary calcium but the argon is radioactive, Argon-40. It takes 11,850 million years for half the radioactive potassium to decay to radiogenic argon.

Radioactive potassium is found in muscle-building foods and in muscles. Amounts are 10-20 times greater than any other radioactive material held in the human body.

RADIOACTIVE RAYS Alpha, beta, and gamma rays are radioactive. When radioactive waves made up of atomic particles penetrate matter they tend to ionize it. Some atoms lose or gain electrons and so are ionized. See **IONIZATION**.

RADIOACTIVE TRACERS Modern science has found many uses for radioactive tracers. They allow detection of critical paths in chemical reactions. Their use in modern medicine has opened whole new disciplines.

Some of the most important radioactive tracers are isotopes of carbon and iodine.

RADIOACTIVE WASTE A major problem in the use of nuclear energy is the disposal of the 'spent fuel' which is still extremely radioactive. There have been attempts to bury fuel elements in the ground in various ways and deposition at sea has been attempted. No viable solution has yet been discovered. At present, some nations attempt to recycle.

There are other sources of radioactive waste than from spent fuel. Some are from milling ores, chemical plants, and medical waste. Radioactive wastes are now found in many landfills. These present a special hazard to groundwater. In 1988, there were a number of instances of medical waste washing ashore on beaches.

Experimentation is underway to use boron or leaded glass allowing the radioactivity to become part of the container. If there were breakage of any sort, there would be no spillage. Other chemical possibilities are under study.

The Australian National University has been conducting studies under Professor Ringwood into the manufacture of synthetic rock fired at volcanic heat. The rock would contain metal oxides mixed with radioactive waste making the waste harmless. See **PLUTONIUM**.

RADIOACTIVITY   Radioactivity is the natural disintegration of isotopes (q.v.). These emit radiation and new isotopes (q.v.) of lesser atomic weight. The process is independent of rock and mineral formation and independent of temperature and pressure variations. All elements heavier than lead, beginning with bismuth have isotopes subject to radioactive decay. Most of the Earth's internal heat is from radioactivity.

Foods contain alpha radiation. A comparison showed fruit to have the lowest levels. Cereals, rank next with 600 times more radioactivity than fruit. Brazil nuts are the highest. They are 14,000 times more radioactive than fruit.

RADIOLARIA   Radiolaria are a class of marine organisms in the Protozoa Phylum. They are shelled, single-celled organisms that secrete opaline silica in the form of relatively long pointed rays.

Radiolaria first appeared in the Cambrian (570-500 m.y.) and are present today. The organisms are primarily planktonic and their skeletons contribute to oceanic ooze.

Radiolarian ooze is composed of the silicious shells of the organism combined with red clay. It is especially abundant in the tropical Pacific and Indian oceans.

RADIUM Radium, a metallic element, is radioactive. The most abundant isotope (q.v.) is Radium-226. It is derived from Uranium-238 and Thorium. This isotope (q.v.) is present in the uranium ores of pitchblende and carnotite.

Uranium decays to radium through 4 intermediate isotopes in a series of emissions of alpha, beta, and gamma rays (q.v.). Radium in turn emits alpha and gamma rays. Half the Radium-226 in a rock or mineral decays to stable Lead-206 in 1,600 years. See **HALF-LIFE**.

Radium has the property of luminescence making it useful for medical applications.

RADON The heaviest of the gases is radon, which is invisible, odorless, and radioactive. It is produced by the decay of radium in the Uranium Series and the Thorium Series. A gram of radium gives off 0.0001 milliliters of gas per day. The isotope, Radon-222, has a half-life of 3.8 days. Radon-222 decays by alpha radiation to Polonium 218. Radon-222 decays by 4 short-lived daughters which include Polonium-218 and Polonium-214. These isotopes are strong emitters of alpha radiation which is a major cause of lung cancer.

Radon weighs 222 times more than hydrogen and tends to collect in enclosed areas, especially in improperly ventilated uranium mines. Radon is 2nd to smoking as a cause of lung cancer. Those who smoked in the presence of radon were 15 times more vulnerable. An estimated 15,000 to 50,000 people die each year from lung cancer from the effects of radon. These are by no means all uranium miners.

Radon seeps from rocks and soils and is therefore ubiquitous. In 1988, the United States Government issued a warning that radon was more widespread than previously thought and that homes should be tested for the radioactive gas. Radon levels can be reduced by subgrade suction, sealing foundations, and increasing ventilation. Radon dissipates in the open air.

It was found that 7 states had household levels that were potentially dangerous. The increased tightness of some energy efficient homes can increase a radon problem if a source exists. The Environmental Protection Agency estimates 15 million households are at risk with radon levels exceeding standards set for uranium miners.

The high risk areas cited are known uranium areas such as the:
- Reading Prong - Parts of Pennsylvania, New Jersey, New York
- North Central - A belt from North Dakota into Minnesota
- Colorado Plateau - Uravan belt of western Colorado and eastern Utah.

The U.S. Environmental Protection Agency has set the Action Level at 4 pCi/l (pico-curies per liter) of air.

An increase in the radon content in a deep water well can be an indication that an earthquake is about to begin. This is very probably the result of a build-up of pressure in uranium-bearing rocks causing them to split and release the gas.

RAFTING Floating or rafting of seeds, animals, and plants is important to their distribution around the globe. Transport may be by ice, plants, animals, in rivers, in the sea, and in the air. Some plants have seed pods adapted to rafting.

RAIN A raindrop is developed by nucleation of water around a dust particle or a salt crystal. The raindrop is suspended in an airmass until precipitation is induced. This usually occurs with a temperature or a mass change or both, allowing gravity to take over.

RAIN SHADOW An area in lee of a mountain range where rainfall is low or non-existent is a rain shadow. The Cordillera stretching from Canada to South America provides an effective rain shadow. The mountains wring the moisture from the airmasses on the windward side.

RAINBOW Raindrops reflect light as prisms (q.v.). When clouds part letting sunlight through, the prisms disperse light so the colors of the Spectrum (q.v.) can be seen. The light is refracted through the drops.

RAINFOREST Dense forests of huge trees developed in tropical areas of high precipitation are rainforests. The trees reach over 60 meters (200 feet) tall as they compete for sunlight. Taller than average trees climb above the canopy and are known as 'emergents'. The canopy of entwining branches have liana vines laced through them, restricting sunlight to the undergrowth. Beneath the canopy only specialized trees, ferns, and ground cover succeed.

Most rainforests are relict and exist as closed systems that once broken do not regenerate. They were plentiful 40 million years ago. Today 1/3 of the Tropical Rainforest is in Brazil, l/10 in Indonesia, and l/10 in Zaire.

There are Temperate and Subtropical rainforests as well. Among the most famous are the redwood forests of northwestern United States. This forest continues into Canada and Alaska but the dominant tree changes from Douglas fir to Sitka spruce. These forests are being extensively and not always judiciously logged.

The major difference between tropical rainforests and other types is the diversity of the tree species. Not only is a large part of the world's biomass in the tropical rainforest but also the diversity and range of plant speciation is the greatest.

Rivers draining rainforests account for most of the freshwater runoff in the world. In addition these rivers deliver 40% of the river-borne carbon to the ocean.

The most critical world environmental problem is the destruction of the rainforests. They are being destroyed at the rate of 5.6 million hectares (14 million acres) a year according to a United Nations estimate. Destruction by fire has increased the carbon dioxide level 8% in a period of 23 years. Half the forests have disappeared in the last 200 years. Africa has seen the greatest loss, about 52% of its forests. The contribution of 'slash and burn agriculture' to the Greenhouse Effect (q.v.) is enormous. It is a global problem.

Long term effects on world climate and the hydrologic cycle (q.v.) have not been assessed. See **AMAZON** and **DEFORESTATION**.

RAINWATER Varying amounts of rainwater are delivered to different parts of the world. The amount depends on latitude, climate, season, nearness to the sea, amount of atmospheric dust, and occluded gases.

Rainwater is a complex solution. Its major constituents are sodium, potassium, magnesium, calcium, chlorine, bicarbonate, and sulfate ions. There are lesser amounts of aluminum, boron, bromine, iron, and silica, plus ammonia, nitrate, and nitrite.

RAISE Raise is a mining term for the cut made in a mine to increase haulage-way for ore removal. It is driven from the bottom upward.

RAISED BEACH The raised or uplifted shore forms a terraced landform. The beach may become raised from glacial rebound or from a lowering of sea level. Raised beaches are common along the shores of Scandinavia. Wave activity has smoothed the terraces and incised new ones. As glacial rebound continues the beaches become a series of steps.

RAJPUTANA The perimeter of the Thar Desert is Rajputana. It is comparable to the Sahel (q.v.) in relation to the Sahara. Desert advance is 0.8 kilometer (1/2 mile) per year. Forests have been cut and the only fuel source is cattle dung. Wherever grass occurs, pasturing is present. Over-grazing is exhausting the grass resource.

The air above Rajputana was and is moist. It is in the path of summer monsoons from the Arabian Sea and air moisture is 4 times that above most deserts and about 80% as much as over some tropical forests, yet rain does not fall.

Warm moist air does not rise but instead sinks creating a subtropical high pressure area. This condition has been documented by Indian and other scientists.

University of Wisconsin scientists discovered that 1/3 of the solar radiation is absorbed by dust. Over a square kilometer there can be up to 5 tons of dust, several times that over a highly industrialized area. Daytime sun is obscured and the surface is relatively cool, limiting updrafts and precipitation. The dust cloud cools quickly at night and the air sinks.

In Rajputana, there are remnants of ancient cultures that farmed 3,000-2,000 B.C. The region had freshwater lakes and moist climate vegetation. Droughts corresponding to expanding Arctic climates occurred, triggering a situation not unlike the Sahel today. Dust bowl conditions grew and cities were abandoned.

The Indus area remained dry to the present and dust enables the desert to grow. Rajputana is 20% of India and at its center is Thar with less than 20 centimeters (5 inches) of rain a year. Cloud seeding experiments failed as the Atmosphere is over-seeded by clays.

RAND 'Rand' is South African for marshy lowland bordering a lake or lagoon. The most famous is Witwatersrand, locale of gold exploitation. The Rand is so important in South Africa's economy, the currency is called the Rand.

MOUNT RANIER Ranier with 4,392 meters (14,410 feet) is the highest of the Cascades in northwestern United States. A seemingly dormant volcano, Ranier erupted 100 years ago spewing pumice over the landscape.

The mountain which stands 2,400 meters (8,000 feet) above its neighboring peaks supports 27 glaciers of which 1 million-year old Emmons is the largest. The glaciers have greatly eroded the mountain, which was probably 300 meters (1,000 feet) higher.

Ranier supports a variety of ecological regimes at various elevations. Dense conifers cover its slopes and and its alpine meadows are vivid with color and life abounds in the Spring.

RAPIDS Rapids are short stretches of river with rough water. They are caused by streamflow over areas of differential erosion or through narrows strewn with boulders. Boulders brought in by high velocity streams break the flow into eddies.

RARE EARTHS The Rare Earths are a family of 15 metallic elements of nearly identical chemical properties. They are not all that rare, since as a group, they comprise 1/6 of all naturally occurring elements. They are not radioactive but often occur associated with uranium and thorium. The Rare Earths have economic importance as high-heat metals and are used in ceramics and optics.

At temperatures above that of liquid nitrogen, the Rare Earth metal oxides can become superconductors. Japan has produced an automobile engine based on yttrium, one of this group.

Major production of Rare Earths is from bastnaesite and monazite (q.v.). Until recently, the United States and Australia produce about 80% of the world's present needs. See **BASTNAESITE, CERIUM, MONAZITE**.

The Rare Earths, Neodymium and Samarium are in strong demand for their use in high intensity permanent magnets. Samarium in 1989 fell short of the demand. World reserves (1988) were 48 million metric tons of REO (Rare Earth oxide).

In 1989 the most important reserves of Rare Earth were (in millions of tons of Rare Earth Oxide):

China	36.0
United States	5.5
India	1.8
Australia	0.72
USSR	0.45

U.S. Bureau of Mines, 1990.

Bastnaesite is mined in China and the United States. The other producers, primarily India and Australia, obtain Rare Earths from monazite (q.v.), which is a by-product of heavy mineral sand operations.

The carbonatites (q.v.) of South Africa and Brazil are Rare Earth sources that have not been entirely evaluated.

RAVINE A ravine is a narrow, steep-sided valley cut by a youthful stream. It is larger than a gully and smaller than a canyon.

RECTANGULAR DRAINAGE The rectangular pattern of drainage occurs most frequently in areas broken by a network of fractures in the bedrock. This pattern is evident in parts of Appalachia, southern Sweden, and Finland.

RECUMBENT FOLD A recumbent or overturned fold has one limb almost parallel to the other. Both limbs are roughly horizontal.

RED ALGAE The most photosensitive of the seaweeds is red Algae. Of this group only dulse and Irish moss are found in intertidal regions. In general these Algae are delicate but they can live in sea depths up to 200 fathoms (360 meters).

Some red Algae encrust rocks with magnesium and calcium carbonate. They were probably important in the formation of ancient marbles and dolomites. See **ALGAE**.

RED CLAY Inorganic red clays at depths over 5,000 meters (16,500 feet) cover 113 million square kilometers (43.6 square miles) of seafloor. The fine clays have less than 30% calcium carbonate or organics.

RED MUD The biggest solid waste disposal problem of the aluminum industry is residue from bauxite processed by the Bayer method. Enormous quantities of red mud are produced each year since a ton is produced for every ton of alumina made.

Red muds are mostly made up of material below 1 micron in size so they are slurried to holding ponds or lagoons near the plants. The lagoon may cover hundreds of acres. Solids eventually settle, even stratify, and the liquor is recycled. The residues are rich in iron oxides and many useful minerals such as titanium and minor amounts of uranium. No economic extraction has yet developed.

In Japan, it has become impossible to establish lagoons for the muds because of space, so residues are being dumped in the sea.

RED SEA The Red, or Erythrean Sea of the Greeks, separates the Arabian Peninsula from Africa. It fills a trough in the Great Rift System that is 2,080 x 250 kilometers (1,250 x 150 miles). As an arm of the Indian Ocean, the Red Sea is almost land-locked between rocky deserts.

Blue-green Algae, ('Trichodesmium erythraeum') are abundant. They are responsible for the red tide (q.v.) when they release a red pigment. The Sea was named for the phenomenon.

The Red Sea marks the early stages of continental break-up. The break-up began in the Oligocene (30 m.y.). The trough, partially filled with lava and was above sea level. Ethiopia was at the south end. As the rift widened, volcanoes dammed the sea, which dried out. Salts 4 kilometers (2.5 miles) thick built up and are now covered by sediment.

Today's Sea dates from 5 million years ago, when Arabia finally separated from Africa. Hot salty water fills pools around hot spots, probably adding to the already saltiest of seas. Evaporation is extremely high. See **RED SEA HOT SPOTS**.

RED SEA CORAL Living coral covers most Red Sea reefs. There are many fish and small invertebrates in the ecosystem as well as more than 100 different coral species. The reefs are of different types:

- Coral Atolls - Sanganab is the best representative
- Fringing Reef - Parallel to the coast. Elongated ridges several hundred meters offshore with intervening shallow lagoons
- Barrier Reef - Still farther out to sea.

Most of the reefs are just below the sea surface. Wingate Reef (Sudan Reef) is noted for its coral variety and fish in abundance. It has been carefully studied.

RED SEA HOT SPOTS Extraordinary 'hot spots' were located in the Red Sea. Gold, silver, copper, and zinc estimated at $500 million have been discovered in the Atlantis II Deep. The iron and manganese have not been evaluated. Sediments in the Deep are unique. They are white, red, green, blue, yellow, and black in color.

The Atlantis II Deep is half-way between Sudan and Saudi-Arabia. The mineral-bearing hot springs are related to seafloor spreading associated with the East African Rift System. See **HOT SPOTS**.

RED SHIFT Movement of a wavelength of light toward the red end of the Spectrum is a 'red shift'. This effect is produced when an astral body moves at high speed away from the observer. See **DOPPLER EFFECT**.

RED TIDE Red tides observed off California and Florida, and in the Red Sea are caused by blue-green Algae ('Trichodesmium erythraeum') which releases a red pigment into the waters.

For a red tide to develop sea conditions must already be set for an algal bloom or proliferation. In addition to pigment exuded by the Algae, light and air are cut off to marine life below by the algal mat which forms. Toxicity from the pigment and a lack of light and oxygen cause massive deaths of marine-life. Hydrogen sulfide from decomposition adds further deaths.

Algae do not photosynthesize rapidly enough to offset the oxygen depletion below the mat. Algae return to normal after a return to the usual sea conditions of the area. This means a reinstatement of the main current flow of wind origin.

The Gulf of California was called the Vermillion Sea because of the plankton blooms. In 1958, the surface was tomato red over a wide area.

In Florida during a bloom in 1946-47 the sea was yellow with plankton and billions of fish were killed. The color of the sea was yellow instead of red due to the species of Algae but conditions were the same.

REDBEDS   Redbeds were a controversial topic for many years.   Although not completely resolved, it is recognized that redbeds indicate oxidation of sediments. Redbeds are completely oxidized so they must have been deposited where the drainage was good and the soils were aerated.

The earliest important redbed sequences were deposited in the Devonian (395-345 m.y.). They include the Old Red Sandstone of Great Britain. Redbeds formed in basins between the Caledonian Mountains (Great Britain).

REDUCTION-OXIDATION   The chemical reactions referred to as 'redox' for reduction and oxidation are important biologically and in mineral formation. There is not an oxidation without a simultaneous reduction. The reaction is caused by a loss and a gain of electrons.

Conditions in a soil profile will be oxidizing or reducing, usually as a result of water table levels. Highly oxidized horizons are rich in iron and aluminum oxides.

REEF   Reef is from 'razif', Arabic for pavement. A reef is usually a shoreline feature. It may be organic or sedimentary. Sedimentary reefs are usually formed from consolidated ancient beaches and are cemented by quartz grains. Most organic reefs today are coral but some ancient reefs, identified as Precambrian, are algal.

There are 3 main reef types:
- Fringing
- Barrier
- Circular or atoll.

Fringing reefs are common, especially along recently subsiding shorelines. Barrier reefs may also be fringing but normally they are of greater extent and are separated from the land by a deep channel. Great Barrier Reef (q.v.) is the most notable example.

Many South Pacific islands are emergent parts of atolls. Organic reefs build beneath the sea surface, often atop volcanic or other ridges. They grow upward on the detritus of earlier colonies of marine organisms. The living portion is always at water levels compatible with growth. Coral polyps and other organisms secrete calcium carbonate, the main reef construction material.

Reef corals are fragile. They can not survive at temperatures below 70° Fahrenheit. Minor salinity changes adversely affect them and they must have a firm substrate. Corals subsist in shallow water symbiotically with dinoflagellates (q.v.). See **CORAL**.

REFLECTION   Reflection is the complement of absorption (q.v.). It is the ability of a mass to repel light waves. Reflection is important in slowing snowmelt especially from glacial surfaces.

REFORESTATION Efforts to reverse deforestation are underway. However, they are insufficient to stem accelerating desertification (q.v.) especially in areas like sub-Saharan Africa.

Pakistan planted 14 million trees in a 10-year period. In Sudan, an irrigated forest has been planted outside Khartoum to alleviate fuelwood (q.v.) problems. This is an area that does not receive even 20 centimeters (5 inches) of rainfall a year.

Village level forestry efforts have been somewhat successful in China and Korea. In Korea, 1/3 of the country has been planted with trees.

A major effort of the United Nations was to reforest portions of the Mediterranean Rim. In Mali and other countries, education has not kept pace with the attempt to reforest and small trees have been cut for fuel. See **FUELWOOD**.

REFRACTION Normally refraction is a distortion or bending of a light wave when it encounters another medium, as light striking a glass. Refraction of ocean waves occurs when waves bend upon approaching an irregular coastline. The waves hit the shore directly. See **REFRACTIVE INDEX**.

REFRACTIVE INDEX Light bends when reflected from facets of a cut gemstone. The angle at which it bends is the refractive index. The same phenomenon occurs when light passes through a natural crystal or prism.

REG The reg is a desert landform. It is a hard pavement of sorted gravel or mixed sand and gravel. Regs are usually near streams or former streams. The most famous regs are Serir Reg of Tibesti in Libya and the regs of Rajasthan (q.v.), India.

REGIONAL METAMORPHISM Regional rock metamorphism occurs when the stresses of heat and pressure within the Mantle are exerted over huge geographical areas. Regional alteration of sediments to quartzite, gneiss, and schist results. The Scottish Highlands are a good example of regional alteration.

REGOLITH The loose weathered mantle directly overlying bedrock is the regolith. In an ideal soils profile, regolith is the C-horizon. Engineers consider the regolith as soil, but complete soil forming processes are not necessarily present.

REGOSOL Azonal soils like those composed of glacial drift, loess, or sands are regosols. No discernible soil profile develops.

REGRESSION The transition of sedimentary deposits from marine to overlying continental is regression. In a geosynclinal sequence. regression occurred when folding and uplifted sediments form a continental platform and caused the sea to retreat.

REGUR On the Deccan Plateau, India (q.v.) soils derived from basaltic lavas are 'regur'. They are dark intrazonal soils, high in montmorillonite clay (q.v.). Regur can attain a depth of 3 meters (10 feet). Similar soils can be found on the volcanic rocks of Parana, Brazil.

REJUVENATION When the erosive capability of a mature or old-age stream is renewed, rejuvenation exists. It results from a lowering of base level or uplift of surrounding terrain. Valleys become more steep-sided and meanders entrench and may become goosenecks (q.v.). Old stream deposits form terraces above the new deeper channel.

RELATIVE DATING Correlations are made among different stratigraphic columns to establish relationships and relative dates of deposition. Correlation is made locally first and may spread to be continent-wide.

Horizons of particularly distinctive rocks are marker beds (q.v.). These may be traced over great distances. Similar beds indicate similar conditions in the depositional environment. Marker beds are particularly valuable if fossilized.

RELATIVE HUMIDITY The amount of water vapor in a column of air compared to amount the air that column could contain at a given temperature is its relative humidity. 100% is saturation. If relative humidity is close to saturation, any minimal cooling may result in precipitation. Relative humidity is measured close to the ground.

RELIEF Differences in landform elevation create a pattern called 'relief'. It results from processes acting upon the Earth's surface. Each process produces a characteristic set of shapes often particular to an elevation.

Tectonic relief results from folding and faulting. Erosion can carve a new mountain range or denude an area completely.

REM The rem is a unit of electromagnetic radiation. It measures the effect X-rays and gamma rays have on living tissue. The dose from an average X-ray is 1/60th of a rem.

Rem is an acronym for Roentgen Equivalent Man. 1 roentgen = the amount of ionizing radiation in a cubic centimeter of dry air at 0° Celsius. See **RAD, RADIATION**.

REMNANT MAGNETISM Magnetism imparted to a rock at the time of its formation and an integral part of that rock is remnant or remanent. It may differ from the present or paleomagnetism of the region.

At formation, the magma contained iron particles that oriented themselves to the Magnetic Field at the time of cooling. These rocks are fossil compasses indicating polar orientation when they were formed.

REMOTE SENSING Geophysicists utilize remote sensing to identify and assess ore bodies. Initially remote sensing relied on hand-held instruments to identify anomalies at the Earth's surface.

More advanced geophysical equipment became airborne. Today, it is really 'remote sensing' using satellites and rockets. From 650 kilometers (390 miles) whole nations can be 'sensed' at a time.

Imagery and computer enhancement have made it possible to determine global agricultural conditions, weather, and sense anomalies leading to mineralized areas.

Remote sensing is also an important part of oceanographic exploration. Sonar and magnetic sensing in the sea have become valuable tools enhancing our knowledge of the oceans.

Remote sensing will play an important part in the monitoring of any arms control agreements. The success of such agreements depends upon monitoring and now possible satellite coverage.

RENDZINAS Rendzinas are intrazonal soils with brown to black surfaces and light gray to yellow subsurfaces. Derived from calcareous marls and chalk, rendzinas develop under grasslands or mixed grassland and forest in humid and semi-arid areas.

RENEWABLE RESOURCES There are 3 classes of organic and inorganic resources. These are:

- The inexhaustible
- The renewable
- The non-renewable.

Solar energy is an inexhaustible resource in human terms. Air is also considered an inexhaustible resource. The nature of their inexhaustibility is omnipresence.

In the case of air, the classification does not refer to quality. In human terms the nature of its inexhaustibility may have to be reconsidered in terms of chemical content and pollution.

Renewable resources are limited but they tend to be maintained. In this category are water, forests, and pastures. These are renewable to varying degrees depending upon a variety of factors. The foremost of these factors is climate and its variability. Human use is an important variable as to whether resources remain renewable or become non-renewable. Interference with the natural laws of replenishment may make them non-renewable.

Only water, soils, and forests are renewed in less than thousands of years and only if conditions of regeneration continue to exist. If the rate of replacement exceeds use, some minerals are renewable. Manganese nodules may be an example.

RENIFORM Reniform means kidney-shaped and is descriptive of some rocks and minerals. Nodules (q.v.) are often reniform.

REPTILE The alligator, crocodile, lizard, snake, and turtle belong to the Reptile Class of animals. Many extinct reptiles (e.g.: Dinosaurs) belong in this class.

Reptiles generally possess scales or horny plates. They have lungs and a heart with 3 or 4 chambers. Reptiles have long been considered cold-blooded but for some species, the evidence suggests warm-bloodedness.

Reptiles resemble amphibians but they differ in development. Reptiles are adapted to land but can spend time in the water. Such is the case of the anaconda, a member of the boa family. The anaconda, largest of all snakes, is found in the Amazon Basin.

The earliest fossil reptiles were found in the Permian redbeds of Texas, Oklahoma, and in the Permian of the USSR. By the end of that period (270 m.y.), they were highly specialized and dominant.

The most important land reptiles were dinosaurs. Dinosaurs persisted until the time of the Great Extinction (q.v.) at the close of the Cretaceous Period (65 m.y.). Many dinosaur fossils are found in the Morrison Formation (q.v.), which extends from New Mexico to Montana and from Colorado to Utah.

RESERVOIR ROCKS Formations containing petroleum, usually under high pressure, are reservoir rocks. They may be limestones, dolomites, sandstones, or salt domes. Some hold only water, however the typical ones contain oil, gas, and water. Internal flow depends on porosity (q.v.). Most have bottom water below oil and gas.

In the Sahara there are 7 great basins with reservoir rocks containing enormous quantities of water at depth. Efforts have been made to tap these sources, notably in Egypt's Western Desert.

RESINS Resins are plant secretions that are often very gummy. They harden on the bark of certain trees especially conifers. In the past, these resins had many uses. They were important in ship maintenance and were called 'naval products'.

Fossil resin or amber (q.v.) is a valued gem and ornamental material, especially when it contains captured insects.

REVERSE FAULT A reverse fault is steeply dipping. The hanging wall (q.v.) has moved up in relation to the footwall. It differs from the thrust fault which has a lower angle of dip.

REVOLUTION Any period of violent change in Earth history is a revolution. Orogenies, or mountain-building events, are also known as revolutions. The Appalachian Revolution closed the Paleozoic Era (225 m.y.).

RHEOLOGY Rheology is the study of plastic, non-fluid flow. This is a type of flow thought to be found in the Earth's Mantle.

RHINE RIVER The Rhine, an important European river, rises in the Swiss Alps near the Austrian border. Fast flowing in its upper reaches, the river slows at Lake Constance. The Rhine flows through the Vosges' fault block mountains, and the granite hills of the Black Forest. It empties into the Atlantic via its delta in The Netherlands.

The Rhine Valley occupies a graben or down-dropped block in the European Rift. The valley is deepening at the rate of 0.5 millimeters per year. It widened 5 kilometers (3 miles) in 40 million years. The Rhine Gorge is the site of Heinrich Heine's 'Lorelei'.

RHIZOBIA   Some bacteria, found symbiotically with legumes, are 'rhizobia'. They are usually in the root nodules. These are the nitrogen-fixing bacteria for which the legumes are famous.

RHYOLITE   Rhyolite, a volcanic rock similar to granite shows indications of rapid cooling. It has a glassy feldspar matrix with small, fine felsic grains and rounded crystals. Rhyolite lava is rich in silica (quartz). It is an acidic igneous rock.

Orthoclase and microcline feldspars predominate in rhyolite. Tridymite and cristobalite varieties of quartz are present.   These varieties only crystallize at high temperatures.

Rhyolite texture is fine and can be porphyritic (q.v.). The rock is pink, red, or light brown to gray. Color-banding is frequent. Rapid cooling yields obsidian; gaseous flows form pumice (q.v.).

RHYTHMITES   Sediments often show cyclical or rhythmic deposition. These suggest seasonal or annual change. The Green River Formation in western United States has 788 meters (2,600 feet) of shale that required 6.5 million years to deposit in freshwater. Periodicity is marked by changes in density, color, and texture.   The formation has reserves equivalent to 100 billion barrels of oil.

Castile Formation, Texas, shows rhythmic deposition of calcite and anhydrite indicating climate changes between dry and less dry.

Coal measures often have cyclical or rhythmic deposition showing climatic shifts and differences in organic content. The deposits of the Black Warrior Formation in Alabama show this rhythmicity, as do many other coal deposits. These sequences are cyclothems.

RIA   The ria is a type of estuary. Its type locality is northwestern Spain where there are a series of fjord-like bays. They differ from the fjord (q.v.) by being shorter and shallower. These narrow bays deepen and broaden seaward. They may have branches.

The Amazon has many rias or submerged courses of what were Pleistocene channels. It does not have a delta comparable to the Mississippi. This may be due to the fineness of the sediments and strong tidal currents. See **AMAZON BORE**.

RICE   Rice is the world's most prevalent cereal (q.v.). It may be grown as paddy or upland rice. The paddy is more important. A paddy (q.v.) of 4 hectares (10 acres) can yield 24,000 kilograms (54,000 pounds) annually, enough to feed 240 people.

RICHTER SCALE   Richter and Gutenberg developed a scale in the 1930's to measure the magnitude of earthquakes. They pre-set a curve against which to measure quakes. The smallest or standard shock was set at 0 and earthquakes noticeable to humans at 2. Quakes causing some damage were 5. At 6 and above there was a lot of damage.

The difference between quakes 2 and 3 was small compared to that between 6 and 7. The most violent type was set at 10.

THE EARTH SCIENCES REFERENCE

The Richter Scale was revised in 1977. Each whole number is now a 10-fold increase. The Alaska quake on the revised scale went from 8.4 to 9.2 and the 1906 San Francisco from 8.3 to 7.9. On the new scale 5 is the equivalent of the explosive shock of 1,000 short tons (907,200 kilograms) of TNT.

RIDGE The spine or core of a mountain range exposed by erosion is of a material resistant to weathering. These rocks are ridge formers. Frequently ridges are of quartzite, a durable metamorphosed sandstone.

In the sea, a continuous high is a 'ridge'. There are a number of oceanic ridges making up the relief of the deep ocean floor. The major oceanic ridges are split by major rifts.

The Earth's 6 principal crustal plates are separated from each other by oceanic ridges and rifts left by seafloor spreading. They average 1,000 kilometers (600 miles) wide. Volcanoes and vents emit lava that fills the floor of the rift forming new crustal material.

In addition to the Mid-Atlantic Ridge (q.v.), there are 2 lateral ridges east and west from Tristan to Africa and South America. According to Wilson, lateral ridges form drift movement trails. There is a corresponding pair connecting Iceland to Greenland and the European Shelf. In the Indian Ocean where 4 continents split from Gondwana, corresponding ridges have been identified.

In meteorology, a ridge is a region of anticyclonic winds around a high pressure area.

RIFFLE Streams often have natural riffles that are small barriers of gravel bars and rocks. These tend to slow flow and sometimes heavy minerals will be deposited. Backed-up water flows at greater than normal speed over these obstructions during low water.

Grooves or riffles are built into sluiceways, inclined troughs, and prospector's pans. They trap gold and other heavy minerals.

RIFT Faults of great magnitude, continental in scale, are rifts. A rift has a host of subsidiary faults. The rifts themselves are usually block-faulted. Many down-dropped blocks have become major rift valleys. Among these are the Rhine Valley and Death Valley.

The East African Rift and associated rift valleys is perhaps the greatest continental system. It extends from Malawi in southern Africa to Turkey. Northeast Africa has been called 'an ocean in the making'. Djibouti is one of the most tectonically active areas in the world. It abuts the triple junction of the Red Sea Rift, the rift filled by the Gulf of Aden, and the East African Rift. Spreading in this area has been operating for at least 23 million years.

Major rifts in the oceans are considered as segments of a Global Rift System (q.v.) and many consider the continental rifts as continuations.

RILL A rill is a small brook or tiny rivulet generated by the impact of rainfall on an unconsolidated surface. Small incisions are made in the surface by run-off. These are rill erosion scars. Rills grow with each rainfall until a gully forms. From the gully, a stream channel can develop.

On a beach, rills are small channels made by outgoing tides.

RING SYSTEM Many planets have ring systems. Evidence seems to show that the Earth had a system at the end of the Eocene (37 m.y.). Earth's ring system is thought to have been similar to Saturn's. The hypothesis is that the system circled Earth's Equator.

Evidence also appears to indicate a close encounter of the Earth with inter-planetary matter about 35 million years ago. The Ring System has been correlated with 'coincidences' occurring at that time. These include major climatic shifts, dramatic increase in micro-tektites, the extinction of Radiolaria (q.v.) and other changes. See **TEKTITES**.

RIO GRANDE RISE The Rio Grande Rise in the South Atlantic Ocean is similar in many ways to Walvis Ridge (q.v.) off southern Africa.

Deep sea drilling on the Rio Grande Rise shows that the oldest Cambrian sediments (550 m.y.) were deposited in shallow waters on a fragment of continent or a subsiding guyot (q.v.).

RIO GRANDE RIVER The Rio Grande River rises in the snows of the Rockies, in the Sangre de Cristo Range near the Continental Divide. Water in the upper reaches is captured in talus and emerges lower down as springs. The Rio Grande flows from arid New Mexico to Texas and forms the border with Mexico.

The river is the 5th longest in North America at 3,034 kilometers (1,885 miles). It drains 471,000 square kilometers (182,000 square miles) with few tributaries. In its middle reaches, the few streams, with flash flooding, are depositing rather than eroding sediments.

Low rainfall and high evaporation have kept the Rio Grande a 'river in jeopardy' for hundreds of years. Waters all along its course have been preempted for agriculture.

RIP CURRENTS Rip currents occur when there is a strong buildup of water between an offshore bar and the mainland. Strong onshore winds develop waves inside the bar. Seaward flow may be sufficient to cut a channel allowing velocity increases.

A rip current is especially dangerous when the offshore bar is submerged. The sea surface has a foam-line as the current moves seaward in the gaps.

Colliding opposing currents also result in a rip-tide. This condition occurs when storm currents encounter longshore currents.

RIP-RAP Broken boulders and rock used as bridge revetments, port protection, and foundations are rip-rap. Stone quarried for rip-rap is the most resistant available in the vicinity of the construction.

RIPARIAN RIGHTS Riparian refers to the location of land along or adjacent to a natural stream or watercourse, or a lakeside. The owner of riparian land has an unrestricted right to water use, except that of shutting off supply to those downstream. Riparian rights were spelled out in Roman Law and continue to be respected.

RIPPLE MARKS Sediments, usually clays, display surface undulations. These are ripple marks originating from current or wave action, or in some cases wind action. Fossil ripple marks resulted when ripples were quickly buried in place and preserved.

RIVER Channeled runoff of surface waters usually begins as small streams. As more streams connect to create a larger volume, a river is born. Rivers collect drainage then transport water and solubles to the sea or to inland lakes. Whenever the velocity slows the river drops its cargo of sands, silts, and muds.

The existence of a river depends upon an availability of water, a surface sufficiently soft for a channel to be cut, and a surface sufficiently inclined to allow gravity flow. The river is the product of the environment and its climate, but it is also a shaper of the landscape.

Drainage always reflects climate and geology. Rivers are the greatest agencies of erosion and deposition. Immense areas have been and are being built from river sediments. At the same time, mountains may be carved from plateaus and great land areas are being denuded by the erosional force of rivers and streams.

RIVER BASIN The entire area drained by a river and its tributaries is its basin. A great river basin will hold a number of smaller basins.

Most large river basins are defined by great rimming falls in a line marking the headwaters areas. The Amazonian fall-line has a horseshoe shape. Sometimes, fall-lines are in descending steps. A river can flow hundreds of miles from its source area and encounter another series of descents as along the Congo or Zaire River. The depositional plain and delta are an integral part of the river basin.

ROARING FORTIES In southern oceans between 40° and 50° South Latitude is a belt of prevailing Westerlies. The winds are very strong and threaten navigation. They have been known as the 'Roaring Forties' since the days of the great sailing vessels.

ROCHE MOUTONNEE Mountain slopes scoured by glaciers look from a distance as though they are covered by sleeping sheep. The French expression 'roche moutonnee' for this landscape became the geological description.

ROCK A rock is an aggregate of minerals. It may be in the form of a massif (q.v.), block, boulder, or cobble and is relatively hard and coherent. Its composition can be described and used to identify and classify it. Subtle differences in chemical composition can yield a totally different rock.

The shape of the Earth and its landscapes are determined by its rocks. Rocks in molten state form its Mantle above which cooled rock forms the Earth's Crust. These rocks determine where water is located and where plants and animals may live. Rocks and the minerals they contain are the material upon which all life is dependent. Modern civilization depends directly on rocks and minerals for energy, food, and shelter.

Rocks are classed by origin:

- Igneous rocks - Of molten origin. May be extrusives (volcanoes) or intrusives (plutons).
- Sedimentary rocks - Deposited in seas or in continental depressions.
- Metamorphic rocks - Transformed by heat and pressure.

Although all rocks began as igneous, 75% of existing surface rock is sedimentary. 52% of surface rocks are shales. Sandstones make up 15%, granites another 15%. Carbonate rocks account for 7%. Rocks are also grouped based upon size, shape, and arrangement of their components and texture.

There are many kinds of rock as many mineral compositons are possible. When recognized, similar rocks are grouped, and given a group name. Some are formed by the gradual change from one to another type.

Surface mineral abundances in rock formations are as follows:

Feldspars	39%
Quartz	28
Clay or Mica	18
Calcium Carbonate	9
Iron	4
Ferromagnesium	2

Although, imperceptible, constant change occurs in rocks. Igneous rocks erode and become sedimentary. Buried igneous and sedimentary rocks are acted upon by heat, pressure, radioactivity, and other forces within the Earth. These forces produce metamorphic rocks that may be subjected to more change. When rocks are exposed, they are altered by subaerial weathering.

Rocks cycles can take millions of years. Rocks deposited in the seas show the episodes of transgressions and regressions of the sea. Evaporites (q.v.) can form in arid areas when the sea retreats.

The oldest rocks so far measured are 3.7 to 3.9 billion years. They are in western Greenland at the mouth of Ameralik Fjord near Godthaab. The next oldest at 3.4-3.5 million years are in South Africa.

ROCK DENSITY Some rock groups have greater density or weight than others. Of igneous rocks, the ultra-basic ones have the greatest density.

Density contributes to crustal pressures. The average density of surface rock is 2.7 grams per cubic centimeter. Mantle density per unit volume is 4.5 grams per cubic centimeter.

ROCKER A short, sluice-like trough or 'rocker' is used in placer mining to separate and concentrate minerals by gravity. It operates like a rocking cradle. As it moves, the lighter materials are thrown to the outside edges and the heavier minerals settle to the center.

ROCKIES The Rocky Mountain Ranges are an integral part of the American Cordillera (q.v.). The ranges are parallel to each other and separated by deep valleys and low plains.

The Rocky Mountain System extends 6,660 kilometers (4,000 miles), from Canada to the Mexican border. Many peaks are over 4,200 meters (14,000 feet). The highest, Mt. Logan in Canada is 6,015 meters (19,850 feet). In North America, it is only exceeded by Mt. McKinley, or Denali, in the Alaska Range. McKinley rises to 6,194 meters (20,320 feet).

The 'Ancestral Rockies' were eroded away 230 million years ago. Prior to them, there were others in the Precambrian (2.3 b.y.). In the range there are volcanic clusters, fault block mountains, and eroded batholiths like the core of Pike's Peak. See **BATHOLITH**.

Sediments were laid down in a geosyncline in the Sundance Sea in mid-Mesozoic (180 m.y.). The sea extended from the Arctic to Arizona and New Mexico. About 50-60 million years ago, upthrusting geosynclinal sediments to between 3,000 and 6,000 meters (10,000-20,000 feet) of elevation created the mountains.

Igneous activity, both intrusive and extrusive with accompanying erosion, all resulted in mountains buried in debris. This period was again followed by uplift (20 million years ago).

ROCKSLIDES The most destructive of mass movements are rockslides, sometimes involving thousands of tons of material. Slides can be lubricated by water or ice. Typically, rockslides occur on undercut steep cliffs. They may be triggered by heavy rains, avalanches, earthquakes, or faulty construction.

ROENTGEN A roentgen is a unit of ionizing radiation which is accepted internationally. It is the amount of gamma or X-ray radiation needed to produce ions with 1 electrostatic unit of electrical charge in a cubic centimeter of dry air at 0° Celsius. The charge may be positive or negative.

ROOKERY A rookery is a breeding or resting place established by colonies of birds and mammals. Seals have rookeries along California's shore.

The word rookery comes from a bird, the rook. Rooks are colonial nesters.

RORAIMA Roraima, on the northern watershed of the Amazon Basin, is a 230,104 square kilometer (138,062 square mile) area where Brazil, Venezuela, and Guyana meet.

The boundary is marked by Mt. Roraima in the Guiana Highlands, a great fortress-like massif. The sediments are Precambrian and similar to African ones. The basement is also diamond-bearing, as in West Africa.

ROSS ICE SHELF In Antarctica between 79° and 82° South Latitude through 20° of Longitude over-hanging the Ross Sea is the Ross Ice Shelf. The ice shelf (q.v.) is unstable and hinged on rocky islands. Glaciologists feel that it could break loose at any time. This is independent of global warming effects. See **GLOBAL WARMING**.

At present the Ross Ice Shelf is 300 meters (1,000 feet) thick. It is subject to calving. The icebergs formed from it are huge.

RUB 'AL KHALI The Rub 'Al Khali (Fiery Heart) in the Arabian Desert is also aptly called the Empty Quarter. This forbidding desert is on the southern Arabian Peninsula and encompasses 500,000 square kilometers (300,000 square miles). It is the largest continuous sand mass in the world. Its dunes are spectacular for their red colors.

Sand pavements have developed on the lower slopes of windward dunes. These differ from desert pavement only in grain size. The sands are coarse-grained and closely spaced giving a smooth continuous surface. The surface is only about a grain thick. Individual surfaces are a meter square and reflect the sun. Once the surface is in place, it is almost impervious to wind. The sands sing when the crust is broken.

Impact craters are found in the desert. One of them, Wabar Crater is 100 meters (300 feet) across. Coesite was found together with meteorites. The occurrence is similar to that of Diablo Canyon, Arizona. The largest meteorite, a chondrite, weighed 5,760 kilograms (12,900 pounds). See **COESITE**.

RUBBER Latex from the Amazon 'Hylea' was first used by Cambebas Indians. They created many articles from it, including sacs or 'seringas' for carrying water. Amazon rubber collectors are 'Seringeiros'.

Rubber does not grow in stands in the Amazon so gathering latex is difficult and time-consuming. Attempts to grow the tree under a plantation system failed because of fungus disease. Dispersed in the forest, isolated trees were affected, but transmission was not rampant. The disease is now controlled at Fordlandia (q.v.).

Rubber became important to industry in the early 1900's and the infamous rubber boom resulted. From clandestinely taken seedlings, the British introduced rubber to South East Asia where it grew successfully in plantations. Today rubber supports Malaysia which produces 43-44% of the world's supply. Liberia, West Africa, grows plantation rubber as its major cash crop.

RUBIDIUM Rubidium is an element in the Alkali Metals Group. Like all members of that Group, it has only 1 electron in its outer atomic shell. Its symbol is Rb and its atomic number is 37.

Rubidium has a radioactive isotope that decays to strontium in a half-life (q.v.) of 4.9 billion years. The ratio Rb:Sr is used in radioactive dating (q.v.), especially of Precambrian rocks.

Rubidium is a photosensitive element whose major use is in electronics and for medical uses.

The element does not form separate minerals but is a replacement for potassium in late-phase pegmatites. Currently the United States is obtaining its supply by extracting it from lepidolite, a potassium mica. The rubidium content of lepidolite is only 1.5%. The Cesium silicate, pollucite, contains up to 3.15% rubidium.

Rubidium may have a potential for use in 'ion engines' proposed for Space travel.

RUBY Ruby is a corundum gem and a precious stone. It is second to diamond in hardness.

The best gems have been found in Mogok Valley, Burma. Burma rubies are reddest and Burma is the origin of the 'pigeon-blood'. Its color is imparted by chromic oxide.

Tanzania produces a rare orange tinted ruby. Thailand and Sri Lanka are also important producers. Rubies are satellite minerals in Brazilian diamond fields but they are not of gem quality.

RUDACEOUS SEDIMENTS Rough sediment components are rudaceous. These include boulders, cobbles, pebbles, and gravels. Compacted and cemented, rudaceous sediments are a puddingstone (q.v.) conglomerate. If rudaceous fragments are angular, the material is a breccia (q.v.).

LAKE RUDOLF Lake Rudolf is the largest of the Great Rift Valley lakes. It is in the Eastern Rift, Kenya. The lake is at 375 meters (1,237 feet) in elevation. It is 265 by 30 kilometers (160 x 18 miles) and at its deepest, in the south, is 120 meters (396 feet).

The only permanent stream emptying into Rudolf is the River Omo draining the Ethiopian Highlands, 500 kilometers (300 miles) away. Intermittant streams from volcanoes to the south are important to inflow. There is now no outlet for Rudolf and its story is like that of Lake Chad (q.v.).

RUMANIAN OIL FIELDS The Ploesti area north of Giurgiu on the Black Sea is Rumania's oil production center. Wells are many thousands of feet deep. Crude from the area looks like molten tar.

Rumania was one of the earliest to produce petroleum and long held a good market share.

RUN-OFF   Rainfall that runs over the surface of the Earth and feeds directly to streams, lakes, and the ocean is run-off. It is the major agency of erosion. In the tropics, run-off periods relate to rainy seasons. In mid-latitudes, snowmelt increases seasonal run-off.

RUPUNUNI The Rupununi are the broad tropical savannas of Guyana. They stretch to the headwaters of the Essequibo River in the Guiana Highlands.

RUTILE   Rutile is a titanium oxide mineral found in igneous and metamorphic rocks. The mineral is mined from placer deposits, many of them in coastal locations. The United States obtains almost all of its raw material for titanium sponge from rutile.

World proven reserves of rutile (in thousands of tons of titanium oxide) are:

Brazil*	66,000
Australia	5,300
South Africa	3,600
India	4,400
Sierra Leone	2,000
Sri Lanka	800
United States	300

U.S. Bureau of Mines, 1988
* Brazil's reserves cited by Bureau are primarily anatase from carbonatite sources.

The United States rutile deposits are on Trail Ridge in Florida. Production slowed almost to a halt when Australian rutile hit the world market. See **TITANIUM**.

Rutile is a satellite mineral in Brazilian diamond sediments. It is in the form of bean-like pebbles with a blue-gray color. They are called 'bagageira' by the Brazilians and considered an indicator mineral for diamond earths.

Rutile is found included in quartz crystals. Rutile usually has a needle-like or acicular form. Rutilated quartz is valued as a carving medium. Included rutile needles are known as 'Venus hair' or 'fleche d'amour' (love arrows).

RUWENZORIS The Ruwenzori Range is on the western edge of the Rift Valley in Zaire and southwest Uganda. Ice-capped mountains rise to 5,089 meters (16,795 feet), the elevation of Mount Stanley. Snow line is at 4,500 meters (13,364 feet).

The snowfield and 4 glaciers feed streams. The Zaire (Congo) River is born in these snows. It formerly flowed to Bahr al Ghazal Basin in Chad, now it flows west and south. The Ruwenzoris form the divide between waters feeding the Albert Nile System and waters to the Atlantic.

The Ruwenzoris are the most extensive range of high mountains in Equatorial Africa. They are located only 48 kilometers (30 miles) north of the Equator.

The structure is a giant horst (q.v.) 100 kilometers (60 miles) long. It was intruded 2 million years ago. It is part of the Great Rift System and the result of block faulting (q.v.). The range rises from the Semliki Plains south of Albert and Edward lakes. The mountains are composed of ancient basement rocks which were upthrust about 2 million years ago. East and southeast are the Toro Ankole Lava Fields. The Semliki River drains the area to Lake Albert along the south horst wall.

'Ruwenzori' means rainmaker and the region does receive about 75 inches annually. The giant Lobelia flourish there as they do on Kilmanjaro. Margherita Mountain at 5,109 meters (16,763 feet) is among 6 peaks over 4,600 meters (15,000 feet) and is covered by dense clouds about 300 days of the year.

Ptolomy identified the Mountains of the Moon as the source of the Nile and suggested they were 3,300 kilometers (2,000 miles) south of the Delta. He was correct in that it was an ancient source. By the time the actual Nile source was discovered, the streams had been blocked by lava or captured. See **NILE RIVER**

RWANDA The African nation of Rwanda is enclosed by Burundi, Tanzania, Uganda, and Zaire. Lake Kivu (q.v.) in the Western Rift Valley forms its border with Zaire. Rwanda is in the watershed on the Continental Divide between the Congo (Zaire) and the Nile river systems.

Rwanda is noted for a forest of bush bamboo and for its mountain gorillas. It is also one of the most populous parts of Africa.

Recently Rwanda has been experimenting with the manufacture of fuel briquettes from papyrus reed. Like many populous areas of Africa, Rwanda is extremely short of fuelwood (q.v.).

San Andreas Fault — Dividing Pacific Plate (Top)
from North American Plate (Bottom)

San Andreas Fault — Western United States
Courtesy of US Geological Survey; Robert E. Wallace, photographer

S

S WAVE The secondary seismic, or 's' wave, is a shear wave. Particles vibrate at right angles, or transverse to the 'p', or primary wave (q.v.). The velocity of the 's' wave is between 4.6-7.5 kilometers (2.2-4.5 miles) per second, depending upon the density of the rock it is transiting. Waves move faster in less dense rocks.

It is conjectured that there are magma pockets where anomalies have been noted in 's' waves. These were recorded from beneath island arcs, oceanic ridges, on young volcanic islands, and in great rift valleys,

SABKHA In a sabkha, a special type of evaporite (q.v.), gypsum and anhydrite form a plain in stages just above the high-tide line. A modern sabkha on the Mediterranean Coast between Alexandria and El Alamein is in a depression between a Recent and a Pleistocene beach ridge.

In the sabkha environment, hypersaline calcium sulfate is saturated. Interstitial waters are increased in salinity by capillarity (q.v.). Calcium and sulfate form from pre-existing lagoonal gypsum which is below the water table. Gypsum nodules are altered to anhydrite.

During the Late Jurassic (140 m.y.) evaporites were deposited on giant sabkhas on the southern edge of the Tethys Sea. The area was barren and saline. Today the region is occupied by Iran, Iraq, and Saudi Arabia. Some sabkhas developed in deep depressions like the Danakil (q.v.) of Ethiopia.

From the center of the Arabian Shield to the Tethys Sea, the prograding plains or sabkhas repeat from west to east over 1,200 kilometers (720 miles). Each episode was followed by a marine transgression.

The sabkha profile is zoned from the bottom up:
- Shelly lagoon phase, above glauconitic sand
- Sandy phase with gypsum crystals
- Large gypsum crystals and banded gypsum in oxidized sand
- Small precipitated nodules of gypsum
- Sand with salt and gypsum formed in supratidal conditions
- Gypsum-halite caprock.

Some giant sabkhas have formed into caprocks. These hold in great oil reserves. Saudi Arabian anhydrite occurs in 4 horizons and is similar to that found in the Trucial States and northwest Iran.

SADDLE REEF Tight-folded mountain ridges rifted at the crest form a saddle. Metamorphosed sediments become ridge-forming rocks or reefs.

Many saddle reefs, especially in ancient rocks, contain gold and other minerals. The mineralization accompanied faulting. Precambrian quartz gold reefs of Witwatersrand, South Africa; Jacobina, Brazil; and Bendigo, Australia are such deposits.

SAGO PALM The sago palm of Southeast Asia is a source of sago powder, a food staple of the area. The palm is an indicator of freshwater.

SAGPOND A small lake developed in a depression caused by faulting is a sagpond. Sagponds are numerous along the San Andreas Fault (q.v.) in California. San Andreas can be traced from the air by the sagponds.

SAGUARO The saguaro ('Carnegiea gigantea') is a large tree cactus found only in the Sonoran Desert of southern Arizona and northern Mexico. It is long-lived, some are known to be 200 years old. It is the dominant vegetation of the region.

The saguaro attains 20 meters (60 feet) and has a columnar trunk with few branches. The pulpy trunk and branches have prickly thorn-like leaves. The saguaro produces a white flower and an edible fruit. It is pollinated by a white-winged dove. Woodpeckers carve holes in the trunk and owls take up residence there.

SAHARA DESERT The Sahara is part of the world's largest desert. It extends from the Atlantic Ocean across Africa to the Red Sea. The desert continues under various names in Asia.

The Sahara covers 1/3 of Africa, an area almost the size of continental United States. It begins at the foot of the Atlas Mountains of North Africa and stretches south to the Niger Basin rim. From the Atlantic to Red Sea is 7,000 kilometers (4,375 miles). From north to south it is more than 2,500 kilometers (1,562 miles). The Sahara expanded to the south by 100 kilometers (60 miles) in a 10-year period as that part of the Sahel (q.v.) became desert. See **DESERTIFICATION**.

The Sahara is a series of tablelands with low hills. The only true mountains are the Atlas, Ahoggar, and Tibesti. There are major depressions and a major canyon. Sand dunes cover 1.3 million square kilometers (0.5 million square miles).

The Sahara is hostile. In Tanezrouft, Algeria, even insects don't survive a sand surface heat of 150° Fahrenheit. Other areas are subject to freezing temperatures. In the Ahoggar Range of central Sahara, temperatures can drop 40° Fahrenheit in an hour. In some parts of the Sahara it hasn't rained in 7 years.

Geology indicates that Sahara was not always desert. Marine sediments of North Africa are thousands of meters thick. Morocco and Spanish Sahara have some of the largest sequences of phosphate rocks in the world telling of a time when the seas covered the region.

Ordovician (500-440 m.y.) rocks have glacial grooves which indicate a more polar position in that Period. Present conditions were initiated with the drying up of Pleistocene lakes and streams.

Surface water is almost non-existent in the Sahara. Populations cluster in oases (q.v.). Some oases support up to 50,000 people on a 30-50 square kilometer (20-30 square mile) area.

Recently, vast underground reservoirs were discovered. There are 7 major storage areas with 15.3 trillion cubic meters of water. In the western half of the desert, reserves are held in the Great Eastern Erg, the Great Western Erg, Niger, Fezzan, and Tanezrouft basins. In the central desert, reserves are in Chad Basin. In the east, the largest reserve of all is in Egypt's Western Desert.

SAHARAN SHIELD The Saharan Shield is an ancient stable craton occupying the western bulge of Africa. Shield rocks are Precambrian (2 b.y.).

Immediately east of the Shield, rocks are only 550 million years old (Paleozoic). Satellite imagery shows a sharp contact between the rock types. The boundary extends into the sea at Accra in Ghana. A similar boundary is found in Sao Luis de Maranhao, Brazil. The grain of the Brazilian Shield rocks matches that of the Saharan Shield.

SAHEL Where the savanna abuts the Sahara on its southern flank is a boundary zone called the Sahel. It is a broad transition belt where great climatic swings occur. The belt extends from 5° to 7° North Latitude. The Sahel reaches west to east from Mauritania to Chad and even includes parts of Sudan, Ethiopia, and Kenya. The belt covers 1/5th of Africa. Monsoon showers are restricted to a very brief period during the year in this semi-arid zone. The position of the Intertropical Convergence (q.v.) governs whether the monsoon-bearing winds can reach the area.

Worldwide cooling can cause the Westerlies (q.v.) to expand pushing the Intertropical Convergence (q.v.) south, blocking monsoonal rains. In an average year, rainfall is between 4 and 24 inches with evaporation as high as 90%. Even these average figures do not tell the story, since there are also years with no rainfall.

From 1870 to 1888, the Sahel was relatively damp, then from 1902 to 1950 there was much drought. In 1973-1974 severe drought was followed by torrential rains that tore away any loose soil. The next 6 years saw no rain.

The violent climate swings adversely affected the ecosystem. The Sahel is marginal with a very delicate balance between drought and survival. Drought and excessive population of humans and animals has damaged the Sahel so much it is losing 65,000 square kilometers (25,000 square miles) a year to the Sahara Desert. Mali appears to be the most vulnerable. The Ethiopian famine of 1986-1987 has been followed by the Sudanese famine of 1988. This trauma is continuing and is accompanied by a fuelwood (q.v.) crisis.

Grass and bush that held back the desert for centuries has been destroyed. The loss is not reversible without a radical climatic shift to a lasting, more moist regime.

SAINT ELMO'S FIRE The phenomenon of a flame from a ship or aircraft during a storm is 'Saint Elmo's Fire'. The flame effect results from a discharge of static electricity. This static electricity gives off the blue glow sometimes observed over power lines.

MOUNT SAINT HELENS Mount Saint Helens, a stratovolcano of the pyroclastic type, is in the Cascade Range of the Pacific Northwest in the United states. On March 27, 1980, the volcano erupted after 127 years of dormancy. Craters formed in the glacial ice. In all, there were about 17 eruptions.

Mount St. Helens exploded May 18 with the force of a 50-megaton hydrogen bomb, ejecting 3.8 cubic kilometers (1.5 cubic miles) of rock. Hot ash rose 19 kilometers (14 miles). With the blast, there were flows of superheated steam, gas, and ash. Mudflows resulted from glacial melt and avalanches occurred.

Prevailing winds carried ash east blanketing the countryside. It reached the East Coast in 4 days. The largest ash cloud was at 19,000 meters (63,000 feet) and was traced around the world. The cloud stayed aloft 17 days.

St. Helens, composed of alternating layers of lava, ash, and debris, built on an older volcano active 2,500 to 40,000 years ago. Modern St. Helens developed 350 to 400 years ago.

There has been swelling of the volcanic plug in the crater since this last eruption and some escape of steam. The pattern is not the same as prior to the last eruption. The volcano is being carefully monitored by the United States Geological Survey.

SAINT LAWRENCE RIVER The St. Lawrence River between the United States and Canada rises in the Great Lakes. After its emergence from Lake Ontario, the river flows north through Quebec Province and empties into the North Atlantic via the Gulf of St. Lawrence.

The St Lawrence River follows the Grenville Fault Line separating the Appalachians from the Canadian Shield. The Shield forms the north shore of the river. The Grenville Fault is the suture line between the ancient plates of Laurentia (q.v.) and Baltica thought to have collided about 440 million years ago.

The river and the Great Lakes became a seaway between Canada and the United States by a recent treaty. The status makes the area subject to International Maritime Law.

SALAMANDER A fossil Giant Salamander was discovered in Switzerland. The reptile lived 250 million years ago and was thought extinct until its living counterpart was discovered in Japan where it has been sold as meat.

The salamander is 1.2 meters (4 feet) long and lives by mountain streams. It is the oldest species with a backbone.

SALAR A salar is an encrusted saline playa (q.v.). Salars are of different types:

- Zoned salars in the Andean Highlands and Colorado Front Range
- Dry silty salars of oceanic origin in the Atacama Desert (q.v.)
- Recrystallized halite in Salar Grande in Bolivia.

Many salars have other economic minerals besides halite. Some are lithium-rich.

The salars of the enclosed Andean basins are very large. The largest, Salar de Uyuni, Bolivia, is 19,000 square kilometers (7,500 square miles). This vast salt marsh is south of Lake Poopo.

SALINA A usually white salina is a salt flat or salt encrusted hollow in an arid or semi-arid region. The salina is also called a salt pan. Salinas result from evaporation of ancient ponds and lakes.

SALINITY All waters are saline but not to the same degree. Salinity is the total dissolved solids in parts per thousand (ppt) by weight contained in water. Freshwater contains salts to a minimal degree. Its potability depends on just how much chemical salt it does contain.

Seawater is considered saline, the average being 35°/00. Seawater differs in salinity depending upon location and depth. Where evaporation is greater than precipitation over the ocean's surface, salinity is higher than average.

Land-locked areas have the highest salinity. The Dead Sea is the saltiest of all seas. In some parts it is a brine. A brine, by definition, contains a higher concentration of dissolved salts than seawater.

Water picks up chemical salts from rocks. When used in irrigation, water tends to become more saline due to evaporation.

SALITRE The Salitre Carbonatite, Minas Gerais, Brazil, is one of many. It, with others in an alkalic complex, is encompassed in a nearly 700 kilometer (420 mile) carbonatite belt. The belt extends north-northwest from the Atlantic at Rio de Janeiro to Goias.

Salitre contains magnetite, phosphate, and titanium. The alkalic rock, salitrite, is an intrusive with 59% aegerine diopside, 30% titanite, 7% microcline, and 4% apatite. The hot springs have temperatures over 26° Celsius (80° Fahrenheit). See **CARBONATITE**.

SALT Salt is essential to the human being, who requires 6.5-7.0 kilograms (16-17 pounds) a year. Chemically, it is sodium chloride and affects the heart, muscles, and cell fluid exchange. The body contains about 8 ounces. It is usually acquired through food.

There is enough salt in the seas to cover the continents with a layer 150 meters (500 feet) thick. Some evaporite deposits are as thick as 2,500 feet.

The United States produces 1.5 million tons a year from the Eastern Salt Basin, New York. Besides the United States, salt is produced in

North Africa, Israel, Jordan, Mexico, and South America. The leading salt exporter is Mexico, with 16 million tons a year, mostly from Baja California. The United States is the greatest producer with 45 million tons annually mostly from brines. The country is not self-sufficient, however, and Mexico makes up the 3 million ton annual deficit.

Halite (salt) mining from the sea and from underground operations is centuries old. In Poland, workers left 80 miles of art galleries carved in salt. Today mining consists of pumping water into the deposit and pumping out brine.

Salt is used to preserve food. It has a number of industrial uses because of its conductivity, usefulness in freezing, and ionization capability. It leads industrial raw materials, ahead of sulfur, limestone, coal, and petroleum. There are literally thousands of uses for salt.

Throughout history, salt dependence was a major consideration in trade, and politics. In the Ancien Regime of France, people were required to buy salt from royal depots. The Salt Tax was one of the major causes of the French Revolution. Napoleon revived it. It was ironic that his soldiers were weakened by the lack of salt in the famous rout from Moscow.

SALT BOILING The Chinese, 5,000 years ago, developed the art of boiling brine. When an egg floats, salts precipitate. Solar evaporation is used in arid areas but in humid ones, boiling is the method.

SALT COINAGE Salt was money for centuries. An ounce of salt traded for an ounce of gold. Roman soldiers were paid in salt and the major highway was Via Salaria extending from Ostia salt pans to Rome.

The most famous caravan routes in the Sahara were to buy salt and gold at Timbuktu. Marco Polo found salt coins with the Great Khan's Seal in the Himalayas. Ethiopia was still using salt discs in the 20th Century. At the turn of the century a bride price in Central Africa was 20 slabs of salt.

SALT CEDAR Salt cedar is remarkable for its evapotranspiration (q.v.) rate. Over a 2.33 million kilometer (900,000 mile) square area of western United States, salt cedars evapotranspirate 75.8 trillion liters (20 trillion gallons) of water a year.

SALT DOME The salt dome has a core of halite. The shape varies, some are mushroom or wedge-shaped, or any shape that fills an available cavity. Pressure can cause salt to flow sideways or upward through cracks or zones of weakness. It is a form of plastic or diapiric flow. Domes often are capped by gypsum or other evaporites.

Since 1901, oil has been produced from salt domes. The salt forms impermeable layers which can contain oil in intervening sediments. Spindletop at Beaumont, Texas, is one of the most famous oil producing salt domes.

SALT LAKE An isolated arm of the sea forms a salt lake or lagoon. The source of salt lakes in the interior of continents is the natural evaporation of water and concentration of salts. This occurs in arid areas when there is no outlet for the lake.

Continental drying which occurred in the Present caused Pleistocene lakes like Bonneville to disappear. Great Salt Lake (q.v.), the remnant of greater Bonneville, has become increasingly saline due to evaporation.

SALT LICK Natural deposits of salt available to wild and domestic animals are 'salt licks'. When natural ones are scarce or unavailable blocks of salt are placed near water holes.

SALT MARSHES Salt marshes are developed around coastal lagoons and salt lakes. The coastal ones are subjected to tidal flow and are especially important breeding grounds for certain marine creatures. They have a special ecology which takes several thousand years to establish. It is fragile and can be easily destroyed.

SALT WEATHERING Desert rocks are often impregnated with salt from former marine sediments or from groundwater. Saline groundwaters have mobile carbonates, chlorides, nitrates, and sulfates. The chemicals react with the rocks they contact.

Salt weathering is important where temperatures reach freezing. Weathering by chemical salts is most effective on porous rocks.

SALTATION Saltation, a process of mass movement particle by particle, is caused by the leaping and bounding of particles in a moving medium such as air or water. Streams carrying a bed load get forward momentum from saltation.

Saltation is essential to sand dune movement. When winds reach 18 kilometers (11 miles) per hour or faster sand creeps. Sand grains bounce forward in leaps. If they encounter obstacles or an area of reduced air pressure, the sand piles up and forms a ridge that may end as a dune.

SALTON SEA Flooding from the Colorado River in 1905 and 1907 caused the depression in the Colorado Desert to fill and form Salton Sea. The sea is 66 kilometers (40 miles) long and 71.6 meters (235 feet) below sea level. Its salinity (q.v.) is well above that of seawater.

The sea covers part of the Salton Trough. Northwest is Coachella Valley and to the south, Imperial Valley.

SALTON TROUGH The great structural depression extending from near Palm Springs to the Gulf of California is Salton Trough or Salton Sink. The area was filled by an arm of the Gulf which isolated and formed a salina (q.v.). It was separated from the Gulf by earthquake damming. Block faulting created a below sea level sink 183 kilometers (110 miles) long and 58 kilometers (35 miles) wide.

Drainage in the Salton Basin is now to Salton Sea. The lower part of the greater Trough area is in Mexico and contains the Colorado Delta.

Old Gulf shorelines are still visible in the area. There are mud geysers or active mud pots testifying to the activity of the region considered to have a geothermal potential.

SALTS Of the soluble chemical compounds, table salt (sodium chloride) is most common. Salts are leached from rocks and soils and transported in solution to the sea or lake. Under arid conditions they precipitate.

SAMPLING A small portion is taken as representative of the whole of a mineral deposit or an economic shipment of ore. It is very systematic. To evaluate cargos, measured amounts (usually over a ton) are mixed and quartered down to a shipping sample. For international shipment such quarterings are carefully monitored and documented.

To sample a deposit 'in situ', the principal methods are to take channel samples, grab samples, and samples at measured intervals. Samples are also taken of tailings and from drill holes.

SAN ANDREAS FAULT The San Andreas Fault is probably the longest fault in North America, 960 kilometers (597 miles). It crosses California from a point north of San Francisco to the Gulf of California.

San Andreas is a strike-slip fault or a fault with displacement parallel to the strike. Activity depth along the fault is up to 33 kilometers (20 miles) and movement is almost all horizontal. In 1857, there was a 10 meter displacement to the northwest.

Movement to date has been 560 kilometers (348 miles). At the present rate it is said Los Angeles will be opposite San Francisco in 10 million years.

San Andreas defines the suture line where the Pacific and North American plates are slipping by each other, edge-to-edge. The fault is not just a single gash but a system. There is also a series of parallel faults in the Gulf of California. Surface evidence disappears in the Colorado Desert but mud volcanoes and earthquake swarms make its presence known.

Farther northwest, in the mountains, the major faultline is identified by sagponds or faultline lakes. San Andreas is part of a system which extends from Mexico to Alaska.

Earthquakes are 10 times more frequent along San Andreas than elsewhere in the system.

SAN FRANCISCO BAY San Francisco Bay is an estuary (q.v.) that once was 1,800 square kilometers (700 square miles) in area. The bay, estuary of the San Joaquin and Sacramento Rivers, has been filled in and built upon. It is now half the size it was when discovered in the 1500's.

There are tides in the estuary of 1.2 to 3.6 meters (4-12 feet). At high tide, water covers plants growing on peripheral flats. There is a salt-freshwater cycle for many sea creatures. Fish and shellfish breed in the estuary and it is a waterfowl refuge.

Urban usage was so extensive, a multi-use plan was developed. It tries to balance human needs with those of nature.

SAND Sand is unconsolidated particles of rock. A grain is larger than silt but smaller than gravel. The size ranges between 0.2-2.0 millimeters. Grains are often quartz, but may be other minerals, especially heavy ones such as ilmenite and magnetite.

Earth-moving estimates of sand yield per cubic foot (0.028 cubic meters) are 144 pounds (65 kilos). A cubic foot of sand mixed with gravel weighs 120 pounds (54 kilos). A short ton (2,000 pounds) contains 4.63 cubic yards of sand. The cubic yard is the American quarry measure.

SANDBAR Waves breaking offshore pile up sand, building a bar or wave-like hill. Offshore islands can ultimately form from these bars. Atlantic City, New Jersey and Miami Beach, Florida are on sandbars.

SANDSTONE A sandstone forms when millions of sand grains become consolidated. They are cemented by silica, by carbonate of lime, or clay. The color is a reflection of the cement and of impurities. They may be white, gray, tan, yellow, brown, green, or red.

SANDSTORM Strong winds lift and carry sands through the air often in eddying swirls. In deserts, sandstorms do the greatest work in reshaping dunes and sandblasting rocks into erosional forms. The storms are legendary and each area has a special name for them such as 'harmattan' of West Africa and 'haboob' of Sudan.

SANITARY LANDFILL Most urban communities have set aside areas for the deposition of solid wastes. These are placed in alternating layers of soil and waste and allowed to decompose. Landfills often contain a fair amount of organic material that becomes subject to anaerobic bacterial decomposition. This can lead to a methane (q.v.) buildup.

In most urban waste there is an industrial chemical component. It is causing the greatest present difficulty with landfills. Some chemicals deteriorate and many are toxic. Many chemicals are soluble and combine with rainwater, so can enter the groundwater. Urban waste disposal is a critical problem and it is becoming more evident.

SANTORINI North of Crete is the 5 island Archipelago of Cyclades. Santorini, or Santa Irene, is the major island. The island was formed by the collapsed volcano of Santorini. Its circular shape reflects the crater walls. The crater is 11 kilometers (7 miles) in diameter or 7 times Krakatoa (q.v.).

Santorini probably was 1,000 meters (3,250 feet) high. The eruption 3,500 years ago had a force estimated at 120 times that of an H-bomb. The volcanic gas and tidal wave that resulted destroyed Crete and its

Minoan Culture. Many authorities believe the eruption gave rise to the Legend of Atlantis.

Iron oxides are still being exuded into the sea where they kill fish and color the waters. Sulfur fumes still escape.

The islands are pumice (q.v.) covered, in places up to 66 meters (216 feet). Remnants of Minoan culture are everywhere and covered by pumice. Walls of old settlements are evident and many artifacts have been recovered from the sea.

Pumice from Santorini was used in building the Suez Canal. Pumice makes an impermeable cement.

SAO FRANCISCO RIVER The 3rd longest river in South America, the Sao Francisco, is entirely in Brazil. The river rises in the Serra da Canastra in Minas Gerais and flows in a broad arc from south to north-east over 3,160 kilometers (1,900 miles) to empty into the Atlantic.

The Sao Francisco River played a great role in populating the hinterland. It is navigable upstream for 315 kilometers (190 miles). Paulo Affonso Falls on the river was the site of the first major hydroelectric facility in Northeast Brazil. It made some industrial devlopment possible. It also brought the region's first real rural electrification.

SAPPHIRE Gem sapphire is a corundum mineral of aluminum oxide and oxides of titanium and iron. Titanium oxide imparts the blue color. The richest deposits are in Kashmir, in the Himalayas at 4,500 meters (15,000 feet). The gems are prized for their cornflower color.

SAPROLITE Weathered bedrock in which original textures and structures are still evident is saprolite. Pegmatites (q.v.) subjected to anaerobic weathering may form relatively deep saprolite. This saprolite material makes hand-cobbing for semi-precious stones relatively easy.

SAPROPEL Sapropel are lagoonal or estuarine deposits with a large organic component. They are composed of an oily material that was distilled under high heat and pressure. It is the result of a diagenetic (q.v.) process occurring at depth.

SARGASSO SEA Sargasso Sea is part of the Atlantic Ocean. The water is blue, warm, and clear. Huge seaweed masses (Gulfweed or Sargassum) float on the surface. The sea is the 'world's largest weed-choked jungle'. It covers 59,570 square kilometers (23,000 square miles) between the Azores and Antilles. Sargasso has no shore. Near its surface, due to the high evaporation, salinity (q.v.) exceeds the average for seawater.

Sargasso Sea is in the Doldrums (q.v.), a belt of little wind or rain. It is bounded on the south by the North Equatorial Current which merges with the Antilles Current. The Gulf Stream is to the north and west and the Canaries Current is east. Circulation of these currents around the Sargasso Sea creates a gyre (q.v.).

The Sargasso Sea itself is relatively shallow. Below it, the ocean is thought to be up to 6.7 kilometers (4 miles) deep and very cold. The Navy is now studying what are considered underwater storms in the deep ocean below the Sargasso Sea. It is thought that these deeps have cold currents from the Arctic and Antarctic, which are mixing. There is also a component from the Mediterranean which is dense, being more saline. Convergence of these currents would create a secondary gyre due to the Coriolis Effect (q.v.).

Sargasso Sea is the spawning ground for American and European eels. Adults swim more than 3,300 kilometers (2,000 miles) to mate and die. Elvers make the return journey to their respective continents.

SARGASSUM Gulfweed or 'Sargassum' is a genus of floating plants sustained by small air bladders. Sargasso Sea has 2 species growing in patches and reproducing by generation from broken shoots.

In the sea, an estimated 4 million tons of 'Sargassum' create their own mat. It is a brownish-yellow in color. The weeds are the habitat of swarms of seahorses, small fishes of the 'Syngnathidae' Family, which are shaped like a horse in the neck and head.

SASTRUGI Sastrugi formations are rough sea-blue surface features of snow and ice carved into pinnacles or burrows by the wind. Sastrugi terrain is very difficult to transit. It is a common landscape in northern Siberia.

SATELLITE Satellites are planetary bodies or moons. The Solar System has more than 30 moons orbiting the planets. The Earth has only one.

Based upon knowledge of natural satellites, artificial satellites were developed and placed in orbit. These orbit the Earth at selected distances and are used primarily for communications.

Remote sensing is now an integral part of exploration. Satellite imagery, especially computer enhanced, has made parts of the Earth known that are difficult of access by land or aircraft.

Natural resources have been revealed by satellite mapping, including some major mineral deposits. Oil and gas will affect surface vegetation giving it a faint yellowish halo. The electromagnetic effects, especially major anomalies (q.v.), reveal regional belts of mineralization and clues to Earth history.

The ability to map vegetation has not only helped exploration but allows for assessments of world-wide harvests and crop yields. Such information can alert planners to problems of diminished yields before harvest time and help avert famine in less favored areas.

SAUDI ARABIA Oil-rich Saudi Arabia occupies part of the Arabian Peninsula. The Arabian Desert dominates the country. Great sand mountains are found in Rub al' Khali (q.v.), the Empty Quarter of the desert.

The wind-blown sands of the desert threaten its oases. Al Hofud is covered each year by about 12 meters (40 feet) of sand. It is a constant shoveling job to preserve the oasis.

Saudi Arabia is one of the richest nations on Earth due to its enormous oil reserves. In addition to these riches, the Arabian Shield is host to a number of other economic minerals.

SAW-TOOTHED MOUNTAINS   Many mountain ranges have saw-toothed ridges. These result from several alpine glaciers plucking the summit regions, cutting cirques, and leaving a row of pinnacles. The peaks of the Wyoming Grand Tetons were formed in this way.

SCABLANDS   Scablands is a local name for part of the Columbia Plateau. Glacial meltwater flowing south cut into lavas and created great canyons or coulees, mesas or buttes. There are many hanging valleys (q.v.) and thick gravel terraces bordering streams. The scablands cover 100,000 square kilometers (40,000 square miles).

SCANDINAVIAN ICE SHEET   The only remnant of the Scandinavian Ice Sheet covers Greenland. When glaciation was at its maximum, the sheet covered Europe to south of Berlin, Warsaw, and Moscow. See **ICE SHEETS**.

SCARP   A scarp, or escarpment, is a cliff-face caused by faulting, slumping, or avalanche. Scarps can look like great battlements or fortresses especially when formed by major rifting. Those bordering the great Rift Valley or the Rhine Valley are good examples.

A crescent-shaped breakaway scarp can often be found where slumping initiates on hillsides. Downslope there will be lesser scarps.

Linear mountain ranges or hills that are subjected to erosion will be marked by long erosional scarps.

SCATTERING   Light waves from the Sun are scattered by tiny particles and gas molecules. The sky's color is related to light scattering as blue is the most easily scattered part of the spectrum. Sunsets reflect the amount of scatter by their color. Shortwaves are more easily scattered than long. SMOG causes so much scatter no particular color shows clearly.

Elementary particles in collision with atomic nuclei and other particles result in energy scatter. This also occurs when particles from Outer Space collide with the Earth's Magnetic Field.

Energy scatter is of 2 types: Elastic and inelastic. If internal energy remains the same, the scatter is 'elastic'. It is 'inelastic' if collisions result in a change in particle energy. Scatter phenomenon, or Compton Scatter, must be taken into account when interpreting scintillometer data to determine radioactivity.

In the oceans, a layer of organisms scatters sound. This Scattering Layer is up to 200 meters (660 feet) thick. It can disturb soundings, as it will supply its own echo. The surface of the Scattering Layer is less than 200 meters below the sea surface at night. By day it may be at several hundred meters.

SCHEME 'Scheme' is British for a development project. Many were initiated during the Colonial Period. Others were set in operation after Independence in association with the new governments. The greatest number were in Africa.

Most schemes resulted in an alteration of ecosystems and many failed because ecological factors were not understood. Developers were unaware of the long-term and drastic nature of some effects. A few succeeded for long periods but deteriorated due to inadequate support. See **GEZIRA** and **GROUNDNUT SCHEME**.

SCHIST A metamorphic rock, schist, is a reworked product of clay, shale, sandstone, dolomite, and various volcanic rocks. 'Schist' means to split (Greek) and the rock is one that readily cleaves along a tabular plane. Micaschist is the commonest variety. Schist occurs widely.

During the metamorphic process, schist is subjected to such crustal stress, it foliates or splits into layers. The foliation is wavy and the included flaky or tabular minerals have a parallel orientation. Foliation occurs with shear stress. The minerals include mica, chlorite, hornblende and talc.

SCHISTOSOMIASIS A parasitic flatworm carried by a snail transmits the widespread disease, schistosomiasis (bilharzia). The snails inhabit slow-moving, weedy, tropical waters and irrigation ditches. They are especially prevalent in the Nile Delta. The parasite, after leaving the snail, lives in water. It can penetrates the human skin. The parasite attacks the liver and bladder.

In the Nile Valley, debility caused by the disease is an enormous economic and social problem for Egypt and Sudan where in some areas, 80% of the population is infected.

Carried by slaves to Brazil, the disease found a snail host along the rivers. Brazilian prospectors working slow-moving streams are at risk. 14 million Brazilians were infected by 1980.

SCINTILLATION COUNTER The scintillometer detects and records ionizing radiation. Radiation is emitted by a phosphor as a series of light flashes or ionized particles. The record is projected on a screen or printed.

SCLEROPHYLL FOREST The sclerophyll forest is composed of low evergreen hardwoods. It is native to warm-temperate maritime climates with hot summers and wet winters.

Tree density depends upon moisture and land use. Cork oak, olive, and pine are dominant. These create a shadeless forest of drought resistant trees. The Chaparral (q.v.) of California is a sclerophyll forest, more lush than average.

SCORIA Volcanic slag formed on the surface of lava is scoria. It contains many impurities. Gas emanating from basaltic flows causes scoria to be powdery and cintery. If scoria is buried for some time, deposits of calcite, quartz crystals, or zeolites may develop in it.

SCOUR Scour is down- and sideward abrasive action which leaves deep traces. Moving glaciers scour and act as huge bulldozers. Sea sediments are scoured by wave action and turbidity currents (q.v.).

SCREE SLOPE The scree or talus slope develops at the base of a hill or mountain. It has a repose angle up to 35°. The coarser and more angular the fragments are, the steeper the slope. As scree builds, it can bury the lower part of a cliff or mountain scarp.

SEA Seas are a part of the World Ocean. All are adjacent to continents except the Sargasso (q.v.). Seas are somewhat enclosed or sheltered parts of the ocean. They have defined boundaries, and are relatively shallow.

Some seas are separated from the oceans by sills. The major seas with enclosing sills are the Bering and Mediterranean. Seas are slightly more saline than the ocean. See **SILL**.

There are 54 recognized seas, some contained within others. The Mediterranean contains 7 smaller seas, probably the legendary ones of the 'Arabian Nights'.

SEA BREEZE The sea breeze is an integral part of the maritime climate. Daytime temperatures warm the land surfaces and a Low Pressure (q.v.) develops that pulls air in from the sea.

SEA CAVES The force of a wave hitting a sea cliff is enormous. Pond states that a wave 3 meters (10 feet) high and 30 meters (100 feet) long strikes a coastal cliff with a force equivalent to 1,675 psi (pounds per square inch). The continuous force erodes softer sediments. It can create caves in relatively short periods of time. Stormwave force is much greater.

The cave develops rapidly from wave impact and the cracking of rock which occurs as a result of the build-up of compressed air within the cliff. Once waves have opened up a cave they tend to cut deeper. If the rock material is readily soluble the process is very rapid. In time the caves can be eroded to arches and columns.

Sea caves are usually fairly small in comparison with the caves found in karst (q.v.) terrain. A large sea cave on the Oregon coast is 450 meters (1,500 feet) long. It is a favored wintering spot for sea lions.

SEA CLIFFS Wave activity creates coastal cliffs, The waves cut into the land and less resistant materials are scooped out. Sea caves (q.v.) may form. Land above the hollowed out area is weakened and slumps. Collapsed material forms a new front which the sea scours again. Meanwhile the coastal front is eroding and the cliff retreats.

SEA ICE In winter, frozen seawater covers 5% of northern seas. In the Antarctic the ice covers 8% of the area. The ice can be in the form of floes or pack ice (q.v.).

SEA LEVEL The reference plane or zero level used to measure an elevation or a depression is sea level. By definition, it has been established as the average elevation of the Earth's oceans.

Changes in sea level can result from changes in the shape of the oceanic basins, whether they become deeper or shallower. The growth of oceanic ridges or their disappearance can cause tremendous amounts of water to be displaced which is reflected globally in the rise and fall of sea levels.

Glacial ebb and flow greatly control sea level. If present ice caps were to melt, world sea level would rise about 60 meters (200 feet) enough to inundate every major port city in the world.

There have been fluctuations above and below present sea level but overall the seas have risen 6 meters (20 feet) in the past 6,000 years. They were still rising in 1965 averaging about 0.6 centimeters (0.04 inches) per year.

In the first part of the 20th century, sea level rose slowly. The level is higher along the western North Atlantic than along the Gulf. Canada and New England are experiencing glacial rebounding, while parts of the Gulf floor are subsiding. It is anticipated that Galveston will be underwater by the year 2,000 if the present rate of sea level heightening in the Gulf continues. See **SEA LEVEL DATUM**.

SEA LEVEL DATUM The sea level datum is a mathematical value for mean sea level. It was derived from an average of hourly elevations of the sea over 20 years.

Sea levels have been gradually rising. The U.S. Coast and Geodetic Survey set the sea level datum for the United States at Galveston, Texas, in 1929. At that location, the datum was an average of the high and low tides at that time.

SEAFLOOR SPREADING Evidence of seafloor spreading has been mounting. The East Pacific Rise (q.v.) is spreading 4.5 centimeters (1.8 inches) a year. The Pacific-Antarctic Ridge is spreading 5 centimeters (2 inches) a year. On average it is thought the Pacific spreading is 10 times more rapid than the Atlantic. See **MID-ATLANTIC RIDGE**.

Mid-oceanic ridges are split by rifts so that crustal plates move away from each other. The rift floor is the center of volcanic activity and new basaltic crustal material is erupted there. As spreading continues more and more new material is erupted pushing outward from the spreading zone.

Different episodes of crustal emplacement show alternating magnetism. These reversals parallel the ridges and show alternating polarity. See **MAGNETIC REVERSALS**.

SEAMOUNT A seamount is any structure rising from the seafloor to a height of 900 meters (3,000 feet) or more. It differs from a guyot in that it may have a peak. A guyot (q.v.) may develop from a seamount if the seamount were emerged long enough for wave erosion to reduce its peak and create the characteristic flat-topped structure.

SEASONS Seasonal changes are noted in higher latitudes because of the tilt of the Earth's axis. The angle is 23.5°. While the Earth orbits, half the globe tilts toward the Sun. For that half, days are longer and warmer due to more direct solar radiation. This is the spring and summer, March 21st to September 21st in the Northern Hemisphere. The Southern Hemisphere is experiencing fall and winter at this same time.

As the Earth's orbit progresses, the relative relationship of the hemispheres to the Sun changes until the seasons are reversed. Although in the Northern Hemisphere the longest day is June 21st and that is the day of alignment with the Sun, it is not the hottest part of the summer. It takes approximately 2 months for the Earth to heat up and radiate its warmth.

SEAWATER CONVERSION Along the Persian Gulf, where there are no viable sources of freshwater. Seawater is evaporated and then condensed to provide freshwater. Oil-rich Kuwait produces 15 million gallons of water a day. Energy costs for conversion would be prohibitive were it not for the country's oil supplies.

SEAWATER SALINITY Seawater in the World Ocean acts as a reservoir of many minerals. This accounts for its salinity. Most of the saltiness comes from sodium chloride, or common salt. The rest is from boron, bromine, calcium, carbon, magnesium, potassium, silica, sulfur, and minor minerals. Sea salinity averages 3.5% or 35 parts per thousand. The salinity of seawater is not uniform. In the Red Sea the average is 4% and in the Mediterranean, 3.9%.

It is interesting that the world's rivers transport practically no sodium chloride. The mineral they most transport is calcium, and this, from whitewater rivers, is mostly calcium bicarbonate.

The major ions found in seawater (in grams per kilogram or parts per thousand) are compared to those transported by rivers:

Ion	Sea	River
Chlorine	19.7	0
Sodium	10.7	0.002
Bicarbonates	1.4	0.06
Magnesium	1.2	0.003
Potassium	0.4	0.002
Calcium	0.4	0.15

THE EARTH SCIENCES REFERENCE

507

Both temperature and salinity affect density. The average is 1.03 grams per cubic centimeter. Warm waters are lighter than cold of the same salinity so warm water floats above cold. The sea's relative density is important to circulation patterns and currents.

SEAWEED Most seaweeds are 'Algae' (q.v.) and are free-floating or planktonic. Floating seaweeds have little air-filled sacs for buoyancy. Others are attached by a holdfast, a suction that clings to rocks and reefs. This sessile type has tentacles to trap food.

Seaweed makes an excellent natural fertilizer and has been so used for thousands of years. In Ireland, Scotland, and Japan, seaweed is a valued food.

SEDIMENT Fragments of matter are precipitated and deposited by water. They can also be deposited by gravity, glaciers, volcanoes, and wind. As the material settles and compacts it becomes a sediment. A sediment may contain a single layer or a series of discrete but related layers. The top and bottom of a layer or stratum are bedding planes. See **SEDIMENTARY ROCKS**.

SEDIMENTARY BASIN The sedimentary basin is a more or less extensive area that has been receiving sediments (q.v.) for long periods. Strata or layers generally dip toward the basin center.

Sometimes a sedimentary basin is confused with a hydrographic basin. The latter drains an even greater area and may well extend outside the basin of deposition. The Paris Basin (q.v.) is an excellent example of a sedimentary or depositional basin.

SEDIMENTARY ROCKS There are 3 major rock types: Igneous, metamorphic and sedimentary. Most sedimentary rocks are marine, having been deposited in shallow seas. They may be composed of pre-existing rock particles, organic debris, or both.

Transgressions and regressions of seas built up piles of marine sediment. Some marine sediments have been uplifted to become parts of high mountain ranges (Alps, Himalayas).

Other sedimentary rocks include:
- Continental sediments formed in local basins.
- Evaporative rocks accumulated as seas receded.
- Layered volcanic ejecta (ash, bombs, and other clastics).
- Conglomerates (boulder, cobble, pebbles) in a sand or clay.
- Organic chemical precipitates.

Sediments tend to be deposited in horizontal or nearly horizontal beds unless folded or faulted. The oldest sediments are on the bottom unless the formation has been overturned.

Once sediments are in place they can be altered by compaction, dewatering, or chemical alteration. They retain much of their original character.

Horizontal and vertical differences can be interpreted in relation to the depositional environment, transgression, and regression of the sea or lake. See **IGNEOUS ROCKS** and **VOLCANIC ROCKS**.

SEICHE   An internal wave (q.v.) oscillating in a body of water is a seiche. It may continue in a lake, gulf, or bay for a few moments or hours. Seiches result from wind, tides, and earthquakes. Seiches last long after the generating force is gone.

The famous Lisbon, Portugal, earthquake set off a major seiche in Loch Lomond, Scotland.

SEIF   The high, long, sharp-crested dune parallel to the prevailing wind is called a 'seif' which is Arabic for sword. Its height to width ratio is 6:1. Some are up to 90 meters (300 feet) high. A seif dune sequence may be hundreds of kilometers long. Seifs are found in the interior of the Sahara and in the desert of Saudi Arabia.

Seif dunes are often in groups with long 'gassi' (alleys) between. These are paved with bare rock. Seifs will result when barchan (q.v.) development is arrested by cross winds.

SEISMIC WAVES   Seismic waves passing through the Earth are induced by earthquakes or other tectonic disturbance. They can be artificially induced on a small scale by highway traffic or on a huge scale by nuclear explosion. Major seismic waves have intensities strong enough to propel them several times around the globe.

Artificially induced seismic waves are used to prospect for oil and minerals. They help to define sediments in a basin. To obtain this data an explosive charge is put in a shallow hole and detonated. Another station some distance away picks up the sound. The intensity and time of arrival of the sound give indications of the rock types.

The characteristics of 'p', 's', and 'L' waves (q.v.) indicate the way waves pass through rock and their depth in the Earth's Crust.

SEISMOGRAPH   The seismograph, an instrument that measures seismic waves, is used to evaluate and pinpoint earthquakes. The seismograph was first used in the 1800's in Italy and was a simple device based upon a pendulum and a weight. Today's equipment is more sophisticated but is essentially the same. It measures the wave intensity and the time of passage through various kinds of rock.

SELENIUM   Selenium, a metalloid (q.v.), is more toxic than sulfur. Its major use is in semiconductors (q.v.). Small amounts are used in glass-making to counter the green cast given by iron. In light, selenium conducts electricity, but not in the dark. It is used in photoelectric cells, fog lights, on buoys, and for automatic door openers. The major source is as a by-product of copper refining. Electrowinning of copper precludes selenium recovery. World resources are set at 80,000 metric tons. Chile, the United States, and Canada share almost half.

Locoweed, a shrub of the semi-arid southwest United States, takes up selenium from the soil. Cattle eating the weed suffer from blind staggers and may die. Animals are only tempted to eat the plant when drought conditions are severe.

Sometimes, Colorado lakes have too much selenium, then the fish become toxic to humans.

SELVA 'Selva' is another name for tropical rainforest vegetation comprised of tall broadleaf evergreens. Selva is used to cover the ecological niche provided by this forest and includes the entire ecosystem. In Brazil the Amazon Forest (q.v.) is Selva. See **TROPICAL RAINFOREST**.

SEMICONDUCTORS Semiconductors are elements that are neither good conductors nor good insulators. They are metalloids (q.v.) and are arranged on the Periodic Table of Elements between the metals and non-metals.

The semiconductors include silicon and germanium which are used in the Computer Industry.

SEQUOIA Sequoias have existed for 350 million years. There are 2 species of these conifers in western United States. They are the rainforest redwoods of the Pacific Coast ranges and the big-trunked sequoias of the Sierra Nevadas.

The coastal redwoods reach 100 meters (300 feet) and are timbered for their valuable wood. Sierra trees are in a belt from west of Lake Tahoe to Bakersfield and there are about 75 stands.

Sequoias belong to the 'Taxodiaceae' Family of conifers. They have a relative in the bald cypress found in southeastern swamps. The sequoias live up to 10,000 years. The famous General Sherman tree is in its prime at 3,000. Sequoias only begin to form cones when about 125 years old, then produce 1,500 or so. Seeds take up to 18 months to mature but may not be shed for a very long time.

SERAC A serac is a large ice wedge at an intersection of crevasses (q.v.). The wedge originates at the front or top of the glacier. It is a shifting ice pinnacle or block with little or no stability. The serac frequently falls and causes avalanches (q.v.).

SERAL COMMUNITY A plant community is seral when its existence provides favorable conditions for a particular plant. The plant is a member of a sere or ecological community in succession or rejuvenation. The seral community may evolve when a shifting cultivation site is abandoned, a fire scourges an area, or a layer of lava is laid down.

The seral community will be colonized first by a temporary assemblage of plants. These will be replaced by others when conditions become right. The community will ultimately be populated by climax vegetation (q.v.). Some communities do not give way readily to climax and pre-climax will persist. If climatic conditions change the pre-climax might become the climax.

SERENGETI PLAIN Serengeti is a large East African plain located mostly in Tanzania, and overlapping into Kenya and Uganda. The plain supports the largest population of game animals in the world. It is a preserve, but population pressures and poaching have exacted a high toll on the wildlife. Droughts have also diminished herds.

SERPENTINE Serpentine is the group name for hydrated iron-magnesium silicates, alteration products of peridotite (q.v.). It is widespread in California, in the Coast Ranges, the Klamath Mountains, and foothills of the Sierra Nevadas. It is especially prominent in Mother Lode Country, California.

Pale green serpentine results from the action of water upon peridotite. It often weathers to a dusty red, reflecting its iron content. California's state rock is mariposite, a member of the Serpentine Group.

SERRA DO MAR The Serra do Mar is the coast range from Rio de Janeiro, Brazil, to Uruguay. The highest peak, Itatiaia, is 2,232 meters (7,323 feet).

The Serra do Mar was a region of early colonization. Slopes were planted to coffee displacing the original forest. These slopes became deeply eroded and the cultivation had to be abandoned. Erosion and natural deep weathering make these slopes subject to great landslides. Major cities, like Rio de Janeiro at the foot of the mountains, experience major landslides in seasons of heavy rains.

SERRA PELADO An extraordinary series of gold deposits was discovered in recent years in Para State in Brazil not far from the fabulous iron ore deposit of Carajas (q.v.). The region was invaded by 25,000 'garimpeiros' or itinerant prospectors. In addition to these, there were more than 300,000 in small camps of up to 30 men. (Women garimpeiros are extremely rare.)

A single camp in the early days was able to obtain as much as 5.6 kilos (15 pounds) of gold a day. They also found diamonds, emeralds, and rubies. All supplies of food, fuel, and tools were flown in.

The major production of gold from Brazil in recent years has been from this region. See **GOLD**.

SERTÃO The Sertão is a vast drought sector inland from the coast in Northeast Brazil. Known as the 'Drought Polygon' it is 1,250 kilometers (750 miles) wide at Brazil's bulge and 1,600 kilometers (1,000 miles) long. The region is subject to great swings in precipitation, from zero to excessive rainfall. 'Caatinga' (q.v.) vegetation covers much of the 5 states that make up the Sertão.

The Sertão is over-populated and pressures on the land are great. Much like the Sahel (q.v.) of Africa, the position of the Intertropical Convergence (ITC) affects the Sertão.

From 1980-1985 the area was affected by drought followed in 1985 by floods so intense 1,000 newly constructed reservoirs overflowed.

Floods are as devastating to the Sertão as droughts. Much has been done to control floods and obviate drought but physical and social problems are enormous. The inhabitants have an extraordinary attachment to the land. Although many leave, they also return in great numbers whenever there is a slight improvement in climatic conditions.

SESSILE Some aquatic plants are sessile or permanently attached to a base. The base may be rock, coral, or other plantlife.

SET An oceanographic term for current flow is set. The set of a current is the direction toward which the current is flowing.

SEYCHELLE ISLANDS The Seychelles are islands in the northwest Indian Ocean. 90 mountain peaks and coral islands stretch over 1,000 kilometers (625 miles) of sea east of Mombasa. The islands were once part of Madagascar (q.v.) but were rifted away.

The Seychelles are fragments of a sunken continent centered on Mahe, an island that is 2/3 coral reef. Mountain peaks are of granite. Mahe, the biggest island, was once covered by rainforest. This has been largely destroyed by settlers, but is still found on mountain slopes.

The Black Parrot and Giant Land Tortoise can still be found on the islands. The 'coco de mer' a coconut palm producing double coconuts is a Seychelle specialty. Copra, dried coconut meat, is the main cash crop and fisheries are important.

SEYMOUR ISLAND Sheltered by Antarctic Peninsula mountains and other islands, Seymour in Weddell Sea, is free of permanent ice. Seymour has become increasingly important to geologists since the discovery of fossil-bearing sediments. Fossil assemblages include primitive marsupials (q.v.). Marsupials are now almost completely confined to Australia.

There are thick sequences of Cretaceous (80-65 m.y.) sandstones and siltstones. Eocene (45-40 m.y.) sediments are in the northern part of the island. Fossil starfish indicate they probably evolved in shallow, temperate Eocene seas (54-37 m.y.).

Continental breakup began 145-100 million years ago and the last portion to break off was Australia (50 m.y.).

SHALE Shale is dense, finely-laminated, fine-grained sedimentary rock composed of silicates and clay minerals. These were deposited in still waters and lagoons. They are fissile, flaky, or friable.

Shale is the world's most abundant sedimentary rock. It is formed from the compaction of muds and silts. These are in thin layers which readily split. Many shales contain petroleum. Billions of barrels of oil are locked up in the Green River Shale (q.v.).

SHARKS Sharks date from Upper Devonian (350 m.y.). They were common in Devonian seas (395-345 m.y.). Teeth and fin spines have been preserved in the fossil record. The skeleton is cartilaginous and not usually preserved.

By the Mississippian Period (345-300 m.y.) there were 300 species of shell-crusher sharks, who fed on Crustacea. Shark speciation was greatly reduced by the Pennsylvanian (300-280 m.y.). Some Eocene (54-37 m.y.) sharks were huge. 'Carcharodon' had jaws 1.8 meters (6 feet) across. Today, the whale shark is the biggest.

The shark has changed little through time except to become smaller. It must swim all the time as it has no skin bladder to allow it to float. In deep ocean waters, the urea content of a shark is in osmotic balance. If the shark enters an estuary it must excrete urea to maintain the balance. See **OSMOSIS**.

Sharks are found in all oceans, although most live along coasts in relatively shallow waters. They are predators and some, like the great white, are dangerous to humans.

SHATT AL ARAB The confluence of the Tigris and Euphrates rivers in southeast Iraq gives rise to the Shatt al Arab. The new stream flows through 190 kilometers of marsh and lake country forming the Iran-Iraq border. It empties into the Persian Gulf. Tides are reflected well upstream on the Shatt.

The marshland is productive of giant reeds which provide for the needs of the 'Reed People' who inhabit the marsh.

SHATTER CONE Shatter cones are made up of fragments caused by meteoritic impact and attendant shock waves. Shatter cones are from 5 centimeters to 2 meters (1 inch-6 feet) long. There are excellent shatter cones in Sudbury, Ontario, Canada, suggesting the Sudbury structure is meteoritic.

SHEAR WAVE The shear or 's' wave (q.v.) is a secondary wave in which particles of air or rock move or vibrate at right angles to the direction of major movement or 'p' wave (q.v.). Rocks shear past each other in faults.

Turbulence is created below jet streams as a result of the transverse nature of part of the flow. The effect is of a shear wave.

SHEET FLOODING Spreading waters cascading over a slope are in sheet flood. The water follows no channel, but covers the entire surface at the base of a mountain. The water spreads over the pediment (q.v.) or alluvial apron (q.v.).

Sheet flooding is prevalent in semi-arid terrains and a major contributor to pediment formation.

SHELL An outer coating or shell is secreted by mollusks (q.v.) and other sea creatures. It is usually, of calcium carbonate. The shell is left as a fossil when the organism dies. Many marine limestones are composed of these fossils.

The shells found in marine sediments are primarily of calcite, although the more soluble aragonite is also present.

The most common are shells from the single-celled foraminifera (q.v.). The minute shells from 'Pteaopids', the floating snails are found in shallow-marine sediments.

Besides the shells of calcium carbonate there are many siliceous shells from Diatoms, Radiolaria, and others.

SHELLAC Tree sap is consumed by insects and converted to resin. The resin thickens and adheres to the bark. Refined, it is shellac.

Not too many years ago, the southern pine forests of the United States were major production centers. India is the major producer today.

SHENSI EARTHQUAKE Enormous sediments of a yellowish silt called loess are found on the Shensi (Shansi) north China Plain. These sediments act to a great extent like quick clays (q.v.) when an earthquake occurs.

The Shensi Earthquake was the most disastrous in Chinese history. This earthquake, in 1,566 A.D., caused the loess cliffs to collapse. Caves carved into these sediments had been inhabited and an estimated 800,000 people were buried. See **LOESS**.

SHIELD DESERTS Tablelands and basin lowlands on sub-horizontal platform strata. They form above the Precambrian basement in shield deserts of the Sahara and Western Australia. Major relief is related to the ancient mountains. Exceptions are the younger intrusives in the Rift Valley and central Sahara.

SHIELD VOLCANOES Convex cones built entirely from basalt are shield volcanoes. The flows come from many fissures and not all from a central crater. Gradually, a central vent emerges (it may have subsidiary vents) and a dome or shield of lava forms. Slopes are gentle ranging from 2-10°. Hawaiian volcanoes are of the shield type.

SHIELDS Shields are stable crystalline masses covering vast areas. They are composed of complex Precambrian rocks. Many of these rocks have been subjected to great orogenic (q.v.) stresses. Ancient mountain ranges have been eroded away. Shields form the core of continents.

The major stable shields are the African, Arabian, Australian, Brazilian, Canadian, Ethiopian, Fennoscandian, and Siberian.

The Canadian Shield extends into the United States. It is the best exposed of all the shields. The Ethiopian which extends into Asia is the largest; the Canadian the next largest. Shields were named for the medieval shield shape of the Canadian mass.

Shields are rigid and have been unaffected by more recent mountain building. They have had some volcanic activity, faulting, intrusion, and erosion. Broadly arched and girdled by mountains, shields are often set off by huge deep-seated faults.

SHINGLE A shingle is a beach or shore with pebbles or coarse gravel. Shingle stones are neatly fitted together (imbricated) with the flat sides up. Many British beaches are shingles.

SHIRE RIVER Great Shire Valley, a deep depression in southern Malawi, contains Lake Malawi. The lake is the source of the Upper Shire River. The Upper and Lower Shire rivers drain the greater Zambezi Basin.

The Upper Shire flows 100 kilometers (60 miles) over a very low gradient before spreading into Lake Malonabe. Emerging from the lake, it flows over 80 kilometers (48 miles), a reach with a series of cataracts. After passing the rapids, the river becomes the Lower Shire which flows 230 kilometers (138 miles) over level plains and through swamps to join the Zambezi River at Chindio.

SHOAL A shoal is a shallow in a body of water, usually indicating a bar beneath the surface. Shoals are associated with schools of fish as plankton tend to flourish in the shallow waters. The plankton are the major source of food.

S.I. The S.I. (International System) of measurement is the new standard. It is based on mathematical formulas and constants.

The meter is = 1,650,763.73 radiation wavelengths in a vacuum corresponding to a change of energy levels in Krypton-86.

The second of arc = 9,192,631,770 radiation periods related to an energy change in Cesium-133. See **ISOTOPE**.

SIAL The symbols for silica (Si) and aluminum (Al) are joined in 'sial' a word describing the continental or upper portion of the Earth's Crust. The Crust is up to 50 kilometers (30 miles) thick beneath continents. Sialic material is largely granitic.

Oceanic crustal thickness is very much less than beneath the continents. Because oceanic crust has more ferromagnesium minerals, it is called 'sima' for silica (Si) and magnesium (Ma), 'sima' (q.v.). Sial is a less dense material than sima. (Note: The chemical symbol for magnesium is (Mg)).

SIBERIA Almost 10% of the Earth's land surface is in Siberia. It makes up 25% of Asia and more than 50% of the USSR. From the Urals in Russia to the Pacific, is 5,000 kilometers (3,000 miles). It is half that from the Arctic to China and Mongolia. Siberia is 25% within the Arctic Circle and 75% is underlain by permafrost (q.v.). This permafrost reaches depths of 450 meters (1,485 feet) and many Pleistocene fossils have been recovered from it.

The West Siberian Plain is considered the world's greatest lowland. Much of the plain is in marsh and permafrost is thick in the north.

Although there are said to be 55,000 rivers in Siberia, there are 4 major river systems: Amur, Lena, Ob-Irtysh, and Yenesei. These river systems are major transportation arteries. They are also obstacles to transcontinental road building but can be crossed on ice during the winter. Siberia has a tremendous hydroelectrical potential because of its rivers. Some major industrial complexes are already being served.

Siberia has 5 major mountain ranges with peaks near or over 3,000 meters (10,000 feet). The Kamchatka volcanic range in eastern Siberia is particularly active.

The Siberian Platform was built up in Early Paleozoic seas (570-550 m.y.). It has abundant marine fossils from trilobites to mollusks. The Upper Paleozoic Platform (520-500 m.y.) emerged and there are fossils of land animals and flora. The Carboniferous tropical forests were responsible for enormous coal reserves.

Siberia has been generously endowed with mineral wealth including the energy minerals. Beneath the West Siberian Plain, oil is estimated at a billion tons and gas at 70 trillion cubic meters. Coal seams are up to 60 meters (200 feet) thick. These hydrocarbons indicate that the region once had a much warmer climate. See **PETROLEUM** and **NATURAL GAS**.

Siberia is also rich in metallurgical minerals. Noril'sk, a Tundra (q.v.) city, supports a population of 250,000. It is near large deposits of copper, nickel, and coal, as well as natural gas. About the only major metal in short supply in Siberia is aluminum. Bauxite (q.v.) is found in neighboring Khazakstan. Siberia's gold rivals South Africa's.

SIBERIAN RAILWAYS For years the only main transportation line was the Trans-Siberian Railway. It served 1,000 locations along 9,600 kilometers (5,482 miles) of track. Its operation cost was $0.02 per mile in 1976. In 1982, the Baikal-Amur Magistral (BAM) Railway was put into service north of and parallel with the Trans-Siberian.

SICHUAN BASIN The Sichuan (Szechwan) or Red Basin of China is drained by 4 major rivers, among them the Yangtse (Chang Jiang). The basin is at an elevation of 500 meters (1,650 feet) has mild winters.

The rainy season is long and a rich agricultural region has developed on the Chengdu Plain. This plain has been irrigated since 250 B.C.

SIDERITE The iron carbonate mineral, siderite is 48% iron and an important ore. It occurs both as a massive mineral and as crystals in druses. Siderite crystallizes in the hexagonal system.

Erzberg Hill, Austria, is composed of siderite and has been mined for iron ore since the 8th Century. Siderite often forms ironstone balls making mining easy.

SIDEROPHILE Siderophile implies an affinity for iron. Some elements are siderophiles. Among these are carbon, cobalt, gold, nickel, and platinum.

SIERRA LEONE In West Africa, Sierra Leone has a narrow belt of Tropical Rainforest (q.v.). It receives 250-375 centimeters (100-150 inches) of rainfall per year. In the upland savanna, forest groves are the traditional home of the elephant and the pigmy hippopotamus.

Mining produces 80% of the GNP (Gross National Product). The major contribution is from diamonds. Sierra Leone has some of the world's richest rutile (titanium) deposits in beach sand concentrations. Iron has been produced from the Marampo Schists since 1926.

SIERRA NEVADAS The Sierra Nevada Range in California is part of the American Cordillera (q.v.). The Sierras are 717 x 133 kilometers (430 x 80 miles) long and have many peaks over 3,600 meters (12,000 feet). Mt. Whitney, in Sequoia National Park, is the highest at 4,393 meters (14,496 feet).

The eastern flank of the Sierras attains 3,330 meters (11,000 feet). The mountains rise directly from the Central Valley floor in the west.

The core of the range is a batholith (q.v.) varying from west to east in composition, from granite to granodiorite. Its geological history is of frequent uplift. Garlock Fault joins the San Andreas and alters the range from its normal NW-SE trend, to west.

SIILINJAVI CARBONATITE The carbonatite complex of Siilinjavi in eastern Finland is mined for phosphate minerals. The complex is part of the great alkalic province of the Kola Peninsula in the USSR. Kola is a major apatite producing area. The alkalic province in Finland is expressed in other carbonatites in what may be an extended belt.

SILCRETE Silcrete, a weathering crust, may be of secreted silica sands, micro-crystalline silica, or more highly metmorphosed silexite (q.v.).

Silcrete crusts are associated with deep weathering and are prominent in laterite regions of Australia. Australian silcretes are up to 5 meters (16.5 feet) thick.

SILEXITE Silexite is a cryptocrystalline variety of silica. It is opaque due to inclusions, has small amounts of quartz crystal or tridymite (q.v.), and is cemented by opal. Silexite only appears in nodules, some very large. Its origin has never been explained.

Silexite appears to result from nucleation. The presence of tridymite implies high temperatures. In the weathered soils of the Catalão Carbonatite, Goias, Brazil, the silexite is boulder size. These boulders are up to 2.5-3 meters (8-10 feet) across.

SILICA Silica is silicon dioxide, a 3-dimensional polymer (q.v.). Each silicon atom is capable of bonding (q.v.) with 4 others.

Sand is an inorganic polymer (q.v.) of silica used to make glass. The glass acts as a plastic and does deform very slowly at average atmospheric temperatures. See **SILICON** and **GLASS**.

SILICATES   Silicates form a mineral group comprised of silicon and oxygen in covalent bonding (q.v.). They are the most important rock-forming minerals. In the Earth's Crust and Mantle, they account for 99% of all rock. Silicates include feldspars, micas, and pyroxenes.

Single-chain silicates join at corners by sharing oxygen ions between different silicons. The crystal structure is of joining tetrahedra (4 faces). Pyroxenes are formed in this way, linked by doubly positive ions mostly calcium, iron, and magnesium. Augite is the most common pyroxene. Double chains give rise to amphiboles of which hornblende is the most common.

There are layered silicates like micas, chlorites, serpentines, and clay. Framework silicates are those in which all oxygen is shared as in quartz and feldspar.

SILICEOUS   If sand or the silica content of a of a rock or mineral is high, it is considered siliceous.

SILICEOUS LAVAS   Acidic lavas are siliceous (q.v.). They are ejected at temperatures between 700 and 800° Celsius, lower than the ejection temperature of basalts (q.v.). Siliceous lavas are more viscous than basaltic and do not flow far. They congeal rapidly often forming crusts over craters. These crusts tend to be exploded away in later eruptions.

Metal deposits are related to siliceous lavas. In the deep basins of the Red Sea many metals are being deposited. These include copper, gold, iron, manganese, silver, and zinc.

SILICIFICATION   Silicification is the process by which organic material is changed to stone by replacement. The replacement of organic material by silica is cell by cell so the plant or animal structure is preserved. Petrified forests were created in this way.

SILICON   After oxygen, silicon is the most abundant element in the Earth's Crust with 27.2%. It is not found in the elemental form, but is present as silica (silicon dioxide). Silica is rock-forming and the most common rocks are silicates. Silica forms crystals as in quartz or is amorphous as in opal.

For at least 4,000 years silica has been important in glass-making which required an ability to handle high temperatures up to 2,000° Fahrenheit (1100° Celsius).

Silicon as a semiconductor (q.v.) has become important in computer chip production. Silicon melts at 1,400° Celsius. As it gets hotter, resistance to impurities decreases. A tiny dust speck will destroy a chip. Allowed impurities serve to increase conductivity in 1 direction only. Some of these impurities are arsenic, boron, indium, or phosphorus. These elements affect the flow of electricity.

Pure silicon (95%) is used as a de-oxidant in copper alloying. Hyper-pure silicon made miniaturization of silicone (q.v.) possible. Silicon may play an important role in superconductivity (q.v.).

SILICON CHIP The silicon chip is a semiconductor (q.v.) that is equal to 50,000 transisters. It must be pure, with less than 5 grams of impurities in a metric ton. The silicon chip has permitted great miniaturization in computer systems.

Pure silicon in 100 millimeter rods is sliced into chips by tiny diamond saws or lasers. Minute chips are etched with patterns. However, if any tiny part does not function on the chip, the chip must be discarded. Chips are wired with gold or aluminum. An aggregate of chips makes up a computer microprocessor.

SILICONE Silicone is a polymer (q.v.) composed of molecules of long chains of bonded silica and oxygen. See **POLYMERIZATION**.

Many silicone polymers have been developed. One such is silicone-rubber which is fire resistant. It also resists corrosion and now most wiring on naval vessels has silicone-rubber insulation.

Since the rejection rate to silicone appears minimal, it is widely used in implant surgery.

SILL Magma flowing along the bedding plane of sediments creates a sill. The Hudson River intrusive sill is extremely thick. The overlying sediments eroded away leaving basalt (q.v.) to form the Palisades. The Great Whin in northeastern England and the Karroo of South Africa are important dolerite sills. See **DOLERITE**.

Ridges can enclose an area in the ocean and effectively dam the bottom currents. The Arctic Sill and the Mediterranean Sill separate their basins from the Atlantic. The Arctic is also separated from the Pacific by the Bering Sill.

SILT Silt is composed of fine-grained particles between 0.0039 and 0.0625 millimeters in size. It is carried by streams as dust particles. Precipitated behind dams, these particles can build up sufficiently to 'silt-up' or fill reservoirs.

SILURIAN The Silurian Period or System (438-395 m.y.) is Early Paleozoic in age. It overlies the Ordovician and precedes the Devonian.

The period opened in the 3rd Ice Age which began in the Ordovician (500-440 m.y.). The ice had retreated by Mid-Silurian. Tillites (q.v.) have been found in Bolivia and Argentina.

The emergence of North America isolated part of the Silurian Sea. It became a vast inland sea where Michigan, New York, Ohio, Ontario, Pennsylvania, and West Virginia are today. Shales and dolomites were laid down in the sea which slowly evaporated. Great deposits of halite (salt), gypsum, and anhydrite were evaporated out.

The Silurian is especially significant as a time when true land plants appeared after the epicontinental seas receded. The seas left great thicknesses of muds and limestone. Reef construction was widespread. Some iron formations have been dated Silurian.

Silurian fossil assemblages contained trilobites, coral, and ostracods, among other organisms. The first true fish appeared.

SILVER The Greeks thought silver a gift of the moon goddess. It is more reactive than gold. Silver crystallizes in the cubic system, and has a hardness of 2.5 on Moh's Scale (q.v.) The metal is usually found in veins. Silver tarnishes when exposed to air and a black deposit of silver sulfide forms on its surface.

Sterling silver (92.5% silver and 7.5% copper) is a popular alloy in the United States. Latin American silver contains 900 grams and is popular for jewelry.

Silver is an excellent conductor of electricity. Silver and zinc batteries are used in missiles and in jet instruments. The batteries are light weight and powerful. Silver-cadmium batteries are used in portable TV equipment. Computer relays are composed of 72% silver and 28% copper. A photograph is composed of millions of tiny silver specks. New technology may displace silver in this use.

The major silver producers are Mexico, Peru, USSR, and the United States. In the United States, it is rarely mined alone, but is worked as a by-product of other economic minerals.

The major sources of silver reserves are (in metric tons of metal content):

United States	31,000
USSR	44,000
Canada	37,000
Mexico	37,000
Peru	25,000

U.S. Bureau of Mines, 1990

World resources in 1987 were estimated at 335,000 metric tons. About 2/3 of the silver is associated with copper, lead, and zinc deposits.

SIMA In the Earth's Crust, the layer subjacent to the sial (q.v.) is the 'sima', from silica and magnesium. Sima is assumed to be high in ferromagnesium minerals and resemble basalt (q.v.). It is associated with oceanic crustal material while sial (q.v.) is considered continental.

SIND DESERT The Sind is the Pakistani extension of the Thar Desert of India (q.v.). The Indus River, a stream exogenous to the area, flows from Tibet to the Arabian Sea. The ancient civilization of Mohenjo Daro (q.v.) is in the Valley northeast of modern Karachi. See **RAJPUTANA DESERT**.

SINKHOLE Sinkholes are funnel-shaped depressions in limestone regions. There are 2 types: Solution cavities from water infiltration and depressions from landslides and cavern roof collapse.

In 1980, a sinkhole developed in Winter Park, Florida. It was 106 meters (350 feet) across and 30 meters (100 feet) deep. A house and a commercial garage were engulfed. The usual Florida sinkhole is much smaller.

SINGING SANDS Walking on dune crests causes sand to slip. A sound is associated with the shifting layers of sand as they are abraded by weight.

Sands sing loudly in the Empty Quarter of the Rub Al' Khali Desert in Arabia. The intensity of the sound depends upon the length of time sands remained undisturbed.

SINTER Sinter is mineral precipitated from a geyser. The material probably escaped with the ejection of carbon dioxide. Sinter may be calcareous (travertine) or siliceous (geyserite).

SIROCCO Hot, dusty winds blow from the desert to the North African and European shores of the Mediterranean. By the time the Sirocco has crossed the sea, it has picked up considerable moisture. When it reaches the Riviera, it is a hot, dust-laden, salty, and very sticky wind. Out of the Libyan Desert, it affects primarily Italy, Spain, and Malta.

SKARN Skarn is the textural term given to a mixed collection of calc-silicates. It occurs as metamorphic rock halos near an intrusive and may contain hematite and magnetite. Altered limestones contain mineralized skarns. The most important ones are ferruginous. In Finland such skarns are worked as iron mines.

SKY The region above the Earth includes the atmospheric envelope and Space. This is referred to as the sky. It appears blue because light is scattered by particulates in the Atmosphere. Blue is the most widely scattered of all visible light. Above the Atmosphere, the sky is black.

SLASH AND BURN CULTIVATION Many primitive communities utilize slash and burn agriculture. They cut and burn the forest to make way for crops. The method prevails in Africa, Asia, and Latin America. It is estimated that 2 billion tons of forest are burned yearly. The deforestation is causing climatic changes, some irreversible.

Land loses fertility rapidly when forest, especially rainforest, is cut. Farmers are forced to abandon sites in less than 3 years and cut another plot. 7 years are required for minimum regrowth. A real fallow could require 20 years. Population pressures tend to have farmers reduce fallow time.

Slash and burn practiced on slopes can be particularly devastating. Among the results caused by run-off are erosion, stream silting, lowering water tables, and acceleration of laterization (q.v.).

In Burma 2.5 million people are dependent upon this type of agriculture. Burmese villages have to be relocated every 4-5 years to insure crops. In Southeast Asia as a whole, clearing is going on at the rate of 33,000 square miles a year.

Much of the rainforest has been replaced by secondary growth, usually scrub and jungle vegetation, since seeds from this vegetation survive the burnings better than those of rainforest flora.

In Ghana (q.v.), rainforest once covered 1/3 of the country. In recent years it has yielded to 'slash and burn'.

SLATE Slate is a metamorphic, schistic rock in finely laminated plates. Slates are metamorphosed shales and mudstones. Some internal minerals are changed to flakes but they are not greatly altered. Cleavage is along bedding planes following relict fissile lines of the shales. Shale colors usually persist in the slates.

Slates are used as roofing material and as paving. See **SHALE**.

SLAVE PROVINCE In Slave Province, Canada, a Greenstone Belt and granites up to 2.5 billion years old are in sharp contact with rocks 1.8 billion years. The younger rocks reveal the life cycle of an ocean basin. The area has been studied for 40 years.

Bear and Slave Provinces are remnants of continental plates located over mantle plumes 800 kilometers (480 miles) apart. The tectonic activity over these hot spots led to a breakup into micro-continents.

SLEET Raindrops form ice pellets as they fall through freezing layers of the Atmosphere. Frozen rain is sleet, a form of solid precipitation. It occurs rarely and its distribution is restricted.

SLICKENSIDES Grooves and scratches on an escarpment face are caused by abrasion. The marks are slickensides resulting from rocks sliding past each other during faulting, landslide, or glacial movement. If faulted, small steps at right angles to the movement may result.

SLOPE Any gradient is a slope. Steep slopes retreat parallel to themselves preserving the slope angle and its approximate size.

Slope stability is an important concern of engineering geologists. Stability is governed by many factors. Some are the:

- Slope angle
- Height of the slope
- Natural vegetation cover
- Underlying bedrock
- Soils, their nature and consistency
- Moisture content of soil and rock.

Inclined distances from point to point are greater than level distances, therefore slope angles must be considered in a survey.

SLOTH The slowest moving mammal is the sloth. It creeps along at the rate of 2 meters (6.6 feet) a minute. An edentate (q.v.), the sloth inhabits the rainforests of Central and South America. It hangs from a tree within range of its food source of fruits, leaves, and shoots.

SLOUGH 'Slough' is British for a creek in the mud or mire of a wetland, marsh or tidal flat. Sloughs are generally at the edge of a floodplain subject to flooding.

SLUICE BOX A trough used for channeling water is a sluice box, a simple device in use on many placers. The trough is made from 3 boards about 2 meters (6 feet) long with 15-20 centimeter (6-8) inch sides. Riffles or slats are built into the trough to slow bottom water and allow heavy minerals to settle. The sluice box is used to rework gravels. Heavier gravels are removed by gravity as the box is angled at about 45°. The remaining material is panned.

SLUMPING Slumping is sediment collapse lubricated by water. Inclined strata or unstable slopes are more likely to slump. Water may be natural groundwater or domestic water from cesspools, irrigation, or leaking pools.

A semi-circular scarp is left on the slope where sediments have been torn away by slumping. It is referred to as a 'slump scarp'.

SLURRY A slurry is a fluid mixture of liquids and solids. A slurry pipeline is the most economic method of transporting some mineral commodities. The minerals are transported in a fluid state.

Today, coal, iron, and phosphates are the most important minerals being transported as slurries. The initial capital investment is great but once in place the system is extremely cost-effective.

One of the world's biggest was installed at Germano Iron Mine in Brazil to transport 7 million metric tons per year of fine ore concentrates to the Atlantic port of Ponta Uba, 404 kilometers (262.5 miles) away. The pipeline is twice the size of that serving Black Mesa Coal Mine in Arizona and 5 times the installation at Savage River Iron Mine in Tasmania. See **PIPELINES**.

SMALL CIRCLE Any intersection of a sphere that does not cut through its center is a small circle. Latitudes, except the Equator, are small circles.

SMELTING Heating rock until the contained metal runs out is smelting. Archaeologists believe it began in Elam on the Persian Gulf (3,500 B.C.).

SMOG Particles are picked up into the Atmosphere by winds. The particles may be ash, carbon from fires, dust, lava, pollen, pumice, seeds, soil, or any material in particulate form. These diverse particulates create SMOG when they hover over an area because the wind conditions are not favorable to remove them. The word 'SMOG' is a combination of SM/oke and f/OG. Moisture in the fog tends to cluster the particulates.

Toxic levels especially from sulfur and nitrous oxides may rise high enough to cause death. Urban areas around the world are most affected. The very tiny particles of aerosols (q.v.) pose the greatest threat. Urban SMOG is dangerous because of the many different chemical particles found in it.

Enclosed basins such as Los Angeles and Mexico City are very vulnerable. Mexico City is considered to have the greatest problem by the World Health Organization. In addition to its population density and enclosed situation, it is one of the major high cities of the world.

SMOG at high elevations is more dangerous because of the photochemical effect from ultra-violet radiation (q.v.).

SNAKE RIVER The Snake River in the northwestern United States has almost twice the volume of the Colorado. It cuts through a Mid-Cenozoic mountain fold belt. Hells Canyon was carved into the Seven Devils' meta-volcanics 7 million years ago. It is deeper than Grand Canyon.

The Snake is a major producing area for Chinook Salmon and Pacific steelhead. The fish lay eggs in the headwaters of the Snake. 24 species are indigenous to the river.

SNOW When water vapor temperature in a cloud is between 0° and 4° Celsius (32°-39° Fahrenheit), snow will form. When the air is not too cold, snowflakes cluster and precipitate.

Snow forms star-shaped 6-sided or hexagonal crystals and needle-like shapes. The flakes change with melting, sublimation (q.v.), and refreezing. Refreezing produces firn (q.v.), an initial step in glacial development. Normally, it is last year's snow that refreezes. The crust of hardened snow is neve, or snow transformed by compaction to a higher density (new lain snow is 90% air space). Snow can form into dunes much like sand. The shapes are similar and so are the winds that create them.

A large part of the Earth is affected by snow. Where the coldest month averages freezing or below, snow may be expected. Half the Northern Hemisphere is in this range. 124 million square kilometers (48 million square miles) are permanently covered, 15.5 million square kilometers (6 million square miles) with ice.

Snow is an efficient water reservoir. In western United States water supplies are dependent upon snows for replenishment.

Snow plays a role in opening up forests to sunlight by breaking off older tree limbs. It also acts as an insulator, keeping the ground surface relatively warm to the advantage of plants and small animals.

Snow is a complex phenomenon and an International Commission on Snow and Ice was formed in 1951 to study both.

SOAPSTONE Soapstone is a variety of talc. It is greenish, oily to touch, and shiny when polished. Soapstone occurs in crystalline schists. It is prized by sculptors as a carving medium. Many primitive people, with unsophisticated tools, have sculpted in soapstone.

Some major works of art have also been sculpted in soapstone. Among these are the statues of biblical figures carved by Aleijadinho, the extraordinary leper of Brazil. The statuary adorns colonial churches in Minas Gerais.

SODA ASH Sodium carbonate or soda ash is a valuable material used in making caustic soda, bicarbonate of soda, and washing soda. It is especially important in the glass industry. There are a myriad of industrial uses. Trona (q.v.) ore is treated to produce soda ash.

SODIUM The element, sodium, is one of the best known conductors of heat. It is a silver-white alkali metal normally occurring in combined form. Sodium is abundantly distributed and chemically active. It can react with water to free hydrogen.

The compound sodium chloride occurs as salt in the sea and in evaporite deposits. Halite is sodium chloride in rock form. Sodium oxide is a compound used extensively in glass manufacture. It is made from trona (soda ash). See **TRONA**.

All plant and animal life require the sodium ion. In animals and humans it combines with body fluids to permit muscles to contract. Most of this sodium comes from salt (q.v.).

SOGNE FJORD The longest and deepest of Norway's fjords is the Sogne on the southwest coast, north of Bergen. Its maximum depth is 1,308 meters (4,290 feet). The fjord is the longest in the world at 220 kilometers (125 miles). It is banked by sheer cliffs that rise to 900 meters (3,000 feet).

Sogne is a branched fjord with 7 major fjords in all. These, in turn, are fed by the Jostedal Glacier.

SOIL Soil is defined as relatively thin earthy layers overlying rock or sediment undergoing weathering. Soil is found directly on bedrock in few areas.

Transitional material is often found in the soil profile. The soil results from physical and chemical action on the rock material of the Earth's surface which has hosted living organisms. Without organic material, it would simply be detritus (q.v.).

Time is a factor in the alteration and buildup of soil. In the first few decades only regolith (q.v.) or weathered rock is present. It may be from a fraction to a few inches thick. In some areas it could take a century to develop 15 centimeters (6 inches). While in other areas, as in Indonesia, soils may develop rapidly. In the case of Indonesia they build rapidly due to the volcanic ejecta, heavy rainfall and warm temperatures.

In the Prairies of the United States, soils have only really begun to be substantial again. They were destroyed in the 1930's. See **DUST BOWL**.

SOIL CREEP Soil creep is the most usual of all mass movements. It consists of a grain-by-grain downslope displacement of earth. A dry flow, not easily detected, it has far-reaching effects from curved tree trunks to damage costing billions of dollars annually.

SOIL EROSION Soil erosion is one of the major hazards of primitive or faulty agriculture. The rich, crop producing topsoils are depleted reducing the amount of arable land.

Erosion has been the most important geological force since the recession of the glaciers, and erosion has been accelerating due to droughts and floods. Sheldon Judson estimated that erosion increased enormously with agriculture and animal husbandry. Agriculture only began 10,000 years ago.

In 1984, the loss of topsoil over newly developed material was calculated at 25 billion metric tons. In the years since 1984 many areas have been subjected to these forces. Drought also fosters the deflation process in many semi-arid basins.

SOIL PROFILE A section or cutaway of soil revealing discernible horizons is a profile. Development, if all horizons are present, shows a gradual transition from surface to bedrock. An ideal profile has 4 major horizons:

- A Horizon - Accumulation and eluviation. Often surfaced by decomposing organic layer.
- B Horizon - Illuviation, deposition of clays, oxides, or salts.
- C Horizon - Decomposition. Rock structure is evident as is mineral content.
- D Horizon - Matrix of unaltered rock.

SOIL WATER Water saturating soils is available to plants. It may be water from rainfall, capillary water held by surface tension, or hygroscopic water held by electrical force as on the surface of soil particles.

SOLAR ENERGY The Sun's energy is derived from high temperature hydrogen (20×10^{6o} Fahrenheit). The sun is a tremendous thermonuclear reactor. The hydrogen atom when it loses its single electron becomes ionized.

Hydrogen only has 1 proton or nucleus. There are so many free hydrogen nuclei, collisions are inevitable. These collisions are strong enough to overcome electromagnetic repulsion which is natural to protons. From the collisions, a kind of helium results.

On Earth, incoming solar energy in the form of short wave radiation is balanced to some extent by outgoing long waves of heat. There is, however, a great imbalance between latitudes. As a result there is a constant transfer of energy.

Earth environment hangs in a delicate balance. A 2% increase in solar heating would create a Greenhouse Effect incompatible with most life. A 2% decrease would bring about an Ice Age.

Efforts to utilize solar energy as a substitute for fossil fuels has been less than successful to date. The number of solar cells required is extraordinarily high and they are still bulky. There is an attempt to create a greater domestic use of this energy, especially in the Sun Belts. See **GREENHOUSE EFFECT** and **ICE AGES**.

SOLAR FLARE A solar flare is a short (l/10 of a second) outburst of energy from the surface of the Sun. Implosion energy is caused by a strong electromagnetic field. 2 streams of cosmic rays are generated, the first from the inward blast and the second from X-rays and gamma rays. The surface area occupied by a flare will vary. The Sun's surface temporarily reaches 100×10^{60} Fahrenheit. The Sun brightens in the visible wavelength by about 1% during flare activity. In the X-ray band, brightness is increased by a factor of 1,000.

Radioactivity is measured in rems (q.v.) and increases at the Earth's surface by a factor of 50 during flare activity. Between 30 and 600 kilometers (18-360 miles) into the Atmosphere, radioactivity is normally at 7 rems per year. This is increased by solar flare activity by a factor of 1,000.

Flares generate electromagnetic storms. The effect of the energy release is to squeeze the Magnetosphere. Storms are felt on Earth and in the Atmosphere. The shock wave generated by the flare is propelled by the Solar Wind (q.v.). It reaches the Earth a day or so after the flare. Sometimes, it arrives within hours. There were 3 large solar flares on August 2, 1972. They created a Canadian power surge and a transformer exploded. These storms can affect currents in powerlines and pipelines.

Flares are followed within hours by aurorae (q.v.) or 'northern lights'. Sunspots (q.v.) associated with the flares have the same 11-year cycle. The sunspots are responsible for interplanetary shock waves. Such waves on Earth release the lights. Ultra-violet emissions cause ionization in the Atmosphere affecting radio signals.

Space flights with astronauts have not been scheduled during the active phase of the 11-year flare cycle. It is believed that 1972 would have been lethal to the astronauts. The geological evidence shows that the 11-year cycle has been operative for at least 600 million years.

SOLAR LAKE Solar Lake in Elath, Israel, is a natural laboratory. It is a ponded lagoon on the Elath Gulf. Elath Gulf is also known as Aqaba (q.v.). It is separated from the sea by a bar. The lake is surrounded by the metamorphic rocks of the Arabo-Nubian Massif.

The hypersaline lagoon receives water at high-tide and in storms. Studies of water residence time in the lagoon show an average of 6 months. The magnesium:calcium ratio increases from 5:2 in the Gulf to from 8:2-10:5 in the lake.

SOLAR PONDS Solar ponds differ from solar lakes only in being artificial. Very salty water is confined in a shallow area. Evaporation from solar energy is relied upon and great saline pans are created. Israel and Jordan have solar ponds as does the United States.

In the United States solar ponds are found at Great Salt Lake, Utah and Salton Sea, California. There is danger that saline waters could leak into groundwater and ponds must be monitored.

SOLAR SYSTEM The Solar System is composed of the Sun, which is a star, and 9 planets which orbit the Sun. The system is in the Milky Way Galaxy (q.v.). Planet Earth is the 3rd nearest to the Sun and has a unique position making possible its World Ocean and life. See **CHZ**.

It is believed that the Sun formed 10-15 billion years ago from a gas cloud and particulate matter. It became disklike when the cloud closed in upon itself from gravitational attraction.

The Sun's rotation began with a faster spin at the center than at the periphery. The velocity grew as the mass and gravity grew. The Solar System has a diameter of 16.6 billion kilometers (10 billion miles). See **BIG BANG**.

SOLAR WIND Streams of charged particles are emitted from the Sun to form thin bands of protons and electrons. The streams contain trillions of particles going out from the Sun in all directions. They travel at extremely high velocity forming a solar wind. Shock waves form at its leading edge.

The Earth is protected to some extent from solar wind by its Atmosphere and Magnetosphere (q.v.). Solar winds penetrate most easily at the poles. As charged particles in the winds come into contact with magnetic field atoms, energy is given off as light. This light creates the auroras (q.v.).

Solar wind is responsible for the streaming tails of comets. The tail streams behind the comet as it moves away from the Sun. Earth has a similar tail caused by the plasma of solar wind.

SOLFATARA The solfatara is a native sulfur deposit resulting from condensation and cooling of hot sulfur vapor from volcanic vents. More than 100 solfataras are found in the Chilean Andes above 5,400 meters (18,000 feet).

Solfataras have been worked in Sicily, Italy, and in the Sierras of California. The Sierra deposit supplied sulfur to the Yerington, Nevada copper works.

SOLIFLUCTION Solifluction is plastic fluid flow of soil saturated with water or regolith (q.v.). Relatively large rocks are carried in suspension. Downslope movement is greater than with creep (q.v.).

Solifluction is a powerful erosion agency. It is most evident in periglacial areas. Permafrost forms an impermeable layer causing soaking of the upper layers of soil during a thaw.

SOLIMOES RIVER The Amazon River is called Solimoes above the confluence with the Rio Negro. The great tributaries of the western Amazon Basin feed into the Solimoes. See **AMAZON RIVER** and **AMAZON TRIBUTARIES**.

SOLONCHAK Solonchak are a group of intrazonal soils containing a high content of soluble salts. Solonchak are semi-arid soils sustaining a salt-loving vegetation.

SOLONETZ Solonetz are a group of intrazonal soils with friable surfaces over an alkaline layer. They are semi-arid soils that support grass. Solonchak soils may be leached and made more alkaline converting them to solonetz.

SOLSTICES The Sun's rays are vertical or 90° to the Tropic of Cancer (23.5° North Latitude) once a year on or about June 22nd. The event is the summer solstice. December 22nd is the winter solstice when the rays are most indirect. The events are opposite in the Southern Hemisphere.

SOLUM 'Solum' is Latin for soil and refers to the upper and most weathered part of a soil profile (q.v.) or the A and B horizons.

SOLUTION Solution is a process in which 2 or more atoms, ions, or molecules are mixed homogeneously. The Atmosphere has gaseous solutions in a gaseous medium, the sea has liquid solutions in liquid, and alloys of metal are solutions in metal.

Solution is an important process in geology. It is a major agency of erosion, deposition, and alteration of rocks and minerals.

SOOT Soot results from burning a light oil, kerosene, or other carbon. Soot particles adhere to chimneys, pipes, or walls forming a soft, velvety-black powder coating. Its size is dependent upon the presence of acetylene in the material burned.

Soot is an important ingredient in SMOG (q.v.). It was the principal component of the London SMOG when coal was the major fuel burned.

Soot is used in inks, for carbon paper, in pigments, and in polishes.

SORBATE Liquids and gases are sorbed, taken up and held by a gas, liquid, or solid as a sorbate. The sorbed substance may be absorbed or adsorbed (q.v.).

SORBENT Any substance capable of taking up and holding another is a sorbent. Charcoal, glass, metals, silica gels, and zeolites are sorbents.

SORTING Natural sorting by size and weight is part of the weathering process. Gravity and streams contribute, operating to transport and deposit detritus. Ocean wave activity is a sorting force. Wind winnowing is a major sorting phenomenon. It plays a great role by deflation (q.v.).

SOUND Sound is a mechanical, radiant energy. It is transmitted by longitudinal waves. The velocity of sound in the sea is a function of temperature, salinity, and pressure. Water is a better conductor of sound than air. Sound travels 5 times faster and farther through water. An Australian depth charge created a sound wave that reached Bermuda in 2 hours 24 minutes (Lamont).

The Greek Pythagoras discovered that music could be analyzed mathematically. He developed ratios for tones an octave or a 4th and 5th apart. He believed the Cosmos could be understood as an harmonic system.

SOUNDING Measuring depths by plumbline or sounding is a common practice in shallow waters. At sea, echo sounding (q.v) is used.

SOUTH AMERICA The continent of South America is the 4th largest. It occupies the southern part of the Western Hemisphere. The continent straddles the Equator and extends to 60° South Latitude. It covers 11.5 million square kilometers (6.9 million square miles).

South America has 9 major physiographic regions. These are the:
- Coastal deserts of the west
- Andes
- Altiplanos or high interior basins
- Amazon Basin
- Shield mountains of Guiana and Brazil
- Central Brazilian Plateau
- Parana Plateau
- Pampas or grasslands
- Patagonian Desert.

The major portion of the continent is drained by 3 great river systems. They belong to a vast inter-communicating system. These 3, the Amazon-Madeira, Orinoco, and Paraguay-Parana-Uruguay-La Plata create islands within the continent when the different systems are in flood. Within Brazil there are other large rivers, the greatest of which is the São Francisco (q.v.).

SOUTHEAST ASIAN RAINFOREST The rainforest (q.v.) in Southeast Asia is 2-tiered primarily with diptocarps in the upper tier. The lower is occupied by bamboos and low trees.

The Eng or In diptocarps only flower every 2-10 years. When they do, they are effusive, producing up to 4 million blossoms per tree. The trees only blossom for a synchronized 2-3 weeks, when they make up for a less than optimal pollinization.

Wet teak forests are found where rainfall does not exceed 187.5 centimeters (75 inches). The teak forests have been the most vulnerable to excessive logging.

SOUTHERN CROSS The star cluster or constellation used by mariners in the Southern Hemisphere is the Southern Cross. The constellation is made up of 4 very bright stars in the form of the Latin cross. There is a 5th star of lesser brilliance.

SOUTHERN PINE FOREST The Southern Pine Forest is a belt of North American conifers, separated from the main conifer belt by a broadleaf forest. Among 10 different species, Longleaf is the most abundant. The Slashpine was sapped for resins, particularly to make turpentine.

Poor sandy soils provide drainage for the heavy rainfall, allowing the pine to flourish in the acid soils. The pines, in turn contribute to the soils acidity.

SOVIET CENTRAL ASIA Soviet Central Asia extends from the Caspian Sea to China's frontier, 2,170 kilometers (1,350 miles). Generally a low-lying area, it has below sea level depressions and extended deserts. Karagiye Depression at 132 meters (433 feet) below sea level is the lowest point. Communism Peak, 7,495 meters (24,590 feet), is the highest. Fedchenko Glacier (q.v.) is in this region. See **SIBERIA** and **USSR**.

SPACE RADIATION True Space begins at the Magnetopause (q.v.) hundreds of thousands of kilometers above the Earth. Space radiation consists of:

- Cosmic rays
- Solar plasma
- Van Allen Belts.

Earth is constantly bombarded by high velocity electrons, protons, and alpha particles from the Cosmos. The major source for the Earth is the Sun, but there is a component from the Universe. See **COSMIC RADIATION**.

Solar plasma is an interplanetary radiation source from outside the Magnetosphere. It is transmitted from plasma tongues and the solar wind (q.v.).

The Van Allen Belts (q.v.) are trapped radiation in the Earth's Magnetic Field.

SPAWN Fish reproduce by spawning. Females deposit roe or eggs, usually in a special area. The females lay the roe and the males later fertilize them. Lagoons and marshes are favorite spawning grounds. To spawn some marine fish swim hundreds of kilometers and often far upstream in rivers.

SPECIES The smallest natural population is the species. It is distinct from similar forms and the population is given a separate name. In the Binomial Classification System (q.v.) the genus to which a species belongs is named first, then the particular species, followed by the name of a scientist who described it, or an honoree. An initial for reference is usually all that is used. An example is 'Ricinus communis L' for the common castor oil plant. The botanist was Carl von Linne (Linnaeas).

SPECIES EXTINCTION Throughout geological history there have been episodes of species extinction. Dr. Schopf of the University of California, Los Angeles, estimates 99.99% of all species that ever lived are now extinct.

During the Permian Extinction (230 m.y.), 75% of all species were lost. The most well-known species extinctions were those of Radiolaria (q.v.) and the great reptiles.

Humans are now contributing to species extinction at an accelerated rate. Tropical forests which cover 7% of the Earth support about 50% of all presently known species and many still unidentified. Rapid distruction of these forests is contributing to species disappearance.

Of the 250,000 species found in the Madagascar rainforest, 75% are not found elsewhere. Already over 90% of that forest has been cut, primarily for cropland.

SPECIFIC GRAVITY Specific gravity or relative density is a characteristic of minerals used for identification. Specific gravity is the relative weight of a mineral in air compared to the weight of an equal volume in water: the density standard.

The dry weight of a sample of corundum (emery, ruby, sapphire) is 2.0 ounces. This is the weight of the mineral in air. In water it weighs only 1.5 ounces, or a 'loss' of 0.5 ounces. The dry weight of 2.0 is then divided by the loss of 0.5. (2.0/0.5 = 4). The specific gravity of the corundum is 4. Specific gravity is not always the same for a given mineral. Impurities can account for discrepancies between specimens.

SPECTRUM 'Spectrum', Latin for image, is an ordered series based upon specific characteristics. Light wave emissions of the Electromagnetic Spectrum are separated into ordered images based upon wavelength and color.

Light is expressed in colors and wavelengths ranging from ultra-violet to infra-red. The spectrum includes visible and non-visible light.

SPERM WHALE 'Cachalot', the sperm whale, grows to as much as 18 meters (60 feet) in length and weighs hundreds of tons. They are the largest toothed whales. They can dive very deeply to reach their prey, squid and octopi. See **WHALES**.

SPHAGNUM 'Sphagnum' is a group of mosses that grow in moist areas of the Tundra and Alpine Tundra. They form a mat on the surface of a swamp adding a mat each season. Layers build up in the swamp until it becomes a bog. Sphagnum finally becomes a fibrous and highly absorbent peat which is used as fuel.

Sphagnum has medicinal uses and was especially important prior to the development of antibiotics.

SPHALERITE Sphalerite is zinc sulfide an important ore. with 55-67% zinc. It crystallizes in the cubic system, has perfect dodecahedral cleavage, adamantine luster, and a hardness of 3.5-4 on Moh's Scale.

Sphalerite is often confused with galena (q.v.), a lead sulfide. It is found in association with other sulfides in limestones. The lead-zinc deposits of Missouri are large and of this type.

Zinc is used to coat iron, a process of galvanization, which protects iron from rust. When zinc is alloyed with copper, brass results.

SPIN Electron spin is a property of elementary particles like the electron, proton, and neutrino. Particles have fixed spin vectors. Spin behavior is an important study of particle physics. It is critical to atomic interaction.

SPINEL The magnesium-aluminum oxide, spinel, has been mistaken for ruby. It is, however, a much softer stone.

The Black Prince's Ruby is in the British Crown. It is an unpolished spinel of 352 carats.

SPINIFEX Porcupine grass or 'spinifex' is ubiquitous in Australian sands. It is a xerophyte (q.v.) dominating the plains. 'Spinifex Triodia hirsuta' and 'Triodia irritans' have sharp-edged, finely pointed leaves capable of cutting humans and animals.

Spinifex covers 1/4 of Australia. It extends along the northwest coast into Queensland and south almost to the Nullabar Plain (q.v.). The pearl bluebush is found on the Plain and feral camels graze on it. True spinifex is a coastal, sand-binding plant.

SPIT A narrow projection of sand or gravel as a ridge into the sea is a spit. They grow seaward when currents permit. Spits may be relatively large. The spit becomes a tombolo (q.v.) if it ties an island to the mainland (Gibraltar).

SPITZBERGEN The largest island in the Norwegian archipelago of Svalbard is Spitzbergen. It is 640 kilometers (400 miles) north of Norway in the Arctic Ocean. Coal was discovered there in 1906 and it has been a coal mining center since.

The glaciers covering the folded and faulted range making up the archipelago are subject to calving. The seas around the area are adrift with icebergs at least 7 months a year, even though the waters are moderated by the North Atlantic Drift. In 1989, a Russian tourist vessel struck one of these icebergs. Fortunately all on board were rescued.

The islands are the habitat of the arctic fox, polar bear, and reindeer. When summer comes many bird species migrate to the many bogs. See **OZONE HOLE**.

SPODUMENE A lithium ore, spodumene, is a complex silicate of aluminum and lithium. Spodumene is usually found in pegmatites (q.v.) and some huge crystals have been found in the Black Hills pegmatites of South Dakota. It is also mined in the Carolinas.

Spodumene (lithium) crystals of exceptional beauty and gem quality have been found at Pala Mine, San Diego County in California.

SPONGES Sponges are plant-like, marine organisms belonging to the Phylum Porifera. Anchored to reefs or the ocean floor as adults they are free-floating as larvae. Colonies of the simply formed tri-walled cells feed using hair-like cilia to capture plankton. Sponge colonies often provide homes for other sea-life.

Sponges first appeared in the Cambrian (570-500 m.y.) and 'Archaeocyathidae' are guide fossils confined to that period. There are over 4,500 species of sponges. Many are used industrially.

SPORE A spore is an individual cell by which a plant may reproduce. Unlike seeds, spores have no protective cover. A single fern may have a billion spores to insure continuity. The tiny specks on molds are spores.

SPRINGS Where groundwater comes to the surface, there is a spring. A trickle or free flowing, a spring may often initiate streams and lakes. Many springs are located at the base of escarpments and are a major source of many domestic water supply systems.

Hot springs occur when groundwaters are heated at depth. They rise to the surface losing minerals as they cool. Hot springs are found in volcanic areas but they occur elsewhere. When accompanied by steam jets, as at Yellowstone, they are fumaroles.

SQUALL LINE The advancing edge of a cold front is a squall line. It can precede a storm by as much as 330 kilometers (200 miles). Squall lines are most notable at sea where they stretch across the horizon.

SRI LANKA Sri Lanka is the current name for the Island of Ceylon, which is in the Indian Ocean off the southeast tip of the Indian subcontinent. It is separated from the mainland by the 53 kilometer (33 mile) wide Palk Strait southeast of Cape Comorin.

History tells us that the Sinhalese Civilization was very advanced and ruled the island over a long period. It was ultimately conquered by the deforestation of the island's rainforest. The present strife between the 2 major ethnic groups on the island is contributing to a modern destruction of the forests. See **DEFORESTATION**.

Sri Lanka is 435 kilometers (270 miles) long and 225 kilometers (140 miles) wide. It is a detached part of the Deccan Plateau (q.v.) and is everywhere underlain by Precambrian basement rocks.

Pegmatites and the Precambrian Khondalite Series is the source for the gems for which the island is famous. The gem province is in southwestern Sri Lanka. The Khondalite also hosts graphite deposits.

Monazite (q.v.) beach sands have an average thorium content of 8-10%. The uranium runs 0.3-0.5% U_3O_8.

STAINLESS STEEL Ordinary stainless steel used for industrial purposes has a content of 18% chrome, 8% nickel, 0.2% carbon in combination with iron. For tableware, carbon is raised to 1% and nickel is not used.

STALACTITE/STALAGMITE Calcium carbonate in solution, particularly in limestone and dolomite areas, may redeposit in caves or confined areas where temperature and pressure are suitable. Precipitation occurs drop by drop allowing crystallization. Crystals growing from cave ceilings are stalactites. Those growing up from the cave floor are stalagmites.

STAND A cluster of trees or plants of the same species is a stand. The stand is limited to an area defineable by its size.

STANDING WAVE A standing or stationary wave occurs when surface waters oscillate vertically between 2 points or nodes with no forward movement. Points of maximum vertical rise and maximum vertical fall are anti-nodes. In large bodies of water the waves are also affected by the Coriolis Effect (q.v.).

The standing wave often occurs between layers of different densities. It may be an internal wave (q.v.) in the sea. Standing waves are often found in lakes and estuaries.

STAR A star is a mass or body in Space made up of a vast amount of tightly packed hot gases. There is such high pressure that the gases emit great energy. This energy is seen from Earth as light. The energy is generated in the core of the star by nuclear fusion.

On a clear night about 4,500 stars are visible from either Hemisphere. If a 3-inch telescope is used, the number becomes about 500,000. There are an estimated 300-500 billion stars in the Milky Way Galaxy (q.v.) and billions of galaxies are estimated.

The Sun is a star with satellites or orbiting planets. Earth is one of these planets. The apparent motion of the stars is relative to the Earth's orbit around the Sun.

The distance to a star plus its intensity accounts for its 'intrinsic brightness'. Comparing it to the Sun it is possible to gain a relative luminosity.

Viewed from Earth, stars appear to twinkle. This twinkling is scintillation. It results from the effect of light, which is particle laden, passing through the Atmosphere. These particles scatter the light. Stars appearing low on the horizon seem to twinkle more.

STARFISH 'Acanthaster planci', the spiny starfish, very suddenly multiplied out of control in the mid-1960's. Starfish attack coral and consume the soft tissue. Coral, in turn, eat starfish larvae and a balance between these species is normally maintained.

Near Guam and some South Pacific atolls the balance between the coral and the starfish was upset. Dead zones in the coral reef allowed a safe breeding ground for starfish. The dead zones were caused by blasting coral to create passages in the reefs, thereby upsetting the ecology.

STATICS Statics is a branch of physical mechanics dealing with equilibrium. Equal weights balance at equal distance from the point of support or fulcrum. This principle was discovered by Archimedes.

If the fulcrum of a lever is moved nearer the larger force, balance is achieved with a lesser force on the opposite side.

STEEL Steel, an alloy of iron and carbon, may be as high as 1.7% carbon. Various metals may be added to give the steel special qualities such as the addition of tungsten for hardness.

Steel production has been changing from the Bessemer Process, which converted pig iron (q.v.) to steel in huge open hearth furnaces. For this process, special coking coals, limestone, and other fluxes (q.v.) were required.

Electric furnaces and other changes have altered the economics, raw material requirements, and fluxes. The industry is in transition. Any method for converting iron to steel is energy expensive.

STELLAR EXPLOSIONS During the past 1,000 years, 5 supernovas, or exploding stars, have been observed in our galaxy. The last was in 1604. Remnants of stellar explosions are sources of intense X- ray radiation.

On February 23, 1987, a supernova was discovered in a Magellanic Cloud (q.v.). It is the closest to Earth in 400 years and the brightest noted since 1885 when a supernova was observed in the Andromeda Galaxy.

The recent event is especially important because the star's behavior is uncharacteristic. Some believe it is a compressing White Dwarf (Type I), others that it is collapsing internally (Type II). Proton detectors picked up neutrino bursts prior to the explosion.

STEPPE Steppes cover 12% of the USSR. They are level, grasslands extending from the western border to the Yenesei River, Siberia. Relief is less than 300 meters (1,000 feet) and the climate is drier than in the American Prairies. Rainfall in the southern part, near the Caspian Sea is only 15 centimeters (6 inches) per year.

STEPPE CORRIDOR The Steppe Corridor is the artery between Europe and Asia. It was Marco Polo's caravan route and Ghengis Khan's invasion route. The corridor is a vast dry and open terrain. See **STEPPE**.

STERILE That which is inert and containing nothing alive is termed sterile. Some soils are considered sterile if devoid of visible plantlife.

STIBNITE The ore of antimony, stibnite, is used primarily to harden lead. 'Hard lead' will contain 4-12% stibnite. The combination of 10-15% antimony is used in linotype machines and others needing heavy type.

Antimony is used to harden bullets. It is also responsible for the blue color in some fireworks. The chief producers of stibnite are Bolivia, China, and Mexico. The estimated world resources of animony are set at 5.1 million metric tons.

STOCK A stock is an intrusion that is similar to a batholith but smaller. The stock may be independent or an exposed portion of a batholith (q.v.). Stocks usually cover less than 100 square kilometers (60 square miles). Some are mineralized. Stone Mountain, Georgia is a granite stock that was intruded 300 million years ago.

STOCKPILE The United States Government maintains a stockpile for strategic (q.v.) metals and minerals. Many metals and minerals formerly produced domestically are now procured overseas. This increases national vulnerability and increases the negative balance of payments.

The stockpile was originally created in response to the disappearance of the USS Cyclops in the Bermuda Triangle March 4, 1918 (World War I). The vessel was carrying a load of manganese. The event showed the United States could not depend upon sealanes for its strategic minerals (q.v.).

Unfortunately, political pressures and expediency have governed the status of minerals and metals in our stockpile. The stockpile does not now adequately reflect a recognition of national vulnerability. In few cases is the lead-time for production of a domestic ore considered a criterion for inclusion or for the size of inclusion. Sell-offs from stockpiles are frequently motivated by politics and not national need or planning.

All major nations maintain stockpiles for national security. Few of the major industrial nations are without a national stockpile plan. Compared with the Soviet Union and many other nations, the United States is poorly served by its stockpile.

STOCKWORK An enclosed body of rock cut by many mineralized veins is a stockwork. Often mineralization is sufficiently great to warrant production.

STOKE'S LAW Particle settlement and sorting are important in the sedimentation process. Settlement velocity differences for particles up to 200 microns in diameter are governed by Stokes Law. This law holds that in a liquid, particles of the same density fall with velocities proportional to the square of their radii.

Larger particles settle a little faster if shape differences warrant. A platy particle has greater drag.

STONEHENGE The archaeological site of Stonehenge on the Salisbury Plain, England, is constructed of blue stones from Pembrokeshire, Wales. Stonehenge was probably a religious and astronomical site. How the great monoliths were quarried and transported remains a mystery.

STONEWARE Dense, durable, non-porous, partly vitrified ceramics fired between 1,200° and 1,400° Celsius are stoneware.

STOPING In underground mines, stoping is common. It involves engulfing and gradually detaching a block of ore.

STORM WAVE An oceanic storm wave is high and short from crest to crest. It can be destructive causing tremendous erosion along coasts. Storm waves accompany the high winds and seas of winter storms in the high latitudes and tropical storms in the low latitudes.

STRAIN Deformation of a body exerted by an outside force is strain. It causes the mass to bind or draw together and be compressed. Rocks are frequently subjected to strain.

Rocks are studied with regard to the forces causing deformation. This is strain analysis which deals with the results and the forces inducing these results.

STRAIT A strait is a relatively narrow portion of a sea between 2 coasts. Some major straits are Bering, Gibraltar, Magellan, and Malay.

STRATA 'Strata' is Latin for beds or layers of sedimentary rocks. A collection of strata with common characteristics and common mode of deposition makes up a formation (q.v.).

STRATEGIC MINERALS Those metals and minerals considered essential for defense and are not produced in the United States are 'strategic'. These may be minerals or metals for which there are unworked domestic sources, usually of only marginal ore grades, but not always. Foreign supplies may be cheaper, at least initially.

High investment costs keep the United States captive to overseas markets. World market conditions have completely governed mineral production. As a result, should the need arise to open a national mine, it would require not only the investment but a relatively long lead-time, which might prove critical.

For some strategic minerals there are no domestic sources at all. For these a dedicated research program for alternatives is required. See **STOCKPILE**.

STRATH The Scottish 'strath' is a wide grassy, lowland valley. A stream may be presently enlarging the valley.

STRATIFICATION Stratification is the parallel or sub-parallel position of accumulating sediments. Layers may be concordant and conform to the layer below, or discordant and show variations of dip (q.v.).

Stratification is both a process and a principle in geology. The strata above are younger than those below unless they have been overturned by later diastrophism (q.v.). Strata may be identified and correlated by type and, if available, by fossil content.

STRATIGRAPHIC COLUMN The stratigraphic column is a graphic display of geological history. It reflects the state of knowledge and the relative age of a particular rock assemblage by describing each stratum (q.v.) in detail.

Each successive stage shown on a stratigraphic column has been given a specific name. The distinguishing features have been catalogued. Fossil interpretation has expanded knowledge of specific environments of deposition. The Geological Table (q.v.) is a summation of stratigraphic columns.

Columns begin at the bottom with the oldest and the Recent to Present on top. Fossil evidence for the past 570-600 million years is good, especially with respect to marine sediments. This evidence has been complemented with radioactive dating (q.v.) back to between 4.4 and 4.6 billion years.

The usefulness of the stratigraphic column has been enhanced by the many extraordinary correlations from area to area. Some have even been drawn from continent to continent as the Karroo sediments separated by the South Atlantic. The principle of superposition (q.v.) has contributed enormously to the development of the stratigraphic column.

STRATIGRAPHIC TRAP Oil and gas may be trapped in sediments and on bedding planes between impermeable strata. Limestone reefs provide stratigraphic traps in lenses of porous material within less porous material.

When sediments are thrust up into an anticlinal fold or down into a synclinal one, the sediments may form pockets of porous material that become suitable traps for oil, gas, and water.

STRATOCUMULUS Clouds that hang low in the sky in dark grey or blue rolls are stratocumulus. They are overhead in winter in the Northern Hemisphere, not producing much precipitation, only overcast conditions.

STRATOSPHERE The Atmosphere is composed of layers and the Stratosphere occupies the level above the Troposphere, which is directly in contact with the Earth. On the average the Stratosphere begins 12 kilometers (7 miles) above the Earth's surface. It extends into Space as much as 50 kilometers (30 miles).

The Stratosphere is characterized by minimum changes in temperature. It remains relatively constant until about 20 kilometers (12 miles) from the Earth. Then a gradual warming occurs. The temperature reaches a maximum at the Stratopause, the contact with the Mesosphere at 50 kilometers (30 miles) into Space.

The ability of aircraft to fly at higher and higher levels is demonstrated by the development of modern aircraft. The DC-9 was a break-through which reached 8 kilometers (4.8 miles). A series of aircraft then kept pushing the limits up to the Concorde's which can fly at an altitude of 18 kilometers (10.8 miles). The MIG fighter aircraft exceeds this.

Jet streams that have speeds up to 480 kilometers (300 miles) per hour occupy the Stratosphere. Their trajectory is mostly from west to east. It is these winds that are responsible for transporting around the globe the particulates erupted from volcanoes.

STRATUM   'Stratum' is Latin for covering or layer. A stratum or sedimentary bed is at least 1 centimeter (1/4 inch) thick. The layer is distinct from the stratum above or below. The distinction may be of lithology (rock type), fossil array, or of a break in deposition.

STRATOVOLCANO   The complex of the shield volcano (q.v.) and the cinder cone forms the stratovolcano. It has layers of lava alternating with layers of pyroclastics and ash. The stratovolcano is usually capped by a cone (Mount Fuji, Japan).

Stratovolcanos begin as shield volcanoes (q.v.) and finally have a cluster of cinder cones. The base of the volcano is very broad.

STRATUS   Stratus clouds are low with a layered-look. Gray in color, they usually produce rain or snow. They are also termed 'high fog'.

STREAK   Streak is the colored mark, or the absence of a mark, made by a mineral on a piece of unglazed porcelain. Streak is a diagnostic tool for mineral identification in the field. Many minerals have very characteristic streaks.

STREAM EROSION   Rocks transported by streams are of varying sizes. Heavy ones sink and are rolled and shoved along the stream bed. Smaller ones are more likely to bounce.

Stream velocity governs the size of the rocks moved in a current. Swiftly moving streams carry larger-sized loads. Very small particles are carried as flocculants or in suspension.

STRENGTH   If strain (q.v.) is increased indefinitely, plastic yield will occur. Soft material gives at yield strength. A brittle material will break at its fracture strength. Overall strength is the capacity of a material to resist the forces exerted upon it.

STRIATIONS   Striations result from abrasion as a glacier moves over a surface. The resulting grooves may be up to 90-100 meters (300-330 feet) long, several meters wide and up to 2 meters deep as are some in Australia. Striations indicate that some tremendous boulders were dragged over the surface by the ice.

STRIKE The strike of a sedimentary bed, dike, fault, or vein is the line of intersection between the structure or bed and the horizontal plane. The strike is normal or 90° to the dip (q.v.). It is a bearing or directional line and the notation is always in terms of the northern half of the compass.

STRIKE-SLIP FAULT A strike-slip fault moves parallel to the strike (q.v.). The lateral displacement or slip is along the strike. The San Andreas Fault (q.v.) is a major strike-slip fault. One side of the fault is sliding past the other along the strike. Displacement is obvious on the Earth's surface where roads and streams are offset.

In global tectonics major strike-slip faults indicate areas where crustal plates are slipping by each other, edge-to-edge.

STRIP MINING Strip mining is an open pit operation. Usually it is employed where sedimentary ore seams can be reached easily after the overburden has been removed. Excavations are made along contours or elevations. Many coal seams have been mined in this manner.

Strip mining has produced great environmental damage in the past. The disturbance of the earth and later abandonment left great scars. Restoration of lands and reclamation are now required by law and in many cases, the restoration has proven to be a profitable investment for the mining companies.

STROMATOLITES Stromatolites are sediments of fossil Blue-green Algae, 'Spongiostromata', with a thread-like structure. The Algae formed mats and secreted calcium carbonate. These mats trapped sediments and organic detritus. The fossils have a concentric structure and the assemblages have formed reefs.

Stromatolites are found in marine, lacustrine, hypersaline, and hot spring environments. From Precambrian (q.v.) to Lower Ordovician (510 m.y.), stromatolites were responsible for the development of great limestone reefs.

Fossils from Africa and North America are as old as 3 billion years. They are present in the 2 billion year old Gunflint Chert of Ontario, Canada.

Stromatolites are forming algal mats today which trap sediments and create columns of mud and dome structures upon which more algae can grow. This sequence can be observed on the Australian west coast in the Shark Bay area.

STROMBOLI The volcano, Stromboli, on a small island off Sicily, is known as the 'Lighthouse of the Tyrrhenian Sea'. Stromboli is a rare volcano type. It is in continuous eruption and has been for 2,500 years.

Rhythmically, gas is emitted which melts material in the crater. The detritus is thrown a few hundred feet up in the air. Fragments are cobble-sized. Not having melted to lava, the ejecta is a form of slag.

STRONTIUM-90 The isotope (q.v.) strontium-90 is a by-product of nuclear reactions. Strontium-90 is similar to calcium in the way it accumulates. It has a half-life of 28 years and a biological half-life of 17.

Since detonations of nuclear bombs began, there has been a steady build-up of strontium in humans. The greatest amounts are found in people from the Tundra (q.v.), Lapps and Eskimos. This may be due to naturally increased cosmic radiation entering polar regions. The increased strontium may be from reindeer milk. The herds graze the irradiated pastures. The source has not been completely studied.

At the end of the Mesozoic, at the time of the Great Extinction of land animals on Earth, there was a deposition of a thin lamina of clay. The clay layer is found distributed very widely in this horizon. This clay, originally described from Italy, is extraordinarily high in strontium-90.

The source of the strontium is thought to have been an astral collision. Some scientists think there is a definite link between the increased strontium and the great species extinction, which also occurred at this time. See **IRIDIUM**.

SUAKIN GRABEN The Red Sea floor drops in 2 stages to the Suakin Graben. It is a part of the Great Rift System that contains the Red Sea. The overall depth of the graben is between 2,250 and 2,850 meters (7,500 and 9,400 feet).

The deepest area is occupied by 2 brine pools, discovered by Research Vessel Valdivia in 1971. Sediments in the pools differ from the usual basalt of deep sea grabens. There are ferromagnesium sediments in the western basin and sulfides in the eastern.

Suakin Deep, off Suakin Archipelago and 40 kilometers (25 miles) south of Port Sudan, contains the most southern of the Red Sea brine pools.

SUBAQUEOUS SLUMPING Subaqueous slumping can result when sediments at or near the repose angle (q.v.) become saturated. A saturated slope is unstable and slumping begins within its layers.

SUBATOMIC PARTICLES There are about 200 identified subatomic particles. These were discovered through the research carried out in accelerators (q.v.). Powerful magnetic fields bombarded atomic nuclei at the speed of light giving rise to the particles. Particle studies became a field in nuclear physics.

SUBDUCTION Crustal material is consumed in the Earth's Mantle (q.v.) by subduction. This occurs in convergence zones, where the lithospheric or crustal plates push against each other. Subduction occurs when the plates meet and one is forced beneath the other. The lower plate is engulfed into the Mantle to be incorporated in magma (q.v.) chambers. The great oceanic trenches following island arcs are also subduction zones.

Subduction, or Benioff, zones are on the oceanic side of a developing continent. Off the American west coast, the Benioff Zone is an active subduction area where the Pacific Plate is rotating counter clockwise in relation to the continent. The suture lines or seams are foci for earthquakes of great magnitude.

Earthquakes in this zone rocked the continent from the Aleutians to Chile in 1986. This is the longest subduction zone on Earth.

Subduction of the Lithosphere is on an enormous scale. The Lithosphere beneath the oceans is less than 200 million years old. No sediments earlier than Jurassic have ever been recovered in cores from either the Atlantic or Pacific.

While the floor of the sea is spreading and emitting new material in one part of the ocean, in another crustal material is being subducted. The subduction rate is estimated to be so great the entire crust could be replaced every 160 million years.

SUBLIMATION Changing water vapor to ice or ice to water vapor with no intervening liquid phase is sublimation. No heat is consumed or released.

SUBMARINE CANYONS Submarine canyons are present on most continental slopes (q.v.). The canyons cut deeply, are V-shaped, winding, with tributaries. They can be like a young narrow stream channel or broad and deep. Canyons may be continuations of continental rivers. Hudson and Congo canyons resemble drowned estuaries.

Submarine canyons are not usually related to rivers but are carved by turbidity currents (q.v.). Sediment-laden currents transfer material from the continental slope to the deep ocean floor. Turbidity currents reach 10-15 kilometers (6-9 miles) per hour, strong enough to scour out canyons.

SUBMERGED COASTS There are many submerged coasts, as a result of global warming and melting of continental ice sheets (q.v.). The coasts of Norway and New Zealand, whose fjords testify to the former presence of the ice, are examples. The Dalmatian coast along the Adriatic Sea is a drowned upland. Islands are often tops of mountains.

SUBMERGED FANS Submerged deltas are found offshore from some major rivers. The Indus Fan covers most of the Arabian Sea north of the spreading ridge. The Bengal Fan from the Ganges-Brahmaputra System is even larger, extending into the Indian Ocean (q.v.)

SUBSEQUENT STREAM A subsequent stream cuts its own valley by selectively eroding the least resistant rock formations and sediments.

SUBTROPICAL JETSTREAM Blowing from the west, the Subtropical Jetstream at an elevation of 14 kilometers (8.4 miles) hovers around 30° of latitude. It is sandwiched between equatorial airmasses and cooler ones from the high latitudes. The Subtropical Jetstream is much weaker than the Polar Jetstream.

SUBTROPICAL VEGETATION Subtropical vegetation is transitional between humid temperate and tropical. The transitional forest is a mix of tropical and mid-latitude species.

The Subtropical in the United States is found in Florida, and in parts of Louisiana and Texas. There are pine species only found in this environment. The magnolia and live oak are common. These forests lack the tiered structure of the Tropical Rainforest.

Broad-leaved evergreen trees are found in Southern China and southern Japan. In China the vast bamboo forests are transitional to grasslands. On mountain slopes in the tropics, the Rainforest merges into the Subtropical, which gives way to the Temperate.

Savannas in subtropical regions are transitional zones. The forests tend to be galleried along streams. Where the climate is more temperate and conditions of humidity and temperature are right the Savanna Woodlands give way to Temperate Forest. See **GALLERY FOREST**.

SUCCESSION Ecological succession is the ordered change through time of floral and faunal communities in any particular geographical area. Primary succession means successful colonization by simple forms which are replaced by more complex ones until a climax community in tune with the soils and climate can be reached.

Secondary succession occurs after a fire or clearing. It permits invasion of specialized forms which survive harsher conditions. After a forest fire, a meadow will develop first. It changes to scrubland before giving way again to forest. This presupposes the conditions for forest survival still prevail. If development is arrested, a new climax community is created at the level of the meadow or scrub forest or anywhere in the chain.

SUDAN The Republic of the Sudan is the largest country in Africa. It is bordered by almost all the nations of Central Africa. Much of the country is within the Sahara and the Sahel (q.v.), but its southern part is in Equatorial Africa. It is of tropical forest and contains the world's largest swamp, the Sudd (q.v.).

Both the Blue and White Nile rivers are exogenous to Sudan but transit the country. Their confluence (q.v.) is at Khartoum. From there, the Nile flows north through the desert to Lake Nasser and the Mediterranean. The only tributary to reach the Nile after the confluence (q.v.) is the Atbara. It is also exogenous to Sudan having its source in the Ethiopian Highlands.

The largest agricultural development program in the world, the Gezira (q.v.), is in the triangle between the Niles just south of their confluence. Gezira cotton is Sudan's major cash crop.

Sudan has a potential for mineral development of its asbestos, chrome, copper, gold, gypsum, iron, and petroleum. The chrome of the Ingessana Hills has been worked somewhat by the Japanese.

Exploration and development require a massive capital investment, some of which has been forthcoming from Saudi Arabians and others. The on-going civil war (since 1956) has hampered any real development.

The Sub-Sahara Savanna Belt is a transitional zone between the desert and the forest. Only a portion lies within the nation of Sudan. The inhabitants are referred to as Sudanese. It is the type locality of the fodder plant 'Sorghum vulgare sudanensis'. See **SAHEL**.

The long talked of Jonglei Canal (q.v.) has been undertaken and since halted by the events of the Civil War. The Canal would shorten the Nile's transit of the Sudd (q.v.) and hopefully prevent great losses of water to evaporation in the vast swamp.

SUDANESE REEF A 50-kilometer (30-mile) long reef is offshore of Port Sudan. It is part of a greater reef system which includes Sanganab Atoll, to the northeast about 25 kilometers (15 miles). The Sudanese or Wingate Reef was used as a laboratory for extensive oceanographic studies in the 1960's.

SUDBURY STRUCTURE The mineralized Sudbury Structure is north of the Georgian Bay of Lake Superior and west of Lake Nipissing, Ontario, Canada. The structure is a kidney-shaped depression measuring 61 x 28 kilometers (37 x 17 miles). Sudbury was affected by extensive volcanic flows. It is famous for its nickel-rich ore.

It has been conjectured by Robert Dietz and others that a meteorite created the basin 1.8 billion years ago. With impact, mineral rich magma welled up in fissures. Dietz predicted the shatter cones that were subsequently found.

Production has reached 34,000 tons a day of ore containing nickel, cobalt, copper, gold and silver. Sudbury supplies 20% of the world's nickel as well as significant copper.

The structure also produces each year 70-80 tons of platinum-palladium (1983). This is the only important western bloc source of these metals with the exception of South Africa. See **PLATINUM**.

SUDD In southern Sudan, the Nile River flows through 830 kilometers (500 miles) of swamp. The swamp is called 'Sudd', which is Arabic for barrier. Swamps between Juba and Malakal are nearly impenetrable with papyrus (q.v.) and water hyacinth. Some of the papyrus reaches 6 meters (20 feet).

In the Sudd, some 33,000 square kilometers (12,000 square miles) are permanently flooded and triple that in the wet season. 50% of Nile water is lost to evaporation or vegetation in the Sudd.

Formerly, there was a large lake in the Juba to Khartoum area. As the lake shrank, a series of swamps developed of which the Sudd remains. The Nile traces a huge semi-circular course through it. The gradient through the swamp is greater than that from Malakal north. See **JONGLEI CANAL**.

SUEZ CANAL Over the last 2,000 years, a canal between the Red Sea and the Mediterranean has been opened and allowed to decline 5 times. Seti I of Egypt began the canal, which was completed by Ramses II. Pumice from Santorini (q.v.) was used in the construction of the present canal which requires great and constant maintenance.

Supertankers are utilized more and more as a result of petroleum economics. These vessels cannot traverse the canal. For a ship able to use the canal on a voyage from Europe to Asia, there is a fuel savings of 75%.

SULFATE When both hydrogen atoms in sulfuric acid have been replaced by metals, it is a sulfate.

SULFIDES A metal in compound with sulfur is a sulfide or salt. Vein minerals in plutonic and volcanic rocks are often sulfides.

Polymetallic sulfides have been discovered on the ocean floor. A deposit in the Galapagos Rift at 2,500 meters (8,250 feet) of depth contains 10% copper, with lesser amounts of lead, manganese, molybdenum, silver, and zinc. The deposit is about 1 kilometer x 200 meters (0.6 miles x 660 feet).

Sulfides have also been discovered on the East Pacific Rise (q.v.) at 21° North Latitude at about the same depth. Such deposits, related to the major rift systems defining crustal plates boundaries, contain 30% zinc and 6% copper.

Metallic sulfides are deposited along convergent plate boundaries. The ores of Kuroko, Japan, the Philippines, western North and South America are examples. The deposits may contain gold.

SULFUR Elemental sulfur is a yellow powder, called brimstone in the Bible. As a gas it has an odor of rotten eggs. Sulfur is mined largely from cavities in salt domes where it is in rock form. It is solution mined by pumping superheated water (250° Fahrenheit) into the mine. The water liquifies the rock sulfur and the liquid is pumped to the surface and allowed to evaporate and recrystallize.

In terms of the Earth's crustal abundance sulfur ranks 16th. After oxygen, it is the most likely element to form negatively-charged ions. The sulfur atom gains an electron to become a sulfide anion which can bond with many different cations to form sulfide minerals. Sulfur is next to salt in abundance in seawater (salt exceeds it by 30 times). A-Additional sulfur sources are sea spray, volcanoes, and hot springs. Rain returns sulfur to the sea.

World resources are set at 5 billion tons. The USSR, Canada and the United States have the largest reserves.

SULFUR POLLUTION Sulfur, a useful chemical can be toxic. Sulfuric acid is a constituent of SMOG (q.v.). It made up part of London's Killer SMOG, which resulted from coal-burning during temperature inversions (q.v.).

Sulfur produces acid rain (q.v.) which stunts plant growth, damages forests, and eats away at limestone monuments from Greece to Agra, India.

150 million tons of sulfur dioxide are released into the Atmosphere annually, 20% of which is over the United States. This is largely produced by power plants and industry. The giant stack above the Sudbury (q.v.) nickel plant accounts for 1%.

SUMERIA   The great ancient nation of Sumeria extended from Mesopotamia (q.v.) to the Indus Valley (q.v.). The felling of the trees and deforestation of Mesopotamia resulted in massive erosion. The Tigris and Euphrates Rivers (q.v.) were so silted, the rivers shifted 215 kilometers (150 miles) to the south.

The only forest that remained to modern times in this vast region were the famed 'Cedars of Lebanon'. Most of these had been destroyed by World War I. The small reserve is suffering from the present war in the region.

SUN   The Sun, a star in the Milky Way Galaxy (q.v.), forms the focal point of the Solar System (q.v.) to which the Earth belongs. The Sun is about 30,000 times the size of the Earth.

Heat is generated by the Sun from thermonuclear reactions, fusing hydrogen to create helium. Temperature at the Sun's surface is 6,000° Celsius and 15,000° at the core. The Sun is burning up at the rate of 4 million tons per second. There is an explosion every second equal to 10 billion hydrogen bombs.

At the core of the Sun are hydrogen atoms fused under cosmic heat and pressure. Sunstorms which result are called solar flares (q.v.). These are flaming gas jets. They shoot up to 160,000 kilometers (100,000 miles) into Space. Fire bridges form and the Sun shines with great intensity. Increased cosmic radiation accompanies solar flares.

The Sun is moving toward the constellation Hercules at the rate of 20 kilometers (12 miles) per second carrying the Solar System with it. It also orbits the Milky Way's hub once in 250 million years at 800,000 kilometers (480,000 miles) per hour.

SUNDA ARC   The Sunda Arc enclosing Indonesia in a half circle is the largest arc structure in the world. It extends from New Guinea to Burma circling Timor. The island arc is followed by the Sunda Trench for 10,000 kilometers (6,000 miles).

The arc appears to be the rim of an impact crater with a diameter of 5,000 kilometers (3,000 miles). The impact is thought by some to have marked the end of the Permian (200 m.y.). It would have rolled the Earth about 120° or 10,000 kilometers (6,000 miles) causing all the continents to drift.

SUNDA STRAIT   The narrow strip of water connecting the Java Sea with the Indian Ocean is the Sunda Strait.

SUNDANCE SEA During the Early Jurassic (170 m.y.), a seaway began developing from the Arctic Ocean along the Cordilleran Geanticline of North America. By Mid-Jurassic (150 m.y.), it had reached what are now Idaho and western Wyoming.

Great limestone reefs were laid down in Idaho. The sea reached a maximum development in Late-Jurassic (140 m.y.) when it covered the northern Great Plains. The size of the Sea fluctuated greatly and there is evidence of its presence in Utah and western Colorado. The sea withdrew as the geanticline to the west rose.

SUNSPOT A sunspot is a dark disklike spot on the Sun's surface up to 16,600 kilometers (10,000 miles) in diameter. It persists an average of 14 days. Between 1840-1841, some spots persisted 18 months. Sunspots are regions of solar flares (q.v.) that light up due to the strong magnetic field. They appear to be related to degassing of the Sun.

There is an 11-year sunspot cycle from peak to peak. Theory says spots are caused by pairs of magnetic lines of force moving from the Sun's interior to its surface. Each pair has polarity, one leading the other across the Sun's surface, until they die out. When they re-emerge, polarity is reversed.

A full sunspot cycle from plus polarity to plus polarity is 22 years. This time frame seems to correlate with droughts on Earth. When sunspots peaked in 1968-69, there was drought in the Sahel (q.v.). When the sunspot minimum (1962-63) occurred the weather in the Northern Hemisphere was severe with the worst blizzards in generations.

Sun spots affect the Earth causing an increase in magnetic storms. These magnetic storms create havoc with compasses and interfere with communications (radio and television). The magnetic storms also induce an increase in rainfall.

At the same time, tremendous quantities of charged particles are ejected into Space. They reflect the Sun's rays so temperatures on Earth drop. They may have contributed to the Mini Ice Ages of the years 1100-1250, 1460-1550, and 1645-1715 A.D.

During the sunspot high in 1968, the Earth's Atmosphere warmed as a result of ultra-violet radiation. Skylab was pulled out of orbit and its debris hit Australia 11 years later.

In 1958, about 200 sunspots were observed. The temperature of the Sun decreased with increasing sunspots. In a sunspot location, the Sun was about 40% cooler (3,800° Kelvin).

SUPERCONDUCTOR Superconductors transmit electricity with no perceptible loss and at very low temperatures. The most important superconductors in the past have been oxides of lanthanum, barium, and strontium. In 1987, a new superconductor of yttrium, barium, copper, and oxygen was created. It is superconductive at 94° Kelvin (-290° Fahrenheit). Experimentation continues especially with silica.

SUPERHEATED WATER Normally, water boils at 212° Fahrenheit. If under pressure water can remain liquid at temperatures much in excess of this. If the pressure is suddenly released the water will 'flash' to steam. This is what happens with geyser (q.v.) activity.

SUPERIMPOSED STREAM The superimposed stream is one that erodes to an earlier surface and continues to maintain its channel. The former structure may be a buried ridge or just alternating soft and resistant sediments.

LAKE SUPERIOR The largest freshwater lake in North America is Superior. It is one of the Great Lakes (q.v.) and covers an area of 82,414 square kilometers (31,820 square miles).

Lake Superior is in a long depression or synclinal trough that was further gouged out by glaciers during the Pleistocene. The lake freezes in winter to such an extent that shipping must await Spring ice-breakers. See **GREAT LAKES**.

LAKE SUPERIOR COPPER Native copper deposits on Michigan's Keeweenaw Peninsula into Lake Superior were worked by the Indians prior to colonization. Since then huge amounts have been produced and the mines are now quite deep. Work ceased because copper in its native state, though rich and pure, is extremely soft.

The ore cannot be cut into with saws or chisels. It is such a conductor of heat and electricity that it cannot be cut by blow-torch. It is so malleable that it cannot be torn into fragments or blasted. It may yield to laser technology.

SUPERNOVA A supernova is an exploding star. It releases enormous energy emitted as heat and light. See **STELLAR EXPLOSIONS**.

1987A, the first close supernova in 400 years, was discovered in a Magellanic Cloud (q.v.). It is the closest exploding star identified since 1604, and the brightest since one occurred in Andromeda Galaxy in 1885. An enormous amount of neutrinos, emitted by the star reached the Earth. They were estimated at 100 billion per square centimeter (0.155 square inches).

SUPERPOSITION Nicolaus Steno in 1669 defined the Law of Superposition. He noted that in any undisturbed rock sequence, the youngest rocks will over-lie rocks that have already been in place.

SURF ZONE The 'surf zone' is that particular area where ocean waves break to form surf. It is between the shore and the outermost limit of breaking waves. Surf waves in Southern California are breaking swell (q.v.).

SURTSEY A volcanic island erupted out of the sea, southeast of Reykjavik, Iceland, on November 13, 1963. It grew to 152 meters (500 feet) in 2 years. It was named Surtsey for the Norse Giant, Surtur, who according to legend brought fire to Iceland.

Surtsey is a surface expression of the Mid-Atlantic Ridge (q.v.). Iceland is the largest part of the ridge to show above sea level.

The volcano became quiet in 1965 and was named a preserve for studies of ecological succession (q.v.).

Succession began with the emergence of a bacteria found in a 1964 ash. Grasses emerged almost immediately on the beaches from rafted seeds. By 1987, there were 12 species of plants and 5 species of nesting birds. The island is still relatively barren.

SURVEYING Physical exploration, measurement, and contouring of the Earth's surface is surveying. It deals with distances, elevations, directions, and limits. Data collected are transferred to maps.

There are many types of surveys all dealing with aspects of the Earth and the landscape. These may be topographical, ecological, or mineral but are not limited to these. Many sophisticated types of equipment are used and these range from the simple plane table (q.v.) to satellites.

SUSPECT TERRAIN Geophysicist, Tuzo Wilson, conjectured that most of the Pacific Coast from Baja California to Alaska was 'suspect blocks of continent'. 2,400 kilometers (1,440 miles) of land west of the San Andreas Fault were rafted from their original area.

Material in the suspect block is an aggregate of unrelated bits of continent. In the San Francisco Bay area 10 different assemblages have been identified. Alaska has similar aggregates of unrelated continental materials that may have been rafted.

SUTURE The resultant seam found in a subduction zone or where continents collide is a suture. Some geologists use the term as synonymous with a major rift.

SWALE A shallow, marshy depression in a glacial moraine (q.v.) is a swale.

SWAMP A swamp is a flat wetland covered with trees, shrubs, and grasses. The soil is thin and readily penetrated by roots. In contrast to a marsh, a swamp is dominated by trees and shrubs. Water may be seasonal.

In northeastern United States swamps are dominated by hardwoods, primarily red maple. Shrubs beneath the trees include the blueberry. On the periodically flooded floor is skunkgrass.

In southeastern United States, the important trees are the bald cypress and red maple. See **WETLANDS**.

SWEET GRASSES There are 4 varieties of grass. They are bamboo, cereal, pasture and sweet. Sugarcane is a major sweet grass.

SWELL In the sea, swell is evidence that waves have traveled beyond their area of generation. As the waves break down or decay, they become swells. Shorter waves die out leaving long ones. Some are strong enough to endanger ships.

Swells are deceptively smooth, but they have great energy. The Southern California swell is generated in the Equatorial Pacific and travels northeast thousands of miles.

SYCAMORE Studies of forest take-up of carbon show that the American sycamore ('Platanus occidentalis') can absorb an average of 750 tons of carbon dioxide (q.v.) per square kilometer. See **CARBON CYCLE**.

SYENITE The rock type called Syenite was named for Syene near an ancient Egyptian quarry. It is a light-colored, coarse-grained, igneous rock. Syenites are associated with alkaline igneous rocks and carbonatites (q.v.). See **ALKALINE ROCKS**.

Syenite has a specific gravity of 2.8 and is light gray to red in color. It contains:

Potash feldspar (orthoclase and microcline)	50%
Hornblende black laths - biotite, augite	20%
Sodium-bearing rocks	20%
Quartz	5%
Apatite, sphene (calcium-titanium silicate)	5%

A monzonite syenite contains a greater percentage of augite. A rare mineral sequence gives the syenites a blue color such as found in some syenites from Scotland, Scandinavian, and the USSR. A Norwegian variety is known as larvakite. Nordmarkite is an alkali syenite also found in Norway. Pulaskite, another alkali syenite is found in Norway and Portugal.

SYLVANIA GUYOT Flat-topped Sylvania Guyot has a common base with Bikini Atoll. The top of the guyot or seamount is 1,282 meters (4,230 feet) below the sea. A saddle connecting it with Bikini is at 1,436 meters (4,740 feet) below the surface. The depth to seafloor is 4,545 meters (15,000 feet).

Samples dredged from the northern part of Sylvania yielded a yellow-brown basaltic tuff covered with manganese oxide. Some tuff was altered to phillipsite, a zeolite. Cracks in basalt breccia reveal apatite from planktonic Foraminifera. The tuff has been 60 million years in contact with seawater and has devitrified.

SYLVITE Sylvite is an important ore of potassium. It crystallizes in a cubic or octahedral habit. Sylvite is mined as sylvinite a combination of sylvite and halite. Salt is sometimes recovered as a by-product. Sylvite is potassium chloride and contains 63% equivalent potassium.

The principal use of potassium is in fertilizers which take 95% of the production.

Efforts to mine sylvite as a source of potassium are being made in comparable mines in Brazil and Congo. Both operations have had special difficulties.

The Brazilian Petroleum Company, PETROBRAS, is developing sylvite reserves from Taquari-Vassouras and Santa Rosa de Lima sub-basins in Sergipe. Reserves are estimated at 309 million tons of 1.7% potassium. Production began in 1984 and 37,000 tons were produced in 1987.

SYMBIOSIS When 2 different species develop a life-style of mutual support, it is symbiosis. The relationship between Algae and coral on a growing reef is symbiotic. Algae through photosynthesis oxygenate the waters and coral supply the carbon dioxide essential to the Algae. To be a symbiotic relationship, both parties must benefit.

SYNCLINE A syncline is a trough created during warping of the Earth's Crust that occurs with folding. Often the downfolded surface corresponds to a depression. Filled with sediments it is a synclinal basin.

The trough or syncline is between 2 crests, or anticlines.

SYRIAN DESERT The Syrian Desert is composed of a million acres of desert that is the result of human activity. Excessive land use destroyed the vegetative cover. There are ruins of more than a 100 cities in the Syrian Desert.

SYZYGY Syzygy is the alignment of bodies in Space. At the end of 1986 there was an alignment of the Earth, Moon, and Sun. This phenomenon occurs every 18.6 years. This event coupled with the solstice (q.v.), affected the tides. On both coasts abnormally high tides were reported which were also compounded by storms.

SZECHWAN CANAL Szechwan (Red) Basin, China, is in sandstone hills. In the 13th Century Kublai Khan finished a 1600 kilometer (1,000 mile) canal in the lower basin and through the Ichang Gorges. The canal, China's longest, connects the Yangtze Basin with the Hwang Ho (Yellow River) Basin.

Uranium Mine — Date Creek, Arizona
Courtesy of Dr. Donald Carlisle, Earth & Planetary Sciences, UCLA

T

TAAL VOLCANO Taal Volcano on Luzon Island, Philippines, has erupted 12 times in the last 200 years. Its collapse created a caldera 3 kilometers (1.5 miles) across. The 1965 eruption emitted sulfurous gases that killed 3,000 people. Its ash covered 100 square kilometers (60 square miles).

TABLELAND The plateau or tableland landform is at least 90 meters (300 feet) above sea level. The tableland is limited by steep escarpments and the surface has a gentle, sloping relief. In southwest United States, the tableland is often capped by a resistant lava. See **MESA**.

TAIGA Flat, marshy, Sub-Arctic forestland is 'Taiga', Russian for land of little sticks. In the USSR, Taiga is transitional between Steppe and Tundra (q.v.) and it extends from Finland to the Pacific. Pine, larch, spruce, and fir make up the forest. Siberian Stone Pine and fir are the most abundant species. Asiatic Taiga is more diverse than the North American.

In North America, Taiga is transitional between deciduous forest or Prairie to Tundra. Taiga covers 1/4 of Canada. The tall pointed spruce is the most abundant species. On well-drained soils, there are white spruce and balsam firs, while black spruce and tamarack are found on less well-drained soils. Willow and alder are found along streams.

Taiga is found in interior and south central Alaska. The western lodgepole pine and the alpine fir are the dominants of the Alaskan forest.

As Taiga grades to Tundra, the trees are smaller. They are inhibited primarily by permafrost (q.v.) and wind. In lower latitudes, Taiga vegetation is found at high elevations.

Most of the Taiga receives an average precipitation of 37-50 centimeters (15-20 inches) a year. The moist climate is due to the low evaporation rate. Taiga forests are underlain by podzol soils (q.v.). Snow acts as insulation and protects seedlings.

From its Taiga forests, Canada supplies 1/2 the world's newsprint. Norway makes up a good portion of the rest.

TAILINGS Tailings are the low-grade materials removed in mining, milling, and refining ores. They result at various stages of ore handling such as crushing, screening, milling, and flotation. Tailings are stockpiled for possible reworking. They can become reserves once more if a sufficient ore grade is present or when technology makes mineral recovery economic.

Tailings from very old mines are often haphazard and the results from different stages are mixed. Some have become environmental hazards because of chemical activity. Many are now being studied to find ways to stabilize and render them harmless.

TAKLA MAKAN The great barren expanse of western China merging into the Gobi Desert is the desert of Takla Makan. It occupies a pear-shaped depression in the Tarim River Basin, an area 1,330 x 667 kilometers (800 x 400 miles). The eastern portion of the basin has an elevation of 600 meters (2,000 feet), the western 1,820 meters (6,000 feet).

On the basin floor a belt of gravels surrounds rock and sand. The area appears pedimented (q.v.). Streams disappear into this gravel and reappear in oases at a lower elevation. Maximum precipitation is only about 10 centimeters (4 inches) per year.

Irrigation waters flow from snows from mountains to the west and south. The mountains include the Tien Shan on the USSR border.

TALC The magnesium silicate, talc, is an alteration product of serpentine (q.v.). It is found in schists (q.v.). The mineral is pearly gray, white, or green with a dull luster. It has a characteristic greasy texture. Massive talc is compact with lamellar crystals. In its harder, more massive form it is called soapstone (q.v.).

The most important talc production in the United States is from deposits in New York and Vermont.

TALUS Slope deposits of accumulated rock debris are talus. Fragments are angular, consistent with closeness to origin. The slope angle is between 26-36°. Talus may form a fan or cone on the lower slope. These can coalesce to form an apron at the mountain front. If fragments consolidate and are cemented, they form a breccia.

TAKU WINDS Winds, known as Taku, blow off the ice cap near Juneau and Douglas, Alaska. They can reach 166 kilometers (100 miles) per hour. These winds contribute enormously to wind chill (q.v.).

TAMARACK The tamarack ('Larix laricina') or eastern larch is a deciduous tree resembling the fir. It sheds its needles in the fall. Tamarack is dominant in the Eastern Boreal or Taiga Forest on the Laurentian Shield. In areas of impeded drainage, the tamarack is the species which invades the muskeg (q.v.) as the bog begins drying out.

TAMARISK The tamarisk, a genus of 'Tamaricaceae', is a coniferous desert shrub found in southwestern United States, where it was introduced. It proliferates along streams and is known as the 'salt cedar'.

TAMBORA Mount Tambora, Sumbawa, Indonesia, had the largest and most deadly eruption (1815) in human history. It emitted 80 cubic kilometers (20 cubic miles) of dust, ash, and gas. There was so much dust in the Stratosphere, there were world-wide climatic effects.

There was snow in June and mid-summer frosts in New England due to the reduction in solar energy. 1816 became known as the 'year without a summer', but it was warmer than usual in Siberia. The eruption was an order of magnitude greater than Krakatoa (q.v.).

TANEZROUFT BASIN   Tanezrouft Basin rivals the Empty Quarter (q.v.) of the Arabian Desert for ruggedness and impassable dunes. The basin extends from mid-Algeria, near Reggane, to the Niger River in Mali. It is about 1,333 kilometers (800 miles) across.

TANG SHAN EARTHQUAKE   In Tang Shan, China, July 27, 1976 at 3:42 A.M., mysterious red and white lights were seen from a distance of 330 kilometers (200 miles). No explanation for the lights has ever been satisfactory. China's worst earthquake since 1556 occurred 16 hours later. There were 2 shocks and an estimated million people were killed.

LAKE TANGANYIKA   Tanganyika in East Africa is one of the Rift Valley lakes. On the floor of the Western Rift, at an elevation of 773 meters (2,550 feet), the lake covers 34,000 square kilometers (13,120 square miles).

The lake is shared by Burundi, Zaire, and Zambia. Maximum depth in the north is 1,310 meters (4,320 feet) and in the south 1,470 meters (4,850 feet). After Baikal, USSR, it is the world's deepest lake. Tanganyika is the world's longest lake at 660 kilometers (410 miles) stretching north-south. Its width ranges from 16-72 kilometers (10-45 miles). The graben which hosts the lake is 25 million years old.

Most of Tanganyika's shoreline is faced with steep scarps. The main inflow is the Ruzizi River from Lake Kivu in the north. The Malagarasi River drains flatlands to the east. Underground flow in the valley also maintains inflow to the lake. Outflow on the west is via the Lukuga River which is seasonal. When the Lukuga flows, it drains to the Congo (Zaire) System and the Atlantic Ocean.

Eruptions in the Virunga Volcanoes (q.v.) caused Late-Pleistocene drainage reversal. Prior drainage was to the Nile River (q.v.).

In Tanganyika, 75% of the fish species are native to the lake.

TANTALUM   The element, tantalum, does not form independent minerals. It is found in the Pyrochlore Group of niobates, in the Perovskite Group of titanates, and in titanium-zirconium minerals of the Zirkelite Group. Tantalum is found in pegmatites associated with columbite and in carbonatites associated with niobates.

Tantalum reserves (in thousands of pounds of tantalum content) are:

Thailand	16,000
Australia	10,000
Nigeria	7,000
Zaire	4,000
Canada	4,000
Malaysia	2,000
Brazil	2,000

U.S. Bureau of Mines, 1990

The United States has only 3 million pounds of economically recoverable tantalum. Substitutes are ususally less effective. The major substitute for tantalum is niobium (columbium). It is used for carbides and superalloys. For corrosion resistance titanium, zirconium, niobium, platinum and glass can be substituted. For high-temperature uses the substitutes are tungsten, rhenium, molybdenum, iridium, hafnium and columbium.

TAPAJOS RIVER One of the major tributaries of the Amazon is the Tapajos. It is one of the purest of rivers, having only 4.0 milligrams per liter of dissolved solids. A major hydroelectric center is just being completed. It is to serve the development of Carajas (q.v.) and other industrial projects, among them an aluminum plant in Belem. What affect the installations will have on water quality is unknown. See **AMAZON TRIBUTARIES**.

TAR SANDS Tar sands are deposits of sand and clay impregnated with oil and bitumen (q.v.). The largest known deposits are at Lake Athabasca on the Saskatchewan-Alberta border in Canada.

The tar and oil sands are about 110 million years old. They hold hydrocarbon reserves that are twice those of Canada's petroleum reserves. Syncrude Canada Ltd. expects to meet 1/3 of Canada's petroleum needs by 1990. At that time the operation should be producing 130,000 barrels of oil per day.

Mining and processing to extract oil from these sands is similar to that of oil shale, but is less costly. The sands have to be strip-mined. 2 metric tons of sand are processed to attain 1 barrel of oil. The residue is a ton of waste. Huge amounts of water are required for processing.

In the Orinoco Basin of Venezuela 150-450 billion metric tons of asphaltic oil are in seams up to 30 meters (100 feet) thick. China also has large deposits of tar sands.

TARN Small, high, mountain lakes are tarns. They are formed either by glacial scour and melting or by faulting. The tarn is frequently found at the bottom of a cirque (q.v.).

Tarns are sagponds over major faults. The are usually aligned and indicate the fault trace. The San Andreas trace in the Sierras is a series of tarns readily seen from the air. The lakes along the Great Rift Valley are much larger. They infill the grabens.

Tarns in the Ruwenzori Mountains and Ethiopian Highlands indicate the secondary faults. Lake Tana, a source area for the Blue Nile, is such a tarn.

TASMANIA In its mountains, the Australian island of Tasmania has many walled lakes or tarns in cirque bowls.

Deep sheets of sandstone cover the east and central part of the island. 165 million years ago the sandstones were intruded by dolerite dikes. Since that time much of the sandstone has eroded leaving the harder dikes as ridges.

TAXONOMY Taxonomy is the classification of plants and animals. Kingdoms of flora and fauna are collected into Orders, Families, Genera, and Species. These are determined by degrees of kinship.

TECTONIC BASIN Tectonic basins result from structural distubances which cause concave sagging on a regional scale. Some are also basins of interior drainage with no outlet to the sea.

Tectonic basin sediments dip toward the center. These basins are enormous is size and may be created by:

- Faulting - Grabens (Great Rift Valley; Death Valley)
- Folding - Basins (Appalachian; Isfahan, Iran)
- Downwarp - Depressions (Lake Eyre, Australia; Chott Djerid, Tunisia).

TECTONIC CREEP Tectonic creep is fault slippage emanating from continuous movement. Such creep is usually not accompanied by earthquakes.

TECTONIC PLATES Relatively rigid areas of the Earth's Crust that are bounded by great rifts are called tectonic plates.

In an attempt to understand plate tectonics, scientists have developed many models. The plates have one of the following types of boundaries:

- Spreading ridges - New material finds its way to the surface
- Transform faults - Plates slide past each other
- Subduction zones - Plate material slides into the Mantle and is consumed beneath another plate.

Plates may be partly oceanic and partly continental, and sizes vary. The largest is the Pacific, including virtually all the oceanic area from the Aleutian Trench to the Pacific Antarctic Ridge, and from the East Pacific Rise to the trenches of the western Pacific.

More than 75 million years ago the North American Plate shoved against the Pacific Plate over-riding it. This collision moved the Pacific Plate to the northwest. Plates supporting the Western Hemisphere are moving west at about 2.5 centimeters (1 inch) per year or 10 kilometers (6 miles) in a million years.

TECTOSPHERE The Tectosphere is the region within the Earth between the surface and the Mantle. It is where crustal plate movement occurs. The region is characterized by large thermal gradients.

TEKTITE The Greek for molten is 'tektos' and from it tektite was derived. A tektite is a rock formed of natural silica glass. Tektites are rounded rocks found in Australia, Czechoslovakia, Indonesia, and in Texas. Their origin is thought to be meteoritic. Their composition differs from obsidian (q.v.).

In Australia, tektites are called 'breeches buttons'. These are bottle green, brown, and jet black. In Texas, tektites are known as bediasites.

TEKTITE II An underwater laboratory is built on a reef off the Virgin Islands. Aquanauts, sponsored by various agencies and NASA, use the lab. The lab was named for the huge number of 'meteoritic' nodules found on the seafloor in the area.

TELEOSTS Teleosts are bony fish with jaw development and a relatively large body mass. Commercial fish are taken from a few orders of teleosts. Humans are having a large impact on the ecology of this fish population. Cod and tuna have been greatly depleted by over-fishing.

TELESCOPE The telescope, an instrument for viewing the heavens, greatly magnifies the viewing field. A new telescope allowing magnification greater than the 200 inch at Palomar Observatory has been constructed of a series of especially angled mirrors. It is at an Arizona observatory.

The first telescope was made in Holland in 1609 and was improved by Galileo. His observations on the relationship of Earth to the Solar System were revolutionary.

TELLURIDE Gold, silver, and copper crystals in aggregate with tellurium (q.v.) form a telluride. The mineral is a dull, soft, and gray mass. The richest telluride source in the United States is in Colorado.

TELLURIUM The element tellurium is a metalloid (q.v.). It is silver-colored and more metallic than selenium. Tellurium is used as an alloy to harden lead and improve the machinability of steel. Tellurium bonds with gold, silver, and copper to form telluride (q.v.).

TEMPERATE FOREST The Temperate or humid mid-Latitude Forest is broadleaf. These forests are on the equatorial side of the coniferous Taiga (q.v.). The Temperate Forest varies in dominant tree type. In northeastern United States, from the Great Lakes to southern New England, the beech, birch, and maple are dominant. In the southern part of the forest the oak and magnolia abound. On poorer soils, the southern yellow pine has taken over.

The central and southern deciduous forest extends to the Gulf of Mexico. It was once the finest and most extensive broadleaf forest in the world with chestnut, hickory, oak, and poplar. The broadleaf trees have largely been cleared.

In southern Chile, there are deciduous trees among the evergreens. The conifers include 'Araucariaceae' unique to the southern Andes. Bamboo forest covers large areas of central China.

There is a belt of Temperate Rainforest which is close enough to the Equatorial Zone to be subtropical. This forest is multi-layered with an undergrowth of bamboo, fern, and palm.

TEMPERATURE The Earth's temperature is a measure of the balance between the heat of radiation absorbed and radiation emitted. The Atmosphere reflects or absorbs solar radiation, reducing the amount reaching the Earth.

Particulates in the Atmosphere cause a Greenhouse Effect (q.v.), or thermal blanket, about the globe. This layer allows visible and ultra-violet light to penetrate to the Earth but absorbs the infra-red.

The Earth's mean temperature at any time is a measure of differential heating. Land and water do not heat to the same temperature with the same solar radiation. There are also great latitude and elevation differences.

Usually surface air temperature is warmer than that at upper levels. The Troposphere or atmospheric envelope extends about 11 kilometers (7 miles) into Space. There is an an average gradient decreasing 3.6° per 300 meters (1,000 feet).

Sometimes a warm airmass overtakes and traps a cooler one at the surface. This creates an inversion in which temperature increases with altitude. If the airmasses remain stagnant, pollutants collect, so inversions are important in SMOG (q.v.) development.

TEN THOUSAND SMOKES When Mount Katmai in Alaska erupted in 1912, it collapsed and became a caldera (q.v.). Just north of the volcano is the 'Valley of Ten Thousand Smokes' composed of fumaroles (q.v.) related to Katmai vulcanism. Many of the fumaroles have decayed since the eruption. See **KATMAI**.

TENOR Tenor is the average metal content of an ore (q.v.) given as a percentage. Tenor tells the economic geologist whether the ore is marketable at a given time. It is also the figure governments use in taxing and certifying ore cargos. Based on the tenor payments and penalties are assessed after a final assay.

TEPHRA Tephra is magmatic material ejected from a volcanic vent. It hardens as it is emitted. The material is classed by size:

- Up to 0.03 centimeters (0.01 inch) - Volcanic Dust.
- 0.03-0.34 centimeters (0.012-0.15inches) - Ash.
- 0.34-3.18 centimeters (0.15-1.25 inches) - Lapilli.
- Above 3.18centimeters - Bombs.
- Very large fragments - Blocks.

Different types of volcanoes produce different and distinctive tephra. See **PYROCLASTICS**.

TERMITES Wood ingesting termites contribute methane to the Atmosphere and may even be a major source of the gas which contributes to the Greenhouse Effect (q.v.). Termites digest cellulose because they host a bacterium in a symbiotic relationship (q.v.).

The methane, which is substantial, is only now being assessed as termite populations continue to grow as a result of the 'slash and burn' cultivation. They are able to increase enormously as their predators are destroyed. They are food for the South American anteater, the 'tamandua', the aardvark in Africa, for birds, and even humans.

Millions of termites are housed in a given pinnacle or mound. Mounds are found in enormous numbers in Africa, Australia, and South America. Termite mounds can be up to 10 meters (30 feet) high. They are formed of chewed leaves and wood cemented with clay. The mounds protect the insects from heat, cold, and dessication.

The social structure in the mound is similar to that of the ant and they, like the ant, raise fungus gardens. The termite is known as the 'white ant' but it is more closely related to cockroach. Like the cockroach it is a living fossil (q.v.). Fossil termites have been dated from 200 million years ago.

There are 5 big termite families, the largest is 'Termitidae'. There are roughly 2,000 species of which 40 are found in the United States. Every year termites do millions of dollars in damage to structures in the United States alone.

Termites are not only negative elements. They serve to restore badly damaged savanna soils so they can in time support grass and trees. In working soils, termites selectively deposit minerals in the mounds, a boon to prospectors.

TERRACE A terrace is a platform, a relict of an older floodplain surface or shore created by stream or wave action. It may be uplifted or incised by stream downcutting or waves on the new shore. Terraces are common along coasts where sea levels have changed. In some areas a series of terraces has resulted from uplift at different periods. Some Scandinavian shores were formed in this way.

TERRAS FIRMES In the Amazon Basin, 'terras firmes' or solid ground is confined to the following areas:

- Land not flooded by rivers or tides
- Higher land, remnants of the Tertiary plateau on the basin floor
- Amazon Plain - Largest sedimentary area in the world

The Plain is really a low plateau with low relief of ridges and 'chapadas' or tablelands.

The Basin is surrounded by higher ground in the form of plateaus and low mountains. These last include the:

- Andean foothills
- Guiana Highlands
- Brazilian Central Plateau.

The Divide between the Amazon and the São Francisco (q.v.) is made up of Cretaceous red sandstone plateaus.

TERTIARY The Tertiary is the 3rd out of 4 geological periods according to an early chronological system. Today the Tertiary and Quaternary periods make up the Cenozoic Era (q.v.). The Tertiary spans time from 60-2 million years ago. It includes episodes of great mountain building, volcanism, and marine deposition.

At the beginning of the Tertiary the North Pole was located north of eastern Siberia near 78° North, 152° East. Polar wandering (q.v.) has brought the Pole to its present position. Enormous shifts in climate accompanied the magnetic ones. It was also a time of great volcanic activity.

In the Paleocene the continent with Europe and North America was still in the far north and the South Atlantic was only 3/4 its present size. Australia and Antarctica were still connected and India had not yet reached Asia. The north polar epicontinental sea was linked to Tethys (q.v) by the Uralian Sea.

By the Eocene Australia, except Tasmania, had broken from Antarctica and the northern continent had split into Europe and America. Glaciation reached sea level in Antarctica. In the Oligocene, the global ocean receded. By the Miocene, Tethys Sea had shrunk as Africa approached Europe and the Alpine Orogeny was initiated. India collided with Asia and the Himalayas began to rise.

The Tertiary is the 'Age of Mammals'. New arrivals included the elephant and the whale. Towards the end of the period humanoid apes appeared in Africa.

TETHYS SEA Tethys was a great sea that covered the Equator in the Paleozoic and Mesozoic times. It separated the globe into 2 hemispheres, north and south. The Alps and Himalayas rose from the Tethyan Trough.

TETONS The saw-toothed Tetons, a Rocky Mountain range, are in Wyoming. The Tetons are 65 kilometers (45 miles) long and rise abruptly from Jackson Hole Valley. Grand Teton, the highest peak, is 4,197 meters (13,770 feet) high. The famous saw-toothed form resulted from glacial erosion which was intense during the last 250,000 years.

The mountains formed 10 million years ago by block faulting. They form an uplifted horst composed of Precambrian greywacke (q.v.). Gneiss and schist dated 2.5 billion years predominate.

TEXTURE Texture refers to the grain size and pattern of a rock or mineral. It may be:

- Coarse - Grains larger than 5 millimeters (1/5 inch)
- Medium - Grains from 1 to 5 millimeters (1/25 - 1/5 inch)
- Fine - Grains below 1 millimeter (1/25 inch)
- Microcrystalline - Below the vision level.

When referring to igneous rocks, texture includes size, shape, and arrangement of the composite grains. These characteristics are related to rock cooling rates.

Grains are phaneritic or aphanitic. If phaneritic they are visible to the eye. If too small to be seen as individual grains they are aphanitic (sometimes felsitic). If all the minerals grains are similar in size, they are termed granular. If grains are much larger than the matrix, they are phenocrysts (q.v.). If phenocrysts are present the material is porphyritic (q.v.). If the material is sandy, it is said to be psammitic.

THALLOPHYTA   Thallophyta are a major phylum of the Plant Kingdom. The phylum includes Algae, Fungi, and Bacteria.

THAR DESERT The desert extending from western India (Rajasthan) into Pakistan is Thar in India. It is known as the Sind in Pakistan. Trade Winds blowing toward the Equator pick up moisture as they pass over the ocean. The moisture remains trapped in the particulates of the airmass and does not precipitate. See **RAJASTHAN**.

The desert is composed of rocky ridges and is separated from the steppes by the Arvalli Range. The through-flowing Indus River has irrigated this floodplain for 5,000 years. Populations have come and gone when the water systems broke down. Dams are under construction to reclaim a vast area.

THECODONTS Considered the ancestor of the dinosaur and the birds, the Triassic thecodonts were early reptiles. They were the first animals to rise on their hind legs. They also had forelegs suitable for grasping. There are 2 orders based on hip joint arrangement. One arrangement is close to that of the bird.

THEODOLYTE A surveying instrument, the theodolyte measures horizontal and vertical angles. Also called 'transits', they have short telescopes that may be inverted end over end. Newer versions have advanced optical systems.

THERMAL POLLUTION Cities are warming world-wide as a result of thermal pollution. The excess heating is the result of the increased use of energy in urban environments. Every use of energy releases heat.

World energy usage is 345 quadrillion BTU's (British Thermal Units). A unit is the heat needed to raise the temperature of a pound (0.37 kilograms) of water 1° Fahrenheit. The magnitude of the microclimatic effect is not fully appreciated. The effect is obscured because of the atmospheric changes which are occuring globally.

THERMOCLINE   The thermocline is a special layer in the vertical profile of the ocean or a lake. In this layer, temperature gradients drop off steeply in a relatively short depth range. The depth to the thermocline varies diurnally and seasonally.

THERMODYNAMIC LAW It is a universal law that heat will disperse toward cold. In accordance with this law, wind and water heated at the Equator tend to move toward the poles.

THERMOMETER The thermometer is an instrument to measure heat. The commonest thermometer has mercury in a glass bulb with a marked column. The mercury responds to changes in temperature and rises or falls in the column accordingly.

THIN SECTION A fragment of rock or mineral is reduced to a 0.02-0.03 millimeter slab to form a thin section. The sample slice is so thin that it is transparent to light when placed on a glass slide. It can be viewed clearly using a microscope.

THINGVELLIR GRABEN Thingvellir Rift, northwest of Reykjavik, is filled by Iceland's (q.v.) largest lake. Faults are on both sides of the valley. The huge rift is a surface expression of the spreading ridge of the Mid-Atlantic (q.v.).

THOLEITIC Tholeitic basalt has little olivine and is rich in pyroxene. It usually has a glassy matrix and is often of orthopyroxene and pigeonite. Tholeitic basalt is assumed to originate deep in the Mantle.

THORIUM The naturally occurring radioactive element, thorium, has a common isotope (q.v.), thorium-232. The isotope can be irradiated to produce uranium-233. Nuclides from thorium-232 decay naturally make up the Thorium Series. Lead-208 is the end product of the decay chain.

Thorium is nearly 3 times as abundant as uranium in the Earth's Crust and 80% of its original abundance is still with us while estimates put uranium at 50%. Primary thorium is found mostly in monazite (q.v.) mined from beach and stream placers. Massive thorium is found in the United States at Lemhi Pass, Idaho, and in Brazil in Minas Gerais. The mineral is also found in veins, carbonatites (q.v.), and some alkaline igneous rocks.

Thorium was widely used to coat gas mantle sleeves of lanterns. They provided a commonly used light enhancer well into the 1960's especially in less-developed areas. Today the major use of thorium is medical and as fuel for the Breeder Reactor (q.v.). See **MONAZITE**.

The thorium oxide resources of the world are estimated at 2.5 million metric tons. The major sources of thorium oxide reserves (in thousands of metric tons) are:

India	292.0
United States	158.0
Norway	166.0
Canada	100.0
Australia	44.0
South Africa	35.0
Brazil	16.0

U.S. Bureau of Mines, 1990

THRESHER Trieste II was able to report on and photograph the United states submarine, Thresher, lost with all hands. Evidence indicates that late winter storms may have changed current regimes around the mouth of the Gulf of Maine. Such a change could trigger a massive internal wave (q.v.). It is conjectured that such a wave destroyed the vessel. Waves of this power and magnitude had been previously recorded. See **INTERNAL WAVES**.

THRUST FAULT A thrust fault is a low-angle, reverse fault. Usually the dip is less than 45°. If less than 10°, it is an overthrust fault.

In Scotland thrust faults have left sedimentary rocks interbedded with metamorphics. Their origin was debated in the 'Highland Controversy' in 1861.

Thrust faulting is evident in the Alps and Rockies. The Lewis Over-thrust in Glacier National Park is a mountain with no roots. It is the vestige of a hanging wall (q.v.). As an erosional fragment such a thrust sheet is a klippe (q.v.).

THUNDER Thunder which accompanies lightning in a storm is caused by an electrical discharge. The electrical energy produces sound waves by causing the air to expand in its channel. The result is the thunder clap.

THUNDER EGG Rounded rocks that have a mineralized core of chalcedony are 'thunder eggs'. The Indians gave them their name. The average thunder egg is 7.6 centimeters (3 inches) in diameter.

Thunder eggs abound in the Chuckawalla Mountains of California and in Oregon.

TIBESTI The Tibesti Massif, northwest Chad and southern Libya, is isolated in a Paleozoic Basin. The mountains are of Precambrian sandstone and have been intruded on the northwest by the Ben Ghnema Batholith along a north-south axis.

The batholith is especially interesting as it varies in rock composition from west to east in the same manner as the California Batholith (q.v.). The batholith dates from 550 million years. It may have risen on a continental margin (q.v.). See **BATHOLITH**.

In the Chadian part of Tibesti a volcanic range rose 5 million years ago. Kmi Koussi Crater, the high point of Tibesti is at 3,395 meters (11,204 feet). It is also the highest in the Sahara. A soda lake, Trou au Natron, is in a crater surrounded by walls of scoria.

Tibesti is cut by narrow gorges which are used as passes. There are inhabited palm grove oases in these gorges. These passes have played an important part in the hostilities between Chad and Lybia.

TIBETAN PLATEAU The Tibetan Plateau is in central Asia, now part of China. The plateau north of the Himalayan Mountains stretches over 180,000 square kilometers (77,000 square miles). The average elevation is 4,000 meters (16,000 feet). Lhasa, one of the world's highest cities, is on the plateau. For centuries it has been the center of a culture and religion.

TIDAL BORE A fast tidal current or translational wave in a relatively narrow, funnel-shaped channel is a tidal bore. Wave heights may be 2 meters (6 feet).

Tidal bores are known in the Bay of Fundy (q.v.), Canada; Turn Again Inlet, Alaska; the Gulf of California; in the Amazon Estuary; and elsewhere.

TIDAL FRICTION Friction exerted by the moon on tidal activity is slowing the Earth's rotation. The slowing rate is almost imperceptible, but days are becoming longer. Scientists tell us that in the Devonian (395-345 m.y.) the day was 21.7 hours.

The Earth's axis is increasing its lean. Whether the lean is from friction or cyclical wobble (q.v.), it will result in major climate changes.

TIDEPOOL Along shorelines where small rock basins are carved by pebbles swirling in the surf, tidepools develop. The tidepools are only exposed at low tide, some only in an abnormally low one. Tidepools are the habitat of a special ecosystem of plants and animals.

TIDES The pull of the Moon's gravitational field upon the Earth together with centrifugal force causes the oceans to rise slightly. Tides are a bulging and sinking of the sea surface.

High-tide occurs twice a day in the part of the Earth facing the Moon. The time interval is now 745 minutes or 12.4 hours.

Occasionally, the Sun's gravitational force is added to that of the Moon and exceptional tides result. These occur when the Sun and Moon are lined up at full or new moon times. These tides are called Spring Tides, a misnomer. In the Bay of Fundy, between New Brunswick and Nova Scotia, Spring Tides can attain heights of 15 meters (50 feet). Coastline shape can affect the special tides.

Twice a month the Sun and Moon are at right angles and a lower than normal or Neap Tide results.

TIEN SHAN RANGE The 'Celestial Mountains' or Tien Shan form the border of Sinkiang Province, China, with the USSR. It is a 2,900 kilometer (1,800 mile barrier stretching to the Pamir (q.v.). Tien Shan is marked by long parallel ridges and long, and deep valleys. The highest point is Robeda Peak at 7,439 meters (24,406 feeet) and the lowest is the Turfan Depression at 154 meters (505 feet) below sea level.

The crystalline basement rocks (300-400 m.y.) of the Tien Shan was uplifted into a fault-block range. The Turfan Depression contains various basins. One Turfan graben contains Issyk-kul, one of the world's largest tarns (q.v.).

TIERRA CALIENTE Tropical Andean climate is affected by elevation. In the warm belt, 'Tierra Caliente', the average temperature is 80° Fahrenheit. The belt ranges from sea level to 1,600 meters (3,500 feet), depending upon nearness to the Equator.

The Tierra Caliente ecosystem varies with precipitation. The range of climates is from rainforest to tropical dry as on the Guajira Peninsula of Colombia. Tierra Caliente and Tierra Templada (q.v.) overlap and the transition is gradual.

TIERRA DEL FUEGO The islands of southern Argentina and Chile extend from the Strait of Magellan to Cape Horn. They form the Fuegan Archipelago and are also known as Tierra del Fuego, or land of fire. The name comes from the enormous grass fires which engulf the area periodically.

TIERRA TEMPLADA Andean climatic zones are divided by elevation level. 'Tierra Templada' is the Temperate Zone between 600 and 1,800 Meters (2,000 and 6,000 feet). It overlaps Tierra Caliente (q.v.) and depending upon its nearness to the Equator, the zone expands or contracts.

Tierra Templada has the ideal elevation in the tropics for coffee cultivation. Where warm, gentle rains fall from March to September and slopes are relatively gentle, the situation is ideal.

Above 1,800 meters is 'Tierra Fria' or the cold zone. 'Nevada' or snowline in the tropics is at 3,000 meters (10,000 feet).

TIGRIS RIVER The Tigris, a famous river of history rises in the Anti-Taurus Mountains of eastern Turkey. The distance from its source to that of its sister river, the Euphrates, is about 160 kilometers (100 miles). The rivers meet in Iraq. See **FERTILE CRESCENT**.

The city of Nineveh was on the banks of the Tigris, while the city of Babylon was on the Euphrates. Many biblical scholars feel the 'Garden of Eden' was located in the Delta.

TILAPIA A fish species, 'Tilapia', was introduced into many African lakes to provide an additional protein source. The fish however, uses its energy in reproduction and doesn't grow to any size. No other fish can compete with its population rate, so it now dominates many African lakes.

Hawaii imported Tilapia for mosquito control and is now plagued with the fish.

TILL Unsorted glacial drift (q.v.), till, is found in most periglacial areas. There are enormous till deposits in Canada and substantial ones in the periglacial areas of the United States. A belt of till crosses 1,300 kilometers (800 miles) of east-central China.

The only evidence of Permian (q.v.) glaciation north of the Equator is the Talchir Tillite of India.

In the Southern Hemisphere there are some striking deposits. Carboniferous till deposits (300 m.y.) cover 10 million square kilometers (4 million square miles) of southern Brazil. They are 1,000 meters (3,300 feet) thick.

In the Flinders Range (q.v.) southeast Australia, there is a belt of till 200 meters (600 feet) thick and over 500 kilometers (300 miles) long.

TILTH The crumbly layer of a soil is its tilth. It acts to break off capillary tubes, thus reducing evaporation from the surface. If a soil is too finely 'crumbed', wind will carry it off. Contour plowing will help protect the tilth.

TIMBERLINE The timberline is the elevation or contour on a mountain slope marking the upper limit of tree growth. A few Tundra (q.v.)

plants survive above the Timberline. Timberline varies with latitude. It occurs higher near the Equator.

The area just approaching Timberline in high latitudes has a special Elfin Forest, known as 'Krumholz' (q.v.).

TIMBUKTU The fabled city of Timbuktu in Mali is 6 miles from the Niger River. Ibn Batuta (14th Century) named it 'City of Gold'. In the 15th Century the oasis city had a university and a large population. One of its important trade items was books.

The Saharan Timbuktu Oasis has an average daily winter temperature of 90° Fahrenheit falling to 56° at night.

Twice a year for centuries, salt from the Taghaza Mines was traded for by merchants from Timbuktu. The mines to the south are a 40-day trip by camel from the city. Salt was brought to Wangara, an arranged meeting site, and traded in silent auction for gold. Cloth, dried fruit and slaves were also traded. See **OASIS**.

TIME ZONES By international agreement, a Prime Meridian was set at Greenwich, England. From it, the Earth was divided from Pole to Pole in degrees of Longitude (q.v.). The 24 hours of the day were calculated from the 180° Meridian or Date Line. A new calendar day beings at this line. Time zones were set up allowing daylight to prevail over a region.

There are 4 time zones in the United States between the east and west coasts. From Vladivostok on the Pacific to the Ukraine in Europe, there are 10 time zones in the USSR.

TIMNA Timna Valley, eastern Sinai, was a copper smelting center at the time of the Pharoahs. Timna Valley is narrow, and branches into the Wadi el Arabah. Wadi el Arabah extends from the Dead Sea to the Gulf of Aqaba. It is an extension of the great Rift Valley of East Africa.

Babylonians destroyed the Egyptian mines, which were reopened by the Romans. After 1,600 years, the Israelis again opened Timna. From 1953, the mines produced copper at the rate of 1 million tons per year. They were closed due to market conditions.

TIN Cassiterite (q.v.), or tinstone, is the principal source of tin. Malaysia has been the major producer with open pit, underground, and dredging operations. Its largest deposit near Kuala Lumpur has produced for about 80 years but is nearing exhausion.

Bolivian tin from veins controlled the world market for many years. The ease of placer operations in the Far East and political unrest in Bolivia changed the picture. Of recent years Amazon Basin placers in Rondonia have been producing from detrital concentrates emanating from Andean tin granites.

China has long been a tin producer. 30 veins in Yunnan Province discovered in the 1980's are reported to have highest grades so far.

The only United States production is from placers in Alaska, and as a by-product from molybdenum production in Colorado. Black Hills pegmatites have not been economically worked for tin for years. At present the United States gets 1/4 of its needs from de-tinning plants.

World resources (1989) were estimated at 9.0 million metric tons. Reserves were distributed among the following producers (in thousands of metric tons of tin content):

	Reserves
Malaysia	1,110.0
Indonesia	680.0
Brazil	650.0
China	400.0
USSR	300.0
Thailand	270.0
Australia	200.0
Bolivia	140.0
United Kingdom	90.0
Canada	60.0
Burma	20.0
Nigeria	20.0
United States	20.0
Zaire	20.0

U.S. Bureau of Mines, 1990

The major uses of tin are electrical and in the production of containers. A possible future use is in superconductivity (q.v.) based on a tin-niobium alloy. See **NIOBIUM**.

TINAJAS Natural rock basins, 'tinajas', found in arid to semi-arid areas, are carved out by intermittent streams. They are pockets beneath temporary waterfalls. The name is Spanish for tank.

Interior basins filled with coarse gravel and sand are natural sinks. Water is held in the gravels and is often fresh and sweet. In the American Southwest, tinajas are often dug out by big-horn sheep or coyotes. These are also called 'coyote wells'.

TITANIUM Titanium, an important metal of the Space Age, is lighter and stronger than steel. It occurs as anatase, brookite, ilmenite, and rutile minerals. Rutile is a common constituent of granites and pegmatites. Anatase and brookite are found in carbonatites (q.v.) as at Magnet Cove, Arkansas and Tapira, Brazil.

As erosional products, rutile and ilmenite are concentrated in black sands. Rutile beach placers are worked in Australia and Sierra Leone. Ilmenite sands have been worked in Florida, India, and Brazil.

In ilmenite, an iron titanate, 50% of the hematite is replaced by titanium.

World resources of Titanium are of rutile (q.v.), ilmenite, and anatase. Together they amount to 200 million metric tons of titanium oxide. These resources are held primarily be Brazil, Australia, India, and South Africa. The world's largest anatase reserve measured 66 billion metric tons and is found in the carbonatites of Araxa, Tapira, and Salitre in Brazil. The Titanium oxide content ranges from 3-23%. From the largest deposit at Tapira the average is 15.6%. Tapira-Salitre have measured reserves of 600 million metric tons of 17-19% according to DNPM of Brazil (1987). See **RUTILE, ILMENITE**.

LAKE TITICACA Lake Titicaca forms the border between Peru and Bolivia at an elevation of 3,750 meters (12,500 feet). It is the highest freshwater lake in the world and the 2nd largest lake in South America after Lake Maracaibo. Titicaca is fed by Andean snows.

The famous Island of the Sun in the lake has ruins of fortresses, palaces, and temples built by Pre-Columbians.

TOBA VOLCANO Toba Volcano erupted 75,000 years ago. Sumatra's Lake Toba occupies the depression left by this largest Quaternary eruption. The caldera is 100 x 35 kilometers (30 x 10 miles). It is estimated that the eruption was 400 times that of Krakatoa (q.v.) in intensity and in atmospheric effects. The emissions were silicious pyroclastics.

TOMBOLO A 'tombolo' is a special type of spit (q.v.). It is a bar of sand or gravel connecting an island to the mainland. The original meaning in Italian is sand hill.

Monte Argentario on the Italian west coast, an Appenine outlier, rises to a height of 600 meters (2,000 feet). It is joined to mainland Italy by 3 tombolos. A tombolo joins Gibraltar to Spain.

TONLE SAP Tonle Sap, Southeast Asia's largest lake, drains through the Tonle Sap River to the Mekong at Phnom Penh, Kampuchia (Cambodia).

From June to November monsoon rains fill the lake and not all drains to the already swollen Mekong which has currents running upstream from rain, wind, and tide. This flow empties into Tonle Sap. For centuries Tonle Sap has acted as a natural flood control agent.

The lake is noted for its freshwater fish, especially carp. When the waters recede fish are easily caught in the shallows.

TOPAZ Topaz, an aluminum silicate, is a constituent of tin granites. Topaz is as hard as spinel, but less so than ruby. It is fragile and breaks easily. Gem topaz is a rich, honey-colored, blue or wine colored crystal. It crystallizes in the orthorhombic system. See **CRYSTAL SYSTEMS**.

The main source of gem topaz is from Brazilian pegmatites. Honey-colored crystals weighing up to 273 kilograms (600 pounds) have been mined. Large blue crystal topazes have been found in the pegmatites of Minas Gerais.

A very rare, flawless, light blue topaz crystal was found near Teofilo Otoni, Minas Gerais. The crystal weighed 35 kilograms (75 pounds). From the rough gemstone, the Princess of Brazil was cut. It was given 221 facets. The Princess weighs 4.3 kilograms (9.5 pounds).

Some fine rare wine-colored gems and blue topazes have come from Siberia.

Topaz rhyolite (q.v.) from Topaz Mountain in the Thomas Range of Utah is a source of small topazes. These topazes are peach color but become clear when exposed to sunlight.

TOPSOIL The humus layer of soil is a mix of rock and organic debris. It is important to plant growth. This important layer of organic and inorganic mix is topsoil. Its contained water is variable and depends upon regional rainfall.

Topsoil is easily eroded if ground cover is removed. For every 2.5 centimeters (1 inch) lost, crop yields are reduced 3-6 bushels (105-210 liters) per acre (0.45 hectares) a year. In grasslands, it can take up to 1,000 years to build an 1 inch of topsoil. If only 1% per year is eroded, disaster can come quickly to agricultural lands.

TOR LANDSCAPE Tor landscape exists where granites have been planed off by erosion. Weathering continued below the surface and selectively eroded the fine-grained, well-jointed, and fissile rocks.

Tower-like rocks or columns are spread over the landscape as small irregular and craggy hills. There is a sharp contact between eroded and fresh rock. Tors are prominent on the British moors.

TORBANITE Torbanite is an oil shale. It has some of the highest hydrocarbon grades in the world. The shale can yield 300 gallons of oil per short ton (1,000 liters per metric ton). Torbanites occur in New South Wales, Australia.

TORDESILLAS A treaty between Spain and Portugal was signed before Pope Alexander VI in 1494 in the town of Tordesillas, Spain. It settled territorial disputes and changed the course of history.

An imaginary line was drawn 370 miles west of Cape Verde Islands. All land west of the line was Spanish, all east of it Portuguese. The Treaty affected colonization patterns in South America, Africa, and the Far East.

TORNADO A tornado or twister is a spinning column of air reaching down from a thundercloud. The airmass, several hundred meters wide, moves up to 500 kilometers (300 miles) per hour and is accompanied by a loud roar. The funnel rotates counterclockwise in the Northern Hemisphere. Its path is unpredictable.

A tornado has a low pressure area at its center. When this passes over a building it causes it to explode from pressure buildup within the building. High winds carry off the debris.

In the United States there are an average of 600 storms a year. Normally, they occur in late afternoon after the Earth has heated up. They are usually in the mid-continent states where airmasses from the Gulf and from the north converge.

TORTURA REED The 'tortura' is a special reed growing on the banks of Lake Titicaca (q.v.). The Indians use it to construct the famous reed boats. 4 bundles of reeds are used, 2 flat bundles for the bottom and 2 thinner ones for sides. If these boats are not left in water all the time, they will last up to 4 years.

TOURMALINE Tourmaline is a complex silicate of boron and aluminum with iron, magnesium, sodium, calcium, and lithium. A rough correlation exists between composition and color.

Tourmalines are prized gemstones with a typical 3-sided columnar crystal. Black tourmaline is common but green, pink, and parti-colored crystals are most sought. The gem crystals are found in pegmatites (q.v.).

The major source of tourmalines is Brazil but beautiful gem tourmalines have been found in Pala Pegmatite in San Diego County, California.

TRACHYTE Trachyte is a lava composed predominantly of feldspar (q.v.). It is grey or even lighter in color. The composition is:

Alkali feldspar	75%
Soda-lime feldspar	10%
Augite	10%

Usually, there are large crystals of sanidine, a potash feldspar, in the matrix. The balance of the rock is made up of a variety of minor constituents. Trachyte easily decomposes.

Trachyte was long used for millstones. It was used in the construction of Germany's Cologne Cathedral.

TRADE WINDS The Trade Winds blow toward the Equator. In the Northern Hemisphere, they blow from the northeast and in the Southern Hemisphere from the southeast.

The Trade Winds are regular and steady winds with velocities between 16 and 25 kilometers (10-15 miles) per hour. The name dates from the era of sailing vessels, when these winds were of prime importance to making headway in low-latitudes. See **INTERTROPICAL CONVERGENCE.**

TRANS-AMAZON HIGHWAY The Trans-Amazon Highway, a gash through the rainforest south of the river on 'terra firme' (solid ground) is 5,000 kilometers (3,000 miles) long. It links the Amazon Basin from east to west, from Altamira, Para, to Porto Velho, Rondonia.

It is part of an eventual network of 15,000 kilometers (9,000 miles). A cut will cross the basin on the north side of the river in the foothills of the Guiana Highlands. From Macapa on the Amazon Estuary, the highway is projected through Roraima to beyond the national park with Pico de Neblina, Brazil's highest peak, and on to São Gabriel da Cachoeira within 200 kilometers (120 miles) of the Colombian border.

TRANS-BAIKAL The Trans-Baikal is a railway link from Baikal to the Sea of Japan a distance of 3,330 kilometers (2,000 miles). Called the 'BAM' it is parallel to the Trans-Siberian Railway (q.v.).

TRANS-MEDITERRANEAN PIPELINE A pipeline from the Algerian oilfields crosses Tunisia, transits the Mediterranean Sea to Sicily, then extends through Italy to the north. The line required very heavy pipe, expecially to cross the Sicilian Channel. The distance is 2,500 kilometers (1,562 miles).

The pipeline links with the European pipeline net. It can carry 12 billion cubic meters (400 billion cubic feet) of petroleum annually.

TRANS-SIBERIA RAILWAY The Trans-Siberia Railway is one of the world's longest. Its construction began in 1891 and the railway was not completed until 1915. It was necessary to construct hundreds of bridges, among them some of the largest at that time. Major Siberian cities are strung along its route. See **TRANS-BAIKAL**.

TRANSFORM FAULTS Transform faults are part of the Global Rift System. The faults are located on plate boundaries. 2 important continental transforms are the San Andreas and the Jordan faults.

The Jordan Fault junctions with the Red Sea spreading zone and extends to the Iranian collision zone. See **SAN ANDREAS FAULT**.

TRANSGRESSION The change from continental to marine sediment is evidence of the sea's transgression. The sediments show the gradual change in the environment. Transgression is a period when seas rise and cover continents or continents subside allowing seas to invade.

TRANSISTOR The development of the transistor, a small electrical device that acts like a valve, has revolutionized communications. The transistor, or semiconductor, amplifies or rectifies current. It is based on the behavior of metalloids (q.v.).

The transistor lead to the development of the computer chip. The metalloids most used in present technology are germanium and silicon.

TRANSLUCENCE The quality of allowing light to pass through a body is translucence. It is an identifying characteristic of minerals and gemstones.

TRANSMISSION Mediums vary in ability to allow wave transmission. The Earth is a poor medium, but water allows light to great depths if there are no scattering agents. Glass allows short waves to pass, but not long ones. Thus, heat builds in greenhouses.

Short wave radiation is transmitted in the Atmosphere better than long. Solar energy penetrates to the surface of the Earth but reradiated energy is sometimes trapped in the lower Troposphere by clouds and SMOG. See **GREENHOUSE EFFECT**.

TRANSPIRATION Moisture evaporating off plants into the Atmosphere is transpiration. This plant characteristic helps retain local humidity. It is part of the hydrological cycle (q.v.).

In some areas, like the Amazon, evapotranspiration contributes much moisture. As a result, deforestation leads to a climate change. The change in micro-climate in Manaos and Belem illustrates this.

In some arid areas, certain plants transpire excessively and soil water is lacking, so these plants actually contribute to the aridity.

TRANSVERSE RANGES The Transverse Ranges of California are perpendicular to the Sierra Nevada. The ranges extend east from the Santa Barbara coast to within (100 km) 60 miles of the Colorado River.

The Santa Inez, San Gabriel, San Bernardino, and Santa Monica mountains make up the Transverse Ranges. The Channel Islands are part of the Santa Monica mountains. The ranges are separated from the Sierras by major faulting.

TRAPROCK In many parts of the world, dark basaltic lavas are called 'trap-rock'. In the United States traprock only means quarry basalt.

TRAVERTINE Travertine is calcareous tufa associated with hot springs and geysers. Stalactites found in caves may be of travertine. It is often mistaken for onyx.

Because it is softer than onyx it is an easier carving medium. Travertine carvings are frequently sold for onyx.

TREE RINGS Trees in temperate climates create growth rings that record the annual cycle. Tropical trees grow steadily so there is no record. In interpreting fossil tree rings, it is possible to determine the paleoclimate since tree growth and rings are related to weather.

Tree rings can be used to determine the relative ages of trees. Some rings are in pairs of light and dark indicating seasons. Others indicate some very old trees. Bristlecone pines in California are 4,000 years old. The dates have been confirmed by radiocarbon dating.

Archaeologists use tree rings to date timbers to determine the age of some ancient structures. These often corroborate the radiocarbon dates (q.v.).

TRENCHES Mid-oceanic trenches are related to the Global Rift System (q.v.). They are located at the edges of volcanic arcs and in earthquake zones. When a crustal plate over-rides another in a rift zone, crustal material is forced through the rift floor into the Mantle.

Trenches are the deepest parts of the oceans. Challenger Deep in the Marianas is 11,022 meters (36,000 feet) below sea level. See **OCEANIC TRENCHES**

TRIASSIC The Triassic (225-190 m.y.) is the earliest period of the Mesozoic Era. The supercontinent Pangaea was still intact. Marine fossils dominated. Of these, the most important were the Ammonites. The first mammals appeared in the Triassic.

Triassic climate throughout a large part of the globe appears to have been semi-arid to arid, probably due to the large landmass area. Some well-known sediments were deposited in the period. These include the Karoo of South Africa and Brazilian redbeds. Similar fossil reptilian fauna are found at both locations. Corals were replacing their losses sustained during the Permian Extinction (q.v.). The important Gondwana fern, Glossoptera appeared in the Triassic.

The huge Tethys Sea (q.v.) covered most of southern Europe and some marine deposits are now found in places like the Dolomites of Yugoslavia.

In Siberia, there are Triassic plateau basalts up to a kilometer (0.6 mile) thick covering 1.5 million square kilometers (900,000 square miles). The flows continued into the Jurassic.

TRIDYMITE Tridymite is a high-temperature (870° Celsius) quartz. It is much rarer than ordinary quartz but is found in some fine-grained volcanic rocks.

TRILOBITE A class of the Phylum Arthropoda, trilobites are related to the lobster and horseshoe crab (q.v.). There were freshwater trilobites, but the majority were marine.

The earliest trilobites appeared about 550 million years ago and became extinct about 200 million years ago. The organism was 10 centimeters (4 inches) long and had a 3-lobed structure. Some had 3 eyes. Adults had 2 sets of legs, one for swimming.

Trilobites are prominent Lower-Cambrian fossils. They are present in shales and fine-grained limestones of the Grand Canyon. They were widespread and are an excellent Paleozoic indicator fossil.

TRIPOLITE Tripolite, or tripoli, is a polishing powder of organic silica. It is made up of diatom (q.v.) skeletons. Tripolite is also called 'fossil flour'. Mineralogically, it is a form of opal.

TRISTAN DA CUNHA The small British Protectorate of Tristan da Cunha is related to a hot spot (q.v.) or plume in the Torres Syncline (South Atlantic). Volcanic eruptions were so great in recent times, the entire population was removed to Britain. When the eruptions ceased, they chose to return.

The Tristan Hotspot is on the axis of the Torres Syncline, a structure in the South Atlantic between South America and the Mid-Atlantic Rift (q.v.). The hot spot (q.v.) has been active for millions of years. With seafloor spreading, volcanic debris has been moving out from the center of activity. There are 2 ridges associated with the hot spot. Walvis Ridge connects Tristan with South Africa. The Rio Grande Rise links Tristan with South America.

TRITIUM Tritium is the radioactive isotope (q.v.) of hydrogen. It is hydrogen-3. The isotope is artificially produced and the nuclide is raw material for fusion reactors. Tritium released by bomb explosion has a half-life of 12 years.

Tritium has been useful in evaluating groundwater reserves. If reservoirs were replenished by rainwater or snowmelt recently, traces of tritium will be present. If tritium is not present, the water supply being mined is geological. Depending upon size and drawdown rate, this supply can be mined out. Many small communities in the southwestern United States depend upon such ancient water supplies.

TRONA Trona is fine, crystalline, yellow sodium carbonate, or soda ash. Trona was discovered in 1938 in Bridger Basin, Wyoming, in the Wilkins Peak Member of the Eocene Green River Formation. Only lately has it been mined on a large scale.

The Green River Formation (q.v.) hosts 42 beds of trona crystals disseminated in shale. These beds are 3 meters (10 feet) thick over 78 square kilometers (30 square miles). Reserves are 260 million tons, or 170 million tons of soda ash (q.v.).

TROODOS MASSIF The massif which almost bisects the island of Cyprus is Troodos. An upthrust of ocean floor material, it is composed of an ophiolite (q.v.) assemblage with overlying sulfides. Typical pillow lavas (q.v.) are present.

The area has important deposits of copper, pyrite, and chromite. Evaporites (q.v.) accumulated when the ophiolite material was exposed.

TROPICAL EASTERLY JET In summer, high pressure airmasses move away from the Equator. They appear locked over Tibet and the Sahara. Air flowing around the eastern edge of the highs has a long way to go and the velocity increases. Jet stream winds blow straight from the east.

At its fastest, the Tropical Easterly Jet is at an elevation of 16 kilometers (9.5 miles). Only the 2 desert highs are stable enough to generate steady easterly jet streams.

TROPICAL CLIMATE The Tropical Zone extends from the Tropic of Cancer to the Tropic of Capricorn. Each side of the Equator has seasonal rainfall with a variable dry season. The temperature difference between the hottest and coolest periods is about 6° Celsius.

On the Köppen Scale (q.v.), tropical climate is divided into Tropical Humid (Af), Tropical Monsoonal (Am), and Tropical Dry (Aw). The coolest temperature for the Humid is 18° Celsius (65° F). There is a narrowing of the belt due to the Subtropical High on the eastern side of oceans. As a result, western continental areas are dry.

Densely forested areas have uniformly high temperatures and heavy precipitation over the entire year. 50% of the world's rainfall occurs in the Rainforest, and at least half is produced by recycling moisture by the forest itself. These heavy rains have a moderating effect on global climate. So-called dry periods in the Rainforest are only seasons of less heavy rainfall.

The humid conditions tend to maintain a relatively even annual temperature, usually 90°-96° Fahrenheit in the Amazon. At night the temperature is only a few degrees less, however, due to the moisture, the nights can feel very cool.

TROPICAL RAINFOREST The Tropical Rainforest is a vast, natural ecosystem. The forests are in the Equatorial Zone with minor inroads into the Subtropical. They cover 23 million square kilometers (9 million square miles). The major Tropical Rainforests are:

- American - Mexico into South America,
- Indo-Malayan - Australia, Burma, Ceylon, India, Indonesia.
- African - Congo (Zaire) Basin to Ethiopia.

Tropical rainforests are characterized by a 3-tiered structure of vegetation. The lowest tier from 0 to 18 meters (0-60 feet) has species ranging from fungi and ferns to relatively tall trees. The middle layer creates the canopy where treetops interweave. At this level the trees are principally from 18 to 36 meters (60-120 feet) high. The topmost layer is made up of emergents or trees that are from 36 to 60 meters (120-200 feet). These trees tower over the canopy (q.v.).

Great diversity of plants and animals exists in the Tropical Rainforest. They contains 40% of all known species. In the Brazilian Amazon, the known species count exceeds 50,000. The Tropical Rainforest is also the world's largest germ plasma (q.v.) pool.

Tropical rainforests originated millions of years ago under different climatic conditions. No new forests are being generated. Present forests are maintained by the constant energy and high temperatures from the Sun and abundant rainfall. The amount of rain differs from forest to forest and within the forests.

The world's main store of carbon is in these forests and they make a great contribution to the carbon-oxygen budget.

The Amazon is in the rain shadow of the Andes and rainfall coming into the area is limited. In Congo, the rainfall depends upon the position of the ITC (q.v.). Deforestation leads inevitably to drier local climates in both these areas.

Forest survival is the result of evapotranspiration (q.v.). Moist cells are created above the trees. Clouds form from this moisture base when thermal conditions are right, usually every afternoon after the Earth heats up. Convective rainfall then occurs. Without this self-production of moisture, these forests would not survive.

The forests have a specialized root mat developed to store nutrients. With deforestation, the nutrients become unavailable for new growth. Rains leach away trace elements from the soils and they become barren of nutrients if not sterile.

Thus, survival of the Tropical Rainforest Ecosystem depends upon maintaining the balance. It is a virtually closed ecosystem in that the forests themselves contribute most of the moisture and nutrients necessary for their survival. The system once broken is succeeded by a different vegetation which rarely leads to a rainforest climax.

Ethiopia was 10% forested 30 years ago, it is now only 4%. The rate of destruction not only of quantity but quality has been increasing in all forests during this same 30-year period. It is estimated that the primary tropical forests are being destroyed at the annual rate of 45,000 square kilometers (17,300 square miles) to logging alone. The major forests affected by logging are those of Indonesia and Sumatra.

On the periphery of the forests, 25,000 square kilometers (9,600 square miles) are annually destroyed in the search for fuelwood (q.v.). An additional 20,000 square kilometers (7,700 square miles) are sacrificed annually for farms and pasture. Central American deforestation has been to make way for cattle to produce beef for export.

In the geological past, tropical vegetation covered most of the Earth. Fossil tropical forests have been found even in Antarctica. Almost all plants including trees have tropical ancestors, even the cacti.

TROPICAL SAVANNAS The Llanos of the Orinoco Valley and Guiana Highlands of South America are typical of tropical savannas. Others are the African Sudan Belt north of the Congo (Zaire) River, and the Veldt of South Africa. There are tropical savannas in Australia and south and southeast Asia. See **GRASSLANDS**.

Tropical savanna climate is transitional between tropical wet and dry. The savanna is characterized by open forest and grassland. Trees are usually galleried along streams. Tropical savannas are located in areas between the Intertropical Convergence (ITC) and the Subtropical Anticyclonic Zone.

The location of the ITC (q.v.) varies. Its presence can block showers or allow monsoon (q.v.) winds with their rains to reach the mainland. Monsoonal winds blocked by the Convergence can leave the area in drought as happens with increasing frequency in the Sahel (q.v.). See **WET/DRY CLIMATE**.

TROPICAL SOILS In the tropics 5 climates govern soil type:

- Equatorial
- Tropical
- Monsoonal
- Desert
- Mountain

In addition to climate, soils are affected by groundwater, vegetation, animal life, relief, and lithology. Beneath tropical savannas, grass roots form mats that act as a buffer to leaching and retard it. This helps create a fragile ecotone (q.v.) that is easily destroyed by over-grazing.

Forests are mostly on poor acid soils from which most nutrients have been leached, so farming cleared land is marginal. None of the farms produce much after 3 years and most must then lie fallow at least 10 to allow regeneration of the soil if the climate is favorable. In many cases the climate deteriorates and soils do not recuperate even after a very long fallow.

The shallow root systems of the Tropical Rainforest allow for immediate intake of nutrients created by the forest itself. Bacteria and other organisms contribute to rapid decomposition. Nutrients are in the vegetation itself, held in the root mat, and are not often in the soils. This accounts for the lack of success of many plantation schemes and permanent agriculture. When widespread clearing precedes planting, soils quickly dry out from evaporation. If the mineral content is right, those soils can become rock. See **LATERITE**.

Tropical soils are not completely uniform. The highly-leached lateritic soils are found on gentle slopes and on unflooded plains. Seasonally flooded areas tend to build up sediments and silts which allow vegetation to flourish on the alluvium. The wetlands, part of every tropical forest, allow for swamp or marsh vegetation. Basin rim soils and slope soils are the most vulnerable and the most attractive to human settlement.

TROPICAL WEATHERING   Tropical weathering is characterized by deep alteration of surface rocks. Soils are leached by rainwaters under tropical and semi-tropical conditions. There is a complex interaction of rainy periods, less rainy periods, and even relatively dry months causing water table fluctuations and with it fluctuations of the reduction-oxidation or re-dox (q.v.) zone. This affects soil formation and weathering.

Deep tropical weathering has been responsible for many mineral deposits. Some of the most important ones are bauxite (aluminum), nickel, and iron ore. See **LATERITE**.

TROPICAL WET/DRY CLIMATE   Between the moist Tropical Rainforest and the Arid Tropical climates is a region which manifests at different seasons the different climate regimes it abuts. It is called the Tropical Wet and Dry Climate. The continents of Africa and South America have the greatest areas affected by this climate. They are also the most populous areas of these continents.

In Africa, a belt of Tropical Wet/Dry known as Sudan or Sahel is located between the Sahara Desert and the Congo Basin. An additional belt of Tropical Wet/Dry known as the Veldt is between the Basin and the Kalahari Desert.

The same relationships are exhibited in the Western Hemisphere. Tropical Wet/Dry Climate is found in parts of Central America and the West Indies. In South America the Llanos (q.v.) of Columbia and Venezuela abut the Amazon Basin to the south. Some of the largest areas of Wet/Dry regime are found in Brazil south of the Amazon Basin. The Campos and Pantanal (q.v.) are the result of this seasonal climate. Areas of Argentina, Bolivia, Paraguay, and Uruguay are also affected.

Tropical Wet/Dry Climate is found in parts of the Indonesian Archipeligo. The northern coast of Australia is similarly affected. In this part of the Globe the pronounced seasonal rainfall is due to monsoonal wind flows bringing summer rains and winter dry seasons. See **MONSOON**.

In Africa and South America the cause is different. As the direct rays of the Sun trace a path between the Tropics of Cancer and Capricorn (q.v.), wind and pressure belts follow. Their shift is only through a narrower range of 5-10° of Latitude and tends to lag the Sun's shift. Small though the shift, the climatic effect can be enormous. See **SAHEL**.

The moist Rainforest Climate is entirely in the Doldrums Belt (q.v.) while the Tropical Wet/Dry is affected by the Tradewinds and Horse Latitudes (q.v.). The Tropical Wet/Dry does not have a wind and pressure belt of its own. It is in the boundary zone between the Doldrums and the Tradewinds.

TROPICS The Tropics of Cancer and Capricorn are imaginary lines drawn at 23°30' North and South Latitude respectively.

The Sun is overhead along the North Latitude line on June 21st, the 1st day of summer in the Northern Hemisphere. In the Southern Hemisphere, the Sun is overhead the South Latitude line on December 22nd. The Tropic circles separate the Temperate Zone from the Tropical.

TROPOSPHERE The lowermost layer of the Atmosphere, adjacent to the Earth's crust is the Troposphere. Unless there is an inversion (q.v.), temperatures in the Troposphere will decrease with altitude. Most weather is directly produced in the Troposphere.

The Troposphere tops out over the Equator at 18 kilometers (11 miles). Over the poles the top is 8 kilometers (5 miles). At the upper limit is a transitional zone or Tropopause. Above the Tropopause is the Stratosphere.

Ozone in the Troposphere is a trace gas which is rapidly building up to levels toxic to life. Ozone (q.v.), as a stratopheric gas, concentrates between 16-40 kilometers (10-25 miles) thus overlapping the top of the Troposphere. The Ozone Layer is important as a shield for the Earth against cosmic radiation.

At times of severe volcanism a layer of sulfates builds up because pyroclastics (q.v.) emit sulfur dioxide at high altitudes. Under ultraviolet light the pyroclastics break down into sulfur and oxygen above the Ozone Layer. See **OZONE LAYER, OZONE POLLUTION**.

TROUGH The region of cyclonic winds around a low pressure area is a trough. If the winds are jet streams, a jet trough can build below them and a trough cyclone can develop.

TROY SCALE The Troy Scale is used to measure gold and silver. 12 Troy ounces = 1 pound. 20 pennyweight = 1 ounce. 1 pennyweight = 480 grains.

TSUNAMI 'Tsunami' is Japanese for a storm wave. It is the oceanic wave accompanying an earthquake. The wave is incorrectly called tidal. The tsunami approaches the shore as a series of walls of water. Dr. Shepard (Scripps) recorded experiencing a tsunami in Hawaii where the 8th wave was the highest.

Earthquakes are frequently generated by volcanic activity at sea.

Energy from the quake travels the sea as low waves with a velocity between 660-830 kilometers (450-500) miles per hour. There may be 6 or more such waves, 8-50 kilometers (5-30 miles) apart. The wave is low, but the distance between crests is long, so lots of water can pile up at the shore. At Krakatoa, the wall of water reached 38 meters (125 feet). The tsunami death toll is high.

From a central base at Honolulu, 20 seismic stations and 40 tidal stations have been set up in the Pacific to monitor and record wave activity. It is still difficult to forecast tsunami heights, but warnings have proven effective.

TUATARA 'Rhyncocephalia' reptiles developed in the Permian (225 million years). The surviving tuatara is a lizard-like reptile with a 3rd eye on top of its head. The present population lives on islands off New Zealand having migrated over a land bridge 180 million years ago.

Early settlers fed their pigs on tuatara, almost making the reptiles extinct. The species is a living fossil (q.v.).

TUFF Tuff is volcanic ash and dust cemented to form a fine-grained sediment. Fragments are under 4 millimeters in diameter. They are usually of pumice and microscopic bits of glass.

Tuffs from rhyolitic or dacitic flows become welded while the fragments are still partly melted. These welded tuffs can be confused with lava flow banding. Welded tuffs form a dense, resistant rock that erodes to pinnacles. Yellowstone Canyon has welded ash flows.

TUNA The tuna is one of the most sought commercial and sport fishes. The fish are migratory. They have been known to school north from Brazil to Nova Scotia where they then take off for Europe. They 'hitch' a ride on the Gulf Stream as one authority put it. Some move into Mediterranean waters.

Tuna fisheries are often the subject of international confrontations. Like all the commercially sought fish, they are at times in danger from over-fishing (q.v.).

TUNDRA The treeless plains around the Arctic Circle abutting the Taiga (q.v.) form the Tundra. It is thin in Europe but in the USSR 10% of the land is Tundra. The Tundra Belt extends across Northern Canada and northern Alaska.

Arctic or Tundra Climate prevails in these northern lands and at high elevations at lower latitudes. In Canada, the Tundra Climate extends well south of the Arctic Circle into the region around James Bay, an arm of Hudson Bay, and to the west into a large area known as Barrenlands.

Tundra Climate is bleak with long cold winters, and no summer temperature above 50° Fahrenheit. The growing season is at the most 2.5 months and precipitation is below 25 centimeters (10 inches). Water is tied up in glaciers at least 9 months a year.

The Arctic Tundra is wind-swept and 75% cloud covered. Surfaces are permafrosted to great depths. The shallow soil above permafrost (q.v.) tends to become water-logged in summer.

In the Alpine Tundra fungal growth is especially prolific. An estimated 2 tons per acre of fungi are produced in these moist soils. Peat develops to a depth of 1-2 meters (3-6 feet) in about 12,000 years.

Flowering herbaceous plants, those with little woody tissue, are common to the Tundra. Moss and lichen compete well. Wildflowers like the anemone, buttercup, and gentian are common. There are bogs (q.v.) and moors with vegetation not considered climax. Birch, willow and a similar vegetation invade drying muskeg (q.v.) on the Canadian moors.

Tundra fauna are specially adapted. They include the lemming, musk-ox, polar bear, caribou, reindeer, snowy owl, and the wolf.

Rock weathering in the Alpine Tundra of the Wyoming Tetons creates great, sorted boulder fields, the largest at the lowest level. Each field has its own plant and animal community.

TUNDRA POLYGONS In the Swedish Tundra, polygons (4-5 sided) with diameters of 10-40 meters (30-130 feet) are found on the surface. Polygon boundaries are trenches. Within larger polygons, there are smaller ones.

How these polygons formed has not yet been established. It is thought that they arise from thermal contraction or dessication. Smaller polygons appear to form from dessication. Once a crack reaches the surface, it becomes subject to ice wedging. Polygons may have resulted from initial frost heave when permafrost began to develop.

TUNGSTEN Tungsten is a valuable metal with a melting point of 3,350° Celsius. The chief ore of tungsten is wolframite, while scheelite is also important.

Worldwide tungsten resources are 6.1 million metric tons of which Southeast China holds about 35%. China produces 50% of the world's supply. 1989 world reserves in thousands of metric tons are found primarily in:

China	1,200
Canada	260
USSR	280
United States	150
Australia	130
Bolivia	45
Korea, ROK	58
Thailand	30
Portugal	26
Brazil	20
France	20

U.S. Bureau of Mines, 1990

The United States now imports 73% of its needs. Domestic consumption increased from 14 to 25.5 million pounds of metal from 1975-1980. The figure is expected to reach 58 million pounds by the year 2000. The use of titanium carbide and other substitutes could reduce this figure.

The stockpile (q.v.) goal of 25,152 metric tons of ore and concentrate is almost attained. The government also stockpiles metal powder, ferro-tungsten and tungsten carbide powder.

In the United States, 70% of the tungsten is used in metallurgy, mining, and construction. It is a major constituent of hardened steels. Tungsten carbide is one of the hardest of all metal alloys. It strengthens high speed cutting tools. 15% is used in electronics. It is favored because of its high melting point.

TUNGUSKA A remarkable explosion occurred in the Tunguska River Basin of Siberia in 1908. The force felled millions of trees and 500 miles away, horses were unable to stand. The shock was felt around the world and the Earth's Magnetic Field was affected.

The atmospheric wave that was generated was recorded at Potsdam, Holland. The wave travelled around the world in both directions.

Tunguska had an oval pattern of destruction. Most authorities calculate that the explosion occurred 3.3 kilometers (2 miles) up in the air. It has been estimated as 1500 times more powerful than Hiroshima. The temperature rose to tens of millions of degrees, such as only occurs with nuclear fission.

Above normal radiation was found many years later. Fused minerals at the site suggest radiation. Other phenomena of atomic sites were found such as the burn patterns on trees, accelerated growth of new trees, and genetic alteration in some plants. The date of this event (1908) was well in advance of the Nuclear Era.

TURBIDITY CURRENTS Turbidity currents are slurries of seawater and sediment. Currents transfer sediments from the continental slopes to the abyssal plains. Turbidity currents, because of their great density, can set up internal waves (q.v.). The effect of such a current is very like an earthquake. The currents may be triggered by slumping, earthquake, or by great density contrasts.

Turbidity currents can be 100 meters (300 feet deep) and up to 5 kilometers (3 miles) long. Studies show they reach an average speed of 10 kilometers (6 miles) per hour, and accelerate downslope.

Turbidity currents have become better known since 1929, when they caused a break in the Trans-Atlantic Cable off the Grand Banks off Newfoundland.

TURFAN DEPRESSION Turfan (or Turpan) Depression is a vast area in northeast Sinkiang on the northern branch of the Old Silk Road through China. It consists of 2 main valleys in the Tien Shan Mountains (q.v.) separated by the Fire Mountains, a long wall of red sandstone hills.

One valley is higher and gravel-filled. The gravel soaks up water from the glaciated mountains. The northern and higher valley is fed by streams and is irrigated. The southern valley drops 153 meters (505 feet) below sea level.

TURKESTAN DESERT The Turkestan Desert is one of the largest Asian deserts. It is in the southwest USSR. The desert extends over 1.94 million square kilometers (0.75 million square miles).

TURQUOISE Copper aluminum phosphate, or turquoise, was so prized by the Egyptians, they made imitations. Turquoise, light blue to blue-green in color, has a hardness of 5-6 (Moh's Scale) and has a waxy luster. It occurs as knobby concretions in veinlets. The best quality in the United States today is from Duval Mine of Kingman, Arizona.

TURTLE GRASS Turtle grass is a flowering plant found in shallow seas. Underwater meadows, 'turtle grass flats', shelter sea turtles. The turtles live off the smaller sea creatures inhabiting the grass.

TVA The Tennessee Valley Authority (TVA) was the largest hydrological modification made up to its time (1930's). It serves a multi-state net with hydroelectric power and flood control.

Many streams were dammed and 26 lakes created. The project transformed the landscape from Tennessee to Mississippi and Alabama in addition to having a major economic effect on the area.

Many archaeological sites were engulfed although attempts were made to salvage material. There were many alterations that resulted in enormous changes in the ecosystems of the region.

TYNAGH MINE The famous lead and zinc mines of Tynagh, Galway, Ireland, contain primary sulfides in place in reef limestones. A few hundred feet away and outside the reef are a narrow band of volcanic tuffs and iron interbedded with carbonaceous shales.

The Red Sea sulfide deposition and that of the Galapagos Hot Spot illustrate what may have been the origin. See **RED SEA HOT SPOTS**.

TYPE LOCALITY The location where a rock type is first found is often considered the type locality. The type locality may be where a rock formation was first recognized or a species of plant or animal first encountered.

Sometimes another locality is substituted as a type locality for a rock formation because a better exposure of sediments or sequence was discovered. Rock type localities are compared with new discoveries of a similar nature to determine age and facies (q.v.) correlations.

Type localities for plants and animals have been of value in understanding distributions and genetic information. Often the type locality is a source of germ plasm (q.v.) for important plant species.

TYPHOONS The name, 'typhoon' is derived from the Chinese word for great winds. A typhoon results from an abnormally low Equatorial Pressure Area. It occurs within a belt which extends at a maximum between 6° and 35° North and South of the Equator. A tropical cyclone results from the low. See **CYCLONE**.

There are about 25 storms a year between July and November in the Northern Hemisphere. The Equatorial Low Pressure Area straddles the Thermal Equator where the Tradewind Belts converge. This area, which moves with the sun, is the Intertropical Convergence Zone (q.v.). This ITC zone and the Doldrums (q.v.) can be 5 or more degrees from the Geographic Equator due to reflective atmospheric forces on the Earth's rotation. These forces can create the tropical cyclones responsible for hurricanes and typhoons.

The Doldrums extend from Eastern Equatorial Africa to the Central Pacific and there are belts of Doldrums off the West Coasts of Africa and Central America.

A typhoon is similar to the hurricane (q.v.) but is of greater intensity. It is confined to the Western Pacific Ocean. The areas most affected are the Philippines, the Ryukyus, the South China Sea and the Taiwan Strait. The storm is developed over water and is accompanied by high seas. It forms a northwest trajectory and progresses in the Tradewinds Belt at about 5-6 miles per hour but on occasion can reach 20 when it encounters Westerly Winds. The internal motion, counterclockwise in the Northern Hemisphere and clockwise in the Southern Hemisphere, is up to 150 miles per hour. The accompanying cloud cover can attain a diameter of 2,000 miles. The eye will be virtually calm with clear skies and maximum winds of up to 25 miles per hour.

U

U-SHAPED VALLEY Glacially carved valleys have a characteristic U-shape. The glaciers plucked rocks from any terrain in their paths. Scouring action left flat valley floors and vertical walls. Yosemite Valley, California, is a good example.

UFO'S UFO is an Airforce acronym for 'unidentified flying object'. All such sightings are carefully recorded and evaluated.

In popular usage, UFO has come to mean flying saucers or craft from Outer Space or other planets. The existence of UFO's is not denied. The explanations for many of them have not been accepted.

UFO's were reported thousands of years ago in China and Egypt. Some sightings result from atmospheric effects but most have never been explained.

UGANDA The African nation of Uganda is in the Great Rift Valley. It is known as the 'Cradle of the Nile'. Victoria Lake (q.v.) source of the White Nile, is in the southeast. The Ruwenzoris (Ptolomy's 'Mountains of the Moon') are along the Western Rift. Mt. Ruwenzori reaches 5,089 meters (16,794 feet).

Uganda is crossed by 2 mineralized carbonatite (q.v.) belts. The easternmost is along the Kenya-Uganda border and west of the Eastern Rift. The western belt is along the Congo-Uganda border and is associated with the Western Rift. This belt is northeast of Lake Edward (q.v.). The western belt extends into Congo (Zaire) and includes the Lueshe Carbonatite.

UINTA BASIN Uinta Basin, Utah, is called Dinosaurland because of the huge number of Mesozoic fossil reptiles discovered there. See **DINOSAUR**.

Uinta Beast (Uintatherian), America's largest land mammal, also left fossils in the Uinta Basin. Uinta roamed the region in the Eocene (40 million years ago).

UINTA MOUNTAINS The Uinta Mountains, Utah, are the only truly east-west range in the United States. King's Peak reaches 4,100 meters (13,528 feet).

ULTRA-BASIC ROCKS Rocks with a silica content of less than 45% are ultra-basic. They are generally dark and dense due to the high content of ferromagnesium minerals. See **FERROMAGNESIUM**.

ULTRA-VIOLET RAYS Ultra-violet rays extend from the violet end of the spectrum of visible light down to 25 Ångstroms in the shortwave range. No boundary separates visible from ultra-violet light, just a gradation.

The Atmosphere protects the Earth from solar ultra-violet rays. These can be harmful to humans, causing skin cancer if exposure to direct sunlight is prolonged. The ultra-violet dosage is cumulative.

Ultra-violet radiation is more intense at high elevations. It is particularly so in high altitude snowfields where there is an additional reflective source. The radiation is greater at High Latitudes in both hemispheres because of the structure of the Earth's Magnetic Field and the snow cover. See **MAGNETIC FIELD.**

UNCONFORMITY An unconformity is a buried irregular erosional surface. It separates younger overlying rocks from more ancient ones below. The horizon represents a gap or hiatus in deposition during which erosion was working on the surface landscape. Frequently sediments overlie eroded basement rocks.

There are 3 types of unconformities. They are the:

- Disconformity - An irregular erosion surface between otherwise conformable layers.
- Non-conformity - Younger sedimentary rocks overlie plutonic (q.v.) ones.
- Angular unconformity. Dipping rocks are overlain by flat-lying sediments.

All are related to the contact between sediments and the underlying earlier surface.

UNDERSTORY   In a tropical or subtropical rainforest (q.v.) plant growth is layered. The understory is all growth beneath the canopy (q.v.).

Rainforests produce $40 billion of medicines annually from the understory. About $20 million are invested annually to study this facet of forest pharmacology. Virtually no money has been invested in the study of the canopy (q.v.) which remains very much unexplored.

UNDERTOW As waves break along a shore, a counter current develops along the seafloor. This current carries fine sediments out to sea.

The velocity of the undertow is related to sea state. Undertows can be extremely hazardous to swimmers.

UNIFORMITY The geological concept of uniformity refers to the internal and external processes operative on the planet. It holds that these processes have been operating throughout geological time at about the same rates.

UNIVERSE The Universe is the sum of all matter and the space it occupies. The matter is made up of protons, neutrons, and electrons. The term Universe has been limited by some to the Milky Way Galaxy (q.v.) to which the Solar System belongs.

Limiting the Universe to our own galaxy implies there are many universes. There are an estimated 600 billion galaxies each containing 100's of billions of stars.

Theory contends that 15-20 billion years ago, the density of matter was infinite. Matter was suddenly released and the Universe expanded and is continuing to do so. There is no empty Space only Space with ionized gases. Between the galaxies, Space is filled with electromagnetic radiation.

The early hot phase is substantiated by the existence of a cosmic microwave background radiation. The Big Bang Theory (q.v.) does not invalidate the existence of the Universe prior to that Cosmic Event. It rather demonstrates a change of form.

Those who contend an ultimate collapse or reversal of expansion assume an 80 billion-year cycle based upon astrophysics. At the end of the cycle another explosion would occur and a new cycle would begin.

UNLOADING When confining pressures are released, rock masses expand and unload layers in slabs or spalls. When granite is released by glacial unloading or other overburden is removed, it spalls in concentric shells. The process is exfoliation (q.v.).

Unloading may take form of minute shedding or huge slabs off the side of a mountain. Unloading effects may be felt to great depths and cause shifting among sediments.

UNKAR SERIES Sedimentary rocks of the 800 million-year-old Unkar Series in the Grand Canyon (q.v.) contain some of the oldest of lifeforms.

UNPAIRED ELECTRONS In an atom most electrons have a single spin direction and are paired with electrons with an opposite spin. Electron-pairing takes place within a single orbital shell.

Where insufficient electrons with opposing spins occur, electrons are left unpaired. Many Rare Earth Elements (q.v.) have this unpairing in the 4f shell.

UNSORTED SEDIMENTS Glacial moraines (q.v.) deposit unsorted sediments of sand, pebbles, cobbles, and boulders intermixed with clay.

UPLAND TROPICAL CLIMATE The climate the Tropics, whether dry or humid, changes with elevation. Tropical mountain climates, as in Brazil, Ecuador, Columbia, India, Kenya, and Peru, are most favorable to humans. Major tropical cities have grown up in these highland areas. Some notable ones are Cali, Columbia; Nairobi, Kenya; and Sao Paulo, Brazil.

Successful tropical agriculture has been carried out in these upland areas. They are famous for the production of coffee, tea, upland rice, and legumes.

UPLANDS All land of measureable relief above sea level is part of the uplands. The exceptions are found in depressions or lands near the sea. Hills, plateaus, and mountains are uplands.

UPWELLING Upwelling to the surface layers of deep oceanic waters is the result of divergence and offshore currents. Strong winds, blowing seaward from the land, build up huge walls of water and blow them across the sea surface. Waves are generated to the right in the Northern Hemisphere and to the left in the Southern Hemisphere.

Displaced surface water is replaced from below and the water becomes a convection cell. Cold upwelling water brings fresh nutrients to the surface. The presence of these nutrients attracts organisms to feed in the area.

Between Cape Mendocino and Point Conception, California, is an upwelling zone. In spring and summer severe northwest winds parallel the coast. Surface waters are pushed out to sea.

Upwelling, brings cold, deep-sea waters with nitrates, phosphorus, and other minerals to the upper layers. When nutrient-rich plumes reach the level to which light penetrates, there is a virtual explosion of plankton (q.v.). The bloom covers miles of sea surface.

Some well known areas of upwelling are found in waters off Peru, Chile, Mexico, the Florida Keys, Madras, Malabar, Walvis Bay, and along the Arabian Coast between Aden and Perim. These are areas of celebrated fisheries.

URAL MOUNTAINS The Ural Mountains in the USSR have long been considered the boundary and gateway between Europe and Asia. The Urals are a series of ranges which extend approximately north-south for 2,000 kilometers (1,240 miles). The mountains are higher in the north near the Arctic Circle. In this part of the system, the climate is Tundra and the mountains have barren peaks or glaciers. Ural slopes are generally covered in mountain forest, principally Taiga vegetation.

In the southern Urals are many notable mineral deposits. among them chromite and iron. On the Siberian side of the Urals, the USSR has its largest iron and steel plant at Magnitogorsk.

URANINITE Uraninite or pitchblende is a polymetallic ore containing 80-90% uranium. Micas, arsenates, phosphates, and sulfates are associated with thorium, radium, and polonium. Uraninite is found at Great Bear Lake, Canada; Colorado in the United States; Czechoslovakia; Katanga (Congo); Portugal; and the USSR. Economic deposits are relatively rare.

URANIUM Uranium is a silver-colored polyvalent metal with 3 naturally occurring radioactive isotopes. U-234, U-235, and U-238. Most uranium in the United States is from carnotite, an uranium-vanadium ore found in Colorado Plateau sandstones. 90% of United States uranium production is from its sandstones. Non-sandstone uranium sources are more prevalent in other parts of the world. These include metasediments in Australia, pebble conglomerate in South Africa and Brazil, and pegmatites in many countries.

Natural uranium contains 99.3% U-238, 0.7% U-235, and a trace of U-234. From crystallization, uranium begins to change in chain-reaction to helium and ultimately to radiogenic lead. The intervening isotopes in the chain are 'daughter elements'.

Uranium-238 has 92 protons and 146 neutrons. Its decay stream gives off helium nuclei or alpha particles. Radiogenic lead has 82 protons and 124 neutrons and has an atomic weight half that of Uranium-238. The half-life (q.v.) of uranium is 4.51 billion years for Uranium-238 and 700 million years for Uranium-235.

It is conjectured that uranium synthesized in galaxies about 10 billion years ago. The oldest dated planetary rocks are 4.6-4.8 billion years. Uranium isotope ratios and the uranium-lead ratio have been useful in dating these rocks.

As a fuel in nuclear energy generation, uranium must be enriched. In this process, the isotope percentage is artificially elevated over natural uranium. This is an expensive process and in the United States has been carried out by the Government. The cost of uranium enrichment has never really been included in the cost to power plants. Even when enriched uranium has been sold to other nations, its cost of production has never been revealed. As long as this continues, the true cost of nuclear energy remains hidden.

URANIUM DAUGHTERS In about 4.5 billion years 50% of the nuclides or elements from radioactive decay of uranium will have become radiogenic lead. Isotopes, the daughter elements, in the decay chain each have a half-life (q.v.). These isotopes belong to the Uranium Series. See **RADIOACTIVE DECAY**.

The Uranium Series is as follows:

Element	Atomic Particle Particle	Half-life	Element
Uranium, U-238	Alpha	4.5×10^9 years	Radium
Radium, Ra-226	Alpha	1600 years	Radon
Radon, Rn-222	Alpha	3.82 days	Polonium
Polonium, Po-218	Alpha	3.05 minutes	Lead
Lead, Pb-214	Beta	26.8 minutes	Bismuth
Bismuth, Bi-214	Alpha/Beta	19.7 minutes	Lead
Lead, Pb-210	Beta	21 years	Bismuth
Bismuth, Bi-210	Beta	5 days	Polonium
Polonium, Po-210	Alpha	138 days	Lead
Lead, Pb-206	Stable		

URANUS Voyager I, in 1985-86, obtained data and photographs which may alter previously held planetary theories. Uranus is the 7th planet from the Sun in the Solar System. It has 4 times the diameter of the Earth and a mass 14.6 times greater. Its Atmosphere is blue-green

(Hydrogen, helium, and methane absorb red light). Uranus has 15 moons and 10 planetary rings (q.v.).

Only Venus and Uranus do not rotate in the same direction as the Sun. Uranus has an 84-year orbit and a 17-hour day. Its Magnetic Field is 50 times greater than the Earth's. Data have not yet been analyzed but the Magnetic Field appears to be oriented 55° to the rotational axis.

URBANIZATION The late 20th Century has seen explosive growth of urban areas. This is especially obvious in the developing nations. The increasing populations have resulted from a great migration from the rural areas to the cities. Shanty towns are common in the midst of great cities. The people in these improvised shelters are lacking in the basics of public health. Communicable disease is rampant.

Cities which have not felt the great migration waves of Africa and Latin America have still felt the problems of increased population. Changing technology has eliminated many employment possibilities and changed work patterns. Migrants can not always find employment.

Population pressure, unemployment or underemployment, crime, and pollution afflict most of the world's major cities, and not just in developing countries. Transportation in large, highly urbanized areas has become a major problem and grid-lock is becoming increasingly common. Transportation contributes greatly to air pollution.

The contribution to global air pollution of the highly urbanized areas is tremendous. It has been said that the air in the major cities has become cleaner in recent years. It is, however, only true in the optical sense. The chemical burden continues to be great.

UREA Urea was the first organic compound ever synthesized. Its discovery by Wohler in 1828 set off a controversy in religious thought. It was felt that man, in creating molecules, was usurping God's prerogatives. The intellectual battle was waged for years.

Natural urea is an end product of protein decomposition. In mammals, it is the main solid from urine production.

Today, the compound urea is most used as a soil conditioner. It contains 46% nitrogen. For fertilizer, urea is produced by compressing carbon dioxide and ammonia (q.v.) under high pressure. The dehydration causes the product to yield urea and water. More than 1/4 of all ammonia (q.v.) is used in the production of urea.

URSA MAJOR Ursa Major (Great Bear) or Big Dipper is one of the most easily recognized constellations in the Milky Way Galaxy. Ursa Major is in the northern sky and 2 of its stars point to Polaris (q.v.).

URSA MINOR Ursa Minor (Small Bear) or Little Dipper is a 7-star constellation in the Milky Way. The constellation is in the northern part of the heavens. Polaris, the North Star, is at the tip of the dipper handle.

The Earth's axis presently points toward Polaris which appears stationary. It has long been a guide to navigators. Latitude can be found by measuring the angle from the horizon to the North Star. This is corrected for the difference of Polaris' location with reference to the Celestial Pole. The Pole is 1 of 2 about which the stars make an apparent diurnal rotation.

USSR The USSR (Union of Soviet Socialist Republics) is the largest political entity. It covers 1/6 of the world. The Soviet Union encompasses 22.4 million square kilometers (8.65 million square miles), 75% of which is in Asia. The USSR makes up 1/3 of Asia and 1/2 of Europe. The nation is roughly divided into:

- Taiga Forest (The world's largest forest) 50%
- Forest/Steppe 20%
- Great Plain (Subtropical) 10%
- Deserts 10%
- Arctic Tundra 10%

Much of the Arctic Tundra is desert since precipitation is minimal and water is locked up in the ice. The Taiga Forest is mostly marshland and permafrosted to great depths. In the northern cold areas depths of from 330-660 meters (1,000-2,000 feet) are not uncommon. One layer of permafrost found in Siberia measured 1,490 meters (4,921 feet). See **PERMAFROST**.

Major rivers in the USSR flow north and south and a number of mountain ranges have the same orientation. Those of the southern border are high east-west ranges. There are 2 inland seas, the Caspian and Aral, and the world's deepest lake is Baikal (q.v.).

The USSR is the only industrial nation that is self-sufficient in energy. For all minerals in short supply, the government maintains a stockpile. In the past 3 decades, exploration and development have greatly decreased outside dependence.

UWEINAT CRATER Uweinat Crater on the Sudan-Libyan border has a diameter of 4 kilometers (2.4 miles). Landsat imagery shows the crater to have surrounding light and dark bands similar to Martian craters. The isolated crater is interesting because there are no other volcanics in the Jebel Uweiwat area. The basement was described originally by surveyors from Shell and British Petroleum. They did not describe the crater. Later explorations defined a ring complex of Paleozoic rocks. The major rock types are metasediments and igneous intrusions of the basement complex.

UYUNI SALAR Uyuni is the largest of the Andean salars (q.v.). It covers 9,000 square kilometers (3,500 square miles) in Bolivia. It has a flat, smooth surface and contains many valuable salts and brines.

Salar de Uyuni is high in the Andes at 4,000 meters (13,200 feet). There is a very low evaporate at this altitude. This implies that these deposits were emplaced when the range was still very young.

Production for Uyuni would be competitive with Chile's output and the proposed production from Argentinean salars of Hombre Muerto and Rincon. These were being evaluated in 1987-1988. The enormous freight rates to the Pacific Coast are a limiting factor. The association of American interests for the development of Salar de Uyuni was called off because of a political impasse in 1990.

Uyuni is the major and richest of the Bolivian salars. The country has enormous lithium and brine reserves. In 1988 the U.S. Bureau of Mines put these reserves at 6 million short tons.

V

VACUUM 'Vacuum' is from the Latin for empty. In physics, a vaccuum is a space that is totally devoid of matter in the solid, liquid, gaseous, or plasma state. An absolute vacuum is probably an impossibility to achieve but the creation of partial vacuums have greatly advanced science and technology.

VADOSE WATER Soil water held in the zone of aeration above the water table (q.v.) is 'vadose'. It is of meteoric origin. Vadose water, originating with rain or snow, fluctuates with precipitation.

VALDEZ OIL SPILL The worst oil spill in modern tanker history occurred in Prince William Sound, Alaska, in March, 1989. The tanker, Valdez, belonging to EXXON, struck a reef and spilled an estimated 462 million barrels (11 million gallons) of oil into the Sound.

The ecological damage to the marine environment and shoreline of the Sound and beyond was enormous. Many species of plants and animals have been affected. The human population dependent upon this environment was disrupted. Some of the world's most valuable fisheries were endangered. Sea mammals were greatly affected. The otter community was decimated. Birds by the millions were lost or injured. It will take years to restore the area at least in part.

The cleanup effort lasted until winter set in. Some effort is still underway in early 1990. It is still too soon to estimate the long term effect on the once rich environment.

VALENCE Valence is a chemical measure of an element's ability to combine with one or more other elements.

In biology, valence refers to the organism's ability to react or unite, as with antigens of the immune system.

VALLES CALDERA Valles Caldera, on the west side of the Jemez Mountains, New Mexico, is an Early-Pleistocene volcano. Its summit was torn off in a violent eruption. After which, the Valles Volcano collapsed in upon itself.

Valles Caldera is more than 21 kilometers (13 miles) in diameter. An estimated 103 cubic kilometers (50 cubic miles) of rhyolitic pyroclasts (q.v.) were ejected.

VALLEY GLACIERS On high mountains, glaciers can develop in small basins. These cirque glaciers tend to move down slope, cutting a channel when they have sufficient mass. It becomes a valley glacier as it moves, scouring a channel. Antecedent stream channels have often been deepened by these glaciers.

The valley glacier moves at different velocities throughout its length, increasing with slope and narrowing of the valley. Shear causes the mass to move along the contact plane. Glaciers carve characteristic U-shaped valleys and build terminal and lateral moraines (q.v.).

VALLEYS Valleys are cut by streams and glaciers. The initial activity creates narrow, steep valleys. Some factors affecting the shape of the valley are the:

- Rock or sediment being cut
- Stream velocity
- Bed load, its quantity, size, and scour capacity
- Relation of the valley to base level (q.v.).

Youthful streams originating in high mountains tend to cut steep V-shaped valleys. Glaciers cut U-shaped valleys (q.v.). More mature streams widen the valleys and the stream has a gentle profile. Valleys can be lengthened by headward erosion and by the building up of a delta area. Deposition of sediments builds a broad valley. They are widened by planation and they may be deepened and widened by valley glaciers (q.v.).

Many valleys are grabens (q.v.) between upthrust ranges. The Rhine flows through such a graben. Death Valley, California is a graben flanked by the Panamint and Amargosa ranges. These mountains are cut by many deep, narrow, V-shaped valleys cut by rapid, youthful streams in flood. Most were cut during a less arid epoch than the present.

The Kali Gandaki River of Nepal has cut the deepest valley in the world between Annapurna Mountain (5th highest) and Dhaulagiri. The valley is 6 kilometers (3.6 miles) deep. The river rising on the Tibetan Plateau flows to the Ganges through a channel cut by an antecedent stream (q.v.).

The Great Valley of California is the largest mountain enclosed valley in the world. It lies between the Sierra Nevada and the Coast Ranges. It, with Imperial Valley, is considered the world's most productive agricultural area. It is almost entirely an irrigated agriculture.

Some Great Valley sediments have been mineralized and some productive oil wells located. Uranium and other minerals including placer gold are found in the area.

VAN ALLEN BELTS A series of electromagnetic radiation belts were discovered by Van Allen in 1951. They are between 1,330 and 66,700 kilometers (800 and 40,000 miles) into Space. The belts of intense radiation are composed of trapped, charged particles held in place by the Earth's Magnetic Field. The region of the Van Allen Belts is in the Magnetosphere.

Some of the particle load held in the Magnetosphere is dropped into the Atmosphere via windows at the poles. The particles set off the 'Aurora Borealis' or Northern Lights.

Knowledge of the Van Allen Belts is critical to Space flights and special flights such as that of the Explorer Magellan have supplied useful data.

VANCOUVER ISLAND Vancouver is the largest island off the Pacific Coast of North America. It is a remnant of Cascadia, a landmass which sank in what has been called a 'convulsion' some 40 million years ago. The event left only Vancouver and Queen Charlotte Islands. Both islands today protect the Inland Passage to Skagway, Alaska, a 1,600 kilometer (1,000 mile) route.

Vancouver's coast is rocky and rugged and has beautiful fjords (q.v.). The island is densely forested and includes the renowned Cathedral Grove.

VARA A 'vara' is an old Latin American length measure still found on Land Grant deeds. It has different values, between 79 and 86 centimeters (31 and 34 inches) depending upon location. In Texas, the vara is 33.3, in California 33, and in Mexico 32.99 inches.

VARVE Lacustrine (lake) or glacial deposits of alternating clays and silts indicate cycles. The combination of a clay and silt layer makes up a 'varve', Swedish for cycle. Varve thickness varies from 1 millimeter to 2-3 centimeters (up to 1.2 inches).

Inflow to a lake may vary seasonally. When it is rapid or when a glacier is melting, large amounts of sand, clay, and silt are deposited. Sand and silt will readily settle and form light-colored sediments. Clays, being lightweight, continue to float and only settle when flows abate. They form the darker sediment layers.

In temperate climate lakes, sand and silt accumulate in summer and clay and organic material in winter. The 2 layers form the varve or 1 cycle. The oldest varved clays recorded were deposited in 13,000 B.C. a radiocarbon date of a glacial epoch of melting.

VARZEA 'Varzea' is Portuguese for the low, fertile floodplain along streams. In the Amazon Basin, the varzea is very broad and silty with an elevation seldom exceeding a few meters (10 feet). It is seasonally flooded. Natural levees built by the river are often forested. Elevated floodplains are limited.

Some Amazon tributaries have virtually no varzea but others like the Rio Negro have varzeas several kilometers wide, much of it covered by 'igapo' forest (q.v.).

VATNA GLACIER Iceland's Vatna Glacier was calved from the Ice Cap and moves at the rate of 1,800 meters (6,000 feet) a year and supplies a number of major streams. Vatna is larger than all the European glaciers combined. It is 900 meters (3,000 feet) thick and covers 8,300 square kilometers (3,200 square miles).

Many volcanic peaks are buried beneath the ice. When an eruption occurs, there is very rapid melting. When the water breaks through, it is as a wall. In 1934, one of these moved at 100 kilometers (60 miles) per hour creating an enormous flood. Eruptions occur at approximately 10-year intervals.

The vast flood leaves behind enormous amounts of glacial debris which can alter stream channels, obliterate meadows, and cause stream capture.

VECTOR A vector is a quantity with a value and a direction. It can be used to define a physical entity, its magnitude (velocity) and direction.

Biologically, a vector is an organism capable of carrying and transmitting disease.

VEGETATIVE COVER Mineral exploration in areas covered by dense Tropical Rainforest has been virtually impossible until the last few decades. Mining had been confined to laterites and placers.

Remote sensors such as SLAR (q.v.) and satellite imagery have made mapping possible. Half the Earth's rainforests are underlain by Precambrian Shield and about 20% of the remainder are in Post-Paleozoic fold belts.

VEGETATIVE ZONES Climate changes with latitude and elevation. These changes have been equated to vegetation zones. These zones are:

- Tundra - Above Latitude 58° and above the timberline at lower latitudes. At the Equator above 2,500 meters (8,250 feet)
- Taiga (Conifers) - Above Latitude 30° and above 1,000 meters (3,000 feet) in the Tropics
- Deciduous Forest - Overlaps Subtropical and above 1,200 meters (4,000 feet) in the Tropics
- Subtropical - From Tropic of Cancer to Capricorn. The forests are more arid than moist. Savanna and gallery forest
- Rainforest/Jungle - Low elevations in moist Tropics and Subtropics.

VEIN Any rock fracture filled with minerals is a vein. If minor, it is a veinlet. If small but associated with a larger vein, it is a stringer. Fractures and faults provide channels for mineralizing solutions.

Unusually thick or large veins or groups of veins are called a lode. The Mother Lode system in California is an example of a series of veins. Usually these are formed in faults where repeated rupture led to later emplacements adding to total thickness.

Most metamorphosed rocks have vein systems that commonly lie at almost a right angle to lineations. Low-grade metamorphism gives rise to carbonates, epidote, and quartz along fractures.

VELDT The grasslands of South Africa are 'veld' or 'veldt'. They are subdivided into high and low. The High Veldt is barren of trees. Grass predominates and produces a root structure that holds water. The grass is tall, up to a meter (3 feet).

Streams in the High Veldt are intermittant and rainfall is in the summer months. It can be as much as 100 centimeters (40 inches). The area is subject to winter frosts.

The Low Veldt is drier with grasses, primarily 'Aristida', forming good pasture with a low carrying capacity. Rainfall is between 12.5 and 37.5 centimeters (5 and 15 inches). See **GRASSLANDS**.

VENEZUELA Venezuela is the 6th most important petroleum producer. The major fields are in the Lake Maracaibo Basin. In 1986, 1.5 million barrels a day were exported at $12.89 each. This was down sharply from the $25.70 of l985 when production was 1.4 million barrels.

Venezuela has 4 different physiographic regions:

- The Andes - Mountains west of Lake Maracaibo. Drainage is to the east via the Orinoco River. 25% of the area
- Llanos or grasslands - From Andes to Orinoco Basin. 33% of the country
- Guiana Highlands - Southern Venezuela and bordering Brazil
- Lake Maracaibo Basin (q.v.).

The Orinoco River System, 3rd largest in South America, rises on the low divide between it and the Amazon on the Brazilian border. The Orinoco is fed from the Columbian and Venezuelan Andes as it flows north. At La Urbana the river begins its eastward flow to its delta on the Atlantic.

The Venezuelan Rainforest in the northern part of the country was reduced by 1/3 between the years 1950-75 as the hinterland was opened up.

Cerro Bolivar, south of Ciudad Guayara, on the Orinoco is the major iron ore mine. It produces 15 million metric tons annually. 80% of this is used nationally the rest is exported.

Los Pijiguaos bauxite mine on the Orinoco is expected to produce a million metric tons a year from a reserve of 235 million metric tons. The alumina refinery is to produce 3 million metric tons a year of metal.

VENTIFACT Desert winds create ventifacts by the abrasion of bedrock and loose sediments. Wind-driven sands and silts sculpt stones to form the ventifact. It is polished, pitted and faceted with sharp ridges.

Experiments have shown that the facets always face the wind. Thus a multi-faceted stone indicates variations in wind direction.

VENUS Of all the planets, Venus has the size and mass most like that of the Earth. Its Atmosphere is 100 times more dense and is predominantly of carbon dioxide.

Volcanoes on the Venus surface have been observed as well as a great deal of lightning in the planet's Atmosphere.

Russian spacecraft have landed on Venus and reported temperatures of about 500° Celsius. This is a temperature at which many metals are molten. The high temperature is related to nearness to the Sun, planetary degassing, and the Greenhouse Effect (q.v.) of carbon dioxide.

On May 5, 1989, the Atlantis, the United States space shuttle, launched the Explorer Magellan on an historic mission to Venus. The voyage will take 15 months and it will be 1992 before data from the Mission become available.

VERKHOYANSK Verkhoyansk in northeast Siberia is the cold pole of the Northern Hemisphere. Temperatures have been recorded at -90° Fahrenheit.

VERMICULITE Vermiculite, a micaceous clay is an alteration product of biotite. It is used industrially as insulation and in agriculture as a soil conditioner. It is common in carbonatites (q.v.). At Phalaborwa South Africa (q.v.), vermiculite has developed on phlogopite in much the same way it has on Iron Mountain, Colorado.

At Dorowa, Zimbabwe, vermiculite in mica-apatite rocks occurs in dikes and stringers. At Catalao, Brazil, the carbonatite has been mined for vermiculite. There is a vermiculate hill 18 meters (60 feet high) the result of weathering. In Uganda, vermiculite also occurs as a residual derived from magnetite-apatite-phlogopite.

VERNIER A vernier is an enhancement of a portion of a main scale on an instrument and has a magnified ruler. On theodolites, it is useful for surveying. The vernier allows rod readings to be subdivided so that errors are minimized.

VERTEBRATES Animals with segmented spinal columns are vertebrates. They first appeared in the sea 250 million years ago. These first fish have an appearance similar to present-day hagfish.

Fossil mammals first appear in the Rhaetic Formation of Europe, at the Triassic-Jurassic boundary (195 m.y.).

VERTISOLS Vertisols, a relatively new soils group, are heavy, dark clays that shrink in dry seasons. The shrinkage is due to montmorillonite (q.v.).

Cotton or Regur Soils of India which extend over 60 million hectares (144 million acres) are vertisols. In Sudan, Badobe Soils cover 40 million hectares (96 million acres). In Australia, 'black earths' cover 70 million hectares (157 million acres).

VESCICLES Empty cavities resulting from gas expansion in volcanic rocks are vescicles. Vescicles have been called 'frozen bubbles'.

Vescicles may have any shape, but in any given rock, they are evenly spaced. Vescicles usually align with the direction of the lava flow. When a rock is completely vescicular, it becomes frothy. Such a rock is then called pumice (q.v.).

MOUNT VESUVIUS Vesuvius, near Naples, Italy, has been erupting intermittently since 79 A.D. when, it engulfed the cities of Pompeii and Herculaneum. That eruption was accompanied by poisonous gas, volcanic dust, ash, and a mud avalanche. Pliny, the Elder, was killed in the attempt to study the effects. The record of the event was made by his nephew, Pliny, the Younger.

Vesuvius grew out of an older volcano, Mount Somma. Vesuvias was covered with groves that flourished in the volcanic soils. In 63 A.D. a series of earthquakes shook the area, then smaller ones followed through the years until the major eruption. A great deal of the pumice and ash that buried Pompeii later was converted to welded tuff. Herculaneum was buried by the mud flow.

VIA SALARIA From Ostia, near Rome, to northeast Italy, is 'Via Salaria'. The road was built by Roman Legions for salt transport. Not only was the salt vital to life in the interior, but Roman soldiers were paid in salt.

LAKE VICTORIA Victoria is the 3rd largest lake in the world. It comes after the Caspian Sea (q.v.) and Lake Superior. Victoria borders Uganda, Kenya, and Tanzania and is astride the Equator at 1,240 meters 4,092 feet). The lake basin developed in Mid-Pleistocene as a result of tectonic flexing of the Earth's Crust. Victoria covers 68,635 square kilometers (26,500 square miles) on a 'sagged plateau' between 2 great branches of the East African Rift. To the north and east are Uganda and Kenya.

Most inflow is from the Burundi Highlands. Outflow is through an old river valley to a low point in the rift wall where the river plunges over Kabalega (Murchison) Falls into Albert Lake and the Albert Nile.

Victoria, an important water source for East Africa, is dotted with innumerable islands. Its average depth is 93 meters (307 feet). The lake is mixed by winds but stratified from January to May. It has 208 known fish species.

Ancient Lake Victoria (Kirunga) was formed during the Miocene by lava flows that created a dam. The lake drained to the west and lasted 22 million years according to potassium-argon dating (q.v.).

VICTORIA FALLS Victoria Falls on the Zambezi River (q.v.), Zimbabwe, bears the African name 'Mosi O Tunya' (smoke that thunders). The falls are 1.6 kilometers (1 mile) wide and the waters fall 106 meters (350 feet).

The falls flow over the basalt cliff into a fracture created slot. The slot is part of series created in basalt joints. These fractures are repeated upstream in the headward erosion which is the pattern of these falls.

Victoria is twice as high as Niagara and 1.5 times as wide. The falls are in a nature preserve maintained to resemble what the area was like when Dr. David Livingston discovered the falls.

VIKING EXPLORATIONS Between 800 and 1400 A.D. the Northern Hemisphere had a relatively warm climate. In Scandinavia there was a population explosion and the inhabitants went raiding. Their forays took them down the rivers of Russia to the Caspian Sea. They founded Greenland in this period. Vineland in Newfoundland was established in 1,000 A.D.

The climate turned cold and Atlantic pack ice made the seas to Greenland and Vineland impassable. Those overseas colonies perished. See **MINI ICE AGE.**

VIRUNGA MOUNTAINS The Virunga or Mfumbiro Mountains consist of 8 volcanoes on a vast lava plateau in eastern Zaire and southwest Uganda. The plateau is in the west branch of the East African Rift. Peaks are between 3,273 and 4,485 meters (10,800 and 14,800 feet). The westernmost is Nyiragongo (q.v.).

Volcanoes on the western end are active and successive eruptions have created billions of cubic meters of lava. From December 1912 to March 1913, a series of eruptions occurred in neighboring volcanoes. The lavas of each were distinctive indicating that they came from different magma chambers.

Earlier eruptions in the Virungas caused sufficient lava flows to build a dam which diverted the ancient Nile. Lake Kivu is a remnant of that river. Kivu's present outlet, the Ruzizi River, flows to Lake Tanganyika (q.v.).

VISIBLE LIGHT The spectrum (q.v.) of light waves includes the visible and invisible. Visible light corresponds to wavelengths between 0.4 and 0.7 microns per second. Light to which the human eye is sensitive is in these visible wavelengths.

VITYAZ The crew of the Russian Research Vessel, Vityaz, measured the Marianas Trench during IGY (International Geophysical Year). The trench measured 10,926 meters (36,056 feet) deep and 1.6 kilometers (1 mile) wide. The same cruise yielded evidence of life from a depth of 11 kilometers (6.7 miles) in the Kermadec Deep.

VISHNU SCHISTS Vishnu Schists in Grand Canyon's Granite Gorge are Precambrian and were laid down 1.7 billion years ago. They were later metamorphosed to form the Precambrian basement. The Vishnu have been intruded by Zoroaster Granites. Later they were uplifted, and exposed.

VOLATILES Volatiles are substances that may change phase from liquid to gas at ordinary temperatures and pressures.

VOLCANIC ASH Volcanic ash, in spite of the name, is not the result of combustion. It is dust-size rock ejected from a volcano. Grains are between 0.25-4.0 millimeters (less than 1/6 inch). Sufficient volcanic ash falling on a given area can cause asphixiation.

Ash, because of its light weight, is carried great distances by winds. In 512 A.D., ash from Vesuvius, Italy, fell in Constantinople (Istanbul), Turkey and Tripoli, Libya. An Irish volcano in 1875 sent ash to Stockholm, Sweden.

Volcanic ash that only travels a short distance and falls on slopes near the crater can pose a threat. Hot ash can move downslope at high velocity. Ashflows have been clocked up to 117 kilometers (70 miles) per hour.

Ash temperatures are hundreds of degrees. They incinerate everything in their path as at Arenal, Costa Rica, in 1968. Such an event is an 'ash avalanche'. A wide swath of forest was destroyed on Mount St. Helens (q.v.) from an ash avalanche in 1980.

VOLCANIC BOMB Chunks of rock ejected from volcanoes are bombs. They are smooth-surfaced and projectile-shaped, having cooled and congealed in transit. A 30,000-ton bomb was ejected from Vesuvius in 1906.

VOLCANIC BRECCIA Volcanic breccia are angular blocks forceably ejected from a volcano by gas pressure. Explosions cause fracturing of country rock and that rock is included in the breccia (q.v.).

VOLCANIC CONE A volcanic cone forms due to buildup of ejecta from the volcano. Cone material is made up of ash, bombs, lapilli, and lava. It tends to stratify due to gravity and weathering. Cone-in-cone structures are remnants of prior eruptions. A volcano may develop a broad central depression or crater in the cone.

VOLCANIC GAS Eruptions are influenced by the ease with which gas can escape the volcano. If gases are confined, the eruption will be explosive.

Volcanic gas is 66% steam, the rest is made up of such gases as carbon monoxide, carbon dioxide, and sulfur dioxide.

VOLCANIC NECK A vent opened during eruption tends to become filled with lava to form a plug. Around this plug, a debris cone forms and acts as a protective wall. When this wall has eroded away, more durable material may still be left. The resulting formation is a volcanic neck or plug. Shiprock, New Mexico, is an example. Some formations are rigid pinnacles. Edinburgh Castle, Scotland, is build on a neck.

VOLCANIC PIPE A cylindrical duct or vent links the magma chamber with the surface. The duct, pipe, or chimney allows gases to escape as well as lava. When lava congeals in the pipe or duct, a volcanic neck (q.v.) or chimney can result.

Pipes, filled with ultra-basic magma rising from great depths, may contain diamonds. These are kimberlite pipes (q.v.).

VOLCANISM Volcanism is a process of Earth renewal. New material is brought to the surface from within the Crust and Mantle. These events are often accompanied by earthquakes. Volcanism is also a mechanism whereby there is a continual degassing of the Earth.

There are 5 major volcano types with many variations:
- Shield - Hawaiian volcanoes
- Stromboli - A continuously erupting volcano
- Vulcanian, Plinian or Vesuvian - Explosive with a tarry lava
- Pelean - Explosive and gaseous
- Katmai - Famous for 'burning sands'.

Billions of tons of material are ejected onto the land or seafloor. Of the 850 known active volcanoes 60% are in the Pacific 'Ring of Fire'. Encircling volcanoes define Pacific Plate boundaries. Unknown numbers are on the seafloor. 10,000 are mapped.

Worldwide, volcanism is episodic with relatively short periods of intense activity. Many volcanoes have been considered inactive only to have them suddenly erupt.

Volcanism is not restricted to volcanoes. Great rifts and fissures, many in the oceans can channel magma to the surface.

VOLCANO A volcano is an individual expression of volcanism (q.v.). It is a hill or mountain ejecting magmatic material from time to time. Volcanoes line great fractures and rift systems and along island arcs. Java in Indonesia has 123 volcanoes, 13 of which are very destructive. Of Kamchatka's 125 volcanoes, 22 are active.

Not all volcano effects are destructive. It is the great island builder of the Pacific. Japan, the Philippines, and Hawaii are volcanic. Extraordinarily fertile soils as in Java are volcanic, ash having contributed many nutrient minerals.

Volcanic eruptions are said to be accompanied by special weather conditions. A special 'stillness' is commonly reported to occur prior to an eruption. Such a stillness occurred November 14, 1959, when a blue-gray mist blanketed Kilauea, Hawaii. It erupted at 8:09 in the evening. The 'fire fountain' leaped 575 meters (1900 feet).

Global as well as local weather is affected by eruptions. If particulates reach the upper Atmosphere, they can encircle the globe. In 1783, volcanoes erupted explosively, in Japan and Iceland. Dust was so great solar heating was cut off and the winter 1783-84 was the coldest recorded in Europe and North America.

Increased dust can reduce temperatures 3°-5° Celsius (6°-10° Fahrenheit). Should the condition persist a few years, an Ice Age climate would prevail.

Since explosive volcanoes emit steam as a major gas, torrential rains can fall in the area. Herculeaneum was buried in a mudslide due to this phenomenon. In recent times similar conditions have prevailed in the Andes.

VOLCANOGENIC ORE DEPOSITS Massive copper and zinc sulfides associated with iron and chert were considered structurally controlled replacement bodies. They are, instead related to a tuffaceous phase of volcanism. Canadian deposits fit into the last rhyolite phase. Kalliokoski (Michigan Tech) found massive sulfides (2.6 billion years old) predating folding.

Sulfide deposition in hot spots (q.v.) in mid-oceanic rifts are a significant indicator of the origin of such deposits as those on the Island of Cyprus.

VOLGA RIVER The Volga River drains the Volga Basin in the Great Russian Plain which makes up 1/3 of Europe. The river rises southwest of Moscow and circles to join the Moscow River east of the city. It is linked to the Moscow-Volga Canal.

The 130 kilometer (80 mile) Volga Canal allows Moscow to be a port. The Volga is linked to the Don and the Mediterranean by another canal. A third series of canals links the Volga to the north to the Baltic and White Seas. In winter, the entire system freezes.

The Volga's course to the Caspian Sea is 3,834 kilometers (2300 miles) long. There are 7 major hydroelectric plants producing 11.5 billion kilowatts of power along the Volga's course. One of the world's largest artificial lakes, Rybinsk, is associated with this system.

VREDEFORT RING A ring is a structure in which a series of dike rocks form large well-defined circles. One of the best described so far is Vredefort Ring, South Africa. It has a diameter of 125 kilometers (75 miles) and is of Cambrian rocks.

The Ring is believed to be the remnant of a meteor crater (q.v.), which has been partially destroyed by erosion.

VULCANO The volcanic island of Vulcano off southern Italy was named for the Roman god of fire. The volcano is similar to Vesuvius and Irazu in Costa Rica. The type is vulcanian or vesuvian. The lava tends to be tarry. Its last major eruption was in 1888.

VULTURE MINE Vulture is one of Arizona's legendary gold mines. It was discovered by chance. Henry Wickenburg, while prospecting, picked up a rock to throw at his stubborn burro and realized it contained gold. The mine is near the present town of Wickenburg.

Mt. St. Helens — Washington, before and after eruptions
Courtesy of US Geological Survey

W

WAD Wad is manganese plus other oxides combined with at least 20-25% water. The material is sooty in appearance and texture. It develops in bog environments.

WADI The Arabic for a dry water course is 'wadi'. The usual wadi traces an ancient stream channel or is the course of an ephemeral stream. Many major wadis in North Africa and the Middle East outline fossil environments which had a more humid climate. In the southwestern United States, these features are known as washes or 'arroyos'.

Wadi El Arabah in the desert south of Sinai is located in a major rift valley. El Arabah is in an extension of the Great Rift System of East Africa.

In times of very occasional rain, wadis are subject to flash flooding (q.v.).

WALLACE LINE In Australia, a major zoogeographical boundary is known as the Wallace Line. It separates Southeast Asian fauna from the Australian. This major ecosystem boundary was discovered by Darwin's contemporary, Alfred Russell Wallace.

WALVIS RIDGE The largest topographic relief features away from the Mid-Atlantic Ridge in the South Atlantic are the Walvis and its counterpart, the Rio Grande Rise. These ridges are transverse to the Mid-Atlantic. Walvis rises from the seafloor off South Africa and Rio Grande is off South America.

WARM FRONT The leading edge of a warm airmass is a warm front. Advancing warm air rises and overtakes the relatively cold airmass ahead of it.

Warm fronts signal the advance of low pressure systems and storms. When a warm front passes or is stationary the Atmosphere is more humid and the temperature is relatively warmer.

WARPING Crustal warping, or epeirogenic activity (q.v.), results in raising or lowering the Earth's Crust on a regional scale. Warping is different from folding (q.v.) for there is no angular displacement. Gentle arching results from forces with insufficient energy for folding.

WASATCH MOUNTAINS The Eocene Wasatch Range, Utah, is of massive limestone that took 11 million years to develop. The mountains form a huge, tilted fault block on the eastern edge of Great Salt Lake.

The ancient shorelines of Pleistocene Lake Bonneville are evident on the slopes of the Wasatch. The cliffs are pink from iron and manganese staining.

The highest elevation, Mount Timpanogos, is 3,660 meters (12,008 feet. Timpanogos Cave is a series of limestone caverns on the mountain's north slope. It is a national monument.

Bristlecone Pine (q.v.) is found in the Wasatch Mountains as well as mountain mahogany. The forests are boreal (q.v.).

WASH In southwestern United States a dry stream channel is a wash, or dry-wash. It is similar to the wadi (q.v.) of the African and Arabian deserts, though those tend to be larger.

Washes are subject to flash flooding (q.v.) especially when there are storms in the headwaters area, sometimes far away. People crossing or working in washes need to be alert especially during the warm summer afternoons, when thunderstorms are prevalent.

'Wash', a mining term, refers to loose gold-bearing alluvial deposits. It includes washed material removed from sluices.

WATER Water is a compound made up of 2 hydrogen atoms and 1 oxygen atom. The size of a water droplet depends on its specific gravity, viscosity, and conditions under which it was formed.

The Earth's water is distributed as follows:

* The World Ocean   97%
* Ice sheets, glaciers, icefields, ice floes   2%
* Streams, lakes, rivers, groundwater, soils   1%

The Earth is 72% covered with water. If the Earth were a perfect sphere, the water would cover it to a depth of 2.5 kilometers (1.5 miles). If present ice sheets were to melt, sea level would rise 60 meters (200 feet), drowning many of the world's largest cities. Global warming by a few degrees Celsius could cause this melting and rise in sea level.

The Atmosphere holds 415 cubic kilometers (200 cubic miles) of water vapor on the average. To create this vapor uses 25% of all the incoming solar energy. Of this evaporated water only about 13% returns to continental areas as precipitation.

Water is unequally distributed over the continents. Each continent has at least one large desert, Africa has 3. Yet, African lakes are reputed to hold 20% of all the freshwater on Earth. Canada has the world's largest supply of freshwater (q.v.), almost 75%.

Water appeared on Earth early, some 4.5 billion years ago. Hot gases and steam were erupted in a great degassing (q.v.). When temperatures cooled to below 212° Fahrenheit, steam condensed to water which filled the lower areas of the planet.

Life depends upon water and the mass of all living things is more than half water. In some plants, water content is 95% and some animals are up to 60%.

Human usage ranges from 2,700 cubic meters per person per year in the United States to 900 cubic meters in some areas.

WATER EROSION Water, in the form of liquid or as ice, is the primary agency of erosion. Water contains chemicals that also further erosion. It is a remarkably powerful agent, carving canyons and valleys.

Oxidation and reduction, processes that are extremely important in weathering and erosion, are dependent upon the amount of water available. The processes relate to levels of the water table and to the wet and dry seasons. See **REDOX**.

Rock weathering (q.v.) is mainly produced by groundwater. Porosity and permeability of rocks together with water determine the rate and type of weathering.

WATER HYACINTH The water hyacinth is a pale violet, lily-like plant. Small bladders allow it to float. It proliferates in warm waters and often creates a continuous mat shutting off air to the water below.

In many countries, where the hyacinth was introduced, it has become a menace to fisheries. It was introduced in India in the 19th Century to decorate gardens. Today, it is choking streams. It has become known as 'the curse of Bengal'.

The hyacinth was also introduced into the Nile, where it is a problem. At one time, in the lake behind Jebel Aulia Dam in Sudan, the hyacinth so proliferated, a great mat resulted. It was so thick it was possible to walk on it. The organic debris created such a biomass huge quantities of hydrogen sulfide was exuded. That, in turn, destroyed lake and river life.

The hyacinth mat has also proven to be an excellent breeding ground for mosquitos. The plant is toxic to all animals but water buffalo, which can graze on it.

Attempts to eradicate the hyacinth from Surinam were made with a $2.5 million spraying at Brokopondo. The herbicide used was 24-D, one of the main components of Agent Orange. The results of the use of the chemical has not been reported.

Water hyacinth is found in Louisiana bayous in the United States.

WATER MEASUREMENT American measurements for water are given in the following units for flow and depth:

- 1 Acre-inch = 3,630 cubic feet
- 1 Acre-foot (q.v.) = 43,560 cubic feet
- 1 Cubic foot = 7.5 gallons (a static measure)
- 1 cfs (cubic foot per second) = 450 gallons per minute
- 1 cfs/day (cubic foot per second per day) = 2 acre feet

WATER PURITY Water from streams supply most domestic water in the United States. Even before industrialization and its pollution of rivers, not all streams were suitable for domestic use.

For a safe and healthy water supply, reliance has to be placed upon water treatment. Billions of liters are purified daily and require enormous quantities of chemicals. Lime and clay are used to remove solids, sulfates of aluminum and iron, iron chloride, and sodium aluminate. Chlorine removes many harmful bacteria.

Spring water from high mountain sources is usually considered pure. However, many springs flow through rocks containing deleterious minerals, so monitoring of mineral content is essential.

WATER QUALITY   Some general guide lines are given for water quality. They are:

- For domestic use - Should not contain more than 500 ppm (parts per million) of dissolved solids
- Irrigation water - Should not exceed 1,400 ppm of dissolved solids.

Sodium content is critical. Too much sodium causes the soil to become sticky. In general water is considered:

- Slightly saline   1,000 ppm dissolved solids
- Very saline   10,000 ppm dissolved solids
- Brine   35,000 ppm dissolved solids

WATER TABLE   The water table is the hydrostatic level or groundwater level of an area. In a region of permeable granular rocks, that level is the upper surface of free water completely filling sediment pore spaces. Depths to this layer depend upon topography and climate.

WATER TREATMENT   Streams, even in supposedly remote areas may not be potable. Almost no water is free from dissolved solids or particles in suspension. Rocks and soils contain minerals and chemicals that may be toxic. See **WATER PURITY**.

There are many ways to treat water but they are basically the addition or subtraction of chemicals and minerals. In water treatment, naturally occurring impurities are removed. These include chlorides, lime, and sulfur.

In many areas, the custom of drinking beer and wine arose because water supplies were dangerous. According to one historian, beer was served for breakfast at Harvard during the Puritan Era.

WATERFALL   A sudden drop in the elevation of a stream bed creates a waterfall. The drop may be caused by a fault or by the difference in erosional resistance of the bedrock. Water falling over a cliff continues down-cutting at an accelerated rate. An eddy forms at the base.

A waterfall is an ephemeral feature. As the water erodes the cliff over which it falls, the waterfall is progressively moved upstream in headward erosion. The erosional process procedes at different rates depending upon the resistance of the cliff-forming rocks. A basin surrounded by a fall-line (q.v.) is being enlarged by this erosion. Eventually erosion causes cliff retreat to a lower slope angle.

Where softer sediments are below a harder covering rock of a cliff, the waterfall erodes caves behind the falls. The Cave of the Winds of Niagara was formed in this way. Eventually the over-hang will collapse accelerating headward erosion.

A spectacular type of waterfall is created when glacial scour cuts off a tributary stream. They can be so high, wind-blown waters are misty. They have the romantic name of bridalveil falls. See **HANGING VALLEY**.

WATERSHED The upland area drained by any part of a river system is its watershed area. Often the area is of forested slopes. The forest contributes to holding water rather than letting it immediately run off.

Watersheds are usually separated by ridges or divides. These are areas between catchment systems. A large basin will have many watershed areas around its periphery. They are drained by tributaries that merge lower in the basin.

WATERSPOUT Funnel-shaped, a waterspout is a creation of wind and water. It is a rotating cloud-filled airmass. The waterspout usually extends from the underside of a cumulous cloud to the whirling cloud of spray at the sea or lake surface.

The winds and formation of a waterspout are a similar to those giving rise to a tornado (q.v.). These 'freak' storms are relatively common in Florida.

WAVES A wave is an oscillatory or undulating motion with a definite rise and fall. It transfers energy in many media. Light waves, ocean waves, and radio waves are the most familiar. Each wave is characterized by its amplitude, length, frequency, and velocity.

Wave energy is reflected in amplitude. It is equal to 1/2 the wave height. Wave height is measured vertically from the base of the preceding trough to the crest of the succeeding wave.

Wavelength is the distance measured from crest to crest. In the electromagnetic spectrum, wavelength is measured in Ångstroms (q.v.). Visible light has a wavelength range from 4,000-7,000 Ångstroms.

The number of waves passing a fixed point in a given period is frequency. It is the wavelength divided by time. Frequency is expressed in cycles per second except in the oceans where it is expressed in meters per second. Wave velocity is calculated by multiplying wavelength by frequency.

Energy created by ocean waves (q.v.) may travel thousands of miles in the sea but the water particle does not. Water droplets trace a circular pattern. The top of the circle is the crest, the bottom is the trough. The water mass moves forward propelled by the wind.

In the sea, wind is the major factor controlling wave height. To obtain 12 meter waves (40 foot), a 100 kilometer (60 mile) per hour wind must blow steadily at least 48 hours over a fetch (q.v.) of 1,500 kilometers

(900 miles). Waves of this magnitude are not uncommon in the North Atlantic in winter.

The progressive surface waves are not the only types found in the seas, bays, and lakes. There are also internal waves (q.v.) and standing waves (q.v.). The ocean is also a medium of transmission of earthquake waves and sound waves.

Ocean waves attack coasts by hydraulic, corrosive, and solvent action. Hydraulic force hits a cliff face, fractures it, and traps air in the rock creating pressure. Compressed air tears the rock apart. When suddenly released, the energy as waves ebbs away. Dissolved chemical solids cause the sea to be slightly acid. Some rocks are easily attacked by this solution. Corrosive action occurs when waves carry sediments capable of abrasion. It creates a notch in the cliff weakening it and causing it to collapse. See **CLIFF**.

Waves within the Earth are termed 'elastic waves' and are set off by earthquakes (q.v.) and explosions.

WEATHER Climate is expressed locally by weather. Weather changes from moment to moment. Pressure, wind, humidity, and precipitation are all important in making the weather.

The Earth has been likened to a giant heat pump being warm at the Equator and cold at the poles. Ocean currents deliver warm waters to colder latitudes. The Ocean transports more heat than the Atmosphere but watermasses move more slowly than airmasses.

Much weather in the United States is the result of the Sub-Polar Westerlies. They bring the cyclonic and anticyclonic airmasses characteristic of Mid-Latitude weather.

Weather, in general over the last 50 years has been the best in about 1,000 years. For a period of equal global mildness, it is necessary to go back 5-7,000 years. However, there is some evidence that present world-wide weather is deteriorating. The weather in North America in 1976 was the coldest in 90 years and the winter of 1976-77 was of record-breaking cold. Above Cairo, Illinois, 3 meters (10 feet) of ice dammed the Mississippi.

The 1980's have shown some warming and 2 major droughts in the United States. Drought in one part of the planet is usually balanced by torrential rains elsewhere. Drought seemed to be settling in over the Prairie in early 1989.

Many scientists believe we are in an Interglacial Epoch and that climatic variability reflected in the weather is to be expected. Drought in some areas and torrential rains in others are characteristic of interglacial epochs. These conditions were recorded in Europe prior to the Mini Ice Age (q.v.).

Other scientists feel that we are on the brink of a great global warming caused by the Greenhouse Effect (q.v.) and the buildup of carbon dioxide and ozone in the Troposphere. The breakdown of the Ozone Layer (q.v.) is another variable in global warming. See **OZONE**.

Climate (q.v.) is the sum total of the weather patterns around the globe. It is these which add up to the cooling or heating of the planet. With modern technology, we are able to monitor events globally. This capability also makes it possible to predict weather and take measures to minimize adverse effects.

WEATHER MODIFICATION   There have been efforts to modify weather in the past decade. The USSR spent more on climate control and weather modification than any other nation ($30 million a year in the 1970's). They routinely seeded with silver iodide crystals to increase rains in crop areas. They have spent a great deal of money in reducing hail damage supposedly using rockets of silver iodide.

In the Soviet Union experiments have ranged from coating glaciers with coal dust in the Tien Shan Range to the diversion of major rivers to the south. The creation of dams and lakes has caused microclimatic changes in parts of the Siberian interior. The goal was to open arable Khazakhstan land to irrigation.

The dessication of the Aral Sea has been in response to the reduction of flow of rivers. The water was diverted to irrigation projects and little allowed to flow to the sea.

Reduced flow to the north will have an effect on Arctic ice packs. Other ramifications are unknown.

WEATHERING   The geological process of weathering encompasses all the forces of erosion acting upon rock surfaces and within soils. Visible changes and new relief forms result from weathering. Rock composition and climate cause the weathering rate to vary.

Weathering takes 3 major forms:
- Biological
- Chemical
- Mechanical.

These processes operate alone or in concert and may act in aerobic (subaerial) or anaerobic (non-atmospheric) conditions. Weathering includes transportation and redeposition as well as decomposition and site changes. Again, the processes work in concert or alone.

Impressive periods of global planation created the great flat-topped mountains of almost equal elevation found in the Appalachians, the Guiana Highlands, and in African ranges. These all have Precambrian cores

The Recent or Present Period is one of great planation and erosion. Earth history has recorded other periods of prolonged erosion on a global scale, sometimes punctuated by mountain building and uplift.

Many minerals are concentrated in the weathering processes. They may be alteration minerals such as clays or secondarily emplaced minerals such as some copper. Or, they may be aggregated layers of precipitated minerals (e.g.: bauxite, iron ore, manganese).

WEDGE Geometrically, the wedge is a solid with a parallelogram for a base and 4 plane faces and 2 triangles. The wedge tapers to one side. It describes the shape of some sedimentary or mineral deposits. In periglacial areas, ice wedges are important weathering agents.

WEGENER Alfred Wegener is considered the 'Father of Continental Drift Theory'. In 1912, he suggested the theory that divided geologists for half a century. Wegener predicted a fault and great lateral displacement between Ellesmere Island and Greenland. When it was discovered, it was named Wegener Fault.

His theory contended that the Earth at the end of the Carboniferous Period (270 m.y.) was composed of a single original supercontinent, Pangaea (q.v.). This world continent was surrounded by a World Ocean. Pangaea began breaking apart in the Permian. By Eocene, a continent (Laurasia) was formed of Eurasia attached to North America through Scandinavia and Greenland. In the south, a continent (Gondwana) contained Africa, South America, Australia, and Antarctica. Laurasia was separated from Gondwana by the Tethys Sea (q.v.).

The implication of Wegener's past geography was that the continents had 'drifted' through geological time. The discovery of the Mid-Atlantic Rift (q.v.), seafloor spreading, and other evidence from the sea corroborated his theory.

WELL Holes bored into the Earth to reach groundwater or petroleum and bring it to the surface are wells. If the hole is simply to test sediments and structures, it is a borehole.

In eastern United States and Europe many communities depend upon wells to supply domestic water. Some wells may tap artesian water (q.v.). In central Australia, virtually all domestic water is from 'bores' or deeply sunk wells.

WELWITSCHIA The South African desert plant 'Welwitschia mirabilis' has a reputed lifespan of a 1,000 years. It grows on flat, stony ground, has a reddish bark, broad leaves, and is short stemmed.

Welwitschia is a 'highly specialized' gymnosperm (q.v.) considered closely related to the angiosperms (q.v.).

Welwitschia begins as 2 lily-like leaves that split as the stem grows to form leaves. It has a long tap root. The circumference can be 3-3.6 meters (10-12 feet) and height 14 centimeters 6 inches).

WENTWORTH SCALE Sediments have been classed on the Wentworth Scale according to size:

- Boulder   Greater than 256 millimeters
- Cobble   64 - 256 millimeters
- Pebble   4 - 64 millimeters
- Granule   2 - 4 millimeters
- Sand   0.062 - 2 millimeters
- Silt   0.004 - 0.062 millimeters
- Clay   Less than 0.004millimeters

WEST AFRICAN CRATON The ancient, stable part of the African continent is the West African Craton. It is composed of the Rigbat and Guinea-Liberian Shields, the western part of the Tuareg Massif, the Anti-Atlas Mountains, and the Ugarta Mountains.

Many basins are contained within the craton. These include Guinea, Taoudenni, Tunduf, and Volta. The Liberian-Nigerian Geosyncline borders the craton on the east and southeast.

WEST INDIES Island groups in the West Indies are emerged portions of a platform 1,267 kilometers (760 miles) long. The islands are Greater Antilles, Lesser Antilles, and Bahamas. The platform rises 455 meters (1,500 feet) from the ocean floor.

WESTERN GHATS In India, a mountain range known as the Western Ghats skirts a narrow coastal plain on the west coast from Bombay to Cape Comorin, 1,600 kilometers (1,000 miles) to the south. In these mountains that average 1,200 meters (4,000 feet) the only gap is in the south. It is Palghat Gap which is 30 kilometers (20 miles) wide.

The Ghats are in the path of the monsoons from the Arabian Sea. These storms bring torrential rains to the region from June to October. As a result, the slopes are forested and the inland plateaus support agriculture.

The upthrust Ghats resulted from the Himalayan collision (200 m.y.). In this event a great rift developed along the continental edge. It was accompanied by enormous flows of basalt. The western edge of the flows was uplifted to dip slightly to the east. This caused the rivers of the region to flow east to empty into Bengal Bay (q.v.) rather than the Arabian Sea.

WETLANDS There are areas where soil moisture is high and the water table is near the surface. Such an area becomes a wetland when accumulated water stands on the surface during part or all of the year. Included in wetlands are areas where the slope is insufficient for drainage and swamps, marshes, and sloughs develop.

The United States Department of the Interior defines a wetland as any lowland area even temporarily covered by at least 2 meters (6 feet) of water.

Freshwater makes up 90% of the wetlands ecosystem. In Florida, where there are the most wetlands in the United States, a lake that averages less than 3 meters (10 feet) deep falls under this classification. The Everglades (q.v.) are the largest single wetland in the United States. This subtropical swamp encompasses 4,400 square kilometers (1,700 square miles).

Wetlands are gradually filling in with depositions of silt and are constantly changing. A meandering stream may fill in a wetland and create another. Earthquakes can change a lake to a swamp or the reverse.

Reelfoot Lake, Tennessee, is now a swamp because of an earthquake on the New Madrid Fault (q.v.).

Many wetlands are drying out naturally, but many are being destroyed. In both cases an ecosystem (q.v.) is threatened. In the United States, there were about 130 million wetlands of which only 30 million remain. Many were drained for agricultural use.

Wetlands are critical in maintaining a balance between wet and dry climates and stemming seasonal floods. Marshes and swamps slow down runoff. They are a natural air-conditioner in Florida, giving off moisture and oxygen. Wetlands are not wastelands but are actually reservoirs of water and should be treated as such.

WHALEBACK DUNES The largest of all dunes are called whalebacks. They have rounded backs and are larger than seifs (q.v.) both in length and breadth. They develop in length parallel to the dominant wind pattern.

WHALES The whale is a marine mammal whose ancesters were land mammals. Presumably, the whale was attracted to the sea by the abundance of available food. Modern whales are of 3 types:

- Plankton feeders
- Fish eaters
- Squid eaters.

Plankton feeders are limited to the colder waters where there are abundant small fish and shrimp. These whales are filter feeders of the baleen type. These are found in the Arctic and Antarctic Oceans. See **KRILL**.

The sperm whale is the largest of the toothed whales, up to 15 meters (50 feet). It has the largest brain of all mammals. It weighs up to 3.6 kilograms (8 pounds). The sperm whale hunts the deep sea for squid. Other smaller toothed whales are fish eaters.

Some whales became icebound off Alaska in 1988 and a massive rescue mission released them. A Soviet icebreaker contributed to the effort. This was not the first time humans have rescued the whale. In 1985, a Soviet icebreaker opened the way for hundreds of Beluga whales to reach the open ocean.

WHEAT Temperate climate wheat with rice and sorghum are the major staple grains of the world. Wheat is a cereal (q.v.) grown in temperate climate grasslands. Per metric ton, tropical wheat requires far more water (8,000 tons) than temperate. Because tropical grasslands are generally drier, the range for wheat is small.

United States wheat, among the best in the world, is the result of hybridization. Russian drought resistant Kubanka was crossed with Russian winter wheat, Kharkov. The hybrid wheat is now shipped to Russia to fill out their harvests.

WHITE CLIFFS OF DOVER The White Cliffs of Dover, England, are composed of chalk. They face similar cliffs across the English Channel on the coast of France.

This chalk was precipitated over 30 million years. Algae and Foraminifera were the catalysts in precipitating calcium carbonate. The Dover cliffs and others along the British Coast are rapidly eroding away from natural and human activity.

WHITE DWARF STAR The white dwarf star is the collapsed state of an ordinary star. The star is dying because its energy source has been consumed.

WHITE GOLD A small amount of platinum is combined with gold to make white gold. Sometimes other metals are used (nickel, nickel-zinc, copper).

WHITE HOLE The White Hole in astronomy is the opposite of the Black Hole (q.v.). It is thought to be matter returning to our Universe together with the energy previously lost in a Black Hole.

WHITE ISLAND In the Bay of Plenty, New Zealand, White Island is built upon a submarine volcano. The volcano and island are over the Tonga-Kermadec Subduction Zone (q.v.). This zone is where the Pacific Plate is sliding beneath the Indian.

White Island was named by Captain Cook. When he discovered the island, it was covered with guano (q.v.).

White Island has been worked for its sulfur deposits and it has been suggested that operations begin again. The original operation and its encampment were wiped out during an eruption.

WHITE SANDS At White Sands, New Mexico, there are extraordinary sand dunes composed entirely of gypsum. The grains, finer than the best beach sand, are snow white.

The source of the sands is the San Andreas and Sacramento mountains. Both ranges have massive gypsum deposits that were formed in an evaporating pan left by the receding seas of 100 million years ago.

The grains of gypsum were carried by the winds to the lowest part of the basin where they weathered to an even finer size. Then they were winnowed and blown into dunes by the southwest winds.

WHITECAP The froth on the crest of a wave is a whitecap. It is whipped up by the wind, which blows the crest forward and over. Whitecaps are an indication that the wind is above 13 knots.

WHITEOUT Ablation (q.v.) causes mists to rise from snowfields creating fog or whiteout. The phenomenon also occurs during a blizzard when high winds whip up the snow.

Whiteouts can cause disorientation and are very dangerous. Mountaineers, in a whiteout, should burrow into the snow for safety.

WILDCATTING Drilling for oil in areas where proven reserves have not been established is 'wildcatting'. Wildcatting has become rare in recent years because of high costs. Even in proven areas the success odds are only 1 in 9 wells.

Onshore cost of a well, exclusive of location logistics was $76,500. in 1978, and an offshore well in that same year was $590,000. They are now appreciably higher.

WILLIWAW Wind gusts up to 100 knots built up on one side of a mountain spill over to the other. This phenomenon is a 'williwaw'. Originally, the name was given to strong winds coming off the Antarctic Ice Sheet and encountered in the Strait of Magellan.

WILLY-WILLIE A violent windstorm in Australia is a 'willy-willie'. It is a cyclonic storm of hurricane force. On the northwest coast of Australia the storms are related to the Intertropical Convergence (q.v.).

WILSON CYCLE Processes balancing the Tectosphere (q.v.) make up the Wilson Cycle. Upper Mantle basalt is depleted and garnet-lherzolite results making the Mantle irreversibly less dense. Continental stability is affected.

The density difference can be 0.2%. This is a considerable difference in Earth composition and undoubtedly causes large effects.

WIND Wind is the movement of air from a center of high pressure to one of low. Wind direction and velocity are governed by the atmospheric pressure areas. Winds range from calm to hurricane force. See **BEAUFORT SCALE**.

Once wind is set in motion by pressure differences, it is acted upon by the Coriolis Effect (q.v.) which tends to deflect it to the right in the Northern Hemisphere. A circulation pattern is set up that creates a discrete airmass. Airmass movement results in wind belts (q.v.).

Circulation is also affected by solar heating. Warm tropical air is transported to higher latitudes and cooler air to lower ones.

Wind is a depositional force. Navaho Sandstone in southwestern United States is a deposit of wind-blown sands. Parts of the Nubian Sandstone (q.v.) of Egypt and Sudan are wind deposits.

In New Mexico. wind is depositing white gypsum sands and forming white dunes. Desert dunes and dunes found on beaches are all wind deposits. See **DUNES**.

Wind erosion is a powerful agency in weathering and deposition. The Wyoming landscape was reduced 45 meters (150 feet) by wind action. Qattara Depression (q.v.) was reduced to 127 meters (420 feet) below sea level by wind scourings.

Wind is also important as a major agency in plant pollination. The pollen is wafted between the female and male trees. Desert winds are the pollinating agency for the date palm. Today human energy is also added in this endeavor.

WIND BELTS Winds blow in definite directions most of the time and are said to be 'prevailing'. Temperature differences between the Equator and the poles generate huge flows. Warm air rises from the Equator, flows toward the poles, cools, and sinks. The topography and shape of the Earth modify the flows.

Wind belts from the North Pole to South Pole are:
- Polar Easterlies
- Westerlies
- Northeast Trades
- Doldrums
- Southeast Trades
- Westerlies
- Polar Easterlies

In the days of the great sailing vessels, the Tradewinds were most important. These winds blow toward the Equator from the northeast and southeast. At the Equator there is a hiatus called the Doldrums, noted for its calm. None of the belts is fixed, they fluctuate in width and latitude.

The United States is most affected by the Westerlies (q.v.) or winds that flow from the west. As they are deflected to the right these winds have a southeast trajectory and bring cold air from the North Pacific and Canada to lower latitudes.

Because of terrestrial heating patterns, monsoonal winds develop in some parts of the semi-tropics. In India, where they are most notable, winds blow dry air from land to sea for 6 months and bring moisture and rain from the sea during the next 6 months.

WIND CHILL Winter winds tend to lower effective temperatures depending upon velocity. This is the wind chill factor. At $30°$ Fahrenheit, in a 10 mile per hour wind, effective temperature will be $16°$.

In the above example the wind chill factor is $14°$. The chart below shows the effect of wind chill at different temperatures and velocities in degrees Fahrenheit.

Temperature	Wind Speeds		
	10 mph	20 mph	30 mph
$30°$	16	4	-2
20	4	-10	-18
10	-9	-25	-33
0	-21	-39	-48
-10	-33	-53	-63

WIND ENERGY Wind has been a source of energy for centuries. Many mechanisms are in use around the world to capture the energy. They are used primarily for raising water from wells for domestic and irrigation use. For wind energy to work efficiently, the winds must be fairly predictable.

It is estimated that 39% of captured wind can be converted to electrical power. Costs presently range from $0.325-$0.10 per kwh (kilowatt hour).

Attempts to create wind turbine systems are relatively modern. By the year 2,000, wind will supply 4% of the energy needs of the United States. In 1983, there were 1400 commercial wind farms in 4 locations in California.

Wind energy is an important erosional force denuding the planet. It is especially operative in desert areas where it has developed great depressions by deflating basin floors.

WIND GAP Mountain gaps, or notches, were cut originally by headward stream erosion. The streams were captured and changed to flow on the other side of the divide, Uplift may have outpaced the stream change leaving a dry channel. Gaps formed by events such as these are further eroded by winds that funnel through at relatively high velocities.

Cumberland Gap was created by this sequence of events. The stream was unable to continue cutting its channel as fast as the land rose, so its course was shifted leaving Cumberland, a wind gap.

Gaps in the Appalachian Mountains provided routes for vehicle transport and trains. They allowed movement West by settlers and were important to the opening up of the Northwest Territory.

WINDOW Geologically, a window is an erosional opening in a thrust sheet, nappe, or fold which reveals more recent or younger sediments. The reverse bedding order indicates an overturning of strata. Windows are common in the Andes, Alps, and Himalayas.

WINGATE REEF Wingate Reef, a coral formation in the Red Sea, is 42 kilometers (25 miles) northeast of Port Sudan and only a short distance from shore. The reef noted for coral and fish is on the average 11 meters (36 feet) below the sea surface. It surfaces only rarely.

WINNOWING The sorting process of winnowing uses wind energy. Fine particles are separated from coarser materials.

Gold has been worked by winnowing where water was not available. Wool or a similar material was used to hold the gold electrostatically while lighter material is allowed to blow away.

WINZE A winze is a narrow, inclined to vertical, shaft or downward excavation connecting different levels in a mine.

WITWATERSRAND BASIN Witwatersrand Basin in South Africa is legendary for its gold. Gold reefs in The Rand were deposited in an intermontane, intercratonic, gently sloping, yoked basin. The basin appears to be a geosynclinal downwarp between granite domes, creating a saddle.

The gold is Precambrian in age. Van Biljon believes the ore is in an ancient embayment along a subduction zone (q.v.) between 2 Archean mini-continents. The Barberton Lineament is considered the suture scar. If this theory is correct, there were break-ups and aggregations of continents throughout geological time.

WOLF CREEK CRATER Wolf Creek Crater of northwestern Australia is considered meteoritic. The crater measures 850 meters (1,800 feet) across. At its center, it is 60 meters (200 feet) deep. Outside walls rise 30 meters (100 feet) from the plain. The meteor impacted the Earth within the past million years. Metal fragments have been found.

WOLFRAMITE A tungstate of iron and manganese, wolframite is 76% tungsten. A monoclinic mineral, wolframite has a high specific gravity and is hard, 4.5-5.5 on Moh's Scale (q.v.).

Wolframite often occurs as a gangue mineral in tin lodes. Bolivia's reserves of tungsten are associated with the tin deposits. The reserves are estimated at 290,000 metric tons. They are mostly a mix of scheelite and wolframite, of pegmatite and vein origin.

China is the major wolframite producer. Europe's most important wolframite mine is Panasqueira in Portugal's Serra Estrela. It has been a steady and important producer for decades. Portugal's production was strategically important in both World War I and II. The United States has minor wolframite production. See **TUNGSTEN**.

WOLLASTONITE Wollastonite is a calcium silicate which is a common mineral in silicious limestones. The mineral is composed of isolated polymerized (q.v.) groups of silica tetrahedra. It is rarely found in pure massive form. There are several massive deposits in California and a very well-known deposit in the Adirondacks of New York.

The major use for wollastonite is in the ceramics industry for the fabrication of tiles and porcelain. It has also been used as an insulator in electronics and as a filler.

The deposit at Willsboro, New York is the major producer. It has a 75% recovery of wollastonite. The ore contains about 15% garnet which is recovered magnetically. Wollastonite reserves in the 1960's were between 3 and 15 million short tons.

WOOD A dense complex of trees which is larger than a grove or stand (q.v.) yet smaller than a forest is a wood.

The hard parts of the tree, its trunk and limbs are called wood. It is used as construction material, as fuel, and in paper production. In the United States alone, in a single year, we use up the equivalent of 230 million trees measuring 30 meters (100 feet) high by 40 centimeters (16 inches) thick.

The forests are renewable only if usage does not exceed the regrowth rate of the same species. At the present rate we are decimating our forests. See **FUELWOOD**.

WOODLAND A woodland is a forested area of widely spaced trees. The intervening area is of low shrubs and grass. The trees do not possess an interlacing of branches so sunlight penetrates to the understory.

WORM HOLE Worm hole is the name astronomers have given to the area between a Black Hole (q.v.) and a White Hole (q.v.). This area is considered the connection between universes.

WRANGELL RANGE In southeast Alaska the Wrangell Range forms a part of the system that extends in an arc from the Aleutians to the Panhandle. The maximum elevation of the volcanic range is 4,900 meters (16,000 feet). The mountains receive heavy snows and are permanently capped with ice. The range has many valley glaciers.

Since 1900, ice has retreated in stages on the Wrangell Range with intermittent ice advances. Mountain streams in some of their upper reaches are braided. These streams eventually reach the Tanana River to the Yukon.

WRENCH FAULT The British refer to strike-slip faults as wrench faults. In the United States 'wrench fault' is reserved for a high-angle, strike-slip fault of great linear magnitude.

In the faulting process, a huge piece of terrain is literally wrenched from its position. En echelon folding may occur as a result of the Earth's crustal movement. San Andreas and the Colorado Wrench Fault are examples.

WULFENITE The molybdenum ore, wulfenite, is an oxide of lead and molybdenum. It is often found in oxidized lead veins.

Wulfenite is tetragonal with tabular crystals sometimes just flat pyramids. It is usually bright orange to red-yellow in color, although it can be green and brown. Especially beautiful specimens of wulfenite crystals have been found in Arizona and New Mexico.

X

X-RAY Electromagnetic radiation in the form of X-Rays have become a useful medical diagnostic tool. These rays are in an energy band from 100 Kev (thousand electron volts) to 10 Mev (million electron volts). X-Rays are in the spectrum (q.v.) beyond Ultra-Violet. They are 10,000 times shorter than visible light.

X-rays are measured in roentgens, named for their discoverer. A roentgen is extremely small. It is equivalent to 1 unit of electrostatic charge in less than 0.001 grams of air. To warm 1 gram of air would take 100,000 roentgens.

Radiation absorbed by the body from X-rays is calculated in rads. 1 rad = 100 ergs of absorbed energy per gram of body weight. It is an individual measure. Humans absorb an average of 7-10 rads a year from cosmic radiation, sufficient to cause disease in some. Miners and others dealing in atomic energy may pick up an additional 12 to 15 rads a year. A lethal one time dosage would be about 500 rads. See **RAD**.

XENO- The prefix 'xeno-' means foreign or coming from a strange source. It is of Greek origin.

XENOCRYSTS Mineral grains in igneous rocks that are foreign to their host rock are xenocrysts. Most can only be seen under a microscope. Larger grains are phenocrysts (q.v.).

XENOLITH An exogenous rock fragment found contained in another rock is a xenolith. In an igneous rock, a xenolith may have become included in the magma when the roof of a structure collapses into a magma chamber below.

The foreign rock fragment may have been altered if the heat and pressure were sufficient. If this occurred, the xenolith will have an alteration halo around it.

XENON Xenon is one of the noble or inert gases found in the Atmosphere. These inert gases were once considered unreactive. Xenon, however, becomes agitated and emits a blue-green glow when given an electrical charge.

The abundance of xenon is calculated at 1 part in 10 million by volume. It is used as an anesthetic for surgery as it is supposed safer than ether. It is, however, extremely expensive.

XENOTIME Xenotime, anyttrium-bearing rare earth phosphate, contains uranium and thorium. Although the amounts are small, they are recoverable. Xenotime is associated with monazite in river and beach sands.

Idaho black sand placers are rich in xenotime. A few placers, formerly worked for monazite, are presently posted for their radioactivity.

XEROPHYTE   Plants adapted to arid environments are 'xerophytes' from the Greek for dry plant. The 3 major types are:

- Drought escapers - Dormant in the seed stage until conditions become advantageous
- Drought dodgers, evaders - Store moisture to use gradually
- Drought resisters - Long tap roots. Some have surface roots.

Many cacti resist germination until especially moist conditions prevail. Creosote bushes maintain a careful spacing between plants by poisoning off too proximate seedlings. The toxin is in the near surface root tips. The Ocotillo (q.v.) is an evader plant while the Mesquite (q.v.) and the Saharan Tamarisk are resisters.

The xerophytes, scrub spinifex and saltbush, are found over half of Australia. From Western Australia into Northern Territory and South Australia, the xerophytic plants include the 'Mulga' and 'Acacia', scrub and adapted shrubs.

Around the Great Australian Bight as far as Kalgoolie, the trees are of the drought-resistant variety of which the 'Mallee' predominates. It is a smaller variety of eucalyptus.

XINGU PLATEAU   The Xingu Plateau with an elevation of 363.5 meters (2,000 feet) is in the geographic center of Brazil. The plateau is between the Rio dos Mortes (River of the Dead) on the east and Rio São Manoelito on the west. On the south are the plateaus or 'chapadão'. On the north is the Amazon Basin. Rapids mark the edge of the Xingu Plateau. They form part of the fall-line of the Amazon Basin.

On the Xingu Plateau, there is a distinctive contact (q.v.) between alluvium and metamorphic rock. This contact marks the southern boundary of the Amazon Basin (q.v.).

The Xingu is only one of many plateaus making up the great Central Plateau of Brazil. This Central Plateau is the divide area between the Amazon Basin and the Parana-La Plata Basin.

XINGU RIVER   The Xingu River crosses the center of the Xingu Plateau (q.v.). Together with its tributaries, the Xingu drains to the Amazon. A major Xingu falls, the Von Martius, is one of the important ones rimming the Amazon Basin.

The Xingu River itself is a major tributary of the Amazon. The Xingu is joined by 4 major affluents, the Morena, the Kuluene, the Batove, and the Ronura. One geographer pointed out that the valley created by the Xingu is as large as all of England.

XYLEM   The inner tissue of land plants is known as xylem. It, together with the phloem (q.v.), is part of a plant's circulatory system. Sap moves upward in the xylem and downward in the phloem.

Y

YAK In Central Asia, the long-haired ox or yak has been domesticated for centuries. The yak provides most of the necessities of life for the Tibetans. The preferred habitat of the yak is over 4,200 meters (14,000 feet).

The yak is also an important caravan animal and it negotiates the high Himalayan passes. A major route is through Tsangpo Valley between Tibet and Nepal. The caravan is en route for 10 days. The trade exchanges grain for salt, fats, and wood.

YAKUTIA DIAMOND FIELDS Diamonds were discovered near Mirny, Yakut, Siberia, shortly after the close of World War II. The gems were embedded in permafrosted soils. The major deposits are located in the middle Lena Basin along the Vilyui River.

The Mir and Udachnaya kimberlite pipes (q.v.) were discovered in the middle reaches of the Vilyui. Diamonds were also found in the upper reaches of the Aldan River, the most easterly major tributary of the Lena. Other discoveries were made in the Anabar and Olenyek sub-basins.

In 1969, the Soviets were claiming to have the largest diamond deposits in the world, greater than those of South Africa. These Siberian deposits are the likely source of Soviet production. This production was estimated at 11 million carats for 1987. For 1989 production was estimated at 7 million carats. See **DIAMONDS**.

YAKUTIA GAS FIELDS In Yakut, in the Vilyui Basin of the Lena River System, Siberia, a major gas discovery was made. Wells were brought in elsewhere but none were as important.

The total regional estimate in 1969 was 12.8 billion cubic meters of gas. See **NATURAL GAS**.

YAKUTSK PLAIN The plain formed by the Lena River astride the Arctic Circle is a permafrosted area. In July and August the area is virtually submerged by surface flooding. In September winter sets in again and surface soils begin to refreeze. See **PERMAFROST**.

YANGTZE RIVER The world's 3rd longest river (Asia's longest) is known in the West as the Yangtze. It has 3 different Chinese names. These are Ta Jiang (great river), Chang Jiang (long river), and Chinsha Jiang (golden sand river).

The Yangtze rises in the high Tangula Mountains of northeast Tibet and flows east across 10 Chinese provinces. It empties into the East China Sea at Shanghai after a 6,520 kilometer (3,430 mile) course.

The Yangtse parallels the Mekong River (q.v.) for some 400 kilometers (250 miles). These rivers are within 65 kilometers (40 miles) of each other. After their courses diverge, the Mekong flows to the South China Sea via Vietnam.

The upper reaches of the Yangtse, above Chongquing (Chunking) are areas of gorges and many landslides. The river receives about 700 tributaries before reaching Chongquing.

The middle reaches are more subdued. At Chongquing the current is 2 meters (6.6 feet) per second. The plains which the river crosses to Shanghai are fertile and productive.

The Yangtse is the major artery of interior China. It is a navigable river for 1,100 kilometers (700 miles) as far as Wuhan. From there smaller vessels can proceed to Ipin, another 1,100 kilometers upstream.

YARDANG Desert winds sculpt troughs between ridges. These troughs have rounded bottoms from which the wind has removed all weak and soft materials. The result is a distinctive landform, a yardang. Yardangs were first described from southwestern United States by Blackwelder.

In the Arabian and Sahara deserts, yardangs can be found between seif (q.v.) dunes. The dunes in the Lake Chad area have some remarkable yardang examples. Yardangs in Asian deserts extend kilometers.

YAZOO CONFLUENCE Amazon tributaries usually debouch into lakes behind great levees along the main stream. The tributaries join the Amazon by way of rios or igarapes (q.v.). This type of confluence is called the Yazoo, named for the way the Yazoo River joins the Mississippi (q.v.).

As the tributaries empty into the lakes, the natural levees are lowered until they are submerged even at low-water. High-water on the Amazon covers these levees. Minor rivers connect the lake to the main river.

In rivers with tributary debouchment similar to the Amazon, there are similar lower courses. Only the lakes are less large.

YELLOW RIVER The correct name for China's Yellow River is Hwang-Ho (q.v.). The Chinese refer to this great stream as 'the river of sorrows' because of the disastrous floods. The Yellow is China's 2nd longest river. It travels 4,800 kilometers (3,000 miles) across northern China. It is the world's muddiest river.

In its middle reaches the river takes a north-south course over the loess plain of Shansi. The muddy sediment, from which it gets its name, comes from this region.

The sediment load, considered the highest of the world's rivers, is 1.6 billion tons a year. This represents the topsoil eroded every year from a 666,000 square kilometer (400,000 square mile) drainage area. The Yellow River drains to the Yellow Sea (q.v.).

YELLOW SEA The Yellow Sea, off the northeast coast of China, is an extended arm of the Pacific Ocean bounded by China and Korea. It is part of the East China Sea, which splits to become the Yellow Sea and the Sea of Japan. The yellow color is due to the mass of sediment contributed annually by the Yellow River (q.v.).

YELLOWCAKE Uranium hexafluoride is the milling product of uranium ore. Traded as yellowcake, it is packed in drums for shipment to government uranium enrichment plants. The product is raw fuel for nuclear reactors.

YELLOWCAKE ROAD The uranium producing areas of Saskatchewan, Canada, are on a hypothetical highway known as the 'Yellowcake Road'. It stretches from north of Saskatoon to Cluff Lake, which has become a major uranium producer.

Uranium production throughout the Athabascan Basin continues to be active. In 1982, about $80 millions were spent in Canada on uranium exploration. It then tapered off to between $30 and $55 millions annually until the world market slowed down.

Canada holds about 15% of the world's resources and 50% of these are in Saskatchewan. Besides the total reserve base, the uranium is generally of higher grade than usually encountered.

YELLOWSTONE CALDERA The largest United States caldera is in Yellowstone National Park. It has a diameter of 80 kilometers (64 miles), and is among the world's largest. It was created in great eruptions within the last 2 million years. Debris was scattered as far away as Kansas.

Twin magma chambers below Yellowstone erupted and formed overlapping calderas. Yellow rhyolite forms the crater walls. The caldera at 2,100 meters (7,000 feet) elevation is nestled among peaks up to 3,600 meters (12,000 feet) on the Continental Divide.

It is assumed that Yellowstone was located above a 'hot spot' or plume. A plume area is 60 times as hot as the rest of the Mantle. The magma chamber contains lava, hot liquids, and gases. Geothermal activity continues in the area. See **HOT SPOTS**.

YELLOWSTONE EARTHQUAKE Yellowstone Basin, the caldera in western United States, was lowered 6.7 meters (22 feet) as a result of the August 17, 1959 earthquake. The tremor caused a great block of rock, 400 meters (1,300 feet) by 0.8 kilometer (0.5 mile), to break off and dam Madison River. 300 geysers erupted and Old Faithful faltered.

A Ranger in Yellowstone Park reported an 'eerie silence' the night before, signifying that the birds had gone. Some bears left before the quake and others were disoriented.

YENESEI RIVER The Yenesei, one of Siberia's great north-flowing rivers, is included in the Soviet plan to divert waters to the Caspian. 15% of the waters of the Yenesei, Ob, and Irtysh are to be diverted.

The Yenesei is on the eastern edge of the Siberian Platform, a stable area bounded by the Yenesei Geosyncline. The river rises in the Sayan Mountains of the south and flows 3,700 kilometers (2,200 miles) to its mouth on the Kara Sea.

Two important Siberian cities are located on the river, Krasnoyarsk and Yeneseisk. Krasnoyarsk is on the Upper Yenesei and Yeneseisk is at the confluence with the Angara River which rises in Lake Baikal (q.v.).

The principal cargos carried on the Yenesei are timber, coal, oil, grain, and building materials. Krasnoyarsk is the chief point of trans-shipment between the river and the railroad network.

YOUTHFUL LANDSCAPE Broad flat uplands, high mountains, and steep-sided valleys are signs of a youthful landscape. The forces creating the landscape are uplift, lowering of sea levels, and stream erosion.

In the youthful landscape, streams move swiftly and cut deeply. There are rapids and some waterfalls. Post-glacial landscapes are youthful. So, too, are landscapes where lava flows have buried the earlier terrain.

YTTRIUM Yttrium is an important alloying element because of its ability to withstand high temperatures and improve forgeability. Yttrium forms highly magnetic compounds.

Yttrium is a relatively abundant in the Earth's Crust. It is a constituent of monazite and bastnaesite, both of which are mined for their Rare-Earths. Yttrium is a by-product.

China became a major yttrium oxide producer in 1986. In that same year a new yttrium extraction plant scheduled to produce 150 tons of oxide per year was set up at Elliot Lake, Ontario. It is a by-product of uranium production.

The world's resources of yttrium-bearing monazite and xenotime are considered large and available worldwide. The major producers of bastnaesite are the United States and China. The United States has many placer resources.

The present authenticated reserves (in metric tons of yttrium oxide) are:

China	720,000
United States	117,000
India	36,000
Malaysia	12,600
Australia	6,900
Canada	3,300
Thailand	600
Brazil	400

U.S. Bureau of Mines, 1990

Yttrium is used in phosphors for television and lighting, in lasers, in ceramics, and for the production of synthetic garnets. The Japanese have produced an automobile engine alloyed with yttrium. These synthetic gems are known as 'yags'.

YUCAYALI-URUBAMBA RIVERS The Peruvian Yucayali-Urubamba river system becomes part of the greater Amazon System when it joins the Maranon. This confluence of the Andean rivers is 1,600 kilometers (1,000 miles) upstream from Iquitos and the Brazilian border.

The Yucayali (Ucayali), not far from its glacial source, skirts Macchu Pichu, ancient monument of the Incas. Before joining the Yucayali, the Urubamba unites with the Apurimac River. All the rivers have their beginnings in Andean glaciers.

YUKON VALLEY The Yukon Valley extends from the Canadian Yukon Territory into Alaska. The Yukon River traces a broad arc across Alaska to empty into the Bering Sea.

The Yukon Valley is exceptional in that it was not glaciated during the Pleistocene. For this reason some of the world's richest gold placers were left in place. The valley was a prime prospecting area during the Alaska Gold Rush.

YUNGAS The semi-tropical valleys of Eastern Bolivia are 'yungas'. They are steep-sided and narrow gorges. The mountains rise abruptly reaching from 66 to 200 meters (2,000-6,600 feet) above the valley floors.

Valley, or yungas, vegetation is subtropical forest and the predominant crops are coffee and coca.

The region is fairly inaccessible. A road from the valleys to the highlands scales 3,400 meters (11,250 feet) in 85 kilometers 50 miles).

YUNNAN PLATEAU The Yunnan Plateau of South China is dotted with many small basins and has many lakes and ponds. The largest lake, Tien Chih, is on the floor of Kunming Basin.

The limestone plateau is pitted with sinkholes. Many collapsed structures in the karstic terrain have become dry depressions.

Waterfall — near Poços de Caldas, Brazil

Z

ZAGHOUAN MASSIF Djebel Zaghouan, a great limestone massif in Tunisia south of Tunis, is a structure trending NE-SW for 9 kilometers (6 miles). It is 3 kilometers (2 miles) wide. Its southeast slopes form an abrupt escarpment (q.v.).

A spring line resulting from thrust faulting is today a water supply for Tunis. When the Romans held Carthage, Hadrian built an aqueduct to transport this water to his city.

ZAGROS MOUNTAINS The Zagros Mountains of Iran extend from the frontier in the northwest to the Strait of Hormuz in the southeast over 1,770 kilometers (1,000 miles). On the west the range drops to the Mesopotamian Plain and the Persian Gulf. In the east, it abuts the high Central Plateau.

The Zagros formed when the Arabian Plate collided with the Eurasian and the Arabian was subducted (q.v.). The suture line is edged by the range. The area is still active and there are frequent earthquakes, largely in the northwestern fault blocks.

ZAIRE The African nation of Zaire, formerly a part of the Belgian Congo, occupies most of the Zaire (Congo) Basin east of the Zaire River. The major tributaries of the Zaire cross the country. The most important and major feeder is the Lualaba which empties into Lake Bangueula to emerge as Luapulu and Zaire rivers.

The mountains of the East African Rift and the lakes of Tanganyika, Kivu, and Edward form the eastern boundary.

Zaire is rich in minerals and famous for its copper which has been mined for centuries. For years, Zaire accounted for 60% of the world's cobalt. 4 carbonatite complexes in a north-south line parallel Uganda and Rwanda. Nyiragongo (q.v.), the famous volcano, may also prove to be a carbonatite. The carbonatite complexes are rich in apatite (q.v.). Pyrochlore is mined from the Kivu area.

Zaire was the world's largest producer of diamonds in 1979 (13 million carats). 70% industrial grade. Up to 1979 all production was alluvial. MIBA, the largest producer, began mining from kimberlite pipes in 1980 and hoped to reach 12 million carats annually even with exhaustion of its alluvial deposits.

In comparison with the rest of Africa, Zaire has rich soils. United Nations officials say Zaire could feed itself and much of Africa's Sahel if it were able to mount the necessary infrastructure. The cost in deforestation and soil exhaustion needs to be balanced in that equation. It is still a world of slash/burn agriculture (q.v.).

ZAIRE BASIN   Zaire (Congo) Basin is a shallow saucer in mid-Equatorial Africa. It has a central elevation of 300 meters (1,000 feet). The land rises gradually to between 900 and 1,200 meters (3,000 and 4,000 feet). The Basin is cut into the Central African Plateau.

Zaire Basin straddles the Equator from 5° North Latitude to 12° South Latitude. The drainage area covers 4,144,000 square kilometers (1,600,000 square miles).

In Katanga District at the southern end of the basin on the Zaire-Zambezi Divide are the famous copper deposits ranking among the world's richest. See **KATANGA COPPER DEPOSITS**.

ZAMBEZI RIVER   The Zambezi, one of the great African rivers, has its origins on the south rim of the Zaire (Congo) Basin in northwest Zambia.

The Zambezi is joined by the Shire 330 kilometers (200 miles) from the Zambezi delta. The Shire rises in Lake Malawi (Nyassa), a lake of the Great Rift System (q.v.) of East Africa.

The Zambezi Delta prograded over the last century and is full of sandbars and mudflats. Since the completion of Kariba Dam in 1958 coastal erosion has taken over. The dam in Kariba Gorge controls Zambezi floods that once spread over the Mozambique Plains. See **KARIBA DAM**.

The Zambezi River is navigable for 660 kilometers (400 miles) upstream from the mouth on the Indian Ocean. Then, 50 kilometers (30 miles) of cataracts are encountered. These are the 'Kebra-brassas' (Portuguese for broken arms).

Dr. Livingston discovered the Zambezi in 1851 at Sheke where Botswana bounds Zambia. He followed a tributary upstream to Angola, then worked downstream to discover Victoria Falls (q.v.). He was the first European to cross Africa from coast to coast.

ZEOLITES Zeolites are a group of hydrated alumino-silicates. There are about 40 naturally occurring crystalline zeolites. Zeolites are found in tuffaceous rocks and there are many deposits in the United States. Zeolites were formed from volcanic glass in reaction with alkaline solutions.

The zeolite crystal structure is of 4-fold rings of silica and aluminum oxide tetrahedra, bounded by cations. This is a relatively open structure and the pores are usually water filled.

Zeolite composition is of an aluminum oxide, with the anion balanced by a cation from a common mineral such as sodium or calcium. Barium, potassium, strontium, magnesium, or iron may be present. Zeolites are relatively hard, 3.5-5.5 on Moh's scale (q.v.), and are often vitreous, or pearly in luster. An interesting characteristic of zeolites is the tendency to intumescence, or swelling.

Presently, the major industrial use of zeolites is as molecular sieves and catalysts. Because they are thermally stable, zeolites have a broad use as catalysts. They are used in petroleum refining, in detergent manufacture, and as absorbers. Some are synthetic. Amorphous zeolites are used for water softening.

Natural ores have potential in pollution control as chemical absorbers since they have a vast internal surface area due to their porosity. They persist over a wide range of temperature and pressure.

A potentially important industrial group, zeolites are being produced synthetically. Japanese production of both natural and synthetic zeolites appears to be the most important at present.   See **CLINOTILOLITE**.

ZERO CURTAIN The 'zero curtain' is a soils boundary. It separates active soils from permafrost (q.v.). It is found where a temperature of $0°$ Celsius persists for 115 days a year and the ground above thaws and refreezes.

ZINC The main zinc ore is sphalerite, often confused with the lead mineral, galena. Both are found in sulfide association. Zinc is the 4th most used metal after steel, aluminum, and copper. It is used to coat iron to prevent rust. The coating process is galvanization.

Sphalerite is common in sulfide deposits in limestones. In the United States, the largest deposits are in Missouri and adjacent states. Zincite, an oxide of zinc, was produced at Franklin, New Jersey for many years.

Metal-rich deposits in the seas off the Pacific Northwest have substantial zinc. These deposits are 400 kilometers (250 miles) off the Oregon Coast. They are at a depth of 2,100 meters (7,000 feet). The muds hold sphalerite with silver and copper. The zinc content is 55%.

As of 1989 the major economic reserves (q.v.) of zinc (in millions of metric tons of zinc content) are found in the following areas:

Canada	24.0
United States	20.0
Australia	19.0
Peru	7.0
Mexico	6.0

U.S. Bureau of Mines, 1990

The world total of resources (q.v.) is estimated at 1.8 billion metric tons. The deepsea resources are not included. In addition to the reserves noted above, the United States has many millions of metric tons of zinc-bearing coal in the midlands, which substantially increase the country's resources.

The major environmental concern with zinc mining is with the co-products of cadmium, lead, and sulfur, which are either toxic or pollutants under certain conditions.

ZINJANTHROPUS Anthropoid fossils given the name, Zinjanthropus, were discovered in Tanzania in 1959. The fossils have been dated 1.75 million years.

The fossils, discovered in Bed I of Olduvai Gorge (q.v.) by the Leakeys, were dated using Potassium-Argon (K-AR). This method is valid for material as old as 5 million years. See **RADIOACTIVE DATING**, **RADIOACTIVE POTASSIUM**.

ZIRCONIUM The chief zirconium ores are zirconite and baddeleyite. Rare zirconium metal has special alloying qualities. Zirconium oxide is used in refractory brick.

Baddeleyite, a relatively rare zirconium mineral, is found in eluvial placers (q.v.) at Poços de Caldas, Brazil. The deposits continue to be worked sporadically.

Zircon is also found in many heavy mineral placers. Trail Ridge, Florida, and beach placers in Travancore, India and Espirito Santo, Brazil have been important sources. The major producer today is Australia with 550,000 metric tons (1989) of zirconium concentrate.

In 1989, major reserves (q.v.) of zirconium (in millions of metric tons of zirconium oxide) were:

South Africa	13.8
Australia	10.8
USSR (estimated)	4.0
United States	3.1
Brazil	1.0
China (estimated)	.5

U.S. Bureau of Mines, 1990

The U.S. has zircon resources (q.v.) amounting to 14 million metric tons contained in titanium sands and in phosphate sand and gravel deposits. The known world resources are put at 60 million tons.

Gem zircon is primarily found in the Mogok Area of North Burma and the Kha District of Indochina. Reddish-brown zircons from Indochina are heat-treated to become colorless.

ZODIAC The Zodiac is a described zone in the night sky which is 16° of arc centered on the ecliptic (q.v.). Most of the Solar System can be seen to revolve around the Sun in this zone.

ZODIACAL LIGHT In the open countryside or at sea, a cone of light appears in the western sky after sunset. It also appears in the east before dawn and has been referred to as the 'false dawn'.

This luminosity appears in definite seasons, after twilight in the Northern Hemisphere from February to April and pre-dawn in October to December. The Germans call it 'Gegenschein' for counter glow. It is refracted and scattered sunlight.

ZOISITE The copper-nickel mineral, zoisite or tanzanite, is a rare blue gemstone of relatively recent popularity. In 1980 the price in Tanzania was $1,000 per carat. The stone is particularly fragile.

ZONAL DESERTS Zonal or low-latitude deserts form an extensive belt from Sahara through Arabia and India to Australia. In South America zonal deserts are confined to the coasts and are backed by high mountains.

ZONE A zone is a sequence of strata with a particular fossil assemblage. The host rock may or may not change at the zonal boundary. Zones have made some stratigraphic correlations easier.

In a mining district the area or region of mineralization is considered a zone.

There are 2 major zones in surface sediments and soils. They are the zone of aeration and zone of saturation. Both are important in the chemical alteration of rocks and minerals. Permeable rocks in the aeration zone do not have their pores filled with water. This is the zone of oxidation. In the zone of saturation, rock and mineral pores are saturated with ground or surface waters. This is the reduction zone.

Where fluctuations of the water table occur during the year due to wet and dry seasons, zones and their chemical activity expand and contract. Special ore development processes require minerals be subjected to the conditions of both zones.

ZOOGEOGRAPHY Alfred Russell Wallace divided the globe into 6 zoogeographical regions, each with its ecosystem with distinctive lifeforms, not found elsewhere. The regions or realms are:

- Nearctic
- Neotropic
- Palearctic
- Ethiopian
- Oriental
- Australian.

See **WALLACE LINE**.

ZOOPLANKTON Marine animals that live as floating organisms are Zooplankton. Often microscopic, the group includes the larval stage of many marine organisms.

Zooplankton, feeding on phytoplankton, migrate vertically in the sea following the light intensity most suited for photosynthesis. In the evening they migrate toward the surface and during daylight hours feed at depths up to 800 meters (2,600 feet) below the surface. See **NANNOPLANKTON**.

ZUIDER ZEE The Zuider Zee in the Netherlands is a shallow bay. The Dutch decided to reclaim a large area and replace saltwater with fresh. The project required 360 kilometers (225 miles) of dike across the mouth of the bay. It was a monumental task to build dikes on the clay seabed.

Tjssel Meer, the lake, was created over 50 years ago. Its object was to protect Holland from flooding and it allowed reclamation of 2,250 square kilometers (870 square miles) of farmland. The reclaimed land is 'polder' (q.v.).

Of recent years the Dutch have been constructing a polder between the lake and Waddensee with a 33 kilometer (20 mile) dike. The dike, Markerwaard, will add 2,330 square kilometers (900 square miles) of arable land.

APPENDIX I

GEOLOGIC TIME				MILLIONS OF YEARS
EON	**ERA**	**PERIOD**	**EPOCH**	
Phanerozoic	Cenozoic	Quaternary	Holocene	
			Pleistocene	
				— 2 —
		Tertiary	Pliocene	— 12 —
			Miocene	— 26 —
			Oligocene	— 37–38 —
			Eocene	— 53–54 —
			Paleocene	— 65 —
	Mesozoic	Cretaceous	Late	
			Early	— 136 —
		Jurassic	Late	
			Middle	
			Early	— 190–195 —
		Triassic	Late	
			Middle	
			Early	— 225 —
	Paleozoic	Permian	Late	
			Early	— 280 —
		Carbon-iferous — Pennsylvanian	Late	
			Middle	
			Early	
		Carbon-iferous — Mississippian	Late	
			Early	— 345 —
		Devonian	Late	
			Middle	
			Early	— 395 —
		Silurian	Late	
			Middle	
			Early	— 430–440 —
		Ordovician	Late	
			Middle	
			Early	— 500 —
		Cambrian	Late	
			Middle	
			Early	— 570 —
Proterozoic	Archaeozoic	Precambrian	Late	
				— 2500 —
			Middle	
				— 4000 —
Archean	Azoic		Early	
				— 4600+ —

Adapted from *Holmes, Edinburgh Geological Society,* 1960
and *Putnam's Geology,* 1975 edition.

Note: Dating is based upon Radiometric estimates.

PERIODIC TABLE OF THE ELEMENTS

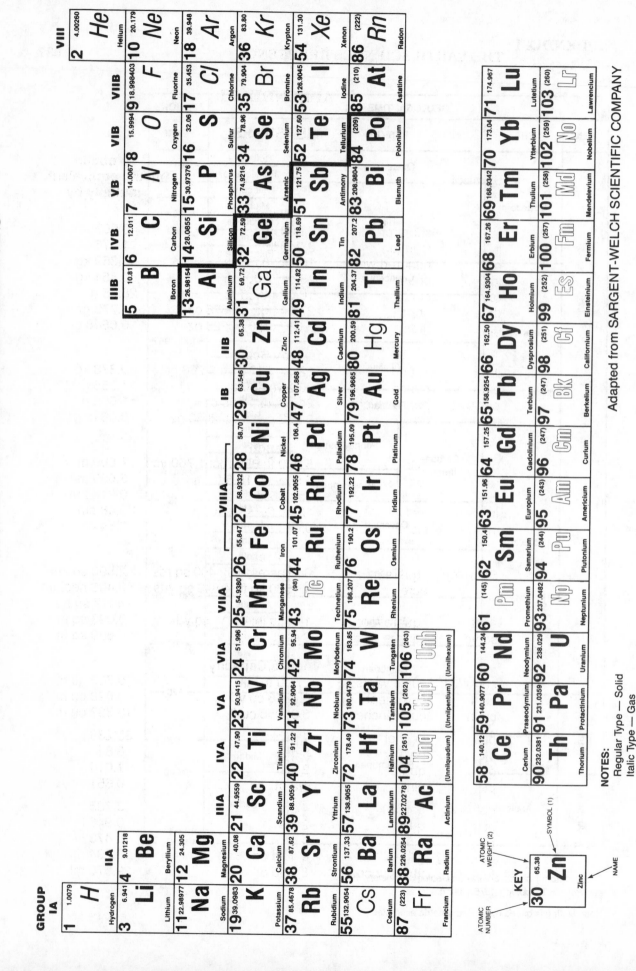

Adapted from SARGENT-WELCH SCIENTIFIC COMPANY

NOTES:
Regular Type — Solid
Italic Type — Gas
Light Type — Liquid
Outline Type — Synthetically Prepared

APPENDIX III

MEASURES

Symbol			To obtain metric equivalent multiply by
		Weight	
st	short ton	2,000 lb	0.907
lt	long ton	2,240 lb	1.016
cwt	hundred weight	100 lb; 0.05 st	45.359 kg
lb/#	pound	16 oz; 7,000 dr	0.454 kg
oz	ounce	16 dr; 437.5 gr	28.35 gr
dr	dram	27.344 gr; 0.0675 oz	1.772 gr
gr	grain	0.037 dr; 0.00228 oz	0.0648 gr
		Troy Scale	
lbt	pound	12 oz; 240 pwt; 5,760 gr	0.373 kg
ozt	ounce	20 pwt; 480 gr	1.555 gr
pwt/dwt	pennyweight	24 grains; 0.05 oz	1.555 gr
gr	grain	0.042 pwt; 0.002083 oz	0.0648 gr
		Length	
mi	mile	5,280 ft; 320 rds; 1,760 yds	1.609 m
rd	rod	5.50 yds; 16.5 ft	5.029 m
yd	yard	3 ft; 36 in	0.9144 m
ft	foot	12 in; 0.333 yds	30.48 cm
in	inch	0.083 ft	2.54 cm
		Area	
Sq mi/m^2	square mile	640 acres; 102,400 sq rds	2.590 sq km
	acre	43,560 sq ft; 4,840 sq yds	0.405 hectare; 4047 sq m
sq ft	square foot	144 sq in; 0.111 sq yd	0.093 sq m
sq yd	square yard	9 sq ft	0.829 sq m
		Volume/Capacity	
cu yd/yd^3	cubic yards	27 cu ft	0.763 cu m
cu ft	cubic feet	0.0376 cu yd	0.028 cu m
cu in	cubic inches	0.00058 cu ft	16.387 cu m
bu	bushel	4 pecks	35.239 l
pk	peck	8 qts	8.8 l
qt	quart	2 pts	1.01 l
pt	pint	1/2 qt	0.551
gal	gallon	4 qts	3.785 l
qt	quart	2 pts	0.946 l
pt	pint	4 gi	0.473 l
gi	gill	4 fluid oz	118.294 ml
fl oz	fluid ounce	8 fluid dr	29.573 ml

BIBLIOGRAPHY

ARTICLES

'Acid rain on acid soil', 1984: Science Vol. 225, p 1424-1434.

Alexander, T., 1975. A revolution called Plate Tectonics has given us a whole new Earth: Smithsonian, Vol. 5, No. 10, p 30-40.

Alfven, H. and Arrhenius, G., 1970. Structures and evolutionary history of the Solar System, I and II: Astrophysical Space Science, Vol.8, p 338-421.

Allard, G. O. & Hurst, 1969. Brazil-Gabon: Science, Vol. 163, p 528-532.

Almeida, F. F. M. de, 1977. O craton de São Francisco: Revista Brasileira de Geosciencias, Rio de Janeiro, Vol. 7, p 349-364.

Almeida, F. F. M. de, 1971. Geochronological division of Precambrian South America: Revista Brasileira de Geociencias, Rio de Janeiro, Vol. l, p 12-21.

Almeida, F. F. M. de, 1953. Botucatu, a Triassic desert of South America: International Geological Congress: Comptes Rendus 19E, No. 7, p 9-24.

Alsop, L. E. & Talwani, M., 1984. The east coast magnetic anomaly: Science, Vol. 226, p 1189.

Alvarez, W., 1984. The end of the Cretaceous: Science, Vol. 223, Vol. 4641, p 1183-1186.

Alvarez, W., et al, 1984. Impact theory of mass extinctions and the invertebrate fossil record: Science, Vol. 223, No. 4641, p 1135-1140.

Amaral, S. E. do, 1971. Geologia e petrologia de Formacao Irati (Permiano) no Estado de São Paulo: Boletim, University of São Paulo, No. 2, p 3-81.

Anderson, D. L., 1984. The Earth as a planet: Science, Vol. 23, No. 4634, p 347-354.

Anderson, D. L., 1971. The San Andreas Fault: Scientific American, Vol. 225, No. 5, p 52-68.

Atwater, T. M., 1970. Implications of plate tectonics for the Cenozoic tectonic evolution of western North America: Geological Society of America, Bulletin, Vol. 81, p 3513-3536.

Audley, C., et al, 1977. Location of major deltas: Geology, Vol. 4, p 341-344.

Averitt, P., 1975. Coal resources of the United States: U.S. Geological Survey, Bulletin 1412, Washington, DC.

Bateman, J. D., 1958. Uranium-bearing auriferous reefs at Jacobina: Economic Geology, Vol. 53, p 417-425.

Bauer, C., 1981. Alumina from alunite, Domestic resources: Mining Engineering, February.

Bolin, B., 1970. The carbon cycle: Scientific American. Vol. 223, No. 3, p 124-132.

Bolt, B. A., 1973. The structures of the Earth's interior: Scientific American, Vol. 228, p 24-33.

Bonnati, E., 1987. The rifting of continents: Scientific American, Vol. 256, No. 3, p. 96-103.

Broecker, W. S., 1984. Ocean: Scientific American, Vol. 249, September, p 146-160.

Brown, L. R. & Wolf, E., 1984. Food crisis in Africa: Natural History, Vol. 93, No. 6, p 16-20.

Budyko, M. I. & Ronov, A. B., 1979. Chemical evolution of the Atmosphere in the Phanerozoic: Geochemisty International, Vol. 16, p 1-9.

Buffey, P. M., 1977. Teton Dam verdict, A foul-up by the engineers: Science, Vol. 195, p 270-272.

Bullard, E. C., 1969. The origins of the oceans: Scientific American, Vol. 221, No. 3, p 66-75.

Bullard, E., et al, 1965. The fit of the continents around the Atlantic: Continental Drift, Philosophical Transactions, Royal Society, London, Vol. 258, No. 1088, p 41-51.

Canby, T. Y, 1980. Water - Our most precious resource, National Geographic, Vol. 158, p 144-179.

Canby, T. Y., 1984. El Nino's ill wind: National Geographic, Vol. 165, No. 2, p 144-183.

Carlisle, J., 1968. Red Tide in California: California Department of Fish & Game, Marine Resources Leaflet No. 2, p 1-4.

Chace, F. M., et al, 1969. Applied geology at the Nickel Mountain Mine, Riddle, Oregon: Economic Geology, Vol. 64, p 1-16.

Chapman, R. W., 1974. Calcareous duricrusts in Al-Hasa, Saudi Arabia: Geological Society of America, Bulletin, Vol. 85, p 119-130.

Chesterman, C. W., 1971. Volcanism in California: California Geology, Vol. 24, p 139-147.

Cole, M., 1960. Cerrado, caatinga, and pantanal; Distribution and origin of savanna vegetation in Brazil: Geographical Journal, Vol. 126, Pt. 2.

Cooke, R., 1965. Desert pavement: California Mineral Information Service, Vol. 18, p 197-200.

Corliss, J. B., 1971. The origin of metal-bearing submarine hydrothermal solutions: Journal Geophysical Research, Vol.76, p 128-138.

Cox, A., et al, 1967. Reversals of the Earth's magnetic field: Scientific American, Vol. 216, No. 2, p 44-54.

D'Assier, A., 1864. Le mato virgem; scenes et souvenirs d'un voyage au Bresil: Revue des Deux Mondes, Vol. XLIX, I.

Dahlin, B. H., 1983. Climate and prehistory of the Yucatan Peninsula, In: Climatic Changes, Vol 5, p 245-263.

Daly, R. A., 1936. The origin of submarine canyons: American Journal Science, Series 5, Vol. 31, No. 186, p 401-420.

Daugherty, A. E., 1966. Marine mammals of California: California Department of Fish & Game, Bulletin, p 1-86.

Dawson, J. B. et al, 1987. Altered former alkalic carbonatite lava from Oldoinyo Lengai, Tanzania: Inferences for calcite carbonatite lavas: Geology, No. 15, p 765-768

De Vletter, D. R, 1955. How Cuban nickel ore was formed, A lesson in laterite genesis: Engineering & Mining Journal, Vol. 156, No. 10.

Deacon, G.E.R., 1958. Upwelling in the Peru and Benguela Currents, In: Proceedings, 9th Pacific Science Congress: Oceanography, Vol. 16, p 78.

Degens, E. T. & Ross, D. A, 1970. The Red Sea hot brines: Scientific American, Vol. 222, No. 4, p 32-42.

Deevey, E. S., 1960. The human population: Scientific American, Vol. 203, No.3, p 194-204.

Denton, G. and Porter, S., 1970. Neoglaciation: Scientific American, Vol. 226, No. 6, p 101-110.

Dietz, R. S., 1972. Geosynclines, mountains, and continent building: Scientific American, Vol 226, No. 3, p 30-38.

Dietz, R. S., 1964. Sudbury structure as an astrobleme: Journal of Geology, Vol. 72, No. 4, p 412-434..

Dietz, R. S., 1962. The sea's deep scattering layers: Scientific American, Vol. 207, No. 2, p 44-64.

Dietz, R. S., 1961. Continent and ocean basin evolution by spreading of sea floor: Nature, Vol. 190, p 854-857.

Dietz, R. S. and Holden, J. C., 1970. The breakup of Pangaea: Scientific American, Vol. 223, No. 4, p 30-41.

Douglas, J. H., 1975. Climate changes, chilling possibilities: Science News, Vol. 107, p 138-140.

Ehrlich, A. H. & Ehrlich, P.R., 1985, The Serengeti: a natural ecosystem: Mother Earth News, 96, p 126-128.

Ellis, William, 1987. Africa's Sahel, The stricken land: National Geographic, Vol. 172, No. 2, p 140.

Emery, K. O., 1977. Marine deposits of the deep ocean floor: Marine Mining, Vol. 1, Nos. l and 2.

Emiliani, C., et al, 1981. Sudden death at the end of the Mesozoic: Earth & Planetary Science Letters, No. 55, p 317-334.

Erichsen, G. E., et al, 1978. Chemical composition and distribution of lithium-rich brines in Salar de Uyuni and near-by salars in SW Bolivia: Energy, Vol. 3, No. 3, p 355-363.

Ericson, D., et al, 1964. The Pleistocene Epoch in deep sea sediments: Science, November.

Ericson, D. B., et al, 1954. Coiling direction of 'Globergerina truncatilinoides' in deep sea cores: Deep Sea Research, Vol. 2, p 152-158.

Fisk, M. R., 1986. Mid-ocean ridge basalts from Galapagos spreading center: Geology, Vol 14, p 204-207.

Ford, T., 1980. Life in the Precambrian: Nature, Vol. 285, May 22, p 193-194.

Frederickson, A. F., 1952. The genetic significance of mineralogy, In: Problems of clay and laterite genesis, American Institute of Mining Engineers, p 1-11.

Funk, B., 1980. Hurricane: National Geographic, Vol. 158, p 346- 379.

Gastil, G. et al, 1975. Tectonics and reconstruction of the Mesozoic of California: Proceedings, International Geological Congress, Section 3, pp 211-239.

Gates, W. R., et al, 1976. Variations in the Earth's orbit, Pacemaker of the Ice Ages: Science, Vol. 194, No. 4270, p 1121- 1132.

Gillson, J. L., 1959. Sand deposits of titanium minerals: Mining Engineering, April, p 421-429

Guerra, A. Teixera, 1953. Formacao de lateritos sob a floresta equatorial no Territorio Federal do Guapore: Revista Brasileira de Geografia, Ano XIV, No. 4.

Guttenberg, Beno., 1960. Low velocity layers in the Earth, Oceans, and Atmosphere: Science, Vol. 131, p 959-965.

Haag, W. G., 1962. The Bering Land Bridge: Scientific American, January, p 112-120.

Hallam, A. 1975. Alfred Wegener and the hypothesis of Continental Drift: Scientific American, February.

Hallam, A. 1972. Continental drift and the fossil record: Scientific American, November.

Hammond, E. M., 1954. Geomorphic study of Cape Region of Baja California: Univ. California, Publications in Geography, Vol. 10, No. 2, p 45-115.

Hammond, P. E., 1980. Mt. St. Helens blasts 400 m of its peak: Geotimes, 25, p 14-15.

Harrison, D. E., 1984. The appearance of sustained equatorial surface Westerlies during 1982 Pacific warm event: Science, Vol. 224, No. 4653, p 1099-1102.

Heezen, B. C., 1952. The origin of submarine canyons: Scientific American, Vol. 63, p 225-240.

Heezen, B. C. & Ewing, M., 1952. Turbidity currents and submarine slumps, and the Grand Banks Earthquake: American Journal of Science, Vol. 250, p 849-873.

Hendrey, G. R., 1981. Acid rain and gray snow: Natural History, Vol. 90, p 58-65.

Herz, N., 1977. Timing of spreading in the South Atlantic: Information from Brazilian alkaline rocks: Geological Society of America, Bulletin 88, p 102-112.

Hiertzler, J. R., 1968. Sea floor spreading: Scientific American, Vol. 219, No. 6, p 60-70.

Heirtzler, J. R. and Bryan, W. B., 1975. The floor of the Mid-Atlantic Rift: Scientific American, August.

Hirsch, R. L., 1987. Impending United States energy crisis: Science, Vol. 235, p 1467-1472.

Houston, B. R., 1971. Industrial clay minerals: Queensland Geological Survey, Rept No. 65, p 1-70.

Hsu, K. J., et al, 1982. Mass mortality and its environmental evolutionary consequences: Science Vol. 216, p 249-256.

Hsu, K. J., 1972. When the Mediterranean dried up: Scientific American, Vol. 227, No. 6, p 26-37.

Humphrey, F. L. & Allard, G. O., 1968. The Propia Geosyncline, a newly recognized Precambrian tectonic province in the Brazilian Shield: International Geological Congress, Prague, Vol. 3, p 123- 139.

Hunt, M., 1988. Titanium: The right stuff for land, air, and sea: Materials Engineering, Vol. 505, p 45-49

Hurley, P., 1968. The confirmation of Continental Drift: Scientific American, Vol 218, p 52-64.

Issar, Arie, 1985. Fossil water under Sinai-Negev Peninsula: Scientific American Vol. 253, No. l.

Jackson, J. K., 1956. The vegetation of the Imatong Mountains, Sudan: Journal Ecology, No. 44.

James, D. E., 1973. The evolution of the Andes: Scientific American, August.

Jordan, T. H., 1978. Compaction and development of the continental tectosphere: Nature, Vol. 274, August 10, p 544-548.

Karig, D. E., 1971. Structural history of the Mariana Island Arc System: Geological Society America, Bulletin, Vol. 82, p 323-344.

Kennedy, G. C., 1959. The origin of continents, mountain ranges, and ocean basins: American Scientist, Vol. 47, p 491-504.

Kent, D., et al, 1971. Climate change in the North Pacific using ice-rafted detritus as a climatic indicator: Geological Society America, Bulletin, Vol.82, No. 10 p 2741-2754.

Kerr, P. F., 1963. Quick clay: Scientific American, Vol. 209, p 132-142.

Kerr, R. A., 1987. Tracking the wandering poles: Science, Vol. 236 (Apr. 10), p 147-148.

Kerr, Richard A., 1987. Another El Niño surprise in the Pacific, But was it predicted?: Science, 13 February, p 744-745.

Kloosterman. J. B., 1967. A tin province of the Nigerian type in southern Amazonia: Technical Conference on Tin, Papers No. 2, p 383-399.

Knight, C. and Knight, N., 1973. Snow crystals: Scientific American, Vol. 228, No. 1, p 100-107.

Krynine, P. D., 1956. Alice in greywackeland: Journal of Paleontology, p 1003-1004.

Kufs, C. & Twedell, D. 1980. Cleaning up hazardous landfills: Geotimes, 25, p 18-19.

Kurten, B., 1969. Continental drift and evolution: Scientific American, Vol. 220, p 54-64.

La Bastille, A., 1981. Acid rain, How great a menace: National Geographic, Vol. 160, p 652-681.

Landwehr, W. R., 1967. Belts of major mineralization in western United States: Economic Geology, Vol. 62, p 494-501.

Larson, R. L., et al, 1968. Gulf of California, A result of ocean floor spreading and transform faulting: Science, Vol. 161, p 781-783.

Latham, C., et al, 1969. The Apollo passive seismic experiment: Science, Vol. 165, p 241-250.

Laughton, A. S., 1971. South Labrador Sea and the evolution of the North Atlantic: Nature, Vol. 232, p 612-617.

Leopold, L. & Langbein, W.B., 1966. River meanders: Scientific American, Vol.214, No.6, p 60-70.

Litherland, M. & Bloomfield, K., 1981. The Proterozoic history of eastern Bolivia: Precambrian Research, Vol. 15, p 157-174.

Lowry, W. D., 1974. North American geosynclines - Test of continental Drift Theory: American Association Petroleum Geologists, Bulletin, 58, No. 4, p 575-620.

Luten, D., 1971. The economic geography of energy: Scientific American, Vol. 224, No. 3, p 165-175.

Macdonald, K. C. , et al, 1981. Crest of the East Pacific Rise: Scientific American, Vol. 244, No. 5, pp 100-116.

MacKenzie, S. D., 1986. Acid rain may trigger Alpine avalanche: New Scientist, Vol. 109, No. 10.

Malkus, J. S., 1957. The origin of hurricanes: Scientific American, Vol. 197, No. 2, p 33-39.

Matthes, F. E. [1930]. Geological history of Yosemite Valley: U.S. Geological Survey, Professional Paper.

Maugh, T. H. III, 1984. Acid rain's affect on people assessed: Science, Vol. 226, (21 Dec.), p 1408-1410.

McCloskey, W., 1985. Along the Chesapeake: Oceans, Vol. 18, No. 3, p 3-8.

McDonald, J.E., 1952. The Coriolis Effect: Scientific American, Vol. 197, No. 5, p 72-78.

McKenzie, D. P. & Morgan, W. J., 1969. Evolution of a triple junction: Nature, Vol. 224, p 125-133.

McKenzie, D.P. & Sclatery, G., 1973. The evolution of the Indian Ocean: Scientific American, May.

McNeil, M., 1982, Panasqueira, Europe's most productive wolfram mine: World Mining, Vol. 35, No. 12, p. 52-55.

McNeil, M., 1980. Brazilian uranium deposits and United States corollaries: Mining Year Book, National Western Mining Conference, p 150-158.

McNeil, M., 1964. Lateritic soils: Scientific American, Vol. 211, No. 5, p 96-117.

Menard, H. W., 1969. The deep-ocean floor: Scientific American, Vol. 221, No. 3, p 126-142.

Menard, H. W., 1961. The East Pacific Rise: Scientific American, Vol. 205, No. 6, p 52-61.

Mero, J. L., 1960. Minerals on the ocean floor: Scientific American, Vol. 203, No. 6, p. 64-72.

Meyer, C., 1985. Ore metals through geological history: Science, Vol. 227, No. 4693, p 1421-1428.

Meyerhoff, A. A., 1970. Continental drift, Implications of paleo-magnetic studies, meteorology, physical oceanography, and climatology; Journal of Geology, Vol. 78, No. 1, p 1-51.

Mierelles, Filho, J., 1985. The perils of deforestation: World Press Review No. 32:33, May.

Molnar, P., 1986. The structure of mountain ranges: Scientific American Vol. 255, No.l, p 70-79.

Moran, J. M, 1975. Return of the Ice Age and drought in peninsula Florida: Geology, Vol. 3, No. 12, p 695-696.

Morrison, C. G. T., et al, 1948. Tropical soil-vegetation catenas and mosaics, A study in the southwestern part of the Anglo-Egyptian Sudan: Journal Ecology, No. 35.

Morrison, P. et al, Eds., 1977. The search for extra-terrestrial life, SETI: NASA, Special Paper 419.

Mullins, H. T. & Rausch, R. F., 1985. Seafloor phosphorites along Central California continental margin: Economic Geology Vol. 80, p 696-715.

Munk, W. H., 1941. Internal waves in the Gulf of California: Journal Marine Research, Vol. 4, No. 2, p 81-91.

Mutter, J. C., 1986. Seismic images of plate boundaries: Scientific American, Vol. 254, No. 2, p 66-75.

Neill, W. M., 1976. Mesozoic epeirogeny at the South Atlantic margin and the Tristan hot spot: Geology, Vol. 4, p 495-498.

O'Hara, J., 1985. The billion $ problem: MacLeans, Vol. 98, p 34.

Padula, V. T., 1969. Oil shale of Permian Irati Formation: American Association of Petroleum Geologists, Bulletin, Vol. 53, No. 3, p 591-602.

Patterson, J. T., 1969, The climate of cities: U.S. Public Health Service Publication, No. AP-59, Washington, DC.

Pecora, W., 1944. Ni-silicate and associated Ni-Co-Mn oxide deposits near Sao Jose de Tocantins, Goiaz, Brazil: U.S. Geological Survey, Bulletin, 935-E, p 247-305.

Peebles, P.J.L., 1984. Origin of galaxies and clusters of galaxies: Science, Vol. 224, No. 4656, p 1385-1391.

Petraschek, W. E., 1973. Some aspects of the relations between continental drift and metallogenic provinces, In: Implications of Contintal Drift to Earth Science: NATO Advanced Study Institute, Vol. I, p 567-572.

Pettijohn, F.J., 1950. Turbidity currents and greywackes: Journal of Geology, Vol 58, p 169-171.

Ploessel, M. R. & Slosson, J. E., 1974, Repeatable high ground acceleration from earthquakes: California Geology, 27, p 195-99.

Prewitt, K., 1984. Methane from anaerobic fermentation: Science, Vol. 223, No. 4640, p 1021-1027.

Price, L. W., 1974. The periglacial environment, Permafrost and man: Am. Assoc. Geographers, Resource Paper No. 14.

Raff, A. D., 1961. The magnetism of the ocean floor: Scientific American, October, p 146-156.

Ramage, C. S., 1986. El Nino: Scientific American, Vol. 254, No. 6, p 76-83.

Rampino, M. & Self, S., 1984. The atmospheric effects of El Chichon: Scientific American, Vol. 250, No.l, p 48-57.

Rampino, M. E. & Stothers, R. B., 1984. Geological rhythms and cometary impacts: Science, Vol. 276, p 1427-1431.

Redfield, A. C., 1961. The tidal system of Lake Maracaibo, Venezuela: Limnology and Oceanography, Vol. 6, No. l, p 1-9.

Reisner, M., 1981. Are we headed for another dustbowl? Readers' Digest, Vol. 118, p 87-92.

Revelle, R., 1982. Carbon dioxide and world climate: Scientific American, Vol. 247, No. 2, p 35-43.

Risser, J. 1981. A renewed threat of soil erosion: It's worse than the Dust Bowl: Smithsonian, Vol. 11, p 119-131.

Rona, P., 1986. Mineral deposits from sea floor spreading: Scientific American, Vol. 254, p 84-92.

Rona, P., 1973. Plate tectonics and mineral resources: Scientific American, July.

Russ, D. P., 1979. Late Holocene faulting and earthquake recurrence in Reelfoot Lake area, northwestern Tennessee: Geological Society of America, Vol. 90, No. 1, p 1,013-1,018.

Sagan, C., et al, 1979. Anthropogenic albedo changes and the Earth's climate: Science, Vol. 206, p 1,363-1,368.

'Sahel will suffer even if rains come': Science, Vol. 224, No. 4648.

Sargent, Bill, 1985, Striped bass and acid rain: Oceans, Vol. 18, No.3, p 8-9.

Schwartz, D. F., et al, 1979. Quaternary faulting along the Caribbean-North American Plate boundary in Central America: Tectonophysics: Vol. 52, p 431-445.

Seliger, H. H. et al, 1985. Climate conspires against oxygen and oysters: Science News, Vol. 127, p. 214.

Seward, F. D., et al, 1985. Super nova remnants: Scientific American, Vol. 253, No. 2, p 88-96.

Sieh, K. E., 1978. Prehistoric large earthquakes produced by slip on the San Andreas Fault at Pallett Creek, California: Journal Geophysical Research, Vol. 83, No. 3, p 309-339.

Stommel, N. & Stommel, E., 1979. Year without a summer: Scientific American, Vol. 240, No. 6, p 176-186.

Stothers, R. B., 1984. The great Tambora eruption in 1815 and its aftermath: Science Vol. 224, No. 4,654, p 1,191-1,197.

Swanson, D. A., et al, 1971. Mauna Ulu eruption, Kilauea Volcano: Geotimes, Vol. 16, No. 5, p 12-16.

Tarling, D. H., 1973. Metallic ore deposits and continental drift: Nature, Vol. 243, p 193-195.

Torquato, F. R. F. & Cordiani, U. G., 1981. Brazil-Africa geological links: Earth Science Review, Vol. 17, p 155-176.

Valentine, J. W. & Moores, E. M., 1974. Plate tectonics and the history of life in the oceans: Scientific American, April.

Vink, G. E., et al, 1985. The Earth's hot spots: Scientific American, Vol. 252, pp 50-57.

Wagner, L. R. [1937]. The Arun River drainage pattern and the rise of the Himalayas: Geographical Journal, Vol. 89, p 239-249.

Waldrop, M. M., 1987. The supernova 1978A shows a mind of its own - A burst of neutrinos: Science Vol. 235, No. 4794.

Waldrop, M. M., 1983. The new inflationary Universe: Science, Vol. 219, p 375-377.

Wesson, R., 1980. New Madrid Fault zone seen: Geotimes, 25, p 17.

West, I., et al, 1979. Primary gypsum nodules in a modern sabkha on Mediterranean coast of Egypt: Geology, Vol. 7, p 354-358.

BOOKS

Abbot, P. L. & Gastil, R. G., Eds., 1979. Baja California Geology: San Diego State Univ.

Abbott, I. A. & Hollenberg, G. J., Eds., 1976. Marine Algae of California: Stanford University.

Abreu, F. de, 1965. Recursos minerais do Brasil. 2nd Ed., IBGE, Rio de Janeiro.

Adams, F. D., 1954. The birth and development of the geological sciences: Dover, New York.

Adler, I., 1971. Atomic energy: John Day, New York.

Ahn, P. M., 1970. West African soils: Oxford Press, London.

Ahrens, L. H., 1965. Distribution of the elements in our planet: McGraw-Hill, New York.

Ainsworth, E. M., et al, 1970. Pacific slope geology of northern Baja California and adjacent Alta California, In Guidebook, American Association of Petroleum Geologists.

Allegre, C., 1988. The behavior of the Earth, Continental and sea floor mobility: Harvard University Press, Cambridge, MA.

Alt, D., 1982. Physical geology, A process approach: Wadsworth Publications, Belmont, CA.

Anderson, M. K., 1987. Siberia: Dodd, Mead, New York.

Arkoll, D. B., 1979. Nutrient recycling as alternative to shifting cultivation, In: Proceedings, Economic Development and Eco-logical Farming: Pergamon, Berlin.

Ashworth, W., 1977. Hells Canyon, The deepest gorge on Earth: Hawthorn, New York.

Austin, M., 1903. Land of little rain. Houghton, Mifflin, Boston.

Aylesworth, T. G., 1979. Geological disasters: Watts, New York.

Azimov, I., 1985. How did we find out about the Atmosphere? Walker, New York.

Azimov, I., 1990. Frontiers: Dutton, New York.

Azimov, I., 1971. Inside the atom: Abelard-Schuman, New York.

Bailey, D. K., 1966. Carbonatite volcanoes and shallow intrusions in Zambia: In Carbonatites, Tuttle and Gittins, Eds.: Interscience, New York, pp 127-154.

Bailey, H. P., 1966. The climate of Southern California, Natural History Guide #17, University of California Press, Berkeley.

Bagnold, R. A., 1941. The physics of blown sand and desert dunes: Methuen, London.

Baldwin, J. L., 1973. Climate of the United States: U.S. Department of Commerce, Washington, DC.

Bannikov, A. G. et al, 1961. Biology of the Taiga: Israel Program for Scientific Translations.

Barbour, K. M., 1961. The waters of the Nile and their control: The Republic of Sudan, a regional geography: University of London Press, pp 109-127.

Barnea, J., 1974. Geothermal power, In: Planet Earth, Readings from Scientific American: Freeman, San Francisco.

Barry, R. G. & Chorley, R. J., 1970. Atmosphere, weather, and climate: Holt Rhinehart, New York.

Basile, R. A., 1971. A geography of soils: Brown, Dubuque, IO. Bascom, W., 1964. Waves and beaches: Anchor, New York.

Bascom, W., 1961. A hole in the bottom of the sea; story of the Mohole Project: Doubleday, Garden City, NY.

Bates, M., 1970. A jungle in the house, Essays in natural and unnatural history: Walker, New York.

Bates, M., 1961. The forest and the sea: Museum Press, London.

Bates, M., 1950. The nature of natural history: Scribner's, New York.

Bates, R. L., 1987. Stone, clay, glass, How building materials are found and used: Enslow, Hillside, NJ.

Bates, R. L., 1969. Geology of industrial rocks and minerals: Dover, New York.

Battan, L. J., 1962. Cloud physics and cloud seeding: Anchor, Doubleday, New York.

Beebe, W., 1934. Half mile down. Duell, New York.

Bell, P. & Wright, D., 1985. Rocks and minerals, Macmillan, New York.

Bentley, W. A. & Humphries, W. J., 1964. Snow crystals: Dover, New York.

Bergaust, E., 1971. Illustrated nuclear encyclopedia: Putnam's, New York.

Berger, M., 1983. Bright stars, red giants, and white dwarfs: Putnam, New York.

Berger, M., 1978. Planets, stars and galaxies: Putnam, New York.

Berger, M., 1977. Quasars, pulsars, and black holes in Space: Putnam, New York.

Berry, L. B. & Mason, B., 1959. Mineralogy: Freeman, San Francisco. Bermann, P. G., 1987. The riddle of gravitation, Revised Edition.

Bigarella, J. J., 1973. Geology of the Amazon and Paranaiba.

Barnes, C. W., 1980. Earth, time and life: John Wiley, New York.

Basins. In: The ocean basins and margins, Pt. 1, pp 25-86.

Billings, C., 1984. Microchip, Small wonder: Dodd, Mead, New York.

Bird, E. C. F., 1985. Coastal changes, A global view: Wiley, New York.

Birkeland, P. W, 1974. Pedology, weathering, and geomorphological research: Oxford Univ., London.

Birkeland, P. W., & Larson, E., Eds., 1978. Putnam's geology, 3rd Edition: Oxford Univ. Press, New York.

Birot, P., 1968. The cycle of erosion in different climates: Batsford, Great Britain.

Blackwelder, E. et al, 1948. The Great Basin, Bulletin, Vol. 38, No. 20, University of Utah.

Blair, C. H., 1986. Exploring the sea. Random House, New York.

Blair, T. A. & Fite, R. C., 1957. Weather elements, 4th Ed.: Prentice Hall, Englewood Cliffs, NJ.

Blair, R. Van Ness, 1975. Mary's monster: Coward, New York.

Blumenstock, D. I., 1959. The ocean of air: Rutgers Univ. Press, New Brunswick, NJ.

Bok, B. J. & Bok, P. F., 1981. The Milky Way, 5th Rev.Ed., Harvard Univ. Press, Cambridge, MA.

Bolin, B., 1974. The carbon cycle, In: Planet Earth, Readings from Scientific American: Freeman, San Francisco.

Bolt, B.A., 1978. Earthquakes, A primer: Freeman, San Francisco.

Bolt, B.A., 1974. The fine structure of the Earth's interior, In: Planet Earth, Readings from Scientific American, Freeman, San Francisco.

Bolt, B.A., et al, 1975. Geological hazards: Springer-Verlag, New York.

Bonavia, J., 1986. The Yangzi River: Passport Books, Lincolnwood, IL.

Bowen, W. L., 1928. The evolution of igneous rocks: Princeton University Press, NJ.

Bramwell, M., 1989. Oceanography: Science frontiers: Hampstead Press, New York.

Branley, F. M., 1984. Comets: Crowell, New York.

Branley, F. M., 1982. Water for the world: Crowell, New York.

Branley, F. M., 1979. The electromagnetic spectrum: Crowell, New York

Branley, F. M., 1972. Pieces of another world, The story of Moon rocks: Crowell, New York.

Breison, R. A., 1961. Research in physical limnology in the Dept. of Meteorology: University of Michigan, 1949-1961.

Briggs, P., 1971. 200,000,000 years beneath the sea: Holt, Rinehart, Winston, New York.

Briggs, P., 1968. The great global rift: Waybright & Talley, New York.

Brindze, R., 1973. Hurricanes, Monster storms from the sea: Atheneum, New York.

Brindze, R., 1945. The Gulf Stream: Vanguard, New York.

Brinkworth, M., 1985. Energy, Tomorrow's World Series: BBC, London.

Brobst, D. A. & Pratt, W. P., United States mineral resources: Professional Paper 820, U.S. Geological Survey, Washington, D.C.

Bronowski, J. & Selsam, M. E., 1963. Biography of an atom: Harper & Row, New York.

Brooks, C. E. P., 1970. Climate through the ages: Dover, New York.

Brown, A. S., 1985. Fuel resources: Watts, New York.

Brown, W. R. & Cuchen, B. W., 1975. Floods: Addison-Wesley, Reading, MA.

Brown, L. A., 1950. Map making, The art that became a science: Little, Brown, Boston.

Bryson, A. R. & Murray, T. J., 1977. Climates of hunger, Mankind and the world's changing weather: University of Wisconsin.

Budel, J., 1966. Deltas, A basis of culture and civilization, In: Scientific problems of the Humid Tropical Zone deltas and their implications: UNESCO, Paris.

Burchill, R. W., 1975. The environmental impact handbook: Center Urban Policy, Rutgers, NJ.

Buringh, P., 1970. Introduction to the study of soils in tropical and subtropical regions, 2nd Ed.: Centre for Agricultural Publishing and Documentation, Wageningen, Netherlands.

Burke, J. G,, 1986. Meteorites in history: University of California, Berkeley.

Burton, R., 1868. Exploration in the highlands of Brazil, 2 vols: London.

Butzer, K. W., 1976. Geomorphology: University of Chicago Press.

Calder, N., 1972. The restless Earth, A report on the new geology: Viking, New York.

Calvin, W. H., 1986. The river that flows uphill, A journey from the Big Bang to the big brain: Macmillan, New York.

Cameron, J., 1976. Afghanistan: IAEA, Vienna, Austria.

Canter, L W., 1977. Environmental impact: McGraw Hill, New York.

Cargo, D. N. & Mallory, B.F., 1974. Man and his geologic environment: Addison-Wesley, Reading, MA.

Carlisle, D., 1980. Possible variations on the calcrete-gypcrete uranium model: U.S. Department of Energy/University of California, Los Angeles.

Carlisle, D., et al, Ed., 1986. Mineral exploration: Biological systems and organic matter: Prentice Hall, NJ.

Carlisle, D. et al, 1978. The distribution of calcretes and gypcretes in Southwestern United States: U.S. Department of Energy/University of California, Los Angeles.

Carmouze, J. P. et al, Eds., 1983. Lake Chad: Monographiae Biologicae, Vol. 53.

Carlson, P., 1980, Biology and crop productivity: Academic Press, New York.

Carroll, D., 1970, Rock weathering: Plenum, New York.

Carson, R., 1962. Silent spring: Houghton, Mifflin, Boston,

Carson, R., 1955. The edge of the sea: Houghton, Mifflin, Boston.

Carson, R., 1951. The sea around us: Oxford, New York.

Caufield, C., 1985. In the rainforest, Report from a strange, beautiful, imperiled world: Knopf, New York.

Chapman, R. D., 1978. Discovering astronomy: Freeman, San Francisco.

Cheney, G. A., 1984. The Amazon: Watts, New York.

Chester, M., 1967. Relativity. Norton, New York.

Clapman, W. B., 1983. Natural ecosystems: Macmillan, New York.

Cloud, P. & Gibor, A., 1976. The oxygen cycle, In: Planet Earth, Readings from Scientific American: Freeman, San Francisco.

Cloud, P., Ed., 1969. Resources and man: W. H. Freeman, San Francisco.

Cloud, P., 1971. Resources, population, and the quality of life, In: Singer, S.F., Ed., Is there an optimum level of population? McGraw-Hill, New York.

Cloudsley-Thompson, J., 1975. Desert life, In: Deserts and grasslands: Hermitage, London.

Coates, D. R., 1981. Environmental geology: Wiley, New York.

Coker, R. E., 1947. This great and wide sea: University of North Carolina, Chapel Hill.

Colbert, E. H., 1983. Dinosaurs, An illustrated history: Hammond, Maplewood, NJ.

Compton, R. R., 1977. Interpreting the Earth: Harcourt Brace, New York.

Compton, R. R., 1962. A manual of field geology: Wiley, New York.

Cook, D., 1985. Ocean life: Crown, New York.

Cook, P. J.. & Shergold, J. H., Eds., 1978. Proterozoic-Cambrian phosphorites: UNESCO, Project 156, Canberra, Australia.

Cooke, R. U. & Warren, A., 1973. Geomorphology in deserts: University of California, Berkeley.

Coombs, C., 1978. Pipeline across Alaska: Morrow, New York.

Cooper, W. W., 1922. The broad-sclerophyll vegetation of California: Carnegie Institute, Publication 319, Washington, D.C.

Corner, E. J. H., 1966. The natural history of palms: University of California, Berkeley.

Corrick, J. A., 1986. Recent revolutions in chemistry: Watts, New York.

Couffer, J. & Couffer, M. 1978. Salt marsh summer: Putnam, New York.

Cousteau, J. I., 1965. World without sun: Harper & Row, New York.

Cox, A., Ed., 1973. Plate tectonics and geomagnetic reversals: Freeman, San Francisco.

Credland,P., 1975.Rivers and lakes: Interiberica, Madrid.

Critchfield, H. J., 1983. General climatology, 4th Ed.: Prentice Hall, Englewood Cliffs, NJ.

Cronin, E. W., Jr., 1979. The Arun, A natural history of the world's deepest valley: Houghton Mifflin, Boston.

Crowell, J. C., & Sylvester, A. G., Eds., 1979. Tectonics of the juncture between the San Andreas Fault System and the Salton Trough, Southeastern California: University of California, Santa Barbara.

Crump, D., Ed., 1983. Nature's world of wonders.

Cvancara, A. 1989. Sleuthing fossils: The art of investigating past life: Johne Wiley, New York.

Dalton, F., 1977. The weather: Wayland, Hove Sussex, England.

Dalton, S. & Bailey, Jill, 1987. Secret life of a forest: Salem House, Great Britain.

Dana, J. D., 1962. The System of Mineralogy, 7th Ed. 3 vols.: Wiley, New York.

Darlington, P. J., 1965. Biogeography of the southern end of the world: Harvard University, Cambridge, MA.

Darlington, P. J., 1957. Zoogeography: Wiley, New York.

Davies, D., 1969. Fresh water, The precious resource: Natural History, Garden City, NY.

Davies, J. L., 1969. Landforms of cold climates: MIT Press, Cambridge, MA.

Davis, K. & Leopold, L.. 1970, Water: Silver Burdett, New York.

De Santis, M., 1985. California currents: Presidio Press, San Francisco.

De Voto, R. H. & Stevens, D. N., 1979. Uraniferous phosphate resources, 3 Vols.: U.S. Department of Energy/Earth Sciences, Grand Junction, CO.

Deer, W. A., Howie, R. A., and Sussman, J., 1966. Introduction to the rockforming minerals: Wiley, New York.

Defant, A., 1961. Physical Oceanography: Pergamon, New York.

Defant, A., 1958. Ebb and flow, The tides of the earth, air, and water: University of Michigan, Ann Arbor.

Delwiche, C. C., 1974. The nitrogen cycle, In: Planet Earth, Readings from Scientific American, Freeman, San Francisco.

Departamento Nacional de Producao Mineral, 1988. Sumario Mineral: Brasilia.

Desmond, A.J., 1976. The hot-blooded dinosaurs, A revolution in paleontology: Doubleday, New York.

Dorst, J., 1967. South American and Central America, A natural history: Random House, New York.

Du Toit, A. L., 1937. Our wandering continents: Oliver & Boyd, Edinburgh.

Du Toit, A. L., 1927. A geological comparison of South America with South Africa: Carnegie Institute, Publication 381, Washington, DC.

Duffey, E., 1975. Grassland life, In: Deserts and grasslands: Hermitage, London.

Dunbar, C. O., 1964. Historical geology, 2nd Ed., Wiley, New York.

Duncan & Swanson, 1965. Organic rich shales of the U.S. and world land areas: U.S. Geological Survey, Washington, D.C.

Eagleman, J. R., 1980. Meteorology, The Atmosphere in action: Van Nostrand, New York.

Ehlers, E. G. & Blatt, H., 1982. Petrology: Freeman, San Francisco.

Ehrlich, P. R., 1986. The machinery of nature: Simon & Schuster, New York.

Ehrlich, P. R. & Ehrlich, A. H., 1990. The Population Explosion: Simon & Schuster, New York.

Ehrlich, P. R. & Ehrlich, A. H., 1972. Population, resources, environment, Issues in human ecology: Freeman, San Francisco.

Eiseley, L. 1969. The unexpected Universe, 4th Ed., Harcourt, New York.

Elliot, J. & Kerr, R., 1984. Rings, Discoveries from Galileo to Voyager: MIT Press, Cambridge, MA.

Ellis, R. H., Jr., 1973. Knowing the atomic nucleus: Lothrop, Lee & Shepard, New York.

Embleton, C. & King, C., 1968. Glacial and periglacial geomorphology: St. Martins, New York.

Englehert, E. A. & Scheuring, A. F., Eds., 1984. Water scarcity: University of California, Berkeley.

Ericksen, G. D., et al, 1970. Preliminary report on the geological events associated with the May 31, 1970 Peru earthquake: U.S. Geological Survey, Circular 639, Washington, DC.

Ewing, M., 1958. The crust and mantle of the Earth: American Geophysical Union, Geophysics Monograph 2.

Ewing, M. & Press, F., 1955. Geophysical contrasts between continents and ocean basins: Geological Society of America, Special Paper, Vol. 62.

Eyre,S.R.,1968. Vegetation and soils, A world picture, 2nd Edition: Arnold, London.

Facklam, M. & Facklam, H., 1986. Changes in the wind, Earth's shifting climate: Harcourt Brace Jovanovich, San Diego.

Falesi, I. C., 1974. Soils of the Brazilian Amazon, In: Man in the Amazon, C. Wagley, Ed.: Univ. Florida, Gainsville.

Fanning, A. E., 1966. Planets, stars and galaxies (revised by D. H. Menzel): Dover, New York.

Farnsworth, E. G. and Golley, F. B., Eds. 1973. Fragile ecosystems: Springer-Verlag, New York.

Fenton, C. L. & Fenton, M. A., 1951. Rocks and their stories: Doubleday, New York.

Ferreira, A. & Pereira da Cruz, M.M., 1985. Geografia fisica, 2nd Edition: Edicoes ASA, Porto, Portugal.

Fetter, C. W., 1980. Applied Hydrogeology: Merrill, Columbus, OH.

Fife, D. & Brown, A. R., Eds., 1980. Geology and mineral wealth of California Desert: South Coast Geological Society, Santa Ana.

Fishman, J. & Kalish, R., 1990. Global alert, The Ozone Pollution Crisis: Plenum, N.Y.

Flenley, J., 1979. The equatorial rainforest: A geological history: London.

Flint, R. F., 1971. Glacial and Quaternary geology: Wiley, New York.

Flora, S. D., 1954. Tornados of the United States: Univ. Oklahoma, Norman.

Fodor, R. V., 1983. Chiseling the earth, How erosion shapes the Earth: Enslow, Hillside, NJ.

Fodor, R. V., 1981. Earth afire, Volcanoes and their activity: Morrow, New York.

Fodor, R. V., 1981. Frozen Earth: Explaining the Ice Ages: Enslow, Hillside, NJ.

Fodor, R. V., 1976. Meteorites, Stones from the sky: Dodd, Mead, New York.

Folsom, F., 1956. Exploring American caves, Their history, geology, lore, and location: Crown, New York.

Forsyth, A. & Miyata, K., 1984. Tropical nature: Scribners, New York.

Frakes, L. A., 1979. Climate throughout geologic time: Elsevier, Amsterdam.

Freeze, R. A. & Cherry, J.A., 1979. Groundwater: Prentice Hall, Englewood Cliffs, NJ.

Galanopoulos, A. G. & Bacon, E., 1970. Atlantis: The truth behind the legend: Merrill, Indianapolis, IN.

Gallant, R., 1986. Our restless Earth, Consultant Dr. George Kukla of Lamont: Watts, New York.

Gallant, R., 1986. The Macmillan book of astronomy, Macmillan, New York.

Gallant, R., 1985. The Ice Ages: Watts: New York.

Gallant, R, 1983. Once around the galaxy: Watts, New York.

Gallant, R. A., 1978. Fires in the sky, The birth and death of stars: Four Winds Press, New York.

Gay, K., 1983. Acid rain: Watts, New York.

Gerasimovsky, K., et al, 1968. The geochemistry of the Lovozero Alkaline Massif: Australian National University, Canberra.

Gibbs, A. K., 1980. Geology of the Barama-Mazaruni Supergroup of Guyana: Harvard University, Cambridge, MA.

Gilfond, H., 1978. The new Ice Age: Watts, New York.

Gillett, K. & MacNeill, F., 1959. The Great Barrier Reef and adjacent isles: Coral, Sydney, Australia.

Gilluly, J. et al, 1975. Principles of geology, 4th Ed.: Freeman, San Francisco.

Gleason, H. A. & Conquist, A. (n.d) Natural geography of plants: Columbia University, New York.

Goetz, D., 1973. Lakes: Morrow, New York.

Golden, F., 1983. The trembling Earth, Probing and predicting quakes: Scribner's, New York.

Golden, F., 1971. The moving continents: Scribner's, New York.

Goldreich, P., 1974. Tides and the Earth-Moon system. In: Planet Earth,Readings from Scientific American, Freeman, San Francisco.

Goldwater, L. J., 1974. Mercury in the environment, In: Planet Earth, Readings from Scientific American, Freeman, San Francisco.

Gorshkov, G. 1970. Volcanism and the Upper Mantle, Investigations in the Kurile Island Arc (Translation), Plenum Press, New York.

Goudie, A. & Wilkerson, J., 1977, The warm desert environment: Cambridge University, London.

Gribben, J., Ed., 1986. The breathing planet: Basil, Blackwell & New Scientist, Oxford, England.

Griggs, G. B. & Gilchrist, J. A., 1983. Geological hazards, resources and environmental planning, 2nd Ed.: Wadsworth, Belmont, CA.

Gross, M. G., 1976. Oceanography: Merrill, Columbus, OH.

Gross, M. G., 1972. Oceanography, A view of the earth: Prentice Hall, Englewood Cliffs, NJ.

Hails, J. R., 1976. Placer deposits, In: Wolf, K., Stratabound deposits: Elsevier, New York.

Hale, G. & McNeil, M., 1967, Impact of water resource development on Western Sudan: Sudan Working Papers, No.21, Lockheed/USAID AFR 359.

Haley, D., Ed., 1986. Marine mammals of eastern North Pacific and Arctic waters,2nd Ed. Rev.: Pacific Search, Seattle, WA. Hallam, A., 1974. Continental drift and the fossil record, In: Planet Earth, Readings from Scientific American, Freeman, San Francisco.

Hargreaves, P., Ed., 1981, The Red Sea and Persian Gulf: In, Seas and oceans: Silver Burdett, Morristown, NJ.

Harrison, C. W., 1972. A walk through the marsh: Reilly & Lee, Chicago, IL.

Hays, D. & Pierson, C., 1957. Uraniferous coal and carboniferous shale in northeast Parana: U.S. Geological Survey, TEM 1097.

Hays, J. D., 1977. Our changing climate: Atheneum, New York.

Hecht, S. & Cockburn, A., 1989. The fate of the forest, Developers, destroyers and defenders of the Amazaon: Verso, London.

Hedgpeth, J. W., 1961. Common seahorse life of Southern California: Naturegraph, Healdsburg, CA.

Heezen, B. C. & Hollister, C. D., 1971. The face of the deep: Oxford, New York.

Heezen, B. C. and Laughton, A. S., 1963. Abyssal Plains, In: The Sea, Interscience, New York, Vol. 3.

Heitze, C. 1977. The Biosphere, Earth, air, fire, and water: Nelson, New York.

Hellman, H. 1968. Light and electricity in the Atmosphere: Holiday House, New York.

Herbert, N., 1985. Quantum reality, Beyond the new physics: Anchor, Garden City, NY.

Hiscock, B., 1986. Tundra, The Arctic land: Atheneum, New York.

Hoke, J., 1971. Ecology, Man's effects on his environment and its mechanisms: Watts, New York.

Howard, A. D. et al, 1978. Geology in environmental planning: McGraw Hill, New York.

Howell, P. P., Chairman, 1954. The Equatorial Nile Project and its effects in the Anglo-Egyptian Sudan, A report of the Jonglei Investigation Team, 4 Vols, Cairo, Egypt.

Hsu, K., 1983. The Mediterranean was a desert: Princeton University Press.

Hubbert, M. K. 1974. The energy resources of the Earth, In: Planet Earth, Readings from Scientific American, Freeman, San Francisco.

Hunt, C. B., 1972. Geology of soils: Freeman, San Francisco.

Hutchinson, C. S., 1983. Economic deposits and their tectonic setting: Wiley, New York.

Iacopi, R., 1973. Earthquake country: Lane, Palo Alto, CA.

IAEA, 1977. Correlation of uranium geology between South America and Africa: IAEA (International Atomic Energy Agency) Vienna, Austria.

Imbrie, J. and Imbrie, K. P., 1979. Ice Ages: Solving the mystery: Enslow, Hillside, NJ.

The Institute of Ecology, 1973, An ecological glossary for engineers and resource managers: Institute Ecology, Logan, UT.

'Inadvertent climate modification, a report of the study of man's impact on climate', 1971. Report before Swedish Royal Academy of Science, 1970: MIT Press, Cambridge, MA.

Iwago, M., 1987. Serengeti: Natural order on the African Plain: Chronicle Books, New York.

Jaeger, E. C., 1956. The California deserts, Stanford University.

Jastrow, R., 1967. Red giants and white dwarfs: Harper & Row, New York.

Johnson, A., 1970. Physical processes in geology: Freeman, San Francisco.

Kahan, A. M., 1986. Acid rain, Reign of controversy: Fulcrum, Golden, CO.

Kalpage, F. S. C., 19 . Tropical soils, Classification, fertility and management: St. Martin's, New York.

Kals, W. S., 1977. Riddle of the winds: Doubleday, New York.

Kandel, R. S., 1980. Earth and cosmos: Oxford, Pergamon, New York.

Kaplan, S. R., Ed. A guide to sources in mining, minerals, and geosciences: Interscience, New York.

Kaufman, W. & Pilkey, O., 1979. The beaches are moving: Anchor, Garden City, NY.

Keating, B., 1972. The Gulf of Mexico: Viking, New York.

Keller, E. A., 1979. Environmental geology: Merrill, Columbus, OH.

Kesler, S. E., 1976. Our finite mineral resources: McGraw Hill, New York.

Ketchum, B. H., Ed., 1972. The water's edge: Critical problems of the coastal zone: MIT Press, Cambridge, MA.

Kirk, R., 1978. Snow: William Morrow, New York.

Klein, H. A., 1972. Oceans and continents in motion, An introduction to continental drift and plate tectonics: Lippincott, Philadelphia, PA.

Knowlton, J., 1985. Maps and globes: Crowell, New York.

Knystautas, A., 1987. The natural history of the USSR: McGraw Hill, New York.

Kraft, K. & Kraft, M., 1980. Volcanoes, Earth's awakening: Hammond, Maplewood, NJ.

Kraft, M. & Kraft, K., 1975. Volcano (Translated by Shepley): Abrams, New York.

Kuenen, P. H., 1963. Realms of water: John Wiley, New York.

Kuenan, P. H., 1950. Marine geology: Wiley & Sons, New York.

Kuhn, G. & Shepard, F. P., 1984. Sea cliffs, beaches, and coastal valleys of San Diego County: Univ. California, Berkeley.

Kuiper, G. P. (Ed.), 1952. The atmospheres of the Earth and planets: Univ. of Chicago.

Kupchella, C. E., 1985. Environmental science: Allyn & Bacon, Boston.

Kurten, B., 1969. How to deep-freeze a mammoth: Columbia Univ., New York.

La Chapelle, E. R., 1969. Field guide to snow crystals: Univ. Washington, Seattle.

Lafond, E. C., 1966. Internal waves: Encyclopedia of Oceanography, R. W. Fairbridge, Ed.: Reinhold, New York.

Lambert, D., 1988. Field guide to geology: Facts on File, New York.

Lambert, D., 1985. Volcanoes: Watts, New York.

Lambert, D., 1983. Field guide to dinosaurs: Diagram Group, Avon, New York.

Lambert, M., 1986. The future of the environment: Bookwright, New York.

Lauber, P., 1986. Volcano, The eruption and healing of Mount St. Helens, Bradbury, New York.

Lauber, P. 1965. Volcanoes, J. P. Eaton, Consultant, Garrard, Champaign, IL.

Lavrishchev, A., 1969. Economic geography of the USSR: Progress, Moscow.

Levenson, T., 1989. Ice Time, Climate, science and life on Earth: Harper & Row, New York.

Levin, H. L., 1981. Contemporary physical geology: Holt Reinhardt, New York.

Levington, J. S., 1982. Marine ecology: Prentice Hall, NJ.

Leet, L. D. & Leet, F., Eds., 1961. The world of geology: McGraw Hill, New York.

Leopold, L. B., 1974. Water-A primer: Freeman, San Francisco.

Leopold, L. B. & Davis, K. S., 1966. Water: Time, New York.

Liddicoat, R. T., 1972. Handbook of gem identification, 9th Ed: Gemological Institute of America, Los Angeles.

Lind, A. W., 1968. An island community, Ecological succession in Hawaii: Greenwood, Westport, CT.

Littlepage, J. D., 1939. In search of Soviet gold: Harcourt, Brace, New York.

Lobeck, Armin K, 1964. Things maps don't tell us: MacMillan, New York.

Long, Captain E. John, 1965. New world of oceanography, Man's new explorations into the mysterious living sea: Pyramid, New York.

Lowe-McConnell, R. H., 1966. Man-made Lakes: Academic Press, New York.

Luce, J. V., 1978. Lost Atlantis: New light on an old legend: McGraw Hill, New York.

Lutgens, F. K. and Tarbuk, E. J., 1979. The Atmosphere, An introduction to meteorology: Prentice Hall, Englewood Cliffs, NJ.

Mabbutt, J. A., 1977. Desert landforms, an introduction to systematic geomorphology, 2 vols., MIT Press, Cambridge, MA.

MacArthur, R. H., 1984. Geographical ecology: Princeton University, NJ.

MacDonald,G.A.,1972.Volcanoes:Prentice Hall,Englewood Cliffs, NJ.

Maher, R., 1968. Shifting sands, The story of sand dunes: John Day, New York.

Marvin, U. B., 1973. Continental drift, The evolution of a concept: Smithsonian Inst., Washington, DC.

Mareschal, J. C. & West, G.F., 1980. A model for Archean tectonism, Pt. 2, Mineral models of vertical tectonism in Greenstone Belts: Canadian Journal of Earth Science, Vol. 17.

Marples, D. R., 1987. Chernobyl and nuclear power in the USSR: St. Martin's Press, New York.

Mason, B., 1958. Principles of geochemistry: Wiley, New York.

Matthes, F. E. [1930]. Geological history of Yosemite Valley: U. S. Geological Survey, Professional Paper.

Matthiesson, P., 1981. Sand rivers: Viking, New York.

Matthiesson, P., 1961. The cloud forest, A chronicle of the South American wilderness: Viking, New York.

Maury, M. F., 1858. Physical geography of the sea: Harper, New York.

McCabe, C. L. & Bauer, C. L., 1964. Metals, atoms, and alloys: McGraw Hill, New York.

McFall, C., 1980. The wonders of dust: Dodd, Mead, New York.

McIntyre, M. P., 1973. Physical geography: 2nd Ed., Ronald, New York.

McKee, B., 1972. Cascadia, The geologic evolution of the Pacific Northwest: McGraw Hill, New York.

McKenzie, D. P. & Sclater, J. G., 1974. The evolution of the Indian Ocean, In: Planet Earth, Readings from Scientific American, Freeman, San Francisco.

McKnight, T. L., 1984. Physical geography, A landscape appreciation: Prentice Hall, NJ.

McKown, R., 1962. The fabulous isotopes, What they are and what they do: Holiday House, New York.

McNeil, M., 1979. Brazil's uranium/thorium deposits, Geology, potential and reserves: Miller, Freeman, San Francisco.

McNeil, M., 1968. Potential for mineral development in Red Sea Hills, Sudan: Sudan Working Papers, No. 6, Lockheed/USAID, AFR 359.

McNeil, M. et al, 1968. Some socioeconomic implications of development project implementation:

Sudan Working Papers, No. 20, Lockheed/USAID, AFR 359.

McNeil, M., 1968. Speculations of results of the possible edaphic changes from proposed Mekong Development Projects: SEADAG Papers, No. 34, New York.

McNeil, M., 1964. Internal waves in the ocean, an annotated bibliography, LR 17669: Lockheed Aircraft, Burbank, CA.

McPhee, J., 1983. In suspect terrain: Ferrar, Straus, & Giroux, New York.

Meggers, B. J., 1971. Amazonia: Man & culture in a counterfeit paradise: Aldine-Atherton, York.

Meggers, et al, Eds., 1973. Tropical forest, Ecosystems in Africa and South America: A compative review: Smithsonian, Washington.

Menard, H. W., 1987. Islands, Birth and death of oceanic islands: Freeman, San Francisco.

Menard, H. W., 1974. Geology, resources, and society, An introduction to Earth Science: Freeman, San Francisco.

Menard, H. W. [1964]. Marine geology of the Pacific: McGraw-Hill, New York.

Meynell, P. J., 1978. Methane, Planning a digester: Schocken, New York.

Mikhailov, N., 1948. Soviet Union, The land and its people: Sheridan House, Kingsport, TN.

Miller, G. T., 1986. Environmental science: Wadsworth, Belmont, MA.

Miller, P. W., Ed., 1980. Disposal effects on groundwater: Primier, Berkeley, CA.

Milne, A., 1989. Earth's changing climate, The cosmic connection: Prism Press, Dorset, England

Milne, A., 1988. Our drowning world, Population, pollution, and future weather: Prism, Dorset, England.

Mitchell, A. W., 1986. Enchanted canopy: Macmillan, New York.

Mohr, E. C. J. & Van Baren, F. A., 1954. Tropical soils: The Hague, Netherlands.

Moorehead, A., 1972. Darwin and the Beagle: Harper & Row, New York.

Muir, J., 1915. Travels in Alaska: Houghton Mifflin, Boston.

Murray, B. C., 1974. Mars from Mariner 9, In: Planet Earth, Readings from Scientific American, Freeman, San Francisco.

Musset, P. & Lloret, A., 1968. Concise encyclopedia of the atom: Collins, Glasgow, Scotland.

Myers, N., 1984. The primary source, Tropical forests and our future: Norton, New York.

Nairn, A.E.M. and Stehli, F.G., Eds., 1973. Ocean basins and margins, In: Vol. I, The South Atlantic: Plenum, New York.

Nakaya, U., 1954. Snow crystals, natural and artificial: Harvard University, Cambridge, MA.

National Research Council, 1971. The San Fernando earthquake of February 9, 1971: National Academy of Science, Washington, D. C.

Nelson, B., 1968, Galapagos, Islands of birds: Morrow, New York.

Neinburger, M. J. et al, 1973. Understanding our atmospheric environment: Freeman, San Francisco, CA.

Newell, N. D., 1974. The evolution of reefs, In: Planet Earth, Readings from Scientific American, Freeman, San Franciso.

Newell, R. E., 1974. The global circulation of atmospheric pollutants, In: Planet Earth, Readings from Scientific American, Freeman, San Francisco.

Niering, W., 1983. Wetlands, Audobon Society Nature Guide: Knopf, New York.

Nixon, N. H. & Nixon, J. L., 1980. Glaciers, Nature's frozen rivers: Dodd Mead, New York.

Nixon, N. H & Nixon, J. L., 1977. Oil and gas. From fossils to fuels: Harcourt, Brace, Jovanovich, New York.

Norris, R. M. & Webb, R. W., 1990. The geology of California, 2nd Edition: John Wiley, New York.

Oakeshott, G. B., 1978. California's changing landscapes: McGraw Hill, New York.

Odum, E. P., 1966. Ecology: Holt-Rhinehart, New York.

Oldfield, M. L., 1983. Tropical deforestation and genetic resource conservation, In: Studies in 3rd World Societies, No. 14.

Oliver, J. E. & Fairbridge, R. W., Eds., 1987. The encyclopedia of climatology; Van Nostrand, New York.

Owen, O. S., 1985. Natural resources conservation, 4th edition: Macmillan, New York.

Padget, S., 1984. Coastlines: Bookwright, New York.

Palmer, E. & Newton, C.W., 1969. Atmospheric circulation systems, their structure and physical interpretation: Academic, New York.

Parker, B., 1984. Concepts of the cosmos: Harcourt, Brace, Jovanovich, San Diego, CA.

Parker, R. B., 1986. The tenth muse: The pursuit of earth science: Scribners, New York.

Parker, R. B., 1984. Inscrutable Earth, Explorations into the science of the Earth: Scribners, New York.

Perry, D., 1986. Life above the jungle floor, A biologist explores a strange and hidden treetop world: New York.

Peters, W. C., 1978. Exploration and mining geology: Wiley, New York.

Pettijohn, F. J., 1975. Sedimentary rocks, 3rd Ed.: Harper & Row, New York.

Pewe, T. L., 1966. Permafrost and its effect on life in the north: Oregon State Univ., Corvallis.

Pewe, T. L, Ed., 1969. The periglacial environment, past and present: Arctic Institute of North America, McGill Univ., Montreal.

Pitcher, T. J. & Hart, P., 1982. Fisheries ecology: Croom Helm, London.

Plucknett, D. L. et al, 1987. Gene banks and the world's food: Princeton University, NJ.

Pond, A. W., 1969. Caverns of the world: Norton, New York.

Popescu, J. et al, 1960. Rivers of the world, Vol. I, Danube, Amazon, Niger and Ganges, Vol. II, Nile, Murray, MacKenzie, and St. Lawrence: Oxford University, London.

Pough, F. H., 1960. A field guide to rocks and minerals: Houghton, Mifflin, Boston.

Powell, J. W., 1961. The exploration of the Colorado River and its canyons: Dover, New York. (Original published 1895).

Poynter, Margaret & Klein, Michael J., 1984. Cosmic quest, Searching for intelligence among the stars: Atheneum, New York.

Pringle, L., 1973. Estuaries, Where rivers meet the sea: Macmillan, New York.

Pringle, L., 1972. This is a river, Exploring an ecosystem: Macmillan, New York.

Pringle, L., 1971. Ecology, Science of survival: Macmillan, New York.

Projeto RADAMBRASIL, 1971-1978. Levantamento de recursos naturais, Vols. 1-22: Ministerio de Minas e Energia, Rio/Brasilia.

Radlauer, R. & Gitkin, L. S., 1985. The power of ice: Children's Chicago, IL.

Ramage, C. S., 1970. Monsoon meteorology: Academic Press, New York.

Ramsey, R. H., 1973. Men and mines of Newmont, A fifty-year history; Ferrar, Straus & Giroux, New York.

Reisner, M., 1986. Cadillac desert, The American west and its disappearing water: Viking, New York.

Richards, P. W., 1952. The tropical rain forest, London.

Richter, C. F., 1958. Elementary seismology: Freeman, San Francisco.

Ricketts, E. F. et al, 1985. Between Pacific tides, 5th Ed., Stanford University, CA.

Riehl, H., 1978. Introduction to the Atmosphere, 3rd Ed., McGraw-Hill, New York.

Ritchie, D., 1981. The ring of fire: Atheneum, New York.

Rittman, A., 1962. Volcanoes and their activity: Wiley, New York.

Rodgers, J., 1982. Life Story of the Appalachians, Mountain building processes: Academic Press, New York.

Rosenbloom, J., 1980. Dictionary of dinosaurs: Messner, New York.

Rubenstein, J. M. & Bacon, R.S., 1983. The cultural landscape: West, St. Paul, MN.

Rublowsky, J., 1981. Born in fire, A geological history of Hawaii: Harper & Row, New York.

Russell, H. R., 1973. Earth, The great recycler: Nelson, New York

Sanders, T., 1985. Weather, a user's guide to the Atmosphere: Icarus, South Bend, IN.

Sattler, H. R., 1981. Dinosaurs of North America: Lothrop, Lee & Shepard, New York.

Sauer, C., 1952. Agricultural origins and dispersals: American Geographical Society, New York.

Sauer, J. R., 1982. Brazil, Paradise of gemstones. Riex, Rio de Janeiro.

Schneider, H. S. & Londer, R., 1984. The coevolution of climate and life: Sierra Books, San Francisco.

Schneider, S., 1989. Global warming, Are we entering the Greenhouse Century: Sierra Books, San Francisco.

Schultz, G., 1975. Icebergs and their voyages: Morrow, New York.

Scorer, R. S., 1972. Clouds of the world: Stackpole, Harrisburg, PA.

Seidel, S. & Keye, D., 1983. Can we delay a Greenhouse warming? U.S. Environmental Protection Agency, Washington, DC.

Serruya, C. & Pollingher, U., 1983. Lakes of the warm belt: Cambridge University, New York.

Settle, M. L., 1984. Water world: Dutton, New York.

Seuss, E., Ed., 1983. Coastal upwelling, its sedimentary record, 2 Vols., Plenum, New York.

Serventy, V., 1967. Landforms of Australia: Angus & Robertson, Sydney.

Sharp, R. P. 1960. Glaciers: Univ. Oregon Press, Eugene.

Shedd, G., 1969. Half-way elements, The technology of metalloids: Doubleday, New York.

Shelton, J. S., 1966. Geology illustrated: Freeman, San Francisco.

Shepard, F. P., 1977. Geological oceanography, Evolution of coasts, continental margins, and the deep sea floor, Crane, Russak, New York.

Shepard, F. P., 1973. Submarine geology: Harper and Row, New York.

Sherwood, M. & Sutton, C., Eds., 1988. The physical world: Oxford University Press, New York.

Shimer, J. A. 1959. The sculptured earth. The landscape of America: Columbia Univ., New York.

Shimkin, D. B, 1953. Minerals, A key to Soviet power: Harvard University, Cambridge, MA.

Shirley, J. C., 1947. The redwoods of coast and Sierras: University of California, Berkeley.

Silk, J., 1980. The Big Bang, The creation and evolution of the Universe: Freeman, San Francisco.

Simpson, G. G., 1965. The geography of evolution: Chilton, New York.

Skinner, B., 1969. Earth resources: Prentice-Hall, Englewood Cliffs, NJ.

Small, R. J., 1970. A study of landforms, A textbook of geomorphology: Cambridge Univ., London.

Smirnov, V. I., Ed., 1976. Geology of mineral deposits: Mir, Moscow, USSR.

Smith, D. G., Ed., 1981. The Cambridge encyclopedia of earth sciences: Crown/Cambridge University, New York.

Smith, H. E., 1982. Living fossils: Dodd Mead, New York.

Spiroff, K., 1959: Seaman's Mineral Tables. Michigan Tech., Houghton.

Stamp, L. D., 1959. Africa, A study in tropical development, 4th Printing: Wiley, New York.

Stanley, S. M., 1985. Earth and life through time: Freeman, San Francisco.

Steinbeck, J., 1951. The log of the Sea of Cortez: Viking, New York.

Strahler, A. N., 1970. Introduction to physical geography: Wiley, New York.

Strahler, A. N. & Strahler, A. H., 1973. Environmental geosciences: Hamilton, Santa Barbara, CA.

Sverdrup, H. U. et al, 1942. The oceans, Their physics, chemistry, and general biology: Prentice Hall, Englewood Cliffs, NJ.

Tallcott, E., 1970. Glacier tracks: Lothrop, Lee & Shepard, New York.

Tangborn, W. V., 1965. Glaciers: Crowell, New York.

Tank, R. W., 1973. Focus on environmental geology: Oxford University, New York.

Taylor, G. J., 1980. A close look at the Moon: Dodd, Mead, New York.

Tazieff, H., 1979. Nyiragongo, The forbidden volcano: Barron's, Woodbury, NY.

Tazieff, H., 1961. Volcanoes: Orion Books, New York.

Thomas, H. E., 1951. The conservation of ground water: McGraw-Hill, New York.

Thomas, M. F., 1974. Tropical Geomorphology: Wiley, New York.

Thomas, W., Ed., 1956. Man's role in changing the face of the earth: University of Chicago.

Trefil, J. S., 1984. A scientist at the seashore: Scribner's, New York.

Trefil, J. S., 1983. The moment of creation, Big Bang physics from the first millisecond to the present Universe: Scribner's, New York.

Trefil, J. S., 1980. From atoms to quarks, An introduction to the strange world of particle physics: Scribner's, New York.

Trewartha, G. T., 1968. An introduction to climate, 4th Ed.: McGraw Hill, New York.

'Tsunamis in the Pacific Ocean', 1970. Proceedings, University of Hawaii: East-West Center, Honolulu.

Turekian, K. K., 1968. Oceans: Prentice Hall, NJ.

Udvardy, M. D. F., 1969. Dynamic zoogeography: Van Nostrand, New York.

United States Department of Agriculture, 1957. Soils, Yearbook of Agriculture, Washington, D.C.

United States Geological Survey, 1986. Mt. St. Helens, Professional Paper 1250: Washington, D.C.

United States Water Resources Council, 1978. The nation's water resources 1975-2000, 2nd nat'l water assessment: Washington, D.C.

Van Andel, T., 1977. Tales of an old ocean: Norton, New York.

Vogt, E. & Hyman, R., 1979. Water witching: Univ. Chicago.

Wagner, R. H., 1971. Environment and Man: Norton, New York.

Wallace, A. R., 1876. The geographical distribution of animals: Harper, New York.

Waltham, T., 1974. Caves: New York.

Walton, W. C., 1970. Groundwater resource evaluation: McGraw Hill, New York

Ward, B. & Dubros, R., 1972. Only one Earth, The care and maintenance of a small planet: Norton, New York.

Washburn, A. L., 1973. The periglacial processes and environments: St. Martin's Press, New York.

Waterton, Charles, 1825. Wanderings in South America: Century, New York.

Wegener, A., 1966. The origin of continents and oceans: Dover, New York.

Weiner, J., 1986. Planet Earth: Bantam, New York.

Weiss, M. E., 1978. What's happening to our climate? Messner, New York.

Wertenbaker, W., 1974. The floor of the sea, Maurice Ewing and the search to understand the Earth: Little, Brown, Boston.

Whipple, J. B., 1985. Forest resources: Watts, New York.

Whiteman, A., 1971. The geology of the Sudan Republic: Oxford University, London.

Williams, T. T. & Major, T., 1984. The secret language of snow: Sierra Club, Pantheon Books, New York.

Wolf, K., Ed., 1976. Handbook of stratabound and stratiform ore deposits, 3 Vols.: Elsevier, New York.

Woodcock, K., 1980. The silicon chip: Wayland, Hove, Sussex, England.

Yang, Z. & Wang, H., 1986. The geology of China. Oxford Monograph No. 3: Oxford Univ., New York.

Young, L. B., 1983. The blue planet, A celebration of the Earth: Little, Brown, Boston.

Young, L. B., 1977. Earth's aura: Knopf, New York.

Young, P., 1976. Drifting continents, shifting seas, Introduction to plate tectonics: Watts, New York.

Yung, P., 1987, Xinjiang, the Silk Road: Islam's overland route to China: Frank, Brownstone, Oxford, England.

Zwinger, A., 1983, A desert country near the sea: Harper & Row, New York.

THE EARTH SCIENCES REFERENCE

GEOGRAPHICAL INDEX

Abay Creek, Ethiopia 69, 385
Abu Qir Bay, Egypt 153
Aconcagua Volcano, Chile 5, 181
Lake Acraman, Australia 280
Acre Territory, Brazil 332, 338
Lake Adabada, Ethiopia 147
Aden 588
Gulf of Aden 96, 481
Adirondack Mountains, New York 27, 410, 437, 619
Adriatic Sea 7, 72, 542
Aegean Sea 7
Afar Triangle 8, 147, 148
Afghanistan 9, 88, 265, 300, 304, 316, 421, 431
Africa 2, 8, 9, 17, 27, 41, 42, 47, 50, 58, 80, 82, 86, 87, 89, 90, 91, 93, 95, 96, 97, 98, 102, 104, 111, 125, 126, 129, 132,143, 148, 151, 154, 157, 159, 164, 167, 168, 170, 171, 178, 179, 181, 188, 204, 205, 208, 210, 211, 212, 217, 220, 228, 229, 233, 235, 237, 242, 243, 249, 251, 252, 260, 264, 265, 271, 272, 273, 275, 281, 293, 299, 301, 313, 319, 326, 327, 331, 332, 337, 338, 346, 347, 348, 358, 368, 373, 376, 382, 384, 395, 409, 410, 412, 413, 414, 418, 427, 430, 433, 443, 444, 453, 455, 456, 463, 470, 473, 475, 481, 486, 487, 488, 489, 492, 493, 496, 499, 503, 510, 515, 518, 520, 540, 543, 554, 59, 560, 561, 566, 571, 576, 578, 584, 590, 605, 606, 611, 612, 613, 618, 629, 630,
Agulhas Current 11, 282
Agung Volcano, Indonesia 11
Ahoggar Mountains, Sahara 15, 156, 185, 384, 427, 492
Air Mountains, Sahara 62, 384
Alabama 31, 116, 295, 394, 480, 583
Alaska 4, 12, 13, 14, 16, 21, 35, 37, 57, 59, 60, 82, 89, 97, 112, 122, 130, 133, 162, 183, 195, 215, 230, 231, 235, 249, 269, 276, 277, 293, 302, 321, 337, 339, 349, 353, 355, 371, 382, 390, 391, 410, 429, 433, 438, 439, 444, 450, 470, 480, 489, 549, 553, 554, 559, 564, 568, 580, 593, 595, 614, 620, 627
Gulf of Alaska 11, 294, 309, 337, 387
Alaska Range 231, 485
Albatross Plateau 13
Lake Albert, East Africa 172, 175, 179, 363, 489, 599
Albert Nile River 179, 357, 386, 488, 489, 599
Alberta, Canada 66, 418, 556
Aldan River, Siberia 623
Aleutian Islands 59, 118, 134, 369, 542, 620
Aleutian Trench 14, 402, 557
Alexandria, Egypt 14, 16, 385, 394, 459, 491,
Lake Alexandrina, Australia 371
Algeria 14-15, 304, 368, 375, 384, 555, 572
Allegheny Plateau 30, 345
Alligator River, Australia 439

Alps Mountains 17, 45, 72, 96, 129, 148, 186, 198, 207, 208, 211, 322, 348, 365, 413, 415, 462, 479, 507, 561, 563, 618
Alsace-Lorraine 234
Altai Mountains, USSR 175, 310, 397, 398
Altamira, Para, Brazil 571
Amapa, Brazil 340, 458, 572
Amazon Basin 17, 18, 19, 23, 33, 34, 72, 76, 77, 78, 80, 91, 98, 116, 120, 125, 128, 158, 166, 182, 183, 196, 198, 209, 235, 251, 272, 273, 280, 294, 322, 332, 340, 345, 349, 403, 420, 432, 444, 458, 465, 470, 479, 483, 486, 509, 528, 529, 560, 567, 571, 573, 576, 577, 595, 597, 622
Amazon Delta 422, 480
Amazon River 4, 19, 20, 21, 23, 33, 41, 50, 52, 61, 71, 72, 75, 76, 91, 98, 105, 126, 129, 183, 209, 251, 272, 292, 326, 332, 342, 370, 374, 378, 379, 411, 422, 423, 431, 451, 480, 528, 529, 556, 560, 571, 595, 597, 622, 624, 627
Amazonas, Brazil 23
Amboselli Plain, Tanzania 305, 318
America 18, 38, 50, 80, 101, 116, 318, 325, 387, 409, 417, 446, 535, 542, 561, 576, 585
American Cordillera 355, 485, 516
Ameralik Fjord, Greenland 484
American Falls 382
Amoricain Massif, Brittany 345
Amu Darya River, USSR 295
Amur River, Siberia, USSR 22, 515
Anabar Basin, Siberia 623
Anak-Krakatoa, Indonesia 23
Anatolia, Turkey 23
Andes Mountains 3, 5, 17, 18, 20, 21, 24, 28, 41, 71, 77, 103, 108, 109, 111, 112, 120, 129, 133, 139, 203, 238, 242, 269, 312, 316, 323, 326, 332, 342, 374, 380, 403, 421, 422, 423, 425, 431, 432, 440, 459, 495, 527, 529, 558, 560, 565, 567, 569, 577, 591, 597, 602, 618, 627
Angara River, Siberia, USSR 25, 48, 626
Angel Falls 25
Anglo-Egyptian Sudan 296
Anglo-Parisian Basin 144
Angola 9, 58, 65, 233, 373, 630
Mt. Annapurna 594
Antarctic 27, 28, 41, 110, 130, 276, 277, 358, 392, 425, 501, 505, 511, 616
Antarctic Sea 358
Antarctic Circle 27
Antarctic Ocean 161, 614
Antarctica 27, 28, 41, 107, 109, 129, 130, 144, 168, 181, 186, 189, 195, 202, 213, 230, 231, 236, 241, 243, 246, 267, 270, 275, 276, 277, 313, 358, 394, 415, 419, 459, 486, 561, 577, 612
Anti-Atlas Mountains 368, 613
Anti-Taurus Mountains 566
Antilles Archipelago 34, 95, 133, 500, 613

Antilles Current 500

Anyatepui Massif, Venezuela 26

Appalachia 30, 31, 116, 429, 437, 473, 557

Appalachian Mountains 4, 28, 30, 36, 41, 87, 157, 196, 207, 275, 291, 362, 366, 390, 402, 405, 427, 437, 438, 494, 511, 618

Appalachicola River, United States 41, 343, 355

Appenine Mountains, Italy 17, 348, 569

Apuan Alps 97

Apsheron Peninsula, USSR 49

Apurimac River, Peru 613

Gulf of Aqaba 31, 33, 96, 245, 526, 567

Aquitane Basin, France 424

Arab Emirates 375

Arabia 191, 240, 257, 258, 284, 296, 378, 418, 413, 474, 520, 588, 633

Arabian Desert 32, 170, 171, 377, 418, 486, 501, 520, 555, 606, 624

Arabian Gulf 431

Arabian Peninsula 8, 32, 33, 281, 358, 392, 431, 473, 486, 501

Arabian Sea 150, 262, 282, 471, 519, 542, 613

Arabo-Nubian Massif 179, 526

Araguaia River, Brazil 33, 50

Aral Sea, USSR 30, 313, 397, 591, 611

Mt. Ararat 33

Araxa, Brazil 51, 95, 388

Arctic 1, 13, 35, 41, 68, 138, 223, 243, 252, 264, 277, 316, 325, 343, 391, 392, 397, 410, 415, 419, 428, 429, 430, 447, 450, 471, 485, 501, 514, 580, 591, 611

Arctic Circle 12, 35, 278, 307, 331, 358, 505, 570, 577, 610

Arctic Current 311

Arctic Ocean 12, 35, 57, 60, 89, 138, 188, 204, 212, 252, 307, 342, 343, 337, 391, 397, 399, 409, 418, 419, 509, 523, 537, 601

Ardennes, Belgium 419

Arenal, Costa Rica 589

Argentina 5, 12, 24, 76, 129, 155, 188, 195-196, 238, 255, 279, 323, 375, 421, 422, 424, 425, 430, 442, 518, 565

Argun River, Siberia, USSR 22

Arizona 73, 104, 106, 112, 119, 121, 122, 133, 191, 205, 207, 211, 239, 249, 281, 339, 346, 353, 363, 378, 426, 428, 432, 452, 485, 486, 492, 522, 557, 583, 603, 620

Arkansas 80, 95, 334, 416, 458, 568

Armagosa Range 582

Arun River, Nepal 28, 152

Arvalli Range, India 562

As Sarat Mountains, Saudi Arabia 318

Asbestos Mountains, South Africa 139

Ascension Island 38

Asia 8, 9, 23, 25, 32, 33, 38, 50, 60, 99, 129, 155, 170, 175, 181, 219, 229, 231, 234, 243, 244, 245, 255, 264, 265, 273, 276, 282, 288, 300, 318, 327, 338, 350, 366, 369, 376, 387, 416, 417, 418, 431, 492, 513, 514, 522, 530, 535, 545, 553, 561, 564, 568, 577, 583, 588, 591, 623, 624

Lake Assal, Ethiopia 147

Aswan Dam, Egypt 39, 40, 273, 374, 386, 392, 394

Atacama Desert, Chile 2, 40, 41, 388, 494

Atakora Range, Ghana 229

Atbara River, Sudan 386, 543

Athabasca, Canada 90, 99, 122, 625

Lake Athabaska, Canada 556

Athabasca Glacier, Canada 122

Athabasca River, Canada 122

Atlantic Coast 41, 130, 131, 404, 416, 424, 438, 441

Atlantic Current 252

Atlantic Ocean 2, 12, 20, 35, 41, 42, 46, 60, 68, 76, 89, 96, 104, 126, 129, 133, 164, 175, 185, 188, 192, 204, 209, 212, 229, 232, 233, 238, 251, 252, 253, 255, 260, 268, 269, 270, 271, 275, 281, 288, 295, 306, 318, 332, 333, 340, 343, 347, 347, 348, 356, 357, 368, 373, 384, 385, 398, 402, 405, 415, 417, 418, 419, 421, 435, 442, 452, 479, 488, 492, 495, 500, 505, 518, 522, 538, 542, 555, 561, 583, 597, 600

Atlantis II Deep, Red Sea 42, 474

Atlas Mountains, North Africa 14, 15, 42, 348, 492

Australia 7, 10, 15, 29, 34, 37, 38, 44, 45, 52, 56, 57, 67, 73, 80, 82, 86, 88, 93, 94, 110, 129, 130, 133, 139, 156, 159, 168, 170, 171, 171, 194, 195, 203, 204, 210, 211, 218, 230, 235, 236, 237, 243, 249, 259, 260, 264, 271, 273, 281, 285, 289, 299, 301, 305, 308, 323, 328, 337, 340, 344, 353, 358, 371, 376, 381, 383, 387, 394, 406, 408, 411, 412, 417, 412, 420, 430, 439, 440, 443, 445, 454, 455, 472, 475, 488, 492, 511, 513, 516, 529, 532, 539, 540, 547, 555, 557, 560, 561, 566, 568, 570, 577, 578, 581, 589, 598, 605, 612, 616, 619, 622, 626, 631, 632, 633

Australian Alps 371

Australian Central Desert 406, 399, 400

Austria 17, 148, 324, 440, 479, 515, 581

Avalon Peninsula 260

Awash River, Ethiopia 147

Ayers Rock, Australia 45

Azores 46, 60, 357, 500

Sea of Azov, USSR 46

Baba Gurger, Iraq 47, 403

Baffin Bay 275

Baffin Island 269, 311

Bagagem River, Brazil 48

Bahamas, Atlantic Ocean 68, 613

Bahia, Brazil 48, 73, 94, 102, 105, 342

Bahr el Ghazal Basin, Chad 488

Bahr el Ghazal River, Sudan 104, 386

Bahr el Jebel River, Sudan 296, 379

Bahrein 48, 155

Lake Baikal, USSR 48, 154, 313, 429, 555, 572, 591, 626

Baikal Range, USSR 320

Baja California,Mexico 49, 88, 121, 355, 390, 402, 427, 496 549
Mt. Baker 97
Baku, USSR 49, 98, 371
Bali, Indonesia 11
Baltic Sea 21, 41, 183, 186, 603
Bananal Island, Brazil 50
Bandai-San, Japan 190
Bandakshan Range 9
Banff, Alberta, Canada 16, 122
Bangladesh 58, 75, 152, 220, 298
Lake Bangweola 126, 629
Barberton Plateau, South Africa 10, 454
Barguzin River, USSR 48
Barrenlands, Canada 580
Batove River, Brazil 622
Bay of Plenty, New Zealand 382, 615
Bay of Fundy, Canada 72, 215, 564, 565
Bear Province, Canada 521
Beaufort Sea 38, 57, 90, 331, 429
Belgium 325, 427
Bengal 607
Bengal Bay 58, 75, 220, 265, 266, 282, 289, 613
Benguela Current, South Atlantic Ocean 58, 373
Beni Basin, Bolivia 322
Beni River, Bolivia 20, 24, 331, 415, 423
Benin, Africa 80
Benin Bight 252
Benoue River 89, 104, 384, 385
Bering Sea 35, 59, 60, 276, 504, 627
Bering Strait 12, 60, 314, 537
Bermuda 60, 133, 277, 371, 529
Bermuda Rise, Atlantic Ocean 60, 371
Bezymiany Volcano, USSR 61
Biafra Bight 252
Bikini Atoll, South Pacific 62, 550
Bay of Biscay 275
Bitter Lakes, Egypt 65
Black Forest, Germany 148, 237, 264, 479
Black Hills, South Dakota 66-67, 197, 312, 533, 568
Black Warrior Basin, Alabama 116, 480
Black Rapids Glacier, Alaska 67, 230
Black Sea 17, 46, 67, 68, 99, 148, 342, 348, 456, 487
Blake Plateau, Atlantic Ocean 2, 68, 253, 295, 340, 370, 401
Blake-Bahama Platform, Atlantic Ocean 357
Blind River, Canada 626
Blue Mountain 380
Blue Nile Gorge 60
Blue Nile River 40, 69, 125, 228, 273, 385, 379, 543, 556
Blue Ridge Mountains 415
Bodele-Djourab Depression 104
Bog of Allen, Ireland 70
Lake Bogoria (Huntington), East Africa 70-71
Bolivia 17, 20, 24, 29, 35, 71, 98, 238, 280, 289, 323, 324, 332, 403, 421, 423, 440, 454,

Bolivia (continued) 460, 495, 518, 536, 567, 568, 569, 571, 581, 591, 619, 627
Bonin Trench 402
Borah Peak, Idaho 72
Borborema, Northeast, Brazil 72, 161, 426
Borneo 289
Bosporus Strait, Sea of Marmara/Black Sea 67
Gulf of Bothnia 118, 199
Botswana 265, 299, 382, 630
Bouvet Island 358
Boulder Dam, Nevada 346
Bradshaw Mountains 106
Brahmaputra River, India/Bangladesh 28, 265, 542
Rio Branco, Brazil 377
Bratsk Lake, USSR 319
Brazil 10, 11, 12, 16, 18, 19, 20, 21, 23, 24, 29, 33, 34, 38, 47, 48, 49 50, 51, 52, 53, 55, 56, 57, 61, 67, 72, 73, 75, 76, 77, 78, 82, 85, 89, 90, 91, 93, 95, 97, 98, 102, 104, 105, 111, 113, 118, 123, 129, 147, 148, 159, 169, 182, 183, 186, 188, 193, 204, 206, 221, 227, 228, 229, 235, 236, 238, 240, 245, 251, 252, 253, 273, 277, 279, 281, 289, 291, 293, 294, 300, 318, 319, 332, 340, 342, 345, 365, 366, 371, 374, 375, 378-379, 383, 388, 404, 411, 420, 422, 423, 424, 430, 435, 436, 440, 442, 443, 444, 447, 453, 457, 458, 460, 465, 470, 473, 476, 486, 487, 488, 492, 493, 495, 500, 503, 509, 510, 516, 522, 524, 529, 550, 552, 555, 556, 560, 563, 566, 567, 568, 569, 570, 571, 572, 574, 581, 587, 597, 598, 622, 626, 627, 632
Brazil Current 76, 77, 188, 195
Brazos Delta, Texas 153
Bridger Basin, Wyoming 565
Britain (See Great Britain)
Brittany, France 1, 345
British Columbia, Canada 13, 82, 97, 132, 134, 213, 331, 429
British Isles (See Great Britain)
Brooks Range, Alaska 12, 231
Bryce Canyon, Utah 439
Bucegi Range, Rumania 96
Bulgaria 148
Burma 58, 135, 289, 348, 363, 428, 487, 520, 546, 568, 576, 632
Burundi 489, 555, 599

Cabo Branco, Northeast Brazil 91
Cabo Corrientes, Mexico 355
Cabo Frio, Brazil 185
Cairngorm Mountains, Scotland 85
Caledonian Mountains 87, 157, 240, 405, 475
California 7, 15, 48, 49, 55, 62, 69, 73, 79, 88, 92, 94, 95, 105, 106, 111, 114, 117, 121, 122, 161, 176, 177, 179, 183, 188, 193, 195, 197, 200, 205, 208, 210, 213, 227, 231, 234, 235, 237, 242, 250, 259, 263, 290, 294,

California 303, 318 328, 333, 342, 343, 349, 354, 364, 366, 368, 369, 371, 387, 390, 392, 403, 416, 428, 446, 460, 474, 485, 492, 498, 503, 509, 510, 516, 527, 533, 556, 560, 564, 573, 585, 588, 582, 594, 595, 618, 619

Gulf of California 13, 49, 72, 120, 132, 188, 252, 342, 417, 474, 497, 498, 564

California Bight 62

California Current 87, 294, 309, 387

Cambodia 348, 569

Cameron Highlands, Malaysia 338

Cameroon 89, 89, 126, 252, 272, 291, 378

Mt. Cameroon 252, 385

Canada 5, 6, 9, 10, 11, 12, 13, 15, 16, 27, 31, 44, 47, 49, 50, 57, 65, 66, 68, 72, 74, 82, 87, 89-90, 95, 97, 100, 103, 117, 102, 128, 133, 169, 209, 213, 215, 222, 229, 235, 239, 243, 244, 247, 248, 269, 276, 295, 302, 311, 313, 315, 318, 328, 331, 336, 354, 362, 371, 375, 376, 379, 380, 383, 388, 390, 391, 409, 410, 418, 427, 429, 439, 444, 445, 450, 451, 452, 453, 455, 470, 485, 494, 505, 518, 512, 521, 526, 540, 544, 546, 553, 556, 564, 565, 566, 571, 573, 581, 588, 603, 606, 617, 625, 626, 627, 631

Canadian Rockies 89, 122, 133, 213

Canadian River, New Mexico 326

Canaries Current 90, 253, 500

Canary Islands 86, 90, 100, 176, 316

Canyonlands, Utah 34, 101

Cape Canaveral 253

Cape Cod, Massachusetts 231, 311

Cape Comorin, India 533, 613

Cape Farewell 311

Cape Hatteras 176, 252

Cape Horn 263, 327, 565

Cape Manuel, Senegal 91

Cape Mendocino, California 195, 213, 349, 588

Cape Mountains, Baja California 49

Cape Province, South Africa 166, 243

Cape Saint Vincent Ridge, Atlantic Ocean 46

Cape Verde Islands 271, 571

Carajas, Brazil 289, 340, 510, 556

Caribbean 41, 96, 149, 271, 294, 295, 392, 400

Caribbean Sea 41, 96. 151, 251, 271, 295, 342, 355, 411

Carlsbad, New Mexico 99, 407, 430

Carlsberg Ridge, Indian Ocean 13, 96, 104

Carolina Outer Banks 145

Carolinas, United States 2, 56, 197, 271, 533

Carpathian Alps 17, 96-97

Carrara, Italy 97

Carrara Mountains, Italy 342

Carswell Lake, Canada 97

Caryn Seamount 270

Cascade Range, North America 39, 55, 97, 112, 133, 266, 317, 347, 438, 471, 494

Casiquiari River, Venezuela 98, 182, 378, 411

Caspian Sea 49, 98, 99, 288, 300, 313, 530, 535, 591, 599, 600, 603, 626

Catskill Mountains, New York 31, 270

Caucasus Mountains 33, 39, 46, 99

Cavanca Range, Mexico 90

Cave of the Winds, Niagara Falls 609

Cayman Ridge 357

Cayman Trench 96

Celebes 207

Central African Plateau 301, 444, 630

Central America 21, 25, 101, 115, 119, 220, 222, 228, 272, 318, 355, 376, 379, 382, 390, 421, 522, 577, 584

Central Australian Desert 45, 412, 519, 612

Central Valley, California 516

Cerro Azul, Mexico 102

Cerro Bolivar 289, 597

Cerro de Pasco, Peru 103

Cerro Matoso 103

Cerro Rico de Potosi, Bolivia 445

Ceylon (See Sri Lanka)

Cevannes Uplift 328

Chad (Tchad) 104, 392, 461, 488, 493, 564

Chad Basin 185

Lake Chad 88, 104, 155, 185, 384, 385, 487, 493, 624

Chagos Fracture 104

Chaillu Massif, Gabon 217

Challenger Deep 574

Chambezi River, Africa 126

Lake Champlain, New York 31, 410

Chang Jiang River, China 515, 623

Changpai Range, Manchuria 109

Channel Islands, California 343, 403, 573

Chapada de Diamantina, Bahia, Brazil 105

Chatahoochee River, United States 41

Chendu Plain, China 515

Chernobyl, Kiev, USSR 241

Chesapeake Bay 168, 414

Chiapas, Mexico 108

Chile 2, 5, 11, 17, 24, 34, 40, 87, 108-109, 111, 112, 132, 158, 175, 176, 197, 208, 248, 250, 259, 270, 323, 324, 369, 382, 387, 388, 415, 440, 452, 495, 527, 542, 558, 565, 588

Chile Rise, Pacific Ocean 13

Chilean Alps 22, 34, 40

Chilwa Island, Malawi 95, 337, 364

Chilwa Lake 337

Mt. Chimborazo, Ecuador 109

China 7, 9, 22, 23, 29, 50, 98, 102, 109, 124, 137, 139, 203, 206, 228, 229, 234, 236, 259, 271, 288, 289, 295, 300, 301, 328, 331, 348, 352, 353, 375, 376, 377, 380, 384, 397, 420, 430, 435, 442, 451, 455, 458, 472, 476, 496, 513, 514, 515, 530, 536, 543, 551, 554, 555, 556, 558, 564, 565, 566, 567, 568, 581, 582, 585, 619, 623, 624, 625, 626, 627

Chinsha Jiang River, China 623

Chongquing (Chunking) China 624

Chott Djerid, Tunisia 557

Chuckawalla Mountains 564

Chugach Mountains, Alaska 121, 231

Chukchi Sea 60

Chuquicamata, Chile 101, 112, 452

Clipperton Fracture, Pacific Ocean 115

Cluff Lake, Canada 625

Coachella Valley, California 497

Coahuila, Mexico 206, 341

Coast Ranges, Alaska 231
Coast Ranges, West Coast 129, 213, 390, 510, 594
Cobalt, Ontario, Canada 118, 237
Colombia 20, 61, 103, 120, 183, 221, 318, 378, 380, 381, 411, 445, 565, 572, 587, 597
Colorado 72, 79, 120, 121, 122, 139, 140, 149, 156, 161, 214, 245, 259, 293, 305, 317, 403, 415, 458, 479, 485, 509, 547, 558, 558, 568, 588, 620 Colorado Delta 121, 497
Colorado Desert, California 48, 121, 364, 497, 498
Colorado Front Range 98, 207, 214, 495
Colorado Plateau 53, 122, 137, 150, 298, 316, 364, 390, 415, 429, 469, 501, 588
Colorado River, United States 28, 121-122, 189, 205, 239, 346, 364, 497, 523, 573
Columbia Glacier, Alaska 122
Columbia Gorge 28
Columbia Icefield, Canadian Rockies 122
Columbia Plateau 53, 122, 137, 150, 301, 319, 327, 423, 438, 502, 588
Columbia River, United States 28, 97, 123, 137
Communism Peak, USSR 124, 530
Como River, Gabon 217
Conakry, Guinea 318
Mt. Concepcion 382
Congo (See Zaire)
Congo Basin 337, 453, 576, 577,
Congo (Zaire) River 41, 89, 104, 126, 132, 144, 166, 175, 233, 291, 306, 337, 483, 488, 489, 555, 578, 588, 629, 630
Congo Submarine Canyon, Atlantic Ocean 126, 542
Connecticut River Valley 81
Lake Constance 471
Mt. Cook, New Zealand 131
Coopers River, Australia 194
Copper Canyon, Sonora, Mexico 132, 236, 264
Coral Sea, South Pacific 133
Cordillera Blanca, Peru 129, 432
Cordillera Central 288
Cordillera Oriental, Bolivia 280, 316
Corsica 163, 275
Costa Rica 101, 151, 288, 601, 603
Costa Rican Ridge 295
Mt. Cotopaxi, Ecuador 136
Crater Lake, Oregon 87, 137, 138, 155, 346
Craters of the Moon, Idaho 137
Crest Province, Mid-Atlantic Ridge 358
Crete 42, 499
Crimean Mountains 46, 99
Cripple Creek, Colorado 139
Crystal Mountains, Gabon 126, 217
Cuba 96, 221, 234, 383
Cumberland Gap 618
Cumberland Plateau 345
Curacao Ridge 357
Cyclades Archipelago 499
Cyprus 132, 233, 408, 439, 575, 603
Czechoslovakia 17, 56, 96, 148, 220, 557, 588

Dahoma Desert 32
Dakotas 9, 145
Dalmatia 301, 542
Danakil Depression 8, 147, 237, 244, 302, 491
Danube Delta 148, 306
Danube River 28, 148, 374
Darfur Province, Sudan 461
Davis Strait, 311
Dawson Creek, British Columbia 13
Dead Sea,Israel/Jordan 149, 155, 175, 237, 245, 313, 347, 378, 496, 567
Death Valley, California 13, 73, 88, 155, 234, 237, 242, 445, 481, 557, 594
Deccan Plateau, India 123, 150, 319, 468, 524
Delaware Bay 268, 414
Mt. Denali, Alaska 485
Derbyshire, England 69
Mt. Dhaulagiri, Nepal 594
Diablo Canyon, Arizona 353, 486
Diamantina River, Australia 194
Djebel Zaghouan 615
Djibouti 481
Djerid Chott, Tunisia 378
Dnieper River, USSR 456
Doldrums Current 188
Dolomites 17, 165, 322, 574
Don River, USSR 603
Dorowa, Zimbabwe 589
Dorset, England 320
Dourbie River, France 239
Douglas, Alaska 544
Dover, England 94, 104, 165, 424, 615
Straits of Dover, England/France 165
Drakensberg Range, South Africa/Lesotho/ Zimbabwe 166, 243
Mt. Dun, New Zealand 170
Dunganab Bay, Sudan 425
Dzungaria, Mongolia 231

East Africa 3, 8, 9, 31, 33, 69, 70, 86, 95, 99, 154, 175, 237, 244, 249, 293, 303, 305, 306, 313, 326, 337, 341, 342, 366, 375, 378, 383, 395, 404, 405, 406, 407, 422, 510, 555, 567, 585, 599, 605, 629, 630
East China Sea 623, 625
East Germany 260, 453
East Greenland Current 311
East Indies 14
East Pacific Rise 13, 115, 141, 175, 262, 263, 268, 295, 319, 358, 401, 417, 505, 545, 557
Easter Island 175
Eastern Desert, Egypt 176
Eastern Drift 252
Eastern Europe 376, 377
Eastern Hemisphere 41, 264, 350
Eastern Highlands, Australia 44
Eastern Rift, Kenya 585
Eastern United States 41, 262, 300, 322, 390, 437, 440, 494, 612
Echo River, Kentucky 339

Ecuador 24, 109, 136, 178, 218, 270, 386, 417, 587

Ediacara Hills, Australia 179

Lake Edward, East Africa 175, 179, 363, 489, 585, 629

Egypt 14, 15, 34, 35, 39, 40, 66, 69, 132, 148, 154, 155, 176, 187, 197, 201, 234, 257, 296, 297, 304, 314, 316, 374-375, 385, 386, 392, 394, 397, 422, 461, 479, 493, 503, 545, 550, 583, 585. 616

El Alamein 461, 491

El Chichon Volcano 108, 171, 387

Elbrus Peak, Caucasus 99

Eldfeld Volcano, Iceland 274

Elephant Island, Antarctica 309

Mount Elgon, Kenya/Uganda 182

Elias Range, Alaska 231

Ellesmere Island 318, 612

Elliot Lake, Canada 613

Elugelab Island, Eniwetok Atoll, South Pacific 185

Emba Basin 304

Emi Koussi Volcano, Tibesti 183

Emmons Glacier 472

Empty Quarter, Arabian Desert 32, 486, 501, 520, 555

England 61, 69, 92, 94, 165, 195, 198, 204, 245, 278, 320, 328, 329, 350, 353, 407, 424, 456, 518, 528, 537, 545, 567, 622

English Channel 185, 391, 424, 615

Eniwetok Atoll, Pacific Ocean 185

Ennedi Plateau, Sahara Desert 185

Equator 24, 27, 35, 38, 42, 87, 89, 114, 115, 124, 125, 126, 131, 134, 136, 143, 164, 173, 177, 187, 188, 218, 243, 257, 264, 270, 282, 286, 291, 318, 328, 329, 335, 352, 377, 385, 386, 392, 423, 456, 482, 489, 522, 529, 558, 561, 565, 566, 567, 572, 575, 579, 584, 596, 599, 617, 630

Equatorial Africa 156, 489, 543, 584, 630

Equatorial Counter Current 188

Equatorial Nile 296

Equatorial Pacific Ocean 550

Er Rif Mountains 362

Mount Erebus, Antarctica 189

Lake Erie, Canada/United States 189, 243, 244

'Erta-ale' Mountains 147

Ervan, Soviet Armenia 33

Erzberg, Austria 515

Espirito Santo, Brazil 67, 77, 632

Essequibo River, Guyana 251, 299, 488

Ethiopia 1, 69, 147, 156, 302, 385, 473, 491, 493, 496, 576, 577, 633

Ethiopian Highlands 69, 147, 228, 385, 386, 407, 487, 543, 556

Mount Etna, Italy 137

Euphrates River, Turkey/Iraq 200, 28, 350, 512, 546, 566

Eurasia 9, 17, 35, 129, 130, 155, 276, 314, 339, 390, 612

Europe 5, 7, 9, 27, 32, 38, 46, 49, 87, 95, 98, 99, 112, 116, 129, 144, 148, 150, 157, 181,

Europe (continued) 186, 190, 208, 210, 229, 230, 233, 240, 243, 253, 264, 273, 275, 278, 280, 298, 300, 301, 305, 308, 314, 321, 325, 327, 338, 347, 348, 359, 368, 369, 379, 393, 418, 428, 430, 431, 431, 440, 446, 451, 452, 456, 478, 479, 481, 502, 520, 535, 545, 561, 567, 574, 580, 588, 591, 602, 603, 610, 619

European Mediterranean Sea 106

European Shelf 481

Mt. Everest 38, 43, 109, 181, 192, 220, 242, 346

Everglades, Florida 192, 404, 613

Lake Eyre, Australia 194, 557

Fairbanks, Alaska 13

Faleme River, Mali 338

Falkland Islands 195-196

Falklands Current 77, 195

Far East 418, 433, 571

Faroe Islands 278

Faroe Ridge 351

Fedchenko Glacier, USSR 530

Fennoscandia 49, 198, 290, 439

Fezzan Basiin 493

Finland 49, 70, 74, 95, 116, 118, 155, 183, 198, 204, 240, 307, 323, 420, 435, 473, 520, 516, 553

Finlay River, British Columbia, Canada 325

Fire Mountains, China 582

Firth of Forth, Scotland 201

Firth of Lorn, Scotland 232

Fitzroy Massif, Andes Mountains 203

Flinders Range, Australia 204, 566

Flores Island 207

Flores Sea, Southeast Asia 207

Florida 24, 30, 48, 57, 60, 67, 101, 133, 192, 205, 253, 258, 271, 322, 340, 365, 404, 427, 435, 447, 474, 475, 488, 499, 519, 543, 568, 609, 613, 614, 631

Florida Current 188, 252

Florida Keys 250, 588

Fordlandia, Brazil 294, 486

Fouta Djallon Massif, West Africa 212, 252, 338, 384

Fram Strait, Greenland Sea/Arctic Ocean 212

France 1, 17, 37, 117, 165, 189, 206, 219, 234, 237, 239, 275, 297, 318, 322, 325, 327, 328, 344, 357, 363, 407, 424, 453, 459, 465, 496, 581, 615

Franz Josef Glacier, New Zealand 212

Fraser River, British Columbia, Canada 97, 212

French Guiana 188

Frisian Islands 448

Fuegan Archipelago 34, 565

Mt. Fuego, Guatemala 101

Mt. Fujiyama, Japan 124, 215, 293, 539

Gabon 104, 203, 217, 457
Galapagos Archipelago 178, 217, 583
Galicia Bank 357
Gambia, West Africa 212
Gambia Mountains 384
Gambia River 212, 252
Ganges River 58, 75, 150, 220, 265, 266, 282, 542, 594
Ganges-Brahmaputra Delta 50, 75, 220, 282, 289, 370, 418, 542
Gangotri Glacier, Himalayas 220
Ganntour Plateau, Morocco 368
Garonne Valley, France 465
Gash Delta, Sudan 153
Gaspe, Canada 409
Gaza Strip 347
Lake George, East Africa 175, 179
Georgia, United States 31, 41, 207, 310, 365, 402, 405, 536
Georgia, USSR 98, 236, 339
Georgian Bay, Lake Superior 356, 544
Germany 5, 22, 148, 237, 247, 249, 260, 264, 344, 381, 406, 430, 452, 502, 571
Gezhouba Dam, China 228, 236
Gezira, Sudan 228, 503, 543
Ghana 12, 151, 228-229, 493, 521
Gibraltar 368, 532, 537, 569
Strait of Gibraltar 229, 362, 537
Gila River, Arizona 121
Glacier National Park 563
Gobi Desert 155, 234, 322, 418, 554
Goias, Brazil 102, 383, 388, 424, 495, 516
Goodnews Bay, Alaska 444
Gore Mountain, New York 220
Gran Chaco, South America 238
Gran Sabana, Venezuela 238, 251
Grand Banks, North Atlantic Ocean 50, 239, 252, 582
Grand Canyon 28, 91, 122, 132, 236, 239, 264, 358, 446, 523, 574, 587, 600
Grand Causses, France 239
Grand Coulee, Washington 137
Grand Mesa, Colorado 156
Grand Teton, Wyoming 561
Granite Gorge, Grand Canyon 600
Great Artesian Basin, Australia 37
Great Australian Bight 622
Great Barrier Reef 44, 52, 133, 411, 475
Great Basin, United States 55, 71, 87, 243, 245, 281, 292, 297, 383
Great Bear Lake, Canada 331, 58888
Great Britain 6, 57, 70, 88, 130, 143, 157, 164, 179, 196, 209, 229, 249, 252, 253, 280, 289, 296, 297, 325, 377, 381, 405, 425, 475, 486, 503, 514, 532, 570, 571, 615, 620
Great Cameroon Volcano 89, 252
Great Glen Moor, Scotland 87, 232
Great Lakes, North America 37, 138, 155, 189, 231, 243, 314, 356, 390, 446, 494, 548
Great Plains, North America 418, 441, 447, 547
Great Salt Lake, Utah 71, 72, 79, 243, 245, 307, 312, 497, 527, 605

Great Sand Sea, Sahara 189
Great Slave Lake, Canada 44, 331
Great Smoky Mountains 415
Great Valley, California 438, 594
Greater Antilles 613
Greece 5, 21, 333, 384, 404, 432, 447, 546
Green Jade River, Turkestan 288
Green Mountain, Utah 162
Green River, Wyoming/Utah 122
Green River, Kentucky 333
Greenland 10, 87, 88, 129, 130, 144, 186, 203, 230, 231, 234, 246, 247, 276, 278, 289, 299, 311, 357, 389, 394, 410, 454, 481, 484, 502, 600, 612
Greenland Sea 212
Guadalquivir River, Spain 343
Guadaloupe Mountains, New Mexico/Texas 411
Guam 448, 535
Guapore River, Brazil 332, 423
Guajira Peninsula 565
Guarapari, Espirito Santo, Brazil 67
Guatemala 101, 136
Guiana Highlands 4, 18, 20, 25, 75, 76, 251, 299, 326, 378, 411, 427, 486, 488, 560, 572, 577, 597, 611
Guiana Massif 345
Guianas 20, 251, 252, 253, 447, 529
Guinea 56, 212, 251-252, 318, 613
Gulf of Guinea 212, 214, 225, 252, 384
Guinea Current 90, 188
Gulf Coast, United States 41, 51, 145, 148, 160, 257, 271, 312, 418, 438, 441
Gulf Stream 90, 133, 188, 190, 212, 239, 252-253, 311, 391, 414, 500, 580
Guyana 75, 251, 253, 299, 486, 488

Hammersley Range, Australia 289
Hangchow Bay, China 259
Harz Mountains, Germany 260-261
Hatteras Plain, North Atlantic Ocean 2
Hawaii 54, 57, 67, 80, 97, 100, 118, 137, 192, 201, 227, 261, 262, 305, 309, 340, 346, 359, 401, 417, 426, 437, 446, 513, 566, 579, 580, 602
Hawaiian Islands 1, 261, 262, 290, 409, 439
Hawaiian Ridge 262
Hawkes Bay, New Zealand 382
Hecla Volcano, Iceland 232, 250, 278
Hector, California 262
Heilung-Kiang River, China 23
Hell's Gate, Kenya 373
Hells Canyon, United States 132, 236, 263-264, 523
Henry Mountains, Utah 311
Herculaneum 599, 602
Hercynian Woods 264
High Atlas Mountains 15, 352, 368
High Plains, North America (See Great Plains) 86, 244, 322, 378, 390, 391
High Qoz, Sudan 308

High Veldt, South Africa 596-597
Himalayas 22, 28, 38, 48, 75, 87, 129, 141,
    152, 192, 211, 220, 242, 265, 265, 282,
    283, 289, 300, 304, 318, 322, 331, 369,
    418, 430, 496, 500, 507, 561, 564, 618, 623
Hindu Kush Range, Himalayas 8, 9, 264, 300,
    420
Hiroshima 582
Holland (See Netherlands)
Honshu Island, Japan 215, 289
Mt. Hood, Oregon 97, 266, 317
Hooghly River, India 220, 266
Hope Sound, Chile 372
Strait of Hormuz 431, 629
Horseshoe Falls 382
Hot Springs, Arkansas 433
Houston, Texas 41
Huallega River, Peru 432
Mt. Huascaran, Peru 45
Mt. Huayco 269
Hubbard Glacier, Alaska 269
Hudson Bay, Canada 10, 122, 186, 190, 231,
    269, 276, 580
Hudson River, New York 168, 270, 518
Hudson Submarine Canyon, Atlantic Ocean
    131, 270, 542
Hudson Strait, Baffin Island/Quebec, Canada
    269
Humboldt Current, Pacific Ocean 41, 270,
    386
Humboldt River, Nevada 328
Hungary 148
Huntington Beach, California 205
Lake Huron 237, 243, 250, 313, 350
Hwang Ho River, China (See Yellow River)
    271, 541, 611
Hyali Volcano 7

Iberian Peninsula 90, 229, 275,27 419
Iceland 87, 118, 203, 227, 232, 253, 267, 269,
    276, 278, 289, 325, 329, 357, 358, 382, 439,
    443, 481, 548, 549, 563, 595, 602
Iceland-Faroe Ridge 357
Ichang Gorge, China 551
Ichtaccihuatl Volcano, Mexico 354
Idaho 72, 118, 131, 138, 207, 264, 298, 393,
    436, 547, 563, 621
Iguaçu Falls 279, 291, 424
Iguaçu River, Brazil 279, 291
Ikursk, USSR 280
Ilheus, Bahia, Brazil 76
Mt. Illampu, Bolivia 280
Mt. Illimani, Bolivia 280
Illimaussaq, Greenland 247
Illinois 206, 362, 610
Imatong Mountains, Sudan 111, 161
Imo River, Nigeria 385
Imperial Valley, California 497, 594
India 5, 47, 50, 53, 56, 57, 58, 61, 76, 75, 102,
    103, 118, 123, 129, 150, 159, 166, 167, 183,
    198, 204, 217, 220, 234, 237, 257, 265, 266,
    279, 281, 286, 291, 298, 300, 301, 302, 307,

India (continued) 318, 319, 320, 343, 355, 366,
    371, 376, 443, 444, 471, 472, 476, 488,
    513, 519, 533, 546, 561, 562, 566, 569,
    576, 587, 588, 598, 607, 613, 617, 626,
    632, 633
Indian Ocean 13, 33, 75, 96, 104, 119, 133,
    150, 166, 188, 202, 209, 232, 243, 281-282,
    331, 332, 338, 348, 358, 370, 371, 376,
    386, 398, 408, 431, 435, 468, 473, 481,
    511, 533, 542, 546, 630
Indian Ocean Current 282
Indiana 381
Indo-Malaysian Archipelago 34, 409, 576
Indo-Malaysian Rainforest 576
Indochina 318, 632
Indonesia 11, 23, 118, 207, 205, 281, 282, 308,
    312, 349, 375, 376, 381, 383, 387, 417,
    470, 524, 546, 554, 557, 576, 577, 602
Indus Gorge 283
Indus River 265, 282, 283, 300, 364, 471, 519,
    562
Indus Valley 576
Ingessana Hills, Sudan 543
Ingur River, Georgia, USSR 236
Inland Passage 249, 595
Ionian Sea 7
Iquitos, Peru 19, 20, 432, 627
Iran 9, 98, 219, 229, 288, 308, 375, 418, 425,
    431, 491, 512, 557, 572, 629
Iranian Desert 284, 418,
Iraq 47, 288, 375, 403, 431, 440, 491, 512, 566
Irazu Volcano, Costa Rica 101, 288, 603
Ireland 53, 70, 200, 229, 248, 253, 342, 435,
    507, 583, 601
Irian Java 381
Iron Mountain, Colorado 293, 458, 598
Irrawaddy Plain, Burma 289
Irrawaddy River, Burma 58, 289
Irtysch River, USSR 391, 397, 515, 626
Isfahan Basin, Iran 557
Islas Hornos 267
Isle Royale 302
Israel 149, 158, 159, 165, 249, 347, 378, 436,
    453, 495, 496, 526, 527, 567
Lake Issyk-kul 565
Itabirito Mountain, Brazil 291
Itaipu Dam, Brazil 147, 273, 291, 340
Italian Alps 165
Italian Archipelago 323
Italy 7, 17, 18, 92, 96, 124, 139, 165, 206, 231,
    288, 302, 342, 345, 427, 446, 453, 496,
    508, 520, 527, 540, 541, 569, 572, 599,
    601, 603 Itasca Lake, Minnesota 362
Itatiaia Mountain, Brazil 510
Ituri Rainforest, Congo Basin 89, 125, 138,
    291, 351, 363
Ivory Coast 248

Jackson Hole, Wyoming 561
Jacobina Range, Bahia, Brazil 16, 94, 492
Jamaica 56, 96, 271
James Bay 269, 580

Jan Mayen Island 358
Japan 86, 124, 202, 215, 219, 287, 290, **293**, 294, 357, 391, 401, 413, 417, 425, 448, **472**, 473, 494, 507, 539, 543, 545, 602
Sea of Japan 406, 625, 626, 631
Japanese Current (Kuro Shio) 87, 188, **294**, 309
Jari River, Brazil 20, 294
Jarilandia, Amazon Basin, Brazil 294
Jasper National Park, Canada 122
Java 228, 312, 349, 602
Java Sea 546
Java Trench 282, 402
Jebel Aulia Dam, Sudan 607
Jebel Uweinat, Sudan/Libya 591
Jemez Mountains, New Mexico 593
Jeraf River, Sudan 296, 386
Jhelum River, India 302
Jonglei, Sudan 296
Jonglei Canal 296, 375, 386, 544
Jonte River, France 239
Jordan 31, 96, 149, 200, 237, 347, 436, **453**, 464, 466, 495, 496, 527
Jordan River 149
Jordan Valley 96, 234
Jos Plateau, Nigeria 385
Jostedal Glacier, Norway 524
Juba, Sudan 296, 544
Judea Mountains 347
Jungfrau Mountain, Switzerland 17
Jura Alps, France 350, 407
Jura Massif, France 297

Kabalega Falls 363, 599
Kaiteur Falls 253, 299
Kalahari Basin 393, 409
Kalahari Desert 299, 373, 382, 409
Kalgoolie, Australia 622
Kali Gandaki River, Nepal 594
Kalingrad, USSR 21
Kamchatka 112, 175, 203, 228, 515, 602
Kamchatka Range 515
Kampuchea (Cambodia) 348, 569
Kansas 87, 625
Kao Lin, China 300
Kara Kum Canal 300
Kara Kum Desert, USSR 300
Kara Sea 397, 626
Karachi, Pakistan 519
Karaganda 304
Karagiye Depression, USSR 530
Karakorum Range 38, 264, 420
Karelia, USSR 198
Kariba Dam 273, 282, 300, 370, 408, 630
Kariba Gorge 300, 630
Lake Kariba 300, 314
Karroo, South Africa 162, 164, 301, 430
Karum Plain 302
Karum Salt Lake 302
Kash Kash River, Turkestan 293
Kashmir 265, 302, 500

Katanga District 588, 630
Katanga Highlands 427
Katmai Volcano, Alaska 302, 559, 602
Katwe Crater, Uganda 302
Kauai, Hawaii 261
Kazun 374
Keeweenaw Peninsula 302-303, 455, 548
Kempyrsai, Khazakhstan 304
Kenai Range, Alaska 231
Kentucky 99, 206, 339, 381,
Kenya 176, 182, 206, 249, 303, 305, 319, 327, 339, 373, 375, 406, 407, 493, 510, 585, 587, 599
Mt. Kenya 244, 298, 305, 479, 484, 510
Kermadec Deep 600
Kermadec Trench 402, 615
Kha District, Indochina 632
Khabarovsk, Siberia 23
Khartoum, Sudan 125, 296, 385, 386, 476, 543, 544
Khazakhstan, USSR 278, 304, 397-398, 515, 611
Khirban Qumran, Jordan 464
Khumba Glacier 192
Khumei, Kordofan, Sudan 304
Khyber Pass 265, 304
Kiev, USSR 107-108, 241
Kigezi Highlands 179
Kilauea Crater, Hawaii 100, 139, 262, 305, 346, 602
Mt. Kilimanjaro 181, 182, 244, 305, 326, 382, 489
Kimberley, South Africa 159, 305, 374
Kimberley Range, Australia 305-306
Kinanpop Plateau 373
King's Peak, Utah 585
Kinta River Valley, Malaysia 306
Kiruna, Lappland, Sweden 306, 336, 455
Lake Kivu, East Africa 175, 306, 395, 489, 555, 600, 629
Klamath Mountains 501
Klamath River 97
Kliutchi Station, USSR 61
Kmi Koussi Volcano 564
Kola Peninsula, USSR 49, 95, 198, 199, 307-308, 460, 516
Komodo Island, Indonesia 308
Kopet-Dagh Range 300
Kordofan Province, Sudan 304, 308, 399, 461
Korea 102, 476, 581, 625
Kos Volcano, Aegean Sea 7
Kosi River, India 220
Kovdozero, USSR 293, 308
Krakatoa Volcano, Indonesia 11, 14, 23, 87, 139, 171, 205, 282, 308, 393, 459, 499, 555, 569, 579
Krasnoyarsk, Siberia 626
Kristna River, India 159, 281
Kuala Lumpur, Malaysia 306, 567
Kuiseb River 373
Kuluene River, Brazil 622
Kunlun Range 413, 421
Kunming Basin, China 627

Kurakorum Range 295
Kure Islands 261, 262
Kurile Islands 290
Kurile Trench 402
Kuroko, Japan 401, 545
Kuro Shio Current 87, 188, 294, 309, 391, 406
Kursk, USSR 309
Kuwait 155, 375, 606
Kuznetz, USSR 310, 398
Kwajalein 310
Kwangsi Province, China 301

La Joya, Peru 170
La Paz, Baja California, Mexico 49
La Paz, Bolivia 20, 280, 454
La Paz River, Bolivia 316
La Plata Estuary 424, 442
La Plata River, Argentina 76, 105, 129, 238,
    421, 424, 442-443, 529
La Sal Mountains, Utah 311
Labrador, Canada 65, 89, 311, 429
Labrador Current 195, 249, 311, 414
Labrador Range, Labrador/Quebec, Canada
    311, 396
Laguna Madre, Texas 312
Lake of the Woods, Canada 10
Lanzarote Island 90, 316
Laos 348
Lappland 306, 412, 541
Laptev Sea, Arctic Ocean 316, 320
Las Canadas, Canary Islands 86, 90
Lassen Volcano, United States 70, 96, 317
Latin America 11, 89, 519, 520, 590, 595
Lebanon 100, 440, 546
Lemhi Pass, Idaho 563
Lena Delta, Siberia, USSR 316
Lena River, Siberia, USSR 280, 320, 515, 623
Leningrad, USSR 415
Lesbos, Greece 432
Lesotho 166, 243
Lesser Antilles 96, 613
Lhasa, Tibet 564
Liberia 260, 487, 613
Libya 156, 189, 190, 215, 260, 302, 376, 392,
    461, 478, 520, 564, 591, 601
Libyan Desert 520
Libyan Desert, Egypt 397, 416
Libyan Erg 189
Lightning Ridge, Australia 408
Limpopo River 370
Lipari Islands, Italy 231, 323
Lisbon, Portugal 323, 508
Little Cameroon Volcano 89
Lituya Bay, Alaska 195
Livingston Falls 126
Llano Estacado, Texas 326
Lock Locky, Scotland 237
Loch Lomond, Scotland 323, 508
Loch Ness, Scotland 232
Mt. Logan, Canada 485

Loire River, France 327-328,
Loire Valley 328
London Basin 424
London, England 92, 407, 416, 528, 545
Long Island, New York 231, 368
Longonot Volcano 373
Lop Nor, Cambodia 328
Los Angeles Basin 416, 523
Los Angeles, California 287, 489, 513
Los Angeles River 205, 437
Los Pijiguaos, Venezuela 585
Louisiana 41, 153, 362, 381, 402, 543, 607
Louisville 381
Lourenco Marques 370
Low Qoz, Sudan 308
Low Veldt, South Africa 596-597
Lualaba River, Zaire 126, 629
Luapulu River, Zaire 615
Lueshe, Uganda 585
Lukuga River 555
Luzon Island, Philippines 329, 553
Lym River, England 324
Lyme Regis, England 278, 329

Macchu Picchu, Peru 20, 627
MacDonnell Range, Australia 15
Mackenzie Bay 57
Mackenzie Delta, Canada 12, 38, 57, 89, 331,
    433
Mackenzie River 122, 331, 383, 390
Madagascar (See Malagasy)
Madagascar Plateau, Indian Ocean 357
Madeira Islands 260
Madeira River, Brazil 20, 332, 529
Madison River, Wyoming 625
Madre de Dios River, Peru 332
Lake Magadi, Kenya 375, 406
Strait of Magellan 333, 538, 555, 603
Magnet Cove, Arkansas 80, 95, 334, 458, 568
Mahe Island, Seychelles 511
Maine 118, 204, 426
Gulf of Maine 285, 563
Malagarasi River 555
Malagasy (Madagascar) 11, 34, 134, 139, 171,
    282, 289, 320, 331, 365, 371, 426, 511, 531
Malaspina Glacier, St Elias Range, Alaska
    337, 438
Malawi (Nyassaland) 9, 94, 175, 337, 338,
    364, 481, 514
Lake Malawi (Nyassa), East Africa 175, 331,
    332, 514, 630
Malay Peninsula 97
Malaysia 78, 182, 306, 338, 343, 375, 487, 555,
    567
Mali, West Africa 309, 324, 338, 384, 476, 493,
    555, 567
Mali Hills 338
Lake Malonabe, Malawi 514
Malta 314, 520
Malvinas Isles 195
Mammoth Cave, Kentucky 99, 254, 339

Manaus, Brazil 19, 20, 21, 24, 75, 125, 379, 447, 573
Manchuria 109
Manhattan Island, New York 270
Manitoba, Canada 269
Lake Manitoba, Canada 9, 10
Lake Manyara, East Africa 245, 341-342,
Mar Dulce 382
Lake Maracaibo, Venezuela 342, 569, 596, 597
Marajo Island, Brazil 422
Maranhao, Brazil 76, 78
Maranon River, Peru 20, 342, 431, 627
Marble Canyon 122
Mt. Marcy, New York 270
Mt. Margherita 481, 489
Marianas 391, 401, 574
Marianas Trench, Pacific Ocean 55, 343, 360, 400, 402, 600
Marie Byrd Land Glacier 231
Maritime Atlas Mountains, North Africa 15
Mt. Markham 178
Sea of Marmora 67
Marmore River, Brazil 20, 332
Marshall Islands 310
Martinique 387, 426-427
Maryland 5, 31, 353
Massachusetts 169, 276, 381, 459
Massif Central, France 239, 363, 424
Mathana Volcano, Aegean Sea 7
Mato Grosso, Brazil 76, 102, 183, 294, 340, 345, 422
Matterhorn, Switzerland 17, 345
Mauna Kea Volcano, Hawaii 261, 262, 346, 359
Mauna Loa Volcano, Hawaii 93, 108, 192, 201, 261, 262, 305, 346, 359
Mauritania 56, 346, 493
Mbei River, Gabon 217
Mt. McKinley 181, 485
McMurdo Sound Station, Antarctica 213, 415
Lake Mead, Arizona/Nevada 314, 346
Meander River, Turkey 347
Mecca, Saudi Arabia 306, 408
Medicine Lake Volcano, Cascades Range 347
Mediterranean Sea 7, 17, 40, 41, 42, 67, 68, 98, 104, 105, 133, 202, 229, 233, 241, 264, 289, 342, 343, 347-348, 363, 368, 378, 385, 443, 461, 491, 501, 504, 506, 518, 520, 543, 545, 572, 580, 603
Mediterranean Rim 342, 347, 476
Mekong River 348, 569, 570, 624
Mendenhall Glacier, Alaska 349
Merapi Volcano, Indonesia 349
Mesabi Range 289
Mesopotamia 200, 288, 350, 546, 629
Strait of Messina 197
Meteor Crater, Arizona 119, 281, 353
Mexico 7, 13, 18, 21, 29, 35, 49, 55, 88, 90, 101, 107, 112, 121, 122, 132, 133, 206, 236, 250, 264, 271, 293, 301, 311, 341, 346, 350, 354-355, 373, 380, 390, 391, 394, 402, 408, 424, 427, 433, 449, 464, 482, 485, 492, 496, 497, 498, 519, 536, 549, 576, 588, 595, 631

Gulf of Mexico 12, 41, 68, 96, 122, 138, 207, 226, 252, 271, 295, 355, 362, 363, 385, 395, 397, 505, 558, 571
Mexico City 55, 80, 287, 354, 355, 415, 464, 523
Miami, Florida 41, 60, 192, 268, 499
Michigan 90, 240, 302, 381, 518, 548
Lake Michigan 243, 303, 313, 356, 444, 453
Michoacan, Mexico 424
Mid-America Trench 402
Mid-Atlantic Ridge 38, 60, 96, 105, 141, 175, 197, 260, 268, 275, 278, 352, 357, 358, 401, 481, 505, 549, 563, 605
Mid-Indian Ocean Ridge 358
Middle East 34, 35, 219, 241, 288, 359, 376, 433, 605
Midway Island 261
Milford Sound, New Zealand 359, 382
Milne Seamount, Atlantic Ocean 2
Milos 7
Minas Gerais, Brazil 48, 76, 77, 102, 105, 291, 340, 365, 424, 465, 495, 500, 524, 563, 570
Mindanao Trench, Pacific Ocean 359-360
Minnesota 9, 90, 362, 469
Mississippi 583
Mississippi Delta 56, 151, 362, 363, 370
Mississippi River 8, 41, 32, 56, 151, 202, 331, 346, 355, 362, 363, 370, 381, 390, 405, 423, 429, 472, 610
Mississippi Valley 327, 346, 356, 362, 363, 438
Missouri 163, 218, 253, 381, 532, 631
Missouri River 8, 331-332, 374
Mitre Peak, New Zealand 359
Mitumba Mountains 126
Mlanje Mountains, Malawi 337, 364
Lake Mobuto-Sese Seko 363
Mogok Valley, Burma 363, 487, 632
Mogollon Rim, Arizona/New Mexico 364
Mohave Desert, California 87, 364
Lake Mohave, Arizona 364
Mohave River, California 364
Mt. Mohinara, Mexico 132
Molasses Reef, Atlantic Ocean 359
Mt. Monadnock, New Hampshire 365
Mongolia 206, 234, 406, 418, 514
Mono Lake, California 15, 366
Lake Monoun, Cameroon 272
Mont Blanc, France 17, 181
Mont Pelee, Martinique 387, 394, 426-427, 445, 602
Montana 83, 103, 111, 132, 207, 410, 444, 453, 455, 479
Montana del Fuego, Canary Islands 316
Monte Argentario, Italy 569
Montelindo River 238
Moray Firth, Scotland 232
Morena River, Brazil 622
Morocco 15, 90, 322, 368, 435, 436, 492
Morro da Mina, Brazil 340
Morro do Ferro, Brazil 465
Moscow, Russia 322, 496, 502, 603
Moscow River 603
Moses Lake, Washington 51, 154

Mountain Pass, California 95, 364
Mozambique 233, 244, 295, 337, 338, 370, 514, 630
Mozambique Plains 300, 370, 630
Muir Seamount, Atlantic Ocean 60, 371
Murchison Falls 363, 599
Mullamullang Cave, Australia 394
Murray River, Australia 371
Mutum, Bolivia 285, 422

Lake Naivasha, Kenya 175, 373
Naferd Desert, Arabia 32
Nairobi, Kenya 319, 587
Namib Desert, Southwest Africa 2, 299, 373, 409
Namibia, Southwest Africa 103, 373-374
Nan Shan Mountains, China 271
Nantucket Island 118
Lake Nasser, Egypt/Sudan 39, 40, 179, 196, 374-375, 543
Lake Natron, Tanzania 375, 405, 406
Mt. Naukluft 373
Nazca Ridge, Pacific Ocean 13
Nebraska 57, 418
Nefta Oasis, Tunisia 378
Nefud Desert, Arabia 32, 378
Negev Desert, Israel 158, 378
Nepal 152, 191, 265, 582, 623
Netherlands 92, 151, 374, 448, 479, 547, 582, 633, 634
Nevada 15, 35, 38, 96, 112, 124, 155, 235, 243, 279, 298, 313, 328, 346, 349, 369, 408, 527
Nevada del Ruiz 380-381, 445
New Brunswick, Canada 72, 215, 565
New Caledonia 118, 221, 318, 383
New England 5, 31, 157, 169, 276, 311, 437, 505, 554, 555
New Guinea 133, 381, 537
New Hampshire 198, 239, 365, 618
New Hebrides 133
New Jersey 21, 52, 247, 336, 368, 409, 469, 499, 518, 631
New Madrid, Missouri 187, 248, 381,
New Mexico 38, 79, 87, 98, 122, 140, 165, 207, 236, 317, 326, 364, 377, 407, 410, 411, 430, 452, 479, 482, 485, 593, 601, 615, 616, 620
New Siberia Island 316
New South Wales, Australia 38, 73, 80, 570
New Valley, Egypt 40, 375
New World 21, 78, 282, 344
New York 81, 90, 157, 164, 169, 183, 220, 258, 270, 275, 276, 339, 368, 382, 410, 469, 495, 518, 554, 619
New Zealand 112, 130, 132, 168, 170, 187, 212, 213, 227, 243, 269, 289, 293, 302, 357, 359, 382, 417, 437, 542, 580, 615
Newberry Caldera, Oregon 232, 390, 398
Newfoundland, Canada 31, 50, 72, 87, 84, 187, 239, 260, 311, 318, 357, 439, 582, 600
Lake Ngami, Botswana 299, 382
Ngorongora Caldera, Tanzania 87, 382

Niagara Falls 381, 599, 609
Niagara Gorge 375, 382
Niagara River 382
Nicaragua 119
Lake Nicaragua 382
Nicaragua Rise 351
Niger 249, 332, 384, 483
Niger Basin 492, 493
Niger Delta 383, 385
Niger Plain 249
Niger River 212, 252, 338, 384, 385, 483, 484, 555, 567
Nigeria 58, 135, 294, 327, 351, 375, 384, 385, 555, 568, 613
Nile Delta 40, 151, 176, 197, 264, 384, 385, 503
Nile River 39, 40, 69, 103, 104, 124, 153, 156, 179, 200, 233, 264, 296, 306, 370, 375, 385-386, 449, 461, 489, 544, 555, 585, 600, 607
Nile Valley 503
90E Ridge, Indian Ocean 386
Lake Ninococha, Peru 20
Lake Nios, Cameroon 272
Lake Nipissing, Ontario, Canada 544
Nisyaros Volcano 7
Nkalonge Hill 337
Nordvest Fjord 203
North Africa 8, 14, 110, 173, 176, 210, 210, 219, 229, 271, 314, 344, 359, 369, 397, 410, 418, 444, 492, 496, 520, 605
North America 1, 12, 21, 30, 35, 55, 59, 60, 81, 87, 95, 101, 112, 126, 129, 130, 133, 139, 150, 155, 181, 184, 210, 211, 226, 230, 233, 236, 240, 243, 269, 273, 275, 276, 294, 295, 298, 301, 305, 309, 314, 318, 331, 339, 352, 354, 355, 356, 368, 369, 376, 390, 391, 393, 406, 408, 417, 418, 427, 428, 432, 445, 447, 451, 452, 454, 455, 482, 485, 498, 518, 530, 540, 545, 548, 553, 561, 595, 602, 610, 612
North American Cordillera 390
North Atlantic Current 90, 391
North Atlantic Drift 253, 532
North Atlantic Ocean 2, 35, 46, 60, 76, 162, 195, 204, 239, 277, 278, 325, 391, 419, 494, 505, 610
North Carolina 310, 406, 426, 441, 460, 462
North Dakota 453, 469
North Downs, England 165
North Equatorial Current 90, 188, 282, 391, 500
North Fork, Colorado 122
North Korea 109
North Pacific Equatorial Current 87, 391
North Pacific Ocean 280, 295, 408, 617
North Pole 35, 37, 112, 173, 415, 448, 561, 617
North Sea 170, 185, 391, 392, 433
North Sea Basin 391
Northeast Brazil 19, 72, 76, 77, 85, 90, 102, 105, 161, 426, 453, 457, 500, 510-511
Northeast United States 286, 549, 558
Northern Australia 387, 439
Northern California 371

Northern Hemisphere 21, 29, 44, 65, 129, 134,
    135, 139, 144, 171, 173, 180, 187, 254, 264,
    275, 329, 350, 389, 390, 392, 393, 399, 400,
    430, 447, 448, 456, 506, 523, 538, 547, 561,
    571, 572, 579, 584, 586, 588, 598, 600, 616
Northern Highlands, Scotland 232
Northern Ireland 53, 87, 123, 444
Northern Province, Sudan 461
Northern Rhodesia 246
Northern Territory, Australia 622
Northumberland, England 245
Northwest Territory, Canada 269
Northwest United States 96, 147, 150, 266,
    301, 361, 470, 471, 523
Norway 5, 27, 103, 104, 117, 118, 162, 198,
    219, 253, 275, 357, 382, 391, 415, 524, 532,
    542, 550, 553
Nova Scotia, Canada 72, 215, 565, 580
Nubia, Egypt/Sudan 40, 374
Nullabar Plain, Australia 110, 394, 532
Nurek Dam, Tajikstan, USSR 147, 394-395
Nyamgasani River 179
Lake Nyassa 175, 332, 616
Nyassaland (See Malawi)
Nyiragongo Caldera, Zaire 388, 600, 629
Nyiragongo Volcano, Zaire 395

Oachita Mountains, United States 44
Ob Dam, Siberia 397
Ob Estuary, Siberia 397
Ob River, Siberia 391, 397, 515, 626
Gulf of Ob, Kara Sea 397
Oblast Region, USSR 339
Ogooue River 214
Ohio 410, 518
Ohio River 205, 362
Lake Okeechobee, Everglades, Florida 192,
    404-405
Okefenokee Swamp, Georgia 405
Oklahoma 87, 416, 479
Oklo, Gabon 104, 203
Old Crow River, Canada 451
Oldoinyo Lengai Volcano, East Africa 95, 375,
    405-406
Olduvai Gorge, East Africa 85, 405, 406
Olenek Basin 623
Olenek Bay 320
Mt. Olga, Australia 125, 406
Olympic Dam, Australia 406
Sea of Oman 283
Ometepe Volcano 382
Omo River, Ethiopia/Kenya 407, 487
Omsk, USSR 397
Lake Ontario 243, 494
Ontario, Canada 118, 237, 240, 269, 336, 380,
    383, 410, 444, 455, 512, 518, 540, 544, 546
Orange River, South Africa 140, 159, 299, 373,
    374, 408-409
Orange River Estuary, South Africa 159
Ord River, Australia 305

Oregon 55, 86, 100, 111, 121, 137, 160, 170,
    232, 266, 268, 318, 346, 353, 361, 383, 389,
    398, 504, 564, 631
Orient 7, 49
Orinoco Basin 556, 597
Orinoco Delta, Venezuela 238, 411, 597
Orinoco Plain, Venezuela 403
Orinoco River, Venezuela 61, 96, 98, 182, 251,
    326, 378, 411, 529, 556, 597
Orinoco Valley, Venezuela 577
Osa Peninsula, Costa Rica 101
Outer Banks, Carolinas 145
Oya Shio Current, Pacific Ocean 414

Pacific Coast Ranges, United States 377, 438,
    529, 509
Pacific Northwest, United States 38, 317, 494,
    631
Pacific Ocean 12, 13, 20, 35, 49, 55, 58, 60, 62,
    101, 108, 112, 114, 115, 118, 122, 129, 134,
    151, 161, 175, 188, 195, 207, 209, 213, 253,
    261, 262, 271, 276, 280, 281, 282, 288, 295,
    319, 332, 342, 343, 344, 349, 350, 357, 361,
    367, 379, 382, 384, 386, 387, 402, 407, 409,
    417, 419, 431, 435, 443, 448, 464, 468, 505,
    514, 518, 523, 542, 549, 553, 567, 579, 584,
    595, 602, 625
Pacific Palisades, California 117
Pacific-Antarctic Ocean 232
Pacific-Antarctic Ridge 417, 505, 557
Padre Island 307
Pakistan 9, 147, 265, 283, 300, 304, 364, 376,
    476, 519, 562
Palestine 464, 466
Palghat Ghat, India 613
Palk Strait 533
Palm Valley, Australia 420
Pamir Plateau 421, 565
Pamir Range 124, 300
Panama 152, 390
Panama Canal 101, 267, 321, 333, 382, 413
Panama Isthmus 101, 314, 421
Panamint Range, California 242, 594
Pantanal, Mato Grosso, Brazil 238, 414
Para, Brazil 19, 33, 75, 422, 451, 510, 556, 571
Para River, Brazil 422, 451
Paraguay 238, 291, 421, 423
Paraguay Basin 442
Paraguay River 71, 76, 183, 238, 332, 345,
    422, 423, 424, 442, 529, 609
Paraiba, Brazil 426
Paraiba Valley, Brazil 404
Parana, Brazil 102, 123, 476
Parana Delta 443
Parana Plateau 53, 76, 123, 150, 279, 319,
    423, 442, 476, 529
Parana River 34, 67, 78, 105, 238, 279, 291,
    332, 423, 424, 442, 529
Parana-La Plata Basin 622
Paranaiba River, Brazil 186

Paricutin Volcano, Michoacan, Mexico 111, 424
Paris Basin 424, 507
Patagonia 129, 155, 425
Patagonian Desert 155, 413, 417, 529
Paulo Affonso Falls, Brazil 500
Peninsula Mountains, Antarctica 28
Peninsula Range, Southern California 88, 121, 427
Pennines 245
Pennsylvania 325, 427, 469, 518
Perim 588
Persian Gulf 33, 48, 200, 282, 425, 431, 434, 506, 512, 522, 629
Peru 20, 24, 40, 45, 87, 103, 129, 132, 158, 162, 170, 178, 183, 202, 242, 250, 270, 332, 342, 386, 387, 420, 422, 431-432, 519, 569, 571, 587, 588, 627, 631
Peru Current 270, 386, 432
Peru/Chile Trench 394
Phalaborwa, South Africa 95, 432, 434, 598
Phantom Valley, Colorado 122
Philippine Trench 402
Philippines 152, 329, 359, 383, 391, 545, 553, 584, 602
Piaui, Brazil 78
Picacho Volcano, Ecuador 136
Piceance Creek, Colorado 149
Pico de Neblina, Brazil 572
Pico Duarte 102
Pike's Peak, Colorado 485
Pilcomayo River, Paraguay 415, 423
Pine Barrens, New Jersey 52
Pine Creek, North Australia 439
Pinnacles Desert, Australia 440
Pinsk Marsh, USSR 456
Po Valley, Italy 446
Pocono Mountains, Pennsylvania 4, 31, 427
Poços de Caldas, Brazil 48, 182, 632
Point Arena, California 195
Point Concepcion, California 62, 588
Poland 49, 96, 218, 254, 456, 496, 502
Polynesia 78
Pompeii 599
Ponta Uba, Brazil 522
Lake Pontchartrain, Louisiana 153, 155
Lake Poopo, Bolivia 495
Popocatapetl Volcano, Mexico 354
Porcupine River, Yukon, Canada 451
Porto Velho, Rondonia, Brazil 332, 571
Portugal 46, 275, 323, 342, 370, 508, 550, 571, 581, 588, 619
Potaro River 299
Potosi, Bolivia 35, 71, 454
Pretoria, South Africa 456
Prince William Sound 122, 593
Pripet Marsh, USSR 456
Pripet River, USSR 456
Provo Lake, Utah 71
Prudhoe Bay, Alaska 12, 13, 57, 428, 433
Puerto Rico 41, 60, 96
Puerto Rico Trench 41, 402
Puna, Andes 451

Punjab 283
Punta Arenas, Chile 415
Puys,France 451
Pyrenees 186, 275, 369

Qatar 155, 375
Qattara Depression 190, 461, 616
Quebec Province, Canada 269, 311, 315, 318, 494
Queen Charlotte Island, Canada 595
Queensland, Australia 44, 170, 532
Queenston Delta 410
Qumram, Jordan 464

Rajasthan, India 476, 562
Rajputana Desert 471
Rand (See Witwatersrand, South Africa)
Mt. Ranier 471-472
Reading, Pennsylvania 469
Red Basin, China 515
Red Desert 322
Red River 362
Red Sea 31, 33, 42, 66, 147, 175, 176, 226, 244, 245, 247, 268, 282, 302, 342, 347, 361, 399, 303, 411, 425, 428, 431, 473-474, 481, 506, 517, 541, 545, 572, 583, 618
Reelfoot Lake, Tennessee 381, 614
Reggane, Algeria 555
Republic of Georgia, USSR 333
Revilla Gigedo, Mexico 391
Reykjanes Ridge, Iceland 268
Rhine Gorge 479
Rhine River 153, 236, 237, 374, 479, 473, 594
Rhine Valley 479, 481, 502
Rhone Glacier 230, 325
Rift Valley, East Africa 31, 33, 70, 95, 96, 147, 149, 175, 237, 244, 302, 306, 337, 338, 363, 373, 375, 381, 386, 397, 399, 481, 487, 488, 489, 502, 513, 555, 556, 557, 567, 585, 605
Rio Branco, Brazil 75, 180, 378
Rio de Janeiro, Brazil 12, 52, 77, 193, 277, 404, 495, 510
Rio del Diablo 378
Rio Doce, Brazil 76
Rio dos Mortes, Brazil 622
Rio Grande, United States/Mexico 41, 354, 355, 482
Rio Grande do Norte, Brazil 426
Rio Grande Rise 401, 482, 574, 605
Rio Negro, Argentina 425
Rio Negro, Brazil 10, 20, 21, 23, 24, 61, 75, 98, 125, 378-379, 447, 528, 595
Riviera 520
Robeda Peak 565
Rocky Mountains, North America 6, 21, 27, 38, 49, 67, 70, 87, 109, 112, 121, 129, 131, 133, 139, 145, 190, 241, 258, 316, 317, 326, 331, 348, 362, 369, 390, 391, 425, 427, 438, 482, 485, 561, 563

Rogun Dam, USSR 147, 394
Romanche Trench 41, 402
Rondonia, Brazil 98, 183, 332, 567, 571
Ronura River, Brazil 622
Roraima, Brazil 75, 251, 379, 486, 571
Mt. Roraima 486
Ross Ice Shelf, Antarctica 277, 478
Ross Sea 478
Roxby Downs Station, South Australia 406
Rotorua District, New Zealand 382
Rub al Khali 32, 486, 501, 520
Lake Rudolph, East Africa 175, 407, 487
Rum Jungle, Australia 439
Rumania 17, 96, 146, 487-488
Rupununi 251, 488
Russell Fjord 269
Russell Lake 269
Russia, USSR (See USSR) 44, 108, 270, 322,
    336, 343, 391, 496, 514, 532, 597, 600, 603,
    614
Lake Ruwenzori 175
Mt. Ruwenwori 585
Ruwenzori Mountains 126, 179, 244, 302, 326,
    363, 488-489, 556, 585
Ruzizi River 555, 600
Rwanda 422, 489, 629
Rwanda Highlands 179
Lake Rybinsk, USSR 603
Ryukus Islands 584

Sabaloka Gorge, Egypt 376
Sacramento Mountains 615
Sacramento River, California 205, 498
Safed Koh Range, Himalayas 9, 265, 304,
Sahara Desert 15, 37, 42, 51, 56, 62, 69, 96,
    104, 110, 155, 156, 157, 171, 183, 185, 189,
    190, 304 327, 338, 346, 365, 384, 385, 386,
    397, 418, 427, 439, 471, 476, 479, 492-493,
    496, 508, 513, 543, 544, 564, 567, 575, 622,
    624, 633
Sahel, Africa 104, 157, 168, 178, 242, 286, 366,
    413, 471, 492, 493, 510, 543, 547, 577, 629
St. Elias Range, Alaska 12, 269, 337, 438
Mt.St.Helens, Cascade Range 72, 97, 108, 266,
    317, 459, 494, 601
St.   Lawrence   River,Canada/United   States
    244, 245, 248, 381, 494,
Gulf of St Lawrence 494
St. Mary's River 405
Salar de Uyuni, Bolivia 24, 323, 495
Salar Grande, Bolivia 495
Salisbury Plains, England 537
Salitre, Minas Gerais, Brazil 495, 569
Salton Basin, California 497
Salton Sea, California 13, 121, 497, 527
Salton Trough, California 88, 121, 226, 227,
    497-498
San Andreas Mountains 615
San Bernardino Mountains, California 563
San Diego Bay, California 449, 571

San Diego County, California 533, 561
San Francisco, California 87, 205, 348, 498
San Francisco Bay 182, 498, 549
San Gabriel Mountains, California 573
San Gabriel River, California 205
San Joaquin River, Calfornia 205, 374, 498
San Joaquin Valley, California 446
San Juan River, New Mexico/Utah 122, 236
San Miguel Island, Channel Islands 403
San Pedro Martyr Range, Baja California 355
Sandwich Isles 195
Sandy Hook 270
Sanganab Atoll, Red Sea 474, 544
Sangre de Cristo Range 482
Santa Ana River, California 205
Santa Clara River, Peru 431
Santa Inez Mountains, California 573
Santa Monica Mountains, California 573
Santa Rosa de Lima Sub-basin, Sergipe, Brazil
    551
Santorini Volcano, Cyclades 7, 42, 87, 459,
    499-500, 536
São Francisco Mountains, Brazil 33
São Francisco River, Brazil 105, 183, 186, 500,
    529, 560
São Luis de Maranhao, Brazil 493
São Manoelito River, Brazil 622
São Paulo Plateau, South Atlantic Ocean 357
Sar-e-Sang, Afghanistan 9
Sargasso Sea 60, 80, 190, 252, 253, 255, 391,
    500-501, 504
Sardinia 275
Saskatchewan, Canada 122, 452, 453, 556,
    625
Saskatchewan Glacier 122
Saskatchewan River 122
Saudi Arabia 33, 155, 189, 234, 236, 306, 318,
    336, 375, 408, 431, 434, 486, 474, 491, 501-
    502, 508, 544, 577
Lake Saugeen 356
Savage River, Tasmania 522
Sayan Mountains, USSR 48, 626
Scandinavia 49, 87, 103, 139, 183, 190, 198,
    203, 209, 277, 248, 425, 427, 471, 502, 550,
    600, 612
Scotland 26, 38, 53, 65, 70, 74, 85, 87, 200-
    201, 226, 229, 232, 240, 248, 253, 318, 323,
    325, 356, 507, 508, 537, 560, 563, 601
Scottish Highlands 87, 248, 476
Sechura Desert, Peru 432
Selenga River, USSR 48
Semliki Plain, East Africa 489
Semliki River 176, 363, 481
Senegal 38, 53, 91, 436
Senegal River 109, 212, 252, 338
Sequoia National Park 416
Serchio River, Italy 97
Serir Reg, Tibesti 476
Serengeti Plain 383, 406, 510
Sergipe, Brazil 144, 551
Serra da Canastra, Brazil 500
Serra do Espinhaco, Brazil 77

Serra do Mar, Brazil 77, 279, 510
Serra do Rabicho, Brazil 422
Serra Estrela, Portugal 619
Serra Pelado, Brazil 235, 510
Sertão, Brazil 33, 85, 105, 510-511
Sete Quedas, Brazil 291
Seven Devils Range 523
Sevier Lake, Utah 71, 72
Sevier Playa, Utah 72
Seward Glacier 337
Seychelle Islands 282, 511
Seymour Island, Antarctica 511
Shari River, Malawi 104
Shark Bay, Australia 540
Mt. Shasta, Cascade Range 347
Shatt al Arab, Iran/Iraq 512
Shenandoah River 31
Shensi Plain, China 513, 624
Shetland Islands 195
Shilka River, Siberia 22
Shire River, Malawi 338, 514, 630
Siberia, USSR 22, 23, 25, 35, 44, 48, 59, 73,
    118, 139, 147, 154, 190, 204, 209, 211, 280,
    310, 313, 314, 316, 339. 370, 389, 397, 440,
    440, 501, 514-514, 535, 561, 570, 574, 582,
    588, 591, 598, 611, 623, 625, 626
Siberian Plain 515
Sichuan (Szechwan) China 515
Sicilian Channel 562
Sicily, Italy 527, 540, 562
Sierra de Encantada, Coahuila, Mexico 206
Sierra Leone 57, 67, 159, 384, 488, 516, 569
Sierra Madre, Mexico 131
Sierra Nevada, California 55, 70, 92, 133, 240,
    290, 313, 348, 366, 368-369, 390, 425, 438,
    509, 510, 516, 527, 556, 573, 594
Sierra Madre del Sur, Mexico 354
Sierra Occidental, Mexico 21, 55, 133, 354,
    424
Sierra Oriental, Mexico 133
Siilinjavi Carbonatite, Finland 516
Silesia 218
Simpson Desert, Australia 519
Sinai Desert 179
Sinai Peninsula 31, 176, 378, 605
Sind Desert, Pakistan 519, 562
Sinkiang Province, China 565, 582
Sino-Siberia 139
Siskiyous Range, California 231
Situk River, Alaska 269
Siwa, Egypt 148
6th Cataract, Egypt 386
Slave Province, Canada 521
Snake River 123, 236, 263, 264, 523
Sobat River, Sudan 296, 386
Sogne Fjord, Norway 524
Sokoto River, Nigeria 384
Solar Lake, Israel 165, 526
Solimoes River, Brazil 20, 21, 75, 125, 379,
    528
Solomon Islands 133
Solomon Sea 133
Songwe Carbonatite, Malawi 331

Sonora, Mexico 132, 236, 264, 390
Sonoran Desert, Arizona/Mexico 250, 296, 492
South Africa 1, 2, 9, 10, 16, 24, 45, 47, 57, 58,
    86, 95, 110, 116, 130, 140, 143, 156, 159,
    161, 164, 166, 171, 177, 179, 199, 206, 208,
    211, 220, 229, 235, 236, 240, 243, 245, 247,
    250, 280, 284, 297, 299, 305, 308, 332, 331,
    333, 334, 366, 373, 383, 408, 412, 414, 428,
    430, 434, 435, 436, 440, 444, 445, 454, 455,
    456, 471, 473, 481, 484, 488, 492, 515, 518,
    544, 569, 574, 575, 577, 589, 596, 598, 603,
    605, 612, 618, 623, 632, 633
South America 1, 8, 13, 18, 21, 24, 28, 29, 34,
    38, 40, 45, 58, 59, 65, 116, 129, 133, 135,
    143, 155, 156, 171, 178, 184, 186, 188, 195,
    230, 233, 236, 238, 251, 252, 261, 264, 267,
    270, 273, 289, 291, 293, 314, 326, 333, 340,
    351, 358, 376, 387, 391, 408, 417, 421, 423,
    424, 427, 430, 433, 447, 454, 464, 470, 481,
    495, 500, 522, 529, 545, 559, 560, 569, 571,
    574, 576, 578, 597, 605, 612, 632
South Atlantic Ocean 58, 76, 195, 271, 358,
    401, 419, 482, 538, 561, 575, 605
South Australia 201, 281, 399, 445, 622
South Carolina 10, 68, 300, 418
South China Sea 348, 584, 623
South Dakota 66, 109, 148, 266, 311, 426, 533
South East Indian Ridge 103
South Equatorial Current 11, 58, 76, 188, 384
South Fork, Colorado 122
South Island, New Zealand 212, 293, 359, 382
South Orkney Islands 195
South Pacific Ocean 22, 62, 185, 209, 212,
    337, 387, 407, 419, 475, 535
South Pole 27, 28, 173, 448, 617
South Sandwich Trench 402
South Seas 411
Southeast Asia 19, 31, 151, 209, 293, 338, 366,
    387, 447, 486, 492, 521, 529, 59, 578, 605
Southeast Indian Ridge 104
Southeast Pacific Ocean 387
Southeast United States 127, 360, 509, 549
Southern Africa 95, 110, 171, 481, 482, 544
Southern Alps, Chile 108
Southern Alps, New Zealand 131, 212
Southern California 87, 105, 121, 180, 182,
    183, 289, 341, 347, 356, 363, 364, 397, 426,
    427, 548, 550
Southern Hemisphere 13, 129, 134, 135, 139,
    143, 156, 168, 171, 173, 187, 188, 254, 258,
    264, 333, 392, 393, 399, 416, 420, 428, 430,
    506, 528, 530, 561, 566, 572, 579, 584, 586,
    588
Southern Karroo, South Africa 422
Southern United States 41, 392, 513
Southwest Africa 299, 373
Southwest United States 27, 30, 36, 86, 190,
    196, 223, 260, 280, 284, 311, 324, 326, 337,
    349, 350, 377, 398, 509, 553, 554, 568, 575,
    605, 606, 616, 624
Soviet Union (See USSR) 37, 44, 49, 61, 98,
    111, 117, 124, 183, 199, 209, 232, 273, 288,

Soviet Union (continued) 309, 339, 340, **360**, 395, 397, 434, 439, 530, 591, 611, 614, **623**, 626

Spain 1, 18, 33, 206, 263, 275, 343, 349, **453**, 460, 480, 520, 569, 571

Spanish Peak, Colorado 161

Spanish Sahara 346, 440, 492

Spearfish Canyon, South Dakota 109

Spitzbergen, Norway 415, 532

Spor Mountain, Utah 61

Spruce Pine, North Carolina 441

Sri Lanka 135, 487, 488, 533, 569

Staffa Island 200, 229

Mt. Stanley 488

Steptoes, Oregon 122

Stone Mountain, Georgia 365, 536

Stromboli Volcano 540, 549, 602

Suakin Archipelago 541

Suakin Deep 532

Suakin Graben 541

Sudan 9, 34, 40, 69, 153, 157, 228, 257, 296, 304, 308, 314, 370, 374, 375, 385, 386, 392, 425, 461, 474, 476, 493, 499, 503, 541, 543-544, 591, 598, 607, 616

Sudan Belt, Sub-Sahara 578

Sudan Reef, Red Sea 474

Sudbury, Ontario, Canada 328, 336, 383, **444**, 455, 512, 546

Sudd, Sudan 9, 191, 296, 385, 386, 543, 544

Gulf of Suez 31, 176

Suez Canal 176, 500, 545

Sumatra 302, 569, 577

Sumbawa, Indonesia 554

Sunda Strait 308, 459, 546

Sunda Trench 546

Sunset Crater 110

Lake Superior 10, 243, 244, 258, 302, 313, 430, 544, 548, 599

Surinam 56, 188, 448, 607

Surtsey Volcano, Iceland 278, 548-549

Susaki Aegena 7

Susquehanna River 168

Suwanee River 405

Svalbard Archipelago 532

Sweden 70, 103, 107, 118, 183, 198, 196, 336, 420, 455, 473, 581, 601

Switzerland 17, 45, 219, 265, 345, 413, 415, 479, 494

Sylvania Guyot 550

Syrian Desert 551

Szechwan, China 551

Szechwan Canal, China 551

Ta Jiang River, China 623

Taal Volcano, Philippines 329, 553

Taconic Range, New York/New England 270, 275

Tadzhik River, USSR 124

Lake Tahoe, California 88, 509

Taiwan 391

Taiwan Strait 584

Tajikstan, USSR 394-395

Takla Makan Desert, China 234, 418, 554

Talmyr Peninsula, USSR 316

Tambora Volcano, Sumbawa Island, Indonesia 393, 544-545

Lake Tana, Ethiopia 69, 385, 556

Tanana River, Alaska 620

Tanezrouft Basin, Algeria/Mali 338, 492, 493, 555

Tang Shan, China 555

Tanganyika (See Tanzania)

Lake Tanganyika, East Africa 125, 175, 306, 338, 555, 600, 629

Tangula Mountains, Northeast Tibet 623

Tanzania 9, 176, 244, 249, 305, 313, 375, 382, 405, 406, 487, 489, 510, 555, 599, 632

Taoudenni Basin 613

Tapajos River, Brazil 20, 273, 556

Tapira Carbonatite, Brazil 460, 568, 569

Taquari-Vassouras Basin, Brazil 551

Tarim River Basin 554

Tarn River, France 239

Tasman Glacier 130-131

Tasman Sea 387

Tasmania 130, 164, 169, 445, 522, 556, 561

Tatar Strait 23

Lake Tear of the Clouds 270

Tehuantepec Isthmus, Mexico 354

Ten Thousand Smokes, Alaska 215

Tennessee 31, 381, 583, 614

Tete, Mozambique 370

Teton Mountains, Wyoming 502, 505, 561, 581

Texas 87, 133, 191, 250, 312, 317, 320, 322, 411, 416, 420, 430, 479, 482, 496, 505, 543, 557, 595

Thailand 135, 206, 340, 348, 487, 555, 568, 581

Thar Desert, India 471, 519, 562

Thomas Range, Utah 570

Thousand Springs Valley, Idaho 72

Tibesti Massif 62, 156, 183, 260, 476, 492, 564

Tibet 189, 265, 283, 519, 564, 575, 623

Tibetan Plateau 109, 348, 564, 593

Lake Tien Chih, China 627

Tien Shan Range, China/USSR 38, 397, 421, 554, 565, 582, 611

Tierra del Fuego Archipelago 21, 24, 133, 195, 267, 333, 355, 565

Tigris River 47, 200, 288, 350, 512, 546, 566

Tigris Valley 350

Timbuktu, Mali 338, 384, 496, 567

Timna Valley, Sinai 567

Timor Island 546

Timor Sea 44

Mt. Timpanogos, Utah 606

Lake Titicaca, Peru/Bolivia 24, 280, 314, 316, 569, 571

Tissel Meer, Netherlands 634

Toba Volcano, Sumatra 569

Lake Toba, Sumatra 569

Tocantins River, Brazil 20, 33, 50, 422

Todd River, Australia 15, 328

Togo 436

Tonga Trench, South Pacific Ocean 59, 402, 602
Tonle Sap Lake, Cambodia 348, 569, 570
Tonle Sap River 569
Topaz Mountain, Utah 570
Topazios Island 428
Tordesillas, Spain 570
Toro Ankole 489
Torres Strait 381
Toskha Canal, Egypt 40, 296, 375
Toskha Depression 48
Mt. Toubkal, High Atlas, North Africa 368
Mt. Townsend, Australia 181
Trail Ridge, Florida 24, 488, 632
Transvaal, South Africa 9, 166, 199, 434
Transverse Ranges, California 427, 573
Transylvania 96
Transylvanian Alps 28
Travancore, India 343, 632
Tristan Volcano 38
Tristan da Cunha, South Atlantic 481, 574
Trombetas River, Brazil 20, 294
Troodos Massif 575
Tropic of Cancer 130, 528, 575, 579, 596
Tropic of Capricorn 130, 575, 579, 596
Trou au Natron, Tibesti 564
Trucial States 491
Tsang Po Valley 623
Tuareg Massif 613
Tuktoyaktut Peninsula, Canada 57
Tunduf Basin 613
Tunguska River Basin, USSR 581
Tunisia 15, 110, 215, 378, 436, 557, 572, 629
Turfan Depression, China 582
Turkan Desert 418
Lake Turkana, East Africa 407
Turkestan, USSR 293
Turkestan Desert 583
Turkey 23, 33, 99, 111, 245, 347, 481, 566, 601
Turn Again Inlet, Alaska 564
Tyrrhenia 14
Tyrrhenian Sea 540

Ubangi River 126
Ucayali River, Peru 20, 342
Udi Plateau, Nigeria 385
Uganda 9, 179, 182, 302, 308, 313, 363, 386, 488, 489, 510, 585, 598, 599, 600, 629
Ugarta Mountains 613
Uinta Basin, Utah 585
Uinta Mountains, Utah 585
Ukraine, USSR 567
Ungava Peninsula, Quebec, Canada 269
United Kingdom 206, 375, 453, 568
United States 5, 6, 8, 11, 15, 28, 29, 30, 35, 36, 37, 53, 54, 55, 56, 57, 61, 66, 69, 87, 88, 89, 92, 95, 97, 98, 100, 106, 111, 113, 116, 118, 121, 126, 130, 132, 133, 134, 138, 145, 147, 150, 154, 156, 158, 159, 160, 162, 162, 168, 169, 171, 175, 187, 192, 199, 204, 205,

United States (continued) 207, 208, 210, 211, 218, 219, 220, 222, 223, 227, 228, 231, 235, 236, 238, 240, 241, 243, 248, 244, 249, 250, 251, 252, 254, 258, 260, 262, 264, 265, 268, 278, 279, 280, 289, 297, 303, 310, 312, 313, 314, 316, 317, 319, 321, 322, 324, 326, 327, 339, 340, 343, 344, 353, 354, 355, 356, 357, 361, 365, 366, 371, 375, 377, 379, 381, 383, 388, 390, 402, 404, 405, 409, 416, 419, 420, 425, 426, 427, 430, 432, 432, 433, 435, 436, 437, 438, 435, 440, 444, 445, 446, 447, 449, 453, 454, 456, 458, 460, 469, 470, 471, 480, 487, 488, 492, 494, 496, 509, 513, 519, 523, 525, 527, 536, 537, 543, 546, 545, 548, 549, 554, 558, 563, 566, 567, 568, 569, 581, 583, 585, 588, 589, 605, 606, 607, 610, 612, 613, 614, 615, 616, 617, 618, 619, 620, 624, 625, 630, 631, 632
Upper Peninsula, United States 237, 344, 455
Upsallata Pass 5
Ural Mountains, USSR 199, 220, 430, 431, 444, 514, 588
Ural River, USSR 304
Urserental Valley, Switzerland 45
Urubamba River, Peru 20, 627
Uruguay 76, 442, 510
Uruguay River 424, 442
Uruque River, Sonora, Mexico 132
USSR (See also Soviet Union) 9, 12, 22, 37, 46, 47, 48, 49, 61, 89, 95, 98, 99, 106, 107, 110, 124, 146, 159, 179, 184, 198, 201, 203, 206, 209, 228, 235, 236, 241, 243, 280, 289, 293, 300, 304, 304, 307-308, 310, 313, 316, 320, 337, 339, 340, 371, 375, 383, 391, 394, 395, 397, 415, 418, 421, 426, 429, 430, 433, 435, 436, 444, 445, 454, 456 460, 479, 514, 515, 516, 519, 535, 550, 553, 544, 555, 565, 567, 568, 580, 581, 583, 588, 603, 611, 623, 632
Urt-Urt Plateau, USSR 300
Utah 18, 34, 61, 63, 72, 114, 121, 122, 132, 138, 162, 207, 219, 227, 236, 243, 245, 298, 300, 311, 403, 418, 439, 452, 453, 469, 479, 527, 547, 570, 585, 605
Uweinat, Sudan/Libya 591
Uyuni Salar, Bolivia 591
Uzbekistan, USSR 397

Vaal River, South Africa 408
Vale de la Luna, Bolivia 316
Valley of the Geysers, Kamchatka 228
Valley of 10,000 Smokes, Alaska 215, 559
Vancouver Island, Canada 87, 195, 210, 595
Vatna Glacier, Iceland 276, 595
Veldt, South Africa 578, 584, 585
Venezuela 20, 25, 26, 61, 95, 96, 98, 101, 183, 238, 251, 289, 342, 375, 378, 411, 486, 556, 578, 597
Gulf of Venezuela 342
Verde River, Paraguay 238
Vermillion Sea 474

Vermont 554
Mt. Vesuvius, Italy 124, 137, 371, 599, 601, 603
Lake Victoria 175, 313, 338, 386, 585, 599
Victoria Falls 599, 630
Vietnam 624
Vilyui Basin, Siberia 623
Vilyui River, Siberia 623
Virgin Islands 558
Virgin Valley, Nevada 408
Virunga Volcanoes 179, 306, 395, 555, 600
Vis River, France 239
Vitiaz Deep, Marianas 343
Vitim River, USSR 280
Vizcaino Desert, Baja California, Mexico 49
Volga Basin 603
Volga Canal, USSR 603
Volga River 98, 225, 603
Volta Basin 613
Volta Grande, Brazil 235
Volta River, Ghana 12, 228, 252,
Von Martius Falls, Brazil 622
Vosges Mountains, France 237, 479
Vredefort, South Africa 486
Island of Vulcano 603
Mt. Vulcano 323, 602, 603
Vulture Mine 591

Wabar Crater, Saudi Arabia 486
Waddensee, Netherlands 448, 634
Wadi el Arabah 378, 567, 605
Wadi Wassat, Saudi Arabia 236
Waiho River, New Zealand 213
Wales 88, 260, 439, 537
Wallaba Forest, Guiana 447
Walvis Bay 373, 374, 588
Walvis Ridge, South Atlantic 401, 482, 575, 605
Wasatch Range, Utah 243, 605-606
Washington 51, 72, 154, 387, 406
Mt. Washington, New Hampshire 198
Wedell Sea 511
West Africa 19, 41, 53, 62, 87, 89, 141, 151, 167, 210, 212, 217, 228-229, 240, 251, 252, 260, 286, 304, 318, 338, 340, 366, 368, 384, 426, 457, 486, 487, 499, 516, 613
West Coast, North America 29, 294, 369, 542
West Coast, South America 24, 369
West Delta, India 220
West Germany 170, 260, 440, 453
West Indian Platform 253
West Indies 101, 176, 267, 271, 613
West Virginia 518
West Wind Drift 77, 188, 195, 282
Western Australia 44, 240, 440, 513, 622
Western Desert, Egypt 146, 176, 479, 493
Western Europe 376, 433
Western Ghats, India 613
Western Hemisphere 5, 9, 41, 65, 264, 266, 350, 452, 529, 557
Western North America 293, 545

Western Pacific Ocean 133, 286, 557
Western United States 92, 100, 112, 115, 127, 132, 265, 266, 292, 316, 430, 438, 480, 509, 523, 625
White Cliffs of Dover 104, 165, 424, 615
White Island, Bay of Plenty, New Zealand 615
White Jade River, Turkestan 288
White Mountains, California 88, 195
White Nile River 69, 125, 175, 228, 291, 385, 386, 422, 543, 585
White Mountains, New Hampshire 198
White Sands, New Mexico 615
White Sea 307, 603
Mt. Whitney 516
Williston Basin, Saskatchewan, Canada 453
Wingate Reef, Red Sea 474, 544, 618
Lake Winnepeg, Canada 10, 89
Wisconsin 90, 302, 410
Witwatersrand, South Africa 16, 414, 455, 471, 492, 618-619
Wizard Island 87, 137, 346
Wolf Creek Crater 619
Wrangell Range, Alaska 12, 231, 620
Wyoming 59, 66-67, 121, 122, 132, 210, 215, 228, 231, 242, 245, 293, 298, 305, 312, 322, 403, 405, 413, 432, 434, 502, 547, 561, 575, 581, 616, 625

Xingu Basin, Brazil 420
Xingu Falls, Brazil 622
Xingu Plateau, Brazil 622
Xingu River, Brazil 20, 21, 622

Yablonovy Mountains, USSR 48
Yakut, Siberia, USSR 315, 623
Yakutat Bay 269
Yakutsk Plain, Siberia, USSR 623
Yalu River, China/North Korea 109
Yangtze Basin, China 551
Yangtze Kiang Gorge, China 353
Yangtze Kiang River, China 236, 515, 623-624
Yazoo River, Mississippi 624
Yellow River (Hwang-Ho), China 228, 236, 271, 423, 551, 624-625
Yellow Sea 625
Yellowstone National Park 86, 210, 215, 228, 231, 258, 268, 384, 397, 405, 424, 432, 580, 625
Yenesei Basin, Siberia, USSR 320
Yenesei River, Siberia, USSR 48, 320, 391, 397, 515, 535, 613, 626
Yosemite Valley, California 92, 193, 228, 585
Yucayali River 627
Yucatan, Mexico 95, 101, 271, 301
Yucatan Peninsula, Mexico 96
Yugoslavia 7, 17, 107, 146, 241, 301, 341, 574
Yukon River, Alaska/Canada 620, 627
Yukon Territory, Canada 231, 429, 451, 627

Yukon Valley 134, 627
Yuma Sand Hills 121
Yunnan Plateau, China 109, 614
Yunnan Province, China 109, 301, 567
Yurang Kash River, Turkestan 293

Zaghouan Massif, Tunisia 629
Zagros Mountains, Iran 229, 629
Zaire (See Congo) 118, 126, 132, 179,
    291, 337, 338, 363, 395, 470, 488,
    489, 555, 568, 576, 577, 585, 600,
    629, 630
Zaire (Congo) Basin 124-125, 164, 230,
    566, 629, 630
Zaire (Congo) River 41, 103, 126, 337,
    475, 488, 577, 629, 630
Zambezi Basin 371, 514
Zambezi Delta 370, 630
Zambezi River 175, 233, 282, 300, 338,
    370, 408, 514, 599, 630
Zambia 9, 126, 132, 249, 300, 314, 337,
    338, 555, 630
Zeberget Island, Red Sea 428
Zimbabwe 103, 111, 161, 166, 243, 248,
    300, 308, 314, 320, 598, 599
Zuider Zee 153, 448, 634

GENERAL INDEX

A-Horizon 81, 260, 280, 454, 525, 528

Absolute Zero 2, 263, 303

Abundance 36, 113, 136, 191, 197, 227, 263, 270, 272, 288, 289, 339, 354, 360, 379, 383, 384, 399, 414, 484, 511, 517, 524, 545, 563, 621, 626

Abyssal Environment 2, 55, 185, 186, 273, 282, 358, 359, 401, 441, 582

Accessory mineral 3, 27, 31, 159, 215, 217, 220, 310

Accretion 4, 153, 401, 443

Acid Rain 4, 5, 107, 149, 333, 449, 450, 460, 546

Actinolite 70

Actinium 6, 212

Adamellite 239

Adaptation 6, 12, 23, 148, 255, 299, 309, 319, 340, 351, 377, 412, 437, 458, 469, 478, 581, 622

Adiabatic 6, 169

Adularia 411

Adventurine 463

Aegerine 337, 460, 495

Aeolian 7, 151, 186, 190, 327, 440

Aeration 8, 29, 90, 91, 144, 271, 414, 427, 441, 475, 593, 633

Aerobic 8, 185, 611

Aeroid 184, 334

Aerosol 8, 107, 262, 416, 523

African Plate 9, 17, 252, 275, 443

African Shield 2, 8, 9, 27, 42, 212, 368, 513

Afro-Brasilia 9, 139, 513

Lake Agassiz (Pleistocene) 9, 10

Age Dating 21, 36, 79, 94, 153, 157, 223, 224, 299, 367, 406, 453, 463, 466, 467, 477, 538, 574, 589, 595, 599

Agate 10, 12, 22, 104, 228, 407, 463

Aggregate 10, 79, 112, 120, 133, 183, 198, 240, 300, 322, 389, 394, 426, 459, 483, 518, 549, 558, 611, 619

Airmass 11, 12, 29, 32, 98, 112, 114, 116, 119, 120, 131, 134, 145, 155, 157, 168, 176, 188, 191, 208, 214, 257, 262, 264, 270, 271, 277, 286, 287, 290, 294, 295, 373, 398, 400, 447, 466, 469, 470, 542, 559, 562, 571, 575, 605, 609, 610, 616,

Alaskite 374, 441

Alabaster 12, 254

Albedo 13, 152

Albite 13, 53, 197, 198, 311, 361, 379

Alexandrite 445

Algae 14, 64, 69, 71, 80-81, 86, 118, 133, 144, 156, 160, 161, 179, 185, 191, 200, 209, 211, 303, 321, 322, 372, 406, 410, 411, 442, 455, 473, 474, 475, 507, 540, 551, 562, 615

Alkaline 15, 70, 85, 86, 95, 103, 198, 212, 239, 247, 259, 261, 293, 296, 307, 325, 334, 368, 434, 435, 444, 452, 487, 495, 516, 524, 528, 550, 571, 630

Alloy 16, 63, 80, 110, 118, 123, 200, 234, 339, 349, 352, 383, 388, 444, 518, 519, 528, 532, 535, 556, 558, 568, 582, 626, 632

Alluvium 16, 31, 33, 49, 97, 107, 143, 151, 152, 154, 156, 159, 181, 185, 188, 220, 235, 238, 251, 266, 283, 306, 326, 343, 412, 437, 441, 463, 512, 578, 606, 622, 629

Almandite 220

Almonds 106

Alnoite 344

Alpha Rays 17, 136, 222, 263, 467, 468, 469, 521, 589

Alpine 17, 99, 114, 271, 345, 368, 472

Alpine Glacier 59, 122, 192, 230, 231, 275, 238, 283, 318, 325, 368, 428, 438, 502

Alpine Tundra 17, 198, 261, 265, 458, 531, 580, 581

Alteration 13, 17, 18, 107, 113, 128, 157, 160, 169, 211, 212, 226, 229, 234, 240, 247, 262, 274, 298, 305, 323, 352, 353, 435, 457, 462, 476, 484, 503, 507, 510, 511, 521, 524, 525, 528, 550, 554, 562, 578, 582, 583, 598, 611, 621, 633

Alternation 111, 124, 138, 142, 208, 215, 314, 315, 437, 445, 446, 494, 499, 506, 539, 548, 595

'Altiplano' 17, 24, 71, 133, 323, 529

Altitude 8, 17, 18, 39, 42, 51, 58, 71, 74, 113, 114, 169, 176, 213, 237, 242, 257, 295, 299, 355, 387, 423, 428, 445, 447, 494, 523, 538, 539, 559, 579, 594, 623, 627

Alumina 18, 56, 113, 252, 300, 473, 597

Aluminum 15, 18, 27, 44, 56, 64, 95, 101, 106, 110, 111, 113, 114, 136, 142, 143, 149, 160, 170, 183, 187, 197, 198, 199, 200, 215, 219, 220, 252, 227, 289, 300, 310, 311, 316, 317, 318, 329, 324, 333, 351, 355, 364, 367, 370, 375, 379, 395, 399, 409, 411, 414, 435, 436, 440, 445, 449, 452, 471, 473, 475, 500, 514, 515, 518, 532, 533, 556, 570, 571, 579, 583, 597, 607, 630, 631

Alunite 18, 56

Amazonite 21, 198, 357

Amber 21, 479

Ambligonite 323

Amethyst 21-22, 167, 220, 463

Ammonia 22, 296, 388, 389, 471, 590

Ammonites 101, 282, 297, 320, 337, 350, 573

Amorphous 22, 93, 105, 141, 159, 360, 408, 517, 631

Amphibole 22, 37, 70, 267, 293, 332, 380, 460, 517

Anaerobic 23, 70, 110, 354, 499, 500, 611

Analcime 435

Anatase 157, 568, 569

Andalusite 310, 460

Andesite 21, 24, 25, 145, 247, 289, 445

Andromeda Galaxy 25, 218, 535, 548

Andromeda Nebula 377

Angara 25, 139

Angiosperm 26, 138, 144, 254, 297, 442, 612
Anhydrite 26, 188, 254, 430, 480, 491, 518
Animal 26, 38, 59, 64, 70, 80, 81, 82, 88, 92, 94, 103, 109, 111, 119, 124, 130, 133, 135, 139, 144, 147, 148, 150, 155, 162, 167, 168, 178, 184, 181, 183, 186, 192, 194, 196, 208, 210, 211, 220, 237, 238, 241, 266, 267, 271, 276, 282, 287, 300, 312, 314, 319, 322, 325, 332, 339, 341, 351, 356, 365, 382, 383, 395, 404, 408, 411, 413, 437, 441, 442, 450, 451, 457, 458, 465, 469, 478, 484, 492, 493, 497, 509, 515, 517, 523, 524, 525, 532, 541, 557, 562, 565, 577, 578, 581, 582, 583, 593, 598, 606, 607, 623, 625, 633
Anion 26, 53, 99, 545, 630
Ankerite 26, 94
Annual 20, 27, 153, 385, 458, 480, 573, 576
Anomaly 27, 36, 96, 139, 242, 268, 309, 311, 336, 419, 457, 477, 478, 491, 501
Anorthite 197, 306
Anorthosite 27, 53, 194, 247, 311, 367
Antecedent Stream 28, 593, 594
Anthozoa 119, 133
Anthracite 28, 66, 116
Anticline 28-29, 78, 122, 160, 199, 208, 221, 284, 286, 336, 341, 392, 458, 481, 538, 551
Anticyclone 29, 155, 391, 481, 577, 610
Antimony 29, 262, 307, 536
Apatite 30, 95, 217, 293, 308, 337, 364, 370, 435, 438, 495, 516, 559, 598, 629
Aphanitic 30, 147, 561
Appleton Layer 195
Apron 16, 31, 49, 326, 512, 554
Aquaculture 32, 273
Aquamarine 32, 61
Aquatic Environment 32, 81, 141, 160, 161, 185, 201, 244, 269, 438, 511, 558
Aquifer 32, 37, 40, 149, 250
Aquitard 32, 37, 326
Arabian Plate 629
Arabian Shield 23, 33, 491, 502, 513
Arable Land 33, 157, 252, 278, 296, 401, 525, 611, 634
Aragonite 33, 66, 93, 163, 365, 513
Araucaria 33-34, 548
Archean Era 34, 90, 161, 229, 234, 248, 271, 337, 439, 619
Archeozoic Era 34, 188, 457, 458
Arch 12, 34, 257, 261, 410, 458, 504
Arching 34, 67, 138, 221, 306, 316, 427, 514, 605
Archipelago 34, 48, 289, 323, 490, 532, 541, 565
Argentite 35
Argillite 35, 36
Argon 11, 36, 136, 148, 247, 299, 301, 309, 389, 453, 466, 467, 599
Arid Lands 15, 16, 34, 36, 49, 68, 75, 76, 78, 79, 86, 114, 153, 155, 167, 190, 204, 208, 219, 234, 261, 284, 285, 299, 301, 309, 316, 338, 351, 365, 384, 412, 426, 428, 430, 445,

Arid Lands (continued) 449, 461, 482, 484, 495, 496, 497, 498, 568, 573, 574, 594, 596, 622
Arkosic 26, 36, 45
Arroyo 36, 605
Arsenates 588
Arsenic 36, 95, 219, 222, 227, 235, 262, 352, 404, 517
Arsenopyrite 132
Artesian 32, 37, 378, 612
Arthropoda 26, 37, 141, 455, 574
Asbestos 37, 90, 140, 244, 360, 543
Ash 28, 38, 61, 97, 108, 111, 113, 136, 137, 171, 179, 190, 196, 207, 210, 227, 288, 305, 312, 371, 381, 382, 406, 432, 435, 452, 494, 507, 522, 539, 549, 553, 554, 559, 580, 599, 600-601, 602 Asian Plate 283, 293
Asphalt 39, 140, 403, 440, 556
Assemblage 39, 179, 289, 360, 413, 511, 519, 540, 549, 575, 633
Astartine 390
Asteroid 39, 139, 171, 192, 288, 354, 474, 541
Asthenosphere 39, 324, 443
Atmosphere 12, 13, 20, 36, 42, 43, 44, 51, 69, 93, 94, 103, 106, 107, 108, 113, 116, 131, 135, 136, 142, 143, 144, 152, 158, 168, 170, 171, 176, 178, 184, 185, 187, 192, 195, 196, 207, 208, 217, 221, 225, 226, 231, 233, 237, 243, 246, 250, 254, 257, 262, 263, 273, 276, 284, 287, 288, 290, 291, 295, 297, 299, 308, 319, 321, 323, 331, 344, 349, 354, 367, 387, 388, 389, 393, 398, 399, 414, 415, 416, 423, 425, 428, 436, 437, 449, 455, 465, 470, 471, 517, 520, 521, 522, 526, 527, 528, 534, 538, 546, 547, 559, 562, 579, 582, 585, 586, 594, 597, 602, 605, 606, 610, 611, 616, 621
Atoll 43, 62, 133, 261, 310, 411, 474, 475, 535
Atom 43, 50, 57, 61, 71, 73, 93, 96, 123, 124, 137, 141, 145, 150, 157, 161, 165, 180, 181, 199, 200, 203, 215, 219, 221, 240, 258, 260, 263, 266, 277, 281, 287, 290, 291, 303, 317, 335, 336, 345, 347, 351, 353, 361, 365, 380, 392, 393, 394, 409, 414, 424, 429, 434, 438, 442, 458, 467, 468, 487, 502, 516, 525, 527, 528, 532, 541, 545, 546, 572, 573, 587, 589, 606, 621
Augen 43
Augite 25, 44, 53, 158, 199, 217, 293, 367, 379, 408, 438, 460, 517, 550, 571
Aulacogen 44
Aureole 128
Aurora 44, 106, 135, 174, 526, 527, 594
Australian Shield 44, 513
Australopithecus 407
Autumn 150, 158, 250, 278, 506, 554
Avalanche 45, 108, 109, 163, 208, 265, 269, 485, 494, 502, 509, 599, 601
Axis 10, 134, 141, 173-174, 177, 180, 187, 233, 275, 315, 335, 336, 344, 367, 389, 417, 448, 455, 448, 506, 565, 575, 591

B-Horizon 260, 280, 525, 528

Bacteria 14, 23, 41, 48, 63, 70, 93, 110, 150,
153, 211, 218, 388, 389, 387, 393, 400, 414,
455, 480, 499, 549, 559, 598, 607 Baddeleyite 48, 182, 632

Badlands 48, 147, 316, 337

Baltic Shield 198

Baltica 494

Bamboo 49-50, 102, 241, 279, 366, 425, 489,
529, 543, 549, 558

Banded Iron formations 49, 291, 294, 357,
455, 458

Banding 43, 204, 205, 211, 233, 247, 352, 365,
407, 454, 491, 591

Bank 19, 27, 50, 125, 159, 202, 216, 235-236,
269, 317, 347, 357, 370, 381, 422, 566, 571

Bar 4, 51, 75, 183, 481, 482, 499, 514, 526, 569

Barchan 62, 170, 300, 395, 508

Barite 51, 142,

Barium 51, 547, 630

Bark 51, 102, 88, 222, 479, 513, 612

Barometric Pressure 51, 52, 264, 286, 387

Barrier 47, 49, 52, 100, 128, 154, 317, 336,
343, 355, 421, 461, 474, 475, 481, 544

Basalt 25, 43, 53, 91, 122, 123, 127, 139, 141,
150, 164, 166, 177, 197, 200, 201, 203, 204,
218, 229, 247, 248, 261, 279, 289, 295, 301,
303, 307, 318, 319, 327, 398, 400, 401, 406,
408, 422, 423, 439, 446, 460, 476, 504, 505,
513, 517, 518, 519, 541, 550, 563, 574, 599,
613, 616

Base Level 54, 154, 427, 477, 594

Basement 62, 77, 134, 150, 152, 171, 179, 185,
212, 251, 317, 323, 331, 346, 384, 385, 386,
390, 422, 486, 489, 513, 533, 565, 586, 591,
600 Basic Rocks 54, 118, 158, 164, 169,
177, 216, 247, 248, 279, 316, 319, 332, 341,
365

Basin 4, 15, 16, 18, 19, 20, 21, 34, 36, 37, 44,
49, 51, 54, 55, 71, 76, 78, 82, 96, 98, 104,
105, 110, 116, 118, 121, 122, 125- 126, 130,
138, 141, 142, 144, 149, 152, 153, 155, 156,
160, 164, 166, 175, 178, 180, 182, 186, 190,
194, 199, 201, 207, 209, 211, 214, 217, 234,
235, 243, 244, 248, 251, 254, 259, 262, 268,
272, 273, 285, 287, 290, 291, 294, 300, 301,
303, 304, 310, 311, 312, 320, 322, 331, 332,
334, 336, 337, 338, 340, 342, 344, 350, 368,
371, 374, 378, 379, 381, 385, 386, 391, 398,
401, 405, 409, 413, 422, 423, 424, 430,
442, 444, 446, 449, 452, 453, 461, 465, 475,
479, 483, 488, 492, 493, 495, 505, 507,
508, 513, 515, 517, 518, 521, 523, 525, 528,
529, 541, 551, 554, 555, 557, 560, 564, 565,
568, 572, 578, 593, 597, 599, 603, 608, 609,
613, 615, 619, 622, 623, 625, 627, 629, 630

Basin and Range Province 55, 68, 88, 121,
156, 240, 268, 438

Bastnaesite 95, 102, 364, 472, 626

Batholith 21, 24, 55, 66, 89, 92, 128, 193, 203,
240, 279, 280, 286, 354, 369, 432, 446, 457,
485, 516, 536, 554, 585

Bathyal Environment 55, 185, 186

Bats 120, 250, 332, 465

Bauxite 18, 56, 92, 160, 219, 229, 251, 252,
253, 301, 318, 370, 440, 473, 515, 579, 597,
611

Bay 46, 56, 62, 153, 183, 215, 252, 259, 265,
266, 268, 269, 275, 283, 290, 320, 356, 371,
372, 373, 382, 383, 385, 389, 414, 480, 498,
508, 580, 610, 633

Bayou 56, 362, 607

Beach 47, 52, 56, 57, 67, 102, 118, 149, 170,
183, 209, 220, 266, 268, 280, 328, 343, 364,
370, 421, 440, 468, 471, 475, 482, 491, 514,
516, 534, 549, 563, 568, 615, 616, 621, 632

Beaufort Scale 57, 218, 271, 300, 616

Bed Load 57, 135, 185, 326, 497, 594

Bedding Plane 117, 163, 237, 295, 314, 507,
518, 521, 538

Bediasite 557

Bedrock 57, 156, 170, 171, 196, 324, 446, 453,
473, 476, 500, 521, 524, 525, 597, 608

Belemnites 320

Benioff Zones 59, 112, 532

Benthic Zone 82, 101, 221, 325

Bentonite 59, 113, 167,

Beringia 59, 60

Bertrandite 61

Beryl 32, 61, 111, 142, 183, 332, 370, 426

Beryllium 61, 111, 466

Beta Rays 61, 222, 467, 468

Bicarbonate 361, 463, 497, 514

Big Bang 62, 173, 587

Big Dipper 174, 590

Bifurcation 61, 98

Bight 62, 252, 622

Binomial Classification 63, 196, 522

Biomass 64, 221, 375, 470, 607

Biome 64, 73, 178, 186, 223, 319, 325, 341

Biosphere 41, 64, 93, 133, 208, 224, 319

Biotite 25, 32, 63-64, 147, 162, 199, 239, 240,
247, 355, 435, 438, 463, 550, 598

Birds 65, 120, 192, 195, 202, 207, 218, 250,
261, 297, 309, 332, 404, 412, 436, 449, 458,
459, 483, 485, 486, 532, 549, 559, 562, 570,
593, 625

Bismuth 65, 468, 588

Bison 59

Bitter lake 66

Bittern 66

Bitumen 66, 556

Black Body 66

Black Hole 67, 615, 620

Black Sands 67, 289, 300, 568, 622

Blizzard 68, 547, 615

Block 68, 123, 150, 154, 190, 196, 197, 209,
229, 230, 237, 240, 258, 268, 304, 307, 316,
320, 342, 345, 390, 401, 422, 431, 479, 481,
483, 509, 549, 559, 601, 605, 625

Block Faulted 68, 91, 154, 197, 258, 259, 268, 345, 369, 481, 489, 497, 561, 605
'Blooms' 68, 438, 442, 474, 475, 588
Blowouts 68, 209, 302, 297
Blue Ground 159, 305, 431
Blue-green Algae 69, 144, 211, 455, 474, 475, 540
Bluff 70, 91, 134
Body 21, 39, 70, 165, 171, 184, 213, 214, 216, 281, 283, 306, 345, 354, 409, 419, 441, 450, 463, 477, 501, 508, 534, 537, 551, 621
Bog 70, 198, 261, 283, 319, 339, 344, 371, 420, 425, 531, 532, 554, 581, 605
Boiling 41, 496
Boiling Point 71, 152, 212, 263
Bombardment 18, 136, 212, 308, 342, 345, 530, 541
Bomb 71, 185, 281, 494, 499, 507, 541, 546, 559, 574, 601
Bonding 71, 92, 106, 114, 137, 178, 260, 266, 287, 351, 361, 365, 367, 414, 516, 517, 518, 545, 558
Lake Bonneville (Pleistocene) 71, 243, 245, 339, 497, 605
Borates 73
Bore 66, 134, 198, 259, 266, 451, 564, 612
Borides 73
Bornite 73, 90, 132
Boron 73, 82, 227, 240, 352, 390, 404, 468, 471, 506, 517, 571
Bouguer Anomaly 74, 242
Boulder 74, 86, 113, 118, 134, 138, 145, 156, 171, 190, 195, 242, 259, 277, 293, 430, 472, 482, 483, 487, 507, 516, 539, 581, 587, 612
Brachiopods 75, 88, 409
Brachiosaurus 75
Brass 16, 76, 532
Brazilia 77
Brazilian Shield 52, 493, 513
Breccia 78, 79, 90, 95, 125, 237, 305, 440, 487, 550, 601
Breeze 94, 164, 319, 356, 504
Brick 79, 362, 446, 632
Brines 71, 73, 79, 109, 147, 165, 226, 227, 258, 287, 302, 323, 333, 356, 375, 435, 452, 453, 456, 461, 495, 496, 541, 591, 608
Broadleaf 102, 190, 509, 530, 543, 558
Bromeliad 80, 187, 279
Bromine 80, 148, 287, 356, 471, 506
Brontosaurus 80
Bronze 16, 63, 80
Brookite 568
Brownstone 81
Browse 81, 162, 241, 366
Bryophytes 81
Bryozoa 26, 81-82, 410
Bush 82, 106, 150, 210, 249, 297, 301, 320, 383, 489, 493, 532
Butte 83, 92, 102, 502
By-product 36, 83, 119, 219, 235, 254, 287, 366, 376, 388, 410, 436, 510, 532, 541, 558, 613

C-Horizon 476, 525
Cactus 187, 492, 577, 622
Cadmium 85, 519, 631
Cairngorm 85
Calcination 101, 322, 460
Calcite 33, 66, 86, 94, 174, 209, 223, 250, 254, 353, 364, 365, 407, 480, 504, 513
Calcium 22, 23, 27, 33, 54, 64, 73, 81, 86, 93, 151, 165, 183, 187, 191, 197, 254, 260, 279, 294, 299, 311, 316, 324, 327, 351, 356, 367, 389, 399, 400, 426, 428, 441, 460, 466, 467, 471, 491, 506, 517, 520, 527, 541, 571, 619, 630
Calcium Carbonate 33, 64, 69, 81, 84, 85, 86, 92, 93, 99, 118, 167, 177, 191, 209, 260, 322, 329, 342, 344, 365, 450, 473, 475, 484, 513, 534, 540, 615
Calcrete 86, 260, 374, 440
Caldera 42, 61, 86-87, 136, 139, 155, 182, 183, 184, 185, 232, 302, 308, 346, 349, 388, 395, 456, 465, 553, 559, 569, 593, 625
Caliche 86, 87, 388
Calm 164, 267, 616, 617
Cambrian Period 37, 82, 88, 101, 110, 119, 177, 211, 221, 265, 343, 379, 409, 419, 439, 468, 482, 533, 574, 603
Canadian Shield 89, 90, 198, 247, 311, 390, 427, 454, 455, 494, 513
Canga 90
Canopy 20, 34, 50, 91, 102, 126, 151, 297, 320, 381, 470, 576, 577, 586
Canyon 58, 74, 90, 99, 105, 127, 132, 137, 147, 156, 166, 185, 212, 213, 233, 236 , 239, 264, 270, 305, 326, 401, 454, 473, 492, 502, 523, 547, 580, 600, 607
Capillarity 56, 91, 92, 193, 200, 236, 491, 525, 566
Capped 32, 87, 91, 92, 105, 134, 142, 170, 182, 296, 323, 329, 350, 408, 440, 491, 496, 539, 553, 620
Capture 92, 262, 386, 474, 489, 595, 618
Carat 92, 143, 160, 229, 234-235, 297, 307, 447, 623, 629
Carbohydrate 92, 218, 400, 420, 437
Carbon 28, 32, 43, 64, 73, 79, 92, 93, 94, 95, 96, 106, 116, 117, 123, 135, 136, 157, 158, 159, 199, 211, 229, 240, 246, 266, 272, 290, 303, 304, 351, 352, 374, 399, 450, 457, 466, 467, 470, 506, 516, 522, 528, 534, 536, 550, 577
Carbon Dioxide 4, 5, 11, 26, 32, 36, 93-94, 110, 124, 133, 152, 159, 178, 221, 233, 246, 272, 276, 314, 322, 344, 354, 416, 437, 442, 470, 550, 551, 590, 597, 598, 601
Carbon Monoxide 94, 107, 123, 416, 601
Carbonate 9, 26, 30, 51, 66, 80, 94-95, 100, 110, 123, 132, 159, 165, 176, 247, 260, 280, 293, 301, 324, 333, 337, 349, 353, 361, 375, 405, 406, 407, 452, 484, 497, 499, 515, 575, 596
Carbonatite 9, 26, 30, 51, 80, 95, 109, 123, 161, 175, 247, 293, 308, 334, 337, 344, 369, 370, 375, 381, 387, 388, 405, 428,

Carbonatite (continued) 434, 435, 458, 460, 473, 488, 495, 516, 550, 555, 568, 569, 589, 598, 629
Carboniferous Period 94, 119, 127, 157, 199, 221, 230, 233, 264, 275, 301, 318, 338, 363, 428, 430, 515, 566, 612
Carborundum 96, 160
Caribbean Plate 119
Carnallite 453
Carnelian 105
Carnotite 96, 468, 588
Carrying Capacity 75, 97, 152, 168, 251, 597
Cascade 196, 230, 257, 259, 279
Cascadia 595
Cassiterite 98, 123, 248, 567
Cataclastics 43, 99
Catalyst 227, 433, 444, 615, 631
Cataract 79, 379, 514, 630
Cattle 82, 108, 151, 170, 223, 251, 296, 421, 509, 577
Cave 34, 68, 92, 99, 100, 101, 165, 167, 201, 229, 250, 254, 299, 322, 339, 372, 407, 464, 504, 513, 534, 573, 606, 609
Cavern 99, 100, 167, 250, 254, 301, 302, 316, 339, 399, 407, 437, 519, 606
Cenozoic Era 72, 101, 119, 123, 162, 176, 188, 189, 209, 281, 350, 434, 436, 514, 550
Centrifugal Force 237, 242, 565
Cephalopod 101, 229, 331
Cerium 102, 365, 369, 449, 472
Cesium 103, 107, 238, 487, 514
Chabazite 104
Chalcedony 105, 108, 294, 407, 463, 564
Chalcocite 63
Chalcopyrite 90, 105, 132, 383, 408
Chalk 94, 105, 119, 138, 209, 424, 478, 615
Chaparral 105-106, 182, 210, 301, 302, 342, 503
Charcoal 7, 106, 528
Charged 17, 21, 44, 45, 106, 180, 219, 221, 227, 287, 334, 345, 350, 394, 438, 462, 463, 466, 527, 547, 594, 621
Chernobyl 103, 104, 107, 241, 439
Chert 108, 408, 540, 603
Chestnut 558
Chimney 109, 159, 374, 417, 440, 519, 601
Chinook 6, 109, 205
Chloride 260, 495, 497, 498, 506, 524, 550
Chlorine 80, 107, 109, 110, 123, 147, 150, 223, 258, 259, 287, 356, 399, 415, 416, 445, 471, 506, 607
Chlorine Monoxide 110
Chlorite 38, 53, 65, 247, 366, 437, 452, 503, 517
Chlorofluorocarbons (CFC's) 8, 107, 110, 206, 246, 497, 408
Chlorophyll 80, 110, 314, 428
Chondrite 110, 353, 486
Chordata 26, 110, 306
Chrome 110-111, 196, 281, 299, 333, 428, 487, 534, 543

Chromite 109, 110, 111, 199, 304, 332, 333, 414, 420, 575, 588
Chromium 110, 111, 136, 183, 355
Chromosphere 111
Chronology 111, 223, 265, 429, 453, 560
Chrysoberyl 111
Chrysotile 37
Cicads 138
Cinder Cone 111, 112, 124, 215, 346, 459, 539
Cinnabar 112, 349
Circulation 19, 114, 166, 263, 273, 276, 301, 315, 355, 399, 435, 500, 507, 616, 622
Circum-Polar Vortex 112
Cirque 65, 113, 119, 212, 345, 502, 556, 593
Citrine 85, 113, 463
Classification 138, 140, 193, 279, 306, 475, 546
Clastics 113, 125, 322, 365, 458, 507
Clay 21, 32, 35, 37, 49, 53, 60, 70, 74, 79, 85, 91, 101, 102, 107, 113, 117, 120, 125, 138, 139, 153, 167, 169, 171, 174, 182, 193, 196, 200, 201, 204, 211, 215, 229, 230, 232, 238, 240, 248, 253, 263, 280, 281, 288, 289, 300, 301, 302, 312, 314, 320, 326, 344, 349, 356, 365, 366, 367, 370, 371, 394, 401, 402, 407, 411, 418, 426, 430, 443, 447, 450, 452, 458, 459, 464, 468, 471, 473, 476, 484, 499, 503, 507, 511, 517, 525, 541, 556, 560, 580, 587, 595, 598, 607, 611, 612, 633
Clear Air Turbulence (CAT) 98-99, 131, 225
Cleavage 36, 85, 114, 204, 206, 212, 258, 333, 355, 360, 361, 441, 460, 503, 521, 532
Cliff 52, 58, 59, 67, 100, 114, 115, 117, 118, 165, 166, 185, 201, 230, 277, 278, 320, 327, 329, 341, 364, 370, 397, 424, 485, 502, 504, 513, 524, 599, 605, 608, 609, 610, 615
Climax 36, 105, 115, 509, 519, 543, 577, 580, 581
Clinopyroxene 70, 217
Clinotilolite 435
Coal 28, 46, 66, 72, 79, 90, 93, 94, 109, 116, 117, 119, 184, 199, 207, 211, 226, 227, 236, 243, 262, 301, 304, 309, 310, 327, 329, 354, 363, 368, 370, 381, 398, 411, 418, 419, 430, 440, 480, 496, 515, 522, 528, 532, 535, 540, 545, 611, 631,
Coarse-grained 153, 162, 217, 233, 237, 239, 327, 333, 365, 374, 379, 380, 401, 486, 504, 514, 550, 561, 568, 618
Coating 214, 257, 389, 425, 532, 563, 611, 628, 631
Cobalt 68, 118, 199, 263, 340, 368, 382, 383, 401, 516, 544, 629
Cobaltite 118
Cobble 56, 118, 125, 154, 242, 483, 487, 507, 540, 587, 612
Coccolith 117-118
Cockroach 119, 325, 560
Cocos Plate 119
Coelenterate 26, 119, 133, 342, 455
Coesite 119, 486
Coke 117, 119, 298, 304, 535

Cold Front 119-120, 214, 385, 533

Colemanite 73

Collision 14, 17, 38, 39, 96, 105, 129, 136, 141, 150, 171, 208, 283, 290, 347, 348, 369, 373, 376, 411, 431, 443, 482, 494, 502, 525, 541, 549, 557, 572, 613, 629

Colloid 22, 120, 151, 182, 451

Collophane 435

Columbite 123, 370, 555

Columbium 122, 387, 555, 556

Column 16, 57, 123, 159, 187, 194, 224, 229, 239, 295, 440, 448, 477, 504, 538, 540, 570, 561

Comet 30, 123, 258, 389, 429, 527

Commensalism 123, 124, 187

Community 17, 63, 82, 96, 115, 122, 123, 124, 178, 326, 323, 356, 383, 499, 509, 520, 543, 575, 581, 612

Compaction 37, 124, 154, 156, 158, 210, 308, 315, 327, 381, 487, 507, 511, 523

Compass 124, 255, 309, 327, 334, 336, 448, 477, 540, 547

Compound 22, 26, 92, 93, 94, 95, 96, 103, 105, 106, 109, 111, 124, 149, 151, 161, 165, 272, 273, 289, 290, 303, 327, 349, 354, 365, 388, 414, 450, 452, 460, 461, 498, 524, 545, 590, 606, 626

Compression 28, 79, 109, 169, 208, 225, 417, 504, 535, 537, 610

Concentration 107, 124, 125, 153, 191, 205, 222, 263, 280, 287, 288, 289, 303, 323, 324, 328, 335, 356, 360, 366, 369, 378, 401, 410, 421, 434, 440, 485, 495, 497, 516, 568, 579, 611

Conchoidal 108, 212, 398, 460, 462,

Concretion 125, 323, 389, 407, 440, 583

Condensation 125, 158, 212, 273, 433, 455, 465, 506, 527

Conductivity 73, 125, 132, 180, 227, 349, 351, 352, 365, 390, 429, 496, 499, 509, 517 519, 524, 529, 548

Cone 87, 111, 123, 137-138, 184, 346, 371, 377, 460, 465, 513, 539, 601

Confluence 21, 33, 75, 125, 279, 296, 299, 332, 362, 379, 384, 385, 386, 424, 512, 528, 543, 624, 626, 627

Conformity 128, 586

Conglomerate 36, 52, 96, 97, 99, 100, 105, 125, 229, 231, 234, 237, 284, 291, 365, 487, 489, 507

Congo Shield 373

Conifer 21, 115, 127, 144, 190, 199, 221, 254, 260, 261, 297, 372, 377, 378, 390, 430, 432, 447, 470, 472, 479, 509, 530, 553, 554, 558, 596

Conodont 127

Consolidation 211, 249, 279, 331, 333, 438, 499, 554

Constellation 25, 128, 333, 439, 455, 463, 530, 546, 579, 590

Contact 90, 125, 128, 220, 303, 308, 341, 493, 521, 539, 570, 586, 593, 622

Continental Divide 76, 105, 122, 129, 332, 431, 482, 489, 625

Continental Drift 12, 38, 44, 129, 177, 225, 301, 357, 411, 419, 422, 457, 546, 612

Continental Margin 59, 85, 98, 128, 130, 134, 164, 197, 226, 289, 348, 401, 417, 443, 564

Continental Shelf 41, 58, 68, 86, 88, 117, 128, 130, 131, 141, 164, 245, 270, 343, 357, 398, 400, 401,

Contour 33, 127, 131, 169, 257, 290, 549, 566

Contraction 131, 249, 295, 411, 581

Convection 39, 130, 131, 142, 143, 152, 154, 160, 176, 225, 257, 268, 411, 443, 577, 588

Convergence 90, 96, 130, 145, 164, 185, 235, 286, 295, 318, 329, 337, 357, 419, 443, 501, 541, 545, 571

Copper 16, 21, 25, 41, 44, 46, 63, 73, 74, 80, 83, 90, 94, 103, 105, 109, 111, 125, 132, 140, 183, 200, 205, 216, 223, 227, 234, 235, 247, 248, 258, 303, 304, 307, 319, 330, 337, 340, 346, 351, 360, 361, 401, 406, 421, 432, 434, 439, 452, 455, 460, 474, 515, 517, 518, 519, 527, 532, 543, 544, 547, 548, 558, 567, 575, 583, 603, 611, 615, 629, 630, 631, 632

Coral 14, 26, 43, 44, 52, 57, 63, 64, 85, 94, 100, 119, 120, 133, 178, 188, 192, 205, 209, 261, 301, 322, 365, 370, 410, 411, 421, 450, 474, 475, 511, 519, 534, 535, 551, 574, 618

Cordierite 183

Cordillera 17, 21, 24, 38, 63, 88, 89, 103, 133, 134, 178, 226, 276, 298, 354, 369, 390, 470, 485, 516, 547

Core 130, 131, 135, 160, 173, 192, 225, 243, 279, 284, 341, 405, 446, 481, 485, 496, 513, 516, 534, 546

Cores 134, 158, 170, 220, 224, 233, 240, 276, 295, 334, 357, 364, 445, 463, 542

Coriolis Effect 134, 143, 180, 237, 254, 286, 295, 392, 399, 501, 534, 616

Correlation 135, 163, 211, 223, 344, 477, 482, 538, 583, 633

Corrosion 100, 135, 227, 444, 518, 556, 610

Corundum 1, 18, 135, 160, 183, 363, 487, 500, 531

Cosmic Radiation 51, 61, 94, 106, 116, 134, 135, 136, 219, 225, 318, 380, 416, 465, 466, 526, 530, 541, 546, 579, 587, 621

Cosmos 39, 47, 67, 128, 136, 139, 163, 170, 171, 173, 174, 436, 465, 529, 530, 546, 587

Counter-current 253, 399, 586

Crab Nebula 137, 377, 459, 466

Crack 100, 139, 161, 203, 214, 229, 240, 326, 370, 371, 403, 444, 445, 449, 450, 495, 496, 550, 581

Craton 77, 128, 138, 229, 362, 373, 381, 454, 493, 551, 613, 618

Creep 138, 497, 525, 527, 557

Crest 78, 123, 129, 138, 285, 358, 491, 537, 579, 609, 615

Cretaceous Period 14, 22, 26, 58, 72, 89, 102, 105, 112, 138, 139, 150, 161, 162, 179,

Cretaceous Period (continued) 209, 239, 247, 248, 253, 261, 297, 326, 334, 337, 341, 343, 350, 354, 355, 362, 372, 385, 392, 408, 411, 414, 418, 420, 421, 426, 479, 511, 560

Crevasse 59, 139, 230, 278, 316, 509

Crinoid 26, 139, 176

Cristobalite 480

Crocidolite 140

Crust (Earth) 38, 99, 128, 138, 141, 160, 163, 165, 173, 174, 175, 184, 196, 198, 203, 207, 215, 218, 221, 226, 227, 228, 232, 248, 259, 262, 264, 290, 298, 302, 307, 311, 312, 315, 324, 339, 341, 357, 360, 363, 364, 369, 379, 389, 399, 400, 401, 408, 417, 422, 427, 443, 462, 481, 484, 485, 503, 505, 506, 508, 514, 517, 519, 541, 542, 545, 551, 557, 563, 574, 579, 599, 602, 605, 620, 626

Crustacean 37, 141, 263, 371, 512,

Crustal Plates 25, 96, 101, 129, 130, 134, 141, 164, 187, 226, 232, 268, 391, 401, 421, 443, 446, 486, 505, 540, 541, 557, 572, 574

Cryptozoic Eon 141, 186, 188

Cubic System 105, 206, 218, 234, 258, 336, 360, 460, 519, 532, 550

Cuesta 142, 266, 398

Cumulous Clouds 18, 113, 116, 142, 5609

Cycles 63, 64, 94, 153, 167, 173, 204, 243, 246, 248, 254, 260, 276, 279, 343, 427, 429, 448, 480, 484, 499, 526, 547, 565, 573, 587, 595, 616

Cyclone 29, 144-145, 205, 208, 254, 271, 295, 329, 398, 579, 584, 610, 616

Cypress 145, 186, 189, 192, 352, 362, 363, 509, 549

D-Horizon 525

Dacite 25, 126, 147, 445, 580

Dahlite 435

Daughter Elements 104, 148, 212, 258, 466, 467, 589

Dawsonite 149

Debouchment 152, 370, 424, 624

Debris 74, 136, 137, 149, 168, 182, 191, 234, 237, 272, 281, 321, 326, 344, 368, 371, 373, 401, 444, 449, 453, 485, 494, 507, 547, 554, 570, 571, 574, 596, 601, 625

Decay 65, 92, 103, 148, 150, 191, 211, 257, 258, 271, 299, 350, 380, 392, 424, 425, 432, 466, 467, 468, 469, 487, 563, 589,

Deccan Trap 123

Deciduous 38, 73, 81, 150, 261, 352, 553, 554, 558, 596

Declination 334, 448

Decomposition 48, 92, 137, 150, 160, 178, 191, 193, 209, 248, 272, 300, 315, 386, 388, 414, 425, 433, 436, 474, 499, 525, 571, 578, 590, 611

Deep Sea 47, 53, 55, 58, 80, 85, 104, 119, 124, 129, 150, 151, 202, 223, 225, 229, 233, 247, 264, 282, 290, 297, 342, 356, 370, 374, 379, 389, 400, 426, 435, 441, 443, 445, 458, 460, 481, 482, 501, 512, 541, 542, 588, 614. 631

Deflation 110, 150, 155, 171, 194, 241, 259, 344, 397, 445, 461, 525, 529, 618

Deflection 134, 334, 392, 616, 617

Deforestation 19, 45, 93, 151-152, 210, 215, 228. 246, 260, 262, 382, 449, 470, 476, 511, 520, 533, 546, 573, 577, 629

Deformation 160, 433, 450, 517, 537

Degassing 152, 298, 344, 399, 547, 588, 602, 606

Delta 19, 20, 23, 40, 56, 57, 58, 65, 121, 139, 147, 152-153, 154, 155, 179, 185, 220, 264, 265, 283, 298, 311, 320, 331, 338, 343, 346, 348, 362, 363, 370, 384, 385, 390, 411, 422, 441, 479, 480, 484, 489, 497, 503, 542, 566, 594, 597, 630

Dendrochronology 153

Denitrification 153

Density 28, 42, 124, 127, 131, 134, 141, 153-154, 163, 165, 177, 201, 207, 213, 214, 219, 242, 253, 264, 274, 279, 284, 285, 290, 291, 364, 380, 400, 417, 429, 451, 456, 460, 465, 472, 480, 485, 491, 501, 503, 507, 511, 514, 523, 534, 536, 582, 585, 587, 597, 616

Denudation 154, 189, 477, 483, 618

Depletion 154, 268, 285, 415, 416

Deposition 16, 28, 31, 45, 116, 117, 124, 132, 140. 151, 154, 160, 164, 185, 195, 196, 203, 207, 210, 225, 229, 233, 236, 239, 245, 248, 249, 265, 274, 175, 277, 301, 315, 318, 325, 326, 327, 328, 343, 344, 347, 360, 362, 370, 388, 392, 425, 432, 440, 453, 458, 463, 475, 477, 480, 481, 482, 483, 484, 499, 507, 508, 511, 525, 528, 529, 534, 537, 538, 539, 541, 560, 574, 583, 586, 587, 594, 603, 611, 613, 616, 618

Depression 8, 18, 40, 48, 54, 68, 82, 87, 110, 126, 136, 147, 152, 155, 163, 179, 187, 220, 229, 231, 237, 244, 245, 257, 302, 304, 313, 308, 323, 331, 336, 342, 353, 365, 385, 388, 397, 422, 450, 449, 461, 484, 491, 492, 497, 505, 514, 519, 530, 544, 548, 549, 551, 554, 557, 569, 582, 588, 601, 618, 627

Desert 31, 33, 35, 39, 40, 41, 44, 45, 49, 51, 58, 64, 86, 87, 88, 103, 109, 113, 129, 134, 147, 148, 149, 155-156, 157, 170, 171, 179, 183, 185, 189, 191, 210, 211, 234, 250, 254, 259, 260, 270, 271, 273, 280, 288, 296, 297, 299, 300, 327, 328, 346, 347, 350, 361, 364, 368, 371, 373, 377, 384, 388, 390, 397, 402, 405, 406, 409, 418, 420, 425, 428, 430, 431, 432, 437, 471, 473, 476, 486, 492, 493, 495, 497, 499, 501, 502, 508, 513, 519, 520, 529, 530, 544, 551, 554, 555, 562, 577, 583, 591, 597, 605, 606, 612, 617, 618, 624, 633

Desertification 96, 152, 157, 168, 241, 242, 366, 413, 476, 492

Detritus 16, 31, 49, 52, 56, 57, 69, 87, 91, 149, 152, 157, 165, 182, 230, 248, 260, 277, 312, 329, 366, 400, 475, 524, 529, 540, 567

Deuterium 157, 259

Devitrification 59, 157, 198, 550

Devonian Period 81, 95, 157, 158, 201, 241, 275, 363, 405, 410, 419, 426, 452, 459, 475, 512, 518, 564

Dew 125, 156, 158, 378, 466

Diabase 158, 162

Diagenesis 117, 158, 367, 409, 415, 500

Diamonds 11, 29, 48, 57, 73, 79, 93, 97, 105, 110, 113, 135, 142, 159, 160, 164, 177, 217, 220, 229, 234, 240, 251, 252, 253, 266, 281, 291, 297, 305, 307, 338, 352, 364, 374, 409, 428, 435, 447, 450, 453, 486, 487, 488, 510, 516, 518, 601, 623, 629

Diapir 160, 165, 208, 248, 443, 496

Diastrophism 190, 186, 275, 342, 411, 538, 595

Diatoms 118, 159, 407, 442, 513, 574

Diatomic 160, 283, 415

Diatomite 160-161

Dicotyledon 138

Didymium 365

Dike 30, 110, 136, 159, 162, 217, 239, 248, 261, 286, 369, 426, 446, 540, 556, 598, 603, 633, 634

Dinoflagellate 162, 475

Dinosaur 162, 189, 194, 211, 221, 230, 288, 336, 470, 574

Diopside 452

Diorite 25, 89, 162-163, 367, 368

Dip 13, 37, 49, 81, 117, 139, 142, 153, 163, 205, 227, 237, 266, 295, 315, 334, 336, 348, 369, 383, 398, 479, 507, 538, 540, 563, 586, 613

Dipole 224, 334, 448

Discharge 20, 75, 125, 126, 148, 163, 179, 321, 415, 443, 564

Discoaster 163

Disconformity 160, 163, 586

Discontinuity 18, 65, 81, 127, 141, 163, 174, 285, 306, 341, 364-365, 405

Displacement 164, 295, 390, 413, 464, 498, 505, 525, 540, 588, 605, 612

Dissolution 99, 185, 191, 213, 245, 280, 301, 329, 339, 353, 365, 399, 495, 506, 608, 610

Distillation 140, 155, 212, 213, 221, 403, 404, 433, 500

Distributary 148, 266, 362, 384, 385, 411, 422, 451

Diurnal 155, 201, 281, 282, 338, 562, 591

Divergence 29, 130, 164, 295, 356, 401, 443, 588

Divergent Margin 130, 164, 443, 446

Diversion 296, 391, 397, 404, 600, 611,

Divide 24, 92, 105, 129, 251, 262, 320, 368, 488, 560, 597, 609, 618, 622, 625, 630

Doldrums 164, 500, 584, 617

Dolerite 162, 164, 296, 301, 338, 518, 556

Dolomite 26, 79, 86, 93, 94, 95, 127, 165, 191, 355, 409, 433, 473, 479, 503, 518, 534

Dome 87, 160, 165, 185, 193, 204, 247, 248, 260, 317, 392, 406, 410, 427, 446, 513, 540, 545, 619

Dominant 39, 127, 144, 192, 199, 241, 251, 329, 340, 390, 407, 409, 411, 422, 432, 470, 479, 492, 503, 532, 553, 554, 558, 566, 567, 574, 596, 614

Doppler Effect 165, 356, 463, 474

Dormancy 137, 261, 266, 424, 432, 471, 494, 622

Down-dropped 154, 209, 237, 268, 315, 365, 390, 422, 479, 481

Downfold 28, 88, 208, 226, 291, 302, 551

Downslope 45, 138, 222, 278, 315, 345, 502, 525, 527, 582, 593, 601

Downwarp 194, 226, 248, 557, 619

Drainage 20, 24, 30, 49, 54, 60, 70, 92, 99, 105, 122, 126, 127, 151, 164 , 179, 190, 192, 194, 198, 205, 234, 259, 262, 272, 273, 301, 306, 312, 313, 316, 331, 339, 348, 362, 370, 372, 378, 384, 417, 429, 444, 448, 465, 470, 473, 475, 482, 483, 487, 507, 515, 529, 530, 554, 555, 557, 569, 570, 597, 599, 603, 609, 613, 614, 622, 624, 630

Drift (See Continental Drift) 129, 168, 230, 253, 299, 313, 325, 328, 373, 419, 444, 476, 481, 546, 566

Drought 44, 76, 97, 101, 117, 167-168, 169, 171, 190, 241, 244, 264, 285, 286, 304, 327, 347, 362, 366, 387, 413, 451, 454, 471, 493, 503, 509, 510, 511, 525, 546, 610, 610, 614, 622

Drumlin 168-169

Druse 169, 223, 515

Dry Climate (See Arid) 40, 55, 80, 93, 102, 105, 156, 169, 203, 208, 210, 241, 250, 260, 283, 285, 286, 295, 302, 304, 313, 315, 321, 344, 363, 366, 367, 373, 376, 385, 393, 404, 405, 409, 420, 430, 445, 447, 449, 452, 454, 455, 471, 474, 480, 492, 495, 497, 525, 535, 554, 565, 576, 577, 578, 587, 597, 606, 614, 617, 618, 622, 627, 633

Dry Lake 55, 156. 194, 302, 308, 328, 364, 404, 414, 445

Dry Season 92, 279, 296, 366, 446, 576, 578, 598, 607, 633

Ductile 85, 333, 351, 381

Dunes 32, 47, 51, 62, 104, 121, 140, 154, 165, 170, 189, 209, 266, 288, 299, 304, 308, 343, 346, 373, 440, 461, 486, 492, 497, 499, 508, 519, 520, 523, 555, 614, 615, 616, 624

Dunite 170

Duricrust 170, 237, 256

Dust 123, 170-171, 172, 173, 218, 227, 238, 257, 258, 260, 271, 300, 304, 327, 377, 387, 389, 393, 401, 407, 449, 469, 470, 471, 518, 520, 522, 554, 559, 580, 599, 600, 602, 611

Dysprosium 199

E Layer 173

Earthquake 13, 59, 72, 97, 108, 117, 119, 121, 141, 160, 174, 175, 197, 207, 223, 266, 267, 278, 290, 293, 311, 323, 349, 374, 375, 391, 394, 397, 413, 416, 419, 434, 464, 469, 480, 485, 497, 498, 508, 513, 542, 555, 557, 574, 579, 582, 599, 602, 610, 613, 614, 625, 629

East African Rift 8, 9, 31, 33, 175, 176, 179,
    232, 237, 244, 303, 305, 313, 331, 337, 341,
    366, 368, 375, 378, 473, 474, 489, 541, 599,
    600, 629
Easterlies 447, 617
Easterly Wave 176, 271, 575
Echinoderm 26, 39, 95, 139, 176, 177
Echo Sounding 177, 503, 529
Eclipse 134, 177
Ecliptic 177, 373, 632
Eclogite 177, 308, 352
Ecology 13, 39, 54, 63, 64, 96, 119, 177-178,
    200, 228, 249, 251, 274, 296, 300, 314, 343,
    356, 377, 379, 387, 390, 404, 414, 418, 421,
    422, 431, 432, 449, 450, 472, 497, 503, 509,
    535, 543, 549, 558, 593,
Ecospace 115, 124, 178, 257, 433, 450
Ecosystem 17, 36, 64, 74, 120, 178, 186, 208,
    209, 224, 241, 257, 261, 314, 332, 336, 340,
    341, 361, 372, 383, 474, 493, 503, 509, 565,
    576, 577, 583, 605, 613, 633
Ecotone 178, 309, 578
Eddy 130, 145, 171, 178, 190, 195, 255, 257,
    282, 391, 446, 472, 499, 608
Eels 190, 314, 501
Effluent 179, 191
Eh 158, 179
El Niño 24, 208, 168, 202, 270, 386-387, 432
Elastic 180, 502, 510
Electricity 26, 103, 108, 116, 117, 124, 174,
    175, 180, 199,
213, 228, 273, 300, 309, 321, 328, 334, 335,
    336, 342, 351, 355, 366, 376, 379, 415, 421,
    436, 438, 442, 444, 462, 463, 466, 485, 494,
    500, 509, 508, 517, 547, 548, 564, 568, 614,
    617
Electrolytes 26, 180
Electromagnetic Field 137, 174, 180, 184, 200,
    207, 219, 225, 280, 321, 323, 335, 357, 360,
    411, 424, 436, 461, 466, 501, 525, 526, 531
Electromagnetic Radiation 42, 57, 180, 436,
    477, 587, 594, 621
Electromagnetic Spectrum 284, 321, 355
Electromagnetic Storms 526
Electron 16, 27, 43, 50, 61, 71, 92, 99, 102,
    103, 106, 108, 125, 136, 137, 180-181, 199,
    200, 222, 257, 259, 266, 272, 281, 287, 320,
    335, 351, 365, 390, 393, 394, 408, 414, 424,
    452, 458, 461, 462, 466, 467, 475, 487, 525,
    527, 530, 532, 544, 586, 587
Electronics 132, 144, 219, 355, 371, 487, 582,
    619
Electrostatics 169, 287, 618, 621
Element 6, 17, 18, 42, 47, 63, 64, 66, 80, 85,
    86, 92, 93, 104, 107, 109, 112, 118, 136,
    144, 148, 164, 181, 199, 200, 203, 205, 212,
    227, 234, 254, 258, 262, 263, 268, 272, 283,
    289, 291, 309, 318, 324, 332, 345, 351, 352,
    360, 365, 380, 390, 393, 414, 429, 436, 450,
    452, 456, 458, 466, 467, 468, 472, 487, 508,
    509, 516, 517, 545, 555, 558, 563, 577, 587,
    589, 593, 626, 629
Elephant 3, 75, 339, 342, 366, 387, 408, 526,
    561
Elfin Forest 182, 567
Eluviation 48, 182, 440, 525, 632
Eluvium 48, 182
Embayment 182, 185, 226, 362, 401, 409, 619
Emerald 183, 281, 510
Emergence 117, 118, 183, 192, 205, 226, 401,
    424, 475, 482, 506, 518, 613
Emergents 90, 470, 577
Emery 1, 135, 137, 183, 531
End product 257, 258, 317, 563, 590
Energy 52, 56, 61, 64, 66, 67, 69, 72, 100, 103,
    106, 123, 128, 131, 135, 136, 143, 145, 149,
    152, 155, 158, 160, 164, 169, 177, 178,
    181, 186, 193, 203, 207, 208, 209, 214, 215,
    219, 221, 226, 227, 231, 246, 249, 255, 257,
    262, 268, 269, 272, 278, 285, 297, 306, 314,
    317, 321, 322, 324, 335, 351, 354, 357, 365,
    375, 376, 377, 380, 382, 385, 387, 392, 394,
    395, 401, 403, 408, 413, 433, 434, 436, 441,
    446, 447, 461, 462, 463, 465, 466, 467, 468,
    478, 484, 502, 506, 514, 515, 525, 527, 529,
    534, 535, 548, 550, 562, 564, 566, 573, 577,
    579, 580, 589, 591, 600, 605, 609, 615,
    617, 618, 621
Environment 6, 14, 21, 23, 34, 39, 54, 62, 70,
    85, 106, 107, 110, 114, 116, 133, 147, 149,
    151, 177, 178, 185, 186, 191, 192, 194, 195,
    205, 210, 223, 230, 246, 248, 257, 262, 266,
    283, 284, 296, 299, 301, 309, 323, 324, 325,
    340, 366, 373, 377, 379, 389, 397, 404, 409,
    410, 418, 419, 420, 426, 428, 430, 445, 450,
    462, 469, 470, 477, 483, 491, 526, 538, 540,
    543, 553, 572, 593, 605, 622, 631
Eocene Epoch 150, 186, 245, 318, 357, 362,
    406, 418, 482, 511, 512, 561, 575, 585, 605,
    612
Eolian 186
Eon 141, 186, 434
Epeirogenesis 186, 184, 605
Ephemeral 86, 187, 194, 281, 413, 605, 608
Epicenter 59, 72, 175, 187, 311, 381, 464
Epicontinental Seas 87, 104, 186, 254, 409,
    431, 519, 561
Epidote 187, 247, 452, 596
Epilimnion 187, 274
Epiphyte 80, 187, 409
Epoch 111, 186, 187, 188, 230, 285, 378, 406,
    418, 435, 436, 438, 594, 610
Equatorial 109, 126, 182, 188, 296, 433, 542,
    550, 558, 576, 577, 584
Equinox 188, 455
Era 111, 188, 189, 429, 434
Erg 51, 62, 156, 179, 189, 461, 465, 493
Erosion 3, 9, 19, 24, 30, 31, 36, 41, 44, 45, 47,
    53, 54, 60, 78, 83, 85, 87, 89, 90, 92, 93,
    100, 104, 112, 113, 114, 117, 118, 122,
    123, 128, 132, 134, 147, 151, 152, 153, 154,
    156, 157, 161, 163, 167, 168, 169, 170, 171,
    182, 185, 186, 189, 190, 197, 199, 207,
    210, 220, 226, 229, 230, 231, 236, 239, 241,
    251, 253, 260, 267, 280, 284, 296, 301,
    302, 311, 316, 315, 316, 322, 326, 327, 331,
    336, 345, 347, 350, 365, 369, 373, 377, 382,
    385, 388, 389, 394, 397, 405, 406, 411,

Erosion (continued) 412, 423, 426, 427, 432, 436, 437, 439, 440, 444, 447, 458, 461, 463, 472, 477, 481, 482, 483, 484, 485, 487, 499, 502, 504, 510, 513, 514, 518, 520, 525, 528, 529, 537, 539, 542, 546, 548, 556, 561, 564, 568, 570, 575, 580, 586, 594, 601, 603, 607, 608, 609, 615, 616, 618,624, 626, 630

Erratics 190, 204, 230, 277

Eruption 14, 86, 89, 92, 108, 111, 122, 136, 137, 141, 160, 170, 171, 176, 177, 179, 184, 190, 201, 204, 205, 223, 228, 268, 278, 283, 288, 297, 302, 305, 308, 317, 323, 331, 346, 348, 357, 359, 369. 371, 381, 387, 393, 394, 395, 401, 405, 424, 426-427, 437, 445, 446, 447, 449, 459, 472, 494, 499, 500, 505, 517, 539, 546, 553, 554, 555, 559, 569, 593, 595, 596, 599, 600, 601, 602, 603, 606, 615, 625

Escarpment 31, 114, 166, 196, 234, 245, 341, 363, 364, 373, 382, 443, 502, 521, 533, 553, 629

Essential Minerals 239, 537

Estuary 72, 75, 201, 203, 214, 217, 355, 397, 424, 442, 480, 498, 499, 500, 512, 534, 542, 564

Ethiopian Shield 513

Ethiopian Zoogeographical Zone 633

Eucalyptus 158, 316, 622

Eurasian Plate 629

European Plate 17, 275, 443

European Rift 479

Eutrophication 70, 191, 244, 405

Evaporation 15, 22, 32, 36, 40, 55, 62, 66, 79, 107, 132, 149, 155, 182, 189, 191, 219, 246, 254, 262, 273, 285, 296, 312, 313, 326, 347, 348, 361, 370, 375, 399, 427, 430, 449, 452, 461, 474, 482, 493, 495, 496, 497, 500, 506, 518, 527, 544, 545, 553, 566, 573, 578, 606, 615

Evaporites 26, 30, 40, 55, 165, 191, 245, 254, 298, 348, 392, 419, 484, 491, 495, 496, 507, 523, 575, 615

Evapotranspiration 19, 20, 41, 91, 116, 192, 496, 573, 577

Evergreens 127, 190, 377, 432, 503, 509, 543, 558

Evolution 6, 139, 148, 169, 192, 193, 222, 265, 267, 372, 377, 411, 459, 509, 511

Exfoliation 193, 203, 240, 284, 587

Exosphere 42

Explosion 38, 86, 108, 117, 136, 137, 171, 190, 193, 218, 279, 281, 282, 287, 307, 308, 312, 319, 323, 331, 344, 377, 388, 392, 393, 394, 405, 427, 437, 446, 508, 517, 535, 546, 548, 575, 582, 587, 601, 601, 602, 610

Extinction 82, 119, 138, 139, 152, 158, 162, 163, 194, 202, 262, 267, 281, 288, 320, 350, 357, 408, 409, 429, 431, 478, 479, 482, 494, 531, 541, 574, 580

Extrusive 25, 215, 225, 279, 301, 380, 405, 484, 485

F Layer 195

Facies 63, 99, 187, 195, 210, 392, 409, 446, 476, 583

Fall-line 55, 19, 424, 483, 608, 622

Fallout 196, 392

Fallow 169, 196, 249, 385, 520, 578

Falls (See Waterfalls) 20, 26, 79, 126, 158, 196, 279, 299, 331, 357, 382, 483, 599, 600, 609, 622

Family 65, 196, 241, 306, 320, 338, 352, 355, 557, 560

Fanglomerate 196

Fan 16, 31, 33, 49, 72, 148, 152, 242, 299, 326, 412, 465, 542, 554

Fault 14, 28, 37, 44, 43, 45, 59, 68, 72, 78, 81, 104, 113, 114, 115, 121, 132, 154, 163, 166, 174, 186, 195, 197, 203, 209, 212, 223, 232, 233, 237, 245, 248, 258, 268, 295, 307, 313, 315, 317, 323, 327, 336, 341, 345, 357, 358, 363, 369, 381, 382, 409, 411, 413, 427, 477, 479, 481, 492, 494, 497, 498, 502, 507, 512, 514, 521, 532, 540, 556, 557, 552, 563, 572, 573, 596, 605, 608, 614, 620, 629

Fault Block Mountains 55, 427, 479, 485, 565, 605, 629

Fauna 64, 82, 96, 101, 104, 120, 179, 299, 302, 314, 340, 349, 406, 409, 442, 543, 557, 574, 581, 605

Feldspar 13, 15, 18, 21, 25, 27, 30, 36, 53, 67, 74, 114, 142, 147, 158, 162, 164, 197-198, 217, 239, 240, 248, 280, 300, 311, 356, 357, 361, 367, 379, 408, 411, 426, 441, 463, 480, 484, 517, 550, 571

Feldspathoid 198, 226, 379

Felsite 25, 198

Felsitic 480, 561

Fen 198

Fennoscandia Shield 49, 198, 203, 230, 513

Fern 144, 187, 199, 227, 233, 261, 279, 309, 314, 430, 458, 459, 470, 533, 558, 574, 576

Ferric Oxide 327, 334, 335

Ferrochrome 199

Ferrocolumbium 123

Ferromagnesium 43, 54, 162, 164, 199, 267, 323, 332, 355, 379, 435, 484, 514, 519, 541, 585

Ferromagnetism 200, 217, 218, 335

Ferromanganese 339

Ferroniobium 388

Ferrous Oxide 327, 336

Ferruginous 125, 134, 170, 317, 361, 407, 520

Fertility 150, 200, 201, 288, 313, 318, 27, 344, 415, 520, 595, 602, 624

Fertilizer 22, 40, 95, 170, 200, 250, 254, 268, 293, 294, 341, 388, 389, 405, 435, 452, 507, 550, 590

Fetch 200, 609

Fine-grained 193, 198, 211, 232, 236, 237, 254, 267, 280, 294, 303, 312, 327, 333, 378, 403, 407, 437, 458, 480, 511, 518, 561, 570, 574, 580, 615

Fire 29, 37, 93, 151, 201, 203, 210, 321, 404, 451, 470, 509, 522, 543, 546, 565

Fireweed 222, 331

Firn 201, 523

Firth 201

Fish 5, 23, 24, 31, 40, 50, 55, 96, 104, 158, 176, 193, 201-202, 209, 215, 230, 239, 270, 272, 296, 309, 314, 338, 349, 374, 386, 387, 391, 400, 410, 413, 414, 465, 466, 491, 500, 502, 505, 509, 514, 521, 545, 547, 556, 570, 577, 581, 586, 587, 594, 601, 605

Fissile 203, 458, 510, 521, 570

Fission 79, 83, 104, 131, 138, 139, 141, 166, 190, 203, 204, 215, 380, 392, 447, 582

Fissure 58, 89, 122, 138, 139, 141, 166, 190, 201, 203, 204, 206, 214, 240, 276, 279, 319, 333, 336, 341, 369, 401, 424, 513, 544, 602

Fjord 201, 203, 269, 359, 382, 480, 484, 524, 542, 595

Flagellate 26, 162

Flagstone 35, 203

Flakes 203, 356, 503, 511, 521, 523

Flash Flood 74, 99, 187, 190, 285, 305, 371, 412, 482, 605, 606

Flat-topped Relief 150, 251, 253, 296, 506, 611. 622

Flint 204, 212, 435

Floes 57, 97, 204, 238, 274, 278, 418, 505, 506

Flood 19, 20, 27, 50, 74, 75, 96, 99, 116, 138, 139, 152, 190, 205, 219, 220, 226, 238, 271, 277, 294, 313, 340, 343, 370, 371, 397, 422, 423, 426, 497, 511, 512, 522, 525, 529, 544, 560, 570, 578, 583, 594, 595, 596, 614, 623, 624, 630, 634

Floodplain 16, 40, 70. 75, 204, 296, 317, 329, 346, 370, 405, 441, 450, 522, 560, 562, 595

Flora 64, 102, 120, 153, 233, 340, 366, 425, 430, 442, 515, 521, 543, 557

Flotation 125, 205, 304, 352, 402, 433, 553

Flowering Plants 16, 18, 144, 222, 253, 261, 269, 442, 492, 529, 580, 583

Flues 207, 227

Fluorapatite 30, 435

Fluorescence 70, 206,

Fluorides 205

Fluorine 205, 240, 266, 355, 404, 435

Fluorite 114, 142, 206, 248, 320, 341, 364

Fluorocarbons 450

Fluorspar 69, 206, 207, 341

Fluvial 185, 190, 207, 245, 284

Flux 82, 174, 206, 207, 293, 323, 535

Fly Ash 207, 227

Flysch 207, 226

Foci 175, 207, 351, 402, 542

Fog 7, 8, 41, 58, 87, 158, 208, 270, 294, 302, 311, 327, 373, 414, 432, 455, 466, 523, 529, 615

Fold 14, 17, 28, 29, 30, 31, 44, 55, 96, 113, 116, 150, 160, 186, 188, 199, 207, 208, 221, 226, 264, 289, 298, 313, 316, 336, 363, 368, 369, 378, 411, 438, 473, 476, 477, 491, 507, 523, 532, 538, 551, 557, 596, 603, 605, 618, 620

Foliation 233, 352, 437, 503

Foothills 20, 31, 76, 115, 244, 261, 337, 369, 403, 421, 438, 510, 560, 572

Footwall 209, 479

Foraminifera 86, 95, 105, 138, 209, 233, 297, 394, 411, 446, 458, 513, 550, 615

Forests 19, 21, 24, 44, 45, 76, 77, 81, 88, 90, 92, 94, 101, 113, 115, 117, 121, 126, 144, 150, 151, 158, 181, 186, 190, 199, 209, 210, 211, 217, 219, 231, 241, 244, 246, 261, 265, 269, 273, 279, 283, 288, 294, 299, 305, 316, 321, 326, 327, 332, 337, 341, 345, 362, 366, 377, 378, 381, 390, 391, 401, 406, 409, 420, 429, 430, 432, 439, 447, 449 470, 471, 476, 478, 486, 489, 503, 509, 510, 513, 514, 517, 520, 523, 529, 539, 531, 533, 543, 544, 546, 550, 553, 554, 558, 576, 577, 578, 586, 588, 591, 595, 596, 601, 606, 609, 613, 619, 620, 627

Formation 47, 160, 186, 193, 195, 196, 210, 224, 226, 258, 286, 289, 291, 294, 297, 307, 319, 345, 348, 392, 398, 411, 412, 418, 419, 430, 454, 458, 479, 480, 507, 519, 537, 542, 606, 618,

Forsterite 428

Fossil Fuel 92, 211, 246, 433, 526

Fossils 21, 22, 41, 45, 60, 82, 85, 87, 95, 101, 105, 111, 119, 126, 127, 135, 139, 144, 160, 162, 163, 179, 186, 191, 192, 195, 204, 209, 211, 218, 221, 233, 236, 241, 246, 248, 264, 265, 277, 278, 281, 282, 295, 297, 320, 325, 329, 339, 343, 344, 352, 372, 404, 405, 406, 407, 408, 409, 410, 411, 418, 419, 420, 448, 455, 477, 479, 483, 494, 511, 512, 513, 514, 516, 519, 533, 538, 539, 540, 560, 573, 574, 577, 585, 605, 632, 633

Fracture 74, 104, 108, 110, 115, 124, 161, 163, 174, 192, 197, 203, 212, 214, 237, 262, 295, 307, 317, 321, 327, 345, 346, 349, 358, 361, 383, 398, 401, 406, 460, 462, 473, 539, 596, 599, 601, 602, 610

Francium 212

Freezing 100, 138, 151, 189, 201, 214, 257, 263, 275, 277, 278, 287, 298, 320, 325, 321, 344, 425, 428, 447, 450, 492, 496, 497, 521, 523, 548, 603

Frequency 180, 195, 213, 227, 283, 430, 462, 609

Freshwater 14, 19, 20, 23, 24, 41, 55, 76, 79, 82, 89, 126, 141, 143, 153, 160, 161, 162, 192, 202, 213, 221, 243, 267, 275, 301, 312, 314, 316, 349, 365, 399, 404, 421, 438, 441, 470, 471, 480, 492, 495, 499, 506, 548, 568, 569, 574, 606, 613, 633

Friable 214, 511, 528

Friction 78, 143, 151, 179, 180, 237, 400, 564-565

Fringing Reef 474, 475

Fronds 199, 230, 303

Front 118, 145, 214, 392, 398, 447, 605

Frost 211, 214, 250, 265, 372, 378, 403, 437, 450, 454, 581, 597

Froth 205, 304, 589, 615

Frozen 428, 429, 505, 521

Fruit 74, 78, 148, 230, 269, 378, 468, 492, 522
Fuel 70, 77, 79, 106, 131, 139, 152, 170, 210, 211, 213, 214, 215, 218, 246, 262, 272, 295, 304, 324, 388, 392, 422, 425, 447, 449, 468, 471, 489, 510, 528, 531, 514, 563, 589, 619, 625
Fuelwood 50, 77, 151, 210, 214, 215, 354, 449, 450, 451, 476, 489, 493, 577, 619
Fulgurite 215
Fumarole 215, 445, 533, 559
Fungi 14, 29, 63, 306, 321, 372, 486, 560, 562, 576, 580
Fusable 351
Fusion 62, 157, 173, 185, 215, 262, 263, 272, 322, 324, 333, 392, 452, 534, 546, 574, 582

Gabbro 27, 127, 158, 164, 217, 368, 400, 460
Gadolinium 199, 217
Galapagos Rift 218, 545
Galaxy 39, 62, 67, 218, 333, 359, 398, 429, 441, 463, 466, 534, 535, 587, 589
Gale 218, 239, 295, 456
Galena 218, 353, 532, 631
Gallery Forest 19, 89, 102, 219, 316, 326, 364, 420, 543, 576, 5964
Gallium 56, 219, 227
Gallium-arsenide 37, 219
Galvanization 532, 631
Gamma Rays 16, 47, 136, 203, 218, 219, 222, 436, 465, 467, 468, 469, 477, 485, 526,
Gangue 197, 206, 220, 619
Gap 135, 199, 264, 265, 586, 613, 618
Garnet 177, 220, 437, 606, 616
Garnierite 118, 220-221, 383
Gasoline 80, 140, 212, 221, 262
Gastropod 101, 221
Geanticline 218, 223, 298, 317, 547
Gel 120, 141, 408, 442, 528
Gelifluction 222
Gemstone 32, 61, 71, 79, 84, 92, 94, 101, 111, 114, 135, 142, 159, 160, 161, 164, 183, 198, 220, 292, 293, 310, 316, 337, 374, 408, 411, 425, 427, 428, 445, 463, 476, 479, 487, 500, 533, 534, 570, 571, 573, 623, 632
Gene 210, 220-221, 349, 372
Genera 82, 196, 202, 306, 420, 557
Genetic 222, 227, 348, 372, 522, 583
Genus 33, 297, 492, 530
Geographic Pole 334, 448
GeomagneticField 224-225
Geomagnetic Pole 225, 448
Geomagnetism (See Magnetism) 117, 225, 429
Geosyncline 13, 23, 31, 34, 124, 186, 221, 226, 239, 298, 315, 363, 409, 430, 439, 457, 476, 485, 613, 626
Geothermal 131, 184, 226-227, 224, 269, 382, 498, 625
Geothermometer 421
Germ Bank 228
Germ Plasm 222, 227-228, 577, 583
Germanium 219, 227, 352, 509, 572
Germination 442, 449, 622

Geyser 41, 72, 227, 228, 268, 278, 371, 382, 405, 417, 498, 520, 548, 573, 625
Geyserite 520
Giant's Causeway 53, 123, 229
Gibbsite 367
Gilgai Relief 229
Glacial Epoch 114, 272, 275, 276, 277, 285, 445, 595, 626
Glacial Plucking 35, 107, 111, 118, 198, 267, 345, 369, 394, 442, 493, 574
Glaciation 27, 30, 33, 35, 49, 65. 74, 79, 88, 92, 97, 100, 108, 114, 117, 119, 122, 131, 132, 139, 152, 153, 160, 167, 168, 169, 183, 189, 191, 195, 196, 198, 200, 204, 230, 231, 237, 245, 246, 249, 259, 267, 269, 270, 273, 275, 276, 285, 299, 312, 313, 316, 339, 342, 343, 345, 368, 389, 394, 412, 414, 420, 428, 430, 431, 437, 445, 449, 459, 471, 476, 486, 492, 494, 502, 505, 506, 523, 549, 556, 561, 566, 582, 585, 587, 595, 596, 609, 627
Glacier 1, 4, 12, 13, 15, 20, 24, 27, 59, 70, 74, 79, 88, 99, 112, 119, 122, 130, 131, 134, 168, 171, 192, 203, 204, 212, 230, 231, 246, 269, 275, 276, 277, 280, 289, 299, 304, 305, 316, 318, 325, 337, 348, 368, 369, 381, 397, 412, 428, 438, 445, 446, 447, 455, 465, 472, 475, 483, 488, 502, 504, 507, 509, 524, 530, 532, 548, 580, 585, 588, 593, 594, 595, 606, 627
Glass 5, 38, 53, 72, 157, 231-232, 260, 279, 317, 322, 323, 324, 380, 426, 429, 435, 441, 444, 456, 462, 468, 476, 508, 517, 524, 528, 565, 573, 580
Glassy 22, 137, 215, 372, 404, 480, 563
Glauconite 232, 245, 247, 491
Glaucophane 70
Global Rift System 175, 176, 232, 237, 243, 244, 242, 357, 358, 382, 401, 443, 481, 572, 574
Global Warming 8, 13, 93, 277, 285, 302, 416, 425, 486, 542, 606, 610
Globergerina 209, 233, 394, 407
Gneiss 34, 36, 43, 90, 193, 233-234, 247, 248, 310, 359, 454, 476, 561
Goethite 234, 289, 323, 406
Gold 13, 14, 16, 24, 29, 31, 36, 39, 41, 44, 45, 49, 54, 55, 57, 58, 66, 69, 80, 82, 83, 89, 92, 95, 96, 105, 139, 144, 159, 170, 196, 200-201, 213, 217, 222, 230, 232, 234-235, 236, 240, 248, 251, 258, 266, 272, 280, 306, 312, 327, 328, 349, 360, 366, 368-369, 370, 374, 381, 385, 388, 394, 406, 408, 409, 421, 428, 431, 434, 439, 440, 451, 453, 463, 464, 471, 474, 479, 481, 492, 496, 510, 515, 517, 518, 519, 543, 544, 545, 558, 567, 579, 594, 603, 606, 615, 618, 627, 614
Gondwana 9, 25, 128, 162, 233, 236, 282, 301, 318, 332, 373, 384, 422, 430, 481, 574, 612
Gorge 121, 147, 225, 228, 236, 239, 263, 279, 299, 300, 305, 316, 320, 341, 348, 373, 381, 386, 406, 407, 551, 564, 600, 623, 627

Lake Gosiute (Mid-Eocene) 245

Gossan 111, 236-237, 323

Gouge 171, 237, 243, 548

Graben 48, 58, 68, 75, 149, 155, 232, 237, 258, 268, 278, 302, 308, 315, 337, 338, 358, 381, 427, 479, 541, 555, 556, 557, 563, 565, 594

Grade 114, 169, 362, 386, 458, 537, 553, 570, 612

Gradient 16, 78, 115, 220, 230, 237, 270, 329, 347, 352, 371, 457, 521, 544, 557, 559, 562

Grain (cereal) 18, 35, 102, 108, 170, 237, 325, 359, 441, 451, 454, 480, 614, 626

Granite 5, 23, 24, 33, 34, 36, 49, 50, 63, 67, 89, 90, 92, 118, 122, 157, 162, 185, 187, 193, 203, 212, 217, 229, 233, 239-240, 247, 248, 249, 260, 264, 278, 317, 320, 332, 337, 345, 352, 353, 354, 359, 374, 379, 385, 426, 427, 432, 437, 438, 439, 441, 462, 463, 479, 480, 484, 511, 514, 516, 521, 536, 568, 570, 587, 600, 619

Granitization 240, 353, 357

Granodiorite 162, 239, 463, 516

Granular 98, 201, 239, 240, 274, 561, 608

Granule 242, 427, 612

Graphite 93, 106, 117, 159, 240-241, 352, 439, 450, 533

Graptolites 26, 88, 110, 158, 241, 409

Grass 17, 81, 82, 102, 108, 170, 192, 210, 237, 241, 251, 261, 314, 359, 366, 382, 383, 425, 441, 454, 471, 493, 528, 532, 549, 560, 565, 578, 583, 585, 596, 597, 620

Grasslands 19, 73, 81, 89, 102, 114, 171, 219, 237, 241-242, 244, 302, 341, 413, 421, 425, 454, 460, 478, 529, 535, 537, 549, 570, 576, 577, 596, 597, 614

Gravel 16, 32, 49, 52, 58, 69, 72, 87, 113, 143, 156, 159, 186, 196, 198, 206, 238, 242, 273, 299, 312, 326, 360, 368, 374, 394, 401, 412, 421, 426, 438, 451, 462, 463, 476, 481, 487, 499, 502, 514, 522, 532, 554, 568, 569, 582, 632

Gravity 3, 17, 27, 74, 92, 120, 124, 138, 178, 182, 189, 200, 205, 214, 217, 218, 225, 231, 242-243, 257, 263, 280, 285, 290, 310, 315, 344, 345, 360, 367, 377, 410, 411, 421, 427, 440, 455, 470, 483, 507, 518, 522, 527, 528, 565, 601

Grazing 109, 157, 168, 241, 341, 382, 383, 413, 471, 532, 540, 578, 607

Great Circle 46, 187, 243, 264, 376, 423

Greenhouse Effect 8, 11, 93, 115, 233, 245-246, 259, 272, 276, 285, 354, 388, 425, 470, 526, 559, 573, 598, 610

Greensand 232, 247

Greenschist 117, 187, 247

Greenstone 34, 90, 232, 245, 247-248, 338, 406, 521

Greisen 98, 240, 248

Greywacke 207, 226, 248, 382, 561

Gritstone 35

Grooves 249, 492, 521, 539

Groundwater 32, 37, 54, 91, 107, 108, 211, 249-250, 254, 273, 283, 301, 310, 326, 328, 341, 353, 361, 404, 407, 412, 437, 453, 468,

Groundwater (continued) 497, 499, 522, 527, 533, 575, 577, 606, 607, 608, 612, 633

Grove 516, 564, 595, 599, 619

Growing Season 169, 250, 309, 325, 580

Growth 88, 128, 169, 210, 213, 273, 290, 297, 300, 322, 366, 395, 411, 437, 442, 462, 475, 521, 566, 570, 577, 580, 582, 586, 590

Guano 250, 436, 615

Guinea-Liberian Shield 613

Gulf 11, 31, 33, 95, 56, 121, 179, 209, 217, 228, 239, 245, 252, 256, 264, 271, 294, 355, 362, 363, 431, 497, 498, 505, 508, 512, 527,564

Gully 48, 82, 147, 473, 482

Gust 616

Guyot 253-254, 475, 482, 506, 550

Gymnosperm 127, 227, 254, 610

Gypsum 12, 26, 96, 100, 101, 191, 229, 254, 261, 364, 430, 452, 491, 495, 518, 543, 615, 616

Gyre 254-255, 391, 500, 501

Habit 48, 69, 142, 218, 220, 234, 217, 258, 360, 361

Habitat 19, 34, 63, 64, 98, 169, 202, 257, 260, 269, 292, 314, 320, 322, 332, 336, 360, 371, 373, 391, 400, 421, 450, 501, 513, 516, 522, 532, 564, 565, 583, 623

Hafnium 556

Hail 18, 257-258, 455, 611

Half-life 70, 103, 104, 258, 287, 299, 466, 467, 469, 487, 541, 574, 598

Halite 191, 258, 491, 494, 496, 518, 524, 550

Halley's Comet 258

Halloysite 215

Halmrolysis 258

Halo 113, 128, 133, 258, 274, 492, 520, 621

Halocline 259

Halogen 80, 108, 259, 287

Halophyte 259

Hammada 156, 259, 461

Hanging Wall 259, 479, 564

Hanging Valley 259, 502

Hard Parts 93, 94, 127, 151, 211, 322, 411, 619

Hard Rock 92, 170, 259, 359, 609

Hard Water 260

Hardness 12, 22, 30, 35, 36, 46, 60, 73, 86, 94, 98, 111, 116, 132, 134, 158, 165, 184, 187, 234, 260, 310, 336, 360, 361, 460, 462, 483, 487, 519, 532, 535, 548, 559, 570, 583, 619, 630

Hardpan 87, 143, 260, 446

Hardwoods 77, 217, 362, 432, 503, 549

'Harmattan' 62, 260, 271, 286, 304, 346, 499

Harzburgite 103

Haze 243, 262, 302

Headland 267, 368, 375

Headwall 59

Headward Erosion 47, 92, 262, 594, 599, 608, 609, 618

Headwaters 187, 213, 262, 331, 378, 382, 385, 483, 488, 523, 606

Heap Leaching 63

Heave 214, 372, 403, 454, 581

Heavens 39, 558, 590

Heavy Metals 226, 263, 334, 339

Heavy Minerals 16, 49, 55, 57, 67, 123, 263, 312, 334, 335, 343, 421, 440, 472, 481, 485, 499, 527, 632

'Heavy Water' 159, 263

Height 19, 22, 138, 142, 200, 208, 254, 259, 262, 274, 301, 375, 405, 419, 431, 446, 449, 497, 509, 521, 564, 609

Helium 17, 43, 62, 222, 263, 272, 283, 297, 389, 414, 525, 533, 546, 589, 590

Hematite 3, 90, 236, 264, 289, 291, 323, 345, 520, 568

Hemisphere 65, 135, 186, 227, 243, 264, 350, 392, 393, 423, 506, 534, 561, 585

Herbs 14, 80, 81, 102, 161, 581

Herds 103, 341, 342, 383, 421, 510, 541

Hexagonal 123, 142, 229, 240, 462, 515, 523

Hiatus 264, 586, 617

High Grade 159, 330, 334, 340, 346, 403, 435, 625

High Latitudes 259, 277, 291, 393, 506, 537, 542, 567, 586, 616

High Pressure Area 29, 60, 168, 175, 254, 260, 264, 267, 324, 387, 471, 481, 534, 575, 576, 590, 616

High-tide 47, 114, 118, 128, 150, 209, 286, 367, 491, 498, 526, 565

High-water 50, 61, 244, 279, 332, 378, 411, 439, 624

Highlands 18, 21, 77, 89, 104, 148, 242, 244, 252, 253, 276, 345, 367, 370, 384, 424, 486, 587, 625

Highway 49, 76, 454, 572

Hills 30, 54, 67, 72, 83, 126, 147, 150, 165, 168, 199, 220, 265, 284, 299, 302, 307, 308, 311, 337, 345, 368, 378, 407, 453, 458, 492, 499, 502, 504, 515, 551, 570, 582, 588, 602

Hinge Point 12, 275

Hinterland 427, 500, 597

Hoar 265

Hogback 142, 265-266

Holdfasts 303, 507

Hollow 214, 495

Holocene 50, 265, 463

Homeostasis 266

Homestead Act 266

'Homo Sapiens' 306, 407

Homocline 266

Hominid 45, 306

Horizon 27, 35, 46, 533, 534, 591

Hornblende 25, 147, 162, 196, 217, 230, 233, 239, 247, 267, 438, 463, 503, 517, 550

Hornfels 267

Horse Latitudes 267

Horseshoe Crab 267-268, 574

Horst 68, 237, 268, 489, 561

Host 136, 208, 209, 248, 359, 368, 369, 374, 524, 533, 559, 621, 633

Hot Spot 38, 41, 46, 218, 225, 261, 263, 268, 229, 279, 290, 361, 400, 417, 446, 452, 474, 521, 574, 583, 603, 625

Hot Springs 46, 73, 145, 147, 184, 202, 226, 245, 268-269, 298, 323, 361, 375, 382, 460, 474, 495, 533, 540, 545, 573

Humanoids 406, 561

Humans 37, 45, 59, 70, 94, 103, 106, 107, 133, 144, 150, 154, 194, 196, 208, 210, 222, 223, 237, 238, 241, 276, 285, 287, 283, 306, 314, 331, 339, 341, 351, 354, 379, 383, 413, 420, 449, 450, 451, 463, 465, 466, 467, 478, 480, 493, 495, 499, 509, 512, 524, 531, 532, 541, 551, 554, 558, 559, 578, 585, 587, 593, 600, 606, 614, 615, 617, 621

Humidity 2, 15, 55, 109, 113, 114, 115, 155, 158, 182, 199, 270, 286, 293, 317, 319, 322, 336, 346, 385, 412, 454, 477, 478, 496, 543, 558, 573, 576, 587, 605, 610

Hummock 229, 372, 405, 428

Humus 102, 116, 271, 326, 447, 454, 570

Hurricane 57, 144, 151, 176, 264, 271, 312, 583, 616

Hydrocarbons 8, 28, 66, 149, 184, 211, 245, 272, 303, 354, 372, 375, 403, 404, 411, 415, 418, 433, 449, 450, 515, 556, 570

Hydroelectric 184, 291, 340, 395, 500, 515, 556, 583, 603

Hydrogen 16, 43, 95, 96, 107, 116, 124, 137, 144, 157, 161, 164, 181, 184, 211, 214, 223, 263, 272, 297, 303, 365, 380, 388, 392, 399, 434, 416, 458, 469, 524, 525, 544, 546, 574, 590, 606

Hydrogen Sulfide 14, 67, 110, 191, 218, 272, 386, 474, 607

Hydrologic Cycle 19, 64, 192, 210, 273, 298, 470, 573

Hydropower 145, 184, 273, 300, 583

Hydrosphere 273

Hydrothermal 303, 368, 452, 457

Hydroxides 53, 90, 143, 160, 197, 262, 300, 334

Hypabyssal 273-274

Hypersaline 540

Hypogene 274

Hypolimnion 274

Ice 13, 12, 28, 37, 45, 48, 59, 88, 100, 110, 113, 116, 118, 122, 123, 130, 134, 139, 141 , 150, 168, 171, 173, 198, 201, 204, 211, 212, 214, 222, 230, 231, 246, 249, 257, 258, 269, 273, 275, 276, 277, 278, 285, 305, 309, 313, 318, 328, 325, 337, 339, 372, 378, 381, 382, 389, 393, 407, 412, 414, 418, 420, 429, 430, 439, 445, 446, 450, 469, 485, 488, 494, 501, 505, 509, 511, 515, 518, 521, 523, 539, 542, 581, 591, 595, 606, 607, 610, 612, 614, 620

Ice Ages 9, 134, 171, 174, 189, 210, 230, 232, 237, 252, 275, 276, 285, 325, 410, 429, 430, 451, 518, 526, 602

Ice Cap 45, 88, 93, 130, 198, 276, 344, 381, 394, 488, 505, 554, 595, 620

Ice Sheet 9, 13, 27, 133, 134, 204, 231, 243, 246, 275, 276, 278, 318, 428, 445, 502, 542, 606, 616

Ice Shelf 27, 86, 128, 130, 277, 486

Iceberg 88, 246, 277, 278, 290, 486, 532

Ichthyosaurus 278, 320, 329

Icicle 278, 381

Igneous Rocks 4, 5, 15, 18, 22, 24, 25, 27, 30, 41, 43, 64, 74, 86, 95, 99, 109, 113, 118, 124, 127, 128, 135, 143, 156, 157, 158, 161, 164, 165, 170, 187, 195, 197, 198, 214, 220, 234, 235, 239, 247, 254, 259, 267, 279, 286, 293, 311, 318, 320, 332, 333, 334, 335, 336, 341, 348, 352, 361, 365, 367, 368, 369, 379, 383, 406, 411, 412, 429, 434, 435, 438, 446, 455, 458, 462, 480, 484, 485, 488, 507, 516, 550, 561, 591, 621

Ignimbrites 38, 279, 302

Ijolite 334

Illuvial 48, 81, 280, 449, 525

Illite 215, 280, 366, 411

Ilmenite 57, 67, 440, 499, 568

Imbrication 280, 514

Impermeability 31, 32, 281, 428, 496, 500, 528, 538

Implosion 281, 526

Impregnation 124, 245, 281, 402, 452, 597, 556

Impression 211

Impurities 108, 113, 125, 213, 227, 499, 504, 517, 518, 531, 608

Inclusion 21, 183, 281, 289, 443, 463, 488, 516

Index Fossil 82, 138, 209, 221, 233, 281, 533, 574

Indian Plate 104, 282, 283, 615

Indigenous 257, 282, 523

Indium 517

'Indricotherium' 282-283

Induration 143, 256, 317, 318

Inelastic Scatter 502

Inert Gases 283, 379, 621

Infiltration 283, 519

Inflow 98, 143, 149, 313, 348, 366, 375, 391, 397, 487, 555, 595, 599

Infra-red 93, 98, 227, 246, 284, 299, 321, 465, 531, 559

Ingot 133, 284, 352

Ingression 284

Inlet 57, 305, 371

Inlier 284, 439

Inorganic 63, 64, 110, 354, 473, 478, 517, 570

Insect 21, 26, 29, 37, 65, 170, 178, 238, 327, 372, 443, 449, 452, 479, 492, 513, 560

Inselberg 156, 284, 308, 365

Inshore Environment 69, 248, 292, 297, 374, 386, 401

Insolation 284-285, 281, 415

Insoluble 223, 349, 403, 436

Insulation 355, 461, 518, 553, 598

Insulator 50, 351, 352, 365, 390, 509, 523, 619

Inter-planetary 482, 526, 530

Interfluve 48, 317

Interglacial Epochs 27, 112, 115, 230, 275, 276, 285, 313, 445, 447, 610

Intermediate Rocks 279, 321, 326, 350

Intermontane 187, 207, 233, 243, 618

Internal Wave 165, 285, 387, 398, 508, 534, 563, 582, 610

International Dateline 285, 350, 387

Interstices 92, 127, 193, 430, 437, 464, 491

Intertidal 59, 80, 286, 325, 380, 73

Intertropical 133, 319

Intertropical Convergence (ITC) 167, 286, 366, 493, 510, 577, 616

Intrazonal 46, 70, 81, 259, 286, 476, 478, 528

Intrusion 21, 27, 30, 69, 109, 128, 157, 161, 162, 193, 195, 232, 245, 258, 260, 264, 279, 286, 293, 305, 307, 311, 317, 328, 334, 337, 338, 341, 357, 359, 362, 363, 383, 426, 427, 429, 435, 446, 457, 462, 463, 484, 485, 489, 495, 513, 514, 518, 520, 536, 557, 564, 591, 600

Invasion 168, 187, 298, 304, 327, 543, 554, 572, 581

Inverse Relief 286

Inversion 41, 184, 286-287, 302, 388, 416, 545, 559, 579

Invertebrate 37, 88, 101, 119, 287, 356, 450, 474

Iodine 14, 80, 286, 356, 388, 467

Ionization 26, 53, 71, 99, 103, 106, 116, 123, 142, 173, 180, 221, 222, 258, 287, 334, 351, 355, 356, 367, 377, 389, 393, 414, 434, 435, 441, 467, 471, 477, 485, 487, 496, 503, 506, 517, 524, 525, 526, 528, 545

Ionosphere 42, 173, 195, 287

Iridium 139, 288, 444, 541, 556

Iron 26, 32, 41, 45, 49, 53, 54, 56, 59, 64, 69, 70, 76, 81, 85, 90, 94, 109, 110, 113, 123, 134, 136, 142, 156, 173, 174, 183, 187, 191, 199, 200, 217, 220, 225, 231, 234, 136, 247, 252, 254, 260, 263, 264, 279, 284, 289, 291, 293, 294, 301, 303, 304, 305, 306, 309, 310, 311, 317, 318, 323, 324, 327, 334, 336, 339, 345, 346, 349, 353, 355, 357, 370, 382, 383, 389, 399, 401, 402, 406, 408, 417, 421, 422, 435, 436, 441, 445, 449, 452, 455, 458, 460, 471, 473, 474, 475, 477, 484, 500, 508, 510, 515, 516, 517, 520, 522, 532, 534, 535, 543, 568, 571, 579, 583, 588, 597, 603, 605, 607, 611, 619, 630, 631

Ironstone 323, 347, 515

Irrigation 40, 98, 169, 228, 250, 288, 305, 371, 378, 397, 476, 495, 503, 515, 522, 554, 562, 572, 594, 608, 618

Island Arcs 14, 28, 47, 252, 261, 290, 291, 293, 342, 401, 491, 541, 546, 602

Isometric System 142, 164, 206, 220

Isostasy 39, 186, 290, 443

Isotope 36, 94, 103, 118, 148, 150, 157, 263, 287, 288, 299, 324, 345, 311, 414, 447, 466, 467, 468, 487, 541, 563, 574, 588, 589

Isthmus 314, 353, 413

Itabirite 291

Itacolumite 291

Ivory 339, 342,

Jacupirangite 293, 334
Jade 293, 380
Jadeite 293, 380
Jasper 289, 294
Jellyfish 26, 119, 179, 348
Jet 294, 416
Jet Aircraft 102, 118, 169, 295, 388, 408, 444. 519
Jet Fuel 140, 295, 304
Jet Stream 8, 11, 12, 26, 98, 112, 134, 167, 171, 286, 295, 387, 456, 447, 512, 539, 542, 575, 579
Jewelry 84, 233, 293, 294, 307, 357, 417, 510
Joint 53, 78, 122, 212, 229, 249, 295-296, 341, 439, 446, 570, 599
Jojoba 296
Jovian Planets 297, 380
Juan de Fuca Plate 97
Junction 195, 268, 358, 572
Jungle 82, 265, 297, 521, 596
Jupiter 39, 296, 300
Jurassic Period 22, 26, 48, 86, 119, 138, 140, 144, 162, 230, 239, 297, 298, 320, 321, 337, 350, 407, 414, 424, 459, 491, 542, 547, 574, 598
Jurassic-Cretaceous Seas 22
Juvenile Water 298, 399

Kame 299
Kangaroo 344, 381
Kaolin 49, 102, 113, 215, 237, 280, 294, 300, 451, 463
Kaolinite 113, 300, 366, 367
Kaolinization 240
Karroo Bush 301
Karst 99, 101, 163, 165,301, 315, 322, 328, 339, 394, 407, 440, 504, 627
Kelp 81, 149, 303
Kelvin Scale 303
Kerogen 78, 303, 304, 395, 410
Kerosene 140, 212, 295, 304, 528
Kettle Hole 304, 450
Khondalite 533
Kimberlite 69, 109, 159, 177, 251, 305, 308, 338, 440, 601, 623, 629
Kinetic Energy 106, 136, 184, 306
Kingdom 208, 287, 305, 306, 332, 442, 457, 557, 562
Lake Kirunga (Pleistocene) 599
Klippe 307, 564
Knickpoint 78
Knoll 307, 308, 315
Köppen Classification 114, 307, 575
Komotitic Pile 248
Kohl 307
Krill 70, 308, 309
Krypton 283, 309, 389, 514
Kupukupu Fern 309
Kyanite 310

L wave 172, 311, 508
Labradorite 53, 74, 158, 217, 311, 361
Laccolith 67, 273, 286, 311-312, 447
Lacustrine 16, 18, 126, 185, 245, 312, 314, 364, 379, 419, 540, 595
Lagoon 43, 48, 67, 79, 107, 117, 178, 185, 251, 310, 312, 355, 360, 418, 448, 465, 473, 491, 494, 500, 511, 526, 530
Lake Lahontan (Pleistocene) 313
Lamination 245, 264, 314, 356, 511, 521, 541
Lamprey 314
Land Bridge 59, 186, 276, 314, 580
Landfill 476, 499
Landform 34, 36, 56, 86, 121, 146, 156, 165, 169, 170, 186, 193, 209, 236, 259, 265, 267, 315, 323, 420, 426, 471, 476, 477, 553, 624, 625
Landmass 25, 127, 128, 129, 130, 137, 138, 139, 164, 181, 186, 225, 236, 275, 277, 282, 289, 301, 318, 320, 357, 363, 398, 421, 422, 444, 459, 574, 595, 612
Landscape 28, 38, 68, 101, 102, 104, 127, 185, 190, 199, 203, 225, 271, 259, 261, 265, 275, 301, 307, 313, 315, 316, 322, 345, 354, 364, 369, 269, 405, 427, 440, 472, 483, 484, 501, 549, 570, 583, 586, 616, 626
Landslide 45, 117, 138, 116, 145, 147, 272, 315, 371, 386, 510, 519, 521, 623
Lanthanum 365, 547
Lapse Rate 390
Lapilli 10, 316, 559, 601
Lapis Lazuli 316
Larvae 29, 32, 190, 268, 374, 414, 425, 533, 633
Laser 37, 263, 309, 317, 392, 444, 518, 548, 626
Latent Heat 184, 317, 334
Laterite 4, 50, 56, 91, 92, 103, 118, 125, 134, 143, 151, 170, 217-218, 220, 251, 252, 317-318, 324, 383, 392, 419, 440, 516, 520, 578, 579, 596
Laths 158, 367, 408
Latitude Effect 135, 318, 400
Lattice 290, 367
Laurasia 86, 128, 318, 422, 612
Laurencium 6
Laurentia 318, 494
Laurentian Shield 90, 554
Lava 1, 4, 5, 22, 23, 53, 54, 67, 68, 82, 83, 90, 92, 95, 99, 100, 111, 122, 123, 124, 138, 142, 147, 150, 154, 161, 166, 176, 178, 179, 189, 190, 201, 202, 203, 204, 205, 215, 229, 247, 278, 279, 301, 298, 301, 302, 303, 305, 308, 313, 316, 318, 319, 323, 333, 337, 346, 350, 359, 361, 371, 373, 376, 377, 382, 395, 398, 401, 405, 408, 418, 423, 426, 432, 437, 439, 446, 460, 473, 476, 480, 481, 494, 502, 504, 509, 513, 517, 522, 539, 540, 553, 571, 573, 575, 580, 599, 600, 601, 602, 603, 625, 626
Lavrakite 550
Lazurite 19

Leaching 40, 56, 63, 91, 125, 170, 182, 196, 223, 254, 280, 317, 319, 352, 382, 401, 440, 447, 452, 528, 577, 578

Lead 36, 58, 80, 150, 218, 220, 223, 253, 258, 262, 263, 307, 353, 368, 401, 416, 467, 468, 469, 532, 545, 558, 562, 583, 588, 589, 620, 631

Ledge 87, 138, 368

Lee 47, 97, 98, 99, 208, 261, 442

Lemming 59, 319, 581

Lemur 320, 332

Lemuria 320

Lepidolite 320, 323, 487

Leucite 5, 15, 195, 361, 458

Levee 51, 65, 139, 448, 595, 624

Lherzolite 616

Liana 320, 470

Lias Clay 320

Liassic 321

Lichen 17, 103, 106, 156, 321, 325, 372, 420, 436, 581,

Light 22, 26, 30, 57, 64, 65, 67, 84, 103, 106, 111, 114, 120, 135, 161, 165, 175, 177, 180, 184, 200, 201, 202, 206, 218, 219, 262, 284, 288, 303, 317, 321, 329, 353, 361, 362, 374, 377, 380, 389, 392, 400, 403, 406, 436, 437, 441, 445, 456, 462, 474, 475, 476, 502, 503, 508, 520, 526, 527, 531, 534, 541, 547, 548, 555, 559, 562, 572, 573, 588, 600, 609, 621, 632, 633

Light Metals 351

Light Years 218, 316, 327, 353,

Lightning 141, 215, 287, 321, 388, 415, 564, 597

Lignite 66, 116, 184, 294, 321-322, 450

Lime 57, 85, 86, 93, 107, 144, 197, 232, 322, 368, 409, 440, 450, 451, 499, 607, 608

Limestone 12, 13, 15, 48, 79, 82, 85, 86, 88, 90, 93, 94, 95, 96, 99, 100, 101, 106, 108, 124, 126, 127, 133, 135, 138, 156, 165, 191, 192, 205, 206, 220, 226, 229, 239, 242, 254, 265, 289, 298, 301, 322, 328, 337, 339, 341, 342, 344, 355, 363, 394, 407, 410, 411, 424, 431, 433, 438, 440, 452, 459, 461, 479, 496, 513, 519, 520, 532, 534, 535, 538, 540, 546, 547, 574, 579, 583, 605, 606, 619, 627, 629, 631

Limonite 70, 125, 234, 236, 289, 323, 458

Lineament 323, 606

'Lines of Force' 207, 297, 323, 334, 335, 349, 547

Lipari 323

Liquid 32, 66, 71, 91, 125, 191, 200, 260, 275, 281, 287, 288, 296, 304, 317, 319, 362, 369, 372, 414, 418, 434, 442, 472, 522, 528, 536, 542, 545, 548, 593, 600, 607m 625

Liquid Petroleum Gas (LPG) 376

Lisbon Earthquake 323, 508

Lit-par-lit 323

Lithium 136, 181, 248, 263, 320, 323-324, 351, 355, 435, 495, 533, 571

Lithology 74, 344, 539, 578

Lithomarge 324

Lithosphere 141, 198, 324, 446, 541, 542

Little Dipper 174, 448, 590

'Little Ice Age' 112, 252, 325

'Living fossil' 119, 202, 267, 325, 336, 378, 404, 408, 484, 560, 580

Llanos 577

Load 16, 21, 75, 91, 124, 152, 154, 168, 198, 265, 282, 326, 328, 385, 539, 624

Loam 326

'Lobelia' 182, 303, 305, 326-327, 489

Lobster 37, 141, 574

Loch 229, 329

Locoweed 223, 509

Locusts 304, 327

Lode 16, 44, 96, 251, 327, 368, 370, 596

Lodestone 124, 327

Loess 280, 327, 428, 438, 476, 513, 624

Logging 217, 252, 340, 470, 529, 546, 577

Long Wave 98, 175, 180, 245, 311, 328, 493, 525, 573

Longitude 225, 286, 328, 350, 456, 567

Longitudinal Wave 529

Lopolith 217, 328, 383

Low Latitudes 17, 270, 286, 390, 428, 456, 528, 543, 562, 570, 596, 616, 617, 633

Low Pressure Area 29, 52, 144, 145, 164, 176, 188, 278, 329, 366, 380, 387, 456, 457, 504, 571, 579, 584, 605, 616

Low-grade 339, 352, 443, 458, 553, 596

Low-tide 51, 81, 129, 286, 343, 371, 565

Low-water 241, 348, 624, 481

Lowlands 71, 76, 77, 116, 205, 238, 242, 326, 329, 337, 348, 427, 438, 442, 471, 513, 515, 595, 606, 613

Luminescence 185, 436, 469, 534

Lunar (See Moon) 137, 247, 308, 316, 342, 374

Luster 36, 46, 108, 120, 267, 329, 351, 361, 398, 403, 429, 441, 460, 462, 532, 554, 583, 630

Lysocline 329

Magellanic Clouds 333, 535, 548

Magma 23, 39, 53, 54, 55, 74, 85, 100, 128, 131, 147, 157, 173, 177, 187, 190, 195, 240, 259, 268, 274, 279, 286, 298, 311, 327, 333, 341, 352, 353, 361 420, 426, 446, 451, 462, 477, 491, 518, 541, 544, 558, 600, 601, 602, 621, 625

Magnesite 94, 333

Magnesium 22, 26, 54, 65, 94, 95, 136, 149, 165, 170, 174, 177, 183, 191, 199. 217, 220, 260, 263, 279, 305, 324, 332, 333, 334, 355, 356, 361, 267, 399, 400, 406, 428, 435, 436, 460, 471, 473, 506, 510, 518, 517, 519, 527, 532, 554, 571, 630

Magnet 174, 200, 327, 334, 336

Magnetic Field 44, 61, 79, 116, 135, 174, 180, 200, 207, 272, 327, 334, 335, 336, 349, 419, 477, 502, 527, 530, 541, 547, 561, 582, 586, 594, 590

Magnetic Lines of Force 297, 323, 334, 335, 349, 547
Magnetic North 334
Magnetic Pole 10, 334, 335, 448
Magnetic Reversals 176, 335, 398, 496, 547
Magnetism 27, 135, 143, 174, 180, 192, 218, 309, 311, 334, 335, 336, 348, 383, 406, 410, 417, 419, 448, 451, 477, 506, 547, 626
Magnetite 27, 67, 135, 174, 183, 263, 289, 293, 306, 327, 336, 440, 455, 495, 499, 520, 598
Magnetosphere 224, 526, 527, 530, 594
Magnolia 186, 336, 543, 558
Mainland 129, 130, 332, 333, 482, 532, 533, 569, 576
Malachite 46, 132, 337
Malleable 85, 132, 333, 338, 351, 548
Mammal 70, 169, 178, 202, 278, 282, 306, 344, 350, 372, 418, 445, 451, 485, 521, 561, 573, 585, 590, 593, 598, 614
Mammoth 59, 211, 339
Mancos Shale 72
Manganese 21, 66, 68, 76, 85, 123, 125, 136, 154, 156, 217, 229, 236, 264, 268, 289, 291, 339-340, 374, 384, 389, 401, 422, 448, 455, 458, 474, 478, 517, 536, 544, 550, 605, 611, 619
Manganite 339
Mangrove 19, 118, 192, 251, 340, 384, 421
Mantle 39, 69, 131, 134, 138, 141, 143, 152, 160, 163, 164, 173, 177, 207, 226, 227, 240, 243, 268, 273, 278, 290, 298, 308, 324, 340-341, 333, 336, 341, 364, 400, 401, 405, 443, 446, 456, 479, 484, 485, 517, 521, 541, 557, 563, 573, 602, 616, 625
'Maquis' 106, 301, 342
Marble 12, 27, 43, 86, 97, 100, 336, 342, 352, 409, 473
Marcasite 349, 450, 460
Margin 226, 290, 342, 347, 351, 417
Marine 14, 28, 31, 32, 37, 43, 59, 70, 82, 85, 105, 117, 118, 119, 127, 137, 141, 150, 151, 154, 161, 162, 163, 176, 185, 194, 203, 204, 205, 206, 207, 208, 209, 211, 213, 221, 226, 248, 265, 270, 282, 284, 295, 297, 312, 314, 329, 343, 348, 378, 379, 385, 400, 404, 407, 409, 410, 419, 421, 423, 424, 427, 430, 440, 468, 474, 476, 468, 491, 492, 497, 507, 513, 515, 530, 533, 538, 540, 560, 572, 574, 593, 614, 633
Marine Layer 87, 208, 294
Mariposite 99, 510
Maritime Climate 386, 503, 504
Marker Bed 58, 209, 344, 407, 477
Marl 73, 119, 207, 247, 332, 344, 461, 478
Marlstone 303
Mars 39, 344, 591
Marsh 23, 62, 63, 67, 70, 109, 182, 192, 198, 238, 261, 344, 354, 362, 371, 382, 429, 456, 471, 495, 497, 512, 515, 522, 530, 549, 553, 578, 613, 614
Marsupial 344, 408, 511
Mass 27, 39, 43, 45, 106, 134, 136, 138, 141, 153, 157, 165, 172, 180, 216, 219, 237, 240,

Mass (continued) 242, 243, 247, 249, 263, 276, 281, 283, 285, 306, 311, 315, 318, 319, 331, 334, 342, 344, 345, 347, 357, 369, 379, 408, 418, 419, 424, 426, 428, 436, 341, 452, 458, 462, 470, 475, 485, 486, 497, 513, 525, 527, 534, 537, 589, 593, 594, 597
Massif 15, 164, 217, 307, 309, 316, 338, 345, 384, 483, 486, 564, 575, 629
Mastodon 339
Mat 191, 303, 474, 501, 531, 540, 577, 578, 607
Matrix 256, 435, 452, 525, 561, 563, 571
Mount Mazama (Ancient) 86, 137, 346, 407
Meadow 120, 163, 260, 423, 472, 543, 583, 596
Mean Free Path 347
Meander 75, 207, 236, 340, 347, 362, 405, 413, 414, 477, 613
Mechanical Force 78, 79, 134, 150, 151, 158, 184, 189, 280, 321, 428, 437, 529, 611
Medium-grained 162, 164, 198, 237, 239, 428, 561
Melange 348
Melt-freeze Cycle 201
Meltdown 107, 241
Melting Point 73, 103, 123, 207, 279, 300, 317, 444, 517, 581, 582
Meltwater 121, 203, 204, 243, 269, 280, 299, 302, 313, 342, 368, 382, 412, 429, 439, 502
Member 210, 221, 291, 348, 418
Membrane 120, 412
Mercury 43, 51, 52, 85, 96, 112, 203, 263, 349, 345, 464, 562
Meridian 46, 54, 88, 286, 328, 350, 423, 456, 567
Mesa 30, 83, 92, 156, 295, 350, 502
Mesosaurus 281
Mesosphere 42, 466, 539
Mesozoic Era 52, 102, 119, 138, 144, 188, 189, 204, 236, 297, 301, 305, 319, 336, 337, 350, 392, 434, 459, 485, 541, 561, 573, 585
Mesquite 350-351, 622
Meta-Sequoia 346-347
Metabolites 350, 351
Metal 14, 16, 18, 29, 35, 36, 39, 42, 54, 60, 63, 76, 79, 85, 92, 93, 94, 100, 102, 106, 107, 110, 112, 118, 119, 120, 123, 127, 132, 140, 181, 183, 192, 201, 205, 206, 212, 218, 219, 221, 222, 223, 225, 227, 234, 247, 259, 263, 268, 284, 289, 302, 304, 319, 323, 329, 334, 338, 339, 349, 351, 352, 355, 359, 372, 383, 388, 390, 401, 402, 435, 441, 444, 452, 458, 460, 461, 468, 472, 509, 515, 517, 519, 522, 528, 535, 536, 537, 544, 559, 568, 581, 588, 597, 615, 619, 631, 632
Metalloid 29, 36, 227, 351-352, 384, 390, 508, 509, 558, 572,
Metallurgical Spar 341
Metallurgy 82, 110, 145, 199, 206, 207, 224, 253, 304, 310, 340, 342, 353, 515, 582
Metamorphic Rocks 64, 352, 356, 360, 372, 406, 437, 438, 455, 462, 484, 488, 503, 507, 520, 521, 526, 563, 596, 622

Metamorphism 17, 22, 30, 36, 55, 70, **86, 89,** 94 95, 99, 112, 115, 126, 127, **128, 134,** 155, 177, 187, 194, 197, 203, 210, 220, **226,** 233, 247, 248, 259, 260, 267, 290, 291, **298,** 304, 316, 331, 336, 337, 355, 360, 368, **408,** 420, 437, 439, 458, 460, 462, 463, **476,** 481, 488, 490, 503, 507, 516, 520, 523, **596,** 600, 609

Metasediments 337, 338, 439, 589, 591

Metasomatism 248, 353, 435, 457

Metavolcanics 523

Metazoa 455

Meteor 122, 135, 288, 353, 389, 603, 619

Meteor Crater 97, 119, 353, 603, 619

Meteoric Water 353, 593

Meteorite 39, 57, 97, 110, 119, 123, 138, **265,** 281, 284, 328, 342, 353, 354, 383, 456, **486,** 544, 557, 619

Meteoroid 171, 354

Methane 201, 246, 297, 303, 354, 375, **380,** 416, 425, 499, 559, 590

Mica 64, 65, 74, 114, 180, 203, 232, 239, **248,** 280, 291, 315, 320, 332, 352, 355-356, **361,** 367, 371, 426, 435, 437, 452, 455, **484, 487,** 503, 517, 588, 598

Micaschist 356, 503

Micaceous 247, 437, 598

Microcline 36, 197, 198, 233, 239, 357, **463,** 480, 495, 550

Microcontinent 357, 521

Microlite 157

Microwave 36, 357, 587

Mid-Atlantic Rift 42, 244, 275, 278, 358, 575, 612

Mid-Continent Rift, Upper Peninsula 258

Mid-Latitudes 129, 131, 155, 174, 176, **257,** 347, 449, 456, 479, 543, 558, 610

Mid-Ocean Ridge and Rift (See Global Rift) 295, 358, 505, 603

Mid-Pacific Rift 358-359

Migma 359

Migmatite 23, 359

Migration 38, 59, 65, 92, 207, 300, 314, **319,** 408, 532, 580, 590, 633

Milky Way Galaxy 25, 62, 67, 218, 333, **359,** 377, 441, 527, 534, 546, 586, 590

Mineralization 13, 98, 108, 124, 127, 136, **154,** 187, 208, 218, 226, 236, 258, 268, 274, **281,** 302, 327, 363, 370, 412, 413, 447, 452, **478,** 492, 501, 520, 536, 564, 585, 594, 633

Mini-Ice Age 275, 445, 448, 547, 610

Miocene Epoch 50, 73, 123, 186, 318, 379, **406,** 446, 461, 561, 599

Mirage 197, 361-362

Mississippi Flyway 207

Mississippian Period 95, 157, 363, 419, **427,** 512

Mist 316, 327, 590, 615

Mobile Belt 9, 138, 229, 363

Mohave Lake (Pleistocene) 364

Moh's Scale 22, 30, 35, 86, 98, 132, 187, **234,** 260, 310, 364, 451, 519, 532, 583, 619, 630

Molasse 226, 365

Molecule 13, 22, 45, 50, 81, 91, 106, 112, 114, 116, 120, 124, 142, 144, 161, 164, 165, 221, 246, 263, 266, 283, 287, 289, 347, 363, 365, 406, 415, 427, 433, 450, 457, 502, 518, 528, 590, 631

Mollusk 22, 26, 33, 66, 94, 221, 365, 379, 425, 426, 513, 515

Molten 130, 137, 173, 179, 221, 268, 279, 286, 302, 319, 333, 341, 357, 420, 426, 439, 442, 462, 484, 557, 580, 598

Molybdenite 98

Molybdenum 98, 248, 545, 556, 568, 620

Monadnock 45, 124, 365

Monazite 67, 102, 335, 365-366, 472, 534, 563, 621, 622, 626

Monocotyledon 138

Monocline 208

Monoclinic Crystal System 142, 197, 411

Monsoon 150, 167, 284, 286, 305, 332, 348, 366, 382, 391, 471, 493, 570, 576, 577, 613, 617

Montmorillonite 53, 59, 215, 366-367, 476, 598

Monzonite 367, 550

Moon 27, 90, 113, 119, 127, 134, 137, 138, 177, 247, 258, 281, 342, 367, 377, 428, 441, 455, 551, 564, 565

Moons 258, 281, 297, 380, 501, 590

Moonstone 198, 411

Moraine 92, 168, 231, 241, 243, 269, 313, 368, 412, 549, 587, 594

Morganite 61

Mosquito 80, 149, 238, 566, 607

Moss 17, 26, 70, 81, 106, 314, 372, 531, 581

Mother Lode 235, 327, 368, 510, 596

Mother-of-Pearl 33, 66, 379, 425

Mounds 170, 209, 238, 420, 428, 446, 550

Mountain Building (See Orogeny) 45, 111, 138, 155, 158, 186, 187, 208, 226, 240, 264, 271, 305, 316, 411, 439, 479, 514, 560, 611

Mouth 22, 79, 121, 126, 152, 259, 270, 289, 291, 343, 370, 371, 563, 626, 630, 633

Mud 45, 51, 58, 59, 67, 68, 73, 79, 112, 113, 135, 159, 167, 192, 233, 245, 247, 257, 269, 302, 312, 315, 340, 354, 361, 368, 370, 371, 372, 381, 387, 394, 400, 401, 409, 426, 437, 444, 445, 449, 473, 483, 494, 498, 511, 519, 522, 539, 540, 599, 624, 630, 631

Mudflats 371, 445, 449, 630

Mudflow 312, 371, 386, 445, 494, 599, 602

Mudstone 35, 226, 521

Muscovite 5, 239, 248, 349, 355, 365, 435

Muskeg 344, 371, 554, 581

Mutation 372

Mutualism 321, 372

Mylonite 372

Nacre 379, 425

Nannofossils 163, 455

Nannoplankton 118, 374

Nappe 374, 618

Narrows 320, 374, 472

Natrolite 375

Natural Gas 28, 49, 96, 140, 184, 208, 217, 221, 263, 272, 288, 304, 322, 354, 362, 368, 371, 375-376, 385, 418, 431, 432, 433, 434, 440, 471, 515, 538, 623

Natural Selection 146, 377, 411

Nautiloids 88

Nautilus 22, 101, 337

Navigation 124, 126, 167, 174, 243, 277, 296, 328, 334, 448, 483, 591

Neap Tide 286, 377, 565

Nearshore 325, 423

Nebula 359, 377

Needle Peak 108, 112, 369, 439

Needleleaf Forest 377

Needles 159, 200, 281, 334, 352, 377, 378, 488, 523, 554

Nekton 379

Neodymium 472

Neogene 379, 446

Neolithic Age 266, 293, 379

Neon 136, 283, 379, 389

Neopilina Galathea 379

Nepheline 5, 15, 96, 198, 293, 361, 379-380, 458

Nepheline Syenite 334, 379-380

Nephrite 293, 380

Neptune 193, 297, 300, 380

Neritic Zone 185, 380

Nesting 38, 162, 478, 540

Neutrino 61, 148, 257, 320, 350, 380, 532, 535, 548

Neutron 17, 43, 61, 65, 73, 93, 104, 157, 203, 263, 291, 380, 393, 394, 586, 589,

Neutron Star 137, 380, 459

Neve 381, 523

Niccolite 118

Niche 177, 377, 383, 509

Nickel 45, 85, 90, 103, 118, 134, 173, 199, 220, 236, 237, 244, 247, 248, 258, 262, 263, 284, 306, 307, 318, 328, 336, 340, 353, 382, 383-384, 401, 428, 441, 444, 455, 515, 516, 534, 544, 546, 579, 615, 632

Nimbostratus 386

Niobates 555

Niobium 95, 123, 145, 247, 334, 369, 387-388, 555, 556, 568

Nitrates 22, 87, 260, 287, 388, 389, 400, 432, 449, 471, 497, 588

Nitric Acid 22, 31, 388, 389

Nitrite 471

Nitrogen 4, 5, 11, 14, 22, 42, 64, 73, 80, 94, 95, 106, 136, 153, 161, 178, 200, 220, 246, 250, 260, 263, 287, 321, 382, 388, 389, 404, 415, 416, 435, 449, 466, 472, 590

Nitrous Oxide 523

Noble Gases 36, 283, 379, 389, 621

Noctilucent Clouds 389

Nodules 68, 125, 204, 264, 340, 374, 384, 389, 401, 478, 491, 516, 558

Nordmarkite 550

North American Plate 97, 195, 348, 391, 443, 498, 557

North Star 124, 174, 448, 590, 591

Northern Lights 44, 526, 594

Notch 117, 610, 618

Nova 392

Nuclear 61, 83, 94, 103, 104, 107, 131, 148, 157, 184, 196, 203, 213, 240, 241, 263, 272, 287, 288, 287, 290, 309, 324, 380, 388, 392, 393, 424, 439, 465, 468, 508, 534, 541, 575, 582, 589, 625

'Nuclear Winter' 171, 288, 302, 308, 387, 393

Nucleation 116, 131, 170, 271, 382, 393, 469, 516

Nuclei 16, 43, 48, 61, 106, 125, 136, 180, 181, 203, 211, 263, 335, 345, 389, 392, 393, 394, 407, 409, 458, 467, 502, 525, 541

Nuclide 143, 148, 394, 466, 563, 574, 589

Nuee Ardente 394

Nummulite 394

Nutrients 22, 24, 29, 33, 40, 90, 91, 103, 115, 116, 161, 162, 169, 191, 196, 223, 251, 270, 271, 273, 287, 294, 308, 309, 326, 341, 351, 374, 385, 395, 400, 406, 436, 577, 578, 588, 602

Oasis 15, 37, 148, 338, 342, 376, 384, 385, 397, 420, 461, 493, 502, 554, 558, 564, 567

Obsidian 5, 22, 29, 30, 137, 231, 232, 372, 398, 426, 459, 480, 557

Ocean Floor 35, 46, 53, 60, 69, 86, 104, 139, 141, 159, 161, 175, 176, 209, 212, 218, 225, 254, 276, 279, 290, 307, 319, 329, 343, 346, 357, 358, 359, 372, 398, 400, 401, 419, 422, 442, 452, 481, 533, 542, 544, 575, 613

Ocher 264, 285, 402, 408

Ocotillo 401, 402, 622

Octahedral 114, 159, 206, 550,

Octopus 101, 531

Offshore 19, 41, 130, 152, 163, 168, 208, 239, 270, 286, 362, 374, 402-403, 404, 421, 426, 440, 482, 499, 542, 544, 588, 616

Ogive 403, 450

Oil (See also Petroleum) 47, 49, 52, 53, 71, 78, 90, 96, 98, 102, 109, 140, 167, 184, 211, 212, 243, 262, 272, 280, 288, 296, 304, 331, 362, 368, 376, 391, 393, 398, 402, 403-404, 413, 430, 431, 434, 440, 444, 479, 480, 487, 488, 491, 496, 501, 502, 506, 508, 511, 515, 528, 538, 556, 570, 593, 594, 613, 616

Oilfields 49, 184, 283, 375, 402, 487, 572

Oil Shale 66, 78, 149, 184, 245, 272, 303, 376, 403-404, 411, 433, 556, 570

Oil Spill 268, 403, 404, 431, 593

Old age (Geomorphic) 16, 199, 341, 397, 468

Oligoclase 351

Oligocene Epoch 320, 406, 473, 561

Olivine 53, 98, 62, 164, 170, 217, 220, 318, 361, 383, 400, 406, 428, 438, 460, 563

Onshore 98, 343, 362, 404, 434, 482, 616

Onyx 407, 57363

Oolites 264, 407, 440

Oort Cloud 407

Ooze 68, 86, 119, 151, 161, 209, 233, 245, 394, 400, 401, 407, 426, 442, 458, 468

Opal 22, 105, 120, 142, 353, 408, 468, 516, 517, 574
Opalescence 411
Ophiolite 408, 439, 575
Ophir 234, 306, 408
Ophitic texture 158, 408
Optics 36, 158, 197, 258, 262, 360, 392, 434, 444, 448, 472, 562
Orbit 16, 30, 39, 42, 111, 123, 173, 174, 177, 180, 181, 199, 258, 272, 335, 359, 365, 367, 380, 393, 409, 419, 428, 429, 441, 448, 455, 461, 462, 501, 506, 527, 534, 546, 586, 590
'Orbital Eccentricity 174, 275
Orchid 187, 261, 279, 378, 379, 409
Order 65, 178, 202, 306, 557, 558, 562
Ordovician Period 66, 110, 138, 343, 409-410, 419, 439, 492, 518, 540
Organisms 14, 21, 23, 25, 37, 43, 59, 63, 64, 67, 70, 81, 82, 86, 93, 112, 118, 120, 123, 124, 126, 133, 144, 145, 150, 151, 156, 160, 162, 177, 178, 191, 192, 204, 205, 208, 209, 211, 222, 257, 268, 272, 297, 322, 354, 372, 374, 379, 394, 395, 400, 407, 409, 411, 426, 441, 451, 457, 468, 475, 502, 519, 524, 533, 574, 578, 588, 593, 596, 633
Orogeny 31, 87, 88, 112, 157, 187, 188, 189, 271, 298, 305, 410, 411, 419, 479, 513, 561
Ortho-pyroxene 563
Orthoclase 33, 36, 74, 142, 197, 198, 233, 364, 379, 411, 412, 463, 480, 550
Orthogenesis 411
Orthorhombic 33, 142, 570
Oscillations 180, 213, 246, 508, 534, 609
Osmium 444
Osmosis 412, 512
Ostracod 297, 519
Outback 15, 82, 412
Outcrop 89, 105, 198, 203, 240, 284, 308, 402, 412
Outer Shell 93, 103, 137, 180, 181, 199, 259, 266, 287, 451, 487
Outflow 252, 391, 555, 599
Outlet 32, 149, 179, 212, 312, 313, 332, 373, 389, 479, 497, 557, 600
Outlier 569
Outwash 231, 412, 428, 458
Overburden 68, 296, 308, 406, 410, 412, 540, 587
Overthrust 199, 208, 307, 413, 434, 563
Overturn 131, 135, 191, 224, 272, 447, 473, 507, 538, 618
Oxbow 346, 347, 413, 406
Oxidation 133, 185, 201, 274, 298, 414, 425, 475, 491, 551, 578, 607, 620, 633
Oxygen 11, 14, 20, 22, 23, 42, 43, 63, 64, 69, 70, 71, 76, 93, 94, 95, 106, 110, 116, 124, 133, 136, 137, 144, 158, 161, 178, 185, 191, 214, 221, 232, 268, 272, 283, 287, 289, 303, 314, 323, 324, 355, 388, 399, 414, 415, 437, 438, 442, 474, 517, 518, 545, 547, 577, 579, 606, 614
Oxygenation 303, 551
Oysters 31, 414, 425

Ozone 80, 107, 110, 111, 415-416, 444, 449, 579
Ozone Layer 42, 80, 107, 110, 111, 206, 285, 388, 415, 416, 524, 579, 610

P-wave 175, 193, 311, 417, 491, 508, 512
Pacific Plate 59, 108, 112, 195, 261, 262, 293, 348, 391, 417, 443, 498, 542, 557, 602, 615
Pacific Rim 25, 112, 134, 191, 261, 363
Pack Ice 35, 204, 418, 505, 600, 611
Paddy 14, 31, 418, 472
Pahoehoe 54, 138, 418
Palagonite 53
Palearctic 418
Paleocene Epoch 27, 138, 163, 186, 418, 561
Paleochadean Sea 104
Paleoclimate 344, 419, 421, 573
Paleomagnetism 143, 225, 419, 477
Paleozoic Era 18, 25, 31, 34, 37, 44, 72, 88, 95, 116, 127, 129, 130, 169, 176, 186, 188, 189, 209, 230, 241, 281, 329, 334, 338, 343, 350, 359, 363, 368, 392, 409, 411, 419, 420, 427, 430, 431, 434, 479, 561, 564, 574, 591, 596
Palingenesis 23, 420
Palladium 436, 544
Pallasite 353
Palm 19, 50, 91, 102, 120, 144, 148, 238, 261, 279, 378, 397, 418, 420, 492, 511, 558, 564, 617
Palsas 420, 428
Paludal 185, 340
Palynology 420-421
Pampas 421, 441, 529
Pangaea 1, 129, 137, 162, 260, 268, 275, 298, 317, 421-422, 431, 574, 612
Panthalassa Ocean 422
Papyrus 422, 489, 544
Parallel 54, 240, 244, 423, 498, 503, 506, 540, 508, 540, 565, 588, 614
Paramos 423
Parasite 22, 48, 81, 208, 209, 503
Particle 27, 28, 35, 36, 39, 43, 44, 45, 52, 57, 61, 73, 79, 81, 99, 106, 111, 116, 120, 123, 131, 135, 136, 137, 143, 145, 150, 151, 170, 171, 180, 196, 197, 200, 203, 219, 222, 224, 236, 237, 257, 260, 263, 300, 314, 320, 324, 327, 334, 345, 347, 348, 350, 367, 370, 377, 380, 389, 393, 394, 407, 408, 424, 427, 436, 442, 452, 459, 458, 461, 462, 463, 467, 477, 497, 499, 503, 507, 512, 518, 522, 523, 525, 527, 528, 530, 532, 534, 536, 539, 541, 547, 589, 594, 608, 609, 618
Particulate 116, 171, 196, 207, 243, 262, 288, 308, 393 449, 520, 522, 523, 527, 539, 559, 562, 602, 471, 478, 541, 549, 577, 597
Patina 156, 157, 425
Pavement 39, 118, 156, 203, 229, 476, 508, 521
Pearl 31, 399, 425
Peat 70, 116, 117, 184, 198, 211, 261, 321, 420, 425, 531, 580

Pebble 52, 113, 118, 125, 153, 156, 158, 229, 242, 280, 312, 412, 414, 458, 487, 488, 507, 5144, 565, 587, 589, 612
Pediment 78, 156, 426, 512, 554
Pediplain 156, 284, 365, 426
Pegmatite 23, 30, 32, 61, 67, 72. 97, 103, 123, 161, 187, 197, 233, 239, 323, 337, 370, 371, 387, 388, 426, 427, 487, 500, 533, 555, 568, 570, 571, 589, 619
Pelagic 50, 69, 83, 233, 426
Pelecypod 66, 426
Peneplain 14, 44, 90, 92, 134, 154, 170, 251, 316, 365, 426, 427
Penetration 30, 219, 222, 226, 231, 283, 286, 287, 321, 359, 374, 380, 400, 441, 467, 494, 527, 559, 588, 620
Penguins 195-196, 270, 309
Pennsylvanian Period 82, 95, 171, 187, 211, 363, 419, 427-428, 469, 512
Pentlandite 383
Perched Water 326, 428
Peridot 428
Peridotite 196, 305, 383, 400, 405, 406, 408, 428, 501
Perigee 428
Periglacial 276, 304, 420, 428, 429, 518, 556, 599
Perihelion 429
Periodic Table 6, 178, 257, 259, 390, 429, 500
Periodicity 170, 171, 228, 419, 429, 445, 480
Perlite 429
Permafrost 118, 190, 222, 249, 277, 320, 331, 339, 344, 371, 420, 428, 429-430, 439, 450, 451, 514, 515, 528, 553, 580, 581, 591, 623, 631
Permeability 32, 37, 148, 193, 279, 327, 430, 433, 607, 608, 633
Permian Period 95, 102, 116, 144, 171, 233, 239, 281, 301, 318, 420, 427, 430-431, 452, 479, 531, 546, 566, 574, 580, 612
Perovskite 174, 555
Petrified 108, 211, 353, 432, 517
Petrochemicals 268, 433
Petroleum 12, 13, 28, 39, 51, 59, 66, 90, 127, 140, 154, 160, 163, 184, 193, 196, 209, 217, 221, 272, 288, 295, 304, 315, 322, 332, 342, 355, 376, 385, 403, 404, 418, 420, 431, 432, 433-434, 440, 442, 479, 496, 511, 543, 545, 556, 572, 597, 612, 631
Petrology 331, 434
pH 5, 15, 107, 158, 179, 197, 332, 334, 434, 436, 454
Phaneritic 434, 561
Phanerozoic Eon 141, 186, 434, 457
Phenocryst 53, 162, 435, 451, 452, 561, 621
Phillipsite 53, 435, 550
Phloem 81, 435, 622
Phlogopite 355, 435, 598
Phonolite 380
Phosphates 30, 88, 95, 109, 151, 200, 247, 254, 293, 301, 322, 340, 344, 360, 362, 365, 368, 370, 391, 400, 401, 405, 407, 428, 432, 435-436, 440, 461, 492, 495, 516, 522, 583, 588, 621, 632

Phosphorescent 64, 162, 436
Phosphorite 322, 435, 436, 437, 455
Phosphorus 64, 250, 308, 436, 517, 588
Photochemical Effect 80, 355, 388, 416, 523
Photon 27, 42, 93, 136, 257, 317, 436, 461, 462
Photosynthesis 30, 69, 92, 93, 110, 133, 162, 185, 202, 246, 303, 316, 400, 437, 438, 441, 442, 452, 474, 551, 633
Phreatic 249, 331, 437
Phreatophyte 437
Phyllites 229, 437
Phytoplankton 24, 94, 161, 349, 374, 400, 436, 438, 441, 633
Picrite 438
Piedmont 30, 41, 196, 337, 438
Piezo-electricity 175, 438-439, 463
Pigeonite 563
Pillar 68, 123, 201
Pillow Lava 53, 54, 218, 247, 408, 418, 439, 575, 591
Pine (See Conifer) 52, 79, 106, 127, 158, 192, 199, 294, 415, 432, 489, 503, 513, 530, 543, 553, 558, 573, 606
Pingo 249, 331, 428, 439, 451
Pinnacle 203, 239, 301, 302, 315, 345, 369, 439-440, 501, 502, 509, 580, 601
Pipes 78, 90, 95, 98, 159, 177, 251, 294, 305, 315, 335, 440, 529, 601, 623
Pipeline 13, 32, 122, 375, 385, 439, 440, 522, 526, 572
Pisolite 407, 440
Pitchblende 468, 588
Pitchstone 231
Plagioclase 25, 27, 53, 147, 158, 162, 197, 217, 239, 240, 31, 361, 408, 440-441, 463
Planation 611
Planet 30, 39, 62, 64, 69, 76, 111, 115, 123, 127, 152, 173, 174, 177, 180, 187, 193, 196, 199, 218, 223, 224, 225, 246, 262, 273, 281, 297, 299, 344, 367, 380, 407, 415, 441, 450, 482, 501, 527, 534, 585, 586, 589, 597-598, 606, 610, 611, 618
Plankton 24, 70, 85, 132, 149, 159, 160, 202, 209, 308, 309, 379, 431, 441, 442, 459, 468, 474, 475, 507, 514, 533, 550, 588, 614
Plasma 49, 284, 442, 527, 530, 594
Plastic 14, 39, 215, 230, 341, 442, 479, 496, 517, 527, 539
Plate Tectonics 9, 16, 17, 27, 58, 96, 97, 101, 104, 112, 129, 130, 141, 187, 208, 225, 226, 229, 232, 235, 254, 268, 271, 279, 288, 290, 295, 401, 411, 417, 443, 446, 481, 494, 505, 521, 540, 542, 544, 557, 572
Platinum 31, 54, 89, 222, 248, 288, 333, 349, 381, 428, 444, 455, 516, 544, 556, 615
Platypus 169, 445
Playa 24, 328, 328, 370, 438, 445, 495
Pleistocene Epoch 16, 59, 71, 97, 104, 116, 121, 163, 189, 198, 230, 231, 243, 245, 275, 276, 283, 302, 313, 317, 339, 343, 347, 386, 406, 441, 445, 446, 447, 463, 465, 480, 491, 492, 497, 514, 548, 593, 599, 605, 627
Plesiosaurus 274
Plinthite 445

Pliocene Epoch 73, 163, 318, 379, 404, **446**

Plucking 35, 108, 112, 119, 267, 345, **369, 394,** 446, 450, 454, 502, 585

Plug 69, 95, 109, 162, 427, 446, 494, 601

Plume 261, 268, 290, 446, 447, 521, 574, **588,** 625

Pluto 123

Pluton 63, 162, 269, 273, 320, 330, 426, **446,** 452, 484, 575

Plutonic Rocks (See Igneous Rocks) 447, 545, 586

Plutonium 107, 241, 281, 447

Poison 169, 272, 341, 348, 388, 405, 450, 599, 622

Polar Airmass 12

Polar Easterlies 447, 617

Polar Front 176, 447

Polar Trough 176

Polar Wandering 336, 448, 561

Polaris 447, 455, 590, 591

Polarity 175, 327, 335, 336, 450, 506, 547

Poles 29, 42, 134, 142, 170, 173, 187, 242, 276, 318, 328, 333, 334, 335, 350, 419, 423, 447, 448, 456, 527, 561, 562, 567, 579, 594. 610, 617

Pollen 51, 65, 146, 154, 222, 420, 421, 448, 483, 522, 529, 617,

Pollucite 103, 487

Pollution 11, 32, 63, 73, 106, 149, 189, 191, 200, 235, 236, 243, 244, 283, 287, 294, 339, 344, 349, 372, 407, 414, 415, 416, 449, 478, 545-546, 559, 562, 590, 607, 631

Polonium 469, 588, 589

Polygon 104, 229, 230, 249, 344, 367, 370, 444, 449-450, 581 Polymer 303, 433, 442, 450, 516, 517, 618, 619

Polyp 25, 119, 450, 475

Pond 149, 192, 202, 238, 344, 450, 474, 495, 526, 527, 627

Pool 42, 221, 226, 247, 302, 403, 449, 461, 474, 541

Population 47, 62, 91, 97, 101, 157, 168, 178, 184, 189, 200, 202, 209, 210, 220, 228, 261, 270, 293, 320, 339, 372, 377, 385, 397, 408, 413, 449, 450, 451, 453, 489, 500, 503, 510, 515, 520, 523, 530, 558, 559, 563, 567, 575, 580, 590, 600

Pore Spaces 92, 127, 271, 350, 365, 428, 430, 437, 451, 608, 630, 630, 633

Porifera 26, 451, 533

Porosity 124, 279, 296, 308, 319, 327, 328, 411, 412, 430, 433, 451, 479, 497, 538, 607, 631

Porphyry 25, 73, 90, 160, 274, 301, 304, 319, 408, 435, 451-452, 454, 480, 561

Poseidon Sea 233, 452

Positron 27, 61, 136, 452

Potash 18, 90, 149, 162, 197, 247, 250, 371, 379, 430, 431, 452- 453, 550, 571

Potassium 13, 14, 15, 18, 36, 47, 64, 143, 183, 191, 197, 200, 232, 247, 280, 299, 308, 320, 324, 351, 355, 357, 361, 367, 369, 371, 399,

Potassium (continued) 411, 435, 452, 453, 466, 467, 471, 487, 506, 550, 599, 630

Potential 175, 179, 181, 183, 184, 402

Pothole 446, 453-454

Power (See Energy) 69, 213, 214, 227, 291, 324, 346, 388, 485, 526, 546, 589, 603, 618

Prairie 108, 331, 454, 525, 535, 553, 610

Precambrian Era 13, 14, 16, 24, 30, 31, 34, 52, 69, 72, 79, 84, 88, 89, 90, 97, 111, 121, 130, 132, 138, 139, 141, 144, 159, 161, 179, 186, 188, 191, 198, 203, 204, 211, 217, 224, 226, 229, 230, 234, 239, 247, 248, 249, 251, 253, 271, 275, 289, 291, 294, 306, 311, 317, 322, 331, 337, 338, 346, 363, 365, 368, 371, 373, 381, 410, 414, 419, 422, 426, 430, 437, 454, 455, 457, 467, 475, 486, 487, 492, 493, 513, 533, 540, 561, 564, 596, 600, 611, 619

Precession 173-174, 255, 275, 455

Present 112, 162, 186, 189, 209, 215, 224, 233, 251, 266, 275, 281, 426, 457, 468, 471, 492, 497, 538, 611

Primate 306, 320

Prism 46, 130, 267, 294, 456, 457, 470, 476

Profile 182, 188, 199, 237, 244, 260, 267, 274, 280, 286, 318, 324, 414, 417, 429, 446, 457, 475, 476, 491, 524, 525, 528, 562, 594

Prospect 360, 402, 410, 457, 614

Proterozoic Era 34, 87, 90, 161, 188, 208, 209, 229, 240, 271, 305, 337, 434, 439, 457-458

Proton 17, 28, 43, 52, 61, 66, 92, 136, 157, 199, 219, 257, 272, 291, 380, 393, 394, 458, 462, 525, 527, 530, 532, 535, 586, 589

Protozoa 22, 26, 206, 374, 458, 468

Psammite 458, 561

Psilomelane 339

Pteridophyte 458-459

Pterosauria 459

Puddingstone 125, 459, 487

Pulaskite 550

Pulsar 459, 466

Pumice 5, 108, 136, 231, 308, 371, 459, 471, 480, 500, 522, 545, 580, 598, 599

Pycnocline 460

Pyrite 41, 132, 289, 304, 316, 323, 349, 369, 383, 408, 414, 437, 450, 458, 460, 575

Pyrochlore 123, 337, 370, 387, 555, 629

Pyroclastics 29, 38, 110, 136, 176, 187, 279, 308, 460, 494, 539, 559, 569, 579, 593

Pyrolusite 339

Pyrophyllite 460

Pyroxene 22, 27, 43, 53, 74, 158, 164, 174, 244, 263, 293, 332, 380, 428, 460, 517, 563

Pyrrhotiite 336, 383

Quadrupeds 320

Quantum 339, 436, 441, 461, 462

Quark 73, 416, 462

Quarry 209, 300, 360, 462, 401, 454, 528, 550, 573

QUASAR (Quasi-stellar Radio Sources) 463, 466

Quartz 15, 21, 23, 25, 30, 57, 58, 74, 85, 105,
    108, 113, 119, 140, 142, 162, 164, 169, 183,
    197, 198, 212, 217, 223, 229, 233, 239, 240,
    248, 278, 280, 281, 289, 291, 294, 327, 349,
    361, 364, 367, 368, 379, 407, 426, 438, 446,
    462-463, 475, 480, 484, 488, 492, 499, 504,
    516, 517, 550, 574, 596
Quartz Monzonite 367, 463
Quartzite 92, 204, 260, 309, 352, 462, 463, 476,
    481
Quartzose 226, 291, 327
Quaternary Period 73, 101, 338, 379, 445, 461,
    463, 560, 569
Quayule 247-248
Quick clay 355, 464, 513
Quick sand 464
Quicksilver 464

Rad 457, 465, 621
Radiation 13, 17, 42, 47, 51, 57, 61, 66, 77,
    103, 105, 107, 108, 116, 123, 135, 158, 170,
    174, 180, 191, 218, 220, 244, 245, 246,
    283, 284, 287, 297, 299, 317, 318, 321, 328,
    334, 335, 344, 376, 377, 415, 436, 438, 463,
    465, 466, 468, 469, 477, 485, 503, 506,
    514, 523, 525, 530, 535, 541, 547, 558, 572,
    579, 582, 586, 587, 594, 621
Radiation Shield 61, 215, 287, 334, 415, 416
Radio 180, 195, 218, 287, 430, 459, 463, 465,
    466, 526, 547, 609
Radioactive Dating 31, 111, 135, 157, 223,
    232, 247, 306, 466- 467, 487, 538, 573, 595,
    599
Radioactivity 47, 52, 61, 66, 67, 70, 77, 94,
    103, 104, 107, 108, 118, 131, 139, 143, 148,
    150, 155, 196, 207, 212, 221-222, 226, 241,
    248, 258, 259, 262, 263, 269, 276, 287, 291,
    297, 334, 344, 351, 361, 372, 376, 393, 457,
    466, 467, 468, 472, 484, 487, 502, 526, 563,
    575, 589, 622
Radiolaria 105, 357, 401, 407, 458, 468, 482,
    513, 531
Radium 143, 468-469, 588, 589
Radon 175, 223, 283, 389, 421, 469, 589
Rafting 16, 469, 549
Railway 77, 109, 217, 234, 332, 515, 572, 618,
    626
Raindrops 386, 469, 470, 521
Rainforest 19, 33, 34, 71, 76, 77, 82, 89, 91,
    109, 116, 126, 151, 178, 209, 213, 215, 228,
    251, 252, 253, 261, 262, 282, 291, 294, 297,
    299, 326, 363, 366, 381, 409, 431, 442,
    458, 470, 509, 511, 516, 521, 522, 529, 531,
    533, 543, 558, 565, 572, 576-577, 578, 586,
    596, 597, 613
Rainwater 82, 87, 137, 279, 339, 470-471, 490,
    575, 578
Rainy Season 183, 238, 241, 279, 341, 394,
    413, 488, 510, 515, 578
Range (See Pasture) 20, 103, 241, 306, 326,
    339, 404, 470 Rapids 19, 97, 147, 332, 363,
    374, 386, 407, 472, 514, 622, 626, 630

Rare Earths 95, 96, 102, 181, 217, 308, 332,
    334, 365-366, 369, 434, 449, 472-473, 587,
    621, 626
Ravine 147, 169, 260, 473
Rays (See Radiation) 44, 99, 164, 173, 184,
    206, 258, 284, 528, 608
Reaction 104, 123, 132, 148, 180, 205, 263,
    272, 281, 309, 320, 333, 352, 379, 401, 415,
    424, 435, 475, 488, 519, 524, 541, 546, 589,
    593, 636
Reactor 79, 106, 107, 130, 240, 241, 263, 380,
    439, 447, 525, 563, 575, 625
Rebound 49, 117, 160, 165, 183, 199, 226, 277,
    296, 471, 505
Recharge 214, 326, 392
Recent Epoch 16, 45, 52, 67, 73, 88, 116, 126,
    177, 186, 203, 224, 266, 275, 302, 337, 341,
    347, 354, 355, 411, 422, 441, 445, 463, 475,
    491, 538, 611
Reclamation 291, 439, 540, 562, 633, 634
Recrystallization 271, 342, 381, 406, 495, 545
Red Mud 473
Red Sea Rift 481
Red Shift 463, 474
Red Tide 14, 160, 387, 473, 474-475
Redbeds 157, 475, 479, 574
Reduction 179, 305, 312, 475, 578, 607, 633
Redwoods 79, 378, 390, 432, 470, 509
Reeds 314, 344, 422, 456, 489, 512, 571
Reefs 43, 52, 59, 63, 64, 99, 120, 132, 209, 235,
    310, 312, 322, 365, 370, 409, 410-411, 421,
    426, 430, 431, 444, 455, 466, 474, 475, 491,
    492, 507, 511, 519, 533, 535, 538, 540, 544,
    547, 551, 558, 583, 593, 618
Refining 140, 403, 433, 444, 513
Reflection 13, 287, 329, 362, 389, 470, 475,
    559, 585, 631
Reforestation 41, 46, 77, 476
Refraction 65, 329, 468, 470, 476, 618, 632
Refractories 110, 111, 201, 300, 310, 334, 406,
    460, 632
Refreezing 45, 249, 253, 278, 523, 623, 631
Refuge 218, 344, 448, 499
Refuse 150, 262
Reg 156, 476
Regeneration 309, 420, 470, 478, 578
Regolith 3, 18, 56, 414, 432, 476, 524, 527
Regression 254, 343, 423, 476, 484, 507, 508,
    519, 615
Rejuvenation 60, 172, 185, 236, 413, 427, 477,
    509
Relative Humidity 155, 158, 270, 477
Relict 470, 521, 560
Relief 28, 44, 99, 117, 134, 142, 155, 156, 163,
    174, 181, 182, 189, 225, 259, 286, 296, 315,
    326, 327, 369, 401, 402, 417, 439, 441, 443,
    458, 477, 481, 513, 535, 553, 560, 578, 588,
    605, 611
REM (Roentgen Equivalent Man) 135, 376,
    465, 477, 526
Remote Sensing 224, 225, 477-478, 492, 596
Reniform 337, 478

Replacement 26, 90, 108, 109, 164, 165, 183, 206, 211, 401, 407, 432, 458, 478, 487, 517, 520, 543, 568, 588, 603

Replenishment 212, 250, 375, 412, 413, 428, 523, 575

Reproduction 196, 309, 413, 492, 530, 533, 566

Reptile 80, 162, 169, 189, 192, 238, 278, 281, 297, 308, 350, 400, 408, 431, 459, 470, 478, 494, 531, 562, 574, 580, 585

Reservoir 47, 160, 191, 210, 213, 322, 331, 342, 355, 362, 374, 391, 399, 428, 430, 431, 479, 493, 506, 511, 518, 523, 575, 614

Residue 206, 262, 317, 473, 556, 598

Resin 21, 66, 250, 442, 479, 513, 530

Resistance 166, 417, 421, 444, 517, 608

Resistant 141, 193, 204, 228, 236, 265, 350, 365, 462, 481, 482, 503, 542, 548, 553, 580, 614

Resources 12, 19, 71, 149, 184, 190, 213, 227, 304, 375, 390, 461, 465, 471, 478, 501, 620, 625, 632

Respiration 93, 437

Retort 78, 404

Retreat 114, 118, 122, 212, 230, 272, 348, 368, 370, 476, 504, 518, 547

Reversals 173, 225, 286, 317, 325, 335, 336, 348, 429, 506, 547, 618

Reverse Fault 413, 479, 563

Reverse Osmosis 345

Revolution (See Orogeny) 173, 213, 219, 316, 359, 367, 417, 479, 618

Rework 23, 169, 420, 503, 553,

Rhaetic Formation 598

Rhenium 556

Rhodium 444

Rhombohedral 36, 86, 162

Rhyodacite 45, 454

Rhyolite 5, 25, 137, 231, 247, 279, 320, 398, 435, 452, 459, 480, 570, 580, 593, 603, 625

Rhythmicity 115, 201, 202, 480, 540

Rice 14, 31, 102, 209, 214, 293, 294, 348, 354, 418, 480, 587, 614

Richter Scale 13, 72, 175, 355, 382, 480-481

Ridge and Rift System 274, 401

Riffle 49, 328, 421, 481, 522

Rigbat Shield 613

Rill 481, 482

Ring Complexes 95, 106, 159, 370, 434, 482, 460, 591, 603

Rings 105, 258, 299, 300, 370, 377, 380, 482, 590

Rip-Rap 482

Rip Current 325, 482

Ripple 91, 483

Rise 140, 164, 176, 239, 282, 357, 358, 398, 401, 409, 592

Riviera 357, 520

Road 118, 133, 214, 404, 454, 515, 540, 599, 627

Rocket 423, 477, 611

Rockslide 19, 485

Rod 132, 289-290, 444, 518

Rodent 238, 314

Roentgen 457, 457, 469, 485, 621

Roots 91, 103, 116, 145, 154, 187, 214, 223, 241, 242, 249, 290, 303, 309, 319, 320, 329, 340, 341, 351, 373, 413, 427, 437, 480, 549, 577, 596, 612, 622

Rotation 26, 143, 177, 187, 232, 255, 275, 312, 344, 367, 392, 441, 456, 518, 542, 564, 571, 590, 591, 609

Rubber 126, 250, 282, 294, 332, 450, 486-487

Rubidium 466, 487

Rubrum 209

Ruby 135, 159, 317, 363, 444, 487, 510, 531, 532, 570

Rudaceous 487

Runoff 19, 32, 41, 204, 231, 278, 301, 313, 363, 399, 412, 470, 481, 483, 488, 520, 609, 614

Rupture 174, 277

Rust 228, 234, 289, 417, 532, 631

Ruthenium 444

Rutile 57, 159, 183, 263, 281, 440, 480, 488, 516, 568, 569

S-wave 175, 311, 491, 509, 512

Sabkha 188, 491

Saddle 119, 482, 550, 619

Saddle Reef 491-492

Sagpond 492, 498, 556

Saharan Shield 14, 493

Salar 24, 323, 495, 591

Salinity 40, 42, 55, 66, 67, 78, 91, 132, 143, 155, 177, 226, 245, 259, 284, 295, 296, 312, 338, 340, 347, 355, 366, 378, 391, 400, 413, 417, 456, 462, 475, 491, 495, 497, 500, 501, 504, 506, 507, 526, 527, 529, 540, 608

Salitrite 495

Salt 24, 15, 40, 53, 62, 79, 94, 102, 110, 124, 140, 147, 149, 155, 158, 160, 183, 191, 194, 198, 226, 244, 255, 258, 259, 287, 302, 312, 323, 338, 340, 375, 388, 398, 399, 400, 430, 431, 435, 436, 444, 452, 461, 469, 474, 491, 495-496, 497, 498, 499, 506, 518, 520, 524, 525, 527, 528, 544, 550, 567, 591, 599, 623

Salt Dome 160, 355, 479, 496, 545

Salt Pan 456, 487, 495, 497, 527

Saltation 167, 497

Saltbush 269, 622

Saltwater (See Seawater)

Saltwater Marsh 344, 497

Samarium 472

Sample 82, 295, 367, 498, 550,

San Andreas Fault 13, 121, 132, 195, 232, 348, 354, 443, 492, 498, 516, 540, 556, 572, 620

Sand Sea 32, 62, 176, 373

Sandbar 499, 569, 630

Sandstone 26, 35, 36, 37, 40, 45, 52, 66, 81, 88, 96, 104, 125, 140, 142, 148, 158, 166, 179, 186, 193, 201, 204, 207, 212, 226, 241, 248, 249, 265, 289, 291, 298, 346, 355, 376, 382, 384, 392, 405, 430, 433, 437, 438, 458, 453, 461, 462, 463, 479, 481, 484, 499, 503, 511, 551, 556, 560, 564, 582, 588

Sandstorm 171, 257, 327, 499

Sanidine 411, 571

Sap 21, 435, 513, 521, 622

Sapphire 135, 159, 500, 531

Sapphirine 183

Saprolite 209, 324, 500

'Sargassum' 80, 500, 501

Satellite 30, 38, 159, 173, 190, 225, 258, 284, 297, 299, 312, 315, 323, 367, 385, 409, 412, 441, 448, 477, 478, 488, 493, 501, 534, 549, 596

Saturation 91, 158, 245, 334, 437, 477, 491, 523, 527, 541, 633

Saturn 297, 482

Savanna 2, 38, 50, 71, 76, 89, 102, 104, 120, 178, 210, 215, 219, 231, 238, 251, 299, 326, 337, 342, 384, 413, 447, 488, 493, 516, 543, 544, 560, 577, 578, 596

Scarp (See Escarpment) 31, 78, 142, 197, 301, 345, 398, 493, 502, 504, 522, 555

Scatter 149, 174, 502, 520, 534, 573, 632

Scattering Layer 502, 503

Scheelite 581, 619

Schist 220, 234, 247, 291, 310, 323, 351, 355, 408, 437, 476, 503, 516, 521, 524, 554, 561, 600

Scoria 54, 460, 504, 564

Scour 135, 140, 155, 171, 190, 231, 249, 259, 313, 368, 369, 397, 483, 504, 542, 556, 585, 593, 594, 609, 616

Scree 504

Screening 133, 200, 350, 494,

Scrub 102, 179, 234, 244, 249, 265, 297, 341, 342, 364, 438, 447, 521, 543, 622

Sea Ice 212, 505

Sea level 17-18, 26, 38, 42, 43, 47, 48, 51, 52, 53, 58, 87, 89, 103, 104, 114, 117, 135, 139, 147, 148, 149, 155, 183, 190, 191, 194, 220, 230, 237, 243, 245, 246, 253, 276, 282, 314, 316, 332, 343, 346, 347, 366, 369, 376, 382, 411, 416, 421, 431, 447, 461, 465, 471, 473, 476, 497, 505, 530, 560, 561, 565, 574, 582, 588, 606, 616, 626

Sea Surface 19, 23, 86, 92, 115, 180, 253, 268, 286, 290, 298, 371, 399, 408, 409, 411, 418, 436, 474, 475, 482, 495, 503, 565, 588, 609, 618

Seafloor 42, 50, 59, 68, 86, 96, 98, 141, 148, 150, 159, 166, 176, 197, 226, 232, 253, 295, 331, 335, 347, 367, 370, 384, 394, 399, 408, 415, 431, 439, 473, 541, 586, 605, 633

Seafloor Spreading 13, 38, 46, 130, 139, 160, 164, 195, 218, 233, 247, 263, 268, 319, 330, 358, 381, 400, 401, 417, 419, 443, 446, 474, 481, 505-506, 512, 542, 557, 563, 572, 574, 612

Seamount 81, 253, 340, 371, 506, 550

Seam 94, 117, 161, 195, 211, 301, 329, 408, 417, 419, 443, 506, 515, 540, 542, 549, 556

Season 30, 92, 150, 169, 173, 174, 179, 183, 187, 191, 201, 295, 305, 309, 327, 332, 391, 411, 414, 423, 446, 450, 470, 506, 510, 531, 574, 576, 633

Seasonal 19, 191, 201, 205, 260, 272, 283, 317, 323, 343, 344, 363, 414, 415, 422, 480, 506, 555, 562, 575, 578, 595, 614

Seawater 19, 28, 53, 54, 79, 131, 144, 153, 155, 157, 160, 161, 162, 191, 225, 226, 247, 258, 263, 283, 295, 312, 329, 364, 374, 386, 387, 399, 400, 401, 414, 418, 438, 495, 497, 500, 505, 506, 545, 550, 582, 633

Seaweed 14, 80, 81, 150, 287, 303, 400, 473, 500, 507

Secretion 221, 321, 450, 451, 468, 479, 516, 540

Section 111, 134, 163, 224, 338, 457

Sedge 102, 192, 344, 422

Sedimentary Rocks 18, 30, 31, 51, 126, 127, 132, 142, 144, 158, 159, 160, 161, 185, 191, 195, 203, 206, 208, 210, 217, 237, 255, 264, 266, 267, 314, 322, 332, 352, 360, 362, 370, 389, 398, 403, 407, 430, 435, 437, 456, 467, 475, 476, 484, 507-508, 511, 522, 536, 539, 540, 560, 563, 586, 587, 612

Seeds 18, 26, 65, 143, 158, 196, 199, 237, 254, 296, 340, 353, 359, 420, 421, 442, 469, 509, 521, 522, 523, 622

Seiche 323, 508

Seif Dune 32, 62, 121, 170, 508, 614, 624

Seismic Waves 27, 117, 141, 175, 187, 193, 219, 225, 307, 311, 341, 355, 364, 365, 395, 409, 421, 442, 464, 491, 508, 579

Selenite 254

Selenium 223, 262, 352, 499, 500, 558

Semi-arid Climate 15, 16, 34, 36, 48, 49, 68, 76, 79, 81, 85, 86, 105, 147, 157, 167, 168, 208, 213, 241, 244, 259, 266, 283, 297, 301, 426, 437, 441, 445, 478, 493, 495, 509, 512, 525, 528, 568, 574

Semi-desert 86, 155, 182, 241

Semi-permeable membrane 120

Semi-precious stones 85, 113, 140, 500

Semiconductors 50, 216, 224, 351, 352, 508, 509, 517, 572

Sequoia 352, 418, 509, 516

Serecite 371

Serpentine 53, 220, 305, 333, 406, 408, 428, 510, 517, 554

Serpentinite 99, 247

Sesquioxides 260, 280

Sessile 241, 426, 507, 511

Sewage 176, 354, 389

Shale 32, 35, 36, 37, 52, 72, 78, 82, 88, 96, 144, 149, 160, 203, 207, 234, 245, 267, 281, 289, 304, 314, 326, 341, 355, 356, 376, 409, 411, 418, 432, 433, 437, 438, 451, 462, 480, 484, 503, 511, 518, 521, 570, 574, 575, 583

Shallow Seas 95, 133, 165, 186, 239, 298, 343, 380, 391, 409, 411, 418, 456, 501, 507, 514, 583

Shallow water 59, 189, 191, 192, 245, 295, 312, 322, 371, 431, 450, 456, 475, 482, 500, 512, 513, 514, 527, 529, 570

Shatter Cone 281, 512, 544

Shear 43, 98, 99, 121, 176, 212, 232, 248, 296, 356, 491, 503, 512, 594

Sheep 59, 196, 236, 241, 382, 475, 583

Shellfish 355, 365, 374, 499

Shell (atomic) 137, 180-181, 199-200

Shells 66, 94, 124, 125, 133, 149, 209, 211, 322, 365, 379, 394, 401, 414, 450, 491, 513

Shield 14, 25, 44, 47, 49, 73, 90, 161, 198, 212, 217, 230, 240, 245, 247, 287, 299, 307, 315, 363, 369, 373, 390, 408, 454, 493, 494, 513-514, 529, 579, 596, 613

Shield Volcano 111, 124, 346, 347, 395, 513, 539, 602

Shielding 219, 287, 310, 334, 335, 415, 416

Shingle 280, 514

Shoal 312, 400, 514

Shock Wave 281, 380, 480, 512, 526, 527, 555, 582

Shore 24, 52, 56, 72, 78, 104, 118, 176, 179, 189, 191, 198, 199, 203, 225, 228, 243, 251, 268, 312, 313, 325, 343, 356, 366, 379, 421, 471, 475, 476, 485, 494, 498, 514, 520, 548, 560, 564, 579, 586, 593, 605, 618

Shortwave 183, 245-246, 287, 328, 436, 502, 525, 573, 585

Shrimp 70, 141, 343, 355, 400, 614

Shrubs 23, 70, 81, 82, 84, 102, 182, 187, 250, 261, 296, 297, 350, 420, 425, 509, 549, 554, 620, 622

Sial 324, 514, 519

Siberian Rift 308

Siberian Shield 25, 299, 513

Siderite 94, 323, 328, 515

Silcrete 260, 516

Silexite 516

Silica 15, 25, 36, 38, 52, 54, 56, 100, 101, 108, 118, 120, 123, 140, 151, 197, 204, 211, 215, 227, 231, 240, 260, 279, 289, 302, 317, 318, 320, 323, 324, 352, 353, 355, 367, 371, 375, 379, 389, 399, 408, 414, 432, 442, 448, 452, 460, 462, 468, 471, 480, 499, 506, 514, 516-517, 518, 522, 547, 575, 585, 619, 630

Silicate 13, 22, 44, 64, 162, 174, 183, 187, 197, 198, 220, 232, 247, 260, 263, 300, 310, 311, 316, 320, 355, 371, 379, 411, 428, 435, 460, 487, 510, 511, 517, 520, 533, 554, 570, 571, 619, 630

Siliceous 102, 108, 125, 146, 160, 161, 170, 205, 226, 370, 407, 468, 513, 517, 520, 569, 619

Silicon 53, 82, 135, 227, 399, 462, 463, 509, 516, 517, 518, 572

Silicone 450, 518,

Sill 35, 60, 98, 137, 158, 161, 162, 164, 229, 245, 266, 286, 301, 342, 343, 348, 447, 504, 518

Sillimanite 183, 310

Silt 16, 19, 40, 91, 104, 113, 126, 152, 153, 196, 211, 238, 300, 312, 326, 327, 362, 370, 371, 378, 385, 400, 443, 483, 495, 499, 513, 518, 520, 546, 578, 595, 597, 612, 613

Siltstone 35

Silurian Period 155, 208, 241, 289, 409, 419, 518-519

Silver 24,35, 41, 54, 83, 90, 96, 103, 124, 132, 165, 201, 213, 218, 327, 345, 361, 388, 432, 454, 455, 464, 474, 517, 519, 544, 545, 558, 579, 611, 631

Silver-iodide 611

Silver Lake (Pleistocene) 364

Sima 324, 400, 519

Sink 238, 497, 568

Sinkhole 101, 301, 315, 322, 394, 520, 627

Sinter 352, 452, 520

Skarn 336, 520

Skeleton 43, 88, 119, 160, 161, 209, 211, 233, 410, 415, 442, 468, 512, 574

Sky 25, 29, 41, 258, 267, 300, 353, 386, 389, 392, 501, 520, 538, 590, 632

Slash and Burn 246, 249, 292, 340, 354, 470, 529-521, 559, 629

Slate 229, 351, 437, 521

Sleet 68, 257, 277, 455, 521

Slickensides 521

Slide (See Landslide) 312, 315, 485, 602

Sloth 372, 522

Slump 117, 502, 504, 522, 541, 582

Slurry 98, 440, 473, 522, 582

Small Circle 243, 423, 522

Smectite 406

SMOG 80, 243, 287, 355, 388, 389, 415, 416, 502, 506, 522-523, 528, 545, 559, 573

Smoke 28, 170, 393, 461, 523

Snail 26, 101, 221, 503, 513

Soapstone 99, 524, 554

Soda 197, 363, 355, 427, 381, 388, 460, 524, 564

Soda Ash 232, 375, 524, 575

Soda Lake, California (Pleistocene) 364,

Soda Lime Feldspar 197, 311, 361, 571

Soda Pyroxene Group 293

Sodalite 15, 195, 316

Sodium 13, 15, 73, 110, 124, 165, 183, 191, 197, 198, 232, 258, 259, 263, 287, 311, 316, 324, 351, 355, 367, 369, 375, 379, 388, 399, 411, 414, 416, 441, 471, 495, 498, 506, 524, 550, 571, 575, 607, 608, 630

Solar Energy 177, 184, 208, 312, 400, 478, 525, 526, 527, 573, 606,

Solar Flare 44, 114, 135, 167, 174, 275, 466, 526, 546, 547

Solar Radiation 13, 168, 171, 219, 245, 284, 344, 367, 393, 415, 416, 471, 506, 559, 586

Solar System 110, 170, 174, 224, 297, 359, 398, 409, 415, 429, 441, 463, 501, 527, 546, 558, 586, 589, 632

Solar Wind 122, 224, 526, 527, 530

Solid 32, 91, 111, 141, 142, 213, 231, 240, 245, 257, 259, 275, 281, 287, 306, 311, 319, 323, 351, 365, 370, 427, 434, 442, 456, 460, 473, 495, 499, 522, 528, 556, 590, 593, 607, 608, 610, 612

Solifluction 137, 277, 527-528

Solstice 528, 551

Solution 15, 22, 82, 90, 91, 92, 98, 99, 100, 104, 119, 127, 154, 165, 182, 183, 187, 190,

Solution (continued) 193, 197, 205, 225, 229, 254, 273, 280, 281, 301, 302, 303, 317, 319, 321, 322, 327, 334, 352, 353, 360, 361, 389, 403, 432, 441, 450, 452, 460, 471, 483, 498, 499, 504, 519, 528, 534, 544, 596, 610, 630

Mt. Somma (Ancient) 599

Sonar 413, 478

Sorting 17, 36, 167, 123, 248, 299, 343, 350, 451, 476, 528-529, 536, 581, 618

Sound 22, 165, 175, 213, 233, 331, 353, 429, 502, 508, 520, 529, 564, 593, 610

Sounding 13, 115, 177, 371, 502, 529

South American Plate 443

Southern Oscillation 387

Spall 193, 439, 587

Spawn 23, 190, 312, 314, 355, 501, 530

Species 19, 22, 26, 34, 39, 45, 49, 64, 65, 77, 82, 97, 102, 106, 120, 133, 139, 152, 162, 176, 177, 192, 194, 196, 202, 209, 222, 261, 262, 294, 329, 332, 338, 339, 340, 348, 350, 366, 376, 383, 394, 409, 420, 421, 426, 431, 442, 450, 470, 474, 475, 478, 494, 501, 509, 511, 523, 530, 531, 533, 534, 535, 541, 553, 554, 555, 557, 560, 566, 576, 577, 580, 583, 593, 599, 620

Specific Gravity 35, 46, 234, 263, 351, 360, 361, 531, 550, 606, 619

Spectrum 161, 165, 177, 280, 288, 321, 456, 470, 474, 502, 531, 585, 600, 621

Sphalerite 85, 114, 164, 532, 631

Sphene 550

Spin 178, 200, 228, 255, 335, 527, 532, 587

Spinel 183, 532, 570

Spinifex 622, 532

Spit 532

Spodumene 142, 323, 324, 533

Sponge 26, 119, 124, 204, 410, 451, 452, 533

Spores 199, 458, 533

Spring 150, 250, 282, 300, 304, 331, 356, 361, 415, 442, 472, 506, 548, 555, 588

Springs 32, 37, 46, 71, 73, 121, 145, 146, 298, 313, 361, 378, 397, 431, 482, 533, 607, 629

Squall 286, 533

Squid 101, 229, 531, 614

Stalactite/Stalagmite 167, 302, 339, 534, 573

Stand 209, 291, 294, 420, 486, 509, 534, 619

Standing Wave 389, 534, 610

Star 25, 39, 61, 67, 111, 120, 123, 128, 135, 137, 218, 327, 333, 359, 376, 380, 392, 429, 441, 448, 455, 459, 466, 527, 530, 534, 535, 546, 548, 587, 591, 615

Starfish 26, 174, 511, 534-535

Stationary Front 214, 605

Steam 107, 117, 154, 166, 190, 215, 226, 228, 331, 333, 371, 387, 403, 404, 405, 437, 494, 533, 548, 601, 602, 606

Steppes 59, 60, 88, 108, 128, 280, 300, 441, 535, 553, 562, 591

Sterility 47, 157, 319, 535, 577

Stibnite 29, 96, 307, 536

Stock 63, 73, 158, 434, 454, 536

Stockwork 536

Storms 18, 49, 52, 60, 68, 82, 114, 144, 149, 189, 205, 225, 254, 257, 264, 270, 277, 285, 286, 321, 329, 380, 393, 398, 447, 456, 466, 482, 494, 501, 504, 526, 533, 537, 547, 563, 571, 584, 605, 606, 609, 613, 616,

Strain 175, 180, 537, 539

Strait 185, 311, 314, 368, 431, 460, 533, 537,

Stratocumulus 538

Stratosphere 8, 11, 42, 107, 110, 415, 416, 538-539, 554, 579

Stratovolcano 124, 215, 317, 347, 494, 539

Stratus Cloud 116, 539

Streak 264, 361, 460, 539

Stress 43, 138, 150, 180, 442, 476, 503, 513

Striations 430, 442, 455, 539

Strike 81, 163, 498, 540

Strike-slip Fault 620, 498, 540

Stromatolites 455, 540

Strontium 487, 541, 547, 630

Subaerial 17, 370, 425, 432, 484, 611

Subcontinent 60, 286, 423, 533

Subduction 17, 28, 59, 97, 108, 275, 357, 401, 408, 417, 541-542, 549, 557, 615, 619, 629

Submarine 18, 55, 58, 125, 130, 160, 166, 197, 258, 257, 270, 285, 308, 342, 343, 361, 370, 402, 542, 563, 615

Submergence 101, 118, 182, 203, 290, 363, 418, 480, 482, 542, 611, 315, 322, 346, 348, 355, 381, 400, 404, 457, 475, 482, 505, 542, 624

Subtropical 22, 26, 28, 29, 32, 64, 89, 92, 105, 115, 118, 149, 151, 186, 192, 196, 205, 210, 213, 215, 228, 253, 254, 258, 289, 293, 297, 301, 317, 318, 336, 340, 356, 391, 372, 420, 430, 448, 470, 471, 542, 543, 558, 575, 586, 590, 596, 613, 627

Succession 231, 509, 543, 549

Sudanese Reef (Wingate Reef) 466, 544

Sulfate 41, 66, 164, 191, 254, 260, 289, 361, 449, 471, 491, 497, 544, 579, 588, 607

Sulfide 14, 29, 35, 41, 63, 73, 118, 132, 236, 247, 272, 301, 303, 307, 360, 361, 382, 383, 452, 519, 532, 541, 545, 575, 583, 603, 607, 631

Sulfur 4, 5, 18, 79, 90, 107, 108, 110, 112, 140, 160, 169, 213, 218, 243, 268, 288, 303, 304, 324, 349, 361, 362, 365, 389, 416, 434, 445, 449, 460, 496, 500, 506, 508, 523, 527, 545, 546, 553, 579, 601, 608, 615, 631

Sulfur Dioxide 579, 601

Summer 27, 35, 106, 120, 158, 173, 188, 203, 244, 270, 286, 295, 299, 300, 307, 331, 344, 347, 356, 393, 431, 471, 503, 506, 529, 532, 554-555, 575, 579, 580, 588, 595, 597, 606

Sun 2, 6, 11, 27, 30, 35, 44, 62, 90, 107, 109, 111, 113, 115, 123, 134, 135, 143, 148, 154, 173, 174, 177, 178, 182, 183, 185, 188, 204, 219, 231, 258, 263, 272, 278, 297, 308, 320, 321, 328, 344, 356, 380, 389, 393, 400, 409, 415, 419, 429, 436, 441, 456, 465, 470, 486, 502, 506, 523, 525, 526, 527, 528, 530, 534, 546, 547, 551, 565, 570, 577, 579, 586, 589, 590, 598, 620, 632

Sunda Arc 546
Sundance Sea 254, 298, 485, 546
Sunspots 279, 415, 526, 547
Superconductivity 263, 303, 472, 518, 547, 568
Supernova 136, 137, 218, 374, 380, 535, 548
Superposition 538, 548
Surf 347, 328, 354, 429, 494, 548, 565
Suspect Terrain 549
Suspension 151, 154, 182, 279, 326, 427, 469, 527, 539, 608
Suture 17, 25, 59, 81, 226, 282, 373, 417, 421, 443, 494, 498, 542, 549, 619, 629
Swamps 70, 82, 116, 117-118, 145, 146, 148, 251, 296, 329, 331, 340, 343, 344, 354, 362, 368, 370, 371, 384, 385, 405, 421, 422, 425, 509, 514, 531, 540-541, 543, 544, 549, 578, 613, 614
Swell 78, 548-549
Syenite 15, 162, 337, 367, 426, 550
Sylvinite 453, 550
Sylvite 550-551
Symbiosis 120, 123, 133, 372, 383, 437, 475, 480, 551, 559
Syncline 28, 122, 155, 208, 221, 286, 302, 538, 548, 551, 575
Syrian Rift 229, 245

Tableland 44, 83, 105, 350, 492, 513, 553, 560
Taiga 73, 115, 127, 190, 199, 209, 309, 339, 377, 390, 391, 429, 553, 554, 558, 580, 588, 591, 596
Tailings 97, 169, 216, 319, 498, 553
Talc 360, 364, 455, 503, 524, 554
Talus 79, 482, 504, 554
Tantalite 123, 370
Tantalum 123, 247, 387, 555-556
Tanzanite 632
Tar 66, 118, 323, 602, 603
Tar Sands 66, 90, 184, 272, 403, 433, 556
Tarn 556, 565
Taxonomy 196, 306, 557
Tectonics 73, 74, 90, 91, 155, 180, 191, 295, 322, 363, 368, 372, 386, 401, 477, 481, 508, 521, 540, 557, 599
Tectosphere 616
Tektite 355, 482, 557
Telluric Currents 174
Telluride 558
Tellurium 96, 352, 558
Temperate 25, 27, 35, 59, 81, 88, 113, 114, 115, 144, 150, 241, 250, 326, 425, 454, 470, 503, 511, 543, 558, 566, 573, 578, 595, 614
Tenor 559
Tension 139, 200, 295, 525
Tephra 559
Termites 178. 238, 354, 559-560
Terrace 16, 19, 24, 58, 60, 70, 117, 183, 343, 358, 364, 423, 440, 471, 477, 502, 560
Tertiary Period 16, 25, 48, 50, 71, 73, 89, 101, 112, 116, 126, 138, 177, 179, 186, 189, 194, 204, 239, 288, 302, 306, 326, 334, 338, 379,

Tertiary Period (continued) 385, 386, 394, 406, 417, 424, 446, 463, 560-561
Tethys Sea 25, 98, 129, 186, 282, 422, 491. 561, 574, 612
Tetragonal 98, 142, 620
Tetrahedra 355, 367, 375, 517, 619, 630
Texture 22, 25, 30, 33, 37, 143, 147, 158, 162, 195, 239, 240, 267, 274, 319, 326, 372, 377, 408, 451, 458, 480, 484, 500, 520, 554, 561, 605
Thallophyta 562
Thaw 100, 138, 151, 214, 249, 275, 278, 319, 321, 344, 425, 428, 450, 528, 631
Thecodonts 562
Thermal Equator 286, 584
Thermocline 187, 274, 285, 562
Tholeitic 408, 563
Thorium 44, 94, 184, 212, 263, 334, 363, 365, 467, 468, 469, 472, 534, 563, 588, 621
Thrust 15, 150, 204, 237, 307, 348, 390, 413, 426, 446, 538, 563, 618, 629
Thrust Fault 197, 409, 479, 563-564, 629
Thunderstorm 18, 120, 131, 142, 164, 187, 188, 210, 257, 258, 271, 286, 321, 564, 571, 606
Tidal Wave (See Tsunami)
Tidal Zone 325, 370, 414, 491, 522
Tidepool 565
Tides 19, 20, 48, 72, 116, 144, 173, 181, 215, 259, 266, 270, 282, 305, 312, 326, 344, 367, 371, 399, 414, 421, 431, 451, 480, 482, 497, 498, 508, 512, 551, 560, 564, 565, 570
Tillite 165, 167, 169, 196, 237, 368, 430, 455, 518, 551, 566
Tilt 183, 233, 448, 455, 506
Tilth 167, 566
Timberline 17, 35, 198, 305, 309, 566-567, 596
Tin 16, 24, 30, 80, 98, 109, 135, 182, 245, 306, 338, 343, 351, 385, 404, 426, 439, 432, 440, 449, 454, 567-568, 570, 619
Tin Granites 567, 570
Tin-Tungsten 351
Tincal 73
Tinstone 98, 567
Titanate 555, 568
Titanite 495
Titanium 3, 18, 24, 48, 80, 90, 95, 102, 263, 288, 299, 293, 333, 334, 335, 355, 414, 460, 473, 486, 488, 495, 500, 516, 555, 556, 568-569, 581, 632
Tombolo 532, 569
Topaz 3, 132, 248, 364, 428, 569, 570
Topography 33, 54, 65, 99, 127, 135, 139, 166, 175, 224, 237, 249, 257, 278, 316, 323, 334, 336, 356, 358, 398, 401, 549, 605, 608, 617
Topset Beds 153
Topsoil 138, 171, 362, 515, 525, 570, 624
Tor 570
Torbanite 570
Tornado 570-571, 609
Tourmaline 3, 248, 426, 571
Tourmalinization 240

Toxic 37, 85, 106, 107, 109, 149, 205, 219, 223, 319, 349, 372, 415, 474, 499, 508, 509, 523, 545, 607, 608, 622, 631

Tracer 287, 309, 392, 467

Trachyte 571

Trade Winds 90, 131, 134, 176, 188, 257, 267, 286, 346, 387, 456, 562, 571, 584, 617

Transform Fault 103, 194, 382, 557, 572

Transformation 153, 173, 213, 214, 352, 390, 425, 442, 443

Transgression 88, 104, 138, 186, 203, 254, 284, 343, 423, 484, 491, 507, 508, 572

Transistor (See Semiconductor) 36, 518, 572

Translational Margin 130, 164

Translational Wave 564

Translucence 106, 160, 254, 258, 321, 407, 451, 572

Transparency 160, 164, 254, 321, 361, 379, 398, 562

Transpiration 93, 169, 573

Transverse 21, 491, 512, 605

Traprock 123, 150, 282, 429, 563

Travertine 86, 51, 520, 573

Tree Rings 79, 88, 153, 573-574

Trench 14, 31, 41, 44, 96, 98, 130, 141, 174, 185, 232, 245, 280, 282, 290, 342, 343, 359, 393, 398, 400, 401, 402, 417, 423, 443, 541, 557, 573, 581, 600

Triassic Period 81, 144, 166, 230, 278, 297, 301, 337, 350, 414, 424, 430, 432, 573-574, 598

Tributary 33, 50, 56, 69, 71, 79, 98, 122, 126, 127, 147, 158, 166, 183, 212, 220, 236, 251, 259, 262, 272, 273, 331, 362, 371, 378, 386, 397, 408, 411, 422, 423, 424, 431, 451, 482, 483, 528, 542, 543, 556, 595, 609, 622, 623, 624, 629, 630

Triceratops 162

Triclinic System 13, 142, 197, 411

Tridymite 480, 516, 574

Trilobites 26, 37, 88, 194, 260, 267, 268, 281, 515, 519, 574

Tripolite 574

Triple Junction 44, 58, 195, 348, 481

Tritium 392, 574-575

Trona 524, 575

Tropical Climate 12, 13, 19, 22, 29, 44, 56, 64, 77, 89, 91, 92, 93, 109, 115, 118, 149, 151, 155, 182, 185, 188, 196, 199, 209, 210, 211, 215, 219, 228, 229, 246, 249, 251, 253, 261, 271, 282, 289, 294, 297, 299, 301, 317, 318, 320, 326, 332, 337, 340, 245, 363, 366, 372, 387, 409, 419, 420, 447, 458, 468, 470, 471, 488, 503, 509, 515, 516, 531, 537, 543, 565, 573, 575-576, 577, 578- 579, 586, 587, 596, 614, 616

Tropical Rainforest (See Rainforest)

Tropical Wet/Dry Climate 579

Tropics 64, 65, 90, 92, 131, 149, 151, 176, 187, 241, 257, 258, 297, 318, 350, 366, 543, 566, 575, 578, 579, 587, 596

Troposphere 8, 42, 62, 94, 246, 416, 538, 559, 573, 579

Trough 58, 120, 176, 188, 212, 226, 227, 232, 237, 248, 261, 285, 302, 373, 409, 461, 473, 481, 522, 548, 551, 561, 579, 609, 624

Troy Scale 235, 236, 262, 332, 394, 428, 444, 579, App III

Tsunami 175, 427, 499, 579-580

Tufa 573

Tuffaceous 603, 630

Tuff 38, 85, 94, 356, 437, 550, 580, 583, 599

'Tule fog' 208

Tumbleweed 18

Tuna 558, 570

Tundra 17, 60, 73, 81, 103, 106, 109, 113, 115, 118, 195, 198, 199, 203, 249, 265, 307, 309, 319, 320, 321, 331, 339, 344, 366, 372, 375, 458, 515, 531, 544, 553, 566, 580-581, 588, 591, 596

Tungstate 619

Tungsten 30, 92, 109, 248, 351, 426, 432, 439, 535, 556, 581-582, 619

Tunnel 32, 94, 122, 140, 167, 219, 319, 445

Turbidity Currents 58, 127, 151, 154, 207, 248, 285, 399, 401, 454, 504, 542, 582

Turbulence 98, 131, 314, 512

Turquoise 582

Turtles 38, 218, 478, 583

Twinning 462

Type Locality 210, 263, 288, 291, 293, 301, 305, 311, 329, 480, 544, 583

Typhoon 144, 267, 584

U-shaped Relief 79, 203, 209, 231, 359, 382, 594

'Uintatherian' 585

Ultra-violet Light 92, 206, 246, 246, 321, 377, 531, 559, 579, 586

Ultra-violet Radiation 42, 51, 67, 93, 122, 206, 247, 316, 370, 415, 416, 514, 465, 523, 547, 585-586, 621

Unconformity 52, 128, 163, 210, 264, 337, 586

Unconsolidated 26, 32, 327, 344, 438, 461, 481, 499

Undergrowth 210, 470, 558

Understory 210, 458, 586, 620

Undertow 586

Uniformity 419, 586

Universe 16, 62, 67, 128, 218, 219, 225, 263, 442, 459, 463, 530, 586-587, 615, 620

Unloading 193, 198, 230, 248, 437, 587

Unreactive 234, 279, 309, 444, 621

Unsorted 167, 368, 566, 587

Updraft 257, 471

Upheaval 98, 113, 221, 429

Upland 65, 77, 78, 82, 89, 144, 203, 240, 265, 297, 326, 337, 365, 480, 516, 542, 578, 587-588, 609, 626

Uplift 14, 28, 30, 31, 96, 117, 160, 165, 170, 183, 185, 186, 170, 198, 207, 234, 236, 239, 251, 260, 265, 268, 271, 280, 282, 283, 323, 343, 357, 363, 365, 369, 410, 427, 443, 471, 476, 477, 485, 507, 516, 560, 561, 565, 600, 611, 613, 618, 626

Upthrust 28, 224, 237, 268, 311, 345, 373, 390, 422, 431, 443, 446, 485, 489, 538, 575, 594, 613

Upwelling 24, 108, 164, 176, 213, 270, 374, 399, 400, 407, 436, 588

Uralian Sea 561

Uraninite 374, 414, 588

Uranium 6, 13, 45, 47, 74, 86, 90, 96, 97, 109, 136, 150, 184, 217, 222, 229, 246, 258, 263, 319, 324, 332, 334, 337, 365, 374, 384, 404, 406, 439, 447, 455, 466, 467, 468, 469, 472, 473, 534, 563, 588-589, 594, 621, 625

Uranium-vanadium 96, 588

Uranus 193, 297, 299, 589

Urban Environment 223, 454, 499, 523, 562, 590

Urea 389, 512, 590

Ursa Major Constellation 174, 590

Ursa Minor Constellation 174, 439, 590-591

V-shaped Relief 542, 594

Vacuum 100, 321, 514, 593

Vadose Water 593

Valdez Oil Spill 404, 593

Valence 266, 429, 436, 593

Valles Caldera 593

Valley 13, 15, 16, 17, 22, 30, 31, 36, 45, 46, 47, 54, 58, 59, 72, 74, 79, 86, 88, 90, 91, 96, 104, 112, 114, 120, 135, 139, 142, 165, 168, 174, 178, 179, 182, 185, 201, 203, 204, 205, 212, 213, 214, 215, 217, 220, 227, 231, 232, 236, 237, 243, 244, 248, 259, 261, 265, 270, 286, 300, 302, 306, 316, 325, 327, 328, 337, 338, 346, 347, 350, 358, 359, 362, 363, 364, 368, 381, 382, 390, 395, 405, 408, 409, 437, 438, 443, 446, 465, 473, 477, 479, 481, 485, 587, 491, 497, 502, 503, 513, 514, 519, 537, 542, 554, 559, 561, 565, 582, 585, 593, 594, 599, 605, 620, 622, 623, 626, 627

Valley Glacier (See Alpine Glacier) 231, 269, 593-594, 620

Van Allen Belts 174, 530, 594-595

Vanadium 96, 140, 262, 588

Vapor 104, 125, 158, 173, 178, 191, 208, 212, 215, 221, 227, 287, 299, 393, 399, 455, 466, 523, 542, 606

Varnish 156, 157

Varve 595

Vegetation 13, 17, 19, 36, 44, 60, 70, 85, 90, 91, 93, 95, 102, 105, 114, 115, 116, 127, 138, 147, 155, 158, 162, 168, 170, 181, 190, 192, 199, 200, 208, 210, 213, 223, 232, 237, 253, 259, 261, 265, 277, 284, 299, 301, 304, 313, 314, 327, 341, 343, 344, 364, 390, 397, 405, 419, 447, 448, 465, 471, 492, 509, 510, 521, 528, 543, 544, 550, 553, 576, 577, 578, 581, 588, 596, 622, 627

Vein 16, 18, 29, 30, 35, 81, 112, 118, 124, 132, 137, 140, 158, 167, 204, 206, 209, 218, 220,

Vein (continued) 235, 236, 247, 266, 268, 273, 274, 286, 327, 331, 342, 360, 369, 410, 426, 519, 536, 540, 567, 588, 596, 619, 620

Veinlet 51, 268, 583, 596

Veldt 567, 596-597

Velocity 16, 25, 40, 91, 100, 109, 143, 159, 177, 185, 200, 204, 213, 218, 269, 281, 303, 306, 311, 312, 331, 341, 356, 362, 364, 380, 412, 413, 417, 456, 459, 482, 483, 491, 527, 529, 530, 536, 539, 542, 576, 579, 583, 586, 594, 595, 596, 609, 616, 617, 618

Veneer 156, 192, 321, 426, 439, 445

Ventifact 597

Vent 87, 95, 215, 218, 228, 233, 261, 268, 319, 333, 346, 369, 405, 424, 427, 439, 481, 513, 527, 559, 601

Venus 590, 597-598

Vermiculite 95, 240, 586

Vertebrate 26, 65, 109, 147, 199, 283, 306, 598

Vertisols 598

Vescicle 23, 53, 598

Vestige 192, 211, 283, 563

Vibration 175, 213, 512

Village 45, 269, 305, 346, 380, 476, 520

Vines 82, 261, 297, 320, 462

Violet Light 120, 283, 585

Viscosity 140, 147, 180, 231, 331, 426, 517, 606

Visible Light 120, 165, 180, 246, 258, 283, 288, 321, 457, 520, 526, 531, 559, 561, 585, 586, 600, 621

Visibility 68, 257

Vitreous 46, 319, 329, 398, 408, 441, 462, 630

Volcanic Arc (See Island Arc) 341, 574

Volcanic Axis 353, 355

Volcanic Belt 41, 160, 360

Volcanic Glass 398, 426, 429, 451, 459, 630

Volcanic Island 38, 43, 46, 90, 101, 141, 289, 353, 417, 446, 482, 548, 603

Volcanic Neck 69, 86, 137, 312, 377, 601

Volcanism 7, 13, 18, 25, 30, 31, 34, 38, 46, 53, 59, 61, 78, 79, 89, 95, 97, 100, 101, 108, 109, 111-112, 113, 118, 122, 124, 128, 136, 137, 138, 139, 141, 147, 152, 155, 157, 160, 166, 171, 182, 183, 186, 189, 190, 196, 215, 227, 228, 231-232, 244-245, 248, 253, 261, 262, 264, 266, 268, 278, 279, 282, 288, 290, 293, 297-298, 302, 303, 305, 306, 308, 312, 313, 315, 317, 319, 320, 323, 329, 333, 342, 344, 346, 347, 349, 354-355, 358-359, 361, 366, 367, 369, 371, 373, 377, 382, 385, 393, 394-395, 398, 401, 405, 408, 411, 418, 423, 424, 426-427, 437, 438, 440, 443, 444, 445, 446, 452, 459, 460, 465, 471-472, 475, 476, 480, 481, 484, 485, 487, 494, 499, 505, 507, 513, 514, 515, 527, 533, 539, 540, 545, 546, 548-549, 553, 554-555, 559, 560, 564, 571, 574, 580, 583, 591, 595, 599, 600-601, 602, 603, 615. 620, 629

Volume 45, 153, 240, 312, 333, 341, 376, 378, 380, 399, 409, 429, 446, 454, 523, 531,

Vortex 112, 176, 311, 315, 316

Wad 605

Wadi 156, 232, 378, 427, 605, 606

Wallace Line 445, 605

Warm Airmass 1, 14, 22, 28, 68, 98, 114, 131, 133, 169, 188, 191, 214, 257, 258, 266, 267, 270, 277, 286, 289, 309, 325, 366, 373, 386, 390, 392, 393, 398, 423, 447, 471, 500, 503, 504, 506, 515, 523, 524, 554, 565, 566, 600, 605, 610, 616, 617, 621

Warm Waters 133, 205, 239, 252, 309, 387, 411, 431, 500, 607, 610

Warm-bloodedness 162, 478

Warping 155, 160, 336, 551, 605

Wash 312, 441, 605, 606

Washed Material 125, 289, 421, 440, 606

Waste 107, 149, 163, 189, 202, 221, 254, 279, 319, 351, 402, 435, 449, 468, 473, 499, 556

Wasteland 62, 614

Wastewater 279, 351, 404

Water Buffalo 342, 382, 607

Water Hole 406, 397, 497

Water Hyacinth 314, 544, 607

Water Table 37, 91, 138, 179, 249, 250, 283, 315, 317, 318, 326, 344, 394, 495, 429, 446, 461, 475, 491, 520, 578, 593, 607, 608, 613

Water Vapor 18, 51, 125, 158, 178, 208, 246, 270, 299, 386, 393, 455, 464, 477, 523, 542, 606

Water-logged 232, 287, 437, 580

Water-loving Vegetation 167, 168, 314, 437

Waterfalls 25, 183, 196, 253, 259, 332, 446, 568, 608-609, 626

Waterfowl 207, 331, 344, 338, 448, 499

Watershed 55, 76, 105, 121, 166, 182, 210, 272, 280, 345, 486, 489, 609

Waterspout 60, 609

Wavelength 26, 120, 139, 165, 180, 219, 261, 328, 357, 458, 465, 466, 514, 526, 531, 600, 609

Waves 22, 34, 52, 56, 57, 58, 60, 67, 78, 92, 98, 100, 114, 117, 118, 123, 124, 139, 167, 170, 175, 180, 184, 189, 193, 195, 200, 213, 218, 219, 245, 253, 259, 283, 285, 311, 328, 357, 360, 364, 366, 381, 387, 389, 400, 417, 436, 440, 459, 462, 464, 466, 467, 471, 475, 482, 484, 491, 493, 499, 502, 504, 506, 508, 512, 526, 529, 534, 537, 548, 549, 550, 560, 564, 573, 579, 582, 586, 588, 600, 609-610, 615

Weather 7, 11, 13, 60, 72, 113, 114, 120, 131, 134, 144, 148, 161, 168, 184, 188, 197, 200, 205, 214, 264, 270, 286, 297, 302, 325, 327, 333, 357, 366, 387, 389, 398, 404, 447, 448, 478, 547, 573, 579, 602, 610-611

Weathered 5, 26, 247, 253, 305, 324, 414, 440, 446, 452, 461, 500, 516, 524, 528, 615

Weathering 17, 30, 47, 53, 56, 57, 58, 58, 69, 73, 74, 79, 82, 87, 90, 101, 106, 113. 150, 161, 189, 196, 186, 200, 214, 220, 224, 236, 240, 241, 247, 254, 258, 280, 284, 285, 295, 317, 321, 322, 324, 356, 371, 382, 389, 406, 411, 414, 425, 428, 437, 446, 457, 481, 484, 497, 500, 510, 516, 524, 528, 570, 578, 581, 598, 601, 607, 611, 612, 616

Wedge 147, 161, 205, 277, 429, 456, 509, 581, 612

Weeds 81, 169, 501, 503, 509

Wegener Fault 612

Weight 18, 35, 91, 92, 116, 117, 123, 152, 154, 160, 168, 193, 203, 205, 217, 226, 230, 231, 238, 242, 257, 263, 265, 276, 277, 282, 290, 291, 315, 322, 331, 345, 355, 361, 362, 380, 400, 428, 443, 455, 464, 468, 485, 486, 495, 520, 528, 531, 535, 589, 601

Welded 16, 38, 141, 255, 580, 599

Wells 6, 32, 37, 47, 60, 98, 101, 102, 117, 154, 175, 198, 202, 223, 226, 249, 263, 301, 382, 392, 397, 403, 404, 421, 437, 439, 469, 487, 612, 616, 623

'Welwitschia mirabilis' 299, 373, 612

Westerlies 145, 176, 267, 269, 286, 325, 366, 393, 447, 456, 483, 493, 584, 610, 617

Western Rift, East Africa 175, 179, 363, 395, 489, 555, 585

Westphalian 95

Wet 19, 200, 241, 253, 285, 326, 366, 367, 370, 437, 445, 503, 529, 614, 633

Wet Season 169, 200, 422, 446, 544, 607, 633

Wetlands 116, 145, 198, 251, 329, 342, 343, 344, 371, 386, 405, 422, 419, 448, 456, 522, 549, 578, 613-614

Whale 37, 70, 229, 291, 296, 308, 325, 357, 374, 441, 531, 561, 614

Wheat 101, 169, 244, 296, 421, 614

Whirlwind 178, 257, 609

White Dwarf Star 535, 615

White Hole 615, 620

White Light 161, 164

Whitecap 123, 615-616

Wildcatting 404, 616

Wilderness 82, 192

Wildflowers 17, 195, 331, 581

Wildlife 238, 269, 344, 408, 510

Willow 219, 442, 553, 581

Wind Chill 554, 617

Wind Energy 143, 617-618

Wind Shear 99, 295, 356

Wind-blown 134, 140, 154, 180, 189, 196, 298, 327, 382, 502, 597, 609, 615, 616, 618,

Window 42, 44, 122, 127, 231, 365, 594, 618

Windward 470, 486

Winnowing 151, 156, 169, 171, 312, 529, 615, 618

Winter 27, 35, 98, 174, 188, 189, 205, 286, 295, 307, 318, 320, 347, 387, 391, 393, 447, 454, 456, 458, 459, 503, 504, 505, 506, 515, 528, 537, 538, 548, 567, 580, 593, 595, 597, 602, 610, 614, 617, 623

Wisconsin Ice Sheet 445

Witching 164

Wobble 173, 174, 231, 233, 565

Wolframite 581, 619

Wollastonite 619

Wood 50, 88, 106, 184, 211, 261, 321, 353, 408, 452, 509, 559, 560, 581, 619-620

Woodland 102, 151, 215, 231, 297, 543, 620

Wool 35, 169, 236, 339, 618

Worm Hole 620

World Climate (See Global Climate) 20, 329,
    462, 554
World Ocean 2, 35, 41, 64, 176, 230, 273, 281,
    398, 504, 506, 527, 561, 606, 612
Worms 26, 179, 441, 455
Wrench Fault 121, 620
Wulfenite 620

X-rays 134, 180, 218, 321, 436, 465, **477, 485,**
    526, 535, 621
Xenocrysts 621
Xenoliths 177, 621
Xenon 283, 389, 621
Xenotime 621-622
Xerophyte 84, 101, 532, 622
Xylem 81, 435, 622

Yardang 104, 624
Yellow Fever 80, 149
Yellow Ground 69, 159, 305
Yellowcake 625
Youthful Streams 473, 542, 594
Yttrium 472, 547, 621, 626

Zenith 448
Zeolite Group 23, 365, 375, 435, 504, 528, 550,
    630-631
Zinc 16, 41, 85, 90, 144, 183, 218, 223, 253,
    262, 361, 401, 474, 517, 519, 532, 544, **583,**
    603, 615, 631
Zincite 631
Zinjanthropus 632
Zircon 34, 142, 632
Zirconium 102, 182, 440, 555, 556, 632
Zirconite 632
Zirkelite Group 555
Zodiac 632
Zoisite 632
Zoogeography 605, 633
Zooplankton 24, 374, 633